D1188038

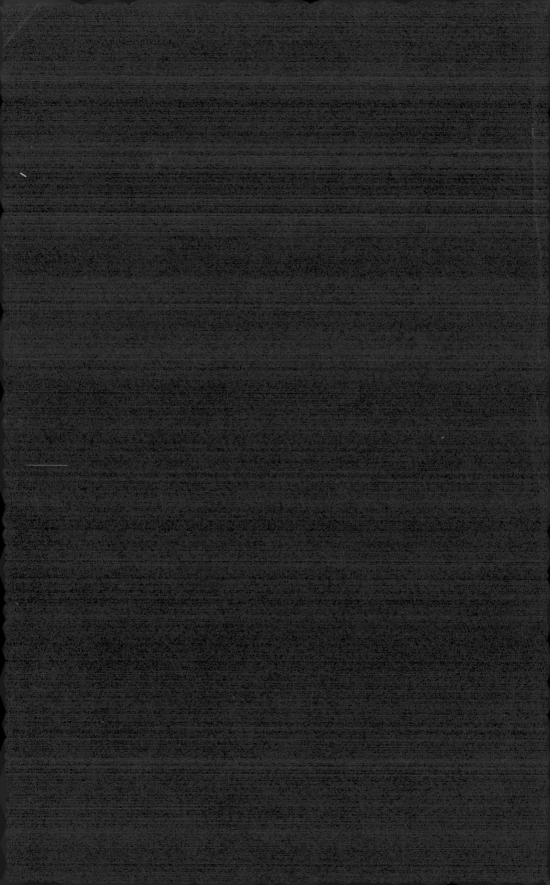

The Pursuit of Reason

Adam Smith

The Pursuit of Reason:
The Economist 1843–1993

RUTH DUDLEY EDWARDS

Foreword by Bill Emmott

Harvard Business School Press
Boston, Massachusetts

To the many people on or connected with *The Economist* who gave me help and ecouragement throughout the long years of this project; to all the *Economist* people, alive and dead, who receive here no or inadequate recognition of their contribution to the paper; and above all to my dear *Economist* friends Gordon Lee, John Midgley and the late Graham Hutton.

First published in the United States by the Harvard Business School Press, 1995
First published in Great Britain by Hamish Hamilton Ltd

Library of Congress Cataloging-in-Publication Data

Edwards, Ruth Dudley.
   The pursuit of reason : the Economist 1843–1993 / Ruth Dudley
Edwards; foreword by Bill Emmott.
      p. cm.
   Originally published: London : Hamish Hamilton, 1993.
   Includes index.
   ISBN 0-87584-608-4
      1. Economist (London, England)—History.   2. Finance—Periodicals—
History.   3. Economics—Periodicals—History.   4. Commerce—
Periodicals—History.   5. Great Britain—Commerce—Periodicals—
History.   6. Securities—Great Britain—Periodicals—History.
7. Great Britain—Economic conditions—Periodicals—History.
I. Title.
HG11.E2E38 1995
330—dc20
                                                            94-34596
                                                            CIP

The paper used in this publication meets the requirements of the American National Standard for Permanence of Paper for Printed Library Materials Z39.49-1984.

Contents

List of illustrations

Foreword

Right from the start, the young *Economist* attracted readers in the young United States; Secretary of State J.C. Calhoun wrote to the editor in 1845 in praise of the paper. Right from the start, James Wilson, Walter Bagehot and the other early editors were fascinated by America and grappled eagerly with the economics of slavery and the politics of the civil war, the business of trade and the principles of the constitution. And right from the start, *The Economist* believed in internationalism, seeing the world as an inter-related political and economic whole rather than as a mere collection of British interests. For all those reasons, the paper's founder would have been delighted but also astonished by how his creation is circulating 150 years later: more than half a million copies sold each week, of which 80% are purchased outside of Britain and the largest slice—45%—in North America.

That international, and above all American, success is what makes it so fitting that Ruth Dudley Edwards's history is now being published in the United States. The book is the story of the paper's long and unending journey, from its founding in 1843 as a small, British campaigning journal with but a few thousand readers, to today's much larger, worldwide, journal that still campaigns and still follows the principles of free trade, personal liberty and rational analysis from facts. It does not stick to those principles merely out of deference to its founder. As I said in my September 1993 speech to our 150th anniversary celebration at London's Reform Club, as editor I have one great advantage over James Wilson: that today's *Economist* has 150 years more experience and more facts with which to confirm the validity of those principles. If experience and facts had proved the principles to be wrong, the paper would have dropped them. But they have not, and it has not.

In that history, and in providing the experience to confirm our principles,

America has loomed large. *Economist* editors, especially the Victorian ones, often found the breadth and depth of America's democracy to be unnerving; and viewing the country from such a distance almost guaranteed misjudgments, most famously Walter Bagehot's dismissal of Abraham Lincoln in 1861 as "unequal to the situation in which he is placed". Yet America has always been *The Economist*'s great hope, a testbed for its own ideas about free trade, capitalist competition and individualism, and overwhelmingly a force for good in foreign affairs. That is also why the paper criticises America so harshly when it sees the country heading in the wrong direction, flirting with protectionism, limiting competition and bashing Japan, infringing liberty and squashing debate through the intolerant disease of political correctness, or else shrinking into isolationist meekness in foreign and defence policy. Such errors are only to be expected from ordinary countries. But from the United States they are at once an outrage and a crushing disappointment.

Now, America remains the centre of our world, based though we are in the centre of London. Its businesses, financial markets, law courts, political processes, diplomatic manoeuvres and even sports together form the main point of reference for all our journalists. Since 1942 *The Economist* has carried a special section called American Survey, yet the country's influence can be found in virtually every part of the paper, and runs thickly through our advertising sales and circulation efforts. British journalists still far outnumber other nationalities on the staff; but if a journalist is not British, the chances are that he or she will be American. Why, in our 150th year we even gained an American chief executive, Marjorie Scardino.

—Bill Emmott

Preface

As I was finishing this book, *The Economist* came into the news and a journalist rang me to ask for a one-sentence summary of its history. I responded with a hollow laugh before stumbling through a brief narrative. What I should have said was: '*The Economist* was founded in 1843 to campaign for free trade, *laissez-faire* and individual resonsibility through the medium of rational analysis applied to facts; its good fortune is that both its principles and its methods remain relevant 150 years later.'

Not that this sound-bite would have kept the interest of this particular journalist: what he really wanted to know was which exciting names had written for the paper over the years and if there were any notable scandals. In this he was at one with many of the staff of *The Economist*, who have been asking me hopefully for years what I have found in the way of sex or violence; until now I have tried to maintain a mysterious silence.

As an institution *The Economist* has its failings, but an aversion to having the truth told about it is not one of them. Typical, I think, was a conversation I had one day with David Gordon, then chief executive. One of David's most endearing if sometimes irrtitating characteristics is that as head prefect he still frequently talked like the rebel of the lower fifth he had been in his days as an *Economist* journalist. I remarked in passing that I did not intend to write much about the last decade or so. 'Why not?' 'Because while you are actually in your jobs, it would hardly be helpful to start analysing your deficiencies as a manager or Rupert's as an editor.' 'Why not? You don't want the book to be bland, do you?'

I hope it is not bland, but this book certainly becomes less detailed or analytical about individuals the closer they come in time: I am a historian, not a journalist. When the paper celebrates its bicentenary, my successor will be able to use freely the transcripts of my numerous interviews with past and present staff, most of whom were extremely frank. I am also influenced by the importance of anonymity in the paper's ethos; it is much too early to study or write about what might have been the effect on the emotional development of the present editor of his relationship with his teddy bear. For the same reason, except in the case of signed articles, I have in all but a couple of exceptional cases preserved the anonymity of *Economist* writers for the last twenty-five years.

The other question I have been most often asked by *Economist* people is 'Do I appear in your book?' I explained some time ago in the staff newspaper that in view of *The Economist*'s dedication to the free market, I would sell space: £50 for a mention, £500 for a favourable adjective and £10,000 for a substantial rewrite. The top offer I received was 50 pence, so I had to make my decisions on other grounds. As the most boring part of any institutional history is long lists of names, I have put the readers' interests before those of the staff. I hope the dedication to this book will earn me their forgiveness.

The Economist paid me a decent fee, lent me the complete run of the paper on microfilm and a machine with which to read it, and also paid the substantial secretarial expenses involved in research, audio-typing and so on. The deal as expressed in the contract was: 'The Economist will give the Author access to company records and personnel. It is understood that in writing the Work the Author is expected to exercise her own independence and judgement. However the author agrees to take serious consideration of any suggestions made by The Economist for changes in the Work.' It is a tribute to the openness of the paper's culture that it never occurred to me that there might be any attempt to censor anything I wrote. I was right: on behalf of *The Economist*, David Gordon and Rupert Pennant-Rea read the book, picked up a few minor factual errors and between them suggested three or four points that might be included and one story that might be left out. In each case, I agreed with them and made the small change involved.

I have dedicated this book specifically to three friends whom I made through the *Economist*. When I first started interviewing for this project in 1981 I visited Graham Hutton, who had been foreign editor in the mid-1930s. As the books recording who wrote what were all destroyed by a bomb in 1941, his extraordinary ability to remember people and identify their writing styles was invaluable. Together we went through several years of the 1930s *Economist*: I have transcriptions of over 100 interviews with him.

Over seven years I became close to him, and *The Economist* and I owe him a great debt for the time and thought he put into helping with this book. Graham died in 1988 and his widow, Marjorie, to whom I became even closer, in 1993. They were both tremendous pursuers of reason and truth whose company I cherished.

John Midgley, foreign editor from 1956 and thereafter Washington correspondent, came over from America in 1982 to talk to me about the paper's history. We spent several days together, talked *Economist* at enormous length and drank a lot of champagne at his club. Like Graham, John is an affectionate reflector on the psychology of his colleagues, and if his memory is less freakishly good than was Graham's, it is more than made up for by his habit of keeping all his correspondence. On countless occasions in London and Washington John has been an entertaining, frank and sceptical sounding-board against whom to test my ideas on people and events. He and his wife Elizabeth have been loving hosts and friends. (John, like Graham, occasionally made a speech about the importance of my remembering that his views were subjective. In the same way David Gordon sometimes fretted that I might be getting to like *The Economist* too much. To all three of them I would point out testily that I am notorious for my preoccupation with telling the truth to and about my nearest and dearest.)

Gordon Lee quite reasonably has demanded at least two paragraphs of unadulterated praise. He was Books editor when I met him in 1974 and began to review for *The Economist*. He is yet another student of those around him and we spent many a long lunch discovering that we shared a similar approach to history and to life and becoming intimate friends. It was Gordon who pointed out to his colleagues in the late 1970s that in view of the deficiencies of the centenary history something serious had better be done for the 150th, and that since there were virtually no written archives, the building up of an oral archive was an immediate priority. He also recommended me for the job. After the kind of hiatus that occurs when you ask busy people to think that far ahead, in 1981 David Gordon and Andrew Knight asked me – entirely on Gordon's say-so – to take on the job.

For several years I was working on the project part-time, conducting an immense programme of engrossing interviews and pursuing written material. By 1988 I was virtually full-time. Two years later, having written about a fifth of the book, I contracted repetitive strain injury and was unable to write or type for almost a year. Delivery dates crashed and the spectre of a history-less sesquicentenary loomed over paper, publisher and writer alike. Many people thought I had developed a psychosomatic ailment to save me from writing this book; sometimes I feared they might be right. I will always be grateful to those friends who saw me through this time, as Gordon did, by the expression of simple faith, and to David Gordon, who provided financial and practical support to get me back to production. Others who helped included Dr Richard Pearson, who diagnosed the condition, various physiotherapists and, above all, Carragh Pittam and Richard Gubbay, chiropractors recommended by David Gordon, and Maureen Cromey, a realistic and witty acupuncturist. Paul Le Druillenec, friend and accountant, and the AIB Bank (particularly Greg Gallivan) also rendered notable practical assistance.

Throughout the years Gordon Lee has been the person to whom I whinged when (in the early days) I found the culture of the paper chilly and arrogant. 'They can't help it, ducky,' he would explain as I arrived in his office expostulating about having been ignored in the lift by two people whom I had met about ten times; 'it's the public school syndrome.' He would then introduce me to some more of the mavericks to cheer me up. (I should add that in the course of time I suddenly found myself happy in the place. I got to know the distinctly non-aloof advertising, circulation, management and other non-editorial people, and once I had been around the place for a long time and had become familiar to enough of the journalists, I got through the editorial carapace and came to understand, enjoy and respect the collegiate atmosphere. So I plead guilty to having become fond of the institution and its staff.)

It was very much in the collegiate spirit that Gordon and three other retired journalists settled in to help me with the last stages of the book. Since I first began to produce piles of typescript, Gordon read it, reread it, talked it through with me and made recommendations that were almost invariably right. He has probably read the book ten times in various drafts and has made it better and given me heart. Gordon was one of the paper's great strategic editors and his friend Andrew Boyd is one of its great sub-editors. I sent Andrew the typescript to ask him if he spotted any errors and it came back expertly subbed. He and Roland Bird (both of whom had consistently encouraged me over the years) voluntarily corrected the galley proofs speedily and brilliantly, and John Midgley spotted some errors. Others on the paper swung into action to get the product out in time. The resourceful Helen Mann, who out of the kindness of her heart has been easing my path on the paper for years, took on the job of transferring innumerable alterations from typescript to disk, helped by Julia Hollands, Julie Reynolds and (from outside the paper) Penny Williams, and triumphed over the immensely complicated logistics of the disk-to-manuscript-to-readers-to-disk-to-publisher-to-galley-proofs-to-proof-readers-to-publisher-to-page-proofs-to-proof-readers-to-publisher process without anyone cracking up or falling out. Others who deserve special mention because they provided particularly notable practical or moral support at one time or another, or throughout, are Carol Howard and her Research Department, Gillian Allen, Susannah Amoore, Geoff Ayres, Katrin Bleckman, Brian Beedham, Patrick Bresnan, Debbie Broxton, Ross Clayton, Pat Coleman, Bob Cooksey, Derek Cutt, the late Lord Drogheda, Bill Emmott, Dudley Fishburn, Daniel Franklin, Des Gorrell, Charles Grant, Nick Harman, Helen Hermanstein, Donald Hirsch, Dave Jones, Andrew Knight, Chris Loughnane, Hugo Meynell, Bob Milner, Aurobind Patel, John Philbin, Joyce Routledge, Marjorie Scardino, Derek Smith, Gerry Stephens, Christina Strupinska, Raphael del Toro, Ines Watson and the staff of the 9th, 10th and 14th floors who uncomplainingly endured my hogging their photocopying machines with hundreds of books and thousands of files. To all the others who were kind, helpful or interested along the way I apologise for not thanking them specifically.

At home my life was changed when I had to find someone to help me do the things my arms were refusing to do. Carol Scott came into my life early in 1990 and gradually took on most of the chores that drove me mad. Apart from sorting out my paperwork, getting the thousands of files of *Economist* archives into some kind of order, keeping files and general administration up to date, putting material on my computer and typing from dictation, she spent hundreds of hours with the microfilm-reader following up my multifarious queries. One small example is that in the early stages she photocopied from the microfilm more than 140 years of indexes so that they could be conveniently consulted. Because of Carol, I was able to follow up themes, ideas and both good and false trails and in consequence vastly enrich the book. Carol has many talents: I particularly appreciate her for being patient, thorough and reliable as well as being calm, easy-going and having an excellent sense of humour. Above all she is temperamentally a problem-solver and has in abundance that quality most prized by Walter Bagehot – sheer common-sense. An old *Economist* hand, Sue Bruce-Smith (and recently also her sister Lizzie Gartside), has typed hundreds of transcripts over the years, has taken a great interest and has been a great pleasure to work with. Pippa Allen came on the scene late and helped a great deal on the audio-typing front at times of crisis. Diana LeCore did splendid work on the index. Angie Mackworth-Young, Judith Harte and Morven Blair provided meticulous help with the page proofs; we decided, for the purpose of clarity, to make a few very minor amendments to some quoted material.

When Andrew Franklin moved from Penguin Books to become publishing director of Hamish Hamilton, I went with him because I liked his enthusiasm for the book. Andrew is febrile, mercurial and confrontational, but his love of books and his instinctive brilliance as an editor make up for everything, and when he believes something is good he is hearteningly generous with praise. When he read the early parts of the book he unerringly pinpointed how it could be made much better, and, swearing as I went, I followed his advice faithfully. His team at Hamish Hamilton have coped with the lateness of this book and have demonstrated technical brilliance as well as good humour in getting it out in time despite the hold-up caused first by my malady and second by Andrew's, Gordon Lee's and my determination to make the book as good as it could be. Charlie Hartley deserves special mention; Keith Taylor is a gem.

Felicity Bryan, ex-*Economist*, who has been my agent for almost twenty years, takes particular credit for my having written this book, for it was she who introduced me first to Gordon Lee. Felicity also shepherded me brilliantly through a little local difficulty halfway through the project. Affectionate and encouraging to her authors and fierce in defence of their interests, she is an author's dream.

This has been a hellishly difficult book; it has been alternately a fearful burden and a job. On the bad days I felt like Sisyphus; on the good I was lifted by the sheer intellectual fun of it all. And I shall never cease to be grateful to the project for introducing me to the wonderful Walter Bagehot.

When I started this project I had the help and encouragement of my parents and my husband. I lost the first two through death and the latter through divorce, but while they were there, their interest and kindnesses were important and much appreciated. My brother Owen made extremely helpful comments about the nineteenth-century section of the book, as well as undertaking some research for me into Scottish newspapers. Neasa MacErlean and Michael Kersse, as always, supportively and intelligently tolerated my intellectual obsessions and cheered every time I quoted Bagehot.

I can mention only a tiny fraction of my many lovely friends, so I am choosing those whose dedication to my welfare extended beyond reasonable limits. Alison Hawkes, James McGuire and Nina Clarke always knew exactly where I was in the production process and how far there was to go and kept urging me along week by week; and Nina, who is also my neighbour, acted as everything from psychotherapist to meals-on-wheels provider. Particular kindnesses were performed by Piers Brendon, Michael Laffan, Aruna and Kuke Khanna, and Deborah Simon. Niall Crowley, the late Brian Inglis, Jill Neville, Janet McIver and Barbara Sweetman Fitzgerald (and inevitably Gordon Lee) were always soothing when I thought I was going mad. Una O'Donoghue constantly cheered me up. And of course John has been a delight.

A number of academics have given me generous help. Sister Martha Westwater's name leads all the rest. Of Mount St Vincent University, Nova Scotia, she is the author of *The Wilson Sisters*, a biography of the founder's six daughters which has been invaluable to me. For the purposes of her research she had spent months and months reading right through over 60 years of the diaries of Eliza Bagehot (née Wilson) – a hideous task, for Eliza's handwriting was awful and the daily entries were almost unbelievably boring ('Got up late as had bad headache. Lady Muck called and told me Mrs Mopp had died. Called on Emilie. Zoe read part of Mr Gladstone's speech to me p.m.' is invented but typical). Aware that there were buried treasures in Eliza's diary, but unable to contemplate a proper excavation, I wrote and threw myself on Martha's mercy. She lent me all the laborious transcripts she had made (of which she had no copy), later sent me the microfilm so I could read the full entries for the periods that most interested me, and throughout sent warm and encouraging messages. Without her help I would have missed some tremendously valuable material.

I am grateful for tip-offs, help and advice to Professors Marian Bowley, Judy Klein and D.P. O'Brien, and to David Kynaston. Robert P. Patterson, a Canadian Bagehot-enthusiast, provided me with a copy of Professor Scott Gordon's invaluable essay, which I might otherwise have missed, as well as his own exhaustive bibliography on Bagehot and banking. Joy Greg (Lady Newsam) has been a great help on Wilson and family artefacts.

Angel Arrese, who is writing for the University of Navarre a PhD thesis on

The Economist from the point of view of journalism and business, spent several days working among the papers in my house and was a great pleasure to swap information and opinions with. I am particularly grateful for the material on early circulation figures which he generously gave me, along with some valuable quotes from American newspapers.

The late David Hubback, biographer of Walter Layton, and my old friend Charles Lysaght, biographer of Brendan Bracken, were extremely helpful with advice and papers. Pat Nimmo gave me a present of a copy of the *Oeconomist*; Keith Parkinson lent me the diaries and account books of his father, Hargreaves Parkinson.

I am grateful to the staffs of the British Library, the British Newspaper Library (Colindale), the Department of Palaeography at Durham University, the Einaudi Institute in Milan, the India Office, the London Library, the London School of Economics, Manchester City Library, the Public Record Office, the Schlesinger Library, Radicliffe College, and the West Sussex Record Office, and to the librarian and all the other staff of the Reform Club.

The following have helped me greatly by talking (or in a few cases writing) to me about their connection with, or their assessments of, *The Economist*: Jean Bird Abrams, Dick Goold Adams, Swaminathan Aiyer, Michael Alderson, John Andrews, Joan Astley, Nancy Balfour, Howard Banks, Paul Bareau, Tom Barton, Francis Bator, Brian Beedham, the late Lord Bensusan-Butt, Graham Billington, Roland Bird, Pat Bottomley, Andrew Boyd, Ronald Brech, Patrick Bresnan, Hugh Brogan, Stephen Brough, Mark Malloch Brown, John Browning, Sir Alastair Burnet, Anthony Cahill, Geoffrey Carr, Iain Carson, John Chancellor, John Chapman, Nico Colchester, Barbara Beck Coulter, Ian Coulter, the late Margot Coville, the late Harold Cowan, Anne and Bernard Crowther, the late Margaret Cruikshank, Edwin Dale, Roland Dallas, Peter Davies, Muriel Davis, Marjorie Deane, the late Tamara Deutscher, the late Lord Drogheda, Walter Eberstadt, Jean Eisler (née Layton), Mike Elliott, Bill Emmott, Nick Faith, Edmund Fawcett, George Ffitch, Dudley Fishburn, Lord Forte, Reggie Forty, Daniel Franklin, the late Lord Franks, Richard Fry, Ruth Galvin, Lesley Gardner, N. A. Gaunt, Harold Gearson, Alfred Geiringer, Doro George, Winifred Glover, Mary Goldring, David Gordon, Anthony Gottlieb, Charles Grant, Clive Greaves, Joy Greg, Johnny Grimond, David Hanger, Nick Harman, Lord Harris, Sir John Harvey-Jones, John Heffernan, Wendy Hinde, Donald Hirsch, Henry Hobhouse, H. V. Hodson, Liam Hourican, Jim Howell, the late David

Hubback, Stephen Hugh-Jones, Marjorie and the late Graham Hutton, F. L. ('Jimmy') James, Lord and Lady Jay, Johnnie Johnson, Houston Kenyon, Shapur Kharagat, Andrew Knight, Keith Kyle, Ann Layton, Christopher Layton, David Layton, Trevor Layton, Gordon Lee, Lord Lever, Graham Lewis, Roy Lewis, Tony Lewis, Pat and Robert Logan, Robin Ludlow, Chris Lydon, Charles Lysaght, Emily MacFarquhar, Ken McKenzie, Lady McNicol, Norman Macrae, Brenda Maddox, Andrew Marr, Peter Martin, Pamela Matthews, Hugo Meynell, John Midgley, Helen Hill Miller, Stephen Millington, the late Bill Mills, Cecily Money, Sir Claus Moser, Richard Natkiel, Annelise Needham, Pat Nimmo, Pat Norton, Padraig O'Malley, E. F. Papp, Aurobind Patel, the late George 'Whacker' Payne, Sophie Peddar, John Peet, Rupert Pennant-Rea, John Plender, Patricia Potts (née Tyerman), Michael Prouse, Matt Ridley, Margaret Rix, the late Lord Robbins, Joe Rogaly, Murray Rossant, Elspeth and Walt Rostow, Senator William Roth, Sir Evelyn de Rothschild, Hugh Sandeman, Marjorie Scardino, Diana Self, the late Bill Shannon, Bill Simmons, Daniel Singer, Chris Slattery, Barbara Smith, Bob Smith, Derek Smith, Peter Dallas Smith, Alison and Peter Smithson, Anne Sofer (née Crowther), Brian de Soissons, Eric Sosnow, Lord St John of Fawsley, Georgiana Stevens, the late Charles Stransky, Bill Taylor, Tony Thomas, John Thorne, Judith Tomlin, Ian Trafford, the late Ian Trethowan, Margaret Tyerman, Mary Tyerman, Robert Tyerman, Sandy Ungar, Nick Valery, Arthur Way, the late E. M. Webb, Caspar Weinberger, Mike West, the late John Wood, Max Worcester, Dominic Ziegler and Taya Zinkin. I appeal to anyone who has been accidentally left off this list not to take umbrage.

I am grateful to the following sources for permission to reproduce illustrations (plate numbers in brackets): Roland Bird (29); the *Guardian* (47); Angela Gibb (25); Hulton Deutsch Collection (frontispiece, 4,5, 13 and 24); Lord Jay (31); David Layton (21 and 27); Lady Newsam (Joy Greg) (6, 7, 8, 10, 14, 15 and 16); Keith Parkinson (28); the *Spectator* (11 and 12). The other illustrations come from *The Economist*.

CHAPTER I

Why

Some try to represent political economy as being a dry, cold, abstract science, which has no warmth of feeling to spare on suffering humanity . . . This is far from the truth; on the contrary, political economy produces feelings so intense for the removal of these evils, that it will not permit us to rest satisfied with mere declamation, but impels us to examine deeply into the whole matter to discover the true causes of this wretchedness, and the mode by which it may be removed, or at least alleviated.[1]

So wrote James Wilson, founder and editor of *The Economist*, in November 1843, in its tenth issue, in an article called 'WIDOW BIDDLE AND THE POOR NEEDLE-WOMEN OF THE METROPOLIS'.[2] Assailing in his typically combative way *The Times* and the *Morning Post*, for bewailing the misfortunes of the suffering poor while offering no sensible remedies, he used the case to demonstrate once again how free trade would alleviate the prevailing and widespread economic distress. His passionate defence of political economy was of a piece with that peculiarity observed by his son-in-law, Walter Bagehot: he was a '*very animated* man, talking by preference and by habit on *inanimate* subjects. All the *verve*, vigour, and life which lively people put into exciting pursuits, he put into topics which are usually thought very dry. He discussed the currency or the Corn Laws with a relish and energy which made them interesting to almost every one.'[3]

It was the combination of a persuasive – even rumbustious – writing style with a near-fanatical devotion to facts that was to give *The Economist* authority and influence from the outset. New papers often fail because they lack a clear identity: about *The Economist* there was no confusion. Its purpose was to further the cause of free trade in the interests of national and international prosperity: its voice was the highly distinctive voice of James Wilson, who announced himself in the prospectus (in the guise of 'ourselves') as having 'very strong opinions, formed after long observation, experience, and reflection, and which the further observation of every day tends only to make stronger'. He did not exaggerate: although he was only thirty-eight and most of his life had been uneventful, he had shown an exceptional ability through reading, listening and thinking to develop his experience into a *Weltanschauung*, from which he established a set of principles that made sense of the great public issues of his time. At root, and directing the conduct of every day of his adult life, was his discovery 'that the only source of certain success, whatever the undertaking may be, is steady, well directed, and unremitting assiduity'.

Wilson was born in Scotland, at Hawick in Roxburghshire, on 3 June, 1805. His mother, born Elizabeth Richardson, died in 1815 after the birth of the fifteenth of her children, of whom five boys and five girls survived into adulthood. James, the fourth son, was too young when she died to retain more than a slight recollection of his mother, whose place was filled for him by his greatly-loved eldest sister, Katherine.

His home seems to have been happy. His father, William, was a well-to-do woollen manufacturer and a well-known Quaker (the family used the 'thee' and 'thou' convention), and he imbued his children with a strong ethical sense and a belief in the merits of hard work. James was to refer to him throughout his life with great respect.

At the age of eleven, James was sent to the Quaker School at Ackworth in Yorkshire, where he was scholastically but not athletically successful. Although popular for his amiability, he had a well-concealed but deep-running shyness that was never to leave him. Discipline at the school was firm: for instance, talking at mealtimes was banned and the children conversed in deaf and dumb language. Yet Wilson was happy there and responded to the demands made of him. Standards were high: he was proud of winning a prize for the best essay on three attributes of God – Omnipotence, Omniscience and Omnipresence. School records report that he displayed 'an unusual passion for figures'.[4]

He left after four years, by then top of the school and set on being a schoolmaster. His father, who gave his children virtual freedom of choice about their careers, sent him to a seminary at Earl's Colne in Essex. After a short time he wrote home in the terms of the parable of the Prodigal Son: 'I would rather be the most menial servant in my father's mill than be a teacher', and he was rescued immediately.

He would have liked to study for the Scottish Bar, but indulgent though his father was, he could not agree to his son taking up an occupation frowned on by the Quakers. There seemed no choice but to go into business, and so, at the age of sixteen, Wilson was apprenticed to a small hat manufacturer at Hawick. A serious-minded youth with great self-discipline, he took easily to autodidacticism and during the next few years spent his spare time in reading a great deal, often late at night, a habit he retained until early adulthood when he became too busy. It was during this period that he acquired a thorough grounding in the principles of classical economics.

His first months at Hawick were spent in mastering his trade with his habitual concentration and thoroughness, whereupon his father bought the business for him and an elder brother, William. They ran it successfully for a couple of years, but Hawick was too small for their ambitions. In 1824, when James was only nineteen, they moved to London, where, with the substantial gift of £2,000 each from their father, they set up the hat manufacturing firm of Wilson, Irwin and Wilson. By mutual consent it was dissolved in 1831 but, under the name of James Wilson and Co., Wilson stayed in the same line of business. He later calculated that by 1837 he was worth £25,000 (the equivalent of £853,000 in 1993): he believed those years to have been invaluable in teaching him about the middle and working classes and about international trade.

By the mid-1830s his domestic circumstances had changed dramatically. Until January 1832 he and his brother had lived with two of their sisters: on the fifth of that month James married the beautiful Elizabeth Preston of Newcastle-upon-Tyne and they moved into a house he had had built for them in Southwark, near his factory. On his marriage Wilson became a member of the Church of England: in the same year his father died in London of cholera.

Wilson had a considerable aesthetic sense, and his wife shared his interest in music (he had played the flute as a boy) and art. Their letters show them to have been a devoted couple, although Elizabeth's recurring ill-health caused him worry and led to enforced separations. They were to have six daughters – Eliza (who married Walter Bagehot) in 1832, Julia in 1834, Matilda in 1836, Zenobia (Zoe) in 1838, Sophie in 1840, and Emilie (her father's biographer) in 1841 – to whom Wilson was a loving and demonstrative father. All six were throughout the whole of their lives to be closely connected to *The Economist* and jointly or severally to own it for 68 years.

By 1836 Wilson was sufficiently affluent to move his family to a mansion in extensive grounds in Dulwich, but in that same year he began to speculate in indigo. He invested most of the capital he had built up through twenty years of hard work, and lost it when the price of indigo fell following the economic crisis of 1837. Having risked more than he could easily afford, he was unable to hold on until better times. By 1839 his personal and business finances were in a critical state.

In his delightful memoir of his father-in-law, Bagehot wrote affectionately of the temperamental failing that led Wilson into trouble on this occasion: 'Mr Wilson was in several respects by no means an unlikely man to meet with, especially in early life, occasional misfortune. To the last hour of his life he was always sanguine. He naturally looked at everything in a bright and cheerful aspect; his tendency was always to form a somewhat too favourable judgment both of things and men. One proof of this may be sufficient; – he was five years Secretary of the Treasury, and he did not leave it a suspicious man.'

Wilson reacted to financial catastrophe with characteristic moral courage and dogged determination. Bagehot was later to remark that Wilson was never to show 'greater business ability, self-command, and energy' than during this crisis. He was able immediately to pay off his personal creditors and to pay half of the demands against his firm. Bankruptcy was avoided through negotiation and the assignment of a foreign property for the remaining half. When some years later the property was sold and failed to make the expected figure, Wilson, although legally in the clear, paid the difference. He was to remain in the hat business until 1844 when he gave it up to concentrate his money and energies on *The Economist*.

His intellectual vitality and preoccupation with public affairs gradually took Wilson far beyond the confines of home and factory. Despite his shyness (which few people noticed) he loved intelligent society and informed discussion of public concerns. Bagehot recorded his often-expressed satisfaction in talking a subject out and noted that conversation used to spur him to develop new but lasting theories on favourite topics. A likeable, well-informed and interesting man, his company was much sought after, and he made many close and enduring friendships.

Crucial to his intellectual development was the relationship he formed in

1836 with his Dulwich neighbour, George Porter, an economist and pioneering statistician under whom the statistical department of the Board of Trade had been established in 1834. Wilson later described Porter's mind – in a term which to him was the highest praise – as the most 'accurate' he had ever known. Wilson himself, in Bagehot's view, was 'a great and almost an instinctive master of *statistical selection* . . . He saw which [figures] were really material; he put them prominently and plainly forward, and he left the rest alone.'

It had been a fortunate coincidence for one of Wilson's gifts that his only sustained period of reading should have coincided with free trade becoming an issue for public debate. In 1820, the merchants of the City of London presented a highly influential free-trade petition to the House of Commons, and the reforming Tory governments of the 1820s were to achieve a great deal in the relaxation of trade restrictions and the simplification and reduction of tariffs.

Wilson came from a family strongly in favour of free trade[5] and the well-publicised disputes between protectionists and free-traders made economics – or political economy as it was then called – his most natural subject of study. What he read then provided the main theoretical basis for his life's work, for, (as Bagehot was to notice) because Wilson never learned to skim reading matter he became reluctant to read at all. If he had to read even a newspaper article, 'it was with as much slow, deliberate attention as if he were perusing a treasury minute'. This was a major handicap to a man moving in the world of ideas, but on the positive side there was never any doubt that what he did read, he understood fully.

His economic thinking was firmly rooted in the classical school. Asked in 1843 by an *Economist* reader to recommend the best books on 'political economy', he listed Adam Smith's *Wealth of Nations* (1776), the works of J.-B. Say, Ricardo's *Principles of Political Economy and Taxation* (1817), James Mill's *Political Economy* (1821), Tooke's *History of Prices* (the first three of the six volumes, published 1838–40) and his friend George Porter's *Progress of the Nation in its various Social and Economic Relations from the beginning of the Nineteenth Century to the present time* (three volumes, 1836–43). He recommended as the best books 'for the common student', Adam Smith's, 'as fixing fundamental principles' and Tooke's and Porter's 'as the most interesting, entertaining, and instructive practical applications of those principles'.[6]

It was a predictable list from a thinking practical man. Adam Smith in 1776 had laid the foundations of English political economy on which David Ricardo constructed an abstract science. In Bagehot's felicitous description, 'what he [Smith] did was much like the rough view of the first traveller who discovers a country; he saw some great outlines well, but he mistook others and left out much. It was Ricardo who made the first map; who reduced the subjects into consecutive shape, and constructed what you can call a science.'[7] The contribution to economic theory of Jean-Baptiste Say, a French businessman turned academic economist, included the concept that supply created its own demand. Mill was a utilitarian philosopher and Ricardo's mentor and spiritual father. The practical analyses of the economist and merchant Thomas Tooke (framer of the free-trade petition of 1820 and later an ally of Wilson's in a currency controversy) and of Porter underpinned the theories of the classical school with a vast array of factual data.

Whereas their predecessors had seen agriculture as the major source of wealth, the classical economists were agreed on the vital importance of manufacturing and the concept of labour as the measure of value. At base lay their conviction that the community as a whole benefited from free competition. All were disciples of *laissez-faire* – a belief that the public good is best served by leaving individuals to look after themselves, since government interference in economic affairs tends to upset the natural checks and balances of wealth-creation. Wilson's *Economist* was to be perhaps the most influential disseminator of this doctrine, through the prism of which it examined and pronounced on the topical issues of the day: its greatest test was to be the Irish famine.[8]

It was the crash of 1837, followed by a prolonged economic depression, that gave the theories of the classical economists an unprecedented relevance. A period of full employment and low prices came to an end when several bad harvests raised agricultural prices and reduced domestic demand for manu-factured goods. Overseas markets could not absorb the extra British indus-trial output and widespread unemployment developed – exacerbated by a fast increasing population (up by almost a third between 1801 and 1831) disproportionately concentrated in urban areas. At a time when Britain was unchallenged as the greatest world economic power, the mass of its people were living in abject poverty.

The focus of grievance was on the high price of bread, a consequence of the operation of the Corn Laws, introduced in 1815 after the defeat of Napoleon to replace the wartime income tax. Foreign wheat could not be imported until the home price had reached 52 shillings per quarter and even then it carried a heavy duty. By the beginning of what was to be the crisis of 1837–42, Britain could no longer feed its population, and the poor – victims of a regressive taxation system – starved. One consequence was a rapid build-up of opposition to the Corn Laws, which, although only one of many protectionist measures, were the most urgently in need of reform.

The headquarters of the new movement were to be in the manufacturing stronghold of Manchester. It has been calculated[9] that the leaders of the anti-Corn Law campaign, later contemptuously labelled by Disraeli 'the school of Manchester', were in fact made up of five distinct groups: the wholly self-interested businessmen who financed the movement in the belief that free trade would increase profits; their humanitarian counterparts who wanted to improve the lot of the lower classes; the pacifists (including Richard Cobden) who believed free trade would bring about an international interest in peace; the London Radicals, utilitarian intellectuals (who included Francis Place and Charles Villiers); and the middle-class radical reformers (including John Bright) for whom free trade was only one campaign among many. Additionally, there were individual free-traders who stood apart from any group. Protectionists lumped them all together as manufacturers bent on destroying British agriculture for the sake of lowering wages at home and increasing markets abroad.

By the late 1830s, Wilson's circle was almost entirely composed of passionate free-traders, his most intimate friends being Porter, John Sibeth (a dedicated amateur politician), and de Brouwer de Hogendorf, a Belgian parliamentarian who provided an invaluable international dimension. Like his brother George* (who would play a major role in *The Economist* in the last quarter of the century), Wilson was ready to take on a public role. He had seen much earlier than most that, since the vast majority of parliamentarians were landowners, they would have to be persuaded to abandon one of their firm beliefs and to recognise that the Corn Laws were quite as inimical to agricultural as to manufacturing interests – an uncommon view. Richard Cobden, who was to be the inspirational leader of the anti-Corn Law

---

*George, Wilson's youngest brother, became chairman of the London-based Metropolitan Anti-Corn Law Association, founded in 1836 and moribund by the end of the decade. He was also a member of the Anti-Corn Law League. *The Economist* (25 March 1969) and recent scholarly works have confused him with his namesake (no relative), the chairman of the League from inception to dissolution.

movement, speaking in 1843 about the late 1830s, reflected that 'most of us entered upon this struggle with the belief that we had some distinct class-interest in the question, and that we should carry it by a manifestation of our will in this district, against the will and consent of other portions of the community'.[10]

Despairing at the way in which so many participators in the controversy had made the issue a matter of class against class, and shocked by what he described as 'the determined and often violent spirit in which all parties have conducted their arguments', Wilson set out on what was to be the first stage in a public career devoted to trying to secure the triumph of reason. His aim was to use facts, interpreted lucidly and rationally, to get through to the lawmakers that repealing the Corn Laws was in the interest of the whole nation.

In March 1839 (the month in which Richard Cobden and his associates founded the Anti-Corn Law League), at the height of his financial troubles and in the midst of negotiations with creditors, Wilson finished a long pamphlet, 'Influences of the Corn Laws, as affecting all classes of the community, and particularly the landed interests'. The partisan, he warned, would not find in it 'one single word declaiming the landowners as selfish, monopolizing law-makers, or the manufacturers as sordid, avaricious beings, grasping at the riches of the great, and treading on the rights of the poor: the subject has already been handled too much in this way'.

The pamphlet's novelty and particular value stemmed from the directness with which he challenged the class-interest orthodoxies head-on and his copious use of statistics and historical fact. His argument was constructed around three propositions:

1) that the Corn Laws had produced consequences 'most prejudicial to all classes of the community, but more especially so to the landed and agricultural interest generally';

2) that the agricultural interest's 'fears and apprehensions of the ruinous consequences' of a free trade in corn were without foundation: in fact landowners would benefit;

3) that while the manufacturing interest and the working population generally would benefit incalculably from repeal, there would be a raising, not a lowering, of the prices of food and labour.

At the core of the argument was the fundamental belief – based on Adam Smith's view that society gains when men compete to better their condition –

that made Wilson a crusader for *laissez-faire*. As he expressed it in his pamphlet, 'the only true theory on national interests' was 'that nothing can possibly be favourable to the whole that is detrimental to a part, and that nothing can be detrimental to one portion that is favourable to another portion'. Or, in a phrase that was to gain widespread currency a century later: 'What's good for General Motors is good for the country.'

He could have chosen no better time to embark on a writing career. Not perhaps until the 1930s debate on Keynesianism and the 1980s debate on monetarism did an economic controversy generate so much heat in Britain – and then among far smaller sections of the population. In the early 1840s (retrospectively named 'the hungry forties'), protectionism was an issue of such widespread significance as to generate a mass agitation. Yet few of the most vocal on either side of the debate even half-understood the issues about which they argued so fiercely.

The free-trade issue was admirably suited to Wilson's eminently practical intelligence. Although he was not the sole originator of the propositions he put forward,* he had thought them through from first principles, talked them through with his associates and written about them with force and conviction. He was never to be a writer of elegance, but, as Bagehot remarked, he was a 'great *belief producer*', and it was this that gave him such a crucial role in transforming the Corn Laws debate from a class question to a national one. Many years later Richard Cobden was to admit that he 'never made any progress with the Corn Law question while it was stated as a question of class against class'.[11]

Reaction to the pamphlet was initially slow, for Wilson had scruples about using influence to get it reviewed in the press,[12] but within a short time it had become widely noticed and favourably received. The editor of the *Leeds Mercury*, the liberal-minded MP Edward Baines, published all 130 pages of it in instalments in his paper. The *Anti-Corn Law Circular* carried an enthusiastic review and Cobden promised that the League would 'make constant use of your valuable work by quotations'.[13] Among its admirers were three influential Whig politicians who were to become lifelong friends of Wilson's: the distinguished and independent-minded William Pleydell-Bouverie, third earl of Radnor, who expressed his delight that 'the Cause has so able and

---

*Wilson's friend G.R. Porter published in the same year a smaller, similar pamphlet, which made much less impact.

zealous an advocate'; the indefatigable free-trade campaigner Charles Villiers (MP and barrister); and his brother George, Lord Clarendon, who was to be in time Lord Lieutenant of Ireland and later Foreign Secretary.

Within a few months Wilson was a public figure, his name known widely within the League and his pamphlet even quoted in the House of Commons by Sir Robert Peel. By the beginning of 1840 it had gone into a third edition and its author was growing in confidence. While writing his pamphlet he had worried that 'the sentences would never come right'.[14] Now, he told Cobden, he was 'watching with intense anxiety the indirect consequences of these pernicious laws on the currency and manufacturers and commerce of this country'[15] and planning a follow-up, published in 1840 as 'Fluctuations of Currency, Commerce, and Manufactures'. In this he explored further his theory that one iniquitous effect of the Corn Laws was to produce sharp price fluctuations. The following year, an article on financial policy which he was writing for the *Morning Chronicle* grew so long in one night as to become instead a 27-page pamphlet called 'The Revenue; or, What should the Chancellor do?' It foreshadowed a distinguished series of writings on currency which were to contribute substantially to the banking debates of the 1840s.

Both pamphlets added to Wilson's reputation as an economics writer of clarity and integrity, whose beliefs – being firmly rooted in broad principles – were always coherent and consistent: as a thinker he was never affected by fashion. Indeed, he had the greatest contempt for those who were: in a trenchant attack on *The Times* in 1843, he accused it of being content to keep 'just a shade in advance in what it deems the most popular line'.[16]

Wilson grew ever busier, as his new social and campaigning responsibilities were added to the demands of his hat business (which involved a good deal of travel within Britain and on the Continent), his statistical researches and his writing. His value as a source of solid information, sound argument and powerful propaganda led many men in public life to want his counsel and his company. It was a measure of his rapid social advancement that as early as the summer of 1840 he was proposed by Villiers and seconded by Radnor for membership of the Reform Club.

The development of political clubs was a feature of the 1830s, following on a Reform Act requirement that voters should be registered. In consequence, Tory and Whig 'registration societies' emerged in the constituencies, and to facilitate the development of party policy and recruitment at national level, the Tory Carlton Club was set up in 1832 and the Whig Reform Club four years later. The Reform also attracted non-Whig reformers like Bright, Cobden and Daniel O'Connell, whose enormous portraits (along with those of Gladstone, Palmerston, Lord John Russell and many lesser contemporaries) to this day loom large in the iconographic pantheon of the club. The Reform's magnificent new Pall Mall premises were opened in March 1841, shortly after Wilson became a member. He was to be a frequent attender for meetings with other enthusiastic free-traders as his public involvement with the campaign grew.

By the autumn of 1841, though he was pleading overwork to avoid being involved by Francis Place in the day-to-day running of the revived Metropolitan Anti-Corn Law Association,[17] he had become involved in its organisation and in strategic negotiations between it and the League, whose attempts to control the Association's activities caused resentment in London. Wilson's friendly links with, on the one hand, Cobden and George Wilson, the League chairman, and on the other with Place, helped to reduce tensions. As economic and social deprivation became more widespread, Wilson's distress and indignation grew. His preoccupation in correspondence with the League chairman was that the energy of the rank-and-file supporters of the League should be harnessed, through imaginative middle-class leadership, to strengthen the anti-protectionist campaign of the propagandists and parliamentarians.

It was not only in his writing that Wilson was a 'belief producer'. He seems to have had a *gravitas* far beyond his years. When he and Radnor became friends, Wilson was a thirty-six-year-old merchant, Radnor an aristocrat who, for twenty-six years in the House of Commons and from 1828 in the Lords, had won widespread respect for his independence in the defence of public against factional interest. Yet, although one must make allowance for Radnor's gentle and unassuming nature (he was said to have been the only friend of William Cobbett never to quarrel with him), his admiration for Wilson and reliance on his judgment and effectiveness are evident in his letters. In due course the nature of the relationship became known to the leaders of the League, and Wilson was asked to bring Radnor and his family more actively into the campaign.

It was primarily, then, in print or behind the scenes as a persuader and recruiter of influential people, that Wilson made his greatest contribution to the anti-Corn Law campaign. Occasionally – though reluctantly – he made public speeches, one of which was given early in 1843 in Drury Lane and reported on illuminatingly by a contemporary:

> I knew that he was closely argumentative, relying more upon statistical figures than upon figures of speech, and trusting more to facts and reasonings than to rhetorical flourishes. He was just the man to test the previously acquired knowledge of the audience. If they listened with interest to plain statements and appreciated a plainly-put point, then they had come to learn and not to be excited by flashes of oratory. And so it proved. They not only listened with deep interest to an address which lasted three quarters of an hour, but repeatedly applauded with enthusiasm when a telling argument was uttered.[18]

The following year he acted as a most unlikely warm-up man for one of the greatest orators and demagogues of modern times, Daniel O'Connell, the legendary figure who in 1829 forced the then Prime Minister, the Duke of Wellington, to open the doors of parliament to Catholics, and who in Ireland routinely addressed audiences of a hundred thousand. Then on trial on a patently unfair charge, he was a hero to English reformers. In the crowd were two university students and future editors of *The Economist*, Richard Holt Hutton and Walter Bagehot. Bagehot wrote to his father that he had witnessed the crowd's 'enthusiastic reception of O'Connell'.

> It was a very imposing sight to see the whole house crammed full as it was in every corner, pit, stage boxes, and galleries, rise at once at his entrance, and remain standing for more than ten minutes, cheering him the whole time, some waving hats and pocket handerchiefs, and very many shouting welcome. What made it still more striking was that the crowd outside, which must, from the loudness of their shouts, have been very large, began to cheer several times under the mistaken impression that he was coming, and the audience inside rose each time and cheered, to the very great annoyance of Mr James Wilson.[19]

Wilson made a speech attacking the belief that agriculture benefited from protection and was greeted with respectful cheers and murmurs of assent. O'Connell, once he could make himself heard above the cheering, had his audience laughing, hissing, yelling and laughing again. His conclusion, that 'the sentiment of England is awakened and abroad; it never will sleep again until the poor are righted, and the rich compelled to be honest', was greeted with 'prolonged and most vehement cheering'.[20]

Wilson's commitment to *laissez-faire* – a doctrine that to twentieth-century susceptibilities seems ruthless – combined with his love of statistics and his unfailing passion for reason, were to lead later to the misconception that he was both dry and unfeeling, charges easily disproved by any sustained reading of his journalism. But on this occasion the highly emotional temperament that the economist kept under restraint completely burst its bonds: whatever irritation he might have felt was forgotten: 'It has seldom fallen to our lot to witness a scene so exciting, so sublime, as was the reception of Mr O'Connell at Covent Garden on Wednesday night... The manly generosity of Englishmen forgot everything but that before them stood a wronged and persecuted man.' And, betraying yet again his sanguine disposition, he continued: 'Let us hope that a new bond of union – no parchment union, but a union of hearts – between Ireland and England will arise from the affectionate reception of Ireland's chief in the capital of England. The interests of the two countries are identical; their grievances are nearly the same; and the same means – the united and firmly expressed determination of a great people – will obtain for them both, in peace, the acknowledgement of their rights and the redress of their wrongs.'[21] (In fact cheap bread was more important for the English poor than for the Irish, whose staple diet was the potato. The tragic irony was that the final spur to repeal the Corn Laws was to come from the fungal infection of the potato in 1845 that brought famine to Ireland.)

Such moments of near-abandon were rare. Wilson was never really at home with the League, being unhappy with what he termed the 'rubbish' spouted by its extremists as well as being by temperament unsuited to participation in a mass movement, however much he approved of it in principle. Yet he backed it loyally. As he put it in 1843 in a letter to Cobden, 'I feel that I, as little as any man, can be supposed to possess any feelings inimical to the League, after the unhesitating way in which from the first I have associated myself with it, – even when in the first place I differed with many of the grounds on which it sought its objects – but I always looked upon those objects as so important that I ever felt disposed to sink all minor considerations, feeling assured that in the discussions which must occur the truth whatever it was would at last be apparent.'[22]

Wilson admired, indeed loved, Cobden – described by Bagehot as a man of 'singular and most peculiar genius' – for his integrity, sensitivity and selflessness. And, although unimpressed by his administrative ability, he thought him 'most valuable in counsel, always original, always shrewd, and not at all extreme'.[23] For the League chairman, George Wilson, he also had great respect. Yet, having a horror of extremism, James Wilson found it distressing to be associated with an organisation whose supporters included the working-class radical Chartists, whose 'creeds and doings', according to one of his daughters, he considered near-criminal and inimical to real progress. In a letter to the League chairman late in 1841, he was preoccupied with the fear that, if rank-and-file supporters were not found an outlet for their energies, they might follow one of the Metropolitan Association's branches and 'run riot into the snivelling and clamorous arms of Chartists'.[24] So although he remained supportive of League and Association activities, Wilson's main work for the cause was conducted over dinners with public men or as a doughty fighter with the pen.

As his reputation and competence as a writer grew, so did his hunger to express himself in print. He wrote for the *Manchester Guardian*,[25] and for at least one Scottish newspaper (in Dundee), as well as for the *Examiner*, a radical intellectual paper owned and edited by a great and witty political journalist, Albany Fonblanque, which had been a powerful inspiration in the great debates of the 1820s and early 1830s about political reform. The world was changing around Fonblanque and the big issues of industrial and commercial policy were not those about which he passionately cared. He was friendly with Wilson and published some of his articles, but he found them too long and upset Wilson by cutting them or postponing publication. For Fonblanque to have given Wilson his head would have swamped his paper, altered it drastically and set up a rival guru in his own pages. But for Wilson, bursting with ideas perfectly in tune with the times and constantly receiving enthusiastic responses to his writing from great men, restrictions on space were acutely frustrating – especially since he was giving his services free. Early in 1843 he began to talk to intimates about setting up a paper of his own.

There was every reason to believe that a healthy market existed for the right product. The *Anti-Corn Law Circular* had a circulation of about 20,000 a week; the League had raised £50,000 and had distributed nine million copies of various anti-protectionist tracts; hundreds of well-attended meetings were being held up and down the country; Richard Cobden, elected to parliament, had taken over from Villiers the leadership of the campaign in the Commons – a development described as 'worth giving way to genius'. And although victory over the Corn Laws seemed not too far away, Wilson felt a strong need 'of a press organ, to maintain the principles of free trade in their widest sense, *apart from and independent of the great popular movement*'.[26] Additionally, this was a period of greatly increasing popularity – and hence prosperity – for the press. Although the stamp duty introduced on newspapers in 1815 was to remain in force until 1855, it had been reduced in 1836 from fourpence to one penny. The circulation of the largest selling daily, *The Times*, climbed from 10,000 in 1834 to 18,500 in 1840 and almost 40,000 ten years later.

There was nevertheless a large element of risk associated with setting up such a paper. For a man who had lost £25,000 only seven years previously, it required a lot of courage as well as optimism to gamble with the modest sum he had so painfully acquired in the meantime. Wilson had little experience as a journalist and none in financing, distribution or printing. In founding a substantial paper dealing with the economy, he would be inventing a new product. Yet the absence of competition was a tremendous bonus, he had belief in himself and he had the confidence of friends: during the spring of 1843 it was Radnor and Villiers who provided Wilson with the encouragement he needed. 'I am sure', wrote Villiers, 'there never was a time when an *independent* organ was more required. We are losing a valuable moment now in not working on the excitement produced in the last six months.' Radnor offered financial backing.

One major issue remained to be settled – the relationship with the League. In June 1843, telling his wife of conversations with Francis Place and Radnor about the paper, he reported: 'I then went to the Club and met Villiers by appointment; – we had a long gossip, and among other things about the paper. He is very fond of the thing, – but from what he said, I fear we shall have some difficulty with the League: – it appears they are extremely jealous of their importance and will want it ostensibly a League Paper, and as such I will have nothing to do with it. I will see Cobden and Villiers at the House to-morrow night on the subject.'[27]

After several conversations with Wilson and Villiers, Cobden wrote to Bright:

James Wilson has a plan for starting a weekly Free Trader by himself and his friends, to be superintended by himself. But he does not intend this unless he can have the support of the League, or at least its acquiescence. He has a notion that a paper would do more good if it were *not* the organ of the League, but merely their independent supporter. But then what is the League to do for an organ? If we start another weekly paper, it would clash with his. Villiers seems to have been rather taken with James Wilson's plan, and it would undoubtedly be desirable to have Wilson's pen at work.[28]

Cobden's initial fears that Wilson's paper might cut across League plans to improve the *Anti-Corn Law Circular* had been allayed by Wilson's assurance that he would aim it at the restricted audience of the landowning and mercantile élite, yet Cobden was still pessimistic about the paper's chances of success. 'I don't like to appear a croaker, though I do feel as one at times. From all that I can learn, Newspapers have been *graves to fortunes* in London, and as a rule those papers started for utility . . . have, without exception, failed. Have you made up your mind to a great and continued pecuniary loss?' Bright, Cobden reported, felt that Wilson would have more usefulness and influence writing in a League paper, 'but I don't like to say anything to discourage you'.

As early as April Wilson had reorganised his life to raise the money he would need. His main financial resources were tied up in his London and Dulwich houses, and he and his wife decided to cut household expenses by letting Dulwich and keeping only two staff in London; Mrs Wilson and their daughters would go to Boulogne for several months. In this way he managed to raise £800, which with a £500 loan from Radnor was enough to get the paper off the ground. The great advantage of having Radnor as the sole financial backer was, as Wilson wrote to his wife, that 'no question will ever arise as to the property, or to whom the benefit of the paper will belong after it shall have risen into a good circulation which I hope it may do in time'. It was to be 85 years before the paper passed out of the ownership of the Wilson family.

Anxious as he was to get the paper going, he was obliged to hold on until the relationship with the League had been sorted out. By late June he was reporting triumphantly to his wife that Cobden had come round completely and agreed that though the paper should be independent, the League should assist in promoting its circulation. 'I think with my great fund of commercial and statistical matter, and very original articles on Free Trade and Political

Economy, there is no danger but a good and attractive paper may be made. You know the facility with which I write on all these subjects, and with weekly practice that facility will increase, and my style will improve, although it is considered extremely good, clear and effective for such subjects at present.' His paper would not do as a League organ, for it 'must be perfectly philosophical, steady and moderate; – nothing but pure *principles*'. Within a few weeks, in August 1843, he had published the 'preliminary number and prospectus' of his weekly sixpenny paper, *The Economist: or The Political, Commercial, Agricultural, and Free-Trade Journal*.* Nowadays an 'economist' is a specialist in a recognised branch of academic knowledge: in James Wilson's world it applied to anyone who approached problems by putting every argument and doctrine to the test of the facts.

*The '*or The*' was altered to '*A*' in May 1844.

CHAPTER II

How

Wilson's intellect was essentially methodical in its habits, ever searching for first principles or fundamental axioms, and then applying them to practice and to actual circumstances. He was fond of trying practical dicta by the test of principle; if principle and practice failed to agree, he would deem that there must be some error in one or other of them, or perhaps in the application of one to the other. A principle, he thought, which is sound in one country must be equally sound in another; if after having succeeded in one place it is found to fail elsewhere, the failure does not prove its unsoundness, but only shows that it must have been erroneously applied to unsuitable circumstances.[1] *Sir Richard Temple, 1882*

'*The Economist*' was not an original title: in January 1821, another Scotsman, George Mudie – a follower of Robert Owen – had brought out a weekly paper of that name. By a delicious irony, the predecessor of the great *laissez-faire* paper was dedicated to utopian socialism. Mudie's paper survived for only a year and it is unlikely that James Wilson ever heard of it.*

The 'prospectus' for Wilson's *Economist* appeared at first glance serious to the point of being forbidding, consisting simply of an introductory article of just under twelve pages, followed by a two-page prospectus that was in effect a detailed table of contents. Liberally laced with the facts and statistics that

---

*Other less cerebral namesakes include the *Oeconomist, or Englishman's Magazine*, the 1799 issue of which included improving literature, extracts from 'Dr Willich's valuable Lectures on Diet and Regimen' and tips on how to avoid consumption; and *The Economist, and General Adviser*, which in the mid-1820s was concerned with domestic advice ranging from how to construct a rat-trap to how to remove chilblains: its 'Weekly Almanack' was crammed with a mélange of statistics on wholesale food prices. Emulators include *The Irish Economist*, which had a short life during the mid-nineteenth century.

Wilson believed were a prerequisite for the forming of sound opinions, the article was more than ten times the length of a leading article in today's *Economist*. It was in fact an historical and economic essay – a kind of mid-nineteenth-century 'Schools Brief' on free trade – which began arrestingly with a lament:

> It is one of the most melancholy reflections of the present day, that while wealth and capital have been rapidly increasing, while science and art have been working the most surprising miracles in aid of the human family, and while morality, intelligence, and civilization have been rapidly extending on all hands; – that at this time, the great material interests of the higher and middle classes, and the physical condition of the labouring and industrial classes, are more and more marked by characters of uncertainty and insecurity.

At the root of this problem, explained Wilson, lay commercial restrictions, all of which tended to 'raise up *barriers to intercourse, jealousies, animosities*, and *heartburnings* between *individuals* and *classes in this country*, and again between *this country* and *all others*'. Other countries had followed England's example of 'short-sighted selfishness', and the consequent threats to her markets and economic well-being led thoughtful men to pay attention to the hitherto neglected science of 'Political and Commercial Economy'. William Huskisson, President of the Board of Trade in the liberal Tory government of the 1820s, had seen that the central political issue was the struggle between – in Wilson's words – 'our rapidly-advancing productive power, earnestly demanding a larger field of exchange, and the principles of restriction and monopoly, blindly and vainly attempting to confine them to their ancient and narrow limit', and (in a telling phrase, very typical of Wilson's writing at its simplest and most powerful) 'that it was a severe contest between intelligence, which pressed forward, and an unworthy, timid ignorance obstructing our progress'.* Through a sustained reform of restrictive legislation and a significant reduction of import duties, Huskisson had brought prosperity, but his resignation in 1827 put a stop to progress and left free-traders without political leadership. In Wilson's view, the agitation for political reform was a distraction: 'the country totally forgot the *ends* of good government in the struggle for its *means*'. Not until the bad harvest of 1838 did free trade again

---

*This phrase has been enshrined on the contents page since 1991.

become an urgent public issue, as its restrictions were seen to work 'mischief to all, benefit to none'.

The remedy was, of course, free trade – particularly vital for Britain, because in no other country did 'so large a portion of the *population* and *property* depend on commerce and industry alone'. Wilson went on to make his case by close analysis and comparison of the effects on supply, demand and revenue of the high duties on sugar and wheat and the low duties on coffee and wool, concluding with the triumphant observation that at home and abroad it was the producers of the two protected interests (West Indian sugar and English wheat) that were in constant distress. How much worse, therefore, would conditions be if Huskisson's reforms had not taken place.

As was often the case with Wilson, a long passage of close economic analysis seemed to free him to take flight into eloquence. It was almost as if, for writer and reader alike, it was necessary to work hard at facts and figures before being permitted to give free rein to feeling: no one was allowed the pudding until he had eaten up his greens. Of all the hundreds of thousands of words Wilson wrote on the good that would be produced by the removal of all restrictions on trade, an almost orgasmic sentence (drastically shortened here) towards the end of his prospectus shows most graphically why a highly emotional man was prepared to dedicate his life to the application of an economic theory:

> If we would convert our increasing population into a source of increased moral and political greatness, instead of constant alarm and uneasiness . . . IF WE WOULD GIVE TO THE OWNER AND CULTIVATOR OF THE SOIL AT HOME THE BEST AND ONLY TRUE SECURITY FOR PROSPERING AMID, AND BY REASON OF, THE PROSPERITY OF THE GREAT COMMUNITY BY WHICH HE IS SO SURROUNDED; we must emancipate commerce and industry from those trammels and restrictions, with which short-sighted jealousies and unwise legislation have fettered them; feeling, at the same time, assured that mutual dependence is the only true and safest guarantee for independence.

It was to public opinion that *The Economist* would be looking to bring about this emancipation, for political parties and their leaders respond to the public will. The public mind was confused and ignorant: the upper classes were tutored in the dead languages, ancient philosophy and history, the middle classes in popular sciences, but no class had been taught 'the principles of

feeding the country, of conducting commerce, of securing national prosperity . . . These important duties have been left to mere accident; it had
indeed been well had ignorance been as unobtrusive, as intelligence has been
neglectful.'

With the country in such a bad state it was necessary for 'every man who
has a stake in the country . . . to investigate and learn for himself'. *The
Economist* had been organised to promote free-trade principles, to minister 'in
other useful ways to the material interests of the country . . . [and] the
advancement of commerce and industry in every form', to be 'a medium of
practical usefulness to commerce, manufactures, and agriculture, on a scale
not hitherto attempted' and also to give the political and general news of the
week.

Then came the prospectus proper, promising 1) original leading articles
applying free-trade principles 'most rigidly' to all the important questions of
the day; 2) articles on some practical, commercial, agricultural, or foreign
topics 'of passing interest; of the state of the revenue, foreign treaties, &c'; 3)
an article on the elementary principles of political economy; 4) parliamentary
reports; 5) free-trade popular-movement reports; 6) news of the week; 7)
commercial news, including market prospects, changes in fiscal regulations,
state of the money market and of railways and public companies; 8)
agricultural advice: 9) colonial and foreign information; 10) law reports; 11)
book reviews; 12) commercial gazette, to include current prices and statistics
of the week; 13) correspondence and answers to inquiries. Additionally, every
month there would be an extra number devoted exclusively to statistics and
the statistical parts of parliamentary papers.

Having briefly spelled out the paper's independence of party or class
interest, Wilson once again got carried away, this time into a peroration
explaining his motives:

> If we look abroad, we see within the range of our commercial intercourse
> whole islands and continents, on which the light of civilization has scarce yet
> dawned; and we seriously believe that FREE TRADE, free intercourse, will do
> more than any other visible agent to extend civilization and morality
> throughout the world – yes, to extinguish slavery itself. Then, if we look
> around us at home, we see ignorance, depravity, immorality, irreligion,
> abounding to an extent disgraceful to a civilized country; and we feel assured
> that there is little chance of successfully treating this great national disease

while want and pauperism so much abound . . . we look mainly to an improvement in the condition of the people. And we hope to see the day when it will be as difficult to understand how an act of parliament could have been made to restrict the food and employment of the people, as it is now to conceive how the mild, inoffensive spirit of Christianity could ever have been converted into the plea of persecution and martyrdom, or how poor old wrinkled women, with a little eccentricity, were burned by our forefathers for witchcraft.

(Almost 150 years later, under the editorship of Rupert Pennant-Rea, a passionate free-trader, a leading article in 1992 attacking protectionism was a great deal snappier, if rather less fun, reflecting the far more standardised style of a product adapted to a much less individualistic age.

> In trade policy, no government is blameless. For reasons that political economists have understood for centuries, almost every government succumbs to pressure from special interests demanding protection from foreign competition: losses may outweigh gains, but those who stand to gain are usually vocal and well-organised, whereas those who stand to lose are not. This protectionist logic works everywhere. America has resisted it better than most. For years it championed the cause of freer trade through the General Agreement on Tariffs and Trade (GATT). Decades of American leadership after 1945 opened markets worldwide. In miserable contrast, the European Community has written the book on new methods of protection.[2]

Yet, quite apart from the 1992 article's uncompromising defence of freer trade and the good it would bring the world, what was even more redolent of Wilson's vision was the accompanying cover picture of a happy, healthy and, no doubt, morally-upright worker in a hard hat with a hammer over his shoulder, smiling broadly under the caption 'GATT WILL BUILD THE WORLD'.)

Even by Victorian standards, James Wilson's prose was often unusually reminiscent of the pulpit. Where other journalists (for instance, leader writers on *The Times*), might moralise, he was evangelical – a deeply religious man whose religion was *laissez-faire*, whose Holy Book was *The Wealth of Nations* and whose Holy Grail was free trade. He believed in God – or rather took God's existence for granted – but carried no torch for any sectarian deity. True to form, even when it came to matters ecclesiastical he was in favour of competition; he did not believe any church had a monopoly of the truth. As if to prove this, the Quaker-turned-Anglican chose the text with which his prospectus began from the writings of contemporary Scotland's most illustrious Calvinist and famous preacher, Thomas Chalmers, who had just led a revolt against government-dictated aristocratic ecclesiastical patronage, and, with 470 other ministers, had set up the Free Church of Scotland. Chalmers's *On Political Economy*, published in 1832, applied Christian ethics to economics, and like Wilson, Chalmers believed that to prosper, a man must be self-reliant. Although the paragraph Wilson quoted had nothing to do with religion, it had everything to do with evangelising.

> If a writer be conscious that to gain a reception for his favourite doctrine he must combat with certain elements of opposition, in the taste, or the pride, or the indolence of those whom he is addressing, this will only serve to make him the more importunate. *There is a difference between such truths as are merely of a speculative nature and such as are allied with practice and moral feeling. With the former all repetition may be often superfluous; with the latter it may just be by earnest repetition that their influence comes to be thoroughly established over the mind of an inquirer.*

(When Chalmers died, *The Economist* praised him for turning against the idea of state aid for religion, for 'the doctrine of *laissez-faire* is equally true in religion and in buying and selling'.)[3]

It was an honest prospectus – honest to a fault in the eyes of Richard Cobden, who was alarmed both by its tone and by the speed with which Wilson had prepared it. He wrote begging Wilson to hold it back until agreement was reached with the leaders of the League. 'I find a strong current against your plan running in the minds of the Leaders; not stronger than in my own mind previous to our last interview, when you convinced me that your plan was the best. Had you shown me the Prospectus before convincing me, I should have been harder to convince – this is *human* and the nature of the Manchester people is *not* superhuman, and their weakness must be regarded. Don't therefore put out your Prospectus until we are fully agreed among ourselves. It can be done, but we must not risk failure by precipitation . . . The first thing asked by the Free-Trade party throughout the Provinces will be "Is this paper recommended by the League?"'[4]

A century later, one of Wilson's most distinguished successors, Geoffrey Crowther, wrongly described *The Economist* as having been, in its early months, 'virtually a house organ of the Anti-Corn Law League'. (Closer to the truth is one historian's contention that it and Edward Baines's *Leeds Mercury* were 'in a sense outriders for the Manchester School'.[5]) Cobden's problem with his colleagues arose precisely because it was not: it was all too clear from Wilson's prospectus that his independence would be as unshakable as his beliefs and that even his own side might find some of his ideas unpalatable. However, Wilson held back and Cobden, in late August and after a lot of effort, persuaded the League Council to agree unanimously to distribute 20,000 copies of the prospectus to leading figures in Manchester and other Lancashire towns.[6]

This was the crucial breakthrough, for, although there was no direct financial benefit, the market outside London opened up. Cobden continued to play his part nobly; a surviving letter to one Robert Haywood of Bolton – to whom he had sent the prospectus – asked him to subscribe and referred to Wilson as 'our early & staunch friend & ally', who would have such control over the paper 'as to be a guarantee for the soundness of its principles & secure it against any party influence'. The letter was presumably one of many.[7]

As a piece of propaganda the prospectus was to prove a stunning success, continuing in demand for several months. (In December Wilson reported that the first impression of over 40,000 being exhausted, he was reprinting 30,000.) But it by no means generated enough subscribers to guarantee that the paper would succeed: indeed it had been in circulation for only a matter of days when *The Economist* first came out on Saturday, 2 September. Leading with more than two pages on 'OUR EXPIRING COMMERCIAL TREATY WITH THE BRAZILS', it made even fewer concessions to its readers than had the prospectus. But to strengthen their resolve there was another text, which took precedence over that of Dr Chalmers and came from another of Wilson's heroes, the political thinker and proponent of ordered liberty, Edmund Burke:

> If we make ourselves too little for the sphere of our duty – if, on the contrary, we do not stretch and expand our minds to the compass of their object – be well assured that everything about us will dwindle by degrees, until at length our concerns are shrunk to the dimensions of our minds. *It is not a predilection to mean, sordid, home-bred cares that will avert the consequence of a false estimation of our interest, or prevent the shameful dilapidation into which a great empire must fall by mean reparation upon mighty ruins.*

(Burke's and Chalmers's epigraphs were to keep their places respectively above and below the table of contents until the end of 1844, when Burke was removed and sent to grace the title page of the annual bound volume and Chalmers was consigned to oblivion.)

Wilson's inexperience showed in the first issue and Cobden, worried, sent him a few hasty tips. 'I find in it a great deal of useful matter', he wrote. 'Can there be a sufficient number of readers with intelligence to appreciate it found to make such a paper pay? . . . First article is too long. It would have been better in *two*. The Brazilian article should have commenced at the top of the second page. The style of this article is too much of an essay for a newspaper. *There should be no preface to a leader*.'[8] John Bright praised 'its business department and arrangement', recommended 'making more of a separation from the preceding part when commencing the articles' and gave it publicity by quoting *Economist* statistics at a public meeting. Wilson noted gratefully 'the very handsome way' in which the provincial press, particularly the *Leeds Mercury*, had noticed the paper.

Presentational aspects of the paper improved as Wilson put good advice into effect, but overall the first issues – unsurprisingly – give an impression of strain. It was not until he was sure the paper would survive that Wilson could take the risk of giving up his hat business, so he had the almost impossible task of running that while producing his weekly paper almost single-handed from his premises at 6 Wellington Street, off the Strand, not far from the City. The only regular contributor in that period of whom anything is known was his wife's brother-in-law, the Reverend William Thorpe, Vicar of Bawtry in Yorkshire, who owned coalfields and was a student of chemistry. On the basis of those credentials Wilson had confidently asked him to provide articles on 'agricultural improvements, geology, agricultural chemistry, etc.', and he provided the occasional article and book review. But, apart from clerical help, the paper was virtually all written and put together by Wilson. According to Bagehot, he used to superintend everything, 'to write all the important leaders, nearly all of the unimportant ones; to make himself master of every commercial question as it arose; to give practical details as to the practical aspects of it; to be on the watch for every kind of new commercial information; to spend hours in adapting it to the daily wants of commercial men. He often worked till far into the morning, and impressed all about him with wonder at the anxiety, labour, and exhaustion he was able to undergo.'

With insufficient help and a fixed number of pages to fill, it was inevitable that recourse was made to padding: for instance, of thirty columns of text in the second issue, six went to books, four of these going to a review of a book called *Personal Recollections of Sindh* ('Of the seven-and-twenty millions who inhabit the British Isles, we will venture to say, not one-twentieth ever heard of Sindh, or knows that about six months ago, at the expense of two battles, much blood, and great treasure, that country was added to our already overgrown Indian possessions. As it belongs to us, however, we may as well know a little about it, and the way in which we got it.') Almost two columns were devoted to crime (Miss Eliza Tabitha Tooth, charged with disturbing a congregation attached to the Wesleyan Chapel in Stoke Newington, was declared by her lawyer to be 'labouring under a delusion which he himself believed to be wholly unfounded, that the members of the congregation had entered into a conspiracy to render her unhappy and miserable'); two to 'Miscellanea' ('A CONCLUSIVE ARGUMENT.– On Sunday, while an itinerant preacher was holding forth at the Broomielaw Quay, on the end of an empty sugar hogshead, near York street, the end of it unfortunately gave way, and the speaker was precipitated to the ground inside the barrel, to the no small astonishment of his auditors, from many of whom his body went entirely out of sight for a few minutes. The circumstances, although no laughing matter to the poor preacher, caused considerable amusement, from the fact that he was lecturing on the passage, "It is easier for a camel to go through the eye of a needle," &c.–*Glasgow Chronicle*.'); three to 'COURT AND ARISTOCRACY' ('WOBURN ABBEY.– The Duke and Duchess of Bedford intend to have company at the Abbey from the week after next until the end of October; and her Royal Highness the Duchess of Gloucester has accepted an invitation from the noble Duke and Duchess, when a distinguished circle will assemble to meet the Royal Duchess. There is a rumour that private theatricals will form part of the amusement provided by the Duke and Duchess at the Abbey for their visitors.'); one column to 'THE METROPOLIS' ('HORSELYDOWN REGATTA.– The annual regatta amongst the free watermen plying at the Old Stairs, was contested on Wednesday, and was in many respects superior to the generality of stairs' wagers.'); a half column to 'THE PROVINCES' ('THE RURAL POLICE.– There appears to be a strong feeling against the continuance of the rural police in Warwickshire, but especially in the neighbourhood of Birmingham.'); and there was a smattering of births, deaths, marriages and bankrupts. It must have been a great relief on both financial and space-filling counts when advertisements spread from the back page into the second last

('H. WALKER'S NEEDLES (by authority the "Queen's own"), in the illustrated Chinese boxes, are now in course of delivery to the trade. The needles
have large eyes, easily threaded, (even by blind persons), and improved
points, temper, and finish. Each paper is labelled with a likeness of Her
Majesty or His Royal Highness Prince Albert, in relief on coloured
grounds.')

The degree to which the paper improved during the next few years is
remarkable: five years on there was not a wasted line. But in the early months
only a few pages of *The Economist* offered material not obtainable from other
newspapers, and much of this was so esoteric as to be unreadable except by a
tiny percentage of readers. In the issue of September 9, the leading articles
were 'RENEWED COMMERCIAL NEGOTIATIONS WITH PORTUGAL';
'MONEY MANIA' (an attack on those urging a vast increase in the issue of
'inconvertible bank notes'); the Reverend Thorpe on 'THE INDICATIONS
WHICH ARE GUIDES IN JUDGING OF THE FERTILITY OR BARRENNESS
OF THE SOIL'; and 'PRODUCTION OF BEET-ROOT AND CONSUMPTION
OF SUGAR IN THE STATES OF THE GERMAN CUSTOMS UNION' (which
ranks with 'THE ECONOMY OF MANURES' as one of *The Economist*'s great
off-putting headlines). In addition there was a short letter from America, a
few columns of useful foreign and domestic commercial, political and
free-trade related news, and almost three columns of valuable statistics on
markets. In fact the paper was a confusing mixture of the invaluable and the
irrelevant.

Apart from the statistics and the free-trade coverage, what made *The
Economist* work even at the beginning was the sheer vigour of Wilson's
intellect, for there was no issue of the paper so weak that it did not yield an
arresting argument, a provocative interpretation or an enlivening attack. On
23 September, for instance, there was a sour little gem tucked away in amid
the foreign news: 'There has been a revolutionary movement in Hayti, and
the black government, in imitation of more important portions of the *white*
world, has issued its manifesto, protesting, in high phrase, its own purity of
motive, and calling on the people to submit to an authority which only exists
for their good.' (Wilson's great amiability was most at risk from anything that
smacked of cant.) And twice in that month he defended head-on a position
that many free-traders shirked – that it was right to trade freely with
countries that still had slaves. (The slave trade had been banned in 1807 and
slavery in the British colonies had been ended in 1833.)

Wilson was never to show the slightest difficulty in reconciling free trade with any moral position whatsoever and was therefore glad, he explained two weeks after founding *The Economist*, to be called on to justify his position on slavery. He made a distinction between the two classes of critics of his position: 'two classes who have always hitherto been so much opposed to each other, that it would have been very difficult ten years since to have conceived any possible combinations of circumstances that could have brought them to act in concert: we mean the West India interest, who so violently opposed every step of melioration to the slave from first to last; and that body of *truly great philanthropists* who have been unceasing in their efforts to abolish slavery wherever and in whatever form it was to be found. To the latter alone we shall address our remarks'.

Their argument he understood to be 'that having once abolished slavery in our own dominions we ought to interdict the importation of articles produced by slave labour in other countries, in order to coerce them, for the sake of their trade with us, to follow our example'. He hoped *The Economist* would be among the last ever to be found 'advocating the continuance of slavery, or opposing any *legitimate* means for its extinction', but felt sure that those adopting 'the opinion quoted above, have little considered either the consequences or the tendencies of the policy they support'. A ban would have to apply as much to gold, silver and copper from Brazil as to sugar and coffee, to cotton, rice, indigo and so on from the Southern states of America as well as to the sugar and cotton of Cuba, thus excluding the raw materials on which millions in Lancashire and Yorkshire depended for a living. Further, in order to avoid providing Brazil with the means to use its slave labour, it would be necessary to ban the export to Brazil of the implements of labour – materials, clothing, food and luxuries. This would also hit British shipping: 'consistency, therefore, requires equally the abandonment of all export trade to slave-producing countries, as it does of the import of their produce; and the effect will carry us even further'. It would also only be right to abandon any trade or manufacture made from slave-grown cotton and so on, so about a half of the present foreign trade even with free-labour countries would have to go: 'when men are prepared and conceive it a duty to urge the accomplishment of all these results, they may then consistently oppose the introduction of Brazilian sugar and coffee and support the present West India monopoly; but not till then'.

There was the additional argument that protecting free-labour societies would incline the Brazilians to believe that we were wrong in saying that free labour is actually cheaper than slave labour. 'We firmly believe that free labour properly exercised, is cheaper than slave labour, but there is no pretence to say that it is so at this moment in our West India colonies; and we undertake to show, in an early number, in connexion with this fact, *that the existence of the high protecting duties on our West India produce has done more than anything else to endanger the whole experiment of emancipation.*' He reported from a recent conversation in Amsterdam the view of a large slave-owner from Dutch Guyana – that it would be impossible to emancipate slaves there while the differential duties on sugar were maintained, 'but abandon your differential duties, give us the same price for our produce, and thus enable us to pay the same rate of wages, and I, for one, will not object to liberate my slaves to-morrow'.

In Wilson's view, 'an entire free trade would do more than any other act to encourage an adoption of our example everywhere'. He finished with a denunciation of well-meant actions that prove counter-productive. Had

> the professors of these opinions ever considered the huge responsibility which they arrogate to themselves by such a course? Let these men remember that, by seeking to coerce the *slave-labour producer* in distant countries, they inflict a severe punishment on the millions of hard-working, ill-fed *consumers* among their fellow countrymen; their own neighbour, whose condition it is their *first* duty to consult and watch: – duty as well as charity ought to be first exercised at home. That is a very doubtful humanity which exercises itself on the uncertain result of influence indirectly produced upon governments in the other hemisphere of the globe, and neglects, nay sacrifices, the interests of the poor and helpless around our own doors, – not only by placing the necessaries of life beyond their reach, but at the same time destroying the demand for their labour by which alone they can obtain them.

He was happy for individuals with conscientious scruples to boycott slave-produce, but, he concluded, wielding the bludgeon even more vigorously, 'do not let them seek to inflict *certain* punishment, and the whole train of vice and misery consequent on starvation and want of employment, upon their poorer neighbours, for the purpose of conferring some *speculative* advantage on the slaves of the Brazils or elsewhere: no man can be called upon as a duty to do so great a present evil, in order to accomplish some distant good, however great – or however certain'.[9]

(More than 140 years later the thrust of the paper's argument on sanctions differed only in detail and in being strengthened by historical evidence. Loathing apartheid, tyranny and cruelty just as Wilson had done, *The Economist* generally – though not dogmatically – opposed sanctions as impracticable and demonstrated a Wilsonian contempt for those who sacrificed innocent people for the sake of moral complacency.[10] Sanctions on South Africa, remarked a leader sub-heading, 'Should be about apartheid, not about feeling good'.[11] The objection was not to the principle of sanctions, but they had 'a dismal record'.

> They are a legitimate way of expressing distaste or despair, but they rarely change the things that cause those feelings. They can all too often be evaded. They sometimes stiffen the backs of the sanctioned and spawn dissent among the sanctioners. Once applied, they are embarrassing to remove if they turn out not to have worked. Yet they remain one of the few extensions of diplomacy available to governments short of war.[12]

Effectiveness was the only criterion the paper recognised as valid. And here it provided its traditional service and investigated the facts. In 1985, in 'WHEN SANCTIONS MAKE SENSE', the 'World Business' section distilled the findings of a scholarly investigation of economic sanctions imposed since 1914 which categorised sanctions according to five objectives and adjudicated on their success or failure. *The Economist*'s contribution was to provide an elaborate score-card for ten out of 108 cases, which in its deployment of relevant statistics differed from the Wilson approach only in its late-twentieth-century sophistication.[13]

In September 1985 President Reagan approved a package of measures against apartheid which included the restriction of certain exports to South Africa: 'No indication was given of what specific reforms the measures are supposed to enforce or what strategy America will follow to secure their enforcement . . . They are so mild as to be little more than a gesture of disapproval, at best a signal that worse will come if the pace of reform does not increase. But worse what?'

The leading article built on the information provided the previous month and tried further to clarify the issue by sketching in the historical context in a few pithy paragraphs:

> Ever since President Jefferson tried to embargo trade with Britain in 1807 –

leading an exasperated American treasury secretary to declare, 'I prefer war to embargo' – America has been a pre-eminent imposer of economic sanctions. Recent victims include Russia, Poland, Afghanistan, Cuba, Nicaragua and now South Africa. Most victim nations are inconvenienced and would prefer the sanctions lifted. Disobedient schoolboys rarely enjoy being beaten. But how much, if at all, will they change in order to avoid pain?

Trade and financial measures against Italy during the Abyssinia crisis of 1935–36 – the first use of international economic sanctions in modern times – led to a plummeting of Italy's exchange reserves but did not liberate the Abyssinians. Sanctions against Rhodesia sapped it of hard currency by scaring away foreign investors and by causing it to sell cheap and buy dear, but it was black armed struggle and world recession which finally felled the white regime. American sanctions against Cuba impoverished the country, but drove it into the arms of the Soviet Union which has sustained Fidel Castro as Latin America's most secure ruler of modern times. The sports embargo against South Africa closed most international competition to its players. Some sports became multiracial. But since the embargo was not lifted, the sanction became a gesture.

The best economic sanctions were those which were specific and imposed by powerful states on normally friendly allies, as with the American financial squeeze that induced Britain to abandon its 1956 Suez adventure.[14]

Pragmatic as ever, in May 1990, the paper scrutinised the issue particularly hard after President de Klerk's release of Nelson Mandela from prison. It recommended playing the sanctions card if that would 'help both these brave men' – a difficult problem, since Mandela needed them kept on to help him to maintain his dominance within the African National Congress, while de Klerk wanted them lifted so as to demonstrate to white sceptics that his policies were bringing tangible rewards. The solution suggested was for the West to help both by saying it would scrap sanctions when three of Mandela's demands had been met: the ending of the state of emergency, the freeing of political prisoners and the allowing home of exiles.[15] In December 1990, with these three things done, the paper recommended immediate lifting of sanctions. The difference from Wilson's approach had been only that Wilson could never have imagined any circumstances in which the sacred tenets of free trade could be set aside even temporarily.)

Wilson's courage never faltered, but the paper's first year cost him dearly.

'Our public men do not know what anxiety means', Wilson – himself by then a public man – was later to say to Walter Bagehot; 'they have never known what it is to have their own position dependent on their own exertions.' He had indeed put everything on the line, the prosperity of his family, the investment of his friend, and his already weakened reputation as a man of business. For the best part of a year, Bagehot noted, Wilson had 'to bear extreme labour and great anxiety together; and even his iron frame was worn and tried by the conjunction'.

Consistently Wilson improved *The Economist*: more and better statistics offered a comprehensive and systematic weekly survey of economic data and such additional features as full copies of commercial treaties made the paper increasingly an invaluable record of the commercial world. Simultaneously, as he expanded coverage of the free-trade movement, which was entering a new phase of popularity, he sought a way of capitalising financially on the relationship between League and paper without in any way compromising his independence. In November 1843 he spelled out to his readers that 'as a journal we are quite independent of the League, and in no way connected with it . . . Still our object is identical. We have laboured, and we *will continue* to labour to maintain and advance, in our own way, those great principles for which we believe, for which we know the League to be single-minded, earnest, and honest advocates.'[16] Yet circumstances made matters rather less simple. The following month Wilson sent Cobden an enormously long, verbose and agonising 'strictly private' analysis of the relationship between the paper and the League along with proposals for the future. He reminded Cobden that during the previous summer he had come to agree with Villiers and Wilson about the 'need of a press organ, to maintain the principles of free trade in their widest sense, *apart from and independent of the great popular movement* . . . I think all that has occurred since, and what we have reasonably to look forward to, in the future, can only tend to confirm those opinions.' The object of the paper could be achieved only 'in the exact proportion in which it is, in the public estimation at least – kept distinct from the League.– Its influence and advantage to the League itself – can only be in proportion as it is known to be distinct.'

There was little doubt that *The Economist* would be of assistance to the League in influencing public opinion and forming a legislative party to pursue first, repeal of the Corn Laws and then, 'the long train of measures and policy, necessarily involved in free-trade principles: – for we must remember that our efforts though apparently at present confined only to one simple act of plain justice – yet in their ultimate tendencies, aim at a change and reform the most extensive that ever was accomplished in the system of a great country:– but a change so plainly to the best interests of all partners, that nothing can resist our success if persevered in'. He was hearing from many men the view that the most profitable use of League funds would be to circulate *The Economist* widely – 'but in such a way as to be least exposed to a supposition' that it was owned by, or dependent on, the League.

Having talked to Henry Warburton (MP, free-trader, philosophical radical and prominent member of the Reform Club) and several others, Wilson had concluded that what was needed was to widen the circulation of the paper, for 'people say that it only requires that it should be known to secure a circulation'. If a '*judicious* circulation were made for a period of *2 or 3 mo*: it seems to be the opinion of those who have suggested the plan that a large portion would continue as subscribers'. If the League were to circulate even one to two thousand a week for two months or so among leading merchants, politicians and parliamentarians, 'it would be a very extensive dissemination of the principles where they would be most likely to take effect': 2,000 for two months would cost only £320.

'It is only however on the ground that the Council of the League may think this a useful way of spending such a sum, that I think they *would ever be justified* in doing it;– & if they do it, there should be no communication with me on the subject, but every means used, that can properly be done to keep the two papers in the public eye, distinct;– and nothing would serve the object of the paper or the cause itself, that had a different effect.' His letter should be kept 'as strictly private communication between us', as there were many on the council, 'and many of our most useful and best friends on whose discretion, neither of us would like to risk much'. Whatever happened, he would 'persevere with the "E" as long as I think it prudent to do so – I have no idea of giving it up at present'.

Wilson kept back the letter for further heartsearching and then sent it with an endorsing postscript that ended bullishly: 'We have a great field opening before us – and with a little patience and perseverance this country will set the example and lead all others to free-trade – *everything tends to this.*'[17]

But most of the letter was uncharacteristically full of repetition, crossings-out and even hints of self-doubt. Indeed were it not for the steady handwriting and Wilson's frequent endorsements of the temperance movement, it would be tempting to guess that worry had driven him to over-indulge at the Reform Club. For, despite the brave words, sales were disappointing and the paper's future was in jeopardy. The paradox was that he could save the paper by making it a League organ, but if it became a League organ it would not be worth saving. The proposed compromise was an uneasy one – and required two honest men to come perilously close to deceit – but it seemed the best available.

As usual, Cobden did his best, but the League Council was slower and less generous than Wilson had hoped. By April, Wilson had exhausted all the money he and Radnor had put into *The Economist* and his friends were mounting a rescue operation. Average weekly circulation in 1843 had been only 1,969 (*Punch* was 3,938 and the *Spectator* 3,557) and in 1844 it was continuing to drop.[18] Henry Warburton wrote to the banker and free-trader, Samuel Loyd, that 'to pay the first cost', it would be necessary to increase circulation by 1,500 copies, yielding £1,500. It looked as if the League and the Liverpool free-traders together would take 500 and Henry Labouchere (Whig ex-President of the Board of Trade) thirty.

After further negotiations, Warburton reported that it would be possible to raise the £750 necessary to keep the paper afloat, with £200 from the League, £25 from Thomas Thornely, a Liverpool merchant, £30 from Labouchere and £145 from Warburton himself. He expected to succeed in raising the remaining £350 from the forty people to whom he was applying. The money would go on distributing 1,500 copies free for six months to potential purchasers. 'Such gratuitous distribution, continued for a time, is understood to be the only effective mode of advertizing a new Newspaper.' An additional plan, suggested by Charles Villiers, was 'for several Gentlemen, Mr Villiers, Mr Thornely, Mr Strutt [Radical MP], and others to write a letter, to be circulated among the presumed friends to the principles of the paper, recommending it to their attention'. Apologising for asking Loyd to sign, Warburton observed that he thought *The Economist* 'creditably conducted; and that at a time when the friends of free trade can find scarcely an unexceptionable channel open to them for the promulgation of their opinions. Villiers, Thornely, and your h.s. [humble servant] are to meet at the Reform Club at 3 o'clock on Friday to consider what can be done.'

The proposed letter ran:

To the Editor of the Economist Newspaper.–

Dear Sir,

In answer to the wish you have expressed, to learn our opinion respecting the Economist Newspaper, as an organ of sound Commercial and Financial views, we have no hesitation in saying, that in this respect it meets with our entire approval. The principles it propounds are those of the best School of Political Economy, and they are illustrated with a fullness of detail, an accuracy, and a power that we have not seen before in any Newspaper.–

We think the paper calculated to be of great service in removing objections honestly entertained by some to the policy of free-trade, and in affording replies to misstatements purposely made by others in support of Monopoly.

We should say, particularly, that the clear and useful way in which the Economist applies principles to practical purposes, added to the great precision of its current information, must render it a publication of the greatest utility to Bankers and Merchants. We shall be very glad to know of its success.[19]

The paper was kept afloat: average weekly circulation in 1845 rose to 2,894. Within a short time Wilson was confident enough to give up his manufacturing business and invest the bulk of his capital in the paper, though he continued with the *Manchester Guardian* and added to his income for a while by providing leaders and the City article for the *Morning Chronicle*. In mid-1846, with the repeal of the Corn Laws, the paper secured another boost. The League was dissolved, its journal ceased publication and all subscribers were sent a circular signed by the League's leaders recommending them to support *The Economist*:* in 1847 circulation peaked at 4,483 and over the next few years settled at around 3,500.† Advertising revenue

*This was the third use by the infant *Economist* of what are now standard marketing techniques: the promotional free or cut-price subscriptions, the celebrity endorsement and the wooing of the subscribers of an expiring publication.

†Although there are no circulation figures for 1854–75, it seems probable that the 1847 figure was not exceeded until 1913. Comparisons with other journals are revealing.
1843 – *Economist* 1,969, *Punch* 3,938, *Spectator* 3,557;
1848 – *Economist* 4,245, *Punch* 7,366, *Spectator* 3,283;
1853 – *Economist* 4,106, *Punch* 7,567, *Spectator* 2,817. In 1993 *The Economist*'s circulation exceeded 500,000; *Punch*, which had failed to adapt to changing taste, had distinguished itself in 1991 by celebrating its 150th birthday and going out of business; the *Spectator*, 165 years old, was on a circulation of around 44,000.

became correspondingly healthy: within a couple of years of its foundation, the paper was furnishing Wilson with a comfortable living. But without Wilson's friends it almost certainly would have foundered: he was too strong-minded to yield to the temptation to sell the paper's soul to the League. It is ironic that the apostle of self-reliance had to fall back on the charity of friends, but since he was a man without false pride, and since his friends were all fighting for the same cause, he was able to accept their help without shame.

That the paper almost went under during its first year was kept quiet. There is no account of any early troubles in the two volumes by Wilson's hagiographer and youngest daughter, Emilie Barrington; indeed in 1928 she stated that 'Contrary to Cobden's fears, *The Economist* had at once a large circulation, and in a short time my father was able to repay what Lord Radnor had kindly advanced.'[20] It may be that Wilson kept the children in ignorance, or it may be family piety: either way it has led to a degree of misinformation. Yet it is clear from Bagehot's discreet but honest memoir that to him Wilson confided something of what he went through.

Too magnanimous a man to resent his benefactors, Wilson's gratitude to Cobden and Villiers was intense. Shortly after the Corn Laws had been repealed, in 1846, he attended a London meeting to promote the Cobden Testimonial. (Cobden's work for the campaign had brought him close to financial ruin: £75,000 was ultimately raised by public subscription.) After reprinting and endorsing 'with great pleasure' the effusive resolutions passed in honour first of Cobden and then of Villiers, he concluded: 'Whatever other names may be justly associated with the repeal of the Corn Laws, and the triumph of free trade, the two which will ever stand foremost and united, alike in the grateful recollections of their countrymen, and in the page of history, will be those of, VILLIERS and COBDEN.'[21] Villiers, like Radnor, was forever to be an object of Wilson's admiration and affection, but his relationship with Cobden was to be destroyed by the Crimean War.

CHAPTER III:

Setting the course

Wilson was a sort of grand journeyman acting upon other persons' ideas.[1]
Spectator

'The extensive and increasing support which this Journal is receiving from
the leading Mercantile, Banking, and Manufacturing Classes, without reference to political party,' Wilson wrote proudly in the final issue of 1844, 'has
induced a constantly increasing care to render the Commercial Department
of the paper as complete and accurate as possible, and thus to combine, with
the discussion of principles, a practical current usefulness, and work of future
reference.' Henceforward, the title of the paper would change from *The
Economist: A Political, Commercial, Agricultural, & Free-Trade Journal* to *The
Economist, Weekly Commercial Times, and Bankers' Gazette. A Political, Literary,
and General Newspaper.*

It was a change that positively trumpeted the extent to which the paper had
found a cohesion, a market and a loyal readership who made clear in
correspondence their appetite for more and more solid information.
Opinions there would always be in plenty in *The Economist*, but what gave it
its primary appeal to men of business was what Bagehot described as Wilson's
'habit of always beginning with the facts, always arguing from the facts, and
always ending with a result applicable to the facts [which] obtained for his
writings an influence and a currency more extensive than would have been
anticipated for any writings on political economy'. No abstract thinker, he
saw political economy as the science of buying and selling, and he wrote
about it in a way that made sense to businessmen.

One of Wilson's great gifts was what Bagehot called 'business-
imagination', which 'enabled him to see "what men did," and "why they did

it"; "why they ought to do it," and "why they ought not to do it."' It was a quality he shared with Cobden. In writing of both of them² Bagehot quoted the remark of the politician and writer Lord Houghton, that in his time 'political economy books used to begin, Suppose a man upon an island', but he observed that neither Cobden nor Wilson did this. Cobden spoke to men of business as a man of business: Wilson wrote 'What they *do* in the city is this' and proved himself a master at making intelligible the 'middle principles' of economics. Most people have no use for the 'extreme abstractions' of any science, pointed out Bagehot, even if they could understand them, but the 'intermediate maxims' are easily understood and easily used. Wilson himself, although 'he did not deny the utility of theoretical refinements . . . habitually and steadily avoided them'. He was a practical man explaining to an audience of practical men those aspects of economics that had practical value; and by applying them to facts he was making the case for the doctrines he wished to disseminate. 'Whether Mr. Wilson was exactly a great writer we will not discuss', said Bagehot, giving the game away. He was not: indeed over-ambition could lead him seriously astray, as with a New Year leader whose opening sentence ran: 'As time pursues her noiseless path, it is a useful thing that periods arrive in the conventional divisions into which mankind, by common assent, have marked the year, when the mind is peculiarly prone, not only to lay plans for the future, but to mark well the experience of the past, – when *anticipation*, however buoyant or sanguine, feels need of the assistance and guide of *retrospection* to determine the principles which shall regulate the practice of the future.' Such lapses were infrequent: for the most part Wilson wrote simply, vigorously and convincingly. Among his admirers was the Duke of Wellington, the practical man *par excellence*, who, although no free-trader, thought highly of Wilson's writings. In later years Wilson was given the job of persuading the Duke in person that the Navigation Laws should be repealed.*³

The nearest that Wilson came to abstraction was in his impassioned defences of his economic beliefs, which he found misinterpreted and defamed

---

*The seventeenth-century Navigation Laws had been modified by the 1840s, but still specified that many products, including grain and wine, could be carried from Europe only by British ships; there was similar protection for British and colonial shipowners in the conduct of trade among the colonies and between them and Britain. Wilson was one of the earliest free-traders to demand the laws' abolition, which he supported in a major speech in the House of Commons in March 1849. They were repealed in 1850.

on all sides. Typical was his anger with *The Times* – a newspaper which seemed to annoy him more than any other and which at various times he accused of hypocrisy, woolly-mindedness and downright inaccuracy.

'Confess the plain fact,' began an 1845 *Times* leader addressed to economists, 'political economy won't do . . . The science may be bottomed in truth, and it may also admit of earthly realization AD 2500. But if you wish yourselves or your grandchildren to see the fruit of your labours, you must cut across. At present the science is neither popular nor effectual. It neither secures the affections, nor raises the wages. It has had a fairish trial, both in talk and legislation, these dozen years; the result is, the Whigs are out, and the agricultural labourers, the chief victims of the experiment, are considerably worse off than ever.'[4]

'This writing is not conceived in an honest spirit', responded Wilson. 'If political economy will admit of realization AD 2500, it does so *now*, and the writer in the *Times* knows it does. To the assertion that political economy – meaning by that word the science propounded by Malthus, Adam Smith, Ricardo, and others – has been applied, "has had a fairish trial, both in talk and legislation, these dozen years" – to that assertion there is only one word in the English language that could be used in giving an answer; but it isn't worth using hard words about the matter. "The Whigs are out," not because they were guided in their conduct by a sound political economy, but because they were *not*.'

The Times had gone on to argue that the only hope of improving the condition of the poor was to persuade the rich to be content with less: 'the clergy are to preach all this unto the rich, and make the poor also demand it of them. This is practical enough; but there is an end for the present of your political economy.' 'It is a maudling way of meeting us', retorted Wilson, 'to say that political economy does not teach us kindness to the poor. Why, neither does astronomy nor navigation . . . "The bonnet to its right use: 'tis for the head;" and so with every thing else.'

While he had no objection to the rich helping or the clergy preaching, he saw nothing 'against the poor looking a bit after their own interests into the bargain, and demanding from the rich, among other things, to be thought MEN – to be treated as men having rights to assert as well as duties to perform; and, since they *do* perform those duties, to have those rights also recognised. This is a part of political economy – *our* political economy; and in respect of half the evils that the *Times* whines over from day to day, but makes no practical proposal to abate, but rather to increase, we beg to say that "it *will* do" – that it is a good natural cure and no quack or temporary remedy.'[5]

Good knockabout stuff like this became more and more a feature of the paper as Wilson's journalistic confidence grew. Using a sledgehammer rather than a stiletto, he dealt comprehensively with those who offended his beliefs. 'The danger which is anticipated from the bad harvest is a danger which political economy cannot overcome', said a *Morning Herald* writer unwisely, eliciting from *The Economist* a growl: 'If this means that a knowledge of the principles of political economy does not enable individuals to cause the sun to shine brightly, the winds to blow gently, and the rains to fall in small quantity, when these things are necessary to bring the crops of particular localities to their most beneficial maturity, it is a truth which even the *Herald* may have found out without having been specially admitted to Ministerial confidence. We admit that there is a limit to the power of knowledge – it is not omnipotent; and we have never heard of any political economists who professed to have any influence over the skies.'

A commonly-made and personally hurtful accusation was that it was inhumane to espouse political economy. It was an issue that Wilson met head-on in a leader called 'THE HUMANITY OR INHUMANITY OF POLITICAL ECONOMY'. Its opening paragraphs spell out simply a defence that is as relevant to the modern *Economist* as it was to Wilson's, for allegations of heartlessness have continued throughout the paper's life.

> There is no inconsiderable school of talkers and writers now-a-days, who seem to forget that reason is given us to sit in judgment over the dictates of our feelings, and that it is not her part to play the advocate in support of every impulse which laudable affections may arouse in us. That the emotions in question are in themselves praiseworthy no one disputes – the motives of those whom they guide are generally as laudable, and hence, by a common fallacy, wisdom is attributed where there is in fact nothing besides humanity of heart and sincerity of purpose. It is these who sneer at political economy, talk of moral and Christian duty, as if the dictates of the latter were at variance with the conclusions of the former, and not unfrequently arrogate to themselves the entire claim to benevolence, kind-heartedness, and charity of disposition.

Moral science and political economy had different functions and connected only where political economy provided the means 'of correcting our notions of duty'. The only test of the morality of actions was whether they produced happiness or the reverse. Political economy could show what the results of many human actions were, and the actions could then be condemned or approved. 'Thus it is that political economy is supposed to conflict with morality, because it demonstrates the conduct which simple benevolence pursues to be often attended by consequences utterly at variance with a benevolent purpose.'[6] And he forthwith launched into an impeccably logical explanation of why recent humanitarian proposals for paying needlewomen a living wage would in the long run lead to greater misery. (That was in 1844. In 1849 *The Economist* was reporting that a Factory Act 'which was to work so beneficially for the women and children, has thrown them . . . out of employment, and increased the labour of the men without increasing their wages'.[7] In 1989 it was explaining that: 'A minimum wage of 25 cents an hour was introduced by Franklin Roosevelt in 1938. It has since been raised 15 times and reached its present level of $3.35 by the start of the Reagan years. Throughout this period, two things have been clear: that a minimum wage reduces job opportunities, especially for the young, the disadvantaged and minorities, and that its effect on poverty is tiny.')[8]

Newspapers or journals are usually written by many hands and over time or across the subject areas inconsistencies of opinion are a common feature: this was not the case with Wilson's *Economist*. It was not just because he wrote most of it and took responsibility for the rest. It was also a combination of an extraordinary memory and absolutely fixed principles. His was no literary memory – 'a full mind constantly occupied with its own contents': it was a mind preoccupied with the present, which yet if triggered off by need, would remember all the details of the relevant previous transaction 'completely, vividly, and perfectly'. Bagehot doubted if anyone ever possessed 'a more useful memory for the purposes of life'. Along with that went the absolute principles that meant that he was sure to approach the same issue in the same way every time. In *The Economist* it resulted in his propounding views on, for instance, state education, factory legislation, famine and slavery that at first glance seemed appalling: there are parallels with the modern paper's attitudes to drugs, overseas aid and sanctions.

But if the critics were harsh, the admirers were encouraging. One S.C. Kell of Huddersfield, concerned that outside Britain, 'the star of protection is everywhere in the ascendant' in Europe, wrote in January 1845 to suggest that a few hundred pounds be raised annually to finance the distribution of free copies of *The Economist* to the public reading rooms in the leading manufacturing and commercial towns on the Continent and perhaps in the United States. He added that it was probable that many of these new readers would then themselves subscribe.

Wilson was delighted, not least because he did not know Kell. In his reply he asked for reader reaction, but mentioned his own enthusiasm for circulating copies in America. He added the information that on a recent visit to a large factory in France he had found 'to our agreeable surprise, that not only was the conductor of it, a regular reader and subscriber to this paper, but that the men in the factory took also a copy to themselves'.[9]

The ever-faithful Earl of Radnor was in the next issue, putting his name down for ten guineas, while Wilson was offering to provide free one-fifth of the copies to be circulated. A month later six more offers were made publicly and a society was formed. Eighteen months later, in August 1846, eleven of its sponsors wrote to the paper to report progress and appeal for further contributions to 'all those who regard a perfectly free commercial intercourse between all nations as one of the surest guarantees of their prosperity and happiness'. *The Economist* had been circulated to reading rooms, newspaper editors and influential statesmen in Europe and America, but the scheme was now in jeopardy: its main support had been the Anti-Corn Law League, now disbanded, which had paid for 200 copies weekly.

A large postbag showed *The Economist* had 'excited considerable interest': hence 'there is little room to doubt, from its talent and efficiency as an advocate of Free Trade, that it has already done much towards removing the prejudice and ignorance which at present oppose themselves to a more liberal commercial system'. Supporters abroad were in great need of ammunition against the protectionists, so the appeal leaders wanted to raise enough to circulate both *The Economist* and a French weekly (*Le Libre-Échange*, which was about to be launched and edited by the economist Claude Frédéric Bastiat, Adam Smith's best-known French disciple).

S.C. Kell provided quotations from foreign encomia. The Mayor of Bordeaux considered that 'all subjects connected with political economy are treated in that journal with such talent, and in such a masterly manner, that much instruction is to be derived from its attentive perusal'; he praised particularly the statistical coverage. The Director of Customs in Naples was reportedly anxious to become a regular reader. From the United States came an endorsement from J.C. Calhoun, ex-Vice President, now Secretary of

State, great orator, leader of the states-rights movement and therefore champion of the interests of slave-owning states, who regarded *The Economist* as 'a very able production on a subject of very deep interest to both countries'. An 'intelligent German' in Leipzig must have caused great delight to Wilson: 'The excellence of the 'ECONOMIST,' and its superiority to other similar papers, is now so much acknowledged, that it has completely supplanted the *Times*, kept hitherto in most of our Museums and Reading Rooms.' And finally came the great man, Bastiat, who was ecstatic:

> May all the nations soon throw down the barriers which separate them.

> One of the most efficacious means of attaining this great result, would be the propagation of the Journal entitled the 'ECONOMIST.'

> There never was a periodical work in which all the questions of political economy were treated with so much depth and impartiality. It is, besides, a precious collection of facts: doctrine and experience mutually support each other in its columns: its diffusion on the continent would have excellent effects, and would destroy at length those anti-British prejudices which have taken such deep root.

The paper's spirit was 'eminently cosmopolite, and diametrically opposed to those usurping and exclusive tendencies which have always distinguished your oligarchy, and which explain and justify the European prepossessions against England'.

A certain incestuousness was creeping in here. Bastiat, the leader of the free-trade movement in France, had followed the fortunes of the League intently, attending their most important meetings, translating the major speeches – including two of Wilson's – and incorporating them into a book called *Cobden et la Ligue*, which Wilson had praised.[10] But that they knew each other does not detract from Bastiat's sincerity. In what it aspired to do *The Economist* was without peer, and for a British journal it was exceptionally cosmopolitan. This was a feature both of Wilson's circumstances and his principles. His business had brought him foreign contacts and friendships: his principles made him an internationalist. And as in all things, he saw internationalism through to its logical conclusion. Here, for example, at the end of a lengthy refutation of calls by *The Times* – among others – for reciprocal trading agreements and concentration on colonial markets, is a passage of his that sums up the attitudes that so delighted Bastiat: 'It would be the greatest folly this country could commit to neglect the great and populous civilized countries around us for the sake of fostering distant and colonial markets, or to neglect the means which we have within our reach of extending our trade, by the adoption of free principles, though other countries may persist in their exclusiveness and commercial hostility. Our example will do more in inducing them to follow the same principles than can ever be expected from negotiations or treaties.'[11] It was an interesting precedent for the attitude the paper was to adopt over a century later to the linked issues of membership of the European Community and the relationship of Britain and its former colonies.

Wilson's and the paper's foreign reputation grew rapidly. In September 1847 he attended an international congress at Brussels – organised by the Belgian Association for promoting free trade – of 'the individuals who, from their exertions and position, are at the head of the politico-economical movements of the world'.[12] The proceedings were reported by 'Our Belgian Correspondent', who was irritated that 'two entire sittings were consumed in the discussion of general principles. The speakers lost themselves in generalising, and the discussions in vapour; they did not sufficiently descend to the practical question . . . It is not necessary to create a school; we must teach facts . . . Each nation represented in the congress had different examples to cite. They ought to have adhered to the matter of practice, and not to theory.' Wilson avoided waffle in his lengthy speech, which included a review of the cotton, iron, woollen and linen trades 'to illustrate the beneficial influence of free trade, and the increased wellbeing of the working population which would assuredly flow from it'. At the grand banquet for foreign visitors, Wilson – 'who has rendered so much service to science', was one of those singled out in the main toast.

The purity of the vigilante of free trade never faltered. When the *Court Circular* reported that 'The Lord Chamberlain has been commanded to announce to the ladies who shall attend the drawing-rooms, and shall be honoured with invitations to Buckingham Palace, that her Majesty the Queen, ever desirous of giving encouragement to the trade and industry of the United Kingdom, and particularly so at this time of commercial depression, would wish to see them in dresses of British manufacture', *The Economist* expressed its deep regret that the Queen's advisers 'had committed her to the exploded fallacy' of encouraging the trade and industry of the United Kingdom by recommending the exclusive use of British manufactures. Not only did this contravene the 'now almost universally acknowledged principle' of free trade; it was a dangerous and suicidal doctrine to promulgate abroad from a nation who, 'more than any other people on earth, depend for the employment of our population upon the consumption of British manufactures in other countries'.[13]

Yet although Wilson was true to his principles, his internationalism had a severe limitation of which he had no inkling – a limited imagination that made him assume that others were as he was. In two essays written long after Wilson's death and making no mention of him, Bagehot put his finger on certain deficiencies that were very true of his beloved father-in-law. Like Adam Smith, Wilson thought 'there was a Scotchman inside every man', which led him to assume the existence of a universal desire to make money and a universal willingness to work hard for it:[14] one might call him a proto-Thatcherite. As the *Scotsman* – over-egging the pudding of his humble origins – pointed out in his obituary, 'he was one of the many examples of our countrymen ... who have raised themselves, by dint of sheer ability and industry, to high positions in the State, from comparatively humble beginnings, and in the face of many difficulties and discouragements'.[15] Indeed classical economics was so dominated by Scotsmen as to have William Cobbett, who believed that man had a propensity to care for others rather than to seek his own well-being, denouncing the whole school with more vigour than elegance as 'half-drunk, half-mad, Scotch vagabonds'.[16]

And along with this inability to grasp the different priorities of other people and other cultures went that great limitation of English political economy pointed out so devastatingly by Bagehot – it was in fact the science of business, developed for the greatest trading nation in history. 'It assumes that every man who makes anything, makes it for money, that he always makes that which brings him in most at least cost, and that he will make it in the way that will produce most and spend least, it assumes that every man who buys, buys with his whole heart, and that he who sells, sells with his whole heart, each wanting to gain all possible advantage.' It was accepted in other countries in direct proportion to their commercialisation.[17]

So despite Wilson's generosity of spirit and great humanity, the 'Scotchman' and the businessman set restrictions on his intellectual and imaginative parameters. He shared with Adam Smith a deep distrust of public educational institutions and displayed a complete inability to see any point in university practices and traditions. 'We will make bold to say that Oxford is a perfect drag upon the age, and a hindrance to real education. It is not *there* that men are educated. Time, no doubt, is spent and tutors paid; but it is when the outer world is reached that *real education* commences – it is when the conflicts of passion with reason, and the struggle for position in life have to be encountered, that the great education of a man commences; and what assistance from without can be given him in that? Absolutely none.'[18] Although there were good grounds for criticism of the old universities, there was more than a hint in Wilson's attitude of 'I went to the university of life', the twentieth-century catchphrase that frequently covers up a sneaking regret at having missed out on a university education. After all, until he was in his mid-thirties, he would have moved almost exclusively among people with a similar educational background to his own. Now he was forty, most of his intimates were university men in addition to being socially his superiors: even a man of Wilson's confidence might develop a slight chip on the shoulder.

In his attitude to the study of subjects that were without obvious practical application there was downright philistinism. In 1848, in a well-deserved assault on Cambridge University's slowness in adapting to the demands of the nineteenth century, he condemned its priorities with a sneer: 'it bestows all its approbation and its more substantial fellowships and livings only on those who acquire a great proficiency in [that] which we must, with some risk of censure for the application of the term, call the art of mathematics and a great knowledge of languages that are no longer habitually used in any part of the globe'. Two paragraphs later, his resentment was directed at 'two ancient . . . very ill-formed languages' and 'the elaborate art of the mathematician'. From his perspective, until now Cambridge had 'slighted and neglected political economy . . . the pride of Britain, [which] has helped to rescue her from the calamities that have fallen on other nations, and has gained for her honour abroad that has never been vouchsafed to anything especially taught at her Universities. Do the Germans and French borrow our classics and our mathematics? No. But they do borrow our political sciences, our free trade theories, and acknowledge that there is no other salvation for society, but in adopting and following the principles of that science which our learned Universities are now only beginning to appreciate.'[19]

Had Wilson been less humane, he would have been less angry with those who failed to follow the one true religion, but the horrors of the hungry forties had turned an amiable man into a ferocious critic. Stupidity and selfishness among those who should know better aroused his particular ire. Though he might hobnob with earls, he had no inhibitions about attacking the British Establishment when its members violated his notions of correct behaviour. The aristocracy elicited an outburst of particular anger in January 1846, when with public opinion won over, the landowning interests in parliament presented the last obstacle to the repeal of the Corn Laws. It was, said Wilson, in a typically trenchant passage, quite simply that they wished to hold on as long as possible to laws which increased the price of '*the especial article which the people buy, and which the aristocratic legislators sell*. They are, in fact, laws passed by the seller to compel the buyer to give him more for his article than it is worth. They are laws *enacted by the noble shopkeepers who rule us, to compel the nation to deal at their shop alone.*' This 'low, mean, sordid' aspect of the matter would be fatal to aristocratic prestige.[20]

Nor did the church escape. Wilson might have become a member of the Church of England, but when it came to religion, he was very much a product of his Quaker background. Clergymen had played no part in his upbringing: he felt for them no more respect than for any other man – indeed because of his loathing of hypocrisy, he frequently felt less. And in addition, he disapproved of any state involvement in the church. In a leading article in 1845 he concluded that 'a clergyman who would keep on a corn law may as well give up his calling at once, for he cannot act consistently in it. The promotor of want, and crime, and cruel death among the poor, is no fit teacher of a religion of love and peace, – no worthy follower of Him who while on earth "went about doing good."'[21] It was unusual for Wilson to invoke the deity: certainly, when it came to the greatest issue of his editorship – the Irish famine – it was Adam Smith, not Jesus Christ, whose counsel he reluctantly followed.

CHAPTER IV:

The crucible:
the Irish famine

Avoiding deaths was not the prime Whig preoccupation: relief would shift the distribution of food 'from the more meritorious to the less', because 'if left to the natural law of distribution, those who deserved more would obtain it'. Thus in the Commons Russell refused to commit himself to saving lives as the prime objective, and some Whig ideologues such as Nassau Senior and *The Economist*'s Thomas [sic] Wilson ('it is no man's business to provide for another') countenanced large-scale mortality with equanimity.[1]

This recent assessment by Cormac Ó Gráda, a distinguished and fair-minded Irish economic historian, is a graphic illustration of how little is known about Wilson or his paper, for of all the issues that he faced as editor of *The Economist*, none caused Wilson as much distress as the fate of Ireland. A perfect example of the tension between his head and his heart, between *laissez-faire* principles and humanitarianism, it preoccupied him and his paper during the late 1840s.

The Great Famine of 1845–9 was the greatest domestic challenge to face British statesmen in modern times: it was one which they failed to meet. Perhaps one million people died from starvation or fever (including, in the late stages, cholera) and between 1845 and 1851 about 1,500,000 emigrated. It was a catastrophe, and it happened on Britain's doorstep to a part of the United Kingdom. If Malthusians saw it as an inevitable fate for an over-populated country, extreme Irish nationalists saw it as genocide; proponents of the cock-up theory of history will probably agree with Dr Ó Gráda that more than anything else what happened to the Irish was a result of desperately bad luck. There had been great hardship at other times from crop failure, but this time there was disaster. The population had virtually doubled over the previous fifty years; dependence on the potato – the main food of over half the Irish people – was greater than ever before; the fungus that destroyed it was of a virulent and unknown strain (the antidote was not discovered until 1882); Britain was stretched first by a bad harvest in 1846 and then by a financial crisis in 1847; and from June 1846 there was a Whig government under Lord John Russell that was ideologically opposed to intervention. Reactions should be seen against the British background, so well exemplified in an episode in 1846 involving those two kindly men of unbending principle, Radnor and Wilson.

Lord Radnor had been stricken by a report in the *Reading Mercury* that 'Mr Moore, steward to the Earl of Radnor . . . informed his labourers, that, *under the circumstances* – that is, I suppose, *considering the dearness of provisions* – although it was usual to lower wages at this time of the year, he should continue to pay 10s a week.' Radnor's consequential letter to Moore had been published by *The Times*. 'I trust,' he wrote, 'that the words in italics are not true. I hope so, not because I object to your continuing the wages therein . . . if the work done is worth that sum, and the men deserve it – but because, if the words, "under the circumstances," meant, or were understood to mean, "considering the dearness of provisions," you were then aiding a most mischievous and unjust delusion, viz., that wages ought to be regulated . . . by the price of provisions.' Supply and demand was the only proper criterion. 'It is sometimes said that a farmer is bound at least to give such wages as his labourer can live upon. I utterly deny that the wages of labour ought to be regulated by the wants of the labourer.' Such logic would reward 'the improvident, the idle, and careless' and would demoralise the labouring classes. Should his labourers or poor neighbours be in difficulties because of the rise of the corn price, 'I may relieve or not, as I like . . . Charity is one thing; wages are another . . . A man should thank me for an act of charity as a gift; for wages he owes me no thanks.'

'The public at large, we believe,' wrote Wilson, 'the readers of the *Economist* and all well-wishers to the independence of labourers, we are sure, will cordially agree with Lord Radnor's opinion . . . The noble Earl has only too truly and clearly expounded, for the ease and satisfaction of the opponents of political science, the principles by which the conduct of individuals is governed and best interests of society promoted. They are disturbed by his letter in their grim self-conceit, and furiously attack the honest nobleman, who courageously speaks truth and wisdom.'[2]

He was just as clear on the Factory Acts. During the 1840s, legislation limited the hours worked in textile factories by women and 13–18-year-olds to 12 hours a day and the hours for younger children under 13 to 6½; in 1847 hours for the former were reduced to 10. *The Economist* was shocked on two grounds: first, by 'the interference of the legislature with industry, with the hours of work, with the contracts between masters and workmen or workwomen; to which we are in all its shapes and forms decidedly opposed' and second, by the flouting of the laws of supply and demand inherent in decreeing what hours people should work. Lord Ashley (from 1851, Lord Shaftesbury, the outstanding social reformer of his day) 'hunts up objects for legislative benevolence from every class . . . with the persevering sagacity of a trapper, and lives in a hallowed round of legislative benevolence, buying the applause of the unthinking by preferred largesses of the public wealth, or the liberties of industry'.[3]

By the early 1860s Bagehot's *Economist*, recommending the extension of child protection measures, was making short shrift of such arguments: 'in defending helpless and ignorant children from the consequences of their own helplessness and ignorance, and the ignorance, if not helplessness, of their parents, we are in reality discharging one of the most natural and normal functions of Government. Indeed, instead of interfering with the principle of free trade, we are, if we use the principle wisely, really enlarging vastly that individual freedom of choice on the part of the working classes, without which freedom of trade scarcely means more than free permission to become the blind instruments of others.'[4]

But for Wilson's generation, economic laws were immutable. Contemplating the records of a contemporary economists' forum, Sir John Macdonnell described its participants as missionaries or proselytisers in an age of 'principles or dogma: [they] . . . were anxious to diffuse "just principles," to "rectify any mistakes," to refute "erroneous doctrines," and to "limit the influence of hurtful publications." I might also describe it as the age of *laissez-faire*, "or the age of individualism"; the age when it was believed that every person is the best judge of his own happiness; when State intervention was regarded as presumably stupid and mischievous.'[5]

The famine was a litmus test of the depth of Wilson's principles: it was a calamity which was to test to the utmost his moral courage (a quality never in doubt), the depth of his commitment to *laissez-faire*, his humanity and his imagination. He could not shrug his shoulders and declare it inevitable as a follower of Malthus might have done, believing that only war or famine could stop population increasing faster than the means of subsistence. Wilson's natural optimism rejected such an apocalyptic vision of the world; he believed that free trade would make the economy grow faster than the population. Sadly for his peace of mind and for the subsequent reputation of his paper, on this issue, more than any other, humanity and doctrine seemed ranged against each other: the unfolding story provides a perfect case-study.

Wilson was passionately interested in Ireland and far more enlightened and better informed than the vast majority of contemporary British journalists, not only through his mastery of relevant economic data but also through personal experience and political contacts. A long semi-autobiographical article written in 1843[6] shows him at the height of his powers, dealing with a topic that engaged both his head and his heart. The issue was repeal of the Union between Britain and Ireland, for which Daniel O'Connell had launched a massive popular agitation.

Being non-political, Wilson explained, his viewpoint was purely 'economical', but he felt it

> as well to clear the way by certain admissions, which, having once stated, our readers may give us full credit for them throughout our argument.
>
> First . . . that Ireland has been hitherto most grievously misgoverned . . . and . . . even now we are reaping the fruits of that unjust, absurd, and wicked, because unchristian system, from which we were finally emancipated in 1829.
>
> Second . . . that since 1829 Ireland has been making rapid progress; and that it requires but continued perseverance in an impartial, bold, kindly, and equally discriminative system . . .
>
> Third . . . that there still exist in Ireland grievances of a very aggravated description . . . A bold, determined, cautious statesman, no matter whether he be Whig or Tory, would deal practically with these grievances . . . and would carry on the imperial government on such a system and in such a spirit, as would give to every Irishman the same advantages, economical and political, as Englishmen and Scotchmen enjoy.

Nevertheless, repeal of the Union would aggravate rather than cure the remaining evils of Ireland, nullify the results of the expected repeal of the Corn Laws and consequently be ruinous to Ireland and disastrous to England; and it might help to bring about the 'social convulsion' which free trade would avert. He would not consider the granting of a local parliament subordinate to Westminster, for those who wanted the Union repealed would never settle for this. 'If one step is made towards an alteration of the "Act of Union", we must go the whole way.' The only real issue was whether an independent Irish parliament, sitting in Dublin, should be responsible only to the crown.

In assessing the strength of feeling behind the repeal movement, Englishmen always forgot the importance of Irish nationality. 'The Scotch and the Welsh are still extremely national in their feelings, but the Irish are *national* throughout the whole structure of their mind, feelings, and physical composition. It may be odd, but it is true, that the Irish are perhaps as intensely national a people as any race that ever existed.'

On Wilson's first visit to Ireland, he explained, shortly after O'Connell's triumph in forcing through Catholic Emancipation, 'anxious to see and hear so extraordinary a man', he had 'pressed amongst the crowd' opposite his Dublin house and heard 'his rich, round, mellow voice' saying – '"I have come from the land of the Saxon and the stranger!" Instantly O'Connell fell fifty per cent. in the estimation of the "Saxon stranger." It seemed an enunciation of intense barbarism. The great advocate of "civil and religious liberty" appeared at the moment an incarnation of intense prejudice and vulgar passion.' Wilson had turned away with 'a feeling of shame and sorrow' that, though Catholic Emancipation was 'a great, a just, and a wise act . . . this "barbarism" should be one of its fruits'. In the intervening years he had often heard O'Connell, 'and being accustomed to that vigorous eloquence and rotund voice, pleading on behalf of Negroes, Jews, and all the rights of humanity, have learned to regard him – despite his many and enormous faults – as a truly wonderful man'. Moreover, having come to know Ireland and the Irish, Wilson could properly estimate that feeling of nationality whose expression sometimes seemed so exaggerated to an Englishman: evidence showed 'that there *was* a time when Ireland was a remarkable country, compared with the rest of Europe', a fact which, 'conjoined with the sad story of Ireland's wrongs, make the Irishman what he is'.

The Irish peasant did not '*live*' at the present moment, but merely existed; 'he lives in the *past* – he lives in the *future*. His imagination is filled with what Ireland was, and with what it may become. And you have but to touch on these two topics, the *past* and the *future*, in order to set fire to his mind, and to make him send up a shout that might rend the heavens, for a Repeal of the

Union.' But repeal would be disastrous, Wilson believed, going on to hypothesise a situation in which all financial and other difficulties had been overcome, an Irish parliament was in charge, there was perfect harmony among all classes and neither Catholics nor Protestants were striving for ascendency. Even then, lacking flourishing cities and a manufacturing population to consume its farm produce, how could Ireland meet its people's need for food and work?

However, should restrictions on free trade have been lifted in Britain, Ireland would share in the consequent prosperity. British manufacturing districts would consume more Irish farm produce in exchange for goods and capital, improvements in agriculture would be followed by commercial development and there would be more jobs in Britain for Irish labourers. 'But Irish nationality would not wait upon this. It would cry to its own Parliament, "Why should we take Saxon broadcloth or Saxon calico, when we can employ our own people at our own manufacturers – let Ireland be for the Irish." The cry would become too strong for anybody to resist', especially since it would seem conducive to the good of Ireland. A hostile tariff would be introduced and capital borrowed to invest in protected Irish manufacturers. 'And for a short time there might be great joy over a short-lived prosperity.'

Then the Irish would find that their agricultural market had fallen off and they were paying more than before for manufactured goods. Smuggling would become a major problem, to be dealt with by a fleet of revenue cutters, 'which would exhaust the Irish exchequer, without being able to put down Irish smuggling'. New taxes would have to be introduced; Irish manufacturers would go bankrupt, with a consequent loss of jobs. 'Meantime, a very bad feeling would grow up on both sides of the Channel, reviving old prejudices now dying away.' This sorry sequence would end in injury to England and in ruin to Ireland, with a possibility of 'a struggle for ascendancy between Catholic and Protestant and the danger of a *religious* war'.[7] Protectionism in the Irish Free State of the 1930s, shameless cross-border smuggling and the Northern Ireland tragedy are but three aspects of recent Irish history that lend credibility to some of Wilson's speculations.

Wilson's anger at the misgovernment of Ireland never abated. The Irish, he wrote in September 1844, were not treated as part of an empire, but as 'a conquered tribe' in 'a subdued province' and were governed by the 'veriest fraction of the community . . . What is the consequence of all this? People without the responsibilities of self-government cannot be expected to exhibit the virtues of free citizens; and they do not. They give no support to the exercise of civil authority. They do not respect partizan judges, nor persecuting magistrates. How could they?' Ireland should be governed by those that knew it, whether it led to federal government, repeal of the Union or 'a thorough and generous amalgamation of the two countries'. For the country could not remain as it was. 'Disunion is always looked upon with pain, but cruelty and injustice must be looked upon with more.'[8]

It was the propensity of governments to vary their policies according to public pressure that most annoyed Wilson, for his dogmatism was imbued with a fierce morality. At a time when Peel's government was dragging its feet on religious concessions to Irish Catholics, he summed up the situation in a manner which could be applied to governments in every country throughout human history:

> When . . . are . . . the admitted and crying evils of a whole nation to be redressed? When the people are driven by the paroxysms of distress, and the sufferings of misgovernment, to a breach of the peace, and unwarrantable outrages; when party spirit quails before national danger; then the government . . . still must not be coerced. Such, would have a bad moral effect. Coercion is turned against the people; and that is not a fitting time to undertake reforms. On the other hand, when the country is quiet and peaceful, and prosperous, then changes are not demanded, and it is unnecessary to undertake them.[9]

Wilson's approved reforms for Ireland were of course limited by his beliefs to the removal of restrictions or – as in the case of the Catholic Church – to the restitution of what he considered to be stolen property.[10] On the general condition of the Irish he was a little more sanguine at the beginning of 1845, attributing recent improvements partly to 'the better habits, prudence, and thrift, resulting from that miraculous conversion to temperance of the most intemperate people on earth but mainly to the improved physical condition of the people, consequent on a renewed demand for their produce in the manufacturing districts of England'.[11]

He was therefore all the more irritated by Daniel O'Connell's 'eternal cry of "give, give"'. In June 1845 he reported on a Commons speech of O'Connell's in which he described Ireland as being in a 'frightful state', with half its population 'so badly fed, so badly clothed, so badly housed, that potatoes, "when they can get them," is their only food, water their only drink, "a blanket is a luxury unknown to them, and decent habitations . . . they . . . never have enjoyed."' Assassinations following evictions increased annually. '"Let only the Queen's government," says Mr O'Connell, "come forward and do something".' Wilson rebuked his hero for saying that government could do good. 'The best government that a people can hope for is one that will do them no harm', and, that being so, a great man like O'Connell should give up such 'clap-trap' and teach his countrymen 'that to themselves, to their own industry, to their devotion to duty and abstinence from crime, they must owe all the advances which they can hope to make in time to come, as individuals or as a nation . . . A lesson on SELF-RELIANCE, taught them by a man of such infinite resources, and whom they, not without reason, so adore, would be the best thing that ever has been done for Irishmen or Ireland.'[12]

Within a few weeks the paper was reporting on the appearance in Europe of what was called the 'American potato cholera and potato plague'. It had been found in Kent, but no reports of it had come in from Scotland or Ireland:[13] they were not long delayed. In mid-October the Prime Minister knew that almost the whole of the Irish potato crop had failed and was convinced that a major disaster was in the offing. With England and Scotland also suffering from potato blight as well as a poor cereal harvest, it was clear that there would be a serious shortage of food in the two islands. 'The accounts from Ireland are appalling and distressing', wrote Wilson that same week. 'The accounts which we receive depict the country as thrown into a state of the deepest despair.' He reacted incredulously to a report by the *Standard* that since the government could do nothing but investigate the facts, the public should give generously. 'What! the Government do nothing to relieve a famine, when a duty on wheat of eighteen shillings a quarter, and on other grain in proportion, stands between it and the famished buyer.' The answer, of course, was – as in Belgium, Holland and Russia – to remove all restrictions on imports. 'It is impossible to calculate the amount of evil which may be averted, and of positive good which may be secured, by an immediate and bold removal of all existing impediments to a free supply of food. If the law be permitted to remain as it is, the future must be to every reflecting man a subject of considerable solicitude and apprehension.'[14]

During these weeks, as anti-Corn Law propaganda intensified, Robert Peel was trying to convert his Cabinet colleagues to that policy. Both he and the Home Secretary, Sir James Graham, his close friend and ally, had been convinced on hearing of the potato blight that repeal was inevitable. As a Peel biographer points out, this was no sudden conversion, but one which had come about gradually over the previous three years.[15] For a Conservative government, the traditional defender of the agricultural interest, even to contemplate removing protective measures, horrified many of their supporters. Over the ensuing weeks, as the public anti-Corn Law clamour grew, Peel strove vainly to win over his Cabinet. The opposition leader, Lord John Russell, who had hitherto favoured an eight-shilling fixed duty, yielded to public opinion and in a letter to the electors in the City of London, his constituency, declared his support for absolute repeal.

The issue of *The Economist* that carried the full text of Russell's declaration is an excellent example of Wilson's mature editorship. It had that single-mindedness that a critic might call monomaniacal. In addition to Russell's text, the leading articles included an analysis of how this development might affect Cabinet policy, a report on trade reverses that blamed them on expensive corn, a statistical discussion of the effects on the price of bread of a sliding scale of duties on wheat, an account of the Bombay Famine of 1812 which explained how relief came from allowing unrestricted export as well as import of grain, and an attack on Peel for depriving the people of bread. And in addition, there was an article on the role of charity in relieving famine that was typical of those that were to earn him an unfair reputation for heartlessness.

When Wilson convinced himself that an unpopular opinion was in the public interest, he often seemed to argue it with a measure of bravado – almost as if a virtue had to be made out of the success of his head in subduing his heart. 'Charity is the national error of Englishmen', he began disconcertingly, '– generally a very mischievous – often a very ostentatious one. Alms-giving is considered by us as the certain panacea for most social evils; and it is by getting up a subscription that we testify our sense of merit, our sympathy for misfortune, and our gratitude for public services . . . a gift of money is the universal salve. It is at once the readiest, the easiest, and the coarsest medicament, – and naturally approves itself to a people at once rich, tender-hearted, and lazy.'

In many quarters there was a strong disposition to apply this same remedy to the threatened suffering – 'a sort of undefined resolution that *something must be done* to prevent our poor from dying of starvation, which, if not rightly directed, may well justify our alarm – for we do not know a more frightful spectacle than that of a number of people tumultuously rushing to do good'. In addition to recommending private charity, organs of public opinion were recommending a parliamentary grant to Ireland of £3,000,000 as well as a programme of public works. He wished people to consider well whether such grants were proper or effective. The problem was not price, but scarcity, so how could this grant help?

> 'Why' (says the charitable), 'it will enable the poor, and those whose little crops have failed, to buy food, which otherwise they could not buy.' Very true, – but it will enable them *only to buy that food which, but for this charitable aid, others not so assisted would have bought*: – that is, it will enable them to take the bread out of the mouths of certain others of their countrymen. It will not augment the quantity of food to be distributed – it will only vary the distribution of it.

Unless the quantity increases, giving money merely raises prices by augmenting customers' purchasing power or bringing more customers into the market; £3,000,000 voted to the Irish would be £3,000,000 voted to the growers of wheat, i.e. first the farmers and then the landlords – 'and is a measure, in consequence, which is certain to be warmly supported, both in and out of parliament'.

No charity would reduce the amount of food consumed by the richer classes, for on that they never economise. So would a parliamentary grant increase the quantity of food available at home? Under the present Corn Laws, only if the price was raised. To distribute £3,000,000 among consumers would certainly enhance the price of wheat so as to bring forward the period at which wheat would be admitted at a nominal duty. This could only be done by raising the price of inferior wheat to a price well beyond its value, so the grant would not increase the food supply till the whole amount had been paid to the landlords. And by that time, the American wheat surplus might all have been bought up by Europe. If the £3,000,000 were now devoted to buying American wheat, a third of the money would go on duty. The only answer was – of course – repeal.[16]

Peel knew Ireland well, having been its Chief Secretary from 1812 to 1818 and Home Secretary from 1822 to 1827. So, although he was already hell-bent on securing the repeal of the Corn Laws, he appreciated that the results would be insufficient to avert disaster: the Irish poor had long depended on the potatoes they grew themselves, and lacked the money to buy even cheap bread. During November, therefore, against Treasury advice,

Peel authorised Baring Brothers to buy secretly from America £100,000 worth of maize and meal – calculated to be enough to feed one million people for forty days. Additionally, Sir James Graham instructed the Lord Lieutenant of Ireland to set up an emergency relief commission to provide jobs, distribute food and control the government depots in which the grain was to be stored.

Although three-quarters of the crop had failed, Graham had correctly predicted in October that famine would not strike for several months. Fear of the disease had led to sound potatoes being put on the market rather than saved for the future; other crops were plentiful and food imports were high. For those with money food was freely available: for those without it, starvation began to loom in the spring. Although great efforts were being made to use public works to provide relief in distressed areas, there were bureaucratic and other delays.

The following month the government corn-depots distributed their supplies for sale at very low prices. Together with its other relief measures, the Peel administration could congratulate itself on having avoided widespread starvation. By the end of June it was out of office. With Whig support the Corn Laws had been repealed at the cost of splitting the Tory Party. Erstwhile colleagues had taken their revenge by voting down the government over a bill designed to control increasing levels of crime in Ireland. On 30 June, 1846, a Whig government under Lord John Russell took power. By mid-August it was clear that the potato crop had failed almost completely.

Wilson had not been idle. Week after week during the spring and early summer *The Economist* had been shaking its head over Ireland, looking at its history, evaluating its condition and coming to further conclusions about the wrongs done to the Irish peasantry by bad government. The more he looked the more horrified he became, and the struggles between head and heart became almost palpable. Did the existence of widespread starvation not prove impracticable the abstract principle that a government should not meddle with the subsistence of the people? On the contrary, it demonstrated 'the propriety of rigidly adhering to non-interference', for it was interference in the shape of the Corn Laws that had caused the problem in the first place. Similarly, it was no part of a government's duty to feed any or all of the people. Since its only funds came from taxation, it could feed one section of the population only by depriving another. If you feed any you have to feed all, and that is beyond any government's control. 'The interference involves the legislature in a task beyond human strength – and knocks out the brains of its assumed wisdom against the terrible wall of national hunger.' The Irish famine 'warns the legislature, if its members be endowed with human feelings, by a piercing and never-to-be-forgotten wail, against all interference with the supply of food for the people. It must leave that to themselves.'[17]

The early stages of the famine and the growing number of evictions had wrought one change in Wilson's thinking; he no longer believed that the Irish problem would be solved simply by the repeal of the Corn Laws and the restoration of civil and religious liberty. If he had a well-developed dislike for English landowners, he had by now an absolute loathing and contempt for their Irish equivalents, under whom he believed the mass of the people to be little better than slaves. At the root of all the evils of Ireland lay the relationship between landlord and tenant: 'Of that, the prevalence of a great corruption of religion, with an extending power possessed by a priesthood, so opposite to the general progress of mankind, is a consequence. Of that, want and idleness and beggary, struggles, for the most wretched means of subsistence, strife and assassination to revenge the dispossession of land, or obtain possession of it, are the fruits . . . To add to the misery of the wretched peasantry of this unfortunate country, the landlords are ably contributing to their bitter draught. Day after day we hear of families, aye, hundreds of wretches, turned out to die in the ditches by their heartless oppressors, the landlords of this country.'

He described emotionally and in detail one such eviction and reflected:

> The enormous evils of such an occurrence will be at once present to the imagination. The vast amount of immediate physical suffering, the destitution of the peasant and those who are dear to him, – the conviction of injustice, the growl of anger at first and the subsequent ripening of anger, in the most energetic and daring of the ousted party, into a feeling of fell revenge, – the brutal attacks and assassinations which follow . . . and these consequences extended . . . to the estates of other landed proprietors . . . the description of them becomes the picture collectively of all Ireland, and explains to us the existence there of vast herds of destitute people, of the rankling feelings of hatred and fear which are common to all classes, and of multiplied and brutal assassinations.

As the reason for these evictions was that the populated land would be more profitable if turned over to pasture, it raised, observed Wilson, an issue which all free-traders should earnestly consider. It was still a correct principle that landowners should make the most of their land and that their relationship with their tenants should be purely commercial. But 'we must insist, with all our free-trade brethren, that this consequence of their principles imposes on them the necessity of examining the tenure of landed property in Ireland, that they may vindicate their own cause, prove the paramount justice of free trade by this other apparent exception, and trace the woes of Ireland to the unjust law from whence they flow'.

Fertile land had been brought from a state of waste by the labour of the dispossessed peasantry, yet the law secured to the owner the property in all that improvement. It must be altered to enforce the rights of the peasantry against the landlord by securing to them the full value of the fertility which their labour imparts to the soil. The right of property might be sacred, 'but when we find that our respect for that of the Irish landlords leads to the impoverishment and degradation of the people, making them at once paupers and criminals', fills Ireland 'with beggars and assassins – when we find that the strong military arm of England is continually called into exercise to keep in awe such a frightful community, and is even ineffectual for the purpose – when we reflect on the enormous expense as well as vast moral degradation which flow from the proper exercise of an individual landlord's power, we are driven, by the numerous practical evils into which the maintenance of the right has involved us, to call in question the right itself'.[18]

He intended another day to go into detail on how to change the law, but a week later he had given up the challenge. 'The law regulating property and the bulk of the people of Ireland are at variance.' The problem would not be solved until the subject had been investigated 'in the catholic spirit of an enlarged and fearless philosophy'. Until that happened, Wilson would avoid further discussing any practical measures. 'Before we can hope to stay the present plague, its source must be more completely opened up.'

Yet throughout the spring and early summer he continued to worry away at the problems of Ireland. Why was there such a small urban population compared to the rest of the civilised world? Why was the labour of the Irish in Ireland far less productive than their labour outside Ireland? The want of a commercial, a manufacturing and a town population was 'the well-head and origin' of Ireland's disorders: how had this come about?

We do not believe that it springs from any original difference in the Celtic and Saxon races. We see no connexion between great animal spirits, with a lively imagination, and dividing the soil into patches. We cannot comprehend the existence of great and varied talents amongst the people, and their comparative ignorance in Ireland of all arts but a rude agriculture. Admitting that the Irish are turbulent, restless and ambitious, we do not see how these qualities explain their acquiescence in mud hovels, rags, and lumpers [a species of potato] . . . We see that, out of Ireland, the Irish attain eminence in every branch of human knowledge. They are, physically, a remarkably well-organised people. They are both strong and intellectual. They are social almost beyond other men. In all the higher walks of art they take a lead . . . they are turbulent and unruly only at home; in the United States they become good citizens, good members of society, frugal, careful men, remitting considerable sums to their relatives at home.

The answer lay in history, in noxious restrictions on Ireland's trade coupled with the seizure and appropriation of the soil and of the produce of manufacturing industry.[19] The following week, examining the record of misappropriation, he examined the landlord–peasant relationship in further detail and took sides even more forcibly than before. By expropriating all the wealth of the country the landowners had prevented the development of a middle class and had injured and oppressed their tenants.

With *The Times* wringing its hands over Irish thoughtlessness, indolence and ingratitude and *Punch* merrily producing cartoons depicting the Irish peasantry as Neanderthal, Wilson's open-mindedness and willingness to learn were remarkable. His well-researched articles were usually between two and three thousand words long and his advocacy of the rights of the dispossessed was heartfelt. Yet within a very short time the tone of the paper's still copious coverage of Ireland began to change. In March 1847, for instance, in an article attacking the principle of state education, the point was proved by reference to the Irish, who for fifteen years had had such a system. 'What are the results? Talkers and writers there are innumerable in Ireland: the judgment of the whole empire is at this moment swamped by their incessant clamour: they are a prodigious multitude of educated counsellors, amongst whom there is no wisdom. Amidst the greatest bounties of nature, they are helpless, and perish; whilst they abound, as their public meetings and numerous well-written journals demonstrate, with all the instruction that school-education can give.'[20]

This was almost certainly written by a new contributor, W.R. Greg, who took a more jaundiced view of the Irish than did Wilson; nevertheless, since Wilson was still in control of the paper, it showed a growing impatience with Ireland, which he often allowed Greg to articulate. Eighteen months later, writing of the tiny and farcical Irish rebellion of 1848 and its aftermath, a leader said irritably that the 'whole affair has throughout preserved the characteristics of Irish agitation: it has been unreal; much vapour and no substance; much acting and no truth'.[21] Daniel O'Connell was no longer an *Economist* hero. Catholic Emancipation was the 'one great service' he had rendered to his country 'and which the remainder of his career was one continued effort to wipe out, cancel, and countervail', for in giving his countrymen a taste for political agitation he had fed them on poison. All that could be done was to put down and keep down agitation and sedition. 'Our mistake has been in supposing that the government of a civilised people will suffice for a savage one.'[22] And in arguing against the rebels being allowed 'the lottery' of an Irish jury trial, Greg showed intense wrath: 'The trial by a jury of our peers is too noble a legacy from our forefathers, too glorious a testimony of our national honesty and worth, too invaluable a bulwark of our freedom and our rights, for us to sit in patience and in silence while it is soiled and dishonoured by a people who too generally (harsh as the expression seems) hold truth to be no virtue, and perjury to be no crime.'

Worse still, Irish disorder was threatening the good name and prosperity of the British Empire. Not only were the peasantry becoming yearly more unmanageable and the landlords more impoverished, but vast numbers were emigrating and carrying with them 'the same insane hatred of the English name, the same calumnious charges against English oppression: till wherever an Irishman has set his foot, England has not only an enemy but a rancorous and untiring missionary of falsehood and ill-will. The rebel, the idler, the assassin, whose turbulent passions we neglected to curb at home, punishes us for our carelessness or feebleness by poisoning against us the minds of his adopted countrymen. And the present state of feeling in America may warn us that this is no light evil.'[23]

Yet less than a year previously Wilson had rejoiced that whatever the 'prejudicial effects' of 'the great sacrifice' which England had made to help Ireland, there had been at least one important consequence – 'of convincing every reasonable Irishman, and the world at large, of the deep interest which is felt by the Government and the people of this country for the welfare of

Ireland'.[24] Now he and many of his compatriots were coming to believe there were few reasonable Irishmen. The British felt that they had shown a new sympathy to Ireland, but they found that they were – to their bewilderment – acquiring abroad, especially in America, a reputation for cruelty and heart-lessness. To this day, it is folk memories of the Great Famine that provide a major inspiration behind foreign support groups for the IRA.

From the point of view of the surviving Irish who had seen family members and neighbours die, only callousness on the part of what they saw as a rich and powerful government could have allowed the deaths of hundreds of thousands of their citizens. And these deaths were very public. In large parts of the country roadside corpses and multiple graves became a commonplace. Those who were themselves spared the more horrifying sights heard about them by word of mouth and ghastly eye-witness accounts appeared in newspapers throughout Ireland and abroad.

From the perspective of the Irish poor, government action was at best ineffective, at worst non-existent. Etched on the memories of the survivors were not the successful initiatives, but terrible images of overcrowded workhouses, closed-down soup kitchens, evictions, fever-victims, coffin ships and death. It has become difficult to understand how Wilson could imagine that England's 'great sacrifice' was acknowledged and warmly appreciated either in Ireland or elsewhere.

CHAPTER V:

No quick fixes

[The Liberal party in England] is apt to hold its creed in a limp, flaccid, nerveless way, which suggests that it either has never thought it out, or is afraid of the conclusions to which hard thinking would lead . . . The Scotch Liberal, on the other hand, is essentially a rationalist, a man who looks directly from cause to effect, who reasons out his principles in his own mind, and once satisfied applies them unflinchingly. The *perfervida vis* of Scotchmen is really to a great extent what the French call having 'the courage of their opinions', and is the precise quality English Liberals are apt to want.[1] *Walter Bagehot, 1869*

From the point of view of British legislators, the Irish famine was an act of God without recent precedent in Western Europe. Lacking any idea of its likely extent or duration, or any idea of how to deal with disaster on such a scale, they threw (by contemporary standards) huge amounts of money at the problem only to find matters getting steadily worse as one crop failure succeeded another. Drawing on his experience as Home Secretary during the 1822 Irish famine, when a mixture of government relief and private charity had kept the death count low, Peel had some success during 1845–6, but he left to the Russell government a bed of nails.

Torn between sympathy and ideology, the Whigs made compromises. Public works were kept going, but under instructions that they be paid for ultimately by local property owners. By the spring of 1847 the government had advanced almost £5,000,000 (most of which was unrecoverable); 750,000 people were employed, on wages too low to enable them to feed their families, doing work which was mostly futile. The scheme was abandoned in March and replaced by soup kitchens, feeding up to three million people, which in turn were abandoned in September. The scheme finally adopted at that time was to apply to Ireland the English Poor Law, which provided the bare necessities of life in workhouses paid for by a rate levied on local landowners. In Ireland, where landlords were poorest where poverty was greatest, it was a recipe for impoverishment and starvation. 'This callous act, born of ideology and frustration, prolonged the crisis', remarked one historian,[2] concluding that the British government chose to push the problems of Ireland into the back seat.

Russell and his ministers would have been deeply wounded by the accusation of callousness, for they were constantly being belaboured by their own supporters for a sentimentality and lack of moral courage that was bound to make everything worse. 'Whatever difficulties and evils governments are called upon to grapple with,' wrote Wilson, 'there are always two distinct modes open to them. The shortest and the easiest, by far the most agreeable, and generally the most popular, is to palliate and apply temporary remedies, which, however, in the long run, invariably aggravate the evil. The course attended with the greatest present difficulty, inconvenience, and, too frequently, popular odium, is that which strikes at the root of the evil, and seeks to destroy its cause. In the former case, every step you take you are further from your point; in the latter case, every movement tends to restore society to a sound, healthy, independent, and prosperous condition.'[3]

(Reflecting on the turmoil and suffering in east Africa in 1981, *The Economist* showed in 'THE KILLER IN THE AID BAG', that it was still prepared to tell harsh truths even at the risk of being branded cold-hearted. Although, in tune with the spirit of a more compassionate and interventionist age, the paper now accepted the need for short-term expedients, it looked hard at their evil consequences. Millions had been adversely affected by political turmoil and war, 'rendering once independent communities helpless and eroding the social and economic structure of entire nations. Aid from the west, while saving hundreds in the short term, has been a contributing factor to this unhappy process.'

> In Ethiopia, Uganda and Somalia, food aid has become a part of the annual cycle – like a third maize crop or unusually generous rains. Because it is available – sometimes late, often not enough, but always available – it detracts attention from the real problems of the region and delays, but does not do away with, the day of reckoning. People come to depend on food aid

as they once depended on their cattle and crops. Governments, no longer responsible for keeping their own houses in order because the international community has shouldered that burden, get away with murder.

The depressing analysis of each part of the region predicted accurately that refugee Ethiopians and Somalians would permanently lose their traditional skills and spend their lives in food queues in refugee camps. Caught in a modern dilemma which Wilson had been spared, it ended rather helplessly: 'East Africa will want more emergency aid next year. Ethiopia has estimated its needs in 1982 at $200m. Somalia wants $300m. Uganda and Tanzania will also require huge subsidies. Without goodwill (and money) from the west many thousands of people will inevitably die. This goodwill cannot be withdrawn. At the same time, however, an effort should be made to call the governments of the region to account.'[4])

In all his labours on the subject of the famine, it is impossible to doubt Wilson's sincerity: his collected writings on Ireland would make a book the size of this one. Week after week he toiled away trying to make sense of the country and its people, hoping that by mastering all relevant aspects of its history and assembling sound agricultural and industrial statistics he might find some method of reclaiming it from what he saw as its increasing degradation and dependence. Fearful in mid-1847 that famine might spread throughout the United Kingdom, he lamented that there 'never was in the social history of any great civilized country a more complicated knot of momentous considerations, affecting its immediate and future destinies, than those in which we are now involved, including as they do the immediate subsistence of the whole of the people, and the necessity of an entire revolution in the characters, habits, and occupations of a large portion of them. How the United Kingdom is to be fed – how Ireland is to exist – to be governed – to be reclaimed morally and physically – are the great objects of present solicitude and future fear.'[5]

A tiny selection of titles of the myriad articles from across the first seven years of Wilson's editorship gives not only an indication of the scale of the paper's concern but also a glimpse of the changes of mood: 'THE MISGOV-ERNMENT OF IRELAND';[6] 'PICTURE OF A WRETCHED COUNTRY – WHAT CAN BE DONE FOR IT?';[7] 'EFFECTS OF THE GOVERNMENT FEEDING THE IRISH';[8] 'IRELAND – ITS PERMANENT EVILS AND THEIR REMEDY';[9] 'THE IMPOSSIBILITY OF FEEDING AND EMPLOYING THE

IRISH';[10] 'WHAT THE IRISH SHOULD DO';[11] 'HOPE FOR IRELAND';[12] 'PROGRESS IN IRELAND'.[13]

(The tradition persists. A small selection of titles and explanatory subheadings from the past two decades shows the paper devoting much labour to giving the facts about famine and aid worldwide – with much informed discussion of related disputes within the European Community, the UN and aid organisations – and showing warm-heartedness as well as hard-headedness. This list is in microcosm a brief history of recent macro-suffering. The 1970s: 'THE FAT YEARS AND THE LEAN' – a commentary on prospects for the forthcoming UN World Food Conference by the internationally respected campaigner against hunger, Barbara Ward, who had been a key figure on the staff in the 1940s;[14] 'THE POOR GET (MARGINALLY) LESS POOR';[15] 'AID NOT TRADE', calling for a Marshall plan for the Third World;[16] 'ENLIGHTENED SELF-INTEREST – Yes, the rich countries should cancel the official debts of the very poorest ones.'[17] The 1980s: 'DISHING THE POOR – Hard cash is better than hard wheat for poor countries. Better still: cut farm prices in Europe, and raise them in the third world';[18] 'AFRICA'S EMPTY BELLY – Help southern Africa with unconditional food aid now – but with conditional food aid later';[19] 'FAMINE '85 – Do-gooders in sandals often do more good in Africa than international civil servants';[20] 'HOW MUCH CAN FOOD AID HELP THE STARVING? The famine in Africa has touched the hearts and pockets of the well-fed as never before. But once the excitement of "Live Aid" wanes, what will the generosity have achieved?'[21]

With the arrival in the editorial chair early in 1986 of Rupert Pennant-Rea, born in Rhodesia and educated there and in Ireland, there was a change not in principle but in emphasis. The fight against waste was waged as vigorously as ever, but the paper seemed more involved in the issue of world hunger, more hopeful of finding solutions – particularly in Africa – and more moved by suffering. In 1987 appeared 'THE DUTY OF CHARITY', which was uncompromising about priorities.

> If Africa comes to expect to be fed, it will never feed itself. A policy of providing food into the indefinite future – a workhouse policy – would be wrong. Yet at moments of vast desperation and many deaths, the world cannot pass by on the other side. Ethiopia is the extreme case, and so must be faced. Even its benighted government will change its mind, or be thrown

out, one day. There are glimmers of hope, for those who seek hard, in Africa's other stricken countries – Sudan, Mozambique, for a start. But without a fight against famine, there will be fewer people to hope for.[22]

India was the role model. 'MALTHUS DEFIED – India's lesson for Africa', described how foreign aid too often resulted in tractors going to people 'who do not know how to repair them, for use on soils that cannot stand their weight; dams providing rural electrification where there are no houses to put light-bulbs in'. Dumped food killed farmers' incentives. Africa should learn from India and prefer 'the motorbike to the Mercedes, the bullock-cart to the bulldozer', learning the skills they were capable of from foreign investors and experts.

> In its latest half-century, mankind has equipped itself to leap clear of history's net. It has discovered new ways to spread knowledge, new types of seed, new medicines, new sources of energy – cheap inventions, available to anyone. Africans, in their enormous, empty spaces, have room to seize the opportunities that lie before the individual, open mind. In the next quarter of a century they could follow Indians towards prosperity, astonishing the world, and themselves.[23]

The titles go grimly on. 'Southern Sudan – HUNGRY BUT NOT DEAD';[24] 'Ethiopia – HUNGER AS A WEAPON OF WAR';[25] 'African Famines – YET AGAIN';[26] 'THE HORN IS EMPTY' – 'Man, not nature, keeps him hungry' was the caption under the photograph of an emaciated African boy.[27] And a few months later, an unusually pessimistic assessment of the gloomy consequence for Africa of the collapse of the Soviet Union in 'TWO DROUGHTS', concluding:

> It will always be difficult for the world's donors to look at starving people and refuse to feed them. But some rich countries are beginning to argue that famines with political causes can only be halted with political solutions: the wars must stop. With attention shifting to the ex-communist world, compassion for Africa is weakening.[28]

In the case of the dying Irish, while *The Economist*'s research into their country's historical and contemporary condition was thorough and fair-minded, and some of Wilson's long-term solutions persuasive, once the Corn Laws had been repealed – and made little difference – he had no more short-term answers. His medium-term answers amounted to little more than a proposal that the people should be allowed to appropriate waste land and support for compensation for tenants' improvements. 'We certainly will not be seduced by any solitary example to play the sentimental, and throw overboard our well-weighed general principles', he had said early on in the famine, and he certainly lived up to that promise.[29] With Adam Smith as the template, virtually every attempt to ameliorate Irish conditions was found wanting. But it is clear that accusations of heartlessness wounded him. 'Never, perhaps, was there a case where it appeared more feasible to disregard the abstract principles of political economy, and listen only to the dictates of sentimental benevolence', he wrote a few months later, for 'the hard-hearted principles of *laissez-faire* were denounced as the principles of *laissez-souffrir*, and the notion of leaving the Irish to struggle unaided by the Government through their misery, was scouted by all but a few political economists, with general indignation.' Yet government interference had merely served to aggravate the situation.[30] In the spring of 1847 there was hurt evident in yet another article about the 'irremedial ruin and degradation' to which Ireland would shortly be reduced if not left to her own devices. It had almost certainly been prompted by a letter from his friend Lord Clarendon, President of the Board of Trade: 'I cannot congratulate you on your article on Saturday. *The Economist* has been some time in labour, but has only produced a *very* small mouse.'[31] It had been his duty, Wilson pointed out, 'at whatever personal sacrifice of feeling' to express dissent, for what was wrong in principle could not be right in practice. 'The science which serves only to navigate a ship in fine weather, and is inapplicable in a storm, is unworthy of the name', he wrote defiantly.[32]

He had many supporters, of course. Radnor wrote a lengthy letter to *The Economist* to protest against the setting up of soup kitchens. It was impracticable and hence false in theory, he explained, to say that it was the duty of a government to provide food for the people; in practice, if attempted, it would lead to injustice and disastrous consequences: 'Charity is a proper motive for the private conduct of individuals, but justice the paramount duty of a government.'[33]

Wilson's friend G.R. Porter rallied round as well – 'heart-sick' at the proposed Irish measures – and his new friend, shortly to be a contributor, W.R. Greg, thought his articles should have a great effect. 'Is it not astounding and alarming, that measures unanimously condemned by all the able and influential organs of the Press, and by all the acknowledged thinkers in the country, should yet be passing in Parliament almost by acclamation, – and that even the very authors and supporters of them should be (as I believe they are) in *their hearts fully aware of their monstrous culpability?*'

Wilson sent Greg's and Porter's letters to Clarendon, who replied that while agreeing entirely 'as to the mischievous tendency (or rather certainty) of the course we are adopting', he still believed it had been unavoidable because of 'the overwhelming character of the calamity' and 'the nature of the people' they had to deal with.

> The best proof of this is that nobody has anything better, even with the benefit of experience, to propose, for you must excuse me for saying that the *Economist* has suggested no plan – the gigantic proportions of our Franken-stein do not add to the stature of your mouse – you *in fact* say *do nothing*, which is exceedingly comfortable for a gentleman writing by his fireside in London, but not at all practicable for a Government having to answer to the humanity and generosity of England for the mortality of Ireland.

Circumstances had forced interference. 'You lay down abstract principles and desire that men should be left to act upon them, which is quite right if ordinary men under ordinary circumstances were in question, but you have to deal with Irishmen . . . It is a great misfortune for us to have such a people under our charge, but we cannot leave them entirely to their own devices at a moment when they are unusually incapacitated.'[34]

Having a benign disposition, Wilson took criticism well and their friend-ship was unaffected. Clarendon became Lord Lieutenant of Ireland in May of the same year and over his five years there sent Wilson about forty letters which added further authoritativeness to the paper's coverage. And while *The Economist* never ceased to deplore any signs of weakness, it gave Clarendon an excellent press when it was possible so to do. 'The Earl of Clarendon is zealously engaged in the arduous work of teaching the Irish', wrote Wilson approvingly in the autumn of 1847. 'He began some time ago to provide them instruction in agriculture. He has now undertaken to illustrate the moral duties. Never since he has been in Ireland has he neglected an opportunity to inculcate the virtues most wanted by the Irish; setting them an example by his conduct of that calmness, simplicity, moderation, and truth telling which they so much require to make them perfect.'[35]

It was a passage illustrative of Wilson's – and indeed imperial Britain's – greatest deficiency: a lack of imagination in dealing with recalcitrant natives and a conviction that all would be well if they could be made into the image of their masters. Scott Gordon's reading of Wilson's character from his portrait is beautifully put: 'He sits stolidly in his chair, his hands folded in finality. His round face is benevolent, but there is the unmistakable mark of doctrine in the eyes, close set and steady, and there is that thin, firm mouth. "There is no nonsense about me," they say. "I know what is right, I work hard, and I do my duty."'[36] And he found it impossible to understand why others were not made the same way. Having first sympathised with the Irish because of British misgovernment, his patience ran out because of their wilful refusal to think or behave like Scots. The more he analysed their conduct as the famine continued – abandonment of jobs in Britain in order to come home and join in the public works; insistence on planting potatoes rather than other crops; following demagogues; and so on and so on – the more sympathy gave way to exasperation and disgust. Who in Britain had given more thought or effort to the problems of Ireland? Wilson had ground away with the statistics, the facts and the doctrine to find solutions and year after year more catastrophes happened. The Irish stayed 'ignorant and turbulent' with apparently nary a fixed principle nor an ounce of common sense between them. Like other contemporaries, he was close to feeling that they were bringing famine on themselves out of sheer cussedness.

'Why can't they be more like us?' Week after week, for 150 years, writers on *The Economist* have been asking that very question as they examine the irrationalities of the world around them. In 1850, by which time his long and wearisome preoccupation with Ireland was virtually at an end, Wilson had found the way. Having scrutinised to the last footnote the 18th Report of the Board of Public Works in Ireland and the 3rd Report of the Poor Law Commissioners for Ireland and summarised them for his readers, he had come to a sanguine conclusion. On some estates with intelligent super-vision, tenants had learned 'sound principles'. Consequently a general rule had emerged: '*Wherever the Irish peasantry are so situated, either by the sub-ordination of their position or by minority in numbers, as to take the tone from those above them and those around them, they succeed and advance.* Wherever they are so far dominant, either in numbers or influence, as to overpower such foreign elements or amendment as may have settled among them, – or where they are without a strong, large and prominent admixture of such foreign superiorities, the failings of their race prevail, and they sink rapidly in social condition.' Being essentially 'an *imitative* being', the

Irishman needed only good example to improve – hence his success abroad.[37]

With the famine at an end and having reached this happy conclusion, Wilson was able to put Ireland aside and get on with his new additional occupations as MP, government minister and polemicist in the raging currency debate. His paper was never to have to face such a ghastly domestic tragedy again, but it often had to consider appropriate policies for dealing with famine in far-flung parts of the Empire, particularly in India. As Wilson's generation gave way to its less dogmatic successors, intervention ceased to be completely heretical, but it was not until the last few decades that the paper again threw itself fervently into the debate on mass starvation. Modern communications bring the dying into every living-room and *The Economist*'s heart and head fight it out.

In 1989 the economics editor, Clive Crook, produced a survey on 'THE THIRD WORLD', a *tour de force* which emulated Wilson's approach to Ireland in seeking to lay down the principles by which a poor country could prosper. In the process he produced a highly coherent explanation of the course of economic history in the recent past along with a robust and limpid defence of classical economics; the argument was shot through with iconoclasticism.

Pennant-Rea once described his paper as 'a "Friday Viewspaper", where the readers, with higher than average incomes, better than average minds but with less than average time, can test their opinions against ours. We try to tell the world about the world, to persuade the expert and reach the amateur, with an injection of opinion and argument. Above all, it's a constant challenge to ensure excellence and to present familiar subjects in a new way.'[38] Clive Crook took a very old and sad subject, one from which most readers shy away, and made it exciting. He had many more resources and much more evidence to draw on than Wilson, but the message was startlingly similar. He was concerned to demonstrate the economic lessons taught by the Third World over the previous forty years. 'For in development,' he explained in his opening article, 'TRIAL AND ERROR', 'more than in any other area of public policy, the facts speak clearly about the links between actions and consequences.'

> When economists give policymakers advice that turns out to be bad, as they often do, their traditional excuse is that unlike proper scientists they cannot conduct controlled experiments. They can never know what would have happened if governments had done something else. But the postwar history

of the developing countries provides the next best thing to a controlled experiment. Governments differed not just in the details of their policies, but in their whole approach to development – and these differences lasted not just for a year or two, but in some cases for decades. The results are now available for inspection.

His message was cheerful. Even the worst cases could become relatively prosperous, if 'just one thing' happened. 'Governments must learn their place.' (This he spelled out later as being to confine themselves to running an effective legal system, good education and health services and an efficient infrastructure.) Although Crook saw a role for governments, he believed they would be well advised to make *laissez-faire* the rule.

> At a guess, government meddling does more economic harm, measured on a dollar basis, in the industrial countries than in the third world. But bad government is a luxury good. The people who live in the industrial countries can afford it, whereas in developing countries any loss of output has to be measured not just in dollars but in ruined lives.

'Advocates of state intervention always love to pose as realists', he remarked in his summarising article. 'Markets are not perfect, they say. If they were, perhaps they could be relied upon to allocate resources properly. But everybody knows they aren't, especially in developing countries, so governments have to step in. Many people would dismiss the arguments of this survey with that and a wave of the hand.'

> These realists are indeed realistic about markets. The price system never works perfectly, least of all in developing countries, so it cannot make all as it would be in some textbook world. But at that point the realists' powers of observation run out. They are laughably unrealistic about governments. In thinking that the state should stroll in whenever markets are flawed, they are making the same mistake that they (falsely) accuse liberal economists of making. They are confusing theory with reality. Surely realists should know that nothing in this world – not even government – is perfect.

The question was whether to rely on imperfect markets or imperfect governments.

> Broadly speaking, the world's poor countries have followed two approaches to development since the 1950s. One of these approaches – far more popular

than the other – deliberately rejected orthodox microeconomics, said that prices did not matter much, and concentrated on the state's role in releasing a variety of macroeconomic brakes on growth. The other left the brakes to release themselves and gave prices (especially world prices) a much bigger say in the allocation of resources. After three decades the experience of these countries answers the question. History chooses the invisible hand.

More than 140 years on, the voice was unmistakably Wilson's.

CHAPTER VI:

The pull of politics

We shall require to have in Parliament new men, who, by study, have
obtained a command over principles, and by practice, a habit of applying
them . . . bold men, who will not shrink from making present knowledge the
basis of legislation. We want men, too, who have faith in principles, who
know that man can only see a little part of every great whole, and who will
fearlessly and trustingly give effect to the discoveries of science, convinced
that they must lead to good, though every turn and winding of the road may
not be within human ken.[1]

When James Wilson wrote in these terms in June 1847, he was already
contesting a parliamentary seat. He had been thinking seriously about going
into politics from the time *The Economist* was little more than two years old.
Two developments had made it possible to go ahead. Changes in the political
scene had made it possible for him to contemplate wearing a party label and
the paper was running smoothly and profitably enough to enable him to take
on the burdens involved in becoming an MP.

In October 1843 – after explaining that he viewed politics solely through
the medium of the 'ECONOMICAL' – he had continued: 'We have only to do
with Sir Robert Peel, Lord John Russell, Mr O'Connell, Mr Villiers, Mr
Cobden, or any other public man, in relation to this one grand consideration.
And Whig or Tory are, of course, objects of the most perfect indifference; we
see the present and future welfare of the empire bound up in FREE TRADE;
and to free trade, therefore, we devote ourselves wholly, exclusively, and
entirely.'[2] Indeed by December Wilson was strongly in favour of a coalition
of free-trade supporting Whigs and Tories. 'If the free traders, "now growing

up into a formidable party" do but steer right onward . . . no fortification or reinforcement of Downing street will avail against them.'3

Although by instinct a Whig, Wilson worked hard at being even-handed. Discussing a debate on the Corn Laws in February 1844, he remarked that 'we shall be as much indebted to the leaders of the present government, and to Sir Robert Peel in particular, for exposing the fallacies and refuting the policy of the fixed duty to which Lord John Russell still adheres for revenue, as we have been to the Noble Lord and his late colleagues for their able exposure of the disastrous and ruinous consequences of the sliding scale'.4

Yet in the same article his loyalties showed when he wrote of 'our severe disappointment at finding a man of Lord John Russell's political standing, of acknowledged clearness of judgment, and of unquestionable sincerity and integrity, giving countenance to a fallacy which we had thought nearly exploded: – "Free trade – very good; but – THE DEBT:" – "total repeal, – unquestionably right and just; but – THE TAXES"'.5 He found it easier to attack Peel, whom in the spring of 1845 he described as 'a great reformer – but only when other men have made reforms safe, and, above all, safe to himself. The whole course of Sir Robert Peel's life has been to oppose every measure, till others had made it ripe for the public, or the public ripe for it, and then, when quite safe, he has adopted it. What other men have conceived, dandled in infancy, watched and nurtured through youth, struggled hard to maintain while fighting its way to maturity and public acceptance – when all the risk of rearing was past, Sir Robert Peel has seized, adopted, and completed. But, no matter how fine the constitution, how promising the ripened manhood, this prudent Minister will have nothing to say to anything while in its *teens*.'6

And again a few months later, in discussing the waning influence of government and public men, he explained it as being a result of their being 'the last to adopt wise principles . . . Ministers, in place of exhibiting the sagacity and wisdom to lead and conduct great public interests, more generally obstruct them, until either public opinion or public exigencies are so strong as to hurry them forward in spite of themselves, and the prejudices of their immediate supporters. Take, for example, the case of Sir Robert Peel, whom all admit to be the most dexterous, and whom many contend is the most able statesman of the day; his official career must be admitted, by his warmest admirers, to have been one uniform course of adopting principles and acts one year which he had vigorously opposed in former years.'7

By the beginning of the following year, having announced his conversion to the true religion, Peel had become a hero: he 'has based his arguments, and defended his propositions, on the fullest admissions of the truth of the doctrines of political economy. To the abstract science propounded by Adam Smith, Sir Robert Peel is the first minister who has given a full and unqualified practical application.'[8] Having seen Peel split his party for a principle, Wilson turned on his foes. While class legislation was 'something to be perpetually disowned and detested ... party morality ... is not one atom better ... It thinks only of faction, when discussion concerns the whole people ... Never was its spirit more truly exemplified than by Mr D'Israeli on Thursday week. He overwhelmed Sir Robert Peel with acrimonious reproaches for deserting his party, utterly regardless of that change being for the benefit of the public.'[9]

Of course Wilson and Disraeli were antipathetic. As Peel had moved away from protectionism, Disraeli – partly for personal reasons – had conducted a vendetta against him in the satirical style at which he excelled. It was he who described Peel as having caught the Whigs bathing and run away with their clothes. 'Sarcasm is a useful enough weapon in its way', commented *The Economist* on Disraeli's novel, *Sybil, or the Two Nations*, 'and no doubt Mr D'Israeli is a master of it. When it happens to be a man's *only* or principal power, however, it becomes almost as great a scourge to himself as it is to others, and, no doubt, Mr D'Israeli labours under the mortification of feeling that, however clearly he shows up in detail the errors of others, he is unable to lay down any feasible scheme of public polity himself, which can command the approval of any half-dozen of intelligent and sober-minded men in the country.'[10]

By the spring of 1846, with Corn Laws repeal on course, Wilson was full of the vision of the new dawn of which he wished to be a part. A new legislative era had arrived, and a

revolution of the most important character is peacefully and quietly taking place ... Traditional influences are giving way to those of knowledge and intelligence. Old parties, bound together only by conventional ties, are broken up, and new ones, knowing a common bond, of well-recognised principles, in accordance with the advanced intelligence of the day, are formed. He who will rule in future, must rule on principle, and not by expediency; in accordance with the improved knowledge of the times, and not by the timid prejudices and fears of conventional cliques.

Though party groupings would be as necessary as ever, they would be formed 'on well-recognised principles of material and social good'.

> Leaders will be as much required as ever; but the claim to such distinction will more than ever be tested by the influence derived from superior intellect, and a strict adherence to wise and well-recognised principles. A political leader in this country now, to preserve his influence, must be in advance, and not lagging behind, the intelligence of the day.[11]

There is a fascinating contrast here with some of what Wilson published – less than five years later – in lengthy, generous and emotional tributes after the sudden death of Robert Peel. (His daughter Emilie wrote that the only time she saw her father with tears in his eyes was when he had read the announcement of Peel's death.) By then Wilson had had three years at the sharp end of politics and the know-all dogmatist had given way to a more sober and humble pragmatist. Peel's 'perfect disinterestedness and his great sacrifices' had made all parties, even those most opposed to him, 'place the most implicit reliance on his intentions'. He would be greatly missed. 'No more memorable example is to be found in history of Mr Burke's aphorism – that to lead, statesmen must follow. Sir Robert Peel had acquired, from much observation, a nice tact in determining the appropriate time to carry a measure.'[12] 'We believe', said *The Economist* the following week, 'there never was a statesman on whose trained and experienced powers, on whose adequacy to any emergency and any trial, both friend and foe, colleague and antagonist, rested with such a sense of security and reliance.' It was hard to avoid erring on the side of leniency, but 'we have been politically opposed to him through life, with the exception of one short episode; and due weight should therefore be attached to the testimony of an antagonist, whose feelings have been often embittered by the contests of party, when we avow that in looking back we can discover some cases in which we now think him right, where at the time we thought him wrong; many in which we can now perceive excuse or justification for conduct which at the time we considered as inexcusable . . . Created of the stuff out of which liberals are made, but born into ranks in which only tories could be found, his whole course was a sort of perpetual protest against the accident of his birth.'

There followed a self-revelatory burst that the younger Wilson would have found heretical. Considering the common criticism of Peel that he showed inconsistency, Wilson's paper suggested that that might be a virtue rather than a defect.

> With the mass even of the most honest and highly-gifted statesmen, political wisdom is the slow growth of years, the product of long experience, of wide and patient observation of experiments tried and failed in, of blunders made, recognised, and profited by. Altered times, new circumstances, past errors, teach their own lessons. Political convulsions bring to light new dangers, and explode old theories; recluse philosophers investigate and perfect subtle sciences which overturn many venerable notions and time-honoured prejudices; and the minister who would be truly wise must hasten to learn all that new discoveries can teach him, however they may shatter the antiquated knowledge of the past.[13]

Life changed quickly in many important ways once Wilson decided definitely to go into politics, an ambition inevitable in a man of action who had become so much part of that world. It was no longer enough to report on and advise politicians from the fringes: he wanted to be one of their number. Once again it was Lord Radnor who smoothed the way and recommended him to try his luck in the Wiltshire borough of Westbury.

Wilson had been eloquent in *The Economist* about the electoral corruption and jobbery of the period. As votes were still cast in public, tenant farmers or tradesmen felt obliged to vote for the candidate approved by their landlord or major customer. The secret ballot might be the answer, but much better would be 'the spread of improved ideas on the proper relations in which men stand to each other . . . Perhaps we may be told that, when these views generally prevail, the millennium will have arrived. We think more hopefully of the world than that.' Worse still was the habit of 'peculiarly "independent" electors' of expecting favours from candidates or MPs. 'To be chosen a member of Parliament is no doubt a great honour, and in this vain world, of course, all honorary distinctions must be paid for in some shape or other. But we will venture to say of those who are or wish to be members of Parliament, and can reconcile it to their feelings to pay for their honours in this gross way, that they are not very likely to be much more refined in looking for repayment to themselves . . . We wish electors could see that "true self-love and social are the same," – that whatever they receive, without fairly and industriously earning it, is taken back from them in some shape or other.'[14]

Now, a year later, Wilson was up against the reality. Westbury's sitting protectionist member intended to stand down at the next election, and though the constituency was strongly under the influence of a Conservative squirearchy, Radnor believed a Liberal could win it. On Wilson's exploratory visit there he explained his political views at great length from an old cart, and encouraged by the reaction, committed himself to the borough and bought a house nearby. His family, who had remained based at Boulogne for over three years, joined him in Wiltshire in November 1846.

The number of qualified voters was tiny – only a few hundred – but the canvassing was intense. Wilson was as thorough in this as in everything. Friends lobbying neighbours on his behalf included Clarendon, Radnor and Villiers and among the obstacles that had to be overcome was disquiet among Whig ministers about articles in *The Economist*.[15] Wilson could almost be accounted heroic in his refusal to trim his own (or his subordinates') arguments. Possibly the paper's most uncompromising *laissez-faire* article appeared only a few months before the general election, sparked off by Ireland yet again but addressing itself mainly to an explanation of which functions a government can exercise with benefit to the community.

> It may be a very unwelcome and humiliating doctrine for statesmen and legislatures to recognise, but it is nevertheless one, the truth of which experience is forcing upon mankind more and more irresistibly every year, that they are much more powerful for evil than for good; that the greatest and most ingeniously devised schemes to better the condition of the world, which have, when adopted, been applauded as the acme of wisdom and the greatest efforts of human intellect, have proved but miserable failures for the objects in view, while they had had innumerable indirect and mischievous consequences never dreamt of or anticipated.

The statesmen with a lasting reputation were celebrated 'only for what they have undone – not for what they have done'. The enlightened men and distinguished statesmen of the age were Huskisson, Lord Sydenham, Peel, Russell, Sir James Graham and Villiers and Cobden.

> But, for what? For contriving wise and clever regulations for society? No. For undoing all that past wisdom had professed to do; for repealing the disabilities and restrictions imposed on Roman Catholics, and for abolishing the test and corporation acts, which were adopted as essential to the

existence and safety of the Protestant Church; for the removal of exclusive political privileges, by the Reform Bill and the Municipal Corporations' Bill; for the abolition of commercial restrictions, by the modification of the Navigation Laws, and the reduction of differential and prohibitory duties at various periods . . . by the total repeal of the Corn Laws . . . All that can be said of the greatest statesman is, that he discovered error and removed it; that he found a country harassed by restrictions and regulations, and that he freed it.

In so far as legislation had tried to improve society 'by regulating or aiding private efforts to obtain a subsistence or to secure prosperity' it had failed totally. 'A continual proneness to interference on the part of governments has been the curse of every country and of every age; and it has just been in proportion as communities have been relieved from that pernicious influence that they have exhibited a healthy prosperity.'

The more enlightened men became, the more they accepted that they were incapable of performing the functions of '"a paternal government," which seeks to aid others to do what experience shows men can only do for themselves'. Would anyone have the presumption to try to improve on the operation of the human frame by meddling with any part of it? The social frame was even more complicated and interdependent and liable to be damaged overall by interference with any part. The 'true secret of the failure of all acts of legislation which seek to promote the prosperity of commerce, the feeding of the people, or the advancement of private interests, is, that they are not only miserably inefficient for the objects they have in view, but principally that they interfere with and artificially supersede the far more perfect laws which Providence has ordained for the moral government of the world.' Among the great natural laws governing the world, the writer recognised 'the strong instinct of self-preservation, natural affection, love of approbation, self-respect, sympathy with misfortune and suffering, and a sense of responsibility and duty to God and our neighbour'. If all or any of these were 'violated, abused, or neglected', suffering and inconvenience would follow, but experience showed that no legislation could prevent individuals from committing such abuses. Therefore,

the great duty of a government appears to resolve itself into an attempt to preserve different parts of society from suffering from the wrongs of others. The more we reflect upon the experience of the past – the more we watch what is now going forward in this country, the more irresistibly are we brought to the conclusion that the only functions which a government can exercise with advantage to society are those connected with the maintenance of order, the peace and security of life and property, and the raising of the necessary funds for those objects; and, moreover, that whenever a government or the legislature step beyond those simple duties, they do so at the hazard of doing much more mischief than good.[16]

The facts were selective and the argument dubious, but Wilson certainly deserved full marks for courage. Once he assumed ministerial office, conflict would arise between the paper's independence and its proprietor's political ambitions, but until then, when he wrote *The Economist*, he expressed his political creed in its purest form, regardless of consequences. His criticisms of the government continued, but Villiers would seem to have persuaded those who mattered that Wilson would vote with the government if elected. He turned out to be excellent at electioneering. He and his family were becoming known in the area and he was happy to explain his ideas clearly and frankly to all and sundry. As his daughter Emilie put it: 'While Ireland in her misery was chiefly occupying my father's pen, he was steadily gaining ground with the electors of Westbury.' An observer remarked that 'Mr Wilson may or may not be the best political economist in England, but depend upon it he is the *only* political economist who would ever come in for the borough of Westbury.'

In June 1847 there appeared in *The Economist* an article on the approaching general election calling for new blood in parliament. It can be read as Wilson's manifesto and it was a decidedly optimistic document. It could properly have been called 'WE ARE ALL FREE TRADERS NOW'. The forthcoming election, he explained, would be fought with little regard to party ties or principles, for the distinction between Whigs and Tories was at an end. With the Corn Laws gone, 'there are no great wrongs to be redressed . . . no flagrant injustice to remedy . . . no general object on which to go to the country. The kingly power is not threatened, the church is not in danger, the aristocracy is safe, public liberty is secure, the Pope is not at our heels, there is no pressing and general demand for any particular species of reform.' Although family and territorial influences would dictate the choice of some candidates, on the whole the next parliament should contain a larger than usual number of 'clever, diligent, thoughtful legislators'.

Ahead lay matters of political expediency, most important being how 'to raise and improve the condition of the lower classes throughout the empire – including unfortunate Ireland'. A related matter was how best to improve the dwellings of the urban poor. While *The Economist* favoured giving the lower classes power over local bodies, it accepted that the majority favoured limiting local authority and extending central jurisdiction. 'Time and the next Parliament must decide the question.' There was also need to improve the condition of the rural lower classes by alterations in the game laws. What was required was that parliament contain men 'imbued with the principles of free trade, prepared at every feasible opportunity to act on them, and resist all attempts to impugn them' in order that the 'condition of the multitude' be improved. Otherwise, 'as time will tolerate no delay, as things not directed to good now run rapidly to evil – if pauperism be allowed to become the rule, instead of the exception, in England as well as in Ireland – if well rewarded employment be not the general lot, we may look for years of misery, ending in turmoil, confusion, and anarchy.' 'The people', he ended solemnly, 'have a great duty to perform: we hope they will perform it honestly, patriotically, and with discrimination, and give us a House of Commons worthy of them, and of the present exigencies of the empire.'[17]

The people of Westbury performed their duty in July 1847, despite a late challenge to Wilson from a Peelite journalist, Matthew James Higgins, who wrote for a variety of newspapers under the pseudonym of Jacob Omnium: the vote was 170 to 149. 'I only hope you may not find attendance in the H. of Cs. a useless as well as a disagreeable occupation', wrote Radnor, less of an optimist than his protégé. 'The new House will be an odd medley, very difficult to manage or to do any good with.'

CHAPTER VII:

'The Up-Line'

The line to Heaven by Christ was made
With Heavenly Truth the Rails are laid . . .
God's Word is the first Engineer
It points the way to Heaven so dear . . .
God's Love the Fire, his Truth the Steam . . .
That drives the engine and the train
In First and Second and Third Class
Repentance, Faith and Holiness . . .
Come then poor Sinners, now's the time
At any station on the Line
If you'll repent and turn from Sin
The Train will stop and take you in.
'The Up-Line', from The Spiritual Railway, *1845**

If Wilson's life as a businessman had given him the experience to make *The Economist* a success, his achievements as a journalist had already earned him respect in influential circles. His reputation for comprehensively and honestly dealing with the major issues of the day was to help towards his rapid advancement in politics.

'Within seven years from the foundation of The Economist', wrote Bagehot in 1860, 'Mr Wilson dealt effectively and thoroughly with three first-rate subjects, – the railway mania, the famine in Ireland, and the panic of 1847, in addition to the entire question of Free Trade, which was naturally the main topic of economical teaching in those years. On all these three

*Carved on a tombstone in Ely Cathedral to commemorate the train driver and stoker killed when the Norwich-to-London train crashed on Christmas Eve.

topics he explained somewhat original opinions, which were novelties, if not paradoxes then, though they are very generally believed now. To his writings on the railway mania he was especially fond of recurring, since he believed that by his warnings – warnings very effectively brought out and very constantly reiterated – he had "saved several men their fortunes" at that time.'

All four subjects singled out by Bagehot were interrelated, particularly the two not yet looked at here, for the railway mania of 1845 was to be a major factor in bringing about the financial panic of 1847. From the point of view of *The Economist*, coverage of these linked topics was to provide a vivid illustration of how quickly it became an important voice in matters to do with banking and the Stock Exchange as well as with politics and trade.

In the early days, the paper's trade information and statistics swamped the few inches accorded to finance. In the first issue, for instance, money market and Stock Exchange prices occupied less than ten per cent of the columns called 'Commercial Markets'. The former had three lines:

> MONEY MARKET.– Though there is a somewhat improved demand for money, owing to the revival of many branches of trade, yet it remains very abundant at little or no improvement of price. Good paper is readily done at 2 per cent.

It also made a brief appearance in the 'Postscript' – the stop-press column dated Saturday morning, the day the paper came out, where it was announced that 'The notice just issued by the Bank of England, with the settled appearance of fine weather, lead to the conclusion that the present abundance of money will continue.'

The Stock Exchange, more favoured, was given a two-column table of current prices: under 'English Funds' were thirteen items, including India Stock, Bank Long Annuities and Exchequer Bills, and under 'Foreign Funds' fourteen, which consisted of the bonds of nine European and five South American countries. The 'Postscript' added a paragraph:

> STOCK EXCHANGE, TWELVE O'CLOCK. There is little change to-day in our markets, and no new feature in foreign or English stocks, except that Consols are nominally a trifle higher, being 95 to 95⅛, having left off yesterday at 94⅞ to 95.

The statistical imbalance was primarily a reflection of Wilson's own priorities, but as he found his editorial feet, became better acquainted with his readers' needs and acquired the resources to meet them, the striking deficiencies were swiftly remedied. Less than six months after its foundation, the paper suddenly and massively increased its Stock Exchange coverage to provide tables of current prices for 31 'Government Funds', 48 'Public Securities of United States of America' (three weeks or so out of date), twelve 'Irish Stocks', five 'French Funds', 41 'Foreign Stocks', 75 'Railways', and 26 'Joint Stock Banks', along with bullion prices and a statement of the liabilities and assets of the Bank of England.[1] And, as time went on, the coverage was further extended and improved.

On the money-market side, there was a distinct advance made in the middle of 1844 when foreign-exchange tables first made their entrance, but it was not until the first issue of 1845 that substantial and systematic coverage was guaranteed by the incorporation in the paper's new title of *Bankers' Gazette*. It says much about the impulsiveness of Wilson's character and the speed and flexibility of his printers that what had been promised the previous week was merely '*The Economist* and Weekly Commercial Times'.

Yet, if it took Wilson some time to acknowledge that there was more to statistics than trade, from the beginning his leading articles showed a keen interest in all aspects of banking and investment. And although on few subjects dear to his heart did he fail to display emotion, it was in connection with railways and railway investment that he became particularly incensed as he strove to stop the government from intervening and the speculators from panicking.

The nineteenth-century passion for railways has no twentieth-century parallel. While the practical advantages were obvious, the greatest appeal was to the sense of wonder: in Britain, railway worship had almost a religious quality. Wilson was less fanciful than many: 'Now, though railways are, on the whole, models of ingenuity, full of wonderful proofs of man's power and skill, they are not made merely for themselves ... If they only, like a tea party, brought people together to pass an hour in pleasant trifling, they would not be made. The purpose of making them is far more earnest. They save the time of the industrious classes.'[2]

By the time *The Economist* was founded, two thousand miles of British railway track, laying the foundations of the trunk system, were already open. The acute depression of 1842–3 had been exacerbated by a standstill in railway investment, but as early as November Wilson was able to announce the 'gratifying' news that railway stock had gone up. Acts of Parliament were required to authorise every line, thus adding substantially to the already heavy development costs of each project. By March 1844 Wilson had noted a number of cases where people who had requested shares had failed to pay for them, thus throwing the burden of expense on those who had. 'All this tends to show what extreme caution and care should be used in such matters to secure perfect success.' But most of his ruminations on railways during that year were focused on the Railway Act introduced by the President of the Board of Trade, William Ewart Gladstone.

Wilson was outraged. 'What a curious thing it is to have a clever, ingenious, metaphysical and abstract man at the head of the trading affairs of this peculiarly practical and matter-of-fact nation', he wrote, denouncing Gladstone for happily supporting legislative acts in direct variance with principle. 'The boast of this country, under all governments, has been that unlike France and many other neighbouring countries, the character of our undertakings was not stultified and destroyed by a system of intermeddling and bureaucracy, so obvious elsewhere.' All were agreed on this. But 'it has seldom been our lot to see contained in any proposition such a mass of antiquated, exploded, and objectionable principle as we find involved in Mr Gladstone's Railway Bill now before us . . . we cannot believe that such a bill will pass in the nineteenth century . . . it abounds with the most unsound principles.' Gladstone sought control over profits and fares, and the right to buy any railway after fifteen years. 'It is impossible to foresee the whole train of mischief which would follow such a measure.' For 'where the most profit is made, the public is best served . . . Limit the profit, and you limit the exertion of ingenuity in a thousand ways by which the public can be benefited and the company enriched.' Examples followed. The answer was competition between railway lines. 'If men see an inducement to invest their money in railways, and will conform with the standing orders of the House, which are strict enough, Mr Gladstone and Parliament may safely enough leave all the rest to people's own care for their own property.'[3]

A slight softening, though no change in principle, was evident a couple of weeks later when Wilson admitted that Gladstone's bill 'points to some things which we have always considered to be evils in our railway manage-ment, and requiring great change . . . the want of facilities for conveying the poorer and working classes'. On foreign railways, particularly those of Belgium, many passengers were of 'the humbler peasantry and working classes'. This was 'not that the Flemish are of a more locomotive or active temperament than the English, for, on the contrary, they are much less so, but that the facilities both in speed, frequency, and cheapness, on their railways, are infinitely greater than ours'. The railway companies needed to recognise the profit to be made from transporting the masses. When they did, they would 'prove peculiarly successful' at meeting the demand if 'untroubled and uncontrolled by official interference'. To his satisfaction, the bill was emasculated in committee, though railways were required to run at least one train daily at a fare of a penny a mile, and the state was given the right (not used for a century) to buy lines after they had operated for 21 years.

(Twenty years later, Bagehot favoured the nationalisation of railways, if done in such a way as 'to diminish their danger, economise their cost, and augment their utility'. He saw no possibility of beneficial competition between railway companies for long periods. 'Intense momentary competition is not only possible but likely. Two boards of directors may quarrel, and may do anything to spite one another for a time, but only for a time. Sooner or later, common sense prevails over ill temper, and the two companies agree what to charge the public; real monopoly becomes invincible, because it is disguised in the forms of seeming competition; it evades the cry which would destroy it, because it looks like the very antithesis of all it really is':[4] he might have been writing about airlines. The British railways were nationalised in 1948, *The Economist* being cautiously in favour. In 1993, however, it had come closer to Wilson's view: it would be right to privatise British Rail, subject to the simultaneous introduction of road pricing.[5])

But by February 1845 there was a new menace to be confronted: speculation had begun to run rife and Gladstone was trying to improve the system of vetting projects with the aim of protecting investors 'against the consequences of imprudent acts. As a principle, we believe there is nothing more objectionable than an attempt on the part of a government to find prudence for a people. It removes a great weight of personal and individual responsibility and caution, and creates a reliance on public officers as the only, however imperfect, substitute. These principles, we think, have been strikingly illustrated by the speculative mania which has existed of late with regard to railway undertakings. Every proposal, without care or inquiry on the part of the public, has been eagerly taken up, and submitted to the railway department of the Board for its consideration and sanction – individual caution has been relinquished, and a public office relied upon.'[6]

Yet again, out of context, it would be possible to read Wilson's articles as unfeeling, but they were anything but. It is more than clear from the emotion he displayed as the mania developed how concerned he was to save others from suffering the kind of financial disaster that had struck him in the late 1830s. His most personal and prophetic article was probably that baldly called 'RAILWAY SPECULATION'. It was an example of Wilson at his best: informed, lucid, sensible, thoughtful – 'belief-producing', the businessman writing for businessmen, or, in this case, the singed speculator delivering the awful warning from the depths of bitter experience.

After putting the positive case for railway investment, he went on: 'Still, we see much, and quite sufficient, to lead us to anticipate enormous losses and intense suffering to which the country will be exposed through these undertakings, whether we look upon them as objects of speculation or of investment.' Most lines in which investments were now being made were less important and would have less traffic than those of the previous decade, and so many were coming into existence simultaneously as to place a severe drain on available capital and greatly increase the price of materials and labour. The money market was as yet unaffected, because of the delay between procuring parliamentary permission and going into operation; hence 'the period when the main bulk of the capital is required is remote from that when the greatest excitement and speculation exists, and no immediate check is therefore experienced by calls of capital'. But when the operations started on these huge projects and, to raise funds, securities came on the market week after week, drawing capital away from London to every part of the country, 'when a combination of other events will no doubt, as in past times, tend to an adverse foreign exchange – if then (and all former experience warns us to expect it) a deficient harvest should occur, an export of bullion take place, and high prices of the first necessaries of life derange business and industry at home, the havoc which these undertakings will create, it is painful to reflect upon'.

> But so it will be. However calm and smooth matters are now, every agency which was silently at work in 1835, to result in the terrors of 1839 and 1840, is as certainly at work now. And just in proportion to our increased population and extended interests, when the next bad harvest overtakes us without any preparation, will be the aggravation of our suffering.
>
> The railways would feel it most of all, for it would emerge that a large

proportion of shareholders were merely speculators unable to pay up the calls; all the weaker undertakings will be suspended for want of capital, and the whole onus of proceeding with them thrown upon a comparatively small number of bona fide holders; and, as with the breaking up of many banks from 1839 to 1843, it will be a matter of marvel and pain to discover the universality of the character of this speculation.

From domestic servants, footmen, and butlers, to titled spinsters and church dignitaries, running through all ranks and professions, the suffering will be more general than on any former occasion. It will be like a universal domestic affliction.[7]

That was written in April. By the summer, the Stock Exchange was in the grip of wild speculation, with shares (often in fraudulent companies) changing hands at enormous profits. The excitement created a market for numerous railway papers, vehicles for a mass of lucrative advertising, which in some cases netted the proprietors over £10,000 a week. *The Economist* was also making money out of what Wilson called the 'furor, or fever', but he had already set the pattern to which the paper has always adhered: the operations of the advertising and editorial departments were completely independent of each other. Another rule of the paper which marked it out from its competitors was its refusal ever to get involved in share-tipping, for 'with every desire to consult the wishes and interests of our subscribers, we must decline to give advice relative to the buying and selling of shares, conceiving that no journalist who values his own character can with propriety do so'.[8]

Where the railway papers fanned speculation, Wilson sought to dampen them with hard facts. The irresponsibility of such organs as the *Railway Express*, *Railway Globe*, *Railway Standard* and *Railway Review* was countered, from October 1845, by a new nine-page section (in a paper now doubled in size to thirty-two pages) called – significantly – *The Railway Monitor*, for 'no paper, which aims at being a perfect commercial organ, embracing questions of trade, finance, banking, &c., in all their branches, can be complete without a considerable and distinct department devoted to the subject of railways . . . we hope, in the midst of the present extravagant excitement and contention of interests, faithfully and disinterestedly to discharge an important duty to the benefit of the public in general, and of our readers in particular'.

He had promised – and delivered – 'an elaborate Review of Railways past, present, and future, with many useful Statistical Tables of Reference:– a careful consideration of the effect of Railways on the national wealth, the productive industry of the country, and their future operation on the MONEY MARKET, and the Capital of the Country'.[9] In fact *The Railway Monitor* was an astoundingly valuable compendium of information, which included weekly figures on companies, lines, finances and traffic: prices were given for 350 stocks for six days a week.

In his lengthy, sober and constructive leaders, Wilson addressed himself to the practical problems being faced by investors. From the outset he urged them to hold back from any new schemes, though of course he stoutly condemned a rumoured government plan to ban any new railway companies. Such a move would drive speculators abroad: 'If mania or speculation, or by whatever other name it be termed, must be at all, we know no theatre where it can be carried on with less mischief to the public in general than on the Stock Exchange.'[10] Existing investors, tempted to sell as stocks fell, were advised to distinguish between real and projected lines. A sound line would recover its value in time: 'It is a good rule to observe, to do nothing where there is not a clear and evident object to be gained by acting; and this is more true at a time of unusual excitement or depression.'[11]

Above all he sought to get through to his readers certain elementary economic facts, such as that there were strict limitations on the amount of capital, labour and materials available for expansion of the railways and all of these were being grossly exceeded. The result would be to deflect these resources from other crucial areas of investment, thus causing a massive distortion in the whole economy: 'If we go on investing so much of our capital in a fixed property not exchangeable, while in doing so we consume so large a quantity of foreign produce, which must be paid for, our imports must at length exceed our exports, and as a necessary consequence, the exchanges will be turned against us and a drain of bullion must ensue; and the scarcity and high price of capital, which is inevitable, will be aggravated by a monetarial crisis.'[12]

As so often, Wilson's analysis was first-class, but his solutions assumed that the mass of mankind, unregulated, would behave like a prudent Scotsman. An example was his proposal that shareholders of companies with new schemes before parliament should combine to persuade their directors to cut their losses before it was too late. It was one of the nostrums that did not work as the mania mounted, investors were ruined, banks failed and the country reeled under a massive credit crisis, compounded by the predicted harvest failure. Wilson drew comfort from knowing and reminding his readers that he, at least, had done his duty. As an example of the unselfconscious way in which he said 'I told you so', this opening paragraph of a first leader in the autumn of 1847 is a classic:

> When the railway mania was at its greatest height, in 1845, we devoted several pages of this journal . . . to show the headlong folly into which the country was then plunging, and the infatuation which had seized the public mind, in believing in the dreams of the interminable railways which, it was asserted, could be made with the existing capital of the country. We took much pains to show the economical errors on which popular opinions were formed, and deductions drawn; and in order to evince our determination not to pander to the agreeable excitement and fever of the time, but rather to warn against the mischief which must infallibly, sooner or later, result from such a course, we then assumed the title to our railway department which it still bears.

Thereafter, no opportunity had been lost to repeat the warnings of what must be the inevitable outcome of the mania, but 'while we had the satisfaction of knowing that many of the more careful readers and thinkers profited by the warning, and disengaged themselves from speculations which could not but ultimately prove disastrous, yet we were sensible that the great masses who read little, and reflect less, would continue to be guided and governed by those whose immediate interests lay in urging forward these rash specu-lations'. Having had no faith in parliamentary attempts to stop the rot, he had long been convinced that only necessity would bring the railway interests to their senses. This time had come.[13] Two weeks later, in a leader beginning 'For upwards of two years we have laboured incessantly to show . . .', he reiterated his advice to shareholders to lean on their directors to persuade them to see sense. 'Gentlemen,' he concluded, 'study your own interest only, and follow it. The country requires and expects nothing else at your hands.'

Though insufficient numbers of these gentlemen followed his advice, Wilson never lost heart. He had to a marked degree the tenacity that distinguishes the successful proselytiser. When his readers or auditors failed to see the truth he sought to communicate, then he patiently reframed the argument and produced more facts in support. Sometimes he showed righteous anger, as when in the autumn of 1848 he pronounced that 'the present prostration and dejection is but a necessary retribution for the folly, the avarice, the insufferable arrogance, the headlong, desperate, and unprincipled gambling and jobbing, which disgraced nobility and aristocracy, polluted senators and senate houses, contaminated merchants, manufacturers, and traders of all kinds, and threw a chilling blight for a time over honest plod and fair industry'. Yet, following the inevitable 'we never failed to warn the public in the plainest terms, and by much-laboured expositions, of the risks . . .', he buckled down again with another lengthy analysis leading to the usual recommendations.[14]

By then the railways were diminishing in importance as an *Economist* concern. Indeed, from within a few months of the introduction of the Monitor in 1845, the collapse of the railway boom had removed much of its purpose. Wilson's measured leaders proceeded alongside a steady diminution in the Monitor's size to a couple of pages or so. It ceased to be a separate section in the autumn of 1870, stayed in the contents list until December 1888 and was then confined to the title-page of each volume until 1934, when, in a sudden leap into modernity, the paper dropped *Weekly Commercial Times, Bankers' Gazette, and Railway Monitor. A Political, Literary, and General Newspaper* from its title and became simply *The Economist*.

CHAPTER VIII

Why Lombard Street ceased being dull, and became extremely excited*

No sooner had he entered the official circle than his extraordinary command of figures made him a species of referee, and it was at length recognized, almost as a self-evident fact, that he had a right to be the Secretary to the Treasury.[1] *Obituary of James Wilson*, Spectator

Parallel with his incomparable work on the railways, Wilson was deeply embroiled in one of the most important nineteenth-century economic controversies, that between the Currency and Banking Schools. As Lionel Robbins (an eminent economist, and friend and long-serving director of *The Economist*), pointed out a century later, by the time the discussion died out in the 1860s, 'there was scarcely a person of eminence connected with banking or with speculation in cognate fields of political economy who had not made some contribution. We have to come forward to the controversies of the inter-war period of the twentieth century before we reach disputes of similar extent or intellectual interest.'[2]

Walter Bagehot's debut in *The Economist* was in February 1857, in the first of twelve articles signed 'A Banker', which sought to make sense of the controversy and make practical suggestions for the future. But these were directed at a relatively specialist audience. Even in 1860, Bagehot, deciding that he could not 'rely on the patience of our readers', chose to say as little as possible about currency in his memoir of Wilson. More than a century later, only students of monetary theory will be interested in the abstract principles

---

*With apologies to Bagehot, chapter VI of whose *Lombard Street* is called 'Why Lombard Street is Often Dull, and Sometimes Extremely Excited'. Because of its location in the City of London, Lombard Street became a synonym for the money market, whose institutions were housed in or near it.

on which the debate was conducted.[3] However, the conduct of the controversy itself is vital for understanding how Wilson and his paper rose so swiftly
to public importance, and if looked at in broadest terms, it makes a
fascinating story. Also, as Bagehot said, 'no subject is more connected with
his memory: he was so fond of expounding it, that its very technicalities are,
in the minds of some, associated with his voice and image'.

Since economics was virtually untaught at English universities until the
1830s, it was an area of study in which Wilson's lack of formal education
mattered little. He was never to become interested in more rarefied aspects of
the subject, but, as with everything else, he mastered basic principles and
basic information and applied the one to the other. When he appeared from
nowhere in 1839 with his first pamphlet on the Corn Laws, the extent of
public interest surprised even him. Although it is impossible to determine
how influential was his contribution to the vast array of literature on the
subject, a very positive indication is given by the coverage he received in 1840
in an important protectionist pamphlet called *An Exposition of Corn-Law
Repealing Fallacies and Inconsistencies*, in which the author, G. Calvert Holland,
challenged in detail the major free-trade works. Charles Villiers was dealt
with in three pages; Robert Torrens (one of the most famous economists of
his day and destined to be a bitter critic of Wilson) in five; the Manchester
Chamber of Commerce in nine; and at the top of the list came Wilson with
one hundred and fourteen.[4]

By the time he founded *The Economist*, Wilson had become as combative
on currency matters as he was on free trade. In his second issue he dealt
summarily with those who disagreed with what was accepted by the Banking
and Currency Schools alike – bullionists to a man – that banknotes should be
convertible, that is, freely exchangeable for gold. The 'Birmingham School',
on the other hand, wanted to print money, believing that industry could be
helped to expand and consequently unemployment be reduced through the
circulation of inconvertible banknotes. 'Among . . . [those] ready with an
infallible cure for all the present ills of our state,' Wilson commenced, 'none,
we think, are more liable to an indictment for gross absurdity at the bar of
Common Sense than a set of wiseacres, who may be entitled the Brummagem
Quacks. Their only chance of escaping a conviction would be on a defence of
monomania.'[5]

Within the year, Wilson was being introduced by John Bright at a League
meeting as 'one of the wisest economists of the age',[6] just a couple of days

after he had written his first lengthy assessment of Robert Peel's proposals for what was to be the Bank Charter Act of 1844.[7] Peel's Act was introduced to prevent any repeat of the financial crisis of 1839, which had arisen when the Bank's stock of gold reserves was severely depleted by a huge out-flow to pay for corn imports. In essence it stopped provincial banks from creating any further banknotes and restricted the Bank of England's note issue to the level of its gold reserves. The most important piece of banking legislation of the nineteenth century, it became the main focus for the long-running disagreement between the Banking and Currency Schools. The most important difference of the many between them was that the former believed that, since banknotes were convertible into gold on demand, it was unnecessary to regulate their issue: the latter believed otherwise, and considered their position vindicated by the Act they had largely fathered. Wilson, of course, saw no need to except banknote issue from the principle of *laissez-faire*: 'Banking, above all other professions, is that which, under entire freedom and non-interference, would soonest be placed in the most perfect position.'[8]

The three leaders of the Currency School were Samuel Jones Loyd (from 1850 Lord Overstone, and henceforward called by that name here), a rich and distinguished banker; George Warde Norman, a director of the Bank of England; and the eloquent and lively Colonel Robert Torrens. The most famous members of the Banking School were Joseph Hume, a great radical parliamentarian but an undistinguished economist; Thomas Tooke, author of the magisterial *History of Prices*; and, after 1844, James Wilson. With the exception of Hume (defeated in 1831 by Overstone) and Wilson, all were members of the élite Political Economy Club, founded in 1821 at the instigation of Tooke to uphold the principles of free trade, with Norman and Torrens among the nine founder members. Limited to thirty-five elected members, it included among its numbers great economists like John Stuart Mill and Nassau Senior and distinguished friends of Wilson like Clarendon, Porter and (from 1847) Villiers: its members met for serious discussion of the crucial economic issues of the day. In view of Wilson's love of informed discussion, it seems surprising that he never stood for election. It may be that by the time he had become a figure of sufficient stature to be a serious contender, he knew he had already alienated too many of the electors.*

---

*Between the 1840s and 1870s, *The Economist* was represented among the membership by several contributors, including Robert Giffen, Sir George Cornewall Lewis, William Newmarch and two of Wilson's sons-in-law, Walter Bagehot and W.R. Greg.

The Currency School believed that the 1844 Act would 'effectually prevent the recurrence of those cycles of commercial excitement and depression of which our ill-regulated currency has been the primary and exciting cause'.[9] Wilson, believing of course that legislation would prove 'a miserable substitution for . . . individual caution', considered the Act would 'endanger more the solvency of banks and very materially and unnecessarily . . . aggravate the evils arising from commercial revulsions and adverse exchanges, to which a great commercial country must ever be less or more subject'.[10]

Neither school had a monopoly of the truth. The Act was to remain unchanged until 1914, but it was not to prove the panacea its defenders had believed, and Wilson was right in believing that there would be a tendency for the Bank's directors now to act less responsibly. There was a hiccup in the spring of 1847, when mismanagement permitted Bank of England reserves to fall too low with embarrassing consequences. Then, in the autumn, a bad harvest and the calls for capital for the railways precipitated a flood of commercial, including banking, failures. A panic and run on the Bank of England ensued, halted by a suspension of the Act to allow it to lend more freely. Select Committees of both houses of parliament were set up to investigate the suspension then and again ten years later when there was a second suspension. James Wilson was a member of, and Overstone gave evidence to, both Commons committees. Though they always found plenty to disagree about, the Currency School had ultimately to admit that the Act could not prevent all panics and the Banking School to accept that it had worked better than it had predicted. In January 1857, while still embroiled in the debate, Wilson wrote to his friend Sir George Cornewall Lewis, then Chancellor of the Exchequer, that 'the practical results are so much nearer to those which I believe sound theory would suggest than any other system that has been propounded'.[11]

The war of words between the economists was at first conducted mainly through pamphlets, for which Wilson, having the advantage of a weekly mouthpiece for his own views, no longer had any need: it was no wonder that he rapidly became the *bête noire* of Overstone and his friends. Considering the criticisms *The Economist* was already levelling at Torrens in May 1844, it is unsurprising that Overstone appears to have taken no part in the operation to keep the paper afloat. Week after week the leaders poured forth with titles like 'MR TOOKE AND COLONEL TORRENS', analysing patiently and at length, and more in sorrow than in anger, the intellectual inadequacies of the Currency School. More galling still was the announcement in May 1847 that in response to 'the suggestion of numerous parties, the Publisher of the Economist has determined to re-print, in the form of a handsome 8vo volume, of about 350 pages, the whole of the series of Articles on the subjects of Currency, Capital, Railway Investments, and the operations of the Bank Bill, which have appeared in the Economist down to the present period'. This appeared as *Capital, Currency, and Banking; Being a Collection of a Series of Articles Published in The Economist in 1845, on the Principles of the Bank Act of 1844, and in 1847, on the Recent Monetarial and Commercial Crisis; Concluding with a Plan for a Secure and Economical Currency.*

In his *Principles and Practical Operation of Sir Robert Peel's Bill of 1844 Explained and Defended Against the Objections of Tooke, Fullarton and Wilson*, Torrens paid Wilson the compliment of describing him as 'the most able of the opponents of the Act', who had 'fallen into some extraordinary misconceptions'. As was customary with opponents in this controversy, he refuted Wilson's arguments in parliamentary language while politely wielding a stiletto. 'My sincere respect for Mr Wilson's talents and attainments leads me to believe that the above passage was written while his attention was distracted by a multiplicity of subjects . . .' Torrens also attacked at some length an aspect of Wilson's maiden speech in the House of Commons, on 30 November, 1847, made in a debate on a motion by the Chancellor of the Exchequer, Sir Charles Wood, 'that a Select Committee be appointed to inquire into the Causes of the recent Commercial Distress, and how far it has been affected by the laws for regulating the issue of bank-notes payable on demand'.

In this speech, Wilson had the temerity not only to challenge the Bank Charter Act and to make an immensely detailed and technical exposition on the currency, but also to propose an amendment (which he later withdrew) that would have limited what he held to be the proposed committee's 'inconveniently extensive' terms of reference. Wood, who was greatly under the influence of Overstone, had quoted from him and Torrens, and Wilson challenged him firmly. 'It contains', said Bagehot, reading it thirteen years later, 'a sufficient account of Mr Wilson's tenets on the currency – so good an account, indeed, that when he read it ten years later, in the panic of 1857, he acknowledged that he did not think he could add a word to it.' But it was not all lucidly expressed principles and statistics: as with his leading articles,

Wilson put something of himself into his speech, this time in the first person singular. Whatever the intentions of those who brought the Act into being, public opinion believed

> that we had thus obtained a degree of safety which had never been connected with any former Act; and I can bear witness personally to the fact, that I have heard many most eminent merchants in the city during the mad mania of 1845 congratulating themselves in the belief that, notwithstanding its influence, they were quite safe from any commercial convulsion in consequence of the operation of that Bill. I have heard some of the most eminent men at the head of some of those great houses which have fallen recently during the last crisis, console themselves by the belief that from its self-acting principle the Bill would save them from the revulsions which had formerly happened, so that they did not think it necessary to exercise the same degree of care and discretion that they would otherwise have felt bound to observe.

And although these expectations had now been modified considerably, they had done much mischief 'by inducing the public to rely too much on its operation, and not upon their own prudence and discretion . . . I believe that every law affecting to protect commerce, and to supply to the public those advantages which should be the result of care and prudence, thus have pro tanto the effect of throwing them for reliance, in seasons of distress, on the provisions of an Act of Parliament which professes to regulate commerce and banking.'

He achieved the distinction of having technical interruptions from the Chancellor of the Exchequer and Sir Robert Peel; he dealt with both of them with aplomb. Wilson had natural authority, and though his subject-matter was dry and he had no gifts as an orator, he had, as Bagehot put it, 'great power of exposition, singular command of telling details upon his own subjects, a very pleasing voice, a grave but by no means inanimate manner – qualities which are amply sufficient to gain the respectful attention of the House of Commons'.

Radnor was proud: 'I cannot resist the pleasure of writing to congratulate you on the success of your speech of Tuesday. I heard it lauded by two persons who heard it, a friend and a foe. And I have just read the observations on it in the *Morning Herald* of this day; which unwillingly commends it in general; but censures a part; in which it is so evidently wrong that the censure only shows its spite. The first step being taken I feel sure you will have no difficulty hereafter and I anticipate your being a conspicuous and useful Member.'[12]

A fortnight later, less than a month after taking his seat, Wilson was nominated to the Commons Select Committee on Commercial Distress: among its twenty-six members were Cobden, Disraeli, Sir James Graham, Peel, Lord John Russell and Sir Charles Wood. It began sitting in May 1848. In Bagehot's view, Wilson appeared to great advantage on a parliamentary committee. Though sure that his own opinions were correct, he had 'essentially a fair mind' and always had the greatest confidence that if the facts were examined, his beliefs would be proved right. He was therefore always ready to probe the facts to the bottom.

> He was likewise a great master of the Socratic art of inquiry; he was able to frame a series of consecutive questions which gradually brought an unwilling or a hostile witness to conclusions at which he by no means wished to arrive. His examination-in-chief, too, was as good as his cross-examination, and the animated interest which he evinced in the subject relieved the dreariness which a rehearsed extraction of premeditated answers commonly involves.

Bagehot judged to be models of their respective kinds Wilson's examination of Overstone before the 1848 Committee on Commercial Distress, of Weguelin (the Governor of the Bank) before the 1857 Committee on the Bank Acts, and several of those before the Committee on Life Insurance, of which he was the chairman. 'And it should be stated that no man could be less overbearing in examination or cross-examination; much was often extracted from a witness which he did not wish to state, but it was always extracted fairly, quietly, and by seemingly inevitable sequence.'

Committee minutes suggest that Bagehot's was a fair assessment, but it is unlikely that Overstone would have agreed; a certain testiness is evident in some of his responses.[13] Looking back in mid-1855, at a time when the future of the Act was under discussion and he was composing a series of letters in its defence to *The Times* under the pseudonym 'Mercator', he declared to his friend G.W. Norman that he had 'fairly met and answered' Wilson's arguments. The row simmered on. *The Economist* attacked the Act and its defenders again in a series of articles from December 1855: 'The whole of the argument in "Mercator's" letter proceeds upon a fallacy so plain and so transparent, and which we thought, since the discussions which took place in

1847 and the evidence taken before the Committee of 1848, had become so generally acknowledged, that it never would have been seriously urged again. That fallacy is that the Bank of England and Banks of Issue generally have the power to increase or contract the circulation at pleasure.'[14] George Arbuthnot, another friend of Overstone's and a senior Treasury official, was infuriated:

> I have some respect for a man who maintains an ingenious argument against facts, but I am utterly disgusted with the way in which the Economist has lately misrepresented facts in order to sustain a fallacy.

Technical arguments about improperly chosen statistics followed.

> This is only one Example of inaccuracy; Every other Example in the Economist is equally falsified.– I intend to draw up a paper putting shortly the arguments of Tooke and the Economist and the statistics by which they are supported, and shewing that the real facts lead to directly opposite conclusions.[15]

(Arbuthnot had appeared in Eliza Wilson's diaries earlier that year, in January 1855, when Wilson brought him and two other Treasury colleagues to stay for a long weekend in the country. 'Mr Arbuthnot is . . . evidently Papa's favourite . . . [He] is like a rollicking little Irishman, though only partly Irish; he has a fund of stories & tells them capitally, in fact his conversation is chiefly a thread of them, linking together every story touched upon with some amusing incident or saying. He seems thoroughly good-natured & kind.'[16]

Simultaneously, the Chancellor was seeking advice from Overstone; receiving it from his official, Arbuthnot, who was relaying information on Treasury matters to Overstone; and listening to the Financial Secretary to the Treasury, his friend James Wilson, Arbuthnot's boss.)

Newspaper conventions of anonymity and pseudonymity could lead to much disingenuousness in public argument. Thus Wilson, writing anonymously in *The Economist*, pretended not to know that 'Mercator' was Overstone, while Arbuthnot, in his 1857 pamphlet attacking Tooke and Wilson, *Sir Robert Peel's Act of 1844, Regulating the Issue of Bank Notes, Vindicated*, criticised as Wilson's the articles published in his *Capital, Currency and Banking* and as *The Economist*'s the Wilson articles of 1855–6. Arbuthnot added a further prudent fiction: what he had described to Overstone as Wilson's misrepresentation, in his pamphlet was said to be error.

Arbuthnot, as befitted a senior civil servant, could be splendidly feline. 'There are some minds, however, so insensible to reason, or so blinded by sophistry, that they will disregard the conclusions of legitimate deduction, and may perhaps consider that the facts on which Mr Wilson's argument is founded, remain to be accounted for. Statistics have extraordinary attractions when they appear to lead to conclusions beyond the reach of ordinary intelligence; they then throw an obscurity over the subject which is mistaken for depth. On minds so constituted, the mistakes of a writer, enjoying deservedly a high reputation as a political economist, must have a fatal influence; it is due, therefore, to the cause of truth, to notice the inaccuracies of the figures quoted by Mr Wilson in support of his opinions.' That having been accomplished to Arbuthnot's satisfaction, he shook his head sadly over his minister's oversight: 'It is to be regretted that the enthusiasm of this eminent writer [Wilson] for a plausible theory should have led him to adopt, without sufficient reflection, figures which appeared to suit his argument, but which, on calmer consideration, he must perceive would lead to directly opposite conclusions.' And in the next paragraph he moved directly into an attack on *The Economist*'s alleged sequence of errors.

Colonel Torrens, still going strong in his late seventies,* declared Arbuth-not's pamphlet 'a master-piece; and as Mr Wilson from his official position may be regarded as the most formidable opponent of the Act of 1844, Arbuthnot's exposure of his fallacies is calculated to render essential service to the good cause'.[17] Overstone wrote approvingly to Arbuthnot, who replied gratefully: 'Thanks to you and [G.W.] Norman, I have learnt a great deal in the progress of my work, and I feel myself a match for a dozen Wilsons. I don't think that he (Wilson) means to be dishonest, but his inordinate vanity leads him to wish to be original and prevents him from retracing his steps when he has made a wrong move. I see that in the supplement to the *Economist* published last Saturday [24 January 1857], he has taken a new position which is even weaker, at least more palpably so, than any that he had assumed before.'[18]

---

*He was to be found in January 1858 in the *Edinburgh Review* ('Lord Overstone on Metallic and Paper Currency') praising Overstone for 'triumphantly' disposing of an 'extraordinary fallacy' of Wilson's and explaining that the 'juxtaposition of elaborate statistics and contradictory conclusions is peculiarly and conspicuously exemplified in the writings of Mr Tooke, Mr Newmarch [William Newmarch, the distinguished statistician who collaborated with Tooke on his revised *History of Prices* and was to be an important contributor to *The Economist* during the 1860s], and Mr Wilson.'

Even when dealing with the most tiresome issues, Wilson's interest was never known to flag, but in October 1856 his most important enemy showed signs of weariness. 'Remember', wrote Overstone to G.W. Norman, 'you live and move in the midst of affairs and are daily surrounded by stirring events and facts pregnant with instruction', while Overstone had much to deter him from 'again plunging into the bottomless abyss of Currency disputes'.

> Moreover do you not perceive – that this subject has now become the peculiar domain of the Fools, the Madmen, and must I add the Rogues of Society . . . I have not read one word of Tooke, nor do I intend to do so. I am very nearly in the same condition as regards Wilson . . . Let things go on in this course, and they will surely present to the public a lesson the force of which may be obscured but cannot be increased by any war of words with Tooke and Wilson – the muddle-headed and the disingenuous. – You will I doubt not steadily do your duty at the Bank – do not fear or hesitate to act in time.[19]

Of course Overstone – the chief begetter of the Act – continued to exert his considerable influence to persuade the Chancellor, Cornewall Lewis, of its virtues. In November 1856 Lewis was reporting that the Bank directors concurred in the view that it should be renewed essentially as it stood, and the economist J.R. McCulloch was exulting that the Act's merits had been recognised before discussions began in parliamentary committees. 'I have not seen Tooke, who no doubt is much disappointed.– But Wilson is a far more dangerous heretic, in as much as he has, to some extent, at least, the ear of Caesar. – I hope Lewis will keep right.'[20]

Caesar was a scholar of ancient civilisations who responded to evidence rather than to pressure. Bagehot considered him 'a shrewd and solid thinker . . . a safe man, a fair man, and an unselfish man' whose underlying concern as Chancellor was '"How much will there be in the till at the end of the year?"' Though he was much more pragmatic and less doctrinaire than Wilson, they were good friends. Their shared talents included an infinite capacity for 'patient labour' and, despite Lewis's great erudition, a determination to make their speaking and writing intelligible. But although Bagehot thought Lewis's judgment sufficient for a great statesman, he felt him to lack the necessary passion. Wilson told Bagehot that once, when he urged something strongly on his Chancellor, Lewis responded: 'No; I can't do it. The fact is, Wilson, you are an animal, and I am a vegetable.'[21]

So while Lewis listened to Wilson's opinions, he was not a man to give them undue weight. 'I have been reading all Jones Loyd's [Overstone's] old pamphlets', wrote Wilson in February 1857;

> they are perfect specimens of taste and style; but the theory so fallacious that I am disposed to give Peel more credit than I ever did before in producing a scheme in the act of 1844, which while it appeared to carry out the doctrines of the currency school, has in reality given a practical effect, more than at first sight is apparent, to the pure Bullion doctrine. The more one reflects upon it, the more one sees that though it may be the voice of Overstone it is the hand of Tooke; but there is much of fiction in its form, which is mischievous and tends to delude.

However, the Act's real evil was that 'it stands now neither upon one principle nor another; it gives up competition, but it does not carry out regulation to the legitimate end.' Yet 'if taken as a compromise I cannot say that in its immediate consequences it is either mischievous or dangerous'.[22]

What bothered Wilson particularly, therefore, was exactly what Bagehot was in 1860 to identify as a great advantage of Peel's Act – that 'it is a sort of compromise which is suited to the English people. It was probably intended by its author as a preliminary step; it undoubtedly suits no strict theory; it certainly has great marks of incompleteness; but "it works tolerably well"; if it produces evils at a crisis, "crises come but seldom"; in ordinary times commerce "goes on very fairly." The pressure of practical evil upon the English people has never yet been so great as to induce them to face the unpleasant difficulties of the abstract currency question.'[23] But Wilson was Scots, and though the notion of compromise no longer filled him with disbelief and horror, his struggle between fixed principles and political realities was evident till the end of his days. 'His theories and his practical views are generally in antagonism', wrote George Arbuthnot to Overstone in 1859, 'but he will be governed by the latter.'[24]

(An interesting example of how far Wilson had moved comes in a letter from Lewis in November 1857 about whether the Indian telegraph should be a monopoly, in which he castigates Peel for having introduced the principle of competition into the railway system: 'If Peel had considered the recondite truth that a straight line is the shortest distance between two points, he would have seen that the principle of multiplying roads between two given points is essentially vicious.' It is clear from the tone of Lewis's letter that he has no reason to expect that Wilson would explode at such an heretical statement).[25]

'I have been thinking', wrote Wilson in April 1857 to Lewis, 'that some very temperately and moderately written articles in the Economist upon the Bank Act of 1844, showing in what respect it is really valuable, and works out sound principles, and in what respect it fails, especially as regards the unsatisfactory position in which it leaves the country circulation, would be useful. Do you see any objection that could be taken at this state of the case to such a discussion? We must do something at all events with the Country Banks; I have been looking into it– the case is as rotten a one as could be presented to a Committee. Have you seen Tooke and Newmarch's new Book? I have sent for it.'[26]

'I see no objection to a series of articles in the Economist such as you mention', responded Lewis. 'On the contrary, I think they would be very useful . . . It is difficult to know what Peel's ulterior policy was, but I have little doubt that what he intended to do, if he could, was to extinguish all Banks of Issue except the Banks of England & Ireland. As this policy seems now pretty generally abandoned, I do not see how we can stand permanently on our present ground . . . The elections have taken several men out of the Bank Charter Committee . . . What do you think of asking Sir J. Graham to take the chair? I am not sure that he would consent, but I really cannot think of anybody else, who is tolerably impartial. Gladstone has become so wild & demagogical that one is afraid of asking him to do anything which requires moderation & judgment.'[27]

The Commons committee to examine the Bank Acts consisted of twenty-two members, including the Chancellor and four of his predecessors – Sir Francis Baring, Disraeli, Gladstone and Sir Charles Wood. Lewis took the chair, and Wilson played a commanding role, examining at length, among others, J.G. Hubbard, G.W. Norman and T.M. Weguelin from the Bank, William Newmarch and the old enemy, Overstone.

This time Overstone was extremely rude to Wilson. His retorts included: 'Really this is hair-splitting, which is not worth the time of the Committee'; 'Take my words as I give them, and do not alter them, if you please'; 'I decline giving any answer to that question'; 'It is not worth while to raise such a question'; and 'that is my defence of the Act of 1844, which I defy your ingenuity to impugn'. Wilson appears to have kept his composure throughout. Later on, under questioning from Lewis, Overstone showed his deep distrust of Wilson. Lewis asked Overstone what he understood to be the meaning of a question Wilson had posed to Weguelin: 'Sir Robert Peel, I think, contemplated that the Act of 1844 should last for 10 years, and no more?' 'I understand that question', replied Overstone, 'to be an endeavour to introduce to this Committee an impression that the Act was intended, in the very words of the question, by Sir Robert Peel in passing it to be an Act to last for 10 years and no longer.' He was asked to explain further. 'When pressed I have stated that when I read that question, it produced upon my mind, especially reading it at the end of the whole of that day's examination, a feeling of very great and painful surprise; and when I read the answer the impression made upon me was, that the witness was so struck by the monstrous character of the question that he put upon it a limited interpretation, which was an exceedingly good mode of getting rid of the difficulty before him.'

'Does not the monstrous character of the question', asked Lewis, 'depend upon the assumption that it means that the Act should simply be repealed at the end of the 10 years, and nothing substituted for it?' – 'It certainly depends upon the assumption that the purport of that question was to produce an impression that there was something in that Act by the intention of Sir Robert Peel in passing it, showing that the Act was to last for 10 years, and no longer.'[28]

'Wilson's mode of examination ... appears to me most audacious and dishonest', Torrens wrote consolingly to Overstone,[29] and the one-sided invective went remorselessly on, exacerbated by a long-drawn-out and hugely complicated dispute between Torrens and the Treasury[30] over the cancellation of Torrens's printing contract for the *Police Gazette*. It was 'not improbable' that Wilson was behind the decision to place the contract elsewhere, postulated Torrens to Overstone. 'From his position, his talents, and his mastery of official and statistical details, Wilson was the most formidable opponent of the Act of 1844. Unscrupulous and audacious, and aiming at the leadership upon the great monetary question of the day, he placed himself in direct, and it might even be said, in malignant hostility to the principles propounded by Your Lordship.'[31]

The enmity was further exacerbated with the arrival in the autumn of 1857 of what is known as the first really world-wide financial crisis, which began in America and spread to England, Europe, South America, South Africa, Australia and the Far East. To avoid the ruin of a number of banks, Lewis and Wilson had the 1844 Act suspended once again to allow the Bank of England to act as a lender of last resort – a matter of great distress to Overstone, who appears to have taken it virtually as a personal affront. The Select Committee, renewed in 1858 when the crisis was over to explain what had happened, exonerated the Act from responsibility for the crisis.

Although Wilson's passionate interest in the currency debate never waned,[32] he ceased to play a key role when his government went out of office in February 1858. It is doubtful if he ever realised the extent of the bitterness he had aroused in his opponents. 'I have had sometimes, unknown to you, to defend you from detractors in your career at home', wrote Radnor's son, Edward Pleydell-Bouverie, before Wilson left London for India in 1859. Wilson's daughter Emilie put this down to the 'buoyancy – a radiancy one might say, in my father's character [that] defied and conquered many difficulties . . . this power to achieve . . . was one which excited envy in the envious and aroused jealousy in the jealous . . . My father was happy, and this, besides his success, was a cause of envy.'[33] This touchingly filial explanation leaves out those characteristics of Wilson's that were taken on by *The Economist* and have made it respected, successful but often disliked. He was clever, well-informed and opinionated and he radiated absolute belief in the correctness of his views – not a popular combination in a country where 'too clever by half' is a term of disparagement.

Yet he certainly did not deserve the loathing felt for him by Overstone and Torrens: nor would he have reciprocated it. He was himself without rancour, an aspect of his character best summed up by Arbuthnot, who had worked so hard against him in the Treasury. After Wilson's death, Arbuthnot wrote to Bagehot approving what he had said in his memoir of Wilson about his time in the Treasury and suggesting an addition.

> You might, with justice to his memory, refer to the very cordial manner in which he discussed subjects with those who acted under him, listened to their objections or suggestions, and often governed himself on them. While he worked as no other Secretary of the Treasury ever worked, so far from depressing others, he encouraged their exertions, co-operated with them, and was always ready to bear hearty testimony to the merits of deserving officers.

Arbuthnot asked Bagehot to mention also

> the generous spirit in which he forgot temporary animosities which are too

apt to arise among earnest men who differ in opinion, and which spirit prevented him from allowing them to operate to the prejudice of the public service. He was eminently tolerant. In my own case, after differences which were enough to ruffle the temper of any man, he soon allowed all personal feeling to subside, and it has been a great consolation to me to reflect that, previous to his departure for India, I had the opportunity of confidential and unreserved communication with him on matters of great public interest, and that we parted with as much cordiality as if there had been no unpleasant passages between us. I had several letters from him from India written in the same spirit, and in the last which I received from him, he enquired about several officers in this Department with whom he had been thrown principally in contact, expressing great interest in matters affecting their prospects of advancement.[34]

It was Wilson's possession of those characteristics, allied to his fundamental pragmatism, that had made it possible for him to keep *The Economist* going in tandem with his political career.

CHAPTER IX:

Independent?

After many fluctuations of repute, he had at length reached an eminence on which he stood – independent of office, independent of party – one of the acknowledged potentates of Europe; face to face, in the evening of life, with his work and his reward; – his work, to aid the progress of those principles on which, after much toil, many sacrifices, and long groping towards the light, he had at length laid a firm grasp; his guerdon, to watch their triumph. Nobler occupation man could not aspire to; sublimer power no ambition need desire; greater earthly reward, God, out of all the riches of his boundless treasury, has not to bestow.[1] The Economist *on Sir Robert Peel, 1850*

Such was the achievement Wilson sought for himself, but on his journey towards this goal his own and his paper's independence often had to be sacrificed. 'James Wilson played the political game for personal gain', says his daughters' biographer. 'He never separated parliamentary success from personal success.'[2] That is a harsh judgment. Wilson was certainly intensely ambitious and he enjoyed social and financial success, but his sense of duty was never in doubt. Ends might sometimes justify means, but the ends remained honourable.

From the beginning, Wilson had made much of the paper's independence of political party, but it had, of course, been a mouthpiece for the doctrinaire liberalism of himself and his similarly inclined friends. It can hardly be denied that Lord Radnor, the paper's financial backer, was given a disproportionate amount of space. In addition to his long letters to the *The Economist*, there were quotations from his letters to other papers, and approving comments were made on a fairly regular basis. For instance: 'We find in the *Wiltshire Independent* on Thursday a continuation of Lord Radnor's admirable letters . . . too good not to be presented to our readers unabbreviated in the leading parts';[3] 'Lord Radnor, with that straightforward patriotic honesty which has ever distinguished him . . . '[4] Yet in fairness to Wilson, he fully agreed with everything he ever published by or about Radnor; he needed all the contributions he could get; letters from a man of Radnor's distinction could only help the paper's prestige; and, perhaps most important of all, he deeply admired and loved him.

With such an emotional man, who was beginning to meet the people he wrote about, it was inevitable that personal feelings would preclude absolute objectivity. Gladstone, for example, who during the 1840s was going through convoluted intellectual and spiritual struggles which manifested themselves in political decisions that often seemed bizarre to onlookers, had one of his tortuous arguments described by Wilson as 'Preposterous sophistry, not to give it a worse name'.[5] Then, a few weeks later, they had personal dealings for the first time. The previous year *The Economist* had reported the existence of a particular American regulation that challenged the thrust of Gladstone's argument in a debate on sugar duties. Gladstone having denied all knowledge of it, *The Economist* had given its source as 'personal communication, in which we are entitled to place the highest confidence'. In February 1845, the *Morning Chronicle*, reporting another sugar debate, quoted Gladstone as saying: 'It now appeared . . . that the whole was a mere fiction, and that the statement was invented for the purpose of deception, or that it was a mere figment imposed on the minds of honourable gentlemen . . . if he was not mistaken, it originally appeared in the Economist newspaper, and he hoped that those who had invented the statement would be more fastidious for the future as to putting such arguments into hon. members' mouths.'

'I am unwilling', wrote Wilson from the Reform Club, 'to believe that you have been correctly reported . . . and I must beg you will excuse me calling your attention to the passage, as it is impossible but that I should feel keenly such an imputation as it contains, it being well and generally known that I was the writer of the articles referred to.' The information had come from an excellent authority on American law, but as soon as doubt was expressed as to the existence of the regulation, Wilson had explained 'in the most conspicuous manner' the status of the report. Clearly, if Gladstone was being correctly reported, he had either not seen the article at the time, or had forgotten it when he made his speech.

I can most conscientiously assert, that in every statement which I have put forth in the journal referred to, I have used the most scrupulous and anxious care that they should be strictly accurate and true; but when it is considered the wide field of investigation of facts and principles, many of which are of the most complicated kind, which are embraced in the leading articles of that paper, it would be more than any one could reasonably hope, to escape altogether from being unconsciously led into error on some point, – which I am certain will be readily admitted and felt by any one who has had such ample opportunity of experiencing as yourself.

If he had been properly quoted, Gladstone would no doubt feel it a duty 'to withdraw the imputation so strongly expressed, or state to me the grounds for such'.

Gladstone responded magnificently:

I cannot be surprised that you should have suffered pain from the statement described as having been made by me, on Wednesday night, in the House of Commons, and I most sincerely regret it.

My language has been, as you suppose, erroneously reported . . . I was not, indeed, aware that you were the author of the articles in question; but I know nothing connected with the Economist which would justify my impugning, in the very slightest degree, the sincerity or integrity of its conductors.

It is not my practice to read the reports of my own speeches, nor to take public notice of any inaccuracy in them; but in a case like this, where personal feeling has been wounded, I shall be desirous to find an opportunity of removing a misapprehension in which others besides the reporter may have participated, which was probably owing to rapidity of utterance or incomplete development of my meaning. At any rate, you are entirely at liberty to make such use of this note as you may think fit.

'Of course, we cannot but express our perfect satisfaction with this explanation, and with the frank and unhesitating manner in which it has been given', began Wilson's delighted response,[6] and henceforward Gladstone was always given the benefit of the doubt. In time they were to be close colleagues, for when Gladstone was Chancellor of the Exchequer between December 1852 and February 1855, Wilson was Financial Secretary and their formal, technical but amicable correspondence demonstrates a happy partnership.[7]

Indeed one of the most passionate defences of any statesman came in June 1855, when Gladstone was publicly reviled for objecting to the continuance of the Crimean War. Wilson's long article refuting Gladstone's argument recorded that he had listened to his two-hour speech with unflagging interest and admiration, and

> we are bound to say that we never heard arguments so skillfully marshalled or so brilliantly expressed, statements so lucid, declamation so impassioned yet so chastened and restrained, and facts and documents so ably collected and displayed irresistibly to suggest and shadow forth the designed conclusion. And if one thing was made clearer than another to our minds as we listened, it was the deep self-conviction of the speaker, and the solemn sense of responsibility under which he addressed his audience. Yet ever since it was delivered that speech has been the object of the most unmeasured invective and the most shameless and perverse misrepresentation. Journal after journal has treated it as a piece of glaring and shallow sophistry, plain to the meanest capacity and prompted by the meanest motives.[8]

That personal loyalty was evident again when he had to follow Gladstone in a debate in February 1857 in which he had attacked Cornewall Lewis's Budget: 'After the relations which had previously existed between his right hon. Friend and himself,' Wilson was reported as saying, 'nothing was more painful to him than to find himself in antagonism to him, either upon that or any other occasion.'[9]

Where Wilson went, so went *The Economist*. So when he had to give up some of his own independence in furtherance of his political career, so too did his paper, which, understandably enough, Wilson saw as his possession, to be used as he thought fit. It had been founded to make money and promulgate free-trade doctrines. Having become sufficiently profitable to finance its owner's entry into parliament, its new role was to help him up the political ladder, which initially he climbed at great speed. Within six months he had a junior ministerial post (a Secretaryship to the Board of Control, dealing with India) and neither he nor his paper was henceforth independent. This appears to have worried only Queen Victoria. In April 1848 the Prime Minister wrote to her recommending Wilson's promotion: 'Mr Wilson's nomination to a Privy Councillor's office may give rise to remarks – a few years ago he carried on the trade of a hatter, & failed. But his integrity has not been questioned and his talents are very considerable. He has provoked the hostility of Mr Cobden & others by the support he gave the government upon the Income Tax & Estimate.'

> The Queen has received Lord John Russell's letter of yesterday. She thinks Mr Wilson very well qualified for office, but doubts whether he is not more useful to the Government as an *independent* supporter by his admirable articles in the Economist . . . the Queen has heard it said that Mr Cobden accuses Mr Wilson of opposing him merely for the sake of office. Should Mr Wilson – who is not reckoned an effective Speaker – not add material strength to the government, the loss of his independent support will be a great disadvantage to it.

And in her diary she assessed Wilson as 'very Liberal, but a clever intelligent man who has supported the Govt. lately'.[10] (He did not become a Privy Councillor until 1859.)

So while *The Economist* was not a slavish follower of the government line, it was by no means a free agent. Criticism was muted and coded. Take, for example, the outbreak of anti-Catholicism that hit Britain at the end of 1850. In response to a papal bull announcing the creation of bishoprics in England, the Prime Minister, Lord John Russell, wrote to the Bishop of Durham denouncing the papal 'aggression' as 'insolent and insidious', resisting any attempt 'to impose a foreign yoke upon our minds and consciences', anathematising those Church of England clergyman who had been introducing their flocks to Romish practices and referring to 'the mummeries of superstition'. *The Economist*, clearly embarrassed at having to endorse a letter that reeked of the kind of bigotry against which it had fought strenuously, reproduced the letter in full and added: 'That speaks for itself. It needs no commendation at our hands.' It then managed some half-hearted approval of a few parts of the letter before applauding Russell's promise to examine whether legislative action should be taken. 'We trust, however, that there is no occasion for new laws on the subject, while old laws hardly need to be brought into exercise. This is a case in which the people may be safely left to avenge themselves against the intruding priests . . . The people are too enlightened, too wise, not to do a more ample justice on the mummeries of superstition if left to themselves, than can be done by the law.'[11]

The people, however, fired by their Prime Minister, promptly began to behave as if a fleet of warships laden with armed cardinals was on the high seas. 'The generous burst of indignation with which the people heard of the

Pope's Bull is fast subsiding', said *The Economist* hopefully. 'Gradually . . . [the nation] has come to perceive that there is no occasion for alarm – that the Pope is a helpless, but not malignant priest – that there is no Roman Catholic Power in Europe to back his manifestoes – that, in fact, his Bull means nothing but a new spiritual organisation of the Roman Catholics, a little new adjustment of the relative rank of Romish Bishops and their flock, giving them an Archbishop and a Cardinal at their heads, with new and more splendid robes, acting in a more imposing manner, to please and beguile.'[12] Over ensuing weeks caution was urged and explanations were made, but still the 'generous burst of indignation' failed to subside. In February the government introduced a bill forbidding Roman Catholic prelates to assume territorial titles in England (it was to fall into desuetude); the distress evinced by *The Economist* in its pitiable efforts to reconcile integrity and expediency was almost palpable. 'We are not now going to argue upon the Papal Bill. It is enough for our present object that the people of Great Britain were all but unanimous upon the subject, be they right or be they wrong.' Having lost the support of the Irish Roman Catholic MPs, the government had fallen (it returned to office when no alternative could be found), yet, explained the article shiftily, it had still been right to pass the bill. Had it not, the opposition would have won an election 'on the double cry of Papal Aggression and Protection', so the upshot would have been worse.

> We do not urge these views as any answer to those who entertain a conscientious and unalterable objection to the present bill. We do so only to those who complain of it as the cause of the present crisis. There are times when public men must abandon views at all risks, in obedience to their conviction. But it is quite plain, that the Government of a country with a representative constitution is simply impossible by men, however great otherwise, at least at the moment, whose views, however right they may be, are so far in opposition to those of the country. No man can hide from himself the enormous dangers of such legislation; but equally no man can be insensible to the still greater dangers of altogether refraining.[13]

It was a woolly, disingenuous but realistic conclusion to an episode in the paper's history that must have given James Wilson some bad moments. Voting for measures he disliked was one thing, but actually having his paper defend them by arguing against fixed principles was another. Although the paper retained its usefulness as a source of information and statistics and its independence on issues that were non-contentious, as a political journal it was overwhelmingly a propaganda organ for the governments in which Wilson served. In Russell's papers, for instance, there is an unsigned note which reads: 'The article in the Economist of the 4th of March [1852] on the Russell Administration appears to be so well and concisely written, that a republication of it in the form of a Pamphlet might prove very useful during the approaching Election. Supposing that to be done, it would be desirable that some addition should be made to it.' And after a few suggestions, the note concludes: 'If these and probably some other subjects which might be suggested, were put together, a very convenient textbook might be arranged, which would prove very useful to candidates when questioned on the hustings.'[14] During the ensuing election, 'the canvassing went on every day except when my father ran up to town for an important division in the House or when any question had to be discussed with his fellow-politicians relative to the line the Economist should take on any special matter'.[15]

With Wilson's special cronies, for instance Earl Grey, the Colonial Secretary from 1846 to 1852, to whom Wilson provided an enormous amount of information and help, the paper was a weapon to be deployed for mutual benefit. In 1850 Wilson writes rather coyly that 'I forgot to call your attention to an article in the Ec[onomis]t this week, on the effect upon the Bank of France & the French Nation of the adoption of notes of a lower denomination than hitherto used . . . It is strongly corroborative of the views you advocated in a very able pamphlet some years ago,– & also of the article in the Ec[onomis]t 8 May 1847;– reprinted at page 200 of "Capital Currency and Banking" [Wilson's book], which, by the way, if you have not got I will gladly send you a copy of.' In other letters in this correspondence, Wilson offers to bring something to the attention of 'our Agriculture Editor', or 'to have the facts, connected with the new rupture at the Cape put plainly before the public. If so, if you will let me have the outlines, I will cause them to be properly elaborated in an article in the Ec[onomis]t.'[16] 'With regard to the Cape,' responds Grey, 'I am upon the whole inclined to believe that the best policy is to be quiet unless any further attack is made by the other side. I doubt whether within the compass of a newspaper article much could be added to what has already been very well put in the Economist.' But a couple of months later he sends Wilson 'a newspaper sent to me by Lord Elgin which contains two remarkable Lectures on the progress of Upper Canada, it might be worth while in the Economist to give a short account of the results'.[17]

And Cornewall Lewis, who had been an occasional contributor to *The Economist* during the 1840s, agreeing with Wilson that a series of articles on the Bank Act would be useful, asks if it would 'be possible to have an article on Coode's Report on the Fire Insurance Duty, containing a summary of his arguments, drawn up for the Economist? I see that people go on repeating the old claptrap about "tax on Prudence!".[18] The following month, therefore, in May 1857, *The Economist's* new columnist, Walter Bagehot, writing pseudonymously as 'A Banker', begins writing about the Act, and an anonymous article appears extolling Mr Coode's paper 'which, as a whole, for its great clearness, thoroughness, and ingenuity, is worthy of the highest praise'.

With Grey and Lewis, Wilson's dealings were straightforward enough. Essentially these ministers were providing useful ideas or information for the paper, and vice versa: there was no clear conflict of interest. But not everyone was prepared to restrict his comments or suggestions to the factual. 'The Economist reasons rather wildly about the approaching extinction of the Whig party', grumbled Russell in July 1852, congratulating Wilson on his election. 'As the Whig party has always been the party of steady progress, that party can never become extinct till no further progress is required – and that time seems a good way off.'[19]

'A change and disruption, too,' had commenced the offending paragraph, 'has taken place in the Whig party, the consequences of which are, we think, likely to be both permanent and of great moment.'

> For a considerable time individuals have been sloughing off from it in both directions. The more sanguine and extreme have gradually associated themselves more and more with the Radical clique; while many of the older, soberer, and more disenchanted, have joined the liberal Conservatives, and many more are prepared to do so, as soon as that party shall assume a definite position and avow a distinct policy. The Whig party, it is felt, has survived its peculiar bond of union and its special topics. It has died of its success, as the Tories have died of their failures. If we except the immediate connections of the Whig leader, there is little to separate the more popularising Whigs from the Manchester school and still less to distinguish the more conservative among them from the party of whom Sir James Graham [the leader of the Peelites] may be regarded as the type.[20]

(The writer of the article was quite right: the word 'Whig' shortly became of historical significance only.)

'For sometime past I have been quite unable to attend to the Econ[omis]t', answered Wilson, 'but I have noticed the articles you refer to & have written to the writer, who like many others objects rather I think to the name of Whig, than to what really constituted our policy & place;– for there is no better progressive reformer, nor accomplished politician though somewhat fastidious as men are apt to be who spend their lives in their own libraries,– than he is. I am writing to him today at great length upon general policies.'[21]

The writer was almost certainly W.R. Greg, who for a decade made an immense contribution to keeping *The Economist* going, by taking up the slack when Wilson's political career came between him and his paper. To what extent Wilson was still involved became an issue in *The Times* a couple of months after he took ministerial office. Under the heading 'The Board of Trade and the Economist', a letter purporting to be from 'A Merchant' complained about difficulty in getting hold of the monthly returns of the Board of Trade immediately on publication. Having sent to the 'Parliamentary Paper-office' every morning for several days only to be told they had not yet been published, to his great surprise 'on taking up the Economist of to-day I find the full returns inserted, together with analytical remarks which show that they must have been in the possession of that paper at an early hour yesterday [Friday] morning, or most probably on Thursday . . . it would appear that the publication is not made fairly and simultaneously, but that the Economist is furnished with an exclusive copy. I am not aware whether this system is an unprecedented one, or whether it is a recognised privilege of some government departments to furnish early copies of their documents either to chosen papers or to private friends; but, whichever it may be, the practice is a bad one, and should be at once abolished. The Board of Trade especially is in no condition to show favouritism.'[22]

A week later, 'A.W.', of the 'Economist office, 340, Strand' defended the Board of Trade from 'these erroneous imputations'. On Thursday the returns had been presented to parliament, with a copy being delivered to every member of parliament the following morning, when they had also reached *The Economist*. The allegations were rehashed in *The Times* at length.

'A Merchant' turned up again on 11 August with another long and similar complaint and yet again on 16 October. This time he quoted 'a business publisher in the City' as also having been told by the Parliamentary Paper-office that the returns were unavailable on a Friday. 'My past experience, however, of the arrangements of the Board of Trade induce me to look at the Economist of this morning, to ascertain whether the publishers of that paper might not have met with success. I there found, I will not say to my surprise, that the returns, occupying three entire pages, were not only inserted, but that they had been furnished in sufficient time to form the subject of a leading article. Whether the Board of Trade was established chiefly for the mercantile community, or for the prior advantage of this or any other paper or party, is, perhaps, under such circumstances, scarcely too harsh a question.'

On 18 October, the issue inspired a lengthy *Times* leader reiterating the complaint that returns refused to others had appeared 'constantly' in *The Economist*. Those refused 'began to think a little why this should be so'.

> Now, it so happened that the *Economist* had been established and very ably conducted for a certain number of years by Mr J. Wilson. This gentleman, observing a great want of practical and accurate knowledge on matters of trade to exist in the lower House, determined to give that assembly the benefit of his knowledge, his assiduity, and his theory of banking. He was returned at the last election for the borough of Westbury. On the expiration of a few months of senatorial existence, and after the delivery of a few speeches well belarded with statistics, Mr J. Wilson took office under the government, and became an employé in this very department – the Board of Trade.

It had been generally understood at the time that he had then given up all connection with *The Economist*.

> The functions of placeman and journalist are incompatible . . . The Economist had passed into other hands. Mr Wilson might occasionally take a sentimental delight in revisiting the scenes of his former labours. Emotions would naturally arise as he walked along the Strand . . . This was excusable – creditable even to our imperfect nature.

The repeated applicants for the returns, however, had put together the facts that Wilson had been editor and proprietor of *The Economist*, that he had disposed of his interest in the journal on getting a job, yet that the returns from his department somehow found their way into the journal he had formerly owned, before they can be obtained by any other applicants.

> He is most unfortunately placed, and great exertions should be made by his friends to prevent the recurrence of so scandalous a job. That Mr Wilson be

never so innocent and unconscious of the whole matter, he will be voted the scapegoat by general consent, and the responsibility will be fastened upon him. He is in this respect a most unfortunate man.

The Times had no desire to rake up a forgotten scandal. However another very recent letter from 'A Merchant' complained of 'a recurrence of the old abuse'.

> Now, this is a little bit of dirty jobbing that must be put an end to at once. This is the second warning that has been given to the parties concerned; it is dangerous to provoke a third . . . If a grand scramble is to take place between all the proprietors and publishers of London journals for prior information from the government boards, we shall be glad to know of the definite inauguration of the new system. In the long run, it is clear the Economist cannot triumph over the rivalry of the exchange and the press . . . It will be in the interests of everyone connected with trade, except that of the persons immediately implicated in this breach of good faith, to turn upon the delinquents. Mr Labouchere [President of the Board of Trade] would do well to investigate the affair in time.

Forced to reply, Wilson's tone was lofty. The 'many personal remarks' were not considered 'deserving of any observation, except so far as it is necessary to show how entirely groundless are the imputations made upon the Board of Trade'. He was 'in no way, and never was', connected with the Board of Trade 'and it is singular that a writer professing to be so well-informed in all the details into which he enters should have made such a mistake'. In the second place 'I have no more connection with, or control over, the accounts referred to than the writer himself.' The allegation was that the accounts were made available to *The Economist* before publication 'through my influence'. In fact the accounts had been available at 5.30 on Friday evening in Bridge Street, Westminster: Wilson had purchased one copy for his own use at 6.00. Two Saturday newspapers contained extracts. The July insinuations were similarly demolished. 'Why "A Merchant" or others have not succeeded in their endeavours to procure these documents I cannot say, but it is certain that in neither case could any blame whatever be imputed to the Board of Trade. There are other statements in the article in The Times of this day equally erroneous, but as they are of no public interest, I forbear any remark upon them, my only object to vindicate a public department from groundless charges with which you have chosen to mix up my name; and I trust, in fairness to the Board of Trade, you will give to this explanation the same prominence which you have given to the charges themselves.'

Henry Hansard, the parliamentary publisher, wrote to the same effect, and 'A Merchant' was reduced to falling back on simple reassertion and contradiction, backed up by another anonymous complainant. 'How spiteful the Times is against the Economist!' commented a correspondent to Wilson. 'I hope you will give it them well.' Quoting this as the lead-in to an *Economist* article summing up the affair, Wilson continued:

> It is not worth our while. Our time and our space are too valuable. Any notice we might take of the 'thinly-veiled jealousy' which has been so long evinced towards us, and the pains we have taken to furnish early, correct, and important commercial information, in that quarter, would only give some little importance to attacks which are otherwise harmless, at least to us, whatever they may be to those who indulge in them . . . People of waspish and irritable dispositions really are not aware how much good they do to those who excite their jealousy and animosity; and, we would add, how silly and contemptible they make themselves appear in the eyes of others.
>
> But there is one little point on which we will make a remark, and we will do so very good-naturedly. We are told that it has excited great merriment amongst some of the frequenters of 'Change [the Stock Exchange] to see the transparent effort which the Times has used to make 'A Merchant' of Cornhill the medium of expressing its own grumblings.

According to Wilson's correspondent 'the Times has forgotten that Friday is a foreign post day, when merchants have something else to do than to send after parliamentary papers which they know will come to them in their own way the instant they are published'. The answer seemed to lie with the inefficiency of *The Times*, which had been late with the extracts from the accounts. 'If so, it is too bad to try to fix a quarrel between the Royal Exchange and the Economist . . . in order to screen personal neglect. But it seems to be understood, and we leave the subject with the feeling of indifference which it deserves.'[23]

(There are occasions when one can see why Wilson could inspire intense dislike and an overwhelming desire on the part of his enemies to prove him guilty of hypocrisy. The inveterate highmindedness can strain credulity. Take his daughter's explanation of why he canvassed so hard to regain his

Westbury seat in 1852: 'It was not chiefly for his own seat in Parliament that he fought so eagerly – interesting though parliamentary life was to him, – it was the fact that the Cause was again in danger. The Tories were in power and England was menaced by Protection being again imposed in some form or other. It was the duty of every sound Free Trader to use every effort to turn the Tories out.'[24] However, ultimately it is clear that though he was not immune to self-delusion, Wilson was no humbug but a man possessed of an attitude to public service that was more typical of his generation than ours. Scott Gordon, who apart from Bagehot is the outstanding writer on Wilson, considered a judgment of R.K. Webb that 'during the great social debates of the early nineteenth century the middle-class "advocates of political economy could never defend themselves satisfactorily against charges of hypocrisy"' and thought the point 'correct in the main, but there never was a man less open to the charge of hypocrisy than James Wilson, and the Economist must stand as a conspicuous, even a great, exception to this judgment'.

There are indeed times when even in his personal life, Wilson appeared to take consistency to a point of near lunacy. In 1850 he wrote to Grey soliciting help for an eighteen-year-old girl whose mother had been executed the previous year for murdering her nine other children in infancy. Abandoned by her father, the girl had been taken in by poor neighbours, to whom Wilson was giving two shillings and sixpence a week for her keep. He wanted help in having her sent abroad, away from local prejudice. 'If you could assist me in getting her disposed of in some way it would be a great act of charity & would save her from an inevitable bad fate.' And then, presumably in fear of a doctrinal rebuke, he adds defensively: 'It is one of those exceptional cases, in which interference can be justified on every ground.– She is the innocent victim of the vices of others.'[25])

Since he avoided discussing what his position was *vis-à-vis The Economist*, we are left unclear as to whether *The Times* had got it right and he was nominally no longer owner. It is a point of merely legalistic interest. He reaped the financial rewards, dictated policy, appointed staff and wrote a great deal. Internal evidence makes it abundantly clear that he was writing regularly for his paper even when Financial Secretary to the Treasury. Emilie records his daily routine during parliamentary sessions in 1848–9. He 'sat many hours of the day and night in the House of Commons. He was a constant attendant; he worked at the Board of Control from 10 a.m. to 4 p.m.; every week he wrote the principal leaders in the Economist, besides generally supervising each number as it appeared; he was, moreover, a weekly contributor to the Manchester Guardian.'*[26] His only relaxation was riding after breakfast, preferably with one or two of his daughters, in Hyde Park on Rotten Row.

*Wilson wrote for the *Manchester Guardian* for at least ten years, certainly up to 1853, when Eliza's diary recorded that while he was recovering from smallpox in April, Julia wrote part of his *Manchester Guardian* article.

CHAPTER X:

Thomas Hodgskin

Placed in the van, the press is necessarily the leader to evil as well as good. The habits of circumspection which attend composition, the necessity of some little reflection, and of contemplating the end, before commencing an article, together with the enlarged knowledge which results from habitually attending to a subject, make the press, on the whole, a guide to much more good than evil . . . But there are times and occasions . . . when the members of the press, sharing the general enthusiasm of newly-gained freedom . . . elated to arrogance by the success they have so much contributed to achieve, vehemently fan a consuming flame that requires to be dampened, and are hurrying society into a fearful conflagration. *Thomas Hodgskin, 1848*[1]

By the late 1840s Wilson had substantial help with the writing and production of the paper. From producing it virtually alone, he advanced to having at least two full-time staff. David Mitchell Aird, who was to be associated with the paper for forty years, acted as manager and, according to Emilie, contributed a great deal of the financial coverage. There was in 1848 a temporary sub-editor (presumably 'A.W.'), who in November was replaced by Herbert Spencer, and part-time, on the economic and social side, was Thomas Hodgskin, an anarchist, whose influence on socialist thought was so profound as to lead the Webbs to call Marx 'Hodgskin's illustrious disciple'.[2] Hodgskin was one of the most original minds ever to work for the paper, the subject of a biography in French by Elie Halévy, yet so thoroughly forgotten that his name appears neither in the *Dictionary of National Biography** nor in the *Economist* centenary volume.[3]

*The deficiency was acknowledged with his inclusion in the *DNB*'s *Missing Persons* volume that appeared in 1993.

Hodgskin was born in 1787 at Chatham in Kent, where his father, a storekeeper at the Admiralty docks, according to his son reduced the family to misery through his selfishness. When Thomas was twelve, his father found him a position on a warship as a naval cadet. He served during the Napoleonic Wars, but in 1812 his deep-seated resentment of the harshness and unfairness of naval discipline led to an outburst against a superior officer. He was retired on half-pay with the rank of lieutenant, and the following year he published *An Essay on Naval Discipline, showing Part of its Evil Effects on the Minds of the Officers and the Minds of the Men and on the Community, with an Amended system by which Pressing* [a primitive kind of conscription] *may be immediately abolished.* Francis Place, who met him around this time and brought him into the circle of Jeremy Bentham and the Utilitarians, described him to James Mill as modest, gloomy, unobtrusive and easily excited and possessing 'some very curious metaphysical opinions'.

From 1815 to 1818 Hodgskin travelled on the Continent, mostly on foot, to study the effects of governments on national character, and his *Travels in the North of Germany*, published in 1820, contains severe criticism of state control and democratically elected representation. He married a German and lived for a few years in poverty in Edinburgh, but in 1822 Place and Mill found him a job as parliamentary reporter on the London *Morning Chronicle*. Hodgskin was an enthusiast for the contemporary movement to provide instruction for working men at mechanics' institutes, already operating in Edinburgh, Glasgow and Liverpool. In 1823 he was a co-founder of the *Mechanics' Magazine* and of the London Mechanics' Institution, which under the direction of Dr George Birkbeck developed successfully and became Birkbeck College. Hodgskin wanted the institution to be funded entirely by the artisans themselves, and strongly opposed a public appeal and the acceptance of a loan from Birkbeck. However, Place, exerting the moral authority of a mentor, persuaded him to tolerate both.

Although at first Hodgskin was the institution's joint temporary honorary secretary, he was soon replaced and he was not elected to the governing body. In 1825 he published *Labour Defended against the Claims of Capital, or the Unproductiveness of Capital proved with reference to the Present Combinations amongst Journeymen, by a Labourer*; in 1827 *Popular Political Economy*, based on a course of lectures on economics he had given at the institute two years earlier; and in 1832 *The Natural and Artificial Right of Property Contrasted*, his last major publication.

He had fallen out with the Utilitarians early on. Where they believed that the greatest happiness of the greatest number was the sole moral and pragmatic test of the value of human institutions, he was a Deist who saw the world as a perfect system determined by natural laws. J.-B. Say provided his motto: 'The laws which determine the prosperity of nations are not the work of man; they are derived from the nature of things. We do not establish, we discover them.' Hodgskin seasoned this with a ferocious individualism that led inexorably to an absolutist condemnation of the existence of government: 'all law-making, except gradually and quietly to repeal all existing law, is arrant humbug'. It follows that imperfections are the result of man's interference. If *laissez-faire* in its moderate form can be summed up as: 'If it ain't broke, don't fix it', then in its purest, that is Hodgskin's form, it is: 'It wouldn't be broke, if it hadn't been interfered with.'

One of Hodgskin's fundamental preoccupations – and it was here that Marx drew from him – was the relationship between capital and labour. He was first inspired in 1817 by Ricardo's seminal *Principles of Political Economy and Taxation*, which attempted to discover the laws which regulate the distribution of the produce of industry between landowners, capitalists and labour. Agreeing with Ricardo's measurement of the value of a commodity in terms of the quantity of labour expended on its production – the labour theory of value – Hodgskin concluded that labour therefore had a moral right to the whole produce: non-working capitalists and landowners were exploiters. It was this view, elaborately developed and trenchantly expressed, that won him a considerable working-class following in London and had him later labelled a 'Ricardian socialist'. His ideas were disseminated in popularised form. An 1831 poem used by the National Union of the Working Classes summarised the message of his first two publications:

> Wages should form the price of goods;
> Yes, wages should be all,
> Then we who work to make the goods,
> Should *justly have them all*;

> But if the price be made of rent,
> Tithes, taxes, profits, all;
> Then we who work to make the goods,
> Shall have — *just none at all*.

Writing about Hodgskin and Robert Owen, the leader of the cooperative movement, who believed that property should be communal, Place remarked:

> The mischief these two men have in some respects done is incalculable. They have, however, set thousands thinking; and difficult as it is, and will be, to eradicate the false notions they have inculcated, yet the thinking portion of the working people having been led by them to believe themselves of some importance in the State, will never cease to think so; and the time will come when they will think correctly on all which concerns their real condition in society.

James Mill was less sanguine, explaining in 1832 to Lord Brougham, the educational reformer who was then Lord Chancellor, that:

> The nonsense to which your Lordship alludes about the rights of the labourer to the whole produce of the country, wages, profits, and rent, all included, is the mad nonsense of our friend Hodgskin which he has published as a system, and propagates with the zeal of perfect fanaticism. Whatever of it appears in the *Chronicle*, steals in through his means, he being a sort of sub-editor . . . These opinions, if they were to spread, would be the subversion of civilised society; worse than the overwhelming deluge of Huns and Tartars.

Particularly worrying were 'the illicit cheap publications, in which the doctrine of the right of the labouring people, who, they say, are the only producers, to all that is produced, is very generally preached. The alarming nature of this evil you will understand when I inform you that these publications are superseding the Sunday newspapers, and every other channel through which the people might get better information.'

Hodgskin would rightly have resented some of Mill's implications, for he never regarded work as the prerogative of the proletariat: merchants, for instance, by moving goods to where their value is greatest, were wealth creators and should therefore be classified as mental labourers. Additionally, as a dedicated follower of John Locke – than whom a 'more thoughtful philosopher never wrote'[4] – the proponent of natural law and the natural rights of man to property, he believed that 'the right of individuals to have to own for their own support and selfish use and enjoyment the produce of their own industry, with power freely to dispose of the whole of that in the manner most agreeable to themselves' was 'essential to the welfare and even to the continued existence of society'. What he denied was that property could be a right conferred by law: 'The law of nature is, that industry shall be rewarded by wealth, and idleness be punished by destitution; the law of the land is to give wealth to idleness, and fleece industry till it be destitute.' But being a believer in inevitable social progress, Hodgskin saw hope in the 'large middle class, completely emancipated from the bondage and destitution which the law sought to perpetuate, [which] has grown up in every part of Europe, uniting in their own persons the character both of labourers and capitalists'.[5]

He planned to write a great work on the nature of law and political obligation, Instead, after 1832, to provide for his seven children, he virtually disappeared from public view, into what Halévy calls *'l'obscurité du journalisme anonyme'*, his long-term fate being to crop up as a footnote in studies of Marx. Writing in the 1920s about the contribution of Hodgskin's 'subversive nonsense' – his mingling of 'embryo-socialist doctrines . . . with anarchic individualism' – to the genesis of modern socialism, one choleric academic concluded that 'Marx, by simply spelling the word "labour" with an initial capital, and using it as a collective noun, or noun of multitude, converted Hodgskin's inflammatory individualistic errors into an alluring justification for a general communistic raid by the massed proletariat upon the property of the aristocracy and the bourgeoisie.'[6] Twenty years later, Bertrand Russell, in *A History of Western Philosophy*, described Hodgskin's *Labour Defended* as 'the first Socialist rejoinder' to Ricardo. Nowadays, the 'Ricardian socialist' tag continues to stick.[7]

Staying with the *Morning Chronicle*, Hodgskin wrote ephemera also for the *Courier*, the *Daily News* and the *Sun*, and until his death in 1869, contributed a weekly article to the *Brighton Guardian*. In 1843 he made a brief essay into the public eye with *A Lecture on Free Trade in Connexion with the Corn Laws*, which argued that the abolition of the Corn Laws would be the first great step towards abolishing law and government. The League appears to have shown no enthusiasm for this argument, but it may have brought Hodgskin to the attention of James Wilson. Alternatively, they may have met through the *Morning Chronicle*, for which Wilson was then a contributor. Either way, by early 1844, Hodgskin had begun his long association with *The Economist*. Brought in initially to review books and pamphlets on economic and social issues, he gradually developed into a leader-writer, particularly on his major preoccupations – education, law, crime and pauperism.

Wilson's acquisition of Hodgskin as a part-time but major contributor is the first example of one of his major gifts as an editor: he recruited exceptional talent.* It was one of his endearing qualities that he sought out original minds and enjoyed the company of people who in many respects were his intellectual superiors. He would have seen Hodgskin as a useful complement. They were in broad agreement on the two issues on which Wilson did not brook opposition: free trade and *laissez-faire*. They were also humane, unusually cosmopolitan for their time and shared a deep dislike of the undeserving rich along with a perception of the middle classes as the key to progress.

Hodgskin certainly added depth, scope and erudition to the literary pages along with a sharpness and combativeness that suited the paper's style: 'Mr Ricardo was more acute than learned; his observation was far superior to his knowledge.'[8] Of course King Charles's head was ever in evidence: 'Those who gave the name of political economy to the science of the Wealth of Nations, did Adam Smith a dishonour and the public an injury. It has no connection with politics, except to repudiate them. Smith overthrew the only systems of politics, or political economy, which had been previously in vogue. One of his great aims was to show that the statesman or politician, by interfering with the production and distribution of wealth, had delayed and deranged its growth.'[9] But he did not have to agree with an author to praise him. A long critical review of John Stuart Mill's *Principles of Political Economy* ended generously: 'we might say that there is throughout the book the want of a guiding principle . . . but we are not disposed to carp or cavil at a work which is undoubtedly the most complete exposition of the whole subject which has yet issued from the press'.[10] And he was wont to range far beyond the predictable. One of his most lively contributions was a review of an indifferent study of the distribution of wealth in the United States which argued that high interest rates were helping to concentrate property in the hands of the few. 'In Europe', posited Hodgskin drily, 'if a similar process is going on, it is checked and tempered by old feudal and aristocratic manners.

---

*This was also an early example of the paper's honourable tradition of employing mavericks: in the 1940s Crowther's discovery, the fiercely Roman Catholic Barbara Ward, and Tyerman's recruit, the passionate Marxist Isaac Deutscher, worked well together. It would be only slightly fanciful to describe Norman Macrae, who joined in 1949, as a late-twentieth-century Hodgskin. The current trend towards uniformity has been reinforced by the retirement of both Macrae and Nicholas Harman, two valuably subversive counterbalances to intellectual fashions.

When a man has acquired a fortune here, he is disposed to enjoy it.'

> He buys land; enters into the rank of the gentry and nobility; gets into
> parliament, perhaps gets a title; builds a fine mansion; entails his estates, and
> places his children amongst the class of those who disperse instead of
> accumulate, and become tributary to the capitalist. The possession of land is
> considered to give dignity and ease; to set a man above labour and make
> usury unworthy of him ... If the founder of a family, from old habits,
> continue to save after he has retired from business, his descendants of the
> next or the after generation are sure to adopt the unthrifty habits of the
> aristocracy. They make settlements, encumber the property, and dissipate
> the accumulation of their ancestor amongst a new set of capitalists. Thus our
> aristocratic manners prevent those enormous accumulations in Europe
> which seem to be possible in the United States.[11]

Hodgskin could be particularly interesting when he strayed from his normal
preoccupations. A leader called 'PRESUMPTION OF THE LITERARY
CLASSES', conceived in October 1848 in a burst of irritation at an article in
the *Spectator*, expressed *The Economist*'s deep-seated suspicion of intellectual
activists and demagogues and its loathing of impulsiveness and violence in the
conduct of affairs. Though written by a philosopher, it would have been
applauded by businessmen, horrified at the disruption resulting from the
revolutions that were sweeping through Europe. Except that it was Western
rather than Eastern Europe, and the tyrants had been conservative rather
than communist, it was a period uncannily like 1989: the citizens of country
after country were toppling their old men in the name of democracy. Already
France had been declared a republic and England was playing host to the
fallen Austrian conservative giant, Prince Metternich, as well as to Louis
Blanc, the French utopian-socialist journalist, whose brief foray into government had ended disastrously with his flight from the ensuing civil war. The
Spectator writer's regret at the failure of the 'leading minds' of Europe to
prepare alternatives to the ancient institutions now under attack set Hodgskin off on a discourse on the foolishness of 'literary men, seized with
ambition and vanity' who recommend 'preposterous' constitutions and laws
worse than what they replaced, thereby hurrying societies 'into all the
turmoil of a mischievous and bloody revolution'. The course of society was
dictated by its own laws, yet the *Spectator* could say about Europe that its
'"people have lost *their confidence in thrones and secular churches, and the leading*

minds have prepared nothing ready to take the place of those ancient powers . . . Ideas of advancement, intellectual, political, and social, are lurking in the leading minds of Europe; but the men who hold those ideas . . . *fear to be explicit, lest they should startle, alarm, or estrange* – they prefer to use their talents in safer and more profitable pursuits" . . . Under a thin disguise of humility', snarled Hodgskin, 'here is literary arrogance in perfection. The *leading minds* of Europe – one of which the writer supposes he possesses, or how should he know what unvoiced ideas are lurking in such minds? – the great literary and philosophical geniuses of the age . . . made no preparation for the events we have witnessed . . . for the very sufficient reason that the said leading minds were, nearly twelve months ago, as uninformed of what was to happen in February last as the most backward minds of Europe.'

No more than anyone else can the 'literary heroes' prepare society for the future, for the role of government is very limited. And here Hodgskin spells out his beliefs in a way that shows him standing foursquare with James Wilson: quasi, rather than wholly, anarchist.

> Governments may preserve peace, see justice done between man and man, enforce obedience to the laws, give security to property and life, but they only do mischief when they step beyond these limits, and pretend, whether administered by ancient dynasties or new *littérateurs*, to rule it by their intellectual, political, and social ideas. Literary men are as susceptible to considerations of this kind as others; and as they are at present in a position, from the breaking up of old authority, to effect a great deal of mischief by exciting unnecessary change and needless alarm, or a great deal of good by calming down effervescence, and chilling impossible aspirations, we trust that they will begin to take a more moderate and rational view of what governments can accomplish, and rather leave society to grow and outgrow present evils, than urge on unnecessary and restless change in political institutions.[12]

There is no evidence about how the relationship between Hodgskin and Wilson was conducted, but it is clear from the pages of *The Economist* that it worked well. Hodgskin added intellectual tone, and though facts, more facts and yet more facts continued to form the backbone of the paper, it became quirkier, less stolid, more cultivated and less prosaic. The pre-Hodgskin *Economist* would not have thrown up a line like 'The writer . . . clings to the idomenean prettiness of Fénelon [the late-seventeenth-, early-eighteenth-century French bishop, mystical theologian and liberal-minded thinker on education and politics]'.[13] But Wilson would not have resisted this development. He might grumble about useless knowledge, but he admired men of real learning. And as an editor he had the great gift of being a relaxed and efficient delegator. When he recruited men of ability he gave them their head.

CHAPTER XI:

The case against the rope

War . . . is bad enough; but it is not all bad, for noble virtues and heroic conduct (which we could wish to see otherwise displayed) are from time to time manifested in it. But about hanging there is no one even insignificant feature which for a moment withdraws the view from its mean, cruel, coarse, vindictive character. Are we wrong, then, in hoping and anticipating, as we certainly much desire, that we are near having seen the end of it? *James Wilson, 1845*[1]

A key example of the difference Hodgskin made comes with the development of the paper's treatment of capital punishment, itself a vital issue in the history of *The Economist*. Wilson's hatred of it may well have stemmed from his Quaker upbringing. He tackled it resolutely but with distaste, determined to force his readers to face the reality of what it involved. In 1845, a round-up of provincial news had the best part of a column on 'EXECUTIONS.–THE HANGMAN IS AT HIS WORK AGAIN'. After describing the lead-up to the public hanging in Ipswich of William Howell, it continued:

> Calcraft having adjusted the fatal noose, and drawn the cap over his face, he continued to move his hands, and pray aloud. Immediately before the drop fell, he said with great emphasis to the mob, 'My dear friends, I die innocent of the crime laid to me – that is all I wish to say to you.' The drop then fell, and the wretched man was launched into eternity without making scarcely a perceptible struggle . . .
>
> An Ipswich paper relates a remarkable fact, proving the inefficiency and positive evils of capital punishments:– 'The magistrates were occupied yesterday for several hours in investigating charges of drunkenness, theft,

&c., at the town hall, committed by persons who came, as several of them said, to "see the poor man hung".'[2]

The following month – at the height of the anti-Corn Law agitation – Wilson wrote a leader commencing: 'The work of death by violence goes on apace among us – here by the hands of the law, there in silence and unseen.'

> We fear legislators do not take sufficient notice of it. It is not likely that *we* at least will be charged with indifference to the public questions which now attract the chief notice of the legislature . . . But we trust, on the other hand, we do not undervalue the moral considerations which enter into the right governing of a state. The times, in particular, suggest some remarks on the sacredness of human life, which is just now being so awfully invaded.

There had been almost a dozen hangings in the previous year, three in the previous week, one more was imminent, another likely. There were weighty arguments denying society the right thus to take life, but the community did not find them unanswerable: 'it is impossible not to believe that these public executions derive some sort of public countenance – are supposed to be a sort of wild justice, necessary for the public good . . . For our own part we shall neither affirm nor deny the right of society to deprive of life a fellow creature. We shall confine ourselves to a view of its expediency.'

It was easy to prove that public executions do no good. The philosopher Francis Bacon said 'in taking revenge a man is but even with his enemy; but in passing it over he is superior'. Capital punishment therefore was not for the exaction of victory over 'a wretched fellow creature', nor for his reform. Its only purpose could be to act 'as a lesson to the evil disposed who continue to live', but the opposite holds true. One onlooker had his pocket picked during a York hanging; Howell's innocent wife had died of a broken heart; twenty people had been squeezed to death at a Nottingham execution; and a lad called Tapping, meeting his death 'with a bold front', was clapped and cheered by seven thousand people.

> It is true that few except those of the lowest class of the community – the lowest in moral feeling, character, or understanding – go to witness executions; but, if these executions are right and proper things in themselves, they are the very people who ought to witness them. It is professed to be for their benefit and warning solely that executions are persisted in, and see the result! They make sport of death, laugh at it, commit their crimes in

the face of it, and while it goes on, are 'planning sins anew.' It does not lessen crime; its proved tendency is to increase it.

Punishment should include the possibility of reform.

> In a world where there is so much idleness, and at the same time so much need for work, we shall surely learn bye and bye that a man may be made a better use of than he is by being hanged.
>
> We cannot conclude without giving expression to the strong feeling of disgust with which we notice the elaborate efforts made by nineteen-twentieths of the newspaper press, to give the character of great events to these detestable scenes. One paper boasts of giving 'twelve columns' of news relating to the trial of Tawell. Another is to have a supplement giving an account of the execution, with all the minutiae of details that can be picked up or invented so as to look genuine. A third glories in giving 'exclusively' a portrait of the murderer; and so on; and these are the instructors of the people! Really, we blush for our profession.[3]

Only a couple of months later, Wilson was too upset to subordinate the moral to the expedient argument. Some juries were taking refuge in verdicts of insanity: 'But the fact is, all criminals are insane' and should be treated kindly and not vengefully. The English criminal code 'is pure unadulterated barbarism. We stand out among so-called enlightened nations, in most unenviable relief, as the hanging nation', yet 'have more criminals for our population than any people among whom records of crime are kept'. So since it simply did not work as a deterrent, surely those who believed hanging was a painful duty would see it should be abolished.[4]

Shortly after particularly disgraceful scenes at a public execution, the Home Secretary placed a temporary ban on public attendance. Simultaneously, meetings were being held in England and New York calling for abolition of capital punishment. Wilson was sanguine: 'when Secretaries of State are beginning to be ashamed of its [hanging] being seen, we surely do not judge erroneously in anticipating that but a little more of it remains to be seen among us'.[5]

The following year Hodgskin drastically changed the emphasis to take account of his long-standing preoccupation with the link between pauperism and crime. It was of overriding importance, he wrote, that industry be set free and the people consequently made prosperous: that would eradicate the crime that stemmed from enforced hunger, enforced idleness, unsatisfactory ill-rewarded work and enforced brutality. Until such conditions operated, a campaign to abolish capital punishment would be bound to fail. However, he continued, taking the issue on to the moral plane that Wilson had deliberately eschewed and putting forward the argument of John Locke:

> We deny totally that the state has any right deliberately and in cold blood to take away the life of a single human being. On the contrary, it is organised to protect life, even the lives of criminals. Admitting all the authority that can be claimed for the often quoted scripture precept, it only goes the length of sanctioning the shedding of blood in retaliation at the time that blood is shed. It does not warrant hoarding up resentment, pouncing on the offender wherever he can be caught, and deliberately, by a slow and settled process, after an offence has been proved against him, taking away his life. The state can have no right which the individuals who compose it have not . . . Two men, or twenty men, or a hundred millions of men, are no more authorised to cheat and steal, and bear false witness, and take away life, than one man.

Like Locke, however, he allowed for a man's right to kill in self-defence, or in defence of his property, 'when the wrong-doer is using the force and violence which he has no right to use'. Consequently, governments were justified in waging a war of self-defence.

> But let the reader mark how much more odious is the offence of the multitude, incorporated into a nation, deliberately taking away the life of an individual, than any common murder . . . In most cases of murder, whether perpetrated from some momentary stimulus to a long-nourished passion, or deliberately planned and carried into effect, the victim is not informed of the intention . . . But when the state puts a man to death, it is done deliberately. He is informed of his coming fate. The very essence of his punishment consists far less in the actual extinction of life, than in the solemn and dreadful preparations for taking it away.

Capital punishment had been instituted in a barbarous age: it was 'merely vengeance securely embodied into law', by those who did not understand its effects. To demonstrate its many evils was one of the noble tasks of modern philosophy.

> That there is some peculiar adaptation in it when ordained by the state to

> repress the horrible crime of murder – that it prevents the commission by
> others of the offences for which it is inflicted – that it saves society from a
> single evil, while it is of itself, and with all its necessary consequences, an evil
> of enormous magnitude – has been proved to be a mere unfounded
> hypothesis – a distempered fancy – a creature of the brain, with no warrant
> from experience, and no sanction from nature.[6]

This and a subsequent leader inspired two enormously long and critical letters discussing the philosophical basis of Hodgskin's view of society and law. In a correspondence column usually dominated by statistical queries or free-trade pieties, they stand as a dramatic testimony to Hodgskin's success in taking the paper intellectually up-market and to Wilson's tolerance in permitting the airing of a metaphysical debate with which he could have had little patience.

(In hopefully predicting the imminent end of capital punishment, James Wilson had been, as usual, much too sanguine. Public executions were abolished in 1868, but it was almost 120 years before the abolition of capital punishment in Britain, a period during which the paper remained resolutely abolitionist. When in 1983, after a landslide Conservative election victory, there was a massive outcry for the return of hanging, Andrew Knight's *Economist* brought out its heaviest weapons in an effort to influence the free vote in the Commons. There was nothing Hodgskin-like about the arguments used in 'CASE AGAINST THE ROPE': they were Wilsonian to an astounding degree, and for the same reasons. The object was to convince the waverers – those who thought hanging a painful necessity – so the case made was expedient, not moral.

> What the pro-hangers hanker for, evidently, is a simple solution to complex
> problems. They think execution is a unique deterrent, that because it is swift
> and sure it closes the endless arguments about crime and punishment, right
> and wrong, and signifies society's absolute abhorrence of certain sorts of
> offence. In practice, it does exactly the opposite.

Facts, figures, every reasonable argument examined and demolished, strong opinions expressed and barbarity denounced passionately – it was one of those articles that shows how in essentials *The Economist* remains unaffected by the passage of time and how enduring are the techniques Wilson employed to counter illogicality and ignorance. Part of the case against executions even revolved around the bad moral effect they would have on the populace at large. 'Those who are tempted to vote yes to hanging', it added grimly, 'must decide whether the duty they would lay on others is one that they would themselves discharge. Would they, if asked by the state, pull that lever and break that villain's neck? If not, they must vote no and lay the subject to rest for the life of this parliament. Every year that passes makes a return to the old barbarity more remote, more unthinkable for a civilised nation, and less useful for a society that wishes to deter crime.'[7] The modern paper used to great effect one of the bonuses of modern technology: it added to the debate a cover picture – a drawing of a Victorian crowd watching a hanging.)

Wilson and Hodgskin were collaborators for at least fourteen years and clearly had a profound influence on each other. Halévy identified those articles that he was certain were written by Hodgskin, but there are many more that bear traces of his influence. Considering Wilson's thirst for conversation on public issues, it is inconceivable that he and Hodgskin did not talk over what interested them both: certainly Hodgskin's articles would have given Wilson cause for reflection. Initially Hodgskin seems to have radicalised Wilson on *laissez-faire* and concentrated his mind on the issue of punishment. Later the roles seem to have been reversed, for in his last few years, Hodgskin shows some signs of pragmatism when he writes about penal reform. There were other minds being brought to bear on the paper, but in its first few years Hodgskin's role was crucial. On Wilson's (and Radnor's) natural aversion to cruelty was built an approach to the whole question of punishment which has been central to *The Economist*'s thinking throughout its history. The issue was constantly placed in the foreground. A classic statement appeared in a leader of 1848 about the decision to spare the lives of the leaders of the ineffectual Irish rebellion. Rejoicing prematurely in this evidence of statesmanship, the article reported 'a gradual and successive abatement and abolition of all the cruel punishments that were originally dictated by feeling or sentiment'.

> Crucifying, breaking on the wheel, impaling alive, torture of all kinds, have been given up. The punishment of death has in several states been wholly abolished, and only reserved in others for murder and treason. Noisome, pestilential dungeons, into which criminals were hurled and left to perish, have almost disappeared, or are only to be be found in a few states that were

to a recent period mere despotisms, and are only reserved for political offenders. Gaols are made as healthy and as comfortable as possible, consistently with securing the person of the prisoner; punishments are nicely graduated and adapted, as is supposed, to offences; and through the whole system of penal jurisprudence public utility and humanity have taken the place of individual vengeance and cruelty. This process is still going on.[8]

Then there was the devastating leader 'CAN THE ARMY BE GOVERNED WITHOUT FLOGGING?', which had been provoked by the death of a victim. Since readers knew 'all the sickening details' that had emerged at the inquest, it would be unnecessary

> to dilate on cats double knotted, on little pieces of flesh deliberately whipped from the body, on blood streaming down the back, on bruised and ruptured muscles, conveying their own agonised inflammation to the heart through all the surrounding tissues, causing disease and death – on the stoical indifference of the victim, or the still more extraordinary indifference of officers who looked on and never cried hold – never even felt his pulse to ascertain if he could bear another lash, while the men in the ranks were fainting at the horrors they were compelled to witness – we shall not dilate on such subjects, however powerful would be their effect in exciting the sympathy and the zeal of every kindly and reflecting man, believing them to be already known to our readers, who are already fully convinced of the desirableness, if practicable, of wholly abolishing the punishment of flogging. Its torturing and brutalising character are too well known to require illustration.[9]

The rest of the article was, of course, a carefully argued annihilation of all prevailing defences of the practice. Interestingly, the paper did recommend 'gentle' flogging in at least two specific instances during Wilson's editorship,*[10] but in both cases it was choosing a lesser evil than capital punishment. There was in 1879 a lapse from the strong anti-cruelty tradition, when an article almost certainly written by D.C. Lathbury, one of the paper's unsuccessful editors, defended flogging in the army in a manner at once callous, high-minded and pragmatic.[11] The paper more or less held its line on capital punishment, though there was occasional slight ambiguity, notably in

---

*The candidates were William Smith O'Brien, leader of the 1848 Irish rebellion, and would-be assassins of the Queen.

the early 1880s when H.H. Asquith was chief leader-writer. When as Prime Minister he allowed the execution of the leaders of the 1916 Easter Rising in Dublin, he was out of step with Francis Hirst's *Economist*, which had urged that in 'punishing the ringleaders the Government, which is surely to blame for their own negligence, would be wise to follow the example of General Botha [who as Prime Minister of South Africa put down an Afrikaner rebellion firmly but mercifully]. There should be no martyrs or heroes or pilgrimages.'[12]

That line was echoed in the 1983 denunciation of capital punishment. Tackling the then fashionable argument that terrorists should be singled out for execution, it said this would 'concede and glorify his case . . . Killing rebels – remember the story of the Dublin Easter uprising of 1916 – can hand them victory.'[13]

If Hodgskin and Wilson were in fundamental agreement, there were noticeable differences on specifics. Attributing most crime to poverty, Hodgskin was not at all satisfied with progress in penal reform. In some of his last *Economist* articles,[14] he was concerned about such deficiencies of the prison system as the damage done by locking up first offenders with hardened criminals and the niggardliness that had prisoners sleeping two or three to a cell. The arguments about the whole nature of punishment were elaborate, and Halévy believes they caused a rupture with Wilson because they were too doctrinaire. Hodgskin did not leave then, but there is supporting evidence of at least some difference of opinion among the staff. In the issue following the last of this series, an article praising juvenile reformatories included the judgment on their major proponent that 'he is wholly untainted with the prevalent weak and morbid humanitarianism; he is interested in the criminal, but he would neither pet him nor spare him; he regards the offender as an object of righteous severity and rigid control; and never for one moment forgets that the injured and innocent community – and not the sinner and the injurer – is the party entitled to primary consideration'.[15]

A reference in a letter from Eliza Wilson to Bagehot in January 1858 identifies Hodgskin as the author of an extreme *laissez-faire* article on the American currency crisis, which was attributed to James Wilson but with which, though he would have been happy with it ten years earlier, he now did not agree.[16] There is no evidence as to whether Hodgskin stayed for long after that; Halévy was unable to identify any of his articles after May 1857. Hodgskin may well have parted company with the paper around that time.

He was almost seventy and it may be that Richard Holt Hutton, the new young editor, found him too much of an unrepentant throw-back to an age that even Wilson had outgrown.

Hodgskin appeared in public in May and June 1858 to give two lectures: 'What shall we do with our criminals? Don't create them' and 'Our chief crime: cause and cure'; his thesis was that crime was caused not by the failings of the individual but by the corrupting tendencies of the law. He then disappeared from view: neither *The Economist* nor apparently any other journal noted his death in August 1869.

CHAPTER XII

Herbert Spencer

The author of the present work is no ordinary thinker, and no ordinary writer; and he gives us, in language that sparkles with beauties, and in reasoning at once novel and elaborate, precise and logical, a very comprehensive and complete exposition of the rights of men in society – those rights that now everywhere engage attention, and are almost everywhere, from being ill understood, the occasion of strife, and, in some societies, the causes of very ruinous convulsions.[1]

So wrote Thomas Hodgskin in 1851, generously and perceptively, in his *Economist* review of *Social Statics*, the first book by his young friend and colleague, Herbert Spencer.

Spencer was born in Derby in 1820 to Nonconformist parents, whose eight younger children died in infancy. His father was a mathematician and teacher; his uncle, Thomas Spencer, a clergyman and radical reformer, an ex-fellow of St John's College, Cambridge, who as part of his battle against pauperism weaned his parishioners away from dependency by teaching them the value of thrift, industry and temperance. An indefatigable campaigner and prolific pamphleteer, he preached at the first and last banquets of the Anti-Corn Law League.

Herbert Spencer, scientifically gifted but poor at classics, lived with his uncle near Bath for three years from the age of thirteen, but refused his uncle's offer to send him to Cambridge: like Wilson and Hodgskin, he was mainly self-taught. After a few months as an apprentice schoolteacher, in 1837 he began a career as a civil engineer, becoming private secretary to the engineering chief of the Birmingham and Gloucester railway. When the railway was completed, in 1841, he lost his job.

By now, according to his friend and biographer, David Duncan,[2] 'he had secured a grasp of mathematical and physical principles, his inventive powers had enjoyed scope for exercise, he had gained a fair knowledge of certain branches of engineering and an acquaintance with the routine of important undertakings, had become accustomed to the management of men, and learnt business habits which could not fail to be useful. His official duties had cultivated his power of consecutive thinking and given him fluency and directness of composition. While affording him opportunities for theoretical speculation, his work did not divorce him from practical interests. On the contrary, it fostered that power of uniting abstract thought with concrete exemplification and illustration so noticeable in his books.'

By that time he had moved from an almost exclusive interest in matters scientific to an absorption with matters political, religious and social. He threw himself so enthusiastically into agitations against the Corn Laws and slavery and in favour of the separation of church and state as to be described by a friend as 'radical all over'. To the *Nonconformist* in 1842 he contributed a series of letters about the laws of nature, arguing that 'natural evils will rectify themselves' with the help of a 'self-adjusting principle': therefore the only purpose of government is to uphold these rights by protecting person and property. The following year he published these letters as a pamphlet called *The Proper Sphere of Government*. Looking back at this period more than half a century later, Spencer wrote of the 'emotional leanings' betrayed in the letters. 'Individuality was pronounced in all members of the family, and pronounced individuality is necessarily more or less at variance with authority. A self-dependent and self-asserting nature resists all such government as is not expressive of equitable restraint. Our family was essentially a *dissenting* family; and dissent is an expression of antagonism to arbitrary control. Of course a wish to limit State-action is a natural concomitant.'[3]

Apart from a brief period in another railway job, just before the market collapsed, his time from 1841 to 1848 was spent in what, fifty years later, he recalled as 'miscellaneous and futile activities mainly spent over inventions, but partly in speculations, political, ethical, linguistic, showing as always the excursive tendency'. His only money-making invention was a binding-pin for sheets of music or printed periodicals. He wrote for the *Zoist* on phrenology and was for a short time a sub-editor on the *Pilot*, the organ of the Complete Suffrage Union. His autobiography[4] tells the story of how he came to be saved by James Wilson from failure and penury. He wrote home in May 1848:

My uncle gave me a letter of introduction to Wilson, the editor of *The Economist*. He treated me very civilly and invited me to tea at his house on Saturday evening. I saw there a very interesting French lady – the Comtesse de Brunetière – who is a daughter of Tallien, one of the notables of the first French Revolution. She is intimately acquainted with all the leading politicians of Paris and gave us some very curious details of the late events. Mr Wilson told us that she had prophesied the leading events of the late revolution two months before they occurred.

Three weeks later he reported on 'a long interview this morning with Mr Wilson, MP, who manifested some interest in my proceedings and inquired how I should like a *sub-editorship to a London weekly paper*. This was put in such a manner as to lead me to suppose he referred to The Economist. Our interview ended with his requesting me to leave my address with him, with the understanding that he would write to me if an opening should present itself.' Spencer presented Wilson with a copy of *The Proper Sphere of Government*, with which Wilson declared himself in sympathy, with qualifications: even Wilson would have drawn the line at Spencer's opposition to government taking responsibility for defence against foreign aggression.

Wilson wrote from Westbury, in November:

> The situation now vacant in *The Economist* Office is that of Sub-Editor, which, while it requires a regular attendance at the office, does not impose heavy duties. You would have a room to yourself, and considerable leisure to attend to any other pursuit, such as preparing a work for the press, especially from Friday night until about Wednesday in the following week. At first the salary would be one hundred guineas a year. If you were disposed to live on the premises you could have a bed room and attendance free. The messenger and his wife live there, and I used to sleep there when my family was out of town, and they attended on me.
>
> If I found that you could contribute leading articles there would be an additional allowance.
>
> The vacancy has existed for some time (it has been temporarily filled [presumably by the mysterious 'A.W.', who had written in Wilson's defence to *The Times* in July of that year]), and as I have about seventy applications for it – to none of which I have replied – you will please say by return of post if you feel inclined to take it, and if so I will appoint a time for you to meet me in town.

Although the salary was low, free accommodation in a central location made the offer attractive. *The Economist*'s first offices had been at 6 Wellington Street (since redevelopment absorbed into Lancaster Place), at the Strand end of Waterloo Bridge; the *Spectator* was at No. 1 and *Punch* at No. 13. Within two years, Wilson had moved his headquarters to larger accommodation nearby, at 340 Strand. For 54 years *Economist* staff occupied the whole of this six-storey, long, narrow building, in the basement of which, at some stage, the paper was printed.

The job was undemanding. 'A journalist', recalled Spencer,

> is usually understood to be one among whose functions is that of influencing public opinion by articles and comments. I had no such function. Replying early in 1849 to a letter from my uncle Thomas, I said – You inquire respecting the particular department of the paper with which I have to do. I cannot better answer than by saying – with all parts except the Leading Articles, Agriculture, Literature, and the summaries that appear under the heads of 'Bank returns and Money Market' and 'Commercial Epitome.' All other matters I have to superintend. I have the offer to write leading articles if I wish to do so; but I refrain from this from the desire to devote all my spare time to my own private writing, which I consider of more importance than the extra remuneration I should obtain by writing for the paper.

And to his mother: 'I manage my work very well so far, and have given satisfaction to Mr Wilson – indeed, I have been complimented by him upon the improvement the paper has undergone, more particularly in the news department, under my administration.'[5]

To a close friend he was more frank:

> I am happy to say that I can answer your inquiries as to my position with tolerable satisfaction. The place suits me on the whole remarkably well, and now that I have got pretty completely acclimatized I have nothing important to complain of and much to approve. In the first place I am almost wholly my own master; scarcely coming in contact with Mr Wilson more than once a month, and this, with my rebellious tendencies, is a great blessing. Then again my work is decidedly light. Even I, with my invincible idleness, am obliged to admit this. On Saturday, Monday, and Tuesday, I have nothing to do but to read through the *Times* and *Daily News* . . . extract what may be needful, and put it aside for subsequent use. On Wednesday and Thursday

my work occupies me from ten until four. Friday is my only hard day, when I have to continue at it until 12½ or 1 at night. This, however, is a very small payment to make for having so much time at my own disposal; permitting me as it does to go where I please, and when I please, during the early part of the week.

There were a few additional perks. Although the paper gave little space to art or the theatre, it often received press tickets, which Spencer used or gave away. 'To the Opera in the Haymarket I had but occasional access; but to the Royal Italian Opera in Covent Garden, I had access whenever the orders were not appropriated by Mrs Wilson, who, as wife of the proprietor and editor, had of course the first claim.' And there were books for review – '(not many, however, for *The Economist* had but small space for literary criticism); and into these I occasionally dipped before they went to Mr Hodgskin'.

On the debit side was 340 Strand. 'Of course the habitat was trying to me – accustomed as I had been to a quiet house and tolerably good air. I see from letters that notwithstanding double sashes to the windows, it took me a week to become so far inured to the eternal rattle of the Strand as to be able to sleep; and I see, too, that for some time I suffered in general health from noise and other causes. Though in the subsequent April I described myself as having become tolerably well acclimatized, yet the insalubrity evidently told upon me.' He was finally driven to find other accommodation in April 1850 when the drains went out of order.

The Economist was far more important to Spencer than was Spencer to *The Economist*. He continued to limit himself to work that could have been done by anyone competent, and had had attributed to him only one leading article – 'A SOLUTION OF THE WATER QUESTION', which made suggestions for improving the quality of London water.[6] And although his attractive personality and originality cannot have failed to make an impact on those round him, the paper was already so individualistic before Spencer even joined as to make any influence he had one of reinforcement rather than amendment. Yet it is no small achievement for *The Economist* to have facilitated the development of Spencer's genius.

'Remembrances of these years of my journalistic life, are agreeable', he wrote many years later.

> Light work and freedom from anxiety made my daily existence a not undesirable one; and some kinds of pleasures were accessible in ample

amounts. The period was one in which there was going on an active development of thought. There then germinated various ideas which unfolded in after years; and of course the rise of these ideas, and in some cases the partial elaboration of them, had their concomitant gratifications of a sustained kind. Moreover, during this interval my existence became much enriched in another way. To the friendships of previous years were now added five* others, which gradually entered as threads into the fabric of my life; and some of which affected its texture and pattern in marked ways. In short, I think I may say that the character of my later career was mainly determined by the conceptions which were initiated, and the friendships which were formed, between the times at which my connexion with *The Economist* began and ended.

It was perhaps just as well that Spencer had made the self-denying ordinance about his function on *The Economist*. Huxley once commented that Spencer's idea of a tragedy was 'a deduction killed by a fact'. Marian Evans described the conflict in practice: 'I went to Kew yesterday on a scientific expedition with Herbert Spencer, who has all sorts of theories about plants – I should have said a *proof*-hunting expedition. Of course, if the flowers didn't correspond to the theories, we said, "*tant pis pour les fleurs*".'[7] Add to that his developing agnosticism, his assertiveness, his unconventionality and his resistance to authority and it is hard to see him as a leader-writer: his soaring mind worked best when pursuing abstract ideas without constraint.

The Economist's role had not been limited to providing Spencer with an easy billet: it also provided him with an environment that helped to develop his individualistic evolutionary ideas. (With the publication in 1859 of Charles Darwin's *The Origin of Species*, some of Spencer's early ideas received retrospective intellectual buttressing: it was Spencer who later coined the phrase 'survival of the fittest'.) Hodgskin, whom he described as his 'coadjutor' on the paper, spent evenings with Spencer and took a deep interest in his projected book. As C.H. Driver has remarked, 'Spencer's

*Marian Evans, the novelist George Eliot; T.H. Huxley, the biologist who was to be the great proponent of Darwinism; G.H. Lewes, a gifted, radical and versatile journalist and writer, who through Spencer met Evans, with whom he was to live for the rest of his life; John Tyndall, a physicist, natural philosopher and populariser of science, who like Huxley believed in applying scientific discoveries to illuminate the nature of the Universe; and Octavius Smith, an independent-minded and enterprising businessman who shared Spencer's opposition to state intervention.

doctrines are, in many respects, so strikingly similar to Hodgskin's that it is not fanciful to assume that the older man to no small degree helped to confirm the younger in the quasi-anarchistic philosophy to which his temperament and upbringing had inclined him and which Hodgskin had spent so many years in developing.'[8] Until his book was finished, Spencer saw few other friends.

John Chapman, a young physician and writer on human nature, who ran a publishing business across the street from *The Economist*, had known Spencer from the mid-1840s and was to publish his book. Spencer's first title was *Demostatics* (from 'Demos', the Greek word for people), which he thought suggested the subject-matter of the book – 'how an aggregate of citizens may stand without tendency to conflict and disruption'. His Uncle Thomas approved, but to his father he wrote that:

> Neither Chapman nor Mr Hodgskin approves of *Demostatics* as a title. They both think that more would be prejudiced against the book by it than would be impressed in its favour.
>
> Mr Hodgskin quite approves of *Social Statics*, which he thinks would be a very good title. I am going to consult with Chapman about it. What is your objection to it? As I am now thinking of it the title would stand –
>
> Social Statics: a System of Equity Synthetically Developed.

In the event the title became *Social Statics: or, the Conditions essential to Human Happiness Specified, and the First of them Developed*. Its declared object was to set forth the doctrine that 'every man has freedom to do all that he wills, provided that he infringes not the equal freedom of any other man'. Wilson's influence had told: Spencer now allowed that in addition to internal policing of people and property, the state should defend itself against external attack. However, he believed that a citizen had the right to refuse to pay taxes if he gave up the advantages of state protection.

In his maturity Spencer was to become a dominating intellectual force, the supreme synthesising naturalistic philosopher, who applied his extensive knowledge of physical and social sciences to justify his belief that evolution made human progress inevitable: nature, not man, set the pace. As a proponent of *laissez-faire* he was so extreme as to have been thought by some critics to be close to nihilism. *Social Statics*, founded upon an elaborate refutation of Utilitarianism, contains most of his later precepts in embryo.

It was natural that Hodgskin should review his coadjutor's book, and predictable that he would do so enthusiastically. More than that, the review contains a particularly strong statement of a major strand in the moral, radical – even spiritual – thinking that underpinned James Wilson's *Economist*. Welcoming *Social Statics* as a fine contribution to the burgeoning science of morality, Hodgskin noted approvingly that it began with

> a refutation of the doctrine of expediency, as assumed by Bentham, to be the rule of conduct for individuals and of states; the existence of a moral sense, or a sense as well adapted to impel men to a proper line of conduct towards one another, as appetite is adapted to impel them to the preservation of the body is shown; the truth is made manifest, that humanity is indefinitely variable, and cannot be made the test of a perfect law; but such a perfect law exists, and can be ascertained, and by that, and that alone, can man successfully steer his course.
>
> Morality is accordingly defined 'the law of the perfect man;' . . . All evil – of course including the moral evil resulting from crime – is evanescent, the consequence of non-adaptation of the constitution of man to conditions, and the constitution is continually changing to adapt it to conditions. Civilisation is the adaptation that has already taken place, and progress means the successive steps of the transition . . . Admitting that the greatest happiness of mankind is the creative purpose; to know how to achieve this purpose, we have to determine the essential conditions on which it depends, and submit ourselves to them.

At the 'head' of these conditions stood 'the social state', for man lived in society, and every individual was a part of it. The task of scientific morality was to ascertain the necessary conditions and state them, 'so that life may be made to conform to them'.

> Individual or private morality, as distinguished from social or public morality, is not at present discussed; the one object being to unfold that primary condition to the greatest happiness, the observance of justice, into a system of equity; to mark out those limits put to each man's sphere of activity by the like spheres of other men; and to delineate the relationships that are necessitated by a recognition of those limits. This is to develop the principles of social statics.

The first principle of social statics and the basis of all justice was that all men have a right and a duty to exercise their faculties within the constraints of the freedom of others. The 'expediency scheme', which supposes 'that man can do something better than observe this principle and its consequences, or something better than obey the orders of his Creator, or comply with the condition of his existence – is true atheism'. Among the many issues addressed were civil and religious liberty, poor laws, state education and sanitary supervision. If Spencer's views on all these subjects were predictable, they were, as Hodgskin pointed out, discussed in a highly original manner. Take the matter of state grants for education, then a matter of tremendous public debate and against which *The Economist*, in many articles by both Wilson and Hodgskin, argued adamantly. (Sample: 'Our objection . . . to this scheme of the State encouraging and assisting education, is, in the main, the same that we make to its interfering with trade or agriculture, whether to encourage and assist, or to regulate and control it. Invariably, that encouragement and assistance tend to degrade the people to be helped and assisted, and to prevent the improvement proposed by the encouragement and assistance . . . To be prized and to be profited by, those who are to be benefited must achieve it for themselves or their offspring.') The same anti-dependency-culture argument was used in opposing virtually every reform from the factory legislation to municipal refuse collection.[9] Hodgskin chose to quote from *Social Statics* a paragraph that illustrated Spencer's sprightly argumentative style. Ironically, in applying the principle of *reductio ad absurdum* to the demands of educational reformers, Spencer neatly summed up what were, a century later, to be the main features of the British welfare state welcomed by *The Economist*: 'having satisfied the prevalent wish for government schools with tax-paid teachers, and adopted Mr Ewart's plan for town libraries and museums, should we not canvass the supplementary proposal to have national lecturers? and if this proposal is assented to, would it not be well to carry out the scheme of Sir David Brewster, who desires to have "men ordained by the State to the undivided functions of science" – "an intellectual priesthood," to develop the glorious truths which time and space embosom?'

> Then having established 'an intellectual priesthood' to keep company with our religious one, a priesthood of physic such as is advocated by certain fee-less medical men, of which we have already the germ in our union doctors, would nicely complete the trio. And when it had been agreed to put the sick under the care of public officials, consistency would of course

demand the adoption of Mr G.A. Walker's system of government funerals, under which 'those in authority' are 'to take especial care' that 'the poorest of our brethren' shall have 'an appropriate and solemn transmission' to the grave, and are to grant in certain cases 'gratuitous means of interment.' Having carried out thus far the communist plan of doing everything for everybody, should we not consider the people's amusements, and, taking example from the opera-subsidy in France, establish public ball rooms, and gratis concerts, and cheap theatres, with state-paid actors, musicians and masters of the ceremonies; using care at the same time duly to regulate the popular taste, as indeed in the case of the Art-Union subscribers our present Government proposed to do?

Although Hodgskin took Spencer to task over his rejection of property rights, overall the review was ecstatic, and very helpful in bringing Spencer to the attention of the thinking public. 'I am quite satisfied with it', he wrote, 'for though the high praise is qualified with some blame, there is not more of this than is needful to prevent the suspicion that I had written the review myself.'[10]

Spencer stayed with the paper for a while, revelling in the new friendships that followed on the success of his book and his attendance at his publisher's soirées. Amusing, considerate and unpretentious, he attracted great affection as well as intellectual respect. As it had facilitated the preparation of his book, *The Economist* facilitated the development of his friendships and the furtherance of his career. W.R. Greg, an exceptionally well-connected journalist, was introduced to Spencer at dinner at the Wilsons. Marian Evans, sub-editor of the *Westminster Review*, worked just across the street and accompanied him to the opera and the theatre on his free press tickets: he tried vainly to persuade her to write novels (she did not get down to *Adam Bede*, her first, until 1858). In April 1852 she wrote of going to the opera 'with my "excellent friend Herbert Spencer," as Lewes calls him. We have agreed that we are not in love with each other, and that there is no reason why we should not have as much of each other's society as we like. He is a good, delightful creature and I always feel better for being with him.'[11] The following month she explained that her 'brightest spot next to my love of *old* friends, is the deliciously calm *new* friendship that Herbert Spencer gives me. We see each other every day and have a delightful *camaraderie* in everything.'[12]

Spencer managed to secure a longer Christmas holiday, 'by arrangement with Mr Hodgskin to do some of his work if he would do some of mine', but the absence of leisure chafed more and more. 'Why', he wondered half a century later, 'did I continue so long to hold a subordinate place? Letters written shortly after accepting it, imply that I originally regarded it as a place which very well served "present purposes;" and one of them dated April 1849, said I "shall probably retain my post until the completion and publication of my book."' Yet two years later he was still in place. In October 1852 he wrote home that he was thinking of preparing an article on 'Method in Education' for the *Edinburgh Review* and getting Greg, one of their major contributors, to present it.

> It is considered by several of my friends that I am throwing away my time in my present position, and that I might with less exertion make more money by original contributions; and at the same time have as much leisure for larger works. . . . This article for the *Edinburgh* will be a kind of experimental test of the safety of the move.

He wrote for the *Westminster Review* and Lewes's *Leader*, but 'caution overruled my ambition' until a small legacy gave him courage to leave. 'Herbert Spencer means to quit his position as sub-editor of the Economist and trust to writing', wrote Evans in April 1853. 'This is *entre nous*. I rather tremble for him – with his nature, article-writing for bread will be worse than he has just now persuaded himself to think. Still this editorship is a horrid *gêne* and tethers him to London all the year, with the exception of a few days' holiday now and then.'[13] The parting in July was amicable. The following year *The Economist* was commenting favourably on an article of his on railways in the *Edinburgh Review* ('well-timed and useful . . . piquant as well as instructive').[14] And in 1859 he was seeking Wilson's advice on finding a government post offering plenty of leisure.[15]

Spencer, wrote Lord Morley many years later, 'had an indefatigable intellect, an iron love of truth, a pure and scrupulous conscience, a spirit of loyal and beneficent intention, a noble passion for knowledge and systematic thought, as the instruments for man's elevation'.[16] These were the qualities that Wilson revered, sought for in his principal recruits and aspired to have as the guiding spirit of his paper.

CHAPTER XIII:

William Rathbone Greg

Walter Bagehot would say that he knew of no more effective current literature than when my father, in conversation, would propound a subject to William Rathbone Greg, who would subsequently convert those conversations into articles, Mr Greg's style being excellent and singularly appropriate to current literature.[1] *Emilie Barrington (née Wilson)*

Spencer's biographer wrote that 'like all the finer natures, [he] shrank from parading the more attractive and lovable aspects of his character – thus permitting an apparent justification for the opinion that he was "all brains and no heart."'[2] William Rathbone Greg, mainstay of *The Economist*'s leader pages for almost a decade as well as for some years its manager, invited similar misunderstanding, being 'inclined to be – or, at least, was felt by an opponent to be – dry, mordant, and almost harsh. These disagreeable prepossessions were instantly dissipated, as so often happens, by personal acquaintance. He had not only the courtesy of the good type of the man of the world, but an air of moral suavity, when one came near enough to him, that was infinitely attractive and engaging. He was urbane, essentially modest, and readily interested in ideas and subjects other than his own.'[3]

His *Economist* debut came probably in 1846, shortly after he came to know Wilson through a correspondence about the Irish famine. It was certainly Greg who wrote the fascinating five-part series in October and November of that year asking 'Who should be blamed for the present condition of society' (a euphemism for mass poverty) – the lower classes, the capitalists, the landowners or the state? Capitalists and landowners were exonerated; the state, by encouraging dependency, bore some responsibility; but most of the blame lay with the lower classes themselves. As was explained in the final summarising article:

> Nobody ever dreams of saying that the English people and government are responsible for the condition of the Turks, or that any merchant on the Exchange is responsible for the sufferings of any individual peasant in Ireland.

Apart from physical evils like disease, against which a man may be unable to guard, according to his – and no one else's – conduct are a man's 'sufferings and his pleasures'.

> On this principle of individual responsibility . . . we have no hesitation in pronouncing, because the masses are suffering, and have long been suffer- ing, without much amending their condition, that they are greatly to blame. Looking to their habits, to their ignorance, to their deference to false friends, to their unshaken confidence in a long succession of charlatan leaders, we cannot exonerate them. Nature makes them responsible for their conduct – why should not we? We find them suffering, and we pronounce them in fault.[4]

Greg saw a silver lining to the Malthusian cloud, believing that the necessity to exercise 'moral restraint' (i.e. abstain from sex) to avoid over-population encouraged self-improvement. (His relationship with Julia Wilson was to demonstrate that he lived up to his principles.) But, along with Herbert Spencer, he saw it as inevitable that this lesson could not be learned without much suffering and premature death along the path of progress. In his fine essay on *laissez-faire*, Scott Gordon concluded that it 'would be difficult to find anywhere a more uncompromising expression of individual responsi- bility than is contained in these articles'. It certainly would not immediately occur to the reader that their author was a distinguished humanitarian and philanthropist.

Four years younger than Wilson, Greg was born in 1809 in Manchester, the youngest of the thirteen children of a rich Unitarian merchant and mill-owning father and an intellectually-inclined mother. His family, plain livers and high thinkers, kept an unpretentiously hospitable home and were benevolent employers to the highest degree: their apprentice-scheme was a passport to a decent life for hundreds of workhouse children. He attended a

Unitarian school in Bristol, where he was taught 'to see nature purely in terms of physical forces. (Unitarians had no truck with orthodox Creationist science, the sort taught in Anglican schools: species were not miraculously created, nor did man stand outside nature.) His masters had even proclaimed the human mind subject to physical law – an idea that Anglicans abhorred, knowing that morality was God's gift, not nature's.'[5] Greg went in 1826 to Edinburgh University, where he and Charles Darwin simultaneously became members of the Plinian Society, in which the religiously orthodox tried to defend traditional beliefs about science and man against the radicals, among whom Greg swiftly became a leader. To his fellow-members Greg read a heretical paper demonstrating that 'the lower animals possess every faculty & propensity of the human mind'. Like so many of his dissenting contemporaries, he was in a constant intellectual ferment, reading and arguing voraciously about government, natural history and society, while developing a fascination with such contemporary Victorian preoccupations as animal magnetism and mesmerism. At Edinburgh he was a fervent proselytist for phrenology, a 'science' which claimed that the shape of the head was determined by the size of the organs in the brain which individually housed such faculties of thought as love and morality.

After two years in which he played a major part in introducing the young Darwin to intellectual dissidence, Greg was summoned home to manage a family mill. His intellectual explorations continued, now extended to literature and philosophy, and through reading and travel he became – for an Englishman of his time – uncommonly well-informed about Continental history, literature and politics.

As a mill-manager, he was soon heavily involved in philanthropic activities in and around Manchester and he identified as the hope of the future the growing middle class leading the anti-Corn Law movement. 'It is among these classes that the onward movements of society have generally had their origin', he said in a speech in 1841. 'It is among them that new discoveries in political and moral science have invariably found the readiest acceptance; and the cause of Peace, Civilisation, and sound National Morality has been more indebted to their humble but enterprising labours, than to the measures of the most sagacious statesman, or the teachings of the wisest moralist.'[6]

In 1835 he married Lucy Henry, daughter of a Manchester physician: six years later her deteriorating health forced a move to the Lake District. By then Greg had had some bruising experiences in public life at election time, concluding with his own defeat as a parliamentary candidate in a particularly disreputable borough. This experience hardened his anti-democratic instincts. Convinced that all classes would fare better under an enlightened and educated oligarchy, he felt the movement for extension of the franchise to be in the interests of none. His viewpoint was disinterested: as Richard Garnett observed, there was in Greg 'an absence of class feeling, even when he may seem to be advocating the cause of a class'.[7] In an essay in the *Westminster Review* in 1845 on 'THE RELATION BETWEEN EMPLOYERS AND EMPLOYED' he denounced any return to the servile relationship between rulers and ruled. New notions about justice had to obtain, but the arrangement was two-sided: both labour and employers had obligations as well as rights. In an exhaustive analysis that drew deep on his managerial experience, he demonstrated that belief in the potentiality of each man whose corollary was an apparently harsh insistence on individual responsibility.[8]

In 1852, Greg was to write an article in *The Economist* called 'ELECTION IMMORALITIES'. At the time, his beloved friend and editor was experiencing a particularly squalid campaign in Westbury. As Wilson wrote afterwards to Cornewall Lewis, only duty 'would have induced me to meet and counteract the dirty work of a four months' incessant canvass, with such a combination against me as I had here. The labour and loss of time and the demoralizing demeaning truths that one had to encounter are too high a price to try even for success . . . I fear there has been an amount of electoral demoralization during the last four months that will cling to the country for many years.'[9] And to Lord John Russell he announced that henceforward one of 'the chief objects' of his life would be to help either extinguish or vastly extend small boroughs, which produced 'the most corrupting and demoralizing practices, which prove equally a curse to the place itself and a disgrace to a representative system': even the old pocket boroughs had been preferable.[10]

On that occasion, Greg was inspired not only by Wilson's concern but by his own memories of electoral excesses. It is a classic example of Greg's *Economist* contributions, bringing to bear on contemporary issues his fastidiousness of intellect and sensibility, his pessimism, his deep spirituality, his eloquence and, in this case, his passionate horror of barbarism.

> Next week will witness one of those anomalous and sadly grotesque spectacles which, perhaps, no country except England can furnish. A great nation, boasting itself – and not without reason – the most advanced and

enlightened upon earth, – rich in material wealth – rich in boundless territory – rich in long descended liberties – rich in all memories which should bind it to live worthily, to think nobly, to act decorously, – is about to proceed to the most solemn and momentous function of its national existence.

Out of thousands of capable men, it was about to choose for a period of six or seven years those 'to whose care are to be intrusted its mighty and varied interests; – to whose integrity and wisdom are to be committed the concerns, moral and material, (as far as Government and legislation can affect them,) of many millions of citizens, and many scores of millions of dependent tribes; – on whose honour and judgment are to depend the character, the comfort, the existence even, of themselves and their children; the progress of many great questions which they have much at heart;– the possibilities of a great future, the continuance of an honourable past'.

It was a task to be 'approached with the utmost gravity . . . discharged with the greatest decorum . . . fulfilled under an overwhelming sense of the wide responsibility attaching to it'. What was required was 'the most careful deliberation, and the most conscientious caution: no selfish motive, no petty passion, no private predilection, should be allowed to interfere where considerations so immense and various are at stake'. Every man should in theory bring to his task 'his most enlightened judgment, his purest honesty, his highest powers'. In practice, however, 'what is it that we shall see?' asked Greg, launching happily into the abyss which should 'make Englishmen blush for themselves and for their country'.

> We shall see a sort of saturnalia – a licensed holiday for all the mean and bad passions of humanity; – we shall see thousands drunk with insane phrenzy – hundreds of thousands drunk with ignominious beer; – we shall see orators busily engaged in rousing envy, hatred, and malignity by every act within their reach – in awakening every furious feeling that ought to slumber for ever, and in deadening and torpifying every controlling principle that should never for an hour be lulled to sleep; – we shall see calumny and falsehood indulging themselves to a degree which in ordinary times they would not venture to approach;– we shall see independent electors selling themselves, some for gold, some for flattery, some for ambition or revenge; – we shall see respectable and noble senators, fawning, cringing, truckling, and lying, in order to obtain a distinction which is only honourable when honourably

gained; – we shall see men who would not steal from a shop, yet complacently pocketing a bribe, and men who, at other times, would counsel no doubtful or disreputable deed, yet now asking a voter to sell his conscience and his country. In a word, we shall witness scenes of low, mean, dirty, shameless iniquity, which will fill us with a double wonder – wonder that so many men fitted to be legislators – high-minded, patriotic, honourable men, who desire a seat in Parliament from no sordid or unworthy motives – should be content to wade to such an eminence through such a sea of clinging and soiling mire.

He called on those to blame for this 'season of riot and licence' – the party managers – to pause, reflect and abandon electoral immorality.

Those men sin against public duty, who, knowing the amount of evil and profligacy almost inseparable, in these days and among our people, from contested elections, get up a contest gratuitously, uselessly, hopelessly, and from sinister and personal views.

Those sin more deeply, and do mischief more widely, than is commonly supposed, who enlist religious animosities into their cause, and, for a casual triumph, give birth to a whole progeny of angry and malignant passions.

Those sin also, who, when their opponents are willing and anxious to forego such exciting and disturbing follies as banners, processions, keeping open public houses, and the like, refuse to acquiesce in such abstinence, lest some of their more worthless followers should be alienated thereby. On them lies a most heavy responsibility.

Lastly, those sin against every principle of integrity and justice, who are content to join with those politicians from whom they differ in everything, in order to defeat those from whom they differ only in a few things. Tories and Chartists who combine forces and stratagems to oust moderate Liberals can scarcely find absolution before any tribunal.

For many readers, the next few days would be fraught with 'just self-congratulation, or much bitter self-reproach, according as they neglect or listen to our earnest appeal'.

> They yet have time
> Their souls to lighten of at least a crime.[11]

(Even these infernal experiences did not persuade Wilson that secret voting should be introduced. 'The ballot would no doubt cure many evils,' he wrote to Lewis, 'but I fear it would introduce others of perhaps a graver importance. It would greatly detract from the public interest in Elections and I fear from public interest in politics and good government. It would go far to destroy that ardent public spirit which is no doubt our best security in the long run.'[12] Or, as Bagehot was to put it more pithily in *The Economist* in 1871: 'It will finally sever the exercise of power from the acknowledgement of responsibility.'[13])

Greg's public writing career had begun in 1840 with a pamphlet called 'Past and Present Efforts for the Extinction of the African Slave Trade'. Two years later he won an Anti-Corn Law League prize for an essay on 'Agriculture and the Corn Law': Lord Radnor paid for its printing and distribution. Reading, reflection and writing began to dominate his life, until, in 1850, his business collapsed. Like his friend James Wilson a decade earlier, he found himself virtually penniless, yet through industrious use of his literary talents he was able quickly to forge a new career, keep his home and support his wife and four children adequately. In 1852 alone he published twelve substantial articles (eleven on economic or political subjects) in the four leading quarterly magazines as well as innumerable leaders in *The Economist*.

The Creed of Christendom, published in 1851, had made his reputation. An uncompromisingly sceptical analysis of the gospels, which drew heavily on German theology, it demonstrated what an obituarist was to call his almost 'rhetorical pleasure in plunging cold steel into the heart of what he regarded as a mischievous fallacy'.[14] Yet while the book was to make him enemies among the orthodox, more perceptive critics appreciated Greg's deep underlying spirituality. *The Economist*'s reviewer, distressed, lauded his erudition and commitment to truth while wringing his hands over Greg's preoccupation with verbal creeds rather than with the truth of Christianity as revealed through the lives of its practitioners.

So if Wilson and Greg had many attitudes and beliefs in common, they differed on religion, where Wilson was content with his unquestioning faith. Yet their friendship was untroubled. (Indeed Wilson sought the company of curious, philosophical and often eccentric minds. He even consorted with thespians – Charles Kean, the actor-manager son of Edmund, was a frequent dinner guest.) Within a few years of their meeting, Greg had become the intimate not just of Wilson, but of his whole family. Greg's wife was both physically and mentally ill and was away from home in medical care most of the time. An affectionate and gregarious man whom solitude made gloomy and depressed, Greg regularly escaped his lonely rural life to take refuge with the lively and sociable Wilsons: from 1850 onwards they provided him with his second home. A man of great charm and amiability, a restful companion who enjoyed life's pleasures, he was particularly happy in the company of women, and was to have a close and influential relationship with all six girls – the future proprietors of *The Economist*. In 1874, the year after his first wife died, he would marry Julia, who had been in love with him for twenty-four years. It was accidental but symbolic that the diary which Eliza Wilson began to keep in 1851 begins with the sentence: 'Herr Greg (von Windemere) der seit dem vorigen Samstag bei uns gewesen war, verliess Westbury.'* (Having come home from finishing-school in Cologne, she was practising her German.)

Greg, called 'Signor' by the Wilson girls, cut a rather exotic and romantic figure. Perhaps because of his wife's insanity and Julia's devotion, he was supposed by contemporaries to have been the inspiration for Mr Rochester in Charlotte Brontë's *Jane Eyre*.[15] The distinguished writer Harriet Martineau, who had been one of his closest friends and who shared his interest in mesmerism, was to accuse Greg of being 'insolent, unbalanced, and a vulgar philanderer', but she quarrelled with all her friends and they had had a political disagreement.[16] Marian Evans, who knew him through his work for her *Westminster Review*, described him in 1852 as 'a short man, with a hooked nose and an imperfect enunciation from defective teeth, but his brain is large, the anterior lobe very fine and a moral region to correspond. Black, wiry, curly hair, and every indication of a first-rate temperament. But when you see him across the room, you are unpleasantly impressed, and can't believe that he wrote his own books.'[17] 'He is very pleasing', she wrote later that year, 'but somehow or other he frightens me dreadfully.'[18]

(Greg and Evans were in any case not cut out to be soulmates. Greg's phrenological studies had led him to the then common view that women's more delicate cerebral organisation betokened 'subtlety and sensitiveness, not strength and tenacity ... the continuity and severity of application needed to acquire real *mastery* in any profession, or over any science, are denied to most women, and can never with impunity be attempted by them;

*Mr Greg (of Windermere), who had been with us since last Saturday, left Westbury.

mind and health would almost invariably break down under the task. And wherever any exceptional women are to be found who seem to be abnormally endowed in this repect, and whose power and mental muscle are almost masculine, it may almost invariably . . . be observed that they have purchased this questionable pre-eminence by a forfeiture of some of the distinctive and most invaluable charms and capabilities of their sex.'[19])

Marian Evans's instinctive antipathy to Greg was not a typical reaction. His popularity supports John Morley's description of him as a personality who produced 'an atmosphere elastic, stimulating, elevating, and yet compos-ing'. Morley thought him unselfish, humble, a 'gay and appreciative compan-ion, and the most amiable of friends . . . His conversation was particularly neat and pointed. He had a lucidity of phrase such as is more common in French society than among ourselves. The vice of small talk and the sin of prosing he was equally free from; and if he did not happen to be interested, he had a great gift of silence.' More than this, like his friend James Wilson, Greg – in Morley's view – 'never fell into the habitual disputant's vice of trying to elude the force of a fair argument; he did not mix up his own personality in the defence of his thesis; differences in argument and opinion produced not only no rancour, but even no soreness'.

For James Wilson, Greg was a godsend – a lieutenant whose instincts and beliefs matched his own in most essentials, who understood his preoccu-pations, grasped his ideas and put them into prose far superior to Wilson's own. Moreover, he wrote 'with that delight which every good workman feels who is conscious of wielding his tools with dexterity. Composition was not to him the toil it is to so many. The expression, apt and lucid, came with the thought. No one who saw the alacrity with which he went to his desk in the morning, full of his subject, and with his first sentence on the tip of his pen, ready to spring on to the blank sheet, could doubt that there was a daily enjoyment for him which is not given to all.'[20] 'Yet', said Morley, 'his fluency never ran off into the fatal channels of verbosity. Ease, clearness, precision, and a certain smooth and sure-paced consecutiveness, made his written style for all purposes of statement and exposition one of the most telling and effective of his day.' A leader assessing in just over one page the parliament of 1847–52, both domestically and internationally, was a small masterpiece of relaxed compression. Ireland received one paragraph:

> Ireland – over-peopled, a prey to famine, with a bankrupt and non-resident
> proprietary, and a priesthood leading the people for their own advantage –

was at that period in a more anomalous condition than ever. That it was dealt with in all respects in the very best manner, cannot be said; but its new condition called for new measures. They were applied, and the extension of the Poor Law and the Encumbered Estates Act, with various advances made by Government, seem to have laid the foundations for substantial improvement. If her proprietary have been in great part displaced – if her impulsive population have been diminished, it is for the advantage of those who remain:– if many have been annihilated, many have found new, and we hope happier, homes in the western world.[21]

As a summary it is pithy, readable, provocative, even if open to the charge of being 'all brains and no heart'.

From his early days as a contributor, Greg was particularly valuable as a commentator on foreign affairs,* for while James Wilson was well connected abroad and a frequent visitor to the Continent, his outlook was essentially that of a man of business, rather than of an observer steeped in European history and culture. Greg's contemplative mind and striking prose added great distinction to the paper's coverage of the upheavals in Europe from 1848 onwards. An example is a savage but fascinating four-page article written in April 1848 and called 'THE FERMENTATION OF EUROPE. WHY WE HAVE NO HOPES FOR FRANCE. WHY WE HAVE MUCH HOPE FOR ITALY AND GERMANY. WHY WE HAVE NO FEARS FOR ENGLAND'.

> The spring of 1848 will be memorable through all time, both for the magnitude of the political events which it has witnessed, and for the unexampled rapidity with which they have succeeded each other. Demands – concessions – constitutions – revolutions – abdications – have trod upon the heels of one another, with a speed which takes away the breath of the beholder.

---

*There is a widespread belief, expressed for instance in two essays in the *Economist* centenary history, in Buchan's *Walter Bagehot* and in *The Collected Works of Walter Bagehot*, that Nassau Senior was responsible for much of the paper's foreign policy coverage under Wilson and Bagehot. Having found no evidence to support this, I consulted two outstanding economic historians of the period. Professor D.P. O'Brien considered that Senior's penchant for recycling material made it almost impossible that *Economist* articles would not have turned up in his collected writings, and the leading authority on Senior, Professor Marian Bowley, had never even heard of the supposed connection. The idea seems to have originated from a clever but mistaken hunch of Graham Hutton, foreign editor during much of the 1930s and author in 1943 of 'Foreign Affairs' in the centenary history.

However, though the world picture looked quite hopeful, the future of France – 'that unlearning and impure country' – looked very gloomy, for she alone 'seems to have learnt nothing, and forgotten nothing; to have forgotten no old watchwords, and learned no new wisdom'. The French people, 'who seem to be as impatient of oppression as they are unfit for freedom', made the fundamental error of confusing liberty with equality.

In the ensuing jeremiad (a genre in which Greg was to specialise: in later life he became famous for a series of despairing essays written under the pseudónymn of 'Cassandra') recent events in the newly-declared republic were analysed. 'In one short month they have run round the whole cycle of tyranny, spent all the resources of despotism, repeated and exhausted all the obsolete contrivances and low stratagems of arbitrary power. They have seized on property, interfered with contracts, threatened the rich, swamped the respectable, broken faith with the national creditor, influenced elections by terror and chicanery, and displayed, in a word, not only all the ignorance, but all the vices, of a fierce and overbearing democracy. *Therefore, we have no hopes for France.*' Of the many causes for despair, the chief was the total lack of moral courage in the French character.

There was hope for the Italians and Germans 'because in both countries the people seek to extort concessions from their rulers, not to supersede them; because they seek to govern in concert with their sovereigns, not instead of them; because, intellectually and morally, despite long ages of degradation, they are a far finer race of men than the French; because, cruelly as they have been oppressed, *they struggle for real reforms*, they demand liberty, not equality'. The Germans indeed were 'a reflective, a peaceful, and a moral race . . . with just notions of real personal liberty'. In England the position was even better, for as well as having healthy traditions concerning government, liberty, order and property, every Englishman knew that here all classes were labouring to improve social conditions.

The wise course for England and Europe was therefore to 'regard France as suffering in the paroxysm of a strange disease and draw a cordon sanitaire around her, till the violence of the malady shall have spent itself, and the danger of contagion shall be past'.[22]

In the more robust world of the mid-nineteenth century, discussion of national characteristics was a respectable pursuit: certainly the depth of Greg's knowledge of Europe, the clarity of his intellect and his biting style added to *The Economist*'s reputation. Prejudice and pessimism notwithstanding, he was an exhilarating writer who did much to strengthen the paper's appeal. Take, for instance, an issue in September 1850, when preceding a leader on the trade and navigation returns and one on the Navigation Laws was Greg's two-page obituary of Louis Philippe. In his assessment of his subject's character and career, Greg looked at the circumstances that had caused this 'crooked and ignoble', but courageous and determined king to abdicate in 1848.

> His nerves were enfeebled by age, and the crisis was fearful, sudden, and supreme. He found himself face to face with an aroused and exasperated people, furious with repeated disappointments, maddened by imagined treachery, sick of deferred hopes. He heard around him, growing every moment louder and more near, the tumultuous roar of an angry populace, whom the recklessness of wild theory, the rage of baffled ambition, the low greediness of gain, the fury of long-smothered resentments, combined to lash into a storm. He could not be unconscious what a fearful retribution his seventeen years of corruption and encroachment had deserved. He could place confidence in no one, for he felt that he had earned the confidence of none; and he was by nature suspicious and mistrusting.

Yet, though Greg's overall judgment of Louis Philippe was severe to the point of harshness, compassion triumphed. 'But peace be to his ashes!' he concluded, '– he met his death with quiet firmness and dignified composure; and had Providence assigned him his lot in humble life, he would unquestionably have been noted as a prosperous, respectable, and able man.'[23]

When on 2 December 1851 the President of the Republic, Louis Napoleon, prevented by the Constitution from seeking re-election, sorted out the political confusion of France by means of a *coup d'état*, Greg's *Economist* leader backed him:

> Louis Napoleon has dissolved the Assembly, relied upon the army, and appealed to the people. He has proclaimed that the Legislative body has ceased to exist; he has closed the Chamber, and arrested a number of the leading deputies; he has issued the programme of a new Constitution; and has convoked the electoral body for an early day . . . For a long period events have been tending to some such issue; and while it is impossible to deny that Louis Napoleon has violated the law, is playing a hazardous game, and has incurred a deep responsibility, it is equally undeniable that there was much

to provoke, and much to excuse, if not to justify, the step which he has taken. He has borne much; he has waited long; and he has now acted with a degree of skill, promptitude, and vigour, which will secure to him much admiration and no little sympathy.[24]

Lord Palmerston, the Foreign Secretary, agreed, and promptly lost his job for welcoming the *coup d'état* without the approval of Queen or Cabinet. In general, British public opinion and the British press, horrified at this anti-democratic development, denounced the usurper out of hand. Since Wilson was part of the government, *The Economist* stayed out of the controversy about Palmerston, who deserved to go, said *The Times*, as a punishment for sponsoring 'a man who had extinguished freedom among the most advanced nations of the continent'. Louis Napoleon himself was furious with *The Times*, whose editor, John T. Delane, explained to the new Foreign Secretary, Lord Granville, that having always tried to teach its readers 'that the extension of English institutions abroad was desirable for English interests and that the thing most to be feared was military despotism we cannot with French facility "Accept the situation" and remain silent when we see all that we have been advocating ever since the Peace overthrown'.[25]

It was a neat encapsulation of a viewpoint to which Greg was diametrically opposed – the notion that English institutions would necessarily flourish in foreign soil. Even Wilson – who in his early days as a journalist had believed that the principles of English political economy were universally valid – had through political experience become much more realistic. Where *The Times* saw press freedom as the *sine qua non* of a civilised society, *The Economist* instinctively made stability its priority. 'The unwillingness which we showed to join in the fierce and unsparing condemnation of the character and proceedings of Louis Napoleon, so universal in the English Press,' Greg wrote at the end of December, 'and our disposition to give him credit for a desire to use his power well, should secure us a patient and considerate hearing, when we warn him of the perils which it is most urgent upon him to avoid, and of the mistakes into which he is most liable to fall.'[26]

(What makes this example of *The Economist* taking an unpopular view even more interesting is that on the same side was the twenty-five-year-old Walter Bagehot. In seven brilliant, excited and often skittish letters from Paris in the obscure Unitarian *Inquirer*, to the dismay of its staid readership and with its editor markedly dissociating himself from Bagehot's opinions, he backed

Louis Napoleon enthusiastically.[27] In one letter he wrote that 'Burke first taught the world at large . . . that institutions are shifting things, to be tried by and adjusted to the shifting conditions of a mutable world – that, in fact, politics are but a piece of business – to be determined in every case by the exact exigencies of that case: in plain English – by sense and circumstances.'[28]

'The first duty of society is the preservation of society', contended Bagehot,[29] and showing very early that preoccupation with national character that was to be so influential in determining his attitude to foreign affairs and to lead him to write *Physics and Politics* (his seminal contribution to the development of Social Darwinism), he went on to explain that the French, being clever and interested in ideas, were unfit for parliamentary government. 'I fear you will laugh when I tell you what I conceive to be about the most essential mental quality for a free people, whose liberty is to be progressive, permanent, and on a large scale; it is much *stupidity* . . . I need not say that, in real sound stupidity, the English are unrivalled. You'll hear more wit, and better wit, in an Irish street row than would keep Westminster Hall in humour for five weeks.'[30] Bagehot, of course, believed the Irish to be congenitally incapable of self-government.

Stupidity, in fact, was 'nature's favourite resource for preserving steadiness of conduct and consistency of opinion. It enforces concentration; people who learn slowly, learn only what they must. The best security for people's doing their duty is that they should not know anything else to do; the best security for fixedness of opinion is that people should be incapable of comprehending what is to be said on the other side.'[31]

What was necessary to keep France from riots and revolutions was 'only such a degree of liberty and democracy . . . as is consistent with the consolidated existence of the order and tranquillity which are equally essential to rational freedom and civilised society'.[32] 'I wish for the President decidedly myself as against M. Thiers [historian and moderate republican deputy] and his set in the Parliamentary World'; he wrote to his mother a couple of days after the *coup d'état*, 'even *I* can't believe in a Government of barristers [he was then unhappily studying law] and newspaper editors, and also as against the Red party who, though not insincere, are too abstruse and theoretical for a plain man. It is easy to say what they would abolish, but horribly hard to say what they would *leave*, and what they would *find*. I am in short what they would call a *réactionnaire*, and I think I am with the majority – a healthy habit for a young man to contract.'[33])

Most of the time Greg possessed in considerable measure that detachment to which *The Economist* aspires. 'No writer of the day', wrote Richard Holt Hutton of him after his death, 'forced Englishmen to look so closely at those French facts which were most disagreeable to them, as Mr Greg.' That many of these facts were equally unpalatable to him is often clear in what he wrote. For instance, in December 1852, after the republic had become the Second Empire and Louis Napoleon had been transmogrified into Napoleon III, Greg considered why those French politicians most popular in England were uniformly hostile to the Emperor. They included among their number men like Guizot and de Tocqueville whom Greg knew and had long admired as writers and politicians, and from whom he 'had been accustomed to take our notions of French interests and French opinions'.

> They formed a galaxy of political and literary talent which shone in the eyes of foreign nations with a lustre which obscured and put out all lesser but more national lights. For the truth we believe to be, that these eminent men with all their brilliancy never had any strong hold on the nation; they were beyond it, above it, apart from it, rather than its leaders or representatives; their ideas and objects of admiration were English rather than French; their talents as writers and speakers gave them vast influence as long as Parliamentary Government prevailed; but they have never inoculated the people with their views; their party was select, but their followers were few.

For a mixture of reasons, including their merits, their faults, their '*Parliamentariness* and therefore the *unfrenchness* of their notions', the 'intriguing character' of several of them, 'the notorious and awful corruption of the Government which they administered in turn; and partly from the deplorable, disreputable, and clumsy catastrophe in which they finished their career, – they are now with five-sixths of Frenchmen the most utterly damaged, discredited, and unpopular party in the country'.[34]

Such home truths did not diminish Greg's popularity in France. He visited Paris regularly, and became an intimate of Madame Mohl (the Englishwoman Mary Clarke), who loathed Napoleon III and whose celebrated salon in Saint-Germain (which Bagehot attended) attracted English, French and Russian politicians, socialites and writers.

At home, regardless of the opinions expressed, the depth and fluency of such articles did much to consolidate and enhance the paper's deservedly high reputation as a source of information on foreign news as well as trade.

From modest beginnings, Wilson had built up a widespread acquaintanceship among Continental merchants and bankers which was a perfect complement to Greg's more literary network. Additionally, from December 1852 when Wilson became Financial Secretary to the Treasury, he had superb sources of information and gossip through his political and social life. As their intimacy grew – and from the early 1850s Greg was far and away Wilson's closest friend – they shared their circles. Greg came to know politicians and Wilson's family met the literati. In 1856, through Greg, the Wilson family met and became exceptionally close to Madame Mohl, through whom they met the smartest Parisian society.

The two friends did not always agree. They differed strongly, for instance, over Austria. Greg, who believed Hungarians to be highly gifted and capable of self-government, supported their desire for independence from the Austrian empire. He had many friends among Hungarian refugees, including the exiled Hungarian nationalist leader Lajos Kossuth, whom he greatly admired,[35] and was seen in some quarters as being involved in 'refugee politics'.[36] Ultimately he came to believe Austria capable of the basest treachery in international affairs. Although Greg's passionate partisanship proved contagious within the Wilson household, where the eldest girls became fervently anti-Austrian, Wilson himself – although hospitable and sympathetic to the Hungarians – refused to become blindly partisan. At one particularly sensitive time – the outbreak of the Crimean War – Greg sent from Paris an article which Wilson referred to the Foreign Secretary for informal vetting. Lord Clarendon denied its anti-Austrian allegations and Wilson proceeded to base on them an article which he subtitled 'GROUND-LESS STORIES AND RUSSIAN INTRIGUE'.[37]

Such differences of opinion were rare and were amicably settled. Wilson was a man who appreciated the virtues of his employees while having a high tolerance for their failings, while Greg perfectly understood that *The Economist* could not ignore the exigencies of its owner's political career. Together they ensured that the paper stayed as independent as was feasible in the circumstances. The handling of the Crimean War was an interesting indication of the latitude allowed as Wilson became more confident of his political standing.

CHAPTER XIV

Moving on

Jimmy Wilson was a worker in connection with the League. He wrote dull pamphlets and made duller speeches, but still he showed some Scotch pertinacity in keeping alive the agitation in the metropolis. When we dissolved our organization and gave up the 'League' weekly organ, a lithographed circular was sent to all its subscribers recommending them to support the *Economist*, which he had previously started, and Bright and I, George Wilson and others, signed the circular. This was the foundation of Wilson's fortune, which was in a sickly state previously. When Wilson entered the Ministry, Mr William Greg became a leading contributor and a sort of *locum tenens* for the proprietor, with whom he was on intimate terms. After a while Wilson, as Secretary of the Treasury, became a dispenser of Government patronage, and he presented Greg last year with the appointment of a Commissioner of Customs, a post involving so little occupation that it will not interfere with his literary labours, but for which he pockets £1,200 a year. Thus the two principal contributors to the *Economist* having secured, the one £2,000 a year and the other £1,200 from the public purse, what so natural as that the paper should be the obsequious servant of the Government, or that the *Economist*'s pages should be employed in assailing the two men who laid the foundations of all this success, if they happen no longer to be in favour with the dispensers of patronage? . . . There is far more corruption going on in connection with the public press than in any other walk of political life.[1] *Richard Cobden, 1857*

Early in 1853, vigorous Russian sabre-rattling at the ailing Turkish empire gave rise to fears that Constantinople itself (today's Istanbul) would come under Russian domination. In July, the Tsar's troops occupied the Danubian principalities, Moldavia and Wallachia (now parts of Romania). By October, Turkey and Russia were openly at war. The British Cabinet was split: the Prime Minister, Lord Aberdeen, was pacific, while the Home Secretary, Lord Palmerston, was bellicose. Worse was Aberdeen's irresolution, which made the job of the Foreign Secretary, Wilson's friend Lord Clarendon, doubly difficult. *The Economist* took a consistent and pragmatic line, summed up in September in 'THE CLOUD IN THE EAST', in a passage so explicit as to be fairly usable as a touchstone against which to test the paper's attitudes to war throughout its history. The article was almost certainly Wilson's: it should be read in the knowledge that Wilson's old allies, John Bright and Richard Cobden, had taken a vehemently anti-war stance.

> No one will accuse us of having ever shown ourselves insensible to the evils of war, or inclined to underestimate its horrors and its criminality. As vigilant guardians of the commercial interests of a great country, our tendency and disposition must naturally be to regard all interruptions of universal amity with even an exaggerated alarm and dislike, and to purchase the continuance of peace at too high a price. But we must not forget that a precarious and ill-contrived peace . . . is almost as fatal and discouraging to commerce as actual hostilities. If negotiations are protracted . . . or if a hollow peace be patched up between the disputants . . . that sense of security so essential to commercial operations will be as effectually destroyed as if a war had actually broken out. No merchants will venture to engage in extensive plans or to count boldly on the future; a chronic uneasiness will hang over their minds; and trade will languish under its paralysing influence.

What was needed was a 'permanent settlement of an ever-recurring difficulty – a final solution, once for all, of a problem that has kept Europe in hot water for half a century. To *avoid* war – considering what war is – is worth every exertion and almost every sacrifice: to *postpone* war, may often be worth no effort or sacrifice at all.'[2]

The contrast of style between this measured policy statement and a typical flight of Greg's eloquence on an allied topic a couple of weeks later makes one grateful that the nineteenth-century *Economist* lacked the homogeneity that now obtains. In 'THE OBJECT OF ENGLISH INTERPOSITION IN THE EAST' he explained, *inter alia*, that if Britain should go to war to defend the Turkish empire, it would not be fighting to uphold an Infidel dominion . . . deeply tainted with the ineradicable vices of indolence, fanaticism, and polygamy . . . We can have no close or native sympathies with a race whose traditions, whose tastes, whose habits, whose pursuits are the very opposite of ours. They are languid and lethargic: we are boiling over with life and energy. They are military: we are commercial. They place the *summa felicitas* in sublime inaction: we in ceaseless and pushing progress. They look with contempt upon our feverish activity and our insatiable greed of gain: we regard with scorn their stagnant and stationary repose, their passive content under remediable evils.[3]

Greg's leaders tended towards the unequivocal: Wilson's illustrate the old battle between heart and head, for although he had steeled himself to war, the Quaker and humanitarian hated the thought. It was an unusual combination: journalists tended to be violently on one side or the other. 'Bloodshed is such a dreadful thing', Wilson wrote in November, 'and war such a critical and doubtful game, that it is impossible not to wish well to the efforts of statesmen to put an end to both.'

No pains should be spared and no opportunity neglected to restore peace and to reconcile the combatants. But in pursuing these righteous and desirable objects, it is of the utmost importance that we should not lose sight either of the requirements of justice or of future dangers. We must not, in our anxiety to quench the flames of war, sacrifice the interests of the injured party, nor must we purchase a present respite from embarrassment and evil by a compromise which can only issue in a return of those calamities at no distant date and probably in an aggravated form, and at a more perilous conjuncture.[4]

In December Palmerston resigned and public opinion, which had turned violently anti-Russian after the sinking of the Turkish fleet, could not be persuaded of the truth – that he had gone over a domestic issue. With Aberdeen undergoing public abuse for cowardice, Greg came very close to attacking him directly, if disingenuously.

We cannot . . . pretend to say what motives may have caused the long endurance, the exhaustless patience, the irrepressible hopes which our Government has shown throughout the dreary history of the last nine months . . . but it must now be pretty obvious to every one that our course has been a mistaken and a mischievous one: and that by temporising with justice and seeking to compromise with crime . . . we have brought both upon ourselves and our allies worse evils, greater expenditure of life and treasure, a more serious and longer struggle, and a more distant and doubtful issue, than if we had from the very outset of the dispute made up our minds to operate with greater vigour and to calculate with less caution.

Yet though *The Economist* said firmly that it was now necessary that condign retribution should be exacted from Russia through war, it lamented that it would not be the real criminal – Tsar Nicholas – who would be punished directly, but the Russian soldiers, who 'on the whole, are as much the victims of the Czar's ambition and injustice as the Turks themselves. They and we are fellow-sufferers by his crime. *Yet it is on these fellow-victims and fellow-sufferers that our vengeance must be wreaked* . . . It is only *through* them that we can reach him.'[5]

In subsequent weeks the paper got down to specifics. The government's duties were spelled out. First, 'to prosecute the war with the most determined vigour, to strike promptly, to strike hard, to strike unceasingly'. Second, 'to make no bad appointments . . . We must not have the lives of our brave fellows squandered, and their efforts paralysed and thrown away by placing over them men, however respectable, venerable, or well-born, whose energies have been impaired, or whose daring has been tamed, or whose character has been rendered obstinate by age . . . To appoint men of known or reasonably-suspected incapacity, on account of their great connections or from political or Parliamentary considerations, would be nothing short of wilful murder.'[6]

Amidst these (tragically unheeded) exhortations were the economic analyses. Britain's previous war, against France, had lasted twenty-three years and had raised the national debt by £585 million. In a fascinating article, 'WAR ON ECONOMIC PRINCIPLES', Wilson compared the figures and conditions for then and now in great detail.[7] And from the Chancellor's right-hand man also came 'THE WAR BUDGET AND ITS PRINCIPLES' – an explanation of how Gladstone was seeking to put into operation in wartime the sound economic doctrines that nowadays pertained in times of peace: 'The two great principles, then, on which Mr Gladstone has based his War Budget as contra-distinguished from former times are, – 1, that the income of the year shall be made to bear the expenditure of the year; and 2, that the commercial and financial policy adopted of late years shall be strictly adhered to.'[8]

Britain and France declared war on Russia in March 1854: it was to take two years of immense hardship for the troops before a victory of sorts and a respectable-looking peace treaty were secured. After forty years of peace and with the military and political command structure still dominated by the aristocracy, Britain had severe handicaps in fighting a large-scale campaign at a distance (even then France provided more than half of the soldiers, and the most effective naval units). *The Economist*'s demands for capable leadership were ignored. Lord Aberdeen remained as Prime Minister; the Duke of Newcastle was Secretary for War; Lord Raglan, the son of a duke, was given command of the unfortunate troops sent out to the Crimea. Not one of them was fit for his job.

While *The Times*, in its finest hour, published harrowing reports from its correspondents illuminating suffering, inefficiency and waste and excoriated the culprits, Greg and Wilson had to bite their lips, publish Raglan's despatches, counsel patience and warn against armchair strategists. Their anger they vented on those they felt to be undermining the war effort by ill-judged public calls for peace. 'We of course', ran one typical attack, 'do Mr Cobden and Mr Bright the justice of believing that they are sincere and honest in their opposition to the war: of their earnestness there can be no doubt.' But this only exacerbated their potential for harm.

> Here are two members of the British House of Commons, whose eminence no one can deny, whose influence with their countrymen used to be great, and deserved to be so, and whose influence Nicholas naturally believes to be great still ... who urge upon the Government, in the most energetic manner, to make peace with the aggressor on his own terms – nay, to end the war on any terms; who, in pathetic language and amid the cheers of the opposite benches, deplore the valuable lives that have been sacrificed, and do not scruple to lay all these at the door not of the man who began the war by his invasion, but of those who were rash enough and Quixotic enough to resist the will of such a mighty monarch.[9]

Cobden took these attacks personally, and bitterly attributed to Wilson and Greg the most dishonourable of motives. He was unfair, for there is no doubt about their absolute personal commitment to the war. Where they trimmed was in holding back their criticism of the government. 'Papa and Mr Greg much excited at the mismanagement of the Army', noted Eliza Wilson in her diary on 21 January 1855. 'Papa called this war "the death-blow of the

Aristocracy".' By then, knowing Lord John Russell to be in the process of bringing down Lord Aberdeen, Wilson felt able to take the plunge: *The Economist* came gravely out of the closet, dressed up in William Rathbone Greg's best cloak. A mass of incriminating testimony about the condition of the army and the management of the campaign 'is now before us' and had to be believed: 'after every allowance has been made by the charity that "hopeth all things" and the wisdom that doubts most things, enough will still remain to fill us with amazement and dismay, and to wring from us the reluctant conviction that our Crimean campaign presents a scene of inconceivable mismanagement and resulting disaster'.

A 'searching investigation and an unsparing reform' were demanded. Those guilty must be found. 'Neglect must be traced home to the negligent; incapacity to the incapable; fraud to the fraudulent; and to every offender must be meted out his due deserts.' All evils in the system must be routed out. It would, however, be difficult to blame ministers, for the country 'never was served by abler or more zealous or more honest men . . . Ministers may have made many mistakes in their foreign policy; they may have clung to peace too long; they may have had much inexperience to get over; but no one can doubt that, from the first moment that war became inevitable, they have laboured with the most assiduous energy to carry it on with all the vigour possible.'[10]

It was not morally a glorious period for *The Economist*, nor could it be while it was so closely tied to a prominent politician, however high-minded. *A fortiori*, ownership as well as editorship of an organ of the press by a statesman was unlikely to be conducive to independence.

Yet, if they committed sins of omission, and suppression, Greg and Wilson told no lies. Their partnership lasted until 1857, during which time, despite his heavy responsibilities at the Treasury, Wilson continued to contribute solid factual pieces, while Greg, from his home in the Lake District or staying with the Wilsons in London, superintended *The Economist* and distilled into elegant essays the conversations he held with his editor on issues and men of the day. The brilliant character analyses of contemporary politicians that were to be such a distinguished feature of the paper under Bagehot were foreshadowed during Greg's time. Two appropriate examples are taken from lengthy pieces Greg wrote in 1852 – before Wilson went to the Treasury – about the men who were to become the two British political giants of the second half of the twentieth century – Disraeli and Gladstone.

Neither political bias nor anti-semitism were elements in the hostile treatment Disraeli was always to receive from *The Economist*. It was simply that his personality was antipathetic to the leading *Economist* figures of his day: Wilson, Greg, Richard Holt Hutton and Bagehot. His outstanding political skills – cleverness, adroitness, subtlety, cunning, flexibility and even wit – could all too easily be seen simply as lack of principle, scruple or seriousness. And his habit of stealing his opponents' policies used to drive them wild.

When Lord John Russell's government had fallen in February 1852, it had been replaced by a Conservative government under Lord Derby, with Disraeli as Chancellor of the Exchequer. Despite his rise to fame within his party as the scourge of Sir Robert Peel over his repeal of the Corn Laws, expediency now persuaded Disraeli to embrace free trade. His anti-protectionist budget provoked a leader in *The Economist* called 'THE STAN-DARD OF PUBLIC VIRTUE. MR DISRAELI'S CONVERSION'.

It was a *cri de coeur* for honour in public life. While consistency had been over-valued in the past, it was 'lax morality' to welcome a change of opinion without considering what had caused it. Inconsistency was in itself neither good nor bad.

> There have been, within recent recollection, some changes so rational, so gradual, so grounded on new knowledge, wider experience, and deeper study, so justified by the purest motives, so obviously honest because attended with much mortification and punished by severe penalties, that we class them among the most indisputable efforts of patriotic virtue. Such was that of Sir Robert Peel from 1842 to 1846. And there have been some changes, also in the right direction, so sudden, so audacious, so utterly unbased upon any additional facts, so inexcusable on the common pleas of previous want of study, so apparently traceable only to the one circumstance of altered position, that it is impossible for the widest charity to elevate them into merits, or to give absolution to the subject of them.

Such was Disraeli's conversion – 'a triumph to our cause which . . . "every one will be glad of, but no one can be proud of"'.

Politicians who gradually become converted from opinions in which they were reared, or who through experience of office learn the errors of their attitudes in opposition, could be forgiven their apostasy. But none of this applied to Disraeli's 'tergiversation' and 'strange recantation'. He had adopted the policy which he had been vehemently denouncing for six years as 'mistaken in principle and ruinous in its result'. And while having no desire to make 'retraction of error difficult' or to hunt Disraeli back 'to his former follies . . . we can give Mr Disraeli no absolution for his obstinate and wilful persistence in untenable opinions; and we can only acquit him of the most frightful and prolonged insincerity, by supposing him guilty of a thoughtless levity in the consideration of the great interests of the nation, which must for ever disqualify him for the position of a leading statesman, and preclude him from obtaining the confidence of the English people'.[11]

Yet Gladstone, who had changed his views on almost every political issue from the time he first entered politics, and who at forty-one was still painfully recanting, was given the benefit of the doubt because of his evident sincerity. Ever since he entered public life

> his mind has been expanding, his powers strengthening, his prejudices weakening, his views becoming more definite, practical, and clear; – and if he is still at times too subtle and refining, if the scholastic character of his intellect occasionally comes out too strongly for his own standing and his country's good, and he draws rather with a fine point than a broad one, this is the result of an original mental tendency which he has done much to correct, and which toil and experience are gradually and incessantly modifying. Cautious and scrupulous to a fault; anxious for practical reforms, but averse from sweeping or systematic changes; a friend to progress from aspiration and reflection, yet attached to the past and the ancient by all those chains which are so binding on the cultured and the tender mind,– he would seem to be qualified above most men to be the chosen and cherished representative of all those who love in ancestral things only what is lovely, who venerate in the old only what is venerable, who wish to prolong no proved abuse, who desire to defend only what is really defensible.[12]

The working arrangement between them was ideal for Wilson, less so for Greg. In the recollection of a niece, he 'was then very poor, and the way of living was of the simplest. I still remember his worn check morning suit, in which, however, he never looked otherwise than neat, and almost dainty . . . he was very punctual in his habits, and very industrious – I think he always worked to the full extent of his mental and physical power.'[13] But even with great industry freelance journalism provided a precarious living.

It was perhaps hope of greater financial security as well as the excitement of a new challenge that made Greg respond positively in 1854 to a proposal that he should co-found and edit a new politically and theologically liberal quarterly, the *National Review*. Walter Bagehot, banker and occasional essayist, was one of its backers and was in the forefront of financial and publishing negotiations. As editor, Greg prepared ambitious plans and promised to invest his remaining slender capital in the project: by December 1854 the review had a publisher and was due to be launched in the spring. Then, in the words of one of his collaborators, 'through certain misunder-standings or mismanagements Greg lost his publishers, and fearing to compromise his relations with the Edinburgh [*Review*], had not spirit to begin again with new people, and retired'.[14] For, as Bagehot pointed out, had Greg failed, 'he lost his whole capital and position. The starting a new Review wd. alienate those by wh. he now lives and of course he said very properly he cd. not do this without a certainty of an equivalent.'[15]

The disappointment had its compensations. As Morley observed, Greg's temperament was 'too sanguine for practical affairs', and as the originator of the project, the philosopher and theologian James Martineau, wrote to a friend: 'His lavish notions had rather alarmed us, – and indeed himself; for on quitting the field he advised us to take up a more moderate scheme, – involving less outlay and requiring smaller returns. So now . . . we revert to what in truth was our notion till Greg came in: a 4/: Review, of about 200 pages . . . Editor (with aid) R.H.H. [Hutton] at a salary'.[16] In the event, Bagehot became co-editor.

The foundation of the *National Review* was an important event in the history of *The Economist*. It not only introduced Bagehot and Hutton to Greg, but gave him a personal interest in their journalistic development. It also provided vital editorial experience for them both, and gave Bagehot the impetus he might otherwise have lacked to write regularly and develop his great natural talent. Greg reviewed the first number in *The Economist* enthusiastically, with a slight hint of wistfulness.

> To belong to no class – to recognise no party, this is the new journal's profession, and we are bound to add, as regards this first number, its practice. Doubtless it is the tendency of truth to assume form, and for forms to become the nucleus of parties: we may live to see new forms and new parties, founded not indeed upon new, but upon revived and liberated truth.
>
> Meanwhile, however, the business is to clear away truth from the wreck of old forms and tottering parties; to clear it away with a reverential, a humble, but a firm hand, not for the sake of creating confusion, but in the hope out of

confusion to restore order. As an agent in this work we gladly welcome the *National Review*.[17]

He was equally generous about Bagehot's anonymous essay, 'The First Edinburgh Reviewers' in the second number. 'It is really a masterpiece of lively, sagacious, and entertaining writing. There is a *verve* and vivacity in the style rarely seen now-a-days; it has even a flavour of Sydney Smith about it; and the author, whoever he may be, promises to supply a want and fill a gap much felt by all editors of periodicals – namely a producer of articles at once sensible, light, pungent, and readable.'[18] (This essay was Eliza Wilson's first introduction to Bagehot: she read it in Paris that November.)

Bagehot's next essay did not impress Greg. 'An article on Gibbon, [author of the *History of the Decline and Fall of the Roman Empire*] with which the Review commences, is neither quite as complete nor as thoughtful as we might have wished. The brilliant historian is clearly no favourite with his critic.'[19] It was a pompous response to a sparkling piece of biographical criticism, a prime example of Bagehot at his most enchanting – before he was obliged to temper his wit and high spirits and assume the *gravitas* required of the editor of *The Economist*. Norman St John-Stevas rightly judged that the Gibbon essay would have earned Bagehot a place amongst the great English comic writers had he never written anything else.[20] Yet it has a serious purpose too: in its assessments of the strengths and weaknesses of *Decline and Fall*, it consistently hits the bullseye.

Two years later the paper was to make amends for Greg's animadversions, when, in a review of Bagehot's *Estimates of Some Englishmen and Scotchmen*, Richard Holt Hutton cited a passage from the essay on Gibbon to illustrate Bagehot's 'rich and buoyant humour . . . [which] consists either in detecting the real incongruities of human life, or in slightly aggravating them in course of delineation, by a mischievous admission of reconciling elements'.[21]

Gibbon apart, the *National Review* greatly impressed Greg; less than eighteen months after its foundation, in his capacity as manager of *The Economist*, he offered its editorship to Richard Holt Hutton. Greg had by then become a Commissioner of Customs, by courtesy of his old friends, Sir George Cornewall Lewis, then Chancellor of the Exchequer, and the Financial Secretary, James Wilson. Hating 'to depend on so precarious a thing as a brain always in thinking order', in May 1856 he had accepted – 'with some loathing and misgiving' – the security of a large official salary and pension and the opportunity to move to London.

CHAPTER XV:

Changing guard

There were three or four great weekly journalists in the nineteenth century
– Cobbett, James Wilson (founder of the *Economist*), Bagehot, and Hutton
(who made the *Spectator* again famous).[1] The Economist, 1916

When Francis Hirst, then editor of *The Economist*, made that judgment in
1916, he ignored Richard Holt Hutton's connection with his own paper. In
1943, in his contribution to the centenary history, he mentioned him in
passing as having been briefly nominal editor. And in the same volume the
essay on the general history of the paper – 'One Hundred Years' – states
firmly that Bagehot was the second editor and fails to mention Hutton at all.

A Bagehot biographer and *Economist* journalist, Alastair Buchan, has a
rather casuistical explanation of why Hutton was not recognised as editor of
The Economist: 'though Greg put the paper together for Wilson during the
latter's spells in office, and though Hutton bore the nominal title of editor,
from 1858–1861, the full responsibility for both policy and management
never left Wilson's hands during his life time and then passed direct to
Bagehot'.[2] The *Dictionary of National Biography* entry, based on a sketch by
D.C. Lathbury, co-editor 1877–1881, describes Hutton as an assistant editor
from 1858 to 1860; Norman St John-Stevas, in *The Collected Works of Walter
Bagehot*, calls him editor; yet the biographical introduction to a recent
collection of his writings describes him as literary editor – a mystifying
compromise, since one of the authors has attributed to Hutton many political
articles in *The Economist*.[3]

Yet Mrs Russell Barrington (Emilie Wilson), clearly states in her biographies of her father and of Bagehot, her brother-in-law, that Hutton became
editor, and indeed her father so describes him in a letter of 1859.[4] So this

confusion would appear to be another example – like that of the supposed service to the paper of Nassau Senior (see footnote on page 161) – of what a tenacious grip folklore can get even on scholars.

Hutton was editor from 1857 to 1861. He was needed because once Greg took up his Customs job in June 1856, *The Economist* suffered. Wilson's political and social lives along with his family responsibilities left him hardly any time to write. Thomas Hodgskin was still in evidence, but he was almost seventy and wrote very little; Greg – manager of the paper as well as chief contributor – could not cope. In December 1856 he asked Hutton, whom he knew quite well by now, if he would be interested in becoming editor: if he wanted the job, Greg would put the proposition to James Wilson.[5] Hutton – whose wife had died in the West Indies and who wished to visit her tomb before marrying again – wrote to his best friend, Bagehot, to tell him of the offer and explain that he was refusing to make himself available for some months.

For all Bagehot's superficial frivolity, *joie de vivre* and slapdash habits, he had the caution and canniness of a good banker. 'I have thought over *very* carefully what you tell me of Greg's offer,' he responded,

> but I cannot think you are acting rightly. You have now an opportunity wh. may not occur again of *fixing* yourself in an established post, likely to be useful and permanent, and give you a fulcrum and position in the world wh. is what you have always wanted, and is quite necessary to comfort in England. I do not think you ought to risk it for the sake of *holiday*. You may have been right to ask it as a beginning of the negociation for it may be a gain to *you* to get it, but it seems to me quite out of the question to make a *sine qua non*. Offers of this kind are not to be picked up in the street every day.[6]

A few days later Bagehot wrote again.

> I am glad Greg has assented to your condition . . . It is no compliment to say that I think you quite capable of writing much better articles than those wh. the *Economist* has had lately – Greg's and a stray one on figures from Wilson now and then – there a[re] few papers wh. have such stuff in them.* It is

*Norman St John-Stevas, editor of Bagehot's collected works, notes: 'In this somewhat elliptical sentence WB is excepting Greg and Wilson from his general criticism, that few papers in recent issues of *The Economist* have any substance ("stuff") in them.'

simple type. I think Wilson must hope they wont be read. He shd. print a heading to that effect at the beginning of the article, if he means to retain any of his present staff – It is beyond all limits – What is to be your part at first, are you a contributor or assistant editor or what?[7]

Hutton returned from the West Indies in April 1857 and visited Wilson at Claverton Manor, his country house near Bath, to talk matters over. 'Papa arranged *Economist* matters with Mr Hutton', noted Eliza Wilson. 'The arrangement', added her sister, Emilie Barrington, 'was that Mr Hutton should be Editor of the *Economist*.'

The appointment was a mistake – an unfortunate mismatch. Hutton was later to be a great editor: from 1861, until his death in 1897, as co-editor and co-proprietor of the *Spectator* with Meredith Townsend, he was to give full rein to his many great qualities – not least his integrity, nobility, intellectual distinction and literary acumen. 'A most tender-hearted, upright, and truth-loving man', said his old mentor, the distinguished theologian and philosopher Dr James Martineau, when he heard of Hutton's death. 'He was indeed all that,' agreed John Morley, 'and we have lost a fine English critic and a beautiful character.'[8] A recent assessment views Hutton as 'the greatest reviewer of the Victorian Age',[9] who published more than 6,000 articles, essays and reviews. He wrote on philosophy, politics, theology, and on the conflict between science and religion, but above all, he wrote magisterially about American, Continental and English literature. 'The over-specialised 1990s might find Hutton's eclectic, interdisciplinary approach either too frightening or too flaky for serious concern', remarked a modern critic. 'But his enduring strength lies in his resistance to the tyranny of reputation and to the tyranny of boundaries set between intellectual disciplines.'[10] Hutton turned the *Spectator* into 'the most revealing guide to the progress of the English mind', is the judgment of one eminent historian.[11] St Loe Strachey, his successor as editor and proprietor, put it neatly when he reflected: 'To Hutton, I think, life was . . . like some High Conference at which he himself was one of the delegates, and not merely a spectator.'[12]

Hutton was perfect for the *Spectator* readership – once memorably described as 'a public sheltered in leafy rectories and in snug villas of rich non-conformists from the headlong decisions and rowdy activity of the world'.[13] As Robert Giffen pointed out in an appreciation of Bagehot, the *Economist* reader was very different. Bagehot's success as editor owed a great deal to the fact that he 'had always some typical City man in his mind's eye; a man not skilled in literature or the turnings of phrases, with a limited vocabulary and knowlege of theory, but keen as to facts, and reading for the sake of information and guidance respecting what vitally concerned him'.[14]

The problem was simply that Hutton was on the wrong paper: he knew nothing of men of business. The mystery is how Wilson and Greg – with their years of experience in manufacturing and trade – could have thought him suitable, for, apart from an academic qualification in political economy, there was nothing in Hutton's background or training that suggested he might have any understanding of the mind of a merchant or a banker. And as an editor, he was still a novice.

Hutton was born in Leeds in 1826, the third son and fifth child of a Unitarian minister, Dr Joseph Hutton, and the grandson of a Dublin Unitarian minister. (Unitarians believed that God was one person: hence they denied the divinity of Christ and the doctrine of the Trinity.) The family moved to London in 1835, where Richard attended the school attached to University College, London and then, from 1842, the College itself. As a Unitarian, Hutton would have been unable to attend Oxford or Cambridge, which still required their students to demonstrate their adherence to Anglicanism by formal acceptance of the Thirty-Nine Articles. Hence University College, founded fourteen years previously with the objective of providing a first-class education untrammelled by religious orthodoxy, was regarded in some quarters as 'godless'.

University College lacked many of the superficial advantages of the older institutions, but at this time it offered a far better education. 'I am sure', wrote Hutton, 'that Gower Street, and Oxford Street, and the New Road, and the dreary chain of squares from Euston to Bloomsbury, were the scenes of discussions as eager and as abstract as ever were the sedate cloisters or the flowery river-meadows of Cambridge or Oxford.'[15]

At University College, London, Hutton took courses in classics, mathematics and natural philosophy and performed brilliantly throughout. 'I think you have heard me speak of Hutton,' Bagehot, his contemporary at UCL, wrote to a relative in their second year, 'and if you have you will know that I consider being equal to him no slight honor.'[16] He graduated in 1845 with first-class honours and the Flaherty Scholarship in Mathematics and Natural Philosophy.

Hutton made deep, permanent friendships. His relationship with Walter

Bagehot, which began when they were both seventeen, was of great intellectual significance to them both. 'All that "pastors and masters" can teach young people, is as nothing when compared with what young people can't help teaching one another', wrote Bagehot in 1852. '. . . So too in youth – the real plastic energy is not in tutors or lectures or in books "got up", but in Wordsworth and Shelley; in the books that all read and because all like – in what all talk of because all are interested – in the argumentative walk or disputatious lounge – in the impact of young thought upon young thought, of fresh thought on fresh thought – of hot thought on hot thought – in mirth and refutation – in ridicule and laughter – for these are the free play of the natural mind.'[17] But Bagehot and Hutton were unusually intelligent and industrious, and they took their play of 'fresh thought on fresh thought' to a higher level than most of their contemporaries. 'Once, I remember', said Hutton in his memoir of Bagehot, 'in the vehemence of our argument as to whether the so-called logical principle of identity (A is A) were entitled to rank as "a law of thought" or only as a postulate of language, Bagehot and I wandered up and down Regent Street for something like two hours in the vain attempt to find Oxford Street.'[18] In their shared fascination with politics as well as with the nature of eloquence, they scoured London in search of great oratory. Parliamentary debates were off-limits, for MPs and peers were in temporary accommodation while Barry's and Pugin's Houses of Parliament were being built, but the Anti-Corn Law League provided opportunities for them to hear Bright, Cobden, O'Connell – and even James Wilson. With their friends they set up a new debating society and practised public speaking, at which neither of them was ever to excel.

Yet Hutton at least never saw it as an equal relationship. There was almost a tinge of self-abasement in the way he expressed to Bagehot his depth of dependency. 'I am certain', he wrote to him in mid-1846,

> that your mind will not feel the want of our daily discussions and conversations on subjects so deeply interesting to both of us nearly so much as mine . . . I have always thought it one of the most happy circumstances of my life that at college I was thrown with a mind so well calculated, not only to afford intellectual sympathy, but intellectual guidance, for to that has your influence on my opinions quite amounted. I have always found myself arrived at the same stage of opinion and progress that you have passed sometime, but through which I am following you, and have always felt that

any beneficial influence I may have had upon you can only be in compelling you to re-traverse and re-consider old ground, while your influence on me has been that of one well able to strike out new paths for himself, on one who requires as an intellectual necessity, the aid of some more original thinker.[19]

A man of great modesty and sweetness of nature, Hutton admired his friend without envy. When he wrote to congratulate him on his first-class degree and scholarship (ill-health had forced Bagehot to postpone his examinations for a year), Hutton enquired if it was 'not curious that *explicitly* our University course has been so very symmetrical and as far as signs go, we shd. be so exactly side by side, I should indeed feel glad if I could think there was the same implicit equality, but that is absurd, the more I am away from you, the more I see how much I depended on you, and what a weak-headed person I am'.[20]

At this time, Hutton was in Germany. Having spent a year in London unhappily studying law, he had gone to Heidelberg, where he tutored James Martineau's eldest son. His frame of mind at that time is indicated in a sonnet he wrote for Bagehot at the foot of a German mountain.

> Dearest companion of my life and thought,
> How often in thy spirit's nobler power
> My weaker soul has aid and comfort sought
> In converse with thee at this twilight hour–
>
> Deep in the solemn mysteries of life,
> Sad in the shade by darkest problems cast
> Thy faith has triumphed in the mental strife
> And light has beamed upon my soul at last.
>
> And now while here beneath the awful shade
> Cast by this barren mountain's rugged face,
> I watch the sullen shadow slowly fade
> As star by star shines out upon its base,
> It seems as though that giant form were doubt;
> Thy thoughts the stars that cast its horrors out.

'Though I don't think it's good at all (it is very young)', he wrote of it to Eliza Bagehot thirty years later, 'it shows you as nothing else could, the strong feeling he excited.'²¹ It also, of course, shows the high moral seriousness of the twenty-one-year-old Hutton, already far down the path of intellectual and spiritual struggle that was to dominate his life. It was during this period that he decided to follow the family calling. In the autumn of 1847 he went to Manchester New College to study under Martineau, then Professor of Mental and Moral Philosophy and Political Economy, and when his mentor and his family moved temporarily to Berlin the following summer, Hutton went with them for several months and along with Martineau studied philosophy – particularly Plato and Hegel.

Martineau's religious tolerance (he was a Unitarian minister) and his belief in the primacy of conscience had a deep influence on Hutton: they became close friends. 'I could never work well and with energy', Hutton wrote to Bagehot, 'without *real* friends near me, to whom my thoughts and attention may sometimes turn entirely. I do not mean simply men one *likes*, but men one loves; and I should be here in a state of quiet apathy, just like yours, if I had not Martineau near me to supply the attractive force that intellectual pursuits must often fail in, when the mind is ill or weary. All your friends you seem to like, but they do not seem to be resources that instantly and spontaneously fill the vacuum that rational, moral, and even religious interests will often leave.'²² It was one of Hutton's great qualities that he could break through his friends' reserve by disarmingly direct expressions of affection.

Hutton 'is one of those deep, fresh, conscientious, and devout thinkers', wrote Martineau of him a decade later, 'to whom external influence and instruction only present the occasion and commencement of a noble and independent inward life'.²³ In ensuing years the twin influences of F.D. Maurice, the writer, moral philosopher and theologian of broad-church Anglicanism, and of John Henry Newman, were to carry Hutton – whose temperament was profoundly Catholic – from the sect of his youth to High Anglicanism. But all through his life he would excel in explaining and reconciling apparently serious religious differences.

However, in the late 1840s he still wished to be a minister – an ambition thwarted because of his oratorical shortcomings: 'he received no call to a permanent charge, his intellectual discourses, adorned by no grace of delivery, failing to secure appreciation'.²⁴

Returning to University College to take an MA in political economy, logic, and mental and moral philosophy, like Bagehot the previous year, Hutton was awarded the Gold Medal. He served briefly as Vice-Principal and Chaplain of University Hall, the Unitarian student residence, taught in a Manchester school, wrote some articles and married Anne Mary, the sister of his and Bagehot's close friend, William Caldwell Roscoe.

It was in November 1851 that he began his career as an editor, when he, Roscoe and Timothy Smith Osler, another University College friend, began helping the historian J. Langton Sanford to edit the *Inquirer*. Sanford and Osler criticised the 'rather optimist and philanthropic politics' of their most benevolent Unitarian readers, Roscoe criticised their literary work from the viewpoint of a devotee of the Elizabethan poets and Hutton offended their Dissenting souls by encouraging them to develop a liturgy and cut down on sermons.

> Only a denomination of 'just men' trained in tolerance for generations, and in that respect, at least, made all but 'perfect,' would have endured it at all; but I doubt if any of us caused the Unitarian body so much grief as Bagehot, who never was a Unitarian, but who contributed a series of brilliant letters on the *coup d'état*, in which he trod just as heavily on the toes of his colleagues as he did on those of the public by whom the *Inquirer* was taken.

Therein, Bagehot 'eulogized the Catholic Church . . . supported the Prince-President's military violence, attacked the freedom of the Press in France, maintained that the country was wholly unfit for true Parliamentary government, and – worst of all perhaps – insinuated a panegyric on Louis Napoleon himself, asserting that he had been far better prepared for the duties of a statesman by gambling on the turf, than he would have been by poring over the historical and political dissertations of the wise and the good'.

> They were light and airy, and even flippant on a very grave subject. They made nothing of the Prince's perjury; and they took impertinent liberties with all the dearest prepossessions of the readers of the *Inquirer*, and assumed their sympathy just where Bagehot knew that they would be most revolted by his opinions.[25]

Hutton, who never shared Bagehot's youthful cynicism, and who was by nature melancholy rather than light-hearted, himself found the letters exasperating, but he also saw their great virtues: he was a man whose critical judgment triumphed over his emotions.

At the end of 1852 Hutton had become Principal of University Hall, a post he had to abandon along with the *Inquirer* in the summer of 1853 when he developed severe inflammation of the lungs. In the autumn he went to Barbados, where he and his wife both contracted yellow fever, from which she died in December.

Back in London, Hutton became editor of the *Prospective Review*, a quarterly of Unitarian tendencies, and the *Inquirer*, for both of which Bagehot occasionally wrote. His friends worried about him. 'He is a first rate German scholar, a capital mathematician, a very fair classic, and writes a very clear and strong style . . .', wrote Bagehot to Crabb Robinson, asking him if he could suggest a suitable job. 'He has been very ill and in much distress of mind, as he lost his wife in Barbadoes, but though from loss of voice, he is unable to teach or preach (his old profession) he is quite equal to anything with the pen and a certain amount of literary exertion would be good for him, independently of financial considerations. He is the sort of man to get on, I should say, in literature for he has great energy and accuracy and is to be depended on for doing any sort of work right which you will agree with me, is not very common.'[26]

The failing *Prospective* was superseded by the *National Review*, and although Hutton was reclusive and 'in feeble health and low spirits', Bagehot persuaded him to join him as co-editor.[27] Their prospectus – offering a platform for free enquiry in literature, politics, and social and religious philosophy – contained a far duller assessment of the English national character than Bagehot had provided in his *Inquirer* disquisitions on the value of stupidity: 'As Englishmen, we place unbounded confidence in the bases of English character, – its moderation and veracity; its firm hold on reality; its reverence for law and right; its historical tenacity; its aversion to *a priori* politics, and to revolutions generated out of speculative data.' And significantly, in its enunciation of its political principles, it included a paragraph that could equally well have done duty for *The Economist*.

> For the working classes we confidently anticipate a social condition far in advance of their present state; we have earnestly at heart the people's happiness and the people's elevation; but we shall not allow our warm sympathies and earnest wishes in this direction to betray us into any faithless compromise of the principles of economic science.[28]

Hutton handled the technical aspects of editing – proof correcting and so forth – and so received £100 a year to Bagehot's £50. He worked in London,

Bagehot in the West Country. That combination of factors may have given an inflated impression of Hutton's importance in the development of a periodical that rapidly became one of the great Victorian quarterlies. In fact surviving correspondence gives a clear impression that Bagehot was in this – as in all other aspects of their relationship – very much the dominant partner.[29] 'I am afraid I covet "*power*" influence over people's wills faculties and conduct more in proportion than I can quite defend', he wrote once to his fiancée.[30] Hutton did not now – any more than he had ever done – put up much of a fight.

Emilie Barrington, who knew them both in their maturity, wrote many years after their deaths a considered assessment of them and their relationship. Their minds were very different: 'any moral or intellectual light came as a flash of truth to Bagehot with this certainty of genius; whereas with Mr Hutton, who had no less a powerful intellect, truths would work themselves out through thought and conscience'. Hutton's conscience was extraordinarily sensitive; Bagehot's influence on him was 'bracing, invigorating, joy-giving; the influence to which he owed, perhaps more than to any other, the power of moving on in life, and of advancing to firmer standpoints'.

> One humorous sally from Walter, one conclusive witty criticism, would clear the air for him, he felt, better than days of solitary pondering and dissection. Mr Hutton had an ample sense of humour wherewith to enjoy any joke against himself, and to feel his mind the crisper for it. In personal intercourse it was most often through the medium of humour that Walter's advice was administered. Mr Hutton accused his own mind of being ponderous and wanting in elasticity, and felt that it was the buoyant elasticity in Walter Bagehot that helped him so greatly. With affections feminine almost in their tenderness and tenacity, his [Hutton's] intellect was remarkable for an insight which, through its uncompromising, crude directness, made his conclusions appear at times almost brutal. Whereas no fault he ever discovered in a friend could make the strength of his affection waver for a moment, his critical acumen made him severity itself when his disapproval was aroused towards faults in others which jarred on his moral sense.

Although he took no pleasure in censure, 'no arguments could ever modify his condemnations. You might plead for extenuating circumstances for any length of time – all the same at the end Mr Hutton would repeat the words with which he had begun the discussion, "But you must admit he (or she) is *dreadful*."'

> The moral disgust he felt for certain defects was incurable, and so instinctive and conclusive was this abhorrence that he did not trouble to give any reasons to justify it, though it appeared strangely opposed to the very Christian spirit which was characteristic of his nature generally. This uncompromising attitude gave his character a quaintness which amused Walter Bagehot, who, when with Mr Hutton, would assume a cynically tolerant view towards most of the weaknesses of human nature. Mr Hutton's earnest devotions and his equally earnest disapprobations made a delightful playground for Walter's humour and satire.[31]

Ironically, by the time Hutton took up the editorship of *The Economist*, Bagehot had become a contributor to the paper and had fallen in love with one of the proprietor's daughters. Having heard of the offer to Hutton, he had had the idea of offering Wilson some articles on banking and had secured an introduction – almost certainly through Greg. Wilson invited him to stay at Claverton, his country house, in January 1857, and as a result of their discussions, on 7 February, the first of a series of twelve letters from 'A BANKER' appeared in the paper. When on his return from the West Indies Hutton travelled to Claverton, he arrived in the company of Greg, the Wilson family intimate, and Bagehot, who was already a frequent visitor. Henceforward, the lives of Bagehot, Hutton and the Wilsons were to be intertwined.

Like Bagehot, Hutton was greatly taken by the family. George Ticknor, the American educationalist and historian, an admirer and friend of Greg, had dinner at the Wilson home in Mayfair in July 1857 and left a vivid picture of his host.

> I dined with Mr Wilson, a member of Parliament, Financial Secretary to the Treasury, owner, and formerly editor, of the 'Economist,' and the person on whom the government depends in questions of banking and finance. He never reads a book; he gets all his knowledge from documents and conversation, as Greg tells me, that is, at first hand. But he talks uncommonly well on all subjects; strongly, and with a kind of original force, that you rarely witness. He has a young wife, and three nice, grown-up daughters [Eliza, Julia and Matilda], who, with Greg, a barrister [Bagehot], – whose

name I did not get, – one other person, and myself, filled up a very luxurious table, as far as eating and drinking are concerned. And who do you think that other person was? Nobody less than Madame Mohl; who talked as fast and as amusingly as ever, full of good-natured kindness, with a little subacid as usual, to give it a good flavor. The young ladies Greg accounts among the most intelligent of his acquaintance, and they certainly talk French as few English girls can; for Tocqueville came in after dinner, and we all changed language at once, except the Master, who evidently has but one tongue in his head, and needs but one, considering the strong use he makes of it.[32]

Emilie Barrington put it more piously:

My father's natural gifts, together with an earnest, delightful nature, and the influence of his official position, made our home attractive to various kinds of interesting people. Walter Bagehot, among the number, found in its atmosphere stimulating conditions, besides the special charm which, from his first visit, my sister had inspired. It seems on looking back a little curious that a person of his notable ability and twice our age should have been treated by us of the schoolroom with so little awe.* One explanation for this seeming irreverence lies in the fact, I believe, that my father's personal influence so completely placed him in the position of great Llama with all his surroundings – without his meaning in the least to occupy such a position – that every one of the family and those who shared the intimate family life, such as Walter Bagehot, Mr Hutton and Mr Greg, gathered as mere satellites round a greater centre luminary.[33]

Wilson might have been a patriarch, but he did not patronise his extended family. When he died unexpectedly in 1860, Hutton, asking Bagehot to write a memoir as a special supplement to *The Economist*, lamented that Greg's *Economist* obituary had given 'no idea of the massive simplicity and geniality of his [Wilson's] social character and tastes, which in a great financier was exceedingly remarkable. Thorough enjoyment of all the more genial sides of life distinguished him, I should think, from Peel and Lewis and Lord Overstone and all those whose interests came nearest to his.'[34] Bagehot took

---

*It was partly because Bagehot shamelessly curried favour with the younger children, pointing out at his first meeting with the three of them that their German governess resembled an egg: 'We at once saw she was like an egg! From that moment he rose in our eyes from the status of a political economist to that of a fellow-creature. He became one of us.'

the point. 'His enjoyment of simple pleasures,' he wrote in his memoir, 'of society, of scenery, of his home, was very vivid. No one who saw him in his unemployed moments would have believed that he was one of the busiest public men of his time. He never looked worn or jaded, and always contributed more than his share of geniality and vivacity to the scene around him. Like Sir Walter Scott, he loved a bright light; and the pleasantest society to him was that of the cheerful and the young.'

But this warmth and geniality brought with it its own complications. Hutton had been editor of *The Economist* for only a few months when Bagehot, to whom Wilson was already devoted, became engaged to Eliza. So in his dealings with Hutton, Wilson was constrained by three factors: Hutton had been selected by Greg; he was Bagehot's closest friend; and in his own right, he was already a Wilson family friend. He was not going to be an easy man to sack.

From Hutton's point of view, if it was an honour to be James Wilson's successor at the age of thirty, it was also a heavy responsibility. From the beginning he recognised some of his own inadequacies. Writing to his friend in September 1860 shortly after hearing of Wilson's death, Hutton said he thought Bagehot 'mistaken in fancying you estimated him intellectually more highly than I did. My very incapacity to deal with his subjects in the same fashion at all, joined to great enough appreciation of the subjects to make me see how powerfully they were dealt with, made his intellect to me most fascinating. I have often on Friday nights walked down to the very end of Pall Mall with him at near three in the morning, merely to get half an hour's more conversation.'[35]

It was not that Hutton was ignorant of economics or politics: it was more that he could neither reflect the central concerns of his readers nor write provocatively enough to grab their attention. Where Wilson gripped with his inspired common sense, Hodgskin with his passionate dogmatism and Greg with his felicitous eloquence, Hutton seemed earnest, moralistic and churchy. He gave little impression of understanding that what took most readers of *The Economist* into their places of work every morning was the desire to make money. It was something that he reflected on in his memoir of Bagehot, when he discussed his friend's dislike of spending money. 'It is curious, but I believe it to be almost universally true, that what may be called the primitive impulse of all economic *action*, is generally also strong in great economic *thinkers* and financiers – I mean the saving, or at least the anti-spending, instinct . . . I suppose it takes some feeling of this kind to give the intellect of a man of high capacity that impulse towards the study of the laws of the increase of wealth, without which men of any imagination would be more likely to turn in other directions.' Lacking such an impulse, for Hutton, transactions seemed to be between God and Man, with the profit motive shackled within strict moral limits.

The following passage is typical:

> Understood in its widest and deepest sense, the principles of free trade are founded on the mutual benefit of *all* kinds of exchanges between those who, possessing different powers and different gifts, wish to gain riches without taking away anything that the other wants. The duty and rights of free trade are founded on the mutual benefit which man can bestow on man, class on class, nation on nation, if none will selfishly grasp at richer equivalents for their own superfluity than, by the natural adjustments of mutual desire, they must receive . . . Nor is there any case so strong for mere physical free trade as there is for the like hearty and unselfish interchange of the intellectual and moral benefits arising from difference of character, opportunity, and culture.[36]

There was nothing unsuitable about the message: it was simply expressed in too abstract and remorselessly high-minded a manner, just as was the injunction that followed an Anglo-French incident early in 1858. In a leader called 'ENGLISH DIGNITY AND FRENCH DICTATION', Hutton asked 'What do we consider true dignity in a case of individual affronts? Surely to act in that calm and dispassionate temper which overlooks all the irritating personal elements of the case, and renders justice as strictly as if there had been no anger, and yet so barely as to avoid all confusion between concessions to hectoring demands, and concessions to equitable rights.'[37]

Nor could he easily produce political invective. This condemnation of *The Economist*'s favourite target was very laboured:

> Mr Disraeli's speech to his constituents, amusing and, indeed, instructive as it is, to read, is not less instructive but much more melancholy to think about. For while the practised skill and the life-like colouring of the great literary artist become only more and more apparent as we examine his sketch of the confusion and party-spirit which pervade the Opposition, – the utter untruthfulness and unreality in that imaginary outline of a firm and

beneficent Government with which he has sought to improve his 'composition,' become only too painfully apparent also. His artistic instincts are far too strong for his sense of veracity; and his picture, which is almost pre-Raphaelite in the 'dissolving' tints of his distance, is obtrusively mendacious and conventional in his attempt at a 'bold' foreground.[38]

(Contrast that with Bagehot ten years later:

> It has been Mr Disraeli's misfortune throughout his main political career to lead a party of very strong prejudices and principles, without feeling himself any cordial sympathy with either the one or the other. No doubt that is precisely the fact which has enabled him on most great emergencies to be of use to his party. His completely external intelligence has been to them what the elephant driver's – the mahout's – is to the elephant, comparatively insignificant as a force, but so familiar with all the habits of the creature which his sagacity has to guide, and so entirely, if it only knew, at its mercy, that all his acuteness is displayed in contriving to turn the creature's habits and instincts to his own end, profit, and advantage, – which, however, cannot be done without also carefully preserving the creature itself from great dangers, and guarding it against the violence of its own passions.[39])

If Hutton's morality tinted his political writing, his theological preoccupations were also evident during his editorship. While there was nothing odd in *The Economist*'s taking note of important contributions to the great religious debate of the mid-nineteenth century, it was inappropriate to give, for example, a more than full-page review to *Sermons Preached at Trinity Chapel, Brighton* by the Reverend Frederick Robertson, whom Hutton had met and been influenced by in Germany.

His literary interests too showed up in the paper disproportionately – if almost guiltily, as in this justification of a review of a new volume from the highly spiritual Coventry Patmore:

> It would scarcely be appropriate to fill the columns of the *Economist* with any extended criticism of contributions to poetical literature . . . But we need not carry out the strict theory of the division of labour so far as to decline to give some brief general estimate of the merits of any work which is likely to attract a considerable share of public attention. In a time when no man of any trade or profession likes to be thought purely one-sided, – when the soldier aims at the culture of the man of letters, and the man of letters

undertakes to discharge many of the duties of a soldier, – when publications devoted to the lightest and most entertaining walks of literature find room for dissertations on Political Economy, there can be no impropriety in one devoted mainly to political and economical studies occasionally passing out of its special sphere to estimate in a few words the works of a rising poet.[40]

The happy family atmosphere which enveloped *The Economist* meant that there was little Wilson could do – at least in the short term – except provide Hutton with as much support as possible. The quality was in any case being raised by Bagehot's contributions – the very first of which attracted a stately fan letter: 'Lord Radnor trusts that "A Banker" will not think him impertinent, if he offers the expression of his great satisfaction at the perusal of the letter in the *Economist* of last night.'[41] During 1857 the intimacy between the Wilsons and Bagehot grew steadily, culminating in November with his engagement to Eliza, with whom Bagehot was ebulliently and demonstratively in love. Although Wilson became temporarily ill and took briefly to his bed at the thought of losing one of his daughters, he was captivated by Bagehot – as much because of his gaiety as his brilliance. The following episode occurred during the severe financial panic of 1857.

18 Novr. 1857

My dearest Eliza,

What do you think your father and myself did the moment you were gone [to Edinburgh, with her mother and sister Sophie for a prolonged course of treatment for headaches] – We went to see the antiquities of Halicarnassus!! They are a set of odd legs, arms and bodies of Greek statues just arrived and alleviated our feelings very much. It happened in this way. We drove past the British Museum on our way home, and Mr Wilson asked if I had seen the new reading room and as I had not, he forthwith took me to see it. We were ushered in to old Panizzi [principal librarian and designer of the room], who was doing nothing in a fine armchair, and he proposed we shd. see the venerable fragments just arrived from Greece. I am not sure, however, that we appreciated them. I have an unfortunate prejudice in favor of statues in *one* piece at least in not more than *six* pieces, and these are broken up very small indeed, and it is a controversy whose arm belongs to whose body – but I believe real lovers of art admire those perplexities. On the whole however we spent our time cheerfully, and in consequence the Chancellor of the

Exchequer and a heap of Scotch bankers were kept half an hour waiting . . . I am a little tired. The affections are always *fatiguing*, then there is the panic which is wearing, and really a trifle anxious, and your father's conversation and what I guess from it lets me so into the interior of matters in which I am much interested that currency becomes an *excitement*.

They had had dinner with an MP friend of Wilson's, who 'gave us a *scrumptious* dinner. Capital wine – and excellent food, tho' not quite in large pieces enough for me. I like to feel I am eating.'

> We talked currency till half past one, and then Mr Wilson and myself walked to Hertford St and stood on the doorstep ever so long, talking of Michel Chevalier* and the double standard in France . . . There were only five of us and a small party is always pleasanter. There is not so much competition for the food. Mr Lowe [Vice-President of the Board of Trade] and the American banker were the others – the latter was instructive.[42]

It was heady company for a West Country banker, made headier still by the opportunity to learn so much at close quarters from Wilson, who in the opinion of a senior Liberal politician, expressed over forty years later, 'in his power of lucidly explaining difficult financial questions, if he yielded to anybody, yielded to Mr Gladstone alone'.[43] Bagehot showed a great desire to prove himself, exulting to Eliza a few days later that 'I think I *have* distinguished myself about "money". I wrote a letter in the Economist 4 columns of leader type. Everything was postponed to it, an article of Mr Wilson's (!!) – one of Hutton's – no end of your sister's literature [Julia and occasionally Eliza used to review books] – and something else. Your father seemed to like it, and Greg said "Better than any of your literary things Bagehot" which is paying a compliment and spoiling it rather. I feel I should like to have more of a reputation about these subjects because you would like it. Of course, I should always have liked it but reputation is not my strongest temptation.'[44] And two days later he announced triumphantly that 'Mr

---

*Chevalier, French economist and free-trader and long-time friend of Wilson's, was instrumental in fostering a pro-free-trade climate that helped to make possible the tariff-reducing 1860 Commercial Treaty between France and England, for which Cobden deserves the main credit. In the mid-1850s, while Financial Secretary to the Treasury, Wilson had several meetings with key French ministers. His daughter Emilie believed that Wilson was an important influence in paving the way for the treaty. Cf. her letter in *The Economist*, 20 August 1927.

Wilson muttered that my letter in the *Economist* last week was written in a "business style", which from *him* I consider great praise. He likes *me*, which is a great point.'[45]

And a paragraph ending a letter to Hutton about *National Review* business is illuminating as to the editor's position *vis-a-vis* his proprietor. 'I am going to write a very short letter [to] the Economist this week stating the argument of my last without reference to Sir R. Peel's act', wrote Bagehot. 'Wilson seems to wish it.'[46] The tone is almost peremptory, but Hutton was not a man to take offence. On the contrary, his intellectual awe of his friend's gifts was expressed at length in the columns of *The Economist*. Reviewing two quarterlies in January 1858 – his own and the *Edinburgh* – Hutton compared their articles on the monetary crisis to the very great disadvantage of the *Edinburgh*.

'The article in the National Review adopts and defends the same currency principles which the ECONOMIST has ever maintained; and brings to the subject so complete a knowledge and so practised a power of illustration, that it will teach many to understand the subject who never understood it before, and may possibly, we think, – though this can rarely happen, – shake the faith of men who have long accustomed their thoughts to run in the ruts of a particular currency system, and shut their ears to arguments that point in the opposite direction.' He summarised the argument of 'this masterly writer', and concluded with the observation that 'whoever will compare the admirer of Lord Overstone's theory who writes in the Edinburgh [it was Colonel Torrens], with the National reviewer, will be glad to pass from the hesitating and sometimes self-confuting admissions of the one to the lucid exposition of the other.'[47]

'He is the greatest puff to his friends that ever was', wrote Bagehot to Eliza. 'He has produced an article on me in the Economist . . . which is quite touching in its eloquence.'[48] '[It] is *splendid*', she responded. 'He *is* a friend worth having.'[49]

Only a fortnight later, Hutton was again extolling Bagehot's virtues in *The Economist*, this time in a long review of *Estimates of Some Englishmen and Scotchmen*, a collection of eight Bagehot articles (on the first Edinburgh Reviewers, William Cowper, Edward Gibbon, Bishop Butler, Shakespeare, Shelley, Hartley Coleridge, Sir Robert Peel and Macaulay) – three from the *Prospective* and five from the *National*. The contents were as dazzling as the title was dull. Hutton did them justice in what was one of the best pieces he ever wrote for *The Economist* – a page and a half in which he gave his considered views on a talent he had been studying for fifteen years.

> There is true genius in these fascinating, and, perhaps, disrespectful estimates, and it is of a somewhat rare kind . . . In the general way a fine critic is personally *invisible*, as it were, in his criticism . . . He enters so thoroughly into the creative mood of the artist he is criticising . . . that he – the critic – only becomes visible where the artist fails. Then and only then he emerges into independent importance, and completes or rectifies the picture which the mind of the artist had left imperfect or incorrect.

Bagehot's criticism was not at all like that; the articles were not written in any mood of sympathy with his subjects.

> He fixes his intellect upon them, but he does not throw himself into their position. Far from trying to bring his mind into the attitude of theirs while he is painting them, – the great fascination of his style chiefly consists in the perfect intellectual independence with which he *resists* the encroachment, while he appreciates the nature of their influence, and keeps them at a distance by vividly representing to himself the scope and limits of their powers. He looks *into* them we may say, but looks into them from the *outside*.

In this sense, Bagehot's estimates were more purely intellectual than any others Hutton knew, and had the consequent defects as well as merits. But they were in no way restricted to the appreciation of intellectual qualities only.

> They are full of humour, which is not, we understand, a quality of the pure intellect at all, and humour, too, of a buoyant and sparkling kind. They show a deep appreciation of many states of mind by no means intellectual; they indicate, for instance, a shrewd knowledge of the world, a keen love of poetry, and a deep sense of the supernatural. But still in every page, almost in every line of this book, you see that the vigilant and restless intellect of the writer is not the subordinate instrument of any of these states of mind. It watches and records all impulses, but it goes into captivity to none. The independent activity of the intellect is a most conspicuous element in the character of the essayist.

'We must conclude', said Hutton after many more acute paragraphs, '"The National Review" is fortunate in having secured in its early days the contributions of a writer so fresh and vivid a genius. His audacity would often provoke rebellion if it were not for the depth of his thought, and his thought would often seem abstruse and dull if it were not for the brilliancy of his humour.'[50]

'I have been frightening myself with studying Mr Hutton's "*estimate*" of your mind in last week's Economist, and getting back some of my old feeling of not being clever enough for you', wrote Eliza.[51] 'I am much amused at the serious way in which you take Hutton's nonsense', responded Bagehot.

> His way of exaggerating the faculties of his friends is the most extraordinary I have ever known. He makes such very small geese into such immense swans. I will talk to you about our minds when I see you. This bank is not a place where one can write metaphysics, but I think you have really the most culture of the two, as I will prove to you, besides the deeper nature. The only thing I maintain is that I have a spring and energy in my mind which enables me to take some hold of good subjects and makes it natural and inevitable that I should write on them. I do not think I write well, but I write, as I speak, in the way (I think) that is natural to me, and the only chance in literature as in life is to be yourself. If you try to be more you will be less . . . Except from the depth and strength of my affection (which at times *alarms* me and *bewilders* me for minutes) I am not worthy of you at all.[52]

'Occasionally smart at the expense of consistency, and flippant to the verge of childishness', observed one otherwise favourable review.[53] These were criticisms that did not trouble Bagehot. 'The Press says I am "childish and indescribably trivial"', he announced to Eliza. 'This is *fame*, you observe – that enlightened appreciation for which authors long.'[54] '*Please* don't be offended at my rubbish', he had begged her early in their engagement. 'Sauciness is my particular line. I am always rude to everybody I respect. I cd write to you of the deep and serious feelings which I hope you believe really are in my heart but my pen jests of itself and always will.'[55]

As Bagehot was at his funniest when writing on solemn subjects, so he particularly enjoyed making serious people laugh. It was no accident that Hutton should have been his best friend and the earnest Eliza his bride. 'I go about murmuring "I have made that *dignified* girl *commit* herself – I have I have"', he wrote in the same letter, 'and then I vault over the sofa with exultation.' His letters relentlessly poke fun at her idols. 'I am going to dine and sleep at Greg's on Wednesday. He is very well. I saw him at the custom house. He had a mild happiness as if he were confiscating goods.'[56]

Bagehot could talk nonsense like nobody else and as the reminiscences of his intimates make clear, it was contagious. The Wilsons were fertile ground. 'What I always like so much here' wrote Bagehot from Claverton, where he was visiting her father and four of her sisters, 'is the mixture of chaff and sense – chaff and currency one might say. I get tired either of sense or nonsense if I am kept very continuously to either, and like my mind to undulate between the two as it likes best. There are some sporting people coming to dinner who will I much fear bring neither sense nor nonsense, but the heavy matter which is compounded of both.'[57] As a biographer put it, Bagehot was '*gamin* foil to the genteel routine of the six sisters. Games of cup and ball with all eyes concentrated in suspense on him to see whether he could screw his monocle into his short-sighted eye long enough to balance the thing, alternated with furious horsemanship, games of cards, and readings from Shelley and Jane Austen. The tendency of the mid-Victorians to mask love behind the language of camaraderie, to divert desire into a sort of teasing sister and brother relationship generally strikes a false note for their descendants. But in this one instance, the ecstatic portrait that both Bagehot and the Wilson sisters have painted of their communal affection had a foundation in reality.'[58]

Even Greg succumbed to the chaff, inspired by travelling in 1860 to Paris with the Bagehots, Julia and Emilie. 'Our Paris visit was not very successful', he wrote to Matilda Wilson in 1860, '– at least to us soberer ones.'

> It produced an enormous crop of bonnets and dresses – with which our room was absolutely *strewn* – but not much else, – except that I had the stomach-ache *en perpetuité*, Emily a sore throat and Julia influenza and measles. We saw, however, an immense deal of Mme Mohl, and I made two or three new acquaintances . . . we croaked together and appreciated each other's hopeless gloom. – You never saw such people as Walter and Eliza for appetite and unpunctuality. They grubbed at 9, at 11, at 2, sometimes at 5, always at 6, and usually again at 11 or 12, with a snack in the interstices. The sofas and floor presented a most distracting chaos of Newspapers, old and new, chocolate, gloves (–generally odd ones) – tea cups, lemonade, pats of butter, statistical returns and Blue books, physic bottles, fragments of bread, half-eaten pears, and the like, all accumulating from the day of our arrival to the day of our departure, and never cleared away. We generally spent half an

hour a day in getting together a quorum to consider when and where we shd. dine, – and another half an hour in settling what to have for dinner. You may suppose what it was to a man of my habits. I got so demoralised with it all that I lost my two purses within a week – mainly from laying them down or dropping them on the floor à la Mrs Bagehot.[59]

If Wilson was King, Bagehot was the Crown Prince. Hutton did his job as best he could and the Wilsons were fond of him, but he was almost an object of pity. When in January 1858 he announced his engagement to Eliza Roscoe, a cousin of his first wife, Eliza wrote to Bagehot that 'Julia is very pleased at Mr Hutton's marriage, and says she hopes he will look less melancholy now, poor man.'[60] 'Julia has sent me Mr Hutton's note to her in which he mentions his approaching marriage', she wrote a week later. 'It is characteristically naive, for he says "She is not very clever nor in any way very striking, I think, but" &c.'[61] 'Mr Hutton's noble, simple nature', concluded Emilie, many years later, 'was not, I think, keenly alive to intricacies in sensitiveness.'[62]

Even with a mediocre editor, there was enough useful material in *The Economist* to maintain, if not increase, its circulation. The Conservatives were in office between February 1858 and June of the following year, so Wilson had more time available. 'I breakfasted with Mr Wilson this morning', Bagehot had written to Eliza when the Liberal government fell. 'He seemed to anticipate glory in opposition and to have a sensation of freedom in having to maintain only what it pleased him to maintain and to have no official etiquette to restrain him; but he will feel the non-arrival of the Treasury bag in a Long Vacation.'[63] During 1858 Bagehot had contributed only two articles to the paper, but he provided several in the spring of 1859: when Wilson became embroiled in canvassing in April 1859, he wrote to his son-in-law that 'Hutton will have to draw from all quarters this week and next. I cannot do anything for him. See what you can.'[64] Bagehot obliged with an excellent article on the state of the City in the week of the outbreak of the Franco-Austrian War.

Estimates of Some Englishmen and Scotchmen had had mixed reviews and been commercially unsuccessful, yet it helped spread Bagehot's reputation in literary circles – where he already had distinguished admirers. One of the giants of Victorian literary criticism, Matthew Arnold, had told Hutton apropos the *National Review* that Bagehot's anonymous essay on Shelley 'and one or two others (in which I imagine that I trace the same hand) seem to me to be of the very first quality, showing not talent only, but a concern for the *simple truth* which is rare in English literature as it is in English politics and English religion – whatever zeal, vanity and ability may be exhibited by the performers in each of these three spheres'.[65] He had also built up a substantial body of articles, essays and reviews – mainly in the *National* and the *Saturday Review* – on economics and politics. The *cognoscenti* would have greatly enjoyed a series in the *Saturday* in 1856 – 'Dull Government', 'Average Government', 'Thinking Government', 'Intellectual Conservatism', 'Responsible Government', 'Inconvincible Governments', 'Shabby Government' and 'Our Governing Classes' – which took his thinking several stages beyond his 1851–2 *Inquirer* articles and put forward ideas which were to be developed in his maturity in *The English Constitution*. Astute, provocative and epigrammatic, they continue his theme of the importance of stupidity in the English character and dullness in parliamentary government, which is 'a test of its excellence, an indication of its success'. The English see politics as a business: 'Steady labour and dull material – wrinkles on the forehead and figures on the tongue – these are the English admiration.' There is no room for the dictatorial disposition in the English Constitution, for the 'English idea is a committee – we are born with a belief in a green cloth, clean pens, and twelve men with grey hair. In topics of belief the ultimate standard is a jury.'[66]

Predictably he made a spirited defence of the dullness of parliament:

> the truth is, all the best business is a little dull. If you go into a merchant's counting-house, you see steel pens, vouchers, files, books of depressing magnitude, desks of awful elevation, staid spiders and sober clerks moving among the implements of tedium. No doubt, to the parties engaged, much of this is very attractive. 'What,' it has been well said, 'are technicalities to those without, are realities to those within.' To every line in those volumes, to every paper on those damp files, there has gone doubt, decision, action – the work of a considerate brain, the touch of a patient hand. Yet even to those engaged, it is commonly the least interesting business which is the best. The more the doubt, the greater the liability to error – the longer the consideration, generally the worse the result – the more the pain of decision, the greater the likelihood of failure . . .
>
> To parties concerned in law, the best case is a plain case. To parties

concerned in trade, the best transaction is a plain transaction – the sure result of familiar knowledge; in political matters, the best sign that things are going well is that there should be nothing difficult – nothing requiring deep contention of mind – no anxious doubt, no sharp resolution, no lofty and patriotic executions.[67]

Among the aspects of political life that he regretted was the pressure placed on members of parliament to have a view on all topics:

The habit of always advancing a view commonly destroys the capacity for holding a view. The laxity of principle imputed to old politicians is, by the time they are old, as much intellectual as moral. They have argued on all sides of everything, till they can believe on no side of anything. A characteristic of the same sort has been observed in journalism. One of our most celebrated contemporaries was asked his opinion on ten great subjects in succession, and on its appearing that he had no opinion, he said, apologetically, 'You see, ma'am, I have written for *The Times*.'[68]

CHAPTER XVI:

The politics of equilibrium

Bagehot knew that the task of his age was to embody and prevent revolution; that is, to promote yet restrain change, so as to direct it. The stolid, cautious, unimaginative members of society will huddle together and do what they can to prevent revolution by merely sitting still; the restless spirits, lit by generous hope or merely fanatical from rancour, will not wait for inching reforms but will want to establish the perfect state by overnight coup. Neither party, neither temperament, will ever have the genius to act at any time in deliberate opposition to its own habit. The only hope lies in the politics of equilibrium, the art by which one or more leading men can move the poised mass a little way toward goals that they dimly see.[1] *Jacques Barzun, 1968*

In January 1859, when Bagehot strode into the political arena with an article in the *National* called 'Parliamentary Reform', politicians and journalists were caught in an argument dominated by prejudice, ignorance, confusion and weariness. Bagehot had the freshness and lucidity necessary to cast new light on what was a venerable but hoary debate.

The House of Commons of this time was an uneasy amalgam of factions, but except on the far reaches of the Conservative Party there was a recognition that the 1832 Reform Act needed to be brought up to date by some extension of the franchise. Minor reforms proffered by Lord John Russell had failed in 1852 and 1854: now Disraeli was pushing for a Conservative measure. John Bright wanted all ratepayers to have the vote: *The Economist*, like most moderate opinion, feared a swamping of the civilised and educated sections of society. In one leader Hutton wrote about the feared precedent:

America is not free. One class alone is represented there, and we see the lamentable result – that the higher and educated classes are a mere drop in the ocean. Fortunately for America the time is not yet come for the existence of 'dangerous classes.' . . . If ever that time does come with an unchanged political system, we can scarcely conceive any alternative between anarchy and an imperial despotism like that of France, or perhaps the former issuing in the latter. Yet this is not because the lower classes are represented, it is because they and they alone are represented, – because *uniformity* was assumed as the basis of all political rights, and then those rights committed to a class which vastly outnumbers all the rest.[2]

There were innumerable ideas abroad for making some concessions while keeping the flood-gates firmly shut, and the debate had assumed a complexity that made discussion confusing. Bagehot's magisterial essay had a cogency and simplicity that clarified the whole debate. In his analysis of the defects of the present system and of the many proposals for tinkering with the Act then under consideration, he claimed to offer impartial criticism and constructive ideas free of any party spirit, though of course his approach was that of the political animal he was by temperament – conservative Liberal or liberal Conservative. 'The true principle', he explained, 'is that every person has a right to *so much political power as he can exercise without impeding any other person who would more fitly exercise such power*.'* That being so, it was the job of a real statesman to try to increase the influence of the 'growing' – i.e. the urban and industrial – parts of the nation as opposed to the 'stationary' – the over-represented landed interest. The working-class voice had to be heard, but a 'democratic revolution' must be prevented. His own proposal was simple if arbitrary: the requirement that in boroughs voters should be householders paying £10 annually should be retained, but in large towns with a substantial industrial population, in order to give the working class a voice, all ratepayers should be enfranchised.[3]

Once again Hutton weighed in incestuously and loyally, devoting most of an *Economist* article on 'THE POLITICAL RELATIONS OF THE EDUCATED AND WORKING CLASSES' to the *National Review*'s publication of 'the first really broad and statesmanlike discussion of the question of Parliamentary Reform that the present crisis has elicited, which bears the most convincing

*Cf. Herbert Spencer's 'Every man has freedom to do all that he wills, provided that he infringes not the equal freedom of any other man.'

witness to the cordial sympathy felt by the most cultivated classes with the political claims of Working Men.'[4]

'Your article is capital and precisely hits the nail on the head', wrote Greg to Bagehot.

> Your dilemma as to the admission of the working classes to the franchise I pressed upon Lord John R. years ago, but the old fogey could not take in the idea. It is true I had no suggestion to offer as to a really effective way out. I think, however, you have now put the case so clearly and forcibly that all men will see that *no* lowering of the franchise will meet the difficulty, and that none that other people will submit to, or even listen to, will give the working classes what they want and ought to have. Whether your plan of solving the difficulty can be accepted I am not so sure. Certainly it must germinate in the mind of the Nation for a year or two, before so novel a proposal can hope to make its way. Still, if well ventilated I should not despair.[5]

A revised and updated version was published as a pamphlet early in March. Robert Lowe, a Liberal politician deeply hostile to working-class enfranchisement, told Bagehot that it was written 'with the insight of a statesman and the moderation of a philosopher': George Arbuthnot, Wilson's Treasury colleague, considered it 'so sensible that it will please no one'.[6] His father-in-law's pride was manifest. 'Everyone speaks in the highest terms of your Reform Pamphlet', he wrote.

> Gladstone is delighted with it, and in mentioning it last night, not at the moment knowing we were connected, spoke in great praise of your former book. Let me have a list of those to whom the Pamphlet was sent. Was one sent to Lord Grey? We are getting into some confusion in the political world about the Reform Bill. The great objection among the Radicals is the non-reduction of the double franchise, and among thoughtful politicians the identity of franchise in town and country, on the grounds I put very shortly in a para. at the end of Hutton's article this week.

He continued with a long and detailed discussion about parliamentary reform and the current debate about gold and silver. 'I wish I had you here to talk over this interesting point. But go on with the articles [on the depreciation of gold]. When shall we see you?'[7]

Wilson decided to hold a dinner at which admirers of the pamphlet could meet its author: among those present were Gladstone, Lord Grey, Lord Granville, Sir George Cornewall Lewis, Robert Lowe (a future Chancellor) and W.M. Thackeray – 'a very fine collection of public animals', as Bagehot described them to Eliza the day before. 'As to reform it will be curious [Disraeli's Reform Bill was coming before the Commons], as Mr Gladstone is going to vote for the ministry, and Lord Grey has recommended Lord Elcho to vote for them; and all the rest of the Parliamentary party are decidedly for Lord John's Resolution. I take it it is a new idea to have a dinner party of both sides on a division night – particularly a division on a fundamental question "affecting the constitution of our country" as one says in articles, and I hope the novelty will prosper.'[8]

Apart from bringing Bagehot firmly into Wilson's political circle, this was the event that began his mutually rewarding friendship with Gladstone. By the time the dinner party was actually held, on 1 April 1859, the Conservative government had been defeated and a general election had been called. *The Economist* fretted over differences among Liberal leaders, particularly about Lord John Russell's having decided that the secret ballot was after all not likely to pose much of a problem:

> We believe that there is no possible alteration in our political institutions which would eventually affect the national character so deeply, and especially the character of the Liberal party so prejudicially, as the ballot. To us, indeed, it is utterly unintelligible how the ballot should ever have become a *Liberal* cry; for if there is any party in the country whose strength, cohesion, and general influence absolutely depend on the publicity of elections, that party is the Liberal party. We object to the ballot, indeed, on no mere party grounds. We hold that it must eventually exert a much more pernicious influence on the national character than even the great evils it is invoked to cure.

And since Liberal views were preferable 'chiefly because they are more truly *national* than any others, because they repose greater trust in the people at large, and give freer play in political matters to the national character', therefore 'any measure which would prejudicially affect the nation at large, would especially injure the Liberal party in the nation'.[9]

The Conservatives failed to secure a clear majority and lost a vote of no confidence in June. Lord Palmerston returned as Prime Minister, with Gladstone as Chancellor. James Wilson, who since 1857 had sat for Devonport, declined his old job but accepted the Vice-Presidency of the

Board of Trade and became a Privy Councillor. A month later he was offered the job of Financial Member of the Council of India – a new job for which his career seemed to mark him out as ideal.

In his thirteen years in parliament, all but three of them in office, Wilson's reputation had grown steadily, without any hiccups along the way. He was fond, said Bagehot, 'of quoting a saying of Sir Robert Peel's, "That the way to get on in the House of Commons was to take a place and sit there."' And that is what Wilson did. Reactions to him were not all favourable. 'In the House of Commons', reported the *New York Daily Times* in 1856, 'his personal ugliness, which is of a most grotesque description, (his head being of the Michael Angelo school, with thin, yellow hair hanging in long, lanky curls around,) and his dull, dreary delivery, made him personally most unpopular.'[10] Yet another contemporary, who remembered him well from seeing him both in parliament and riding in Rotten Row, described him as 'a man of striking figure and appearance – with flowing flaxen hair, just of the hue familiar to him who has dwelt amongst the fair lasses of his beloved native Teviotdale. But he had also high and commanding features of the true Norman type, which were as prominently developed and keenly cut as those of the first Pitt, Castlereagh, Sir James Graham, and the late Lord Derby. And that protuberance of the lower brow, to which the phrenologists give the title Individuality, is as marked in him as in the busts and medallions of Michal Angelo Bonarroti himself.'[11] However, even the *New York Daily Times* writer acknowledged Wilson's 'vast store of commercial and financial information, always ready for delivery, [which] made him of service to the Government . . . He is a man of intense industry and considerable power.'

'The Corn Laws had been repealed,' wrote Bagehot, 'the pitched battle of Free Trade had been fought and won, but much yet remained to be done in carrying out its principles' (particularly as regards the sugar duties and the Navigation Acts), 'in applying them to articles other than corn, in exposing the fallacies still abundantly current, and in answering the exceptional case which every trade in succession set up for an exceptional protection'.

> These were painful and complex matters of detail, wearisome to very many persons, and rewarding with no *éclat* those who took the trouble to master and explain them. But Mr Wilson shrank from no detail . . . He was able to do an important work better than any one else could do it, and, in English public life, real work rightly done at the right season scarcely ever fails to meet with a real reward.[12]

There was, too, that extraordinary capacity for work that had enabled him to found *The Economist* while running his factory. Discussing his iron constitution, Bagehot referred to the intensity with which he worked:

> Although his hours of labour were so very protracted, yet if a casual observer happened to enter his library at any moment, he would find him with his blind down to exclude all objects of external interest, his brow working eagerly, his eye fixed intently on the figures before him, and, very likely, his rapid pen passing fluently over the paper. He had all the labour of the chronic worker, and all the labour of the impulsive worker too.

('A Sunday in a Scotch Hotel', wrote Wilson once to Cornewall Lewis, 'is the best of opportunities for getting up any amount of arrears of correspondence. You may go to Church once . . . But if you have scores of friends in the Town and on every other day of the week asked to dinner three deep, you have no chance of seeing anyone or asking to be seen on a Sunday. This is therefore the twenty-fourth letter I have written to-day.' It was also immensely long.)[13]

Wilson's first ministerial job – from 1848 to 1852 at the India Board of Control, the government department which supervised the activities of the East India Company – had given him a foundation of knowledge on which he continued to build even after he moved on. At the Board he had run the Finance and Revenue Departments, had developed a state guarantee to encourage English investment in India and had been the driving force behind the development of the Indian railway system: Emilie remembered him planning the railway lines on the dining table at home. He had also made Indian friends: in the autumn of 1851, Eliza recorded in her diary a visit of several days from Pier Ibrahim Khan, Seid Abdoolua and two servants and the interest and curiosity aroused among the locals.

Additionally, Wilson had been made the government representative on committees dealing with his particular interests – the most important of which investigated the economic and colonial aspects of reducing duties on sugar. 'Of the latter, indeed,' said Bagehot, 'he became so fully master that some people fancied he must have been in the trade; so complete was the familiarity which he displayed with "brown muscovado," "white clayed," and all other technical terms which are generally inscrutably puzzling to parliamentary statesmen.'

Hansard records Wilson's steady performance in the House of Commons as a speaker on topics of almost unrelieved dullness: 'Copper Ore Duties',

'Spirits in Bond', 'Malt Tax' and 'Milling Trade (Ireland)' are a small sample. And in 1852, when he was in opposition and more free to choose those debates in which he participated, they were 'The Budget', 'Sugar Duties', 'Sugar-Producing Colonies' and 'Free Trade'. 'Papa brings on a motion on sugar tomorrow night', wrote Julia to Greg; 'we go to hear him; we feel a purely dutiful interest in the subject.'[14]

As Financial Secretary to the Treasury Wilson was in charge of the financial detail of national expenditure, which included dealing with the minutiae of shepherding financial measures through the House and answering questions on the civil estimates. The multiplicity of subjects on which he was required to provide figures can be indicated by taking just one month – January 1854 – when they consisted of: Customs Officers, Post Office Arrangements, Duchy of Cornwall, Kingston-upon-Hull Bribery Commission, Colonial Postage, Export of Arms, Exchequer Bills, Dublin Hospital, West Surrey Electors and Copper Coinage for the Colonies.

The Economist, of course, faithfully represented all of Wilson's concerns, for they were all relevant to the men of business. He neither sought nor shirked coverage of his speeches, which were reported in exactly the same manner as anyone else's. The paper may have lost because Wilson could devote so little time to it, but it gained through the authoritative nature of its information and the prestige of its proprietor.

When his party came back to power in June 1859, Wilson was more than ready for a change. He had been offered the Vice-Presidency of the Board of Trade in 1855, and had refused, as the then convention would have required him to stand for election again and he feared he might lose. The following year the Secretary of State for the Colonies, Henry Labouchere, ex-President of the Board of Trade, had offered him the governorship of the Australian colony of Victoria, which Wilson was happy to take. They had reckoned without the Queen:

> The Queen has received Mr Labouchere's letter, and hastens to express her opinion that Mr Wilson would not be at all a proper person to be Governor of so large and important a Colony as Victoria. It ought to be a man of higher position and standing, and who could represent his Sovereign adequately . . .
>
> She wishes further to observe that Mr Labouchere should in future take care that, while he tries to ascertain the feelings of people as to their

accepting the offer of a Colonial appointment, before he submits them to the Queen, that these enquiries should be made in such a manner as not to lead these persons to *expect* the appointment, else, if the *Queen* does not approve of them, the whole odium of the refusal will fall upon her.[15]

Eliza Wilson bleakly recorded the follow-up.

> *19 May 1856* Papa learned that the Queen had objected to his being given the Governorship of Victoria.
>
> *20 May 1856* Papa sent his resignation to Ld. Palmerston.
>
> *23 May 1856* Papa called on Ld. Palmerston who persuaded him to retain his office.

In the winter of that year Palmerston suggested Wilson to the Queen for 'a well-paid and agreeable position secure from the effect of changes of administration' and for which 'he would be extremely fit'.[16]

> *8 November 1856* Papa wrote to Mama, J. & me to give separately our candid opinion & feeling about accepting the Chairmanship of the Board of Inland Revenue.

As Palmerston had half expected ('Mr Wilson, however, is known to wish for some promotion in political office & that may render him disinclined to go to the Board of Inland Revenue.'), Wilson refused. Although he thought it 'a good pillow', he 'did not wish to lie down'.[17] In June 1859, however, when Palmerston asked him to become Financial Secretary yet again, Wilson refused. He wanted a less demanding job and he hoped that by taking the Vice-Presidency of the Board of Trade, in due course he would get the Presidency.

Only a few weeks later, Sir Charles Wood, Secretary of State for India, wrote to the Queen that 'in the present financial state of India, it is very desirable to send to that country some person well versed in such matters who may carry with him the financial knowledge acquired by the experience of this country'.

> The means of doing so will be by sending out as the fourth member of Council who is ordinarily a lawyer, a person versed in financial matters under whom the departments of the Indian government may be formed. Your Majesty's government entirely concur in the expediency of this course & Sir Charles Wood would humbly submit to your Majesty the name of the

Honourable James Wilson, the Vice-President of the Board of Trade as a person certainly qualified for such a post.[18]

The financial crisis in India was a result of the conflict generally called the Indian Mutiny, which broke out in 1857; the last flickerings of revolt were not extinguished until 1859. There had been mounting discontent among conservative Indians over the inroads of westernisation, and the annexations of Oudh and other princely states; and the Bengal army had been alarmed by stories about the imminent introduction of new cartridges greased with beef and pork fat (which would outrage both Hindu and Muslim soldiers). The appointment of too many British officers to Indian regiments had also had frustrating effects on Indians' promotion. After the conflict (in which, in fact, more Indians fought alongside the British than against them) various reforms were belatedly carried out, one of them being the takeover by the British government of the vestigial powers of the East India Company; in place of the President of the Board of Control was now a Secretary of State for India.

The *Economist* line had been predictable, urging the necessity of firm but just action: the Mutiny had been 'the revolt of an army' not 'the hatred of a people'. The paper had always reflected the attitude of the more evangelically inclined of the British administrators in India, who believed in ruling a colony in the interests of the inhabitants rather than just for profit. The 'essence of the warning we have just received', said Hutton in *The Economist*, is 'the duty of governing these "dim common populations" not for our sake, but for their own, with a single eye to India's welfare'.[19] However, his strong support for the modernisers meant that there was little sympathy for the conservative reactions which their activities often aroused in India. The 'arbitrary usages' of Indian civilisation were a matter of perplexity – almost affront. 'Caste itself', wrote Hutton – 'at first no doubt taking its rise in the natural affinities of kindred and nationality – had been hedged in and defended by a multitude of the most absurd and superstitious usages which, unfortunately for the Hindoos, were burdens that not only their fathers and they had been quite able to bear, but most anxious to parade, to foster, and to increase.'

> Instead of rising up in indignant revolt against the network of fretting observances which the lapse of time gradually introduced into the usages of caste, the Hindoo mind abjectly accepted and sanctified them . . . Arbitrary custom overrides everything and constitutes itself their only religion. What

is morbid in the Englishman is natural in the Hindoo. Dr Johnson's fidgetty anxiety to tread on every paving-stone in his daily walk, might have spread into a new caste-law in India, and imposed itself on thousands of feeble minds as an indisputable rule of piety.

This irrational conservatism, colliding with the rational conservatisms of science and art, was bound to be defeated.

> To create a circulation of *classes* – a social power by which the *lowest* rise into independence, so that the whole frame of society is periodically renewed, is characteristic of that humane civilisation which England, and England alone, has introduced into India. Nothing short of her influence could ever break through the baleful influence of an obstructive caste-conservatism, and a vast system of physical as well as moral superstition.[20]

But though the paper might castigate irrational native practices, it was quick to denounce as hypocritical the popular newspapers that had attacked caste, for supporting 'social and legal distinctions between Englishmen and natives'. Their attitude and language appealed 'not to the right pride of Englishmen, but to that haughty and almost insolent inclination to "cow" an inferior race to which we are all as Englishmen, from our high national position, in no slight degree liable . . . it is an argument not in favour of recognising boldly, what no one can ignore, the superiority of the English character to the Oriental, but in favour of *stereotyping that superiority as an institution*, and so repressing the rise of the native caste beneath'. The evil of all 'caste-conservatisms' was that they 'shut out hope and emulation'. There was 'caste enough, and too much, even in England. But we have little of this hopeless and petrified sort.' The 'rabid' Anglo-Indians (this term then meant British residents in India) were savagely crying out for an arbitrary Oriental-style policy. 'Should we ever establish designedly an *English caste* in India, – in other words, should we ever systematically attempt to rule the people through the worst part of their nature by adopting that worst nature for ourselves, – we should sign the doom of our Indian Empire; and no manly Englishman could in his own heart wish to see that doom delayed.'[21]

The words were Hutton's, but the sentiments were passionately shared by Wilson, whose concern for India was warring with his perception of his best interests. He was undecided about whether to take the job, he told Wood, because 'while I have every motive to remain as I am, in a position in which I have at command everything in life I could desire, with a safe seat in Parliament as long as I desire to occupy it, with the enjoyment of what I regard as the best society in London, because the most intelligent and intellectual, and in the midst of a public political career with which I have every reason to be in every way highly satisfied, all of which *and much more* must be suddenly torn to pieces and abandoned if I accepted such a service. Still if it were presented to me under circumstances which made it assume the character of a public duty, I would be prepared to give it a favourable consideration, and would not lightly allow personal sacrifices, however great, to stand in the way of my undertaking it.'[22]

'Your father gives a very amusing account of the interior of the Board of Trade,' wrote Bagehot to his wife almost a fortnight later, 'but he thinks more of India than of anything else.'[23] Initially unhappy about the idea, Bagehot acquiesced when it became clear that Wilson believed 'that in even *attempting* to sort out the finances of India 'he would be doing the greatest and most lasting public service that it was in *his* power to accomplish'. Accepting the office on 11 August on the understanding that he would be in effect Indian Chancellor of the Exchequer, Wilson spent until October acquiring a thorough briefing from politicians and merchants around Britain. 'I have learned a great deal about India the last two months', he told Cornewall Lewis as he left. 'I have lived almost exclusively among ex-Indians of one kind or another and have heard all views. The difficulties do not diminish by better acquaintance. *Time, distance*, and divided authority, with the sacrificing consequences of procrastination and shirking responsibility and the tendency to get rid of difficulties by compromise or delays are fatal elements in the character of the Gt. of India. The best man for India is he who will *act*, and trust for approval.'[24] Other last-minute responsibilities included saying goodbye to friends, colleagues and constituents, visiting Hawick (where he was made an Honorary Burgess) and presiding at the wedding of his fifth daughter, Sophie, to William Halsey, a junior official in the Indian civil service whom Wilson appointed as his private secretary.

He leant heavily on his senior son-in-law. 'Your husband is very tired', Bagehot reported. 'I sat up late last night with your father about his will which was a cheerful topic . . . It is clear I must stay over Sunday, probably till they go.'[25] He had agreed to be nominated along with three Wilson brothers as a trustee for Mrs Wilson and her daughters. More than that, as Wilson explained in his farewell letter to Cornewall Lewis, who was now Home

Secretary: 'My friend Bagehot has undertaken a sort of general superinten-
dence of *The Economist* and Hutton remains Editor under him. Will you
kindly allow Bagehot to call upon you occasionally?'

With his wife and daughters Matilda, Zoe and Sophie (Julia and Emilie
were to join them later), Wilson left England on 19 October. He reached
Calcutta by the end of November and went thence (partly on a railway line he
had planned ten years previously) to join the Viceroy (since 1858), Lord
Canning, on his tour of the Upper Provinces of India – an experience he
enjoyed greatly and which gave him the opportunity for extensive consultations with revenue officers. Richard Temple, whom he recruited on to his
staff* shortly afterwards, later provided a sketch of Wilson in India, which
vividly brings out what Bagehot called his 'experiencing nature' as well as his
passionate – almost visionary – approach to political economy. 'I became
much attached to him,' Temple wrote in 1882, 'and whether as master,
teacher, or friend, he made an impression which time cannot weaken.'

> He was of the middle height, with considerable breadth of chest and
> shoulder, his physical frame indicating strength and endurance. His age was
> fifty-four years, rather late perhaps for a man who proceeds to India for the
> first time; still he seemed to bring with him an abundant stock of freshness
> and vigour. His complexion was light and the broad prominent brow,
> overshadowing the eyes, gave an intellectual cast to the face. He had a keen
> perception of every object that met his view, a habit of casting observant
> looks in all directions, and an extraordinarily retentive memory of what he
> saw, heard or read.

Temple found him grave while intent on work, but bright and vivacious in
society.

> He delighted in India, and regarded her resources with hopeful interest, her
> people with sympathy, her scenery with admiration, her antiquities with
> curiosity. Nothing, he said, could be imagined more intensely interesting
> than India; with the ancient cities, the relics of decayed dynasties, the
> thronging population, the bustle of trade at every corner, the expansive
> plains bounded by alpine ranges affording a climate for new varieties of
> production, the large rivers, the magnificent canals irrigating the country,

*Temple, in 1868, became a successor of Wilson's as Financial Member of the Council.

the careful agriculture with cultivation up to the roadside, the thrifty and economical habits of the people bent on active and profitable pursuits.

Temple found it both instructive and amusing to accompany Wilson on his walks in the suburbs of Calcutta during the early morning.

> He would observe every Native garden that we passed, talking about the natural habitat, culture and uses of the trees or plants. He would often stop at the wayside booths or shops, discussing the manufacture, prices and style of the wares. He would note the carts, drawn by bullocks and laden with produce, on their way to the capital, also the men and women carrying head-loads of articles to market. Then he would ever and anon exclaim that the country seemed bursting, as it were, with vitality and industry.

The fairs and especially the central market of Calcutta 'offered to him an extensive scope for economic reflection'.

> He would watch the piece-goods and fancy-wares from Europe, the Oriental stuffs made in far-off cities, the flowers and vegetables brought by railway from gardens distant hundreds of miles, the game snared or shot in forests and marshes. He regarded all these goods, indeed, with the eye of an economist, in reference to their uses, but having a lively imagination he recognised their beauty also. If a thing seemed beautiful he felt all the more zealous in promoting its usefulness; if a thing was useful he appreciated it the better from its being beautiful also.

Wilson speculated much in conversation on the role of trade as an agency for bringing about peace among men and nations, a view he pressed strongly on a Scots missionary who visited him to urge 'the importance of cultivating kindly relations with the Natives'. He was tremendously anxious to understand India 'as she actually was'.

> While keeping in recollection the broad traits of human nature, as common to mankind in all times and places, he was especially desirous to realise to himself the idiosyncrasies, aptitudes and tendencies, even the prejudices, of the Natives. Although the people had to be led gently towards the paths of economic science, yet he wished to show the tenderest consideration towards the thoughts and sentiments springing from their historic antecedents. He hoped also to evince that moderation and restraint which befitted the peculiar position of the British as foreign masters of an eastern empire.

Such in brief was Wilson, the first scientific economist who had ever visited India. He probably learnt more of the Country in a very short time, than any person who ever landed on its shores, and his general information extended daily.[26]

While Wilson immersed himself in the work of trying to extinguish the deficit and set Indian finances on a sound footing, back in England, Bagehot was valiantly coping with the domestic and professional responsibilities handed over to him. 'The great change of late to me', he wrote in January to his sister-in-law, Zoe, 'is that having the Economist to look after I come to London and call on public characters and sit (like Jet [Emilie's dog]) with my mouth open hearing what they say. I do not say much myself, though I think if I was fifty and a cabinet minister, *would* not I talk platitudes? It must be such a pleasure to say that two and two make four and see people take it in or seem to as a new truth, and *then* to say they make five and find people swallow that too. I am sure if they treated me in that way, I shd. not say anything. I shd. assent – for I consider old people and great people have a right to it – and besides it is *easy*.'[27]

Although he put a brave face on it, Bagehot found his new responsibility onerous. The job of keeping *The Economist* up to standard was a heavy addition to those of full-time banker and co-editor of the *National Review*, and though Wilson had introduced him to a wide range of political contacts, he still felt himself an outsider. Hutton struggled on, but needed a great deal of help. 'Mr Wilson used to write the economical and financial articles in the paper mainly himself', wrote Bagehot to Gladstone, 'as well as direct its general policy; and both these departments have now in *some sort* fallen to me, but I of course, independently of all other differences, feel beyond measure the want of that *living* knowledge which his habits of public life gave him.'[28] Still, the very fact that he could confide his problem to the Chancellor of the Exchequer and ask for and receive advice on suitable material for the paper showed that he was going about his job with great *éclat*. And Wilson was writing to Bagehot as well as sending him copies of all his official correspondence, so as matters developed in India, *The Economist* proved exceptionally well-informed. (Richard Temple also contributed five letters from India.) Indeed Bagehot felt so close to Wilson as to have the 'constant habit of referring to his mind and keeping up a sort of mental dialogue with him'.[29] Having such a deep understanding of the intellect that had conceived the paper and directed it for seventeen years protected Bagehot from the likelihood of major errors of judgment.

Neither Bagehot nor Wilson worried about how *The Economist* should handle the problem of discussing its proprietor's activities in India, which were followed with keen interest by men of business at home. 'You must deal with my speech and my policy as you think best, without thinking of *me* at all', wrote Wilson in February after bringing his budget before the Legislative Council. 'At this distance I may be treated as a stranger.'[30] While *The Economist*'s Indian coverage was obviously pro-Wilson, it was geared as far as possible towards the factual and in that Bagehot genuinely approved of Wilson's policies, there was no conflict of interest. (Indeed among the natural constituency of *The Economist* there was much enthusiasm for Wilson's plans: one of his many fan-letters came from that eminent man of business, Prince Albert, who wrote that in Wilson's financial statement and plans for a paper currency, he had 'treated most important but most difficult questions in a masterly manner which would not have been possible but for your strong belief in the unalterable truths of the laws of political economy taught by abstract science'.)[31] When Sir Charles Trevelyan, Governor of Madras, made public his opposition to Wilson's budget – an indiscretion that almost torpedoed Wilson's well-presented and well-received schemes for retrenchment and new taxes, caused a major row in India and England and led to Trevelyan's recall – Bagehot kept his cool despite his personal feelings. *The Economist* analysed Trevelyan's criticisms fairly and in depth and concluded in a measured fashion:

> Sir C. Trevelyan thinks there is danger in the course Mr Wilson has taken. But is there not greater danger in his own course? He has told the natives of Madras that new taxes which are unjust and unnecessary are about to be levied upon them. He has used his authority as local Governor to spread this doctrine. He has hinted that he expects the natives will rebel. Who will be to blame if they do rebel? Surely the ruler who was intrusted with an authority over 30,000,000 of people, and who incited them to resistance.[32]

'The way you have treated the Trevelyan matter was fair, reasonable, and dignified', commented Wilson, whose private comments on Trevelyan were forgiving but comprehensively damning. (They knew each other well, having worked closely together and disagreed at the Treasury. Trevelyan had featured in Eliza Wilson's journal in January 1855, on a working visit with George Arbuthnot and another colleague, as the girls' favourite of the three:

'Sir C. Trevelyan is assistant secretary to the Treasury . . . His pedantry & unpredictability make him very unpopular with his collaborateurs, but in private his gentlemanlike manners, genialness, genuine goodness & the universality of his knowledge & interest make him a very pleasant & instructive companion. At least the impression he produced on us was such & though his moralizing may sometimes have a touch of pedantry, it is so genuine & so modest as to do one good *malgré soi* & make one feel how much more thoughtful & unworldly he is than the generality of those one is in the habit of meeting.'[33]

Wilson had expected trouble from him in India, but 'never that he would proceed to such extremities'. He had for years considered him scarcely responsible for his actions, 'having so impulsive a mind, so ill-balanced, with such an overweening confidence in himself . . . with a large smattering upon everything but profound in nothing; with a dull apprehension but the most dogged obstinacy I ever saw: and with an inordinate vanity and love of notoriety to be gratified; without the slightest judgment or discretion or forethought, or calculation of consequences: all these characteristics lead a man so heedlessly into danger and control him so completely as to leave him hardly a responsible being'.[34] For his part, Trevelyan believed Wilson 'had neither religion nor gentlemanly feeling, but only what he thought worldly wisdom', was unscrupulous in achieving what he wanted, and prepared to sacrifice the future of India to bolster his reputation and enable him to return home as Chancellor of the Exchequer, and was a byword in England for selfish egotism.[35] The rights and wrongs of the controversy are complex. The Secretary of State for India, Sir Charles Wood, was virtually forced by Lord Canning to recall his great friend Trevelyan, and, primed by Trevelyan, made it clear to both Canning and Wilson that he thought Wilson had acted hastily and applied English ideas unsuitably.

There are only a few letters between Bagehot and Wilson that deal in any detail with the affairs of *The Economist*. Two concerned the emergence of a competitor, which in its first issue referred to *The Economist* – not by name – as a 'journal of respectability' in which 'political, literary, and even agricultural topics take precedence of those of a commercial character'. 'The opposition to the Economist has appeared and is called "The Money Market Review,"* price 6d. *un*stamped [stamp duty was 1d. per copy]', Bagehot

---

*It ultimately became transmogrified into the highly successful *Investors Chronicle and Stock Exchange Gazette*.

informed Wilson. 'But you need be under no apprehension about it [as it is dull] and feeble in the extreme – not giving a tithe of the information the Economist gives on business subjects, and written in a very inferior way. I am generally on the dismal side on all subjects, but I am cheerful about this. I am sure it will have no effect on us. Mr Aird [first manager, then publisher, of *The Economist*] says it will be advantageous.'[36]

'About the *Economist* and your threatened opposition,' wrote Wilson in a letter that crossed Bagehot's,

> I am very glad to see that in every way it holds its own so well: its writing is certainly as a whole very good and its views sound. One number only I complained of because it consisted in a great measure of an extract from my speech and another from my Minute. The more I see of life and public life, the less I like to see my name prominently to documents. Throughout the late contest I never put anything in the shape of a Minute but always in the form of a despatch from the whole Govt. It removed that unhappy personal characteristic to all public proceedings which Trevelyan could not resist; the passion of seeing C.E. Trevelyan to documents has been his ruin. So pray say nothing and admit nothing, that looks like a personal puff or undue pushing forward of me . . .
>
> But to return to the *Economist* and the opposition. I don't fear the opposition but I am sorry you lose your City correspondent [unidentified]. But it won't answer, and in six months he will come back if you can make room for him. My advice would be take no notice whatever of it: if they try to goad you into controversy don't be tempted. It will only give them importance. And by this means you will not make an enemy of any one connected with it. I have seen this tried before: it is almost impossible it can succeed. All you can do is to keep a good lookout, as you and Hutton have done, and go on the even tenor of your way.[37]

That same letter of Wilson's, written in July 1860, went into considerable detail on recent developments and the progress he had made on his five major objectives: the extension of taxation to the trading community; the establishment of a paper currency; the reorganisation of the financial system, including annual budgets, estimates and audits; the introduction of a cheaper and more efficient police system and consequent reduction of the native army; and the introduction of public works and roads to promote increased production of cotton, flax, wool and European raw materials. (He had come a long way from the quasi-anarchic Wilson of the 1840s.) He reported that he was far advanced with all but the fifth objective, which was inchoate.

> But you will call it a very large order. However, you have no idea of the increased capacity of the mind for undertaking a special service of this kind, when removed to a new scene of action, and when one throws off all the cares and engagements more or less trivial by which one is surrounded in ordinary life, and throws one's whole soul into such special service, and particularly when one feels assured of having the power to carry it out. I cannot tell you with what ease one determines the largest and gravest question here compared with in England, and I am certain that the more one can exercise real power, there is by far the greater tendency to moderation, care, and prudence.

Wilson was again too sanguine: he died on 11 August, 1860, at the age of 55, from dysentery aggravated by overwork. He had been ill in June and July but had stubbornly disregarded advice to leave the dangerous climate of Calcutta for a time. Two days beforehand, when he knew he was dying, he was visited by Lord Canning, to whom he talked 'chiefly about some private arrangements, and then a little about public matters – the Currency Bill, the Military Finance Commission, etc . . . He said that he knew how it must end . . . I was much struck by the tone in which he spoke of public matters;– not a word of self, or of his own name, or share in the work at hand; and yet with great hopefulness of the success of most of the machinery which he has set at work. It was very touching.'[38] And taking devotion to duty almost to a level of self-parody, on the day of his death almost his last words were 'Take care of my Income Tax.' His funeral on the following day was said to be the largest ever held in Calcutta, where a statue was raised to him.*

('I BOAST THAT I AM OF THIS RACE AND BLOOD' was the first singularly inappropriate inscription on this slightly more than life-size marble statue. Later, no longer wanted in Calcutta, it was shipped to London

---

*His job was offered first to Bagehot, then to his old Treasury colleague and crony of Lord Overstone, George Arbuthnot; it was accepted by the Financial Secretary to the Treasury, Samuel Laing. When Laing resigned two years later the post went to Sir Charles Trevelyan. The Wilson family were distressed, and Bagehot wrote on 8 November, 1862, a long article in *The Economist* criticising the appointment though noting that 'the conductors of this journal cannot profess to be impartial'. Subsequent letters and reassurances from Sir Charles Wood salved the wound; Wood even sent to Bagehot a letter from Trevelyan speaking warmly if inconsistently of Wilson's virtues and achievements.

in the care of the Standard Chartered Bank, with whom Wilson's connection as one of its first directors was so tenuous that his daughter did not even mention it in her two-volume biography. Perhaps not knowing that the relationship was more apparent than real, the bank kept him outside their headquarters for many years along with a plaque reading: 'THIS STATUE FORMERLY STOOD IN THE DALHOUSIE INSTITUTE WHERE IT WAS ERECTED BY THE MERCANTILE COMMUNITY OF CALCUTTA AS A TRIBUTE TO THE PUBLIC SERVICES OF THE RIGHT HONOURABLE JAMES WILSON 1805–1860 FOUNDER OF THE CHARTERED BANK OF INDIA, AUSTRALIA & CHINA AND SUBSEQUENTLY FIRST FINANCE MEMBER OF THE VICEROY'S COUNCIL'. In 1990 *The Economist* heard not only that the statue was in London but that the bank wanted to get rid of it, so James Wilson was transported to the Economist Tower, where it was felt he could stand gravely on the surrounding 'Plaza'. Experts warned against his marble being exposed any longer to the weather, so unenthusiastically it was agreed that he must live inside in a corner.

The modern *Economist* is known in artistic circles for its encouragement of modern art, which festoons its walls and appears regularly in exhibitions of sculpture outside and paintings and sculpture inside. Much of what turns up is to the untutored eye very bizarre indeed. The fifteen-storey building the paper inhabits itself dates only from the early 1960s and is remorselessly minimalist. It would be difficult to find a more magnificently incongruous object for these surroundings than this dour-looking, highly conventional piece of high-Victorian art. Yet, after a shaky start ('Isn't he *ugly?*' was the initial general response), Wilson has gradually become an important icon. Coins (real – or at Christmas, chocolate) are dropped in his outstretched hand to cheer him up; on his birthday and his wedding anniversary he gets a buttonhole; at Christmas he is given tinsel necklaces; special occasions produce presents of ties and hats, and the ebullient receptionist, Patricia Coleman, involves him in general conversation and acts as his spokesman. In the exhibition to mark the 150th anniversary of the paper's foundation, he stands in the centre on a red soapbox, continuing his crusade. His new inscription says simply:

JAMES WILSON

BORN HAWICK 1805

DIED CALCUTTA 1860

MANUFACTURER, JOURNALIST AND PUBLIC SERVANT

FOUNDER IN 1843 OF THE ECONOMIST)

There was a mixed fate for Wilson's Indian reforms. His currency plans, for instance, were damaged. In 1861, Bonamy Price, later Professor of Political Economy in Oxford, wrote furiously to Richard Holt Hutton: 'I am perfectly savage this morning. That . . . Wood has been ear-wigged by Overstone, and upset Wilson's glorious scheme in India. It is a public disgrace, and calamity. Never before were scientific power and practical political talent so combined as in Wilson: and the last Indian Minute was the glory of his life. And to be overthrown by such contemptible, despicable twaddle, as that a paper currency must vary in quantity as if it were metallic. My wrath now overflows on you and Bagehot. You were the guardians of Wilson's fame: and you never would let me do anything to set forth the power, the truth and the accuracy of that unrivalled paper on a paper currency. And now the one distinctive greatness of his life is gone. I am glad you are not in my way to-day; you would find me dangerous.'[39] His income tax, too, suffered, being dropped for a time after the five-year trial period. In the long run, however, many of his achievements were lasting. Sixty-seven years after his death, a review in *The Economist* of Wilson's biography inspired a long letter from an academic at the University of Bombay, who had written a book on Indian finance. Wilson was 'the first and pre-eminent founder of present-day public finance in India', who had 'a place in Indian finance comparable only to that given to Alexander Hamilton' in America.

It is a permanent wonder to students of the subject how any public servant could have achieved in eight months what he did and that, too, with so much success . . . Not only did he introduce a new system of taxation, an improved system of budgeting, and laid the basis of our paper currency system, but he introduced a proper system of accounting and a system of police. Wilson has so stamped his figure and character on Indian finance that we can never think of it without him. He served the interests of India with conspicuous efficiency and a zeal particularly his own. He saw things had to be done and done quickly, and he had the strength to do them, brushing aside formulas and conventions. Indeed, to many, his greatest and most lasting work is in Indian public finance.[40]

The main reaction to his death, noted Bagehot later, was 'That he should have left a great English career *for this!*', yet ironically it was India that gave Wilson the opportunity to prove himself a man with greatness in him. Bagehot, inevitably, provided the best epitaph: 'He was placed in many changing circumstances, and in the gradual ascent of life was tried by many increasing difficulties. But at every step his mind grew with the occasion. *We* at least believe that he had a great sagacity and a great equanimity, which might have been fitly exercised on the very greatest affairs. But it was not so to be.'

A month after Wilson was buried, Eliza Bagehot's diary records: 'Walter stayed at home to write for the *Economist*. At one o'clock we saw Papa's death in the *Times*. Julia found it and called me and we both ran to Walter's study.' The *Times* notice was reproduced in a black-edged issue of *The Economist* along with a statement that 'The conductors of this journal do not feel that they can at present do more than record this mournful event in the words of others. It has come too suddenly upon them. If they should themselves say anything on the subject, it must be hereafter and deliberately.'[41] Bagehot found himself 'bewildered' and suffered deeply. 'I never really contemplated the contingency of his death', he wrote to Sophie's husband, William Halsey. 'He had so much life, vigour, energy, that it was and even still is – peculiarly difficult to me to connect him with that idea.'[42] It was a theme picked up by his *Economist* colleagues: 'The whole thing is terrible beyond expression, the more so that I cannot reconcile the idea of death with Mr Wilson in any way', wrote Hutton. And Greg thought Wilson 'the last man in the world with whom one could connect the idea of death'.[43]

'All I implore of you', wrote Hutton to Bagehot, 'is to let some worthy notice be taken of his life and character in the *Economist*, *and soon*, before the warmth of public sentiment is quite cooled concerning his sad end. If you delay long this will be so in the *outer* world. And I feel very strongly that something is due to him in his own paper, as I am sure you will do.' At Hutton's further suggestion, the paper did him proud, with a fourteen-page supplement in November: 'MEMOIR OF THE RIGHT HON. JAMES WILSON by his son-in-law WALTER BAGEHOT, ESQ.'[44] Bagehot also performed his filial duty in *The Economist* over the next few years by keeping a close and critical eye on developments in Indian finance. Yet although in the short term he did much to keep Wilson's name alive, paradoxically, in the long term he had much to do with the eclipse of his reputation in England. Financial Secretaries to the Treasury are not remembered long by posterity, but founders and editors of great magazines often are. Wilson was not entirely forgotten, but he was seen as a forbidding and pedestrian figure compared to his glittering son-in-law.

Yet if Bagehot was, as he has been memorably described, Victorian England's most versatile genius, Wilson was the embodiment of her most striking virtues. He was self-reliant, self-made, successful, diligent, strong-willed, thorough, honourable, genial, tolerant and charitable in human relations, a loving family man and a loyal friend. Trevelyan's impugning of his motives does not convince, for a man of unscrupulous ambition could not have won the intense regard of men like Bagehot, Greg and Hutton. As an editor, he had the requisite passion, principle, talent and doggedness to get the product right. As a recruiter of staff he encouraged talent – even genius – and he was unafraid of unorthodox opinions or quirkiness of intellect. Not all of them were a great success on the paper, but the very roll-call of Thomas Hodgskin, Herbert Spencer, William Rathbone Greg, Richard Holt Hutton and Walter Bagehot is evidence of the extraordinary breadth of vision of the hat-manufacturer from Hawick. It was he too who had set the internationalist tone of the paper and set up a splendid network of correspondents at home and abroad. No one would have been more distressed than Bagehot to know that his own paper failed to recognise that its success was more due to its founder and first editor than to anyone else.

Bagehot soon realised that he could not long continue to act as executor of Wilson's estate, head of his family and custodian of his newspaper from a base in the West Country. Most weeks he went to London on Wednesday afternoon, returning late on Saturday evening. He had also had to cope with the problem posed by his dearest friend's inadequacies as editor. In December 1860 Hutton wrote to a friend to say he was applying for an educational post and needed a testimonial.

> The step is the more necessary for me as Bagehot has almost made up his mind to come to town and devote himself in great measure to the Economist,– with an ultimate view, I imagine, to Parliament. This would not necessarily dispense with me but it would prevent any chance of an

improving position at the *Economist*, and perhaps curtail my general *influence* in the politics, which I should not like. However if I do not succeed, I shall still be able to work on at it if I please. Literary work is not without interest, but it is not what one could wish; and the general principles of Jowett's essay on Casuistry have a good deal of application to it as a profession.[45]

Although this is the only direct evidence that Hutton had chafed at constraints on his freedom of expression, his subsequent career corroborates it strongly. There was, for instance, the passage in an 1861 article that could not have appeared while Wilson was alive and a minister in Palmerston's government:

Lord Palmerston has twice within the week had to reply to an attack upon his political ethics; in neither case has he been wholly successful, and in one case very much the reverse. With all his high qualities, his political morality is not of the most scrupulous kind. He is a utilitarian, and like most statesmen who have been acclimatised to the atmosphere of the joint responsibilities of a rather miscellaneous Cabinet, his treatment of all questions hinging on individual responsibility is, to say the least, free.[46]

It was almost as delicately put as the veiled attack contained in a leader Wilson had written in 1843, while he was still politically a free agent.

Sir Robert Peel is not a *corruptionist*, and personally will have nothing to do with anything like a job. Lord John Russell's character stands as high; and though the reputation which Lord Palmerston bears is that of being more adroit and versatile, we have no right to impute to him anything which would be unworthy the character of a gentleman.[47]

Nor, under Wilson the politician, could this swingeing judgment have appeared: 'The nation has little reason just now to be proud of either of its great parties, – either of the Conservatism which is strong only in cowardice, or the Liberalism which is bold without belief.'[48]

Yet though Bagehot's rein was looser, it was still a rein. Bagehot's strong pragmatic streak was always likely to baulk at Hutton's overwhelming tendency to moral censoriousness. The difference between them was to be clearly demonstrated in the way *The Economist* and the *Spectator* dealt respectively with the American Civil War.

Bagehot moved to London in April 1861. In early summer he became

THE POLITICS OF EQUILIBRIUM 225

editor, the problem with Hutton having been posthumously resolved by James Wilson. He, it emerged, had been approached in Calcutta in 1859 by Meredith Townsend, editor and proprietor of the *Friend of India*, who wanted to start a newspaper in England. Wilson advised Townsend to try to recruit Hutton, believing the kind of paper Townsend envisaged to be far better suited to him than was *The Economist*. In due course Townsend bought the ailing *Spectator* and on meeting Hutton, he was so impressed that he offered him not only the co-editorship but the co-proprietorship. It was a perfect solution to both Hutton's and Bagehot's problems. Hutton and Townsend had complementary interests and gifts and were to work together harmoniously and most successfully until Hutton's death in 1897: Bagehot was far better off running *The Economist* alone. And since the offices of the two papers were but a few yards apart, the two friends could offer each other constant support and companionship.

CHAPTER XVII

'He was like no one else'

Tell me who is Mr Bagehot? you spoke as if you knew him. He was lately most complimentary to me in print. And how do you pronounce his name? Bagot, or Badgeot, or Badgs-hot or (Gallice), Bargeo? *John Henry Newman, 1867*

Newman's friend responded with 'Baige-ot', making confusion worse confounded.[1] The name should be pronounced 'Bajot', the 'g' being soft, as in badger, a fifteenth-century variant.[2] People dislike revealing their ignorance, so his unpronounceable surname was a major cause of Bagehot's failure to achieve the level of posthumous fame his genius deserved. Another was that for the greater part of his working life he edited the anonymous and forbidding *Economist*. A third was his early death, a fourth the sheer difficulty of categorising him. He was a banker, editor, essayist, journalist and failed politician, who wrote on economics, education, history, law, literature, politics, religion and social psychology. His books cover an odd range of subjects under deadly titles, those published during his lifetime being: *Estimates of Some Englishmen and Scotchmen*; *The English Constitution*; *A Practical Plan for Assimilating the English and American Money, as a Step Towards a Universal Money*; *Physics and Politics or Thoughts on the Application of the Principles of 'Natural Selection' and 'Inheritance' to Political Society* and *Lombard Street: a Description of the Money Market*. To the uninformed of the present generation, they sound like part of a job-lot lining the walls of a public house or restaurant with a library decor. A fifth reason, therefore, is that his subjects seem complex and heavy. At the same time, self-important intellectuals instinctively dismiss him as lightweight, sensing perhaps his antipathy to what they stand for. As Augustine Birrell, Liberal politician and man of letters put it, Bagehot 'hated dullness, apathy, pomposity, the time-worn phrase, the greasy platitude. His writings are an armoury of offensive weapons against pompous fools. The revenge taken by these paltry, meaningless persons is to hiss *paradox* whenever the name of their tormentor is mentioned.'[3] Also against Bagehot is 'that specialists do not lightly forgive their colleagues for competence in other fields'[4] as well as the assumption of this age of 'experts' that the polymath is by definition superficial. Yet Francis Hirst, editor of *The Economist* from 1907 to 1916, was not being fanciful when he ranked Bagehot as a journalist with Cobbett, Hazlitt and Morley, as an economist with Bastiat, as a 'political speculator' with Mill or Bryce and as a literary critic with Matthew Arnold.[5] Then there is the narrowness of modern readers; few of us are attracted by the notion of reading about both the money market and Social Darwinism, the English constitution and the poetry of Shelley. And there is of course the added presumption that academic progress will have long ago rendered Bagehot's ideas on all his areas of interest out-of-date.

More than sixty years after Bagehot's death, William Irvine observed that a 'quiet body of readers are aware that in his time Walter Bagehot decently occupied a prominent position in the financial world, that he made money unobtrusively, that he gravely edited a grave journal and wielded a powerful influence in the "City," that he published a few sedate tomes in later years and a few dashing essays in youth, and that in middle life he wrote dignified love letters to his future wife. What could relegate a man more rapidly to oblivion?'[6]

Irvine's splendid appraisal demonstrated the brilliance and fascination of his subject, but failed to rescue him. Almost thirty years on, in 1968, the distinguished historian Jacques Barzun tried to determine why a man frequently described as a genius should remain 'a shadowy figure in that part of the public mind where reputations are considered settled' and put his finger on what was by then a key element: 'if a man has been dead nearly a hundred years and is "well-known" without being known well, a certain impatience arises at the mere mention of his name. It would be better for him to exchange his ambiguous position for one of complete obscurity. It is easier to pull Kierkegaard out of nowhere and establish his complex presence than to revise our judgments of those who have only half entered the Pantheon, whose nose and cheekbone only are showing.'[7]

Barzun was introducing the historical volumes of *The Collected Works of*

Walter Bagehot, *The Economist*'s stately tribute to its most revered name. Though well-edited, beautifully produced, and a treasure-chest for those prepared to open it, the fifteen uniform navy-blue volumes did little to attract the unconverted. Like the editor of the *Works*, Norman St John-Stevas, the paper's luminaries sought to bring their great man to a wider public. Prime Ministers and ex-Prime Ministers were hauled in to pay tribute. In 1967 Harold Wilson unveiled a blue plaque on 12 Upper Belgrave Street, where Bagehot lived from 1861 to 1870; Edward Heath spoke at the launch of the political volumes in 1974, while Harold Macmillan did the honours in 1978 for the economic and Margaret Thatcher for the miscellaneous and last volumes in 1986. She quoted from President Woodrow Wilson, one of Bagehot's most devoted admirers.

Perhaps such attentions from the great and the old merely serve to give an impression of Bagehot as the object of veneration of an 'Army of Fogies' (one of his appellations for the Conservative Party). It is an unfortunate fate for someone whose gaiety and boyishness persisted throughout his life, yet it has helped to distance him further from those who might be induced to sample him not for his common sense, which the respectable continually stress in an off-putting way, but for his sheer ability to invigorate his readers in any generation. One of his contemporaries observed to Richard Hutton that one seldom asked Bagehot a question 'without his answer making you either think or laugh, or both think and laugh together'. His writings have the same effect.

It is rare to find any attentive reader of Bagehot who does not develop an enormous affection for him: as Francis Hirst put it simply, he was 'a wonderful man'.* Yet his devoted admirers face enormous obstacles to their evangelism. It is a frustration akin to that of the man who believes he has found the secret of life but cannot persuade anyone to listen to it.

Bagehot himself would not have minded that subsequent generations took little notice of him. 'I am afraid I am callous, possibly proud, and do not care for mere general reputation', he wrote once to Eliza. 'Of course it wd. be a pleasure if it shd. come, but it is a thing which no sane man ought to make

---

*A notable exception is the poet and critic C.H. Sisson, whose *The Case of Walter Bagehot* (London, 1972) demonstrates that without a sense of humour and the capacity to recognise a generous spirit, it is possible to misunderstand Bagehot from first to last. The only merit of this feeble book is in its amusing allegation that it is the 'affable, matey tone about his work which has made thousands of mediocrities feel at home with him'.

necessary to his happiness, or think of but as a temporary luxury, even if it shd. come to him. First rate fame – the fame of great productive artists is a matter of ultimate certainty, but no other fame is. Posterity cannot take up little people, there are so many of them – *Reputation* must be acquired at the moment and the circumstances of the moment are matters of accident.'[8]

His wit was often savage – particularly in his younger days, before maturity softened, and public responsibilities trammelled, him – but it always had the serious purpose of enhancing the vividness of his imagery. Take this unforgettable description of a retired Lord Chancellor: 'There is a glare in some men's eyes which seems to say, "Beware, I am dangerous; *noli me tangere*." Lord Brougham's face has this. A mischievous excitability is the most obvious expression of it. If he were a horse, nobody would buy him; with that eye, no one could answer for his temper.'[9]

But though he especially enjoyed making fun of worthy, serious-minded people, Bagehot was only incidentally mischievous. As his introspective joy came from what he called 'playing with my mind', so his eagerness to provoke through his writing was the extrovert side of the same coin – he played with the minds of his readers. He let his quizzical eye rove around every aspect of his experience and in his early, freelance days, no section of society was safe from demolition. 'If I were asked what the great distinction was between educated people and others,' he wrote in an *Inquirer* article, 'I should say that the former have filed their opinions and that others keep them loose. A common man takes every subject as it comes; if you ask about the planets he says they are planets, if you ask him about the fixed stars he says they are fixed. On every topic he has a short, thick, little opinion, which he, on a sudden, expectorates in conversation. But he has nothing more.'[10]

It is interesting to contrast this sharpness with the more measured tone of the *Economist* editor, sixteen years later, when he addressed the Metaphysical Society on 'The Emotion of Conviction', and treated of the same topic.

> Persons of untrained minds cannot long live without some belief in any topic which comes much before them. It has been said that if you can only get a middle-class Englishman to think whether there are 'snails in Sirius,' he will soon have an opinion on it. It will be difficult to make him think, but if he does think, he cannot rest in a negative, he will come to some decision. And on any ordinary topic, of course, it is so. A grocer has a full creed as to foreign policy, a young lady a complete theory of the sacraments, as to which

neither has any doubt whatever . . . Most persons who observe their own thoughts must have been conscious of the exactly opposite state. There are cases where our intellect has gone through the arguments, and we give a clear assent to the conclusions. But our minds seem dry and unsatisfied. In that case we have the intellectual part of Belief, but want the emotional part.[11]

If the second passage lacks some of the verve of the first, it contains more wisdom – not simply in its appreciation of the doubts of middle-age, but in its greater tolerance of human frailty. There was a marked contrast with the young Bagehot, who had so much resembled those college youths who, 'never having tried their own strength, have not yet acquired a fellow-feeling for weakness'.[12]

Yet if Bagehot disliked ignorance, he was no intellectual snob. As his ready admiration for James Wilson demonstrated, intelligence and the ability to learn from experience were qualities he admired deeply. His writing is full of apposite contributions to never-ending debates about men and society, passages that stop the reader in his tracks as he recognises their relevance to his own – or indeed, to almost any – time. Many of these occur in his long essays, a medium which gave him ample scope for discursions on the human condition. Dilating on Bagehot's 'free-handedness' as a writer, Birrell felicitously described this aspect of his achievement. 'He practises no small economies . . . He writes like a gentleman . . . [and] is full of pleasant surprises and delectable speculations. He leads you into a pleasant country, and delights you with a variegated landscape.'[13] An excellent example is how rumination on the state of Europe in 1863 led Bagehot to open a *National Review* article with:

Tranquillity can never be the lot of those who rule nations. Glory they may have; the praise of men; the approbation of their own consciences; the happiness which springs from the full occupation of every faculty and every hour; the intense interest with which dealing with great affairs vivifies the whole of existence; the supreme felicity of all allotted to men – that of feeling that they have lived the life and may die the death of the truest benefactors of their race. All these rewards they may aspire to; but *repose*, a sense of enduring security, comfortable and confident relaxation of 'having attained,' of being safe in port, of everything 'being made snug,' which enables a man to say to his soul, 'Soul! thou hast much peace laid up for many years: eat, drink, be merry, and sleep;' – these blessings are not for either sovereigns or statesmen, at least not for those of Europe in modern days.[14]

And his last major work, the unfinished 'Postulates of English Political Economy', yields a classic example of an immutable political truth: 'All governments like to interfere; it elevates their position to make out that they can cure the evils of mankind. And all zealots wish they should interfere, for such zealots think they can and may convert the rulers and manipulate the state control.'[15]

Fortunately for the readers of Bagehot's *Economist*, although the brevity of leading articles and the solemnity of the paper exercised a brake on his talent, he still seized every opportunity to soar from the particular to the general: 'Nothing can exceed the torture of being constantly told "on the best authority" a vast variety of inconsistent rumours, the mass of which must be lies, but some one of which may possibly have some truth in it. Every person of any influence in such matters knows that the truth at the moment is imparted only to a very few persons – who are generally reticent, and selected because they are reticent – and that therefore the mass of grave and plausible persons who affect to know so much are usually impostors, and know nothing.'[16]

Often, too, there are passages which, with only minor adjustments of language, could be applied to specific events or situations pertaining long after Bagehot's time. For example, in *The English Constitution*, when Bagehot illustrates an assertion by reference to Aberdeen's replacement by Palmerston in 1855, as valid an example would be the replacement of Chamberlain by Churchill in 1940.

> Under a cabinet constitution at a sudden emergency this people can choose a ruler for the occasion. The great qualities, the imperious will, the rapid energy, the eager nature fit for a great crisis are not required, are impediments – in common times . . . By the structure of the world we often want, at the sudden occurrence of a grave tempest, to change the helmsman – to replace the pilot of the calm by the pilot of the storm . . . at the Crimean difficulty . . . We abolished the Aberdeen Cabinet, the ablest we have had, perhaps, since the Reform Act – a Cabinet not only adapted, but eminently adapted, for every sort of difficulty save the one it had to meet – which abounded in pacific discretion, and was wanting only in the 'daemonic

element'; we chose a statesman, who had the sort of merit then wanted, who, when he feels the steady power of England behind him, will advance without reluctance, and will strike without restraint. As was said at the time, 'We turned out the Quaker, and put in the pugilist.'[17]

In 1991, with Margaret Thatcher and John Major, of course what happened was the reverse.

On Whitehall, about which he writes often and amusingly, Bagehot – writing about the eighteenth century – could have been briefing the writers of the 1980s television programme, 'Yes, Minister': 'But the ultimate issue of business is not the part of it which most impresses the officials of a department. They understand how business is conducted better than what comes of it. The statesman who gives them no trouble, – who coincides with that which they recommend, – who thinks of the things which they think of, is more satisfactory to his mere subordinates than a real ruler, who has plans which others do not share, and whose mind is occupied by large considerations, which only a few can appreciate, and only experience can test.'[18]

And writing in the 1860s about recent failures in foreign policy, with only the slightest modification he could have been enlightening critics of British policy towards the European Community:

> But ... [are] the English people ... not above all nations divided from the rest of the world, insular both in situation and in mind, both for good and for evil [?] Are they not out of the current of common European causes and affairs? Are they not a race contemptuous of others? Are they not a race with no special education or culture as to the modern world, and too often despising such culture? Who could expect such a people to comprehend the new and strange events of foreign places? So far from wondering that the English Parliament has been inefficient in foreign policy, I think it is wonderful, and another sign of the rude, vague imagination that is at the bottom of our people, that we have done so well as we have.[19]

In his ability to cast a cold eye on his fellow-man, Bagehot was likened by Hutton to a naturalist: a better comparison might be a lepidopterist. Another great friend, William Rathbone Greg, described his mind as 'about the most peculiar I ever came into contact with, – very powerful, very suggestive, and very passionless'.[20] Both men were ardent, romantic spirits who, much though they loved and admired Bagehot, were temperamentally ill-equipped to understand that a penchant for scientific detachment and a remorseless eye for the incongruous and the absurd do not necessarily imply an absence of passion. Nor does the ability to see clearly the point of view of someone else imply an absence of conviction: it is more likely, as in this case, to come from imagination and insight.[21]

To take examples from the opposite end of the spectrum, who but Bagehot could have so pithily illuminated the cast of mind of both underwriters and fanatics? The former came up when, on holiday in Cornwall, he and Eliza visited the tiny, rocky harbour at Boscastle. 'I suppose', he wrote, 'we ought to think much of the courage with which sailors face such dangers, and of the feelings of their wives and families when they wait the return of their husbands and fathers; but my City associations at once carried me away to the poor underwriter who should insure against loss at such a place. How he would murmur, "Oh! my premium," as he saw the ship tossing up to the great black rock and the ugly breakwater, and seeming likely enough to hit both. I shall not ask at Lloyd's what is the rate for Boscastle rocks, for I remember the grave rebuke I once got from a serious underwriter when I said some other such place was pretty. "Pretty! I should think it was" he answered; "why it is lined with our money!"' How typical of Bagehot that he should have written this for the *Spectator*, a journal whose readership would have found the preoccupations of an underwriter about as antipathetic as those of a prostitute.[22]

Considering the fanatic mind, Bagehot took as an example the seventh-century Muslim military leader, Caliph Omar, who burned the great library of Alexandria because '"All books which contain what is not in the Koran are dangerous; all those which contain what is in the Koran are useless." Probably no one ever had an intenser belief in anything than Omar had in this.' In such a case a 'hot flash seems to burn across the brain. Men in these intense states of mind have altered all history, changed for better or worse the creed of myriads, and desolated or redeemed provinces and ages. Nor is this intensity a sign of truth, for it is precisely strongest in those points in which men differ most from each other. John Knox felt it in his anti-Catholicism; Ignatius Loyola in his anti-Protestantism; and both, I suppose, felt it as much as it is possible to feel it.'[23]

This essay is a splendid and memorable insight into the fanatic mind, and one most valuable for a present-day observer of Islamic fundamentalism. There is only one thing wrong with it: considerable inaccuracy. Bagehot cites

Gibbon as his source, whereas Gibbon had discussed the story only to jettison it. And the alleged words of Omar that Gibbon quoted before discarding them were not as given by Bagehot but read: 'If these writings of the Greeks agree with the book of God, they are useless and need not be preserved: if they disagree, they are pernicious and ought to be destroyed.'[24] None of this deleteriously affects the essential truth of the passage, but it is a graphic example of Bagehot's carefree attitude to detail. Knowing and loving literature as he did, he quoted and misquoted freely with the abandon of a cultured man rather than the concern for accuracy of a scholar. In the same spirit he frequently quoted and even misquoted himself without identifying the source. As a proof-corrector he was hopeless, and though he well understood the meaning of figures, his attitude to them was cavalier.

The tendency to be slipshod was exacerbated by his extreme (though initially self-imposed) busyness. 'You see,' he wrote once to a friend, 'I have hunting, banking, ships, publishers, an article, and a Christmas to do, all at once, and it is my opinion they will all get muddled. A muddle will *print*, however, though it won't add up, – *which is the real advantage of literature.*'[25]

Of course the very variety of his experience and interests added greatly to the appeal Bagehot made to receptive minds. His devout admirer, Woodrow Wilson, who kept on the wall in his study a drawing of a photograph taken of Bagehot in his maturity, believed his appearance to be 'a sort of outer index to the singular variety of capacity which has made him so notable a figure in the literary annals of England. A mass of black, wavy hair; a dark eye, with depths full of slumberous, playful fire; a ruddy skin that bespoke active blood, quick in its rounds; the lithe figure of an excellent horseman; a nostril full, delicate, quivering, like that of a blooded racer; such were the fitting outward marks of a man in whom life and thought and fancy abounded; the aspect of a man of unflagging vivacity, of wholesome, hearty humour, of a ready intellectual sympathy, of wide and penetrative observation.'[26] It was a description of which his sister-in-law Emilie approved, except that she dissented from the use of 'ruddy'. Her amplification, written almost forty years after he died, conjures up something of the magical impact he had on the Wilson family when he rode into their lives in 1857.

> He had a very fine skin, very white near where the hair started, and a high
> colour – what might be called a hectic colour – concentrated on the cheek
> bones, as you often see it in the West country. Such a colour is associated
> with soft winds and a moist air, cider-growing orchards, and very green, wet

grass. His eyelids were thin, and of singularly delicate texture, and the white of the eyeballs was a blue white. He would pace a room when talking, and, as the ideas framed themselves in words, he would throw his head back as some animals do when sniffing the air. The way he moved, his voice, everything about him, was individual. To us Walter was ever *Walter* – and that meant something quite unlike anybody else.[27]

It was an individualism developed through suffering. The effects on this gifted and affectionate child of living with a periodically mad mother and a severely retarded half-brother were the enhancement of his intuition, tolerance, lucidity and humour. 'We live in a rough world, and it is dangerous not to know that it is rough', he said once. And certainly the vicissitudes of his family life also introduced him early on to some of the harsher realities of human existence.

For an editor of *The Economist*, Bagehot's pedigree was impeccable: he was even born in 'The Bank House'. The Bagehots were traders, the Stuckeys were bankers and the two families dominated the prosperous Somerset town of Langport. In 1824 they allied themselves through the marriage of Thomas Watson Bagehot and Edith Estlin, née Stuckey, and the subsequent appointment of Bagehot to a partnership in the Bristol and Somersetshire Bank, popularly known as 'Stuckey's'.

At the time of their marriage, Thomas was twenty-eight; Edith, ten years his senior, was a beautiful widow with three sons. Thomas and Edith had two children, but the first died at three years of age. Walter was born on 3 March 1826 and while he was very young one of his half-brothers died and another was killed in an accident; the survivor and eldest, Vincent Estlin, was feeble-minded. Edith, a woman of great wit and *joie de vivre*, was driven into the first of her bouts of insanity. 'Every trouble in life is a joke compared to madness', Walter Bagehot was often to say. It was to dominate most of his life, for Edith predeceased him by only seven years.

A rare and disguised reminiscence shows how early he adapted to the role of chief consoler. 'A child of my acquaintance corrected its mother, who said that "they should never see" two of its dead brothers again, and maintained, "Oh yes, mamma, we shall; we shall see them in heaven, and they will be so glad to see us." And then the child cried with disappointment because its mother, though a most religious lady, did not seem exactly to feel that seeing her children in that manner was as good as seeing them on earth.'[28]

Even to intimate friends, Bagehot was never able to talk freely about his mother's condition, but like many private men he often revealed a great deal in his public utterances. In a sympathetic and sensitive essay on the poet William Cowper, written when he was only twenty-nine, Bagehot talked with familiarity and pain about the circumstances that bring on episodes of madness. The ultimate cause 'is of course that unknown something which we variously call pre-disposition, or malady, or defect. But the critical and exciting cause seems generally to be some comparatively trivial external occasion which falls within the necessary lot and life of the person who becomes mad. The inherent excitability is usually awakened by some petty casual stimulant, which looks positively not worth a thought – certainly a terribly slight agent for the wreck and havoc which it makes.' Great general problems were 'too impersonal, in truth, to cause the exclusive, anxious, aching occupation which is the common prelude and occasion of insanity'.[29]

It was, of course, the impossibility of predicting what would reactivate Edith's insanity that placed a particular burden on a highly-strung boy, yet he coped magnificently. His letters home show not only his anxiety and deep concern, but also a refusal to evade the issue. This was partly because of her influence. In 1845 she wrote to him that 'there is nothing like "speaking the truth from the heart" even where people differ, and between parents and children these are the only discussions which really make correspondence interesting and valuable for time and eternity'.[30] So when in the following year she wrote him some deluded letters, he responded honestly and critically.[31] Very like her in many ways, he was more successful than anyone else in dealing with her attacks of irrationality or morbid melancholia: humour and imaginative sympathy were his main weapons.

To this responsibility was added that of coping with his adult half-brother. At six he was writing their joint thank-you letter to an aunt. At nine, according to a contemporary, he was '"doing sums" with about twenty clocks all ticking in unison and striking to the minute around him (such being Vincent Estlin's whim of the hour), while his mother read *Quentin Durward* in as high a key and as rapidly as was possible, for the benefit of poor Vincent'.[32] Yet his efforts to answer Vincent's questions were a training-ground in patience and clear communication. In a letter of 1851 to his mother, he was to illustrate his failure to explain to Parisians a recent event in English politics by the sentence: '"You don't explain it to me" as Brother would say.'[33]

Though such experiences were frequently a cause of great anxiety and agony of mind, nevertheless in many respects Bagehot had a very happy childhood. His mother was a remarkable woman, remembered by one of the Wilson sisters as possessing 'great charm and fascination. She had a power of infusing life into the atmosphere about her, of making it indeed vibrate with a sense of activity and movement, very contagious in its effect. Her presence gave a feeling of zest to the living of life. Her intellectual vivacity brought into family life a keen relish for intellectual pleasures; she never failed to show an unselfish devotion to the interest of others, and, best of all, she stimulated the existence of all those about her with the invigorating tonic of humour . . . Her voice in speaking I recall as one of the most delightful I ever heard.'[34]

Bagehot was to say that she understood his jokes better than anyone else – indeed, their shared sense of humour could take her from delusion to reality. He once told of an occasion late in her life when during breakfast she decided she was incapable of speaking. Unable, however, to endure being deprived of conversation with her son, she wrote something on a slate, hung it round her neck and stood at the door of his study gazing at him silently. He looked up, saw her thus bedecked and both of them burst out laughing; this restored her to normal conversation.

Not only was Edith well-informed and interesting about many subjects, particularly literature and religion, but she was a free and critical spirit who observed the people within her circle with a discriminating eye, sharing her observations with her son. When he was only sixteen she was writing to him *à propos* a neighbour: 'I scold her much for caring totally (unlike you and papa and *me* now) about people and their attentions. She has always got some little fad about "cold manners," default of courtesies and enquiries, and fresh peccadilloes of the kind she punishes by a cross proud look (*entre nous*), and then – there they are – all turned to icicles and send each other to Coventry! . . . How one does wish to expand the good in humanity, to repress the bad, and raise all hearts and minds above the petty jealousies of life, and fix them upon the sublime views of the immortal soul and its life to come and which is to last for ever!!'[35]

If she was yeast, her husband Thomas was ballast – solid, dependable, affectionate and a man of fixed principles. He had grounded himself well in history, philosophy, politics and the other interests of a cultivated Victorian gentleman. Bagehot used to say that he could get immediately from his father any detail of English political history during the preceding fifty years. Thomas Bagehot believed in steady industry and the acquisition of a thorough foundation of knowledge from an early age and he guided his son's reading and general education. To the sixteen-year-old Walter he wrote that education was like a tree:

> The roots must be deep and firm if the trunk is to grow high and its branches spread widely, and all its parts must grow together. A man's character must be gradually forming religiously, morally, and intellectually . . . If one part of the character be forced too much, it will generally be at the expense of some strength in another, and I often think that we may trace some of the faults of young and old collegians to the too exclusive pursuits of collegiate honours. In saying this, however, I know you will think that I under-rate the exertions that must and ought to be made by them. Temperance is all I wish to inculcate and a wide view of the blessings of education founded in wisdom and virtue. Every day do I feel how much I have lost in not having had such an education as I wish to give you, and you need not therefore fear that anything will be wanting on my part to secure to you its advantages.[36]

Although in adulthood Walter enjoyed some leisure pursuits (he used to ride furiously to hounds, loved playing battledore with the young Wilson girls and during his time at *The Economist* played chess regularly at the Athenaeum with Richard Holt Hutton) he was always to maintain that 'business is much more amusing than pleasure'. So while as a small child he rode his pony with the recklessness that was to distinguish him as a horseman, climbed trees, played games and had the limited companionship afforded by his sickly cousin Watson ('Watty', who had been adopted by the Bagehots when his parents died), none the less the chief concern of his young life was the acquisition of knowledge. First with a governess, then at Langport Grammar School and always under the watchful tutelage of his father, he had acquired before the age of thirteen a precocious knowledge of English literature, Latin, French, history and politics. 'We are all going on very well without you,' he wrote to his mother when he was twelve and she was in London 'and Papa and I have such nice chats about Sir R Peel and the little Queen. Papa has quite made up his mind since he had read our friend the Duke's speech that the Queen did quite right and blames "The Right Hon. Baronet" for making the ladies of so much consequence since they could only use the ladies' privilege of railing against everybody and everything.'*[37] (Though Walter Bagehot was never to be narrowly partisan, his father had imbued him early with instinctive sympathy in politics for the Whigs, and in economics an absolute belief in the virtues of free trade.)

Already, his range of intellectual interests was unusually broad for his age: it was to be extended when in 1839 he was sent to Bristol College, chosen by his father because of its general excellence and Unitarianism. Edith Bagehot, a member of the Church of England, thought it 'heretical' and would have preferred a normal public school: it was Bagehot's good luck that his father's religious principles prevailed.

Bristol College was liberal in outlook and introduced its pupils to subjects taught in very few schools in Britain at that period: its curriculum included medicine and science. In his three years there Bagehot studied classics, German, Hebrew and mathematics. The headmaster, Dr James Prichard, his mother's brother-in-law, was an ethnologist of distinction who entertained his young relative frequently at home. There Bagehot heard conversations about 'the Arrow-headed character and the monuments of Pentapolis'[38] and craniology ('Concerning the skulls, I hope I am pretty well master of the leading divisions. One of Mr Booth's boys has lent me a couple of skulls, and with the aid of a number of Chambers's Information for the People, I am I hope qualified to understand most of Dr Prichard's Craniology.')

Bagehot's years at boarding school were a time of unremitting industry. As he struggled, usually with success, to be at the top of every class, in his spare time he read widely in literature, politics and history. His letters home are a detailed account of his intellectual journey: in contradistinction to those he wrote as an adult, they tended towards the heavy and earnest. He had a couple of friends, but otherwise stayed as remote from the rest of the boys as they would let him; occasionally his refusal to play provoked them to violence. Accustomed mainly to adult company, he felt mild disdain for his contemporaries. As one of his biographers points out, throughout his life corporate action, mass enthusiasm, left him cold.[39] Although the kindest of men, he was never to have any instinctive feeling for the sufferings of the

*Bagehot is referring to the 'Bedchamber crisis'. The Prime Minister, Lord Melbourne, had gained the trust of the nineteen-year-old Queen Victoria and had surrounded her with Whig Ladies of the Bedchamber. When Melbourne resigned in May 1839, Peel refused to form a ministry unless the ladies were replaced: he therefore refused office and Melbourne stayed in power. The Duke of Wellington had defended Peel in the House of Lords.

common people and his passionate objection to the extension of the franchise to the uneducated owed much to a fastidious aversion from the uneducated masses.

It was at University College, London – where he went in 1842 at the age of sixteen and a half – that the latent boyishness, frivolity and mischievousness of Bagehot was to emerge. Once again the accident of his father's Unitarianism proved to be of great educational advantage to his son, saving him from a narrow and lax curriculum in Oxford or Cambridge. (Bagehot was later to dismiss Oxford colleges contemptuously as 'hotels without bells'.) To the subjects which he had already studied were added moral, natural and political philosophy, logic, and even that most newfangled subject of all, political economy.

Better read and more stimulating in conversation than his contemporaries, Bagehot attracted a group of highly intelligent and serious-minded young men, of whom Richard Holt Hutton was to be most important to him. He still showed no enthusiasm for the majority of his peers; in the debating society he had a reputation for superciliousness. Hutton described how 'his satirical "Hear, hear" was a formidable sound in the debating society, and one which took the heart out of many a younger speaker. And the ironical "How much?" with which in conversation he would respond to overstatement, was always of a nature to reduce a man, as the mathematical phrase goes, to his "lowest terms."'[40]

Bagehot did not so much prize erudition as cherish quality of thought: sloppy, woolly thinking was to irritate him profoundly all his life. His distaste was well summed up in a letter he wrote to Hutton some years later, attacking him for being unduly kind in a review: 'There is a pale, whitey-brown substance in the man's books, which people who don't think take for thought, but it isn't.'[41]

Allied to that was his unusual freedom from concern about the opinions of others. He was to write once that 'you may talk of the tyranny of Nero and Tiberius: but the real tyranny is the tyranny of your next door neighbour', yet he was himself unusually free of any moral or intellectual inhibitions imposed from without his close circle. The best and brightest of his comrades acted as a spur and an inspiration, his gifted and eclectic teachers introduced him to new worlds, and his explorations of political life in London with Hutton developed in this provincial boy a taste for the centre of power. Despite suffering from acute anxiety about examinations as well as intermittent ill health (he had a weak chest and suffered from eye strain and frequent headaches) which forced him to take an extra year over his degree, his academic results were brilliant: first-class honours in his BA in 1846 and the Gold Medal for moral and intellectual philosophy at his MA degree two years later.

While studying for his MA, Bagehot contributed three substantial essays to the *Prospective Review* – a Unitarian quarterly which had published Richard Holt Hutton's first essay. His debut in 1847 was a review of *Festus*,[42] a thirteen-thousand-line poem by Philip James Bailey, based on the legend that inspired Marlowe's *Doctor Faustus* and Goethe's *Faust*. In it there were already examples of his gift for the encapsulation of an idea in a striking phrase. Insisting on the importance of punishing the criminal (while deploring the barbarities of the law in earlier times), he pronounced: 'In the notions of our ancestors, the sacred desire for a righteous judgement upon the criminal may have been turned by human imperfection into a savage hatred towards him. But one extreme is no better than another; and do we not live among thousands who are ready only with their tears, when stripes also are needful?'[43] One of the editors of the journal, John James Tayler, a Unitarian minister, theologian and ecclesiastical historian of considerable distinction, wrote to his friend James Martineau that Bagehot's mind was obviously 'diligently cultured and disciplined' and praised the essay's 'high-toned morality'.[44]

Quite as precocious, opinionated and equally *de haut en bas* was his lengthy essay the following year on 'The Currency Monopoly',[45] in which he subjected to close scrutiny writings on the Currency and Banking Schools controversy by Thomas Tooke, Colonel Torrens and James Wilson. As a moderate supporter of the Bank Charter Act and of its suspension in 1847, Bagehot found fault with all of them, but even more interesting were his pronouncements on *laissez-faire*, then being put forward by *The Economist* as an unmitigated good.

Bagehot had become a reader of *The Economist* from the time he began to study political economy for his MA, but though he agreed with it in principle on *laissez-faire* as on free trade, his stance was infinitely more moderate. Although appreciating why 'money-making men' were suspicious of government interference, he feared this was a sentiment 'very susceptible of hurtful exaggeration':

In the minds of many at this day it stands opposed to the enforcement of moral law throughout the *whole* sphere of human acts susceptible of attestation: to the legislative promotion of those industrial habits which conduce to the attainment of national morality or national happiness at a sacrifice of national wealth: to efforts at a national education, or a compulsory sanitary reform: to all national aid from England towards the starving peasantry of Ireland: to every measure for improving the condition of that peasantry which would not be the spontaneous choice of the profit-hunting capitalist. Whoever speaks against these extreme opinions is sure to be sneered at as a 'benevolent sentimentalist': and economists are perpetually assuming that the notion of government interference is agreeable only to those whose hearts are more developed than their brains: who are too fond of poetic dreams to endure the stern realities of science.[46]

Bagehot – as always – was in fact arguing for common sense: when faced with extremism he excelled at *reductio ad absurdum*. In another area – taking issue with James Wilson – he remarks that 'it is certainly very strange to find a distinguished practical man of business like Mr Wilson laying down the old doctrine of the Bank directors that inconvertible bank notes could not be depreciated, no matter at how low a rate of interest they are issued. Why those who hold this doctrine do not go further, and maintain that everybody should be allowed to issue debased coin *ad libitum*, is more than we can understand.'[47]

Through the serious and dense matter of this essay one can sense Bagehot's amusement at the excesses of political economists, particularly Tooke. Not yet confident enough to make fun of such people in public, in private he wrote to his mother, about Tooke's book, that 'a political economist in a rage is an amusing sight: his violence is so meagre, and he has no rhetoric or eloquence to cover it with, and make it seem decent'.[48]

The last essay of the trio, also published in 1848, was a review of John Stuart Mill's *Principles of Political Economy*. It showed more humility than Bagehot had displayed in dealing with the currency controversy, where the tone in which he took issue with Tooke, Torrens and Wilson was patronising – the young man shaking his head impatiently at the follies of his elders. In the case of Mill he showed a healthy respect for a remarkable mind and acknowledged him as a great thinker whose writings ranked him with Adam Smith and Ricardo. He had had to wrestle with it: 'I am in much trouble about John Mill, who is very tough and rather dreary',[49] he wrote to a friend, but he found the struggle rewarding. Significantly, he admired the strength of Mill's desire for the 'mere discovery of truth'[50] and the honesty with which he had faced opinions opposed to his own: 'The false colours of prejudice and passion have no place in an intellect so thoroughly achromatic.' But apart from challenging him on certain of his theories, he criticised Mill's work – as he had criticised *Festus* – for the absence of a moral dimension. He regretted also indistinctness and diffuseness of style, occasional dogmatism where there was ground for doubt 'and an excessive averseness to subtle speculation'.

None of these was a criticism that could ever be made of Bagehot himself. Discursive he might be: obscure or rambling never. Already at twenty-two he had in abundance that power to clarify his arguments that was to make him a writer of genius. He had the intellect and industry to master even the 'tough and rather dreary' thinkers across the spectrum of the humanities and social sciences and explain their ideas in a manner at once simple and sophisticated. Of the wide range of linguistic tools that he used, analogy and paradox were two of his favourites. In the Mill essay, for instance, he explains his view that the working classes could be converted to financial prudence and hence prosperity through education because 'instruction is to the mind what the telescope is to the eye. To an uncultivated intellect what is distant will always be invisible, but a well trained mind is habitually able to look into the future, and to deal with the absent as though it were present.'[51] And in treating of economic thinkers he addresses the paradox of Adam Smith and David Ricardo (which he was to develop at much greater length later in his career): it was the bookish Smith who was the 'common sense' thinker; the abstract thinker was the businessman Ricardo . This would have been surprising 'if we had not known how little outward circumstances avail against the intrinsic aptitudes of a strong mind'.

In the same article he again condemned – on moral and pragmatic grounds – the extreme exponents of *laissez-faire*. It was wrong to keep wages down to the lowest possible level: capitalists 'have no more right to be greedy and avaricious than any other class, and it is discreditable to the economists to teach that such conduct is not hurtful to the public and indefensible in itself'. The upheavals of 1848 had clearly made him think long and hard about the need to improve the lot of the 'lower orders': 'Whatever be the evil or the good of democracy, in itself it is evident that the combination of democracy and low wages will infallibly be bad.'[52] 'The only valid security against the rule of an ignorant, miserable and vicious democracy, is to take care that the democracy shall be educated, and comfortable, and moral ... The most important matters for the labouring classes, as for all others, are restraining discipline over their passions and an effectual culture of their consciences.'[53]

Disciplining passion: it was a preoccupation of Bagehot's at this time. His mother was deteriorating; within a few years he described her to a close friend as subject to 'a good deal of habitual delusion and aberration, which, I fear, will end in ultimately disqualifying her for society'.[54] Bagehot had, he said, 'suffered a good deal when I first put this steadily before me'. Worse, he had had to face up to that appalling reality at a time when Richard Holt Hutton was abroad and their close university group had fragmented; as well as his usual health problems he had had to endure long periods of great depression, and there is strong evidence to suggest that he feared for his own sanity.[55]

Intellectually he was frustrated. From November 1848, in accordance with a long-standing agreement between him and his father, he laboured through the dreary process necessary to become a lawyer.

At that time, those wishing to be barristers had neither lectures nor examinations. The only means by which an aspirant could acquire the necessary knowledge was to become a clerk in the chambers of a practising barrister; the qualification was gained through membership of an Inn. The work was tedious, detailed and involved much copying.

Bagehot's first period as a pupil was spent with a conveyancer. Being industrious, he tried hard and took what interest he could in the subject, but for a man who had spent six years in an intellectual ferment, and whose main failings in his work were boredom with minutiae and a tendency to the slapdash, it was a dismal occupation: after six months with the conveyancer he slightly improved his lot by moving to chambers where the principal specialised in common law and special pleading.

He was a contemptuous member of Lincoln's Inn. Almost twenty years later he described how the Benchers ('old and rickety and much addicted to port wine')[56] admitted newcomers to the Bar:

> The process was then this: all the students dined in Hall during term, and the only attempt on the part of the Inn to test or augment our legal knowledge consisted in certain exercises, which we had to 'keep', as it was

called, in due rotation . . . A slip of paper was delivered to you, written in legible law-stationer's hand, which you were to take up to the upper table, where the Benchers sat, and read before them. The contents were generally not intelligible: the slip often began in the middle of a sentence, and by long copying and by no revision the text had become quite corrupt. The topic was 'whether C should have the widow's estate?' and it was said that if you pieced all the slips together you might make a connected argument for and against the widow. In old time I suppose there used to be a regular 'moot', or debate, before the Benchers, in which the students took part, and in which the Benchers judged of their competency. Probably this sort of examination, by publicly putting a nice case and publicly arguing it, was very effectual. But in 1850 the trial 'case' had dwindled down to the ever lasting question, 'whether C should have the widow's estate?' The animated debate had become a mechanical reading of copied bits of paper, which it was difficult to read without laughing. Indeed, the Benchers felt the farce, and wanted to expedite it. If you kept a grave countenance after you had read some six words the senior Bencher would say, 'Sir, that will do'; and then the exercise was kept . . . If you laughed you had to read the 'slip' all through.[57]

While engaged in this dispiriting combination of sham and drudgery, there came into Bagehot's life a new friend who was to have a profound effect on the development of his character and career – the poet and scholar Arthur Hugh Clough, who had resigned his fellowship at Oriel in Oxford because he could no longer accept the Thirty-Nine Articles. Strongly backed by Bagehot, Clough had been given the headship of University Hall, recently founded as a residence for University College, London undergraduates. He was unsuited for the job and left in 1852, but in the meantime he had changed the course of Bagehot's life. Hutton thought that Clough had 'a greater intellectual fascination for Bagehot than any of his contemporaries', because of his preoccupation with truth and the difficulty of obtaining it. 'He had a straining, inquisitive, critical mind', wrote Bagehot of his friend after his death; 'he scrutinized every idea before he took it in'.[58]

Clough had had what Bagehot considered the misfortune to come up against two of the most influential and vibrant intellects of his time – Dr Arnold of Rugby and John Henry Newman. Arnold's great success was in raising the spiritual sights of the ordinary English boy – 'the small, apple-eating animal whom we know' – to a consciousness that life was solemn and full of great intellectual and moral problems. 'The common English mind is too coarse, sluggish, and worldly to take such lessons too much to heart', judged Bagehot, but they had a destructively strong effect on the 'susceptible, serious, intellectual' Clough. From Rugby he had gone to Oxford, then in the emotional turmoil created by Newman, 'a consummate master of the difficulties in the creeds of other men . . . a nearly perfect religious disputant'. As Norman St John-Stevas puts it neatly, Clough had been 'pulverized by Dr Arnold and winnowed by Dr Newman'.[59] He was paralysed by doubt in a manner well summed up in these lines from his poem 'Amours de Voyage':

> *Action will furnish belief* – but will that belief be the true one?
> This is the point you know.

Bagehot, whose mind was set in the same sceptical cast as Clough's, studied the spiritual ruin that was his friend and determined not to go the same way. As he said in his essay on Clough: 'it is not desirable to take this world too much *au sérieux*'. Clough, he concluded, should have been told 'to take things easily; not to try to be wise over much; to be "something beside critical;" to go on living quietly and obviously and see what truth would come to him'.

Bagehot had grasped this imperative through facing his fears as honestly as he had faced his terror about inherited madness. In that case he had concluded it was a matter of will. Now before he could decide on which career would assist him towards a sane existence, he had one more seminal experience to undergo. 'Very unwell mentally and bodily',[60] he was persuaded by a friend to spend some time in France: he arrived in Paris in August 1851.

It was his second visit to Europe (in 1844 he had been to Belgium, Germany and Switzerland with his Aunt Reynolds). He had adequate French and enough contacts to afford him a stimulating experience intellectually and there was a growing political crisis to excite him. He became absorbed in the struggle between Louis Napoleon and the Assembly, whose members were resisting his pressure to change the Constitution so as to allow him a further term of office. Bagehot's admiration for Louis Napoleon's strength of character at a time of general weakness and vacillation in French political life grew steadily. He had nothing but contempt for the idealists and revolutionaries who abounded among the politicians and the press. He believed with Edmund Burke that 'politics are but a piece of business'.[61] His imagination was stirred and his spirits raised to a point of intoxication when the President staged his *coup d'état* early in December, arrested thousands of his opponents and swiftly put down the left-wing rebellion that followed.

Bagehot's physical courage – so evident in his vigorous riding and hunting – had him walking the streets at a time when sensible Parisians were lying low at home. The cavalier in him – that important facet of his character that set him apart from his more earnest and religious friends – which had been so long suppressed by worry and ill health, surfaced triumphantly in the centre of Paris. 'A Cavalier is always young', he wrote a few years later. 'The buoyant life arises before us rich in hope, strong in vigour, irregular in action; men young and ardent, framed in the "prodigality of nature;" open to every enjoyment, alive to every passion; eager, impulsive; brave without discipline; noble without principle; prizing luxury, despising danger, capable of high sentiment.'[62] It was in that spirit that he assisted the rebels with the building of barricades, 'which I found amusing', he wrote to Hutton. 'They have systematized it in a way that is pleasing to cultivated intellect. We had only one good day's fighting, and I naturally kept out of cannon-shot. But I took a quiet walk over the barricades in the morning, and superintended the construction of three with as much keenness as if I had been clerk of the works.'[63] And to Henry Crabb Robinson, an elderly man of letters whose intimate friends included several of the leading writers in Britain and Europe and a fascinating conversationalist whose breakfast parties Bagehot used to attend, he wrote mischievously: 'I was here during the only day of hard fighting which we have had and shall be able to give lectures on the construction of a barricade if that noble branch of Political Economy ever become a source of income in England.'[64]

Bagehot had seemingly ceased writing for publication once he began his legal studies. It was his French experience that was to give him the stimulus to find himself as a journalist, or rather as a gifted and lambent commentator on politics. His exhilaration with his new experiences needed the public outlet which he found in the sober *Inquirer*. The dominant theme of his articles was that stability matters above all. 'By the sound work of old-fashioned generations, by the singular pains-taking of the slumberers in church yards – by dull care – by stupid industry, a certain social fabric somehow exists – people contrive to go out to their work, and to find work to employ them actually until the evening, body and soul are kept together, and this is what mankind have to show for their six thousand years of toil and trouble.'[65] To that need all else had to be sacrificed: including, if necessary, civil liberties and freedom of the press. The French national character – 'excitable, volatile, superficial, over-logical, uncompromising'[66] – was not conducive to a system of parliamentary government on the English model, for would not 'any large and omnipotent Assembly resemble the stormy constituent and the late chamber rather than business-like formal ennui-diffusing parliament to which in our free and dull country we are felicitously accustomed?'[67] 'The English had the stupidity necessary for both steadiness of conduct and consistency of opinion.'[68] What was deplorable was the kind of liberal opinion that ignored reality: if Louis Napoleon's solution did not suit, then critics should offer a practical option rather than finding fault, but it would have to be a system that would work, that would be accepted by 'a wilful nation' and must preserve the stability of French society.

The message was a conservative one for such a young man and was addressed to an audience who found heretical not only its content but its tone. Bagehot had only contempt for his worthy readers: 'bald-headed people . . . [who] don't comprehend anything which is not erroneous',[69] and his cavalier mood exacerbated his arrogance. The net result was a typical Bagehot paradox. Like those of today's left-wing politicians who have realized that a well-cut, sober suit can hide the radicalism of their beliefs, Bagehot covered up the essential conservatism of his central message with the irresponsible language of youth. The style of the letters was described by Woodrow Wilson as being conducted 'at a spanking, reckless gait'. Even Crabb Robinson, an admirer of Bagehot's, was horrified by the obvious cynicism and flippancy: ever afterwards he described him to Richard Holt Hutton as 'that friend of yours – you know whom I mean, you rascal! – who wrote those abominable, those most disgraceful letters on the coup d'état – I did not forgive him for years after.'

Bagehot returned to England wholly unrepentant, buoyant, happy and with his future decided on. For a long time he had been plagued by indecision. His mother wanted him to come home to work in the family bank, and although he was anxious to look after her he feared the stultification of life in a small community. His father had wanted him to practise at the Bar, which carried the great bonus of living in London. Duty and prudence triumphed, for he feared a living as a lawyer might be uncertain and he had come to the conclusion that he could care for his mother while keeping boredom at bay through part-time journalism. His articles might have been unpopular – John Morley, the great radical, was one of those horrified by them – but they had created a stir and there was no doubt about his talent as a descriptive writer and analyst. And Paris had taken him off the academic treadmill. His experiencing nature had blossomed and his genius as a synthesiser of data across the spectrum of contemporary knowledge was becoming evident. His ruminations on constitutional issues, on national character, on democracy, on the development of societies were those which were later to infuse his writing in *The Economist*: he was now ready to undertake a totally new experience and to apply himself to it with his customary industriousness.

Although Bagehot was never to practise as a lawyer, his period of study had not been wasted. The blend of his habitual diligence and intellectual curiosity had ensured that he acquired a grasp of the law that added further breadth to his understanding of the structure of English society. Perhaps even more important, he had observed from the inside that an institution commanding great public prestige could be at its core a farce: 'All established customs will find grave people to defend them, and ingenious reasons are soon found for them', he was to write when discussing the law. 'No one likes to admit that a magnificent and an ancient institution, from which he gains glory, is a mere "sham" and empty appearance.'[70]

It was Bagehot's ability to employ his cold eye to strip away the façade and expose the reality of the institutions of the state that was to make him a commentator of genius: it was to be augmented by his often savage wit. In 1849, describing to his father the formal presentation to their Chancellor of University College London graduates, he reported that the event had gone off well but the Chancellor 'was not quite up "to the swing of the humbug" and did not comport himself with much dignity or éclat. His method of proceeding was to lurk behind the door and when anyone was announced to rush out and shake hands with him greedily. A good many people took him for a waiter and wondered at the intensity of his affection.'

Self-importance had become Bagehot's bugbear. The charade performed with such pomposity at Lincoln's Inn had produced a scepticism, even agnosticism, that left nothing sacred – even great scholarship. In one of a number of delicious asides poking fun at academia, he writes that 'when a great author, a Grote or a Gibbon, has devoted a whole life of horrid industry to the composition of a large history, one feels one ought not to touch it with a mere hand – it is not respectful'.[71]

Naturally, even the profession that Thomas Bagehot took so seriously was not spared: 'Here I am in my father's counting house trying (and failing) to do sums and being rowed ninety-nine times a day for some horrid sin against the conventions of mercantile existence', he wrote in January 1853 to a friend. The first stages of understanding of banking were a sore trial to him. The father was a model of punctuality and precision: the son uninterested in accuracy to the point of carelessness. 'I am going on in a very torpid state of mind myself', he wrote to Hutton. 'I have devoted my time for the last 4 months nearly exclusively to the art of book-keeping by double entry, the theory of which is agreeable and pretty but the practice perhaps as horrible as anything ever was. I maintain too in vain that sums are matters of opinion – but the people in command here do not comprehend the nature of contingent matter and try to prove that figures tend to one result more than another which I find myself to be false and they always come different. But there is no influencing the instinctive dogmatism of the uneducated mind.'[72]

There were, however, advantages to mercantile life: 'There is some excitement in it, if this does not wear off – always a little to do and no [we]aring labor which is something towards perfection.' And when he had mastered the preliminaries, he began to come into his own. Banking was in his blood; in addition to his father he had been close to two banking uncles who had also had distinguished careers in the wider financial world. Vincent Stuckey had been a clerk in the Treasury from 1797, had risen to be head of the Bill department and was briefly private secretary to Pitt until he went back to Langport and the bank in 1801. Under him the bank had expanded considerably and had fourteen branches. The London branch of Stuckey and Reynolds was run by Uncle John Stuckey Reynolds, who in an earlier incarnation had been a high-flyer in the Treasury; he had returned to banking because of scruples about the moral danger of worldly achievement.

Bagehot's quick intelligence and his unparalleled ability to get to the heart of the matter were tremendous assets. A relative of his reminisced about an appearance before the bank committee at Langport representing a 'luckless, hair-seating manufacturer', on behalf of whom 'I tendered – in aid of some rather short securities – a heap of policies on his life of long standing'; he was discomfited by the question with which Bagehot broke the silence – 'Henry, will your client undertake to *expire* as part of the arrangement?'[73]

Enhancing all his gifts and infusing all his judgments was an exceptionally subtle understanding of human character which expanded and deepened as the years went by, coupled with a profound psychological insight into how people operate individually and collectively. All these qualities were to make him a good banker and the experience of banking was to make him a better writer. No one else was ever to explain so limpidly the simple essence of banking transactions: 'Credit means that a certain confidence is given and a certain trust reposed. Is that trust justified? and is that confidence wise? These are the cardinal questions. To put it more simply – credit is a set of promises to pay; will those promises be kept?'[74] Many articles in *The Economist*, and *Lombard Street* itself were to reflect that experience, crystallised in crisp, clear and often memorable prose: 'The essence of deposit banking is that a very large number of persons agree to trust a very few persons or some one person.'[75] Bagehot had no particular regard for the challenge of banking: 'Any careful person who is experienced in figures, and has real sound sense, may easily make himself a good banker. The modes in which money can be safely lent by a banker are not many, and a clear-headed, quiet, industrious person may soon learn all that is necessary about them.'[76]

From 1856 he began to write regularly on English and French banking. His major concern at the time was how to ensure that commercial banking was safe: 'There are three conditions which seem essential to the maximum of security. We may be safe without them, but it is clear that we should be safer with them. First, a large property ought to become liable for our money when it is lent. Secondly, we should be able to ascertain that, while the loan lasts, that property continues liable – *a fortiori*, that it continues to exist. Lastly, the banker – the actual practical man who regulates and reinvests our money – should be so thoroughly remunerated that his clear interest is rather to retain his position by employing our money well than to risk it by employing it ill.'[77]

Bagehot's most significant economic publications at that time were the series of twelve articles by 'A Banker' in *The Economist* in 1857–8 and an essay in the *National Review* on 'The Monetary Crises of 1857'. Interesting reflections on national character in that essay included the suggestion that French trade 'is so little based upon borrowing or trust, that it is not exposed to a panic such as Lombard Street and Wall Street have experienced'.[78] He added weight to his analysis by adducing in support his anonymous self in *The Economist*.

By 1861, when Bagehot succeeded Wilson as director of the paper and Hutton as its editor, the industry of this gifted polymath had earned him several distinct reputations. First had been the laurels he had won and the brickbats he had sustained for his literary essays: to those published in 1858 as *Estimates of Some Englishmen and Scotchmen* had been added several further substantial pieces, including essays on Dickens, Milton, Thackeray and Scott. Discussing Bagehot as a writer on literature, William Haley remarks that his reputation reflects his practical judgment and misses his romantic imagination: he is seen to have both feet on the ground and his hands in his pockets – shrewd, sober and sensible.[79] No one who read even a handful of his literary pieces could see him in so limited a way – at the very least he was whistling while he walked.

The majority of these essays were written for the *National Review*, which he co-edited from its foundation in 1854 and edited from 1862 until its death two years later. It was here too that he published most of his long profiles of great statesmen and demonstrated his great talents as a historian – not one who finds and interprets original material and produces works of scholarship, but one who explains the past in such a way as to help us understand the present and the future. His extraordinary sense of history had been evident in many of his literary essays in just the same way as his deep familiarity and imaginative sympathy with great literature was evident in his other writings.

His historical sense infused his writings on politics, for he viewed the recent past of a living politician with the historian's detachment as well as with the coherence and perspective that usually come with the passage of time. During the 1850s he had produced extremely distinguished long essays on English statesmen – Lord Brougham and Sir Robert Peel – which were a portent of the brilliant character sketches that were to illuminate the pages of *The Economist* throughout his editorship. Sir Robert Peel – nearest of all men to Bagehot's definition of a constitutional statesman: 'The powers of a first-rate man under the creed of a second-rate man'[80] – gave Bagehot scope *inter alia* to dilate fascinatingly on the nature of administrative power. Lord Brougham – the great excitable reformer – was brought to life in a series of delicious images, one of the most telling being with the aid of a passage from Lord Tennyson's *Godiva*:

> I waited for the train at Coventry;
> I hung with grooms and porters on the bridge
> To watch the three tall spires;
> And there I shaped the city's legend into this.

'Lord Brougham would not have waited so. He would have rushed up into the town; he would have suggested an improvement, talked the science of the bridge, explained its history to the natives. The quiet race would think twenty people had been there.'[81] In that essay too was demonstrated Bagehot's genius for painting the backdrop of history in a way that has deep resonances for later generations. Take, for example, the opening to his masterly account of the malaise that gripped Britain in the first half of the nineteenth century and which also rings true for the decade after the Second World War: 'The years immediately succeeding the great peace were years of sullenness and difficulty. The idea of the war had passed away; the thrill and excitement of the great struggle were no longer felt. We had maintained, with the greatest potentate of modern times, a successful contest for existence; we had our existence, but we had no more; our victory had been great, but it had no fruits. By the aid of pertinacity and capital, we had vanquished genius and valour; but no visible increase of European influence for it.'[82]

Added to this, he was a respected banker, having been manager of the Bristol branch (he resigned after Wilson's death but kept the secretaryship) and subsequently supervisor of the London branch, while maintaining an interest in Langport. As a writer on economics he was esteemed as a frequent contributor to *The Economist*. As a commentator on politics, he made a reputation in his 1856 series on government in the *Saturday Review*. Then in 1859 had come the pamphlet on parliamentary reform that had excited so much interest among the well-informed and with James Wilson's help had brought Bagehot into a wide political circle. It was after that period that he had begun to write frequently in *The Economist* on matters political.

Bagehot hated foolishness as much as he despised humbug, whether in politics or economics, and in the realm of finance he took as harsh a view from an early age as did his father-in-law. (Bagehot was himself a model in this regard; he was not only extremely prudent with money – he hated spending it.) 'We wish somebody would write something on the *duty* of common sense. Many divines patronize other virtues, ingenious speculators are florid on out of the way obligations, but all neglect the duty of not concerning oneself with affairs which one can't manage, and of managing appropriately those which one does manage. And yet this is worth something. The happiness of how many families, the welfare of how many children, depend on it.'[83] Then, applying himself to Lord Overstone's vestigial theory of a trade cycle (which Bagehot was to develop over the next decades), he reflects on the fear that a period of a low rate of return on investment inexorably leads towards irresponsible investment: '"John Bull", says someone [himself], "can stand a great deal, but he cannot stand *two* per cent."'* He goes on to look at the morality of the matter: 'People won't take 2 per cent; they won't bear a loss of income. Instead of that dreadful event, they invest their careful savings in something impossible – a canal to Kamchatka, a railway to Watchet, a plan for animating the Dead Sea, a corporation for shipping skates to the Torrid Zone.' He hopes that this time sense will prevail: 'that people will be wise – that capitalists will exercise a discretion – that merchants will not over-trade – that shop keepers will not over-stock – that the non-mercantile public will bear a reduction in income – that they will efface superfluities, and endure adversity, and abolish champagne; but unless self-denial is exercised, and judgment put forth and common sense exerted, the case is hopeless. One of two alternatives must be taken. If the old, and tried, and safe investments no longer yield their accustomed returns, we must take what they do yield, or try what is untried. We must either be poorer or less safe; less opulent or less secure.'[84]

It was a pithy summary of what James Wilson had been preaching for nine years in *The Economist*.

---

*This is an interesting example of how Bagehot's ideas were crystallised. In 1848, in his essay on J.S. Mill's *Principles of Political Economy* (*WB*, xi, p. 190), he referred to a contention of Fullerton's (author of *On The Regulations of Currencies*) that when interest is as low as two per cent 'capital habitually emigrates, or . . . is wasted on foolish speculations, which never yield any adequate returns'. By 1852 he had turned it into an anonymous epigram: 'John Bull, as it has been wisely observed, can stand a good deal, but he cannot stand 2 per cent.' (*WB*, ix, p. 300) Then in *Lombard Street*, in 1873, he refers to the saying 'John Bull can stand many things but he cannot stand 2 per cent.'

CHAPTER XVIII:

The changing face of *The Economist*

I can say with truth that it has constantly happened to me that when unable, either from want of knowledge or from other circumstances, to come to a conclusion, I have resolved to postpone the consideration of the matter till I had seen what the next *Economist* said about it; and I have reason to know that more important persons than myself used constantly to consult him.
Lord Granville (Foreign Secretary 1851–52, 1870–74, 1880–85), 1877[1]

It was a physical relief for Bagehot to take over fully at *The Economist* in 1861 and move to the Wilson house in Upper Belgrave Street. Because of his banking, journalistic and domestic responsibilities he had been taxing his always frail physique by commuting by rail from his rented house at Clevedon, on the Somerset coast, east to Bristol, south to Langport and a long way east to London. His wife's diary frequently records him falling asleep on the train and overshooting his station.

Living in London, he could also more easily enlarge his network of contacts, although he was never to concentrate simply on those who might be useful to him in his capacity as editor of *The Economist*. He had represented himself to Eliza as highly selective about social intercourse: 'It is inconceivable to me to like to see many people and even to speak to them. Every new person you know is an intellectual burden because you may see them again, and must be able to recognize and willing to converse with them.'[2] And he certainly hated chit-chat: 'at London dinners you talk nothing; between two pillars of crinoline you eat and are resigned'.[3] Yet there was enough good company available for Bagehot to have an active social life. While journalists and men of letters like Hutton had a tendency to stick to their own kind, Bagehot's insatiable intellectual and human curiosity inclined him towards interesting people in several circles. He was at ease at breakfast with Gladstone, taking tea with George Eliot or Lady Waldegrave, dining with the banker and scientist Sir John Lubbock, or playing chess with Hutton at the Athenaeum.

Bagehot was Wilson's executor, and manager, editor and principal writer on business subjects under the terms of the agreement drawn up with Wilson's trustees – of whom he was one. Although opposed to *The Economist* having a salaried editor (he believed that only someone with a stake in the paper could be relied upon to conduct its affairs honestly), as a trustee he was precluded from taking any financial interest in the property. He was paid £400 a year for editing and managing, the going rate for writing, and additionally he received half the profits above £2,000 a year. (Little financial information is available on the nineteenth-century *Economist*, but we know that in 1862 it yielded £2,197 and in 1872 it achieved a record profit of £2,765. In a memorandum on family finances Bagehot observed that Wilson had reckoned his income from the paper at £3,000, inclusive of his salary as manager, editor and principal writer, with the actual profit from the property itself being around £2,000. 'The old accounts in Mr Wilson's time are not very clear; regarding the property as I know he did as a very delicate and confidential one, I think he did not care to put down the figures in a way that might give hurtful information, if by chance communicated to wrong persons' – presumably Greg or Hutton.[4]) Bagehot had to answer to no one except the paper's proprietors – his adoring wife, mother-in-law and sisters-in-law. There were co-trustees, but they left everything to him. Unlike Wilson, he had no political colleagues peering over his shoulder; unlike Richard Holt Hutton, he had no proprietor or proprietor's son-in-law to interfere. Editorial policy reflected his own position, which he described as 'between sizes in politics'. Nominally a liberal, his opposition to change for change's sake and his Burkean concern for giving priority to preserving social stability brought him close to the heart of conservatism. In truth he did not have the makings of a good party man. He was too sceptical, too sardonic, and too interested in truth. It was probably as fortunate for him as it was for the paper that his attempts to get into parliament were unsuccessful.

In 1860 Bagehot failed to get the nomination for London University; then in 1865 Wilson's great friend Charles Villiers suggested first that he stand for Dublin, an idea he rejected, and then that he try for Manchester. His only chance, Bagehot told Gladstone, of being selected for Manchester, was to have it recognised through the help of an 'intellectual certificate' that he had given much time and labour to the commercial and economic subjects which so absorbed that city's voters.[5] 'If thorough acquaintance with economical science, extensive and accurate knowledge, ready and practical habits of business, and a conciliatory disposition, go to fit a man for the representation of these great national interests,' wrote Gladstone in response, in a letter designed for publication, 'it certainly appears to me that your fitness must stand without dispute in the first rank.'[6]

In mid-June the *Manchester Guardian* reported that Bagehot was in the running: the 'proprietor of *The Economist*, a gentleman of independent property and position, favourable to the amendment of the representation but not the lowering of the suffrage and whom they believe will be well qualified, from his intimate acquaintance with commercial subjects, to represent this important constituency'.[7] At the public selection meeting in July a letter was read out from W.R. Greg, whose personal and family reputation still stood high in the city. He recommended his friend as 'a man of business, a shrewd economist, a subtle and sagacious thinker, with unusual practical faculties' who would 'speedily make for himself a position in parliament'.[8] Bagehot – reputedly the best conversationalist in London, but an uninspiring public speaker – gave a poor address and retired: the reputation of *The Economist* did not stand sufficiently high for the home of free trade to welcome its editor regardless of his deficiencies.

Bagehot had written five years earlier with personal feeling about the problems faced by a sceptical would-be orator: 'We are in the habit of speaking of rhetoric as an art, and also of oratory as a faculty, and in both cases we speak quite truly. No man can speak without a special intellectual gift, and no man can speak well without a special intellectual training. But neither this gift of the intellect nor this education will suffice of themselves. A man must not only know what to say, he must have a vehement longing to get up and say it. Many persons, rather sceptical persons especially, do not feel this in the least. They see before them an audience, – a miscellaneous collection of odd-looking men, – but they feel no wish to convince them of any thing. "Are they not very well as they are? They believe what they have been brought up to believe." . . . You may easily take away one creed and then not be able to implant another . . . Another kind of sceptic is distrustful . . . "It is of no use; do not hope that mere arguments will impair the prepossessions of nature and the steady convictions of years."'[9]

There was more against him than being a poor speaker. The previous month he had presaged his own defeat in a stirring *Economist* article. Called 'Politics as a Profession', this was a lament that large cities never chose the young unless they were locally connected. If the small constituencies were to be swept away and the large cities would not oblige, how would future ministers get into parliament? – 'young men, that is, who have nothing to recommend them but talent, honesty, independent means, laudable ambition, and a resolution to devote themselves to the most honourable and arduous of all professions – young men who are neither extreme radicals, nor millionaires, nor younger sons of peers or great statesmen, nor members of mighty county families?'[10] Reporting his failure to his parents, he observed that despite Gladstone's recommendation, 'Manchester could not "see it" . . . They said, "If he is so celebrated, why does not Finsbury elect him?"'[11]

The following year Bagehot did secure the nomination to Bridgwater, a small borough in his native county of Somerset. This time he lost by 7 votes in a poll of 595. He had campaigned enthusiastically, but was defeated by the constituency's traditional corruption, which later the Bridgwater Bribery Commission estimated always to affect three-quarters of the voters in that constituency.

Having lost because of his refusal to bribe the electorate, Bagehot nevertheless felt obliged to indemnify his agents for illegally spending £800 more than the legally permitted £700. He knew that if he did not pay up he would – in his own locality – be seen to be mean and a bad loser. Yet having paid that unauthorised sum and knowing that therefore his agents would feel indemnified the next time around, he felt unable to accept the nomination a second time. The constituency was disenfranchised by the Bribery Commission. Bagehot was left £1,500 poorer and without a seat, but with the consolation that his integrity was intact.

Not long into the campaign he had realised that he would almost certainly lose the election; purity lost votes. He gave the commissioners a diverting example of how this realisation had dawned on him during an encounter with a disarming rustic, who explained: 'I won't vote for gentle folks unless they do something for I. Gentle folks do not come to I unless they want something of I, and I won't do nothing for gentle folks, unless they do something for me.'[12]

Bagehot's painful experiences were to lead him to adopt the view that the best method of deterring candidates from corruption was to award the seat to the highest-polling candidate on the list who was proved to be free from corruption. 'You must give the purity-party a chance of the seat or you do nothing. You must say to them – "be pure yourselves; coerce into morality those who wish to bribe; look well after every inferior agent; do not let a farthing dribble where it ought not – AND you shall have your reward; *your* member shall be returned." The party with a legitimate majority will then have a legitimate advantage; if it is thoroughly pure and if it is efficiently detective it will win.'[13]

In 1867 Richard Holt Hutton tried yet again to secure the London University nomination for Bagehot but failed, largely because Bagehot lost his head in his election address and alienated Conservative voters by his attack on his *bête noire*: 'Mr Disraeli, indeed, believes that by influence and corruption the mass of the new voters may be made to aid him. But I do not believe that a government based on influence and corruption is possible in England.'[14] Having been rejected in the home of free trade, in his home county and in his old university, Bagehot gave up his parliamentary ambitions. He subsequently refused to stand for mid-Somerset in 1868 and for Liverpool in 1873.

There is no doubt about the depth of his disappointment. In 1870, in a paper to the Metaphysical Society, he offered himself as 'an example of utterly irrational conviction'. Having described how he lost Bridgwater, perforce refused to stand for the next election and saw another Liberal candidate elected, he concluded: 'I have of course ceased to have any hold on the place, or chance of being elected there. But for years I have the deepest conviction that I should be "member for Bridgwater;" and no amount of reasoning would get it out of my head. The borough is now disfranchised, but even still, if I allow my mind to dwell on the contest, – if I think of the hours I was ahead in the morning, and the rush of votes at two o'clock by which I was defeated – and even more, if I call up the image of the nomination day, with all the people's hands outstretched, and all their excited faces looking the more different on account of their identity in posture, the old feeling almost comes back upon me, and for a moment I believe that I shall be member for Bridgwater.'[15]

Despite Bagehot's and *The Economist*'s adherence to liberalism, his sceptical mind and search for simple truth kept the paper more independent than most of its contemporaries. Great changes in the press had come about in the previous decade with the abolition of the advertisement duty in 1853, stamp duty in 1855 and paper duty in 1861: an immense proliferation in newspapers resulted. In 1855, for instance, the *Daily Telegraph* was founded and the *Manchester Guardian*, the *Liverpool Post* and the *Scotsman* became daily papers. Sales rocketed overall, though the changes were not necessarily to the advantage of an expensive weekly like *The Economist*.

Most daily papers, including the *Telegraph* and the *News*, cost one penny; *The Times* cost threepence; *The Economist* cost eightpence. The profitability of the paper had gone up after the abolition of stamp duty, as the price was kept at the same level. Otherwise the tax abolition made little difference. Indeed there was more risk of competition, for example with the appearance in 1859 of the weekly forerunner of the *Investors Chronicle* and in the late 1870s with the emergence of the *Statist*.

The press was read almost exclusively by the middle and upper classes. It was not until the 1880s, when Forster's 1870 Education Act, providing for almost universal elementary education, had borne fruit, that there was a working-class market: the pioneering paper of the popular press – *Tit-bits* – was launched in 1880.

The dailies were primarily concerned with politics, particularly speeches, both in parliament and outside it, which were often reported in full. Additionally, some attention was given to the church, to business and to sport. *The Economist* was different. There the emphasis was on business: 'it is among . . . [men of business] and among them only that *The Economist* will ever circulate, and political articles would injure the paper, if they excluded necessary business matter or if they were not such as men of business would care to read. But if properly written they are a material support to the paper and strengthen its circulation. Indeed if politics were abandoned there wd. be a universal impression that the paper had changed its character and was going down.'[16] Thus wrote Bagehot in 1873 and throughout his editorship his eye was always firmly fixed on his typical reader. It was under Bagehot that, for instance, coverage of literature virtually ceased.

Economist editors have varied widely in their ideas about which – if indeed any – books should be noticed in the paper: it is an area where an individual's private intellectual interests particularly tended to surface. (Under the literary editorship of the ex-defence correspondent and omnivorous reader Gordon Lee in the 1970s and early 1980s, there was a nineteenth-century flavour to the 'Books' section's lavish coverage of literary biography and military history.) Books also can be easily squeezed out when there is pressure on space, or they can be a useful filler when material is short. A comparison of the quantity and subject-matter of book-reviewing under the first three regimes shows wide divergences. In the whole of April 1856, with Wilson and Greg in charge, the 'Literature' section filled in total thirteen-and-a-half columns – almost seven pages. Notices of the quarterlies – particularly Bagehot's and Hutton's *National Review*, the *Westminster Review*, the *Edinburgh Review* and the *Quarterly Review* – occupied three columns; Lieutenant-General Monteith's KARS AND ERZEROOM: *with the Campaigns of Prince Paskiewitch in 1828 and 1829, and an Account of the Conquests of Russia beyond the Caucasus* was allocated two. Slightly more space was given to a biography of Sir Robert Peel, full of heretical accusations against 'Economists', and to SYRIA AND THE SYRIANS; *or, Turkey in the Dependencies* by Gregory N. Wortabet, 'of Bayroot, Syria', while slightly less space went to the translation of Comte de Montalembert's WHAT IS TO BECOME OF ENGLAND? *The Political Future of England*.

The eclectic choice reflected the reality that Wilson never read anything but official papers, while Greg occupied a rarefied atmosphere intellectually far above and too eccentric for *Economist* readers. The reviews generally were leaden and heavily reliant on enormous slabs of quotation; an exception was the lively review of the book on Syria, which included a passionate denunciation of 'the deplorable condition of . . . Mahommedan females' and 'the utter want of education which must make the life of an Eastern woman one of inconceivable tedium and monotony'. Julia Wilson, perhaps?

In April 1860, under Richard Holt Hutton, total coverage was down very slightly to six-and-a-half pages. The first week's issue devoted a page primarily to four pamphlets on political reform, but included short reviews of the letters of the eighteenth-century *littérateur* Horace Walpole (a 'complete and reasonably cheap edition of Horace Walpole's Letters has long been a desideratum'), a collection of poetry and a new edition of the *Canterbury Tales*. Almost four columns the following week, one on the poems and essays of Hutton's and Bagehot's old friend William Caldwell Roscoe; two plus on *Travels in Eastern Africa; with a Narrative of a Residence in Mozambique* (including a passionate tirade against the evils of slavery), and one-and-a-half columns reviewing the *Edinburgh Review* and – incestuously – the *National Review*. Four columns again in the third week: one-and-a-half to a further review of *Travels in Eastern Africa*; onc plus devoted to *Biographies of Lord Macaulay Contributed to the Encyclopaedia Britannica* and just over one column

262 THE PURSUIT OF REASON

to a pamphlet called 'American Security. Practical Hints on the Test of Stability and Profit, for the Guidance and Warning of British Investors'. Even by Hutton's standards the three columns of reviews in the last week of the month must have been particularly perplexing to men of business. The lead review was on a French translation of the first volume of an Italian work on the papacy and Rome; almost two columns were devoted to a pamphlet about the army volunteer movement and one to a two-volume novel called *The Cousin's Courtship*. Hutton being the man he was, the reviews were excellent, but few had anything to do with the tastes or preoccupations of the paper's readers.

In April 1863, under Bagehot, there were three weeks with no book reviews whatsoever: the fourth ran to just over one page – entirely devoted to *Dialogue on the Best Form of Government* by Sir George Cornewall Lewis. (Five years later the policy was even more self-denying and stern: April yields just one book review, less than a column-and-a-half in length, on R.H. Patterson's *The Science of Finance*. In April 1874 there was not a single review.)

These developments are a vivid example of two aspects of Bagehot's professionalism as an editor: he gave his readers what they – not he – wanted, and he had no need to resort to 'padding' – a term he himself invented. 'I hope to be able to deal in some way with the book [*Some Leading Principles of Political Economy Newly Expounded*] in The Economist,' he wrote to its author, J.E. Cairns, in June 1874, 'but I shall not at all be able to deal with it as it deserves for a newspaper is not a good place for discussing any abstract arguments which require a precise use of terms and which presuppose a good deal of previous training and previous information in the reader. Particular points can be popularized in a newspaper when circumstances direct attention towards them – but a whole subject cannot be connectedly treated, – whereas it is the particular characteristic of your arguments that they require to be considered in their relations with one another and with much else. Want of space too, has made me abandon the special literature Sup[plemen]t. of the Economist; but you may depend on it I will do all I can to bring before the public the *rare* point of such a book as this.'[17]

Taking the first week in April in the same three years – 1856, 1860 and 1863 – for detailed comparison, the strengths and weaknesses of the paper under each of the three editors and the extent to which Bagehot rapidly improved it become clear.

On 5 April 1856, Wilson was in ministerial office and Greg was struggling to fill up the pages: the Crimean War had just ended and a peace treaty had been signed the previous day with Russia. Out of a total of 28 pages, more than three were occupied by the opening section – '*The Political Economist*'. Greg led with 'The Peace Malcontents', a leader which carefully suppressed his and Wilson's reservations about the way the war had been conducted. Rather disingenuously, he explained why those dissatisfied – for various reasons – with the peace treaty should accept it. He concluded: 'For ourselves, in the sentiments with which we regard this peace, satisfaction far outweighs all opposing and modifying feelings. From the outset of the contest, as our readers are well aware, we have strenuously and perseveringly maintained that our cause was just, that our policy was sound, that our ultimate success was certain if we did not halt or falter by the way. We have steadily denounced all suggestions of premature pacification, or hollow compromise, or unworthy despondency, or weak fatigue; and if we now appear among the rejoicers and congratulators, it is because we hold the main purpose of the war to have been substantially attained, and because, though we may have anticipated more brilliant success, we did not expect that it would come so soon; and therefore if our first feeling was one of slight disappointment, our second and deliberate feeling is one of cordial and unfeigned content.'

The next three articles were brief, uncontroversial and factual: 'The Revenue Accounts', 'Crossed Cheques on Bankers', and 'The Trade of February'. 'Italian Indications' was longer and livelier and a typical *Economist* rumination on trouble abroad: Italy could be rescued from tyranny and violence if the great European Powers exercised reason. The best remedy for the violence characterising Italian nationalist opposition to foreign rule was to buy Lombardy and Venice from Austria. Greg then got into his utopian colourful stride: 'This done, everything else would follow as a matter of course. A rich and prosperous State, of second magnitude, would be formed in the North of the Peninsula, – free, constitutional, and flourishing because free; an object alike of envy and of example to all others. Austria would thus be cut off from the South of Italy; and misgovernment there would cease as if by magic . . . Can no statesman, of all those assembled at the Conference, be found to initiate such a solution of the chronic difficulty? – a solution which would immortalise at once his name, Italian redemption, and European peace.'

'Factory Legislation' was classic James Wilson. His blood was up: the

House of Commons had been wasting its time discussing 'trifling, vexatious, costly, wasteful, and absurd' regulations.

> The real history of the Factory Act, put in a sentence or two, is this. New machinery came into use, by which careless or ignorant people were injured, or which by its own nature broke and destroyed lives and limbs. In this there is nothing extraordinary. Man is perpetually learning new arts, which bring with them new dangers, and keep him in perpetual pupilage . . .
>
> The factory workers, however, not being on good terms with their masters, and being supported by a set of theorists and gentlemen who had imbibed a ridiculous prejudice against manufacturers . . . made a great fuss about being liable to such injuries, and required that the Legislature should protect them. Compassionate noblemen, tinctured however with class prejudices against manufacturers, and demagogic parsons, who were more anxious to increase their influence than promote piety, aided a few leaders of the factory hands, and so the Legislature was induced to make a law about easing machinery, enclosing drums, providing hooks for bands, &c., &c.

The lawmakers had failed to realise how wrong was this meddling. 'The members of the Legislature are even worse than the Bourbons [who had learnt nothing and forgotten nothing]; for they not only repeat, they exaggerate, if it be in a somewhat different direction, the errors of their predecessors, and, by multiplying frivolous laws, are making obedience to all their enactments absolutely impossible.'

The 'political' section ended (apart from a half-page of revenue statistics) with 'OFFICIAL INTELLIGENCE OF PEACE':

> Foreign-office, March 31, 1856.
> The Hon. Spencer Ponsonby arrived at the Foreign-office this morning from Paris, with the definitive treaty for the restoration of peace, and for the maintenance of the integrity and independence of the Ottoman empire, which was yesterday signed at Paris by the Plenipotentiaries of Her Majesty, of the Emperor of the French, of the King of Sardinia, and of the Sultan, and also of the Emperor of Austria and of the King of Prussia, on the one part, and of the Emperor of all the Russias on the other.

'*Agriculture*' occupied less than half a page and mainly discussed the weather ('. . . we have a change which promises more genial gales with rain . . .'), the debt French cattle breeders owed their English equivalents and the encouraging tests of an Arachide-nut cake, palatable to both sheep and cattle. The one-page '*Literature*' section was followed by a little over half that space on the '*Imperial Parliament*'. The paper no longer printed full accounts of debates – merely summaries of the most relevant developments. The headings this week were 'PEACE WITH RUSSIA', 'SALARIES OF THE COUNTY COURT JUDGES', 'REFORM OF THE CORPORATION OF THE CITY OF LONDON', 'DRAWBACK ON MALT', 'BANK NOTES', 'MEDICAL PROFESSIONAL BILL', 'THE FACTORIES BILL', 'BLOCKADE OF THE RUSSIAN COAST', 'DIRECTORS OF JOINT STOCK BANKS', 'DRAFTS ON BANKERS BILL' and 'THE EXPORTATION OF IRON'.

'*News of the week*' ran to over two pages, led by 'COURT AND ARISTOC-RACY', which, along with information about royal levees, had quite useful business information ('Colonel Sir H. Rawlinson, KCB, has been appointed to succeed General Sir George Pollock as one of the nominated Directors of the East India Company'; 'An influential deputation has waited upon Lord Palmerston on the subject of the wine duties'). 'METROPOLIS' consisted of two sections. First: 'Health of London during the Week' – numbers of deaths and births registered in London compared to the years 1846–55, followed by immensely detailed weather reports from the Royal Observatory in Green-wich. Second: 'Drury Lane theatre. – The English Opera company is drawing crowded houses. The performances are of a first-class character, and Miss Dyer has appeared in the *Bohemian Girl* to very great advantage.' The bulk of this section was taken up by 'FOREIGN AND COLONIAL'. Based on a mixture of press clippings and information from Wilson's widespread commercial network, these items were highly variable in quality. The detailed information on France was of the kind that made *The Economist* invaluable to its discerning small readership. ('Business in Paris has been extremely stagnant. The best sorts of flour, which on Wednesday fetched 89f 50c per sack of 157 kilogrammes, sold on Saturday for 88f.'). There were brief entries on Austria (summarising the state balance sheet for the year to 31 October 1855); and on the United States ('specie exported 273,661 dols; total exportation, 1,607,502 dols.'). The 'West Indies' report was fascinat-ingly varied: 'The agricultural advices are generally satisfactory . . . Exchange was quoted for sixty days at one and a third per cent. Premium. The disturbances at Demerara had ceased. A militia has been formed, the number of persons already enrolled being upwards of 1,000.'). No firsthand report had come from the Cape of Good Hope: 'The journals received from the

Cape colony down to the 7th February represent the state of the frontier as still one for anxiety . . .' The paragraph on Australia opened vividly: 'By way of Valparaiso a few *Sydney Morning Herald*s, dated the 4th January, have come to hand, being a fortnight later than the accounts received by the Lightning.' India and China between them ran to one-and-a-half columns: 'Foochow dates are to the 4th instant. There is little change in the price of tea.' The week to 22 February in Calcutta had been 'characterized by much dullness and want of animation'; however interest rates were likely to be lowered in Bombay 'as the large importations of bar silver continued to arrive by the Suez steamers'. Details of tea transactions from Hong Kong and Chinese and Indian exchange rates *vis-à-vis* England concluded the commercial information and were immediately and absurdly followed by obvious – if brief – padding: a short list of strikingly irrelevant aristocratic births, marriages and deaths.

'COMMERCIAL AND MISCELLANEOUS' was a very accurate description of what followed, for the section included the average amount of banknotes in circulation in Ireland to mid-March, the state of duties on sugar imports into France from French colonies in India and the Americas, the declaration of ten shillings per share return on the Australian Royal Mail Navigation Company, an announcement by the Chancellor of the Exchequer that – as with British companies – a government duty would be payable on French policies undertaken in England, the presentation of a favourable report by the Housekeeper's Life Assurance Company, details of grain prices and a statement of deposits at the United States Branch Mint in New Orleans in February.

A tiny section headed 'To Readers and Correspondents' conveyed two messages:

> Q.Q.Q., in Paris. – 'Favour us by sending us a specimen. What you propose will be very welcome if reasonably well done.'
> H.E.P. – 'Our correspondent's communication shall appear next week.'

After this light relief, the paper moved on to two pages of '*The Bankers' Gazette*' and more serious matters, providing an avalanche of figures on 'BANK RETURNS AND MONEY MARKET'.

'*The Commercial Times*' was a catch-all running to over five-and-a-half pages. It covered 'FOREIGN MAILS' ('Destination: Lisbon, Madeira, Brazil, B. Ayres, and Falkland Isles; mails despatched from London: 9th of every

month; when expected: April 16'), 'Mails Arrived' ('On March 28, Cape of
Good Hope, per steam frigate Styx, via Falmouth'), 'WEEKLY CORN
RETURNS', 'COMMERCIAL EPITOME', 'IMPORTS OF GRAIN AND FLOUR
INTO LONDON', and 'SPIRIT OF THE TRADE CIRCULARS'. In this last item
eight circulars were featured, of which that of Messrs Powell and Co. of
London was the most general: 'A moderate scale of business, at nearly
unaltered prices, has been the general character of the leather market during
the past month; for although the political position of the country, as to its
warlike aspects, was somewhat doubtful, yet there existed a universal feeling
of almost confidence, that the termination of this state of uncertainty would
be peaceful, so that not any provision has been made by purchasers for
military purposes'; and that of Mr T. Thorburn of Glasgow the most specific:
'Bar iron has declined about 10s per ton, and the quotations are 8*l* 5s to 8*l*
10s, rails 7*l* 15s to 8*l*, at which there is a good demand.'

'*The Gazette*', which followed on, consisted of a column-and-a-half of
tightly-packed information on dissolved partnerships, sequestrations, bankrupts and declared dividends, followed by the 'COMMERCIAL TIMES', a page
of statistics called 'Weekly Price Current', headed by a note that 'the prices in
the following list are carefully revised every Friday afternoon, by an eminent
house in each department'. The statistics covered all available varieties of
ashes, cocoa, coffee, cotton, drugs and dyes, dyewoods, fruit, flax, hemp,
hides, indigo, leather, metals, molasses, oils, provisions, rice, sago, saltpetre,
seeds, silk, spices, spirits, sugar, tallow, tar, tea, timber, tobacco, turpentine,
wool and wine. The section's last column was a statement of comparative
imports, exports and home consumpion between 1 January and 29 March
1855–6, showing the stock on hand on 29 March in each year – for the Port
of London – of sugar, molasses, rum, cocoa, coffee, rice, pepper, raw
materials and dyestuffs.

'*The Railway Monitor*' – by now a sadly shrunken one-column section –
contained 'RAILWAY CALLS FOR APRIL', 'EPITOME OF RAILWAY NEWS'
(at home and abroad), 'RAILWAY AND MINING SHARE MARKET. LON-
DON' and was followed by '*The Economist's Railway Mining and Share List*' and
'OFFICIAL RAILWAY TRAFFIC RETURNS'. Then came five pages of
'*Accounts Relating to Trade and Navigation*' for January and February 1856 –
three tables, 'I. IMPORTS INTO THE UNITED KINGDOM', 'II. EXPORTS
OF FOREIGN AND COLONIAL MERCHANDISE FROM THE UNITED KING-
DOM' ('Silk Manufacturers of India: – Bandannoes, Corahs, Choppas,

Tussore Cloths, Romals, and Taffaties – 54,646 pieces exported in 1855, 52,216 in 1856') and 'III. EXPORTS OF BRITISH AND IRISH PRODUCE AND MANUFACTURES FROM THE UNITED KINGDOM'.

Finally, there were three pages of advertisements, including six shipping notices ('DANUBIAN PRINCIPALITIES, CONSTANTINOPLE and the CRIMEA. – The navigation of the Danube having reopened, the STEAMERS of the Imperial and Royal Danube Steam Navigation Company have RECOMMENCED RUNNING. For particulars and time tables see "Bradshaw's Continental Railway Guide"; or apply to Draper, Pietroni, and Co., 31 London Wall.') and railway company notices. Visitors were sought for three artistic events – Italian Opera at the Lyceum, English Opera at Drury Lane and 'for Gentlemen only' the re-opening of Dr Kahn's 'celebrated Museum, which has been elegantly re-decorated and enriched by many interesting additional objects . . . Amongst the new features of high interest will be found a magnificent Full-length model of a Venus, from one of the most eminent of the old masters.' There were advertisements for false teeth, bedsteads ('from the plainest japanned deal for servants' rooms, to the newest and most tasteful designs in mahogany and other woods'), oats, brooms, shirts, suits, doormats, jewellery, baths, beer and Schweppe's Malvern Seltzer. Most interesting of all – indeed the most engrossing part of the whole paper – were the medicine advertisements, full of wild claims, euphemisms, delphic utterances and doomladen warnings. White's MOC-MAIN LEVER TRUSS for the treatment of hernias was a vast improvement on 'the use of the steel spring, so often hurtful in its effects'; Jozeau's Copahine or Saccharated Capsules were 'the best remedy for a certain disorder (see "Lancet" of Nov. 6 1852)', while 'FRAMPTON'S PILL OF HEALTH' was a vital resource for every housekeeper and head of family in the land: it cured the temporary sickness occurring in families 'more or less every day', including the effect of over-indulgence at table, and was truly excellent in dealing with the manifold ailments of the Victorian female – 'removing all obstructions, the distressing Headache so very prevalent with the Sex [James Wilson could have benefited from handing it round at home]: Depression of Spirits, Dulness of Sight, Nervous Affections, Blotches, Pimples, and Sallowness of the Skin'.

But there were more serious medical problems than constipation to be addressed. An advertisement for a series of pamphlets by distinguished medical men set the tone with a verse from Cowper:

Read ye that run, the awful truth,
> With which I charge my page;
A worm is in the bud of youth.
And at the root of age.

Saml. La Mert, MD offered 'Nervous Debility: its Causes, Symptoms, and Cure' and 'The Science of Life: or, How to Ensure Moral and Physical Happiness', while a Member of the Royal College of Physicians submitted 'An Essay on Spermatorrhoea'. The palm has to be awarded to J. L. Curtis's treatise on the 'Causes of Premature Decline in Man, with Plain Directions for perfect Restoration. A Medical Review of every form, cause, and cure of nervous debility, impotency, loss of mental and physical capacity, whether resulting from youthful abuse, the follies of maturity, the effects of climate or infection, &c., addressed to the sufferer in youth, manhood, and old age: with the Author's observations on marriage, its duties, and disqualifications; the prevention and cure of syphilis, spermatorrhoea, and other urino-genital diseases'. The pamphlet came with a prescription for 'a disinfecting lotion for the prevention of all secret disorders' and an encomium from the *Naval and Military Gazette*:

> We agree with the author that, so far from works of this class being objectionable in the hands of youth, or difficulties being opposed, every facility should be given to their circulation: and to strengthen our opinion we need but refer to the recent distressing events at our military and scholastic academies at Carshalton and Woolwich.

The *Chronicle* was quoted as saying that, should youth put the pamphlet's precepts into practice, 'One cause of matrimonial misery might they [sic] be banished from our land; and the race of the enervate be succeeded by a renewal of the hardy, vigorous spirits of the olden time.'

Such advertisements are typical of those appearing in countless Victorian publications, but there is a pleasing incongruity about their appearance in a paper dedicated to the interests of scientific truth. Yet *The Economist* was true to itself in the areas that mattered. Spurious medical claims were one thing, dubious financial advertising another.

To the contemporary eye what is most striking about the 1856 paper is the sheer unreadability of most of it. It was no longer the crusading journal of the early days, propounding in page after page the philosophies of free trade and *laissez-faire*. Thirteen years on, believing the first cause won and viewing the second more pragmatically, the paper was largely a collection of specialist fact-sheets, geared to the needs of several disparate groups. But while the worlds of the banker, the silk importer, the flour miller, the farmer, the speculator and the manufacturer might touch only tangentially, those who read *The Economist* could rely on its information and expect to find at least some interesting general reading among the leading articles. (The length of the leaders usually ranged from about 800 to 2,400 words, though Wilson had been known to run closer to 4,000. By the end of the century they had stabilised at around 1,250, not much longer than today.)

Four years on, in April 1860, there was no change in size, the fact-sheets were essentially the same and substantial changes were not immediately apparent. Yet the more general parts of the paper already strongly reflected the interests of the new young men and '*The Political Economist*' had more than doubled in size. The one-page leading article – 'THE BILL BROKERS AND THE BANK OF ENGLAND. Is a Compromise Possible?' – was a racy piece on a rather esoteric issue in which Bagehot crisply reported the reasons for the dispute, explained why it was of public interest, summed up the rights and wrongs of the matter and proposed an eminently sensible compromise.

Hutton almost certainly contributed the three-column '"THE SITUA-TION" CALMLY REVIEWED' which followed – a solid and conscientious piece reviewing the Italian question so calmly and reasonably as to be soporific. Even more sedating for the general reader was the five-column 'MR WILSON'S PLAN FOR A PAPER CURRENCY IN INDIA', wholly composed of long extracts from his speech. Things livened up with another Bagehot piece: more than a page on 'SOME FALLACIES ABOUT REFORM', which was concerned to demolish the notion that all men who met certain minimum standards of literacy and numeracy had a natural right to an equal voice in the government of the country. 'In any other scientific question, no one would think of arriving at a decision by the votes of a majority of a body composed of the highly skilled, the moderately skilled, and those who had merely acquired the rudiments.' A way would be found to increase the franchise sensibly: 'there is a vast fund of good sense and public spirit in the English people, and let them once be persuaded that a system which gives to the workpeople of a single large contractor or manufacturer, a voice in the constitution equal to the united voices of all the merchants in the Royal Exchange, is not only unsound in itself, but is not the only available means of giving the working classes any voice in the constitution at all and there will yet be hope of modifying our constitution on a basis that shall endure for ten times the period for which the new Reform Bill is warranted to secure peace and quietness to the Government.'

The next three columns consisted of a long extract from James Wilson's speech on the cause and cure of the Indian deficit and the full text of a correspondence between government and Chambers of Commerce *à propos* the working of the commercial treaty with France.

Other than the two-page '*Literature*' section, the rest of the paper was little changed. Three years later, well into Bagehot's editorship, the quality of the leading articles in the slightly shorter political section was more even and the emphasis on finance more marked. The issue of 4 April 1863 led with a trailer for the following week, when the paper would include 'a Survey of Finance, showing the present state of the Revenue and Expenditure of the country, the changes in both during the last twenty years, and the principles which should regulate their course in future'. This issue began with a substantial analysis of 'THE STATE OF THE REVENUE', analysing in great detail the UK revenue for 1862, which had exceeded his estimates. The Christian socialist and writer Charles Kingsley inspired 'MR KINGSLEY ON EMIGRATION AND MANUFACTURING SELFISHNESS', a highly diverting piece of classic Bagehot mischief attacking Kingsley's tendency to jump to conclusions. 'Mr Kingsley,' it opened, 'notwithstanding his connection with a Christian Church and his residence in a civilized community, has many of the instincts of a Red Indian. The Old Adam is very strong within him.'

> For some reason or other, he is possessed with a fierce dislike and an incurable suspicion of all manufacturing employers of labour. Probably in his youth he drank in all the calumnies which were then current in London society and among Southern country gentlemen against Cotton Lords, and he still believes them to be the ogres and oppressors they were then represented. Perhaps in his infancy his father, like Hannibal's, swore him upon some Druid altar in 'Wessex' to undying hatred against a class whom he has persuaded himself are God's enemies and the people's as well as his own.

Bagehot's detailed and critical running commentary on the progress of the American Civil War continued with 'THE GROSS MISCONDUCT OF THE FEDERAL GOVERNMENT IN THE CASE OF THE PETERHOFF' and was followed by a short article on a relatively technical subject: 'MR GLAD-STONE'S BILL FOR THE ISSUE OF STOCK CERTIFICATES PAYABLE TO BEARER', then by 'THE PRUSSIAN CRIME' – an angry piece about the activities of one 'M. Von Bismark-Schonhausen', recently appointed Prime Minister of Prussia, who was to become one of *The Economist*'s *bêtes noires*: 'The Prussian Government is rapidly earning the reputation of being the most contemptible in Europe', the article opened, and it continued with a highly readable explanation of the crisis over the Polish insurrection and a savage attack on the 'evil' of Prussian involvement.

The quality of the paper had already risen sharply, because of Bagehot's emphasis on issues relevant to his readers, the excellence of his sources of information and the brilliance of his writing. The strides made in financial coverage had had their reward in the increasing importance of banking advertisements, which included the Bank of Hindustan, the Chartered Mercantile Bank of India, London, and China, the Union Bank of Australia and the Oriental Bank Corporation. There were, too, minor improvements to the specialist parts of the paper, but Bagehot was at work on a major overhaul, which was still in its early stages. Most important to this was the transformation of statistical coverage.

CHAPTER XIX:

Putting figures to it

> Many have an impression that Statistics are dull and uninteresting but such
> can only exist with those who are contented to look on long arrays of figures
> without reading them and learning the result, or the truths they teach. As
> well might we take up a volume, turn over its pages, and without reading one
> word pronounce them a mass of uninteresting *black* and *white*. To those who
> *read* Statistics, who read the results exhibited by figures, who find what new
> truths and facts they develop – what old prejudices and errors they dissipate;
> they are not only instructive, but afford the deepest, and often the most
> *exciting interest.*[1]

This ardent passage comes from Wilson's introduction to *The Economist*'s
first statistical supplement, which provided twenty tables covering a vast array
of historical data on population, revenue and trade. During his editorship,
Wilson hurled at his readers all the useful figures he could find, determined
that they should understand that there was probably 'no science of greater
importance to all other sciences than Statistics'. Reason and speculation were
all very well, he averred, but had to be tested by experience. Particularly 'in
regulating and guiding us to correct principles of trade, commerce, and
intercourse with other countries' the science of statistics had done more 'to
wipe away those intricate masses of cobwebs which narrow prejudices,
unworthy jealousies, unchristian animosities, and inflamed passion, had
contrived to weave between different countries in the world, than all the
reasoning or arguments otherwise have accomplished'. Similarly, more had
been done by the recently established Statistical Department of the Board of
Trade 'to advance the great interests of our country and of the world at large,
by the aid which facts have given to free-trade doctrines during the last ten or

twelve years, than could have been accomplished by the annual re-appearance of a Smith or a Burke, with all their cogent reasonings and burning eloquence for half a century to come'.

Wilson was an amateur number-cruncher, whose clarity of mind and immense capacity for detail had enabled him to make intelligent use of the inadequate data available. Bagehot was different: he hated detail, yet possessed unusual statistical insight and was no less determined than Wilson that *The Economist* should be the leading statistical journal of its day. Among his innovations were regular banking and budget supplements, an annual *Commercial History* and the *Investors' Monthly Manual*. And if he lacked Wilson's ardour, and better understood the limitations of numbers, he had in plenty an intellectual appreciation of the vital importance of lifting the science of statistics on to a sophisticated, professional plane. One of the leading Victorian statisticians, Robert Giffen, a close colleague of Bagehot's, was a great admirer of his 'quantitative' sense – his knowledge and feeling of the 'how much' in dealing with the complex working of economic tendencies.[2]

> Much economic writing is abstract, and necessarily so. You can say, for instance, that import duties tend to diminish trade between countries, and that duties on imported articles, when the same kind of articles are being produced at home, are peculiarly mischievous; or that fluctuating exchanges are injurious to trade. But in the concrete world there is something more to be done. Here the 'how much' is very often the only vital question. Fluctuating exchanges may be injurious to trade, but then they may be more tolerable than the evils incidental to some remedial course you propose. Import duties may also have to be tolerated as less injurious or more practicable than some other form of taxation; and even import duties which are protective may in given circumstances have to be accepted, for the sake of revenue or to prevent the mischief of too sudden changes.
>
> In dealing with concrete things, then, and the applications of his science, the economist must know where to place his emphasis – to be able to measure one evil against another and one force against another. And the sense necessary for this was Bagehot's in an unusual degree.

It was, thought Giffen, a quality whose value could not be over-estimated; it fascinated him that it co-existed in Bagehot with 'a repugnance to minute detail, including an aversion to manipulate figures, all but amounting to inability to "add up". The petty detail which most people find easy enough was beyond measure irksome to him; and the irksomeness was aggravated, when I knew him, by weak eyesight. But columns of figures are not statistics, though they are the raw material of statisticians; and this Bagehot fully proved by his remarkable appreciation of the numerical element in economic problems, all the while he had these technical difficulties in his way. In this quality he was second to no statistician I have ever met, and infinitely superior to most.' He was, in Giffen's view, an exceptionally good judge of statistical tables and the results they demonstrated. 'He knew what tables could be made to say, and the value of simplicity in their construction. He had an intense dislike of that vice of almost all amateur statisticians, and not a few experts, the attempt to put too much into their tables.' Additionally, he insisted that although you chose the most accurate of your clerks to prepare accounts and tables, you then had them checked by an expert, who would spot a flagrant error overlooked by mechanical compilers.

In developing the paper's statistical coverage, Bagehot's main ally was William Newmarch, a Yorkshireman, and yet another of those upwardly-mobile practical men to whom the nineteenth-century *Economist* owed so much.[3]

Born in 1820, Newmarch left school early. With – as *The Economist* put it coyly in his obituary – 'few of the advantages that a middle-class education now affords', he 'was mainly indebted for his association when very young with men in the active pursuits of business life'. He was a clerk first for a stamp distributor and then with the Yorkshire Fire and Life Office, graduating in 1843 to the position of second cashier in a Wakefield bank. 'Marrying young, and anxious for a wider scope for the exercise of a talent for the study and discussion of economical subjects, Mr Newmarch removed to London' in 1846 as second officer of the London branch of the Agra Bank and shortly afterwards also joined the *Morning Chronicle*. His talent and understanding of banking and currency came early to the attention of the great men in the field, particularly Wilson's old friend Thomas Tooke, and in 1852 Newmarch had the distinction of being elected unusually young to membership of the Political Economy Club – of which Tooke had been a founder. He fitted in. An historian of the club, Sir John Macdonnell, described Newmarch as a recruit to the Old Guard of individualists and *laissez-faire* stalwarts among the predominantly and increasingly agnostic membership. Macdonnell thought him a speaker 'of consummate lucidity and perspicuity, one who would have adorned any legislative assembly.'

By 1863, when Bagehot recruited him, Newmarch had for several years been a senior manager in the insurance industry, and in 1862 had become manager in the banking-house of Glyn, Mills, & Co. A man of immense energy, he had additionally developed a reputation as a useful financial journalist and a first-rate statistician, particularly in the trade and banking field. He had spent several years helping Tooke with the fifth and sixth volumes of his *History of Prices and of the State of the Circulation from 1792*, and his prestige rose dramatically in 1857, the year in which their publication coincided with Newmarch's vigorous evidence to the Select Committee on the Bank Act, in which, quite naturally, he ranged himself on the Tooke and Wilson side of the currency controversy.

The volumes were a superb reflection of what Giffen considered Newmarch's special forte – throwing light through statistics on problems related to the theory of business, especially banking – and on the applications of political economy to the real world. The volumes' scope was immense, but, said Giffen: 'Whether it is the effect of the gold discoveries in bringing new resources into the money market, and giving a vast impetus to trade, or the effect of a great movement of migration on the trade of old and new countries alike, or the financial consequences of a great war, Mr Newmarch is at home in the discussion.' He was, Giffen believed, the populariser of the idea that it is possible to generalise daily changes in the movement of business and relate them to the working of the laws of human nature. Tooke's and Newmarch's volumes were highly influential among economists both at home and abroad, and Newmarch received what was for a City man a very rare honour – election as a Fellow of the Royal Society.

Years after Newmarch's death, a member of the Political Economy Club, speculating on why many severe judges had thought so highly of him, suggested that it might have been due to 'his tremendous energy . . . his mastery of his business as a Bank Manager, and the downright vigour and rigour of an old-style, hard-headed economist'.

Palgrave told the story of how when he was editing *The Economist* he attended the Club sometimes at Newmarch's invitation. 'At one of these dinners the Governor of the Bank of England, past or present . . . was pluming himself on the way in which the Bank had passed through the crisis of 1866 without infringing the Act of 1844. The amount of Bank Notes held during the worst time then was exceedingly small. Palgrave had himself rather wondered how, considering the amount of Notes which they must have had in their tills at their various country branches at Manchester, Birmingham, Liverpool, and elsewhere, they had any left for Threadneedle Street. Newmarch soon settled the question. He took up the thread of discussion as the Governor left it. Casting aside his aspirates in his excitement, he said: "You did not break the Act, and I'll tell you 'ow you did it. You sent the 'at round Lombard Street every night, and we all paid in all the Bank Notes that we 'ad, and we drew them out again the next morning. That's 'ow you did it." '4

Certainly Bagehot was a long-standing admirer of Newmarch. In 'Monetary Schemes', an article he published in the *Saturday Review* in 1856,5 discussing an article of Newmarch's in *The Economist*, Bagehot described him as one of the 'ablest observers of our monetary phenomena'. And when in 1859 Bagehot wrote his seminal pamphlet on parliamentary reform, he made good use of Newmarch's paper, 'On the Electoral Statistics of the Counties and Boroughs in England and Wales during the Twenty-five Years from the Reform Act of 1832 to the Present Time',6 of which he said: 'We cannot speak too highly of these most admirable statistics. No pains have been spared to make them complete, and extreme judgment has been shown in the selection.'7

An enthusiastic member of the Statistical Society, Newmarch was proud of the progress that had been made in developing statistics as a science. It had arrived, he asserted in 1861, at a kind of intermediate point, from which the way up to a higher level could be seen – 'the least doubtful result of our experience being the discovery that the most solid progress is made by guiding ourselves in the main by close observation of facts, and by employing speculative and hypothetical reasons under the most cautious conditions, and always with distrust and reserve'8 – verily an ideal collaborator for Bagehot.

Newmarch's first and best-known job for the paper was to devise and prepare the annual *Commercial History*, heralded in *The Economist* as 'a careful Digest of the leading Merchants' and Bankers' Circulars in the different branches of trade, Lists of New Companies, Returns of Prices, Accounts of the Banks of England and France, &c. The object of the Supplement being to place in possession of our readers a Commercial History of 1863 worthy of preservation and adapted for reference.' Both in the *Commercial History* and in his many specialist articles in the paper itself, he contributed much more than facts and figures. In addition to what his *Economist* obituarist described as his skilful 'superstructure of reasoning', he brought to the paper the most modern statistical ideas and refined them to its purposes.

In the beginning, most *Economist* tables displayed only absolute values, but in such a way that the reader could easily see how that week's or month's value compared with previous ones. The text usually referred to the increases and decreases from one period to the next. Yet this information was of limited value. 'Merchants and manufacturers', wrote the economist, logician and statistician, Stanley Jevons, in 1862, 'are of necessity intimately acquainted, by experience or by tradition, with such periodic fluctuations as occur in their own branches of industry. By the skill and rule-of-thumb knowledge which each one acquires in his own pursuits, they make allowance for such variations, and thus very rude comparisons of prices, stocks, and sales enable them to detect irregular changes in their own market, which is all that they require.

'But this unwritten knowledge of commercial fluctuations is not available for scientific purposes, and it is always of a very limited extent.'[9] Jevons's aim in his analysis was to mimic the merchants' reasoning and set out the natural course of commerce in order to identify the extraordinary, finding out the nature of the yearly variation due to natural causes as opposed to extraordinary circumstances. Using prices quoted weekly in *The Economist*, Jevons developed a price index: Newmarch, who had already done trail-blazing work in this field, published price indices in the first issue of the annual *Commercial History Supplement* in February 1864, commenting: 'In the plan of these tables we have followed the methods laid down by the authors of the two last volumes of the "History of Prices" (by Tooke and Newmarch), and lately adopted by Mr Jevons in his able pamphlet "A Serious Fall in the Value of Gold Ascertained".' In 1869, in a two-and-a-half-page letter to the paper[10] on the depreciation of gold, Jevons discussed Newmarch's work on gold prices, acknowledged that they had developed the idea of price indices simultaneously and referred gratefully to 'Your invaluable Annual Review'. *The Economist* was the first newspaper in the world regularly to publish a price index.

From the beginning of Bagehot's editorship, many *Economist* tables included a column showing the increases or decreases over the previous week, month or year. Percentage changes and price indices then appeared as common features of Newmarch's *Commercial History*. The *Statist*, founded by Giffen in 1878, the year after Bagehot's death, used empirical averages and percentage changes and in 1886 had a price index designed by Augustus Sauerbeck, who admitted his debt to Jevons and Newmarch. *The Economist* and Sauerbeck indices were to have no competition until the appearance in 1903 of an official wholesale price index.

The Economist was paid the supreme compliment of imitation, and not just by the *Statist*: it was the model for the American *Commercial and Financial Chronicle* (whose aim was 'to give readers a classified, accurate, trustworthy record of all the movements in commercial and financial affairs'). And by the late 1880s all three journals frequently tabulated percentage changes of volumes and values. The staple was, however, the absolute increase or decrease from a previous period – what modern statisticians call 'first differences'. The preoccupation was with 'tracking change' – as Judy Klein points out in her *History of Practical Dynamics and Time Series Analysis*. *The Economist*'s table of contents referred to tables of values not as 'current prices', but as either 'price current' or 'the movement of prices'. 'In addition to stressing changes in values, some tables were arranged to emphasize the relative time framework of the calendar year . . . The values for one week, one month or one quarter were displayed' to give a feel for seasonal variations.

'The first use of the statistics', explains Professor Klein, 'was for financiers to compare one week's values with another, but the same data connected in a longer series could also be used by "public men" to give clues to the causes of economic fluctuations – hence tracking ups and downs of trade, and the tendency for good years to follow bad years in succession, produce the notion of "cycles of trade".' So these statistical innovations were to bear fruit for Bagehot, for instance, in the contribution he was to make to the theory of the trade cycle.

Judy Klein analyses developments from the early days of *The Economist*. Her table of the nature of quantitative reasoning in nineteenth-century journals is a graphic demonstration of what a pioneer Wilson had been:

Quantitative emphasis	Title	1st date and place
tabulated weekly, monthly data	*The Economist*	1843 – London
for trade, finance, commerce	*Statist*	1878 – London
	The Commercial and Financial Chronicle	1865 – New York
practical algorithms for handling vital statistics	*Journal of the Institute of Actuaries*	1886 – London
descriptive statistics – empirical, mathematical	*Journal of the Royal Statistical Society*	1839 – London
science, mathematical philosophy	*Philosophical Transactions of the Royal Society*	1665 – London

Professor Klein draws attention to the strong connections between the journals and their respective readers. Indeed, the world of statisticians was even smaller than that of the economists. The seriously interested met each other at what James Wilson assured his readers was the most attractive of all 'the literary or scientific societies in London – the Statistical Society (Regent Street). The meetings are held Monthly, from November to June inclusive in each year, when the papers which are read, and the discussions which arise thereon, are of the most interesting character.'[11]

Newmarch was in turn secretary and President of the Royal Statistical Society, editor of its *Journal* and assistant to Bagehot. Giffen became assistant editor of *The Economist* in 1868, and editor of the *Journal of the Royal Statistical Society* in 1876; he founded the *Statist* two years later (the latter regularly published proceedings of the Royal Statistical Society, which in turn published excerpts from supplements to the *Statist* on financial and commercial history). Stanley Jevons, a Fellow of the Royal Society and the Royal Statistical Society and in the late 1870s Professor of Political Economy at University College London, was friendly with Bagehot ('Possibly it may be worth naming that I have heard the Chancellor of the Exchequer and *two* Governors of the Bank of England speak of your book on the Gold discoveries with very great respect and praise', Bagehot wrote to him in 1866, in a letter designed to be a reference backing his application for the Cobden Professorship at Manchester),[12] and shared with him an alma mater. He was a relative of Bagehot's friends and family lawyers, the Roscoes; he appeared in *The Economist*'s letter pages and was possibly an anonymous contributor. (In

1866 Bagehot had asked him to write occasionally for the paper.[13])

Many of the statisticians also met each other at the Political Economy Club: 'Our members with rare exceptions have been busy men, merchants, judges and practising barristers, journalists, scientific soldiers, professors, millionaires, Government officials, ministers of State, Bank of England, or private bank directors . . . It would be difficult to imagine a more diverse, nondescript assemblage of diners, all, if socially of one class, more on an intellectual level, more willing to listen or talk, and abler.'[14] The members (limited to thirty from 1847 until 1904) met to dine briefly and discuss 'some doubt or question on some topic of Political Economy'. Bagehot, a member between 1864 and 1877, Greg, 1867–1881, and Newmarch, 1852–1882, were compared by a contemporary:

> Mr Newmarch was perhaps a statistician rather than an economist, but he was master of economic science, as then apprehended, and very positive in the enunciation and application of its principles. He was voluble and often excited in discussion and it was curious to watch the blood colouring his temples and forehead as his vehemence developed. He had long been secretary, was entire master of its business and was always present. I revert to stricter economists in naming Mr Bagehot. We met on Friday evenings, not a convenient day for the Editor of the *Economist*, but he came as often as he could and was always a welcome debater. If I venture to say that he was perhaps too frequently betrayed into the examination of differences and discriminations of the second order every reader of his writings can appreciate without accepting the criticism. His manner of speech was correspondingly finical and fastidious but his intervention in discussion was always stimulating and acceptable . . . Another clear and vigorous debater among us was W.R. Greg, author and reviewer – the W.R.G. of endless pungent paragraphs on topics of the day. Like his brother-in-law, Bagehot, he had a very large knowledge of literature and of business, but whilst Bagehot went on refining Greg was prompt and decisive and, if his nail may not always have been the right one, he always hit his nail and hit it on the head.[15]

It was almost certainly Newmarch who defined the 'true statistician' in an *Economist* article not long after Bagehot's death. He was 'not the man who seeks out figures to support his case, but rather he who, having perceived the bearing of the main facts on the subject he proposes to elucidate, then patiently works out his figures, examining and testing them the more scrupulously in proportion as they appear to support his case, and accepting the conclusions to be derived from them only after having satisfied himself completely not merely of the correctness of his calculations, but of the correctness of the conclusions he has deduced from them; and who, finally, is willing to throw aside the most dearly cherished theory, the moment it becomes doubtful whether it is entirely supported by facts.'[16]

It was a description of which Bagehot would have approved. He, however, took a more subtle – more 'finical' – view, never sharing the conviction of his father-in-law's generation that absolute certainty could be achieved. In 1876 he addressed himself to the limitations of statistics in an essay in the *Fortnightly Review*.[17] Political economy, he pointed out, was an abstract science which laboured under a particular disadvantage: 'Those who are conversant with its abstractions are usually without a true contact with its facts; those who are in contact with its facts have usually little sympathy with and little cognisance of its abstractions. Literary men who write about it . . . are like physiologists who have never dissected; like astronomers who have never seen the stars; and in consequence, just when they seem to be reasoning at their best, their knowledge of the facts falls short. Their primitive picture fails them, and their deduction altogether misses the mark.' On the other hand, 'those who live and move among the facts often, or mostly, cannot of themselves put together any precise reasonings about them'.

> Men of business have a solid judgement – a wonderful guessing power of what is going to happen – each in his own trade; but they have never practised themselves in reasoning out their judgements and in supporting their guesses by argument; probably if they did so some of the finer and correcter parts of their anticipations would vanish. They are like the sensible lady to whom Coleridge said, 'Madam, I accept your conclusion, but you must let me find the logic for it.' Men of business can no more put into words much of what guides their life than they could tell another person how to speak their language. And so the 'theory of business' leads a life of obstruction, because theorists do not see the business, and the men of business will not reason out the theories. Far from wondering that such a science is not completely perfect, we should rather wonder that it exists at all.

Statistics had helped by giving tables of facts that kept theoretical writers on the right lines, yet problems remained. Writers with no practical experience often misunderstood the material: 'At the outset there is a difference between the men of theory and the men of practice. Theorists take a table of prices as facts unsettled by unalterable laws; a stockbroker will tell you such prices can be "made". In actual business such is his constant expression. If you ask him what is the price of such a stock, he will say, if it be a stock at all out of the common, "I do not know, sir; I will go on to the market and get them to *make* me a price."' Statisticians made tables in which 'artificial tables run side by side with natural ones; in which the price of an article like Honduras scrip, which can be indefinitely manipulated, is treated just like the price of consols, which can scarcely be manipulated at all . . . In most cases it never occurs to the maker of the table that there could be such a thing as an artificial . . . price at all.'

Then there was the problem of comparing prices of commodities of varying quality. The *Gazette* average of corn was compared incessantly, as if quality was constant. Corn this year might be vastly superior to that of last year, yet the tables compared the two 'without noticing the difficulty. And when the range of prices runs over many years, the figures are even more treacherous, for the names remain, while the quality, the thing signified, is changed. And of this persons not engaged in business have no warning.' Even the best statistical tables were no substitutes for a true knowledge of the facts: 'they do not, as a rule, convey a just idea of the movements of a trade to persons not *in* the trade'.

> It will be asked, why do you frame such a science if from its nature it is so difficult to frame it? The answer is that it is necessary to frame it, or we must go without important knowledge. The facts of commerce, especially of the great commerce, are very complex. Some of the most important are not on the surface; some of those most likely to confuse *are* on the surface. If you attempt to solve such problems without some apparatus of method, you are as sure to fail as if you try to take a modern military fortress . . . by common assault: you must have guns to attack the one, and method to attack the other.

Bagehot had need of help in developing the statistical armoury and it was to strengthen him as a writer on finance. Yet although experience was to add richness and greater technical competence to his economic writing, from a very early stage in his life as a banker he had a precocious grasp of the fundamentals of the world of money which no amount of experience or accumulation of detail could obscure. It was one of his greatest intellectual strengths that having grasped a general principle, he never lost sight of it, for his were real truths – not matters of doctrine: they were rooted in the timeless realities of the human condition.

CHAPTER XX

'A "new cut" into things'*[1]

Much has been written on panics and manias . . . but one thing is certain, that at particular times a great many stupid people have a great deal of stupid money. Saving people have often only the faculty of saving; they accumulate ably, and contemplate their accumulations with approbation; but what to do with them they do not know. Aristotle, who was not in trade, imagined that money is barren; and barren it is to quiet ladies, rural clergymen, and country misers . . . [our scheme] for preventing improvident speculation . . . is, not to allow any man to have a hundred pounds who cannot prove to the satisfaction of the Lord Chancellor that he knows what to do with a hundred pounds. The want of this easy precaution allows the accumulation of wealth in the hands of rectors, authors, grandmothers, who have no knowledge of business, and no idea except that their money now produces nothing, and ought and must be forced immediately to produce something.[2] *Walter Bagehot, 1856*

The year following that observation, Bagehot was able to view the 1857 panic at first hand as a banker and at second hand through the eyes of the Financial Secretary to the Treasury. After a period of very hard work, he wrote to Eliza in January 1858 that the crisis was all over and 'everybody has *too* much money. It is really a very ridiculous world. The last few times I have been here everybody was on their knees asking for money – now you have

---

*James Bryce wrote to Emilie Barrington in 1914 of Bagehot: 'He always made, as Aristotle says of Plato, a "new cut" into things. Whenever he touched anything he brought up a crop of new ideas on a subject that had seemed trodden hard, just as a shower of rain in the South African Karroo will bring up grass and flowers.'

nearly to go on your knees to ask people to take it. Neither of these two extremes is very pleasant.'

> Being besought is not unagreeable intrinsically – but when a man is very earnest for money, you begin to suspect he is 'in difficulties' and ought not to have it, and in the other case it seems demeaning the majesty of money to ask – or beseech – human beings to take it. You look at a hard eyed bill broker and think what is this man created for, if *not* to take money. Still the present state of things has the advantage that there is no tension of mind in managing your business while it lasts. You need not follow a man with your eyes when he takes away your money and think '*Will* he ever pay me?' – I own I like the *sensation* of safety.[3]

Almost twenty years later, he remarked in his second and last essay on 'The Postulates of English Political Economy', that if stated plainly, it would probably be new to many people that 'a very great many of the strongest heads in England spend their minds on little else than on thinking whether other people will pay their debts. The life of Lombard Street bill brokers is almost exclusively so spent.'[4]

Bagehot had published only literary and political articles between 1853 and 1855, but from 1856, during the five years before he became editor of *The Economist* in 1861, he had published extensively on finance – mainly on banking and currency. For the *National Review* he wrote essays in 1857 on 'The Crédit Mobilier and Banking Companies in France'[5] and the following year on 'The Monetary Crisis of 1857'.[6] But while he enjoyed working some of his ideas out at considerable length, Bagehot usually reserved the long essay for literary topics or profiles. When he wrote about money, brevity was more appropriate: a literary man would read a fourteen-thousand-word article; a businessman would be unlikely to get through more than a couple of pages.

To the *Saturday Review* in 1856 Bagehot contributed five short pieces ('Money', 'The Crédit Mobilier', Monetary Schemes', 'Sound Banking' and 'Unfettered Banking'), but the following year he had his serious break-through into financial journalism with his twelve 'A Banker' letters in *The Economist*. After a brief lull, and to provide essential backup for Hutton, from 1859 he began to write increasingly frequently on financial matters: by 1861 he was writing the money leader virtually every week.

As Bagehot's experience of business increased, so did his determination to get through to his readers – to become 'the belief producer' that James Wilson had been. It had always been a preoccupation of his: he prized clarity above all other stylistic virtues, observing in 1852 that 'the knack in style is to write like a human being. Some think they must be wise, some elaborate, some concise; Tacitus wrote like a pair of stays; some startle, as Thomas Carlyle, or a comet, inscribing with his tail. But legibility is given to those who neglect these notions, and are willing to be themselves, to write their own thoughts in their own words, in the simplest words, in the words wherein they were thought.'[7] That professionalism which he displayed to such a marked degree as editor of *The Economist* was particularly noticeable in the deliberate way in which he amended his style to suit his non-literary audience. Richard Holt Hutton would later lament that Bagehot's later writing lacked the buoyancy and elasticity of the early years, yet the refinements he made did not go against the grain.

Giffen, who came to work with him as late as 1868, found him still labouring 'to be conversational, to put things in the most direct and picturesque manner, as people would talk to each other in common speech, to remember and use expressive colloquialisms. Such Americanisms as the "shrinkage" of values he had a real liking for, and constantly applied them. I have known an eminent German economist so caught by this style as to imagine that Bagehot was a self-taught businessman and not a scholar.'[8] Yet Bagehot's scholarship was a key element in bringing economic and financial matters alive. What his father-in-law had done with his heart, he did with his head. As Jacques Barzun said, he performed his miracles of animation through the use of his historical sense: 'He is always "applying the historical method" (which includes the biographical).'[9]

It was that historical sense that he brought to the theory of the trade cycle, developing through reading and observation an explanation of how the economy swung between boom and collapse. His argument was broadly that a period of prosperity leads to increased consumer spending, optimism makes credit more easily available, so the stupid money goes looking for good returns; this encourages schemes which compete for further capital and scarce resources, thus raising prices and interest rates, which affect confidence and hence in the event of, for instance, a bad harvest, precipitate a crisis. The ensuing depression reduces the cost of resources and money, so credit improves as time passes, people forget, spending increases, John Bull gets fed up with 2% and the whole cycle starts all over again.[10]

Bagehot refined and developed this theory week by week and sought to drive its lessons home to his readers – both high and low. He directed telling advice at the Bank of England during the period of stagnation that followed the 1857 crisis and was exacerbated by a bad harvest in 1860 and the outbreak of the American Civil War in April 1861. In September of that year he published an article called 'The Duty of The Bank of England in Times of Quietude'. The Bank's duties 'in times of quiet and plenty are at least as important as those which fall to their lot in times of scarcity and disaster. The duties of a time of ease are quieter and tamer and less conspicuous, but they have ultimate consequences as momentous, whether for evil or good, as those of an awful momentous crisis. It is in times of plenty that the seeds of disaster are scattered; it is in times of plenty that there is an opportunity for financial discretion. During the extremity of a crisis, and even for a long previous period, the course of the Bank of England is scarcely *optional*. A definite course of conduct is chalked out before it by pressing necessity. But in times of quietude there is a choice really open to it. It can actually select the policy which it desires; and it is, therefore, very important to consider which it should select.' What the Bank directors had to do was 'to move with the market, or *after* the market, but not to move too rapidly'. They should be augmenting their reserves 'against a day of future difficulty'.[11] And when the signs of expansion appeared in 1863, *The Economist* sounded many a note of caution. In the *Commercial History of 1863*, 'prudent observers' were warned to be ready 'for contingencies the exact date of which is alone uncertain'. 'Credit', the paper warned, 'was the life of trade, but every sudden growth of new credit is always tainted with an admixture of evil.' Trade would probably flourish in 1864, but then there was the possibility that a long period of dear money would lead to the gradual failure of any trade that had been fostered by 'undue credit'.

Bagehot was to publish in *Lombard Street*, in 1873, the fruit of twenty years of experience of, rumination on and writing about banking and the world in which it operated. A key stage of development in his thinking came through his experiences as both banker and journalist during the period encompassing the City's first 'Black Friday' – 11 May 1866 – when Overend, Gurney & Company Ltd closed its doors to depositors and precipitated a major panic: *The Economist*'s forebodings had been justified. A byword for respectability ('grave old gentlemen . . . spoke of "Overend's" with a curious solemnity and almost under their breath'[12]), Overend's had latterly moved from straightforward bill-broking to more long-term investments – borrowing short and lending long. In July of the previous year, to raise extra capital, the partners had turned the firm into that relatively newfangled entity – a limited company. At the time Bagehot publicly welcomed this development on the grounds that it would require Overend to publish to its shareholders the state of its old and new kinds of business. 'For many years it has been a matter of public notoriety that this firm transacted business not at all in general of an illegitimate or unprofitable character, but still of a sort different from those conducted by bill brokers "pure and simple" . . . we have heard many people with *real* money say that they should like to know the proportion between the pure bill broking business of Messrs Overend, and the *extra* and accessory business which their large superfluous means had led them also to undertake. *Now* we shall know this.'[13]

The hint that all was not well was necessarily guarded: as he explained to his readers after the crash, 'we could not say what we then believed, and what was generally known, that the old firm had by most reckless management reduced one of the most profitable concerns in England to one of the most losing concerns. We can only say what we can *prove*, and though we thought this as much as we now think it, we could not say it in print without legal consequences.'

(In the 1970s and 1980s *Economist* readers also had ample hints about a dubious bank. A report in 1978 called 'ENIGMA VARIATIONS' speculated on the mystery of the ownership of the Bank of Credit and Commerce International, revealed that the Bank of England was preventing it from opening more than the 45 British branches it already possessed, and discussed its association with Bert Lance, President Carter's budget director, who had been forced to resign after a financial scandal the previous year.[14] When BCCI hit the headlines in October 1988 with the arrest of several of its staff in the US on charges of laundering drug money, *The Economist*'s report from Washington and Karachi was extremely detailed and frank. 'Among the world's banks', it began, 'BCCI has an unorthodox image. It is a secretive outfit with a complicated corporate structure. Most of its banking offices are controlled through holding companies in Luxembourg and the Cayman Islands, places not noted for tough banking regulation.'

Particulars of ownership followed, and the involvement of Bert Lance was again discussed. This broad hint was followed by:

> For years there have been rumours that some of BCCI's staff were suspected of being involved in shady deals. When asked about this recently, a BCCI official brushed it off as racism. BCCI, he pointed out, is a third world institution – owned by Arabs, run by Pakistanis, and patronised by dark-skinned people from poor countries. Is it any wonder that the white men who dominate international banking look down their noses at it?
>
> Those noses are now longer and steeper.[15]

In January 1990 the comprehensive 'HOW BCCI GREW AND GREW', written in Washington, Tampa and London, included information about investigations into the bank, exchange-control violations and more about Bert Lance. Readers were also told about BCCI's troubles with regulators in the United States and reminded of the freezing of its number of British branches in 1978.

It was no wonder that the tone of the leader on the collapse of BCCI in July 1991 was minatory about the failures of auditors and regulators and dismissive of claims for compensation. 'No bail-out' read a sub-heading.

> Depositors with BCCI are clamouring for compensation beyond whatever pay-out they will get from their deposit-insurance funds. Governments should resist pressure to bail them out with taxpayers' money. In banking, as in other financial supervision, a licence to operate cannot be treated as if it implies a government guarantee. Some of BCCI's customers had chosen the bank quite deliberately: they risked money in order to obtain above-market rates of interest or to hide their assets from tax authorities. Foolish, greedy or badly informed, their decisions have to be their choice, made at their risk.[16]

Or, as Bagehot had put it in relation to the scandal of his day: 'The plain truth is that Overend, Gurney *un*limited, for the sake of high interest took bad securities, and in consequence someone must reap the due consequence of that badness.'[17])

The inevitability of reaping the consequences was one of Bagehot's recurring themes: someone always had to pay for a bad decision. If John Bull was not content with 2% and speculated, John Bull risked losing his money – and deserved to. No *Economist* reader had an excuse for not having foreseen trouble.

Some months after the 1866 panic was over, reacting to the fact that there was a great deal of money lying idle 'craving for a safe and not extreme income, if only it knew where to find it', he set out in two deliberately simplified articles in *The Economist* the basics of investment:[18]

> The primitive considerations in money are two. First, whose labour do you propose to get a share of? Secondly, what is your certainty that you will get a share in it? Persons who want to understand the income [sic], should sit with folded hands, should lock themselves into a room until they can answer these questions plainly, and to their own satisfaction; . . . These questions raise two distinct topics of reflection, which must be kept apart or the subject is in a maze: the efficiency of the industry in which the investor proposes to take part, and the guarantee which the investor has that if he lends his money he will really get a share in that industry.

He proffered some general cautions as precepts to the investor:

> First, have nothing to do with anything unless you understand, *at least* believe you understand, and stop for any time and whatever anyone may say till you are sure you do understand it. If you find it baffle you long, have nothing to do with it, for probably you may not apprehend it after all.
>
> Secondly, divide your investments. It will be evident from what has been said that every mode in which money can be employed has some attendant risk. This taking a share in industry is a delicate process to those who *can* know but little of industry . . . Thirdly, we should warn investors against the advice of others. It is quite right to take counsel, to hear what is to be said, and to use it as ground for a decision. But it must be used to aid the intellect, not to supersede the discretion. Most advisors counsel what is safe for themselves, but then they suppose a competency which probably the person advised does not possess.

The broker should be trusted to tell the investor *when* but not *what* to buy, for he might have 'an interest in deciding wrong, and has at least a far less interest in deciding the matter rightly than you the investor have'.

The same rules of common sense held good for bankers, for whom Bagehot produced practical wisdom with great regularity and commendable patience, pointing out again and again that the essence of banking was trust, and that one should lend money only if one had good reason to expect the recipient to repay. One of his most telling *Economist* articles – and one which should provoke a wince from many international bankers today, as they still labour under their burden of Third World bad debt – was called 'The Danger of Lending to Semi-Civilised Countries'. Written in 1867, it questioned the wisdom of making a large loan to Egypt. What perturbed Bagehot was the tendency to 'lend to countries whose condition we do not know, and whose want of civilisation we do not consider, and, therefore, we lose our money'. The problem was, he began, that few people had any appreciation of the risk of lending 'to a country in a wholly different state of civilisation . . . The primary conditions of national good faith are three – a continuous polity; a fixed political morality; and a constant possession of money.'[19]

The Bank of England was in a different category: it was the lender of last resort and therefore had a special role, particularly in a panic such as that of 1866, brought about by a loss of confidence in credit. Recognising its nature, on Black Friday itself, Bagehot wrote a note to the Chancellor, Gladstone, to stress how matters stood at the grassroots. 'A complete collapse of credit in Lombard St and a greater amount of anxiety than I have ever seen.

'Large orders for notes are sent from the country by Country bankers, and the notes are going down this evening . . . There is much foreign money in London invested in bills . . . I fear this money will be withdrawn from a general apprehension that English credit is not to be relied on.'[20] Bagehot was one of those Gladstone consulted on whether Peel's 1844 Bank Charter Act should be suspended to remove the restriction on uncovered note issue to fourteen million pounds.

A week later, with the Act suspended and the panic over, Bagehot gave almost three pages in *The Economist* to a luminous explanation of the whole panic, addressing what he considered the four key issues: 'Why was there a Panic?' ('Last Friday no one knew who was sound, and who was unsound. The evil was not an over expenditure of capital such as at other times, as in 1847, has caused a panic; nor a drain of bullion which, except for admirable management, in 1864 would have caused one, but a failure of credit from intrinsic defect. Suspicion got abroad not because our whole reserve of bullion was too low to support the credit of the country; not because our annual expenditure had dangerously surpassed our annual saving; but because the lenders of money were *suspected* of misusing it; because the most celebrated of old houses evidently had misused it; because no one knew who else might not be to blame; because all persons under obligations to pay on demand felt they must strengthen themselves because the floating peril might come their way, and if they did not they might perish. The panic of 1866 was, to speak strictly, a credit panic – not a capital nor a bullion panic. And this is why there was such need for the suspension of the Bank Charter Act.');[21] 'The Suspension of the Bank Charter Act' ('had it not been broken this month, it would have been repealed next'); 'Conduct of the Bank of England' (given by Gladstone 'a letter of liberty . . . not a letter of licence', their conduct had been 'sound, cautious, and admirable', except in respect of their hesitation about lending on government security); and 'What will happen now?' ('though the immediate future must be chequered and painful, the worst bitterness of the panic is already spent and past'.) More than a century later, this article has a breathtaking immediacy and authority.

From 1868, although Bagehot continued to write the general economic articles in *The Economist*, most of the financial journalism was written by Robert Giffen. Bagehot had become seriously ill in December 1867 and took several months to recover; he was never to become strong again. He had therefore had to hire an assistant.

Giffen was yet another self-made man.[22] He was born in 1837 in Strathaven, Lanarkshire, the son of a grocer who was also an elder of the Presbyterian Church. Educated at the village school, with his elder brother John he ran the Sunday School library, read voraciously and wrote anonymously articles and poems for a newspaper in Hamilton, the nearest big town. At the age of thirteen he was apprenticed to a lawyer and spent a good deal of his time in Glasgow during the next seven years, where he attended two sessions at the University. He transferred to a commercial house, but in 1860 decided to become a journalist. After two years as a reporter and sub-editor on the *Stirling Journal*, he came to London as a sub-editor on the *Globe* – an evening newspaper that had once been edited by James Wilson's old enemy, Colonel Torrens, and which until 1869 was a vigorously liberal organ. In 1866, now married to a Glaswegian, he became assistant editor of both the liberal *Daily News* and John Morley's *Fortnightly Review*: the journals to which he contributed as a freelancer included the *Spectator*.

For Bagehot, Giffen was an ideal choice on professional and personal grounds. They saw eye to eye on the important issues and they already had a friendly relationship. As early as 1861 they had been in correspondence on technical matters to do with the National Debt[23] and about an article of Bagehot's on the American Constitution.[24] A letter of Giffen's in January 1865 mentions their having met to discuss his plan to abolish all banking restrictions to issuing banks.[25] By the middle of that year Giffen was sufficiently well-known and they were on sufficiently good terms for Bagehot to apply to him for a testimonial to help him in his attempt to win the Manchester constituency nomination. 'It would be presumptuous', wrote Giffen, 'in expressing an opinion as to your qualifications for Parliament, to want to connect that opinion with any particular constituency. But of the qualifications themselves neither I, nor, as I believe, any one who knows you can have any doubt whatsoever; and undoubtedly they point, of themselves, to the class of our great commercial and manufacturing constituencies in an especial degree. If thorough acquaintance with Economic science, and accurate knowledge, ready and practical habits of mind and a conciliatory disposition, go to fit a man for the representation of these great national interests, it certainly appears to me that your fitness must stand without dispute in the fittest rank.'[26]

In 1867 Giffen had written an important article on the National Debt and had become a member of the Statistical Society, of which he would become President in 1882. His skills as a statistician were already being recognised widely. That same year the President of the Poor Law Board, G.J. Goschen (Chancellor of the Exchequer, 1887–1892), asked Giffen to help with an historical retrospect and with statistics for the Local Taxation Report to the Treasury.

To Bagehot he was a great blessing: they helped to develop each other's statistical skills and in politics and on matters to do with the City they were close enough for Giffen to become in many ways Bagehot's alter ego. At this stage of his life Giffen was a moderate liberal and was passionately in favour of free trade: as an economist he was a Ricardian and committed to laissez-faire. He was also a man of cultivation, common sense and gregariousness who would become a mainstay of the Political Economy Club, to which he was elected shortly after Bagehot's death. One of his admirers recollected years later that sometimes in conversation with Giffen 'some one present was able to clench and condense his argument by quoting one of the lapidary phrases with which the Wealth of Nations abounds. The effect was always the same. Beaming with pride and pleasure Giffen would exclaim, "We are none of us wiser than Adam Smith!" . . . in matters of statistics we are none of us wiser than Robert Giffen . . . The sagacity with which Giffen perceived and avoided the pitfalls of statistics amounted to something like instinct, not to be transmitted by statistical testament.'[27] One of his excellent characteristics was to appreciate another man's gifts and he was to write movingly of the joy of drinking 'of the champagne of Bagehot's wide discursive talk, full of humour and sidelights on every subject he touched'.

Giffen's reflections on the nature of journalism sound a warning note about being too literal-minded about who wrote what in *The Economist* – even in the days before the heavy subbing that is now the norm.

> Discussions arise and pass away, and what each man did in them it is not easy to trace. This is plain as regards what passes in conversation and private notes; but even in journalism it would not be easy by a collection of articles, assuming that the articles themselves on passing topics would be interesting enough to collect, to give a notion of what a particular journalist did. Sometimes it happens that a man with a special knowledge of a particular subject cannot write upon it when the occasion arises, because he is busy with something else; so that his ideas have to be filtered through another mind if they are made public at all. Sometimes much of his own writing has to be on subjects not specially interesting to him, and where he is perhaps the funnel for another man's ideas. Thus the articles of a journalist, apart from their fugitive character, which is an obvious drawback, may be a very imperfect representation of his contribution in the shape of ideas to a particular journal.

As editor, Bagehot was in a good position to avoid writing 'another man's ideas on another man's subject instead of his own, though he could not altogether escape the necessity of writing on what did not much interest him; but he could not escape at all the necessity of passing on favourite subjects and ideas to others.'[28]

The list of favourite subjects was long. He was, said Giffen, 'as far as possible from giving the idea of a man with a special genius for a subject and much absorbed in it . . . our business talks, though having for end and object the conduct of a political and business newspaper, always travelled much wider than the record. Not to speak of his interest in literature and philosophy, he had the keenest interest, for instance, in the essential differences of system between English and Scotch law and English and Scotch forms of local and judicial administration, a subject which grew out of some business topics in the beginning of our acquaintance; in the art of money making, as distinguished from mere knowledge and skill in economics and the methods and subjects of business; in the working of personal motives of revenge and the like, as they affected the great game which was constantly playing before us in the City; similarly, in politics, in the personal element, the personal and family relationships of our public men, which he believed to have far more effect on the course of politics and parties, and the making or marring of careers, than the outside world supposes.'

> I only mention a fragment of the things about which he was intellectually curious, and which were yet far enough away from the special subjects before us . . . Bagehot undoubtedly possessed the quasi-omniscience so necessary in the highest journalism as well as the best literature in an unusual degree, and as such he could not be primarily an economist as the world understood him. He was something very much greater – a thinker of some new ideas of great value in the science, and a describer of the modern world of business, which is so different from the world of business that existed only one or two generations ago, and which alone could be in the minds of earlier writers on political economy; and he was all this in part *because* the study of political economy formed only a portion of his intellectual interest.[29]

Giffen became City editor of *The Economist* in 1870; he left the paper at the end of 1872,[30] becoming City editor of the *Daily News*, and in 1876, additionally editor of the *Journal of the Statistical Society*. He stayed friendly with the Bagehots, and probably continued to contribute to the paper. By this time Bagehot had other help. Eliza mentions a Mr Ellis, who was on the staff at the time of Bagehot's death, and Edward Johnstone, a financial journalist and later to be editor, also wrote for the paper.

The 1866 crash had been followed by the – to Bagehot – now predictable period of virtual stagnation, followed by a boom, which began in 1868 and continued until 1873. Danger signals flashed in 1870 as a consequence of events in France. Napoleon III, whose virtues and failings had been fascinating Bagehot for twenty years, declared war on Prussia for what Bagehot thought to be reasons of 'mortified vanity'. ('Probably no great ruler, so little scrupulous as Louis Napoleon certainly is, ever so deliberately and inexorably gave judgement as it were *against* himself. Did ever any man before, who had succeeded so well in accumulating power, succeed equally well in surrendering it again? Did ever before a vaulting ambition show as cold a sagacity in leaping down from a height as in scaling it?'[31]) He lost the war, the Empire collapsed and the Bank of France suspended payments in cash. With large sums of foreign money being diverted to London, Bagehot feared a repeat of 1866. He decided to put into the form of a book the ideas that he had been hammering home in *The Economist* for years.

Ill-health, grief (his mother died in 1870) and his many professional preoccupations prevented him from publishing *Lombard Street* before the spring of 1873. What emerged was a great monument not only to Bagehot, but to the newspaper that had afforded him the freedom to refine his ideas and bring them to maturity without interference of any kind.[32]

The primary audience to whom Bagehot wished to get through were those who ran the various institutions which in effect ran the money market – 'the various kinds of City men, the merchant, the stockbroker, the banker, [who] were all living figures to him', as Hutton put it: Bagehot loved to 'dissect, with that realistic humour of which he was a master, the relative bearing of their disturbing passions and conventions on that instinct of gain which forms the sole basis of economical reasoning'.[33] Knowing these people as intimately as he did, he realised that many of them – high and low – lacked a sense of the wheel in which they were cogs. As Giffen pointed out, the 'conception of the London money market as an organization does not seem to have occurred to anyone before'.[34] A grasp of the workings of that unofficial organisation was a prerequisite for grasping the ideas Bagehot wished to sell – hence that exercise in clarification and demystification that has made *Lombard Street* a classic for over a century, when some of the issues raised by it are no longer topical.

'I venture to call this essay "Lombard Street",' he began, 'and not "The Money Market", or any such phrase, because I wish to deal, and to show that I mean to deal, with concrete realities. A notion prevails that the money market is something so impalpable that it can only be spoken of in very abstract words, and that therefore books on it must always be exceedingly difficult. But I maintain that the money market is as concrete and real as anything else; that it can be described in as plain words; that it is the writer's fault if what he says is not clear.' What was more, it was 'by far the greatest combination of economical power and economical delicacy that the world has ever seen'.[35]

Part of the attraction of *Lombard Street*, and what was to bring it to a far wider audience than Bagehot could ever have imagined, was his positively romantic attachment to the world he described. Bagehot wrote about the City 'like a lover', observed the Liberal politician and essayist, Augustine Birrell.[36] Then there was the immediacy of his language, deliberately geared to his ideal City reader: 'in turning over the pages of *Lombard Street* at random', remarked Giffen, 'I find such phrases as "money-market money", "borrowable money", "alleviative treatment", "one of these purposes is the meeting of a demand for cash"; and sentences like this, "Continental bankers and others instantly send great sums here, as soon as the rate shows that it can be done profitably", where the "instantly" is grammatically superfluous though it helps to drive the meaning home. For such awkwardnesses Bagehot not only did not care, but he was even eager to use them sometimes if he thought they would arrest attention . . . the meaning must shine through the words.'[37] It is an approach often forgotten by critics of the modern *Economist* who accuse it of lapsing into a demotic or vulgar style.

Lombard Street described in a masterly way how the machinery of the money market worked, how its various cogs – from the Chancellor of the Exchequer to rural joint-stock banks – interconnected, as well as explaining the whole psychology of buying and selling money. It is the light it sheds on men and money that made the book timeless, but it also had an immense practical effect. Bagehot's mission to persuade the Bank of England to act as a central bank had met and would meet great resistance from within, but he proved to be the driving force for change. He would almost certainly still be dissatisfied with the calibre of people running the Bank,* but by the 1890s his vision of its necessary position in the money market had been generally accepted and put into effect.

Shortly before Bagehot died, Sir Stafford Northcote, Chancellor of the Exchequer in Disraeli's government, asked F.E. Welby, head of the Treasury's Finance Branch, to seek Bagehot's advice. His problem was that the Treasury was finding it expensive to borrow money to fund the floating debt; there were insufficient resources to finance new educational and social legislation. The government security, the Exchequer Bill, invented in the late seventeenth century, had limitations that made it deeply unpopular to the modern money market. Anxious that Bagehot should be given credit for finding the solution, Welby wrote years later to *The Economist*: 'He answered promptly: The English Treasury has the finest credit in the world, and it must learn to use it to the best advantage. A security resembling as nearly as possible a commercial bill of exchange – that is, a bill issued under discount,

---

*It is too early to pass judgment on the performance of the team that took over in 1993: Governor Eddie George and his deputy, Rupert Pennant-Rea, 14th editor of *The Economist*.

and falling due at certain intervals – would probably be received with favour by the money market, and would command good terms.' Despite opposition from the Bank of England, Northcote went ahead and devised the floating security of Treasury Bills.

In the weeks before he died, Bagehot commented on the details of the innovation in *The Economist*, of course without mentioning his involvement. During his Budget speech the month after Bagehot died, while referring to the successful issue of the Bills, Northcote added:

> While speaking on this subject, I cannot avoid making a passing allusion to the name of a gentleman who took a great interest in this as in many other economical measures, and who, by his able advice, contributed not a little to the successful adoption of the scheme in question; but who has very recently, to our regret, been removed from us, and by whose death I am sure England has sustained a great loss. I refer to the late Mr Walter Bagehot, who was well known to Members of this House, and whose reputation extended over the country.

Bagehot's invention 'was of great service at the time,' wrote Welby in 1912, 'and it has been of infinite service as an established security which has met successfully for more than a third of a century the financial emergencies of the country in both peace and war'. So far, the Treasury Bill has outlived its originator by more than a century.[38]

CHAPTER XXI

The experiencing nature

Bagehot never visited America, and he understood far less about it than he supposed. It is a relief to turn from his purely political articles to those in which he probed the crisis of the Civil War for the lessons it had to teach about constitutions, democracy, and politics in general . . . Indeed, these 'constitutional' articles provide the fascinating spectacle of Bagehot, not exactly arguing with himself, but by means of the American question working deeper and deeper into his subject, until he is ready fully to articulate some of the most characteristic doctrines of *The English Constitution*. We see the interplay of his English preoccupations with American circumstances, and Bagehot growing in wisdom as a result. *Hugh Brogan, historian and ex-*Economist *journalist, in* America and Walter Bagehot

Though he was a genius, Bagehot had his journalistic lapses. He was often a poor prophet and sometimes he completely misread political developments. His underestimation of Disraeli was his major failing domestically; his misreading of the American Civil War his worst abroad.

Many commentators were to see the American Civil War as a simple matter of human rights, but *The Economist* had a far more complex attitude, rooted in its long torment over slavery. Wilson had been passionately opposed to what he described as 'the curse and the crime of slavery', yet in the 1840s he had been convinced that efforts to suppress it were proving counter-productive. After thirty years of effort, he believed, it appeared that making the slave trade illegal was increasing cruelty, suffering, misery, wretchedness and death. Parliament should consider 'whether our whole system is not based in an erroneous estimate of its power', for 'whether we view the African slaves penned up like so many cattle in the barracoons on the coast, awaiting the accidental arrival of the slaver – the owner nicely calculating and weighing the chances of gain against the cost of subsistence in the interim, not only as regards the whole number, but more particularly with respect to the weaker constitutions, and thus determining who he will leave to perish of sheer want, and who he will still maintain on the *chance* of a sail; or whether we view them, after being hurried surreptitiously on board, with a total disregard to their personal or physical safety, and the middle-passage undertaken, attended with such appalling circumstances, that we had the best evidence that, on an average, the numbers landed safely are little more than the half of those embarked; or whether we finally consider the circumstances under which they are landed on any part of the coast, and secreted until a favourable opportunity offers of safely removing them, and all the time exposed to the greatest misery and deprivations; – we see in the whole result of our present system nothing but a frightful aggravation of all the horrors which our efforts are intended to remedy.'

Experience proved that 'there is no risk, no hazard so great, that it will not be encouraged by a prospect of a certain amount of gain. And, therefore, it would appear that all that we can expect in the future, by carrying out the same policy, however far, and however strictly would be merely a continuation of our past experience – that every increased effort we make to suppress the traffic by these means will not succeed in its object, while it exposes the slave to increased suffering, torture, and mortality.'

In 1988 *The Economist* was to cause a furore with 'GETTING GANGSTERS OUT OF DRUGS', using very Wilsonian arguments.

> Young men in the ghettoes and millionaires' daughters up at Oxford die horribly of it. Wherever it spreads, crime rates soar. Policemen are murdered for it, politicians suborned for it. Central Americans buy whole governments through it. Lebanese and Afghans nourish their feuds with it. The traffic in illegal drugs . . . has become a main tragedy of this age. The trade was created in its present worst possible form because democratic politicians fell into a well-meant confusion of policy 20 years ago.

Supply had been made highly illegal, some demand was not – 'exactly as during America's prohibition of alcohol in the 1920s, and thus with the same results. Gangsters market the stuff to people who feel no guilt about buying from them.' Drug smuggling had become the world's most profitable business. The answer was to legalise drugs, while controlling and discouraging their use.[1] The futility of spending billions of dollars on fighting drug-trafficking has been a constant for several years, with the arguments being driven home by the power of facts and figures. To *The Economist*, the case is rational and therefore incontrovertible. To public opinion and hence politicians, reason can seem immoral: with drugs, as with famine and slavery, the superficially hard-hearted – because unpalatable – views of *The Economist* have often required great moral courage to propound.

The point about relative supply and demand was also at the core of Wilson's argument. He believed that the slavery issue distorted the truth about the relative economic conditions of Africa and America.

> It never for one moment entered the minds of those who sought to redress the great existing evil, that Africa had a vast uncivilised, unemployed and unfed population, while America and the adjacent islands possessed, as they then existed, an ample opportunity of affording civilisation, employment, and support to that race.

The evil was not in the removal of African labourers to the West, which was a positive good, but wholly in the condition to which they were there consigned.

> Abolish slavery, and the slave-trade is stripped of all its gravest objections. Abolish slavery, and place common precautionary regulations on the transport of African labourers, and at once you confer the greatest blessing on them, by introducing them to civilisation, employment, and means of support. Had the subject been rightly understood in 1806, neither our colonists, not the Government, nor the Philanthropists of the day, would have adopted the course they did. It is against the interests and objects of all to maintain slavery and abolish the slave-trade.

It would have been in everyone's interests to have abolished slavery but to have regulated and encouraged free immigration from Africa to the West.

> The system of slavery has only been adhered to, and would only be long adhered to, in any country where the supply of labour is not equal to the demand. The history of the world proves most indisputably that all the objects and motives of maintaining slavery have vanished, as soon as the supply of labour was sufficiently abundant . . . Our present policy is at war with itself, and with the interests of all the parties concerned. It accom-

plishes not its end, but aggravates into a monstrous evil what might be a most legitimate good under proper regulations.[2]

Experience in government was to temper Wilson's attitude; in the early 1850s in *The Economist* he admitted there had been considerable success in suppressing the slave-trade by force, but he continued cautious in relation to slavery in the Southern states. Although anxious to help 'our transatlantic brethren to cleanse themselves from that leprous spot of slavery which tends to make their whole system hideous', he believed that expediency required a gradual approach to eradicating slavery there, for unlike in the West Indies, there was no sovereign power to compel the Southern planter to free his slaves. Emancipation 'must be brought about by discussion, enlightening them as to their true interests; it must be adopted from their own free will; and they must take measures to make it safe and advantageous to all. They must provide for the absorption of the present race of slaves by the rest of the population, or, for their establishment out of the country . . . The sagacity of the Americans may be trusted to meet and conquer this difficulty.' It was a view shared, at that time, by Abraham Lincoln.

W.R. Greg, in 1853, took the argument further. England might abhor slavery, 'but it is a different question whether our abhorrence is a justification for making common cause with the enthusiasts of the Northern States in a crusade against slavery in the Southern States. The party in the North feels the pollution and the degradation which inflicts the whole society; but we have no more business, as a nation, to take up the cause of the Abolitionists in the United States, and declare a war of opinion against the Southern planters, than we have to take up the cause of Mazzini and Kossuth, and assail the Government and people of Austria and Russia.'

Where would such a moral crusade stop? What about Turkey, Egypt, Russia and the Gold Coast? There were 3,204,093 slaves owned by about 3,000,000 people, and valued at 1,200 millions of dollars. 'How can such a mass be emancipated? Where are they to go? How are they to live? How could they be employed? They could not get their own living. Are the planters to vacate the land for them? Are they to give their estates up to their slaves? Are they to become the servants of the Negroes? Immediate and unconditional emancipation is simply an impossibility.'

The declaration by an anti-slavery meeting that immediate and unconditional emancipation was the duty of the masters in the states was not to be surpassed for impracticability 'by any project hatched in the world either inside or outside of Bedlam':[3] Greg was his usual optimistic self.

The tone changed dramatically under the editorship of Richard Holt Hutton. Cassandra had been replaced by an evangelist, whose major concern was that in both America and England, 'the public sentiment with regard to slavery has become much less healthy, defined, and vigorous'. In America the South was growing in strength, while in England, though anti-slavery views remained unchanged, they were held 'languidly' and 'influential organs of our public opinion put forth arguments discouraging altogether the effectual resistance we have hitherto offered to the extension of the slave-trade'.[4]

In 'THE SLAVE TRADE AND ECONOMICAL LAWS' he became downright heretical. 'There is nothing more fatal to the spread of sound principles in Political Economy than their forceable application to questions quite beyond their proper field. Mr Hutt's speech on Monday night is virtually an elaborate attempt to prove that the principles of Free Trade apply to the traffic in slaves, – at least as much as they apply to the traffic of spirits or opium or any other article. That the traffic is most iniquitous, he, of course, admitted. But he maintained that it was only possible for those to check it who had access to the sources of *the demand*, and he vehemently deprecated as useless any attempt to cut off the supply.' (Hutt, who in the late 1840s had the full support of Wilson, was at least more consistent than *The Economist*.)

> Moreover, in applying this line of argument, he held language which we very often see used in relation to economical science, and which, probably, does more to render this branch of science distasteful to ordinary people, and to gain it an undeserved reputation for false and ostentatious pretension, than any application, however rigorous, of its proper and just principles. 'It was impossible for this country,' said Mr Hutt, 'so long as high prices were given in any part of the world for the importation of African slaves, to arrest this kind of merchandise in its progress to the market. Why was it that in this country, with all the means of prevention they possessed, they abandoned high duties on such articles as spirits and tobaccoes? Because they found it impossible to prevent the operations of the smugglers; *and they might as well arm a fleet or announce legal penalties to prevent the flow of the tides, or the revolutions of the seasons, as attempt to stop by similar means the operation of that great law of commercial intercourse, the law of demand and supply.*'

Hutton protested against such language. 'It is simply a blunder to speak of a moral law like that of demand and supply, as in any way analogous to those inexorable physical laws which determine the "flow of the tides" and the "revolutions of the seasons". The law of demand and supply is simply a law of *tendency*, the others are laws of absolute necessary connection. Demand supplies a motive which *tends*, in the absence of serious impediment, to bring forward a supply; but such impediments may be interposed, in almost any number, by appeals to motives having an opposite tendency in the minds of those who could alone furnish the supply. No possibility of such impediments exists in the case of the laws of the tides and the seasons.'

Interference was wrong, and therefore generally very difficult, if undertaken on behalf of the consumer alone, 'but it might be right, and therefore often very practicable, to interfere on behalf of those whose rights are invaded by unscrupulous attempts to satisfy that demand'. This was the case with the Slave Trade.

> The truth obviously is that the sphere of economical science extends only to the operation of self-interested tendencies, where no universal principle of equity intervenes to restrain the actual development of those tendencies; and the principles of commercial freedom take the far higher ground, that it is, in general, where human rights are not invaded, *wrong* to interfere with the natural relations of demand and supply, – not Mr Hutt's very erroneous ground that it is impossible to do so.

Hutton continued with a great number of facts demonstrating how successful had been the policy of suppressing the trade, his argument having many parallels with the paper's attitude to sanctions: the criterion was success. It was impossible to over-estimate 'the moral effect on the world of England's visible earnestness of purpose in suppressing the slave trade. The weaker powers, who need her goodwill, follow at once. The stronger are shamed into neutrality.'[5]

The following year, 1859, America was in crisis and the Union seemed about to collapse. Hutton saw positive benefits: 'with the separation between the Northern and Southern States of America, we trust that a new era may open for Africa'. With the help of the North it would then be possible to eradicate the slave trade to America. 'Confessedly we have failed hitherto, because, and only because, the American Government has shamefully shirked its duty. The only flag which covers the trade is the American . . . If once we could effectually stop vessels under the American flag the trade would cease.'

Lincoln's administration was deeply pledged to the effectual suppression of this traffic and it would be a long time before the Southern Confederacy had anything resembling a navy. 'In the meantime, if we draw close our relations with the North, the combined opposition of England and the Northern States to the Slave Trade will interpose in the way of its renewal an obstacle too formidable for the Southern Confederacy to overcome.'[6]

Hutton's straightforward moral loathing was a much simpler response to the issue of slavery than was that of his great friend, for Bagehot's eye was cast as coldly on slavery as on any other human phenomenon. While he abominated it, emotion did not affect his views. Greg had pointed out in one article that Negro slavery in America had come about as a 'substitute for the murder of the slow Indians in the mines': like the papacy, and many other institutions and practices 'that now plague society', it had originated in a desire to do good. Similarly, Bagehot saw it as having had benefits at certain stages of development. In new countries, he wrote in 1861, it was the only means available of providing leisure:

> By the irresistible influence of superior leisure and superior culture, the Virginian slave-owner acquired a singular pre-eminence in the revolutionary struggle, moved the bitter jealousy of all his contemporaries, and bestowed an indefinite benefit on posterity. But even this beneficial effect of slavery, momentary as it was, was not beneficial to the Union as such: it did not strengthen, but weakened the uniting bond; it introduced an element of difference between state and state, which stimulated bitter envy, and suggested constant division. In the correspondence of the first race of Northern statesmen, a dangerous jealousy of the superior political abilities of the South is frequently to be traced.

However the biggest price paid for the short-lived benefit of slavery had been

> immeasurably more dangerous to the Union than the benefit itself. As we all perceive, it is tearing it in two. In the progress of time slave-owning becomes an investment of mercantile capital, and slaves are regarded, not as personal dependents, but as impersonal things . . . The owner . . . is often brutalised by working them cruelly; he is still oftener brutalised in other ways by the infinite temptations which a large mass of subject men and subject women inevitably offer to tyranny and to lust.[7]

It was a theme he was to return to several years later, informed by the events of the American Civil War, when he wrote about the development of societies in *Physics and Politics*.

> Refinement is only possible when leisure is possible; and slavery first makes it possible. It creates a set of persons born to work that others may not work, and not to think in order that others may think. The sort of originality which slavery gives is of the first practical advantage in early communities; and the repose it gives is a great artistic advantage when they come to be described in history . . . Refinement of feeling and repose of appearance have indeed no market value in the early bidding of nations; they do not tend to secure themselves a long future or any future. But originality in war does, and slave-owning nations, having time to think, are likely to be more shrewd in policy, and more crafty in strategy.

Yet this gain is bought

> at a ruinous after-cost. When other sources of leisure become possible, the one use of slavery is past. But all its evils remain, and even grow worse . . . Wholesale slavery, where men are but one of the investments of large capital . . . is the slavery which has made the name revolting to the best minds, and has nearly rooted the thing out of the best of the world. There is no out-of-the-way marvel in this. The whole history of civilisation is strewn with creeds and institutions which were invaluable at first, and deadly afterwards.[8]

The major difference between Hutton and Bagehot was over the relative importance of slavery in the American Civil War. Hutton whole-heartedly took the side of the North. Bagehot saw matters otherwise. He spelled out his position in response to an argument of John Stuart Mill's which stated, 'in a very clear and succinct form the view now prevalent in England as to the bearing of the victory of the North or of the South respectively on the prospect of Negro Slavery and gives us an opportunity of pointing out wherein and why, we consider that view to be altogether mistaken, and founded on the combination of an error and an oversight'. *The Economist* shared 'to a very great extent, the usual sentiments of Englishmen' on slavery and entertained 'no doubt whatever that in particular slavery, as it exists in the confederate states of America, is a grievous economical error, a blot upon their civilisation, a bar to their progress and (independently of all con-sideration for the negro himself) a source of deplorable demoralisation to the rich whites who own slaves, and of still worse degradation to the poor whites who do not'. Where the paper differed from Mill was as to the means, not the end. 'Mr Mill thinks that the surest and most salutary means are to be found in the subjugation of the South; – we think, on the contrary, these means are to be looked for in its independence. It is because we wish well to the United States that we desire their liberation from the guilt and the burden of African slavery. It is because we wish well to the Africans – because we are ardently bent upon their immediate improvement and ultimate emancipation – that we wish for a dissolution of that union which has hitherto crushed them down by its banded, undivided, and resistless might.'[9] Sometimes Bagehot's propensity to paradox led him down peculiar paths.

Where he had got it wrong was pointed out the following week in a long letter from Professor J.E. Cairns of Queens College, Galway, an Irish economist who that same year produced a book called *The Slave Power*, a powerful statement of the Northern case, which became highly successful in both England and America. When Cairns died thirteen years later, Bagehot wrote that 'the characteristic of Mr Cairns's mind was a tenacious grasp of abstract principles. He applied to the subjects of his life exactly the sort of mind with which a great judge applies the principles of law to the facts before him; and he applied it under more difficult circumstance, for, in the principles of positive law, a judge can absolutely be guided by previous precedent, whereas a thinker in the moral sciences has to make his principles, as well as to apply them.'[10]

A man of original mind, moral courage and considerable prescience, Cairns took Bagehot's argument apart. Bagehot had posited that 'the independence of the South would offer a fairer prospect for the speedy extinction of slavery in North America than its subjugation, on the grounds that, the South being once a separate State, with fixed boundaries, the further extension of slavery would be impossible, and the area of the institution being thus circumscribed, its immediate decline and ultimate extinction, in conformity with the principle pointed out by Mr Mill, might be looked for as the natural result; whereas, by the success of the North, followed by the restoration of the Union, the South would once more have at its command the power of the Federal Government, with which it would be able to push its aggressions as before into adjoining territories.' On the contrary, argued Cairns, the facts suggested the absolute opposite – a slave power pushing into vast new territories. A Northern victory on the other hand, 'whether it be followed by a re-establishment of the Union under the *régime* of a Republican Party, or (which appears to me more desirable) the curtailment of the area of the Confederation to the limits of the Mississippi, cannot fail in either case to give a death-blow to slavery'. A Northern defeat was impossible without European intervention: what was to be feared was not the complete triumph of the North but a partial success which might allow a compromise.[11]

The Economist on the American Civil War was almost entirely Bagehot[12] – a reminder of how crucial to the paper is the personality of a strong and opinionated editor. Throughout the course of the Civil War, Richard Holt Hutton in the *Spectator* was taking an implacably anti-Southern position while his best friend maintained his ambivalence a couple of doors away. In September 1861 Harriet Beecher Stowe wrote a formal letter to Lord Shaftesbury complaining about the British attitude to the Civil War: he sent the letter to the press. Hutton agreed with her; Bagehot defended the role of Britain.

> Mrs Beecher Stowe says that our *sympathies* are astray, and the *Spectator* alleges that we are *meditating* wrong. As far as we can extract any distinct charges from the long letter of the American lady, she declares that we have been false to our anti-slavery antecedents; that we have encouraged and wished success to the rebels; and that we have acted thus out of a mean regard to our own pecuniary interests;– in truth, that we wish success to the South because we are anxious about our supply of cotton, and prize this above all higher consideration. That a transatlantic abolitionist should transmit such reproaches is natural enough. That an English journal should adopt and repeat them is less explicable and less excusable.[13]

He took particular exception to the view that the British lacked sympathy with the North because of their interest in cotton supply and were 'backing up the South because we want their crop more than we disapprove their institutions; in a word that, as one of our contemporaries indicates, we have stopped our ears with cotton wool against the cries of the maltreated slaves. The accusation on the part of Mrs Stowe might have passed over as a natural ebullition of irate disappointment; but it ought not to have been reiterated and supported by a journal like the *Spectator*, so respectable for its moral earnestness, so distinguished by its marked ability. Nothing in the language or conduct of this country since the beginning of the contest has ever given warrant for the sneer.'[14]

Bagehot himself fairly summarised in August 1863 what he wanted from the war:

> The end which has ever been wished for by us has been one singularly different from that desired by the zealots for the Federals, or the zealots for the Confederates. We could produce rather strong invectives from our contemporaries who entirely sympathise with the Federals, charging us with Confederate predilections, and equally strong invectives from our contemporaries on the opposite side charging us with Federal sympathies. What we have always wished is –
>
> First. That the South should be independent . . .
>
> Secondly. Though we wish the South to be independent, we wish it to be weak . . . We wish that the area of slavery should be so small, that, by the sure operation of economical causes, and especially by the inevitable exhaustion of the soil which it always produces, slavery should, within a reasonable time, be gradually extinguished.
>
> Thirdly. For obvious reasons, we wish that these results should be obtained as soon, and that Civil War should cease as soon, as possible.[15]

And he was, of course, in favour of Palmerston's stance of cautious neutrality.

In Hugh Brogan's view, *The Economist* throughout read like a politer version of *The Times*: 'Both start by taking a strongly anti-Southern position, on the assumption that the war is about slavery, which is anathema to both. And both evolve away from this attitude quite steadily until the war is nearly over.' Bagehot, as Brogan makes clear, showed no grasp of how important the Union was to Americans and his attacks on the North for protectionism seemed on a moral par with the assaults on the South for slave-holding. Part of his ambivalence was a result of an aesthetic objection to Northerners. In 1852 he had asked Arthur Hugh Clough if he expected 'to find America "instructive"? I should think for a visit it wd. be very much so. I rather like that rough active pecuniary life, but I doubt whether it wd. be *perfect* for a very long time. Besides, they are so dyspeptic.'[16] It was not that he was a snob in the normal sense of the word, but he found distressing what he saw as American – and particularly Northern – immaturity and absence of cultivation: 'the American nation', he wrote once, '. . . has no correct measure of its own strength. Having never entered into close competition with any other nation, it indulges in that infinite braggadocio which a public school so soon rubs out of a conceited boy.'[17]

Brogan's view is that Bagehot's main source on the Civil War was *The Times*, augmented by hints from Downing Street. There is certainly independent evidence that he was influenced by politicians. In March 1861 the Secretary of War, his friend Sir George Cornewall Lewis, wrote to him that he had 'never been able, either in conversation or by reading, to obtain an answer to the question, What will the North do if they beat the South? To restore the old Union would be an absurdity. What other state of things does that village lawyer Lincoln contemplate as the fruit of victory? It seems to me that the men now in power at Washington are much such persons as in this country get possession of a disreputable joint stock company. There is almost the same amount of ability and honesty.' 'After nearly three years of experience', commented Bagehot after quoting this letter, 'it would be difficult to describe Washington more justly.'[18]

Over four years Bagehot produced in his political and military comment on the Civil War what Brogan fairly describes as a 'long train of . . . fatuities'. So in terms of week-to-week military and political coverage there was little to choose between *The Economist* and *The Times* in terms of good information or sound prediction. It is a reminder of how even the best journalists can be well and truly misinformed by being too close to the centre of power. However there was much that was interesting nonetheless in his commercial coverage. Bagehot was, for instance, as Brogan points out, laudatory of Samuel P. Chase as a finance minister, whereas *The Times* failed to recognise his quality and went on predicting American economic ruin.

Similarly, Bagehot's general commercial coverage was excellent. There had been a panic in the winter of 1860–61 and when Fort Sumter was fired upon and Lincoln proclaimed a blockade, it had serious implications for British trade. Yet Bagehot did not share the consequent hysteria. Brogan points out, for instance, that Bagehot came much closer than his contemporaries to realising that the collapse of the Lancashire cotton industry and the resulting famine were the outcome not of the blockade but of the glut of the pre-war years caused by massive over-production and over-investment.

Most striking of all was Bagehot's generosity of spirit. Having even less respect for their leaders than he had for the American people, he had in particular been grossly unfair to Lincoln throughout the war. Typical was his dismissive assessment in December 1861 that: 'The President is unequal to the situation in which he is placed. He has received the training of a rural attorney, and fortuitous concurrence of electioneering elements have placed him at the head of a nation';[19] and in October 1862 he wrote of the 'astonishing absence of statesmanship, and indeed of ordinary political sagacity, which has distinguished the Washington Government from the outset of the Civil War'.[20]

He made up for all this in a marvellous tribute published after Lincoln's assassination, showing his recognition at last of another 'experiencing nature':

> Mr Lincoln, by a rare combination of qualities – patience, sagacity, and honesty – by a still more rare sympathy, not with the best of his nation but the best average of his nation, and by a moderation rarest of all, had attained such vast moral authority that he could make all the hundred wheels of the Constitution move in one direction without exerting any physical force . . . We do not know in history such an example of the growth of a ruler in wisdom as was exhibited by Mr Lincoln. Power and responsibility visibly widened his mind and elevated his character. Difficulties, instead of irritating him as they do most men, only increased his reliance on patience; opposition, instead of ulcerating, only made him more tolerant and determined.[21]

But even though his conversion to Lincoln was hasty and belated, there were other redeeming features of *The Economist*'s coverage. As Brogan put it, if Bagehot 'could sometimes be wrong, he was never silly'. During the course of the war he learned a great deal and in reflecting continually on constitutional differences of the two nations he prepared himself to write *The English Constitution*. Like *Lombard Street*, this book was evidence that his association with *The Economist* was fundamentally of great benefit to him.

It is easy to regret that the burdens of his editorship along with his banking responsibilities between them put a stop to Bagehot's work as a literary critic, and it is easy (though wrong) to dismiss as ephemera much of what appeared in *The Economist*. But as Brogan shows in the case of the American Constitution, the process of reporting on current affairs was for Bagehot a crucial way to develop his own thought. He needed to have a practical application of abstract principles to reach his conclusions, and the Civil War was a perfect laboratory test of the workings of America's Constitution in practice, particularly since it bore so much on his own preoccupations with reform of the franchise. Here is Bagehot in *The Economist*, rehearsing the ideas which would be developed at much greater length in the *National Review* later that year.

The Constitution of the United States was framed upon a vicious principle. The framers were anxious to resist the force of democracy – to control its fury and restrain its outbursts. They either could not or did not take the one effectual means of so doing; they did not place the substantial power in the hands of men of education and of property. They hoped to control the democracy by paper checks and constitutional devices. The history we have sketched evinces the result; it shows that these checks have produced unanticipated, incalculable, and fatal evil, but have not attained the beneficial end for which they were selected. They may have ruined the Union but they have not controlled the democracy.[22]

But eleven years later, in November 1872, he was hailing the re-election of General Grant as an indication of 'the immense fund of common sense and conservative feeling which exists in the American democracy'. General Grant might be unexciting, his deficiencies might be very well known, and his administration, as a whole, be unimpressive, but Greely, his opponent, was an unknown quantity and 'the hard English political sense of the Americans began to reassert itself'. Under Grant, America had been feared abroad and quiet at home: it would be inexpedient to swap him for a man 'not fully trusted'.

These were obviously the thoughts of the majority of men in the Northern States, and they are the thoughts of sensible business-like persons, not inclined to change for the sake of change, not given to dreams, not liable to weariness of their rulers – persons, in fact, who are as like Englishmen and as unlike continental democrats as it is possible to be. That is most satisfactory to this country, which at heart dreads the vacillation, unsteadiness, and caprices which it attributes to democracies, much more than any consistent line of conduct they could possibly adopt. We can negotiate and arrange matters, and find a comfortable *modus vivendi* with people who are so steady and so intelligible – or to use an expressive word, which we do not mean to be depreciatory, so *ordinary* – as the American electors.

Even more educational for Bagehot was what had happened with the newly franchised.

There never was in the history of democracy so dangerous an experiment as that of entrusting full electoral power to nearly four millions of black persons, but just emancipated from actual slavery, totally uneducated, and

hungry for material advantages ... Many observers were gravely apprehensive that this enormous crowd of capricious, ignorant, and prejudiced men
might render political steadiness in the Union all but impossible, might
make and unmake governments, or pursue Utopias, or submerge all politics
in a fierce and irresistible demand for an agrarian law. The result has
dissipated all these apprehensions.[23]

It was a result deeply reassuring to a man who had feared disaster in Britain
from the 1867 Reform Act.

Bagehot's fascination with the American Constitution inspired ten substantial articles in *The Economist* between April 1861 and July 1863, following on
from his criticism of the American political system in his 1859 pamphlet on
parliamentary reform. The earliest of these were used in his long article in
the *National Review* in October 1861.[24] This article was hostile, but as
Bagehot studied the American Constitution through the Civil War and the
ultimate victory of the North, he learnt much to amend his attitude. In May
1865 he began a series on the 'English' – meaning British – constitution in
the new *Fortnightly Review*, edited by George Henry Lewes. George Eliot
(Marian Evans), Bagehot's friend Sir Francis Palgrave and Anthony Trollope
also contributed to the first issue. Bagehot's nine articles, 'THE CABINET',
'THE PRE-REQUISITES OF CABINET GOVERNMENT, AND THE PECU-
LIAR FORM WHICH THEY HAVE ASSUMED IN ENGLAND', 'THE MON-
ARCHY', 'THE MONARCHY (CONTINUED)', 'THE HOUSE OF LORDS',
'THE HOUSE OF COMMONS', 'ON CHANGES OF MINISTRY', 'ITS
SUPPOSED CHECKS AND BALANCES', 'ITS HISTORY, AND THE
EFFECTS OF THAT HISTORY' appeared between May 1865 and January
1867. (By the latter date Lewes had been succeeded as editor by John Morley,
who was to make the *Fortnightly Review* a monthly journal of great dis-
tinction.)

In their lack of reverence, these articles had echoes of the young Bagehot.
Memorable images abounded, for example: 'as a man's family go on
muttering in his maturity incorrect phrases derived from a just observation of
his early youth, so, in the full activity of an historical constitution, its subjects
repeat phrases true in the time of their fathers, and inculcated by those
fathers, but now true no longer. For, if I may say so, an ancient and
ever-altering constitution is like an old man who still wears with attached
fondness clothes in the fashion of his youth; what you see of him is the same;

what you do not see is wholly altered.'[25] As one biographer put it: 'with the ironic simplicity of Hans Andersen's child, he set out to describe what the old man looked like without his clothes'.[26] In such constitutions as the 'English', he explained, 'there are two parts (not indeed separable with microscopic accuracy, for the genius of great affairs abhors nicety of division); first, those which excite and preserve the reverence of the population – the *dignified* parts, if I may so call them; and next, the *efficient parts* – those by which it, in fact, works and rules'.[27] For a constitution to be successful it must first gain authority and then use it. The 'English' constitution's characteristic merit was that while 'its dignified parts are very complicated and somewhat imposing, very old and rather venerable . . . its efficient part, at least when in great and critical action, is decidedly simple and rather modern'.[28] The Queen was the head of the dignified part, the Prime Minister head of the efficient part: as truly as the Americans, the British had an elective first magistrate.

Bagehot's method of bringing reality home to his readers often shocked. Anthony Trollope was one of those who strongly objected to his constitutional articles. There must have been many who thought his article on the monarchy close to *lèse-majesté*. Bagehot's very language while discussing the crucial importance of the monarchy brought its occupants down to size; 'it is nice to trace how the actions of a retired widow and an unemployed youth become of such importance'.[29] His explanations of the nature of its appeal were as timeless as his observations on the many different aspects of the English constitution: 'Royalty is a government in which the attention of the nation is concentrated on one person doing interesting actions. A republic is a government in which that attention is divided between many who are all doing uninteresting actions. Accordingly, so long as the human heart is strong, and the human reason weak, royalty will be strong because it appeals to diffuse feeling, and republics weak because they appeal to the understanding.'[30]

Like *Lombard Street*, *The English Constitution* was to become a classic. Indeed the editor of Bagehot's *Collected Works*, Norman St John-Stevas (now Lord St John of Fawsley), has become a ubiquitous presence as a medium for Bagehot, whose opinions are quoted on issues that range from a Select Committee's right to force Robert Maxwell's sons to face questions, to the proper fate of the Duchess of York.

Bagehot and *The Economist* are inextricably fused. His books draw together many of the ideas he developed as a journalist, and they continue to attract new generations of fans. Yet his achievement for *The Economist* was perhaps of equal importance. He took James Wilson's creation, broadened it, deepened it, enriched it and made of it a product with a life of its own. Bagehot got the formula right, won for the paper a solid reputation and made it so sturdy that it could live without him.

CHAPTER XXII

After Bagehot: trial and error

All the interests connected with banking and the money market, from the Directors of the Bank of England down to the smallest discount establishments, will miss the acute criticism, the steady guidance, the admirably lucid reasonings, which made the *Economist*, on its own ground, a power in the business world. And this power was strengthened by moral forces. The *Economist*, under Mr Bagehot's management, never fell under the shadow of a suspicion. Its censures were often severe, and its warnings to the public could not fail sometimes to damage the repute of insecure investment. But the anger of the irritated investor, or of the disappointed speculator, never took the form of an impeachment of the motives of the critics. Even in Capel Court, where the belief in human virtue is scarcely developed, a suggestion that Mr Bagehot's praise or blame was anything else than strictly impartial would have been scouted as an absurdity.[1] *Obituary of Bagehot in the* Examiner

'I scarcely know anyone that could have been severer to me than poor Bagehot's death', wrote W.R. Greg to Lady Derby, 'though why I should call him poor I really don't know, for his end was just the peaceful, easy, unexpected one we should all wish for ourselves, if only it had come twenty years later.'

But he was quite a unique man, as irreplaceable in private life as he was universally felt to be in public. He had the soundest head I ever knew since Cornewall Lewis left us, curiously original, yet without the faintest taint of crotchetiness or prejudice or passion which so generally mars originality. Then he was high-minded and a gentleman to the backbone; the man of all I know, both mentally and morally, *best worth talking things over with*; and I was besides deeply attached to him personally. We had been intimates and *collaborateurs* in many lines for twenty-five years; so that altogether there is a great piece gone out of my daily life, and a great stay also – the greatest in fact. There is no man living who was, taken all in all, so much to me . . . The family all loved him and leaned upon him as he deserved, and he was the trustee, guardian, and executor of us all.[2]

Since 1868, when Bagehot's health took a turn for the worse, it had been deteriorating for several years: he suffered frequently from colds and influenza and his chest was weak. His condition was worsened by the draughts in his study in the new house he and Eliza had bought in 1876; William Morris had failed to deliver the promised curtains and in March Bagehot had caught a bad cold. It was typical of his conscientiousness that in March 1877 he had turned this into a fatal illness by insisting on travelling as promised to spend Easter at Herd's Hill with his father, an ailing widower of seven years' standing.

Eliza thought him improved on 24 March.

> I spent the morning on the bed by him & cut a new copy of Rob Roy for him to read. Mr Brooke came at 9 & 2 & was satisfied that his bronchitis was rather better. Walter spoke often of his extreme weakness, increasing as the day advanced. I spent aftern. on sofa behind curtain so as not to disturb him & wrote to Mr Batten and Mr Wm. Coles for him. About 4 he asked me if I 'had been down to the parlour today'; he exerted himself with his pillows & would not let me help him, saying, 'let me have my own fidgets,' but called me to him & soon fell fast asleep across the bed – breathing loud & hard. This gradually quieted & I went down and told his father and aunt the change for the better had come – then knelt by him to count his pulse at 5:25 . . . while I counted, a little purple came on his lips and he became still and white; I called his aunt – then poured brandy down his throat. She said – it is of no use & I knew that he was gone.

His father, reading the tributes in the newspapers and the letters of sympathy, said: 'I should never have known how great a man Walter was, had I not survived him.'[3]

Wilson had bequeathed his estate in trust to his widow and six daughters, and after their deaths to their children. Bagehot was executor and co-trustee with Wilson's brothers George, John and Walter. During Bagehot's lifetime, he had naturally undertaken most of the trustees' work, not only for reasons of proximity but also because he was a banker, though it is clear he kept closely in touch with George Wilson. (A diary entry of Eliza's in 1905 records her having Bagehot's letters to George Wilson read aloud to her.) When Bagehot died almost all of the burden fell, at least initially, on George Wilson. (Though John Wilson makes occasional appearances in Eliza's diary, he seems to have played a very minor role in the sisters' affairs.)

The major and urgent requirement was to find an editor acceptable to James Wilson's widow (who was to survive until 1886) and six daughters, all of whom lived in London, as well as to their trustees. Of the sisters, Eliza and Julia, as the most senior and – through marriage – the most closely concerned with the paper, carried the greatest weight, but there were frequent consultations with Matilda, Zoe, Sophie (when she was not abroad) and Emilie.

The sisters were to feature in the life of *The Economist* for a very long time. Five lived to be over eighty: Julia, the most shortlived, died in 1911, Eliza in 1921, Matilda in 1922, Zoe in 1923, Sophie in 1926 and Emilie not until 1933, five years after the sale of *The Economist*. They were known by a later editor, Francis Hirst, as 'the dear old ladies', and although rarely seen in the office, they were an object of fascination to successive generations on the staff and together formed the subject of a recent biography.[4] An even later editor, Donald Tyerman, wrote that there 'is no more picturesque feature in the history of any modern newspaper than the gentle proprietorship of these long-lived ladies'. It was, of course, highly unusual for such power to be even nominally in the hand of women, but by Victorian middle-class standards the Wilsons had had a feminist upbringing. And, of course, the male trustees were always there in the background.

There was nothing uniform about the sisters: their intellectual and spiritual differences are a vivid illustration of the curiosity, range and vitality of Victorian thought. But together they had suffered a second serious bereavement which, like the loss of their father, also brought with it a decline in social consequence and opportunity. It had hurt that James Wilson, who was set fair to become Chancellor of the Exchequer and a peer, had died at fifty-five before receiving any formal recognition. Now Bagehot, whose personal reputation brought the great and famous to his dinner table, and who was held in the highest regard by senior politicians, had died at fifty-one before being offered any prizes. For the second time, the sisters' worlds contracted.

If they were essentially *rentiers*, they were *rentiers* with a deep interest in their property. They all took seriously their responsibilities as their father's legatees, but Eliza had the added burden of being Bagehot's widow. Serious-minded, a dedicated reader of *The Economist*, the *Spectator*, the quarterlies and new essays and literature, she was to busy herself during the forty-five years of her widowhood with keeping alive Bagehot's name and reputation. She was a *de facto* highly effective literary editor, who enlisted to the cause of keeping Bagehot's name before the public a wide range of distinguished people (including a succession of *Economist* editors) who found it impossible to refuse to help. The great Cambridge economist, Professor Alfred Marshall, was unable in 1885 to turn down Eliza's request to him to write a preface to Bagehot's fragmentary work, *The Postulates of English Political Economy*, despite his reservations: he explained in a private letter a few years later that he thought Bagehot 'most brilliant, but very hasty and in reading him I alternately agree and admire much and differ and admire a little'.[5] The diary references abound. Here are a few samples among many:

> *24 July 1878* Drove to Mr Hutton's office to discuss with him asking Mr Giffen to edit conjointly Walter's Economical Essays.
>
> *15th November 1880* I made out lists of Economist articles for 'Biographical Studies' aftern.
>
> *3 July 1885* [Letter from Sir John Lubbock] with his preface for Postulates of Political Economy Students Edition.
>
> *17th April 1889* Took Emilie to see Miss Browning aftern. and went to see Mr Johnstone about republishing Walter's papers on the currency.
>
> *7th August 1909* Mr Hirst and Mr Withers dined here and I talked with the latter about his preface to 'Lombard Street'.

Although, as guardian of her late husband's reputation, Eliza was the sister most intimately concerned with *The Economist*, Julia had also a deep personal interest. The most intelligent of the Wilson sisters, whose book reviews in the 1850s had been well up to *The Economist*'s standard, she was also the mother of the designated heir to the great tradition. Her son, Walter Wilson Greg, born in 1875, was intended by his family to enter *The Economist* and ultimately become its editor.[6] Julia too had to endure a long widowhood: W.R. Greg, ailing when Bagehot died, began to decline mentally and physically shortly afterwards and died in 1881.

Matilda had been Bagehot's favourite sister-in-law, frequently accompanying him to such occasions as Lady Waldegrave's Sunday-afternoon gatherings. They were both enthusiastic cardplayers: Bagehot noted approvingly that she had 'the true gambler's spirit . . . her temper was affected when she lost'. Open, generous, vital and musically gifted, Matilda was popular and much concerned with secular philanthropy. At the time of Bagehot's death, she was still living with her mother. In 1887, at the age of 51, after Mrs Wilson's death, Matilda married Matthew Horan and spent the rest of her life in socialising and doing good works in Kent and London.

The fourth sister, Zoe (Zenobia), was intelligent, earnest, intense and gloomy. In 1868 she had married Orby Shipley, a Church of England clergyman and a crusader for prison reform. During the 1860s Shipley had become one of the high church radicals – known as the 'Ritualists' – who wished to see the Church of England disestablished in order to free it from interference: he backed the introduction into the Anglican Church of such Roman Catholic practices as incense-burning and candle-lighting.

Orby Shipley was an intensely combative individual who published many polemical tracts. Both he and Zoe entered the Roman Catholic Church the year after Bagehot's death, whereupon Shipley had to give up the priesthood. He and his wife spent the rest of their long lives primarily in the enthusiastic practice of their religion. He was a prolific, she an occasional, essayist. Her publications in *The Dublin Review* included articles on 'Tractarianism and Ritualism' and on religion and literature. Like Eliza and Matilda, Zoe was childless.

Sophie was a sociable individual, who in 1859 had married William Halsey, an Indian civil servant and an amateur gambler, whom James Wilson hoped to keep financially stable by taking him to India as his private secretary. The financial difficulties of the Halseys were to be one of the main burdens which Bagehot had to bear as a trustee for the family. They remained in India (with occasional escapes to England for William and many escapes to Europe for Sophie) until 1883, when William went to Australia on an enterprise which proved unsuccessful. By 1889 they were settled in London and back in the close family circle. Three of their children reached adulthood: one of them, Sybil, was to marry Michael Colefax and become a famous society hostess.

The youngest sister, Emilie, was the toughest and the most domineering. Ruminating on their relationship in 1854, when Emilie was only thirteen, Eliza fretted in her journal about 'the folly of my weakness in regard to Emy, which is doing her great harm by increasing the wilfulness of her character. I hesitate in forming a judgment & even when formed have no decision in carrying it out, giving her thereby an opportunity of having continually her own will, the effects of which are to make it difficult to her to submit to others & to implant or rather increase the vanity which a sense of decided vigour of mind has already impressed her with.'

Neither Eliza nor Emilie fundamentally changed. Eliza stayed indecisive and intellectually passive and leaned heavily on the judgment of others. Intensely energetic and ambitious, Emilie painted and wrote diligently despite having very slight talents. She had married, in 1868, Russell Barrington, an artist and a decent and helpful man with some involvement in Liberal politics, whose chief claim to fame appeared to be that his mother was the daughter of an earl. Emilie had two children: Guy, who was born in 1869, was mentally somewhat retarded, and Ivo, born in 1871, survived only four months.

Emilie was to find her solace in intense relationships in the world of art. She was friendly with the Pre-Raphaelites and with the individualistic allegorical painter, George Watts, to whom she became obsessively attached after Bagehot's death in 1877. 'I have told him', she wrote later,[7] 'that he had done something for me in filling the terrible gap which my brother-in-law's death made in our lives.' Indeed Emilie set up house next door to Watts in Melbury Road in Kensington in 1879 in a house bought by Eliza, who after Bagehot's death often lived with the Barringtons and was under her sister's thumb. The relationship with Watts deteriorated after his marriage at the age of 69 in 1886: his wife resented Emilie's intrusive presence, fought with her bitterly and eventually succeeded in distancing Watts from her. She annotated a copy of Emilie Barrington's book on her husband with the words 'poisonous snake' over her name on the title page.[8]

Emilie was to duplicate much of this relationship with Frederick Leighton, President of the Royal Academy, from the early 1880s until his death in 1896. Although some contemporaries record Leighton as having, like Watts, chafed under the more egregious aspects of Emilie's devotion, the objects of her affections owe her a debt for contributing markedly to their posthumous fame. In the case of Leighton, Emilie would seem to have been a major force in turning his magnificent house into a museum. She wrote a biography of him[9] as she had of Watts. In old age she was to perform the same service for her two earliest heroes: in 1914 she published *The Life of Walter Bagehot*, and in the following years a nine-volume edition of his works; and in 1927, in her mid-eighties, a two-volume biography of her father, *The Servant of All*.

Unlike her ephemeral novels, Emilie's essays into biography are of considerable use to posterity, particularly in the case of Bagehot and Wilson. Hagiographical she might have been, but she had a concern for documents and facts and published in those volumes many letters which would otherwise have been lost forever when after her death her daughter-in-law burned the family papers.

Emilie also had an eye for the more human aspects of her subjects. There was, for instance, a telling description of how James Wilson's combination of a deeply emotional nature along with a Scottish reserve showed itself as he left for India. Of the farewell she wrote: 'the moment of actual parting with my father alone I retain clearly and vividly. In an outburst of affection for him I threw my arms round his neck and kissed him; he did not respond, but stood quite still and looked beyond and away. A curious pained expression passed over his face, the look that proved the last I was ever to see. The thought perhaps that in a few weeks half the world would be between him and his three children had struck his mind with painful vividness.'[10] Then there is her really rather sharp and clever speculation about the relationship between Bagehot and Richard Holt Hutton. 'Though Mr Hutton was so devoted and intimate a friend, I doubt whether Walter confided much of his home trouble to him. He stayed at Herd's Hill before and after Mrs Bagehot's death, and he must have known of her mental infirmity; but she did not take to him, notwithstanding Walter's endeavour to make them friends. Mr Hutton's noble, simple nature was not, I think, keenly alive to intricacies in sensitiveness. He would have had to be told of the pain, and might have been too explicit in expressing his sympathy, and that would not have suited Walter's nerves. Walter most openly mentioned it to those who understood more instinctively, but who did not *discuss* it with him.'[11]

Quoting John Morley on 'the impossibility of conveying to those who did not know him the originality, force, acuteness, and, above all, the quaint and whimsical humour of that striking genius', Francis Hirst, reviewing the Bagehot biography in *The Economist* while editor, wrote that there were 'one or two chapters, and many scattered paragraphs, in which Mrs Barrington has achieved this impossibility. It may not be a perfect portrait, but it is a real likeness.'

Emilie's biography of Bagehot is an incomparably better book than her two-volume study of her father, written when old age had taken its intellectual toll on her: *The Servant of All* is virtually unreadable. Every time she wearies of developing the narrative or following through an idea, she throws into the pot long and often extremely dull letters about the minutiae of government.

The anonymous *Economist* reviewer of her biography of her father, seeking to pay proper tribute to the book's subject and author alike, while doing no damage to scholarship or truth, talked generalities, quoted wisely and ended with the best compliment he could muster: 'Many interesting points of contrast and of similarity between the situation then and now will strike the reader of Mrs Barrington's pages which contain not only much attractive personal detail of an Early Victorian Household of the Upper classes but also many sidelights on contemporary history.'[12] Nonetheless, despite the book's manifold failings, Emilie Barrington's decision to undertake such a project at such an advanced age in response to the discovery of many of these worthy – if unexciting – letters in a disused cupboard, was an act of typical courage. Domineering, febrile, irritating she may have been, with an inflated idea of her own talents, but from the historian's perspective she is a great unsung heroine of *The Economist*. So also is Eliza, without whose banal, almost unintelligible and infuriatingly terse diary (she gave up the introspective journal very early on), this period in the paper's history would be a virtual blank. She provides enough clues to reconstruct the essence of the story of how the stricken proprietors sought to carry out their responsibilities honourably and the errors they made along the way. Until Bagehot's death there were hardly ever any references to the paper in her diary. From then on, it became a major subject.

> *Good Friday 31 March 1877* Russell [Barrington] went to London . . . to take Mr Greg's article which J[ulia]. & E[milie]. had seen written for The Economist, but found that Mr Hutton had written a much better one which they used.

This obituary appeared on 31 March – on the second occasion when *The Economist* came out black-edged. 'England has lost this week', it began, 'a man of singular power as a political, economical, and literary thinker, and the loss is one in which our own readers must unfortunately bear their full share.'

> And in saying a man of singular power, we do not use the word 'singular' as a mere superlative to express a high degree, but in its more exact sense as expressing a very rare – and, indeed, an almost unique – kind of power, of

which we do not know that we could anywhere find another equally well-marked example. Mr Walter Bagehot, whose essays on finance, on banking, on economy, and on politics, have long been so familiar to all the leading statesmen and politicians of England and to many of those of France and Germany, died this day week at Langport, after two or three days' illness, at the early age of fifty-one.[13]

The vivid, affectionate and wide-ranging assessment of Bagehot's achievements that followed was in marked contrast to the skimpy obituary in *The Times*, an organ which had ever had a distant – when not downright unfriendly – relationship with *The Economist*.

Noting how typical it was of English 'social ideas and ways of thinking' that Bagehot's death was almost unnoticed by the daily press, the Irish journalist E.D.J. Wilson remarked that *The Times* had given him 'something about the measure of the tribute that would be paid in the regular way to a deceased Rear-Admiral or Colonial Bishop'.[14]

Eliza's diary is blank for most of April, but May and early June show intense activity on the *Economist* front. In addition to the sisters, there were consultations with three of the five husbands: W.R. Greg, Orby Shipley and Russell Barrington. Other key *dramatis personae* were Richard Holt Hutton, ex-editor; Robert Giffen, ex-City editor; William Fowler, a lawyer who seems to have dealt with *Economist* business, a currency expert and later an MP; and R.H. Inglis Palgrave, a family friend and a well-known banker and statistician. And above all, there was Uncle George Wilson, who had been a colleague in London of his brother James in the old Anti-Corn Law League days, and who took his duties as a trustee with deep seriousness, despite being based in Scotland in the Wilson family home town of Hawick. He was a well-respected businessman locally, who had coped stoically in 1873 with the loss of almost every penny he possessed and was gradually returning to prosperity.

Robert Giffen was first on the scene in Eliza's diary: on 27 April 1877, he paid a long call 'by appointment' and brought with him the proposed title page of Bagehot's pamphlet on silver. He was back a few days later, 'to give me particulars of the people on the staff of the Economist – Mr Hutton came at 12.30 & stayed luncheon'. On 7 May, 'Mr Fowler came at 3 to talk over the Economist & met Mr Ellis and Mr Johnstone with Uncle George. Mr Greg came at 5 & talked with us & Emilie dined here.'

> *10 May 1877* Mr I. Palgrave came here & proposed ed. scheme for
> Economist to Uncle George.
>
> *12 May* Mr Hutton came at 11.30 & gave his opinion on Mr Palgrave's
> scheme. We discussed Economist . . . Mr Palgrave met the family here at 3.
> Julia & Mr Greg came at 5. We talked all day about the Economist.
>
> *13 May* Uncle George collected the family opinion on offering Mr Fowler &
> Mr Palgrave a small share in the Economist.
>
> *14 May* Mr I. Palgrave, Mr Greg, Uncle George & Russell breakfasted here
> – & then went to see Mr Jevons [by now Professor of Political Economy at
> University College London] & Mr Giffen – returning towards 4 to meet the
> family – Mr Fowler also came & we discussed Economist.
>
> *15 May* Mr Giffen called morng. & I offered him the editorship of
> Economist – Mr Palgrave came too & walked away with him & returned to
> Yarmouth.
>
> *17 May* Mr Giffen called morng. & accepted the editorship of Economist,
> the details to be settled with Mr Palgrave & Mr Hutton.

Eliza exchanged letters with Palgrave concerning 'the negociation about
Economist' and wrote to Uncle about the 'arrangement'.

Consultations continued.

> *23 May 1877* Uncle George . . . Zoe & I went at 1.15 to Mr Hutton's office
> & talked about Economist & then went to Ect. office & saw Mr Ellis, Mr
> Aird [publisher/printer] & Mrs Stubberfield [housekeeper].

The following day, Uncle George went back to Scotland, leaving Eliza to
write to a Mr Moffat about Sophie's marriage settlement; she wrote again
asking Moffat's consent to sell one-eighth of *The Economist*, again with
further details, and secured his consent on 12 June. Uncle George wrote
asking 'What did Ect. owe Walter?' and William Newmarch sent 'engrossed
copy of minute of Political Economy Club on Walter's death'. Meanwhile,
there were hitches and consultations about *The Economist* between Palgrave,
Russell Barrington and Eliza, between Greg, Barrington and another family
lawyer and Giffen, and between Palgrave, Hutton, Greg and Barrington.

> *31 May* Russell & Greg lunched here. Mr Greg & Julia came to tea. Much
> discussion about Economist . . . Mr Giffen wrote, declining offer we made
> for remuneration after 7 years.
>
> *1 June* Mr Greg & Russell spent morn. here discussing Ect.

2 June Mr Palgrave & Mr Hutton met Mr Greg here morng. & we discussed plans for Economist. Mr Hutton wrote down another offer for Mr Giffen – which Russell took to him & talked over before dinner.

(Russell Barrington had assumed an important role: indeed that same day Eliza had written to Uncle George 'proposing that Russell shd look after the office': this seems to have been a non-starter.)

There are no details of the revised offer, or any reasons given for Giffen turning it down – though they were presumably financial – but he seems to have rejected it that evening: no further negotiations were held. Albert Chapman, who joined the paper as office-boy in 1898 and wrote a memoir in 1942, mentions that he heard 'on very good authority' that Giffen was very disappointed not to become editor, but it is clear from Eliza's diary that relations between them remained excellent and nothing dulled his affection for his old editor, as he made plain in two important assessments of Bagehot. One, 'Bagehot as an Economist', was published in the *Fortnightly Review* in April 1880.[15] Thirty years later, he provided the Bagehot entry for the *Encyclopaedia Britannica*,[16] a less personal piece than his earlier article, but nonetheless a warm and generous tribute.

Chapman's engaging explanation for why Giffen founded the *Statist: a journal of practical Finance and Trade* is that it was a 'solace' for losing out on *The Economist*. Certainly, it was a financial solace. From 1878 until well into the twentieth century, the *Statist* was *The Economist*'s main rival and provided quite serious competition: Chapman recalls that when he joined *The Economist* in 1898, the editor, the advertisement manager and the company meetings manager used to scan the editorial and advertisement columns in the *Statist* every week.

If, during the years that followed their refusal to be financially generous enough to secure Giffen, the proprietors suffered regrets, there was ultimately cause for relief. Although as a writer and as head of the Statistical Department of the Board of Trade he had a career sufficiently distinguished to gain him a knighthood, many of his views became – in *Economist* terms – heretical, though 'until his retirement [in 1897]', observed the paper's obituarist in April 1910, 'he remained an uncompromising Free Trader'. He had offended *The Economist* by becoming in old age 'a great advocate of increased armaments and of an expansive imperialism' – anathema to Francis Hirst, then editor. And towards the end he committed the final wickedness:

he did a complete about-turn and demanded the imposition of corn duties. However, said *The Economist* generously, 'Sir Robert Giffen was always more than a statistician, and the City still remembers a powerful letter of his which practically snuffed out Bi-Metallism as a practical project for this country.'

The search for an editor continued and was speedily successful:

> *5 June 1877* Mr Palgrave & Russell again here at 11.
>
> *6 June* Mr Greg, Orby & Russell went to see Mr Hutton aftern., who proposed that Mr Lathbury shd. edit Economist conjointly with Mr Palgrave.
>
> *7 June* Mr Hutton called . . . Mr Palgrave came at 5 to say that the arrangement with Mr Lathbury was completed.

The same day, Eliza wrote to Giffen 'announcing new editors of Economist' and to Lathbury 'on becoming Editor of the Economist'. The following day she wrote to Moffat (presumably cancelling the plan to sell part of *The Economist*) and received an answer from Giffen. Flurries of correspondence with Palgrave and Uncle George followed and the excitement died down for a while.

The Economist often seems to have a positively perverse lack of information on, or interest in, its past luminaries. In 1910 Sir Robert Giffen's death was thought to merit three-quarters of a column, yet a few years later much less space was allocated to the two people who became editors in his stead. The two notices read simply:

> By the death, in his ninety-second year, of Sir Robert Inglis Palgrave, a notable figure is lost to the world of banking and of economic literature. In 1875 Sir Robert gave evidence before a Select Committee as a representative country banker; from 1877 to 1883 he edited *The Economist*, and since then has published many works dealing with banking and economic subjects, besides editing the 'Dictionary of Political Economy'.[17]

Lathbury got even shorter shrift, although he was given a headline:

MR D.C. LATHBURY.

> We regret to announce the death, in his 93rd year, of Mr D.C. Lathbury, who from 1878–1881 was joint editor of *The Economist* with Sir R.H. Inglis Palgrave and after 1881 was a regular contributor for many years.[18]

Robert Harry Inglis Palgrave was born in 1827, the third son of Sir Francis Palgrave, a lawyer and historian and son of Meyer Cohen, a member of the Stock Exchange. In 1823 Robert's father had become a Christian and had adopted the surname of the mother of his wife Elizabeth, daughter of a country banker. Robert's eldest brother, Francis Turner Palgrave, was a public servant in the education department, a poet and the compiler of *Palgrave's Golden Treasury*. He was a friend of Walter Bagehot's: 'I met here . . . in Normandy . . . an old friend of mine, Palgrave . . .', he wrote in 1863 to a sister-in-law, 'and he has expounded the cathedrals and made us understand a little. He is just married to a young wife of a Unitarian family, after writing poetry about a million women, and publishing much of it.'[19] Another brother, William, was to become a famous traveller in the East, a diplomat, and for many years a Jesuit. The youngest of the four, Reginald, became clerk to the House of Commons.

R.H.I. Palgrave entered the bank in Yarmouth of which his grandfather was a partner, at eighteen, having become familiar with it during his time as a pupil at Charterhouse: 'in the family it was thought desirable that a boy intended for the business should spend at least some part of one of his holidays thus'.[20] By the time he became editor of *The Economist*, he had written an essay on the local taxation of Great Britain and Ireland which had won the Taylor prize of the Statistical Society, *Notes on Banking in Great Britain and Ireland, Sweden, Denmark, and Hamburg* and *An Analysis of the Transactions of the Bank of England for the years 1844–72*. He also contributed to banking journals: indeed in May 1877 he wrote an obituary of Bagehot for the *Banker's Magazine*. He was not an inspiring writer. 'The weekly articles in *The Economist* on the most important political and financial questions of the day', he wrote, 'have been of great value in assisting the formation of a sound public opinion on many subjects, and Mr W. Bagehot's services to the businessmen of his time will be long remembered with respect and honour.'[21]

By this time Palgrave was prominent in the Yarmouth bank of Gurneys Birkbeck Barclay, Buxtons & Orde, had been married since 1859 to the daughter of one of the partners and, in 1875, like Bagehot, had given evidence on banks of issue before the Select Committee. He had become friendly with Bagehot through family connections and their professional interests. They exchanged warm correspondence – mainly on banking matters – and Palgrave occasionally wrote for the paper. In 1874 he contributed on a non-banking subject in a leaden article called 'The Claims of Science and the Claims of Democracy', arguing against extending the opening hours of the Royal Botanic Gardens. Bagehot approved of the sentiments: 'I am afraid that the democratic tendencies of the age and not least of this Government are much opposed to the true interests of science.'[22] What he made of the prose is not recorded: 'it is to be hoped that the public will see the desirability of being satisfied with the present very ample allowance of opportunity for visiting the Botanic Gardens at Kew, and that they will not insist on acting over and over again the fable of the goose and the golden eggs for the sake of a little present pleasure' was the stirring conclusion to Palgrave's piece.[23]

On his own subject, however, Palgrave commanded great respect. Bagehot was 'most happy' to print a long and highly statistical and technical letter from him in 1875, defending the status quo in the controversy over whether the state should issue banknotes. Bagehot had argued trenchantly with Gladstone over his belief that country banks had been largely responsible for the 1866 panic, but he worried about the conflict between his roles as editor and banker. 'I would rather you shd. put your name to it as I am very anxious to keep the Economist from even seeming to be an advocate of the subject', he wrote to Palgrave,[24] and the piece duly appeared in the correspondence column.[25]

To the proprietors and trustees, who knew of Bagehot's respect for Palgrave as well as appreciating the importance to *The Economist* of preserving its high reputation in the banking world, Palgrave must have seemed in some respects a highly attractive proposition. As an extremely specialised writer based in Norfolk, he was not a practical proposition as sole editor; but, with Giffen out of the running, and with Hutton's recommendation of a candidate for joint editorship, the proprietors were satisfied.

Relevant information on Daniel Conner Lathbury is as sparse as that on Palgrave.[26] The eldest son of the Reverend Thomas Lathbury, an ecclesiastical historian of sufficient distinction to be featured in the *Dictionary of National Biography*, he was born in 1831 and educated at King's College, London, and Brasenose College, Oxford, where he won fame for his brilliance and debating skills, became President of the Union and was nicknamed 'the British Lion' because of 'his fearlessness and courage', as well as his 'tawny locks'.[27] He went through the same farce at Lincoln's Inn as had Bagehot, and like him never practised. He married a daughter of Bonamy Price, Professor of Political Economy at Oxford from 1868 until his death twenty years later. Price had been a friend and admirer of James Wilson, after whose death he wrote to W.R. Greg that Wilson had 'left no equal behind him for the combination of science with practical genius'.

Lathbury was a highly principled and industrious journalist – 'an eminently useful and trustworthy man' in the view of the famous historian ('Power tends to corrupt and absolute power corrupts absolutely'), his intimate friend, Lord Acton. Lathbury was 'an excellent man', according to the great journalist, J. Robertson Scott.[28] 'You never saw a man more frank, cheery, and well-conditioned', Acton told Gladstone's daughter, Mary. He was the man Acton consulted when he felt doubtful about anything: Lathbury 'steadies and encourages me'. Lathbury had written a great deal for the *Daily News* and the *Pall Mall Gazette*, and Acton claimed to have been negotiating with Delane, the *Times* editor, to get him a job, when *The Economist*'s offer came up.

'When I first met them in 1898', wrote Albert Chapman, 'they were very old men [Lathbury 67, Palgrave 71] . . . Sir Robert Harry Inglis Palgrave was a man who built up a considerable reputation as a writer on banking and kindred subjects. I only saw him once or twice. He seemed to me to be a man of considerable physical vigour. He was a rather heavily built man with a fresh complexion and large features. His handwriting was small and neat . . . Daniel Conner Lathbury was a leader writer of considerable ability for many years. When I first met him in 1898, he appeared to be a very old man . . . Lathbury was a rather short man with a sedate appearance. He wore spectacles and always walked as if deep in thought. He was a competent leader writer on political, education and religious subjects.'

Chapman's attitude to *The Economist* was uncritical to the point of hagiography, so his ruminations on the Palgrave–Lathbury interregnum seem positively iconoclastic: 'To my mind a joint editorship of any paper is never satisfactory. You can seldom be sure that two people will be of one mind on all subjects. In times of trouble one may be tempted to shelve responsibility on any line of conduct. Interest in the paper may decline. Readers like to know who the editor is and to feel that he is speaking to them out of his own mouth. With a joint editorship you have a job to know who is who. The proprietors of *The Economist* may have regarded their joint appointment as a purely temporary measure until they could make a more solid and enduring appointment.'

Since he was the repository for *Economist* folklore, Chapman's guesses are worth recording here, though in this case he seems to have been generally off-beam. There is certainly no evidence that the proprietors saw the joint editorship as a stopgap: indeed Lathbury and Palgrave must have seemed to be perfectly complementary.

The relationship with the proprietors started smoothly. Palgrave, from Yarmouth, corresponded with Eliza; she corresponded with Uncle George in Hawick, who was presumably in touch with both editors. Lathbury was close at hand and Eliza became quite friendly with him and his wife. In July, a couple of weeks after making the appointments, George Wilson came to London again and rushed about on family business for a few days, doing accounts, talking to Fowler, Aird and Lathbury and visiting the office. The new regime settled in and the family sat back for a few months. Something was causing concern by November, when Hutton and Greg visited Eliza specifically to discuss the paper and some toing and froing followed. The activity then died down for a few months, but flared up the following July, when Eliza begged Uncle George 'not to postpone coming', Julia and Greg wrote to her about the paper and Eliza wrote to Fowler. Part of the worry was about finding a third trustee: Greg's suggestion of Sir John Lubbock came to nothing.

Eliza soldiered on as the chief sister-in-charge. Relevant letters were sporadic, visits occasional. In November she wrote to Palgrave about a 'mistake in Economist'. In December, although 'Upstairs all day with headache & cold – I saw Mr Lathbury in my boudoir aftern. & had a long talk about the Economist'. Palgrave came for a talk in February, and Lathbury called the next day '& made some propositions respecting the Investors Manual'.

It was time for Uncle George to descend again. Palgrave was notified and came to London to meet him.

> *4 April* [Eliza to Uncle George] returning lawyers' bill & memorandum for arrangement about Mr Palgrave's share of Economist.
>
> *14 April* [Greg to Eliza] enclosing proposed prospectus of Ect.
>
> *15 April* [Eliza to Uncle George] asking him to stop the prospectus.

Those cryptic words are the last we hear from Eliza about Palgrave's plan to buy a share in the paper. Do they mean that there was a proposal to turn the paper into a limited company? Certainly later evidence shows that Eliza's attachment to the memories of her father and husband, coupled with her hesitant and conservative disposition, were to be blocks to selling the paper.

1. James Wilson

2. Flattering portrait of the Rt. Hon. James Wilson, MP, by Sir John Wilson Gordon, presented in 1859 to Mrs Wilson by the Royal Academy of Scotland

3. Ceramic plaques of the Hon. Charles Villiers, MP, and William Pleydell-Bouverie, 3rd Earl of Radnor

4. Richard Cobden

5. Herbert Spencer

6. William Rathbone Greg

7. Eliza, Julia and
Matilda Wilson

8. Walter Bagehot

9. 340 Strand, home of *The Economist* 1845–98

10. The post-1860 proprietors. Mrs James Wilson (*left*) and her six daughters, (*clockwise from right*): Eliza (later Bagehot), Emilie (later Barrington), Zoe (later Shipley), Julia (later Greg), Sophie (later Halsey) and Matilda (later Horan)

R.H.HUTTON

11. Richard Holt Hutton

12. John St Loe Strachey

J.ST.LOE STRACHEY

13. Herbert Henry Asquith

14. Eliza Bagehot in middle age

15. Emilie Barrington in middle age

16. Walter Wilson Greg

17.
The Economist staff
in 1916 at the
farewell tea-party
for Francis Hirst.
Back row, left to right:
Mr Alexander,
Rex Lambert,
J. E. Allen,
M. H. Flood,
H. S. Whitcombe,
E. T. Brown,
A. H. Chapman.
Front row, left to right:
H. W. Kirk
Mary Agnes Hamilton,
F. W. Hirst,
Gilbert Layton.
Foreground:
E. M. Webb

The Economist,

WEEKLY COMMERCIAL TIMES,

Bankers' Gazette, & Railway Monitor.

A POLITICAL, LITERARY, AND GENERAL NEWSPAPER.

Vol. IV. SATURDAY, MAY 16, 1846. No. 142.

CONTENTS.

THE POLITICAL ECONOMIST.

THE CORN LAWS REPEALED BY THE HOUSE OF COMMONS.

NEW AND SERIOUS DANGER IN THE HOUSE OF LORDS.

At four o'clock this morning the final vote for a repeal of the Corn Laws was taken in the House of Commons. It was carried by the largest majority which has appeared in any stage of the bill. The numbers were—

For the third reading........................... 327
Against 229

MAJORITY, NINETY-EIGHT.

The majority, on the 28th of February, for going into committee, after a debate of three weeks, was *ninety-seven* in a house consisting of *five hundred and seventy seven-members*. The bill has ultimately been passed in a house consisting only of *five hundred and fifty six* members by a majority of *ninety-eight*, being an increase of *one vote*, and a relative increase of *five votes*. The numbers in the three great divisions which have taken place were :—

	For going into Committee February 28.	For the Second Reading March 28.	For the Third Reading May 16.
House ...	577	516	556
For ...	337	302	327
Against ...	240	244	229
Majority ...	97	88	98

The debate was most appropriately concluded by Mr Villiers, who has the merit of having been the first member of the legislature, who since the law was passed in 1815, proposed its entire repeal. For seven successive years Mr Villiers has renewed his motion to that effect, and considering the reception which his motion has hitherto received, it must be a matter of the highest gratification to that honourable gentleman, as it will be to the country at large, that he this morning concluded so triumphantly, a work begun and persevered in with a fearless reliance upon the truth and justice of a great principle. As far as the House of Commons is concerned, the work is completed, and it is devoutly to be wished that nothing may occur which can again bring it under discussion in that branch of the legislature. That, however, must depend upon its fate in the House of Lords.

Last week we expressed a confident belief that no effectual opposition would be offered to this Bill in the House of Lords, and that any attempt to mutilate or alter it, even in committee, would prove unsuccessful. We sincerely regret that from what has transpired during the present week, we are compelled materially to modify those views, and to express a serious apprehension that more recent occurences have placed the measure in greater jeopardy than it has been since its first proposal. From the first moment the policy of the Government became publicly known, it has been evident, that a large number of those opposed to it, have been materially influenced by the impossibility of forming a government which would give effect to their views. In December, Lord Stanley, the only party to whom they looked refused to do so. Up to a very recent period, while the language held by that noble lord has indicated a strong disapproval of the bill, it was generally understood that he would not lend himself to any scheme for embarrassing the Government. As long as this was the case, there existed no motive for those who disapproved of the bill to press their opposition. To many it appeared a mere idle exhibition of feebleness to carry an amendment without seeing a probability of forming a government that could give effect to it. On this ground many who were really opposed to the bill, were even more opposed to any course which would only end in a fruitless amendment, and a collision with the House of Commons.

For the first time, it has been positively stated, during the present week, and industriously circulated, that Lord Stanley has consented to form a ministry if required to do so, in the event of the rejection of the Corn Bill by the House of Lords. Whether this be true, or whether the rumour has been circulated for the purpose of influencing the determination of those who are still doubting as to their course, it is hard to say ; but certain it is, that the opinion is now most confidently entertained, that not only will an amendment in committee be proposed, but that it will, in all probability, be carried ; in which case, it is said that Lord Stanley will be sent for, and requested to form a government.

Another reason that has been assigned for the greatly altered tone of the Protectionists during the last week, is a sudden discovery that the country is apathetic and heedless about the measure. This is the old difficulty which has ever been encountered between the country and their lordships. If the country is quiet, and exhibits no unusual excitement, it is charged with apathy ; if, on the other hand, there is a strong exhibition of popular feeling in favour of a measure, then is it objected that it is inconsistent with the dignity and deliberative character of the House of Peers to yield to clamour. If ever there was a case to which neither of these charges applied, it is the present one. For seven years the most powerful and successful organization which has ever existed in this country for any object, has been unwearied in its efforts, heedless of personal sacrifices, and exhibiting a devotedness to a cause without parallel in the history of the country. The last public act of that organized body was to pledge itself to an expenditure of a *quarter of a million*, if still necessary to carry its cause to a successful issue. But the most remarkable fact connected with the public agitation for free trade, and one which more than any other is calculated to inspire every reflecting mind with the highest respect for the purity of the motives of those who lead it, was, that the moment the Government announced their determination to carry this policy into practical effect, the agitation of the League was suddenly and immediately suspended, while the organization itself remains more powerful and extensive than ever. Up to the last moment when agitation could be useful, by informing the public mind, it was persevered in. As soon as it could be construed into intimidation, it was suspended. Since the Legislature has taken the question into consideration, with the sincere desire to settle it, there has not been one public meeting, or any act which could be construed into a wish to overawe their deliberations. On this score, their lordships will be left without excuse.

But we must own, that, after the most careful consideration of all the consequences of a defeat of this important measure in the House of Lords, we are wholly unable to discover any advantage, either temporary or permanent, which the Protectionists can derive from it. Suppose the measure rejected ; and even suppose that Sir Robert Peel thereupon would resign, which we think impossible, what then ? If Lord Stanley were to form a government based on a fixed duty, what is he to do with the House of Com-

There were good reasons for the family to be worried. Giffen's *Statist* had started; for the first time in almost forty years, a competitor was to be reckoned with, and this at a time when the product had gone downhill. Both editors had deficiencies, but events were to show that it was the political coverage that was causing most urgent concern. Palgrave called on Eliza in July; Greg wrote her a letter, whose subject was 'Economist – his views, on Uncle George's'; they talked things over the next day and Eliza communicated Greg's opinion to Uncle George. There was another lull; Uncle George came in March 1880 and with Eliza talked to both editors. In October the plot thickened.

> *6 October 1880* [Uncle George to Eliza] Who are Asquiths.
>
> [Eliza to Palgrave] Who is Mr Asquith.

In mid-November Uncle George arrived again: this time he meant business.

> *28 November* 1880 Uncle George read over Walter's paper concerning the family property.

A new player entered. Meredith Townsend, Hutton's co-editor and co-proprietor at the *Spectator*, came with his wife to dine: the following morning he breakfasted with Uncle George.

> *4 December* Mr Palgrave spent the morng. with Uncle George & agreed to take Mr Johnstone as assistant editor. I talked with them 1½ hours.
>
> *6 December* Uncle George saw Mr Johnstone about the new arrangement.
>
> *9 December* 1880 Uncle George saw Mr Lathbury at Ect. office & gave him his dismissal at three months notice.
>
> *10 December* Mr Hutton & Mr Askwith [sic] dined here.
>
> *11 December* Mr Johnstone lunched here. Uncle George & I saw him in my sitting-room & Uncle G. engaged him as assistant editor for the Economist. We all dined at Park Lodge [chez Greg].
>
> *31 December* [Uncle George to Eliza] with copy of agreement with Mr Johnstone. Mr Hutton dined with us. He recommended Mr Asqwith for the political writer on the Economist.
>
> *1 January* [Eliza to Uncle George] agreement between Mr Palgrave and Mr Johnstone.
>
> *15 January* Mr Palgrave here all morn. talking about the Economist. [Eliza to Uncle George] my interview with Mr Palgrave.

What had gone wrong was neatly summed up by Lord Acton's remark to Mary Gladstone in July 1880, that Lathbury's articles in *The Economist* 'seem to me excellent in tone, judgment, and impartiality'. Acton, who had had a disastrous political career in the 1860s, had represented the rotten borough of Carlow in Southern Ireland from 1859 to 1865 and had been described by the *Carlow Sentinel* as being 'as much acquainted with the interests of a commercial community as a resident in Nova Scotia entitled to vote by proxy'.[29]

Acton was Catholic, aristocratic, Italian-born, priggish, supercilious and a denouncer of English philistinism. He saw politics as being like religion: 'with me, a party is more like a church, error more like heresy, prejudice more like sin, than I find it to be with better men'.[30] He was about as far removed from a man of business as could be found in the Liberal Party. So too was Lathbury, a prominent member of the Church of England and a follower of the Oxford Movement, who was to go from his co-editorship of *The Economist* to the editorship of a Church of England weekly, the *Guardian*, from which he was also fired: 'he made his name during his brilliant editorship of the *Guardian* from which he was dismissed ostensibly for denouncing the policy which led England into the Boer War, also for giving rein to his opinions on various debated Church matters', explained an obituarist.[31] Subsequently he founded the *Pilot*, which survived for four years. In his seventies, he published lives of Dean Church and Gladstone, helped with the preparation of the *English Hymnal*, edited *Correspondence on Church and Religion of W.E. Gladstone*, and failed to finish his *History of the Catholic Movement in the English Church*. One of his obituarists wrote that his 'exquisite humour, his gentleness, but, above all, his disciplined and Christian temper, made him incapable of bitterness and narrowness of view'.[32] And bearing in mind his reputation for what the *Spectator* called 'magnificent honesty and independence', it is doubtful if he would have been prepared to bend much to his proprietors' wishes.

Reading the political coverage during Lathbury's tenure of office, one feels for Uncle George, fuming in Hawick. In recommending Lathbury, Richard Holt Hutton, who had failed as editor, was offering someone in his own image but lacking his own exceptional gifts as a writer. It was not that Lathbury did not cover foreign and domestic politics thoroughly (and he did have some good outside contributors): it was that his priorities and perceptions were different from those of his readers and his own writing often seemed infused with piety. To *The Economist*'s readers, accustomed for years to having their familiar fare spiced with sparkle, malice and wit, it must have seemed like a clerical takeover.

Take the head-shaking over 'The Degradation of Political Manners' in the wake of the political divisions over the Eastern Question. The new extreme partisanship was deplored: neither the government nor the opposition deserved the assaults they received. 'Public opinion, vexed and bewildered by all this noise and violence, stood, as it were, amazed and inarticulate, making no intelligible sign. For the time the only question seemed to be who could cry loudest, and call the Grand Turk or the Czar, as the case might be, by the hardest names.' Customs and restraints of public life had been abrogated: there had been unwarranted impugning of the integrity of English gentlemen and statesmen. The press, hitherto superior to American or French journalism in its standards, had in some cases descended to 'odious and abominable slanders'. Worst of all, there was a tendency, even in parliament, to abandon 'political decorum'; there had been a 'new spirit of disorder . . . manifested in sundry random and mischievous debates'. This should cease.[33]

Sometimes one feels Lathbury chafing under the restrictions of this commercially minded organ. 'This is not the place to speak of the great questions opened out by Cardinal Newman's speech on his elevation to the Sacred College', he writes wisely. 'But that elevation is in itself too remarkable an event to be passed by quite without notice, even in the *Economist*.' It had personal, theological and also intellectual importance 'as constituting an indirect tribute to Cardinal Newman's extraordinary eminence in literature . . . he . . . has done for English theology, in its literary aspect, what Pascal and Bossuet did for French theology; and when to this is added the singular beauty of his life – its sincerity, its consistency, its modesty – it is not wonderful that his countrymen, Protestants and Catholics alike, have regarded the act of the Pope as an undesigned but appropriate expression of the admiration they have themselves felt, without having opportunity to express it'.[34] Wilson or Bagehot might have decided to write about Newman in *The Economist*, but they would have found a plausible way of justifying the decision.

Not only were Lathbury's concerns wrong for his Mammon-driven readers; his writing was often dull. A good example was an issue of the spring of 1880, when a general election was being fought by the two giants of British politics – Disraeli (by now Lord Beaconsfield) and Gladstone. The events were highly dramatic. Beaconsfield, expecting to win, had dissolved parliament as a calculated risk, yet early returns were indicating a Liberal victory: though there was more polling ahead, the only question was how big would be the majority. *The Economist*'s response was to express its rather arcane worry that Liberal electors still to vote who had been fearful of helping to bring in a weak government would be in the dark about the correct next step. There was now no doubt that 'a Liberal Government will succeed with the present government before the session is many days old. Whether that Government shall be weak or strong depends upon the elections yet to come. An elector who, in presence of such a choice as this, hesitates whether to vote for the Liberal candidate, must be unfortunately familiar with the non-natural use of words if he styles himself a Liberal any longer.'[35] With every daily paper confidently forecasting the Liberal victory, it is difficult to envisage how any Liberal businessman anywhere could have found himself in a dilemma over how to vote.

This article was followed by three solid but wearisome leaders on France, Ireland and Prussia. The French article required readers to care about the treatment of the Jesuits in France and its impact on the relationship between the Executive and the Senate; the Prussian piece analysed for them with relentless rigour the key points of the new German Imperial Judicature Acts. They were a far cry from foreign coverage under Wilson or Bagehot, both of whom recognised that their readers' prime concern about happenings abroad was how their pockets would be likely to be affected. The Irish article looked at the cases made in the *Nineteenth Century* – for and against Home Rule – by two Irishmen, the barrister Justin McCarthy and the journalist E.D.J. Wilson respectively. The appraisal was technically competent and fairminded and spent much time analysing hypothetical deadlocks between an imperial parliament and an Irish parliament: 'We should be exceedingly sorry to see the good sense of the English and Irish people put to so severe a test. Under Home Rule the only way to avoid this result – and this by no means an assured way – would be to set up an organic law with a Supreme Court to interpret it.' There could hardly have been a more depressing contrast to Bagehot's style. A few years previously, for instance, a Home Rule demonstration in Limerick that had turned ugly had inspired him to offer his readers a series of both thoughtful and highly entertaining reflections on human nature and national characteristics:

Ireland . . . is almost as soon put out of conceit even of the dreams of her agitators as other nations are with their achievements. Even in England we no sooner obtain one thing than a party springs up which shows how utterly inadequate it is, and how we ought to obtain another before we ought to be satisfied, and if we gain that other, then there is immediately a third object to put forward which goes beyond both. But in Ireland this form of political discontent, which is indeed – where it arises gradually and naturally – of the very essence of all progress, works prematurely. The people do not even wait till they have got one thing to begin to feel that it is not enough. They are conscious of satiety even before they have secured anything – except a cry. Home Rule was the most popular of all cries a few years ago. Now it is evidently beginning to appear humdrum to the Irish party of excitement . . . The Irish get impatient of the uniformity of even a prosperous agitation, and for this very good reason, that it is not so much the thing agitated for that they want, as the agitation itself.[36]

Typically, he put these observations in context:

It is not specially characteristic of Ireland that the extreme party should feel the highest indignation and anger against any evidence of power and popularity advanced by the more moderate party which asks, though in less unreasonable language, for some of the same objects which the extreme men also demand. In every country the extreme party is most irritated against the party which comes nearest to itself, but does not go so far. But it *is* probably characteristic of Ireland that the moderates after they have won their victory over their assailants, do not venture to improve the occasion by exposing the despotism and imperiousness of their adversaries, and vaunting their own comparative constitutionalism and reasonableness, but rather pass over the *contretemps* of the riot in profound silence, as if convinced that the more they dwell on the violence and unfairness of their assailants, the more the popularity of these assailants will increase, and the popularity of the moderates diminish.

And having developed the point further to show that the popularity of Home Rule was to do with the Irish liking for opposing the existing order, he concluded that the truth was 'that almost all effervescence against civil restraints in matters not obviously moral, is popular in Ireland. And as this is so, Home Rule must be regarded as deriving its popularity hitherto, quite as much from its general irreconcilability with the existing order of things, as from representing any new order of things with which Ireland would really be content. The Union may be unpopular in itself, but it is also unpopular because it represents the established order.'[37]

That might not have gone down too well in Limerick, but it was certainly calculated to get them nodding and smiling in Lombard Street. Lathbury's unrelieved, serious, rational fairmindedness was a drab contrast. Here, from April 1880, are the most interesting statements he could find to make about the two great gladiators.

Gladstone had won the election with the unprecedented barnstorming 'Midlothian' campaign in which he stumped the country indulging in what has been called 'Brobdingnagian' oratory, savaging the whole six-year foreign-policy record of Beaconsfield's government. He had been roused to fury in 1876 over atrocities committed by the Turks in Bulgaria in their attempts to restore order after nationalist uprisings. Motivated by fear of Russia, the Conservative government had followed traditional British policy in supporting the integrity of the Ottoman empire, but events in Bulgaria changed the picture. Gladstone published *The Bulgarian Horrors and the Question of the East*, demanding Turkish withdrawal 'bag and baggage', and won over public opinion almost single-handed. Beaconsfield – who had been making militaristic noises – backtracked, Russia went to war against Turkey in April 1877, an armistice was concluded in January 1878 and at the great Congress of Berlin, in mid-1878, secret deals between states produced a result that satisfied the British government's main wish – that Turkey, although forced to cede territory, should not pass under Russian domination. Beaconsfield came home from Berlin to great popularity, but it soon waned. Then, while new economic problems arose, two imperialist adventures – against the Zulus and the Afghans – went wrong in 1879.

After an election dominated by passion, rhetoric and accusations of unprincipled and immoral conduct, the dreary conclusion offered by *The Economist* was that the result had been decided by 'the distaste' felt for Conservative foreign policy. 'Englishmen have shown that they do not care for the things Lord Beaconsfield cares for, that they do care for things about which Lord Beaconsfield is indifferent, and that they are not to be taken in by fine phrases, when the results which they describe turn out to be contemptible.' As a piece of invective it was a sad comedown from Bagehot.

It was a shame that Bagehot was not around to write about Gladstone's

Midlothian campaign. Twenty years previously, in a fine essay in the *National Review*, he had mused about him as an orator: 'He has the *didactic* impulse. He has the "courage of his ideas." He will convince the audience. He knows an argument which will be effective, he has one for one and another for another; he has an enthusiasm which he feels will rouse the apathetic, a demonstration which he thinks must convert the incredulous, an illustration which he hopes will drive his meaning even into the heads of the stolid. At any rate, he will try. He has *a nature*, as Coleridge might have said, towards his audience. He is sure, if they only knew what he knows, they would feel as he feels, and believe as he believes. And by this he conquers. This living faith, this enthusiasm, this confidence, call it as we will, is an extreme power in human affairs. One *croyant*, said the Frenchman, is a greater power than fifty *incrédules*.'[38]

Because of its blind spot, *The Economist* was always far better on Gladstone than on Disraeli: empathy promotes understanding more effectively than hostility. Lathbury was no exception. One of his better pieces was a thoughtful explanation of his view that, had the Liberal majority not been very large, Gladstone would not have been a good choice as Prime Minister: 'In such a case the duties of a Prime Minister are hardly distinguishable from those of a leader of Opposition. There is the same demand for prudence and finesse, the same want of opportunity for doing anything great or decisive, the same necessity for calculating votes and avoiding anything that can, by possibility, alienate a doubtful friend or confirm a wavering enemy. For leadership under these conditions Mr Gladstone is not fitted.' Even in present conditions there were apprehensions about his leadership among some Liberals. How would he deal with the Eastern Question? Would he allow his sympathy for Russian backing for the oppressed nationalities of the Balkans to cloud his judgment of British interests? The writer was sanguine: 'Hitherto, Mr Gladstone's foreign policy has been judged by what it was when he had no keen interest in the question at issue. It may be – we are inclined to think it will be – a very different and a much more energetic policy when he has to deal with questions to which he attaches the highest importance.'[39]

It was an honest article, but a bland and vague conclusion, like so many of those in the more than three years of Lathbury's political editorship: he was chicken to Bagehot's red meat. And while it is unfair to hold up Bagehot as the standard by which *Economist* writers should be judged, the fact was that readers noticed a dramatic decline in quality and entertainment value. With circulation dropping, Lathbury had to be replaced. Again, Eliza managed to maintain good relations with a disappointed man; she was still socialising with the Lathburys in old age, and according to Chapman, Lathbury continued to contribute for many years. (One can find him unmistakably here and there: 'The late Dean of Westminster was so living a figure in England, and especially in London, his popularity was so wide and his influence so great that we are impelled to mention his death even in the *Economist*', began a leader several months after Lathbury was fired.[40])

This time Hutton had done better: Askwith, Asqwith or Asquith, as Eliza variously described him, was no well-meaning milksop: he had what Bagehot would have called 'a masculine intelligence'. In an article in January 1883 ostensibly about 'The New Radicalism', *The Economist* produced a seminal article on the evolution of liberalism that showed how far Wilson's paper had developed since he founded it forty years earlier. The article was prompted by a speech of Joseph Chamberlain's: the writer was almost certainly Herbert Henry Asquith, for it has his breadth and historical sense allied to the freshness of a young mind. It concerned 'the magnitude of the change which has come over the temper and aims of English Radicalism. The purely negative theory of the functions of government which was almost universally accepted by Radicals thirty or even twenty years ago, no longer commands the assent of their successors to-day. The advanced Liberals of the last generation regarded it as an axiomatic truth that the duty of the State begins and ends with the protection of life and property and the enforcement of contracts, and that the moment it steps outside this narrow sphere it is sure to make disastrous mistakes and cause infinite mischief.' It was a principle 'held by historical writers as little Radical as Macaulay; by philosophical thinkers like J.S. Mill; by practical reformers, like Cobden. It afforded a logical foundation and gave coherence and consistency to the various articles of the Radical creed. The doctrines of non-intervention in foreign policy, of Free-trade in fiscal matters, of voluntaryism in religion and education, found in it, if not their common source, at least a common point of contact. But it requires very little observation of current politics to see that the principle of *laissez-faire* is no longer in the ascendent. A strong belief in the power and duty of the State to render active service in the improvement both of the social and the material condition of the community is characteristic of the new school of Radicals.' The example cited was Joseph Chamberlain's advocacy of free public education; the logical conclusion was that the state should become responsible 'not only for the maintenance of order, but also, to some undefined degree, for the distribution of comfort and social well being'.

> We do not know how far Mr Chamberlain would carry his principle, nor is it necessary to trace out the very wide and very dangerous applications of which it is capable. Abstractions have very little influence in English politics, and the attitude of both the old and the new Radicals has been determined by practical much more than by speculative considerations. In the early part of the century the State interfered everywhere, and, as a rule, its interference did more harm than good. Abroad, the country was being perpetually involved in controversies in which it had no real interest and saddled with responsibilities for which it received no corresponding benefit. At home, a vicious poor law and absurd fiscal system paralysed the industry of the community, and artificially distorted the course of trade. Naturally, there-fore, the more strenuous reformers, impressed with the mischief which had resulted from the injudicious activity of Government, sought to confine its functions within the narrowest possible sphere. This work was necessarily for the most part destructive, and though excess of zeal sometimes led them into great mistakes, as in their opposition to the Factory Laws, their vigorous and persistent crusade against the follies of paternal government was of lasting service to the country.

Conditions were now utterly changed – 'a generation's experience of perfect industrial freedom has brought with it new wants to be supplied and new evils to be remedied'.

> The rapid increase and new distribution of population, the altered relations of masters and workmen in every branch of industry, the growing risks to which the social structure is exposed from the ignorance of the masses and the recklessness and cupidity of individuals – all these things have given rise to a set of problems – sanitary, educational, and industrial – which can be solved, if at all, by the direct action of the State alone. Hence the very same class of minds which a generation ago were somewhat over-impressed with the mischiefs of Government interference, are now somewhat over-impressed with its possible benefits. The work which lies before the reformers of to-day is almost entirely of a constructive kind, and it is not

unnatural that they should at times be tempted to exaggerate both the capacities and the responsibilities of the State.[41]

That was in essence the agenda accepted by *The Economist*, which made clear the following year the means by which such ends were to be achieved: 'Liberals who have faith in the permanent value only of political change that is brought about by evolutionary processes can have no objection to accept, as defining their attitude towards the leading public question of the hour, certain words used in Midlothian by the present Prime Minister when leading the attack against the late Beaconsfield Government. "Emancipation and enfranchisement," said Mr Gladstone in 1880, "have been the mottoes of the Liberal party; progress qualified by prudence; trust in the people, above all, qualified only by that avoidance of violent change, that avoidance of ill-considered change, which is really necessary in order to give due effect to the principles of Liberalism, and to ensure safety in the work of progress."'[42]

CHAPTER XXIII

Herbert Henry Asquith

It is never safe to pronounce a confident opinion as to the outlook in Ireland, that Alsatia of the civilised world, in which all the best-established laws of political and economic science seem to lose their validity, and to be persistently reversed. The Economist, *10 February 1883*

It was against the touchstone of prudence that *The Economist* was henceforward to evaluate the reforming ambitions of politicians. During the first half of the 1880s the paper was fortunate to have current political preoccupations scrutinised by Herbert Henry Asquith, its chief leader writer, who was to be a Liberal Prime Minister from 1908 to 1916.

Asquith was one of the most brilliant minds of his generation.[1] He was born in 1852, the son of a Lancastrian Nonconformist and small employer in the woollen industry, and his father's death when he was eight caused a domestic upheaval; in 1864 his uncle John Willans (a son-in-law of the Liberal MP Edward Baines, who had been an early fan of James Wilson) took the two Asquith boys to live with him and sent them to the City of London School. In 1869, at just 17, Asquith won one of the two Balliol scholarships; at Oxford he had a glittering academic career as well as becoming – like Lathbury – President of the Oxford Union, where his exceptional skills as a debater were used to full effect. In 1874 he was elected to a Fellowship at Balliol and simultaneously became a student at Lincoln's Inn and a pupil in the chambers of Charles Bowen, later to be a fine judge.

Asquith was called to the Bar in 1876 and married the following year. It was poverty that forced him to supplement his meagre legal earnings through lecturing and journalism. One of his jobs was as a lecturer in political economy for the London Society for the Extension of University Teaching, which required him to address groups in London suburbs. As a 16-year-old he had won a prize for a paper on Mill's political economy and the whole subject area of free trade was of enormous interest to him, but economics in general, in which he was largely self-taught, interested him only slightly.

As a journalist he had much to offer. His wide reading and broad spread of knowledge was complemented by an extraordinary memory: 'his knowledge was not, as with so many, locked away at the back of the mind, available indeed in the long run, but after some fumbling with the key. It was producible on the instant in black and white, without blur, indecision, or inaccuracy.'[2] He was also an admirably lucid writer.

His journalistic mentors were Richard Holt Hutton and Meredith Townsend, joint-editors of *The Economist*'s neighbour, the *Spectator*. 'One of them (Townsend)', he wrote in his autobiography, 'occupied the lower, and the other (Hutton) the upper, floor in their dingy office in Wellington Street, just to the north of Waterloo Bridge.'

> Ostensibly they had nothing in common: Townsend, with his courtly Anglo-Indian air, tapping his snuff-box, and walking up and down his room, emitting dogmatic paradoxes: Hutton, more than short-sighted, looking out on external things through a monocle with an extra-powerful lens, and talking with the almost languid, donnish air of one who had in the old days breakfasted with Crabb Robinson, and sat at the feet of Arthur Clough. I was often in and out of this curious laboratory, passing from one floor to the other, and now and again forgathering in colloquy with both of the respective occupants. There would be a free and animated clash of discussion, usually about the subjects of the forthcoming number, always ending in an *entente cordiale*; and they would return to their dens, and each set to work to hammer out in totally different styles their joint handiwork.[3]

(It was no wonder that such a happy partnership had had no qualms about recommending a joint-editorship to *The Economist*.)

For the *Spectator*, Asquith wrote about political, social and economic matters, a combination which made him a natural for the paper next door. In his memoirs, Asquith says that he wrote for *The Economist* almost every week until 1885 one of the two leading articles; his biographers say he seemed to have had a regular retainer of £150 per year.[4] A shred of evidence in Chapman's memoirs confirms the general impression that Asquith's relationship with *The Economist* was distant: a crossed-out sentence mentions a printer's boy collecting Asquith's leaders and taking them to St Clement's Press.

What did he write? His biographers mention only free trade as a subject, and there were certainly between 1881 and 1885 a number of very well-argued and well-informed pieces attacking protectionism. But to an over-whelming degree, evidence suggests that most of his articles for *The Economist* reflected the abiding domestic preoccupation of the Liberal government during that period: Ireland.

Ireland had forced itself high up the agenda during the 1870s. In 1874 a Home Rule party had won 59 seats in the House of Commons. Its members developed a policy of obstructing parliamentary business by filibustering, in order to force the government to heed its demands. The party flourished in the deteriorating political and social situation in Ireland after an agricultural crisis in the late 1870s. Steady improvement in conditions had given way from 1877 to one disastrous, and two poor, harvests, which by 1879 had brought about the worst suffering since the Great Famine. Complemented by a depression in Britain and a consequent fall in earnings from exports and migrant labour, the distress proved a breeding ground for land agitation and violence. In 1880 a National Land League was formed, with the immediate objective of securing a fair deal for tenants, and the long-term aim of creating a peasant proprietary. Its president was the brilliant young Protestant landlord and Home Rule MP, Charles Stewart Parnell.

For a parliamentarian, observed Roy Foster,[5] this 'involvement in the Land League meant riding a tiger'. For along with calls to withhold rents inevitably went threats and actual violence. The League's most popular weapon was the boycott, which succeeded in keeping empty those properties from which tenants had been evicted. Although the League theoretically eschewed violence, the success of the boycott inevitably depended on lawless elements in the community exacting vengeance on those who let or rented a property following an eviction.

Parnell's accession to the leadership of the Irish Home Rule party in 1880, coupled with a rising number of ghoulish and bloody agrarian outrages, rattled Westminster. Before the arrival of Asquith, *Economist* articles on Ireland might best be described as being in the category of 'Why? oh why?':

> Why is it, for example, that even in the districts where the police force is largest, no one has been arrested for 'appearing in any disguise.' When

tenants who had paid their rent had been carded or mutilated, it has always been by men with faces blackened so as to avoid recognition. It is to be presumed that this is a sufficient disguise to constitute a misdemeanour, and if so, why have none of these men been arrested during their progress and punished, at all events as severely as the law will allow? Some, again, of the provocations to unlawful meetings and of the injuries done to farms took place in broad day, and in the very presence of the police. Why, with scarcely one exception, have the offenders against this provision been left to go free? . . . This particular offence of going about at night disguised might certainly have been put a stop to if a sufficiently numerous constabulary had been distributed with sufficient skill and handled with sufficient vigour. Is it to be believed, for example, that if some man of proved resolution . . . had been sent down as Special Police Commissioner to the disturbed districts with instructions not to let a single band of men with blackened faces escape him, and with authority to enrol as many additional constables as he thought necessary, the instances of actual outrages would not have been very much fewer? It might have turned out that the highest penalty which can be inflicted for misdemeanour was too trifling to deter men from going about disguised. But if it had been so, this would have constituted an excellent case for demanding the infliction of severer punishment.[6]

This reads like Lathbury – well-meaning, civilised, rational and with no idea of how life was lived by those who conducted their affairs by the light of emotion and often of desperation, not that of reason. What Asquith had to offer as an alternative to handwringing and unexceptionable philosophical generalisations ('Law is only respected in so far as it has the power to prevent crimes or to punish them.'[7]) was a passionate interest in Ireland and a great understanding of both the law and the Liberal Party. He looked at the facts, interpreted them through his knowledge and understanding, formed opinions and presented them clearly.

Of all the major writers in the paper during the nineteenth century, it was Asquith who most resembled Bagehot, whose writing he knew well and greatly admired. What was almost certainly his debut has Bagehot's crisp and brutal realism: 'The landowners have long been known to be a very small body as compared with their tenants, but it has now been proved that they are weak as well as few. The weakness of a class can be protected by law, but in a democratic country it can only be turned into strength by the class itself becoming larger. If the possession of land in Ireland is to be permanently secure, the number of those who possess it must be increased.' There was to be an Irish Land Bill. What must be avoided in such legislation was 'the natural desire of the legislator to make the remedy pleasing instead of effectual'. This could be done by buying up vast numbers of estates and making them over to their tenants. Unfortunately, many of these farms could not be profitably worked; prosperity would require consolidation and hence widescale emigration for those for whom there was no place on the land.[8]

It was a bracing introduction to one of the issues with which he would be concerning himself in *The Economist* with great regularity. A couple of weeks later, he addressed himself to the Irish Chief Secretary's Protection Bill, which included a proposal to suspend the Habeas Corpus Act in certain districts of Ireland. Asquith was never happy with coercive legislation and he went to great lengths in this article, as in many others, to consider alternatives and make practical suggestions as to how they might work. In principle he considered that there were three prerequisites necessary to justify the suspension of the Habeas Corpus Act: 'It should be shown, first, that the permanent law is insufficient to put down agrarian crime; next, that this permanent law cannot be made adequate to the need; and lastly, that the exceptional law which it is proposed to introduce is reasonably likely to do the work.' He scrutinised the evidence and considered the case to be made.[9]

James Wilson viewed the Irish despairingly from the perspective of a 'Scotchman' – a man of business and enthusiast for progress through self-help. Bagehot viewed them as he viewed all the peoples who came within his ken – as a part, though a rather diverting part, of his anthropological studies. For a man with a profound sense of humour and a love of paradox, the Irish made a nice change from the Prussians. To Asquith, the Irish, and more so Ireland, represented a legal problem, and the great strength of his contributions lies in his remarkable forensic abilities. There can have been few aspirant English politicians who acquired – before ever entering parliament – such a first-rate grounding in the Irish question. *The Economist* may claim some credit for providing the platform on which Asquith was to develop his views on an issue which would bedevil his political career to its very end.

Many of the concerns of well-intentioned English statesmen were evident in the highly cerebral Asquithian dissections of the urgent and complicated problems posed by Ireland, distinguished by a certain patrician brutality. In two articles in March 1881,[10] he was concerned to tidy up what he saw as 'loose language' used about 'the need of remedial legislation', for 'the Irish tenant farmer is not the victim of injustice or wrongdoing. The law under which he lives is more favourable to him than similar laws in England, Scotland, or France.' His only grievance was poverty, caused by a shortage of land. The landlords were not responsible. Therefore, to take any of their land without their consent or without adequate compensation would be 'at best, disguised robbery . . . The coming Land Bill will have to be judged, first, on the score of justice, and next on the score of policy.' On the latter score, it would be 'prudent' for parliament to try to tackle 'some at least of the causes which have brought Irish tenants to the pass in which they now are'. Ireland could be treated differently from England or Scotland: 'exceptional cases may be benefited by exceptional treatment'. It would be unwise to force upon the Irish people stronger economical meat than they are yet prepared to digest. There was an important qualification to be made, 'for although in one sense Ireland is behind England and Scotland in point of civilisation, in another sense she is very much ahead of them. The diseases which are bred of the rottenest of advanced societies have already taken hold of Irishmen. They are infected by the revolutionary ideas which are so prevalent among continental nations.' The Irish Land Bill therefore had to be judged according to 'the justice of its dealings with the landlords and the expediency of its dealings with its tenants'. What he rejected out of hand was the notion that the present generation of Irish landlords should suffer 'because the Irish tenants, say of Cromwell's day, were robbed . . . If the possession of land for two centuries, and its peaceful descent from father to son, or from vendor to purchaser, does not confer an indisputable title, there can be no such thing to be had.'

Week after week Asquith scrutinised the bill, an attempt to improve on Gladstone's largely ineffectual 1870 Landlord and Tenant (Ireland) Act, which required landlords to pay some compensation to tenants for improvements, while giving them – in theory – security of tenure if they paid their rent. The 1881 Irish Land Act was designed to give what were known as the three f's: fair rent, fixity of tenure and free sale; it set up a land court and a land commission, among whose responsibilities was the establishment of fair rents, and it provided a certain amount of money to help tenants buy land.

Throughout most of 1881, Ireland took precedence in *The Economist*, providing the subject of the only domestic political leader two weeks out of three. Alongside the detailed analysis of the Land Bill ran two other major Irish issues. The first was the continuing agrarian outrages, which, as Asquith had feared, coercion measures had failed to suppress. The Chief Secretary, who had originally intended to arrest 'only "dissolute village ruffians"', had ended by seizing an MP, a Catholic priest, and the Secretary of the Land League: yet this had failed to strike general terror into the population. This was inevitable. 'The Irish, though impulsive and, therefore, liable to sudden excesses of panic as well as of heroism, are a brave people, and a people singularly fond of notoriety.' The government were compelled to make the conditions of those imprisoned easy, 'to discuss almost every case in Parliament, to allow any amount of newspaper comment, and to promise almost once a week that when the country is quiet the prisoners shall be set free. The Irish, therefore, are not terrified by arrests which expose them to little inconvenience, which make them widely known and popular, and which are certain not to continue longer than will entitle them to be returned as martyr candidates to Parliament.'[11]

Like all good Liberals, Asquith hoped that when the virtues of the Land Act were perceived the agitation would die down. In 1879 the Conservative government had 'treated the land agitation as though it were of no more importance than the Home Rule agitation – as though, in other words, the chronic insecurity of the Irish farmer, brought home to him with exceptional emphasis by a succession of bad years, were only on the same footing in point of practical urgency with the vague aspirations of the Irish nation for a more distinctive and conspicuous position in the Empire. For this want of insight we have paid the penalty in the enforced suspension of civil liberty in Ireland, and the loss of a whole session to the people of England and Scotland.' But when the new law had been passed and got to work, the problem would be solved, for 'A community will not continue to be agitated for the mere pleasure of agitation.'[12]

The civil liberties issue concerned him deeply. He agreed with a report from a Select Committee of the House of Lords advising the suspension of the Irish jury system 'for a limited time within a limited area, and in regard to crimes of a well-defined character'. However his article argued against the popular English view that Ireland would be better off without juries altogether: 'if nations could be governed upon abstract principles that might be true, or rather a trained and paid jury of barristers, solicitors, and magistrates, might beneficially supersede the present juries selected by

haphazard. The legal system has, however, other ends to secure besides
scientific justice, and one of them is the contentment of the people.'

The Irish would be bitterly affronted by the abolition of a system
'considered in all the highly civilised countries as a guarantee of liberty,
and now established in every country of Europe, not excepting Russia'.
Besides, in most non-agrarian cases, Irish verdicts were probably much the
same as in England, 'sometimes unreasonable, now and then grotesque,
but in the immense majority of instances accurate and fair with a leaning
towards mercy'. The advantages of the jury system were that they gave the
people confidence in the administration of justice, and let them bring
principles of law, 'in themselves rather hard and unbending, into accordance with the opinion of the times. This is done even in England through
secondary verdicts and recommendations to mercy, and sometimes acquit-
tals in the teeth of evidence – as for example in a great proportion of trials
for infanticide, and on the whole it is not injurious that it should be so.
Laws never work well where they are out of accord with the national
conscience.'[13]

Concern about civil liberty waned as the Liberal Party ran out of patience
with Parnell's negative attitude to the Land Act: in the view of *The Economist*,
the legitimate grievance having been removed, the League stepped up its
agitation, deliberately set out to wreck the Land Act and courted its financial
backers, the American Fenians, 'by open professions of sympathy with their
ulterior aims'.[14] In mid-October 1881, Asquith welcomed the arrest of
Parnell and, on his calling for a rent strike, the outlawing of the Land League.
Asquith now rejected any scruples about civil liberties: 'the time has at last
come when the ultimate resources which every organised society holds in
reserve to maintain its unity and protect its existence must be drawn upon
and brought into play'.[15] Taking the argument further, he backed the policy
which was to deal 'liberally' with that part of the agitation that was natural
and well-founded, and 'to repress, soberly but firmly, so much of it as was
sinister and insincere'.[16] It was an issue which brought out very clearly *The
Economist*'s consistent position on freedom. In line with the Bagehot view that
the first duty of government is to maintain order, Asquith wrote that if it was
inconsistent with the principles of liberalism to resort to force, there was, 'as
Mr Chamberlain points out, no escape from the conclusion that "Liberalism
cannot defend the freedom which it is its object to establish, and is powerless
to protect the majority against the anarchy and disorder which are fostered by

an irreconcilable minority." Everyone must share the hope that the need for coercion would soon pass away, and that parliament could then follow up the Land Act by other necessary improvements. 'But it must first be made possible for honest men to pursue their business in peace and to pay their debts without fear.'[17]

Although the land courts continued to operate with some success, the violence still increased in amount and in brutality and Asquith hammered away in *The Economist* about 'the immediate and paramount duty of the Government . . . to prevent and punish actual crime'. Yet he supported the renewal of the Coercion Act only as a regrettable temporary expedient to enable the Land Act to work: 'the substitution of the arbitrary action of the Executive for the regular and equable pressure of the law is an evil which can only be compensated for by the strikingly beneficial results': he sought and examined alternatives.[18]

It was a most appropriate time to have a lawyer – and a political lawyer at that – as a chief leader writer. Another important politico-legal issue was about the fate of Americans arrested in Ireland under the Coercion Act. The British government and public opinion were much exercised over the question of the Fenian Brotherhood, the Irish-American organisation which had sent several hundred Civil War veterans to Ireland in 1867 to stage a revolution. Though this turned out a fiasco, the Fenians and their sister movement, the Irish Republican Brotherhood, remained an important force in Britain, Ireland and America, where their public voice was the political organisation, Clan na Gael. The deep suspicion in which Parnell was held was to an extent a reflection of his perceived close association with Fenianism. On a visit to America in 1880, he had collected $200,000 and had formed an alliance with Clan na Gael and the Land League in the struggle for land and constitutional reform.

Although Irish-American groups were to provide financial, moral and some political support to revolutionary movements in Ireland, up to and through the 1916 rising, the War of Independence and the present IRA campaign in Northern Ireland, Irish-American organisations supporting irredentist activity have had several changes of name over the past century; the most important now is NORAID (the Irish Northern Aid Committee) which has provided large sums of money to the IRA. Yet though the Fenian organisation is long dead, the hold it took on the public imagination has not been relaxed. To this day 'fenian' is a term of abuse in Northern Ireland, one which the rawest British Army recruit will quickly come to recognise as meaning a supporter of the Provisional IRA.

The names have changed but the issues have not. As Asquith put it, in April 1882:[19] 'as a rule, the American Government is composed of born Americans, and born Americans regard Irishmen for the most part as the Arab regarded Europeans, as uncomfortable, unaccountable works of God, whose destiny is not a happy one. American politicians are, however, quite aware that . . . the Irish vote is an important one, and they are willing, with the Fall elections coming on, to run a certain risk to catch it. They are ready, therefore, to protest that Americans, whether by birth or naturalisation, if arrested under the Coercion Act, ought to be released or tried.' The problem was to reconcile security (bearing in mind that no Irish jury would convict a man arrested under the Act), justice and the need to keep the American government friendly. 'Irish-American hostility is at all times troublesome enough; but if the Government of the United States were hostile, it would become a very serious danger', with the possibility of having to garrison Canada. Asquith agreed with the government that, though the American protest was unreasonable, all those arrested should be permitted to return to America or face trial in Britain. This was a classic article in the best *Economist* tradition of setting the facts down, putting the evidence in context, analysing it dispassionately and reaching a strong opinion, in this case with the added bonuses of legal knowledge and historical perspective. Thus American protests were looked at in the light of past protests from Britain over the treatment of its citizens abroad. Englishmen, Asquith pointed out, would have been sure to think in similar circumstances that, 'in asking that their countrymen be brought to trial or released, they are asking for the most reasonable thing in the world'.

The absence of jingoism and the anxiety to see the other country's point of view did not denote weakness. The toughness always evident in the paper under Wilson and Bagehot was a strong feature of the Asquith approach. If the government should find it necessary to refuse the American request, 'all classes should unite in their support. No friendliness can make it wise to allow to the subjects of a foreign Power the right of unrepressed agitation; nor ought the foreign Power to plead for any privilege so fatal to the possibility of amity. All it can fairly ask is a humane treatment for its subjects.'[20]

CHAPTER XXIV

Settling down

The infusion of this [Scotch] spirit, which may be described as sternness, but is really the result of a stronger habitual relation between thought and action, is precisely what English Liberalism wants to give it bone.'[1] *Walter Bagehot*

The advent of Asquith had certainly added sinew and zest to the political section of the paper, which under Edward Johnstone's direction was now more geared to the interests of the readers. Johnstone himself is a rather enigmatic presence in the paper's history: he was to be the longest-serving and least publicly-known of all its editors. For facts about his life one is dependent on obituaries in *The Economist* and the *Scotsman*[2] and a very few reminiscences by contemporaries.

One of the three Scots editors (the others being James Wilson and Alastair Burnet), Edward Johnstone was born in Moffat in 1844 and worked for a while in an office there. At the age of twenty-two he went to Edinburgh, where he began working for the *Scotsman*, which eight years later sent him to London as financial correspondent and then manager of its London office. An unidentified contemporary wrote: 'I remember as if it were yesterday a comely, fresh-faced young southern Scot . . . coming to me at the *Times* office with a letter from Mr Charles Cooper, the editor of the *Scotsman*, introducing him to me and asking me to help him along if I could. At that time he was attending to the financial portion of the *Scotsman* London letter. I liked his appearance, and gave him a letter to the manager of the *Economist*.'[3] Simultaneously Johnstone was writing on finance for Morley's *Pall Mall Gazette*. He wrote financial leaders for Bagehot, and clearly appealed to Uncle George. A man with his feet on the ground, his liberalism was of a practical kind – a totally different beast from Lathbury's spiritual woolliness. From Johnstone's installation early in 1881 as Palgrave's assistant, the relationship with the proprietors jogged along apparently peacefully for some time. The main *Economist*-related concerns to surface in Eliza's diary in 1881 were with production and – as always – the fate of old friends.

> *2 April 1881* [Palgrave to Eliza] Mr Newmarch has had an attack of paralysis.
>
> *28 May* [Emilie to Eliza] Mr Greg very ill physically & mentally.
>
> *2 August* Called at Ect. office, took Mr Palgrave's books & saw Mr Johnstone.
>
> *16 August* Uncle George spent day at Ect. office arranging Aird's business.
>
> *23 August* Uncle George out all day. We played whist with him eveng. & settled that Mrs Stubberfield must be moved upstairs at Ect. office.
>
> *16 November* Heard that Mr Greg died about 9 a.m. yesterday.

Greg's obituary in the paper with which he had been so intimately connected was a model of impersonality.

> The death of Mr William Rathbone Greg has removed from us a thoughtful Economist and a keen observer. A brilliant style joined with careful research gave a prominent interest to Mr Greg's work, among which may be mentioned the 'Essays on Political and Social Science,' 'Literary and Social Judgments,' and 'Rocks Ahead; or the Warnings of Cassandra.' Mr Greg possessed eminently the courage of his opinions – a quality far from common among the present generation of writers and thinkers, and to be valued accordingly. He was born in 1809. In 1856 he became a Commissioner of Customs; from 1864 to 1877 he was Controller of the Stationery Office. The recently published volume of Mr Greg's 'Miscellaneous Essays' makes us the more regret that the list of his published works has now been brought to a close.[4]

> *10 December* 'Mr Palgrave lunched here & Uncle George had him for business in my sitting-room after – settling to publish the Economist ourselves & to leave the printing only with Mr Aird'
>
> *12 December* 'Uncle George saw Mr Aird morng. & arranged to leave him the printing of Economist but do the publishing ourselves'.
>
> *18 December* Eliza to Johnstone 'with list of misprints in Economist'

Rumblings of trouble began early the following year, 1882, when, following several of the usual entries, there was a crisis.

Uncle George came to town and interviewed Palgrave and many meetings and much correspondence followed. Did Uncle George and Eliza discourage Palgrave from his proposal to give up his Yarmouth job and home? Or did he change his mind later? There is no evidence.

Normal routines were soon resumed. Eliza pointed out to Johnstone a 'mistake in quotation of Bengal Central Railway'. In October Eliza and Palgrave corresponded about the 'attack of Daily News on Economist' and Eliza and Uncle George about 'printing', the 'proposed advt of Trade Supplemtns to Ect', 'Ect literature' and ominously, Uncle George's concern about 'Bad style of more articles'.

What was upsetting Uncle George now, it would become clear, was the standard of the Palgrave side of the paper. The problems with the Lathbury–Palgrave partnership had by no means been on all on Lathbury's side: an instant decline had been evident in the coverage of the money market. Yet in the memorandum which Bagehot had written in 1873 on the conduct of *The Economist*, and which Uncle George read over on 28 November 1880 before sacking Lathbury, he could scarcely have been more emphatic about the importance of proper coverage of that area. Writing in 1873 about the paper's decline in profitability in the years after the 1866 panic, Bagehot had attributed it to 'the dull state of the money market which was so motionless for nearly four years, that there was nothing to tell the public about it . . . my reason is that when the money market began to afford points of interest, the Economist at once recovered its position and its profitableness. The other papers made nothing of their chance at all. Every other part of the Economist must now be considered second to that which concerns the money market, as far as the profitableness of the paper is concerned. It was always of the first importance but at the outset of the paper the discussions on commercial legislation and especially on Free trade probably equalled it. But now free trade has long been established; important Commercial legislation is exceedingly rare, and nothing of general interest can ordinarily be written about them. The natural changes in trade are all which can now be discussed, – and of these the changes in the money market are the most important because they affect all men of business.'[5]

It was no wonder that, with this as Holy Writ, Palgrave should have applied himself to doing everything in his power to compensate for the loss of Bagehot's particular quality in dealing with that market.

Labouring to fill the shoes of a genius, Palgrave did his best – and unquestionably, the *Bankers' Gazette* part of the paper was distinguished under his editorship. For instance he greatly improved the banking supplement which Bagehot had begun in 1861 as a collection of half-yearly bank reports – adding a full and classified table of the British banks. Although given to pushing ideas on bank reserves and the bank rate that were far ahead of their time, some of his leaders on technical problems were to become part of standard banking literature.[6] Even more vital for the paper, his integrity was as far beyond question as his competence as a student of market technique: 'in all discussions as to the Economist it must be remembered', Bagehot had written in 1873, 'that the main part of its reputation (and therefore its income) depends on its supposed *honesty*'. That legacy was of incalculable importance. Yet, though Palgrave could uphold Bagehot's moral standards as financial editor, he fell far short of him as a writer. A general reader even now can enjoy Bagehot's ruminations on the money market: only aficionados could take much pleasure in Palgrave. 'Business in the City is still characterised by the dullness which has now lasted so long, and to which at present there seems as if no immediate termination could be assigned', was a typically arresting opening to a first leader in 1881.[7]

Palgrave also made the mistake of allowing the money market to dominate the paper even when its condition did not justify giving it such priority. By contrast, in the six weeks before Bagehot became terminally ill, the leading article was twice on politics ('THE MEETING OF PARLIAMENT AND THE EASTERN QUESTION', 'THE LIGHT THROWN BY THE PARLIAMENTARY BLUE BOOKS ON THE EASTERN QUESTION'), once on state finance ('THE ESTIMATES FOR 1877–1878 AND THE STATE OF THE REVENUE') and the other three times on the money market – in each case for a very good and specific reason. 'THE VERY PECULIAR PROSPECTS OF THE MONEY MARKET' discussed the problem posed by the ebbing away of bullion in the Bank of England at a time when trade was slow and there was no increase in demand for money – the raising of the Bank of England rate would therefore be insufficient to attract bullion: 'foreigners remit here according to what they find they can themselves make here, and not according to what the Bank of England or any other bank is charging'. In that article of only half-a-column, Bagehot's contagious curiosity about the 'what-ifs' of the money market were communicated in uncluttered prose. More personal still, though few readers could have known it, was the dry factual announcement on 24 February of Bagehot's invention – 'THE NEW TREASURY BILLS', an innovation of great importance to many readers. The third article – 'THE

PROPOSED ROYAL COMMISSION ON THE STOCK EXCHANGE' – was feisty and controversial.

A year later, under Palgrave, over the same period the money market was in the prime position five out of six times: it was displaced only by a foreign policy crisis on which the paper had strong views. Two of the money market leaders might conceivably have taken prime position under Bagehot – the reduction in the bank rate to 2%, and a thoughtful, if technical, analysis of the Bank of England's historical role as a discounter of bills. The other three articles sought to grab readers' attention with these opening sentences: 'The position of the money market has altered but slightly during the present week';[8] 'There is but little alteration in the position of the money market this week as compared with last, except perhaps a slight hardening of the rates';[9] and 'No alteration was made in the bank rate this week.'[10]

Before the Palgrave issue came to a head, there erupted what in the next century would be a common occurrence: a crisis with the printer. David Aird, who had been with the paper virtually from its inception, fell out with the new management. In 1846 he had been described as manager; later he had become publisher and printer; in 1877 he had met Eliza several times to discuss the small volume of Bagehot obituaries he was printing for her; in December 1881 Uncle George had taken publishing away from him; now, in January 1883, Palgrave was writing to Eliza about 'Mr Aird's attack [crossed out] demand for 200'. This is the last reference to Aird until December 1885, when Uncle George wrote to tell Eliza of his bankruptcy. It was a sad end to a relationship of almost forty years. In 1927, in her biography of her father, writing about the 1840s, Emilie had written about Aird's efficiency and whole-hearted devotion to Wilson.[11]

Life at the paper under Uncle George's interventionist regime was certainly more action-packed than had been customary.

> *3 March 1883* [Uncle George arrived] Talked over his idea of getting Mr John Morley to edit the Economist. He dined here with Orby & Zoe.
>
> *4 March* Julia came at 11 & Emilie read her the proof of Mr Morley's memoir of Mr Greg in studio.

Even by the standards of Eliza's diary, this is a particularly infuriating entry, for nothing more is said about Uncle George's idea. John Morley, who between 1867 and 1882 made a great success of the *Fortnightly Review* and between 1880 and 1883 was a fine editor of the *Pall Mall Gazette*, would have been a fascinating but extremely risky choice. A man of unquestioned integrity, he was in some respects strongly in the *Economist* tradition. Harold Laski once related that Morley, finding him reading his book on *Rousseau*, wondered 'whether it would not have been better for the world if Rousseau had never been born. When people put emotion in the place of reason they lead the world to the devil.'[12] Yet he lacked a certain rugged pragmatism. A friend of Bagehot and Greg, he was the kind of high-minded person whom Bagehot loved to tease. 'I often ventured to say to him,' wrote Morley in his slightly priggish way, '"You have only one defect; you do not feel the inherent power and glory of the principle of Liberty."'[13] Nor, one imagines, did the men of business, who would, in any case, have seen Morley, politically, as a dangerous radical. Moreover, it is impossible to see his idealism being able to accommodate the commercial priorities of most *Economist* readers, nor his vanity sitting happily with an anonymous journal that put figures before ideas. He was probably never offered the job; in any case, at this stage of his life, his sights were firmly set on the House of Commons. He remained friendly with Eliza and, more than twenty years on, was to have an important influence in the choice of an editor. Although Uncle George's idea about Morley as editor had died a quick death, it is clear from Eliza's diary that he still sought to oust Palgrave. He got his way:

> *14 July 1883* Mr Palgrave called morn. — has resigned.
> [Palgrave to Eliza] Resigning editorship of Economist.
> *16 July* Julia, Zoe & Orby dined here. Sophy & Matilda came eveng. to discuss Mr Palgrave's resignation of editorship of Economist.
> *17 July* [Eliza to Uncle George] asking for time to think.
> [Eliza to Mr Fowler & Mr Hutton] asking for interviews.
> *19 July* [Uncle George to Eliza] His views after consulting co-trustees – enclosing Mr Johnstone's letter stating his position.
> All the family met here at 12 to discuss Uncle George's letter.
> *20 July* Sophy & Mr Hutton dined here. Orby came eveng. to discuss the Economist position with Mr Hutton. Mr Fowler called morn. & lunched here. Accepted Mr Palgrave's resignation.
> *22 July* The family held a meeting in my room towards eveng. & heard a paper Orby had written & wishes to send to the trustees.
> *23 July* Russell & I wrote a letter to Uncle George. I took it to Mama & Thurloe Square. Brought back Julia to dinner to discuss it.

24 July [Eliza to Uncle George] answer recommending the acceptance of Mr Palgrave's resignation & the appointment of Mr Johnstone as chief editor of the Economist.

1 August Uncle George saw Mr Johnstone & offered him the editorship of the Econ.

16 August [Palgrave to Eliza] gives up Editorship of Economist in Sept.

Palgrave was to have a career of distinction as a writer on banking, as the editor of the three-volume *Dictionary of Political Economy* ('a great undertaking . . . our warm congratulations, and their warmth is not lessened by the veteran author's connection with this journal', wrote the *Economist* reviewer in 1908[14]), as a member of the 1885 Royal Commission to Enquire into the Depression of Trade and Industry, as a Fellow of the Royal Society, a Justice of the Peace, and – in 1909 – a knight. Indeed he was such a pillar of his local community as the Yarmouth director of Barclays that he was given the Honorary Freedom of Great Yarmouth in 1910.

Johnstone's good fortune lay in his timing. Had he succeeded Bagehot immediately, he would have been a severe disappointment. As it was, he came as a relief after six years of worry and turbulence. 'So far as his position as a journalist can be estimated by one in the same line as himself,' wrote his *Economist* obituarist, 'I may perhaps be allowed to add that Mr Johnstone never sought prominence. His ambition was limited, and, perhaps, wisely limited, to doing his utmost and best to maintain the credit of the *Economist* as a clean, impartial and faithful newspaper, devoted to the higher interests of finance. In this I think he succeeded. He never pretended to be a great writer, never pushed himself forward in society or in political life, but steadily endeavoured to maintain the paper laid down by its founder and its first editor . . . It was no light task to follow a man whose original thought had enriched our whole system of political economy, and had raised his newspaper to a position of almost unique authority. But Mr Johnstone undertook the task and left the paper after 26 years, with its old reputation unimpaired. In many respects the two men differed widely; but they were alike in soundness of judgment, in mastery over the principles for which they stood and, above all, in their loyalty to the paper and its traditions.'[15]

CHAPTER XXV

The fallen idol

Mr Gladstone . . . is undeniably defective in tenacity of first principle. Probably there is nothing which he would less like to have said of him, and yet it is certainly true. We speak of course of intellectual consistency, not of moral probity. And he has not an *adhesive* mind; such adhesiveness as he has is rather to projects than principles. *Walter Bagehot*, 'Mr Gladstone', National Review, *July 1860*[1]

On the face of it, Johnstone might seem a poor substitute for the great Morley, who became Secretary of State for India, and ended his distinguished career as a viscount and a holder of the Order of Merit. Johnstone was a humble backroom financial journalist, whose friends were in his own milieu, while Morley was famous and influential. Yet Johnstone was almost certainly by far the better choice. The proprietors' primary objectives were to save the reputation of the journal and protect their investment. Prudence was paramount: by playing safe, at the very least they could rely on holding on to the core of their readers and advertisers. Morley, when crisis hit the Liberal Party in 1886, was to be on the opposite side from that espoused by *The Economist* or its natural readership.

A man with a very clear view of his own deficiencies, Johnstone built up around him a tiny staff and a group of reliable, regular contributors. It was on the business and financial side that he would himself primarily contribute, but he had a considerable impact on the political side by attracting and encouraging contributors of quality and giving them their head. On contentious issues he knew exactly where the paper should stand: he was indeed a man of fixed principles. Nor did he fear controversy. It was early in his editorship that the paper had to choose between its traditional beliefs and its hero: Gladstone espoused Home Rule for Ireland and *The Economist* abandoned Gladstone.

When Johnstone took over in 1883, no conflict was in sight. Like Lathbury, Asquith commented on the Liberal government critically, but from the point of view of a sympathiser. He had long since, according to his great friend R.B. Haldane, set his sights on becoming Prime Minister, and his politics – on the radical wing of the Liberals – were broadly in line with those of his leader. On Ireland, however, he took a rather tougher law-and-order line than Gladstone. When Parnell and two other MPs were released from jail without any apparent guarantees of good behaviour, Asquith, perturbed, pointed out the necessity in dealing with Irish affairs 'constantly to keep in mind the effect which our policy will have upon the mind of a people who are at the same time, and in an almost equal degree, imaginative, ignorant and keenwitted'.[2]

If Chapman is right, besides the weekly contribution from Asquith and the occasional one from Lathbury, other political writers included Asquith's Oxford friend Alfred Milner, who was also to have a public career of considerable importance. The young Milner – 'tall, dignified, and grave beyond his years, weighing evidence on every subject, anxious for the maintenance of absolute justice, eager to organize rather than to influence, and fearful to give generous impulses full rein'[3] – was another penniless barrister, who earned his living on the *Pall Mall Gazette* until in 1885 he resigned, concluding that journalism 'neither suited him nor he it'. It was in that same year – shortly before the crunch came on Home Rule – that Asquith's legal fortunes took a turn for the better and enabled him, too, to give up journalism. But until then, although authorship is sometimes difficult to identify, the dominant *Economist* voice on Ireland sounds like Asquith's.

The paper's main criticism of the government was that, in its dealings with Parnell, it had a tendency to subordinate the restoration of legality to political expediency. In view of Asquith's later career, it is absorbingly interesting to read what are almost certainly his assessments of the great political leaders of his time. Whatever his qualifications, his long-standing admiration for Gladstone was unbounded. Parnell, however, he distrusted and disliked from the outset, accusing him of 'unscrupulous perversions of the meaning of the Land Act' and speaking of the 'irritation and disgust' engendered by his paralysis of parliamentary procedure, his degradation of public life and the harassing and insulting of Gladstone.[4] Yet, while he doubted his motives and his sincerity, the violence of the Fenians was to make Asquith, like so many other Liberals, recognise the stresses under which Parnell had to labour. Scrutinising the pressures Parnell also faced within his own party, Asquith began to moderate his antipathy.

'MR PARNELL AND HIS PARTY' was a particularly fine example of *The Economist*'s high-quality Irish coverage. Michael Davitt had made a speech advocating the nationalisation of the soil as the solution of the Irish land question. Having contemptuously examined specimens of the 'fallacies which pervade Mr Davitt's speech', Asquith concluded that the speech proved that 'we have in Mr Davitt an agitator of the old-fashioned Irish type; possessed, heart and soul, with a genuine and all-absorbing enthusiasm; outspoken alike in his enmity to the English Government and in his denunciations of crime and outrage; not afraid to publish his real aims, and commit himself to a large and yet definite scheme'.

> Nothing could well be in greater contrast to Mr Parnell's cold and carefully-restrained rhetoric; his habitual economy and reserve in the use of generalities; the studied ambiguity in which he wraps his most important declarations; his sensitiveness and apparent deference to the hostile environment in which he has to work; the almost ostentatious indifference to the conventional artifices of a popular leader with which he conceals his singular power of conciliating rivalry and subduing insubordination. It is probable that Mr Parnell, who is not a man of ideas or of creative faculty, could never have laid the foundation on which the Land League was built up. It is certain that Mr Davitt, with his concentrated and, so far as we can judge, single-minded enthusiasm, could never have formed or kept together the Irish parliamentary party.[5]

And while quite a few political newspapers might have printed a leader of that quality, what *The Economist* had over the competition – at its best – was the combination of first-rate political comment with complementary analysis of the facts and figures behind a political proposal. A few pages later in that issue, therefore, there was a further leader, looking in as much detail as possible at the validity of Davitt's rather vague costings for his proposal: 'We have endeavoured', it concluded, 'to deal with Mr Davitt's scheme without partiality. No subject is more a "burning question" than the settlement of the Irish Land Question; but it is matter for deep regret that a man who has devoted the time and attention to it which Mr Davitt has can only produce a plan which involves a thinly-disguised communism, and is thus opposed to the first principles of economic teaching.'

At the end of 1883 Asquith wrote an article summing up Parnell's career, which he believed had now reached its zenith. There was little more he could do, now that he had delivered all possible economic benefits to his followers. Irish independence was impracticable, since it would make the peasantry 'members of a poor State', a prospect with little charm for a people 'whom untoward circumstances, habitual poverty, and a habit of contrasting them- selves with richer races, have made singularly, and, indeed, unintelligibly, sordid and grasping'. The Irish 'had never risen in any determined insurrec- tion; as, of course, had nationalism been their first passion, they would, being a brave people, have long since done'. Parnell might therefore well have reached the zenith of his authority.

> He is a very able man in his way, abler probably than Englishmen think, for they are not accustomed to his type, which is common enough upon the continent, but his ability will not of itself give him power. There is a gulf between him and Englishmen – who always demand humanity in their leaders – which nothing will ever bridge; while his hold over Irishmen, though singularly strong, is partly due to accident . . . Perhaps in all Ireland there is no man who, either in his powers or his weaknesses, in his speech or in his bearing, in the character of his intellect, or in the instincts of his heart, is so little Irish as Mr Parnell. He rules because his followers, with the quick instinct of a melancholy people, have discerned that his faults and capacities exactly supplement theirs, that he supplies precisely what they lack; but the condition of ruling in that way is that leader and led shall have common objects. Irishmen and Mr Parnell are ceasing to have them, for the ground is clearing, until he at heart can desire only one thing – separation from Britain, which they at heart regard as a counsel of perfection, always to be praised and defended, but not exactly to be sought.[6]

It is an extremely astute assessment of Parnell and – where his personality was concerned – more right than wrong. But Asquith, as he continued to write sporadically about Ireland, greatly underestimated the impact Parnell was to have, not just in Ireland, but through the medium of Gladstone, on the domestic political canvas of Britain.

Almost from its foundation, *The Economist* had had an intensely personal relationship with Gladstone, one of those men, as Francis Hirst expressed it when writing of both Gladstone and Disraeli, 'of such infinite versatility that each fresh critic finds a new aspect on which to found his estimate of their characters'.[7] The paper's consistent underestimation of Disraeli severely limited the quality of its coverage, but wrestling with the phenomenon of Gladstone stretched many a fine *Economist* mind to its limit over a period of more than fifty years and drew forth some exceptionally good journalism.

Political opponents at first, the paper had been partial to Gladstone ever since 1845, when he wrote his generous-spirited apology to Wilson for maligning *The Economist* in the House of Commons. Serving under him as Financial Secretary to the Treasury, Wilson had become a warm and affectionate admirer.

Although himself in office, Wilson had defended Gladstone heroically – if anonymously – when he fell out with the government over the Crimean War. While disagreeing almost completely with Gladstone on the war, yet 'it devolves upon us the advocates of war, to protest against the pitiful unfairness shown to the advocate of peace; and we should despise ourselves were we unable to do justice to the character, or to appreciate the reasoning, of a formidable opponent.'[8]

A few months later, in 'MR GLADSTONE UNDER AN ECLIPSE', Greg, regretting another Gladstonian philippic, explained that Gladstone had 'no sincerer admirers than ourselves; none, we believe, who can more fully enter into the peculiarities of his mental constitution; none who better comprehend the sources of those estimable qualities which so endear him to his associates, or who possess more accurately the key to those idiosyncrasies which so often fill the hearts of his antagonists with sinister and malignant joy'. They had had to defend him against those who could not believe 'that a subtle mind can be an honest one, or that a man who goes so far wrong can yet fancy all the time that he is going right'.

Gladstone's greatest enemies were his brilliant intellect and – even more dangerous – his sensitive conscience: 'The more imperious the sense of duty, the more scrupulous and commanding the conscientiousness, the more does it need to be enlightened and controlled by a sound judgement and correct instinct. All extreme sensitiveness is apt to degenerate into morbidity; – sensitiveness of conscience more surely than any other. And when once it has passed the limits of moderation and sobriety, it presses all the other powers of thought and character into its service; it blinds its victim to all other considerations; it enables him unconsciously and unfeelingly to trample upon all other principles; it takes the bit between its teeth, and guidance or restraint are thenceforth hopeless.' His loathing of war, and his religious objections to fighting for unbelievers against a Christian Power, made him lose sight of the nobility of the cause, and 'all that was wise, stern, and statesmanlike gave way before the feelings of the gentle and polished philosopher whom such barbarism revolted; and of the humane lover of his species whose very soul was harrowed by the bloodshed and the suffering around him'.[9]

Gladstone's kindness to Bagehot and the great liking and intellectual respect they felt for one another maintained the tradition of closeness to *The Economist*, though there continued to be many areas of disagreement. On the Eastern Question, for instance, Bagehot was an uncompromising non-interventionist, as much opposed to Gladstone's policy of encouraging nationalist uprisings in the Balkans as to Disraeli's attempts to prop up the Turkish empire. 'Time out of mind', the 'subject races of Turkey . . . have been despotically governed,' he wrote the month before he died 'and an indefinite time must elapse before the results can be effaced from the race'.[10]

Not long after Bagehot's death, the paper squarely declared its political stance in an apologia with a whiff of the self-justification of the insecure editor.

> It has of late been more than once our misfortune to take a different view of the duty of the English Government in regard to foreign affairs to that taken by the Liberal party as expounded by its Parliamentary leaders. We call this a misfortune because, though the *Economist* is not, and never has been, a party journal, it is, and always has been, a Liberal journal. Its conductors have always believed that what are vaguely, but not inacurately [sic], called Liberal principles are demonstrably true, and that the prosperity and greatness of England are largely owing to her steadfast adherence to them over a long series of years. Under our system of Government some deference to party combinations is indispensable, and for that reason a journal which professes to advocate Liberal principles is bound not lightly to put itself in opposition to the interpretation placed on them by the Liberal leaders. Occasions of departing from that interpretation may arise, but they ought not to be sought for, nor to be lightly taken hold of.[11]

The paper urged that Gladstone, rather than Lord Hartington (who had led the Liberals in the House of Commons from 1875, when Gladstone had resigned the party leadership) should lead the Liberals into the election: 'We say this with no disrespect to Lord Hartington's leadership ... but in a general election the qualities which Mr Gladstone possesses are of supreme importance. They are qualities which will do more than anything to make victory sure, and being such it is a matter of obvious prudence in the Liberal party to secure the possessor of them for their leader.'[12] In general, the coverage was rather flabby. Lathbury agreed with Gladstone that the first business of the electorate was to get rid of the existing government, continued questioning his foreign policy, regretted the damage done to individual liberty by his concessions to the temperance movement, and showed some unhappiness that Gladstone, while maintaining his opposition to Irish Home Rule, had mixed up the issue with the extension of local government and thereby, perhaps unwittingly, encouraged the notion that Home Rule deserved an inquiry. Still, he concluded, reporting on the unnecessarily high moral line Gladstone had taken on a particular issue: 'The fire within him is not fully kindled until it is touched by some moral argument. This is no small part of the extraordinary influence which he exercises over men, and to complain of it would be as unreasonable as it would have been for the Israelites to find fault with Samson for not cutting his hair before going out to fight the Philistines. Mr Gladstone must be had on his own terms or not at all.'[13]

Asquith wrote often about Gladstone from the eye of the apprentice politician and he was often quite prophetic. Taking stock, for instance, in January 1883, he remarked that even the many respectable people who thought Gladstone to be a 'dangerous and untrustworthy statesman' were 'immensely proud of him' as 'a national possession' and were deeply apprehensive lest anything 'shorten the days or impair the powers of the one man of genius who still remains to give elevation and dignity to our public life ... Mr Gladstone's supremacy is as different as possible from that of the Metternichs and Guizots.'

> His political method is inductive, not deductive; he is, of all statesmen, in the least degree the slave of formulas and systems, and there is probably no instance of a man of the same age, and of anything like the same intellectual powers, who was equally accessible to ideas, equally open to the lessons of experience, equally free from regret for the past and a dread of the future. Mr Gladstone's ascendancy is thus not that of one who stands solitary and

isolated, dominating his contemporaries by the force of an imperious authority. It is rather that of one who, with the exceptional sensitiveness and quickness of genius, feels and responds to, and is therefore enabled to control and direct, the opinions and the emotions of his fellow-countrymen.

The risks such a personal ascendancy brought with it were twofold. It had a somewhat paralysing effect on colleagues and any other leader, and further, while through personal allegiance he had kept party and public support for his Irish policy, 'the superficial unity which Mr Gladstone's influence preserves in his party may become deceptive and unreal'.[14]

Asquith stopped writing some time in 1885, but towards the end of his time with the paper – in January 1885 – he assessed Gladstone in the light of his seventy-fifth birthday and the fiftieth anniversary of his first assumption of office. After a retrospective summing-up, he saw no reason for Gladstone to fear the verdict that history would pronounce upon 'the superficial inconsistencies of his long career, when the passion and prejudices of contemporary partisanship have cleared away'. And then, after a lengthy encomium, came the peroration:

> A late convert to the Liberal creed, or, at least, recognising only late in life that its fundamental doctrines were implicitly involved in his own political faith, he has for nearly twenty years controlled the policy and determined the fortunes of the Liberal party. Twice at least during that period – in 1868, when he declared in favour of the dis-establishment of the Irish Church, and in 1876, when he began the crusade against Lord Beaconsfield's Eastern policy – his individual initiative has, so far as we can judge, changed the course of history. At the present moment, amid many blunders and failures for which the public insist on holding others responsible, his Ministry is maintained, not only in office, but, to appearance, in the confidence of the people, by the fact that, so long as he is at his [sic] head, the country is governed by the one man of indisputable and universally acknowledged genius who is to be found in the English political arena . . . Nor are feelings of this kind by any means confined to his own followers . . . until Mr Gladstone retires from the scene, his personality will remain the dominant factor in English politics.[15]

Dominant he certainly was, but Gladstone was by now dogged by domestic and foreign problems and internal party divisions. He was to be brought down by the Irish Nationalists, who were impatient with the Liberals' refusal to accept the principle of Home Rule. In June 1885 the Irish MPs backed the Conservatives – who had become committed to the principle of a peasant proprietorship – and defeated the government in a Commons vote: Gladstone resigned. Lord Salisbury's caretaker government delivered the price for Parnell's support with the 1885 Ashbourne Act, which made five million pounds available for loans for land purchase: it was the first step in a process which was during subsequent Conservative governments to make many millions of pounds available for a redistribution of land ownership.

In late 1885 the Liberals won exactly half the seats in the Commons and the Irish Nationalists increased their strength from 61 to 86. Shortly after the results were announced, rumours began that Gladstone had been converted to Home Rule.

The Economist had always been implacably opposed to Home Rule. Wilson thought the idea mischievous and destructive: Bagehot believed that both islands would suffer if the Union were dissolved, and he also saw with great clarity the problem posed by the Scots in the North of Ireland: 'Ireland contains two *peoples*', he wrote in 1867, '– one Irish, or, if they like that word better, Fenian, and another which, though calling itself by many names, is, in character, in creed, and in social circumstances, substantially Scotch. Not only is there no unity between these races, but there is no possibility of any. The hatred of a Venetian for an Austrian is feeble compared with the hatred of a Tipperary peasant for a Northerner; the pride of a Virginian to a Negro is gentleness compared with the pride of a Protestant of Ulster to any "native" whatsoever.'

> The two peoples differ radically in race, creed, and civilisation, in their fundamental theories of land, in the tendencies of their dreams, in their notions of social organisation – in everything, in short, which has ever divided mankind. They have waged an internecine war for six hundred years, during which they have built up a popular literature of hostility; they renew this war in streets and alleys every year, and they are ready at this moment as ever to fight it out, if only England would let them, 'to the bitter end'.[16]

Yet, like his predecessors and successors on the paper, Bagehot was harshly condemnatory of many aspects of the British record in ruling Ireland and supported enthusiastically all measures designed to allay traditional grievances about, for instance, the established church. Bagehot also saw clearly in

1871 that the partial devolution of power proposed by supporters of Home Rule was but an interim measure: 'It is in fact as plain as common sense can make it to all who look at the condition of Ireland with impartial eyes, their "Home Rule" would be but the first step in a series of virulent disputes as to the political relations of the two Islands, which could hardly end except in separation, or reconquest with all the evils that that would bring in its train. The Home Rule party would certainly be imprudent, but they would be far more logical, if they were to raise a cry at once for an independent Irish republic.'[17]

With the whole question of Home Rule, two issues particularly offended *The Economist*. It believed that neither the Irish people nor their representatives knew what they meant by Home Rule: 'They are not electing statesmen with a clear idea of the steps to be taken,' wrote Bagehot in 1874, 'but politicians who tend to vote for a particularly ill-defined and vague proposition, to please their constituents, once a year, and for all the rest of the year to vote as they are bid by the party which may be most likely to grant such Irish demands in small matters as most nearly affect them.'[18]

The second great cause of grief was the the disorderliness of the Irish representatives and their disruptive effect on the House of Commons. At its very best the paper was capable of making a big imaginative leap and grasping that people might choose to be negative or irrational, but in general, throughout its history, it displays a mixture of irritation, bafflement and sometimes even outrage that people can be so blind to reason. If its most absurd manifestation was James Wilson's inability to understand why starving peasants in the west of Ireland would not pull up their non-existent socks, Bagehot's annoyance with the inability of the Irish electorate to think through policy matters coherently was almost as ludicrous, especially in view of his evaluation of the Irish national character.

After Asquith left (he won a seat in the 1885 election), *The Economist* began to show nervousness about Parnell's new strength now that both parties were in need of his support. It took consolation from a belief that even what it considered the irresponsible elements in both parties – the Conservative Lord Randolph Churchill and the Liberal Joseph Chamberlain – would wreck their chances if they tried to outbid each other for Parnell's support. Parnell had 'in that spirit of imperious insolence which characterises all his dealings with England, and, perhaps, to some extent accounts for his influence in Ireland, contrived to give his scheme of "legislative independence" the appearance at once of an insult to the intelligence of English statesmen, and an aggression on the interests of English working men, who, between them, will have the final settlement to this question'.¹⁹ *The Economist* was particularly enraged with Parnell that week, for he had perpetrated the gravest heresy of all: he had announced that the Irish parliament he wished to create would be there to protect Irish industry, which obviously would require the establishment of 'a protective tariff against English and Scotch goods'.²⁰

The post-Asquith *Economist* was horrified by the Irish party's ability, first, to undermine the order that existed in the House of Commons, and second, to appeal to the basest power-seeking interests among the major parties. The Lathbury skirts were drawn aside whenever this squalid amorality had to be scrutinised. Like the most rational and sanctimonious of *Economist* writers over the years, Lathbury was so high-minded he appeared to live in a moral igloo.

By December 1885, rumours were abounding that Gladstone was meditating a *volte face*, but *The Economist* was quietly confident that this was impossible. Assessing the results of the 1885 election it concluded that Parnell could secure Home Rule from neither party, for 18 Tories were Ulster Unionists and many others would never vote for Home Rule. In exchange for an alliance with the Liberals, giving Gladstone a majority exceeding 150, Parnell would certainly want Home Rule. 'Yet Mr Gladstone, whatever his secret views as to the best government of Ireland, can hardly grant that, he stands pledged to the lips against that, and so do most of his followers, Mr Chamberlain included, and he is nearly certain to offer something much less sweeping . . . Mr Gladstone, whatever his own ideas, rarely goes quite beyond the plans which his followers will accept, and we may, we think, therefore take it as certain that Mr Parnell's proposals will be rejected by both parties.'²¹ It was a bad misjudgment. Only a week later *The Economist* was hit by the great betrayal and had to announce the 'startling' news of 'the publication of a scheme of Home Rule of Ireland, to which it is announced that Mr Gladstone has given his assent. There have for some time past been vague and floating rumours that the Liberal leader, impressed with the significance of the Irish elections, has come to the conclusion (which was dimly foreshadowed in his Midlothian manifesto) that the time has arrived for a substantial concession to the demands of the Nationalist party.' But nothing on this scale had been expected. What was clear was that no business could be done until the problem of Irish government was solved, since the Parnellites held the balance of power: 'We may well differ as to the course which a statesmanlike policy would prescribe, but we cannot ignore the obvious fact that ... things cannot possibly remain as they are.' Yet 'the objections to tampering with the supremacy of the Imperial Legislature, to exposing the loyal minority to confiscation and oppression, to handing over to men a vast proportion of whom are ignorant fanatics the control of police and the power of indulging in fiscal experiments, have never yet been fairly encountered or satisfactorily answered ... The Irish have certainly made great advances in the power of tenacity and in the capability for disciplined and united action; but we see little evidence of the development of the higher faculties of foresight, insight and self-control. These familiar considerations, which we have often pressed on our readers have not, in our judgment, lost anything of their relevance or their cogency.'[22]

The paper had manfully pulled itself together by the following week.

> Are we not all a little over-timid about this Irish struggle? We all assume in argument – certainly we have frequently assumed in this paper – that if Mr Parnell controls about eighty or more votes, he must be able to dictate to the British Parliament; but is that strictly true? It certainly was true while the ancient British parties were contending on tolerably equal terms; but is it equally true now, when upon this subject they are perceptibly drawing together?
>
> If we understand the position – and the *Economist*, it should be remembered, cares only for the moderate and responsible statesmen on either side – the revelation, whether accidental or designed, of serious Home Rule projects being entertained by statesmen of the first rank, has elicited from both sides a strong expression of distaste, amounting, in fact, to a positive refusal to sanction those projects. The Tories absolutely refuse to follow their leader if he goes in that direction; while the Liberals, if we are to state the exact truth, murmur that they will not follow even Mr Gladstone, unless they are compelled by the constituencies. In other words, pending a dissolution *ad hoc*, the result of which no one even pretends to forecast, the two parties have drawn nearer to one another, and are determined that the Irish proposal, as presented in the crude form of an independent Irish Parliament, shall be rejected.[23]

There were, the leader accurately pointed out, few genuine Home Rulers in

Britain, and ironically, the example selected was John Morley, who was 'sincerely convinced . . . that this experiment ought to be tried; but the majority who would vote for it are influenced rather by disgust than by friendship for Ireland'.

Week by week, the paper expressed disillusion, hurt and increasing hostility. Why was Gladstone equivocating? It was hardly likely 'after the daily and nightly study which (he tells us) he has given to the subject that his mind is not made up, one way or the other, with regard to the Parnellite demand for a separate Irish Parliament'.[24] He had filled many Cabinet posts, they said when he took office in February 1886, 'with even more than the customary disregard for the expectations of the public, and for the apparent claims and capacities of the statesmen concerned'. They welcomed, however, John Morley's appointment as Chief Secretary of Ireland, since if a scheme of Home Rule was on the agenda, 'it is obviously right that the Minister for Ireland should be one who (unlike any of his colleagues) has been for years a consistent Home Ruler himself'. Mr Gladstone was still being evasive, merely speaking of examining 'some other method' of solving the Irish problem than a new coercion act: 'unless he can show that half the news which comes to us from Ireland is unfounded, how can he justify leaving the helpless and the unprotected at the mercy of their oppressors, while his other and better "method" is being examined or invented?'[25] In the same issue they fought the threatened Home Rule proposal in a thoroughly *Economist*-like fashion. 'CAN IRELAND AFFORD HOME RULE?' asked one article. A page of statistical calculations later, the answer was that granting to Ireland 'an independent and self-supporting Administration, which would contribute its due quota to the Imperial expenditure' would add two million pounds to the Irish tax burden: 'It would be interesting to hear from those who advocate a disruption of the legislative union whether Ireland is prepared to pay such a price for it, and if so, how the money could be raised.'[26]

This preoccupied condition of British politics was also evident in the contents pages of the paper. 'LONDON AND IRELAND', 'THE IRISH SPLIT', 'THE CONTRIBUTIONS OF SCOTLAND AND IRELAND RESPEC-TIVELY TO THE IMPERIAL EXCHEQUER', 'THE TAXATION OF IRE-LAND', 'IRISH SECURITIES', 'TWO ERRONEOUS IDEAS ABOUT IRELAND', 'IRISH RAILWAYS IN THE PAST HALF-YEAR' and 'HOW IRISH STATISTICS (?) ARE MANUFACTURED' all appeared within four weeks in February and March 1886. The last item was a savage attack on an article by Robert Giffen in the *Nineteenth Century* on 'The Economic Value of Ireland', which was not only vague, but appeared to suggest Ireland was in a healthier economic state than the paper believed. Was the article 'an elaborate joke, or is it intended to be read seriously?' The critical vocabulary included 'loose', 'erroneous', 'misleading', 'blunder', 'wrong', 'conjectural', 'distorted', 'misrepresent', and 'serious discrepancies'.[27]

Week by week, in article after article, every opinion or alleged fact or opinion supporting Home Rule was subjected to scrutiny and vigorous challenge. One of the most interesting from the perspective of a century later was the condemnation of the notion of giving 'some form of Home Rule . . . which should leave Ulster either a separate State, or a province under the British Parliament'. Attractive though the idea was because of the danger of Ulster rising against the authority of a parliament in Dublin, it could not work: it would, 'even for this country, be too illogical. If Ireland is not a nation, Ireland has no claim to Home Rule in any shape or form, and without Ulster Ireland is not a nation. She is scarcely even a geographical expression.' Secondly, the majority of the Irish would 'peremptorily reject' any such solution and from their standpoint, would be right. They wanted not 'provincial liberties, but a national position' and were convinced 'as we believe erroneously – that when once masters of their own revenues, they will be able to terminate, or at least materially to diminish, the chronic poverty of Ireland, to construct arterial drains, to "foster" manufacturers, and to "encourage" trade'.

Thirdly, 'England would derive scarcely any benefit from the arrangement. Ulster is not Protestant, but Protestant and Catholic; the Catholic population would sympathise actively with the South, and it would soon be necessary to garrison and police the North as heavily as we now do the whole island. Those who advocated the plan are at heart thinking that the Orangemen are strong enough to coerce the Catholics; but then that is precisely the situation which with our principles of government we should be bound to prevent.'[28]

Towards the end of March the calm broke, with the resignations of Joseph Chamberlain – advanced Radical, ex-Mayor of Birmingham, President of the Local Government Board of Trade – and of George Trevelyan (son of the Charles Trevelyan who had undermined Wilson's position in India) – who had been Irish Chief Secretary from 1882 to 1884 – to fight Gladstone's Home Rule proposals. *The Economist*, which was doing an excellent job as a

Cassandra, was quick to see the seriousness of the Liberal split.

Since Home Rule had not been an issue in the general election, a dissolution of parliament would almost certainly be necessary before such a measure could go through. Now, instead of two parties going to the country, there would be five:

> There are, first, the Parnellites, who will reject every man opposed to Home Rule, and who, besides controlling eighty-six seats in Ireland, possess one in England, and throw a most influential vote in from thirty to fifty-eight more, the latter being the number in which they themselves claim to possess great power. There are, secondly, the Tories, who will this time lose the Irish vote, and may, therefore, return to Parliament with somewhat diminished numbers. There are, thirdly, the Gladstone Liberals, who desire to grant Home Rule, who will be assisted by the Irish in the boroughs, who are dominant in Scotland and Wales, and who will, therefore, probably prove to be the largest section in the House. There are, fourthly, the Hartington Liberals, or Moderates, who desire to support Mr Gladstone and the Liberal party generally on most subjects, but who are so completely severed from them by their dislike of Home Rule, that they are almost as distinct as Tories. They will . . . be numerous enough to form an appreciable party in the House . . . And fifthly, there will be the Chamberlain Liberals, that is, all Radicals who remain Radicals, but are most unwilling, even on Mr Gladstone's recommendation, to grant Home Rule.[29]

The following week *The Economist* bit the bullet in an article on Gladstone's personal position. It was necessary to face the 'calamity' that to vote against Home Rule meant ending Gladstone's great career: anti-Home Rule Liberals had to choose openly between their principles and their leader. For many Liberals, who had felt 'most keenly the effect of that personal magnetism', to tell him that he must stand aside would seem 'a blasphemy, and to all must involve a degree of suffering, in which we sympathise most deeply'. Yet the deed had to be done. 'Those Liberals who oppose Home Rule must recognise that it is a proposal so large and so far-reaching, that if it is wrong, no leader, not even Mr Gladstone, can be worth so much either to the party or the country as to justify non-resistance.'

Ireland had been the scene of Gladstone's failure.

> He has proposed to give equality to the Catholic Church, secure tenure to tenants, and wide suffrage to the people; and the Irish Catholic Church has

become more irreconcileable, the Irish land has become more unsaleable, the Irish people have grown more openly hostile, and determined on secession from Great Britain . . . The situation is most abnormal, yet from it there is no escape. Those Liberals who propose to defeat Mr Gladstone must consider that whatever their respect, or admiration, or affection for their opponent, he is in their judgment leading an army to inflict a mortal wound on Ireland, and a dangerous one upon Great Britain. There is no refuge from that conclusion, and it is one which must overpower any consideration for any individual, however illustrious he may be either in his character, his services, or his career.[30]

When Gladstone's scheme 'for which the country has been waiting with feverish expectancy' was unfolded, *The Economist* declared its worst fears realised. 'It is a scheme which, while professing to maintain the unity of the Empire, makes directly towards disintegration; which professes to have for its object the establishment of more harmonious relations between Great Britain and Ireland, but which will only strengthen and embitter the antagonism that exists; and which, while it seeks to ameliorate the condition of Ireland, would hand that unhappy country over to the strife of rival factions, the bitter play of religious animosities, and to the keener conflict of class hatreds.'[31] (The overwhelming fascination of the issue is graphically illustrated in Eliza's diaries, which show unprecedentedly sustained involvement on the political front. During a week when she was ill with what her doctor had diagnosed as a slight case of diphtheria, the senior *Economist* proprietor had her nurse read to her Gladstone's 3 hour and 25 minute Commons speech on the Home Rule Bill.)

The paper's extreme distress of mind led to one of its more interesting constitutional articles the following week, when it addressed itself to the problem of Gladstone's pre-eminence and the 'temporary breakdown of the British system of Cabinet government', a system that 'has gradually come to be regarded among us as the key of our administration, and the check not only on the folly or caprice of Parliament, but on the rashness or unwisdom of any individual Minister'. This applied even to a Prime Minister: 'Much of completeness, and something, perhaps, of genius, is often sacrificed for the compromises such a system compels, but much also of personal rashness, personal obstinacy, and personal want of insight is thereby rendered innocuous.'

In the present instance, Gladstone had failed to treat the Cabinet as a committee of colleagues, but without any consultation had laid before them his complete plan: 'The Ministers must accept them or break up the government.' The paper was not prepared to bring against Gladstone 'the usual charge of seeking a dictatorship. All men like their own way, especially when they are full of years, conscious of successes, and surfeited with adulation, and we do not believe that Mr Gladstone, though more masterful, is more arbitrary than his rivals or his colleagues. But . . . on this occasion the usual check upon rashness provided by our Executive tradition . . . has been entirely wanting. Mr Gladstone did not take the country into his confidence at all, and he took his committee of colleagues very little . . . Whatever may be the ultimate result, a great event – one of the greatest in our history – had occurred through the volition of one man, who, in spite of all our elaborate constitutional checks, had made himself for this occasion the Government . . . A kind of presidency has been substituted for the traditional English scheme, and its first result has been a proposal, which may yet be carried, for abandoning one of the three kingdoms of which the country is composed.'[32]

Week after week, the extent of Gladstone's perfidy became an ever-greater source of distress. He addressed a manifesto to his Midlothian electors, which was read by 'moderate men of all parties with sorrow and indignation. It is a direct, and, indeed, avowed appeal from the educated to the ignorant, from experienced politicians to the multitude of electors, from Parliament to a plebiscitum.' Furthermore, Gladstone had thrown out a 'dangerous hint' that if he carried his bill he might offer Home Rule to Scotland and Wales: 'that is to say, he, in the middle of a great struggle, without public demand from any side, offers to transmute the Kingdom of Great Britain into a federation, and thus to undo the successful result of a policy persevered in ever since English History began . . . we do accuse him of believing that he has now attained a position at which he is at liberty, with no pressure from circumstances and no consultation with colleagues, to formulate constitutions for Great Britain from the depths of his own mind.'[33]

Under Wilson, in the early days, the paper had been a weapon in a crusade: now it was employed in a war. The campaign against the fallen idol continued apace. In May alone there were seven articles assailing Gladstone's Irish proposals from different angles, ranging from outraged indignation at his lack of principle to detailed examination of small print.

Wilson and Bagehot had evinced distaste for the more intransigent Ulster Protestants, and they have had few fans on the paper in the twentieth century, but in the climate of 1886 *The Economist* saw Ulster as a mother of heroes: 'It certainly does not lie in the mouths of the Home Rulers to say that because she occupies, so to speak, only a corner of the island, she has no claim to stand by herself. They have no hesitation in contending that if Wales desires to separate her administration from that of England her desire ought to be granted. But relatively to England, Wales is infinitely smaller in every way than is Protestant Ulster to the rest of Ireland, and how can those who cry out for sectional Home Rule here consistently stigmatise it as intolerable in Ireland.'[34]

The Home Rule Bill was defeated on its second reading in June, parliament was dissolved and an election was called. There was relief when it became clear that Gladstone was fighting the election on the straightforward issue of his bill. With considerable glee the leader writers addressed themselves to the matter of the likely effect of the Irish vote in Britain. The previous December, Gladstone had been extremely bitter when, at the dictates of Parnell, the Irish vote had gone Tory. He had declared this to be a wrong principle: 'What we want in this country,' he said, 'is the voice of Ireland from Ireland, and the voice of England, Scotland, and Wales from England, Scotland, and Wales. But this is not the voice which some of the counties of England have been returning. Lancashire has returned a voice. She has spoken, but if you listen to her accents, you will find they are strongly tinged with the Irish brogue.' It had, added Gladstone, given rise to 'a very serious question . . . whether the voice of this country shall in this manner be falsified'.

'At the coming election the Irish vote will be cast solid for Mr Gladstone, and the tinge of the brogue which six months ago sounded so unpleasant to his ear will then seem only to lend an added charm to such constituencies as declare in his favour.' Fortunately, the *Economist*'s detailed analysis of the number of natives of Ireland resident in each county demonstrated to its satisfaction that, 'in reality, the much-boasted power of Mr Parnell to sway the elections as he thinks fit is largely a delusion. If the constituencies will only take the trouble to assert themselves, they can easily show for how little his attempts at dictation really count.'[35]

The *Economist* writers had always done their homework when it came to detecting inconsistencies in Gladstone's behaviour, and their strong Liberal tradition gave them excellent sources of information. They spared no effort in getting their readers ready for 'one of the most momentous elections of modern times'. Their attitude to Gladstone continued to harden: in late June they were talking about the dangers of his 'continued dictatorship . . . He will be as fully master as an American President, with this great difference, that he will be master in Parliament as well as in his Cabinet . . . That is the most urgent fact of the situation, more urgent even than the danger of Home Rule, and it should be thoroughly explained to the electors.'[36]

Throughout the campaign the commentators pored over Gladstone's texts like a bunch of scholars scrutinising the Dead Sea Scrolls, infusing all their detailed analyses with their profound knowledge of their target. In that same week in June in which they discussed the constitutional implications of a Gladstonian victory, they addressed themselves in detail to the omissions in Gladstone's speeches of information about the financial aspects of Home Rule, a deficiency which of course they remedied at great length. 'THE DEAD BILL' began with an old story 'to the effect that at a reception at Stafford House, when somebody said that the Dowager Duchess of Sutherland ought to marry General Garibaldi, it was objected that the General had a wife living. "Oh, that does not matter," was the reply, "Gladstone is here, and we could easily get him to explain her away." And nobody, it seems to us, but the dialectic genius capable of explaining away Garibaldi's wife could explain away the extraordinary distinctions which, in his recent Midlothian speeches, Mr Gladstone had drawn as to the issue on which he asks us to vote . . . Mr Gladstone's curious and subtle phraseology is . . . tainted with a most significant ambiguity. He is, in reality, seeking to cajole people into voting for a bill which he assures them is dead – knowing well they would not vote for it were it alive – by the simple device of muddling their minds over the distinction between principle and policy.'[37]

Disillusion brought them to bitter attack on Gladstone's integrity. *The Economist* stopped short of actually calling him a liar, but came very close. He hit his lowest point in its estimation when he assured English labourers that Home Rule would induce all Irishmen to return home and thus remove them from the British labour-market. It was doubly mean – 'the meanness of offering a bribe, and the added meanness of seeking to buy votes by promises and predictions which are impossible of fulfilment'.[38]

It was with a palpable sigh of relief that *The Economist* greeted Gladstone's defeat. The Liberal Party was instructed to accept loss of power with resignation, to abjure Home Rule, to 'endure such proposals as its adversaries may carry for the good government of Ireland, and to recommence the long postponed legislation for the benefit of the United Kingdom'. The electorate had not only voted against Home Rule: it had voted for giving 'English and Scotch affairs . . . the measure of attention which for some years has been denied them, and which the Irish declare they shall never receive until Home Rule has been conceded'.[39] The writers' distrust of the Grand Old Man had reached such a pitch that they worried momentarily that he would try to hang on to power despite the overwhelming rejection of his policy. Their fears were unjustified. With only 191 followers and the unreliable support of 85 Irish Nationalists, there was little Gladstone could do against 317 Tories and 77 Liberal Unionists. Indeed as *The Economist* pointed out with mingled sadness and relief, his personal ascendancy had greatly declined: 'Mr Gladstone has not convinced the people he is right; on the contrary, the result of his great effort, in many respects a wonderful one, has been to convince a heavy majority of them that he is wrong. He has not read their feelings aright, though he was supposed specially to understand them; he has not addressed the right arguments to their intelligence, and he has failed, often in cases where he personally intervened, to touch their imaginations.'[40]

It was a sign of the extraordinary manner in which the Irish question turned British politics upside-down, that the paper should have exhaled a sigh of relief that Lord Salisbury would henceforth be dealing with Ireland. Only four years earlier it had found a speech by Salisbury on the subject 'very melancholy . . . to read', calling as it did for the conquest of Ireland before any further attention was paid to alleviating grievances. 'The plan would involve a degree of severity, an amount of bloodshed, a confusion of the innocent with the guilty, which by a people like ours, and in a country so near and so visible as Ireland, would never be tolerated. It would be necessary, if smooth phrases are cast aside, to shoot down every Irishman in Ireland who refused to obey the Courts or to pay rent, or to be evicted, and every Irishman in England who actually sympathised with him, and to continue doing this whenever outbreaks occurred for at least a generation.'[41]

That was almost certainly written by Asquith, four years before he was converted to Home Rule and thirty-four before – as Prime Minister – he took notorious and counter-productive punitive action in Ireland by permitting the execution of leaders of the 1916 rebellion. Now Salisbury was committed to the extension of peasant proprietorship and *The Economist* was aligned with the Liberal Unionists, whose mission was two-fold: to stop undue coercion in Ireland and expel Gladstone's Irish policy from 'the Liberal pharmacopoeia'.[42]

CHAPTER XXVI

St Loe Strachey

It was not for a slight cause nor with a light heart that we separated ourselves from our leader and from the comrades with whom we had so often marched to battle, and even now we would not think harshly of them, and we are ready to believe that, having made this extraordinary and rapid change of front, they have at least since been able to convince themselves of the wisdom and justice of the course they have taken. But we complain that they do not try to convince us too, and we say that, as long as this is the case, for us the acceptance of this new creed which they have embraced would be a shameless apostasy unworthy of any honourable man; or, we should add, of any temperate and cautious one. *Report of a speech by Joseph Chamberlain,* The Economist, *5 October 1889*

There were 12 more long years to run of the quarrel between Gladstone and *The Economist* over Home Rule. It is impossible to determine definitely who had written the bulk of the leaders immediately after Asquith's departure, but it was almost certainly Lathbury. An obituarist wrote that 'he had been a follower of Mr Gladstone, but doubts seem to have weakened his allegiance before the Home Rule Bill made him a Liberal Unionist; he went so far, indeed, as to speak for the Conservative candidate in his own division in Surrey at the General Election in that year'.[1] That picture ties in closely with the growing disillusion of the wounded disciple evident in *Economist* coverage of Gladstone. Lathbury was known, as editor of the Anglican *Guardian*, for his 'firm and clear opinions', and there he gave no quarter when an issue of principle was involved. In Gladstone's Irish policy, Lathbury saw a stark, moral issue.[2]

Henceforward, the battle was conducted on the paper's behalf by a tough new recruit, John St Loe Strachey, already installed as Asquith's successor at the *Spectator*, who would at the end of the century succeed Hutton and Townsend there as editor and proprietor. Strachey was to be one of the four longest-serving and most influential political writers for *The Economist* in its first 60 years (the others being Wilson, Greg and Bagehot).[3]

Born in 1860, Strachey was the second son of Sir Edward Strachey, a prosperous Somerset baronet. His family had an intellectually distinguished history and his uncles included John Addington Symonds, a writer, Sir John Strachey, an Anglo-Indian administrator and Sir Richard Strachey, a lieutenant-general; Lytton Strachey was his cousin. He was educated mainly by his father in their lovely country house, and, like Bagehot, he had an understanding of ordinary rural people which was to help him to see how the Conservative Party appealed to working-class voters. In 1922, in his autobiography, he wrote at eloquent length about the culture which formed him: 'I may class myself as thrice-blessed in being brought up in Whig ideas, in a Whig family with Whig traditions, for in spite of the stones, intellectual and political, that have been thrown at them, salvation is of the Whigs.' This was not 'the Whiggism of the Whig aristocracy as represented by modern Tory historians, or by the parasitic sycophants of a militant proletariat', but that which had sprung from such 'true Whig principles' as the Bill of Rights and 'the Glorious Revolution of 1688' and had its origin in the party of Cromwell and John Milton, 'the party which even in its decadence flowered in England in Chatham and in William Pitt, and in America in Washington, John Adams, and the founders of the Republic. Whig principles to me mean that the will of the majority of the nation as a whole must prevail, and not the will of any section, even if it is a large section and does manual work. These are the principles which are in deadly opposition to Jacobinism and Bolshevism', under which, 'as their inventors proclaim, true policy must be made to prevail by force, or fraud if necessary . . . But though the will of the people, be it what it may, must prevail, the Whig claims absolute liberty in all matters of personal opinion and of conscience . . . These are the true Whig principles, and in these I was brought up.' It was a romantic defence of the political creed to which James Wilson and many of his inheritors came by a variety of routes.

Strachey's father, who directed his intellectual development as Thomas Bagehot had Walter's, was, the mature Strachey concluded, one of the best of Whigs: 'Moderation, justice, freedom, sympathy with suffering, tolerance, yielded not in the form of patronage but in obedience to a claim of right which could not be gainsaid – these were the pillars of his mind.' Although pro-free-trade, he did not see it as the ultimate panacea, and he transmitted idealism rather than doctrine to his son. Like Thomas Bagehot, he was passionately interested in politics 'and he followed every turn of the political wheel'. Profoundly well-read, he had several distinguished friends including Hutton (who like him was a disciple of the rather mystical divine, Frederick Maurice) and Townsend, and he was a contributor to the *Spectator*.

After a period as a clergyman's private pupil, Strachey was sent to live with an uncle at Oxford. He entered Balliol nine years after Asquith, read history, got a first despite having a poor relationship with the dons, made many friends and was converted from republicanism and socialism and recruited to membership of the free-trade crusade. His counsellor was Bernard Mallet, whose father, Sir Louis Mallet, was an economist, a famous civil servant and a disciple of Claude Frédéric Bastiat and of Cobden, whose official secretary he had been during the negotiations for the Commercial Treaty with France. Bernard Mallet had learned at his father's knee to look upon political economy 'not as something to be applied only to trade, but something which concerned our morals, our politics, and even our spiritual life. Though it no doubt involved Free Trade, what both the Mallets pleaded for was "the policy of Free Exchange" – a policy entering and ruling every form of human activity, or, at any rate, everything to which the quality of value inured, and so the quality of exchangeability.'[4] Young Mallet argued that socialism should be tried if everything else had failed, '*provided one was not convinced that the remedy would prove worse than the disease*. But he went on to explain to me, what I had never realised before, that the enlightened economists took no responsibility for the existing system. They held instead that the present ills of the world came, not from obeying but from disobeying the teachings of Political Economy.' Louis Mallet, a pillar of the Political Economy Club, to which his son and Strachey would be elected in the late 1890s, held that much harm had been done because 'we call the policy Free *Trade*, and so have narrowed it and made it appear sordid. If, like the French, we had called it Free Exchange, we should have made it universal and so inspiring.' Strachey rapidly became a true believer, coming to understand that 'Political Economy, properly understood and properly applied, is not a dreary science, but one of the most fascinating and mentally stimulating of all forms of human knowledge.'

In 1884, Strachey settled in London and began to read for the Bar, but he soon found his true vocation. In his teens he had contributed two sonnets to the *Spectator* and while at Oxford had written articles and reviews for the *Saturday Review*, and occasional pieces for the *Academy* and Morley's *Pall Mall Gazette*. Late in 1885 he asked his father to give him a formal introduction to the *Spectator* editors, and he went to see them at No. 1 Wellington Street and was given some books to review. He 'was actually hailed as a "writer and critic of the first force"', and became a regular contributor. In the political convulsion of 1886, which split families rather as Suez did 70 years later, Strachey's father and elder brother remained Liberals with Gladstone while he followed Chamberlain and Lord Hartington into the new Liberal Unionist Party. 'My conversion was not in any way sought by my new friends and chiefs at the *Spectator* office, though they at once took the Unionist side. I have no doubt, however, that my intercourse with Hutton and Townsend had its effect, though I also think that my mind was naturally Unionist in politics. I was already a Lincoln worshipper in American history and desired closer union with the Dominions, not separation. I was for concentration, not dispersion, in the Empire.' There was no falling-out with his father, though they both supported their causes fiercely.

During the 1886 election Strachey acted as agent for a Somerset neighbour, Henry Hobhouse (a friend of Eliza Bagehot's), and on his return to London he was asked by Hutton to help out while Townsend was on holiday. His first leader, dealing with the election results, had a conclusion that would have been perfect for *The Economist*.

> Conciliation or Coercion was the cry everywhere. And yet the majority of the new voters, to their eternal honour, proved their political infancy so full of sense and patriotism that they let go by unheeded the appeals to their class-prejudices and to their emotions, and chose, instead, the harder and seemingly less generous policy, based on reason rather than on sentiment, on conviction rather than on despair. As the trial was severe, so was the honour due to the new voters lasting and conspicuous.[5]

Within a few weeks Strachey became the weekly leader writer and holiday understudy at the *Spectator*, 'a mixed post which, by the irony of fate . . . had just been vacated by Mr Asquith'. At the proprietors' suggestion, he gave up the Bar in exchange for a guaranteed salary, the right to do what outside work he liked and a promise of a half-share in the *Spectator* when one of them retired or died.

Strachey gave up the other journals to which he had previously contributed, but in addition to his *Spectator* work he took on leader writing for the *Standard* and the *Observer*, occasional pieces for the *Manchester Guardian*, the co-editorship of the *Liberal Unionist* and a weekly article for *The Economist*.

> Mr Johnstone was not only a great editor, but a very satisfactory one from the contributor's point of view. He told you exactly what he wanted written about, and then left you to your own devices. As it happened, I generally was in entire agreement with his policy, but if I had not been, it would not have mattered, because he had made it so very clear to one, as an editor should, that one was expressing not one's own views, but the views of *The Economist*. Whether they were in fact right or wrong they certainly deserved full consideration. Therefore, full exposition could never be regarded as taking the wrong side.
>
> Though *The Economist* was less strongly Unionist than I was, I cannot recall any occasion on which my leaders were altered by the Editor.[6]

Looking back on nine or ten years with *The Economist*, Strachey could remember only one comment from Johnstone. 'Mr Johnstone, though so great a journalist and so sound a politician, was not a man who had paid any attention to literature. Possibly, indeed, he did not consider that it deserved any. When, however, the complete works of Walter Bagehot . . . were published, Mr Johnstone asked me to review them for the paper.' Strachey, a great admirer of Bagehot, was delighted, and wishing to say something to 'make people "sit up and take notice"'. In regard to Bagehot's 'perfection of style', he declared it worthy of comparison with Robert Louis Stevenson, 'who at the time was held to be our greatest master of words. Mr Johnstone, with, as I fully admitted, a quite unnecessary urbanity of manner, apologised to me for having altered the article. He had, he explained, left out the passage about Stevenson. But mark the reason! It was not because he thought the praise exaggerated, but because he feared that Mr Bagehot's family might think that the writer was not properly appreciative of Bagehot's work if he compared it to that of Stevenson!'[7]

With an active member of the Liberal Unionist Party writing the leaders on domestic politics, *The Economist*'s position hardened. In April 1887, for instance, the paper's attitude to coercion in Ireland was very different from that which Asquith had regularly propounded: where he had seen coercion as a last resort, Strachey seemed positively enthusiastic. In 'MR GLADSTONE'S APOLOGY FOR OUTRAGE', Gladstone and Morley were denounced for their speeches against the Criminal Law Amendment Bill: 'If Mr Gladstone's apology was unscrupulous, Mr Morley's speech . . . was, in truth, far more sinister and dangerous.'[8]

Gladstone's capacity to provoke seemed limitless. One of his most serious offences was his attack on the Irish constabulary for acting 'with oppressive illegality' and thereby causing a mob to resist the law. His new creed was: 'When you dislike a law, don't trouble to alter it, simply disobey it.'[9] He was 'possessed with a kind of fury, which is leading him from indiscretion to extravagance'. His language 'must increase the disorder in Ireland, and it must finally dissolve the ancient Liberal Party'.[10]

The old reprobate was a mesmerising object of study as he rampaged around the country and spread himself over the monthlies and quarterlies with heretical opinions backed by suspect facts and figures. The core of the paper's main ideological difference with him was laid bare in March 1888. Strachey then wrote one of his finest articles in response to Gladstone's contribution to *Contemporary*, which exposed the frightful truth that Gladstone, at the end of his long and great career, had become not only a Federalist but a Federalist 'of what are called in America "State-Rights Opinions"'. It was an issue about which Strachey felt particularly passionate: Lincoln was his hero, and he had always disapproved of Gladstone's defence of the rights of the Southern states. The cause which Gladstone was pressing was 'federalism of a poor and badly-jointed kind. Throughout he shows, as he did during the American Civil War, that the very idea of a State as it has been understood by all eminent political thinkers, and all who have claimed for themselves the title of patriots, is entirely foreign to his sympathy.'

> He sees nothing in a State to die for. The utility of those common laws, common taxes, common modes of executive action, common interests and common hatreds, common aspirations and common ideals, which bind a State into a vast corporate entity, breathing one breath, and inspired with one soul, is entirely invisible to him. He maintains, as it were, that a bundle of sticks is as good as a beam, that a group of congregations is the equivalent of a Church, that a common crowd, if it only stands together in peace and amity, is a corporation. He does not see at all, or rather care at all, that 'autonomy,' so far as it exists in any portion of a State, must be a distraction from the unity of that State, and from the safety and duration of its vitality. He thinks particularism no source of weakness, far less of decay, and would

far rather that Greece suffered than that Athens and Sparta should give up their individuality. He affirms, for example, that slavery was the cause of the American Civil War, and does not see, or care, that slavery was that cause, because only of the State Rights system; that if America had been an undivided nation, slavery must either have been universal, or have been abolished, and that it could never, therefore, under that condition, have been a cause of war at all.

Arguments followed about Gladstone's examples of Utah, Germany, Austro-Hungary and France, all of which promoted a 'federalism without any clear idea of the first conditions of a working unity . . . Mr Gladstone, while keenly alive to the feeling of nationality, appears utterly obtuse alike to the value and the claims of a formed and organised nation.'[11]

The intellectual and moral rift between Gladstone and a newspaper which had always made social stability a priority had become a ravine. A few months later *The Economist* even succeeded in taking issue with him over his speech on market gardening and fruit growing at the Hawarden Flower Show. It was 'a very pleasant and a very readable essay. Mr Gladstone has many charming things to say about the love of flowers and the devotion of the poor in our towns to something that reminds them of the country, and of course says all he has to say with consummate grace and skill.' However, 'the glorification of spade labour makes a very pleasant rustic idyll, but in reality any great extension of spade labour is utterly opposed to the whole tendency of modern agriculture'.[12]

There was genuine distress at the spectacle of the *enfant terrible*. 'Those who delight in the game of catching Mr Gladstone out,' said a leader in the autumn of 1888, 'and who find pleasure in the spectacle of one of the greatest of living statesmen attempting partly to explain away, and partly to justify statements made by him, with a complete disregard of accuracy, must have found his recent political speech at Wrexham very pleasant reading.'

> To those, however, who, though they entirely disagree with Mr Gladstone, are above all things anxious that he should not end his political career by stooping to conduct which no political necessities can justify or make worthy of a great statesman, the perusal of the speech in question is in the highest degree painful . . . If we judge Mr Gladstone's later methods of controversy impartially, it must be confessed that they are not only unworthy of a statesman of his eminence, but that they would have to be condemned wherever encountered and by whoever employed.[13]

In December 1889, his version of Irish history was inducing in *The Economist* 'a feeling of positive bewilderment . . . So preposterous are the misrepresentations of fact, so perverse and inconsequential the citations of history, and so topsy-turvy and irrelevant the political analogies it contains, that the speech seems almost like an oratorical nightmare.'[14]

'Enough is enough' was the message of their tribute to Gladstone on his 80th birthday in January 1890. Yet it was a gracious message: in offering congratulations, the leader said that it was, 'not for readers of the *Economist*, however apart they may have drifted from Mr Gladstone in politics, to forget his services to political economy and public finances'.

> We have often been compelled to criticise the details of his plans, but he has been the truest and most successful of Free-traders, has so rearranged the Queen's taxes that they have ceased to press on the springs of industry; have steadily kept in view the reduction of the Debt, has raised more perhaps than any man the financial credit of the country, and has strengthened, in season, and out of season, that real 'sheet-anchor of English finances,' the general horror of a deficit in the great annual account. These are true services, and we have no intention of joining the crowd who, because Mr Gladstone has fallen into a great error, deny that he ranks among the foremost figures of our time, and receive tidings of his good health with the growl of discontent.

However, if Gladstone came back into office, though he would by that time be 82, he would be setting out to get through a piece of legislation of great controversy and detail; it would be exceptionally fatiguing work which would, 'we feel confident, overstrain even Mr Gladstone, even should he retain, as his followers feel so sure he will, all his faculties unimpaired'.[15]

One of the charges being levelled against Gladstone is one to which members of the left are as vulnerable today – and which was addressed trenchantly by Joseph Chamberlain, who 'did a signal service in insisting upon what may well be called the common sense of coercion. It may be tiresome for the speaker to go over the old commonplaces as to the necessity for putting down resistance to the law of the land, but for all that the true principles must be kept clearly before the country, in order that public opinion shall not become enervated and debauched by the specious appeals made to it in the name of humanity, and by the denunciations of those who carry out the law as tyrants and oppressors . . . it is only one kind of coercion which Mr Gladstone and his friends ever care to denounce. The Gladstonians are never tired of denouncing coercion by the law, and no instance in which a man has been forced by the law to do something against his will, however petty, escapes their notice. When, however, the coercion is not by legitimate authority, but by the National League, which enforces its unwritten law with a promptitude far greater, and by a code of punishment infinitely more ruthless than any administered by judges or police officers, no voice is ever lifted among the Gladstonians in condemnation . . . Coercion is apparently only to be condemned when it follows due process of law.'[16]

'It is a grave aggravation of the many evils attending the discussion on Home Rule that eloquence or good writing about it have become impossible. The subject is, in reality, so limited, the arguments have been so thrashed out, and the illustrations available are so few, that orators, publicists, and audience are alike exhausted.'[17] So too, is the modern reader. And yet the whole wearisome debate over Home Rule provided the opportunity for the paper to address itself to a vast range of timeless political issues: law and order; the structure of the United Kingdom; the rights of regions; individual liberty; the nature of Cabinet government; parliamentary procedure; the economics of devolution; the nature of tribal and religious conflict, and many others. Reading the relevant leaders from 1880, when Home Rule began seriously to distort the priorities of government, one has a sharp appreciation of the solid quality of James Wilson's creation and the high quality of the people it attracted, even at its weakest. Lathbury and Palgrave might have been comparative failures as editors, but they had knowledge, intelligence and integrity. Edward Johnstone's paper was often pedestrian, but it was never in danger of losing the essential core of readers who relied on the paper for honest information and opinions consistent with great liberal principles. Sir John Clapham[18] thought *The Economist* close to becoming 'Unionist partisan' at this time, but it never became partisan to the extent of losing its intellectual integrity and it made noble efforts throughout to set out the Gladstonian case honestly before tearing it apart: it is a superb historical source.

One major question about the split was who had split from whom. On this Chamberlain, who was fast becoming the paper's new hero, and who was another great performer on the stump, fought an unremitting battle. Gladstonian Liberals charged Liberal Unionists with deserting their principles – a charge which stung *The Economist* painfully. A leader which was classic Strachey on classic Chamberlain declared that this charge 'no doubt tells with a people like the English, who admire party fidelity, and Mr Chamberlain was therefore right, at the risk of creating weariness, in answering it once more'. In a 'most stirring passage' in a speech in Morley's constituency, 'he reminded the Radicals of Newcastle that five years ago their policy was to redress the grievances of Ireland through the Parliament at Westminster, and to maintain the law and repress crime and outrage . . .'

> 'Have you changed your opinions? If you have not changed your opinions, then I say that should be now your policy which was your policy then, and if you have changed your opinions, perhaps when you talk of traitors and renegades you had best look for them amongst those who have abandoned their principles, who have surrendered their position without firing a shot or without even a council of war, and surrendered it to the enemies of their country.'

That, said Strachey, was the whole truth upon that point in a nutshell. 'If there is any discredit in changing an opinion, or deserting a party, or revolutionising a policy, it attaches solely to those Liberals who suddenly, at the bidding of a chief, abandoned views held steadily ever since the Reform Bill, broke loose from all leaders except one, and surrendered a seventh of the population of the kingdom and a fourth of its area, if not to "enemies of their country", as Mr Chamberlain says, at least to those who profess to hold its greatness, its objects, and even its existence in no regard. The Gladstonians may be entirely right in their new policy, but it is a new one, a leap in the dark, a jump into the unknown. The Unionists alone are standing upon ancient Liberal principles, and there never was a charge made against a party more gratuitously unjust than the allegation that they have ratted.'[19]

The wearying sequence of charge and counter-charge was dramatically punctuated in November 1890, when Captain Willy O'Shea, citing Parnell as co-respondent, won his divorce from the wife whom the Irish Nationalist and Liberal Party leaders had long known was Parnell's mistress. *The Economist* reacted to this sensational development by making it the subject of a fourth leader (admittedly in a week when there was important financial news) and treated of the matter with extreme distaste: 'It is not the province or the custom of the *Economist* to comment upon cases in the Divorce Court, but the verdict pronounced by a jury this week against Mr Parnell may gravely affect the organisation of political parties, and must, therefore, be discussed.' He would certainly have to retire for a time as party leader. 'It is true that the

Irish Revolutionists seem disposed to support him, and that the Catholic Bishops, who guide the more orthodox Home Rulers, may be unwilling to interfere . . . Catholic bishops have defended too many profligate Kings to be greatly shocked by the conduct of an agitator who may still be of use to the cause they are upholding.'

The Economist would not complain if Parnell's party backed him, they said, with a sudden softening of the priggish tone. 'Every nation must judge for itself whether it can dispense with a leader or not, and it is quite certain that if Englishmen were engaged in a great war they would not dismiss a new Nelson on account of his conduct in respect to a future Lady Hamilton.' However since he was bound to alienate the puritan section of the Liberal Party, by staying as leader he would undoubtedly wreck the cause of Home Rule: 'The effect on the elections of such a trial, with its revelations about fire escapes will, especially in Scotland . . . therefore, be very grave.' When it became clear to Parnell that those committed to Home Rule would want him to go, he would go: 'Mr Parnell is not the man to lead after such a hint has been conveyed to him', said the leader, demonstrating that the paper understood Parnell as little as it did the Irish Catholic bishops. Trying not to crow, it predicted a poor look-out for the post-Parnell party. No one else would have his 'hold over the imagination of the Gladstonian party', who saw in him 'a man who was never willingly a Jacobin, who disliked the Plan of Campaign, who thought the constitutional method the only one which would work, and who superseded instead of aiding the American party of dynamite and force. Whether they were right is another matter.'[20]

Gladstone duly wrote to Morley explaining that Parnell's continuation in the leadership would render his own 'retention of the leadership of the Liberal party, based as it has been on the prosecution of the Irish cause, almost a nullity'. This letter was shown to Parnell, who ignored it; and his party split noisily and viciously.

The ensuing imbroglio caused great satisfaction to the opposition. Gladstone was criticised for illogicality: if Ireland had a right to choose her own rulers and manage her own affairs, why was he denying her autonomy in the choice of leader of the Nationalist Party? Parnell's conduct after the divorce case had demonstrated to the country 'the wisdom and prudence of the attitude which has been taken up by the Unionists since 1886'. It had been revealed that Parnell was 'politically untrustworthy and unscrupulous; that he is utterly reckless as to the means he employs when a personal advantage is to be gained; and that instead of being the sober, level-headed conservative of the Gladstonian myth, he is a man who is perfectly willing to fan the embers of Fenianism and sedition in order to score a point against his antagonists'. The ordinary elector would be feeling 'like a man to whom an accident has suddenly revealed the unsatisfactory character of the guide who was to have led him along the edge of a precipice'. And the way the split in the Nationalist Party had been carried out showed that 'the Southern Irish are wholly given over to the spirit of faction, and that they have no notion of settling a dispute by the weapons of reason, argument and discussion . . . We have been repeatedly told that the moment a Parliament assembles on College Green we shall see two orderly constitutional parties established; but after the disgraceful scenes of last month, it is impossible not to doubt the truth of this picture . . . the task of defending the union has been very greatly facilitated by the course of recent events.'[21]

The hope that Gladstone would now realise that Home Rule was unattainable in the near future was dashed in the course of the next year. His political minders were urging him to keep off Ireland and speak about reforms endorsed by the Liberal Party, yet in a great speech at Newcastle in October 1891 he 'ran over all the subjects upon which the [National Liberal] Federation had passed resolutions, and said upon each a few patronising sentences but his heart was evidently far away . . . He spoke upon all of them without cordiality, and even with reluctance.'

> He did not care about the foreign policy of the Government, only remarking that Egypt, which was occupied by his own order, was an embarrassment; he was languidly jocular about economy, which recalled to him, he said, the days of his youth; he was anxious only that Parliaments should be shortened so far as they 'justly and wisely' could be; he was indifferent about the liquor trade, hoping only that this generation would see it 'reformed' in some methods not indicated; he was unhopeful about land reform, though he wished the land to be 'enfranchised'; he was not hostile to the House of Lords, unless, indeed, they threw out his Irish Bill; and he was not in earnest upon the question of shorter hours, rather doubting if, in the case of the over-worked trades, they might not be accompanied by shorter pay. It was not until he reached Ireland that his voice swelled and his figure dilated, and he gave himself to his subject as the one which really filled his mind. Once upon that he soon made it manifest that his mind was unchanged, that he

still believed in the 'union of hearts,' that he still considered Ireland an oppressed land, and that the reflection of five years had only so far altered his convictions as to induce him to expand his concessions by surrendering the Irish police to the New Government to be established in Dublin. He intended, it was clear, still to make Ireland the one subject of his efforts when he returned to power, and to postpone all other 'reforms' until Ireland had been cut out of the area of British Parliamentary action.

He had, reflected *The Economist* lugubriously, probably benefited that week by the sudden death of Parnell, who had become such a divisive force in Irish nationalist politics.[22]

The Economist searched for all the consolations it could find. Perhaps Parnell's followers would blame Gladstone for his untimely death and vote against him in the election next year. Why should he win a majority of the House of Commons when he had failed to convert any Unionists? How could a Home Rule Bill be got through the House of Lords, since the peers disliked Home Rule more than they feared abolition? If Gladstone did decide to abolish the Lords, it would be a long process.[23]

The Conservatives and the Liberal Unionists (whose seats had dropped from 77 to 46) together won 314 seats in the ensuing election: the Gladstonian Liberals won 272, which with the support of the 80 Irish Nationalists gave them a comfortable majority. Gladstone made Asquith Home Secretary, and Asquith's successor at *The Economist* took stock of the Prime Minister. Strachey thought that a future historian would be chiefly perplexed about the origin of Gladstone's power. '"Mr Gladstone," he will say, "was, in 1893, the acknowledged dictator of the Liberal Party, and as that party possessed a sufficient majority in Parliament, was, in a sense rather continental than English, the actual head of the State . . . he was supreme in his own Cabinet, dictated the principal objects to which his colleagues should direct their energies, and arranged the order of importance to be attached to each measure."'

The historian would consider that Gladstone's success was due partly to his personal qualities: eloquence, great knowledge, 'a certain dominance of nature which impressed and alarmed all who came in contact with him', and to an entire independence of all colleagues as well as to 'a loftiness of moral character, which greatly influenced a people accustomed to regard respectability of the higher kind as a qualification even for great office'. The puzzle was why he fascinated the multitudes: he was no tub-thumping patriot, and though the poor thought he was on their side, there was little evidence that this was so. The historian would conclude that he probably owed his popularity to his 'genuinely democratic tone about the intelligence of the people. Latterly he even exalted the impressions of the masses, which must always be vague and general, above the thoughts of "the classes", as he called them, and this, in a country where everyone fancies himself looked down on by somebody else, greatly soothed a widely-diffused feeling of wounded pride.'

> The 'people' thought they were understood as by a friend, and, with characteristic goodness of heart, stood by their friend under all circum-stances, and without caring for the consequences, which half of them thought Mr Gladstone must understand much better than they. They did not ask so much for acts in proof of friendship as for a certain bearing, and, above all, for the absence of any evidence of a supercilious judgement. Americans have always exhibited the same desire for a 'friendship' in their rulers, just as jurymen love friendly Counsel, and it is probable that the newly-enfranchised classes in England were unusually sensitive as to any opinion passed on their worthiness to exercise their new power. This, at least, is the most probable explanation of the ascendancy exercised by a man of complex character, who was certainly never understood by the classes who raised him to such unquestioned supremacy among the followers of his policy.[24]

Gladstone pushed his Home Rule Bill through the House of Commons by a spectacular display of tenacity and ruthlessness. One of his weapons was the guillotine, introduced into parliament in the previous decade to reduce the paralysing effect of the Irish party's obstructionist tactics. This development had caused much heart-searching; but Asquith, in *The Economist*, sickened by the abuse of the privilege of full discussion, had eventually backed the introduction of a method of preventing a minority from tyrannising a majority, despite misgivings about introducing coercive authority into par-liament.

The change in the rules eased the business of parliament, but during the Home Rule debate frustration at the imposition of the guillotine led to hand-to-hand fighting on the floor of the House. Strachey blamed addi-tionally the weakness of the Speaker (Irish members had long been shouting

'Judas' at Chamberlain without being penalised). Horrified though he was at the scandal for the House of Commons and the country as a whole, there was some comfort to be drawn by a Unionist as enthusiastic as himself: 'though a certain number of English members may have been engaged in the *mêlée*, the chief combatants belonged either to the North or the South of Ireland. The incident was in this sense a useful object lesson, and showed clearly the bitter antagonism of the two Irelands, whose existence it is part of Mr Gladstone's fixed policy to ignore.' His relentless use of the guillotine indirectly led to the fighting. 'The old-fashioned notion that free speech is a safety-valve for party passion is not far wrong . . . Pressure of an arbitrary and tyrannical kind was week after week during the present month applied to the Opposition, and at last the inevitable explosion took place. That is the long and short of the whole affair.'[25]

The Home Rule Bill passed its third reading in the Commons by 34 votes on 1 September 1893: it was defeated in the Lords a week later. Gladstone wanted to dissolve parliament and appeal to the country, but was dissuaded by colleagues anxious to see the Newcastle reform programme through. His vague threats to the Lords were unconvincing; the country, said *The Economist*, felt a sense of relief at the rejection of the bill: 'The electors are heartily tired of Home Rule, and the raising of such questions as Parish Government and Church Disestablishment will still further tend to the disappearance of interest in Home Rule. Mr Gladstone will find when once the attention of the country has been diverted from Home Rule, that it will be exceedingly difficult to bring it back again to a subject at once so tiresome and so threadbare.'[26]

The following March, after a disagreement with his Cabinet over the need to build more battleships, Gladstone resigned. Conflict apart, he was 84, his sight was failing and so was his health. *The Economist*, acknowledging 'the greatness of the personality that is passing out of our political life', said an honourable goodbye.

> During the past eight years it has seemed to us a matter of public duty to condemn almost all Mr Gladstone's political actions. Nor can we refrain even on the present occasion in stating our belief that since 1886 his influence on affairs has been highly injurious. To appear to ignore our political hostility to Mr Gladstone, or to slur it over, would be as foolish as it would be unworthy, and we may be sure that Mr Gladstone himself would

be the first to admit that any attempt to disguise the profound feeling of distrust with which so many have regarded, and still regard, his more recent political attitude would be out of place. After 1886, both in opposition and in office, Mr Gladstone, in our opinion went far astray from the true path of statesmanship.

A list of his misdeeds followed. 'But though we have been obliged to say so much lest we should appear to agree with those who consider that the death or retirement of a political opponent can fittingly be made the excuse for insincere and groundless eulogium, we are not blind to how much our public life owes to Mr Gladstone. Mr Gladstone's purely personal influence on politics has been distinctly a good one, for it has been one which has never been tinged by selfishness or by sordid and petty views.'[27]

The paper soared to rhetorical heights when Gladstone died four years later, which is more than can be said for Eliza, whose diary entry read:

> *19 May 1898* Very wet & cold. Miss Mary Greg called aftern. & Mrs Eustace Greg at tea. Emilie went to meeting of the Peoples' Concert Society at Mrs Bevan's [?] Princes Gardens. Dr Herbert Parry in Chair. Mr Gladstone died in Hawarden Castle at 5 a.m.

'A darkness that can be felt has enveloped the land on the death, after months of intense suffering, of its most illustrious citizen', began *The Economist*. 'There is no distinction based on party feelings; a common sorrow animates all. We feel as though we had lost a splendid possession, as though we were bereft of a magnificent treasure. And so, indeed, it is; for what treasure is there in the world comparable with that of a great man? . . . when a powerful and noble mind is withdrawn from men, no loss can be greater . . .'

> It was not merely Mr Gladstone's fine intellectual gifts, his power of debate, his eloquence, his varied learning which made him such a power in the nation, and which compelled the unqualified admiration of his foes. It was the subtle force called personality in which these attributes were blended; it was the impalpable quality which we term magnetism for want of a better name.

Death concentrated their minds on the historical context. Gladstone had entered public life 'at a time when new ideas were "in the air", and his peculiar intellectual constitution enabled him gradually to assimilate these ideas, and relate them to the traditions in which he had been reared. This process, carried on through life, seems to us to have been the chief source alike of his strength and weakness.'

> He was always assimilating, always relating new to old, always endeavouring to weave new facts and old traditions. He was thus essentially the statesman of a transition era, whose function it was to prevent the shock of new and old by a timely and noble kind of opportunism. But in so doing he sometimes failed to distinguish between the solid mountain of facts and the cloudland of fancy.

Determined not to appear sentimental, the leader went dutifully through the successes and failures of Gladstone's political career, but it grew impatient, and ended with a fine Victorian flourish.

> But let us end with the note we struck at the beginning, the human note. While criticism will busy itself with Mr Gladstone's deeds; while it will as surely frown upon his support of the South in the Civil War as it will acclaim his prescience in denouncing Turkish rule; while it will note his too sanguine expectations as regards the national futures of Italy, and his impossible Irish projects, while venerating his name as financier, reformer, and leader of men; while, we say, historic criticism will weigh Mr Glad-stone's political career in her balances, his bereaved countrymen will treasure up his memory as a great man, as a noble and splendid product of the historic soil of England.[28]

Edward Johnstone had paid Gladstone the supreme compliment: not only were the pages on which the leader appeared black-edged, but 'WILLIAM EWART GLADSTONE' took precedence over 'THE MONEY MARKET'. (In the days before 'THE MONEY MARKET' was automatically given priority, the deaths of James Wilson and Bagehot were given pride of place and a black-rimmed front page; in 1901 Queen Victoria received the accolade of an entirely black-edged issue, but failed to make the first leader, as did in 1910 Edward VII, who was further downgraded with only two black-edged pages. By 1936, the paper had been revamped and the money market banished to the back pages, so George V had no competition for first leader. But instead of black-edged pages, he was awarded a black-edged box with

GEORGE THE FIFTH

KING-EMPEROR: 1910–1936

over the appreciation: his son received equal treatment, with

KING GEORGE VI

1936–1952

'Geoffrey Crowther, 1907–1972' was the caption to a black-rimmed photo-graph on the cover, marking the death in office of the chairman of *The Economist*, who had previously been its managing director, and before that, probably its greatest editor since Bagehot. It was a far more generous tribute than that paid six years earlier to Lord Layton, editor 1922–38, co-proprietor from 1928, chairman 1944–63 and a man of some importance in both national and international affairs: he got no cover, no photograph, no black borders, just two columns on the sixth page.)

Almost a century later, in April 1992, the paper carried Gladstone's picture on its front cover, with the caption 'A PROPHET FOR THE LEFT'. It was a touch irreverent, in the manner of the present-day *Economist*. The GOM looked as high-minded and unyielding as ever, but his jacket was festooned with yellow and red roses (yellow being the colour of the Liberals and the red rose the emblem of the refurbished Labour Party). He stared loftily over the microphones with which he was being assailed, clearly brooding on the fact that in the British general election the Conservatives had just won a majority for the fourth time in a row. 'When William Gladstone', it began rather awkwardly, for it seems *lèse majesté* to refer to him so informally, 'pitched into the Tories on one of his first great radical reforms (to open up the franchise to working men), his rebuke silenced their scoffing in the Commons: "You cannot fight against the future. Time is on our side." Britain's Labour Party has been fighting the future for a quarter of a century; and at last the future has plainly won. That is the message of four consecutive election defeats. It is the Conservative Party, not Labour, that has built its programme upon what is to come. Labour has been the defender of what is past or passing. As the grim prospect of another five years or so in opposition sinks in, Labour will have to endure creative self-destruction if it is to get to grips with this fact.'

The Labour leadership, those 'latter-day Bourbons', failed to realise their party had outlived its times. The Tories had become the main engine of change since the 1960s. 'Arguably, the last dramatic initiative mooted by Labour was the reform of the trade unions proposed in 1968–69. The Wilson Cabinet flunked it.' Since 1979 the Tories had transformed Britain's industrial relations; they were reforming the public sector; and John Major sought a classless society. The answer for the left was to out-radicalise the Tories, for the Conservative Party 'still has deep roots in vested interests. It still happily contemplates a country in which those educated in private schools belong to a separate and privileged caste and disregards the plight of the least gifted.' It was complacent about an old order of vast inherited wealth, about the human misery and waste of almost three million unemployed, and while paying obeisance to competition and free market forces, supported a protectionist EC common agricultural policy that 'would have made Disraeli blush'.

The concluding section had the heading 'Welcome the Whigs' and was essentially a statement of what *The Economist* of the 1990s stands for. It was presented with the clarity and absolute conviction that distinguished the paper under Rupert Pennant-Rea, editor from 1986 to 1993. Not since Francis Hirst, who was fired for his uncompromisingly pacifist opinions during the First World War, has an editor been as lacking in doubt as Pennant-Rea. It is a feature of the times: no one ever accused the nineteenth-century *Economist* of being woolly in its liberalism, but the historical context during much of this century has frequently engendered doubt and hesitancy among thinking people, and this has inevitably affected even such opinionated people as tend to write that paper. But since 1945, Britain has sampled political experiments across the spectrum from radical left to right, and handwringing is out of fashion. Against that backdrop, a man of fixed principles can more easily flourish. The only important question to be asked about *The Economist*, observed Geoffrey Crowther in its centenary year, 'is whether it is the same river, coming from the same source and moving towards the same sea, whether James Wilson and Walter Bagehot, if they could have stayed so long with the bark they launched and steered, would also have found themselves where *The Economist* is to-day'.[29] Pennant-Rea's paper's creed, expressed in the guise of a programme for the left, was in fact a programme for what Crowther described memorably as 'the extreme centre', which, with lurches here and there, has been generally adhered to over a century and a half. It passed the test.

> Another radical philosophy does exist, one that was there before the Labour
> Party was formed, almost a century ago. It is time for the left to go back to it,
> and to embrace those old Whig beliefs that survive in all three parties that
> have gone begging for a proper party champion ever since Labour displaced

the Liberals in the 1920s. How to define them? As a philosophy, first and foremost – a compassionate but individualistic creed that produced the great Victorian reforms. This creed was both more suspicious of the state and less class-obsessed than the socialism that later swamped it. Enough of its spirit lingers in both the main parties of the left – the Liberal Democrats as well as Labour – for it to inspire a new generation of British radicals. The alliance between the two parties will not come together quickly or easily; politicians of the left will have to learn new ways of working together. Already, though, some prominent Labour men are talking about creating a cross-party convention to agree on constitutional changes – exactly the kind of reform the Whigs would have lauded.

What would be the policies of a new, unsocialist, left? The idea of personal freedom, and the political rights of individuals and local communities against the centralising powers of the state, would be central to them. They would include support for proportional representation, a freedom-of-information bill and a more open style of government in Whitehall. So far, so easy: but personal freedom also implies free markets – and the left will have to learn to revel in them again. A radical competition policy will set the left against agricultural protectionism and industrial cartels. It would also tackle the restrictive practices of the professions; the fixes that keep the courts impeded by under-trained judges, the universities clogged up with life-tenured academics, and the hospitals in awe of Napoleonic consultants.

Neither personal freedom nor free markets will ensure freedom of opportunity unless Britain offers enough of the ladders that create a working meritocracy. Radical proposals for improving state education and the training of young school-leavers ought to make a mockery of the Tories' half-hearted steps in the same direction. They could, for instance, trump the Tories' conversion to Europe, by vowing to give every British child a working grasp of one continental language.

One thing more: the left must offer real hope to the have-nots; no realignment of the anti-Tory opposition can begin to make sense unless it harnesses the loyalties of the lowest paid or unpaid. But that requires the left to face up to the shortcomings of the Welfare State. State benefits have not stemmed the decline of Britain's inner cities, nor the emergence of a pitiful underclass. The dishing out of state cash has left people passive, without enough choice. The revamped left should look urgently at ways of giving the poor real choices about where they live; how their children are educated;

and above all, how they can start earning again. This points to giving them the buying power of state-financed vouchers. The quantity of state cash available will always be a problem, and here, too, the left will have to be realistic. If voters refuse to support higher-tax parties, then the truly poor can be helped only through programmes that are more rigorously selective.

If much of this has a Thatcherite ring, or sounds suspiciously like a leader in *The Economist*, so be it; Margaret Thatcher was in many ways a great radical, and this newspaper was founded in Whig opposition to the stick-in-the-muds of the day. Many on the left will question the wisdom of a radical party that reflects in any way such a tradition. But they should ask themselves: is their problem one of image – or are they secretly frightened of radicalism itself? The aftermath of defeat is a frightening time for losers. But with boldness a new and radical opposition could rise from the ruins. Come back, William Gladstone, the saddened left has need of you.[30]

CHAPTER XXVII:

Turning the century

I felt then that I was becoming connected with a very important publication which possessed a great reputation not built in a day. It gave me inspiration from the start and I feel I must say it has been a great help to me in the course of my life. Its steadiness and integrity have been to me a light shining in any darkness that came over the world and it has truly been a guiding star.
Albert Henry Chapman, writing in 1942 of 1898

Albert Chapman first heard of *The Economist* when he started work at Smith's Bookstall on Mortlake Station: 'The Bookstall manager picked it out from amongst his many newspapers and said to me, "You will have to watch this paper because about three times a year they have a double number and charge double price". The charge per copy then was 8d. so the double number was 1s. 4d. The danger was, he said, that the double number may pass unnoticed as *The Economist* had so many larger numbers during the year some of which were not charged double price. He was referring to the two Banking Numbers in May and October and the Commercial History in February each year. Apart from this there was the Monthly Trade Supplement for which no extra charge was made.'

After three years, in 1897, Chapman joined the paper as an office boy on six shillings a week, hoping for opportunities for promotion. He thought himself very fortunate: 'I felt that The Economist was no ordinary newspaper but that it was one of the leading journals of the world. This knowledge made all the difference to my work. I felt I could tackle any task, however hard.'

When, more than 40 years later, during the Second World War, a few individuals were trying hastily to put together a modest celebratory volume of essays for the paper's centenary in 1943, the deputy editor, Donald

Tyerman, asked Chapman to provide the basic material for their joint effort: 'A Hundred Years'.

The result was an uncritical, but deeply touching, reminiscence by a man who was brought up with and retained the values of a respectable working-class Victorian, while the institution which he revered expanded and changed radically around him, without lessening his devotion. It is also a source of great historical importance for the editorships of Edward Johnstone and Francis Hirst.

The premises in which Chapman began working had been little changed in 52 years of occupancy. 340 Strand was a long, narrow building with five floors and a basement – wholly occupied by *The Economist*. Every week the new issue was placed in the front window, with the leader pages opened out. Inside, a circular staircase rose between the five front and five back rooms. The basement, in which first David Mitchell Aird and later a Mr Meredith had printed the paper, was now empty: Clement's Printing Works (later to be known as St Clement's Press) had taken over the job. The front room on the ground floor was occupied by the five business and publishing staff: the manager, H.W. Kirk; the advertisement manager, M.H. Flood; Horace Whitcomb, the company-meetings manager; Kirk's assistant, and Chapman, the office boy.

Howard Kirk was the business manager and was therefore in charge of the books – keeping track of cash, circulation, advertising revenue, subscribers and general accounts. The few surviving records show him to have been meticulous, accurate and possessed of that beautiful copperplate handwriting that adorned Victorian ledgers. Additionally he dealt with the printers and received callers. According to Eric Gibb, who joined the paper in 1906, Kirk was the soul of loyalty, but apt to be suspicious of strangers: 'When a new face appeared at the counter he scrutinised it carefully, rather like a Scotland Yard man sizing up a suspect. Once a stranger walked in and asked him whether *The Economist* was a monthly or a weekly paper – a curious question which raised a sharp suspicion in his mind. "What do you want to know for?" he asked, giving nothing away. I remember, too, a stranger asking to see the editor and being looked over by him with great suspicion. It was the first visit to *The Economist* of the next editor-but-two, Walter Layton.'[1] Kirk had joined in 1892 and stayed with the paper for more than half a century. He made no waves but, like Chapman, he helped to keep a Victorian presence in existence on the paper for almost half-a-century after the old Queen died. He was one of 'the old fashioned gentlemen', said one of his later staff, Edward Mafeking Webb, who found him most agreeably paternal.[2]

Michael Harry Flood, the advertisement manager, had joined in 1896 and stayed for over 30 years. Chapman thought him 'quite a character in his day with an imposing appearance and a great capacity for securing business. During the company promotion booms I have seen him bring in as many as four or five prospectuses week after week to be advertised in the Economist. He was always lively and quite added to the good feeling which always seemed to prevail.'[3] His opposite number was the company-meetings manager, who persuaded companies to pay *The Economist* for space in which to report their annual general meetings. When Chapman arrived at the paper, the job was occupied by James Probert, who left shortly afterwards to join the *Morning Post* and was succeeded by Horace Whitcombe. Whitcombe was briefly an apostate, departing to start a paper called the *New Saturday*, but its decease after ten months sent him back to his old job, for which, if Chapman's memoirs are to be relied on, he was over-qualified: 'He was a very well informed man and could write well. I used to talk with him a great deal and find him extremely interesting. He could talk on most of the leading questions of the day.' The fourth occupant of the room – Kirk's assistant – left after three months and Chapman was promoted into his place.

The room behind this HQ was used for storing waste and parliamentary papers, which were carefully indexed. 'Mr Johnstone used to go through these occasionally and turn some out.' Johnstone had the first floor front room, overlooking the Strand – which, when occupied by Bagehot had, according to the housekeeper, been 'a well furnished apartment, with a nice sofa': the waiting room was at the back. In the room above Johnstone was the only other member of editorial, the assistant editor, Walter William Wright, who had been with the paper from about 1883.

From the time Johnstone took over as editor he appears always to have worked with only one assistant. Chapman believed that under Palgrave and Lathbury and in Johnstone's early days A.J. Wilson was an assistant editor, although Eliza never mentions his name, the only members of staff who feature in her diaries around that time being 'Mr Ellis', 'Mr Nash' and 'Mr Duguid'. However, since Eliza never mentions Walter William Wright either, and Chapman had a great respect for facts, there is no reason not to assume that Wilson probably did at some time work on a paper for which he would have seemed tailor-made. A man of great ability and probity, he went on to be founder in 1891 of the *Investor's Review* and was described as 'the knight, without fear or reproach of City Editors', by his contemporary James Mill.[4] Certainly he was a financial editor of great integrity: when on the *Pall Mall Gazette* in 1875, like the few other journalists who knew Disraeli's government intended to buy shares in the Suez Canal company, he took no advantage of the information and thereby passed up a fortune.*

Chapman said that Walter William Wright had joined at roughly the time when Johnstone became editor, spending nine years in the business department before succeeding the resident assistant editor, Charles Duguid, in 1892. Wright had started his working life in the railway service and then, having drifted into journalism almost by accident, worked his way up by sheer effort. Chapman was impressed at how hard he worked. As well as writing articles, he did a great deal of statistical work, producing the Banking Numbers and much of the *Commercial History*. 'He was a most lovable man,' said Eric Gibb, 'and I remember him with affection more than fifty years after his death.' Mrs Brooker was housekeeper, and she and her husband, as caretakers, occupied the building's remaining rooms. Outside the front door, sitting on a box, was an old soldier, who sold the *Westminster Gazette* every evening and 'used to guard our front door from the incursion of intruders. He was quite a well-known figure to people who passed in and out of the office.'

Chapman used to spend a lot of time upstairs with the Brookers.

> They were nice homely people and, as I write, I can see Mrs Brooker spotlessly clean. She always looked that in the mornings when I used to arrive to find her busy dusting and cleaning. She was never demonstrative and you scarcely felt her presence. She used to dress in the afternoons and take her walks abroad in and around the Economist office. She used to talk with me a great deal and tell me all she knew about The Economist. These talks have helped me to build up my story. They enabled me to sense the atmosphere of family life that weaved itself around The Economist. Mr Brooker had poor health. He could not go out. But he used to get up every day and sit by the fire smoking his pipe. I used to go upstairs and see him and talk with him in my spare time. I did this very often . . . Mrs Brooker before

---

*The centenary history is quite definite about A.J. Wilson's time on the staff, but the information came only from Chapman's folklore: the 1943 book is equally definite about the substantial contribution of Nassau Senior, who never wrote for the paper at all.

she came to 340 Strand was a servant in Mrs Bagehot's household and used to relate to me many stories concerning the six sisters . . . When I joined The Economist in June 1898 . . . Walter Bagehot had been dead 21 years. Yet Mrs Brooker . . . used to constantly talk with me about Mr Bagehot. Indeed I felt she was anxious to make me feel at home in my new surroundings and it seemed to me as though Mr Bagehot was still living in the memory of the people who were working on The Economist.

She told Chapman how 'Mr Bagehot, as she always described him, used to keep his coachman waiting outside seeming to forget the passage of time so deeply was he absorbed with his work.'

Chapman was fascinated by the proprietors.

It may here be appropriate if I weave into these impressions the picture of Mr Johnstone surrounded by the six daughters of the Right Hon James Wilson the founder of The Economist. In the lively interest displayed by these old ladies in everything appertaining to The Economist is an episode which I often dwell upon. They loved their Economist literally and truly. They kept the light of their father's lamp burning brightly and also the deep love and admiration of Mrs Walter Bagehot for her husband and father and the way the other five sisters shared that love is a story that Sir Hugh Walpole or any other novelist could write a novel. At this time in the year 1898 the lives of the old ladies were drawing towards eventide, but a really beautiful evening. Now they could still read their Economist with admiration and with a critical eye. So much so that postcards used to arrive from one or the other telling Mr Johnstone of any mistakes in the spelling of words that appeared in The Economist. Mr Johnstone used to read these postcards with an amused twinkle in his eye. It just showed that the old ladies were keenly alive to any weaknesses in the compilation that may be apparent in their much loved journal . . . I did not know them all I only saw three out of the six but Mrs Brooker told me of their strength and weaknesses so that I really felt I knew them well.

In addition to being sent their weekly free *Economist*, the sisters received 'certain other newspapers mostly illustrated ones', which Chapman despatched to them. 'They evidently liked this way better than ordering direct from a newsagent and it gave the office staff an opportunity of looking through these papers before they were posted. Everything possible was done by The Economist to consider the happiness and comfort of the old ladies whom we loved with a profound admiration. It is quite conceivable that the newspapers sent to them were continued to be sent round the beautiful family circle.' Orby Shipley ('the well known disciple of Edward Bouverie Pusey one of the most influential men in the Church of England. There is what is known as the Orby Shipley Missal for use at Holy Communion') was sent the *Guardian* and the *Tablet* – respectively Church of England and Roman Catholic. In 1942 Chapman could still remember all the addresses to which he used to send the papers.

Precedence was clear: Eliza was 'the most important old lady as regards The Economist . . . She was getting on in years when I first saw her. I saw her fairly frequently as she used to make occasional visits to The Economist office. She continued this practice up till the time of her death in 1921. She lived to a great age. The days she was known to be paying one of her visits were set apart as "great days". I used to obtain fleeting glimpses of the great lady as she came up in her brougham. She was always carefully ushered into Mr Johnstone's sanctum.' Julia, 'the wife of William Rathbone Greg the well known writer on philosophical subjects', ranked second. Chapman was particularly interested when Mrs Brooker told him that Greg had chosen to be buried in Mortlake Cemetery, in Chapman's own neighbourhood. While writing the memoir, Chapman visited the grave. 'Mrs Greg was as active as her sister Mrs Bagehot in the interest she displayed in The Economist. I never met Mrs Greg.'

She was also important as the mother of Walter Wilson Greg, who was being groomed, against his inclination, to become editor. He had read modern and medieval languages at Cambridge, but failed to get an honours degree and was thus debarred from reading moral sciences, which included political economy, to prepare him for financial journalism. The problem was solved by Eliza, who with Julia in the autumn of 1897 visited Cambridge and 'had tea with Professor Marshall & explained Walter's position, he joined us & we went to see Mrs Marshall'. (The formidable Mrs Marshall used to teach the students her husband refused – which included all women.) By the time Chapman joined the paper, Greg had almost finished his year of reading economics and was about to join a bank to gain the right kind of practical experience.[5]

Chapman had little information on the other sisters. He had once seen Sophie Halsey's husband – 'a nice old gentleman with a kindly manner'. He knew that Emilie Barrington lived with Eliza, had an artist husband and later wrote the Wilson and Bagehot biographies, and that the sisters used often to stay with Matilda Horan in Kent and with Eliza either in London or in the country. 'The old ladies lived to a ripe old age. Mr Hirst used to speak of them as "The Dear Old Ladies". And that is how I like to remember them.'

Less symbolically important and less romantic, but of more practical importance, were the trustees. In 1883 George and John Wilson had at last begun the lengthy process of appointing a replacement for Bagehot, as well as one for Walter Wilson. By 1885, for the first time in five years, they had a trustee based in London, a Wilson nephew, James Gibb. He was, said Chapman, 'a tall man of striking presence with a small grey beard', 'very astute', and he audited the books of *The Economist*. An underwriter, he worked in the firm of Bray Gibb and Co. Hawick, however, remained dominant, with another Wilson nephew, James Glenny, a manufacturer, 'a thin man rather bent with sandy hair. I used to see him when the Trustees met in London.'

All appears to have gone smoothly between proprietors, proprietors' husbands, trustees and Johnstone from the beginning. A modest, kind and genial man, Johnstone was ideally equipped to deal with the sisters, and he was reassuringly calm and reliable. He worked five days a week and spent his leisure time in the Scottish pursuits of golf and shooting. Eliza's diaries show occasional social and professional contact with him and his. She and her mother went to St Mary's Church in October 1884 to see his son (he had four daughters and two sons) marrying a Miss Lund and called on the bride a couple of months later; he occasionally dined with her; she sent him lists of errors or misprints; he wrote from Edinburgh in 1886 to announce his mother's death; he helped her with Bagehot's papers, and wrote a preface to a new edition of Bagehot's *Universal Money*. He received a few other mentions, including:

> *29 August* [Johnstone to Eliza] asking whether he shd insert obituary notice to Uncle John Preston, brought by Mr Absolm [sic] to office.
> *30 August* [Eliza to Uncle George] with Mr Johnstone's note to notice of Mr P.

The notice did not go in. The family always stayed out of the paper. With the sole exception of Emilie – and that was to mark the end of an era – none of the trustees or sisters had their deaths as much as mentioned in *The Economist*.

> *14 November 1886* [From the Continent, Eliza wrote to Johnstone enclosing a letter for inclusion in *The Economist*.]

This was an extraordinary event, but Eliza, worrying about poverty in London, had been inspired by Continental experiments to suggest a philanthropic scheme which she thought might appeal to men of business. Headed 'DISTRESS IN LONDON', her letter appeared over the signature 'E.B.'. There was not a single response to it. William Fowler, on the other hand, writing in the same issue to defend the half-sovereign against the abolitionists, stirred up tremendous controversy.

Then in 1890 came the bombshell.

> *30 July 1890* Uncle George came & told us that Mr Johnstone wants to have a share in Economist.
>
> *4 August* Uncle George had a family meeting all aftern., coming up with Matilda from Kent.
>
> *5 August* Russell lunched with Uncle George. Family meeting at 4 when Uncle G. read Mr. Johnstone's proposals.
>
> *6 August* Lunched in garden. Uncle George & Wm Halsey joined me there after tea. J. E. & Walter had tea with Mrs De Morgan & they went to exhibition of modern pictures at the Guildhall ... Uncle G. Jas. Gibb, Sophy & Wm dined with us. J. Gibb did the part of 'Devil's Advocate' against giving Mr Johnstone a share in Ect. in perpetuity.
>
> *7 August* Sent for Matilda, who lunched here with Uncle George. We discussed scheme & all signed paper authorising Uncle G. to give Mr Johnstone 1/7 or 3/16 of Economist.

Johnstone received 3/16, though not in perpetuity. The deal was highly complicated; it took almost two years to complete the indenture of variation of trusts. James Gibb prevailed: the proprietors retained the right to repurchase the shares after the deaths of Johnstone and his wife.

It was back to business as usual. In July 1893, Walter Greg, in his last year at Harrow, came up early for the Duke of York's wedding day and with his mother, Eliza and a large party watched the procession from the *Economist* office. In 1894 Johnstone wrote to Eliza that Mrs Stubberfield, the long-serving housekeeper, whom a contemporary described to Chapman as having been 'a Victorian lady with lovely flowing curls', wished to retire. (Chapman also mentions her nephew, M. Absolon, 'a very powerful looking man with a fresh complexion and a luxurious white beard', as having been 'very prominent in the management', and as having had a role in developing the Banking Supplements in 1877.)

Further drama developed, and Eliza's diary demonstrates graphically the problems caused by having six proprietors and three active trustees, of whom two were in Scotland: letters flew about like confetti. Nor was it any longer possible to resolve matters quickly by having Uncle George dash down to London to sort everyone out: he was now in his eighties. And Hutton, Eliza's traditional adviser, was ailing and bereaved. (He died in September 1897. Nothing appeared about him in *The Economist*, and in the *Spectator* in place of an obituary there appeared as the leading item a brief announcement of his death, with a few details, concluding with the curious sentence: 'His colleagues are forbidden by pledges which they cannot break, either to write a memoir of him, or, within the range of their influence, to permit any one else to do so.'[6] St Loe Strachey, although he later wrote copiously about Meredith Townsend in his autobiography, reluctantly continued to honour his pledge to Hutton.) Yet what appears to emerge from several elliptical entries is that Eliza, through delaying and other blocking tactics, was instrumental in maintaining the status quo. (Various references in her diary to Johnstone and a daily newspaper tie-in with Chapman's information that Johnstone played a prominent part in setting up the *Daily Express*, founded in 1900 by Arthur Pearson to 'be the organ of no political party nor the instrument of any social clique': its first managing director was Edward Henderson Johnstone, his eldest son. Had Johnstone thrown his lot in with the *Express*, he would have found himself high and dry three years later, when Pearson enthusiastically adopted the protectionist cause.)

There was some kind of unspecified new arrangement, but it involved no change in ownership. Uncle George promised to continue looking after *The Economist* and Eliza, for her part, promised to continue to 'superintend' it. Whatever his disappointment at not increasing his share beyond 3/16 to 5/16 (as he had proposed), Johnstone was quite prosperous. The circulation throughout his editorship had hovered between a low of 3,003 (1894) and a high of 3,490 (1890): the norm was between 3,100 and 3,200. Circulation figures exist for 1876 onward, Bagehot's last full year as editor (he died in March 1877), when it ran at 3,690, dropping to 3,503 the following year and then steadily downwards until 1881. Advertising revenue in 1876 was £3,129; it fell to £2,850 in 1878, but afterwards the trend was more often up than down and by 1898 was £7,790. Bagehot had estimated that the profit in 1862 was £2,197, rising to £2,765 ten years later. Further information on profits is not available, but with the circulation holding more or less steady, and advertising revenue having more than doubled since Bagehot's day, they must have been substantially higher. Along with the other proceeds of James Wilson's estate, they were enough to keep the six sisters in suitable style and at a time when a working-class man could marry on £100 a year, Johnstone lived comfortably on £400 salary and 3/16 of the profits. After the turn of the century, he had the luxury of a motor car and a chauffeur.

He was a quiet man, with a routine as fixed as his principles. According to Chapman, he would arrive at the office at about 8.30:

> He was always wrapped up in a heavy overcoat. He had his lunch in the office and seldom went out all day. On his arrival I had to take all the post in to him and the newspapers opened. He would go through the pile of letters and select the important ones which he opened himself. It was my duty to keep all the business correspondence separate from the editorial. After he had gone through them he would mark any letter that was pointing out an error or raising a question with a query E.J. mark which meant that the person concerned would have to appear before him with the answer. The business letters were taken to Mr Kirk and the editorial to Mr W.W. Wright the Assistant Editor.
>
> After perusal of letters Mr Johnstone settled down to read the newspapers which came from all parts of the world. This would keep him busy until 11 am when he would ring for the papers to be cleared away which had to be done expeditiously. He would then settle down to writing with a break of an hour for lunch. He would write most of the afternoon until 5 pm when he used to leave for home. He invariably wrote a leader or two each week and two or three business notes. This was his method of work until the close of his editorship in 1907.

A few friends used to call to see him and go out with him regularly, those thought by Chapman to be closest being Alexander Mackay, General Manager of the Law Union and Rock Assurance ('a tall man of fine presence'), J.P. Croal, then editor of the *Scotsman* ('a typical Scot, bluff and burly'), G.D. Wansbraugh, who smoked a fine cigar and wore a grey tall hat, and Mr Roper, manager of Singer Sewing Machines. They seemed glamorous to Chapman, but by the standards of most editors of *The Economist* they were an undistinguished group. Johnstone showed no ambition to move with the great or get involved with public affairs. This was to contribute to obscuring his achievements as editor. In so far as he had any reputation in *The Economist* of the twentieth century, it was as a nonentity who had produced an honest but boring paper.

Certainly Johnstone's paper was far less interesting than had been Bagehot's or would be Hirst's, who took over in 1907. But the times were dull, apart, that is, from the jingoist and anti-jingoist excitements of the South African war. Aside from the fireworks engendered by Gladstone, domestic politics failed to excite and the press suffered. By the turn of the century, wrote Stephen Koss, 'the larger vessels of the political press were becalmed, and the smaller ones were sinking. "Journalism had become like most other such things in England, . . . somewhat sleepy and much diminished in importance," G.K. Chesterton remarked in his novel, *The Napoleon of Notting Hill* (1904).'[7]

Even the economists were affected by this diminishment of intensity. Sir John Macdonnell, considering the third phase of the Political Economy Club, from 1883 to 1901, noted the tendency of members to avoid purely abstract questions and take instead as the basis of discussion comparatively small issues and highly technical topics treated from the point of view of the expert. 'I ventured to call the first period [1821–46] the age of principles; the second the time of transition; I might describe the third as the period of socialism without doctrines. I might, some would say, more accurately define it as a time of pacific anarchy. It is as if a mercantile house of long standing, once owning ocean-going vessels and making great ventures across the seas, had, sobered by age, quitted this hazardous business and gone into the safer coasting trade.' It was also a period distinguished by greater modesty than before. 'Mr Lowe [Robert Lowe, Chancellor of the Exchequer 1868–73] said, in 1876, that the work of Political Economy seemed nearly done. The discussion in this period [*circa* 1910] would suggest that it has only begun.'[8]

The principle on which Johnstone operated his coastal trade was to farm out most of the leader columns to a stable of regular contributors, tell them what he wanted written about and print what they gave him. They knew his stylistic requirements. 'He never wasted a word of his own, or allowed his contributors to waste theirs; he had a hatred of tautology, and his bitterest reproaches were reserved for those whom he suspected of writing for "lineage".'[9] A comparison of the discursiveness of St Loe Strachey's autobiography with the crispness of his *Economist* contributions lends support to this assessment.

Strachey shares with Thomas Hodgskin and William Rathbone Greg the distinction of being one of *The Economist*'s three most important political writers to have been left out of the centenary history: he is also the most famous. In Strachey's case it is puzzling that Chapman failed to mention him, for he had stopped writing for the paper only a short time before Chapman arrived and as editor and proprietor of the *Spectator* he had become a famous figure in journalism. In 1897, after Hutton's death, Strachey had become Meredith Townsend's partner, and by mid-1898, at Townsend's request, he had bought him out. One of Chapman's duties was to take a copy of *The Economist* along to 1 Wellington Street every Saturday morning to exchange for a copy of the *Spectator*, but though he 'always enjoyed my Saturday morning chat with the publisher', he never gleaned any information about Strachey. It is possible that it was to the advantage of neither paper for it to be too widely known that they shared chief political writers almost without a break from 1881 to 1896, when Strachey briefly took on the editorship of the *Cornhill Magazine*. In his autobiography, Strachey put up an ethical defence of anonymity which also serves to explain how such a system permits someone to write differently for different audiences. 'The public are apt to suppose that anonymity is the cloak of misdoing, and I have often heard people declare that in their opinion every leader-writer should be forced to sign his name. As I once heard it picturesquely expressed, "The mask should be torn from the villain's face. Why should a man be allowed to stab his neighbour in the dark!"'

> As a matter of fact I am convinced that anonymity makes, not for irresponsibility but for responsibility, and that there are many men, who though truculent, offensive, and personal when they write with the 'I', will show a true sense of moderation and responsibility when they use the editorial 'we'. The man who writes for a newspaper very soon gets a strong sense of what is right and proper to be said in that particular organ, and he instinctively refuses to give way to personal feeling and personal animosity when he is writing, not in his own name, but in that of his newspaper.

Strachey had grown greatly in stature and even stronger in opinions during the decade in which he wrote for *The Economist*. The unevenly educated young man from Somerset who had been a misfit at Oxford had become a figure of importance in politics and society. In 1887 he had married Amy Turner, whose mother, a daughter of Nassau Senior, had a salon in South Kensington where Amy had met many great men, including Bagehot. This connection reinforced Strachey's natural *laissez-faire* and free-trade inclinations as well as opening up to him a much wider world. Simultaneously, through his involvement with the Liberal Unionists, he had come to know most of their leaders and was particularly friendly with Chamberlain. The Stracheys were highly sociable and their friends came from many different circles, even including Fabians like George Bernard Shaw and the Webbs, with whom they used to go cycling – a pastime that had become a world-wide craze. Their Unionism had been reinforced by a visit to Ireland in 1890, when they were overwhelmed by the beauty of the country, appalled by the damage caused in the South by riots and deeply impressed by the liveliness of Belfast commercial life.

Strachey's second major preoccupation during his period with *The Economist* was his commitment to 'democratic Imperialism'. 'To me,' he wrote in 1922, 'the alliance of free self-governing Dominions which constitute the British Empire, has a sacred character. It has rendered great help to the calls of peace, civilisation and security, and it will render still more. I feel, further, that throughout Africa, and throughout India, we have done an incomparable service to humanity by our maintenance of just stable government.'[10]

It was not an attitude that would have found favour in *The Economist*'s early years. Even though Wilson had ended his career as a colonial official, like Bagehot he cared about the expansion of trade, not of territory. Bagehot was instinctively isolationist in foreign policy and objected to the expenditure of Britain's human resources abroad. 'Lord Melbourne's habitual query, "Can't you let it alone?" seemed to him,' wrote Hutton, 'as regarded all new responsibilities, the wisest of hints for our time. He would have been glad to find a fair excuse for giving up India, for throwing the Colonies on their own resources and for persuading the English people to accept deliberately the place of a fourth or fifth-rate European power – which was not, in his estimation, a cynical or unpatriotic wish, but quite the reverse, for he thought that such a course would result in generally raising the calibre of the national mind, conscience, and taste.'[11]

Yet Bagehot would not have dissented from Strachey's view of the British achievement. 'We are pre-eminently a colonizing people', he wrote in 1865.

'We are, beyond all comparison, the most enterprising, the most successful, and in most respects the best, colonists on the face of the earth. We have the largest colonial Empire in the world. We have governed it, not always no doubt with foresight and sagacity, but assuredly, during the last three quarters of a century at least, usually with mildness and invariably with liberality.'[12]

At the time Bagehot wrote this, although Britain was indeed extending the principle of colonial self-government (the Colonial Laws Validity Act of 1865 considerably increased the powers of colonial legislatures), it was also still extending its imperial territory. Between 1851 and 1871, acquisitions included Basutoland, part of Burma, Lagos in Nigeria, Berar and Oudh in India, Queensland, British Columbia and the former territories of the Hudson's Bay Company. In January 1877, to Bagehot's disapproval, Disraeli made Queen Victoria Empress of India, adding a powerful symbol to the growth in imperialist enthusiasm for making Britain great. Public opinion was excited by tales of adventure and heroism and much was made of successes in imposing civilised standards on strange societies. In 1874, for instance, in ending the Ashanti War, Sir Garnet Wolseley extracted from King Koffee a promise of free trade and the ending of human sacrifices. It was a Scot, John Kirk, consul-general in Zanzibar, who in 1873 persuaded the Sultan to abolish slave-markets and the export of slaves. Disraeli, having stolen the Liberals' clothes in the field of social reform, set out to corner the imperial market, yet such was the spirit of the times that it was Gladstone who in 1882 ordered the military occupation of Egypt – a supposedly temporary measure which stretched out for a lifetime. Some of the annexations were unenthusiastically authorised by British governments when British traders or mineral prospectors penetrated remote territories, got into trouble, and then demanded protection from the mother country. Some were spurred by competition from other major powers. In the early 1880s, the 'scramble for Africa' forced the pace; and the British Empire was not to reach its territorial apogee until after the First World War.

Imperialism could be defended with both moral and pragmatic arguments, and it swept along people of all classes and most political persuasions. But complacency duly accompanied success – and was bolstered by an (often exaggerated) idea of the relative harshness of other colonial regimes. An *Economist* article written in May 1886, just before Strachey came on the scene, positively glowed with national self-satisfaction.

Most of the political difficulties of the British people arise just now from their virtues . . . But for British scrupulousness foreign policy would present few problems, for there are many combinations, all, we admit, slightly unprincipled, under any one of which they could take their own way, keep Egypt or give up Egypt, regain their full importance in Europe, and have their pick of the few remaining unoccupied countries of the world. A determined alliance with Germany, to be maintained whether Germany were right or wrong, would of itself secure for the present those results. But for their desire to grant liberty to all under their flag the British would never even hear of discontent in India, for the discontent that is audible comes from limited and powerless classes, and the powerful populations in the great peninsula have no pressing grievance, except their own numbers, and no intention of facing the British army. But for the right feeling against such a course in Parliament the want of soldiers would be no trouble, for British pay and kindly treatment would attract an ample supply of effective mercenaries, even if a wisely-arranged conscription did not give the Government Asiatic soldiers by tens of thousands. An army of Janizaries could be formed of children from the lowest classes of India with little expense and no resistance. And but for their virtues, their reluctance to employ Courts Martial, their forbearance under provocation which would rouse other nations to fury, and their generosity, there would be little seriousness in the Home Rule movement.[13]

It was natural that Unionists tended to be also imperialists, and Strachey took up the position from the highest of motives: 'though I was always so ardent a supporter of the British Empire and of the Imperial spirit, I was not one of those people who thought that the mere word "Imperialism" would cover a multitude of misdeeds'.[14] His principled commitment was clear in his relentless criticism of Cecil Rhodes, the champion of British imperialism in southern Africa, founder in 1880 of the De Beers diamond mining concern and in 1887 of the British South Africa Company, which took over the territory later known as Rhodesia, and premier of the Cape Colony in the early 1890s. In 1888, aiming to win friends who would help him to obtain a charter for his company, Rhodes gave £10,000 to Parnell for the Irish Nationalist Party and contributed lavishly to the funds of the Liberal Party, who were theoretically anti-imperialist. He got his charter in 1889, founded Salisbury (today's Harare, capital of Zimbabwe) in 1890 and took control of the rest of the territory at breath-taking speed. Strachey never forgave Rhodes, as he told him to his face when he was dying, for giving money to the Irish enemies of Britain and the Empire. He regarded him as an arch-corrupter and one who thereby did great harm to the democratic Imperial ideal, and he scrutinised his behaviour minutely.

The Johnstone/Strachey *Economist*'s imperialism was a departure from the past in its desire to encourage imperial federalism and attack any mani-festation of what Strachey decried as 'State Rights', a concept he had deeply deplored since boyhood when he first learned about the American Civil War. But, as with Ireland, his coverage of the imperial issues was well-informed, clear and readable. He fought particularly hard against the policy of 'developing' Africa by imperial chartered companies, as this, he foresaw, meant that the nation would get all the disadvantages arising from an expansion of the Empire, and none of the advantages.[15]

The combination of Strachey's view on chartered companies and his implacable hostility to Rhodes was to reach its *Economist* climax in 1896 when Rhodes was forced to resign from the Cape Colony premiership as a consequence of the Jameson Raid. Dr Leander Starr Jameson, Rhodes's Scottish lieutenant in the Chartered Company, shared his leader's aim of breaking the Afrikaner (originally Dutch) government that controlled the Transvaal. He and Rhodes championed the 'Uitlanders', the English-speakers who had come to form two-thirds of the white population of the Transvaal since the discovery of gold around Johannesburg. By making it hard for these people to obtain citizenship, the Afrikaners (then often called Boers) kept political power in their own hands – and pursued a very conservative policy. Strachey had taken a well-balanced position in *The Economist*, spelling out the context: 'These two ideals for the organisation of civil society, the Ultra-Conservative and the Ultra-Progressive, cannot easily exist side by side, and one need not wonder if that of the majority clamours for supremacy in spite of all questions of abstract and legal right'; yet he pointed out that the Uitlanders were not entirely reasonable 'to expect to be instantly and without any sacrifice on their part put into the possession of the citizenship of a country which the Boers acquired for themselves not without labour and peril'.[16] When tension built up in Johannesburg, and an Uitlander rebellion seemed imminent, Jameson led 470 mounted police into the Transvaal – where, however, they surrendered when Boer troops encircled them (while the Uitlanders did not rebel after all). President Kruger, who had been one of the Boers' victorious leaders in the 1880–81 war (in which the Transvaal regained its independence, although remaining under British suzerainty), handed over his prisoners to the British authorities. His conduct, said Strachey, 'has been in a high degree generous and pacific'. (According to his wife, Strachey had been excited by the Jameson Raid and initially thought it justified, in which case he was making a very clear distinction between his personal views and *The Economist*'s.) Strachey's hero in this episode was his friend Joseph Chamberlain, Secretary of State for the Colonies between 1895 and 1903, who had instantly condemned the Raid in public (though, to say the least, he had played an equivocal part in its gestation):

> His firm and statesmanlike attitude is indeed the only bright spot in a discouraging and disagreeable business, and gives us confidence to hope that the future action of the British Government in the complicated circum-stances that have arisen in the Transvaal will be wise and farseeing and to our credit as a nation. Meantime, it is impossible not to feel that the future of South Africa as a whole has been gravely compromised by the events of the last few days. It is clear that if British South Africa is to obtain its highest political development, and to take the place in the Empire which it deserves, the various colonies and communities which it contains must be federated and united after the model of Canada. But to carry out this plan the goodwill of the Dutch population is necessary.[17]

Rhodes and Alfred Beit, a German turned British imperialist, his close friend and business partner in De Beers and the Chartered Company, were in that same month obliged to resign as directors of the company because of their complicity in the Raid. Strachey published a philippic against the Chartered Company: the resignations would make little difference, he said, since Rhodes and Beit were still the largest shareholders and as powerful as ever, without being trammelled by having to keep the imperial government happy. It was the Chartered Company that ought to be deposed: its history 'is the most effective object lesson which could be imagined as to the danger in our day of mixing up pecuniary adventure and politics, and trusting sovereign powers to any commercial association whatsoever'.[18]

Strachey stopped writing for *The Economist* shortly afterwards, but the *Spectator* did its duty: it provided Johnstone with yet another recruit: 'In appearance Mr William Clark was rather on the short side, inclined to stoutness. His head used to be buried in his shoulders', wrote Chapman. He called on Johnstone on Tuesdays and produced his leader about Thursday. 'He used to write his own manuscript in a beautiful handwriting with no alterations. I do not believe he made many alterations in proof. What he wrote invariably remained as written . . . I only spoke to him once, asking him if he would like some blotting paper. He replied, "I never use blotting paper".'

During Clark's two or three years with the paper, he demonstrated what Chapman rightly termed 'a very pronounced critical faculty', expressed with considerable robustness in the authentic voice of the pre-Strachey *Economist*. Johnstone had unwittingly permitted Strachey to take the paper slightly off course: Clark was in its natural tradition. And if he was not quite isolationist enough to have entirely satisfied Bagehot, he was pragmatic, sensible and forceful in a way that would have delighted Wilson. The author of a Fabian essay on the Lancashire cotton industry, he had the essential approach of a man of business: he always added up the figures that went with a policy. 'The *Economist* has never been able to believe entirely', he wrote in February 1898, 'in what may be called the plantation theory of colonisation which Mr Chamberlain is understood especially to favour. It is very doubtful whether the trade of any uncivilised region in the tropics, especially if inhabited by naked negroes, is worth the expense involved in its conquest, garrison and gradual reduction to industrial order, and quite certain that the trade will not be valuable for many years after settlement . . . Nevertheless, we feel obliged to join the chorus of those who advise the Government to stand firm in West Africa, and not give up any territory to which they have a clear right, even if they are threatened with European war.'

The reasons given for this were political: Europe was in 'an unusual and most aggressive temper' which did not allow for reasonable negotiation. 'The nations, particularly France and Germany, deceived, as we think, by false analogies, have made up their minds that they can suddenly become rich by possessing tropical colonies, and are straining every nerve to obtain vast tracts of land, which they cannot populate or, indeed, use, but which they fancy, if reserved exclusively to themselves, will provide them with limitless markets for their growing manufactures.' Compromise or arbitration were out of the question, for France, 'misled by our previous weakness or indifference, thinks that if challenged we shall abandon our "pretensions," and as our only pretension is to our own ground, we must, if challenged, fight. There never was a war with less cause or less chance of profit, but still, if we surrender our own under a threat, we shall very speedily find that we have nothing left to surrender. The nations of the Continent are not asking for West Africa only, but for all the dominion they can get.'[19]

Another *Economist* Old Boy, Alfred Milner, Chairman of the Board of Inland Revenue, had been sent to South Africa as High Commissioner in the spring of 1897. Milner had served in Egypt from 1889 to 1892 under Evelyn Baring, later Lord Cromer (consul-general 1883–1907), whose impressiveness as a colonial ruler – in all but name – had converted Milner to imperialism. (Cromer had by 1895 also become a mentor and close friend of Strachey.) Milner, an excellent administrator, was no diplomat, and within a year, alarmed by the build-up of armaments on which Kruger had embarked after the Jameson Raid, he was writing to Chamberlain that war was inevitable unless there was reform in the Transvaal. With Cecil Rhodes back on the board of the Chartered Company and busily stirring up anti-Kruger feeling in South Africa, tensions mounted again. Even before matters came to a head, William Clark had launched an all-out, sardonic attack on Chamberlain's colonial policy in 'GRABBING FOR POSTERITY'. He began with the observation that Chamberlain 'plays many parts, and he generally contrives to overdo them. When he was leading the Radical party with his so-called unauthorised programme 12 or 13 years ago, he told his hearers that they would be unwise to trouble their heads with foreign and Imperial questions, which were really devised on purpose to prevent them from comtemplating [sic] the great domestic theme of grassy acres and milk-bearing cows. But since he went to the Colonial Office, Mr Chamberlain has forgotten these rural affairs, and has gone to the opposite extreme of directing John Bull's eyes to pathless wildernesses and far-off islands where, he tells us, we are to "peg out claims for posterity." . . . Why should we hanker after "every bit of the globe which, so to speak, comes into the market"? Expansion may be a good or bad thing, in regard to which each case must be judged on its own merits. But that expansion, or grabbing, as it is vulgarly called, is a necessary and wise trade policy is a proposition that only needs stating to be refuted. That it has imposed on Mr Chamberlain must give us a measure of Mr Chamberlain's statesmanship.'[20]

It was a radical change from Strachey's reverent attitude to Chamberlain, and it caused some flutters in South Kensington:

2 *February 1899* [Eliza to Johnstone] Mr Clarke on Chamberlain. [Since

Uncle George had died in December, although James Gibb and James
Glenny were still trustees, a greater burden had fallen on Eliza.]
5 February 1899 Drove to the Spectator office aftern. & had a long talk with
Mr Townsend about his office arrangements. Called on Mr Johnstone &
[illegible] at the Economist office.

Eliza is unlikely to have been egging Clark on: indeed his tone as regards
Chamberlain seems to have moderated subsequently, but the line adopted on
the continuing trouble in South Africa was courageous. The Uitlanders were
demanding protection, Kruger was obstinate and Milner was impatient. *The
Economist* was strongly anti-war: 'We are told by noisy people, who know very
little of what they are talking, that "Imperial interests" require this or that,
and that if we stand any more nonsense from the Boers our South African
Empire will be ruined. If that were true, if a few thousand Boers could really
endanger British rule in Africa, we should have to infer that the British South
African Empire was the weakest known in history. We have a great regard for
our Canadian friends, but we may mildly suggest to them that this is our little
affair, and that we think we can settle it. We do not think it dignified or wise
to hint by resolution that the fate of the British Empire depends upon
whether a certain number of miners and capitalists on the Rand are to qualify
for the vote during seven years or five. Do not let an exaggerated Imperialism
make us ridiculous before the world. Our Empire was not built up that
way.'[21]

And true to the classic *Economist* style, he called for 'a firm, but reasonable
and good temper'. No one could want war, for it was in no one's interests.

War broke out in October 1899, following the rejection of a Boer
ultimatum which had arrived shortly before a British ultimatum was due to
reach Kruger. The Conservative government was united: the Liberals were
split. On one extreme, as a 'pro-Boer', was David Lloyd George, a
little-known Welsh MP who, as Roy Jenkins put it, 'made his reputation as a
man of the left by this starry-eyed championing of a community now almost
universally regarded as the most reactionary in the world'.[22] On the other
were the Liberal imperialists, a group that included Asquith. In between was
the Liberal leader, Sir Henry Campbell-Bannerman, who was instinctively
opposed to war but was trying to hold his party together. Morley was on the
anti-war wing. Anti-Boer feeling had built up in England and anyone who
questioned the merits of the war was reviled as 'pro-Boer'. Most of the

Liberal papers were in the imperialist camp: among the few exceptions, the editor of the *Daily Chronicle*, H.W. Massingham, and most of his staff were replaced by imperialists in November. The only remaining exceptions were the *Manchester Guardian* and, from 1901, the *Daily News*, which changed course after a Quaker takeover.

Johnstone stuck to his guns: *The Economist* never reneged on its view that the war had been unnecessary. However, now it had started, the task was to win. 'We ought not to have been at war at all,' wrote Clark, three months into the fighting, 'but we are; and the sole duty imposed on the Government which has made that war is to carry it on with vigour and celerity.'[23] A major concern was to dampen down the passionate quarrels caused by the war and by disputes about the terms of an eventual settlement. 'This is a war,' he wrote during the first phase, when the Boers were invading the Cape Colony and besieging Mafeking, Kimberley and Ladysmith, 'the first in which England has been engaged since 1815, in which the duty of Englishmen is to wait with fortitude, to be as silent as is consistent with our manners, and to compel the military executive, as opinion can compel it, to regard the campaign as a great one, and if that is possible, to overdo rather than to minimise reinforcements.'[24]

With the tangible success that came with the second phase of the war, Clark preached generosity. There should be no 'injudicious severity', he wrote after the relief of Mafeking, should the Boers abandon the war. 'The Transvaalers can only be called rebels by putting a strained interpretation on the word; they have fought as fairly as a semi-civilised people can be expected to fight, and the fact that they defeated us at first is no reason for revenge. They ought to be pardoned, if only because their resistance has probably doubled the defensive strength of Great Britain, which in view of the expansion of the Empire and continental hostility was very much to be desired, and might under other circumstances have been difficult to secure.'

'His articles on the South African war were widely discussed', said Chapman, 'and people used to sometimes ask when we were going to get our windows broken.' But Clark died on holiday in Herzegovina in 1900 and the savage and individualistic element went out of the coverage of the war. When a peace treaty was signed in May 1902, the leader applauding its sensible terms was bland in the extreme. 'The satisfaction which every Englishman must feel at the restoration of peace is more profound than the danger escaped may seem to justify ... The Boer resistance was unexpectedly obstinate, but to overcome it was, at the worst, only a matter of time. And against this must, it is said, be set the training our troops have received, the experience gained by the War Office, and the evidence given of the colonial determination to fight side by side with England whenever their co-operation is needed. Something might be offered by way of criticism upon all these supposed gains, but it may be enough to point out that even if they are all as great as they are represented, Englishmen may still be heartily glad that they are not forced to reap them any longer.'[25] Yet the strength of the paper's opinions was not diluted. There was, for instance, in 1901, an uncompromising leader on a Commons debate on black labour in South Africa, making it very clear that, for *The Economist*, 'pro-Boer' simply meant 'anti-war', and that it was plain – and good economic sense – that what the black worker needed was 'the right inducement, which was a good wage, agreed with his employer, and a taxation which he could not wholly avoid'. If black superstitions about 'bogeys, spooks, and the like' meant that he would not work in mines, however high the wages, then labour must be imported, 'under proper guarantees and careful guardianship'.[26]

'The dignity of labour is never preached with so much conviction as when the congregation is composed of native Africans and the pulpit is occupied by a mine owner', was the tart opening to a leader the following year on 'NATIVE LABOUR IN RHODESIA', which had echoes of William Clark along with the *Economist*'s basic humanitarianism. 'Never, moreover, is it so hard to produce the desired impression.'

> The native is a victim of that universal form of idleness which consists in not caring to do unpleasant work for inadequate pay. His wants, unfortunately for employers, are few and easily satisfied, and having got, or if necessary earned, enough for his maintenance, he does not care to earn anything more. The directors of the British South Africa Company are naturally grieved at this indifference to money and money's worth. The native seems to be an admirable example of that frugal contentment which has been so much praised by poets. But frugal contentment is not at all the temper which the British South Africa Company wish to encourage. The reports of the interviews which the Native Commissioner has held with the chiefs show that he is chiefly occupied in engendering a Divine discontent.

The Commissioner had tried to persuade them of the delight of labour. 'If they will only work, they will have better lands, better crops, better cattle, better sheep, and more money with which to buy wives.' They were deaf to his eloquence: 'indeed, he himself supplies us with one not quite inadequate reason for their indifference. The chiefs, he says, replied, not that their people liked idleness better than work, but that they "wished to work in places at which they did not die in such numbers." An abnormally high rate of mortality seriously interferes with the enjoyment of the attractions set out by the Native Commissioners.'[27]

In the last few years of Johnstone's editorship the quality of coverage of foreign affairs, including South Africa, deteriorated, but for most of his time with the paper it was frequently very high. *The Economist* had not merely used the services of the *Spectator*'s political writers: it had also, for many years, used one of its editors, Meredith Townsend, as a major contributor on foreign affairs.[28] Born in Essex in 1831 and educated in Suffolk, Townsend had left school at 16, well grounded in classics, to teach in misery in Scotland. He was rescued the following year by a family friend, the editor of the *Friend of India* at Serampore, near Calcutta. At 21 he became its editor, at 22 its proprietor. For a time he also edited the *Calcutta Quarterly Review* and the *Annals of Indian Administration* and was a *Times* correspondent. His support for enlightened policies was valued by two successive Indian pro-consuls, Lords Dalhousie and Canning, but Townsend was no government stooge. Nor did he live in an expatriate cocoon. He went to great lengths to understand India, learned several Indian languages well and Hindustani fluently, and became an intimate friend of his Brahmin munshi (language teacher). Ill-health drove him back to England, having been pointed by James Wilson towards the *Spectator* and Hutton: his association with *The Economist* started with the death of Bagehot.

'He wrote a weekly article for a number of years under Mr Johnstone', recorded Chapman. 'He used to deliver it himself on Wednesdays. He used by-lined sheets of paper for his Manuscript. He was a short stoutish man who used to wear a clerical hat. He could write on most subjects with a critical pen.' Strachey narrowed the field somewhat. 'Townsend ... was specially interested in Asia and the Asiatic spirit and foreign affairs ... [and] knew a great deal about diplomatic history and about war by land and sea, as must every man who has lived long in India.' What interested him primarily was 'what might be called the scenery of life and politics. Townsend looked upon life as a drama played in a great theatre and seen from the stalls.'

He was honourable, high-minded, kindly and generous, despite being extremely sharp-tongued: 'He barked but he never bit.' Once Strachey had become sole proprietor of the *Spectator*, he took some risks, the circulation doubled and profits increased dramatically. But Townsend was never jealous, for he had, like the *Economist* proprietors, 'preferred the atmosphere of the Three-per-cents'. Strachey keenly admired Townsend's intellectual gifts. 'It is my honest belief that he was, in the matter of style, the greatest leader-writer who has ever appeared in the English Press. He developed the exact compromise between a literary dignity and colloquial easiness of exposition which completely fills the requirements of journalism. He was never pompous, never dull or common, and never trivial . . . No one could excite the mind and exalt the imagination as he did. And the miracle was that he did it all the time in language which appeared to be nothing more than a clever, competent man talking at his club. He used no literary artifice, no rhetorical emphasis, no elaboration of language, no *finesse* of phrase. His style was easy but never elegant or precious or ornamented. It was familiar without being commonplace, free without discursiveness, and it always had in it the note of distinction . . . He never appeared to preach or to explain to his readers . . . his writing at its best was in form perfect journalism.' His faults were an undue liking for the sensational ('with a sense of half-reality, half make-believe . . . Townsend transformed his quiet life into one long and thrilling adventure'): he might say 'very dangerous and even very absurd things – things which became all the more absurd because they were, as a rule, conveyed in what were apparently carefully-balanced and carefully-selected words'. As a journalist, he liked definiteness. 'Qualifying words were an abomination to his strong imagination.'

Of Townsend's hundreds of contributions to *The Economist*, one of the finest appeared during the reign of Lathbury and Palgrave. Called 'WHAT ENGLAND HAS INFLICTED UPON INDIA', it was a startling change from most of the Indian coverage, which, when it was not focusing on finance, ruminated about how to make the natives see reason. Even Bagehot had added little distinction: India seemed not to excite him.

It was unjust, began this article, to admire the advantages of English rule in India without stating the disadvantages. These were not those commonly cited: India was not being impoverished by paying a vast tribute to Great Britain (it was small), by loss of trade (it was 20 times higher than under the great Moguls), or by the extinction of industry (new industries like tea, indigo and jute were far more profitable than the muslin manufacture killed off by

British competition). Three evils had been inflicted upon India, but they were intellectual, not economic.

> The first and greatest of these has been the unintentional but inevitable suppression of intellectual progress in its natural, and therefore hopeful, grooves. The English have not been without care for their subjects' minds, but their care has been not to develop them but to wrest them violently into unnatural directions. They have insisted that the natives shall eventually cease to be Asiatics and become Europeans. They have taught them English literature, English mechanics, and Western science, have rewarded progress in those departments exclusively, and have judged every man according to the degree in which he has made himself intellectually an Englishman. Above all nations, Indians are moved by influence from above, and consequently all intellectual power has been exerted in a direction in which nine-tenths of its force is wasted, and all originality has disappeared. Native poetry, native philosophies, native theologies, have all died under the cold breath of the Northern wind, and in their stead we have a generation of students, chiefly on the coast fringe, wasting powers which are sometimes extraordinary upon imitations, upon English poetry, English literature, English political thought – with the result that they occasionally produce things as clever as the Latin verses of Milton, and about as useful to themselves and to mankind. Fettered in a language which they understand without feeling, and in a system of thought which they only borrow, the educated natives become mere copyists, develop no original power, and pour out whole libraries of poor, though often correct, English, for which no human being is the better.

In 100 years, among a people of rare intelligence, no original mind had made itself visible to the world. The old learning had disappeared, and the majority of the upper classes had become markedly less cultivated: culture, in fact, of any genuine kind, had been superseded by an English whitewash.

> This is an enormous evil, and it extends to every department of thought till we never now see a great native politician or financier, or architect, or original artist of any kind whatever. The higher thought of the whole people in all directions lies crushed, and its originality is extinguished. That would be the result, even in this country, if the only road to fame or power lay through Latin; and the Indian, besides being far more susceptible than the

Englishman, has far less mental relation to him than we have to the ancient Romans. The pivot of thought is different. It is noticed that natives in Pondicherry often become 'dark Frenchmen,' and they could have taken much from Arabs, but no one except a Chinese is so unlike an Englishman as the educated native, who talks English without an accent, and writes a tongue which, except when he is in a satirical mood, is like English with the tone and the melody alike gone out of it. We are producing a generation of imitators, amidst whom creative thought is dying away, till a nation of philosophers can only produce commentators, a most poetic people have given up original composition; and a race which has covered a continent with magnificent structures never produces a striking building.

The second evil had been to extinguish the hope of careers, 'and therefore the main inducement to become great'. The warlike nations of India had produced not only great – but original – soldiers, 'but we have prohibited war and refused military service until it is vain for a native ever to expect to command a corps of cavalry, much more to command in chief in an independent expedition'. They had produced great politicians, like Akbar, 'but we shut up the political road to them all unless they like to become mere debaters in a deliberative council. That is not the native ideal. He desires to be original, to make his will executive, to *octroyer* [bestow] great reforms, and, above all, to govern; and we are compelled by the necessity of the position to refuse all these things. No native can any longer attain a throne, or even a satrapy, and in practice he is shut out from the politics of his own country altogether, while the Empire at large is not thrown open to him.' It was the same with architecture, engineering and teaching. 'The single inspiriting occupation left to them is that of making money' – an occupation disdained by the better-born – yet unless they were Parsee, their wealth did not give them status: 'The native Baring, the native who buys all the opium, the native who is bullion dealer for a continent, is counted above the herd. The hope of distinction as the man himself reckons distinction, the hope of fame through works which may live for ever, the hope of executive power, are as extinguished under British rule as military ambition. The salt of life is taken out of the mess, and an ambitious Indian lad, full of half-developed power, is in a more hopeless position than an Armenian under St Petersburg, or an Algerian under Paris.' Partly perceiving this, every viceroy had tried to open careers to natives, but not the careers they wanted. 'The man . . . who could govern a province as the Maharajah of Jeypore does must content himself with a magistracy. We believe this evil eats out half the good ambition of the upper classes, and depresses every rank of the community above the very lowest.'

And if that were not enough, there was thirdly the fact that the British conquest had 'profoundly demoralised the relation betweeen governors and governed. The old native Governments were, and are popular. Oppressive and bad as we think them, they suited the popular taste, they allowed all to rise, and they kept up a vivacity and vigour of life in which the people delighted.'

> Their courts were splendid; their capitals full of bustle, chances, and excitement; their provinces scenes of incessant adventure; life under them was full of colour, opportunity, and pleasurable conflict. Now all is calm, just, and 'leaden'. A race without grace, without love of splendour, and with a hatred of adventure and intrigue, consulting no one, responsible to no one, appearing and disappearing like shadows from a northern sea, issues incessant orders, levels all grades into equality before itself, taxes with iron rigidity, and presses incessantly but silently towards objects with which its people at heart do not sympathise in the least. Justice – then why is the white man our ruler? Equality – why should there be equality when the Brahmins came from the mouth of the Creator, and the Sudra from his foot? Wealth – what particular good does wealth bring us who can live on anything, if we have only the social dignity which these barbarians refuse? These are the thoughts of natives, and the consequence is a dislike of the Government as foreign and unsympathetic, which is rapidly altering the character of the people, killing out their great quality, loyalty, and making them suspicious, sullen, and distrustful of the slightest attempt to reform, or guide, or tax them ... this distrust ... increases rather than diminishes with the fidgetiness of the Government, which always suggests to the people that England holds India because she is enriched by holding it, and may yet obtain from it some more plunder ... A quiet, enduring, but dully taciturn hatred of their Government as alien in race, in motives, and in objects, is the third great disadvantage inflicted by Englishmen upon the people of India.[29]

The men of business apparently took this onslaught on received wisdom, published in November 1879, stoically: it did not generate a single letter to the editor. However, another characteristic Townsend assault a couple of weeks later, on what he saw as a seven-year mishandling of relations with Afghanistan, provoked a most interesting response. Townsend had attacked the record of successive governments in bringing about the situation which had led to the second Afghan War (which had begun in 1878 and was not to end until 1881), although his harshest strictures were reserved for the Disraeli government then in power. ('When a Government has neither the wisdom to do right, nor the skill to do wrong successfully, it is idle to talk about supporting it. It is powerless to do anything but mischief, and to support it is simply to enable it to do more mischief.')[30] This had elicited a reply from the Duke of Argyll, who had been Secretary of State for India from 1868 to 1874, defending a particular aspect of the Liberal record. 'The fair and impartial tone of your article on the Afghan question,' he began, '. . . will give to all its statements a weight very different from that which is attached to similar statements in journals more purely political.'[31]

The letter is a useful reminder that despite its small circulation, *The Economist* was extremely influential. Prince Albert had been perhaps its most aristocratic constant reader, but an eighth duke was an interesting status symbol, though a duke most untypical of his kind. Argyll, an amateur scientist and a man of considerable intelligence, known as 'the Radical Duke', had been a keen free-trader from the 1840s, was a colleague of Wilson's in government and was admired by John Bright. Still, his long and helpful missive from Inveraray was an encomium worth having: the modern advertising department would have had an interview with him in their promotional film. The letter also made a nice change from the norm, for most were highly technical, anonymous, or both.

Spectator staff served *The Economist* well for over 20 years: between Asquith, Strachey, Townsend and Lathbury, Johnstone had sound – sometimes brilliant – contributors on the political side for most of his term as editor. Yet politics clearly took second place to Johnstone's main preoccupation, to provide his readers with honest and useful financial information at a time when it was in ever-greater demand. Under Bagehot the greatest strength of the paper's financial coverage had been the money market: Johnstone's forte was the Stock Exchange.

CHAPTER XXVIII:

Selling integrity

In many respects, *The Economist* was the Stock Exchange's antithesis. The markets are mercurial, *The Economist* was as firm and unshaken, in good times and ill, as the Rock of Gibraltar. The Stock Exchange, mirroring the propensities of its clients, tends often to take the short view, because jobbers are concerned with the state of their books . . . *The Economist* on every question took the long view; for that was *The Economist*'s book. When the market's approach was narrow and one-sided, *The Economist*'s was wide and balanced . . . At moments when investors were painfully preoccupied with the one in the many, *The Economist* remained steadily insistent on the many in the one. *Hargreaves Parkinson, ex-Stock Exchange editor, 1943*[1]

Around the time when Edward Johnstone took over, Britain's economic situation was changing portentously. 1873 had marked the peak of the trading boom, which was followed by a long period of comparative depression that hit manufacturers and producers, not consumers. Not only was there increased competition from Germany and the USA in the export markets, but improved communications and transport encouraged imports. But though producers (particularly in agriculture) suffered from cheap competition, the consumer inevitably benefited. Additionally, a reversal of the pre-1873 inflationary trend helped to push up real wages and until the turn of the century the majority of the population – already profiting from social reforms – enjoyed a real improvement in their standard of living. Britain continued dominant in the field of foreign investment, investing more than a third of its capital overseas and outstripping all its competitors put together. As a provider of short- or long-term capital at home or abroad, the late-Victorian City of London had no serious rivals. And with the world increasingly following Britain's long-standing example by adopting the gold standard, London, the greatest market in gold, came to be known, in David Kynaston's phrase, 'as a kind of universal switchboard in the settling of trading and financial matters'.[2] To corroborate this he quoted Francis Hirst, who, writing in 1911 when he was editor of *The Economist*, described the City as 'the greatest shop, the greatest store, the freest market for commodities, gold and securities, the greatest disposer of capital, the greatest dispenser of credit, but above and beyond, as well as by reason of all these marks of financial and commercial supremacy, it is the world's clearing house'.[3]

Charles Duguid, City editor of the *Morning Post*, who had been Johnstone's assistant from 1889 to 1892, wrote in 1904 almost as limpidly about a component part of the clearing house: 'The Stock Exchange has been described as the mart of the world; as the nerve-centre of the politics and finances of nations; as the barometer of their prosperity and adversity; and so on. It has also been described as the bottomless pit of London, and as worse than all the hells. Perhaps, however, the Stock Exchange can best be defined and described as a market. Just as Smithfield is the market for meat and Covent Garden the market for flowers, fruit, and vegetables, so is the Stock Exchange the market for stocks and shares.'[4]

The Stock Exchange had come into its own after the Companies Act of 1862, which brought the principle of limited liability on to the Statute Book; Bagehot's *Economist* had seen clearly the virtues and vices of this development. Taking a retrospective view of the progress of the joint-stock company, the paper observed in 1863 that the gradual abolition of unlimited liability had given a vast stimulus to joint-stock enterprise, 'and the anticipations of loss to such as transact business with Companies framed under the Limited Liability Act have not been realised, owing principally to the wholesome rules usually adhered to by the public with regard to the limitation of calls on the capital of such Companies'.[5] By the beginning of the twentieth century the company system was dominant in British industry and banking. The balance of power was tipped in favour of shareholders, who cared about dividends, rather than of entrepreneurial individuals. The *rentier* class, who lived comfortably on income rather than earnings, were absorbed in the struggle to maximise the returns on their investments with the minimum of risk. Good advice was urgently needed.

The Economist's coverage of the Stock Exchange had been initially perfunctory, but within a few months of its foundation, in February 1844, it carried extensive and rapidly growing statistical tables on prices for domestic and foreign government funds, securities and stocks. The wild speculation that attended the railway mania was well reported and analysed in the 'Railway Monitor' and in Wilson's leaders and there was even the occasional splash of colour in the reporting: the most amusing example, 'THE STOCK MANIA', with the sub-heading, '"Who put my man in the stocks?" – *King Lear.*"', was reprinted from the *Glasgow Citizen*.

> In King Lear's time such an occurrence appears to have been rare. Everybody is in the stocks now. Needy clerks, poor tradesmen's apprentices, discarded serving-men, and bankrupts – all have entered the ranks of the great monied interest. Persons to whom Goldsmith's village preacher were a Croesus, bravely pledge themselves in black and white, on rolls of enduring vellum, to bridge over mighty rivers, to perforate the Grampians, the Pyrenees, or the Appenines, or hew down mountains of stubborn granite, and level spacious valleys with viaducts of stupendous masonry!
>
> Bold assumption this of a power mightier than that which the mightiest monarch wields! We swale [melt away] with wonder at the thought of it. The genius of modern speculation, armed with a hollow scroll for a truncheon, effects more conquests than ever were achieved by the sword. A tiny slip, marked with a few cabalistic scratches, is the talisman with which she works. O sovereign power of paper!

Two paragraphs full of such imagery as 'castaways on the bare sea of poverty', 'fleshless ghosts . . . pointing the way to veritable treasures' and 'bleeding ankles' climbing 'the thorny steep of fortune' were followed by 'Oh, ye sifting committee men who try the merits of rival projects, little do ye dream what huge and multifarious results hang on your decision! What dreams of new dresses – of costly sideboards – of elegant villas at the coast – is it your high privilege to realise at once or dissipate for ever!' And so on.[6]

Neither Wilson, Greg nor Hutton had much familiarity with the Stock Exchange as an institution: Bagehot, of course, knew it intimately. His response to the boom engendered by the 1862 Companies Act was to launch in 1864 the *Investors' Monthly Manual*, which aspired to list 'the highest, lowest, and latest Price of ALL Stocks during the month, Railway Shares, Banking Shares, and other Securities; the mode in which their Dividends are payable, their four last dividends, &c. &c.; so as to give all the information so important at all time to Investors, and so especially important just now when prices are so fluctuating. The Manual will include Stocks dealt in at the Provincial Exchanges as well as in the London Market.' In a shrewd marketing ploy well ahead of its time, the manual was distributed 'gratuitously' with the first issue, while succeeding numbers were sold at 6d. to such *Economist* subscribers 'as do not intimate their wish not to receive it'. (In an article in the centenary history, Hargreaves Parkinson, editor of the *Financial News* and ex-deputy editor of *The Economist*, pointed out that this procedure 'anticipated by nearly seventy years' that 'adopted by His Majesty's Treasury on the conversion of 2,000 millions of War Loan in 1932, when all holders who failed to "intimate their wish" to the contrary were deemed to have converted their stock'. It was yet another example of the nineteenth-century *Economist* using marketing ploys more associated with the modern paper.)

It was an extraordinary pioneering effort. 'We have had great difficulty in getting together this mass of information,' wrote Bagehot, 'and have to tender our best thanks, in a very great number of instances, to the public offices, consulates, great mercantile houses connected with foreign Governments, and many other competent persons, for the kind and ready information they have given us'; where information was 'imperfect . . . we hope in subsequent numbers to enlarge it carefully, and to make it entirely complete'.[7]

The *Manual* was a money-spinner. In 1876, the year of the first surviving circulation records, it sold 36,535 copies (not many fewer monthly than the 3,690 weekly average of the mother paper), adding a further extra advertising revenue of £228.7s.6d. to the £3,129.9s.6d. earned by *The Economist*. It was constantly improved, adding company reports, details of new issues and, from 1879, the yield of every dividend-paying security at the latest market price of the month, refined in 1883, when Johnstone took over, to make allowance for redemption where necessary. As Parkinson observed, that alone 'was a Herculean task which none of the *Manual*'s devoted servants who, in the days before calculating machines, scarcely slept at all in the hectic interval between the end of each month and the appearance of each new number, were ever likely to under-estimate'. During a lifespan of almost 66 years, the *Manual* faithfully recorded everything of interest to investors, and it provides a superb chronicle of the economic history of the period at home and abroad. Its circulation never went below a monthly average of 2,500 until the 1890s, when increasing competition, from dailies like the *Financial News* and the *Financial Times* and journals like the *Investor's Review*, steadily impinged. By

1913 the circulation was down to a monthly average of 1,296 and continuing downwards; the *Manual* was finally killed off in 1930.

Johnstone was a faithful follower of Bagehot in several important respects, particularly in probity, respect for facts and dogged opposition to waste in public expenditure; and also in the belief that investors should take personal responsibility in financial matters, and that what was wanted, as Bagehot wrote just before his death, was 'not more paternal interference in Stock Exchange affairs but less'.[8] Here, of course, Bagehot and Johnstone were at one with Wilson.

In the view of his *Economist* obituarist, writing in 1913, Johnstone in some ways faced more difficulties than his predecessors, for he became editor just at the time when financial journalism was growing in popularity, and 'old methods were giving way at the advent of a newer, "snappier" school of writer . . . and there was a danger that the English Press might become shallow and subservient to outside interests – the mouthpiece of financiers and share-pushers, the enemy, instead of the friend, of the investing classes'.

> To some extent journalism was contaminated by this touch of the company promoter, but as we look back over the history of the last 30 years we can fairly say (on comparing it with other systems) that the English financial Press might have fallen much further. We do not wish to overrate in this matter the power of one man; but those financial writers who knew him will, we think, agree that Mr Johnstone, simply by the force of his example, exercised a very wholesome and restraining influence on the development of this form of modern journalism. He was above all things critical, and he believed that the first function of the financial writer was the critical function. He realised, as most of us do realise, the force of the old dilemma. 'If you are so clever that you can advise other people to make money, why do you slave at the page instead of making money for yourself?' His answer would be that he did not pretend to make money for other people, though he might show them how not to lose it. He did not claim to have a supply of 'good things' up his sleeve; the most he could do was to keep tight hold of certain governing principles, and apply them to the facts of every case as it was presented to him. It was no duty of his to make his readers' fortunes, but he might, and he did, guide them clear of blunders, and point out the traps that had been set for unwary feet. For this work of critical financial writing Mr Johnstone was pre-eminently fitted.

A man of 'natural shrewdness and of a keen, penetrating judgment', though cautious, he was not timid. '"I have given far too many knocks in my time", he once said to a contributor, "to be troubled when they hit back." He had, if the phrase may be allowed, a very Scotch mind – a mind which could see through fallacies, distinguish the essential from the unimportant, and lay bare the weakness of a bad case for everyone to understand.'

> Whether it was an alluring prospectus or the dodge of a company promoter, an unsound Budget, a monetary fallacy, or a blunder in economics, Mr Johnstone could criticise with deadly force, and in language which was powerful mainly because it was clear, simple and terse . . . His own style was direct, forcible, and unassuming – and the style was the man. In the whole of his career he never criticised a venture without giving the ground of his objections, never gave a blind 'tip,' or permitted the insertion of a puff. Business could come or go – he never allowed considerations of additional income to sway the opinions of the paper. He stood, if we may say so, for the only sound type of financial journalism; and many of those who came in contact with him in his active career remember his work to-day as the test and standard by which to judge the quality of their own achievements.[9]

Johnstone had helpers on the financial side, so it is not possible to tell who wrote what in the financial and business pages. Chapman mentions a 'Mr Baker' (who assisted in the early years 'on stock exchange matters'); H.W. Wheeler ('a financial writer of considerable ability who could write on almost any financial topic needing skilled treatment. He was a jovial personality with a great capacity for hard work. He died in February 1920 at 68 years of age'); and J.S. Mann (a contributor 'for some years', who wrote occasional leaders and business notes and 'was a well known figure in the office'). The contributors' lists for the period 27 September to 15 November 1924 attribute to Mann 14 'Notes of the Week' (six on China, others on India, Mexico and Japan) and book reviews on Australia and on disarmament; he went on writing for the paper until 1925. The overall tone was often stern and admonitory. 'PARASITES OF THE STOCK EXCHANGE' considered stockbrokers operating outside the Exchange and prophesied serious results should the practice increase: 'The tone of commercial morality, especially amongst subordinates, will run very great risk of being decidedly lowered, and the fruits of this may be painfully apparent.'[10] In 'THE VIRTUES AND VICES OF OPTIONS' (an option being 'the price paid for the right to demand or to deliver a certain amount of stock at a given price within a certain definite period'), options were examined from 'the standpoint of business morality . . . they foster a form of speculation which already flourishes too abundantly. They do this not only directly, but also indirectly, as, owing to the way in which they limit loss, they encourage people to speculate in stocks and shares who otherwise would be restrained, not so much by a positive prudence as by a negative timidity. But it is evident that one can be as effectually destroyed by a poison taken in regular and known quantities, as by a large draught taken heedlessly.'[11]

In 1890, the paper's worst fears were realised. The great Baring banking house got into severe trouble as a result of over-speculation in South America; its liabilities were over £20 million. In 1866 Overend, Gurney had been let go to the wall: this time the Governor of the Bank of England intervened before the crisis was made public and raised a £7 million guarantee fund, thus staving off a panic and allowing Barings the opportunity to recover and – in time – reconstruct itself as a joint-stock company. This outcome was seen as a triumph: Johnstone was unimpressed. A leader which drove the money market into second place said:

> It is impossible to withhold sympathy from the victims of misfortune, even when they have brought upon themselves the ills that befall them. Nevertheless, we feel unable to join unreservedly in the chorus of condolence which has been raised this week over the collapse of Messrs Baring Brothers.
>
> It is, indeed, a pity that such a great house should have been brought low, but it would have been still more to be regretted if the punishment for the errors that have been committed should have fallen, not upon those responsible for them, but upon innocent parties. Had Messrs Baring Brothers been able to shift the burden of their South American obligations upon the investing public they would now have been standing erect; and without indulging in any recriminations, it must be admitted that they did not neglect to use all the means in their power to rid themselves in this way of their liabilities. The subject is not a pleasant one to pursue in present circumstances, and we would rather not speak of the market devices that were employed to attract investors. Our opinion as to these was expressed freely and strongly enough at the time, and no good purpose is to be served by going back upon them. We cannot, however, profess to feel sorry that the efforts to induce the investing public to come to the relief of Barings have

proved ineffectual . . . In no unkindly spirit . . . we feel bound to say that it is better that things should have turned out as they have done, than that the Barings should have succeeded in relieving themselves from the evil consequences of their own rashness in the pursuit of wealth, at the expense of confiding investors.[12]

Later that same year, in 'THE BUSINESS MORALITY OF THE STOCK EXCHANGE', there was cause for more general rebuke. 'In times like the present, when the bubble of inflation has been pricked, the public begin, with chastened sadness, to seriously take account of the results of their operations on the Stock Exchange. A rough profit and loss account is made out . . . and the result . . . too often is to show, that while they have got the experience, the "House" has got the money. For this, of course, the public have, no doubt, themselves largely to blame . . . the speculative public . . . take a "fancy," . . . in much the same way as if a horse were concerned instead of a security, and in these circumstances their operations are seldom to be differentiated from pure gambling.' They should have known that the cards were stacked against them: 'in the "House," . . . the shearing of the lambs seldom comes to an end'. Where the public was being swindled, the Committee should deal rigorously with the abuse.[13]

The need to punish wrongdoing in the Stock Exchange was a frequent cry: it was parallelled a century later in the leaders dealing with Lloyd's of London. The minatory tone and the absence of fear about offending vested interests were as marked as ever. After several scandals and alleged frauds in the 1970s and early 1980s, the repeated failure of Lloyd's to introduce certain crucial reforms that would safeguard the 'names' (the individual members who back the market with their wealth) against exploitation or fraud by agents, was denounced as 'morally wrong, and economically short-sighted'.[14] In 1991, looking at the sequence of devastating liabilities (asbestos and pollution claims; professional-indemnity insurance of executives of bankrupt American savings-and-loan institutions; the fire on the North Sea oil platform, Piper Alpha; the Alaskan oil spill from the Exxon Valdez and so on), the paper was enraging the chairman of Lloyd's by predicting that unless new names were spared the potential disaster of unlimited liability, it would be a case of 'ask not for whom the Lutine bell tolls. It tolls for Lloyd's.'[15]

Contemplating the notion of the demise of a great institution three centuries old, which in 1900 had underwritten half the world's insurance, there was no evidence of sentimentality. In a climate in which recession-hit clients demanded cheap premiums, 'while governments, judges and juries are saddling insurers with huge bills for environmental clean-up or compensation for personal injuries', either premiums would rise sharply or 'another way must be found to pay for the sins of the past'.

> It is tempting for Lloyd's to use this general background as an excuse for its present plight. Tempting, too, to accuse doomsayers of exaggeration, while assuming that its presence is so vital – to the City of London, to Britain, to world insurance – that something will always be done to keep it going. But the hard fact has to be faced: if Lloyd's does not change, it will die. Investors will not put up their money, clients will not offer their business – and both will be right to hold back. Death will probably be slow, and painful. And, though Lloyd's matters, it no longer matters enough for others to want to rescue it.[16]

Even more scathing was the treatment of fraud and Lloyd's.

> Nothing stimulates claims of sharp practice more quickly than losing money. Ten years ago Lloyd's seemed riddled with crooks, yet the 'names' who provide its capital complained little – because most were making profits. Now that many face huge losses, cries of skulduggery have multiplied. Yet reform in the 1980s means that Lloyd's is much cleaner than it was.
>
> Some of the loudest moaners are among the 50-odd Conservative members of Parliament who are names. They are wailing for better investor protection or market management. So where were they in the 1980s? Many were fighting (successfully) to preserve Lloyd's tradition of self-regulation and give it immunity from most lawsuits. It would be hard to find a clearer case of people hoist with their own petard.[17]

One way to start the restoration of confidence in the institution was 'full disclosure. For too long, Lloyd's has covered up when it should have opened up. Claims of wrongdoing must be quickly and publicly investigated; computer records must be made available; any malpractice must be punished.'[18]

The paper has always been true to its radical roots in its instinctive dislike of the perpetuation of privilege or the cover-up of wrongdoing by old-boy networks. That applied to Lloyd's: it also applied to the nineteenth-century

Stock Exchange Committee, of which Johnstone's *Economist* made frequent stringent criticism, finding particularly objectionable the fiction that it was simply a club with which the public had nothing to do.

> Charity is one thing and business is another, and any attempt to mingle the two is likely to lead to confusion and worse. We have heard a great deal too much latterly of the assistance which has been lavishly granted to the weaker brethren on the Stock Exchange, to enable them to avoid the straightforward and businesslike course of publicly declaring themselves defaulters when they cannot meet their liabilities. Since the conspicuous precedent was set at the time of the Baring crisis, the financial world has suffered from an epidemic of well-meant, but ill-advised bolstering up. In that case, of course, some intervention was necessary in order to prevent a panic, although opinions still differ as to whether it was not carried further than was called for . . . But now that it has become fashionable to apply the same principle to all sorts of petty difficulties, a considerable amount of harm is done without any excuse or compensation, and at the mid-monthly settlement last week, benevolence of this sort was carried to a positively ridiculous extreme. We call it benevolence, because those who were chiefly responsible for it have posed, and have been duly applauded, as benefactors who had come to the rescue of insolvent, but deserving, members of the 'House'; and though we may suspect that a good deal of it was prompted by motives that were not altogether disinterested, we are very willing to acknowledge that good-nature and kindly *bonhomie* enter largely into the mutual relations of the Stock Exchange fraternity, and are responsible for much of this misplaced charity.
>
> Benevolent or not, however, the system is bad. It is bad for markets, bad for the Stock Exchange, and worst of all from the point of view of the public interest.

Many failures had been expected: only ten had occurred, giving rise to a feeling of artificial security and an unwarranted rally in prices. 'As a natural consequence, markets were in a more unhealthy condition than ever – instead of being purged and cleansed by the excision of the centre of irritation, they had been poulticed and coddled and galvanised into an appearance of vitality.'[19]

Yet the overall coverage seemed always fair, often friendly and bespoke great familiarity with the institution. Issues addressed included the problems of the City police in dealing with 'a large body of shouting and gesticulating brokers and dealers' outside the main door of the Mining Department,[20] the attitude of the Stock Exchange Committee to the innovation of the 'tape',[21] the suicide of a member after the Kaffir (South African mining shares) collapse[22] and a competitive 50-mile 'tramp' in the rain to Brighton.[23]

A great test of Johnstone's editorship – and one that he passes triumphantly – was his coverage of major frauds. Aylmer Vallance, assistant editor to Walter Layton in the 1920s, later wrote a book about swindling, and his frequent use of *The Economist* as a source for the late nineteenth and early twentieth centuries[24] demonstrated the paper's contribution to keeping the world of investment on the straight and narrow.

In Johnstone's time there were no longer issues of principle about whether investors should have legal protection: that was a *fait accompli*. Questions thenceforward concerned the extent and nature of that protection. 'All the law can do', said the paper in one of a series suggesting urgent improvements in the Companies Acts to deal with fraudulent company promotions, 'is to endeavour, to some extent, to impose the safeguards which any intelligent investor would provide for himself.' What no amount of legislative interference in business could do was to 'prevent the loss of money by those who, regardless of considerations of prudence and common sense, allow themselves to be caught by the first tempting bait that is set for them'.[25]

The warnings given to those who were sensible enough to read *The Economist* were startlingly frank and often splendidly ironic. Eric Gibb, a connoisseur, credited Johnstone with 'pawky humour' and this is a good description of the prevailing tone of 'THE PROPOSED PURCHASE OF ITS OWN SHARES BY THE ROCK LIFE ASSURANCE COMPANY'. It observed that at a meeting of policy-holders, the chair was occupied 'by Mr Bidder, QC, a gentleman who, we understand, does not generally preside over the proceedings of the company, but of whose forensic talent the directors no doubt thought it wise to avail themselves, in order that their case might be presented to the policy-holders with all the skill of a practised advocate'.

> Possibly, it may be unjust to judge of Mr Bidder's effort by the meagre report of the proceedings which is, apparently, all the company have thought it necessary to submit to absent policy-holders. One would have thought that in a matter of such vital importance as this the directors would have taken care that all that was said both for or against their proposal was

fully reported. They, however, do not seem to have seen the matter in this light, and it is possible, therefore, as we have said, that the condensed report does not do full justice to Mr Bidder. We must, however, take what the directors have been pleased to give us, and we are certainly not a little astonished to find that, in their opinion, as expressed by Mr Bidder, the Rock Office, as at present constituted, is one which insurers ought to shun. For, according to them, it is an office in which policy-holders are unfairly mulcted for the benefit of shareholders.[26]

The paper was being deliberately hard on poor Bidder, whose remit included having publicly to defend an indefensible scheme against a recent savage attack in *The Economist*. (Seven years later it was able to demonstrate the precariousness of the company's finances, 'the inherent viciousness of this phase of the Rock's financial policy' and 'the need to prevent legislative sanction ever being given to such conduct again'.[27])

Another QC to come under the lash was a Mr Pope, who, on reading an investigatory committee's report on a company of which he was a director, said 'he would like to go away and hide his head. The pity is that such an eminent lawyer as Mr Pope should have accepted a position, the duties of which he was either unable or incompetent to fulfil, for the story told by the committee is one of the most discreditable that has ever been published in relation to the affairs of a joint-stock company.'[28]

There were all too many such stories, which were revealing about the stupidity and greed of directors and shareholders alike. Late-Victorian Britain was in the grip of what the paper called 'a company-promoting mania', in its way as bad as the railway mania half a century earlier, and protective legislation was still in its infancy and being introduced only as scandals proved it necessary: 'There has never been a time when the necessity for caution and inquiry among investors before subscribing to new companies was greater than it is now, when promoters and promoting agencies appear to have come to the conclusion that no project is too wild, no business too trumpery to be converted into a joint-stock company.'[29]

The worst cases were the financial massacres of the innocent, as exemplified by the case of the Liberator group. This sensation was the result of a criminal conspiracy devised and run by Jabez Spenser Balfour, who, with the aid of respectable and well-rewarded Nonconformist stooges, ruined thousands of families who put their savings into a building society which used them for crazy speculation.

The directors have practically admitted that they were mere tools in the hands of Mr Jabez Balfour, and that their idea of fulfilling the responsibilities of their office was to accept and ratify whatever that worthy chose to place before them. Such a scandalous dereliction of duty certainly deserves exemplary punishment.

But even more extraordinary have been the admissions of the chartered accountants, who recognised fully the dangerous courses into which the companies were drifting, but contented themselves by writing their protests to the directors, and allowing those protests to be withheld from the shareholders. Their plea that an exposure in the early days of the scandals would have brought about the ruin of the companies is contemptible, in view of the fact that by their reticence the ruin has become enormously greater and more widespread . . . It will be interesting to see what steps the Institute of Chartered Accountants may see fit to take in the circumstances to which we have referred . . . Chartered accountants claim very special privileges. What are they supposed to do in return for those privileges?

The Companies' Winding-up Bill, once condemned as an unnecessary piece of legislation, had had its utility proved, for the prospect of the publicity engendered by the Official Receiver's examination 'is certainly acting as a deterrent to men who would [otherwise] be only too ready to sell their names at so much per annum'.[30] Further attacks on accountants and demands for punitive action by the Institute against their guilty members finally elicited a satisfactory letter from the Secretary of the Institute – a tribute to the paper's influence. ('Auditors are capitalism's handmaidens', observed 'WHO WILL AUDIT THE AUDITORS?' in 1989. 'Unless they provide, and are seen to provide, accurate, honest and impartial information on companies, the whole structure of competitive market economies will be threatened.'[31])

Week after week, suspect schemes were closely examined and readers warned off. Ernest Terah Hooley, regarded as a financial genius until he went bankrupt in 1898, became more seriously dishonest from 1900 and was finally sent to prison in 1912, had every scheme he produced examined beadily: 'it is to be regretted', said one of several uncompromising leaders in 1897, 'that in his zeal for the investing classes, Mr Hooley has committed himself to the formation of a "corner" [in Australasian frozen meat], which has more than the usual elements of uncertainty to commence with, and the practical certainty of ultimate failure'.[32]

During Hooley's bankruptcy proceedings it emerged that he had incurred great expense in hiring titled directors. 'Investors have often been warned', sighed *The Economist*, 'against putting their trust in ornamental directors and sinking their commonsense at the invitation of men with handles to their names, who degrade the titles they have inherited or acquired; but they have seldom had such an object lesson in the art of the decoy duck as the Hooley companies appear likely to furnish.'[33] However, the paper had earlier that year already fingered the man who was to be the greatest decoy duck of all: Lord Dufferin, first Marquess of Dufferin and Ava, KCB, GCMG, GCB, now retired from a glittering career which included being successively Governor-General of Canada, Ambassador to Russia, Ambassador to Constantinople, Viceroy of India, Ambassador to Italy and Ambassador to France. If any one article illustrates the greatest virtues of Johnstone's editorship (and the distinction of his style, for it is almost certainly his), it is 'THE DIPLOMAT IN THE SPHERE OF FINANCE'.

> British diplomacy has had no more brilliant representative in modern times than the Marquess of Dufferin and Ava, in whom the inherited wit of the Sheridans is combined with the culture and the experience acquired by long service in many countries and at many Courts. When, therefore, Lord Dufferin passed over from diplomacy to finance, by accepting the position of chairman of the London and Globe Finance Corporation, a good deal of curiosity was felt as to how he would acquit himself in his new sphere of activity and interest. It was quite certain that he would impart to the discussion of business matters some of that grateful [sic] eloquence and readiness of repartee which has obtained for Lord Dufferin a reputation not inferior to that which his diplomatic achievements have earned for him; but it was not so obvious that he would exhibit that financial grip and grasp of detail which is supposed, more or less accurately, to characterise the chairmen of joint-stock companies. In the few public appearances which Lord Dufferin has made in his new capacity of financier he has shown a disposition to deal lightly with hard facts and figures, mainly leaving them to his colleagues; but, like the skilled diplomatist that he is, he has displayed conspicuous ability in making rough places plain, and in glossing over apparently difficult points in such a way as to impress the average shareholder with the conviction that things are really much better than they look, and that 'everything is for the best in the best of all possible' enterprises.
>
> Lord Dufferin is, therefore, to be credited with the introduction of a new

and agreeable element in the usually dry discussion of joint-stock finance, a departure which was rather strikingly in evidence at the meeting the other day of the British America Corporation. In the hands of an ordinary company chairman it is not too much to say that the facts disclosed at the meeting as to the position of the undertaking would have appeared extremely unsatisfactory, but Lord Dufferin had no difficulty in persuading the shareholders that what might seem disappointing incidents in the brief history of the corporation were really blessings in disguise. The British America Corporation, we may remind our readers, widely advertised its prospectus just about a month ago, though the £1,500,000 of capital asked for was only to be accepted from shareholders in the London and Globe Finance Corporation.

The *raison d'être* of the Corporation was difficult to discover. Why could not its object – to buy and develop mines in several parts of the world – have been attained more effectively by an issue of London and Globe capital? Two explanations had been hazarded: 'one that the underwriting and financing of the new Corporation was intended to provide a profit out of the pockets of the London and Globe shareholders, to inflate the profit and loss account of that company, and to increase the sum available for distribution; the other that two sets of fees for largely identical boards are better than one set. Neither explanation, however, is conclusive, and we can only regard the inception of the British America Corporation as a conundrum which it is better to give up.'

The Corporation's record was scrutinised and found seriously wanting, but the directors were unperturbed: 'That only tends to show how rapidly Lord Dufferin's colleagues have acquired his diplomatic way of looking at things. Most other directors, even in this case-hardened age, would be just a little disconcerted in having to inform a body of shareholders that, of the principal purposes for which their capital had been invited, one had been definitely abandoned, and another was still in the stage of negotiation; but now that the really diplomatic manner has been introduced into the company-creating business, there is no telling what developments may follow.'[34]

By the middle of the following year the business (now promoting another new company) was described as having 'arrived at a burlesque stage now, if it had not done so before, and it is inconceivable that any self-respecting prudent invester [sic] should regard the latest scheme evolved from the fertile imagination of Mr Whitaker Wright as worthy of serious consideration and pecuniary interest.'[35] Wright, who was openly living a life of extravagance on a par with that of his spiritual descendant, Robert Maxwell, was pursued by *The Economist* – and apparently only by *The Economist* – as relentlessly as Hooley. Eventually his gambling in mining shares landed him in serious trouble when the threat of a South African war started a stock-market slide: Dufferin had much to smooth over in addressing shareholders. Disaster followed, and in January 1901 Dufferin – already grief-stricken by the loss of his heir at Ladysmith – had to explain publicly to shareholders that he had been quite unprepared for two circumstances: first, 'that the company had a great number of bitter opponents, which, I suppose, is the case of all companies; and, in the next, that our Stock Exchange interests were not only far more complicated and extensive than I had imagined, but that nobody who had not been brought up to the business could ever hope to master its intricacies'.

> On this discovery, it naturally occurred to me that it might be my duty to withdraw from my post of chairman; but, in the first place, it is not so easy for a man in my position to lift his hand from the plough when once he has taken hold of it, and, in the next, I perceived by many signs that my resignation was the very thing that your opponents were anxious to bring about, and that it would be followed by the immediate depreciation of your securities.[36]

So everything had been left to Whitaker Wright, who then managed to lose £500,000 in a Stock Exchange gamble and thus bring down the company.

> Thus, apparently, the sole purpose which Lord Dufferin's connection with the undertaking has served has been to cover with a cloak of respectability the essentially speculative character of its transactions, and to inspire investors with a confidence in it which they would not otherwise have shown. His name and reputation have been regarded as a guarantee, if not of solvency, at least, of straightforward, honest management. But it has all along been a perfectly delusive guarantee, because he knew nothing at all about the management, and was conscious all the time that he did not know anything. How he could have consented to play such a part it is hard to understand. It is nothing to the point to plead, as he does, that a business with which two such eminent persons as Sir William Robinson [CMG,

KCMG, GCMG, ex-Governor of Western Australia] and Lord Loch [KCB, GCMG, 1st Baron, ex-Governor of Victoria, Milner's predecessor as High Commissioner in South Africa] had been connected was one in which he felt he might legitimately engage. We have no right to assume that either of these eminent persons was such a simple figure-head as he admits he has been; nor, even if they were, would their fault extenuate his.

(Lord Dufferin's plight was a lonely one: Robinson had died in 1897 and Loch in 1900.)

> That one who has in many highly responsible positions rendered valuable services to his country should in his later years have so far demeaned himself as to become, for a monetary consideration, the passive tool of a scheming financier every one must regret. But regret it as we may, the fact that in doing so he has injured many innocent people, and sullied his previously unblemished record remains, and it would be idle to attempt to blink it.[37]

Dufferin died early in 1902, and thus escaped seeing Whitaker Wright in the dock. The *Economist* obituary paid tribute to his intellectual brilliance, high cultivation and 'indescribable charm of manner' and regretted that his last days had been 'clouded and embittered by the melancholy outcome' of his business experience. 'Lord Dufferin chivalrously remained with the company until the end, and there can be no doubt that he was a heavy loser in consequence, for, as he said in a deeply pathetic letter, which has since been published, "I am nearly ruined, and, of course, many other persons are involved in the same catastrophe." That such a record as that of Lord Dufferin's should have had for its final moral the extreme danger which lies in the acceptance of directorial responsibilities, especially in connection with speculative companies like the London and Globe groups, is one of the saddest eventualities that it is possible to conceive.'[38] It is a moral which nearly a century later still seems lost on the titled. 'Of course I knew Maxwell was a rogue, a bit of a pirate', said Lord Donoughue – admittedly, compared with Dufferin, a rather downmarket peer – (ex-journalist, ex-economics adviser to Harold Wilson and James Callaghan, and ex-board member of the Economist Intelligence Unit), explaining in 1992 his close association with two of Maxwell's pension-fund-robbing investment companies. 'But I did not know him as well as is being alleged, and I did not know he was a crook. With hindsight I regret it. I don't wish to make an excuse for myself at all, but I'm not an experienced City person. I was an academic and a writer.'[39] Only the names change.

In 1902, in the course of Whitaker Wright's examination under the winding-up procedure, he gave a useful insight into the venal climate of the financial press: 'It is well known in the City that all the financial daily press and those who publish the reports of transactions on the Stock Exchange and call attention to them . . . will not assist companies in any shape or form unless they have consideration in some form or other.' His system was to have his brokers sell shares cheaply to his press targets and then buy them back at a higher price. These transactions had been carried out with three journalists on the *Financial News*, one on the *Financial Times* and the editors of both.[40]

In a thoughtful article in 1913 on the way in which financial journalism had changed from 1890 onwards, Francis Hirst's *Economist* mused on corruption. 'There is not . . . much risk of biased information printed unconsciously by the newspaper editor. He is too well skilled in the art of recognising the preliminary puff and the veiled advertisement to let much of it get into the columns of his paper unknown to him. But the Press, generally speaking, is not so scrupulous regarding the purity of its editorial columns as some of the comments we have perused on this new controversy might suggest. There are degrees of depravity. First blackmail, then puff, then the suppression of facts which would be inconvenient to advertisers and the insertion of those which are favourable. Lastly, there is the negative vice of abstention from criticism.'[41]

On the evidence available, Johnstone's *Economist* seems to be beyond criticism on all these tests. The only area where the faintest question mark arises is that of mining investment. Metal mining, as *The Economist* spelled out in 1888, is 'at best . . . an essentially uncertain operation . . . no prudent person should risk in such ventures more than he can afford to lose without serious inconvenience'.[42] There were, however, all too many imprudent people about who were attracted by the notion of becoming rich overnight from the yields of unproven mining ventures – mainly pursuing gold – in Australia, India, South Africa, South America and other exotic places.

The Economist initially dealt with mining as it dealt with any other kind of investment, using whatever information was available to a London-based financial journalist. By the mid-1890s, however, Johnstone had recruited as 'our special correspondent', later 'our special mining correspondent' and later still 'our special mining commissioner', J.H. Curle, author of *The Gold Mines of the World*, a journalist of considerable eminence. Curle's reports from all over the globe were exhaustive and authoritative. According to Chapman, his articles created a lot of interest and acted as a great stimulant to sales. 'Many people used to call at the office hoping to meet him but we were never able to arrange a meeting.' In 1898, for instance, his articles included a series of eleven invaluable first-hand reports from gold mines in Western Australia. Number x, written in June in Kalgoorlie and published in September, dealt with 'MENZIES, LADY SHENTON, SONS OF GWALIA, THE MURCHISON', which included such information as:

> The White Feather mines have a few patches of gold left, but they are being rapidly gouged out. Robinson, which I inspected, had some small patches on which it actually paid several dividends, but which are now quite done. Indeed, the condition of the mine is appalling, hardly a ton of ore developed, and that unpayable, while the reef dips up and down in all directions. I am surprised, therefore, to hear that the chairman of the company stated at a recent meeting that the mine was looking better than ever, and that more stamps were required, a statement which was endorsed by another director, who had recently inspected the mine.[43]

The same article dealt with the prospects of the Sons of Gwalia, which could be 'a great mine' if the lode continued to carry good gold when it entered the sulphide region: the mine would be most capably managed. Capable management was not to prove enough to save a mine whose ore chutes eventually proved not to go deep enough, but for a few years it made a great deal of money for its managing firm, whose driving genius, Herbert Hoover, Curle met on his visit to the Sons of Gwalia.

Hoover, a gifted young mining engineer, who in his later incarnations as a humanitarian and then as President of the United States (1929–33) was to be friendly with Francis Hirst, quickly gained Curle's admiration and became a close friend and travelling companion.[44]

Curle accompanied Hoover on his tour of outlying mines in Western Australia in October 1903 and on a visit to the Transvaal in 1904, and during part of 1906 Hoover sublet his London apartment to him. Hoover impressed and was accessible to journalists (and indeed published anonymous articles in the *Financial Times*), so, as his biographer, George Nash, puts it, Curle was only one of several 'Hoover-boosters', but he was probably the closest and most influential. Curle, in Nash's view, often acted in his columns as a mirror of Hoover's thinking and provided a great deal of information on Hoover's firm – Bewick, Moreing. In mid-1903 he listed seven properties in Western Australia associated with Bewick, Moreing, and said of them that there were 'no better worked mines in the world'.

But Nash's conclusion is that there was no corruption involved, and that Hoover deserved the good publicity: he was appreciated by journalists fed up with incompetents and charlatans. Like other journalists, Curle overrated a number of Bewick, Moreing mines on which shareholders later lost money, and he was also himself a shareholder in their particularly disastrous operation in Lancefield, Western Australia. But it would seem that at worst all he did was to become anonymously a propagandist for a fundamentally honest man who made some mistakes in a highly risky business. Certainly it casts no shadow over Johnstone's reputation. Like Wilson and Bagehot, Johnstone spotted the gap in the market: his outstanding achievement was to turn his paper into a great investigative financial journal of absolute integrity at the time when such an organ was badly needed.

Because he was with the paper so long (just under a quarter of a century); because he followed Bagehot; because he kept a low profile and hardly anything was written about him; and because Eric Gibb, who joined the paper in 1906, found him well past his prime – 'an elderly editor (who was said to have had a stroke)' – and made him rather a figure of fun, Johnstone's reputation has been that of a dull caretaker.

'I have ... occupied the editorial chair for 17½ years', wrote Geoffrey Crowther in 1956 in a valedictory article. 'This is a long time – I take pride in the fact that it is a longer time than was served by any of the most distinguished of my predecessors. James Wilson, the founder, conducted the paper for just over sixteen years, Walter Bagehot for seventeen years and five months, and my immediate predecessor, Lord Layton, for sixteen years and nine months. Thus four editorships out of a total of only eight, have lasted between sixteen and eighteen years. It is a long time – and, in my judgement, long enough.'45

That passage illustrates two things with great clarity: how little the paper knew of its own history and how undervalued was Edward Johnstone's 23 years and seven months of editorship. Crowther was extremely precise about the dates of the predecessors with whom he compared himself, but because he did not know of Hutton's editorship, his information was seriously inaccurate. Wilson had served less than 14 years, Bagehot less than 16. Crowther, who was driven by a compulsion to stay on longer than had Bagehot, therefore put in more time than necessary. Johnstone, described by a man of the discernment and wide experience of St Loe Strachey as a great editor, was dismissed out of hand: Crowther saw no need even to mention his name.

CHAPTER XXIX:

Fighting the future

It is Dangerfield's great merit that he shed no tears for the age that had gone. Its virtues seemed golden only in the harsh reflected light of the Western Front. In fact it was a cruel, selfish and backward age, wedded to social and philosophical attitudes which no longer made sense. The civilized Asquithian serenity was simply a veneer, concealing depths of injustice and passion which were smashing through the surface even before the guns began to roar. Liberal England was not killed; it died a natural, if unpleasant, death; and Dangerfield wrote its appropriate epitaph. *Paul Johnson, preface to 1966 edition of George Dangerfield's* The Strange Death of Liberal England

Edward Johnstone's reputation had inevitably suffered by comparison with that of Bagehot: such is the usual fate of the invaluable consolidator who follows the brilliant innovator. (Donald Tyerman, who succeeded Geoffrey Crowther – regarded as the greatest twentieth-century editor of *The Economist* – was to have the same problem.) Johnstone was also to be compared unfavourably with the young and dazzling Francis Hirst, who was appointed in 1907 and shook the paper up to dramatic effect. Forty-six years later, *The Times*'s obituary of Hirst described him as having taken over 'a stereotyped paper, then in the seventh decade of its life, designed primarily to instruct the business community'.[1] It was natural that to later generations the sparkling and highly political editorship of Hirst and the tragedy of the manner of his departure should have obscured the solid virtues of his predecessor.

The tendency to underestimate Johnstone was compounded by the effects on the paper of his poor health during his last few years as editor and the loss of some of his finest writers, including Strachey, Clark and Townsend.

Additionally, he had lost his building. In September 1900, 340 Strand had to be vacated to allow its demolition as part of an improvement scheme: the staff moved to Granville House, Arundel Street, Strand, where they stayed until the paper changed hands in 1928. Chapman thought Johnstone settled down 'tolerably well', but shortly afterwards he had a stroke which damaged his arm. He used a dumbbell to try to get back its use, but his condition continued to deteriorate and in Chapman's view he never seemed the same afterwards. However, he managed to carry on until February 1907 and during his last few years the paper still published some combative and entertaining journalism.

Two important new contributors were Talbot Baines and J.E. Woolacott. According to Chapman, Baines wrote a weekly leader on European – and particularly Russian – affairs during Johnstone's last four years: 'He wrote in foolscap sheets in very bad handwriting. He always left his articles until the last minute. I have known him come in on the afternoon of press day and produce two leaders in about four hours.' At a time when Russia was in turmoil domestically and in grave trouble abroad (most notably in a losing war with Japan over Korea), *The Economist*'s coverage was balanced, competent and well-informed – less than memorable, but worth reading. For instance, commenting on the Tsar's failure to respond to a petition from ill-treated workmen, Baines remarked sharply that autocracy, 'like every other form of government, has its special obligations. Under all other forms some channel exists in which those who think themselves oppressed can make their voices heard. There is some Chamber in which the working class have a share of representation, however small, and can, on occasion, make that share audible.'

> In Russia alone there is nothing of the sort; in Russia alone is the Sovereign the sole source, whether of justice or of mercy. And, therefore, in Russia alone has the Sovereign no right to refuse to consider in his own person the prayers of his subjects . . . Even a Czar cannot have things both ways. If he is an autocrat, he must behave as an autocrat, or have his incapacity for his place and function demonstrated to the world.[2]

The Baines line throughout was traditional *Economist*. When the Russian Baltic Squadron, *en route* to the war in the Far East, fired in absurd panic on British trawlers near the Dogger Bank, killing and wounding crewmen, the paper's advice was to be calm but firm. Adequate apologies and compensation would be accepted – otherwise, it might properly be necessary to declare war.[3] As for the divisions rending Russia – the Tsar should see reason, he should ignore his 'reactionist' advisers, institute moderate reforms and cut the ground from under the revolutionaries. Sanity should prevail.

> That in the end the Russian nation will achieve freedom with order may, indeed, be hoped, and with some confidence, expected. Nor does there seem any likelihood that it will ever relapse into the condition of sullen subjection to a despotism working through a corrupt and incompetent bureaucracy from which it has emerged. But the chances . . . that the possession of constitutional liberties might be reached without political and economic convulsion have dismally faded.[4]

Again according to Chapman, J.E. Woolacott, who was on the staff, wrote many of the articles spearheading *The Economist*'s sharp attack on the crusade launched by Joseph Chamberlain in 1903 in favour of imperial protectionism. An able and versatile journalist, for five years Woolacott wrote for the paper every week about two articles and one or two notes. He left at an unspecified date to become City editor of the *Daily Tribune* and later took up a job on the *Statesman* of Calcutta.

There is insufficient evidence to indicate who wrote which of the leaders assailing Chamberlain. Many of them have a wit highly reminiscent of Johnstone: all of them are pugnacious. Certainly, together Johnstone and Woolacott made the paper an effective and brutal weapon in a debate that tore apart the Conservative and Liberal Unionist Parties and seriously damaged their coalition government. Chamberlain triggered it all. In advocating a tariff reform that was to bind the Empire more closely together through preferential duties, Chamberlain had emulated Gladstone by undergoing an apparently sudden change of heart that turned a well-disposed *Economist* into a bitter enemy. It was an issue that had already broken his long friendship with St Loe Strachey.

A.J. Balfour, who had taken over from the ailing Marquess of Salisbury as Prime Minister of the Conservative and Liberal Unionist government in July 1902, tried vainly to avert a Cabinet split. Among those who left the Cabinet in early autumn was Chamberlain, who embarked on a dynamic public campaign that was strongly reminiscent of Gladstone's 20 years earlier.

For more than two years the issue of tariff reform dominated British politics, producing *inter alia* a reunification of the Liberals, who had split over the South African war. Asquith and his fellow-imperialists, who had been calling themselves the Liberal League, came back under the banner of Sir Henry Campbell-Bannerman to fight for free trade. As Chamberlain stumped the country, Asquith followed in his tracks, answering each speech with devastating effectiveness. To the dismay of Chamberlain's followers, even such dedicated Unionists as the Duke of Devonshire (known as Lord Hartington until 1891) chose to give free trade priority over Home Rule and vote Liberal. Nor did *The Economist* hesitate. As it remarked with satisfaction after the Liberals triumphed in the general election of January 1906 with an overall majority of 84: 'The conflict has lain in a very marked degree between Protection and Free-trade. The fiscal policy of the last 60 years has been enthusiastically challenged and enthusiastically defended, and the new Government will do well to bear this fact in mind when they are shaping their programme. Englishmen, as has been said again and again, can only give their minds to one thing at a time.'[5] If Chamberlain were right in saying that the Unionist Party was 'the one effective barrier against Home Rule,' observed another leader, 'Mr Chamberlain is the man who has done most to pull that barrier down. But for him, though the majority might have gone, the party would have remained.

> It would have been strong in the unity of its members and in the ability of its leaders. The disrupting element of Tariff Reform would not have been brought into it, and in the absence of that element one Unionist statesman after another would not have been forced to retire from office, nor would every Unionist member have been made uncertain whether his worst foes might not be those of his own household.[6]

The titles of just a few of the relevant leaders tell of the depth of the paper's hostility. 'THE CANTING AND RECANTING OF MR CHAMBERLAIN',[7] 'THE IMPENDING UNIONIST WRECK',[8] 'MR CHAMBERLAIN'S GYRATIONS'[9] (an article on Chamberlain as 'political prestidigitateur' that provoked a bitterly anti-*Economist* article in the *Scotsman*, which Charles Wilson sent down to Eliza), 'MR CHAMBERLAIN IN DESPERATION',[10] 'MR CHAMBERLAIN'S EQUIVOCATIONS',[11] 'MR CHAMBERLAIN'S INACCURACIES',[12] 'MR CHAMBERLAIN'S RECKLESS PROMISES',[13] 'MR CHAMBERLAIN'S MAKE-BELIEVE',[14] and, just before the 1906 general election, 'MR CHAMBERLAIN'S APPEAL TO CREDULITY'.[15]

When Chamberlain died in 1914, after years of paralysis following a stroke, Francis Hirst, whose devotion to free trade was rock-like, was magnanimous: *The Economist* does not number pettiness among its faults. Having summarised Chamberlain's career and its culmination in overwhelming defeat, followed by the gradual falling away from his tariff reform programme, he wrote that 'even those who are most opposed to it have felt acute sympathy for the sufferings and misfortunes of an extraordinary man, who will rank high among modern politicians for nimbleness in debate, for adroitness in counsel, for power as a platform speaker, and above all, for a courage and resolution which never faltered even when fortune turned irretrievably against him'.[16]

So on the major issues Johnstone did right by his readers to the very end. Yet he was certainly stale, and the paper was badly in need of a transfusion of new talent and fresh ideas. 'The editing of the paper was a little mechanical', recalled Eric Gibb. 'One of the first things the editor said to me after I joined gave me the right line.'

> 'Remember,' he said, 'that if I reprinted this week the corresponding number of last year, nobody would notice it.' That was his pawky humour; but a fair parody of the facts. Every Monday, first thing, we turned out last year's volume to see what advice we had given to the nation twelve months ago; and we were inclined, *mutatis mutandis*, to repeat it. Apart from the saving of labour it ensured a consistent policy, but it had its pitfalls. Once in a note on a firm's results in 1907 I followed the line of 1906, and the firm complained that I was wrong. 'Last year,' it said, 'you made the same mistake and you apologised.' That was true; and so, having repeated last year's mistake in one number, we repeated last year's apology in the next.

(Johnstone had a precedent for repetition. In *The Economist* of 29 February 1848, for instance, 'THE SLAVE TRADE AND SLAVERY' was absolutely identical to an article that had appeared almost three years earlier.[17])

The total staff of *The Economist* when Gibb joined in 1906 amounted to eight: 'but one was sacked for unpunctuality, and then there were seven'. (In 1964, when he wrote his reminiscence, the figure had reached 165 full-timers; in mid-1992 it was 286.) In 1907 Chapman moved from the business side to be the statistical department; he was described by Reggie Forty, who knew him from the late 1930s, as a statistician of 'the scissors and paste brigade'. He would take, for example, clippings from the *Financial Times* about share prices or exchange rates and stick them on a sheet of foolscap paper: if necessary, he would write something that joined the clippings together and made them seem like original *Economist* material. It was, observed Forty, entirely typical of Chapman that his major outside interest was cricket statistics: he knew Wisden back to front.

Chapman collated and calculated for almost 60 years, while around him gifted statisticians like Walter Layton pushed forward the frontiers of the subject. Yet he was invaluable. Roland Bird described him as 'a human computer', who made mistakes only very rarely and who was immensely industrious and cooperative : he was the mainstay of the *Investors' Monthly Manual* until it was wound up in 1930. Pressure from concerned family and *Economist* management persuaded him to retire in 1958, but he kept coming in to the office, armed with his big fountain pen, working away solidly. 'What can we do with Chapman?' asked the desperate editor, Donald Tyerman, of E.M. Webb, who had worked with him for over 40 years. 'He won't go.' It took until 1961 to stop him coming into the office and he died shortly afterwards. Thirty years later some of his contemporaries still feel guiltily that in persuading him to stop working they broke his heart and so caused his death.

David Eric Wilson Gibb joined the editorial staff after the family had given up the dream that young Walter Wilson Greg would follow in the family footsteps: he had chosen instead the path of literary scholarship. Chapman recorded that Greg was an occasional contributor, whose articles were 'of the deeply intellectual and scientific type ... after perusing them, one could justifiably assume that he may have felt that he was not quite suited for the hurly burly of an Editor's life'. The 23-year-old Eric Gibb had no obvious credentials other than being a Wilson relative and son of a trustee. 'I had never written anything for print; had no experience of newspapers; knew almost nothing of finance or economics. But I prepared myself by reading a book on money by Professor Jevons, and it seemed to me that he had put the whole science of political economy into a nutshell, leaving nothing for anyone else to say. The book in fact made a qualified economist of me. But Jevons or no Jevons, mine was a queer appointment.'

In fact Eric Gibb was a very good choice. Although he stayed only for three or four years, leaving to join the insurance firm of Bray Gibb and Co., he was to be a valued friend of the paper for more than 60 years, staying closer to it after its sale in 1928 than any other descendant of the Wilson family. For almost six decades he was an informed, lighthearted commentator on banking, insurance and legal topics and acted as an unofficial supervisor of the paper's general coverage of the insurance business; he also provided sardonic and trenchant pieces on whatever quirky subjects took his fancy. His style was distinctive and amusing, his sense of humour quintessentially English – low-key, ironic, fastidious, discursive and literary. Leafing through old *Economists*, it is always a great pleasure to come across a Gibb article – often, particularly during the rather solemn period of Walter Layton's editorship, the only skittish barque on an ocean of worthiness: satire was far more a feature of Johnstone's paper than that of many of his successors.

Take, for instance, Gibb's contribution to a 1936 episode in the protectionist debate. Following the example of Italy and Switzerland, France had devalued its currency and simultaneously relaxed import restrictions and reduced tariffs; Holland was offering to follow suit if other countries reciprocated. Neville Chamberlain, Chancellor of the Exchequer, instead of offering reciprocity, had announced that no changes were being contemplated in 'the system of very moderate protection which we have established'.[18] In its first leader, 'A CHANCE FOR STATESMANSHIP', *The Economist* had magisterially denounced the British response. The following week Gibb provided 'JEEVES AT THE TREASURY'. Jeeves – known to have been Bertie Wooster's speech-writer – had agreed to help his new boss, the head of the Treasury, with a speech welcoming the adoption by the French of 'the policy we have made our own' – of encouraging international trade and breaking down economic barriers. 'Sort of welcoming the prodigal son, if you follow me.'

> JEEVES: Entirely, sir.
>
> CHIEF: I've got something here that I've jotted down. It goes like this. The event must have come, I say, like the cracking of ice at the approach of a warmer season to the Polar explorer whose ship has been frozen for many months into immobility.
>
> JEEVES: If it would not be taking a liberty to say so, sir, the metaphor, or to speak more correctly the simile, would appear to be strikingly felicitous. Mr Wooster at the height of his faculties as an orator could not unaided have expressed himself with such poetic feeling.
>
> CHIEF: Glad you like it, Jeeves. I thought it wasn't bad myself. Can you think of anything to go with it?
>
> JEEVES: If I might make a suggestion, sir, I would advocate following it up with an extract from the poets.

CHIEF: Got anything in mind?

JEEVES: Yes, sir. I would recommend, after your reference to the ice, that you commit yourself with some firmness to the statement that the hounds of spring are on winter's traces.

CHIEF: Rather neat that. Your own, Jeeves?

JEEVES: The poet Swinburne's, sir. *Floruit circa* 1896. In early life he embraced Republican principles which rendered him unpopular in the Highest Quarter; but subsequently he enjoyed a not inconsiderable vogue, and it would be safe to hazard an excerpt from his works.

The Chief then sought a solution to his difficulty. What if he was misconstrued as meaning that British tariffs and quotas would be reduced? Some people might fail to see the difference between British and foreign quotas and tariffs. Should he simply follow up the cracking ice and the hounds of spring with a declaration that 'if anything is to happen to British tariffs and quotas they are going up'? Jeeves advised against such an uncompromising procedure. Foreigners, being of a sourer disposition than the British, might proclaim themselves suspicious of 'the *bona fides* of His Majesty's Government. Many of them, I understand, are somewhat ill-disposed to British statesmen as a class and have at times gone to the length of openly charging them with hypocrisy.' He recommended 'the employment of what might be termed the *oratio obliqua* rather than the *oratio recta*'. There would be no immediate cause of offence, but later on it would be possible to point to a *caveat*.

JEEVES: Employing the cracking of the ice and the hounds of spring as a *terminus a quo*, or starting point, I would recommend your envisaging the explorer stationed on the deck of his vessel.

CHIEF: Or bridge, Jeeves?

JEEVES: Certainly, sir, on the deck or bridge, whichever you prefer. He is concerned that the ice should crack in the right places. It would, in fact, be foreign to his policy to encourage any cracking of ice to his own detriment. The theme could also be further developed so as to explain, or at least indicate, that HMG contemplated the removal not of all tariffs and quotas, but merely those of an excessive or unjustifiable character. It will, of course, be necessary to state very precisely that none of our tariffs and quotas fall into the latter category. But if any sour-minded foreigners make any ill-advised suggestion for the lowering of British duties, you can invoke your imagery of cracking ice and hounds of spring as equivalent to an emphatic *nolle prosequi*.

    CHIEF: Thank you, Jeeves. Most helpful. It looks as though you are going to be invaluable here.

    JEEVES: I endeavour to give satisfaction, sir.[19]

Like all good satirists, Gibb was enraged by foolishness and injustice and his offensives against idiocies, inefficiencies and injustices perpetrated by the Establishment helped to keep *The Economist*'s image radical. For instance, in 1949, reviewing in a leading article a textbook on criminal law, he gave low marks to lawyers for their contribution to reform, and continued: 'But if there is something to be said for the lawyers there was nothing to be said for the bishops.'

> When Romilly, in 1810, brought in a Bill to abolish the death penalty for 5s. thefts, the Archbishop of Canterbury led six other bishops into the 'No' lobby and contributed seven ecclesiastical mites to the successful defence of savagery. The record of the Anglican Church, says Mr Radzinowicz, is that it never led in any important movement for reform. When one contemplates the wrongheadedness of the governing classes, one can only say that Parliament and the ecclesiastics allowed to the Society of Friends and men in the humbler ranks of society a monopoly, in this province, both of statesmanship and of Christianity.[20]

Politicians and bureaucrats fared no better. In 1948 he explained the deficiencies of contemporary legislation thus: 'Parliament half bakes a Bill and calls it an Act. A civil servant finds a bit of it that is underdone. It is pushed, unobtrusively, back into the oven, re-emerges for a moment and returns for another cooking when the next chunk of raw dough is discovered.'[21]

    The dottier aspects of English law were a constant stimulation to Gibb. There was the absolute legal requirement that an alderman of the City of London – 'decorative in silk breeches and frills' – be on the premises while trials were being held at the Old Bailey: 'let him step out of the building for five minutes and the engine of the law seizes up'.[22] In 'BEAUTY AND THE BENCH' he discussed the requirement in fatal injury claims for the judge to assess a widow's remarriage prospects: 'The plaintiff goes into the witness box and the judge in the discharge of his duty has a good look at her. He may like her appearance, or he may find her unpleasing. Opinions will differ, and naturally some judges are better judges in this sphere than other judges; but each must do his best in the light of his own taste and experiences. He must mark the plaintiff's looks to the best of his ability.' If she gets only gamma minus, she will win full damages; beta or beta plus would cut them by 20% or so.

> In the rare event of an alpha or alpha plus stepping into the box, the judge is in a cruel predicament. As a man of the world he surmises that before her marriage the plaintiff had a queue of suitors. As a man of sentiment he knows that many young men must have remained single for her sake, still carrying through the years her image in their hearts. Remarriage will certainly be open to her as soon as she wishes it, and it looks as though the judge must stifle his feelings, knock 100 per cent off the dependency value and award no damages at all.

The lesson was clear. For weeks or months before the action a good-looking young plaintiff should concentrate on her appearance, scouring the shops for the most unbecoming and ill-fitting dress; the colours should clash – 'they cannot fight each other too fiercely for her purpose'; she should eschew the hairdresser and borrow a pair of glasses with very thick lenses.

> Nature may have given her a voice like Cordelia's, but she must try to shout her evidence raucously and make her answers to counsel's questions as waspish as possible. If, when she leaves the box, the judge says to himself 'what a dreadful woman', she will have scored a triumph and secured her hundred per cent.[23]

(The other side of that particular coin was illustrated by the effect Dr Mary Archer's appearance had in 1987 on the judge presiding over the libel action her husband Jeffrey took against the *Star* newspaper. The judge's description of her as 'fragrant' and the implication of his summing-up that no man married to a woman of such attractions could have, as the *Star* had alleged, visited a prostitute, was to cause general hilarity: indeed, five years on, the word 'fragrant' is usually used by the British chattering classes jocosely. *The Economist*'s sardonic 'UNFRAGRANT' commenced with a parody of Humbert Wolfe's classic verse ('You cannot hope / To bribe or twist / Thank God! / The British journalist / But seeing what / That man will do / Unbribed, there's no occasion to').

> You cannot hope with bribes to budge
> The strict, impartial British judge,
> But seeing what the chap will say
> Unbribed, who needs to anyway?

Not Mr Jeffrey Archer, for one. It would have taken a contrary-minded jury to resist the summing-up in the libel case that ended on July 24th in a unanimous verdict and £500,000 damages for him . . . at the expense of the *Star* newspaper. Most libel plaintiffs against newspapers win their suit. But no man has ever earned more, from the gutter press or anyone else, for not visiting a prostitute. And not many judges have ever shown a jury more clearly than did Mr Justice Caulfield what he thought and they ought to think of the press, the prostitute and the rival versions of the non-affair set before them.[24]

Account books surviving for the period 1917–28 show that Gibb wrote on average six or seven articles a year: during the year from 5 April 1941, the date from which the earliest surviving contributors' book starts, he wrote five. By the early 1960s he was down to a couple a year and his last appears to have been his 1964 reminiscences of 1906. Having written for the paper for so long, Chapman had observed 20 years earlier, 'his personality can be said to have welded itself into The Economist'. A modest shareholder from 1929, when the paper changed hands, he was appointed in 1934 to the board of directors, on which he served for over 30 years.

Chapman considered that Gibb's combination of common sense and writing ability would have made him an excellent editor, 'but the tide of destiny' swept him instead into insurance-broking. He was briefly *de facto* editor. 'Not very long after I joined the staff,' he recalled when he was over 80, 'a series of mishaps made me for a few weeks acting editor of the paper, and anything could have happened.'

> But the good old system held, and we turned out the standard articles, telling the world in one number what to think of the Kaiser, the new reign in China, the gold in the Bank of France, the state of the Australian Stock Exchange, the nitrate industry and the position in Ambula. Where it all came from and where Ambula is Heaven only knows. But nobody complained.[25]

According to Chapman, in February 1907 Johnstone 'literally just drifted out of the office. I heard nothing of him. He did not, as far as I am aware, correspond with any one at the office during the remaining five [sic] years of his life.' Eliza Bagehot sent a wreath when he died in December 1913.

Eliza's diary for 1907 is missing, so there is no record of the prolonged deliberations about Johnstone's successor. During the seven-month interregnum that followed, the paper was in the charge of the assistant editor, the lovable and hard-working Walter William Wright, who kept Johnstone's editorial machine running with the help of Gibb and the freelancers; even Walter Wilson Greg weighed in with a couple of leading articles. Chapman believed that Wright, who had been on the staff for almost a quarter of a century and had been Johnstone's assistant for 15 years, hoped to be editor; but, unsurprisingly, the trustees and proprietors were looking for a fresh start.

'The Trustees of The Economist', commented Chapman with considerable understatement, 'were not a body that did things in a hurry.' Speculation was rife during several months of interregnum and the announcement of the appointment of the 34-year-old Francis Wrigley Hirst caused great surprise in the office. Wright seemed to take it to heart, said Chapman; 'soon after his health broke down, and he died in November 1908 at 52 years of age'.

Hirst's credentials for the job were splendid. The son of a prosperous Yorkshire wool-stapler, through his mother he was a second cousin of Asquith, whose elder brother was Hirst's housemaster at Clifton. In 1891 he won an open scholarship in classics to Wadham College, Oxford, where his brilliance (he took a double first in classics) was matched by his popularity; in 1896 he was elected President of the Union. He was a glittering figure and the best scholar among the remarkable Wadham generation that included F.E. Smith (from 1922, Lord Birkenhead – Lord Chancellor 1919–22, Secretary of State for India 1924–28) and John Simon (from 1940 Viscount Simon, Home Secretary, 1915–16 and 1935–37, Foreign Secretary, 1931–35, and Chancellor of the Exchequer, 1937–40), who were to be Hirst's lifelong friends despite their very different political views.[26] Although he was to be notorious throughout his life for unbending principles, Hirst also possessed a genius for friendship: his innumerable friends included academics, chess-players, economists, fishermen, politicians, tennis-players and writers, obscure and famous. *F.W. Hirst By his Friends*, published in 1958 five years after his death, included affectionate assessments by the great classicist and peace campaigner, Gilbert Murray, by the US ex-President Herbert Hoover and by Arthur Ransome, the famous children's novelist. 'His friends put up with, from him, what they would not tolerate in others,' wrote his friend and *Economist* colleague, Molly Hamilton, in 1944, 'because he is not only an individual of delightful distinctness but endowed with a very high degree of personal charm, as well as a "pawky" humour there is no resisting. It is one of his most attractive traits that, rigid as he is in doctrine and capable of bearing gladly the most shocking bores if they have the right opinions, he sticks to his friends through thick and thin, and forgives them every kind of deviation: once accepted, you can think pretty well what you like.'[27]

At Oxford an important influence for a future editor of *The Economist* had been Francis Ysidro Edgeworth, originally a classicist, by now Drummond Professor of Political Economy, who had recently given up the Tooke Professorship of Economic Science and Statistics at King's College, London. Edgeworth, whose economic thought had been much influenced by Stanley Jevons and, later, Alfred Marshall, viewed economics from a mathematical perspective and was an inspiration for the development of the formal and mathematical treatment of economic theory. 'He was', said John Maynard Keynes, 'a man of the highest gifts and greatness of nature which failed in some way of complete fruition.'[28] So he founded no school, but he made a major contribution to the measurement of economic value through the use of index numbers. He excited the attention of the young Hirst and 'encouraged me to write an article for Palgrave's *Dictionary of Political Economy* on the "Tabular Standard" by way of supplement to his own admirable article on "Index Numbers"'.[29]

After Oxford, Hirst spent some time at the London School of Economics and in 1899, like Bagehot and Lathbury before him, was called to the Bar. Unlike them, he practised for a while, but soon realised the law was not his *métier*: he had no capacity for detachment. His passionate interests were politics and economics; his talent was writing. He wrote with the clarity of the classical scholar, and took as his guideline the dictum of that great journalist John Morley: 'The first business of a writer is to make his meaning plain. Style without lucidity is an offence.'

In politics, Hirst was firmly in the tradition of Cobden and Bright, to whose political views he was even closer than had been James Wilson, whose support for the Crimean War had alienated them. He had won the Cobden Prize essay competition in 1899, was a leading member of the Cobden Club and the main progenitor of *Fact versus Fiction*, its 1904 onslaught on Joe

Chamberlain's 'raging, tearing campaign' for tariff reform. The previous year he married Cobden's great-niece, Helena; they were later to live in Dunford House, Cobden's old home in Sussex. Their doormat read 'Peace, Free Trade and Goodwill'.

While editor of *The Economist* Hirst stood for parliament in a Suffolk consituency. 'I well remember', wrote Chapman, 'how excited I felt at the prospect of Mr Hirst entering Parliament. When he went down to Sudbury for the six weeks' canvass he used to take with him small pamphlets he had prepared. I well remember one entitled "Unfurling The Standard at Haverhill". In it Mr Hirst indulged in poetry which told the electors what a Tariff Reform policy would mean to them. It was just a few lines as follows:–

> They will tax your meat. They will tax your bread
> They will tax your clothes. They will tax your bed
> They will raise the prices of all that you buy
> Your wages will fall and your wife will cry
> When you can't get food and you can't get warm
> You'll know the meaning of Tariff Reform.

But alas Mr Hirst's message did not prove acceptable to the electorate of Sudbury and he did not get elected for Parliament. This did not dismay him as he still had his pen and he soon got down to his criticisms of what he regarded as injustices in the conduct of public affairs.'

Hirst's grandfather had once said to Hirst's father: 'Alfred, always be against war; nine times out of ten you will be right, and the other time it will not matter.' This was a precept fully accepted by his grandson Francis, whose sister Helen observed that he 'agreed with Sydney Smith that "the greatest curse which can be entailed upon mankind is a state of war"'. Consequently Hirst hated imperialism, which he believed to be a threat to peace, violently opposed the Boer War and was a founder member of the 'League of Liberals against Aggression and Militarism'. His triplet of modern villains at this time were Rhodes, Chamberlain and Milner. Gladstone, whom he had heard speak at Oxford, Sir Henry Campbell-Bannerman, leader of the anti-war Liberals, who said of imperialism: 'I hate the word and I hate the thing', and the high-minded and uncompromising Lord Morley were his triplet of modern heroes. Gladstone was a hero also for his fiscal policy and achievements, of which Hirst had an unrivalled knowledge. To a popular life of Gladstone by Wemyss Reid, Hirst had contributed some chapters on

Gladstone's commercial and financial record, based on a thorough study of parliamentary debates. Morley, who was writing a vast life of Gladstone, then employed Hirst to read and analyse all the financial memoranda and correspondence in the archive at Hawarden Castle. This material ultimately formed the basis for *Gladstone as Financier and Economist*, which Hirst published in 1931;* in the meantime, like his interest in statistics, it was an indication of his intellectual rigour and a splendid preparation for editing *The Economist*.

By 1907, Hirst was a highly regarded writer and journalist. Starting while still at Oxford with a contribution to the much-talked-about *Essays in Liberalism*, of which he was also joint-editor, he followed with *Local Government in England* (with his Austrian lawyer friend Franz Josef Redlich), *Adam Smith*, *Trusts and Cartels*, and, anonymously, *Arbiter in Council*, an analysis of the economic follies of war. Additionally, he had written regularly for the anti-war *Speaker*, edited by his friend the great journalist J.L. Hammond. In mid-1906 it was bought by the Joseph Rowntree Social Service Trust (Cocoa Quakers, like the Cadburys), who initially intended to make Hirst editor: in the event the editorial appointment was delayed and early in 1907 given to the legendary H.W. Massingham, under whom the *Speaker* was metamorphosed as the *Nation*.

It was Morley who recommended Hirst.[30] It was said at the time, recalled Chapman, that when Morley was told he would have made a good Chancellor of the Exchequer he was said to have retorted that the same purpose would be served by making Hirst editor of *The Economist*.

Despite Morley's unflinching support for Home Rule (at this time safely on the back burner) and a view of the world far more radical than that of the early-twentieth-century *Economist*, his protégé was accepted. Hirst's warmth and charm were to make him very important to the sisters, whom he called 'The Dear Old Ladies'; references to visits, postcards and letters from 'Mr Hirst' are frequent in the diary of Eliza, who was 75 in 1907. 'I well remember my meeting with Mr Hirst when he visited the office for the first time', recorded Chapman. 'He was rather powerfully built, tall with very fair hair. He seemed very pleasant . . . Mr Hirst was one of the illustrious band of liberal journalists prominent at that time . . . My own feeling was that the

---

*He was the second *Economist* editor to have written a book on the Grand Old Man: Lathbury's *Mr Gladstone* (London, 1907) was a short ecclesiastical biography.

Trustees of The Economist had made an excellent choice for their new Editor. Mr Hirst was young with the promise of a good number of years before him and just the right age to develop and further enhance the reputation of the paper. Mr Hirst was a man of strong convictions with no axe to grind and one felt that he would always call a spade a spade.'

He certainly did that: there was no fudging of opinion in Hirst's paper. But from the outset, there were signs of his fundamental deficiency as a journalist and political commentator: he had a completely closed mind, having, as his friend and ex-colleague Molly Hamilton put it in 1944, 'a notable ability to close his eyes to events, feelings and developments . . . a faculty specially marked in the economic sphere. *Laissez-faire*, for him, is a religion.'[31] Or, as another contemporary wrote sourly in 1937 of pre-war Oxford: 'We listened with detached sympathy to . . . the do-nothing economists represented then, as to-day, by Mr Francis Hirst.'[32]

It was a suitable opening to his editorship that in his very first week, one of his leading articles was called 'THE TRIUMPH OF THE HORSE'. As befitted the gifted classicist that he was, he told of how scholars 'who contend with perennial ferocity generation after generation as to whether there was any such person as Homer, enter with equal fury into the equally insoluble problem whether Homer, or the person or persons who wrote the Homeric poems, had ever seen a horse ridden by a man in the ordinary way'. More important was the fact that primitive man's first use of the animal was to harness it to a chariot. 'In other words, the first and most wonderful invention of all, an invention as important to transit by land as the oar, the rudder, and the sail to transit by sea, was the invention of the wheel. From this everything sprang, the cart, the carriage, the railway train, the bicycle, and the motor car.'

When railways were introduced, most people believed the horse to be doomed. 'Never has scientific foresight been more completely deceived. Every new railway gave new employment to horses and for every animal that was taken out of a stage coach, two or three extra ones were required to bring to and fro from railway stations goods and produce that had never before been able to find a market.' Yet with the arrival of the motor-bus and the motor-car 'the sentence of commercial death did seem at last to have been passed upon the horse', which seemed likely to be gradually driven, first from the streets of the town and then from the roads of the country. A few surviving steam ploughs and harrows might linger on backward farms, and 'in the parks of great landed proprietors horses and ponies might still provide innocent recreation for country gentlemen'. Yet once again the horse was coming through triumphantly. Luckless investors had had a severe lesson: 'We cannot help feeling a little ashamed of the critical ability of the hardheaded race of Englishmen, and the still harderheaded race of Scots, when we read the statement made at the meeting of the London General Omnibus Company . . . that no motor omnibus has yet been invented that can be made to pay. It seems rather astounding that among all the new companies which were floated, and among all the old companies which gave out huge orders for motor-cars, not a man could be found capable of arriving by a simple calculation at the fact that the new vehicles could not possibly be made to pay.' There was now a significant revival in the demand for horses. 'Well-to-do people who sold their carriages and converted their coachman into a chauffeur are now reverting to the more ancient mode of conveyance. They find, apparently, that speed may be bought at too high a price, and we are informed that job-masters, cab proprietors, saddlers and other "ruined industries" are beginning to hold up their heads again. It is an ill wind that blows nobody any good.'[33] (Johnstone, 30 years his senior, had had a motor-car and chauffeur for a decade.)

'For him the world about 1860–70 had the shape it ought to have,' said Molly Hamilton, 'and he somehow convinced himself that this shape could be brought back, or rather, that in fact it now existed if only people would open their eyes and not entertain ridiculous notions.' In 1912 'THE VALUE OF SPEED' summed that up. In transport, the railway train and electric traction (trams and underground trains) were a good thing: 'mechanical invention had done vast good with few, if any, disadvantages to balance'.

> The melancholy foreboding of old-fashioned conservatives like the Duke of Wellington, to whom railways spelt national decadence and ruin, proved almost wholly unfounded . . . Almost equally wonderful and beneficial was the bicycle, a supplementary boon which has immensely extended the activity and range of active people. At first the bicycle was a fashionable luxury of the rich; now it is a means of innocent and healthy enjoyment for all classes, and an indispensable necessary of daily life to many for whom this time-saving machine provides profitable work at a distance from their homes. The cycle is also a factor in distribution – invaluable to shopkeepers who cannot afford a horse and trap.

But two later inventions had brought 'no such certain or unmixed gain'. The motor car 'gives far more pain than pleasure, far more annoyance than comfort . . . the benefits of the few are obtained at an utterly disproportionate cost to the many'. The sight of 'motor-car luxury' incited labour unrest.

> Of the flying machine, it may be said that so far it offers all the disadvantages
> of the motor-car with none of the advantages. The high flier may commit
> either suicide or homicide, or both. If he tries his luck often he is sure to
> come to grief. Its only claim so far to consideration is that it has added, like
> the submarine, to the horrors and terrors of modern warfare.[34]

(Hirst's consistency was awe-inspiring. In 1945 he was still wholly antipathetic to the motor-car, 'the most pernicious of modern inventions'.)[35]

Hirst was in fact a perfect example of Bagehot's definition of a Conservative: 'While the Liberal turn of mind denotes the willingness to admit new ideas, and the perfect impartiality with which those ideas, when admitted, are canvassed and considered, the Conservative turn of mind denotes adhesiveness to the early and probably inherited ideas of childhood, and a very strong and practically effective distrust of the novel intellectual suggestions which come unaccredited by any such influential associations.'[36]

This passage appeared in 'THE CONSERVATIVE VEIN IN MR BRIGHT', an article inspired by a powerful speech made in 1876 against the enfranchising of women by the crusader for universal male suffrage. Six years later, in a tribute to Bright, another *Economist* leader-writer considered his 40 years of absolute consistency in public life. Unlike most men of unbending conviction, he had neither been left behind by the march of events, nor ended his career as others did 'by fatiguing their contemporaries with the monotonous iteration of familiar catch-words and worn-out formulae'. This was because Bright had started so far in advance of the current opinion of his own generation 'that he has never been passed, or even overtaken'.[37] The problem with Hirst was that he had started behind his own generation and applied to every changing event the beliefs of Cobden and Bright, which he held to be immutable. Female suffrage was a classic case.

CHAPTER XXX:

The editorial dame

By what strange artifice or cosmic whim,
By what upheaval of the natural frame,
By what deep surgings on the horizon dim
Emerged at length the Editorial Dame?

. . .

Into a world where Adam reigned supreme;
Into a sphere where prejudice dies hard,
By infiltration or such subtle scheme
She forced his hand and played the fateful card.

And if at times her clothes seemed rather queer,
Her hair untidy or her skirt askew,
She yet achieved the object held so dear:
The chance to air a woman's point of view.

With stately poise and erudition sure,
With strident voice and self assurance blind,
She demonstrated to the more demure
The sweet omniscience of a super mind.

And if each day she disappeared from view
(Her absence marked by silence hard to bear)
Perhaps she'd found a neighb'ring tannic brew
To share with colleagues equally 'aware'.

Or in some restaurant smart, or grand hotel, –
Behind a 'bombe suprême' or glass of wine,

Had thrilled an audience privileged to dwell
On implications human and divine.

And if, because of this, she seemed to show
Some slight contempt for those outside her 'set',
Her sense of things mundane is clearly slow;
(She's not thrown off her 'authorism' yet!)

But with the mellowed influences of time,
These less attractive moods may pass away,
And then (oh! thought voluptuous and sublime)
These able ladies will have come to stay!

'THE EDITORIAL DAME', *undated, by 'Hopeful', an anonymous* Economist *poet*

It was not until the 1920s, under the feminist Walter Layton, that *The Economist* made up its mind finally about the rights and the role of women. From then onwards it was consistently to be in advance of public opinion in its editorial line. After 1938, under Geoffrey Crowther's editorship, it put its policies into practical effect: women were given encouragement and opportunities remarkable in the newspaper world. Crowther not only liked and respected women; he recognised them to be cost-effective. 'You can get a first-class woman', he used to point out, 'for the price of a second-class man.' Anonymity helped: it is difficult to imagine that in the 1940s and 1950s, the overwhelmingly male readership would have received with equanimity the information that a high proportion of the paper's journalists were women: indeed the American Survey, from its inception in 1942, was always predominantly female. Individual women built up their own networks and broke down prejudice inside and outside the paper, step by step. Mary Goldring (Oxford), who joined in 1949 with experience as a technical journalist, was taken on to write about industry from the point of view of changing manufacturing practices. She was the only woman in the business section – 'the back of the paper'. When one of her supercilious young fellow-journalists at an early editorial meeting instructed her to fetch something, Roland Bird, the business editor, told him never to speak to her like that again. Quickly she found a niche on technical matters, having to combat not only the male chauvinism within industry but also the view of the majority of management that journalists should use the tradesmen's entrance.

Goldring dealt with this by dressing and acting grandly: her clothes were couturier and her manner assured. Starting as the dustbin, who was given all the jobs the young men despised, she invented the job of air and science correspondent, learned the hard way about the enormous technical advances of the 1950s and by the time the young men had realised that aviation, atomic power and so on were exciting, she was unchallengeable. She found a whole new readership and source of advertising for the paper, enraged the aircraft industry by the strength of her criticisms (she was, for instance, a prime enemy of Concorde, which she thought not a good enough aircraft for the money), caused arguments at board meetings between Lord Drogheda (fighting the corner of the highly effective aircraft lobby) and Donald Tyerman, who defended her strongly, and was to stay for 25 years, the last eight as business editor; her post-*Economist* life has been as a distinguished BBC presenter and freelance economist. Mary Goldring's pioneering work in explaining the unfamiliar in terms the ordinary reader could understand created the climate which spawned the Science and Technology section.

Until Layton's arrival, though the paper was often quite radical in its ideas about women's talents, rights and prospects, there was little consistency – no agreed dogma. More than with the majority of controversies, what most counted were the personal idiosyncrasies, experiences and attitudes of the proprietors and editors. The relationships that Wilson, Greg, Bagehot and Hutton had in their various ways with the Wilson girls made their own contribution. While the prevalence of headaches and other ailments no doubt bore out the prevailing view of intellectual Victorians that the female nervous system was extremely delicate, the sisters' intelligence, range of intellectual interests and their considerable knowledge of politics meant that they were taken much more seriously than many of their contemporaries – hence the forays into print of Julia and Eliza in *The Economist*, Zoe in the quarterlies and Emilie in biography and fiction.

In the paper in the early days, women were rarely discussed. Greg occasionally gave vent to horrified expostulation at the notion that woman might wish to abandon her 'sacred sphere'. He became particularly excited in 1850 at the news that some American women wanted equal access to professions. Would they give up their noble calling as wives and mothers 'to become incompetent surgeons – third-rate physicians – shallow lawyers – wordy, inconsiderate, and excitable senators – hasty, impulsive, and dis- credited ministers of state?' Yet he was in favour of reform of unjust aspects of the law of property, divorce, and child custody.[1] Thomas Hodgskin pondered what to do about the grim time some women were having in their sacred sphere. In 'A HINT. – CRUELTY TO WOMEN', in 1853, he reflected on the huge daily volume of police reports concerning the fining or imprisoning of men for violence towards women, and worried that 'the classes who habitually ill-treat women' were unlikely to see such reports, since they rarely read newspapers. In a conclusion typical of his attitude to punishment, he argued that: 'It is in truth little better than a waste of suffering – a sort of gratuitous cruelty – to inflict punishment as an example, and not make the infliction known. We would hint, therefore, to all concerned, that every instance of punishment for ill-treating women should be shortly but emphatically described by the police authorities, printed on large posting bills, and displayed on the walls and thoroughfares of all places where it is likely to be useful . . . The State neglects its duty much more by not carefully spreading this instruction amongst them than by not establishing schools and teaching some people the rudiments of the arts.'[2]

It was not until Bagehot became editor that serious attention was given to the status of women, not only because issues such as female education and suffrage were on the agenda by then, but also because his fascination with human character caused him frequently to dwell on the distinctions between, and relationships of, men and women.

He believed women to be clever, but to have two major intellectual deficiencies. First was their innate delicacy: exposure to 'an outspoken literature' could have an extremely pernicious effect on the delicate 'moral constitution of the female mind'.[3] Second was the female inability to think in abstractions.[4] But after prolonged exposure to myriad intelligent women, he began to allow for the possibility of progress: if a woman was 'placed in an intellectual atmosphere, in which political or other important subjects are currently passing, you will probably find that she can talk better upon them than you can, without you being able to explain whence she derived either her information or her talent'.[5] Even the problem of abstractions could be overcome up to a point, he had decided by 1864: a woman's mind 'could comprehend abstractions when they were unrolled and explained before it but it never naturally created them; never of itself, and without external obligation, devoted itself to them'.[6]

Bagehot wrote about women with a rare sympathy: few men of his generation would have shown such understanding as he did in his 1862 essay about the great letter-writer, Lady Mary Wortley Montagu, whom he described as 'that most miserable of human beings, an ambitious and wasted woman'.[7] His *Economist* articles on women's issues were to become increasingly radical. Take, for instance, in 1868, 'THE PROPERTY OF MARRIED WOMEN', in which he dealt briskly with the opposition to a bill to give married women the same rights over their property as single women. (In the Wilson family, Bagehot had experience of marriage settlements. In his capacity as *de facto paterfamilias* in 1874 he was to take his duty so seriously that he held up the wedding of his friend W.R. Greg to Julia Wilson until the mislaid marriage settlement was found.) This bill, he said, 'seems to be thought by some of our contemporaries a very fearful omen of the revolutionary temper of the times . . . We confess we are not in the least alarmed.'

There was an excellent precedent, Bagehot wrote: the Northern states of America had almost all adopted this principle, without any injury to the family. Interestingly, one advantage which he cited about the removal of what he calls 'the very unwise and unjust proprietary disabilities under which married women are placed' was to make married women less protected: in acquiring power over their own property they would be obliged to take responsibility for their own debts. 'We do not doubt that this new care will seem at first a very great burden to Englishwomen of the middle class educated in English ways of thinking. It will seem to take much of the softness and safety from their lives. It will possibly diminish the charm of manner which belongs to a protected existence – the charm which women share at present with children. But we do not doubt that it will, on the whole, give more to women than it takes away. The sense of responsibility in which they are so often wanting is a great training for character.'[8]

Toughening women up was a theme to which he returned with increasing frequency, as he did to the idea that it was urgent to discover 'what women's special qualifications *are* for practical life, by doing all in our power to develop those feminine powers which have hitherto lain idle for want of culture'. He backed enthusiastically the proposal to set up a women's college at Cambridge; women needed to be taught the habit of independent study. 'If lads are too seldom encouraged to grope their own way through difficult subjects without being prompted and led at every turn, we may say that girls are never encouraged to do anything of the sort at all – nay, that they scarcely ever have the opportunity of doing so, since the habit of their intellectual as of their moral education has been the attitude of *dependence*, instead of the attitude of original enquiry and research . . .'

> There has been, and is still, an idea that a girl is more 'feminine' if she waits passively to be 'told' her way through a difficulty, than if she applies her whole energies to unravel it for herself; and everything, both in her external surroundings and her moral relations, is usually adapted to increase and deepen the sense of dependence, which almost ranks indeed as a feminine virtue . . . it seems reasonable to suggest that *all* intellectual culture, so far as it is really intellectual, aims at removing this absolute dependence on authority, and at teaching the intellect to trust laws rather than persons.

What women needed more than the intellectual conditions were the moral conditions of creative force – 'the habit of sounding their own mental problems for themselves, of judging rapidly for themselves in emergency, of relying upon themselves to prosecute a train of thought or study once begun'. Therefore *The Economist* 'earnestly' desired to see this educational experiment 'fairly made'.[9]

In 1865 Bagehot had rejected John Stuart Mill's call for female suffrage as impractical, for 'out of the two or three million women who he would thus endow – including half-a-million of maid-servants – not above ten thousand would have any political opinions at all, or any *political preferences* for one candidate over another; and that in consequence to give them votes would merely be giving extra votes vicariously to their fathers, their husbands, their masters, their lovers, or their priests'.[10] Only three years later, *The Economist* was discussing women's suffrage seriously. 'Is there evidence that political prudence, political sagacity, and political conviction are sufficiently widely-spread amongst women, or any class of women, to make their votes an element of value to the state? If so, such of them as can be fairly assumed to possess these qualities should have the franchise.'[11]

Five years later again, in 1870, John Bright's brother, Jacob, introduced a bill to allow rated female householders to vote: it passed a second reading. Bagehot committed *The Economist* to female suffrage:

> No doubt the notion of women having votes is a very considerable innovation; it is contrary to recognized usages and habits in a more than ordinary degree; as in all questions between the sexes, there is a difficulty in making them the subject of common reasoning at all – people taking for

granted that the settled rule is the law of nature, and having a difficulty in conceiving any substantial change in the common relations of life. But the innovating tendency is now so strong as to have overcome this initial difficulty; people are really willing to review the inveterate custom by which women have been kept from voting, as well as other customs which regulate their legal and social position.[12]

There were no valid reasons to object to the bill. It removed an anomaly; at worst it would add only a small number 'to the mass of indifferent and corrupt voters'; and if the measure led to a more general suffrage for women it would be because the experience proved to be favourable, and that would be a good undeniable reason for change. He also made a point which could have been tellingly used against his own women-folk in the anti-suffrage position they took up after his death; 'it is said that women of the class to whom the Bill applies do not, as a rule, care for votes. We see no sufficient evidence for this, no evidence certainly that there is not a large number who would care; but if it were true, the opinion of the class has little to do with it. It is a question mainly of individual privilege, and we should obviously be careful how we permit some tax payers not only to forgo their own privileges, but those also of their neighbours.'[13]

The more thought Bagehot gave to the question of women, the more radical he became. In 1874 he chided those who were fearful of the decision of the Convocation of the University of London to open degrees to women; 'One would suppose by what one reads that what the University had done was to force women into duties for which they are totally unfitted, and into the midst of the conflicts of public life.' In fact change would come about gradually: a few able and enterprising women, who might otherwise take up 'rash movements', would have their minds opened. Higher education bred moderation. Education would make women less, not more, forward and presumptuous. 'Of course we do not mean that a higher education will not qualify the women who gain it to do much that at present they cannot do; nor that many of the new occupations for which they will be so qualified will not be occupations now monopolised by men. That is a result not only to be expected, but to be greatly desired.'

Women were already immensely important in nursing and midwifery and should be trained for full efficiency. They were also particularly well suited to treating women's and children's diseases. They were recognised as 'admirable telegraphic operators and might be equally admirable analytic chemists and apothecaries'. He denounced the idea that education would make women less feminine. 'Is it ignorance which causes feminine grace, or rather, which prevents it?' The University of London should go ahead. 'The frivolity of women is one of the greatest causes of vice and frivolity in men. If we can but have a generation of women somewhat less dull, and somewhat less inclined to devote themselves to silly occupations, we hope that not only their children but their husbands and brothers will be the gainers.'[14]

The paper held to his line when, a few weeks after his death, parliament approved of the granting of medical diplomas to women, leaving doctors feeling indignantly 'that they are selected for a sort of special disgrace, by being thus made what someone termed the *corpus vile* on which the experiment of enlarged calling for women should be tried'. *The Economist* leader reiterated the Bagehot theme about women complementing men rather than competing with them, and called for the opening-up to women of all suitable diplomas and degrees. The importance of giving women access to teaching at the highest level was stressed, for there were 'no better, because more patient teachers than women'. And, carelessly proffering a splendid piece of *Economist* esoterica, it cited the case of a woman in Dublin who had been by far 'the best "coach" in nautical astronomy to be found in the Irish capital, yet she had, and at that time could have had, no degree to attest her competence to the world'. In law, if they mastered the dry technicalities, women could make admirable conveyancers, or even advisers on equity and on commercial law. As for medicine, the difficulties of risking serious wounds to women's delicacy had already been surmounted in nursing.[15]

The following year, intervening in the heated controversy as to whether men and women should be educated separately or together, the paper came down once more on the radical side: 'If female education is ever to be well arranged, women and men must learn to understand, to gauge, and to respect each other's intellects, and this they will never do till they have been subjected to the tests of a similar education, and have found out the precise points upon which their capacities are either different or unequal, the exact finger post at which they ought to part in the race of educational life. Only in competing for the same degrees can this priceless discovery be made.'[16]

But although the Bagehot line was held on women's education and on the Married Women's Property Act,[17] female suffrage was a different matter. The Wilson girls had been in favour of female education; Eliza was a benefactor of two Cambridge women's colleges – Girton and Newnham – and Emilie was much involved in pressing for the opening up to women of trades and professions. Yet the sisters all set their faces against female suffrage or any form of female involvement in politics. The issue had disappeared from the public view in the 1870s, but it reasserted itself in the mid-1880s. In February 1886 Eliza rejected an invitation to join the Women's Liberal Association, and when Millicent Fawcett asked her to join the General Committee for Women's Suffrage in 1889 she refused. Eliza, Julia and Emilie were three of the 104 signatories to the 'Appeal against Female Suffrage' which appeared in the June 1889 issue of *Nineteenth Century*; Sophie signed a later appeal, and the sisters' biographer suggests that neither Matilda nor Zoe had the necessary status to have their signatures sought.[18]

The following month Mrs Fawcett published in the same journal 'Female Suffrage: A Reply'. She cited in support of her case many of the men who had had 'the most formative influence on the current of thought, political or otherwise, in England during the last twenty-five years', including John Stuart Mill, Charles Darwin and Walter Bagehot.[19]

This cut no ice with the ladies or with their paper; perhaps 'dear Walter' was tacitly believed to have gone too far. When the suffragette campaign hotted up in the 1890s, *The Economist* stated its position with admirable clarity. 'PARLIAMENT AND FEMALE SUFFRAGE' responded to the presentation of a petition to the House of Commons with the opening line: 'We have no sympathy with the cause of female suffrage.' Should such a 'legislative revolution' come about 'under existing conditions, the country would at once declare that its mandate had been misread'. The tactics of the advocates of female suffrage were deplorable: 'It is neither reasonable nor decorous for petitioners to scold Parliament as to the proper exercise of its legislative functions, and to attempt to force it to take a particular line of action.'[20]

Once Bagehot's influence had faded, the paper had lost interest in women's place in society: no substantial articles had appeared for almost 20 years prior to this one. However, the suffragette movement was busily putting the issue back on the agenda.

If women barely existed for Edward Johnstone's *Economist*, they were a vital influence on Francis Hirst's. Not only did his editorship coincide with the high point of suffragette agitation, but one of the small team of journalists he recruited was Mary Agnes Hamilton, known at Newnham College,

Cambridge, as a powerful debater and seasoned controversialist with a taste for 'clear hard thinking' and a dislike of sentimentality; in 1929 she was to become a Labour MP and Clement Attlee's well-regarded Parliamentary Private Secretary. Hirst was happy with able women: two of his sisters were of high academic distinction and held university teaching posts, and his wife, to whom he was very happily married, was charming, intelligent and outgoing. But no one could convert him from the view that women were in essence irrational and therefore should not be allowed the vote.

In *The Economist* Hirst fought the suffrage movement with two main arguments. The first was that it would be undemocratic 'that a political revolution of the first magnitude, which would place the present electors in a minority in almost every constituency of the United Kingdom, should be rushed through a Parliament elected not at all on this issue under the aegis of a Premier [Asquith] who stoutly declared his opposition to the project at the last election'.[21] 'A true democrat,' responded a reader in the following week's issue, 'it seems to me, is merely one who holds that every person who has the misfortune to live in a particular country has, naturally, the right to a voice in determining how the affairs of that country shall be managed. This being so, it would obviously be his duty to vote for any measure which tended to secure that end.'[22] 'We do not see,' rejoined Hirst, who had introduced the endearing practice of conducting a public dialogue with some of his correspondents, 'why a democrat should not be scrupulously democratic about the means he adopts to attain his ends.' (In Switzerland, where women did not get the vote in federal elections until 1971 – and in local elections, in some cantons, not until much later – experience was to show that a requirement that existing voters approve the measure was a first-rate method of keeping the franchise male.)

The second major argument against female suffrage was suffragette militancy. 'Why, it has been asked, should they not have the franchise? They are intellectually as fitted for it as men, and morally they are probably better fitted for it. They are as capable of managing their own property as men and they have shown equal capacity in the conduct of local and philanthropic affairs.' While there was no obvious answer to these questions, women were likely in time to overcome the opposition to such a great change, but rightly or wrongly the suffragettes, 'in the opinion of many of us, had reinforced the theoretical argument against women's enfranchisement by a practical argument of great and invisible force'. They had demonstrated 'that women may possess a kind and amount of political passion which is very rare among men. It is hardly possible to conceive of a group of men going about annoying Ministers and breaking up public meetings in the way with which the Suffragettes have made us so unpleasantly familiar.' The suffragettes behaved like hooligans, but their social position was entirely different.

> They have education, they have refinement – when not following their self-chosen occupation; they are forward, when it suits their purpose, in claiming the courtesy due to their sex. What is it that allows or compels them to lay aside these qualities, and to become – on a sudden and for a particular object – the shrieking, struggling, fighting viragoes of the Ladies' Gallery and the Albert Hall? Is it something in the very constitution of their sex, something which at times can make women more reckless and more formidable than men, because in men these qualities are found only in a particular, and that the lowest class, but in women there is seemingly no safeguard against their appearance in quite unexpected quarters?[23]

Q.E.D.

'"Democracy or Disorder" you head your article,' commented a reader, 'but you show singularly little appreciation of the cogency of the alternative. Disorder is not a disease, but a symptom. Order is an excellent thing, but it is not the highest good, and to desire that order should be maintained when any considerable section of the community is smarting under an intolerable sense of injustice, is certainly not to desire the welfare of the State ... Your argument would have been equally valid against the Reform Bill, or against the repeal of the Corn Laws. It is, indeed, a stock argument which Conservative obstruction has brought against every democratic reform.'[24]

Hirst was unmoved. When the Liberals were returned in January 1910 mainly on the issue of the rejection by the House of Lords of Lloyd George's 1909 'People's Budget', he could continue his 'democratic' argument about the absence of a mandate. A 'conciliation bill' was brought in offering an enfranchisement of about 1 million women (there were then 7 million voters on the register) which, to Hirst's pleasure, was adroitly scuppered by the government. The militancy of the suffragettes increased. The Women's Social and Political Union (WSPU), run by the Pankhursts, organised more and more dramatic demonstrations. Another election at the end of 1910 failed to make female suffrage a major question; nonetheless the conciliation bill was brought in, again early in 1912. It was voted down, in *The Economist*'s view, because of revulsion against militant methods, thus providing a lesson which would have 'a salutary effect on public morals and public work. It proves again that the choice of means is as important as the choice of ends in public as in private life.'[25] Hirst had cause for more rejoicing as further parliamentary initiatives proved unsuccessful, and as the militancy escalated, so did *The Economist*'s rhetoric. Resisting threats became the central argument.

> We only give way to threats when the force behind them is irresistible, even then men often prefer death. It is by these threats, accompanied by physical force of an overwhelming kind, that the Russian government is now trying to deprive Finland of its liberties. It is by these threats, accompanied by persistent military force, that the Turks held down Macedonia. Even a member of Parliament who was favourable to woman suffrage is inclined to vote against it when his life and his family is threatened . . . If the right of small minorities to govern by violence and outrage is conceded, what becomes of the rule of majority government, stretching from the parish meeting to the House of Commons? And remember, it is upon majority rule alone that a civilised democracy can rest. If a handful of angry folk are to insult and badger the Speaker, the Prime Minister, and everybody who has been placed in authority by constitutional methods, then on every council and committee in the kingdom a violent woman may equally claim to rule and govern the majority of her colleagues.[26]

The suffragettes, he believed comfortably, had also alienated women: 'It is surely natural that women should resent this attempt to inflame the strong against the weak, and to destroy the social ties and conventions upon which their own security and happiness depends. The sanctity of solemn vows, the ties of love and family affection, honour, romance, the privileges of the weak, the chivalry of the strong – these are constituent elements in the social fabric which speak to the majority of women and men with overwhelming power.'[27]

Hirst's complacency was rudely shattered that same year, 1913, when his beloved wife Helena, 'deeply stirred by the Pankhurst campaign, took part in a Militant demonstration; threw a stone at a Minister's window and was arrested. He was deeply upset; the publicity was hateful; moreover he held that a compact had been broken – the agreement that he would not figure on any anti platform and she on no suffrage one. Poignant at the time, this rift, in the end, deepened their unity.' In response to an appeal from Hirst, his friend John Simon acted as a mediator.[28]

In his scintillating *The Strange Death of Liberal England*, George Dangerfield described 'the Women's Rebellion' of 1910–14 as 'above all things a movement from darkness into light, and from death into life . . . its unconscious motive was the rejection of a moribund, a respectable, a smothering security . . . Woman, through her new awareness of the possibilities of an abstract goal in life, was, in effect, suddenly aware of her long-neglected masculinity.' That security, to which Francis Hirst, the epitome of Liberal England, was blindly trying to hang on, was being abandoned by many elements in society. What women were forswearing was 'in the worst sense of the word, a *feminine* security'.

> The legacy which their Victorian predecessors had bequeathed them was a purely negative one – the legacy of conscious adaptation to the role of Perfect Wife. The Victorian woman was the angel in the house . . . the helpmeet who conceived children in submission and without desire, the eternal inferior. Her whole career lay in marriage, her security was founded in her husband's ability to provide for her, her ambition satisfied itself in helping him along his path through the world.

The wives became submissive tyrants; the women without husbands filled their drab existences with 'good works, gossip, hypochondria, and religion'. Consciously or unconsciously, pre-war women realised that 'by living only in relation to a single man, woman had become separated from her own womanhood, and, by fair means or foul, she must get it back again'.[29] Bagehot had the imaginative sympathy to understand much of this: Francis Hirst could not.

When war broke out next year, even the most militant women threw themselves enthusiastically into war work. Under Hirst's successor, the phlegmatic Hartley Withers, the paper appears to have shown no interest, let alone fervour, about women's suffrage. Under '*DIARY OF THE WEEK*', in June 1917, was recorded:

> TUESDAY, JUNE 19TH. – Money in request at 4½ per cent and over. Discount market unsettled and rates lowered ⅛ to ¹⁄₁₆ per cent. 'Over the counter' sales of Treasury bills resumed. Rate of interest allowed by Bank of England to clearing banks for three-day loans reduced from 4½ to 4 per cent. Sir D. Haig's despatch on winter campaign published. Majority of 330 for Woman Suffrage. German titles dropped by members of Royal Family.

All-Russian Congress of Workmen's and Soldiers' Delegates opened in Petrograd. Sale of German bank offices realised £260,500.[30]

That bill, to give women over 30 (and all men over 21) the vote received the Royal Assent in February 1918 and in December 1919 the first woman to take her seat in parliament arrived after a by-election.* *The Economist* relegated this historic moment to '*EVENTS OF THE WEEK*':

> DECEMBER 1ST. – Premium Bonds debate. Viscountess Astor takes her seat in Parliament.[31]

In 1927, under Walter Layton, the following paragraph dealt with the next great advance:

> *Women and Franchise.* – The Prime Minister, in an answer to a question in the House of Commons on Wednesday, disclosed the decision of the Government to honour the pledge given by the Home Secretary two years ago that women should be placed on the same footing as men in respect of the franchise. Legislation to this end will be introduced next session, and the result will be the addition to the voting register of about three million women between the ages of 21 and 30 and a further large number of women over 30, who are at present excluded by the property or other qualifications. We do not anticipate that the change will have any revolutionary effect. The younger women will, as the older women have done, divide their votes among the three political parties in roughly the same proportion as the men. But it will increase the liability of the electorate to sudden waves of emotion, and will add substantially to the size of unattached sections, which sway elections. It may be argued theoretically that the interests of the State would be best served by the fixation of 25 as the lower age-limit both for women and for men voters. But since women have been admitted to the franchise, it is clearly only a matter of time before the two sexes were placed upon the same basis, and since the age limit has been placed at 21 for men, there is no longer any logical ground for opposing the Government's proposal.[32]

---

*Constance Markiewicz, who had been elected to parliament from Ireland in 1918 as a Sinn Fein candidate, never took her seat.

All passion was spent. *The Economist* of Withers and Layton carried useful statistical information about women's work and pay and proposed moderate reforms, even tut-tutting in 1932 over France's failure to enfranchise women. It was not until the Second World War, with the mass entry of women into work, that debates about women's rights became again frequent and controversial. On matters like equal pay and employment opportunities, *The Economist* was radical and tough. Several of the most feminist articles were written by Donald Tyerman, then deputy and later editor. The war had given the community, he said as early as 1941, 'the chance to start again on a fairer and more efficient foundation; and over a great part of paid employment, there is little doubt that the only obstacles to "equal pay for equal work" are the prejudices which have hitherto compelled women to seek their living only through a narrow funnel of ill-paid jobs'.[33]

Three years later the editor, Geoffrey Crowther, was co-author of an uncompromising declaration that 'equal pay should become the general principle, to be applied as soon as possible except in those cases where it would not be in the interests of the women themselves. And in furtherance of that principle, the state, which is now almost the worst discriminator, should throw the whole weight of its example and its influence in favour of equal pay.'[34]

From April 1941, records show who wrote what, otherwise it would be impossible to determine whether the many articles dealing with women's rights were written by men or women. Although a high proportion of the wartime (1939–45) journalists were women, they wrote in what Bagehot would have called a masculine style. Most identifiable, because most personal, was Barbara Ward, an inspirational and radical influence on the paper, particularly in her role as Geoffrey Crowther's social conscience. Typical was a feisty onslaught on Harold Nicolson, husband of Vita Sackville-West, who in the House of Commons had opposed the idea of female diplomats for the traditional reasons (women's ineptitude in economic and commercial affairs, their unsuitable mental and emotional make-up; foreign opposition; marital complications), 'adding whimsical excursions into history in support of his view that "the irruption of women into diplomacy has always been disastrous"'. She counter-attacked. It was not true that women with trained minds were 'more emotional or instinctively unstable than men with a corresponding education. "Failure of a Mission" is proof of this. Sir Nevile Henderson's feelings about the Nazi bosses were a determining factor in his disastrous conduct of affairs.* If Mr Nicolson must rake up history, Catherine the Great, Elizabeth or Maria Theresa overshadow his "Helen of Argos".'[35]

Optimism reigned: the post-war world would see women forging ahead in all walks of life. 'Now, more than ever, a woman's place is in the House', observed a male writer commemorating Lady Astor's parliamentary silver jubilee. The period of probation was over and women must now be treated as equal in every respect.[36]

It soon became clear that the new dawn was not yet breaking, and that post-war progress in the advancement of women was slow. This was not true on the paper, where women had equality in all but pay. Indeed Crowther was in many respects an extraordinarily enlightened employer. When Patricia Norton had her third baby and breast-feeding precluded her from coming into the office, he arranged for a car to drive her and the baby to and from the office three days a week; the baby divided her time between the roof of the Ryder Street building and the caretaker's flat. Crowther and his successor, Donald Tyerman, were approachable and flexible about family responsibilities. But along with this went an assumption that men should be paid more than women because they either had, or would have, family responsibilities. Equal pay was for government, big companies and trade unions.

Some of the women simply did not think about money: Nancy Balfour was independently wealthy; Margaret Cruikshank and Pat Norton had well-paid husbands; others were simply so grateful for equal intellectual opportunities that they felt it churlish to demand fair remuneration as well. Salary levels were secret and negotiated individually and women tended to be less pushy than the men. Market forces ruled, and until the climate changed in the 1970s, few of the women, however able, could easily have found such satisfying jobs elsewhere.

Nor did women realise how badly paid they were compared with men. A confidential salary list from 1953 tells the story. Of editorial departmental heads, gross pay (salary plus expenses) was: Nancy Balfour (American Survey £1,200;) Roland Bird (Business World, and also deputy editor £2,500); Marjorie Deane (Statistics £875); Norman Macrae (Home £1,750); Donald

---

*Henderson was British Ambassador in Berlin from 1937 to 1939. An arch-appeaser, he went so far as to attend Nazi Party rallies at Nuremberg as a gesture of goodwill. Enthusiastically pro-Munich, it took Hitler's occupation of Czechoslovakia in March 1939 to dampen his optimism about the prospects for good Anglo-German relations. *Failure of a Mission* was his apologia.

McLachlan (Foreign £2,000). Of the 15 next most senior journalists, the six women had an average salary of £830; the nine men £1,076. And the most diffident were the worst paid (that also, of course, applied to men).

Lack of much public debate reduced post-war *Economist* coverage of women's issues. What was said was remorselessly reasonable. So women's magazines were filled with nothing but '*Kinder, Küche, Kleider* [clothes] – and cosmetics'. Never mind. It might be that they fostered a false romanticism that made marriage more difficult, yet 'against that must be set the fact that the counsels of these periodicals are making marriage smoother, homes brighter, food better and clothes smarter. At a time when so much is heard about the wickedness of the Press, even Mr Randolph Churchill would surely agree that the women's magazines, at least, are on the side of the angels.'[37] 'Some of the economic disabilities of women are indeed inseparable from their dual potential as wives and as workers', concluded 'THE FEMINISTS MOP UP'; 'but others are certainly unnecessary. While none of them is so grievous that it is worth being chained to the railings for, it would be a pity if for that reason – or conversely, because feminism is too much identified with extremism – interest in the movement should die altogether. A sensible and moderate programme deserves to command general support.'[38] In the 1950s, these dispassionate leaders were written by women.

(The complaint that as it got older *The Economist* became, if not more vulgar, more demotic, is borne out by the contrast in the women-related headlines of the 1940s and those of the 1950s. 'THE DISTAFF SIDE' was the most skittish of the earlier group. Otherwise, they read like a series of titles of dreary pamphlets from the Ministry of Labour: 'WOMEN'S PAY', 'THE RIGHTS OF WOMEN', 'RESTRAINT OF WOMEN', 'WOMEN'S LAND ARMY', 'WOMEN ENGINEERS', 'THE OLDER WOMAN', 'DOMESTIC SERVICE', 'A WOMAN'S PLACE', 'CARE OF CHILDREN'.

There was a cautious attempt in the early 1950s to liven things up: 'VOTES AND VEILS IN THE MIDDLE EAST', 'A WOMAN'S WORLD?', 'LABOUR LOST BY LOVE' (graduate women marrying and giving up work), 'THE FEMINISTS MOP UP', 'BRITISH WOMEN SIZED UP' (changes in average female body-shape) and 'BRAINS AT THE SINK', and a shortlived descent into the embarrassing with 'PETTICOAT BATTLEGROUND' (the women's magazine circulation war) and 'INDUSTRY'S PETTICOAT REVOLUTION'. From the mid-1960s titles became more factual again: 'EQUAL PAY AGAIN', 'GETTING THE MOST OUT OF WOMEN', 'WHAT WOMEN WANT', 'ON

EQUALITY', 'WOMEN'S WORK', 'TALKING LIBERATION', 'POLITICS IS WOMEN'S WORK', 'THE UNDERDEVELOPED SEX', 'WOMEN AND CHIL- DREN LAST' – with the odd lapse again into lumbering 'ladies-God-bless- 'em' lingo: 'UNFAIR RULES FOR FAIR SEX'; 'ROY'S PLOY FOR THE LADIES'. (In fairness, this was a period during which the Conservative Party came out with a well-meaning pamphlet about improving women's lot and called it 'Fair Shares For the Fair Sex'.)

Because there were so many women on the paper, it was more conscious of women's issues than most serious journals. But in the post-war years most women's concerns were written about by women, which tended to make the treatment less rather than more radical. *Economist* women were honorary chaps writing for chaps: they were not tempted to produce propaganda suitable for the *Guardian* 'Women's Page'. In any case, women's issues took up an infinitesimal amount of their time. Pat Norton, Frances Chadwick, Barbara Beck, Sarah Hogg, Brenda Maddox, Emily MacFarquhar, and very occasionally Mary Goldring or Felicity Bryan, might produce facts and figures to back the rational case for encouraging women to develop their talents, but such pieces were incidental to their main jobs – as business or political writers. Their arguments were made dispassionately and always in a tone of complete reasonableness. The only sign of the personal in several dozen of their articles came in 1963 from Pat Norton, who had produced and successfully brought up three children during her quarter-century with the paper. The Minister for Health was proposing to prevent women from working for six weeks after childbirth. 'POSTPARTUM WORK BAN' had an irascible tone: 'It looks as if the Government and the House of Commons are about to make fools of themselves by imposing a quite unwarranted restriction on individual liberties.' It was a matter entirely for the woman; 'the mother who really needs public concern on her behalf is the "non working" one with a new baby, other small children to look after and the housework to do. Compared with this, work in an office is a rest cure.'[39]

It was a young man, who on and off for almost 30 years has been Barbara Ward's successor as the social conscience of the paper, who made the most uncompromising and fiery feminist statement and brought the *Economist* women out of the closet. Nick Harman was awash with radical attitudes when he arrived on the paper; his deep admiration for the talented and highly attractive Barbara Smith, one of the paper's most distinguished foreign- department journalists, fired him with anger about injustice to women.

'Masculine prejudices about feminine capacities should more often bring rage to female tongues and blushes to bearded cheeks', he wrote in 1964. 'For ages before the Ministry of Labour this week produced its figures on the need to make better use of women workers throughout the economy . . . it was obvious that the rankest waste of talent in this country (and, to be fair, in most countries) was the waste of woman-power . . . family attitudes, and the entire social ethos of a nation and at least three generations of parents, teachers and pupils, must be changed before it becomes regarded as normal for a young girl to aim at a career in industry.' Progress lay in industrial far-sightedness. 'But businessmen can hardly be expected to consider such remote and indirect sorts of benefit in their employment policies.' So the cause of the woman technologist and manager in industry must for the time being be advanced by propaganda. 'The contribution of *The Economist* to this is that, of its full-time, London-based editorial staff of 40, 13 are responsible women.'[40]

Two years later, after Alastair Burnet had become editor and the paper had moved to right rather than left of centre, another radical man produced a memorable article. Norman Macrae, whose huge talent was to make him one of the paper's greatest assets and most distinguished names, exhibited in 'EQUAL PAY AGAIN' his unrivalled gift for turning cherished beliefs on their heads. Like James Wilson, another good-natured man of fixed principles, Macrae could be relied upon to prove conclusively that in giving a starving child a piece of bread one was likely (a) to cause it to choke to death, and (b) indirectly to bring about the death of thousands more. Was equal pay for equal work good? No. The Conservative government in the mid-1950s had aimed to give a lead to private industry by introducing it for civil servants and teachers. The result had been to disperse resources to young girls rather than to experienced teachers. The acceptance of the principle of equal pay would probably push up women's rates in industry, thus adding to cost-inflation, which was bad. If more married women were attracted back to work it would be good. But the unskilled, young, short-service girls would more probably benefit, which would be bad. A much better approach would be to overturn the apprenticeship system, develop training schemes that suited women, abolish the requirement for women to retire at 60, reduce or abolish employers' compulsory national insurance contributions for part-time workers, and increase family allowances to undermine employers' feeling that 'family men' needed more money.

Three of the four steps suggested above would add to the national income, while the fourth (higher family allowances) is socially desirable in its own right. Taken together, they would add far more to women's real lifetime earnings than would the corny gesture of proclaiming 'the principle of equal pay', while reflecting smugly that nobody can really define what it means. These are the reforms that intelligent feminists should be pressing for.[41]

Did many readers notice the paper abandoning a policy it had endorsed for 25 years? Probably not, for, when it comes to variations in the approach to women's rights, confusion in the post-war *Economist* indicates division about means, not ends. But there were upheavals within the paper. Alastair Burnet's arrival had meant not just a move to the right, but a change from the deliberately pro-woman climate of Crowther and Tyerman; simultaneously, the burgeoning feminist movement of the mid-1960s was raising women's consciousness. Some of them were no longer content to be cheap and grateful. Emily MacFarquhar, a gifted member of the foreign department who was the paper's China expert, was a tough American. When a long-serving colleague whom she admired and liked was fired by Burnet for taking too much time off to look after her children, MacFarquhar had a blazing row with Burnet over the manner of the woman's dismissal and they maintained a cold war ever afterwards. MacFarquhar became a self-appointed shop steward for the women and fought for equality on many fronts, for instance, life insurance provisions, non-discriminatory wording of advertisements and, with much more difficulty, pay. When she had joined in 1965 she had dined out on having been told that she would be paid less than if she were a man. Ten years later being underpaid made her angry and she wrote to the new editor, Andrew Knight, to say that now that the Equal Pay Act was coming into effect, she trusted she would be paid no less than people with similar qualifications. After a tremendous row nothing happened for several weeks; she consulted, but did not call in, a lawyer, and was given a substantial pay rise without any acknowledgement of the principle. Knight displayed his habitual quality of holding no grudges and even forgetting rows: MacFarquhar acknowledges the paper's great strength, under all modern editors, in its treatment of women.

By and large, *The Economist* has been the best kind of paternalistic employer, and nowadays women get equal pay. Most important of all, since David Gordon became chief executive, women have been actively encouraged on the business side of the paper. In 1986, a Texan lawyer, Marjorie Scardino, was appointed head of *The Economist* in America; in 1987, Helen Alexander, a graduate of the INSEAD business school, was appointed international circulation director. No one would raise an eyebrow at the notion that in the future there might simultaneously be a female editor and (as there now is) a female chief executive. Yet the aura of the place is male, the format of the large editorial conferences favours those experienced in the male tradition of debating, and the paper's image is overwhelmingly male; few women read it.

The 1980s saw two important changes in the coverage of women: it became more overtly feminist and was once again written by men as well as women. In 1982 'DAUGHTERS OF THE NON-REVOLUTION' was the lead: the cover showed a depressed-looking schoolgirl standing in front of No. 10 Downing Street.

> Consciousnesses have been raised, laws have been passed, damages have been won. But more than a decade after the first advances of the feminist revolution, its gains in most western countries are looking slim. Recession is a partial explanation. It is not the only one.

The article assailed the economic waste and social injustice of discrimination, recommended positive recruitment (searching out female talent and coaxing it into politics and other hitherto male preserves), positive selection (giving preference to the under-represented when all other qualifications were approximately equal) and such institutional changes as bringing in flexitime and job-sharing in industry and making parliament work sensible hours.

> The liberation that women have won so far too often means freedom to do a double job. The Russian babushka who gets to queue for hours for her family food, after she has finished clearing snow off the Moscow streets, is an extreme example. Working women in the west are better off, with their late night supermarkets and dishwashing machines, but they are still among society's losers. Today's wives may put up with things as they are. Their daughters will not.[42]

It was a woman who provided coverage of the gradual erosion by Islamic fundamentalists of women's liberties in Pakistan that drew protests from the embassy,[43] but it was a male 'Islam Correspondent' who continued the attack with a long and detailed denunciation of the betrayal of Islam manifest in anti-woman prejudice.[44]

The effects of working in a feminist environment are particularly noticeable in the foreign coverage. In 1986 a young single woman undertook the survey of the Arab Gulf Co-operation Council countries and produced *inter alia* a memorable indicator of female liberty: how much you could see of the local women.

> In Oman, all sorts of bits are visible – the legs of those in western dress, the stomachs of those in saris, and the faces of most of them. Among some of the tribes in the interior, however, the women still wear masks. In Kuwait, Bahrain and the UAE, working women usually wear western clothes, though fairly modest ones; most women in the street wear a black cloth covering their head and clothes, but generally do not cover their faces. In Saudi Arabia and Qatar, you do not much see women at all. The Saudi Arabian ones you see are, in the words of a Sudanese expatriate, 'wrapped up like maize'; their faces, as well as their heads and bodies, are covered.

Emma Duncan is of the generation that does not find it necessary consciously to write as if she were a man. 'As a liberated western female,' she ended this section, 'this correspondent is horrified by the lives of the women in the Gulf. Some of them don't much like it either. But after a conversation with a female Saudi PhD who said she had no desire to swap places, your correspondent had to admit that there might be two sides to the story.'[45]

Some of the men make their feminism equally clear. In his Japan Survey,[46] Nick Valéry wrote that Japan 'wastes one of its greatest assets by clinging to feudal notions about the role of married women'. The Africa correspondent, in an article beginning 'The lot of African women is not only unfair, it also costs Africa money', lambasted the behaviour of men,[47] and the Washington correspondent wrote a deeply sympathetic piece about how Hillary Clinton, an 'intelligent, successful person by anybody's standards', had been forced to 'change her clothes, re-style her hair and wear a vacuous smile'.[48] It is an impressive record, and even Francis Hirst must be given credit for being a pioneer in hiring a woman and making of her a close friend.

CHAPTER XXXI:

The Oxbridge influx

'What's left to us, then?' said Nigel. 'To a generation tired of life?' said
Hugh. 'Surely, it's obvious.' He paused. Then as others still looked to him
he gave a shrug of his shoulders. 'Death,' he said. 'That's all.' *Mary Agnes
Hamilton*, Dead Yesterday, *1916*

It was Hirst who turned the paper away from relying on old pros and
established the twentieth-century tradition of bringing in young Oxbridge
recruits. From his period *The Economist* ceased to be written mainly by the
kind of people who would have chosen to read it; instead it became the
province of those confident and bright enough to write about anything. In
the process it both gained and lost.

He appears to have inherited six people: Howard Kirk (manager), Mike
Flood (advertisement manager) and Horace Whitcomb (company-meetings
manager) on the business side and Walter William Wright, Eric Gibb and
Albert Chapman in editorial. 'So Mr Hirst had only a few bricks to work
upon so he had to cast round to find straw to make more bricks', observed
Chapman.

During Hirst's nine years as editor, there were a few changes on the
business side. Edward Mafeking Webb became office boy in 1915, having got
the job through his officer in the Church Lads' Brigade, a relation of the
assistant editor. Kirk was given an assistant called Alexander (first name
unknown), and when Horace Whitcomb died in 1915 he was replaced by his
son Harold, who stayed until his sudden death in 1937. The hereditary
principle was observed also on the editorial side. When Walter William
Wright died of pneumonia in November 1908, his son Alexander joined the
staff, 'sat at his father's desk and practically took up the work where his father

left off'; some time after war broke out in 1914 he left to join the *Morning Post* as assistant City editor.

Hirst modelled his editorship on Bagehot, for whom he had a profound admiration, seeking to impose his own stamp on the whole paper and broaden its scope and authority. Like Bagehot, he had an enormous range of interests, mixed in stimulating intellectual circles and travelled abroad, so he gave to the paper a new freshness and vigour. A natural innovator, he abandoned the stable of outside leader-writers, wrote two or three major articles every week and set about building up a staff. Chapman is precise about who joined, but vague about when and for how long, so only in some cases can one be specific about chronology. Additionally, since Hirst chose staff who were mainly in agreement with him and dictated the party line on all controversial issues, it is rarely possible to identify conclusively who wrote what. He chose the brightest, best and youngest available, he treated them as friends and equals, and the *Economist* office became a lively, happy place, teeming, said Chapman, with 'activity and interest'. Hirst's paper was a significant step forward in the direction of the modern, collegiate paper, albeit one controlled by a dictator.

According to Chapman (though no one else mentions it), Hirst had been City editor of the *Daily Tribune* (a liberal newspaper founded in January 1906, which collapsed in February 1908), was replaced there by *The Economist*'s J.A. Woolacott, and brought with him to Granville House from the *Tribune* one Alexander Mackay Stewart, who used to write Stock Market notes and work with Walter William Wright on Stock Exchange and general financial subjects.

In 1908 the 29-year-old polymath Hilton Young became an assistant editor. Educated at Eton and Cambridge, President of the Union, friendly with E.M. Forster and others of the Bloomsbury set, with a first in natural sciences, he was yet another retired barrister. After a brief period studying international law at the University of Freiburg, he became a financial journalist and joined *The Economist* primarily to write financial leaders. He was wholly in line with Hirst on the need for economy in public expenditure. The epigraph to his *The System of National Finance*, published in 1915, was from David Copperfield:

> Mr Micawber conjured me to observe that if a man had twenty pounds a
> year for his income and spent nineteen pounds, nineteen shillings and

sixpence he would be happy, but that if he spent twenty pounds one, he would be miserable. After which he borrowed a shilling of me for porter and cheered up.

The book was nostalgic for the days of the great frugal finance ministers, 'who would turn the labels on a dispatch-box to save the public money': Gladstone was 'their flower . . . They have passed from the scene. Now in Elysium it is theirs bitterly to lament the wastage of Ambrosia, for profligacy had followed.' Margaret Thatcher would undoubtedly have considered Hilton Young 'one of us'.

In 1910 Young was an unsuccessful Liberal candidate, and in that year he left *The Economist* to become City editor of the *Morning Post* and London correspondent of the *New York Times* financial supplement: in 1911 he published *Foreign Companies and Other Corporations*. He was later to become a Spinozan pantheist, a war hero, a Liberal and then a Tory MP, a member of the British delegation to four League of Nations Assemblies, editor-in-chief of the *Financial News*, and the second of the three Financial Secretaries to the Treasury to have worked on *The Economist* (Douglas Jay would be the third); in 1935 he went to the House of Lords as Lord Kennet.

After Wright's death in November 1908, Eric Gibb became deputy editor, and, perhaps to replace Young, Hirst brought in as another all-purpose writer his own *alter ego*, J.E. Allen, his friend of 20 years with whom he had been at school and at Wadham and had shared chambers in the Inner Temple, where they entertained countless anti-imperialist Liberals: in 1913 Allen was to marry Hirst's sister Helen. Allen had stood unsuccessfully as a Liberal candidate in 1905 and 1906, was the author of *County Elections* and was highly knowledgeable and opinionated about public finance. After the war he wrote *The War Debt* and was co-author with Hirst of *British War Budgets*; during the 1920s his letters to *The Economist* included a complaint about plans to introduce a levy on capital[1] and a recommendation that lorries using the public highway should be required to pay a toll.[2]

Very early in his editorship, in February 1908, Hirst visited Cambridge where, in Professor Alfred Marshall's Social Discussion Society, he heard the 24-year-old Walter Layton speak learnedly on economic aspects of the Licensing Bill then going through parliament. The previous year Layton had taken a double first in the new Economics Tripos at Cambridge, had won the Gresham Studentship in Economics at Caius College, had, like Hirst in 1899, won the Cobden Prize, and had just finished a major statistical analysis of railwaymen's wages for the main railway union. At Hirst's request Layton provided *The Economist* with 'THE LICENSING BILL AND SOME ANOMA-LIES',[3] an article of staggering technical competence and a suitably solid first contribution from a future editor and proprietor: shortly afterwards he agreed to join the paper part-time.

Until 1914, Layton (judged 'modest and unassuming' by Chapman) came up to London to write leaders for Hirst and more importantly, to develop the statistical side of the paper, which had progressed very little since the innovations of Bagehot, Giffen and Newmarch. The combination in Layton of the Nonconformist work ethic and a desire to explore his ability to its limits compelled him to take on far too much. He recalled over 50 years later his crushing programme of work in the winter of 1908.

> Tuesdays, Thursdays and Fridays at *The Economist*, where I set to work to revise the fifty-year-old Price Index Number, initiated a regular compilation of the profits of Joint Stock Companies, compiled the first index number of the volume and value of our foreign trade and made other statistical innovations in addition to ordinary leader writing. Two courses of lectures at Cambridge on Mondays and Wednesdays as well as coaching private pupils; a weekly tutorial class of the WEA [Workers' Educational Association] at Portsmouth every Saturday night, and another one at Leicester on Wednesday evenings, both of which involved long railway journeys, and the correction of students' essays on my slow Sunday trek back from Portsmouth via Brighton to London and Cambridge.[4]

In January 1910, in Switzerland with his fiancée and her family, he had a nervous breakdown, after which he cut down on obligations and reduced his commitment to *The Economist* to one day a week.

A statistician of considerable promise, at Cambridge he progressed from being an assistant lecturer to A.C. Pigou, Marshall's successor, to a university lecturership. He specialised in the economics of industry and labour as well as public finance and developed into a first-rate applied economist. Alfred Marshall, concerned about Layton's health, wrote to him in 1910:

> If you could make the same thoughts answer for:
>   1 Part of your duty to *The Economist*,
>   2 Part of your lecture work and,

3 A few short books or rather a collection of essays, I think your work would have a high quality and the chance of your breaking down through overstrain would be diminished. If you try and ride three horses at once I fear for your health . . . I think Bagehot worked somewhat on those lines and I am inclined, being a mere old fogey, to support as a motto, Live up to Bagehot![5]

Layton accepted Marshall's advice and used his academic work on the history of wages and prices not only in his Cambridge lectures, but at *The Economist*, as the basis for the Newmarch lectures he gave at University College, London and in the articles that were adapted in his *An Introduction to the Study of Prices*, published in 1912. This little book became a classic: in 1934 and 1938 the second and third editions were published with Geoffrey Crowther as co-author.

To have the opportunity to cut his journalistic teeth on *The Economist* was of incalculable importance in determining the course of Layton's and the paper's future. As for Hirst, Layton was a perfect recruit, helpful, industrious and thorough; his enthusiasm for female equality could be overlooked in view of his soundness on free trade and his pioneering achievements in a field of great importance to the paper's readers. Marshall described him as 'unequalled among the younger British economists in realistic study'. One of the first jobs he and Hirst undertook together was the modernising of the paper's index number, a statistic that fascinated Hirst in its role as 'a sort of barometer of trade. A rise in prices may herald speculation and business activity, or it may follow them, whereas a fall in prices may be either an effect or a cause of depression.' They set about reconstructing the index number Bagehot had first published in 1873, which had been based on the wholesale prices of 22 key commodities and had since then been used by statisticians all over the world to trace the general movement of prices.

It was originally an ingenious but simple contrivance. The price of each article at the current date compared with its price at the standard period (1845–50) was expressed as a percentage; and the sum of these percentages constituted the index number. Thus, taking the standard period as 100, *The Economist* index number for 1873 was 134, which meant that the general level of wholesale prices had risen 34 per cent., and the value or purchasing power of gold had fallen to a corresponding extent.

However, by 1907 it was necessary to incorporate new key commodities like rubber and jute and to alter the weight given to some commodities; 'iron, for instance, is much more important than lead, and cotton than flax. In a good index number, therefore, a rise or fall in the price of iron or cotton has more influence on the whole index number than a rise or fall in lead or flax.'[6]

Layton and Hirst were an excellent partnership. Hirst understood the needs of his readers as Bagehot had done, and, also like Bagehot, he had found the right person to provide them with the figures they would find most useful. But Layton's time was too limited to do the laborious work of providing regular statistics, and after Alexander Mackay Stewart had left, in April 1911, Layton's younger brother Gilbert joined the paper and, said Chapman, 'immediately began to produce statistics and write articles as if it were like rolling off a log'. Because of lack of family money (Walter had won scholarships all the way) Gilbert Layton had gone straight from school into the banking house of Brown Shipley and Co. At *The Economist* he took charge of the twice-yearly Banking Supplements, the index number and the statistical and factual side of editorial. According to the only surviving pre-1941 contributor's list, in a seven-week period in 1924 Gilbert contributed 11 leading articles, 20 notes of the week and three articles for the Banking Supplement; the subjects were almost all statistically-based, from root crops to excise duties, from industrial profits to Uruguayan railways. Lacking his brother's driving ambition, Gilbert was to stay an unassuming but invaluable linch-pin of the paper for the next 46 years, in his later years as an avuncular general manager.

Another Layton connection was his Cambridge pupil and friend, Dudley Ward, one of the group of high-minded young radicals, wedded to peace and reform, which included Layton and his fiancée, Dorothy Osmaston. When in November 1909 Ward won a Fellowship at St John's College, he and Layton celebrated by going to Grantchester and bathing in the river with Rupert Brooke. (Ward was to live for many years in The Old Vicarage in Grantchester, now owned by Lord (Jeffrey) Archer, about which Brooke had written a famous poem.) Ward joined *The Economist* in 1910 to write leading articles and banking notes and left in 1913 to undertake what he described in *Who's Who* as 'research work in Germany'. More accurately, he was on a peace mission, despatched by Francis Hirst and financed by two rich Liberals (John Brunner and Ernest Schuster), to counteract the scaremongerings of the yellow press by acting as a press correspondent 'with the object of promoting friendly relations between Germany and England'. His qualifications for the job were, as Hirst put it, that he was 'an honest journalist' and 'a real lover of peace'[7] (also, he was married to a German). Brunner gave a lunch at the National Liberal Club to introduce Ward to representatives of a number of provincial newspapers, which he hoped would use his despatches. During the war Ward worked in the Treasury – for a time on external finance under Keynes – and was recognised as a man of great ability.[8] He was involved in various post-war organisations for sorting out Europe and became manager and a director of the British Overseas Bank. The Cambridge connection was strengthened through correspondence with John Maynard Keynes, whose first known letter to a newspaper, signed 'J.M.K.', went to *The Economist*. Intended simply as a letter to the editor on free trade, its substantial elaboration on an editorial theme earned a fee of £1. 10s.[9] Keynes occasionally contributed and throughout his life engaged in vigorous correspondence with the paper.

The 24-year-old Leonard J. Reid arrived early in 1912 to write on politics (mainly domestic, the records suggest) and stayed for 20 years. From a Liberal academic and literary background (his father was Professor of Ancient History in Cambridge), he had emerged, said his *Economist* obituary, with 'a remarkable combination of enthusiasm with exceptional clarity of style and literary quality'.[10] He was to become a technically well-equipped financial journalist, but his main interest was in the effects of finance and economics on politics. A good amateur cricketer, 'he was always ready to discuss the pros and cons of any particular game' with Chapman. He became assistant editor after the war and stayed until in 1932 he became City editor of the *Daily Telegraph*. He was one of the most popular members of the staff; Graham Hutton remembered him from the 1930s as 'awfully nice' and his obituary spoke of his loyalty and 'the healing effect of his kindly and gentle nature'. Hutton described him as very able and utterly reliable with his facts – 'a clearer-upper who got all the dirt out of the corners', and particularly good on the American economy. Journalism came easily to him, recalled Chapman. 'I remember one day he went up to Lord's and came home on a lovely summer's day to sit in *The Economist* and write a leader on The Putumayo Rubber Atrocities. He felt so strongly about it and poured forth his indignation in an *Economist* leader. Yes Mr Reid was a lovable man.'

It was rage rather than indignation. The article was a response to the publication in July 1912 of a report by Sir Roger Casement,* a great humanitarian despite being an employee of the Foreign Office, on the treatment of native Indians in the Putumayo district of Peru by agents of the Peruvian Amazon Company. Casement had earlier exposed the hideous ill-treatment by European employers of native labour in the Belgian Congo. 'A more gruesome story of continued and systematic oppression by barbarous methods has not been revealed in recent times', wrote Reid. 'The horrors of Congo pale before those of the Amazon.' To enforce the collection of rubber, the agents employed terrorism and torture of men, women and children.

> We do not propose here to enter into the harrowing details of suffering. Suffice it to say that brutal floggings (in many cases with fatal results) were varied by semi-drownings, starvation, confinement in a diabolical type of stocks, specially designed to give acute and continued pain, and other refinements of torture equal to the infernal masterpieces of the Spanish Inquisition, not excluding burning victims alive. Many of the tortures cannot be described in print, but we may give one extract from Sir Roger's report of one of the 'milder' punishments.
>
> 'Men and lads, rubber collectors or fugitives from its collection, were suspended by a chain fastened round the neck to one of the beams of the house or store. Sometimes, with the feet scarcely touching the ground and the chain hauled taut, they were left in this half-strangled condition until life was almost extinct. More than one eye-witness assured me that he had seen Indians actually suspended by the neck until, when let down, they fell a senseless mass upon the floor, with tongues protruding.' Elsewhere he states that women and girls were frequently subjected to this torture, while the victims were frequently flogged and mutilated while in this helpless and agonising position. There existed, in fact, an orgy of devilish cruelty run wild.

In its visceral loathing of cruelty and its determination not to allow its readers to shirk the issue, this was a blast in the great tradition of James Wilson and Thomas Hodgskin. In the Johnstone tradition was the denunciation of irresponsible directors, who this time included a baronet and a director of two well-known London banks.

*Casement was hanged in 1916 for his role in the Irish Easter Rising.

> We trust we may assume that the English directors and shareholders of this company were blissfully ignorant of the state of affairs in Putumayo for at least some time after their acquisition of the enterprise. Ignorance cannot altogether remove their responsibility. The pleas of ignorance by those who are bound to know is indeed a poor, miserable and shameful plea . . . Here, in a remote forest region, we find a British company, through its accredited agents, enslaving, torturing, and squeezing money from the life-blood of defenceless men, women and children. It has been a scene of torture, murder and massacre; but Mr Acland, for the Foreign Office, disclaims all responsibility.

The Indian population had fallen from 50,000 in 1906 to 8,000 in 1911. Reid urged support for the fund opened by Casement and hoped, that, *pace* Acland, the British government would put pressure on Peru.

> The noble work of the chivalrous Sir Roger Casement must not be allowed to fail. It must be backed up by the whole influence of Great Britain. So far the Peruvian Government appears to have connived at the proceedings of men who ought long ago to have been in the dock. If these horrors are not stopped and the perpetrators punished, the right of the Peruvian Government to remain in the comity of civilised nations will not easily be upheld at the next Hague Conference.[11]

Chapman records two others who were on the staff for a short time under Hirst: C.K. Hobson, brother of Oscar (a great financial journalist and occasional contributor to *The Economist*), later at the Board of Trade, and for a short time in 1916 21-year-old Richard Lambert, a classical scholar of Wadham, who was to be editor of *The Listener* from 1928 to 1939 and an expert in media communications.

Hirst's most unorthodox recruit was the vital Mrs Mary Agnes (Molly) Hamilton, cigarette-smoking, opinionated, committed to her career, absorbed in politics and separated from her husband – in short the very epitome of the kind of modern woman of whom Hirst completely disapproved. In her autobiography, *Remembering My Good Friends*, and one of her novels, *Dead Yesterday*, she painted a vibrant picture of the serious-minded, idealistic pre-war generation from which Hirst had drawn his recruits.[12]

One of six children, Hamilton was born in 1882 in Manchester, and brought up there and later in Aberdeen and Glasgow. Her mother, of Quaker background, was brought up from her early teens by a friend of John Bright and was sent to Newnham, after which she taught botany at Manchester High School for Girls. Her rationalist father, Robert Adamson, who ended his career as Professor of Logic and Metaphysics at Edinburgh University, was a reformer, an enthusiast for sexual equality, and an intimate of Gilbert Murray and of C.P. Scott of the *Manchester Guardian*.

After nine months staying with a German professorial family and attending the University of Kiel, she went as a Scholar to her mother's old college at Cambridge, where she read classics, history and economics and took the equivalent of a second in Part I and a first in Part II. (It was not until 1948 that women were admitted to membership of the university and granted degrees.) Like Layton and Hugh Dalton (Labour Chancellor of the Exchequer from 1945 to 1947, and destined to be a close friend from 1929 and, if Graham Hutton was right, her lover[13]) she was affected by the 'noble influence' of the idealistic political philosopher Goldsworthy Lowes Dickinson. Excluded from Marshall's lectures, but instructed in his *Principles* by his wife, 'dull and repressive of wandering curiosity or thought connections', Molly Adamson was stirred by speeches of the undergraduate J.M. Keynes. The political climate was dominated first by the Boer War, then by tariff reform; the debates in the college 'Political', modelled upon the House of Commons, were intense and Adamson excelled; she was, said her Newnham obituarist, 'one of those students whose doings reverberate for succeeding generations'. Her college contemporaries were 'serenely confident' about their futures. 'Confidence in the world order of which our lives were somehow to be part was the basis of our mental and moral outlook ... Axiomatically we believed in progress. We had a sense of duty, of right and wrong, of good and evil, which appeared to us instinctive and was, we assumed, natural to man. About the universe, we felt an unquestioned and fundamental assurance. Differing in detail, we yet shared an ultimate philosophy so much taken for granted that it was hardly examined.' Like virtually all the people with whom Hirst had surrounded himself, they were 'chock full of conscience, social and individual'.

> We saw ourselves as going out to fight, as best we could, on the side of the battalions of light and hope. For that fight we girded ourselves with zest and with confidence in the issue. We got tremendously excited about inequalities and injustices. Ardently, most of us hoped for great economic, social and

political change and improvement. The wrongs of the poor were vividly with us, so were the wrongs of the Irish and the Boers, the Finns and the Indians. We crusaded for causes of every kind.[14]

In 1905, the year after she graduated, Molly Adamson married C.J. Hamilton, who had graduated from Cambridge in 1901 with a first in the Moral Science Tripos and had become a lecturer in Political Science at University College, Cardiff; she lectured there in history for a while. The marriage was a disaster which formed the basis for *The Last Fortnight*, a novel she published in 1922, although she never as much as mentioned her marriage in her autobiography; neither remarried, but in their *Who's Who* entries neither of them mentioned the other.

By the time she joined *The Economist*, around 1912, Molly Hamilton had worked on Poor Law reform and on a land inquiry set up by Lloyd George, the Chancellor of the Exchequer, and had translated a study of French tariff policy as well as a book on Austria-Hungary by Hirst's great friend, Franz Josef Redlich. A versatile writer, she had already published a *Junior History of Rome*, *Greek Legends* and a novel and had had some journalistic experience. The main male character of *Dead Yesterday*, her novel about the outbreak of war, published the year in which she left *The Economist*, is the acting editor of a liberal weekly organ of opinion. Chapman believed the book to be written around the staff of *The Economist*. 'Several members of The Economist staff were depicted in the novel as characters. It was easy to recognise them.' Hamilton herself said that she drew 'faithfully, a group of youngish persons, very much like those comprising the set in which I lived', which is not quite the same thing; she had an extremely active life outside the office. Nearly 80 years later it is impossible to identify any of the characters with any degree of confidence, but there are passages that reflect the social gulf in the office right up to the Second World War.

Nigel, charming, clever, superficial, arrogant and bored with life, is standing in for a lengthy period for Davis, the rather prosaic editor for whom he has contempt.

> 'What is it, Mr Brown?' He half turned round in his chair to look at him. In the hierarchy of the office, members of the editorial staff were addressed without prefix, as Matheson, Jeffries, Robinson; while the clerks and advertisement staff retained it. Nigel, of course, was Mr Strode to everyone, but that was a different matter. Matheson and Jeffries lunched together and

addressed each other as Bill and Walter; Matheson dined with Mr and Mrs Jeffries at Putney. Robinson, equal in official status, did not exist outside the office. The other two sometimes lunched with him and occasionally even supped on press day; but no one called him anything but Robinson. It was felt – but never said – that though he was all right, Mrs Robinson might be difficult and not quite up to the delicate standard of Putney. On the other hand, Robinson was far the ablest of the three: Fleet Street was full of substitutes for Matheson and Jeffries, but Robinson was indispensable. So in his way was Mr Brown. Mr Brown moved from one foot to the other.

'It's about Mr Jenkins, sir.'

'Jenkins?' Nigel was for the instant at a loss. Then he recovered.

'Oh, yes, the advertisement manager. What about him? Sit down, Mr Brown.'

Mr Brown looked at the indicated seat, but made no motion towards it. To have sat down in the editor's room would have disturbed his sense of values; for an awkward job of this kind he preferred to stand.

'It's like this, sir. For some time past I've been afraid Jenkins hasn't been running quite straight . . . I knew he'd been in money troubles . . . I've had my suspicions about the ads for some time.' He hesitated.

'Well?' said Nigel, still in the dark.

Mr Brown stared at the portrait of Mr Gladstone over the fireplace.

'Taking commissions on the ads, sir. Putting up the rates to advertisers and pocketing the difference.'

The cashier entered into a detailed explanation, which made the point clear even to Nigel, who had never troubled to master the technical side of the paper: and further showed that Jenkins's defalcations all dated from the period of Davis's departure. Mr Brown handled this point delicately, but he observed that Mr Davis used to go through all the accounts on Saturday morning, and 'a thing like this couldn't have escaped his notice: he is wonderful with figures, is Mr Davis.' Nigel never came in on Saturday: he had not even realised that Davis regularly did so. But, of course, Davis was a creature with no life outside the office. Nevertheless, to realise that Jenkins had so quickly taken advantage of the slacker hand at the helm caused him a moment of anger. It was not lessened when Mr Brown stated that Jenkins was a very useful man: to dismiss him would be awkward for the paper.[15]

Jenkins was summoned.

Nigel looked at the advertisement manager. He was a little man rather like a rat in appearance, with sleek hair, shiny, pimply face, weak, pursed-up mouth and pale, shifting eyes. In his dapper city clothes, light spats and white-edged waistcoat he looked an absurd, incredible vehicle for a passion that swept manners and security and decency away: one of the ten thousand colourless suburbans who came up to town day in, day out, did the same things week after week and year after year, and kept up an appearance. With his eyes pink and swollen behind his dimmed glasses, he was a forlorn but also a ridiculous figure. Nigel watched him carefully flick a speck of dust off his trousers, and marvelled at it all. Jenkins, the type of machine-made modern life at its poorest; the product of a cheap and hurried schooling, evening classes, the city and suburban trains; born and bred behind dirty lace curtains in a jerry-built house, with no hope in the future of anything but such another house, in a quarter where every house was as like its neighbours as were a row of peas in a pod; imprisoned from his earliest breath in a false respectability whose maintenance was the only religion that had ever been instilled into his mind . . . Jenkins was the typical wage slave, bound to a more dreary servitude than that of the manual worker he despised. One could picture his drab existence from start to finish, were it not so hopeless that to do so even in imagination was depressing.[16]

A sense of difference between the editorial and the business side of a newspaper is a fact of life: in Britain, in the twentieth century, it was exacerbated by those differences in education which make for the greatest gaps between the classes. Until Hirst, of the six editors, only Lathbury had been to an ancient university (Oxford), and three (Wilson, Palgrave and Johnstone) had been to no university at all. Additionally, three of the six (Wilson, Bagehot and Palgrave) were businessmen and Johnstone had come up the hard way. Only Hutton and Lathbury, both unsuccessful editors, had come to the editorship solely through the intellectual route. Hirst was to start a new pattern: the domination of Oxbridge. His successor, Hartley Withers, was an Oxford man; Layton and Crowther were Cambridge and Tyerman, Knight, Burnet and Emmott Oxford. Rupert Pennant-Rea, Trinity College, Dublin, was the only twentieth-century appointment from outside the charmed Oxbridge circle, and TCD is hardly plebeian.

The many intellectual and social advantages of an Oxbridge education inevitably accentuate the gulf between the educated and less educated.

Wilson would have had much in common with Hirst's business staff: to Hirst and his young Oxbridge recruits they were a race apart who did not know their alpha from their omega.

The division became less acute after the Second World War, but to some extent it exists on *The Economist* even now. Yet there are always some people who cross the divide and imperceptibly draw the two parts of the paper closer together. In the last decade, it has helped that the chief executive, David Gordon (Oxford), had transferred from editorial and could spar on equal terms with the most arrogant journalist ('a highly intelligent and adorable guy,' said one normally critical commentator in 1984; 'it is lovely having one of your own up there'.) In recent years also, the patrician courtesy and wit of Hugo Meynell (Sandhurst), who started in 1963 in advertising and rose to become deputy managing director in 1973, made him at ease with everyone, while the non-Oxbridge investment-journalist-turned-defence-correspondent-turned-literary-editor-turned-surveys-editor, Gordon Lee, provided alcohol and sympathy to all those in distress in the organisation, be they despairing intellectuals or disconsolate members of the postroom. Crossing the divide is a job that can be done only by the socially confident or naturally egalitarian. In Hirst's editorship, the job was done by the equable Gilbert Layton and the jovial Mike Flood, who used to throw themselves into renditions of Gilbert and Sullivan for half an hour at a time. Layton, an amateur performer in musical comedy, who like his elder brothers Wilfred (a professional organist) and Walter had been to choir school, would start a song in the editorial office: Flood would pick up and join in from the room at the end of the corridor shared by administration and advertising.

A fragment of correspondence between Robert Woodbridge and Gilbert Layton, 20 years later, is an excellent reflection of Layton's style and personality.

WOODBRIDGE & SONS
Solicitors

5, Serjeants Inn,
Fleet Street,
London E.C.4

20 December 1933

My Dear Gilbert,

I am a Liveryman in the Worshipful Company of Cooks which is a City Guild as you probably know. I understand I am to be elected to the Court in the near future. The Clerk to the Company Mr Clifton Sherrard is my Cousin and has written to me today asking me to give the names of two references to whom he must apply formally. I hope you will not mind my giving your name.

Believe me,

Yours sincerely,

Robert W.

Layton's response:

I must truly confess I am deeply concerned
To be told that a man I have always admired
Has been living on money he never has earned
And with underworld crooks has for some time conspired.

It's too awful! A lawyer a liveried crook!
I'll never believe it – it cannot be true.
I think at your letter I'll take one more look,
Why, of course, you're among quite a different crew.

As a liveried cook, not a crook, you aspire
To let the world know how your spare time is spent,
Not with golf, or the beagles, but close by the fire
Making soufflés and soups with demeanour intent.

Chacun à son goût. Yours is a quaint hobby.
Why aren't you a Vintner or Cooper or Mercer?
But a livery man, I suppose, my dear Bobby,
Must be his own cook, or his liver gets worser.

Were you an accountant or banker or such,
I might cherish some qualms in consenting to tell
What I know about you. But it don't matter much
Whether lawyers cook books, and so everything's well.

21–xii–1933   G.C.L.

Under Hirst's editorship the circulation and advertising climbed steadily and deservedly, for he improved the product radically. For a start, it increased in size substantially. Bagehot's 1876 paper, like Johnstone's of 1893, consisted of about 28 pages; by 1906, Johnstone's last year, this had risen to around 40, mainly accounted for by the new lucrative branch of advertising, formal reports of company general meetings. Hirst's paper went up by another 16 or so pages, of which most were used to accommodate the considerably enlarged political and financial coverage. In appearance, however, even Hirst's paper was little changed from that of James Wilson; the major innovation had been Johnstone's introduction of display advertising on the front page; in February 1885 Apollinaris mineral water was the pioneer.

Apollinaris occupied its exclusive position until April 1886, occasionally ringing the changes. In March readers were informed that it had been granted the '*HIGHEST AWARD*' by the jury at the London International Health Exhibition 'Over all other Mineral Waters, Natural or Artificial'. The *British Medical Journal* was quoted: 'APOLLINARIS reigns alone among Natural Dietetic Table Waters. Its numerous competitors appear to have, one after another, fallen away.'

The BMJ spoke too soon. That same month another mineral water occupied Apollinaris's space. Friedrichshall, 'the well-known Aperient Mineral Water', which was of 'considerably greater strength and efficiency than heretofore', was to be taken in doses of a large wineglassful, and Sir Henry Thompson, FRCS, pronounced that he 'knew nothing at all equal to Friedrichshall. The LONGER it is taken the SMALLER is the quantity necessary to effect the purpose.'[17] Sir Henry was quoted in turn, though less specifically, by Apollinaris, on 1 January 1887. 'Probably our travelling fellowcountrymen owe their attacks of fever more to drinking water contaminated by sewage matter than to the malarious influences which pervade certain districts of Southern Europe. The only water safe for the traveller to drink is a natural mineral water.' Within a few years mineral waters had given way to more appropriate advertisers, mainly insurance companies, and the front page of *The Economist* was that much duller.

The advertising pages had also become duller. Patent medicines had given way to portmanteaus and new-fangled technology like the typewriter and the telegraph. But the content of Hirst's paper was full of zest and stimulation. It reflected his well-stocked and curious mind and the great charm of his personality as well as the lively staff he had gathered about him. His approach to his readers was more personal than any editor before or since. For instance, when he went abroad, he used to present afterwards in *The Economist* his personal impressions in the first person over his initials. In January 1909 he wrote three articles about his first visit to the United States, beginning with 'IMPRESSIONS OF AMERICA – BUSINESS AND BUSINESS MEN IN THE UNITED STATES'.

> It is difficult to visit New York without feeling that what philosophers call 'the effective desire for accumulation' constitutes a more general, potent, and overmastering impulse than in any great city of Europe. The hurrying multitudes that rush from a half-finished breakfast to the neighbourhood of Wall Street and crawl back exhausted to subway or elevator in time for dinner and bed are all hustling up an endless ladder in the vague hope of resting one day in happy leisure on the roof of fortune. Far be it from me to deny that the majority enjoy the ascent. It is exhilarating if dangerous.

He then gave his readers a slightly abridged version of 'The Story of the Galley Slave', a sketch by the American humorist George Ade about the businessman who was always about to retire but always had one task left to do and who ultimately died with a ticker tape on one side of his bed and a stenographer on the other. There was, said Hirst, 'really something to admire in the prodigious energy, zeal, and activity of the American fortune-maker. From railwayman, or factory hand, or office boy to President is quite a usual story. Ruthless concentration on the business, infinite capacity for work and the love of it, partly for the sake of getting on and wholly to the exclusion of other interests and pleasures, are the qualities that tell at first. From among those who are not exhausted or killed in this preliminary ascent there emerge a few great organisers or manipulators like Rockefeller, Carnegie, or Morgan.' The bad side was that ambition often made subordinates disloyal, but he praised the American determination to encourage the capable and industrious. He was also impressed by American generosity. The miser was 'a rare bird' and spendthrifts abounded – especially among women.

> But there is probably more civic munificence, notably in the endowment of education, than anywhere else in the world. In spite of all the organised corruption there is an immense deal of public spirit. If there is too much private spirit in public life there is also a splendid manifestation of public spirit in private life. One meets with it everywhere. It is part of the energy and devotion that New York and New England have inherited from pirate patriots and pious protestants, or drawn from the exhilarating air of America.[18]

'THE BANKER, THE PIONEER, AND THE SPECULATOR' followed and

offered for his average business reader a most illuminating comparison between the two banking capitals. New York was 'the banking and speculative centre of the United States': London was 'the world's mart and exchange'.

And in 'THE UNIVERSITIES AND THEIR PRESIDENTS' he was favourably impressed by the importance of universities in national life, which he attributed to some extent to the average American university being less powerful than Oxford or Cambridge. 'The rather exclusive caste with its innumerable degrees that files out of Oxford and Cambridge is but faintly reproduced in the American system by Harvard and Yale, whose mannerisms are sometimes imitated by the youthful universities of the West, and often caricatured by the American humorist.' Diligence was a feature of American universities because few students were from prosperous homes. Even at Harvard 'there is far less of the dilettantism and indifference to the practical business of life than is to be found in the extravagant sets at our fashionable colleges'. There was, too, much greater emphasis on politics and political economy. 'The large universities have quite a number of economic lecturers, who often specialise on live subjects, such as railways, banking, or industrial corporations. Thus the students are constantly reminded of the various lines of business into which they can enter in order to earn a living after they have taken their degree.'[19]

His reactions to America show clearly that though Hirst might be, as Walter Layton and Geoffrey Crowther put it in their joint obituary,[20] 'a Victorian Liberal born too late', he was no young fogey. Though he came from a prosperous background, it was one built on hard work and thrift, qualities he greatly respected. One of his virtues as a journalist was the combination of his great intellectual qualities and his businessman's instincts. Nor was he a Little Englander. He might want to keep England Victorian, but he was no more a cultural than any other kind of imperialist and he made enduring friendships abroad as well as at home. Some of his trips abroad, oddly enough, were to visit battlefields, for he had a deep interest in military history.

One distinguished foreign recruit whom Hirst brought to the paper was Franz Josef Redlich, the great authority on English local government (with whom Hirst had collaborated), who was a member of the Austrian parliament from 1907 to 1918 and was to be briefly Finance Minister twice (1918 and 1931), as well as for several years a Professor of Comparative State and

Administrative Law at Harvard: during the First World War he was a dedicated pacifist. Redlich's association with the paper did not survive Hirst's removal, but Luigi Einaudi's did: he was to stay as an Italian correspondent until after the Second World War, when he became President of the Republic of Italy.[21] The scanty correspondence in the Einaudi archive suggests that he became a subscriber in 1908, when he was teaching economics at the University of Turin and was a prolific contributor on economics to Italian newspapers. In March 1908 he wrote a letter to *The Economist* criticising and amplifying its coverage of the Italian budget. By the summer he was a paid contributor, earning £6. 5s. 0d. in August. From then on he was a constant; his work for the paper included – certainly in the 1920s – the Italian entry in the annual *Commercial History*.

Most of Einaudi's surviving correspondence with *Economist* staff takes the form of routine communications. Proofs were sent with a printed note saying: 'The Editor of The Economist [in Gothic type] begs to enclose a proof and will be glad to have it returned as speedily as possible' and cheques were accompanied by, for example, 'The Editor has pleasure in enclosing herewith Cheque for £6: 5: – in consideration of your contributions to the "Economist" during August.' The payment forms were largely unchanged from Hirst's day up to the Second World War, but they were insufficiently deferential for Albert Chapman, who when he wrote with similar information to Einaudi added 'esteemed' before 'contributions'. (In 1961 the paper published one of its rare obituaries:

> *Luigi Einaudi*, scholar-statesman, liberal economist and second president of the Italian Republic from 1948 to 1955, who died on Monday, was surely the most distinguished of all foreign correspondents of *The Economist*, for which he wrote regularly from Italy in the years before the last war. *Albert Henry Chapman*, who died on Friday last week, was certainly the longest-serving member of *The Economist*'s staff, which he joined in June, 1897, and took leave of only in January this year, after a loyal lifetime's work.[22])

Einaudi's cache demonstrates how the paper became more businesslike. A 1931 letter from Pearl Wallace (later Mrs Leonard Reid), Walter Layton's secretary, requests him in future to send his correspondence twice monthly, to arrive on the first and third Thursday of each month. 'If, however, in the interval between your letters, any event of outstanding importance should occur which, in your opinion, merits immediate notice in our columns, perhaps you would be good enough to send a short note covering that particular item of news.' A letter from Douglas Jay, assistant editor in charge of foreign correspondents, is also engagingly redolent of ancient courtesies.

July 19th 1935.

Dear Professor Einaudi,

We greatly regret the erroneous printing of the word 'colonies' in the *Economist* of July 6. This was due to the indistinctness of the word after your ink correction. We enclose the copy so that you may see how the mistake arose.

We have inserted a correction in this week's paper.

Yours sincerely,

The enclosed copy shows that, for foreigners at least, subbing could be very heavy even then. Here, sentence by sentence, is part of an Einaudi paragraph compared with what appeared in the paper after Jay had dealt with it.

EINAUDI That, whatever is the cause, activity is better is evident from the unemployment figures, which are down to 755.349 at the end of May against 941.257 at the same date last year.

ECONOMIST Unemployment had fallen to 755,349 at the end of May, against 941,257 at the same time last year.

EINAUDI The call to the colony [corrected by Einaudi indecipherably to 'colours'] of 600 to 700 thousand more young men has obviously eased the labour market; but unemployment statistics never could be literally trusted.

ECONOMIST The dispatch to the Colonies of 600,000 to 700,000 more young men has obviously eased the labour market; but the unemployment statistics could never be literally trusted.

EINAUDI I dont wish to discuss the technicalities of their compilation and to guess the reasons why, against a total unemployed figure rising sometimes over the one million mark the number of subsidized men was in 1934 only 155.650 on the average.

ECONOMIST Compared with a total unemployed figure rising sometimes to over 1,000,000, the number of men receiving relief in 1934 was only 155,650 on the average.

EINAUDI The point is that there is a vast difference between different countries. What in an highly developed industrial country would be an appalling figure, one or two million men begging for bread on the streets, or living on the dole, is very much less staggering in countries, like Italy or France, where people live mostly on their farms or small shops or are independent artizans.

ECONOMIST In countries like Italy or France, however, where people live mostly on their farms or in small shops or are independent artisans, the total may not be as alarming as it looks.

Jay's memory is different.

An . . . eminent . . . occasional contributor was our Italian correspondent Luigi Einaudi, then a professor of economics, orthodox free-trader, and critic of Mussolini. I was particularly enjoined by Layton not to alter a single word of the rather odd English in Einaudi's Italian letters, since any change might land him in serious trouble with Mussolini . . . I was forced to leave Einaudi's in all their semi-grammatical oddity. Some readers must have been puzzled . . . But twenty years later, in the post-war world, when Einaudi became President of Italy, Head of State, having survived Mussolini and the war, I met him on a visit to this country, and he cordially thanked the *Economist* staff for their help in enabling him to out-live Mussolini and preserve his economic conscience at the same time.[23]

Jay is half-right: Einaudi material that in any way bore on politics went uncorrected. For instance, 'SIGNOR MUSSOLINI'S IMPORTANT SPEECH', a report of 'the most pointed and timely of Signor Mussolini's economic speeches' since 1926, reported straightforwardly a large number of foreign exchange regulations and then tip-toed into the wider issue in a highly individualistic style of which normally Jay would have made short work. 'In industrial and financial circles there arises from time to time a vague feeling that Signor Mussolini may turn Socialist. Business opinion is in favour of corporativism, but it would be very much more favourable, were there not some misgiving about a certain mystic affinity between corporativism and Socialism. Utterances by young philosophers and old syndicalists cause uneasiness. Signor Mussolini, however, has allayed these fears. He is not moving, he affirms, towards State capitalism or State Socialism. But, he says, nevertheless, that Italian bankers, financiers, capitalists, industrialists and agriculturists have done all they could to force him and the State towards State Socialism. They have done business badly, and when they have lost their depositors', creditors' and shareholders' hard-won money they have asked for State aid . . . If he chose, he adds, he could turn State capitalist or State Socialist. But it would be the fault of the capitalists and bankers and financiers, not the fruit of his own will.'[24] This was typical of the highly skilful and intrepid political tightrope-walk that Einaudi conducted from 1922 to 1943 between his readers' need to understand what was going on and his own desire to evade the attentions of a touchy dictator. His association with *The Economist* was well-known, and on occasion, he had to go so far as to disassociate himself from its editorial line.[25]

During the war he managed to provide a few articles, posted from Switzerland, and his last contribution was a signed letter in 1946, when he was Governor of the Bank of Italy, arguing against a threatened French annexation. 'We are now a conquered country and expect penalties to be imposed. But the renunciation of the Upper Roya Valley offends tradition, national sentiment and just economic interests. If necessary, this area, kept a part of Italy, could be made a free zone. But to carry out the proposed unjust awards is truly the best method of reviving fascism and nationalism which, in my opinion, were dead in Italy as from July 25, 1943 [Mussolini's fall].'[26]

As well as the recruitment of first-class foreign commentators, Hirst also attracted lively readers. One of the great attractions of Hirst's *Economist* was the correspondence columns. 'I hold more strongly than ever that it is the first duty of the Press, and a duty still honoured by our great provincial newspapers as a rule, to print letters – provided they are reasonably interesting, concise, and grammatical – indifferently and impartially, whether they come from supporters or opponents', he wrote in his valedictory article.[27] His controversial opinions livened up his readers, with some of whom he conducted a dialogue.

One engaging exchange in May 1913 was about the principle of compulsory military service, to which Hirst was bitterly opposed.

A WORKMAN ON COMPULSORY SERVICE.

Sir, – Your leading articles are usually written in such sober language, and your grasp of public affairs so great, that as a workman I am a bit puzzled to understand what you have said in your issue of April 19th *re* Col. Sandy's Bill.* There are two sides to the matter – the side of the leisured classes, and the side of the working classes – neither of which has been properly put before the public; the disposition of everybody seeming to be to push the duty of national defence on to somebody else.

Now, in 1886, in connection with another matter closely akin to this, I parcelled out society into seven distinct classes or strata as follows:-

Class I. – All those whose names appear in Burke [*Burke's Peerage*].

Class II. – All those whose incomes are above £10,000 a year, but who are not mentioned in Burke.

Class III. – All those whose incomes are over £1,000 a year and under £10,000.

Class IV. – All those whose incomes are above the income-tax limit and under £1,000 a year.

Class V. – The working population, and includes all whose incomes are below the income-tax limit.

Class VI. represents disease-ridden aliens and others, depredators, loafers, able-bodied mendicants, vagrants, and undesirables generally.

[Class VII represented 'physical failure, exhaustion and destitution'.]

He estimated the annual number of suitable men becoming 18 to be 150,000.

Now, Sir, most of your correspondents are gentlemen of University education, and it may seem presumption on the part of a *bona fide* workman to address you at all, but the first question I would ask is, is the splendid heritage bequeathed to us by our forefathers worth preserving? And if so, are we all doing our best towards that end?

Classes V, VI and VII were providing by far the bulk of the defence forces. Might not each of the classes I, II, III and IV form a battalion of its own, 'to vie in healthy rivalry with those of the classes below them? Where there's a will there's a way, and I have yet to learn that the annual waste of manhood

---

*A proposal – which was voted down – to compel all males, except those specially exempted, to enter the army at 18 and serve at intervals for four years. *The Economist* had written of it that, abroad, conscription was 'the chief cause of revolutionary discontent . . . British employers of labour may be reminded that there is a group of Socialists in England which advocates the arming of the democracy for the purpose of destroying capitalism and overthrowing the social fabric. This is rather different from the idea propagated in some London newspapers that by compulsory service the labouring classes will be disciplined into a state of submissive obedience to their superiors. A notion less in conformity with the facts has never been propagated.'

that I have mentioned is intentional. – I have the honour to be, Sir, your obedient servant, JOHN HENRY KING.

53 Marple street, Nottingham, April 25th'

> [It is very pleasant to find a *bona fide* working man reading and appreciating the *Economist*, even when he does not always agree with us . . . why should hard working taxpayers, who support a military and naval expenditure of 74 millions, be treated as an 'annual waste of manhood'? Some of us think that freedom from the slavery of compulsory service and from military rule is no small part of 'the splendid heritage bequeathed to us by our forefathers'. ED, *Economist*][28]

'I am grateful to you for having published my letter,' replied King, 'and more so for your appended note, because I believe that this matter cannot be too much threshed out. I may say that I go the library every Saturday afternoon, and though I scan a great many other papers and reviews, I never fail to look at the *Economist*, because I consider its political articles to be the fairest and the best to be found there.' The term 'annual waste of manhood' had been a clumsy way of expressing his belief that 'there is no want of pluck on the part of those forming Classes I., II., III., and IV., and that if facilities were given, many of them would gladly shoulder a rifle in defence of these isles'. At present classes V and VI were providing 96 per cent of the rank and file of His Majesty's forces.

> Now, Sir, we can quite understand a gentleman in any of the first four classes viewing with repugnance the idea of his sons having, for any purpose, to mingle on equal terms in times of peace with the likes of us, or of joining a force that is known to be almost entirely composed of us; but if the force were designated by another appellation, and were composed entirely of the sons of those forming that particular class, do you not think we should hear less of this shortage of men? Say the 1st Essex Gentlemen Sharp-Shooters; the 2nd Surrey Gentlemen Sharp-Shooters; the 3rd Middlesex Gentlemen Sharp-Shooters; or the 4th Kent Gentlemen Sharp-Shooters. In such a case each county would have four companies – a company for each particular class – which in time would grow to half battalions and probably to battalions.
>
> As long as human nature is what it is, there will always be distinction of class, and to tell the gentlemen of, say, Class II., that if they wish to display

their patriotism they must go and herd with, say, those of Class VI. in times of peace is to fetter their natural aspirations.[29]

Hirst appended no comment to this letter, which to modern eyes reads like a leg-pull, but was almost certainly serious. Almost 80 years later, 'THE CLASS OF 1992' had the introduction: 'The British are notoriously obsessed with class. But what is it? In the first of an occasional series, we show that class is not disappearing, merely evolving.' It provided five rival ways of dividing the British into class categories, which included the market researchers':

A   Professional/senior managerial
B   Middle managers/executives
C1 Junior managers/non-manual
C2 Skilled manual
D   Semi-skilled/unskilled manual
E   Unemployed/state dependants

the 'despairing effort of one American Marxist, Erik Olin Wright, to make modern society fit his theories':

Bourgeoisie
Small employers
Petit bourgeoisie
Expert managers
Expert supervisors
Expert non-managers
Semi-credentialled managers
Semi-credentialled supervisors
Semi-credentialled workers
Uncredentialled managers
Uncredentialled supervisors
Proletariat

and the approach closest to that of Hirst's correspondent, John Henry King - that of the sociologist, Lord Runciman, who sought to reflect the distinctions the British actually make:

Upper class
Upper middle class
Middle middle class

Lower middle class
Skilled working class
Unskilled working class
Underclass

Embedded in this excellent analysis of social and economic changes in the old order was a look at how the racing aristocracy pursued 'their mission to keep hoi polloi in their place'. As befits an institution awash with the products of exclusive public schools and Oxbridge, *The Economist* loves to poke fun at the privileged. Royal Ascot, it explained, still managed to preserve exclusiveness through 'Sir Piers Bengough – Eton, the Hussars and now Her Majesty's Representative at Ascot'.

> First you have to spot a notice inviting applications in the court and social columns of the top people's newspapers, *The Times, Telegraph* and *Independent*. Then you have to be sponsored by someone who has attended the royal meeting on at least eight occasions. Then you have to pass the office's internal vetting scheme, which excludes undesirables ('you know, people who haven't paid their training bills'). You are checked for credit-worthiness and vetted for security.
>
> Even then you are still not through. Those who have been before get priority; new applicants have first to be lucky in a ballot. Despite these obstacles, 18,000 applied for entrance badges last year, though the number who got them is regarded as a class secret.[30]

'What are the qualities that make a good journalist', Hirst asked once. 'Candour and courtesy should be on one side of the shield', he answered; 'independence and a sense of responsibility on the other. Without these four possessions a journalist is in danger of becoming a charlatan, a boor, a mercenary, or a conceited ass. If he possesses these, if he remembers not to distort facts, or to disguise them, however unpleasant, not to mistake rudeness for courage, not to allow his pen to be guided by paymaster or advertiser, then he may become not rich indeed, or famous, but very useful to society and helpful to progress.'[31] Those principles shone, like his personality, through Hirst's *Economist* and inspired respect. Year by year the paper's stature grew along with that of its editor. As a writer on finance and statistics Hirst's reputation was high, and like Bagehot's his *Economist* writings formed the basis for a series of books. In 1911, at the invitation of his friend H.A.L.

Fisher, the distinguished historian and Liberal stalwart, he published *The Stock Exchange – A Short Study Of Investment and Speculation*, which went into four editions.

The following year came an update of the great work of James Wilson's friend, G. R. Porter, *The Progress of the Nation in its Various Social and Economic Relations from the Beginning of the Nineteenth Century*, which acknowledged the substantial contribution of Mary Agnes Hamilton on local government and Walter Layton on wages and prices. The main part of the book, on domestic industry, had been 'executed by members of the staff of *The Economist* under my supervision, and as nothing on this scale has been attempted before we can fairly claim the indulgence of the reading public. The figures – taken from official sources – have been so carefully tested and revised that errors must have been reduced to a minimum.' Hirst had himself provided a chapter on foreign trade, on new developments in transport and communications, on coinage, banking and insurance, and on public revenue and expenditure. 'A concluding chapter, in the preparation of which I have had valuable assistance from my friend Mr. W.T. Layton, deals with the difficult problem of the growth of national wealth and capital.' And finally, in the section dealing with valuations of capital growth, Hirst had used the system devised by Robert Giffen, which, he pointed out, resembled Newmarch's work in *The Economist* in 1873. The incestuousness of the world of statistics extended well beyond the grave.

Another cooperative effort was *The National Expenditure of the United Kingdom*, for which Hirst wrote a preface and which was published in 1911 from the *Economist* office.

> Shortly after the publication of Lord Charles Beresford's* open letter to the Prime Minister demanding another orgy of wasteful expenditure I submitted to Mr Asquith and to the Chancellor of the Exchequer a memorandum – in the compilation of which I was greatly assisted by my colleagues on the staff of the *Economist* – on the actual and prospective state of our finances, with special reference to the size and cost of the Navy. That memorandum is the basis of the little book I am herewith presenting to the public in the hope that it may be the means of promoting large economies in the public service.

*Beresford was an Admiral of the old school, who over the years fell out frequently with the Admiralty, approving of reforms which he himself initiated and violently opposing those of others.

Hirst was always intensely exercised about public waste: 'There is always room for economy. There is always need for criticism of public departments, for the simple reason that in a public department there is no responsible person who has any pecuniary interest in keeping expenditure down, or even in making sure that the public gets value for money received and spent.' Something could be done for the taxpayer if the Treasury had 'a thrifty and resolute chief . . . When Gladstone was in his prime he contrived to infuse his own stern sense of responsibility for public monies into almost every department of the State. In those days officials in the Army, the Navy, and the Civil Service were rewarded not for advertising themselves in the newspapers, not for associating themselves with costly projects, not for inventing grand displays at the national expense, but for maintaining efficiency in their departments and saving money by vigilance and foresight.'

CHAPTER XXXII:

Peace, retrenchment and reform

There must . . . be a rule of reason in these, as in all other matters. No country ever completely failed to take any precautions at all against the possibility of war, and no country can ever make itself completely secure. Somewhere between the two extremes lies the reasonable course and the duty that the country owes to itself is, in the light of the evidence of the new nature of war, to review its precautions and decide which of them are reasonable. *Geoffrey Crowther, 1945*[1]

'Peace, retrenchment and reform' – the three objectives for which Hirst crusaded – were all threatened by the acceleration of the armaments race. Military expenditure was 'a dead weight that depresses employment, curtails credit, and taxes both income and capital';[2] in his life within and without *The Economist*, he worked single-mindedly against the armaments race. He was ghost writer to the like-minded Sir John Brunner, who in 1911 had become President of the National Liberal Federation (founded in 1877 by Joseph Chamberlain as 'a real Liberal parliament outside the Imperial Legislature'); together they worked for lower expenditure on armaments and for friendship with Germany, which they wanted brought into the *Entente* with France and Russia. Hirst fed his *Economist* readers column after column of opinions and facts, more facts and yet more facts. Typical was a brief note of 1909.

THE GERMAN NAVY AND THE BRITISH NAVY. –

As some people in the City appear to be almost as much frightened as the *Standard*, which talks of a hundred million loan, and suggests that our naval expenditure should be 82 millions, we may, perhaps, usefully mention two or three sets of facts and figures. In the last ten years we have spent some 300 millions on our Navy; Germany, some 108 millions on hers. Our expenditure is now about 34 millions; that of Germany, 17 or 18 millions. The tonnage of our effective war ships is about 1,852,000; that of the German, about 628,000. Those who fear a German invasion really ought to be given a safe conduct out of the country. We think the scare has been worked up by interested parties.[3]

In 1862 Bagehot had laid down the basis for *Economist* thinking on defence in a pamphlet called 'Count Your Enemies and Economise Your Expenditure',[4] an expansion of an article in the paper called 'THE LIMIT OF DEFENSIVE OUTLAY'.[5] His approach would have been endorsed by James Wilson; and it would almost certainly have been acceptable to all his successors, with the exception of Hirst, who did not believe in the existence of enemies.

> When military men or naval men, or, far worse, enthusiastic amateurs of war by sea or land, insist on the necessity of such and such things . . . it is of no use objecting. They say: 'England is not safe without these things. Would you endanger our country? Would you risk our homes and families? Would you not like to be secure yourself?' Such rhetoric is unanswerable for the best of all reasons, that it half-convinces oneself.

Objections started only when the bill was presented.

> On a sudden the history of late years then strikes you very vividly. First, the Admiralty took away some money with which it made wooden ships; and then it 'discovered its error', and acknowledged that wooden sailing ships were useless; so it asked for additional money and made wooden *steam* ships with much *éclat*. And I for one was convinced that it would be alright, and that England was now safe. But in less than a year the Admiralty discovered its error again, and pronounced all wooden ships, whether steam or sailing ships, to be useless; so it abstracted further money and constructed 'iron-plated ships' . . . which cost almost fabulous sums apiece; and now 'the Admiralty is discovering its error' again, or something like it, for it wants more money, and is making what I must call naval *nondescripts* . . . things more like an ugly insect than a ship . . . I know (though it is a matter of prophecy, I am assured of it as if it had happened) that as soon as we have made one sort of these ugly and indescribable things, we shall be told it is of no use, and that we must make another more ill-favoured and indescribable still.

(A century later Mary Goldring was a scourge of that same mentality, lambasting extravagant and inefficient weapons. One of her roughest campaigns was against not the Admiralty, but the RAF. The Canberra bomber was going out of service, and needed an urgent replacement, for until the Polaris submarine came into service in the late 1960s, some means 'other than parcel post' had to be found to deliver British nuclear weapons.[6] Instead of providing the requisite 'fish-and-chips type of aircraft', which the Australians would also buy, the TSR 2 had been chosen: 'Sophisticated, wicked-looking and narrowly specialised, TSR 2 is caviare to the general.' The Australians had opted instead for the Americans' TFX, for countries 'do not spend 2½ million on each single aircraft unless they possess nuclear weapons; and someone in Whitehall should have noticed that the Australians do not have them'. The TSR 2 would have a fighting chance of reaching its target, though it was unclear whether it had the range to reach any target worth hitting. 'What kind of pig in a poke have we bought?' she asked. For £400 million, or roughly twice what the first British atom bomb had cost, 'the country gets an aircraft that is neither flesh nor fowl, an aircraft that fills the role neither of the Canberra nor of the V-bombers'.

> Most of the blame rests squarely on the air staff, which conceived the specification for the aircraft; but some must attach to the Ministry of Defence and its scientists who allowed the air staff to get away with it. Who authorised a tree-top bomber planned to attack targets behind the enemy lines (including, if the air staff is to be believed, objects as small and mobile as tanks), but then chose the most inflexible aerodynamic shape to do it? Who decided to opt for navigation systems that must be slow and expensive to develop, and then neglected to incorporate the one device that would have given the aircraft flexibility in speed and range: namely, 'variable geometry' wings which could change shape in flight and permit an exclusively supersonic aircraft to fly when it chooses as slowly as a butterfly?

It was an expensive monstrosity.[7])

Examining the argument that scientific progress made it necessary for expenditure to continue to rise, Bagehot observed: 'Great attention and wonderful inventive power has of late been invested in the arts of destruction. No sooner is one invention perfected than a second takes its place. What was a superior way of killing people in 1859, is a most inferior way, a quite *passé* and useless way in 1862.' With all the expenditure, the nation was barely keeping pace with science, which suggested that 'science is very adequate to expend money, but very inadequate to defend a country'.

The army and navy were maintained for three main reasons. 'First, to defend our colonies and commerce in distant countries. Secondly, for the aggressive expeditions which are more or less necessary in foreign warfare, and serve to keep our enemy at home. Thirdly and principally, for the defence of our own shores.' Government should be able to deal with each use of army and navy separately and with the whole collectively. 'They ought to be specially precise with the *third*. What is the maximum force which it is at all likely may be brought against us, and what is the disposable force with which we are prepared to meet it?' Until it is known what is the aggressive force against which protection is necessary, it is impossible to gauge whether resources are sufficient or insufficient.

The true test of whether something new should be made was that some foreign nation 'has already made, or is actually making, some new things of the same sort, or something which requires this new sort to resist it'. It should be made clear publicly, in parliament, 'that our armaments are, as a mathematician would say, only *functions* of foreign armaments; that if foreign nations increase theirs, we shall as a principle increase ours, so that they will gain nothing; and if foreign nations diminish theirs, they will incur no risk as far as we are concerned, for we shall at once diminish ours too . . . The really pacific *nature* of England is not comprehended anywhere abroad, because the considerations which regulate the amount of our armaments are only half divulged, and are supposed on the Continent to be in fact offensive, while they really and truly are defensive.'

Johnstone's *Economist* strongly pushed the Bagehot line: 'ADMIRALTY WASTE AND INEFFICIENCY' had a very familiar ring. 'Every twelvemonth the public is bewildered to hear that some system of management has been prevailing in Whitehall for the last forty years, which it is difficult to imagine any sane First Lord tolerating for a fortnight.' These deficiencies might or might not have been remedied by Lord Charles Beresford's Intelligence Department. 'The Admiralty has been the subject of too many scandals in regard to inefficiency and waste to make scepticism as to its reform anything but very natural.'[8]

After five years' work and expenditure, complained 'OUR REFORMED

ARMY' in 1905, the result was: 'An army absolutely unfitted and unprepared for war, a public absolutely ignorant of the character and needs of the Empire to which they belong.'[9]

One of the constant inefficiencies continued to be precisely what Bagehot had pointed out. The military would neither count nor realistically assess their enemies: instead, they responded to panics about foreign threats. 'About the only business which in this country is never transacted in a businesslike manner is that of military preparation', complained Johnstone's paper in 1888. What usually happened was that because of economies, or an expansion of demands, or a temporary shortage of recruits, an insufficient proportion of the armed services were retained at home to meet an emergency.

> Some officer trusted by the public suddenly warns it, either in a speech or a letter, that this is the case, the country wakes up to the deficiencies in its armament, and there is a scare more or less severe. Questions are asked in the House of Commons, there is a debate in which every weakness is exposed, and then the Government, with apparent reluctance, but real pleasure, comes down and asks for a few millions to be expended in fortifications, or in ironclads, or in an increase of pay and allowances, to attract more and better recruits. The money is invariably voted, and then the country, almost without inquiry as to what has been done with the new supplies, sinks back into torpor, until some event once more provokes it to inquire into the condition of the defences, when the same process is repeated, with the same result.[10]

There was nothing new about the armaments-related inertia-panic-inertia cycle. In 1862, it was Richard Cobden's pamphlet – 'Three Panics, an historical episode' – that had partly inspired Bagehot's pamphlet. In 1913, Hirst brought his hero's polemic up-to-date in *The Six Panics and Other Essays*. He did not discuss how his paper had reacted to these various alarms: it is instructive to do so.

Cobden's and Hirst's first panic had been precipitated in 1847 by a letter in *The Times* from the near-octogenarian Duke of Wellington calling for a strengthening of defences against a popularly-expected French invasion. In response, the Chancellor of the Exchequer, Lord John Russell, announced a rise in income tax from 7d. to 1s. to increase armaments and reorganise the militia along the lines propounded by Wellington. (Condemning 'the unseemly discussions', based on no reality, that had been reviving 'feelings of national antipathy, jealousy, and suspicion', Wilson's *Economist* regretted Russell's financial proposals and the 'unfortunate tone' and 'doubtful taste' of his lengthy speech about the comparative naval and military strength of England and France.[11]) Public protests and the abdication of Louis Philippe, the improbable putative invader, brought about a U-turn within ten days, and in the following year began a gradual reduction in military and naval expenditure.

The second panic was caused by the *coup d'état* of Louis Napoleon in December 1851: 'It was now discovered that Louis Philippe, the ogre of the first panic, had been a peaceful quietist, a complete contrast to Napoleon, around whose terrifying personality the new alarms gathered.' (In 'BLESSED ARE THE PEACEMAKERS', Wilson's and Greg's *Economist* denounced the irresponsibility of the press – *The Times* was being particularly frightful – for pouring forth 'columns of the most unmeasured and virulent abuse against the French Government, the French army, and the French nation, as if their express object was to create animosity on one side of the channel and exasperation on the other'.[12]) A bill brought in by Russell to enlarge the militia was defeated on an amendment by Lord Palmerston intended to increase its scope, and the government fell. The combination of the death of Wellington in September, reviving nostalgia for great military feats against France, and the acceptance by Louis Napoleon of the title of Emperor in December, activated more invasion rumours. (*Economist* articles sought to dampen down foolish speculation. With Wellington dead, military reforms of which he would have disapproved might now be considered in the light of technical progress. 'Possibly the maintenance of such a force provokes quite as much as it repels aggression.'[13] As for the French, their war party was very small, comprising 'chiefly a few ambitious soldiers, a mass of journalists, and a race of politicians'.[14] England was stronger than France in every respect. Other states 'have more reason, on account of her exceeding strength, to dread her than she has to dread any one of them. But, happily for her and for them, the bonds of peace have strengthened as her power has grown.'[15])

Ultimately, despite the best efforts of *The Times* and most of the press, commercial interests turned against the fomenters of discord and the hysteria began to die down. Next year Britain and France united to fight Russia in the Crimea.

The third panic came against the background of the transition of the 1850s from sailing ships to steam vessels and culminated in a growing belief in 1859 that the French navy was much stronger than the British. There were alarmed speeches in parliament ('panic-mongering' in Cobden's and Hirst's view) and the naval estimates were sharply raised. (This time *The Economist* was on the side of increasing expenditure: Wilson was the absentee owner, Hutton was editor, but 'ARMAMENT AND DISARMAMENT' was classic Bagehot. A cool assessment of relative strengths and weakness, it concluded that prudence required the building up of the fleet, regardless of Louis Napoleon's intentions. For 'if we remain as unready and as inadequately defended as we are for one month longer, we are dependent on French forbearance, not on English strength – on what Louis Napoleon may choose to do, not only our means of preventing him from doing what he chooses. And, *secondly*, the pacific temper and conciliatory behaviour both of France and of its chief, will bear a pretty exact proportion to the state of our national defences. They will respect us if we are strong and ready; they will affront us if we are weak and unprotected. As King John says:-

> How oft the sight of means to do ill deeds
> Makes ill deeds done.'[16])

From 1862 the navy had been built up, fears were allayed and naval and military estimates began gradually to be reduced from their all-time high.

Hirst blamed the fourth panic on one of his *bêtes noires*, W.T. Stead, 'a clever journalist who indulged an unfortunate talent for sensations, [and who] restarted the old business of Naval Panicmonger in the *Pall Mall Gazette*'. Pressure mounted on Gladstone's troubled government, income tax was raised from 5d. to 6d. in November 1884 and the following month a sum of £5½ million to be spread over five years was announced by the First Lord of the Admiralty, after which the agitation died down and the press lost interest. (Johnstone's *Economist* applauded the spending of the five million, considered it should be spent in only two years, and blamed both political parties for allowing naval defences to fall into a 'comparatively backward condition'.[17])

Hirst's 'Fifth or Dreadnought Panic' concerned a technological development in the building of warships: both Britain and the United States designed all-big-gun battleships early in the twentieth century. First to be completed, in 1906, the British 'Dreadnought' set the pattern for the warships of the navies of the world for almost 40 years and provided their generic name. 'The Dreadnought', in Hirst's view, would be 'marked down by the recording angel as a double offence against the British nation and against the human race'.

British superiority in battleships was to be one of the decisive factors in the 1914–18 war, but for the eight preceding years the numbers to be built were a subject of vicious political argument. There were three main camps: the Tories, in opposition throughout the period, who could never have enough; the mainstream Liberals, who, being in government, juggled defence and financial priorities; and those who were essentially pacifist and who believed that the building of offensive weapons made war more, not less, likely.

In 1906, to Hirst's delight, Sir Henry Campbell-Bannerman's new administration slowed down the Dreadnought building programme, partly because of the Prime Minister's loathing of instruments of war and partly to encourage arms reductions at the 1907 Hague conference.* (*The Economist*, just coming to the end of Johnstone's editorship, was once again on the other side from Hirst. Though it admitted that armaments were costly and potentially destructive, and that they were apt to be quickly superseded by newer inventions, in Europe, at least, they had not 'multiplied wars. They may deserve all the reproaches that the Prime Minister heaped upon them last Monday, but when we come to consider what the charges amount to, we have to admit that Europe has never been so peaceful as since the international race began.' Governments seemed more afraid of going to war 'in proportion as the cost and magnitude of the engines which war will bring into action become greater and more impressive . . . The strong man armed can afford to disregard a sneer which may prove unendurable to those whose strength is less visibly assured.' The paper feared that the example which Campbell-Bannerman had decreed England should set was not calculated 'to make much impression on the Powers she will shortly meet at The Hague'. Foreign powers would not take Britain's disarmament rhetoric seriously unless she suspended shipbuilding and laid down no more Dreadnoughts, but this could not be done.

---

*The Hague conferences were another stage in the process of reaching international agreement to reduce the risk of war and to ameliorate its effects, begun in 1864 with the Red Cross-inspired Geneva Convention. The first – convened by the Russians and attended by 26 nations – met at The Hague in 1899 and *inter alia* set up a permanent court of arbitration – the Convention for the Pacific Settlement of International Disputes; in 1907 the second made the arbitration principle compulsory. Both failed in the attempt to limit armaments but their successes strongly inspired the creation of the post-war League of Nations.

Englishmen are not at all anxious to see foreign navies brought closer to their own. They believe that the circumstances of their position make the maintenance of a certain standard of relative strength at sea essential, not merely to their safety, but to their existence. And, holding this view, they do not pretend to judge of the circumstances of other nations . . . When we are told, as of late we have been told by some of our own countrymen, that this insistence on adequate maritime preparation argues a foolish distrust of humanity, we can only reply that we take humanity as we have hitherto found it. It may be undergoing some great and unsuspected change. The reign of self-interest may be drawing to a close, and the advent of an international millennium may be at hand. All we can say on this head is that we see nothing to justify the roseate picture.

Until 'domestic prophets' were proved to be right, 'we prefer to trust to the commonplace teaching of experience. So long as human nature remains what it has been in the past . . . we shall continue to think that England must remain supreme at sea, and that in order to remain supreme at sea she must regulate her shipbuilding by the shipbuilding of other Powers. War may be "the most ferocious and futile of human follies," but there is a futility far surpassing the futility of preparation which shocks and surprises the Prime Minister. It is the futility of want of preparation.'[18])

Balfour's Tory opposition and much of the press continued highly critical of Campbell-Bannerman, whose resignation and death in 1908 removed the most powerful force for disarmament. The following year Asquith's government increased the naval estimates in order to keep pace with German shipbuilding. By 1911, with Winston Churchill in belligerent mood as First Lord of the Admiralty, Hirst was completely at odds with the mainstream of the Liberal Party. He was – understandably – particularly contemptuous of the 'Sixth or Airship Panic' – the 1913 version of an outbreak of UFO hysteria, when invasion fears were exacerbated by claims that German Zeppelins were flying over Britain with malign intent.

The Economist, along with the *Daily News*, the *Manchester Guardian* and Massingham's *Nation*, were the tiny proportion of the press representing the views of Lord Morley and his couple of allies in the Cabinet. In the interests of peace and retrenchment, Hirst worked indefatigably on comparative financial, military and naval statistics – with a single-mindedness reminiscent of the young James Wilson.

In the preface to *The Six Panics*, Hirst described his object in writing the book as having been not so much 'to prevent the recurrence of false alarms in the sensational press – for no reasonable man can hope to do that – as to prevent the abominable waste of public money in which a successful panic always ends. It is all-important that the governing classes and the leading statesmen, who are trustees for the nation and for the public funds, should feel ashamed of the hoax which has now been practised upon them so often. If this little book serves to supply them with a defensive armour against the arrows of future panic-mongers, I shall be very well satisfied.'

The trouble was, as Bagehot had put it in discussing Cobden's attitude to defence expenditure: 'Sensible men have a well-founded suspicion of those who repeat the same unvarying dogma under many varying circumstances.'[19] And it did not matter how high the naval estimates were; Hirst, like Cobden, would always think them too high. 'If the recent additions, which had raised our naval estimates from 32 to 44 millions, had not been made,' he wrote passionately in 1911, 'there need have been no increase in the death duties, and no super-tax, and no land-tax; or, again, the whole of the duties on tea, coffee, and cocoa might have been swept away and substantial reductions made in the income-tax; or, again, the money might have been used for destroying the slums in the towns of Great Britain and Ireland, and erecting model dwellings, or making playgrounds and open spaces. In a few years there would have been no slums left, and the physical strength and happiness of the whole population would have been marvellously improved.'[20]

'The *worst event* which we can fairly anticipate', Bagehot had laid down, 'is the event against which, as reasonable men, we should provide.'[21] It was not an approach Hirst could fruitfully adopt, for he was incapable of believing in the depths of his soul that the seemingly enlightened world in which he lived could ever throw up the circumstances that would produce a European war. He refused to see any solid basis for the Anglo-German tensions that had existed for decades.

Until Hirst, the paper had taken a realistic but not unfriendly attitude to Germany. Bagehot disliked Bismarck, but he recognised his extraordinary achievement in welding together the German nation. Reflecting in 1870 on the conclusions to be drawn from Germany's success in the Franco-Prussian war, Bagehot had remarked that no doubt 'Germany may become, or try to become, a great naval power, and she may be a worse rival for England on the sea than France. But as yet this danger is in the air; Germany has, as yet, no fleet which we need fear, and we may deal with this danger when it comes.'[22]

Johnstone's paper did not get over-excited in January 1896, when the Kaiser sent a telegram to Kruger congratulating him on 'maintaining the independence' of his country against the Jameson Raid; it was couched in terms that implied that Germany would be prepared to interfere to protect the Transvaal. 'An open quarrel between Great Britain and Germany is so improbable,' said *The Economist*, 'and would indeed so closely resemble a quarrel between a tiger and a shark, that it would be wrong to ascribe too much importance to this ill humour . . . Every nation has its own pivot, and we must not forget, in considering the attitude of Germany, that her rulers have a most difficult part to play in Europe, with a people who are not entirely satisfied as to their wisdom, and that they are justified by the universal precedent in thinking first of the interest of their own State, to which, in their judgments, the interests of Great Britain are very often opposed. They make a mistake in showing so much temper in Zanzibar and elsewhere; but, after all, the intercourse of international society must sometimes be varied and made more interesting by the unamiability of some of its component parties.'[23]

It was not in the interest of Germany to go to war with Britain, the paper reassured its readers in 1900; its interest in the British Empire was restricted to South Africa, which it would not try to annex since it would not be able to defeat the Boers. Austria would be a reluctant ally, and France and Russia would be 'eagerly watching an opportunity – the former to recover her provinces and prestige, the latter to bring down a military strength which she regards as menacing'. Britain had no reason to provoke Germany into a war: 'Englishmen have no instinctive or historic dislike of Germans, with whom they have never fought a war. The South African idea which, no doubt, was once entertained in Germany, being abandoned there is no point at which the political interests of the two States come into collision, while though the trade rivalry may grow bitter we certainly shall not wage a great war in order to extinguish it. Rival tradesmen are often bitter in their comments on each other, but they do not come to blows in the street.'[24]

Five years later the message continued the same. 'No responsible statesmen in either country will ever, we may be sure, work for the coming of that Anglo-German naval war which is the bogey of certain alarmists in England, and the hope, we are afraid it must be said, of a certain school of German publicists, enthusiastic for the "expansion" of their nation oversea.

We have no motive for aggression on Germany, and her commercial rivalry with us assuredly could not be eliminated, or even permanently affected, even by a decisive British victory over her fleets.' There might be reason for apprehension 'not so much of war as of war scares' because of certain aspects of the German naval programmes, especially when reflecting that 'overseas commerce is not protected by battleships, but by cruisers . . . Still, it is fair to remember that Germany believes in the policy of conspicuously displaying her naval strength, that battleships display it in the most impressive form . . .'

> She has created a vast overseas commerce and a magnificent mercantile marine, and she is perfectly entitled to make such provision as seems good to her to protect them and to impress the world with her ability to do so, and to enforce her just claims.

The truth was that both pro- and anti-Germans in England were inclined to forget that 'Germany' was an abstract expression which could be interpreted in different ways.

> Those who most strongly deprecate British suspicions of Germany are apt to identify the nation with the pacific, energetic, practical German men of business or of learning, who are not in the least anxious to get the better of us except in the peaceful rivalries of research or commerce. Those who fear German aggression have in their minds the efforts of a group of patriotic Chauvinists, largely under the influence of a particular school of historians and economists, who believe in colonial 'expansion', protected markets, and the encouragement and fostering of commerce and industry by the Government, and who seem to hold that the prosperity of German trade is, and ought to be, inseparable from the presence of the German flag. History does not bear them out, and their peculiar theories are generally discredited by British political economists. But they are powerful at Berlin . . . This is the party that denounces the Anglo-Japanese alliance as reserving the Far East for exploitation by Great Britain and Japan; that hopes for a Russo-German counter-alliance which could only tend to the partition of China.[25]

For all *The Economist*'s tendency to believe – against most of the odds – that reason must eventually triumph, it has been saved by a certain earthy realism from falling too often into the silliness of the utopian intellectual. A paper which has to devote much of its attention to commodity prices keeps its feet on the ground. 'What men of business want to know is', wrote Bagehot in 1867 in 'FRANCE AND THE MONEY MARKET', at a time when France was feeling threatened by the two new nations of Germany and Italy, 'will there be a general war or will there be a general peace?'[26] Sober analysis is what the readers want. But on the question of war what they got from Francis Hirst was dominated by wishful thinking. When the tortured Kaiser Wilhelm II – a man permanently torn between the liberal values drummed into him by his forceful English mother and the macho Prussian values pressed on him by his immediate circle – visited England late in 1907, *The Economist* positively drooled over Queen Victoria's grandson, England's 'best friend' in Germany.

> It is easy to overrate the part which the link of blood and early association plays in the relations of Sovereigns with one another, but it is equally easy to give it less than its due weight. When a great Sovereign can recall the 'ties of close relationship and many dear memories of bygone days' that unite him to Edward VII, when the 'remembrance of a beloved mother' [with whom in fact he had a very difficult relationship] can carry him back 'to the earliest days of a happy childhood spent under the roof and within the walls' where he is now a guest, only an exaggerated scepticism can believe that these things count for nothing.

The Kaiser had told his audience at the Guildhall that maintaining good relations between Germany and England '"as the main prop and base of the peace of the world"' was his aim 16 years previously '"and history, I venture to hope, will do me the justice that I have pursued this aim unswervingly ever since."' There have been moments, indeed, in the course of those sixteen years when the Emperor's methods may not have seemed the best that could have been chosen for the furtherance of this aim. But that is no reason for doubting his sincerity.' The European outlook was brighter than it had been for a long time, assisted by increasing commercial ties. And while it would be pleasing if the Germans came to an arrangement with Britain to reduce the size of the two navies, if it proved otherwise, there should be no irritation or suspicion. 'Nothing has done more to disturb our friendship with European Powers than the disposition occasionally shown in England to regard the action of another Government in thinking only of its own interests, and shaping its policy with exclusive reference to those interests, as necessarily implying hostility to us . . . The influence which really makes for peace is the conviction, which is happily growing stronger, that peace is the interest of everybody. That conviction may not be enough to secure the desired result in all cases, but, even if it should prove inoperative in this or that instance, it remains the one real foundation on which a new and better state of things can be built up.'[27]

Better again was the visit of King Edward VII and Queen Alexandra to Germany in 1909, which 'should go far towards breaking down the deplorable misunderstanding which has long been troubling Europe. The brilliant and stately reception of the Royal party, the hearty welcome accorded them in the streets, the cordiality of the speeches at the State banquet, make an excellent beginning towards impressing the popular mind and altering the tone of much professedly patriotic but really mischievous and inflammatory journalism . . . the special cordiality with which it has been invested on both sides should intensify the pacific significance popularly ascribed to it, and abate the theatrical bogey which has been conjured up for the purpose of another raid on the Exchequer . . .'

> Is it too much to hope that we may cease to build specifically against Germany, and against possible combinations of Germany with some grotesquely incompatible Power . . . Germany claims, not unreasonably, that she is only bringing her fleet up to a level corresponding with her shipping and commerce. If she has a suspicious and restless war party in high places and among Pan-German enthusiasts, we also have our believers in German spies and in a corps of German waiters, prepared on the outbreak of war to seize every London railway terminus, and our prophets of invasion who ignore not only our Navy, but the elementary conditions of the manoeuvring of a huge transport flotilla.

The royal visit had diminished the dangers, 'and this diminution should be reflected in mutual reduction of naval expenditures'.[28]

The year before war broke out, cheered by a measure of agreement among the Great Powers about how to solve the Balkan crisis (anti-Turk alliances among various Balkan states were adding to tensions between anti-Serbian Austria-Hungary and pro-Serbian Russia), Hirst had reached a state of buoyant optimism. 'After four or five years of diplomatic friction and naval competition between the British and German Governments, a fair prospect has at last opened out for that sort of friendly business understanding which has long been advocated in the pages of the *Economist*. It has always seemed to us a sufficient condemnation of the policy pursued by the Foreign Office after the conclusion of the *entente* with France,* that it has involved so huge an additional application of national capital to the machinery of destruction. Dreadnoughts have grown into super-Dreadnoughts; torpedoes, submarines, cruisers have been multiplied; new naval stations have been fortified; docks have been broadened and deepened.' However, private letters from Berlin and Vienna 'strongly confirm the view that a rational cooperation between England and Germany, so happily begun during this Balkan crisis, will lead, if pursued with wisdom and statesmanship, to a fresh era of peace in Europe'.[29]

Francis Hirst was not unusual in failing to predict a European war: the memoirs of those young at that time almost unanimously speak of a golden summer shattered by the thunderbolt of unimaginable tragedy. Molly Hamilton spoke of her set, in July 1914, being almost completely unaware of what was coming to them; and in August when it did come, being dumbfounded. 'I was to be told, in 1917 and after, that they [her set] are incredible; I find it hard, now, not to endorse that view. But they were actually as I had described them, earnest, politically minded, but invincibly ignorant and unprepared.'[30] They knew nothing of foreign affairs: in Hamilton's novel, the clever liberal Nigel finds his journal under attack.

> Nigel knocked the ash of his cigarette neatly into his saucer.
>
> 'Of course,' he said lightly, 'I don't pretend to understand foreign policy.'
>
> Looking up, he found Mrs Leonard regarding him with an expression that was almost stern.
>
> 'Does that seem to you a very serious lapse?'
>
> 'Very,' she said shortly. 'Very serious indeed.'
>
> 'But why?' he asked. 'Domestic affairs are surely infinitely more important – to say nothing of their being both interesting and more or less intelligible, which is more than I can say for foreign policy.'
>
> 'Hasn't it occurred to you that domestic affairs are, at any moment, at the mercy of foreign policy? And largely because so many people, especially so many Liberals, think, like you, that it's none of their business; don't understand, don't try to understand, and therefore can't criticise, much less guide?'

*In 1904 an Anglo-French *Entente Cordiale* was signed: it settled several colonial bones of contention and agreed that Egypt and Morocco would be under British and French influence respectively. The 1907 Anglo-Russian *Entente* settled disputes over Afghanistan, Persia and Tibet.

Nigel moved rather restlessly in his chair. He began to wish that Mrs Leonard were not so intelligent. He felt comfortable and at peace in an atmosphere beautiful, restful and potentially romantic; why must her brain so inexorably work?

'Peace, retrenchment and reform,' he murmured, ashamed of the shibboleth, but too happily lazy to trouble about that.

'Ah – how you say that! Have you ever thought what it means? The *New World* is keen about social reform, I give you credit for that; but aren't reformers always put off because their schemes cost too much money? How can we get the money – in any country in Europe – if we have to go on pouring millions into armies and navies? And how can you stop pouring in those millions unless foreign offices work for peace? Instead of which, the continuity of foreign policy is a continuous risk of war.'

Nigel sat up. Mrs Leonard's tone was so eager, her face so grave, that he felt that all this was, to her, very important. If he showed that to him it didn't matter, he would earn her contempt.

'I am afraid the difficulty with me has been a rather stupid one. The kind of Liberal who is always making a row about Morocco and Persia and Denshawai and Miss Malecks, and all that, puts me off dreadfully.'

'Oh, you "all that"!' Mrs Leonard exclaimed.

'They haven't thought it out,' he went on. 'They want us to reduce armaments and be the *preux Chevalier* of Europe at the same time. I'm all in favour of intervention; but to intervene one must be strong. If our civilisation – which after all, is the highest in Europe – is to count, we must use it to help other peoples who are struggling—'

'Ah, but wouldn't it tell much more effectively if we were definitely always on the side of peace? I don't mean vaguely, as a pious aspiration, given up when there is any difficulty, anything that looks like an affront to our *amour propre* or a danger to our exported capital, but as a definite policy?'[31]

Nigel had always looked upon foreign policy as being like mathematics: 'a thing most ordinary people had better leave alone', and even in a journalist it was hardly surprising in the world before the Great War. Anglo-French, Anglo-German, even Anglo-Russian relations, were comprehensible in simple terms, but without enormous dedication the small print of their relationships was virtually beyond understanding. Few other than a handful of politicians, journalists and Foreign Office officials could have known enough about the Balkans to understand that they could create the greatest war of all time.*

In the 1990s the average *Economist* reader will have seen countless clever maps, graphics and pictures that make it possible to develop a picture of what is going on in the old Yugoslavia; television and other modern communications will have given him a sense of international affairs and an understanding that the collapse of one ism – such as communism – is likely to lead to outbreaks of others, like nationalism and fundamentalism. In 1914 the *Economist* readers had to rely on prose of varying accuracy and readability which was often out-of-date.

Two extracts make the point. The first comes from one of two two-page signed letters from Hirst's Viennese friend Franz Josef Redlich, which were published on 1 and 8 August 1914 but had been written before the Austro-Hungarian ultimatum. Headed 'AUSTRIA-HUNGARY AND SERBIA', they attempted to explain the historical background to violent Serbian nationalism. Authoritative, intelligent and fair-minded, and invaluable to those greedy for information, to the ignorant they were inevitably so full of numbingly unfamiliar detail as to ensure that no Nigel would ever get through more than a paragraph.

> There is a tripartite division of the Southern Slavs between Austria, Hungary, and Bosnia-Herzegovina. In Austria dwell the Slovenes, pure in

*When on 28 June 1914 a Bosnian Serb assassinated Archduke Francis Ferdinand, heir presumptive to the Emperor of Austria-Hungary, in the Bosnian capital, Sarajevo, Austria-Hungary saw an opportunity to crack down on a Serbia whose nationalist aims were seen as a threat to the multinational Habsburg empire. To provide the excuse for a preventive war (for which support had been rather vaguely promised by the Kaiser), the Austrians on 23 July presented a 48-hour ultimatum. Serbia accepted nine out of 11 demands and offered to submit the outstanding issues to arbitration. Arriving home from his annual cruise on 27 July, the Kaiser instructed his bellicose Foreign Office to tell Austria-Hungary that war was now unjustified, but he was too late: on 28 July Austria-Hungary attacked Serbia. Germany's initial hopes for 'the localisation of the conflict' ended with Russian mobilisation. On 31 July Germany sent Russia a 24-hour ultimatum demanding that it should halt mobilisation and France an 18-hour ultimatum requiring it to promise neutrality should there be a Russo-German war; both were ignored. Germany declared war on Russia on 1 August; on 2 August it demanded from Belgium free passage across its territory; on 3 August it declared war on France; on 4 August it invaded Belgium. Britain, which had a treaty obligation to defend Belgium, declared war on Germany the same day. During August Japan declared war on Germany, Austria-Hungary on Russia, Japan and Belgium on Austria-Hungary and Germany, and France and Britain on Austria-Hungary. On 5 September Britain, France and Russia signed the *Triple Entente* agreeing not to make a separate peace with Germany. The two sides were respectively called the Central Powers and the Allies.

Carniola and mixed with Italians and Croats in Trieste, Gorz, and Istria. In Hungary the Southern Slav race has exclusive possession of Croatia and Slavonia, no less than three-quarters of the people being Catholic Croats and one-quarter Orthodox or Serb. Moreover, more than half a million Serbs live in the Southern districts of Hungary itself, where they often form the most prosperous section of the town community. Finally, Bosnia and Herzegovina have from time immemorial down to the present day been occupied exclusively by the Serbo-Croatian stock. Since the Turkish occupation, indeed, the members of the three confessions – Catholic Croats, Serbs, Moslems – have been almost like three independent peoples. Yet they all speak the same language, though in writing the Serbs used Cyrillic, the Croats Roman letter-writing. The whole population is under 2,000,000 – i.e., 400,000 Croats, 600,000 Moslems, and 800,000 Orthodox Serbs.[32]

Nowadays, a Nigel will be cosmopolitan and interested in going beyond the pictures on his television screen. He will have within his *Economist* all the explanatory maps and graphs he needs to understand anything complicated. He will have enough basic knowledge not to get lost and he will want to make sense of it: with the help of a snappy style, his attention will be held. 'WHEN COUNTRIES SPLINTER' was the sombre title of the leading article in June 1992, but the cover was a still from the Marx Brothers film *Duck Soup*. 'In the days when Groucho Marx ruled Freedonia,' it began, 'the real world was divided into 65 countries.'

Today the United Nations has 178 members, and the numbers grow by the day as Bosnians, with Macedonians grunting at their trotters, follow Croats and Slovenes in a Gadarene rush to statehood. Last weekend Czechoslovaks went to the polls as citizens of one country; next time they may be voting in separate elections as Czechs and Slovaks. Meanwhile, far from turbulent Europe, Canadians have been trying to keep Quebeckers from seceding – and are finding in the process that Canada's Indians and Inuit now also want self-government. Self-determination, that basic principle of democracy, is getting out of hand. In some places at least, 'Duck Soup' has become a turkey shoot.[33]

Hirst was no Nigel, yet he too failed to see the war coming – because he refused to see any war coming. He took exactly the same position about the civil war being threatened over the granting of Irish Home Rule. In the teeth of bitter opposition from the Conservative Party, Asquith's Liberal government had pushed Home Rule through the Commons in 1912: the Lords had rejected it, but could only delay it, because the 1911 Parliament Act had removed their right of veto. Since 1910 the issue had been tearing Ireland apart, with the Ulster Unionists threatening civil war if Home Rule was enforced and the Irish Nationalists predicting revolution if it was not. The situation had been rendered more alarming by the formation of the Ulster Volunteers, matched in the South by the Irish Volunteers. By the summer of 1914, with Home Rule about to come into effect, both these forces were armed, sections of the Conservative Party and the British Army were openly sympathetic to Unionist intransigence and threatened violence, and the Nationalists were becoming more militant in the face of rumours that partition might be the compromise.

Under Hirst *The Economist* had undergone a U-turn on Ireland: the mouthpiece of St Loe Strachey's uncompromising Unionism had taken the Morley line on Home Rule – though without the Morley passion. The proprietors seem to have borne this patiently, though a letter of January 1914 from Charles John Wilson in Hawick suggests they can hardly have been happy. He wrote to protest about the government being put in the position of having 'to order the troops of Britain to fire upon those whose only crime is that they desire to remain under the British Government'. This was 'hardly thinkable . . . Now, why should the two predominant parties in the State not join hands and say that the Catholic part of Ireland shall have Home Rule as they desire, of course, by a Parliament always subordinate to the Imperial Parliament, and let the Protestant part of the North-East remain directly and exclusively under the Imperial Parliament.' Both sides must want to avoid this: 'the Ulster men' would not want to be first in 'setting the heather on fire'.[34]

Hirst was obdurate. 'Men like the Prime Minister and Lord Morley,' he wrote in May 1913, 'and, in fact, all their older colleagues, have been Home Rulers . . . since 1886. Nearly all their younger colleagues were Home Rulers in 1894. And for 10 years the whole party was out of office, largely, as it was supposed, through the unpopularity at that time of Home Rule. Therefore, if Mr Asquith were to abandon the Bill, he would be guilty of a double treachery – first to himself and his colleagues, and, secondly, to his Irish allies.' What the Ulster Unionists must do was to accept the will of the people.[35] He did not address himself to what should be done if they refused;

presumably he thought it impossible. When the King summoned relevant politicians to Buckingham Palace because of his concern that 'the cry of civil war is on the lips of the most responsible and sober-minded of my people', Hirst rebuked him for taking such a dangerous interventionary course, and with much quoting of Bagehot, implicitly advised His Majesty to stay out of politics if he knew what was good for the monarchy.[36]

Hirst 'knew and cared much more about foreign issues than any domestic one, except public economy', said Molly Hamilton. Indeed he had been to Bosnia only two years previously. 'His own first foreign journey had been to Austria. There he had made what was to be a lifelong friendship . . . with Josef Redlich. For him, certainly, the Austro-Serbian conflict was alarming, though I am not sure that his view was not faithfully expressed by the *John Bull* poster – "To hell with Serbia!"'

> There was an argument in the *Economist* office about the subject of the leader for the last week in July. The staff – at that time Leonard Reid, Gilbert Layton, A.W. Wright and myself – thought it must be about Ireland, where armed rebellion seemed to be preparing and there had just been an affray in which the King's Own Scottish Borderers were involved. F.W.H. insisted that it must be about the expiry of the Austrian ultimatum to Serbia – which we had forgotten. Even he, however, was calmly planning a summer holiday which was to take him to the battlefields of Europe. He was going to Waterloo, to Sedan, and so on. I can see him, now, in the brown linen suit which a very hot day and the imminent prospect of departure made suitable.[37]

By 31 July, when Hirst wrote two major articles for the issue of Saturday 1 August, there was no longer any doubt that the crisis was grave: the Irish 'affray' was relegated to fourth leader (the third being 'THE STOCK EXCHANGE CRISIS DAY BY DAY'). By this time the Admiralty had cancelled dispersal orders to certain squadrons of the First British Fleet in order to keep it complete. The bourses had closed in Vienna, Budapest, Brussels and Paris on the 27th and in Berlin on the 29th; seven firms had failed on the London Stock Exchange, which was closed on the 31st; Bank rate had gone up from 3% to 4% on the 30th and to 8% on the 31st. In 'THE WAR AND THE PANIC', Hirst explained that the yellow press and *The Times* were trying to drive the government into a European war, helped by Churchill's 'deplorable' action in giving a 'sensational order to the Fleet, as if, forsooth, whatever happened, any British Government was entitled to plunge this nation into the horrors of war, in a quarrel which is no more of our making and no more our concern than would be a quarrel between Argentina and Brazil or between China and Japan'. Fortunately, he said, the instincts of the business and working classes were utterly opposed to those of *The Times*, whose 'poisonous articles' were encouraging the Russian government to expect British support. Much was due to the great efforts made in England and Germany during the last two or three years to re-establish the old friendship 'which ought never to have been disturbed'. The general feeling of the nation was 'that we should observe strict neutrality', thus enabling Britain 'if the worst comes to the worst – to mediate effectively between exhausted combatants'.[38] In 'THE FINANCIAL SITUATION AT HOME AND ABROAD' he condemned as the most deplorable mistake the closing of the London Stock Exchange: 'Nothing, indeed, could have given a more dramatic touch, and nothing could have testified more clearly to the impossibility of running modern civilisation and war together than this closing of the London Stock Exchange owing to a collapse of prices, produced not by the actual outbreak of a small war, but by a fear of a war between some of the Great Powers of Europe.'

Molly Hamilton's novel describes the scene in the newspaper office after war had been declared and Morley and two Cabinet colleagues had resigned. The banks had extended the 3 August Bank Holiday until the end of the week.

> 'Of course,' Robinson was saying in his loud unmodulated voice, 'the Banks, I mean. Simply lost their heads and thought of nothing but themselves.'
>
> 'Banks?' Matheson looked up. 'Who cares about the Banks? This is the end of civilisation.'
>
> 'What I want to know,' piped in Jeffries, in his slow clear drawl, 'is why those fellows resigned? What on earth did they think we could do: sit and wait till Germany had walked over the others and then came on and walked over us? The French Army is no good, is it, Matheson?'
>
> 'The men are all right,' Matheson looked up, 'but the whole system's rotten with corruption. I wouldn't guarantee that anyone's got a boot that fits him . . . And as for going off to Alsace, it's madness, sheer madness.'
>
> 'Oh, I don't know,' cried Jeffries. 'The Belgians are evidently much better fighters than we thought, and we shall be on the spot in no time.'

Nigel had greeted them with a nod and paused to listen as he hung up his hat. But he did not feel much inclination to join in. They had gone off on to points of details, which were not the points that interested him. Matheson got up.

'I understand there will be official papers out tomorrow or Friday,' he said. 'The negotiations. . . . But not, I'm afraid, in time for us to handle them?'

'Oh no,' said Nigel quickly. 'We want, this week, to handle the thing broadly . . . .Come in, in an hour or so, Robinson, and we can discuss what we ought to say about the financial situation.'

'You'll have to try to convert him, Robinson,' murmured Jeffries as the door shut.

'Oh, he'll see the point all right. The editor's jolly sharp, knows a lot more about finance than you think. You should see him dictating on the Exchanges – you know how Davis used to have to work it all out? Well, Strode just sits there and dictates as clearly as if it were A B C.'

'Yes,' said Jeffries, 'his mind's wonderfully quick, isn't it?'

'Another thing,' Robinson went on, 'about him is he knows what the week's topic is going to be – Davis never did. But the *New World*'s on it every time now. . . . Davis was a crank in some ways: I'm glad he's not here. He'd take a queer line; like you, Matheson.'

Matheson shrugged his shoulders.

'I don't take any line,' he said, 'but I don't expect everything to stand on its head. People will want profits just the same; look after their own interests just the same; and say to all the others, "You began it, yah!" That's all we're doing.'

'Well,' cried Jeffries eagerly. 'So they did begin it.'

Matheson, who began to move away, cut across his eagerness. 'All right, Bill,' he said. 'You'll be a good journalist in time. Suggest to Strode a leader called "They began it" – he'd like it. Only you must phrase it better.'

With characteristic courage, Hirst made no concessions to the pro-war fever that was sweeping the country. His leader on 8 August was a magnificently uncompromising statement of an already unfashionable view. 'Since last week,' it began, 'millions of men have been drawn from the field and the factory to slay one another by order of the war lords of Europe. It is perhaps the greatest tragedy of human history.'

> We have watched the increasing rivalry of armaments with consternation, we have implored our Government to convene the nations of Europe, and seek to arrest the mischief before it was too late. It is now too late. The explosion has come. Look where you may you can see no ray of comfort. Death, anguish, starvation, and despair are written over Western Europe. As if the Balkan wars had not been enough, hell has been let loose among the most civilised nations of Europe. It is the triumph of diplomacy over common sense, of force over reason, of brutality over humanity.

In his bitter analysis of what had brought it about, the only tiny consolation he could offer was that the government's stated aims were 'to defend the small nationalities of Europe against aggression and oppression'.

> We must all strive during this war to keep our tempers. Those who strove to prevent it and those who strove to promote it are animated by a common patriotism, by a common desire to mitigate the sufferings of the poor, and the disasters which have befallen manufacturers, merchants, shipowners, and shopkeepers in all parts of the country. The present is black, and the future is hidden in impenetrable gloom. The Germans, both in the Empire and in Austria, are a brave and resolute people. They are now surrounded and outnumbered, but they will fight with a desperate energy which forbids us to be certain of success. Central Europe will be deluged with blood, and whether the war ends through economic exhaustion or not, commercial prostration is certain for all the combatants, and the longer the war lasts the more acute will be the distress and the longer the process of recovery. In the opinion of many shrewd judges, a social upheaval, a tremendous revolution, is the certain consequence.

And with an outbreak of the old unfounded optimism, he added that it might perhaps 'be the last time that the working classes of the Continent will allow themselves to be marched to destruction at the dictates of diplomacy and by the orders of their war lords'.[39]

CHAPTER XXXIII

Freedom and responsibility

[Rupert Brooke died of blood-poisoning at Scyros in April 1915.] He was buried on St George's day, by moonlight: and above his head, on the white wooden cross, an interpreter had written in Greek – 'Here lies the servant of God, sub-lieutenant in the English Navy, who died for the deliverance of Constantinople from the Turks.' . . . with his death one sees the extinction of Liberal England. Standing beside that moonlit grave, one looks back. All the violence of the pre-war world has vanished, and in its place there glow, year into backward year, the diminishing vistas of that other England, the England where the Grantchester church clock stood at ten to three, where there was Beauty and Certainty and Quiet, and where nothing was real. Today we know it for what it was; but there are moments, very human moments, when we could almost find it in our hearts to envy those who saw it, and who never lived to see the new world. *George Dangerfield*, The Strange Death of Liberal England[1]

6 March 1916 [Walter] With statement.
14 March [Eliza to Walter] Answer to statement.
17 March [Walter to Eliza] Answer.
22 March [Walter] Hartley Withers.

With these elliptical entries Eliza dates the time when Hirst finally became too much for the most important trustee, Walter Wilson Greg, grandson of James Wilson and son of William Rathbone Greg. By now Greg was well on the way to making his reputation as an outstanding Shakespearean scholar and bibliographer, already sufficiently distinguished to be elected to the club where his Uncle Walter Bagehot had so often played chess with Richard Holt

Hutton, and where his Aunt Eliza and other old *Economist* hands had influence.

> *31 January 1910* I wrote several letters asking friends to vote for Walter when he comes up for election at the Athenaeum on Feb 14th.
>
> *7 February* Sir Inglis Palgrave & Sir Robert Giffen about Athenaeum election.
>
> *14 February* Walter elected to the Athenaeum 261 votes 3rd on list.

When he was knighted in 1950, the *Daily Graphic* wrote that 'for nearly sixty years, Doctor Greg (now seventy-five) has worked on parchments and old documents, studying watermarks and the habits of scribes, to separate the truths from the falsehoods'. His problem with Hirst was not the matter of truth or falsehood: it was emphasis. As Walter Layton put it many years later: 'the Wilson Trustees, though understanding Hirst's pacificism and the paper's critical attitude about the Government's conduct of the war, did not share his views. On the contrary they became increasingly embarrassed at finding themselves responsible for pacifist opinions. Criticism may be justified and necessary in wartime; but unless you are prepared to make a compromise peace you may only produce "alarm and despondency" and achieve nothing except a weakening of morale.'²

The sacking of the editor was handled in a highly civilised fashion. As editor he was by Eliza's side a couple of days after the decision had been taken:

> *25 March 1916* R[ussell Barrington] went to Taunton & motored Lord & Lady Bryce* & Mr Hirst here to lunch. We all went to a meeting at the Town Hall when Lord Bryce spoke & afterwards unveiled the tablet put up by the town on the house where Walter was born . . . A great many people came here to tea after the meeting (50).
>
> *27 March* The Bryces & Mr Hirst left for London after breakfast.

Hirst did not leave until July, by which time he had been able to organise a new venture. In the meantime – and for the rest of her life – he continued his warm relationship with Eliza.

---

*James Bryce, friend and admirer of Bagehot, Regius Professor of Civil Law at Oxford 1870–1893, MP from 1880, Irish Secretary 1905, Ambassador to the United States 1907–13, Order of Merit 1907, Viscount 1914; author of a classic study of the American Constitution – *The American Commonwealth*.

Hirst's use of *The Economist* to denounce war, waste and the suppression of civil liberties had been tolerated for a surprisingly long time, for, as Molly Hamilton put it, to have condemned war in 1914, 'without, at once, going on to cite 1914 as the exception that proves the rule, was to invite at best a drawing away of skirts and more often a "Yah, pro-German!" "Always a pacifist, but heart and soul with the government in *this* most righteous war" – in this phrase of C.F. Masterman's, the second half carries the emphasis, and so much emphasis that it annihilates the first. Our emphasis was on the first half.'³ She depicted the climate vividly in the novel she was writing during her last years at *The Economist*:

> 'Of course might is right,' he said. 'How can you tell which side is right except by its winning? I can't see any other criterion . . . If the Germans were to beat us – which is inconceivable – they'd prove themselves the better men, and that's all there is in it, as far as I can see.'
>
> This was too much for Nigel.
>
> 'I disagree with you entirely,' he said. 'I can't admit for a minute that it's simply a case of force against force. We are fighting for an idea – the idea of freedom and respect for treaties. What idea are the Germans fighting for?'
>
> No one answered.
>
> 'Aren't the Germans fighting to defend themselves against Russia?' Daphne threw in.
>
> 'That's no doubt the excuse they give their own people . . . But we *are* fighting for an idea,' Nigel went on, 'and it's because of that that you find heaps of people who hate war ordinarily enthusiastic for this war – men like Sir Anthony Toller [fictional] and all the other men of letters and professors – Gilbert Murray [rationalist friend of Hamilton's father as well as of Hirst] and Bridges [Robert Bridges, the Poet Laureate], and so on – and young men who hate the idea of killing going off to fight. They're not in love with force – they hate it. This is a war against war: that's why all the pacifists are in favour of it.'
>
> 'Pacifists always have been in favour of war when it comes to the point,' said Lois. In the general laugh that accepted this remark Daphne's protest went unheeded.⁴

The 1914–16 period was probably only the third occasion in the paper's life when no one would have been surprised if the windows had been smashed. The first had been during the South African war and the second at the height of suffragette militancy. (The fourth was to be during the 1956 Suez invasion, which Tyerman's *Economist* opposed.) Francis Hirst's moral courage is one of the great legacies he left the paper.

His first sacrifice to his beliefs was Walter Layton, on the day war was declared. Layton, drawing on his experience in 1904 as assistant secretary to the Royal Commission on the Supply of Food and Raw Materials in Time of War, had spent the previous afternoon explaining to a packed Cambridge lecture hall what kind of measures the government could take to keep merchant ships at sea. Arriving at *The Economist*, he soon found himself 'entirely out of sympathy with the editor. Turning up the file for 1871 to see what had happened in the Franco-Prussian war, I came across a despatch sent from Paris by a correspondent who had lived through the siege. In the course of his letter he said that from beginning to end of the war no bank in Paris ever closed its doors.'

> I took the article in some excitement to the editor and suggested that we should reprint this extract to help to restore confidence on the financial front. He brushed it aside with the remark that 'Grass will be growing in Lombard Street before the end of the year.' I sadly left the office and did not return until I was appointed editor three years after the war ended.[5]

Hirst's wartime *Economist* represented the views of a tiny segment of public opinion – the rump of those whom his friend F.E. Smith had dismissed early in 1914 as 'Sir John Brunner and the old whining brigade'.[6] He was now even more out of step with the journal closest to him, the *Nation*, for unlike Hirst, Massingham admired both Lloyd George and Winston Churchill and believed the neutrality of Belgium was a great moral issue. Additionally, *The Economist* was an unattractive bedfellow for the large socialist element within the surviving pacifist movement. Molly Hamilton was the exception; she stayed on the staff although now a member of the Independent Labour Party, and, outside work, mixed with anti-war people like Bertrand Russell and the Bloomsbury set, whom Hirst would have found unfathomable. 'Anyone who has any truck with Socialism must be intellectually flabby,' he remarked to Hamilton *à propos* his friend Lawrence Hammond: 'It was like him not to notice that the imputation also covered me; he was entirely innocent of any intent to wound.'[7]

In August 1915 she wrote an impassioned letter to the paper, signed with her initials, expressing the hopes of what would nowadays be called the peaceniks:

SIR, – While the Press of all countries inculcates hatred for the enemy, and tries to persuade its readers that some end never specified is to be gained by the expenditure of your last shilling and the shedding of the last drop of the blood of our youngest and strongest, there is an unmistakable change in the tone and temper of private conversation. To the plain man and woman something of the unholy reality of war has been forced home after a year of endurance. There is hardly anyone now who is not asking, 'What is it all for, this agony and degradation?'

That this is happening here we know for ourselves. It is also happening in Germany. Last week's Nation contained some extracts from private letters of German soldiers . . .

'All of us, even those who at the beginning were the keenest for the fight, now only want peace, our officers as well as us. Convinced as we may be of the need to conquer, enthusiasm for the war does not exist for us. We do our duty, but our souls are suffering. I cannot tell you the suffering we endure.' – *A German Soldier to a Swiss Professor.*

'The longing for peace is intense with us. At least, with all those who are at the front, forced to kill and to be killed. The newspapers say that it is not possible to stem the warlike passion of the soldiers. They lie, knowingly or unknowingly. Our pastors deny that this passion is abating. You cannot think how indignant we are at such nonsense. Let them hold their tongues, and not speak of things they do not understand. Or, rather, let them come here, not as chaplains in the rear, but in the line of fire, with arms in their hands. Perhaps then they will perceive the inner change which is going on in thousands of us . . . They speak of a Holy War. I know of no Holy War. I only know one war, and that is the sum of everything that is inhuman, impious, and beastly in man, a visitation of God and a call to repentance to the people who rushed into it, or allowed themselves to be drawn into it.' – *Another Letter.*

Again, in the *Hamburger Echo* of July 29th there is a violent attack on certain members of the German Social Democratic party who are 'ready to find excuse for the militarism of every country save their own.' Similar reports come in letters from the other belligerent countries. The censored Press has no room for them, but they prove the existence everywhere of a real recognition not only of the horror, but of the futility of war. Can this recognition, purchased at such a price, not be brought home to the Goverments? [8]

While Hirst seemed as exercised about abstract principles and waste of money as about individual suffering, Hamilton's focus was on people. *Dead Yesterday* has its longueurs, but among its strengths is her scathing indictment of those of her journalistic and intellectual contemporaries who felt revitalised by the excitement of war, but found excellent reasons to stay at home. Nigel, allowing himself to be persuaded of his journalistic indispensability, helps with recruitment:

> He could pass safely from the horrors of the battlefield, thus eloquently delineated, to the causes that made it inevitable, essential for a nation that still held its head high, to take part in those horrors. For a rustic audience they could be simply and broadly sketched – the long-planned malevolence of Germany, the innocence of Belgium, the heritage of England's glorious past. From the motives an easy transition carried him to the future: a free world, expanding in the sun that shone upon it, once the dark cloud of Prussian militarism was swept aside. To every man the call was clear and insistent. Honour had made it impossible for the nation to stand aside. Now every day was proving more clearly that this was not only a war of ideals, but of self-defence; a war for existence in which every man who was a man must take his part.[9]

His equilibrium is only slightly shaken by the lack of enthusiasm for the cause shown by a soldier home on leave.

> 'You've been too near it, you know,' said Nigel lightly. 'After all, I believe one has a better sense of proportion at home.'
>
> Captain Toller was evidently slightly irritated. He got up and stood with his back to the fire.
>
> 'Twenty kilometres of corpses, burning like dead leaves, does rather put one out of focus, I dare say,' he said.[10]

Yet despite Hirst's isolation and the upheavals of wartime, the circulation dropped only slightly, from an average of 4,504 in 1913 to 4,369 in 1915, for even if business readers might find the leading articles not to their taste, the financial coverage and commercial information was still invaluable.

Four days after war was declared, 'A PLEA FOR PREVENTING CORRUP-TION AND WASTE DURING THE WAR'[11] began Hirst's detailed – and usually constructive – campaign against inefficiency and corruption in the conduct of the war. More interesting, because *sui generis*, was his onslaught against the erosion of civil liberties. 'If anyone had suggested a month ago that a Radical Government would suddenly proclaim martial law in Great Britain and Ireland after a brief adjournment of Parliament,' he wrote within three weeks of the outbreak of war, 'such a person would have been classed by unanimous vote with the inmates of lunatic asylums.'

> And yet we read in the *London Gazette*, August 14th:- 'At the court at Buckingham Palace, the twelfth day of August, 1914. Present the King's Most Excellent Majesty in Council. Whereas by the Defence of the Realm Act [DORA], 1914, his Majesty has power during the continuance of the present war to issue Regulations for securing the public safety or the defence of the Realm subject to and in accordance with that Act: Now therefore his Majesty is pleased by and with the advice of his Privy Council to order, and it is hereby ordered, as follows.'

The country was 'now entering upon a period of government by procla-mation – proclamations of war, proclamations interdicting all commercial intercourse with Germany and Austria-Hungary, proclamations postponing the payment of debts, proclamations forbidding coal exports, proclamations altering the monetary system, and so forth. But the martial law proclamation and the Press censorship now established will assuredly bring home to the English people for the first time since Napoleonic times, the meaning of a Continental war and the vital bearing which military intervention in foreign disputes may have upon the liberties of the subject and the rights of self-government.' He recognised that in the event of invasion, there might be a temporary necessity for arbitrary military rule 'and the loss of privileges which have existed since the Magna Carta', but the ordinary tribunals of law and justice could have dealt with what were in this proclamation. He examined extensively its provisions, which included sweeping rights to requisition property, expel people from their neighbourhood, punish tres-passers and those withholding certain information from the military or unlawfully publishing military information and arrest people without a warrant on suspicion of acting, or having acted, or being about to act 'in a manner prejudicial to the public safety or the safety of the Realm, or upon whom may be found any article, book, letter, or other document the possession of which gives grounds for such a suspicion'. Trial would be by court martial, from which apparently there was no appeal.

Since this was a proclamation 'which so far as we can see puts an end to all the safeguards that have hitherto existed, and places everybody at the mercy of Army officers', it should be put into intelligible English and circulated among the entire population.

> It would be quite easy for anybody, without any evil intent and without the slightest idea that he was doing anything wrong, to fall under military suspicion, to be seized without warrant, searched for suspicious papers, carried before a court of martial law and condemned to imprisonment without appeal, and perhaps even without a public hearing.

Parliament should elucidate the matter and ensure that at the very least there could be an appeal to a jury against a court martial decision. 'Otherwise what is the use of the Magna Carta and the Habeas Corpus Act? It may be necessary that there should be a Press censorship, and that news about British troops, which may be read by any Belgian or Frenchman, should be suppressed in Great Britain. It may be necessary that in a country which swarms with Law Lords and Lords of Appeal and High Court Judges and County Court Judges and Magistrates of all kinds, military tribunals should be set up with extraordinary power.' He hoped instead for an amended Act and a more reasonable proclamation.

> Even if the Attorney-General and the Solicitor-General and the Lord Chancellor and the Secretary for War and the First Lord of the Admiralty and the Home Secretary are all agreed as to the propriety of this proclamation, we shall still maintain that it contains many unnecessary and objectionable features which strike at the very roots of law and liberty. We must beware lest in pursuit of Belgian Neutrality, or Servian Independence, or even the Balance of Power on the Continent, we sacrifice the ancient rights and privileges of Englishmen.[12]

No one could accuse Hirst of being a man who believed that the ends justified the means.

In November he was assailing Sir Stanley Buckmaster, Solicitor-General, the Press Censor, for wishing to extend his authority over the discussion of foreign policy: that would ensure that the government was in the dark about 'the legitimate desires and expectations of the people of this country in regard to a settlement'. Buckmaster had pointed out the danger of offensive opinions upsetting neutrals. The danger of quotations, pointed out Hirst, could not be overcome, for foreign papers could manufacture whatever opinions they liked and attribute them to British politicians or the press.

> The other day the German Government, in order to encourage the German people, distributed a quotation from the *Economist* to the effect that 500,000 textile operatives in Lancashire were out of work. The figure we actually gave was 12,000, and was taken from the *Board of Trade Gazette*. What then is the use of being nervous when your enemy invents his quotations? It is quite true that foolish articles and false or inflammatory language may do harm in neutral countries. But if the British Press were muzzled, and compelled to sing in chorus like the German, with a band of trained professors, the effect upon neutral opinion would be much more mischievous, and we doubt very much whether a Government whose views had to be popularised in this way would long remain popular.[13]

Reviewing J.B. Bury's *History of Freedom of Thought* in January 1915, Hirst saw no evidence that the author 'had contemplated the possibility of a war encroaching upon that freedom of thought and speech which Milton placed above even the right of trial by jury: "Give me the liberty to know, to utter, and to argue freely according to conscience, above all other liberties."'

> The idea that a Liberal Government would restrict freedom of political discussion as well as news in time of war, and would hand over offenders with the sanction of Parliament, to Courts-Martial, had evidently not occurred to our learned author, and we cannot wonder that he was unable to foresee the Defence of the Realm Act as an incident in a war of liberation![14]

The Economist has always cared about civil liberties, though seldom seeing the issue in quite such black and white terms as did Hirst. Bagehot took for granted that it was important to preserve the liberty of the individual – but not at all costs. 'A free Press, a Parliament, and the other little comforts of a free people', he wrote from France in 1851, 'are not appreciated here and now – people want to be quick and to mind the shop – and perhaps they are right – for though journalists deny it, leading articles may be bought too dear.'[15] Government's first duty was 'to ensure the security of that industry which is the condition of social life and civilized cultivation'.[16]

The principle of the need, above all, to secure the state, normally underpinned, for instance, the paper's thinking on the Official Secrets Act. In 1930, three London newspapers announced that the Cabinet had decided to arrest Mahatma Gandhi, and the government invoked the Official Secrets Act. The journalists were exonerated. 'Undoubtedly the Government blundered', observed *The Economist*. But, in the relentlessly reasonable tone of the Layton paper, it concluded: 'Whether any amendment of the Official Secrets Act is desirable there is room to doubt. No one wishes to weaken the powers of the authorities to deal with espionage or improper disclosure of State secrets.' But if the Act was to stand, there should be an assurance that its powers would be used only 'in big and serious cases', and the Prime Minister should publicly clear the journalists. 'An incidental reflection suggested by the affair', it concluded sagely, 'is that, all circumstances being considered, improper leakages are surprisingly few.'[17]

Layton always tended towards undue optimism about the good sense of authority. Eight years later, in 1938, his paper had to face the fact that the government had been widening the use of the Official Secrets Acts and had thus presented a 'menace' to journalists' 'traditional liberties'. On this occasion the paper took a much tougher line. 'The Press is broadly content with the freedom afforded it by the law of the land. But the degree of discretionary power given to the executive arm by the Official Secrets Act in its present form is dangerously wide. *Raison d'état*, undefined, is an element foreign to Britain's juridical tradition.'[18] Later that year, with Crowther as editor, the paper went further: 'not least among disquieting devices which limit Press discussion of the conduct of administration, civil as well as military, is the labelling of all sorts of subjects as official secrets. So used, the Official Secrets Acts, originally passed to provide means of combatting espionage and the leakage of important information to alien Powers, are, at the best, irritating, and, at the worst, redolent of the malpractices of eighteenth-century Governments.'[19]

From the outbreak of the Second World War, the paper published extremely useful summaries of defence measures, 'to provide a useful tabulation of legislation and other acts of governmental and semi-governmental bodies arising out of the war'.[20] This time it had none of Hirst's automatic hostility towards DORA, although it kept a sharp eye on the balance of security and liberty. It was pleased to report three months after war had broken out that MPs from all parties had demonstrated 'zealous' concern for civil liberties by limiting the exceptional powers of the Official Secrets Act to espionage and related cases, and bringing in changes to wartime Defence Regulations. 'The chief objection to the original Regulations was that the powers taken to limit the expression of opinion were too drastically and too widely drawn – even on the assumption that conditions of grave emergency had to be provided for.' So far, there had been no wide use of DORA to suppress criticism of policy.

> It is wholly to the good that this should be the case in a war that is being fought in defence of liberty. It is a sign of sanity and national confidence. Conditions may come when the nation's safety will not permit such a measure of tolerance, more especially if publicists forget that their duty to be circumspect is a corollary of their right to speak their mind. But free speech and the rule of law are the firm foundations of democracy in war as in peace. They cannot be surrendered.[21]

Churchill was rebuked by Tyerman, late in 1943: 'Pleading for all-out effort in the war, he belittled by way of example the undue attention paid, say, to the rights and wrongs of procedure in juvenile courts. Here the Prime Minister, democrat and Parliamentarian by nature and life-long experience, surely nodded.'

> The distinguishing mark of free nations at war, despite the dire compulsions imposed by military and economic needs, is the constant care still taken for individual liberties . . . If it was needful, for safety and order in India, to imprison the Congress leaders without trial, it is imperative that the proceeding should be regarded as, at best, a necessary evil – and, perhaps, that it should now be asked whether the time for *habeas corpus* and open trial has not arrived . . . It is part of the process of winning the war, with all its hateful necessities, that the soul of democratic law and order should not be surrendered.[22]

Other editors have followed suit, in peace and war. When in 1971 the Home Secretary, Reginald Maudling, decided to deport Rudi Dutschke, a German student and political activist, Alastair Burnet's paper, although supportive of the Heath government, objected – rather pragmatically – to the decision and the manner in which it had been taken. 'A strong, civilising Home Secretary is a central figure in any successful government. He is judged not so much by the manner in which he handles the great issues but on his treatment of difficult civil liberties cases. On almost all of these cases the harsh decision can be guaranteed to win the plaudits of the less liberal elements in our society. But, as some of his predecessors found, they can do grievous damage not only to this country's reputation, but also to those of Home Secretaries and governments . . . The Dutschke case is the first difficult one to have arrived on Mr Maudling's desk. It has not, on the evidence available, gone well for him.'[23]

Andrew Knight's editorship initially showed a different emphasis – an updated version of James Wilson rather than of Francis Hirst. Bitterly attacking the illiberalism implicit in the high taxation, high subsidies, protected state monopolies, anti-market Labour government, 'Are the ordinary freedoms of the individual British citizen now intolerably curtailed? An unfortunate example to the rest of the democratic west?' enquired his paper in 1975 during his first year as editor. 'Capitalism in its rawest form 150 years ago clearly infringed many people's liberty, not to mention their dignity. Not everyone was free then to go to school, or to visit – let alone pay for – a doctor. So social democracy prospered – and with it the power of the state. Simultaneously some private power groups were – rightly – cut down to size. Others, eg, trade unions, were – wrongly – allowed to amass power. Now state compulsion has shifted the balance once again against individual freedom, helped in its work by computers, cowardice, bumbledom and bureaucracy.'[24]

A couple of months later, Knight was perforce to have his attention focused on a different facet of the civil liberties issue. In October 1975, in the House of Commons, Jeff Rooker, a Labour MP, asked the Speaker for guidance on 'a question of privilege': it was clear from his tone that he was one of the many people who find the paper irritatingly opinionated.

> There appeared in *The Economist* of 11 October a most detailed article about a draft Report of a Select Committee of this House which, in fact, does not meet until Wednesday of this week. The report in *The Economist* gives in detail the amount of money which it is proposed to raise by means of the wealth tax. Full details are given. No member of the Select Committee has seen the draft Report. No hon. Member has seen the draft Report.
>
> In the past the editor of *The Economist* has not been slow in coming forward to give advice to Members of this House. There have been complaints from time to time about Governments making statements

outside the House instead of in the House. Hon. Members certainly have a right to be the first to be informed of the contents of the Select Committee Reports. I should like you to consider this article, Mr Speaker and to give a ruling.[25]

The following day the Speaker ruled that a motion relating to it should be given precedence over the scheduled day's business. The House of Commons thereupon agreed to a motion by the Leader of the House: 'That the matter of the complaint be referred to the Committee of Privileges'. *The Economist* reported this development at the end of an irreverent article discussing the activities of the Radcliffe committee (whose membership was 'as safe and uniconoclastic as could be drawn up in the basements of the civil service department, where a list of great and good citizens is maintained for just such delicate missions'), set up in the wake of the government's failure to stop publication of Richard Crossman's diaries to consider what principles should govern publication of memoirs by former ministers. 'This group of potential authors of governmental memoirs meets in secret session in the cabinet office, under the guidance of a senior official from the Ministry of Defence, on an undisclosable number of occasions . . . to receive evidence from unnamed witnesses, who have themselves been assured that their views will never see the light of day. Informed sources are unquotably suggesting that the conclusions of Lord Radcliffe's committee might conceivably be ready for Christmas.'[26] The principle of parliamentary privilege, as an anonymous expert was later to explain in *The Economist*, was 'essential but too often its practice is embarrassing or . . . counter-productive'. Its scope was so broad (technically, until 1971, it had been an offence to report parliament at all) that it was rarely invoked and it was both uncertain and unpredictable: equally unpredictable were the possible punishments, which included imprisonment or a reprimand at the bar of the House.[27]

In their prime, James Wilson had been a distinguished member of Select Committees and Bagehot a valued expert witness. Andrew Knight, who four days later would be celebrating being 36 years old and one year in the editor's job, was hauled up on 28 October before the Committee of Privileges to justify himself to 12 MPs who took their role extremely seriously; his task was made no easier by the knowledge that the proceedings would be published verbatim by Her Majesty's Stationery Office. He had to uphold the dignity of his paper, avoid compounding the offence and defend Mark Schreiber (now

Lord Schreiber), the journalist arraigned along with him. (A nice coincidence was that the leaked draft report was that of the Select Committee on a Wealth Tax, which was chaired by the mid-1930s *Economist* assistant editor, Douglas Jay.) The issue was blurred, certainly as far as some of the Labour members of the committee were concerned, by the fact that in addition to writing – primarily on the then particularly contentious issue of taxation – for *The Economist* part-time, Schreiber was a special adviser to the Leader of the Opposition, Margaret Thatcher, who had inherited him from Edward Heath (he resigned from this job afterwards; and *The Economist* decided to stop employing any journalists with outside advisory interests).

Schreiber denied having known he was committing a contempt of the House and refused to disclose his sources. Knight regretted the contempt, took responsibility as editor and admitted confusion:

> There is no doubt that in retrospect it was a contempt of the House. By way of explanation and not by way of extenuating circumstances, the decision to run it in the form it was printed was taken on Thursday afternoon. I cannot remember the exact time, but it would have been between lunch time and tea time. I would crave your indulgence to explain what is involved in producing the newspaper at that particular time. In a way that no other comparable magazine in the world works, the Editor and his small staff read every single page and every single note going into the newspaper between those hours. We send a far greater proportion of the magazine to press at a later hour than others do, and this article in the form it went into the newspaper was one of those articles. I cannot pretend I really concentrated hard on this particular article, saying, 'Do I or do I not? Where can I get legal advice?' There was no legal advice to be had. We print in Slough, not London. In those circumstances, there was some confusion in my mind, but I was aware there might be a question of contempt.

Knight combines candidness (on which he was complimented in committee) with inveterate self-justification: he is notorious for his habit of answering at great length criticism from the most obscure sources. So later in this examination he worried about what he had said. 'I do not want to give the impression that I am a confused editor on Thursdays', began a long explanation of why he had not been clear about contempt in this instance. Later he became crisper.

Mr Knight, you knew at the time you finally approved the publication that it was a contempt of Parliament?

I did not say I knew. If one could put percentages on it, it was probably 60–70 per cent., but it was not a time when one could ring up counsel for advice. I was surprised when Mr Rooker asked this question on Monday.

You now accept that it is not in the public interest to publish documents of this kind?

No, I do not.

Do you claim it is in the public interest that you as an editor should feel free to publish information based upon what is from the point of view of this House a forbidden document?

The question is: to whom it is forbidden. The Speaker at the beginning of every session asks that the ancient and undoubted privilege of Parliament be protected. The question of privilege and the lack of rules concerning the privilege situation has been debated in the past. Indeed, Members of this Committee have themselves said in the House that the present lack of definition of privilege, and even the word itself, call for changes. In Erskine May [the bible of parliamentary procedure] it is laid down that 'improper obstruction' or 'substantial interference' with the working of a Select Committee should be deplored and prevented and should be treated as contempt. All I can say is that in the past few days I have spoken to a number of members of the Select Committee on a Wealth Tax including Members of both major parties and my first question has been: 'Has your work been obstructed, or do you feel there has been any improper interference?' I have yet to come across any Member who feels the work of the Select Committee has been obstructed or interfered with.

If you had known it was a contempt would you still have published the article?

Not if I had been 100% certain.

This was hardly conciliatory. The committee's report found Knight 'blame-worthy in deciding to publish what he knew was a draft committee document, and reckless in deciding to go ahead when he suspected that he was acting in contempt of parliament', and it found Schreiber 'wholly irresponsible' for failing to keep the information confidential and further in contempt of the House for refusing to name his source. Regretting that they lacked the power to fine *The Economist*, the committee recommended that Knight and

Schreiber be excluded from the precincts of the House for six months. 'They recognise that this may impede their journalistic and advisory activities, but nevertheless consider such exclusion to be justified.' Knight published the report, along with the analytical outside expert's view, in *The Economist* and reprinted the public statement he had given the press, which had drawn attention particularly to:

1. The unclear definitions, and the unpredictable application, of parliamentary privilege . . .

2. The conflict that arises when select committees are used, and encouraged, to promote public debate over a politically controversial tax. We welcome this use of select committees, but draw attention again to contradictions that it has given rise to in this instance . . .

3. The confidentiality of a journalist's sources which the committee condemns, but which we feel must be maintained.[28]

The ensuing publicity was one-sided and marvellous, especially for a publication whose arrogance usually makes it unpopular with its contemporaries. Why, asked Alan Watkins in the *New Statesman*, were Knight and Schreiber 'placed in the position of having to answer questions – sometimes fatuous, sometimes impertinent, sometimes both – addressed to them by a collection of bores, windbags, proven incompetents, ministerial rejects and political derelicts?' 'A body of the most senior MPs in the Commons', wrote the *Sunday Times*, 'last week cast itself as a collection of fragile political virgins, facing a fate worse than death by exposure to public opinion. The trick is ridiculous, but also alarming.' Bernard Levin wrote in *The Times* of 'the curious passion the House of Commons seems to have for making a collective ass of itself'. Others piled in: 'END THIS ABSURD CHARADE' (*Evening News*), 'MUMBO JUMBO' (*Daily Mail*), 'ONCE MORE INTO WHAT BREACHES' (*Guardian*), 'PRIVILEGE RULING SEEN AS FREEDOM THREAT' (*The Times*). The political editor of the *Sunday Mirror* appeared in the letters column of *The Economist* suggesting that, should the suspension go ahead, it might be a good idea for the press to leave parliament unreported for the relevant period.[29]

On 16 December the chairman of the committee moved the acceptance of the report, but the House voted instead, by 64 to 55, for an amendment 'regretting the leakage of information' but recommending that no further action be taken. The most important result of the affair had been to force a two-and-three-quarter-hour Commons debate and bring the whole issue out of mothballs. The paper allowed a personal tone to creep into its brief report, which ended:

> *The Economist* thanks those who spoke or voted for the amendment; those many other MPs who expressed support but who understandably preferred the company of their families to staying up late on the night; and the national and regional press which was a brick.[30]

Erosion of civil liberties is hydra-headed. In 1982, three years into the Thatcher era, the emphasis had changed again. Commenting in 1982 on plans to update emergency legislation should war between Nato and the Warsaw Pact look imminent, 'OH NO YOU DON'T' reported with satisfaction on a statement by the head of the Press Association that 'censorship during the transition to war (as opposed to war itself) was not on'.

> The PA, of course, had not been asked for its views by the civil service team planning its takeover in time of emergency. Nor had the rest of Fleet Street. It had not crossed the bureaucrats' minds that such a scheme might be unworkable, even though press and public are clearly less pliable than in the deferential days of 1939 when the Emergency Powers (Defence) Act shot through parliament a week before the outbreak of war.[31]

Fiercer still was the language used next year to approve a report proposing safeguards for the rights of those affected by anti-terrorist legislation and to condemn an 'ill-drafted and anti-libertarian' criminal evidence bill. 'The best way to subvert a liberal society is to terrorise its government into denying due process of law to its citizens; that, at least, is what most modern political terrorists think. They call it "unmasking the true face of repression", and if they can bring it off (as they almost did in Northern Ireland in the 1970s, until Britain changed its ways – sometimes under pressure from the European court of human rights) they can drive a wedge right to the heart of the legitimate state.'[32]

The Pennant-Rea paper was harsher again, experience having shown that governments could not be trusted. It was outraged in 1987 when the Thatcher government took legal action against *Spycatcher*, the memoirs of the ex-MI5 agent Peter Wright, and gagged the British press by injunction. As a rule, although *The Economist*'s cover pictures and the advertisements may vary from one region of the world to another, the editorial contents are the same for all regions. Now an exception was made. In the copies distributed in Britain, the *Books and Arts* section began with an almost blank page, which contained only the section heading, a review title ('MY COUNTRY, WRIGHT OR WRONG'), details of name, author, publisher, number of pages and price and, in the middle of the page, in a box:

> The Economist has
> 1.5m readers in 170
> countries. In all but one
> country, our readers
> have on this page a
> review of 'Spycatcher',
> a book by an ex-MI5
> man, Peter Wright. The
> exception is Britain,
> where the book, and
> comment on it, have
> been banned. For our
> 420,000 readers there,
> this page is blank – and
> the law is an ass.[33]

Pennant-Rea's *Economist* called for both a Freedom of Information Act and a Bill of Rights. In 1988 it condemned 'the presumption that official information should be kept secret unless the government, or the law, deems otherwise. That is the wrong way round. Government information should be open unless there is good reason for keeping it secret.'[34] Later that year it recalled that, before she became Prime Minister, Thatcher had attended a seminar where it was suggested that Britain should have a Bill of Rights 'to protect it from tyrannical governments'. '"When," bridled the future prime minister, "did a Conservative government ever trample on the liberties of the subject?"' While Britain was not 'a notably unfree, undemocratic country . . . should the prime minister ever ask her question again, "October 1988" will do as an answer'.

> In this one month the government has banned radio and television from interviewing the representatives of legal organisations in Northern Ireland; sacked workers at GCHQ, its communications-interception station, for

refusing to leave a trade union; prepared to reverse the burden of proof in criminal trials for those found with a knife or whose hands have traces of explosives, and to end (at once in Northern Ireland, later in mainland Britain) a suspect's right to stay silent when questioned by the police without having damaging inferences drawn in court as a result.

There was nothing particularly Tory about this. 'Labour's record includes removing the right of entry to the country of East African Asians with British passports, and laws that allowed staff to be sacked if they did not join a closed shop.' Governments had too readily meddled with civil liberties for their own 'administrative convenience, prejudices or political needs'.

> Why do British governments behave in this way? Mainly because they have no incentive to do otherwise. Britain was early among the nations in recognising that representative institutions such as parliaments can keep a government in check. It then rested on its laurels. It was slow to notice that once legislatures fell into the grip of party machines, parliament alone could not stop governments acting in an overmighty fashion. Where other nations have bills of rights, consitutional courts, a separation of powers, federalism or referendums, each designed to constrain governments, Britain has a void.

A partial answer was a Bill of Rights.[35]

The Economist annoys a lot of politicians at home; it makes even more enemies abroad, and many of them ban it. In 1971, there was a rather amused look at press censorship abroad, complete with league-table of recent *Economist* bannings. 'The unfortunate men whose job it is to scan foreign newspapers to prevent subversive material from entering their countries seem to have been in a more lenient mood this year than they were in 1970 – at least so far as *The Economist* is concerned. Whether the rules they supposedly work by have been relaxed or whether *The Economist*'s reports have been thought less corrupting than in the past there is no way of knowing.' While 50 out of 52 issues were known to have been banned in one country or another in 1970, the figures were down to only 18 in the first 11 months of 1971.

> Like the ancient Mariner, the Iraqi censor generally stoppeth one in three. Last year he was well ahead with a ban on 19 issues; this year he is in the lead again with ten. But although Libya ran a close second last year in the first flush of Colonel Qaddafi's enthusiasm by banning 14 issues, this year the

colonel's men have drawn the line at only one. Thus Spain, the good old faithful, which led the field in 1968 and 1969 and came third last year by banning 12 issues, has moved up to second place with a modest score of four. Morocco, which was the winner in 1967 but did not score at all in 1969 and 1970, is back this year with two. The king's bloody birthday party in July saw to that. [King Hassan had crushed a coup attempt.]

This form of censorship tended to be unpredictable. While the Spanish censors were concerned simply to keep off the bookstalls any criticism of General Franco's regime or news of 'unflattering' events in Spain, the Iraqis were as sensitive about news of 'their Arab brethren or the Israelis or the Iranians' as about themselves. Some governments preferred to buy up all the copies rather than be accused of banning them.

> However irritating it may be for Spaniards, Iraqis or others to be deprived of their copy of *The Economist*, they are more fortunate than those who never have the chance to buy it at all. In the Soviet Union and eastern Europe, for example, foreign newspapers are imported by a government agency for distribution to certain government offices, libraries and carefully selected bookstalls in hotels where foreigners stay. No news comes out about the occasions when the governments concerned feel it wiser not to let *The Economist* reach the desks of the senior civil servants.[36]

The story was brought up to date at the beginning of 1992 in 'POLITICALLY INCORRECT – Where to be safe from The Economist'. 'Saudi Arabia's new year's gift to *The Economist* was an open-ended ban. The Saudis were probably upset by a report in our Christmas issue which said that some Muslims considered the Saudi monarchy un-Islamic. If past bans are any guide, this one could keep Saudi Arabia *Economist*-free for six months.'

Until then, 1991 had seen fewer bannings than usual; only 11 issues out of 51 were banned outright by a total of 18 countries, of which 17 were Arab and the 18th was Malaysia. It was a considerable improvement on 1970. 'An indefinite ban shows that a government is really miffed. More often censors ban individual, politically incorrect issues.' Thus, in 1991:

> * Tunisia banned *The Economist* for questioning allegations of an Islamic plot to overthrow the government.
> * Syria objected to a cover calling Israel's prime minister the 'Father of Palestine'.

* Morocco was angered by a map showing that the Western Sahara did not belong to it.

* The United Arab Emirates (UAE) banned an issue in June for reasons that remain obscure, and another in September – apparently for describing the Bank of Commerce and Credit International (BCCI) as the emirates' favourite bank.

* Kuwait banned an issue in September which suggested that the ruling family had learnt nothing from the Gulf war, and two in October for reasons that were not explained.

* The entire Arab world, with the exception of Lebanon, Jordan, and Egypt, banned an issue containing a survey of the Middle East; Egypt allowed the issue to be distributed, minus the survey.

* Malaysia banned two issues in May for articles that looked at its government.

Some governments chose delayed distribution as an alternative. Malaysia did this three times in 1991 because it disliked an accusation that it had an 'economic policy that took wealth from the Chinese and gave it to the Malays'. At the time of writing, the 23 November issue was still blocked from Malaysia, because of an illustration, in the science section, of a naked man. 'Other delayers were Indonesia (which did not want to read that its troops had massacred civilians in East Timor) and Kenya (which did not appear to agree that there was "Something rotten in Kenya").'

> A gentler form of censorship is to snip or blot out material that governments hold to be subversive or offensive. This is done by armies of people working for the distributor to instructions from the censor's office. In 1991 advertisements for alcoholic drinks were blotted out in most Muslim countries, as were those showing too much female flesh. The Saudis cut out articles critical of the royal family, Kuwait ones that reported its mistreatment of Palestinians. The UAE cut out articles on the BCCI. The Indian censor blotted out maps showing Kashmir to be disputed territory. Welcome to the new world order.[37]

Bagehot, commenting on the banning of the paper in France in 1869, provides the laconic coda: 'If The Economist would make a revolution, what would not make a revolution?'[38]

Hirst had some progress to report on the civil liberties front in the spring of 1915. 'We have often harped on the utterly un-English policy of hushing up or suppressing reports which are either known to the enemy through the neutral Press, or if made known to them through the British Press would have no military value. We have also protested over and over again against any attempt to prevent the views of the critics of the Government finding expression. Last August and September our observations on the Defence of the Realm Act, and the substitution of Ministerial or martial law for judge and jury received no echo. At last it was taken up in the House of Lords, then in the Press, and now, happily, the constitutional guarantees of liberty have been practically restored.' Yet parliament was a worry.

> The House of Commons . . . is still inert and lifeless under the deadening effects of a hollow 'political truce,' and the Front Opposition Bench policy of reserving all criticism until the end of the war (and then, we suppose, roasting the Government for mistakes which an intelligent Opposition might have done something to prevent) is largely responsible for the disrepute into which the House of Commons has unfortunately fallen. The Civil Service Estimates suggest that a pursuit of superfluous expenditure might have had very valuable consequences . . . publicity is the guardian of efficiency and economy. Daylight is unpopular with every bureaucrat.[39]

Worse was to come. Next month Asquith's government, suffering from criticism of the munitions shortage and the generally poor performance of the War Office, was reorganised as a coalition with the addition of one Labour MP as well as some of the Conservatives. And ministers began to talk of introducing compulsory military service.

'Do you feel as much stirred as I do about the wickedness, and folly, and shame of introducing compulsory service?' asked Hirst of C.P. Scott, editor of the *Manchester Guardian*. 'I feel that this, with Protection, the Censorship, and a military bureaucracy would make England no place for people like me . . .'

> I am enjoying a little rest at this delightful place [he was staying in the West Country, in Tavistock], and am not sorry to see the organised hypocrisy of Liberal Imperialism based upon the unholy alliance of Jingoism with Socialism falling to pieces.
>
> Will not this Coalition Government be weak and discredited from the start, without any common purpose or object?
>
> Will not a general election be necessary after all?

Are not horror and disgust about the war prevailing everywhere? and is there not a reaction against the foul Northcliffe* pogrom of people with German names.

P.S. Why should all of us Britons be ruined because a little group of Liberal and Tory Imperialists has taken the idiotic resolution of destroying the German nation?

What a poor thing is the Cadbury Press!†⁴⁰

Scott's reply spoke of the need to resist Germany's aggressive imperialism and to keep a strong defence force post-war. He was vague about conscription. 'The present outcry for compulsion is clearly manufactured,' responded Hirst, 'the object being to discipline and enslave the working classes and to keep down Ireland. Dr Clifford [a Liberal Baptist] who with Lloyd George preached the Holy War now renounces the idea of transplanting German institutions and especially the curse of military conscription . . .'

What right has the state to enslave men and ship them to unknown destinations to be slaughtered? . . . From the sole standpoint of winning the

---

*Alfred Harmsworth, 1st Viscount Northcliffe, had created or acquired *inter alia* the *Daily Mail*, *Daily Mirror*, *Observer*, *Sunday Dispatch* and *The Times*. 'Some little time ago an Englishman happened to take lunch at a little hotel not very far from Carnarvon,' wrote Hirst a few days later in a splendid tirade. 'In this home of political enlightenment he took up the *Daily Mail*, and afterwards asked the proprietor whether he formed his opinions and gathered his facts entirely from that paper. "No," he replied, quite indignantly: "I read *The Times*, and my wife takes in the *Daily Mirror*, and on Sunday we have the *Weekly Dispatch*." The visitor then explained to this simple Welshman that all his information came from one factory, and that to correct *The Times* by the *Daily Mail*, and both by the *Weekly Dispatch* is simply a case, as the City would say, of pig on pork, and of pork again upon pig. To mistake public opinion for the articles fabricated by one newspaper proprietor and distributed like soap advertisements through dozens of newspapers by journalists whose successes consist in writing out the opinions of their proprietor, and in the provision of such popular sensations as may contribute to the circulation and improve the advertising revenue of the newspaper trusts, is a favourite error of second-rate politicians. Whether the unfortunate hacks are called upon to summon Lord Kitchener to office or to drive him out, to hail Mr Churchill as a saviour of the country or as a public danger, to shout for Tariff Reform or to proclaim the virtues of free food, there is a certain type of man, shallow, noisy, and worthless, who will change his opinions as nimbly as the *Daily Mail*, and be confirmed in them as *The Times* goes lumbering after. Infinite mischief has been done, and will be done, by the Harmsworth Trust.' (*The Economist*, 29 May 1915)

†The Cadburys, chocolate manufacturers and social reformers, owned the liberal *Daily News*. Laurence Cadbury became a shareholder in *The Economist* after his friend and ex-teacher, Walter Layton, organised its purchase in 1929; Dominic Cadbury became an *Economist* director in 1989. In 1930, Layton became Chairman of the *News Chronicle* (the merged *Daily News* and *Daily Chronicle*).

war and emerging with a complete social and economic disaster at home I
see every reason to combat conscription with all the forces in our power.
There is nothing I think in your letter which goes against this view.[41]

That last sentence illustrates perfectly a point Hamilton made about Hirst.
'His power of seeing what he wishes to see and not seeing that which is
disagreeable gives him a heroic pertinacity, sometimes unhappily in sheer, if
quite unconscious, obscurantism. It was, later, to enable him to entertain the
most romantic notions about what was going on in Nazi Germany; it made
him furiously angry when Winston Churchill insisted on drawing up
Germany's armament budget. This convenient visual trick extends, of course,
to the opinions of his friends: those he does not care for he simply treats as
non-existent.'[42]

Hirst's campaign against conscription began a few days later with 'PUBLIC
OPINION AND COMPULSION' – an attack on the role of the Northcliffe
press. 'Prussian militarism is at all costs to be crushed. What becomes of this
high moral purpose if we proceed to adopt the accursed system for the
destruction of which we have already sacrificed hundreds of thousands of
men and hundreds of millions of money? Let the Coalition beware of
mistaking newspaper articles for public opinion.'[43] A week later came 'THE
WAR AND MR LLOYD GEORGE' and 'THE IDEA OF COMPULSION',[44] while
the next week 'THE PROPOSED DICTATORSHIP' launched a savage attack
on Lloyd George, about whom Hirst had ambivalent views. He had
disapproved of Lloyd George's propensity for redistributing wealth, but had
been heartened by his pre-war opposition to Churchill's naval expansionism.
Now he was outraged. 'Mr Lloyd George's substitute for the British system,
which we have hitherto pursued in war and in peace, is a French dictatorship.'
Lloyd George had gone on to argue the necessity of compulsory service,
which, he claimed, had been 'the greatest weapon in the hands of democracy
many a time for the winning and preservation of freedom'. In this he echoed
Churchill, who wanted the state to have 'complete control over the lives and
property of its fellow-countrymen. The rights of the State, he says, over all its
subjects are absolute. Fortunately for us in Great Britain that has been untrue
since the Magna Carta, and is untrue now.' But had the present-day
statesmen justified their claim to such a degree of confidence? 'There is as
yet no sign of economy or self-denial in the upper branches of the
Administration.' There followed a long assault on waste and administrative
failure.[45]

'I fear that nearly all the Liberal journalists and newspaper proprietors can easily be got at and persuaded', Hirst told Sir John Brunner, seeing himself as the only reliable press campaigner against 'military slavery'. Brunner provided him with money to produce 'a good strong well argued pamphlet' against conscription[46] and in *The Economist* he ground away, week after week. 'CONSCRIPTION AND ARGUMENT',[47] 'PARLIAMENT, THE WAR COSTS, AND THE CRY FOR COMPULSION',[48] 'AUTHORITY AND REASON'[49] and 'COMPULSION, CONSCIENCE, AND BUSINESS'[50] were just a few, and the correspondence columns were alive with the subject.

All his pleas got nowhere. In July 1916, in the week before he left, 'THE CABINET CRISIS AND PERPLEXITIES OF FAITH' bitterly attacked Asquith for having 'ruined a great party' by 'subordinating everything to the supposed duty of holding office with political opponents'. His summary of the year of Coalition is suitably bleak.

> The Press renewed its attacks upon the voluntary system and upon Free-trade; protectionist taxes were adopted and passed in the autumn. Finally, through the machinations of Mr Lloyd George and Lord Derby, supported by two powerful newspaper trusts, Mr Asquith was induced reluctantly and by degrees to accept the principles of conscription, first for single, then for married men, subject to protection for conscientious objectors. Meanwhile, Sir Edward Carson had resigned, in connection, it is believed, with the Salonika Expedition, and later on Sir John Simon left the Government on the conscription issue, thus assisting in the formation of a new Liberal and Labour party, which is gradually assuming more and more political importance. The misfortunes of the Mesopotamian Expedition might have produced another crisis if they had not been overshadowed by the appalling administrative incapacity which permitted a revolutionary outbreak in Dublin. The results are now seen in the attempt to patch up a settlement of the Irish question. Then came the catastrophe which deprived the country of Lord Kitchener.* This week Lord Selborne has resigned, because he thinks it dangerous in the present state of Irish feeling to establish a Parliament in Dublin. Mr Runciman is invalided, so that the country is temporarily without a Secretary of State for War, an Irish Secretary, a Lord Lieutenant, a President of the Board of Agriculture, and a

*Lord Kitchener, Secretary of State for War, was drowned in June 1916 when HMS *Hampshire* was sunk by a German mine.

President of the Board of Trade, while the Munitions Minister is for the time being employed in Irish diplomacy.

A long moral tirade followed, ending in a blast of Hirstian optimism. 'We hold very strongly that a fresh and vigorous Administration could easily be formed, which by military, naval, financial, and diplomatic action would bring this war very speedily to a favourable conclusion. It will not have escaped the notice of our readers that four eminent and independent peers have openly expressed in our columns their concurrence with our criticisms of the diplomacy which doggedly refuses to discuss peace overtures even in the Cabinet. If our circulation and letter-bag are any test, their views are rapidly gaining ground in business circles.'[51]

In his last issue he wrote a powerful appeal to the new Secretary of State for War, Lloyd George, on behalf of conscientious objectors. Describing one particularly harrowing case of injustice affecting 34 men, he complained of the absence of any regret from a minister 'that such treatment should have been meted out to men who stand for convictions drawn from the Sermon on the Mount and the life of Christ'.[52]

He was allowed to go out in style with his highly personal 'VALE-DICTORY'.

> An association of nearly nine years with *The Economist* has created very real, if indefinable, bonds of sympathy with thousands of readers at home, in the colonies, and in foreign countries, although one is personally acquainted with only a few. So many friendly letters have been exchanged, and the relations of the Editor with his readers and correspondents have for all these years been so agreeable, that I must allow myself the pleasure of saying to them a grateful farewell; for after next week my responsibility for *The Economist* will cease, and I shall turn to another task.

Since the beginning of the war, it had been 'difficult and even hazardous' for an editor who believed 'that truth and patriotism ought somehow to be reconciled. Whether I have in any way succeeded others must judge: but I can at any rate say that, while I have strongly criticised sections of the Defence of the Realm Act, my relations with the Press Censors have been of the best. Indeed, on only one occasion during the whole course of the war has *The Economist* met with any criticism from that quarter; and on that occasion a satisfactory explanation was given.' Looking at the present and the future, he thought the financial fabric of Western Europe to be 'in imminent peril, and in a few more months it will no longer be possible to disguise the bankrupt condition of several great nations. Civilisation as we have known it and representative institutions are doomed unless, through the exertions of individuals, the rights without which an Englishman, at any rate, will hardly care to live, are speedily restored.' To that end, freedom and independence had to be won back for parliament and press.

> One last word I owe to *The Economist* and its readers. I have been accused by The Times financial editor of imparting to *The Economist* a 'distressingly pacifist' policy. In plain English, I am accused of being a peacemaker. The accusation is not distressing to me. I plead guilty to the charge. It has been my principal object during the past year to prepare the public mind for peace by separating passion and fiction from reason and fact; and if I could believe that I had hastened its advent by one day, and saved the precious lives and limbs that are lost in 24 hours, I should feel myself to have won a prize worth all the titles that Emperors shower on their favourites and Ministers on their supporters. That the negotiation of peace is a difficult task I admit; that the attainment of an honourable and lasting settlement is beyond the reach of a competent diplomacy I deny. That it is desired by all the belligerent nations I feel certain, and the fact that the circulation of *The Economist* has touched its heights during the past few weeks may serve to indicate the feeling of our business men.[53]

A marvellous photograph shows the gathering of his staff at Hirst's house in Campden Hill Square on a Saturday afternoon that summer, when they presented him with a chair, on which was inscribed:

> In token of our esteem and affection we the undersigned members of the staff of The Economist regretting Mr F.W. Hirst's resignation of our editorial chair present him with another in the hope that it may support him in his continued and untiring efforts for the cause of peace and freedom.

> Justum et tenacem propositi virum
> Non civium ardor prava jubentium
> Non vultus instantis tyranni
> Mente quatit solida

The verse was from Horace (Ode III 3 1); the most appropriate translation is:

> The man who is tenacious of purpose in a rightful cause is not shaken from his firm resolve by the frenzy of his fellow citizens clamouring for what is wrong, or by the tyrant's threatening face.

Hirst had persuaded a group of like-minded people (Sir Hugh Bell, the great ironmaster, and two Radical *laissez-faire* and anti-war MPs) to put up the money for a new weekly which he called *Common Sense*. 'The views to which the paper was dedicated were anything but those of the average commonsensical man,' remembered Molly Hamilton, 'but Francis Hirst invariably, and with a blandness that often deceived the unwary, assumes that his opinions are those of all rational human beings.'[54] He took two members of staff with him – Hamilton and Alexander, assistant to Howard Kirk, the manager. E.M. Webb, the office boy, was too sensible to accept his invitation and stayed and took Alexander's place. *Common Sense* – which functioned as a kind of pacifist HQ – lasted about four years.

Hirst's successor, Hartley Withers, had already been connected with *The Economist* for almost a quarter of a century, having begun to contribute occasionally in the early 1890s.[55] Born in Liverpool in 1867, the fourth son of Henry Hartley Withers, 'gentleman', at Westminster he was a Scholar and school captain and at Christ Church, Oxford, he was a Junior Student. He took a first class in classical moderations and in 1890 a third in *literae humaniores*, that same year becoming a temporary assistant master at Clifton College, where Hirst was still a pupil. Withers left to become a Stock Exchange clerk and contributed now and then to the *The Economist* and *Spectator* as well as to the *Pall Mall* and *Westminster Gazettes*.

In 1894 Withers joined the City staff of *The Times* and for five years from 1905 was City editor. It was during this period, at the age of 42, that he made a start on what was to be his most distinguished career – writing books about money and the City. Between 1909 and 1942 he produced 21.* His writing benefited greatly from the breadth of his intellectual background and classical training: he was a master at using literary allusions to add immediacy, interest and humour to his writing. His witty choice of epigraphs, for example, was

The Meaning of Money, Stocks and Shares, Money Changing, Poverty and Waste, War and Lombard Street and *International Finance* were written before he became editor of *The Economist*; *Our Money and the State, The Business of Finance, War-Time Financial Problems* and *The Case for Capitalism* while he was editor.

one of the delights of his books. *The Meaning of Money* was prefaced with a quote from Goethe:

> Grau, theurer Freund, ist alle Theorie
> Und grün des Lebens goldner Baum.
>
> [Grey, good friend, is all spent theory
> And green the golden tree of life.]

George Savile, Marquess of Halifax, a brilliant seventeenth-century political polemicist, provided one for *War and Lombard Street*:

> Wise Venturing is the most commendable Part of human Prudence. It is the upper Story of Prudence, whereas perpetual caution is a kind of underground Wisdom that doth not care to see the Light.

An Essay upon Publick Credit, published in 1710, launched *Stocks and Shares* with: 'I am to speak of what all People are busie about, but not one in Forty understands', and Alexander Pope's contribution to *War-Time Financial Problems* was:

> Blest Paper credit! last and best supply!
> That lends Corruption lighter wings to fly!
> Gold imp'd by thee, can compass hardest things,
> Can pocket States, can fetch or carry Kings;
> A single leaf shall waft an Army o'er,
> Or ship off Senates to a distant Shore;
> A leaf, like Sibyl's, scatter to and fro
> Our fates and fortunes, as the winds shall blow;
> Pregnant with thousands flits the Scrap unseen,
> And silent sells a King, or buys a Queen. (*Moral Essays*)

The Quicksands of the City, and a Way Through for Investors was a splendidly incongruous though appropriate vehicle for Shakespeare's 'Out of this nettle, danger, we pluck this flower, safety.'

Of those 21 books, *The Meaning of Money* is the best-known. In it Withers's aim had been 'to meet the difficulty experienced by the average reader in understanding that part of a newspaper City article which deals with the money market. It has been compiled with as little reference as possible to other books, and chiefly expresses views and facts gathered from practical men at work in the great machine which it describes . . . The difficulties of the subject are very real to its writer, who has consequently aimed earnestly at clearness, risking platitude and iteration to achieve it. Its shortcomings will be pardoned, by considerate readers, on the ground of the limited leisure in which it was written.'

Limpid, literate and witty, the book was instantly and deservedly successful. As his *Times* obituary was to note, Withers's 'active and powerful mind was accurate, realistic, sceptical, and critical' and he had used his twenty years in the City to understand 'the movement of every cog' in its financial machinery. 'The quest taught him what perhaps no one had ever clearly learned before, the true economic interaction of all the organs of finance – Treasury, central bank, deposit banks, accepting houses, brokers, and merchants', and with the application of his literary ability, produced 'a great book, epochal in finance'. *The Meaning of Money* drew rave reviews from journalists and even from academics. In the *Economic Journal*, the quarterly organ of the Royal Economic Society, the book was given the accolade of a review by the chairman of its Editorial Board, Professor Edgeworth, Francis Hirst's statistical mentor, who particularly liked Withers's ability 'to put himself in the position of those who have not yet lost through familiarity the sense of wonder which the modern monetary system is calculated to excite in the ingenuous mind'.[56]

The book's whimsical, caustic quality enlivened and clarified the most unpromising subjects: his list of United Kingdom invisible exports to the United States included 'Pleasure, social amenities, titles, and art treasures' (Americans in England 'are anxious to cut a figure in what is called Society, and the lavish expenditure in which they indulge is believed to be of some assistance to this ambition. All this expenditure here on their part has the same effect on the balance of Anglo-American indebtedness as an English export. It is also well known that the scions of ancient English families frequently find wives among the attractive daughters of America, and the big dowries that the latter bring with them amount to a considerable annual charge on the United States.') and 'Family affection'. ('Many of the English, and especially Irish, settlers in America regularly remit sums to their parents and families in England, taking nothing in return but affection and gratitude. Every one who has read "Some Experiences of an Irish RM" remembers the picture of McCarthy, the horse-dealing farmer who charged Mr Bernard Shute £45 for a mare, saying, "She's too grand entirely for a poor farmer like me, and if it wasn't for the long weak family I have, I wouldn't part with her for twice the money." The long weak family was explained by Mr Flurry Knox to be "three fine lumps of daughters in America paying his rent for him".')[57]

'His style', observed Chapman judiciously, 'would have gladdened the heart of Walter Bagehot.' Hirst gave Withers a two-part review in *The Economist* and paid him a similar compliment, noting that Withers combined a theoretical capacity with a practical instinct and a well-trained intellect with a long and sympathetic association with men of the financial world.[58]

Withers would have been the first to admit that he stood on Bagehot's shoulders. For instance, discussing the role of the Bank of England, he referred to the belief that under the Bank Charter Act of 1844 it was required merely to carry out its legal responsibility with regard to its note issue and otherwise act like a normal bank. 'This, in fact, was the view long entertained by an influential section of the Bank's Court of Directors, and its fallacy was exposed in that most brilliant of all essays in practical economics, Walter Bagehot's great work on "Lombard Street". Bagehot not only exposed the fallacy, but killed it, buried it, and damned it.'[59]

Within a few months of becoming a successful author, Withers entered Eliza's diary as a tender of the sacred flame, providing a new preface to *Lombard Street* and negotiating with the publisher on her behalf.*

Between then and becoming editor of *The Economist*, Withers wrote five more books and provided the major contribution to a publication by the US National Monetary Commission called *The English Banking System*. (The other substantial section was provided by the ex-*Economist* editor, R.H. Inglis Palgrave, pushed out by Uncle George 27 years previously.) He spent a short time as City editor of the *Morning Post*, moving in 1911 to Seligman Brothers, the merchant bankers. In 1915 he went into the Treasury with the title of Director of Financial Inquiries, to head a statistical and information bureau. In his *Economist* obituary of Withers, Eric Gibb speculated that, for a man of almost 50, the atmosphere of a government office must have seemed restrictive: 'It was certainly with relief that he returned to financial journalism.' Chapman recorded that Withers had written for *The Economist* at

---

*The tenth edition of *Lombard Street* (1892) had additional notes by Edward Johnstone; the 1910 edition had an introduction and corrigenda by Hartley Withers and the 1915 edition had notes revised by A.W. Wright, of *The Economist*. It was translated into Italian by Luigi Einaudi.

fairly regular intervals during Hirst's time, so that he was transferring into familiar territory: from the point of view of the proprietors and trustees, he was a welcome safe pair of hands.

The third Oxford-educated editor – and the first not to be fired – Withers was older than any of his predecessors or successors. After the excitement of the Hirst years, Withers's style came to Chapman as rather an anti-climax.

> After the very active nine years The Economist had just passed through it seemed now as if Mr Withers was going to steer it through calmer waters. A period of quiet may at times be a good thing for a newspaper provided it is soundly edited and Mr Withers was a man of the type that would write on his chosen subjects in an interesting and attractive manner. He was a different type to Mr Hirst with different methods of work. Mr Hirst would, perhaps, walk across the park and arrive at the Economist office about 11 o'clock, whereas Mr Withers would walk along the passage at 10 o'clock each morning and would invariably leave the office about 5 o'clock. Mr Hirst did not seem to work to a time table but Mr Withers seemed as regular as clockwork in all that he did.

Searching in some desperation for telling personal details, Chapman fell back on Withers's dog.

> Both men were fond of walking and I always used to like the picture of Mr Withers when he used sometimes to leave on Friday afternoon with his knapsack on his back and his much loved and faithful companion 'Ginger' walking by his side. When he used occasionally to bring 'Ginger' up to the office the dog would wander from room to room as the staff were working. Yes under Mr Withers we all continued the happy family we were under Mr Hirst.

(Jimmy James, who joined as an office boy in 1920, was similarly stuck for detail: almost all that he recalled of Withers was that 'he used to come in on Saturday morning and bring his dog with him and we used to have to give the dog a saucer of water'.)

Eric Gibb was more discerning as well as being less under the spell of Hirst. 'It is nearly thirty years now since he left *The Economist*,' he wrote in his *Economist* obituary of Withers, 'and there are few left today who worked with him while he was editor. But for those fortunate ones who passed their early manhood in his companionship, his memory still means a great deal. No editor ever had more completely the devotion of his staff, or better deserved the great affection in which they held him.' But then Withers and Gibb must have suited each other admirably. Withers's 'quick, keen mind,' wrote his *Times* obituarist, 'which ran to a sardonic humour and an unfettered enjoyment of the caustic jest, made him too intolerant of mediocre thinking to afford satisfaction in doing business with average minds'. Typical – and as timeless as many a Bagehot jibe – was his comment when in 1918, in response to an allegation by a general that the Prime Minister and members of his government had made incorrect statements in the House of Commons, the government proposed a two-judge tribunal to examine the evidence: 'Seeing that lawyers are, by their training, specially disqualified for discovering facts, and consequently have to be helped by juries of common sense folk whenever questions of fact have to be decided, a worse tribunal for the purpose could hardly be conceived.'[60]

Paul Einzig, one of the great names in British financial journalism, provided forty years later in his autobiography[61] corroborative evidence of Withers's decency as well as paying an extraordinary tribute to the reputation of Withers's *Economist*.

Einzig arrived in London in 1919 at the age of 22, with little money and no English friends. Born in Transylvania and brought up in a backwater, in 1917 he had decamped from his prosperous home to Budapest, where he met writers, politicians and bankers and graduated from the Oriental Academy. His desire to come to England lay 'in my irresistible urge to be in the centre of things', for foreign newspapers had made him aware that Hungary was itself a backwater. 'Why just in London of all places? Why not in Paris, or Berlin, or New York? It is hard to say. I think it must have been mainly because I developed an immense admiration for the only English financial newspaper I knew at the time – the *Economist*, copies of which reached Budapest through Switzerland through the War and which I saw regularly from 1917 onwards. I was impressed by the competence and dignity that characterised the *Economist*.'

Einzig had already published signed articles in various Hungarian financial newspapers, but with little sense of achievement. 'In his biography of Marcel Proust, G.D. Painter explained his hero's strong desire to penetrate into the most exclusive French aristocratic set on the ground of his determination to be accepted "where acceptance would be most difficult". That is precisely how I felt when I decided to take the first opportunity to go to London and to learn enough about conditions there to be able to write for *The Economist*. The difficulty of my task attracted me irresistibly.'

He arrived on 29 November 1919. Within a couple of days he had bought a secondhand portable typewriter, had written an article and had set off to find *The Economist*. 'Even as I was walking down Kingsway towards my destination in Arundel Street in the afternoon of December 1st 1919, I kept debating with myself the wisdom of this obviously premature move. I knew perfectly well that it would be more sensible to try something less ambitious – if indeed I had to try something at once – and defer my approach to *The Economist* until after I had gained experience by writing for less important newspapers. But my impatience got the better of my considered judgement. For nearly two years it had been my ambition, amounting almost to obsession, to see an article of mine printed in *The Economist*.'

The article concerned the economic aspects of the Hungarian communist experiments under Bela Kun during the spring and summer of 1919*, about which Einzig had rightly assumed there was no first-hand information within the British press.

> After much hesitation, having been several times on the point of changing my mind, I mustered all my courage and entered Granville House, where the offices of *The Economist* were situated. That it was a small, unpretentious and old-fashioned building, not at all up to my expectations, did not in any way mitigate the awe I felt on looking at the great name on the door . . . In the inquiry office I asked timidly if I could see the editor. My pulse was beating considerably faster than usual. I doubted if he would even receive me . . . Why should he, a prominent and busy man, spare me even a few minutes of his time?

In fact, Withers saw him immediately.

> I was astounded at the unexpected simplicity of the room to which I was ushered. I had been used to showy offices in Budapest, so I expected to find the Editor of *The Economist* in a magnificent room adorned with impressive

*In March 1919, with Czech, Romanian and Serb troops occupying two-thirds of Hungary, Bela Kun's promise to provide Russian forces to fight the Romanians helped to give him power. His 'soviet republic' imposed doctrinaire Bolshevism by means of terror and antagonised most of the population. In August he and his government fled and Budapest was taken by Romanian forces. Within a few months the Allies had persuaded the Romanians to leave and imposed (temporarily) a democratic form of government on Hungary.

art treasures, antiques or oriental rugs. Instead, I found myself in a medium-sized room containing absolutely nothing to impress the visitor. But Withers himself impressed me very much. He was fully up to my expectations. It is true he was a frail figure with a benign countenance and with an unpretentious personality. Yet at that moment I could not have imagined anyone more awe-inspiring than the Editor of *The Economist* behind his crowded desk with an unmistakeable air of quiet authority about him.

I shall never forget the friendly way in which he received me, his welcoming smile as we shook hands, as if he were really pleased to see me, a total stranger, a shy young man wearing a brand-new trench-coat which I had just bought because I thought it looked very English with its belt. He must have realised how nervous I was and did his best to put me at my ease.

Withers had difficulty with Einzig's spoken English and told him to leave the article and come back the next day. After a sleepless night Einzig returned.

> Withers received me with a friendly smile and said:
>
> 'I spent several hours last night in correcting your English . . . I should very much like to use it. But I don't know you. Could you give me any references?'
>
> My heart sank. I had to tell him that I was not in a position to give him a single reference, since he was the first Englishman I had met in this country apart from shop assistants, hotel staffs and suchlike. I suggested that he could inquire about me at the British Consulate in Bucharest . . .
>
> After a bare moment's hesitation he replied:
>
> 'Oh, well, I think I can trust you.'

The preamble to the article in *The Economist* of 13 December 1919 was: 'Bela Kun's experiment has been more scientifically valuable than Russia's experience of Bolshevism, because in Hungary it is much easier to trace causes and effects and the connection between theory and practice. Hungary provided a better laboratory test. We are enabled to put before our readers an examination of this experiment, made by a financial writer who witnessed it on the spot.'

> My pride then knew no bounds. The wording of the preamble, and implying as it did that *The Economist* considered it an achievement to have been *enabled* to publish *my* article, was almost incredible.

Being without a bank account, when Einzig received his £8 cheque, he handed it over to the London School of Economics in payment of his first fee for the course he was about to take. 'On a later occasion when I called again to pay my fee – this time in cash – I heard [the same girl] . . . whisper to another girl clerk: "this is the man who paid his fee with the *Economist* cheque."'

Emboldened by his success, Einzig went on to write a few pieces on Hungary and Romania for other newspapers and in January 1920 even succeeded in having an article on 'The Monetary Economy of Bolshevism' accepted for the *Economic Journal* by J.M. Keynes, who, with Withers, was the only editor to take the trouble to correct Einzig's English. Two other articles on aspects of the Hungarian communist experiment exhausted the possibilities of *The Economist* for the moment (he was to publish a total of five such pieces between 1919 and 1922), and his limitations of subjects and language led to a long period of 'disheartening reverses . . . When month after month I received back one rejected article after another I was able to keep up my hopes and my determination to struggle on because I always felt that, having succeeded in placing an article in the *Economist* immediately after my arrival in England, I was sure to be able to be successful in the long run.'

In September 1923 Einzig was foreign editor of the *Financial News*, having spent two years as Paris correspondent, during which time he gained a doctorate from the University of Paris. *The Economist* published a long and critical but friendly notice of a book he had based on his thesis on the movement of prices in France since 1914 – a subject dear to the heart of the then editor, Walter Layton. 'Dr Einzig's book is full of ideas and provocative to thought', the review concluded.[62] In June 1926 Einzig initiated a column in the *Financial News* on the money market, which he was to make famous and influential. 'There was apparently much agonized discussion as to what the column should be called,' said the paper's biographer, 'but in the end the name of Walter Bagehot's renowned study of the City was deemed worthy.'[63] Some time in the 1930s, when 'Lombard Street' and his other journalism had made him an established star in financial journalism, along with his many books (by 1939 he had published more than Hartley Withers), he ran into Withers, who was then semi-retired. 'Just at that time I was thoroughly unpopular in certain banking quarters with which he had close and friendly relations as Editor of their quarterly magazine. So I asked him whether he realized the grave responsibility he had incurred in letting me loose in the

British financial Press. I told him that, had it not been for his patience in taking the trouble to correct my article, and for his kindness in trusting me in spite of inability to give references, I should probably have lost confidence in my prospects during the period of my reverses and would have given up the struggle and returned to my native country. He replied laughingly that he was quite prepared to shoulder his share of the responsibility for my success in establishing myself here.' *The Economist*'s decency during the Second World War to distressed foreign journalists was to evoke in its turn similar outbursts of gratitude.

'Mr Withers started in quiet fashion', explained Chapman. 'He did not cause a flutter in any dovecots. He just plodded steadily on from week to week writing one and sometimes two critical leaders.' He was a more interesting editor than this makes him sound, and one who quickly won the respect of his readers. In June 1917 his predecessor, Sir R.H. Inglis Palgrave, wrote to Eliza Bagehot 'approving Mr Heartly [sic] Withers Editorship'. Circulation rose from 4,723 in 1916 to 6,170 in 1920. The paper had, of course, become much more orthodox in its attitude towards the war. In December 1916, hailing as an important event a German expression of a desire to negotiate for peace, *The Economist* observed that it might be 'a mere stratagem designed to gain time, so that our enemies may improve their defences on their Western front and consolidate their measures for aggression in the Balkans, or it may be a kite flown for the benefit of public opinion in Germany or in neutral countries, or even in the nations against whom she is fighting', yet it was probably 'a confession of internal weakness' resulting from the military losses of 1916. If Germany was ready 'for a peace that will satisfy the victims of her aggression, and protect civilisation in future against similar attempts to ride rough-shod over international decency and justice, the prestige of Prussian militarism will be shattered'.

> Since, however, it is extremely unlikely that this consummation so devoutly to be desired is yet in sight, our only policy is to take all possible measures for the vigorous prosecution of the war, with our confidence confirmed by the signal of distress that our enemies have run up to the masthead.[64]

Hirst would have hated even more the ringing patriotic paragraphs that began 'FINANCIAL HEROISM' in October 1917.

> We live in a heroic age, in which the greatest contest ever fought by the

nations of the earth is being carried out with a display of courage by the combatants on both sides which is probably unparalleled in history . . . The courage with which the combatant forces of the Allies have fought for liberty and justice, and the existence of civilisation, is only paralleled by that with which those of the Central Powers have fought for ruthlessness and the rule of force, for domination and destruction.

England had a special cause for pride, 'seeing that the army with which we are now regularly beating the well-trained German legions has been almost entirely improvised out of a population devoted to civilian pursuits, and nourished on civil and pacific ideas . . . The courage, tenacity, and endurance with which this war is being waged by the fighting men of the world is only another example of the unknown stores and resources which human nature had at its disposal when this great crisis in its history called them out.'

Yet this was not tub-thumping: the purpose of this high-sounding rhetoric was to lead into a castigation of waste and inefficiency at home that would have had Hirst nodding in agreement. 'We are of the same blood and bone as those who are daring all things in the trenches and in the minefields for the cause of progress, and yet in the fourth year of war we are still very far from doing what is our plain duty in the field of financial warfare. Why should this be so? We believe that it is due to lack of imagination, deficient grasp of economic facts, and the failure of our leaders to put our financial duty clearly and continually before us.'[65]

Thousands of people who, if they had had the opportunity, would have fought as well as anyone, 'continue to waste on self-indulgence and fripperies money that is needed for the war. It is more than high time that we should put this right, and that the heroism which is fighting our battles at the front should be supported by some attempt to imitate it by those of us who are left at home in the use that we make of our money.' It would be financial heroism to save as much as possible in order to subscribe to War Loans.[66]

This was a theme that Withers plugged relentlessly. 'AT THE FRONT AND AT HOME' condemned 'the extravagance of women in the matter of dress, which has seemed to increase as the war has gone on'; it had been 'a very unworthy set-off to the excellent work for the war by which they have won acknowledgment to their right to a vote. The worst of this extravagance on their part is that it is flaunted in the streets, and so is a very visible bad example to all those to whom War Savings missionaries are appealing. But though feminine extravagance thus has palpable and very unfortunate effects, there is no reason to suggest that it is greater than the even more inexcusable wastefulness on the part of men who ought to know better, because their understanding of money matters is, or ought to be, in most cases, greater than that of women.' This 'thoughtless and ignorant extravagance is raising the cost of the war, and producing a very critical and dangerous spirit among the working-classes which is expressing itself in crude and inequitable proposals for taxing capital which appear to be based on the belief that the capitalist, as such, is growing rich out of the war'.[67]

Withers's coverage of the war was heavily focused on money. Space, of course, was at a premium. Hirst had greatly increased the size of the paper: the actual number of pages for the whole of 1905 were 2,148, for 1913 3,030, but they had fallen in 1915 to 2,408 and in 1918 to 2,004. Therefore, if the normal statistics and essential factual information were to be provided, it was necessary greatly to restrict political coverage. Withers's major theme, apart from the need to eliminate waste in public and in private, was his belief that taxation rather than borrowing should be the means of paying for the war effort. Otherwise, he feared the onset of dangerous inflation.

CHAPTER XXXIV

The wasting disease

Dryden thought that 'no Government has ever been, or ever can be, wherein timeservers and blockheads will not be uppermost'. Without going all the way with him, we may safely contend that the financial achievements of our war Governments do not encourage us to increase official control of the Money Market. *Hartley Withers, 1923*[1]

Withers, recalled Gibb, had 'shocked some orthodox bankers by the simple thesis that every loan creates a deposit', a principle that made him 'specially sensitive to the possibilities of inflation in wartime, and his main work on *The Economist* was to give warning after warning of what inflation meant and declaration after declaration that it could start as easily from a ledger entry as from a run on the printing press'.

> 'Inflation,' he said, 'is the tree up which I bark.' It was not then an easy thing to persuade either all economists or all bankers that a currency could be inflated by bank credits, and there was a tendency to treat Withers's reasoning on this matter with a slightly superior scepticism. Events justified his warning so completely that he has to some extent suffered the fate of many men before him whose arguments were challenged by one generation and dismissed as truisms by the next. But the force of his influence in those war years was beyond question; and as we look back to 1921 we can fairly claim for Withers that if the world's politicians had continued to heed the warnings he gave week after week in *The Economist*, and had acted on them with the necessary courage, most of our economic problems would be far less baffling than they actually are in 1950.[2]

An article in July 1917 greatly stirred up his readers. 'FINANCE, FOOD, AND

INFLATION' discussed the statement by Andrew Bonar Law, Chancellor of the Exchequer, introducing a Vote of Credit for £650 million: 'it is possible to gather, with more or less confidence in our ability to follow him, that in the first 35 days of the financial year the average daily expenditure exceeded the Budget estimate by two millions a day; in the subsequent 77 days the average daily excess over the estimate was one million; and over the whole period – that is, the first 112 days of the current financial year – the average daily excess was 1,384,000. In this period the total expenditure was 6,795,000 per day, against a Budget estimate of 5,411,000.' The grand total was £1,171 million; expenditure for the year might run to £2,500 million. 'But before we allow ourselves to be terrified by these figures, we must remember that the Government's policy of financing so much of the war by inflation has multiplied and debased the currency to an extent, and with results, to which we have been for many months calling attention. Three thousand millions now is probably equivalent to less than two thousand of pre-war millions, and the income of the nation must have been increased, on and in paper, by at least 50 per cent.'

> We note with satisfaction that public interest in this evil policy is being aroused, and that its discussion is spreading to the non-technical papers . . . Better still, even ex-Ministers have now perceived that inflation, which has been an ingredient in war finance for nearly three years, is a fact to be reckoned with. Mr McKenna [Chancellor from May 1915 until Lloyd George's overthrow of Asquith in December 1916], having called attention to the general agreement, in the reports on labour unrest, that foremost among its causes is the general rise in prices, went on to say that the main cause of that rise is not profiteering, but 'inflation due to the high expenditure, and that the remedy is to be found in close control of that expenditure.'

Withers questioned the efficacy of this cure: in Germany, where expenditure was lower, inflation was higher.

> The cure for inflation is to force or induce the people to restrict spending and hand over their money in taxes or loans to be spent on the war, instead of manufacturing fresh currency by the printing press or through the banking machinery. Of the two methods taxation is obviously preferable, and Mr McKenna, having acquiesced in the late Budget, must share the

responsibility for its lamentable failure in that respect, and consequent addition to the debt charge, on which he laid belated stress.

The government had gone over to Alice in Wonderland economics: it had multiplied currency, put up prices and caused industrial unrest, which it now proposed to allay by fixing the price of the loaf at 9d. and subsidising this from the taxpayer's pocket or through further inflation.[3]

'One of the pleasant consequences of inflation', commented Withers six weeks later, 'has been some very interesting correspondence on the subject lately published in our columns. Some of this has been critical of the view expressed in *The Economist* – namely, that since the Government has failed to tax us with the vigour that was required, or to make a sufficiently effective appeal to investors to save their money and place it at the disposal of the Treasury for the war, a round-about and inequitable means has been chosen of enforcing restriction of consumption by manufacturing currency for the purchase of the goods and services needed for the war.'

> This process has been carried out, partly by the issue of Treasury notes to a much greater extent than was required to take the place of the gold which has been called in from circulation, partly by a great increase in the coinage of silver, but chiefly by the Government's policy of financing the war by selling securities to banks and by inducing the banks to make large advances to their customers in order to take up War Loans. When the banks lend money to the Government, either by subscribing to War Loans, by purchasing Treasury Bills or Exchequer bonds, or lending against Ways and Means advances, nobody's purchasing power is reduced as it is when the ordinary citizen pays taxes or subscribes to War Loans out of saved money.

Instead purchasing power was increased.

> The banks give the Government the right to draw cheques upon them, and these cheques, when handed by the Government to contractors and others to whom it owes money, are paid back into the banks, and so increase the amount of banking deposits which are potential currency, because they give the holder the right to draw cheques against them. Consequently, the process known as inflation, by which we mean an increase in currency more rapid than the increase in the production of goods, has been set up, causing a rise in prices that makes the war more costly, imposing considerable

hardship on those least able to bear it, and raising a dangerous feeling of unrest in industrial circles.

He responded in detail to several correspondents and concluded with evidence from the Commission of Inquiry into Industrial Unrest showing that the outstanding cause was rising prices:

> These extracts very largely confirm the view that has been for many months expressed with wearisome iteration by the *Economist*. We have to induce the public to believe that the only source from which the war's needs can be provided, apart from borrowing and credit operations abroad, is the current production of the nation; that the whole of its current production, except what is needed for the maintenance of our health and efficiency, has to be handed over to the Government for the prosecution of the war if the war is to be prosecuted to the best of our ability and on the soundest and cheapest lines; that this process can be best brought about by taxation and by continuous, vigorous, and effective appeals to investors to save money so that they may hand over their buying power to the Government, and no longer continue, as in peace time, to claim the energies of the producers of the nation for the supply of their own comforts and enjoyments.[4]

The term inflation used in relation to economics had first appeared in 1864 in an American dictionary (Webster) but was first found in an English source in the 1880s. Even during Withers's tenure as editor the term needed to be explained to non-specialists. As late as 1917 he was describing it as a 'somewhat obscure expression'.[5] In a book based on a series of lectures given at the London School of Economics, Withers gave his usual clear definition, supported by a example used by H.S. Foxwell, Professor of Political Economy at the University of London, and one of the contributors to the *Economist* debate on inflation.

> Professor Foxwell, in the course of a lecture on Inflation, lately gave an excellent illustration of the effect of the quantity of currency on prices from a remark of Dr Johnson's. When told that in Skye twenty eggs might be bought for a penny, Johnson observed: 'Sir, I do not gather from this that eggs are plenty in your miserable island, but that pence are few.' There it is in a nutshell. If currency is scarce, prices are low. If it is plentiful, prices are high. By inflation I mean an increase in the currency more rapid than in the volume of commodities and services that the community is producing.

When this takes place, if at the same time what is called the velocity of the circulation – that is, the pace at which money is turned over – remains the same, it is impossible to avoid the conclusion that a rise in prices must happen.[6]

In *The Economist* the discussion was conducted on a slightly higher plane. Responding to a letter from T. B. M., a well-known banker, claiming that 'this inflation theory is an old pet of professors who do not like such a simple axiom as supply and demand', Withers made an uncompromisingly monetarist statement. Where T. B. M. believed that an increase in the money supply followed on price rises, Withers held that 'the inflation theory, in the sense in which we hold it to be true, is directly based upon the quantity theory of money, which in turn is directly based on supply and demand. According to it, if you multiply currency – that is to say, all forms of money (including cheques) which are taken in payment by the community for commodities – faster than you multiply the supply of commodities, the result is a rise in prices. This follows because the increased currency causes an increase in the effective demand for goods, which can only be effective if those who make, or wish to make, the demand have currency ready wherewith to pay for the goods. If there is more currency available for the purchase of a relatively smaller amount of goods, the goods to be bought will command a larger amount of currency; that is, the buying power of money will fall, and prices will rise. So stated, the theory seems to be an unassailable platitude.'[7]

The 'wasting disease of modern economics' is how Rupert Pennant-Rea and Bill Emmott (both later to be editors) described inflation in their dictionary, the *Pocket Economist*,[8] a volume in which, in appropriate *Economist* tradition, they sought to demystify the jargon of economics. 'Economists differ in their analysis of the causes of inflation, and therefore in their prescribed cures. MONETARISM holds that inflation can be reduced only by slowing down the growth of the MONEY SUPPLY: in the words of Milton FRIEDMAN, "inflation is always and everywhere a monetary phenomenon". Many KEYNESIANS tend to believe that inflationary pressures can exist independently of monetary conditions; to run a modern economy at low inflation and low unemployment, they say, governments need an INCOMES POLICY.' In 1917 Keynes was in the Treasury and not yet in the public eye and Friedman was five years old. Withers was extrapolating his views on inflation from the quantity theory of money, first developed by such philosophers as John Locke (in the seventeenth century) and David Hume (in the eighteenth) to oppose the mercantilist view that exports should be maximised and imports minimised. Distinguishing between wealth and money, quantity theory underpinned the free-trade position by arguing that mercantilism led to more money and thence to higher prices, but did nothing to increase wealth.

An unapologetic populariser, Withers did not claim to invent any theory, he founded no school, he never became a guru and he received no lasting recognition, but he performed a remarkable job in helping to educate an influential audience into an awareness of uncomfortable truths. In particular, through his signed journalism, his lectures, his books and above all, through his relentless campaign in *The Economist*, he conducted a valiant and influential crusade against 'the old mediaeval dodge of depreciating the currency, varied to suit modern needs'.[9]

Although affected by changing economic views about causes and cures, to an editor, Withers's successors were anti-inflation. In the April before the Second World War, Crowther's *Economist* began a relentless campaign. 'INFLATION AHEAD?' enquired how best to go about defence borrowing. 'Can it be done without inflation?' There were three approaches. 'The first is to allow the competition for the available supplies of labour and capital to force up prices and wages – the classical form of inflation.' This would be inflationary and inequitable. 'The whole experience of the decade 1914–24 is against its adoption.' The second – the reduction of consumption by increasing taxes – was 'a clumsy weapon': what was actually necessary was to restrict not all, but certain specific, forms of expenditure that competed with rearmament needs. The third – 'direct control and rationing of those varieties of labour and raw materials which are in short supply', under a Ministry of Supply – was the answer.[10] Two decades of economic crises had wrought a great change in *Economist* orthodoxies.

Two months later 'DRIFTING TOWARDS INFLATION' stressed urgently that the problem of wartime finance, 'if left alone, will not stand still; it will solve itself by the method of inflation, which has always hitherto been considered the worst way'.

> It has been the custom in this country, ever since the end of the War, to congratulate ourselves on the self-restraint and wisdom we showed, in greater measure than any other European country, in our war finance.

Germany has been pointed out as proof that the aftermath of social disturbance produced by unsuccessful war finance can be worse than that of unsuccessful war itself. But it would now appear that the Germans . . . have learnt the lesson better than we have ourselves. They are mobilised for war finance; we are still drifting without any visible objective, plan or leadership.[11]

Complacency was again the target at the beginning of 1940. 'Since the outbreak of war,' began one typical article, 'there has been an impressive unanimity of testimony that inflation must and will be avoided. This sentiment has been heard from the Chancellor of the Exchequer, from politicians of all parties and from independent authorities. This unanimity is all to the good.' While it was possible to see some advantages to strictly limited rising prices, 'that way lies the primrose path'.

Inflation, if it comes, will come so imperceptibly, so independently of any decision of authority, that it can be relied upon to take an ell for every theoretical inch conceded to it. The danger is that we shall get a sizeable inflation while protesting that we want none; if we say we should like a little, we shall get an infinite amount.[12]

Keynes incurred displeasure by reassuring the public in a broadcast in September 1940 that there had been no significant degree of budgetary inflation.

The most that can be said is that, through a conjuncture of circumstances, we have been able to avoid the difficulties of war finance in the first year of war – though not as completely as Mr Keynes would have us believe. The most significant point in his broadcast is that 'this second year is, in truth, the first year of the real war for Britain.' There is not the slightest reason for relaxing the pressure of opinion for a courageous and comprehensive financial policy.[13]

The duties of consumers continued to be hammered home in true Withers-like fashion. Savings propaganda was condemned for placing its emphasis merely on the total of money subscribed. 'There is also a tendency to bless with the patriotic label private individuals' subscriptions to War Loans which represent no genuine abstention from consumption at all. The whole cast of Savings propaganda needs to be quite radically altered. The individual should be told that his duty is to reduce his consumption by every possible means. He should have the lesson driven home to him on every hoarding that every act of consumption uses shipping space and labour – the two scarcest of commodities. Once he has economised as much as he can, it matters very little what happens to the money he saves thereby.'[14]

However, Withers's analysis of the major cause of inflation was out – swept aside by the tide of economic fashion. In 'BANK CREDIT AND INFLATION', Crowther looked at 'old-fashioned Quantity Theory' and subjected it to a masterly analysis in the light of recent economic trends. His conclusion was that the 'quantity of money in existence begins to look like a factor of very secondary importance – a mere by-product of the technical means selected to accomplish more fundamental processes'. What was fundamental was the volume of expenditure.

> After the war, too, whether the need of the moment be to avoid inflation or deflation, the monetary managers will be wise to keep their eyes fixed on expenditure and to worry about the quantity of money only in so far as it can be expected to influence expenditure. The volume of credit clearly has important consequences for the banking system; but for the community as a whole its importance is very much less than had hitherto been supposed.[15]

In 1945, four months after Germany's surrender, Wilfred King* warned that 'the menace of inflation in Britain is greater now, and the defences against it are probably weaker, than at any time in the past six years. It will be hard to convince the public that this is so. In the early years of the war people were told so often that the inflation bogey was just round the corner, yet never caught a clear view of it, that they have grown sceptical about its very existence.' Yet inflation had been avoided because the lessons of 1914 had been learned, and the defences of penal taxation, physical controls and rationing and price control had been erected. The worry was now that the 'tired and ignorant' public would no longer make the necessary sacrifices to avert this danger. Since Britain had never had runaway inflation, 'its people are not imbued with that wholesome fear of it that is bred in every Continental'.

---

*King was an outside contributor from 1943, while with the *Financial News*. A great authority on the London discount market, he joined *The Economist* in May 1945 to work on the Business World and from the following year combined this with the editorship of the *Banker*.

> Horror stories about the German, Austrian and Russian inflations after the
> last war, or about the Greek and Chinese inflations in this one, are useless as
> propaganda in this country. The man in the street is firmly convinced that
> that kind of thing cannot happen here. And in this he is certainly right.
> Inflations of that type result from a breakdown of public administration or
> civil discipline, so that the Government, lacking an effective tax machine,
> has no alternative but to pay its bills by creating new money. And as prices
> rise, each fresh creation has to be larger than its predecessor: at the climax of
> the German inflation in 1923, the government doubled the note circulation
> in a single week, whereupon the currency became entirely worthless.

In law-abiding Britain, with its long tradition of heavy taxation and efficient
fiscal machinery, there were no such dangers, but this was no reason to
minimise those that did exist.[16]

Alec Cairncross, in 1946 briefly on the Business World staff between civil
service jobs,* provided a detailed guide to measuring inflation along with an
entertaining definition: 'Inflation is one of those distracted words, like
coordination, to which the ordinary man turns when he feels that there is
something wrong somewhere: it implies malaise in the movement of prices.'
His conclusions, however, were solemn. Inflation since 1939 had been
controlled, but that success owed 'as much to the stability of the British
temperament as to any native skill in monetary and economic management.
That skill will have to face its severest tests during the early post-war years; if
it fails, temperament will give way to temper, and the causal processes of
price inflation will then be free to destroy the fruits of patience.'[17]

The prophecies were coming true in 1951. In 'INFLATION'S GALLOP',
Tom Kent (who joined the Home Department in 1950), offered only a grim
prospect. Rapid worldwide inflation was underway and the collective proposals of the finance ministers of Western Europe were 'no more than jejune
generalisations'. It was no longer possible for the British people to choose
whether or not they would have inflation. 'The germ is already in the

---

*Sir Alec's long and distinguished career in academia and the public service has included being
Head of the Government Economic Service from 1965 to 1969. His daughter Frances joined the
paper in 1974 and has been successively editor of the Britain section and environment editor.
Other examples of fathers-and-children who have featured editorially in the twentieth-century
Economist are Denis and Hugh Brogan, Alastair and David Buchan, Fred and Donald Hirsch,
Walter, Margaret and Christopher Layton and Bernard and Daniel Singer.

bloodstream; it is gradually incubating; and the period of development will not be over for many months yet.'

There was no good news. As so often, *The Economist* felt duty-bound to offer its readers the Scylla/Charybdis choice.

> Once inflation is in the bloodstream, the choice of the form it shall take – suppressed or open – is a cruelly difficult one. To choose suppression now means shortages and queues; it means that there will be more rationing, production controls and allocations; that the incentives to work hard and to change jobs in response to changing demands will be weakened; that stocks will be run down and productivity fall as workers wait for materials to turn up; that yet more rigidities and inefficiencies will be built into the British economic system; that the rearmament effort will probably, in spite of the controls, be weakened, and exports of consumer goods will almost certainly fail to make up the gap left by the inevitable reduction in engineering exports.

That was what had happened in 1946 and 1947. Also against suppression was that there was no end to it, and that in the then climate of trade union demands it would not work. 'To attempt suppression, to tie the economy up in red tape, and then to have rocketing prices after all – this would surely be the worst of both worlds.'

Yet the evils of letting inflation run its course were just as great.

> If the first are economically debilitating, the second are socially corrosive. For over a decade, British economic policy has, in substance, refused to choose between these unlovely alternatives. The result is that we have had a bit of each. There has been enough congestion to make the economy dangerously rigid and inefficient – but not enough (save at intervals) to bring about open economic disasters. There has been a fall in the value of money, rapid enough when looked at in retrospect, but not sufficient at any time to produce social revolt. With inflationary pressure no more than it has been in the last five years, or with the special disciplines of wartime, such an ignoble compromise will work. It is very doubtful whether it will work with the much greater inflationary pressure that is now in prospect.

He then produced Scylla and Charybdis's big brother. The right policy was 'to let the inflation that is already in the bloodstream work its way out in rising prices (with all the hardships and difficulties that that involves)', but then to prevent a fresh crop by using 'all the old-fashioned remedies – by monetary policy, by restriction of credit and by public retrenchment'. Politicians might think it impossible to sell such a programme to the electorate. 'That is their business; but it is the economist's business to warn them that the alternative may well be an economic and social disaster to which past history in these islands provides no parallel.'[18]

Despite the occasional lull, worries about inflation have continued to be a dominant concern of the paper. 'Inflationary cares infest this epoch,' wrote Norman Macrae in 1959, 'and they are unlikely silently to steal away.'[19] Wage increases had become the bogey, but by 1970, in Burnet's paper, there was a challenge from the right. Milton Friedman had metamorphosed the despised quantity theory of money into monetarism. 'Is it not right, ask the extreme monetarists on the right wing of the Conservative party, that all inflations are preceded and wholly caused by a rise in money supply, so that incomes policies are superfluous?' 'TIME TO STOP INFLATION' contended that: 'No, in Britain it really is not quite right – and for an orthodox reason of economic theory that now seems to be as evident as an open barn door.' And, like Crowther nearly 30 years earlier, the paper proved by analysis of recent financial data that the money supply was of secondary importance. Yet it was not being dismissed out of hand. Along with the incomes policy, the paper recommended a reduction in the money supply.

Hyper-inflation was the fear by 1974: even if wage limits held, 15% inflation loomed. The tone was apocalyptic, lacking the old confidence that the natural solidity of the British people would ensure they muddled through.

> No country which has sustained a rate of inflation of over 20 per cent for long has been, or has remained, a democracy. South American countries run inflationary economies only with authoritarian governments which dictate the distribution of income. Without dictatorship the social strains of over-rapid shifts in income from the weak to the strong tear society apart. Few countries have ever sustained rates of inflation of 10–20 per cent for more than two years. Governments either react violently to the crisis of double-figure inflation to pull prices back down, or lose all control. Of 63 countries experiencing inflation between 1960 and 1972, the maximum number in the 10–20 per cent band in any one year was seven. Only one country, South Korea, stayed in the band for more than three years, and only two countries, Iceland and the Philippines, stayed in it that long. The

countries that went into 100 per cent a year hyper-inflation included some in Latin America where an actual majority of people seeking paid employment cannot get it. Once a hyper-inflation has broken through, a large excess of job-seekers over vacancies really does not automatically cure it.

Britain was entering the danger zone where inflation could not be stopped by deflating demand without bringing about intolerable unemployment. 'Unless the Government has the strength to enforce direct controls over wages and prices, the only exit is through the roof.' It was crucial that in the forthcoming election, called by Edward Heath over the issue of who ruled Britain, the Conservative government rather than the striking coal miners should prevail.[20]

In fact the government lost, but, like all the major world economies, Britain 'scrambled down from the peaks of threatening hyperinflation'. The opposition leader, Margaret Thatcher, denounced formal incomes policies out of hand. 'A year ago next week,' reported Knight's paper in April 1980, 'Mrs Thatcher's government was elected with the firm belief in strict monetary control as the primary nostrum for Britain's endemic inflation. With wage and price inflation both around 20%, confidence has subsided to the point where honest and unremarkable reservations by a treasury minister have been uproariously greeted as open revolt. All that poor Mr John Biffen admitted this week was that there is no God- or Friedman-given 18-month lag between a slowdown in money growth and a drop in inflation.'[21]

Yet the single-mindedness of the Thatcherite government worked and, for a time, most governments were monetarist. Inflation ceased to be a major worry for *The Economist* until 1990, when 'THE WORLD'S NEXT INFLATION' warned that the old enemy was 'poised to strike back', and fretted that the Group of Seven (finance ministers from the seven major capitalist economies) failed to realise that it should be their main priority.[22] Human nature and politicians being what they are, in an age of recession a little modest reflation no longer frightens the horses, but it frightened Pennant-Rea, that Robespierre among economists, who could no more be deflected from the path of fiscal righteousness than could James Wilson before politics corrupted him. His *Economist* revived an ambition expressed by the equally strict Tom Kent during Crowther's editorship. In 1951 Kent fought the developing orthodoxy that inflation was inevitable: that was 'not an acknowledgment of economic determinism but a political judgment that the will to control inflation has disappeared. Six years of postwar experience seem an inadequate basis for quite so pessimistic a conclusion.'[23] Forty-one years later the paper supported calls for zero inflation with a vision of 'a crunchier, less opaque world in which performance is more justly rewarded; in which the manpower devoted to the business of managing money becomes less extravagant; in which companies can plan for the longer term because the outlook for costs, prices and margins, cloudy at any time, is at least spared the cloud of inflation. The price mechanism, the heart of the market economy, will again work over time and not just for today. Big prizes; and the more that people can be persuaded to drop their addictive habits now, the smaller will be the pain before those prizes are won.'[24]

CHAPTER XXXV:

War and peace

Had these men any quarrel? Busy as the Devil is, not the smallest! They lived far enough apart; were the entirest strangers: nay, in so wide a Universe, there was even unconsciously, by commerce, some mutual helpfulness between them. How then? Simpleton! their Governors had fallen out; and, instead of shooting one another, had the cunning to make these poor blockheads shoot. *Thomas Carlyle*, Sartor Resartus, *quoted in* The Economist, *1919*[1]

Although the anti-inflation crusade was a new preoccupation for *The Economist*, Withers was also loyal to the hardy perennials. In September 1918 'MILITARISM AND BOYCOTT' represented three: free trade, internationalism and magnanimity in victory. 'It is, or appears to be,' it began, 'a common fallacy in England that on all political and all economic questions all Germans think exactly alike. Apart, however, from the intrinsic unlikelihood of 70 million beings holding the same views on any subject that ever engaged the attention of created man, there is evidence of a wide diversity of outlook in the German people, and it will be a fatal error in our diplomacy if we forget or deliberately ignore the differences of belief and of interest which divide the various sections from each other. The art of dealing with your enemy is not to provide him with a common ground on which all classes can take their stand, but to emphasise the points of difference, and widen instead of filling up the breaches which must exist in a large, scattered, variously occupied people.'

Germany had now given up hope of winning:* 'with a truer realisation of American man-power, with the submarine laid aside in the cupboard where dead hopes are left to rot, with Austria growing more restive, with food scarcer than ever, and with the morale even of the Army impaired, the civilian has little to sustain him through the dark hours, and he will be sustained only by a desperate sense of common peril'. The German military leaders were therefore calling on their people to fight for survival, claiming that the Allies' quarrel was with every single individual, not just with the leaders. As always, *The Economist* made the strongest possible distinction between the moral responsibility of leaders and led.

> German militarism and German militarists – the Kaisers, Crown Princes, and Hindenburgs [Field Marshal and, since 1916, Supreme Commander on the western front] – are like a man who has committed murder, and knows that he has already incurred the extreme penalty. To such a man nothing is too heavy to endure, nothing too rash to be attempted. There is no half-way house for him, and failing an out and out escape he has no clemency to look to. That is the position of the ruling gang in Germany, for unless they can lead their country to victory their day is done, and their power broken. In their calculations, so long as there is the faintest chance of relief, no price is too high to pay themselves or to exact from their subjects, and their natural obvious course is to persuade their subjects that they are all in the same boat with the same danger threatening everybody.

It would be inexcusable to help the German ruling classes with this game: 'Surely this talk of a boycott and these official films which declare war for ever on all German trade are devices that play straight into Hindenburg's hands, for their most certain result is to stiffen the resistance of commercial classes in Germany, and fill up the breach between traders and militarists.'

---

*The German U-boats had almost brought Britain to its knees early in 1917. In April it lost a quarter of all the ships leaving British ports and food and fuel were running short; Lloyd George then introduced a highly effective convoy system. By the end of 1917 the Germans and Austrians had smashed the Italian army at Caporetto, and the military collapse of Russia (now under communist rule) had brought them the Ukraine's coal and iron and Romania's oil. They could switch whole armies to the western fronts, where in 1918 the Germans crossed the Marne and nearly reached the Channel ports. Although the United States had declared war on Germany in April 1917, a whole year passed before large American armies entered the fighting in France. It was only on 3 August 1918 that *The Economist* could hail 'the timely appearance in the field of America's manhood, fighting with the freshness and dash of those who have just buckled on their armour, and yet with all the steadiness and wary resource of seasoned veterans'.

The governing classes had the noose around their necks; the trading classes 'are not, or need not be, in the same position. They still have factories, their experience, and the remnants of their foreign trade to care for, and though their difficulties must in any circumstances be very great, not even a crushing defeat need rob them of all their interest in life, as it must and shall rob the military gang that rules from Berlin.'

> But if England and the other Allies agree to a definite policy of boycott, if we declare beforehand that all our efforts in war, and at the peace conference, and in the subsequent peace, will be devoted to making it impossible for Germany to do business with anybody, then we simply cross the t's and dot the i's of the Hindenburg manifestos. We are . . . filling the business men of Germany with the same desperate motives for resistance as already inspire the generals and the dynasty. The effect will be not merely to prolong the war, and swell our casualty lists, but to decrease the prospect of that crushing victory over German militarism which is the beginning and the end of our war aims. We shall, in fact, be recruiting for the Hohenzollerns [the ruling dynasty].

The leader concluded by noting that in a recent speech the Prime Minister had declared himself in favour of a League of Nations,* 'with the wise proviso that "victory is essential to sound peace". He said also that "if after the war Germany repudiates and condemns her perfidy, or, rather, the perfidy of her rulers, then a Germany freed from military domination will be welcome into the great League of Nations."' Such a promise was wholly inconsistent with the suggested boycott: 'If Mr Lloyd George had expressly repudiated this wild doctrine and intimated England's willingness to trade with Germany, after our objects – restitution, reparation, and security – have been fully provided for, he would have done much, by undermining the power of German militarism at home, to bring nearer the date of the victory that we are determined to secure.'[2]

'WHAT SORT OF PEACE?' asked the paper in October 1918 during negotiations among the Allies. It was concerned that doubts existed over

---

*The main object of the League of Nations was to keep the world peaceful through international cooperation. At the 1919 Paris Peace Conference the Allies accepted a League Covenant which included provisions for arbitrating disputes, for collective action in the face of aggression and for negotiations on armament reduction, and set up an assembly, a council and a secretariat. Germany joined the League in 1926 (and withdrew in 1933). The United States never joined.

British attitudes to President Woodrow Wilson's Fourteen Points:* protectionist pressure was being put on Lloyd George. Reminding its readers of working-class resentments at high prices and profiteering, it asked how they might react after the war, if the manufacturers now 'beating on the doors of the War Cabinet and using all their influence to snatch a tariff victory at a khaki election' persuaded the War Cabinet to frame its peace proposals to fit a high protection tariff 'which must keep prices of all commodities above their proper level and increase the profits of the privileged manufacturers'. High food prices would make aggrieved consumers say '"I have lived through a profiteer's war to emerge into a profiteer's peace", which is just the kind of peace that they are least likely to appreciate or endure.'

> We want a clean peace, and we want it not only in foreign but in domestic policies. Without such a peace at home and abroad the revival of a more terrible war between nations and between classes is inevitable, but it can never be achieved if the war's end is made the profiteer's opportunity, and under the pleas of patriotism tariffs are introduced to swell the profits of protected manufacturers and increase the burden of the harassed consumer. We are coming to the great crisis of the world's history, and whether we take the right path or the wrong depends mainly on whether we look forward in a sensible or in a narrow and reactionary spirit. An American story tells of a financier who spent the Judgment Day in cornering harps, and the same attitude of mind is shown by those manufacturers who envisage the Peace Council, which is laying the foundations of a new and permanent peace, as a place where they can hatch a tariff for the greater profit of their own business.[3]

(Times had changed: businessmen were no longer the natural allies of free trade. Nor are they now. In 'AFTER THE MARKET' in November 1992, a first leader deploring the fashionable swing against the market capitalism of the 1980s instructed Bill Clinton not to listen to businessmen. 'For perfectly understandable reasons, they want just one thing from government: prefer-

---

*Wilson's Fourteen Points were proposed in January 1918. They included acceptance of the principle of absolute freedom of the seas, the establishment of a 'general association of nations for the purposes of affording mutual guarantees of political independence and territorial integrity to great and small states alike' (that is, a League of Nations), and – the third point – the 'removal, as far as possible, of all economic barriers and the establishment of an equality of trade conditions'.

ence. Every industrialist invited into the White House will make a persuasive case for special assistance. New industries seek subsidies and protection from competition so they can establish themselves in the markets. Their slogan is: invest in tomorrow. Old industries need the same, to avoid the need for retrenchmment. Their slogan is: export goods, not jobs.'

> It would be nice to help them all; but, as Adam Smith pointed out more than 200 years ago, you cannot extend preference to everybody. Each measure of assistance puts a tax on other producers and on consumers at large.[4])

Fighting on the western front ceased on 11 November 1918 with the armistice between Germany and the Allies. Many emotional accounts have been written of the extraordinary scenes in London on Armistice Day, when the crowds, as Molly Hamilton put it, 'were drunk with peace, not victory'. *The Economist* was dead sober, though a tinge of feeling did penetrate 'THE MONEY MARKET'.

> Anticipations of stringency have not been fulfilled; money has been difficult to find in the mornings, but has 'come out' in the afternoons, and pressure due to the transfer of funds to the Bank of England by applications for the French loan has been satisfactorily avoided. The discount market was in a dead-alive condition. It is a time at which the boldest monetary propheteers admit that they cannot see ahead, and business was on the smallest possible scale. Peace and victory bring general relief and thankfulness, and sufficient for the week is the blessing thereof.[5]

The leading article, 'AND NOW TO BUSINESS', opened with a blunt paragraph which is one of *The Economist*'s classic statements about war.

> With deep thanksgiving we chronicle the victory, secured by the signing of the armistice terms last Monday, of the cause of liberty and justice, and the end of the slaughter of the best men of the greatest nations of the earth. That such a war should have been the only means by which they could settle their differences is a sufficient proof that the civilisation under which we lived until 1914 was a mockery. Civilisation in anything like a true sense of the word has to be created. How are we going to face the problem?[6]

(This disillusion was a sad contrast to the great Whig hopes expressed in Wilson's belief of 1843 that 'morality, intelligence, and civilization have been rapidly extending on all hands'.[7])

Twenty-seven years later Geoffrey Crowther's 'ANCIENT SACRIFICE' was less blunt but more human, though there was castigation of 'the sins of blindness and indolence and complacency that encouraged the aggressor – sins from whose taint none is free'. But he allowed that it was right that there should be 'a brief pause of rejoicing. "Speak ye comfortably to Jerusalem and cry unto her that her warfare is accomplished and that her iniquity is pardoned."'

> The second thought – the deeper and more lasting – is for those who will not come back, for those who will not grow old, as we that are left grow old.* For this country (though not for others) they are mercifully fewer than in the last war. But human life is not to be computed statistically, and of all war's wounds an empty heart is the only one that time does not heal. To the gallant dead, many memorials will be established and consecrated with a sincere and universal resolution to see their task finally accomplished. But, just as Lincoln said of the soil of Gettysburg, it is not for us to dedicate memorials, it is rather for us, the living, to be here dedicated to the great task remaining before us, and to find in its acomplishment the only lasting proof that they neither lived in vain nor died forgotten.[8]

Withers's article became passionate on a familiar theme. 'Building a new world is an exhilarating task that will occupy, we may hope, the best intellects and the most honest spirits among us for many a year of blunder and achievement, ending in something like success. But it cannot be begun until our output of goods and services is secured and the day's daily bread is granted to us.'

> During the war we have worked under conditions of economic recklessness which were partly inevitable and mostly criminal. The nation knew that whatever the price of victory that price had to be paid; this knowledge has been exploited by politicians, officials, and profiteers – both employers and workmen – and the nation has met the bill. Now we have to get back to the business basis under which the test of industrial achievement is not the

---

*From Laurence Binyon's *For the Fallen*. The verse reads:

'They shall grow not old, as we that are left grow old;.
Age shall not weary them, nor the years condemn.
At the going down of the sun and in the morning
We will remember them.'

satisfaction, at any price demanded, of the needs of consumers able to exercise choice. A great output, wisely and equitably distributed, is the only means to the economic security on which our work-building schemes and hopes must necessarily be based.

He registered disgust at the political manoeuvres now preoccupying British political leaders, who were shaping up to a general election. 'President Wilson and M. Clemenceau have marked the occasion with words befitting it, showing that the age of war and diplomatic trickery is over, that mankind's wounds have to be healed, and that the nations must work together to that end. Mr Lloyd George has been dancing on the political tightrope': he had been toying with protection. The role of the individual citizen was to continue to exercise self-control in spending and subscribe to government loans.⁹

The Economist was enraged by the rhetoric of the 1918 election campaign. 'At ordinary times there is something pathetically pleasing about the spectacle of a man thoroughly satisfied with his own performances. One feels that in a world full of disappointment and half-achieved ideals it is something that anybody should be able to feel that he has done a big thing well; and it is one of the many drawbacks of a critic's job that he should so often be compelled by his invidious duty to point out that the big thing might have been done a good deal better.'

It was reasonable that everyone should be throwing up their hats because of the task done on behalf of 'liberty and a decent ideal of international behaviour against military autocracies believing only in the mailed fist'. Britain had every right to be proud of its achievement 'on sea and land and in the factory and the field'. But it was another matter 'when we find the men who have been in the position of leadership arrogating to themselves the merit of this achievement, because it was, in fact, carried out largely in spite of the blunders and short-sightedness of the Government that ruled us during the war. Their record was one of reckless extravagance combined with pitiful cheeseparing, diplomatic bungling, and mismanagement at home that was more than once in danger of producing such exasperation as to impair the efficiency of our war effort.'

> Democracy has so far failed to bring the right men to the top; if it continues to fail on this all-important point it has evil days ahead of it. The men who led us in the war did their best, and we have good reason to thank them for

their courage and tenacity. But courage and tenacity are qualities that are common enough in these islands. Any office boy can refuse to believe in the possibility of his own defeat. And it does not augur well for the solution of the difficult problems of reconstruction when we find our present rulers blowing a blare of trumpets about their war performances as if they and not the country had been responsible for victory.

Lloyd George claimed that financing the war had been a great achievement, yet that was won by the enormous financial strength with which the country started the war, 'thanks largely to the Free-trade policy which Mr Lloyd George now threatens to modify, and by the elasticity of our banking system which the Labour Party proposes to spoil by nationalisation'.

The financial delinquencies had led to a rise in prices 'that set all classes at loggerheads, and produced a profiteering spirit both among employers and workmen that has been a black stain on our war record'.

> At this moment of triumph and relief it is not a pleasant task to recall these sins of omission and commission on the part of men who did their best according to their lights. But when these men claim that their best was so good and their lights were so illuminating that they are the only people fit to be trusted with Government of the country, it is high time to protest against so pessimistic a doctrine, and to urge the country to do some thinking for itself and to apply the necessary spur in the direction of improvement, if as seems is only too likely, our political machinery is so far incapable of finding a better set of substitutes.

The Labour MP, Arthur Henderson, had said that 'nothing is better calculated to drive the masses of the worker in the direction of Bolshevism than the triumph of reaction at the polls'.

> A policy of reaction, complicated by doles, is one that seems likely to lead to serious trouble, and to retard that industrial recovery on which our financial strength depends. The problems before the country call for statesmanship, not vain-glorious boasting. If they are met in the right spirit and with the hard work, good will, and co-operation that the war brought out in spite of our rulers' muddling, we shall deal with it as successfully as with the threat of German aggression. But lighthearted self-satisfaction and political juggling at the top seem to show that the country will, as usual, have to do its own work.[10]

The election held in December 1918 was an overwhelming victory for Lloyd George's Coalition,* although his section of the Liberal Party had won fewer than half the government seats. Yet he had been the focus of the contest, and the triumph reflected the majority view that he had won the war and he would now create 'a country fit for heroes to live in'.

Like Hirst, though for different reasons, Withers was ambivalent about Lloyd George. The December 1916 leader which discussed his replacement of Asquith as Prime Minister showed sympathy for Asquith and a patchy and reluctant appreciation of his successor's virtues. Having acknowledged the outgoing government's failings, it forgave them. 'When the war broke out the Ministers then in power were at the end of an arduous spell of labour, which had already entitled them to a high place among our constitutional reformers and constructive statesmen. They had done great work, and they were tired men. They made a great effort to face this Titanic crisis, and it is a marvel that they achieved what they did. Then came the Coalition, and with it difficulties and hesitations, and the lack of stimulus that is given by a strong Opposition. With tired men still in most of the most responsible offices, vigorous action was hardly possible.'

> When, therefore, we hope for better things from a change of bowling, it is because we believe that the country has throughout been asking for what it is now likely to get, namely, vigorous government and a strong lead in the great effort that lies before it.

The danger was that the new leaders would 'give us violence instead of vigour, and recklessness instead of courage; but they will be restrained by the power of an able and patriotic Opposition'. Lloyd George had a good and bad record; the hope was that he would respond to the gravity of the crisis.[11]

In 1918, although grateful for victory, the paper had not learned to love the Prime Minister. Apart from his failure to toe *The Economist*'s line on war-finance, his braggadocio and deviousness were traits that did not appeal to Withers. But on the major issue facing the Prime Minister, the need to bring about a lasting peace, their outlook was similar, indeed more similar than Withers could have realised, for throughout the election and the

*The results were: Coalition 478 (Conservative and Unionist 335; Liberal 133; Labour 10); non-Coalition 229 (Conservative 23, Irish Unionist 25, Liberal 28, Labour 63, Irish Nationalist 7, Sinn Fein 73, Others 10).

negotiations Lloyd George voiced hard sentiments against Germany in order to be able to act soft. More than was contemporaneously realised, he did much to control France's territorial demands, to reduce the demands on Germany for financial reparations, and to keep the punitive parts of the Peace Treaty of Versailles as vague as possible in the hope that in the future wiser counsels would prevail. Behind the scenes, during the Peace Conference, he stirred up liberal demands for conciliation. It was as a part of this campaign that J.M. Keynes published an attack on reparations in the seminal book *The Economic Consequences of the Peace* in December 1919.

The Economist viewed reparations as a red herring. 'Whatever we may or may not receive from Germany, our duty remains the same. We must make up our minds to work out our own salvation, which involves working hard, spending as little as possible, and saving as much as possible, so that manufactured and inflated credits may give way to real saved capital.'[12] Its French correspondent, discussing a common view 'that Germany should be bled white', noted that even France – 'and France has been encouraged to have large hopes – realises that it is bad policy to kill a creditor who owes you money'.[13] Its German correspondent worried about inflation.[14]

Keynes's case against the economic aspects of the Treaty was 'unanswerable', judged *The Economist* in a full-page review of his book. It described as 'brilliant' his chapter on Europe before the war, in which he explained 'the delicate system of economic interdependence on which we relied in 1914'. Another chapter 'shows how over the whole Continent of Europe that system has been shattered by the war. It is the contrast between these two pictures which gives point to his exposition of the Treaty, and dignifies with a tragic significance the futility and impossibility of its economic provisions.' In his final constructive chapter Keynes dealt 'with the revision of the terms of peace and the rehabilitation of Europe, which then, and only then, may become a practicable proposition', reproduced a scheme he had originated the previous year for the cancellation of inter-Allied indebtedness, and produced 'concrete conditions for an international loan'.

> All these proposals are susceptible of criticism or modification in detail, but in their general outline they are the one alternative to dissolution and economic collapse in a great part of Europe. Mr Keynes recognises that before any of these hopes can be realised there must be a change of Government and a change of heart in every Allied country, and it is to the formation of the general opinion of the future that he dedicates his book.[15]

A leader demurred only slightly. In the course of feeling its way towards what 28 years later would be known as the Marshall Plan, it declared that 'Prostrate Europe cannot recover without help, and the great difficulty to be solved by the countries that can give help is how to see that it gets into the right hands.' More particularly, as *The Economist* had often urged, 'we should cancel all the indebtedness of the Allies to us, in view of their weaker financial position and the greater strain that the war threw on them, and should then ask the United States to fund our debt to them into a forty or fifty year loan, with an option to fund the interest for a few years'.

> We still prefer this solution to Mr Keynes's, for we believe that we can afford it if we work and reduce extravagance, and it is in accordance with our proud financial traditions. We ought long ago to have recognised that, as Mr Keynes says, 'if these great debts are forgiven, a stimulus will be given to the solidarity and true friendliness of the nations lately associated,' and acted towards our debtors in this sense.[16]

'He could see the world's economic and financial system as a whole,' Norman Crump (later banking editor of *The Economist*) wrote of Withers many years later, 'and explain it in words intelligible to the ordinary man who, by reason of the war of 1914–18 and its aftermath, had perforce to seek an understanding of economic affairs.'[17] There was no better time for *The Economist* to have been led by a clear mind, focused on finance.

In September 1921, 'obeying', as Gibb put it, 'some strange restless instinct that was part of his complex fascinating personality' and 'much to the regret of the proprietors', Withers took up a lucrative offer to become editor of the financial supplement of the *Saturday Review*: he stayed for only two years, after which he combined business and authorship. 'He may hardly be described as a great editor', observed Norman Crump fairly enough, but he was a good editor, who improved the paper's image and circulation, kept it true to its principles and produced a great deal of shrewd and far-sighted economic coverage. As Crump concluded, Withers's real legacy 'was to the generation of financial journalists who came after him. How great this was may be seen by contrasting the arid, technical City article of 50 years earlier with the broad view taken by those writing at the time of his death' in 1950. Yet that assessment makes him sound excessively like an innovator; like Johnstone and Hirst, Withers continued the tradition of Bagehot by trying to explain the world of money clearly and practically.

In October 1919, Withers wrote an unusually personal – indeed passionate – article which is the nearest he came to a valedictory. In style and emphasis as well as content, it was the product of a man whose roots were firmly in Victorian England, but who looked squarely at the future in a manner both realistic and prophetic: it provides a link between the old and new style of editors. Withers (banker and financial writer) was the last of the line dominated by men of business or City specialists. Henceforward editors were economists (Layton, Crowther and Pennant-Rea) deeply interested in politics, or political journalists (Tyerman, Burnet and Knight) who had to understand economics to understand politics. Emmott combines both.

In 'IS IT PEACE?', Withers considered the idea of the League of Nations from a typically practical point of view. Picking up three phrases from a Lloyd George message to a meeting of the League of Nations Union, he observed that:

> Noble ideals, enlightened opinion, and awakened consciences are splendid phrases and splendid things, and without them the world can never move an inch along the path of progress. But the business of the cobbler is with leather, and we make no excuse for putting the peace problem on a much lower plane, and harnessing the League of Nations' Pegasus to a market cart. As a matter of plain business the League of Nations has got to be made a success if we are to survive. If we do not harness this Pegasus to our market cart, there will be no market, no cart, and no goods to put into it.

It was not only true, as the Prime Minister had said, 'that civilisation can no longer afford to squander its time and treasure on destruction'.

> If it were only a question of being a little poorer or a little richer, those among us who have a sneaking – or, in some cases, a frank and hearty – affection for the old system of national glories based on international hatreds might fairly argue that we do not know what we can afford until we try, and that everything depends on whether it is worth while to pay the price. But what we have lately gone through, and the price that we have paid, and have still to pay, are trifles compared with the next effort to be made if we allow the race in armaments to begin again after a few years of breathing space.

He quoted a 'fine speech' in which Asquith had observed that 'for all our new and deadly apparatus – aeroplanes, submarines, tanks, and the rest – the world is only just beginning to learn the alphabet of destruction'.

When the whole alphabet has been mastered, and the world has got well into the grammar, and has acquired a smattering of the language of destruction, it seems likely that there will not be much of the world left to talk it. If we are going to turn the best energy of all the scientific ingenuity that we can muster or train into inventing and perfecting new and horrible weapons, and devote our best labour and most costly materials into making them and marshalling them for the next fray, the life of the ordinary jogtrot individual, who really makes history by leading a decent life and leaving successors to do likewise, is likely to be one of over-taxed destitution, probably ending in a war which will be infinitely more ruthless than the last one in the matter of civilian destruction.

War had for a long time been a ridiculous tragedy. There was some point in an angry man killing someone who had annoyed him, but as killing became organised and developed on a national scale, it lost all pretence towards sense. And then, in a curious *Economist* twist, the leader swung straight into a vindication of financial interests, who had, in the matter of war, 'on the whole, a clean record'. While financial considerations might sometimes have been behind small wars, finance was usually on the side of peace, 'not only because it knows that war is destruction, and destruction does not pay, but because it also knows that international amity and co-operation are good for business, and make for that general prosperity on which alone finance can thrive. It may be a sordid point of view, but it is one which helps forward that material prosperity without which the best ideals cannot make much progress.' While the bellicose press accused international finance of pacifist leanings, the pacifists accused it of fomenting war. The truth was probably midway between the two: the financier wanted peace for reasons of business, but sometimes recognised that business was not everything and that war had to be faced in the last resort.

> The financier, like the rest of us, is really quite human. He wants business to be good, but he has this great advantage, from the point of view of the community, that he cannot prosper unless we all prosper, and he knows it. International finance and commerce have done more than any other human agencies to bring the nations together for their mutual benefit. They can do great work now in making the mutual benefit of the nations a firm basis of peace.[18]

CHAPTER XXXVI:

How can I help?

Happiness only consists in the development and use in each man of his capabilities, and capabilities mental and physical when left unexercised decay and die . . . The question to hammer out is this, what is there worth doing in life, how can I help? *Walter Layton, circa 1906*[1]

The main theme of 'IS IT PEACE?' – the need to make the League of Nations effective – was the main item on the agenda for the next two decades in the paper's life. It was a period during which Walter Layton strove vainly, through *The Economist* and through his own prodigious efforts in the public service, to make reason dominate the international stage.

Layton was a tremendous acquisition, by far the most distinguished man ever to take up the job and with an international network of high-level contacts beyond the wildest aspirations of most journalists.[2] He had gone into the war as a rising academic and had swiftly become a public servant of such achievement that in 1919, at the age of 35, having turned down a knighthood, he was given the high distinction of being appointed a Companion of Honour. Other young risen stars like Arthur Salter, Josiah Stamp and even J.M. Keynes had been awarded lesser honours, but then Layton was a protégé of Lloyd George.

Briefly at the Board of Trade, he had then, in April 1915, joined the secretariat of Lloyd George's new Munitions of War Committee as a statistical expert on labour supply. When the Ministry of Munitions was set up the following month, Lloyd George took Layton with him and made him Director of Requirements and Statistics. Layton developed methods of collecting reliable information on which to establish munitions priorities and mobilise the economy to meet demand from the front: it was principally through his use of Layton's weekly progress reports that Lloyd George ran his department so effectively.

Layton proved to be a first-class civil servant, both because of his intellectual gifts and his ability to get on well with everyone from immediate colleagues to generals: he became in effect Lloyd George's personal assistant, accompanying him to Cabinet committees and abroad for meetings with the French Minister of Munitions and with Sir Douglas Haig, the Commander in Chief. He had a good relationship with Lloyd George's successors at Munitions, but kept up his close relationship with his old chief; in 1917, he went with him on his prime-ministerial visit to a conference in Rome to sort out Allied supplies to Russia. That same year Layton was by far the youngest member of the Milner Mission to Petrograd, whose leaders included the old *Economist* hand, Lord Milner (now a member of the War Cabinet), and General Sir Henry Wilson, later Chief of the Imperial General Staff.

In his war memoirs, Lloyd George provided a typically feline account of the failure of this mission to realise that a Russian revolution was imminent. Milner, 'by temperament and training a bureaucrat . . . knew nothing of the populace that trod the streets outside the bureau. He did not despise them. He just left them out of his calculations.' Wilson, exclusively a professional soldier, took no 'cognisance of the people, except the specimens who joined the Army. He judged these entirely by the canons of discipline. The supreme test of discipline was saluting the officers. He saw with his own eyes that the Russian soldiers passed that test superbly. Mutiny in the Army was therefore remote . . . He had strong political prejudices, but they were sectarian in their origin and all irrelevant to the Russian situation. He hated Papists and Irish Patriots [he was to be assassinated in 1922 by Irishmen] and he encountered neither amongst the Russian soldiers or civilians.' Thus Wilson agreed with Milner that there was no immediate danger of an upheaval in the immediate future. The delegates 'came away fully convinced there would be no revolution till after the War. Sir Walter Layton was perhaps an exception. When asked on his return, "Are they keen on the War?" he replied, "No, they are much too busy thinking of the coming revolution." His official report, however, dealt only with Munitions – and properly so – and the War Cabinet were therefore not informed of the conclusion to which he personally had come.'[3] The Tsar had abdicated within a week of the return to London of the Milner Mission in February; by the end of 1917 Lenin's Bolsheviks were in control and Russia was out of the war.

In the same year the Foreign Secretary, A.J. Balfour, led a mission to the United States with Layton as the chief representative of the Ministry of Munitions. An observer of the mission found most impressive of all 'the slight figure who reminded me externally of the Greek professor in Bernard Shaw's *Major Barbara*. Before the war he had been a don at Cambridge, a teacher of economics, and he retained this senior laboratory manner of an expert who counts on holding attention . . .'

> He devised the organizing of America for destructiveness as an engineer might deliberate lining a leaky tunnel with copper and there was as little pretension in his manner as there was sentiment or doubt. His accent was cultivated, he was obviously a university man, but he had come to the top by mental equipment. 'Mental equipment' means many things, but plainly he was not of those remote emissaries who go in for cerebral scroll-saw work. He managed his mind as a woodman manages his axe. The exact swing and drive and bite of it could escape no one, and for all his almost plaintively modest demeanour he had instant arresting power.[4]

Layton's lack of personal ambition and his selfless desire to serve impressed everyone. When Churchill took over as Minister of Munitions, Layton offered his resignation on two grounds, first, 'because it would give you a much clearer field for building according to your own plans. My position here is, I believe, a rather unique one in Government departments and has depended very largely on my personal relations with the Minister on the one side and the heads of departments on the other. For it has been largely left to me to follow up supply and co-ordinate the effort of the departments . . .' Second, because he felt that being only 33 and 'A1' physically, he should join up.

'If you want to go you can go', wrote Churchill. 'You will be followed by my curses and as soon as you are in uniform the War Office will order you back to your post, which is here.' Layton was soon a full member of Churchill's Munitions Council, later chairman of its inner cabinet, the Clamping Committee, in which he was involved in national economic planning. He visited France behind the lines in style with Churchill and spent a great deal of time in Paris at countless Allied conferences on munitions supplies. After the war he was involved in drafting the military and economic clauses of the Treaty of Versailles and was the British representative on committees discussing armaments limitation.

Much of Layton's life was to be spent in what to most people would appear dull work in frustrating circumstances. As with his war work, he was to spend much of the rest of his career in a miasma of national and international secretariats, committees, sub-committees, commissions, councils and conferences, most involving hard work and many leading nowhere. Yet one of the greatest and most indefatigable international public servants of the first half of this century, Arthur Salter, writing in 1966, considered that in all his experience of international conferences, he had never seen anyone equal to Layton in the combination of 'arduous, skilful, and successful work, a selfless concern for the success of the conference and what he considered the most valuable of its possible achievements – and a subordination to this object of any publicity or recognition of his own efforts'.[5] At home and abroad Layton was a man liked, admired and relied on by almost everyone with whom he dealt, but he lifted no one's spirits. His intensely emotional centre was obscured by his carapace of shyness, austerity and highmindedness. Lady Violet Bonham Carter, Asquith's sharp-tongued daughter, once told Graham Hutton that on spotting Layton one evening arriving in white tie and full decorations, she had thought: 'Here comes the handsomest little grey mind in Europe.' It was an unfair judgment, for Layton's mind was of exceptional quality, but it had a ring of truth. His intelligent and well-informed biography is tedious and his own memoirs, written in old age, were too boring to find a publisher. *Dorothy*, the book he wrote to try to assuage his grief after his wife's death, showed a little of the passionate nature he kept hidden throughout his public life, but soon degenerated into earnest accounts of her good works with committees and worthy causes.

Had it not been for *The Economist*, Layton's post-war career would have been mainly a study in failed projects and dashed hopes, for even the *News Chronicle*, on which he was to spend a major part of his energy during the 1930s and 1940s, did not survive. Already, by the autumn of 1921, he had suffered two major setbacks. Having eschewed a return to academic life, he had become the highly-paid Director of the Iron and Steel Federation and shortly afterwards – at Lloyd George's request – had taken a year's leave of absence to take over from Arthur Salter as Director of the Economic and Financial section of the League of Nations. His main League job was to organise a huge international financial conference, which, although successful in getting 39 countries – including Germany – around the table, produced very little constructive thinking. And on his return to the Federation, Layton realised he disliked the job and was out of sympathy with his employers.

The three trustees, Walter Wilson Greg, Eric Gibb and Sir Lawrence Edward Halsey (a relation of Sophie Wilson's husband William Halsey), offered Layton a contract for five years to edit and manage *The Economist* and the now ailing *Investors' Monthly Manual*. His contract required him to 'obey and comply with all lawful orders and directions given to him from time to time by the proprietors' and to use 'his best endeavours to promote and maintain the success and reputation of the newspapers and the interests of the proprietors'. He was 'generally' responsible and in control of production of the newspapers, of content and rates of payment, of the hiring and paying of staff (though he had to give the proprietors information about them and their rates of payment if required) and could do whatever he considered 'bona fide and to the best of his judgment conducive to the interests of the proprietors'. An interesting clause was that prohibiting him from divulging 'the authorship of any unsigned article or contribution or the source of any information appearing in the newspapers without the consent of the person or persons contributing or supplying the same except to any person lawfully authorised to demand the same'. He could take on outside work in his leisure time, as long as it did not involve editing, assisting in editing, or promoting any other newspaper or periodical: if the business was sold before the end of December 1926 compensation would be paid. His salary, which represented a considerable drop for him, was to be £2,000 a year, with a fifth of the excess net profits of the newspapers over £6,000, which seems roughly to have been an increase of around £1,000 on Withers's remuneration. (Bagehot had been on £400 a year with half the profits above £2,000 – an average of £780: the Sauerbeck price index shows the average index 1866–77 at 100 and that of 1922 at 131.)

'The Proprietors of the Economist have appointed Mr Walter T. Layton, CH, CBE, Editor of the paper, and he will take up his duties early in the New Year', was the announcement in the paper in December 1921; there was no valedictory from Withers.[6]

All that survived of *Economist* business records after the office was bombed in a German air raid in May 1941 was several ledgers in the fireproof safe. The first three record only the paper accounts, circulation and revenue from advertisements for *The Economist* and the *Investors' Monthly Manual* from 1876. From 1917, however, records also include balance sheets and detailed figures on general and literary expenses, printing and folding, wages and salaries and sales accounts and subscriptions.

Taking 1920, the last full year of Hartley Withers's editorship, the picture was extremely healthy. Rounding up shillings and pence to the nearest pound, the profit for the year was £14,089; this included a loss of £751 on the *Investors' Monthly Manual*, which competition had sent into a steady decline: it was axed in 1930. Withers received one-third of net profit over £6,000, giving him £2,696, and Howard Kirk, the manager, one-tenth of net profit in excess of £7,000, giving him £709, leaving £10,684. After deduction of tax, £8,310 was left, every penny of which was divided between the Wilson family ($^{13}/_{16}$ – £6,752) and Edward Johnstone's executors ($^{3}/_{16}$ – £1,558).

Hartley Withers had a basic salary of £1,000, so in 1920 he earned a total of £3,696. Journalists' remuneration appeared in the ledgers under 'Literary Expenses': business staff came under 'Wages'. H.W. Kirk earned £500 a year, which with his profit-share brought his total to £1,209; Mike Flood, the advertising manager, between salary and commission earned £1,119; and the company-meetings manager, H.S. Whitcomb, was on an impenetrable mixture of wages and commission, apparently being reduced by sub-payments to subordinates, which was earning him well into four figures. His assistant, H. Bernard, was on £338, Chapman on £252 and the secretary and third member of the Whitcomb family to have joined the staff, Miss D. Whitcomb, was on £208.

The literary staff had basic salaries on top of which they earned extra according to output. Although the social superiors of Kirk, Flood and Whitcomb, they were paid far less. Then (as until recently), though editorial created the product and themselves as a cut above the rest of the staff, it was those who brought in the advertisements and managed the paper who called the financial tune. With extras, Gilbert Layton's salary of £360 came to £535, Leonard Reid's £300 came to £470, Roydon C. Hopkins (who wrote on all aspects of business) made up his £252 to £421 and the editorial secretary, Miss Gower, earned only her £192 salary.

Subtracting staff salaries and extra earnings (£2,618) from the total of literary expenses (£4,257) leaves a total of £1,639 in payments to outside contributors, individual payments to whom are listed month by month in the 1917–29 records. For that period, therefore, there is firm evidence of who were the writers, but not what they wrote, except for those who appear elsewhere on a list of contributors for a six-week period in late 1924.[7]

In 1920 there were 92 outside contributors, of whom just over a third contributed only one article, slightly more four or more, and 15 were sufficiently regular to receive retainers. Old contributors included Gibb (2 contributions – an exceptionally low number for him) and J.S. Mann (12), who went back to Johnstone's time (Mann ceased contributing in 1925) and from Hirst's, Dudley Ward (7) and Hilton Young (1). People who were then distinguished or would be in the future included Sir William Ackworth (5), probably the greatest expert in the world on the relationship between railways and government; Luigi Einaudi (promoted that year to a retainer); Paul Einzig (2); Victor Gollancz (1), later a famous publisher; P.D. Leake (2), an accountant who provided *Who's Who* with one of its oddest entries ('... has given much time and thought to economic subjects, including national taxation; has formulated a complete scheme for a flat-rate produc-tion tax as the natural and least harmful source of revenue taxes'); Dominick Spring-Rice (2), banker, journalist and Secretary of the Political Economy Club; William F. Spalding (9), a major authority on banking and foreign exchange; and Barbara (later Baroness) Wootton (5), economist and social scientist, and one of five female contributors. In addition to Einaudi, Gibb, Leake, Spalding and Dudley Ward, Layton inherited several people who stayed with him for years.* There was also F. Harcourt Kitchin, a writer on banking and economics and an expert on insurance, who had been plucked in 1908 from the City office by his great friend Moberly Bell, managing director of *The Times* (about whom he later wrote a book), to be briefly and ineffectively an assistant editor in 1908. Kitchin had a spell managing the *Glasgow Herald* and then came south again to edit the *Board of Trade Journal*. Withers, who had known him when City editor of *The Times*, took him on in April 1917, but Kitchin left in November; he remained an outside contribu-

---

*Those who can be identified (or whose speciality can be inferred from the fragmentary contributors' list of 1924) included D. Sanford Cole (shipping), H.G. Crockett (agriculture), David Evans (coal), Arthur Greenwood, economist, Labour MP and later a minister, T.E. Gregory (later Professor Sir Theodore, a world-class currency expert and adviser to foreign governments), Otto Grimstvedt, (Norway), A.N. Jackman (mining), C. Kains Jackson (cereals), Walter Landells, Stock Exchange broker, J.E. Levinsky (Poland), Robert Crozier Long (Berlin), Percy Martin, at various times foreign correspondent to many English newspapers (South America), D.E. Protecdicos (Greece), Per Skiold (Sweden), H.A. Siepmann (Hungary), Josiah Stamp, famous economist, statistician and international public servant, J.A. Stevenson (Canada and the US), F.W. Tattersall (cotton), A. Thodey (Australia) and Hartley Withers himself, who wrote between 8 and 12 times a year during the Layton years for which there are records.

tor. Chapman, who remembered Kitchin writing for *The Economist* during Johnstone's editorship, found him exotic. 'He was a versatile writer of novels under the nom-de-plume of Bennet Copplestone', explained Chapman. 'I always felt that Mr Harcourt Kitchin had too many irons in the fire. He always seemed so busy with scarcely time for rest. I did not hear where he eventually ended but I did hear that his health broke down and his brain became unstable. I understand he was rendered poor by being over-insured. The high premiums which resulted made him a comparatively poor man while he was alive.'

> Mr Harcourt Kitchin's life, although he was successful, seemed to me to have a rather tragical close. It might have been a different story had he not have made the mistake of accomplishing too much. It is a difficult thing always to be a dual personality and in this instance it was not a case of two hearts beating as one.

Withers passed on to Layton a solid property and Layton applied himself to improving it, but he did nothing rash. Although his editorship was to be of profound importance to the paper, and although he was probably the person to whom it owes most thanks for its survival and continued independence, change and reform were undertaken slowly and with caution. Chapman remembered his arrival and 'the businesslike manner in which Walter Layton started his editorship. The staff were invited into his sanctum. He shook hands and greeted us cordially saying how pleased he was to become Editor and asking us to see him if we were in any difficulty. It was a nice gesture and we then returned to our tasks of doing all we could to assist in the production of *The Economist*.' Most of the staff, of course, already knew him from his pre-war time with the paper.

As was customary, no heads rolled. Indeed, other than secretaries, Hopkins, who left in January 1928 after at least 11 years with the paper, was the only existing member of staff to leave before the paper changed hands. Since the policy of distributing every last penny of profit meant there was no money available for expansion, Layton could do little to augment the staff. In the six years after taking over he added only three people. In 1922 he took on a part-timer, Ifor L. Evans, a Cambridge graduate in economics and history, who the following year became a Fellow of St John's College, but who remained with the paper for four years. A versatile young man, he is shown by the fragmentary contributors' list to have written 'THE WORLD'S PRODUC-

TION OF CEREALS' and a review of Mill's *Autobiography*. (From 1934 he was Principal of the University of Wales, Aberystwyth.) In 1923 Layton employed an extra secretary, Pearl Wallace and Hargreaves Parkinson, who was to stay with the paper until 1938 and to conclude his career as editor of the *Financial Times*.

Parkinson was a Lancastrian who had been educated at Blackpool Grammar School, King's College, London and the London School of Economics; he had been badly wounded during the war. When Layton recruited him he was 26 and his work experience had been exclusively in the public service, first in the Department of Overseas Trade and then with the National Savings Committee as assistant press officer. 'Short, stocky, still speaking broad Lancashire,' wrote Layton in his unpublished memoirs, 'he came to me from the London School of Economics. He had been inspired by the figures of profit of public companies which we had just started to compile and publish regularly. He was anxious to write a doctoral thesis on the subject and asked if he could have a seat in the office where he would be surrounded by the original material. He offered to put his researches at the disposal of *The Economist*. I readily consented and before many weeks had passed he too had joined the staff and had started his distinguished career in financial journalism.' Layton wanted him to set up an intelligence branch, for, typically, he was determined to give the paper a solid base of factual information. Layton had no interest in superficial improvements; he concentrated on fundamentals. From the foundations laid by Parkinson would come the library (later research department) and the Economist Intelligence Unit, which became a major research and consultancy organisation after the war.

Parkinson, industrious and methodical, and as Tyerman put it in an obituary, with 'an honest devotion to facts plainly and fairly set down for ordinary folk to understand, and a dogged sense of responsibility to his paper and its readers', was a perfect choice. In May 1926 the Intelligence Branch went public:

ECONOMIST INTELLIGENCE BRANCH

In order to meet a demand from many of our readers, we have made arrangements which will enable us to supply statistical or other information from our records, and to answer economic inquiries. A fee will be charged (with a minimum of half-a-guinea) to cover the cost of any special work involved.[8]

Between July and December 1926 it earned £221, which went some way towards the salaries of Parkinson (£399 a year) and a secretary (£124). 'From the moment this branch was formed,' said Chapman, '*The Economist* seemed to develop to a very marked extent. Information on all sorts of questions was sought and information that was exceedingly valuable came back in return. The paper became known to an even wider circle and the staff found that they were kept busy in assisting to deal with the multifarious problems that had to be solved.' The Einaudi archive bears him out. A letter of June 1926 on *Economist* writing paper – overstamped 'INTELLIGENCE BRANCH' – read:

> Dear Sir,
> May I venture to trouble you on two matters in which your assistance would be greatly valued?
>
> (1) We have been asked whether it is possible to obtain a copy, in English, of 'The Italian Bank Note Reform Decree'. I do not know whether you will be able to identify the Decree from this apparently somewhat vague description, but if a copy could be obtained and sent to us, we should be obliged. If no copy in English be available, we could arrange for the translation of an Italian copy here.
>
> (2) We are interested to see from time to time, in your articles, references to an Index of Italian Stock Exchange Values. We are wondering whether it would be possible to publish this in our Monthly Supplement, mentioning, of course, its source. Should we be troubling you unduly if we were to ask for the *total* monthly figures from March, 1924 to date? If you would also be kind enough to indicate the address of the authority issuing the figures, we might write direct to them to make arrangements for the mailing of this Index to us regularly in the future.
>
> > Yours faithfully,
> > The Economist.
>
> > p.p. H Parkinson
> > Intelligence Branch.

The Intelligence Branch appears to have taken responsibility for the annual *Economist Commercial History* and at least some of the supplements, including the monthly Trade Supplement which Parkinson started in 1923. In January 1933 it acquired an effective librarian who also compiled the half-yearly indexes and catalogued books and parliamentary papers. ('The burning out of our premises in Bouverie Street in the raid on London on May 10 1941, was enough to break Mrs Andrews's heart,' recorded Chapman, 'as practically all the library she built up with so much care was lost.') Material stretching back almost a century had included a substantial number of books (including those in a bookcase which had belonged to Bagehot), records and statistics, a complete set of company prospectuses dating from 1898, records of industrial profits and capital issues from 1912, correspondence, most of the paper's ledgers and the back issues, as well as what had been added under Parkinson, his successor, Walter Hill, and Vera Andrews herself.

The paper was so disheartened by the disaster that there was no attempt to build up a proper library again. Today it has a highly professional research department consisting of 14 people occupying cramped accommodation, who depend on essential reference books and modern communications technology. The lost volumes of back issues were replaced, in many instances through the generosity of readers, but other than essential legal documents, no archive has been maintained since the fire. The few ledgers which survived the fire were lost for a long period and recovered by accident. Most of the staff – like the recently departed chief executive – merrily throw almost all their papers out every time their filing cabinets fill up.

Steadily, Layton added to the team of outside contributors, particularly in the area of overseas correspondence, for he was determined to increase the geographical spread of foreign coverage as well as to make it less exclusively financial.* He expanded too on the home side, bringing back as regular contributors Hirst's colleagues J.E. Allen, Mary Agnes Hamilton (now a specialist correspondent on the Labour Party) and C.K. Hobson; even Francis Hirst himself made an appearance. Layton added numerous experts on everything from individual commodities to civil servants' wages.†

---

*During the 1920s his acquisitions included correspondents on Argentina (H. Hallam Hipwell), Austria (Grenfell Brothers and Dr Georg Tugendhat), Czechoslovakia (J. Emlyn Williams), Denmark (E. Woldbye), France (Bampton Hunt), Holland (S. Bromver), Hungary (Eugene Havas), Japan (S. Okabe), India (R.W. Brock), New Zealand (Professor J.R. Condliffe), South Africa (A. Cooper Key), Spain (R.M. Cereceda), Switzerland (Egmond d'Arcis-Juvet), Yugoslavia (A. Vidakovic) and the League of Nations (H.R. Cummings, head of the League's London office).

†Those whose areas of expertise can be identified include R.B. Ainsworth (wages), C.D. Cassidy (Hong Kong), Sir Robert Donald (press), Lt. Col. R.J. Drake (a much-decorated thinking soldier), David Finnie (accountant and later well-known company doctor), C.P. Fitzgerald (commodity prices), Grenfell Brothers (stockbroking experts – later Morgan Grenfell), D.A.E.

Interesting names on the list include Mark Abrams, the pioneering market researcher; Professor Arthur Bowley, statistician; Per Jacobsson, Layton's young Swedish colleague at the League Secretariat, who was later to run the Bank for International Settlements and then the International Monetary Fund; Lewis Namier, the historian; H. St John Philby, explorer, whose son, Kim Philby, would be one of the paper's most famous correspondents; Professor Charles Rist, international currency and banking expert, later Governor of the Bank of France; Dennis Robertson (later Professor of Political Economy at Cambridge); and Mary Stocks, economist, journalist and later public servant and peer.

In addition to Parkinson, two great finds were Nicholas (E.H.) Davenport and Aylmer Vallance, both gifted and both rather exotic personalities in respectable worlds; they began by writing respectively about oil and shipping, later joined the staff and later still became well-known – in Vallance's case to the point of notoriety. Layton's most remarkable coup, however, was his acquisition early in his editorship of Professor Arnold J. Toynbee, now out of fashion, but then developing a reputation which was ultimately to gain him worldwide guru-status; Toynbee wrote one leader and two or three notes every week until the outbreak of the Second World War.

These, however, were piecemeal improvements made by cheeseparing, and they had only a minor effect on sales. In 1919, 1920 and 1921 the government had bought 500 copies weekly, raising circulation to over 6,000 in 1920 and 1921: during the rest of the Wilson ownership, that figure was achieved only once, in 1927.

'A family Trust . . . is not an instrument well fitted for the management of an important journal of opinion', wrote Layton years later. 'With every decade that passes its members get more scattered and out of touch with the paper and with one another.'[9] In the case of the Wilson inheritance, the

Harkness (economist, later Permanent Secretary of the Northern Ireland Ministry of Finance and head of the Northern Ireland Civil Service), H. Wilson Harris (League of Nations expert, editor of the *Spectator* 1932–53), H.H. Harrison ('American cotton crop', 'Irish Free State problems'), Ralph Hawtrey (Director of Financial Enquiries at the Treasury), Hubert Henderson (economist, public servant, editor of the *Nation* 1923–30), William Hurcomb (subsequently Permanent Secretary, Ministry of Transport), Arnold McNair (later President of the International Court of Justice), Hugh Quigley (electricity industry), George Recknell (life assurance), Sir Henry Rew (agriculture policy), R.J. Stopford (Martin's Bank), Raymond Street (cotton industry), Raymond Gram Swing (American correspondent in London) and Dr Georg Tugendhat (oil and Austria).

fragmentation was accelerating fast. Sophie's husband, William Halsey, had died in 1902; Matilda's husband, Matthew Horan, in 1903; Julia in 1911; the surviving two husbands, Russell Barrington and Orby Shipley, in 1916; Eliza in 1921, the year Layton took over; Matilda in 1922; and Zoe, and Sophie's son Willie, the following year. Julia's share had been left to her son Walter Wilson Greg, Eliza's to Emilie, Matilda's to Sophie's grandson Noel Halsey and Zoe's mainly to the general estate. The trustees were anxious to sell and in 1925 began the long legal process necessary to make it possible; among Layton's papers is a draft memorandum and articles of association of The Economist Newspaper Ltd, dated as early 11 May 1925. By the time 'Re Wilson's Trust and Other Trusts Greg v Halsey 1925 W. No. 3742' reached the courts, Sophie had died, leaving her estate to her children in a complicated settlement.

An order of the Chancery Division, dated 22 March 1926, approved the scheme which formed the basis for a contract of 20 May 1926. The Wilson and Johnstone trustees agreed to sell the newspaper business and assets to The Economist Newspaper Ltd, which in turn allotted to the Wilson trustees 7,800 of its 'A' ordinary shares and to the Johnstone trustees 1,800 'B' shares' – both valued at £1 each – and an ebonized board with 'The Economist Newspaper Limited Registered Office' written in gold was duly fixed to the office door.

In the meantime Layton was looking for backers, and he found them easily enough from among his vast network of friends from academia, civil service days, the League of Nations and the Liberal Party. His initial group included Sir Henry Strakosch, an expert on currency, a member of the Financial Committee of the League of Nations and chairman of the Union Corporation of South Africa, and Laurence Cadbury, Layton's ex-pupil, managing director of Cadbury Brothers and a long-time admirer. In 1926 Cadbury's brother Henry, managing director of the *Daily News*, offered Layton its editorship, which Layton refused because he would have had to give up his three main occupations: editing *The Economist*, undertaking jobs for the League of Nations and trying through Summer Schools and *Yellow Books* to develop policies to revitalise the Liberal Party. However, in 1927 Layton accepted Cadbury's invitation to join the board of the *Daily News* as financial and policy adviser.

The sum required to buy the paper was expected to be about £60,000, but the smooth progress of negotiations was halted by the emergence of a competitor. Brendan Bracken, a member of the board of the printers and publishers, Eyre & Spottiswoode, and founder in 1926 of the *Banker*, was in acquisitive mood. He had just bought the *Financial News* when he began looking covetously at *The Economist*. 'According to legend,' said his biographer, Bracken approached his neighbour, James Wilson's granddaughter, Sybil Colefax, at a party. '"I suppose you are sentimentally attached to your holding," he remarked tentatively. "Oh, no," she replied, "I find it a very dull paper and feel no attachment to it at all."'[10] When competitive bidding had driven the price up to £100,000, Layton went to call on Bracken. 'He could not have received me in a more friendly spirit and at once said that of course his friends assumed that I would remain as editor. As he had nearly doubled the price against me there was something of the bear-hug about this embrace.'

The flamboyant, mysterious and Tory Bracken was not a man Layton could implicitly trust to uphold the traditions of *The Economist*, yet Bracken readily accepted the argument that editorial independence was essential to the paper, and he proposed joint ownership, a course of action that left him with the resources to add some more titles to his stable, including the *Investors Chronicle*. The Wilson trustees supported Layton's demand for an inbuilt guarantee of editorial independence, and it was agreed that his group would have three directors, including the chairman and vice-chairman, while the newly formed Financial Newspaper Proprietors Ltd (FNP, in which Eyre & Spottiswoode held a controlling interest) would have two, including the managing director.

The news was announced in the paper in July 1928.

THE ECONOMIST

> The present week has witnessed an important event in the history of this journal. On Monday, July 9th, the Court approved an application by the trustees of the Wilson Trust for permission to sell *The Economist*. Thus for the first time in its eighty-five years of life a change takes place in the ownership and control of *The Economist*.

The press notice which had appeared on 10 July was then quoted verbatim. Having very briefly covered the paper's origins, it explained the trustees' reasons for selling. 'It was felt, however, that if the control of *The Economist* were to pass either to a newspaper group or to any particular financial interest, a reputation built up on independence of judgment and unfettered criticism would be jeopardised. Arrangements have accordingly been made by the purchasers which will ensure the complete editorial independence of the paper.' Voting shares would be divided equally between FNP and 'an influential group of individual shareholders'.*

> Both parties are anxious to maintain the traditional character of *The Economist*, and it has, therefore, been agreed that the articles of the company will provide for the appointment of a board of independent trustees with the following functions:
>
> (a) They will have the right to veto the appointment or dismissal of any Editor of *The Economist*, the Editor to have sole responsibility for the policy of the paper so long as he retains his office;
>
> (b) They will have the right to veto the transfer of voting shares in the new company;
>
> (c) They will be represented on the board.
>
> By these and other provisions which will to a considerable extent be modelled on the articles of *The Times* Holding Company, the independence of *The Economist* will be amply safeguarded.

'The *locus classicus* [best example] for editorial arrangements with proprietors', wrote Robertson Scott, an aged editor, in the 1950s, 'is Geoffrey Dawson's plan with *The Times* on starting his second term of service [in 1923] . . . Wickham Steed urged him to make for himself "a bomb-proof dug-out"!' The arrangement involved the establishment of a committee solely concerned with safeguarding future transfers of the controlling shares in *The Times*, 'to ensure, so far as is humanly possible, that the ownership of *The Times* shall never be regarded as a mere matter of commerce, to be transferred without regard to any other circumstance to the highest bidder or fall, so far as can be foreseen, into unworthy hands'. Members of the committee were the Lord Chief Justice, the Warden of All Souls, the

---

*The first independent shareholders were: Lord Cowdray (head of Pearson's), 7,500 ; W.W. Greg, 7,000; Laurence Cadbury, 5,000; Lionel Nathan de Rothschild and Anthony Gustav de Rothschild (bankers) jointly, 5,000; The Rt. Hon. Walter Runciman (businessman, Liberal MP, Financial Secretary to the Treasury 1907–8, President of the Board of Trade 1914–16), 5,000; Baron Schroder (Schroder's merchant bank), 5,000; Sir Henry Strakosch and Joseph Kitchin jointly, 3,000; The Hon. R.H. Brand (Lazard Brothers), 2,000; Ernest Simon (businessman, ex-Lord Mayor of Manchester and Liberal ex-MP), 2,000; Henry Graham White (ex-member of Executive Committee of the League of Nations Union, Liberal MP), 1,500; Walter Layton, 1,250; Sir Laurence Halsey, 500; and D.E.W. Gibb, 250.

President of the Royal Society, the President of the Institute of Chartered Accountants and the Governor of the Bank of England. Without giving any reason, they could give or withhold consent to the transfer of shares: they were required 'to have special regard to the maintenance of the best traditions and the independence of *The Times* and the elimination of consideration of personal ambition or personal profit'.[11] By extending this approach to cover the hiring and firing of *The Economist*'s editor, Scott said, Layton and his advisers had made him 'the best safeguarded Editor in Europe'.

More than 60 years later, 'the best traditions and the independence of *The Times*' have not been proof against commercial realities. In 1981, when he took over from the Canadian Roy (later Lord) Thomson what *The Economist* called the 'rich man's burden' of the unprofitable *Times* and its sometimes profitable sister, the *Sunday Times*, the Australian Rupert Murdoch (*inter alia* owner of the *Sun* and of *The Economist*'s exact contemporary, 'the all-human-life-is-there-especially-the-sexier-parts-of-it *News of the World*',[12] also born in 1843) gave various sweeping assurances about the preservation of editorial integrity in order to avert a reference of his bid to the monopolies commission. Andrew Knight's *Economist* was unworried about possible proprietorial interference with editorial strategy: editorial opinion was a different matter. 'All involved with Times Newspapers should be on their guard to maintain the independent tradition, under a proprietor whose record of political interference with his editors is considerable. These guarantees must be made to stick and publicised – when necessary by the national directors* – if broken.'[13] Headshaking was in order a few weeks later, with scepticism growing about the Murdoch guarantees. 'There is a world of difference between the commercial and marketing policy of a paper – with which a proprietor will and should involve himself – and the integrity of the journalistic function, the newsgathering and editorialising. This integrity has been fought for and won on most British newspapers since Hitler's war, but it can easily be surrendered under commercial duress.'[14] Within a year the paper was commenting that Murdoch's chief defence of his infringements of editorial freedom 'is that nobody really expected him to

---

*These had replaced the old *ex officio* group and consisted of the Lords Dacre (alias Hugh Trevor-Roper, the historian), Greene (previously Sidney Greene, General Secretary of the National Union of Railwaymen), Robens (ex-Chairman of the National Coal Board) and Roll (chairman of a merchant bank and previously an academic economist and senior civil servant).

honour such pledges anyway, which is true'.[15] The following month saw the sacking of Harold Evans, editor of *The Times*, who 'stage-managed his own departure quoting Mark Twain. He might better have spent his time reading Dr Faustus. It is clear that those who sup with the Mephistopheles of popular journalism are likely to find themselves eaten by breakfast time.'

> Mr Evans's dismissal was prolonged by the ambivalence of *The Times*'s 'independent national directors'. They exist as a court of appeal for an editor against his proprietor. They have clearly not been used as such by either the proprietor or his departing editor. They spent much of the week wondering why.[16]

(Four of the journalists who dominated *The Economist* in 1982 were eight years later to be pre-eminent in Murdoch's News International. The editor, Andrew Knight, had become that group's executive chairman; his deputy, Norman Macrae, was a *Sunday Times* columnist; his political editor, Simon Jenkins, was (until 1992) editor of *The Times*; and his UK editor, Andrew Neil, was editor of the *Sunday Times*. And Knight's predecessor as *Economist* editor, Sir Alastair Burnet, had been an independent director of Times Newspapers since 1982. All this incest adds piquancy to the comments of the various organs on each other. There in April 1989 is 'Atticus' in Neil's *Sunday Times* noting that the previous Wednesday's bad trade figures had hardly been mentioned in *The Economist*. 'Sadly, *The Economist* is no longer regarded as essential reading on the British economy. This is why.' Then *The Economist*, a few months later, refers to the *Sunday Times*'s 'Rottweiler politics', 'downmarket drift' and endless proclamation of the wonders of Murdoch's Sky television,[17] prompting its target to take out a whole-page advertisement in the following week's *Economist* stressing their policy similarities, pointing out the wider choice of viewpoints available in the *Sunday Times*, and suggesting that the motivation for the attack was a dog-in-the-manger attitude to the Murdoch papers' employment of Jenkins and Macrae as columnists.[18])

The Times having fallen to Murdoch with scarcely a whimper from the national directors, there was nervousness within *The Economist* when in the late 1980s Murdoch set his sights on its part-owner, the *Financial Times*.*

---

*In 1934 a complex reorganisation had the FNP's assets taken over by Financial News Ltd, in which Eyre & Spottiswoode, in the guise of the Eyre Trust, continued to hold a controlling interest. In 1945 FN Ltd took over the *Financial Times*, which consumed the *Financial News*. In

'DRACULA ABOARD' reported Murdoch's refusal of his invitation to the forthcoming *FT* centenary dinner. 'But he will be there in spirit, as most of the 700 guests know only too well. The Australian-American newspaper magnate now owns 20.6% of Pearson, the newspaper's parent company. An intriguing tactical campaign for control of the pink paper is under way.'

> So far, Captain Murdoch has refrained from sending in his boarding party. A takeover of Pearson would probably cost him another £1.6 billion ($2.8 billion); and, because he also owns *The Times*, would run smack into Britain's monopolies commission. Instead, he has drawn his ship alongside Pearson's galleon, made it fast with grappling irons, and smilingly asked if he can be of help. Pearson's managers are eyeing him askance, holding a steady course and hoping against hope that the man-of-war will float away.

The sympathetic but critical manner in which the paper went on to deal with its co-owner was a good illustration of the healthiness of their relationship. Murdoch's ambition to back an American edition of the *FT* was at odds 'with the sober-suited, product-oriented strategy of the *FT*'s managers'. Having outlined *FT* objectives, the article commented: 'Cautious though it may seem by Murdochian standards, the *FT*'s spending spree will test a management which is lightly staffed with the necessary talent and which has only a shaky grasp of the foreign markets it is tumbling into.'[19]

Although there is mutual respect between *The Economist* and the *Financial Times*, there have always and inevitably been tensions; there are areas in which they compete. Advertising is a source of constant and accepted rivalry, but there was, for instance, great resentment on the part of *The Economist* when in 1978 the *FT* announced plans to publish a weekly edition in the United States just when *The Economist* was there embarking on a major and costly circulation drive. Protestations from Alan Hare, chief executive of the

---

1957, because of bad relations with the chairman, Brendan Bracken, the Eyre family sold to S. Pearson and Sons just over 50% of FN Ltd. At the head of the Pearson empire was the third Lord Cowdray, whose grandfather had founded the firm and whose father had been one of Layton's backers. (Cowdray's late father's shares were transferred to him in 1935; he sold 2,500 to the Crowther family in 1952, acquired 250 in 1952 and hastily shed his entire holding in 1957 after the FN deal.) Pearson's manifold activities include oilfield equipment, banking (Lazards), book publishing (Viking Penguin, Longman), fine china, Madame Tussaud's waxworks and local newspapers (the Westminster Press). In 1967 the Financial & Provincial Publishing Company was created to oversee the FT Ltd, the FN Ltd (which then ceased to exist) and the Westminster Press. The following year it was renamed S. Pearson Publishers, the parent company remaining S. Pearson & Son which subsequently shortened its name to Pearson.

FT and one of its representatives on the board of *The Economist*, that no appreciable damage would be done, were coolly received. Ten years later the 'DRACULA ABOARD' writer, with his glee well-concealed, recalled that the *FT* had 'tried in the 1970s to launch a business magazine in America called *World Business Weekly*. The venture was an instructive flop. American managers did not want an international alternative to their more parochial business magazines.' The *FT* made handsome amends by giving its 20,000 or so subscribers to *The Economist* for the relevant period after *World Business Weekly* went out of business.

In general, the *FT* is pleased with the profitability and high reputation of *The Economist*, but less enthusiastic about its ventures into ancillary activities where there have been some burnt fingers. Yet *Economist* management see diversification as essential to long-term health. This underlying difference of opinion led to a public row in 1986, when the *FT* refused to approve consent to a large increase in *The Economist*'s borrowing limit, which had previously been approved by the board, including the *FT* members present, and submitted to all shareholders for their approval. At *The Economist*'s annual general meeting, Lord Blakenham, chairman of Pearson and of the *FT* (but not on the *Economist* board), used his voting power to block the relevant resolution. 'Although this corporate matter is bound to have an effect on the relationship between Pearson/*FT* and *The Economist*,' wrote Evelyn de Rothschild (then chairman), David Gordon and Rupert Pennant-Rea in a joint statement to *Economist* employees, 'the staff of the newspaper and of Economist Publications, our new colleagues at Business International, and our other group employees should be assured that it does not in any way adversely affect our business – in terms of cash, of management or of independence. We are not a controlled subsidiary of Pearson and remain an independent company.'[20] The memorandum went on to observe that 'This particular kerfuffle will soon die down'; and so it did.

Essentially, there is mutual respect, even affection and much cross-fertilisation. For instance, Lord Drogheda, variously managing director and chairman of the *FT*, was also deputy chairman of *The Economist*, sat on its board from 1941 for 48 years and shimmered effortlessly from one institution to another, using an office in the Economist Tower for several years towards the end of his life. Joe Rogaly of the *FT* started out with *The Economist*, whose deputy editor (Nico Colchester) and managing editor (Susannah Amoore) are imports from the *FT*. David Gordon, although an

Economist man all his journalistic and business life, was, as its chief executive, an *FT* nominee, with a seat on the *FT* board. His predecessor, Ian Trafford, came from the *FT*.

The relationship works because of mutual trust, so the prospect of Captain Murdoch was a serious threat. 'He will drag *The Economist* downmarket', said the pessimists. 'Nonsense,' said the optimists: 'the Trustees are there to protect the editor from all such pressures.' 'There is no Trust that cannot be broken', said some of the pessimists. 'When it comes to it,' said others, 'you'll find that the Trustees will succumb. Look at *The Times*. The Great and Good always succumb to swashbucklers.'

In the event, a cunning hook-up with a Dutch firm and consequent new share issue reduced the Murdoch holdings in Pearson, and in 1990 his man-o'-war was seen floating away from the Pearson galleon on a wave of global debt. For the moment *The Economist* remains safe, but the question stays open about whether the security offered by the trustees could be fully effective in really desperate times.

'The agreement adumbrated above,' wrote Layton in his *Economist* article about the 1928 transfer of ownership, 'confers very important powers on a body of independent trustees. The right to veto the transfer of shares – with a view to preventing control being acquired by persons who might use it for improper purposes – follows the precedent set by the *Times* and the *Spectator*. But the present scheme goes farther, and gives to the trustees a voice in the appointment or dismissal of the Editor.'

> In the long history of *The Economist*, which has played no small part in moulding the tradition of British financial journalism, full responsibility has resided in the hands of the Editor. It has, in fact, been the chief asset of *The Economist* that its editorial policy has been entirely free from external pressure or control. This independence, which is our most cherished inheritance, will continue under full and adequate safeguards.

Whatever is said about the legal safeguards, what is vital is that the trustees are people of moral substance, who care about the paper and who are fit for battle if required. Yet there is little sign that those criteria have been identified as the prerequisites. *The Economist* as a newspaper may mock the Establishment, but it would be hard to find more identikit Establishment figures than have been the trustees. Every one of the 14 who have been appointed came equipped with a title, and several of them were chosen for seemingly irrelevant reasons. And of the ten who have ceased to be trustees, all but three died in office.

Walter Layton, as befitted such a busy man, saw no reason to encourage any *esprit de corps* among the original trustees. Sir Laurence Halsey, who lasted until 1945, had been a Wilson trustee; Sir William Beveridge and Sir Josiah Stamp were, with Layton, part of the tightly knit group of radical Liberal ex-civil servants, and Sir Alan Anderson, son of the great pioneering doctor, Elizabeth Garrett Anderson, was by contrast a power in the world of shipping and finance, who became Conservative MP for the City of London in 1935. A letter he wrote nine years after being appointed says much about the importance of the trustees in the life of the paper at that time.

> 26th. April, 1938
>
> Dear Layton,
> Will you please ask your Secretary to let me know who are my co-trustees of the Economist and to send me a copy of the Trustee Deed which I will return when I have had a look at it.
>
> Yours sincerely,
> A.G. Anderson

When the first vacancy occurred with Stamp's death in 1941,[*] there was no set procedure for filling it. Layton had suggested Keynes to the managing director, Brendan Bracken, who agreed but forgot to tell the chairman, Sir Henry Strakosch, until Strakosch had already written to the three surviving trustees suggesting the appointment of Sir Charles Hambro, managing director of Hambros Bank, and, like Alan Anderson, sometime director of the Bank of England. Anderson thought Hambro 'an excellent choice', Halsey thought him 'very suitable' and Beveridge offered no opinion.

Surviving correspondence shows that Hambro, who remained a trustee for 22 years, never really got a grip on what the appointment was about. In a friendly letter of 1952 commenting on names suggested by Geoffrey Crowther for a replacement for the deceased Anderson, he included the following:

> Bilsland I know. He is on the Dollar Exports Council. A first class name in

---

*See appendix for list of trustees.

Glasgow and a very talented person. If you want a Scot, you could hardly get a better one.

I do not know whether there is any benefit to The Economist in having a shipping man except that they are all internationally minded. We have lost one in Alan Anderson and I am wondering whether my colleague at the Bank of England, Basil Sanderson, might not be a suitable replacement. In the Shipping World he is tops . . . In private life he is a great gardener and although past middle age, still plays a first class game of tennis.

Ten years later an artless suggestion made to the then chairman, Walter Layton, evoked an almost testy response from that mild-mannered man. Agreeing unquestioningly to the terms in which the trustees' position was secured in a proposed *Economist* reorganisation, Hambro continued: 'I would again like to question whether or not the present would not be a good opportunity to do away with the Trustees. I feel that the Economist is so well established in the world today and its name stands so high everywhere, that I wonder whether we are necessary to you, however much we may feel proud of being a means of forwarding the prosperity of the paper. However, I bow to the better judgement of you and your Board on these matters.'

'I and my Board . . . are not at all disposed to do away with the Trustees', replied Layton. 'Far from this being a "good opportunity" I have in the past twelve months been vigorously selling the Economist charter to the Shaw-cross Press Commission and there is quite a prospect that the Commission will make recommendations in the hatching of which the Commission's ideas will have been influenced by our experiment.'[21]

Part of the problem was that, in his anxiety to secure names who would shed lustre on the paper, Crowther, who after 1945 effectively chose the trustees, made the appointment seem more of an honour than a duty. Writing to Sir Robert Sinclair in 1952, he explained that 'The Trustees' duties might, in certain circumstances, be quite responsible. But they are never likely to be arduous. The Trustees met in person at the time of my appointment in 1938 and again informally about two years ago when they lunched here. But otherwise the business (which normally consists only of approving the occasional stock transfers) is conducted entirely by correspondence, and so far as I know nothing has ever arisen in the twenty-four years that the present company has been in existence that has occasioned any argument.'

Relations between the three authorities set up by the constitution – Trustees, Directors and Editor – have, in fact, always been most harmonious. Indeed, by far the most onerous duty of the Trustees is to keep an eye on what the paper is doing.

I very much hope that you will be able to give us a favourable answer. The present Trustees are two administrator-academics [Sir William Beveridge and Sir Oliver Franks] and a banker. We feel that, for proper balance, we need an industrialist, though one with some experience of public affairs, with a judicial temperament and without any political commitments. We are all agreed that you answer the specification more exactly than anyone else we can think of. In addition to that, it would give us all – and me most particularly – the greatest personal pleasure if you would agree to be associated with us in this way.

Sinclair, a man with an academic and wartime-civil service background, appears to have been a conscientious trustee during his 25 years. He and his co-trustees (Lord Franks, ex-Ambassador to Washington, Sir Frank Lee, ex-Permanent Secretary of the Board of Trade, and Lord Harcourt, ex-Economic Minister to Washington, senior figure in banking and insurance) were unanimous in objecting to a suggestion in 1965 that the *Financial News* might buy up some ordinary shares, thus giving them more than half the capital and making *The Economist* technically a subsidiary. But Sinclair's relationship with the paper raises two issues. First was the reason for choosing him rather than names suggested by the trustees themselves. Protesting all the while that it was for the trustees to choose their new recruit, Crowther effectively vetoed two of their candidates for lack of public eminence: 'we rather felt', he wrote of one of them, 'that since we had all had to look him up in *Who's Who*, that was in itself a disqualification'. Another letter of Crowther's demonstrates another potential pitfall of recruiting men of affairs: conflict of interest. Sinclair was chairman of the Imperial Tobacco Company.

On the day he wrote happily accepting ('as I think you know, I have been a warm admirer of the newspaper for many years'), Sinclair wrote a separate letter to Crowther complaining about a 'NOTE OF THE WEEK' headed 'DID YOU GIVE HIM CIGARETTES?' in which Pat Norton discussed new evidence that smoking was linked to lung cancer.[22] Crowther, then editor, wrote: 'I am more than sorry for the unfortunate coincidence that led to your longer letter. Since you are now about to be one of the trustees I can explain a little bit more about the internal mechanism than I might otherwise think it right to do in loyalty to my colleagues. I did not myself see this Note until the proof stage, when I raised at once the advisability of it. On reading the Note itself I felt it dealt reasonably and objectively with the matter of legitimate public interest and that it might be a worse failure of duty on my part to censor the Note than to pass it. I did, however, raise an objection to the title, but I allowed myself to be persuaded by the argument that in Christmas week a reference to a widely printed advertisement might be considered permissible, and even a sort of compliment to the success of that particular item of publicity. Perhaps I was wrong and it went further than a joke should have done. If so, I am sorry.

'I understand of course your reluctance to engage in public controversy on the subject, but if any of your associates would like to write me a Letter to the Editor – which could of course come from a private address – I shall be delighted to print it.'

That was craven enough: much worse was Crowther's unprompted obeisance as chairman. Writing to Sinclair in 1964 about the proposal to offer the editorship to Alastair Burnet (Tyerman was being eased out early), Crowther added:

> You will have seen the Note entitled 'Huff Puff' on page 24 of the current issue. I assure you that it will not have made you any angrier than it did me, and I have sent off a very sharply worded note of protest. At any other time, I would have feared that it would make you decide to have nothing further to do with *The Economist* – and I don't know that I could have blamed you. As it is, I hope and pray that it will make you the more interested in seeing that such silly and irresponsible (and uncalled-for) things do not get into the paper in future. I need hardly say that I did not even know that the subject was to be broached when I spoke to you on Wednesday – or, indeed, until I opened the paper yesterday morning.

The offending item was:

CIGARETTES

HUFF PUFF

An agency of the United States government is trying to compel American cigarette manufacturers to mark their packages with an indication that smoking may damage the health (see page 43). This is a sensible prescription that should be made obligatory in Britain too. While smoking continues, it is desirable that those who sell cigarettes should continue to compete; that is why *The Economist* has opposed those who would like to ban cigarette advertising. But the manufacturers should also – all of them – have to advertise the fact that their product can be noxious.[23]

This episode is a perfect example of Crowther's lack of moral courage, a quality which Tyerman – who had nothing like his abilities as an editor – possessed in abundance. If he did protest about the article (which is questionable), he was, as chairman, improperly challenging editorial independence – for which he should have been rebuked by Sinclair, as trustee.

There was no evidence of nervousness in the paper's dealings with its most important trustee, Oliver Franks, who was festooned with more honours (including a peerage and the Order of Merit) than all his colleagues put together. Announcing in 1982 that Franks would head the inquiry into the government's conduct prior to the Falklands war, 'BRING CANDY' told the famous story of the 1948 Christmas Day broadcast in Washington, 'in which various ambassadors were asked in pre-recorded interviews what they would really like as a present. The French envoy pleaded for world peace. The Russian ambassador for freedom for those enslaved by imperialism. Sir Oliver Franks began: "Well, as a matter of fact, it's very kind of you. I think I'd quite like a small box of candied fruit".'[24] That was affectionate, but when Franks's report appeared, it was heavily criticised for its exoneration of ministers for numerous errors of judgment. 'Historical inquiries', concluded 'WALKING ON WATER', 'are seldom satisfactory as a means of ascribing praise or blame. The Franks committee was established in the heat of the moment to re-establish the authority of a government at war and to expiate the guilt of past errors. These functions it has performed . . . But it has left history with as many questions as it has answered.'[25]

Perhaps some punches were pulled, but nonetheless, it cannot have been easy for Andrew Knight, a man inexorably drawn to the great and famous, to publish what was essentially a negative judgment on the inquiry. Yet there would have been no risk of Franks flouncing off in the manner that Crowther appeared to expect of Sinclair. One of the trustees for 41 years from 1946, and their unofficial chairman for a quarter of a century, Franks was the kind of man who gets the Establishment a good name. He took his duties seriously and saw them clearly. The trustees became closer to the paper during the 1970s and thereafter, meeting the editor at least annually and being privy to his and the chairman's thinking when the paper was facing commercial difficulties, or, on one occasion, required their firm intervention with the *FT*. Franks's bible was the last part of paragraph 41 of the Articles of Association, which says that, when coming to their decisions on share transfers, the appointment of an editor or any other matter, the trustees should 'have regard to the importance of maintaining the best traditions and present general character of The Economist newspaper and to national rather than personal interests'. Not all his colleagues had done the job well, he considered: in his view a trustee should have broad experience, solidity of judgment, strength of character, the ability to make up his mind and also be prepared to give himself time to think. One might add that they should be in good health; characteristically, but untypically for a trustee, Franks resigned five years before he died. In a world of corporate raiders, Layton's far-seeing fortifications require to be manned by fit people with specific personal qualities.

The transition from the Wilsons was carried out with sensitivity and harmony. Of the three Wilson trustees, Sir Laurence Halsey continued as a trustee under the new regime, and Greg and Gibb became respectively major and minor shareholders. A fortnight after the announcement of the sale, Layton published a rather disjointed effusion from Emilie Barrington, stringing together quotes from various relevant figures of the 1840s. '*In view of the change in the proprietorship of the "Economist,"*' said the introduction, '*the following letter from Mrs Barrington, youngest and sole surviving daughter of the Rt. Hon. James Wilson, in which she gives some intimate details relating to the origins of this journal, will be of special interest to our readers.*'[26] Five years later Layton published the only obituary *The Economist* ever gave a Wilson daughter: even the death of Eliza, who had taken a keen personal interest in the paper right up to the end, had not been noted.

> *Mrs Russell Barrington*:- A link with the past has been broken this week, by the death, in her ninety-second year, of Mrs Russell Barrington, the sister-in-law of Walter Bagehot, and the only surviving daughter of the Rt. Hon. James Wilson, PC, MP, who founded *The Economist* in 1843. Mrs Barrington was a novelist and essayist; she was not only Bagehot's biogra-

pher, but also the editor of his works; and she was an artist, and the friend and biographer of Watts and Leighton. Her latest task was accomplished in the course of the last few days with the publication of Bagehot's letters to her sister, afterwards his wife, which Mrs Barrington edited. Readers of *The Economist* will share our natural regret at the loss of one whose life was so closely associated with the life of this journal, and with the lives of its founder and famous contributor.[27]

She had been two years old when, 90 years previously, *The Economist*, which kept her in comfort all her life, was founded.

CHAPTER XXXVII

Keeping the faith

Who would true valour see,
    Let him come hither;
One here will constant be,
    Come wind, come weather.
There's no discouragement
Shall make him once relent
His first avow'd intent
    To be a pilgrim.

John Bunyan. Chosen by Walter Layton for his wife's memorial service in 1959

Layton's great achievement was to have his *Economist* read widely in the corridors of power abroad as well as at home. It was cautious and 'slightly on the dull side of solid' – but it carried great weight. *Economist*s went to the foreign offices and the central banks abroad rather than to the bookstalls; they were, in a felicitous phrase of Graham Hutton's, 'highly influential copies'. The paper gained in importance because Layton was important, and because the interlocking circles in which he moved gave him extraordinary access to information, the dissemination of which in turn increased his and his paper's influence. And if that influence, thrown as it was behind a series of mostly lost causes, failed to achieve its grander purposes, it made a serious contribution to the education of the middle ground and the encouragement of international understanding. The desire to help suffused everything he did. Hutton once described Layton's staff as 'a caucus of knowledge and concern' – people steeped in awareness of the horrors of the Great War and determined to do all within their power to bring about lasting peace and a fair society. Certainly they could have had no leader more dedicated to duty and more determined to make clear to *Economist* readers where, in turn, their duty lay; Layton's sheer selflessness and decency shone out from his relentlessly worthy pages.

A major concern of Layton's *Economist* was the forwarding of concerted international action to tackle the economic problems of a world hard hit by the war. First it was necessary to resolve the major economic issue of the first half of the 1920s – that of the gold standard.[1] Before the war, the gold standard had underpinned the currencies of virtually all trading nations, resulting in fixed exchange rates; £1 was exchangeable for $4.86. The wartime inflation that had so troubled Withers had weakened the pound and in 1919 the gold standard had had to be suspended. All political parties, the Bank of England and the City wanted a return to the pre-war status quo as early as possible, and the government had obliged with a deflationary financial policy which pushed up the value of the pound and also the level of unemployment. Without further legislation the return to gold would have occurred automatically at the end of 1925; by the end of 1924 it was obvious to informed observers that negotiations to smooth an earlier transition were afoot. It was evident from the sudden and secret visit to America of the Governor and Deputy Governor of the Bank of England, noted *The Economist* in January 1925, that the exchange situation between the two countries had reached a critical phase. 'Distinguished bankers are not likely to be taking an ocean trip amid winter gales for the sake of their health.' The decision to return to the gold standard should be taken early rather than late. 'Provided the policy does not involve any drastic or seriously disturbing movements of prices, the predominant opinion of the country is that the restoration of the gold standard affords the surest and, indeed, the only practicable guarantee against renewed violence of exchange fluctuations.'[2]

If the tone seems wary even for Layton, it was because he was under pressure. In his dispiritingly cagey unpublished memoirs he confides that, while editor,

> I made full use of the editor's free hand in making of policy. This was not always pleasing to the Board and the Trustees. In the early 20s, for instance, the underlying economic issue of the day was the struggle to get back on to gold at the old dollar rate of exchange. *The Economist* consistently held that if gold convertibility was the aim it should be at a more realistic rate. Not all the trustees were pleased. Then as now, the editor of *The Economist* was an

influential figure, and I was constantly being asked to undertake jobs by such men as Montagu Norman, the Governor of the Bank of England, who was the driving force behind the return to gold. We nonetheless maintained our line on gold. More to the point, one of Layton's most important potential backers, Sir Henry Strakosch, was vehemently opposed to any form of devaluation, which he described as 'more appropriately called repudiation'. Repudiation, 'pure and simple' was, to Strakosch, unthinkable.[3]

So Layton was taking a courageous line but with a conciliatory veneer. His conclusions were expressed in an opaque style and he tried to soften the impact of his unsavoury opinions where possible, as in his pious expression of hope that the return to gold should occur under the governorship of Montagu Norman, 'a leader who has won in quite an exceptional degree the trust, confidence, and affection of the City'.[4]

Yet if to the Strakosch camp Layton's line was dangerously unorthodox, there was another perspective from which it would have seemed heartless and pusillanimous. Nicholas Davenport, for instance, believed 'that the policy of going back to gold sprang from a sadistic desire by the bankers to inflict pain on the working class'.[5] Keynes was mounting a vigorous attack on the social implications of a return to gold, and Layton, as one of the few economists in a position of real influence, was one of a tiny number of people equipped both to understand Keynes's argument and to make it widely known. But Layton always looked at the political implications of economic policy, and practised the art of the possible; so in this debate he went, as he was always to do, cautiously and only part of the way with his old colleague.

Behind the scenes, as Layton would almost certainly have known, Winston Churchill, then Chancellor of the Exchequer, had read and listened to the few critics – all outside government – who wanted a managed currency, believing as they did that one tied to an inflexible standard would hit industry and the already high level of unemployment. In response to an article by Keynes in the *Nation*,* in February 1925, Churchill had written to his

---

*In 1923, the purchase of the *Nation* (full title: the *Nation and Athenaeum*) was brought about by Keynes with money from Laurence Cadbury, Arnold Rowntree and Ernest Simon; the economist Hubert Henderson was installed in H.W. Massingham's place. The board of directors consisted of Keynes, Layton and Rowntree, described by Beatrice Webb as 'a group of Liberals whose bond of union is their belief in the possibility of finding a progressive policy in national affairs which is not based upon a collectivist dogma'. In 1931 the *Nation* was merged with the left-wing *New Statesman*, symbolising, observed Robert Skidelsky, 'the fact that historic Liberalism had run its course'.

controller of finance, Otto Niemeyer, what Keynes's biographer describes as 'perhaps the most savage indictment of the Treasury and Bank ever penned by a Chancellor of the Exchequer'.[6] 'The Treasury', it began, 'have never, it seems to me, faced the profound significance of what Mr Keynes calls "the paradox of unemployment amidst dearth". The Governor shows himself perfectly happy in the spectacle of a Britain possessing the finest credit in the world simultaneously with a million and a quarter unemployed . . . The community lacks goods, and a million and a quarter people lack work. It is certainly one of the highest functions of finance to bridge the gulf between the two. This is the only country in the world where this condition exists.' If it was true that the financial policy that had been pursued was correct and that high unemployment was permanent and inevitable, that was 'one of the most sombre conclusions ever reached'. Yet he could see no way of handling financial and credit policy to bridge the gap 'between the dearth of goods and a surplus of labour; and well I realise the danger of experiment to that end. The seas of history are full of famous wrecks. Still if I could see a way, I would far rather follow it than any other. I would rather see Finance less proud and Industry more content.'[7] In the end, as usual, the Treasury and the Bank of England prevailed over the scruples of a politician who was out of his depth and did not know his own mind.

The Economist approved Churchill's confident mien when he announced the news in his end of April Budget. 'Great Britain has made its gesture to the world in the grand manner: "Gentlemen, the war, with its temporary interruption of our mutual affairs, is over. We have the honour to pay in our accustomed manner if so be that your account is in credit in our ledgers." Mr Churchill is to be congratulated on his courage in taking the step in this decisive way.' However, there was no doubt as to the real architect of this policy. 'The decision announced last Tuesday is the crowning achievement of Mr Montagu Norman.'[8] ('Twenty years later Churchill told his doctor, Lord Moran, that the return to gold had been the biggest blunder of his life: "Montagu Norman had spread his blandishments before him till it was done, and had then left him severely alone."'[9])

It was Layton's appreciation of where power really lay that led him to be protective of Churchill when, three months later, Keynes produced 'The Economic Consequences of Mr Churchill', a pamphlet excoriating the Chancellor for allowing the exchange rate of sterling to be set ten per cent

too high: this would inevitably lead to similar reductions in wages. 'ECONO-
MIC INCONSEQUENCES' was the unusually severe retort.

> In the present depressed and depressing condition of our chief export
> industries it is much to be deplored that certain distinguished economists
> should disturb the public mind by attributing far too much effect to our
> monetary policy as a cause of the depression.

The facts were other: international trade was slack for several reasons,
including post-war impoverishment and political disputes, and, domestically,
production costs were too high, especially in sheltered industries like coal.
The temper of the article rose when it came to Keynes's attribution of
present distress to the return to the gold standard and therefore to Churchill.
The mere use of the pamphlet's title 'shows how far its brilliant author has
been led astray from his usual detachment and clear-sightedness. For no one
knows better than Mr Keynes that Mr Churchill had not much more to do
with the restoration of the gold standard than the Serjeant-at-Arms . . . In
hurling his thunderbolt at the innocent Mr Churchill, when all parties have
been pledged to the policy which he happened to carry out, Mr Keynes allies
himself with disappointed politicians; in saying that our monetary policy is
the real source of our industrial troubles, he shows symptoms of falling into
the dangerous habit of concentrating the attention too closely on one branch
only of the science of which he is so distinguished an exponent': recent
statistics were adduced in evidence. Layton's prime concern was with the
dangers of boat-rocking: even his friend Josiah Stamp was rebuked for having
claimed in the Coal Inquiry Report that 'the special plight' of the coal
industry had been exacerbated since March by currency policy.

> His opinion is entitled to the highest respect, but he can hardly suppose that
> it is practical politics to propose to abandon the gold standard: and this
> being so, it was somewhat inopportune, at the present crisis, to lay so much
> stress on a view which is so likely to be misunderstood. We have not yet seen
> evidence that countries with low exchanges are, in fact, driving us out of
> international markets, either in coal or in general foreign trade.

And as so often with Layton, patriotic political reasons for defending the new
status quo led to a loyal conclusion: Churchill had 'laid bare once more the
fraud on the wage earner that is perpetrated by depreciating the currency'.[10]

Hoping that reason would triumph at home, Layton, like most of his contemporaries, assumed that the British economy would somehow adjust to meet the demands placed upon it by an overvalued pound. 'The old orthodoxies about the dangers of high wages are being forgotten', wrote Keynes in 1930. 'How far the old notions are being overlooked even by the orthodox themselves, and in the homes of the orthodox, is shown, I think, by what happened on the occasion of the return to the gold standard in 1925, when it was believed ... by the Governor of the Bank of England, the Secretary to the Treasury, and the editor of *The Economist*, that it was possible to increase real wages some 10 per cent by an arbitrary act without producing any untoward consequences – a conclusion which would have shocked, more than one can say, their predecessors in these offices of fifty years ago.'[11] The most immediate 'untoward consequences' were to be an exacerbation of the struggle between capital and labour: union leaders were not minded to respond to calls for wage reductions. Not for the first or last time, the battle-ground was to be the coal industry.

The story of *The Economist*'s attitude to miners begins with the triumph of heart over head and ends with the triumph of head over heart. In the early years of his editorship, before he became softened by the pragmatism induced by political office, one of the issues on which James Wilson had been notably unyielding was that of the wickedness of Factory Acts and other protective legislation. There had been just one exception to his paper's blanket condemnation of interference between master and man, woman or child. Horrified by the scale of mining deaths caused by inadequate ventilation ('The loss of lives by the hundred, at every turn, broken hearts and blighted hopes, are matters *not* of arithmetic and calculation'), the paper had announced that, in view of the expense of protective measures, there was no chance of general improvement without 'legislative interference'. In the contract between coalowners and coalminers 'there is no sort of equality, and therefore no justice ... we are not such pedants in science as to arrest ... by any formula of ours about interference in private affairs, the proved necessity of the central government coming forward to say that the lives of industrious, if not enlightened, of useful, if lowly, subjects, are of a value sufficient to make them exercise the whole power of the State for their preservation and protection'.[*12]

---

*This was a technically well-informed article, almost certainly written by Wilson's occasional contributor, his wife's brother-in-law, the Reverend William Thorpe, coalmine-owner, student of chemistry and Vicar of Bawtry.

By the mid-1920s there was a long and bitter history of obstinate conflict in the coal industry. Hirst's old friend Lord Birkenhead once remarked of the miners' leaders: 'I should call them the stupidest men in England if I had not previously had to deal with the owners.' After several post-war clashes, in 1925 another was averted by the provision of a temporary subsidy to avoid wage cuts and the setting up of a royal commission of people who knew nothing about the coal industry, under Herbert Samuel, a senior Liberal politician, to consider methods of raising mining productivity. In March 1926 the commission recommended better working conditions, a number of organisational reforms and immediate wage reductions. The owners' demands were exclusively for lower wages and longer hours, both of which the miners rejected outright. *The Economist* agreed with the commission, but was sympathetic to the desire of the miners to resist a policy which might mean 'permanent loss of employment, the break-up of homes, and the migration of perhaps tens of thousands of miners'. It was easy for those 'who think in terms of economic abstractions to say that this policy is inevitable, but anyone who appreciates the human aspects of the problem, the tragedy implied in the wasted skill acquired after years of labour or in the breaking up of social ties, will sympathise with the reluctance of the delegates to give even an inch of ground'. The only other option was to continue the subsidy, but that would be folly. 'The longer the subsidy lasts the more difficult it becomes to get rid of it. It delays the economic processes by which the mining industry must put itself into a condition of efficiency and of ability to compete.' It would be foreign competitors who would benefit.[13]

At the end of April the subsidy ran out: when the miners rejected wage cuts and local rather than national agreements, the owners locked them out. The Trades Union Congress weighed in and a General Strike began at midnight on 3 May 1926. Layton was the first of four *Economist* editors to circumvent a printing strike, and he did it personally. Between them, he and his tiny staff typeset text and printed it on a Roneo duplicator. There was a temporary hitch when they ran out of 'e's, giving Layton and Leonard Reid some fun in recasting the leading article. The 'EMERGENCY NUMBER', costing only 3d., came out on 8 May.

> For the first time in eighty-four years 'The Economist' is unable to publish its normal weekly issue. In the present sheet we have endeavoured to summarise for the benefit of our British readers the more important economic features of the situation and market movements. Arrangements

will be made to maintain the continuity of 'The Economist' records and reports as soon as circumstances permit.

BRITAIN UNDER A GENERAL STRIKE.

The country has entered on one of the most far-reaching industrial conflicts in history with amazing coolness. The public may demand a more complete explanation than they have yet had as to the events of the last few fateful hours and the reason for breaking off negotiations; but the Trade Union Leaders must bear the main responsibility for calling into use a weapon which cannot be employed without challenging the constitutional principles in which they themselves believe.

The constitutional theme dominated respectable opinion, but, characteristically, Layton's prose lacked any sense of outrage. While stressing that men returning to work should be protected against victimisation, he had no desire to see the unions broken. 'The urgent need is to find a way to resume negotiations while tempers still remain cool.'

The Economist was pleased by, but did not gloat over, the collapse of the General Strike, which had failed 'because the endeavour of a minority to impose its will on the Government and compel it to agree unwillingly to terms which it considered unreasonable broke against the rock of national solidarity. In spite of widespread sympathy with the hardships that the mining community must face, it was universally realised that it would be a shattering blow to the nation if its Government were to fail on an issue of this kind. The British constitution is far too deeply founded on the will of the people for failure to be possible, and the Government quickly put the issue beyond doubt by the firmness of its actions and the efficiency of its improvised services':[14] it was the paper's traditional call for stability above all. The miners, however, were still out, and as usual, Layton bent his efforts to try to find a solution. Throughout July, with Seebohm Rowntree, he laboured over compromise settlements which ultimately were wrecked by an equally well-meaning but much more muddled intervention by a collection of churchmen.

'The only methods of making a recurrence of last year's crisis absolutely impossible', said *The Economist*, months after hunger had forced the miners to capitulate, 'lie in the creation of channels in which a new spirit . . . could function, and the building by cooperation of better machinery for negotiation. Instead of taking these facts as the guiding star of their policy, the Government have chosen a course which, by rallying all the suspicion and reviving all the bitterness which time was beginning to allay, will effectively kill the new spirit and obstruct cooperative effort.'[15] Layton was right. The miners eventually, in 1947, achieved their long-term aim of nationalisation ('Coal is no longer King, but a pauper requiring costly public assistance', observed Roland Bird, doubting if nationalisation was likely to bring about efficiency),[16] and, in 1974, to the lamentations of *The Economist*, they avenged their old humiliation by bringing down a Conservative government. Ten years later Margaret Thatcher turned the tables, and Andrew Knight's *Economist* called for government action to ensure a strike-free future for coal.

> The biggest danger in this winter's collapsing strike is that it will harden Britain's tribal loyalties. Tory supporters could bask in their revenge . . . Militant miners' supporters could conclude that the next struggle will need to be even more bitter, and meanwhile prepare for that day by baying at the 'traitors' in the trade unions and Labour party. Britain will then have learnt nothing, forgotten nothing. Some time in the 1990s, its economy even feebler, it will have another miners' strike, perhaps led by a then 55-year-old Marxist called Arthur Scargill.

The only answer was to open up the coal industry to competition. Government should declare that:

> Coal is just another commodity, like oil or cabbages. It requires no extraordinary skill to produce. It does not have the social importance of health or education, nor the natural-monopoly qualities often ascribed to the railways. It has no place in the public sector. Only the folk memories of the miners' strike in 1926 made the Labour government put it there in 1947 and successive governments keep it there ever since. We will sell some pits to private investors; and we will give away others, preferably to their miners, sometimes with a fixed-term subsidy.[17]

Tory governments went part of the recommended way and, in due time, on 13 October 1992, the closure of 31 pits and the loss of 30,000 jobs was announced. 'Last session', Bagehot had written in 1859, after some labour upheavals, 'there was rather a *romantic* notion of the working man – next session there will be nothing of the kind.'[18] In 1992 the opposite occurred. *The Economist* missed the mood of the country, which on this swing of the pendulum found the few surviving miners extremely romantic. *The Economist* – and Rupert Pennant-Rea's *Economist* to a marked degree – has been more Roundhead than Cavalier, so coverage of the miners was relegated to the 'Britain' section ('King Coal is not dead . . . something will survive', it said in a slightly surprised tone[19]), while blue-rinsed Conservative ladies from the Home Counties complained to their MPs about the betrayal of a fine body of men.

Pennant-Rea was not an editor who bent to fashion: 'Michael Heseltine's bungled announcement of his pit-closure programme in October harmed his political reputation', began a leader in January 1993. 'Now it is in imminent danger of harming something more important: Britain's chance of cheap, efficient energy. Mr Heseltine, the president of the Board of Trade and the minister responsible for energy, seems bent on devising a crowd-pleasing retreat. He must be reminded that keeping pits open will mean higher prices for consumers and fewer jobs in industry outside coal mining.' However, the sound of marching Tory matrons had been heard even on the 13th floor of the Economist Tower and healthy disputes had followed, so a concession was made to public opinion. 'Given the bungle, there is a case for running down coal rather more slowly than ministers originally intended. As economic recovery gets under way, the government would then be less vulnerable to charges that it was throwing miners on to the slagheap.' But an even more competitive energy policy should be sought: coal should be privatised sooner rather than later.[20] In the modern *Economist*, coal is a commodity: it is the consumer who is King.

Throughout the rest of the 1920s Layton toiled away at the coalface of the various movements for international cooperation. The free-trade debate in the late 1920s offers a perfect illustration of the manner in which his various roles interconnected. In 1927 he was appointed as a British delegate to the World Economic Conference in Geneva. He laboured over papers pushing the case for maximum reduction of tariff barriers, which were published anonymously along with others in an *Economist* 'Economic Conference Supplement' just before he went to Geneva.[21] At the conference he scored a personal triumph: the *Manchester Guardian* described how, 'ruddy and of a cheerful countenance, his keen, youthful face suffused with enthusiasm, [he] delivered at the opening of the conference the most weighty of a series of weighty utterances and has since been unable to escape the attentions of pressmen and portraitists. No suspicion of political ambition mars the purity of the motives of this disinterested theorist who seems to be at home with all the humbler duties of the producer and trader no less than with the more grandiose problems of economic evolution.'[22] During the conference he sent *The Economist* a cautiously optimistic 'From a Special Correspondent' report,[23] and on his return, pleased that the conference had recommended a policy of seeking tariff reductions, he published a second 'Economic Conference Supplement'.[24] He could not avoid including his name in the list of delegates: otherwise, it appeared nowhere in *The Economist*'s coverage.

In the month preceding the 1929 general election, a supplement on 'The Case for Free Trade' was designed to oppose the protectionist arguments of a section of the Conservative Party. Walter Layton had stood as a Liberal candidate three times during the 1920s – unsuccessfully, like Bagehot and Hirst before him – but now the argument was put in general, not party political, terms. Having made, perforce, the usual national-interest case and brought it up to date with detailed evidence, there was, by Layton's standards, a passionate conclusion: 'A great movement is on foot in Europe towards a saner fiscal policy, and from that movement Britain above all nations stands to benefit. *It is almost inconceivable that any British Government should choose this moment for a British backsliding into Protection, which would deal a death-blow to that movement and would lead Europe back into the rut of exclusive and embittered nationalism, which was the most dangerous legacy of the Great War.*' The article went on 'to lift the matter for a moment on to a broader and a higher plane. A writer in a great American publication recently said:- "Suggest to an American or an Englishman that he has no right to create tariffs, which, while of dubious benefit to himself, are ruinous to this or that group of foreigners, and he would stare in genuine amazement at the suggestion that the ruin and misery of foreigners is any concern of his or should influence his conduct in the slightest degree."' This gave food for thought: economic interdependence had grown to such an extent that it was 'no longer possible or desirable to consider policy on purely national lines. Britain, from her own viewpoint, of all nations, can only be prosperous in a prosperous world, and the broader view goes hand in hand with the narrower. *The policy of economic liberalism is Britain's tradition and her mission to the world. It is the only policy which harmonises with the world's desire for Peace and Security.*' It was in the power of Britain, while helping herself, to help the peoples of all the nations who had suffered from 'the narrow nationalist policy of trade restrictions ... *If Britain now refuses to stray from the path of true economic statesmanship, history may say of her that she saved her own people by her fiscal constancy and the world by her example.*'²⁵

Throughout this and similar campaigns, Layton enhanced the *Economist*'s already well-discharged function as a paper of record by his practice of publishing detailed reports on international economic and political developments. The chronic international ulcer caused by differing views about the scale of German post-war reparations was one of the problems which, year after year, received remorselessly comprehensive and constructive coverage. In 1924, for instance, when a committee of experts, under an American chairman, General Charles G. Dawes, produced a revised schedule of reparations based on Germany's supposed ability to pay, *The Economist* produced a sixteen-page 'Reparations Supplement'. 'The publication of the Experts' Reports, followed closely by the General Elections in France and Germany,' said the introduction, 'without any doubt means that the Reparation problem is about to enter upon an entirely new phase. The question is one of such fundamental difficulty, and the Nations of Europe have been so often disappointed, that we dare not put our hopes too high.' Yet, since conditions were particularly propitious, it seemed 'a suitable moment to present to our readers a summary of the Experts' Reports ... and to accompany it by an historical summary of the whole question'.²⁶ Five years later, the Young Plan, the successor to Dawes, again scaled down the wartime Allies' demands and effectively freed Germany's finances from Allied control. One of the Young Committee's proposals was for the setting up of the Bank for International Settlements (with which Layton was to be closely involved), designed to act, at first, mainly as a clearing house for the payment of reparations and war debts: *The Economist* provided a lengthy summary of the Bank's statutes.

Then there were the supplements on individual countries. The 'Roumanian Supplement' in 1929 is a good example of the breadth and weight of contributors. The contents and authors included: Greater Roumania (anonymous), Economic Policy (Virgil Madgearu, Ministry of Industry and Commerce), Public Finance (Mihai Popovici, Minister of Finance), The National Debt (Savel Radulescu, Head of the Economic Division of the Ministry of Foreign Affairs), Banking (Aristide Blank), Agriculture (A. Nasta, Professor at the Agricultural High School, Bucarest) and Foreign Trade (Our Bucarest Correspondent). Nothing of this kind would be published today. For many years, *Economist* surveys or supplements on foreign countries have been written from a severely independent viewpoint, without any contributions by the country's ministers, officials or politicians.

Politically, Layton's paper was an organ of propaganda for decency and common sense in relations between factions and nations. The old *Manchester Guardian* once published a leader with a sentence which was much mocked by Malcolm Muggeridge in his cynical days: 'It is greatly to be hoped that men of moderation and goodwill may come together, and wiser counsels prevail.' A more perfect summing up of what Walter Layton and his *Economist* stood for would be difficult to find. Layton, however, added his own twist. 'If Layton felt at a late hour on Thursday', wrote Douglas Jay, 'that the young leader-writers were too emphatic, and there was not much time or space to correct them, he used simply to add the words at the end: "Time alone will show." "Will Hitler desist from further aggression?" we would ask. "Time alone will show," added Layton, altering the entire tone of the article.'[27]

At the root of Layton's deficiencies as editor was the simple fact that he was not by instinct a journalist. His mission was to explain, not entertain. His *Daily Telegraph* obituarist remarked that 'he never seemed . . . entirely at ease in the rush and bustle of Fleet Street, with its daily need for quick decisions, unruffled and kindly though he always was to those about him. His temperament was more that of a senior civil servant, and an admirable one at that.'[28] Worse yet, he thought like a conscientious academic: congenital fairmindedness and reluctance to make snap judgments are serious handicaps in the world of newspapers. A leader writer recalled the disaster that befell the *News Chronicle* on the night of the 1938 Munich Agreement.

> That night, exceptionally, Layton thought it was his duty to come into the office and settle the leader with us. We discussed and discussed it from every angle, while edition after edition went out without any leader on the subject and when it did appear, in the latest editions, it was too indecisive to have any value. What was needed at that moment from the *News Chronicle* was a blast like Churchill's in the debate in the House of Commons a few days later, 'A total and unmitigated defeat'.[29]

The implications for *The Economist* were less serious: under Layton it was primarily a learned journal of trustworthy fact and deliberate conclusions. And if the conclusions too often lacked bite, the substance of the economic and political coverage was invaluable, not least because – as in Bagehot's day on the domestic stage, and now also internationally – the editor's integrity was an acknowledged fact. Layton's paper was, in essence, a lengthy, reliable and unique weekly brief on world facts and figures. In the late 1930s, next to *The Times*, *The Economist* was the British newspaper most quoted by leading American papers. Every week the American Embassy cabled a 1,000-word summary to the State Department. Readers who were heads of governments included Manuel Azaña (the Premier of Republican Spain), Heinrich Brüning (German Chancellor 1930–32, who had also been a contributor) and Benito Mussolini, who described himself, when Layton interviewed him in 1932, as the paper's 'most constant reader'.[30] Franklin D. Roosevelt was another regular, the only one of that foursome who, in 1943, was in office and in a position to send a cable on the occasion of the centenary luncheon:

> Hearty congratulations to you and your associates on the Centenary of *The Economist*. There will be ever-widening opportunity for services in the difficult years that lie ahead, and adequate understanding of the economic interdependence of nations will be necessary to ensure peace in a free world. In the great task of economic enlightenment *The Economist* can play a significant part.[31]

Eric Gibb was the unwitting cause of an incident which showed how seriously the paper was taken abroad after only three years of Layton's editorship. In December 1924, the Prime Minister, Stanley Baldwin, had made a statement about the possible need to safeguard particularly threatened industries, which left him and his Chancellor, Winston Churchill, in danger, thought *The Economist*, of being 'stampeded by forces behind them, and too strong for them, into the morass of Protection on whose edge they are now so perilously playing'. The appearance of Churchill, the great proponent of free trade, as a defender of protectionist proposals had been 'the *bonne bouche* of the House of Commons debate': the paper was unimpressed with his 'adroit' efforts to represent himself as 'a bulwark against the excesses of his Protectionist colleagues', although that had indeed been the case. Lloyd George, who was then back in favour with *The Economist*, but already past his zenith (having lost, in 1922, the premiership which he was never to regain), argued against protection: 'The worst of proposals like that of the Government is this: it is taking the mind of the country away from the method of confronting the most dangerous competition which we are ever likely to be confronted with by substituting this vicious, false, artificial, barren scheme for a real method of confronting our difficulties.' Tinkering with tariffs was dangerous. 'The more that we philander with the barren doctrine of trade restraint and tariff juggling, the further away shall we be from facing the problems which must be solved before our industry and our trade can return to a satisfactory degree of activity and prosperity.'[32]

This debate – in particular, the ministers' mocking response to Lloyd George – had inspired Eric Gibb to venomous satire in 'SUCCESS', which began by considering the wreckage of unnecessary failures strewn over the path of history.

> Regularly by the roadside we find the remains of men who had the world before them, who started with the opportunity of splendid careers and great fortunes, but turned their back on their own chances and threw everything worth having away for the sake of some idea, some cause, some enthusiasm, which they allowed to seize hold of them and make them into monomaniacs and laughing-stocks to their generation.

Examples included Socrates wasting 'his and other people's time, in idle chatter at the street corners, and at the end dying absurdly over a drink of hemlock', Rembrandt 'starving among riches, simply because he would not paint the pictures that the public wanted', Milton 'dragging out a miserable existence and selling his life's work at the finish for a price that any unskilled labourer could earn to-day in a fortnight', and William Wilberforce surrendering his political career 'for a few hundred thousand black men whom he had never seen, and who could not have disturbed the peace of mind of any sensible, well-regulated man'. Even 'the most sensible of us to-day, in contemplating these now famous lives, must find it hard to realise how absurd they really were to their contemporaries', for all of them had become famous later. 'We see the truth far more clearly when we think of the thousands of others who threw away everything without achieving fame either in life or in death' and see the 'foolish risks the idealist runs when he throws away substance for shadow, and what a ridiculous, pitiable figure he really cuts'.

Fortunately 'such self-inflicted failure' was now rare. The House of Commons, for instance, was mainly 'an assembly of realists who appreciate the Career at its proper value, will allow no nonsense to stand in the way of its achievement, and when one door to advancement is closed will jettison all the things that need to be jettisoned before another door can be tried . . .'

> In a recent debate on Free Trade, our truly representative Prime Minister

was heartily amused at the spectacle of a middle-aged politician belonging to a beaten – almost exterminated – party, expressing the same old beliefs in time of adversity that he had expressed in the day of success. As an honest but experienced man he was naturally tickled by the thought of a politician not merely out of office, but hundreds of miles away from any prospect of taking office, refusing to recolour and revarnish the outward appearance of his beliefs to a more fashionable and popular shade.

Baldwin's picture of 'the stranded idealist' distancing himself ever further from a successful career (meaning Lloyd George) had evoked happy laughter in the House of Commons. That acknowledged master in the art of self-advancement, Winston Churchill, in his great speech, 'highly applauded as one of the greatest of a great rhetorical life, set out in unanswerable arguments the philosophy of the realist; the politician who faces things as they are, and understands that the duty of a successful man is to succeed'.

> It is true, he said in effect, that having throughout my life been an ardent believer in Free Trade, I have now joined a Government that believes in Protection, and have been put up by my colleagues to argue the case for Protection. We are all politicians cut from the same block, and we can often amuse each other for an evening by charges of inconsistency, and by quotations that are meant to be embarrassing; but we are all in it together, and we all of us understand pretty well the rules of the game. I am different from most politicians, certainly, but the only difference is that I am cleverer, and manage to spend practically all my time in the House of Commons on the right-hand instead of the left-hand of the Speaker.

Since politics represented real life in miniature, average citizens would find it conducive to peace of mind to know 'that our country is run not on fanciful or foolish principles, but by those who work upon the sound practical doctrine that "things are in the saddle and rule mankind"'.

> And yet – when you have pondered again this Christmas the birth and beginnings of Christian Faith, and in the light of that revelation you turn back to modern conditions and contemporary personalities, to whom do you doff your hat – to the brilliant figure of the successful realist, or to the obscure idealist ridiculously living and (still more ridiculously) dying in his unshakeable belief?[33]

By Gibb standards, this was pretty heavy-handed, but it proved too subtle for Central Europe. Walter Layton recalled the story forty years later. The paper's correspondent in Vienna, Dr Georg Tugendhat,* a member of the staff of the *Neue Freie Presse*, was rung after midnight a few days later by his proprietor, whose copy of *The Economist* had just arrived. Tugendhat 'grumblingly asserted that he had been woken by the telephone call, but his boss insisted that he must dress and come round to the office at once and write an article for the next morning's paper, that an important thing had happened in the political attitude of *The Economist* and that he must explain it'.

> In a matter of minutes a sleepy journalist arrived at the office and he was immediately informed by his employer that *The Economist* had turned protectionist and was no longer fighting the free trade case. If this implied the paper was representing the City of London that was staggering. Tugendhat, who had previously lived in England for some years, hastily read the article through and had the difficult task of explaining . . . that this was just two columns of satire and it would be difficult to write an article explaining the satire in German. The proprietor . . . was one of the best informed Austrians about English economy. If he was deceived, how many more of our foreign readership would fall into the same trap?

The incident taught Layton 'very forcibly to appreciate that when half the sale of *The Economist* is in overseas countries you cannot possibly make use of prolonged satire without running a great risk among *Economist* readers – a moral which one has to learn about the Press generally. I told the staff to be very sparing in the use of satire.'[34]

(In 1965, while writing his memoirs, Layton came across this article and sent it to Gibb. 'I'd sent you in the article,' remembered Gibb, 'whether on your initiative or not I don't remember, and you asked me to see you. I obeyed, and you told me that you couldn't possibly publish some of the things I had said about Churchill, but you had difficulty in cutting out the light ones. You must have succeeded, but the article reads pretty snug to-day. I must have been an even more unpleasant person then than I am now.')

---

*Whose son Christopher Tugendhat would be successively a *Financial Times* journalist, Conservative MP, European Commission vice-president and businessman.

CHAPTER XXXVIII:

Unreason abroad

The knitted woollen statue of Walter Layton in Trafalgar Square is coming unravelled. *Beachcomber*, Daily Express, *1937*

Another oblique compliment came in 1933 from Adolf Hitler's cabinet in Berlin. In March Layton had interviewed Hitler (whom he found rather unimpressive), Joseph Goebbels and Dr Hjalmar Schacht (the Nazis' financial *éminence grise*, whom he had come to know well when they served together on the Organising Committee for the Bank for International Settlements), and had written critical but not denunciatory articles in the *News Chronicle*. His *Economist* staff had been augmented on the foreign affairs side by two young men who were fiercely anti-Nazi: Graham Hutton and Douglas Jay. Jay had left his sub-editing job on *The Times* partly because he could no longer bear the paper's deliberate watering down of the grim news reported by its Berlin correspondents. Just before he left, he had read a report on the Reichstag Fire* which convinced him that the Nazis were responsible.

In August *The Brown Book of the Hitler Terror and the Burning of the*

---

*On 27 February 1933 the Reichstag (German parliament) building was burned down. Hitler blamed the communists and assumed emergency powers next day. President Hindenburg, 85 and dying, had reluctantly made him Chancellor on 30 January; but the Nazis had no majority in the Reichstag (and never, in any free election, got one). Suspension of all civil rights after the fire helped them to win more seats – but still no majority – in the March election. A cowed Reichstag, with many members either in concentration camps or in hiding, then gave Hitler full dictatorial powers. By July Germany was a one-party state, openly committed to brutal suppression of dissent and persecution of the Jews. Many observers believed the fire to have been started by the Nazis themselves; in Germany, Layton met distinguished proponents of this theory. A mentally retarded Dutchman, Martinus van der Lubbe, was made the main scapegoat and, with four others, was committed for trial at Leipzig in October.

*Reichstag** arrived at the *Economist* office at a time when Jay was 'seething with this feeling that the whole British public was being deceived about Hitler'. 'The whole book,' wrote Jay years later, 'including the treatment of the Reichstag fire, only confirmed in my mind the view of the Nazi leaders, which I had derived from *The Times*'s Berlin correspondents . . . in post-war years when apologists for Baldwin and Chamberlain have argued that nobody could have understood the Nazis' intentions fully before 1938 and 1939, I have noticed that these apologists become sceptical when I reply that it was all perfectly clear in 1933.'[1]

Layton was away on holiday and no one else was minded to worry about upsetting City readers, so Jay's uncompromising review was left intact. 'The orgy of barbarism and brutality which heralded Herr Hitler's regime', it began, 'was at first only known to the outside world through stray newspaper reports and unverified rumours. Lately, however, the process of investigation and verification by reliable inquirers has been carried a long way; and the main facts may now be regarded as established beyond all reasonable doubt.' The full-page leading article summarised the book's contents in graphic detail and concluded: 'The confirmation by full and reliable evidence of the worst suspicions that have been felt about the Reichstag Fire and the Hitler Terror is bound to produce a shock of revulsion and horror throughout the civilised world. It will also raise the question whether the right to equality of status among the nations can be claimed by a Government which disregards the ordinary canons of justice and humanity in revenging itself on its own fellow-countrymen.'[2]

Within a few days Layton's holiday had been disturbed by a letter from Count Schwerin von Krosigk, the German Minister of Finance, one of the Nationalists briefly in Hitler's government, with whom Layton had had a good relationship during the Reparations talks of 1931.

> Dear Sir Walter,
>   The September 2nd issue of your journal, The Economist, in an article entitled 'The Hitler Terror', accepts without criticism or reservations the one-sided account contained in 'The Brown Book of the Hitler Terror and

---

The Brown Book, although adorned with the names of Albert Einstein and other reputable figures, was compiled by a team of communists, whose 'proof' that the Nazis burnt the Reichstag was fraudulent; but the book's major theme, the 'Hitler Terror', was solidly based on hideous fact.

the burning of the Reichstag Building.' Far-reaching conclusions are drawn from that account without waiting for further confirmation.

As you know, for many years I have had the highest admiration for you and your journal. It is therefore the more to be regretted that you should now have thought fit to publish a one-sided judgment of the situation in Germany – views that are bound to give grave offence in quarters who shared with me a respect for you which will now be seriously impaired.

Yours sincerely,

von Krosigk

PS – I am sending this letter to the press for publication.

v. K.

Layton came hurrying up to London, where his staff feared rebuke for behaving recklessly and letting him down. But, although he was upset, that was not Layton's style. Even-tempered and tolerant of the human weaknesses of others, he once voiced the philosophy that 'when milk has been spilt it is less helpful to cry than to mop it up'; even less helpful was 'to break the jug that held the milk'.[3] After much discussion he wrote the following response:

September 14, 1933

Dear Count Schwerin von Krosigk,

The attitude of the *Economist* in commenting on matters affecting Germany, such as reparations, the war guilt question and disarmament, during the ten years of my editorship is, I hope, a sufficient guarantee that I would not willingly misinterpret the German situation. I, therefore, greatly regret that you should consider that it has been unfair in its judgment of recent events in the article of which you complain – a regret which is deepened by the recollection of the confidence which has been established between us in various negotiations in which we have hitherto been engaged.

In the circumstances the only way that I can suggest of meeting your objections is to ensure that a full and unbiased report of the case for the prosecution at the forthcoming Leipzig trial is published in the *Economist*, and to attend the trial personally in some at least of its stages so that I may form a first-hand impression of the proceedings.

If this course commends itself to you and your Cabinet colleagues, I will discuss the necessary facilities for my visit with the Embassy here in London.

Believe me.

Yours sincerely,

W.T.Layton

September 15, 1933

Dear Sir Walter,

I can do no more than reaffirm the good understanding which existed between us and which was due in no small part to the views on German problems which you put before the public, and I willingly acknowledge that your attitude towards German problems makes it impossible to imagine that you have in any way tried to give an intentionally false picture of the German situation. Indeed, it is your own general attitude and your peculiar knowledge of German affairs both at home and abroad which naturally led us to expect from you a particularly impartial view of the internal development of the new Germany. But the regrettable fact remains that you allowed the *Economist* to publish a one-sided judgment, which has caused the reactions in Germany which I mentioned in my last letter.

As the Leipzig trial is open to the public it is possible for anyone to give an objective account of it.

Layton published the correspondence in full under 'Letters to the Editor'. 'It is hardly necessary to say that the significant absence of any pressing invitation to the Editor to be personally present at the trial in no way affects our intention to present an unbiased account of the proceedings at Leipzig and to comment on them without fear or favour', was the opening to the substantial defence of all Jay's comments which followed: 'as regards the "Terror," it is not denied in Germany that the Nazi revolution has been accompanied by murders and acts of cruelty, nor that the Government is still responsible for systematised oppression of liberty – *e.g.*, the concentration camps. The responsible leaders of Germany must be under a strange delusion if they fail to recognise how deeply stirred and shocked the world has been by these aspects of the new regime. – ED. *Econ.*' was the ending.[4] Jay was instructed to write a weekly column on the trial, which was reported in great detail, without comment. Indeed comment would have been superfluous. Gems included the following exchange between one of the accused, Georgi Dimitrov, a Bulgarian communist politician in exile, who exercised his right to question witnesses, and Hermann Göring, who took umbrage at Dimitrov's line of questioning.*

---

*Georgi Dimitrov ran the Comintern for Stalin from 1935 to 1943, and was installed as Prime Minister of Bulgaria after the Russian army's arrival in 1944. Göring, in 1933, was President of the Reichstag, Minister of the Interior, and Prime Minster of Prussia.

Göring: You are a crook and your place is the gallows.

Dimitrov: Are you afraid of my questions, Herr Minister Göring?

Göring: Get out, you crook. You wait till we get you out of the power of this
court.

   Dimitrov was then removed by order of the President.[5]

'By Christmas, when the trial ended,' wrote Jay, 'not merely Layton but a
good number of *Economist* readers, were, I believe, no longer in much doubt
about the real character of the Nazi leaders.' Certainly, though the leader
marking the acquittal of four of the accused was not pure Jay, it was judicious
rather than cautious. 'Though most German opinion', it concluded, 'wel-
comes the verdict as proof of the impartiality of German justice, the Nazi
Party and its organs in the Press have bluntly described it as "a miscarriage of
justice" and as a sign of the survival of obsolete canons of Roman law in the
German judicial system. These must be replaced by the "true law," which
"has its roots in the feeling of the nation." The future of Germany in the
years immediately ahead will largely turn on whether this attitude is to
prevail or whether the Government will be strong enough to ensure the
maintenance of those canons of abstract justice which are essential to any
civilised community if the social order is not to degenerate into sheer and
undisguised tyranny.'[6]

   What made the paper particularly valuable abroad was its coverage of
'abroad', for it was under Layton that it strongly developed that paradox that
has led to global success: it has flourished in inverse proportion to Britain's
importance in the world. Under Layton there was a growing perception of
the reader as English-speaking but not necessarily English; by the time war
broke out in 1939, half of all the copies were going abroad. Solidly rooted in
Britain and expressive of British liberal principles though it continued to be,
The Economist increasingly came to report the world in the manner of a
multinational board where English is the lingua franca.

   Thus, for example, in the 1920s, coverage of Russia was undertaken on a
scale and in a manner as enlightening for a Frenchman or an American as for
an Englishman. Ivan Maisky, a member of the staff of the Soviet Embassy in
the 1920s, reminisced much later about his relationship with Layton. 'One of
our great successes was the maintenance of good contact with that highly
influential weekly – Liberal in outlook – The Economist, which had
considerable influence in the City. Its editor was the well-known journalist

and economist, Walter Layton, later to be Lord Layton, and an important statesman.' He was 'a Liberal, not of the 19th but of the 20th century, and well understood the mutual interdependence – both economic and political – of the contemporary world powers'. Maisky found Layton very interested in the Soviet Union both as a market for Britain and 'as a new form of economy, the first of this kind in the world. We crossed swords many times and [had many] lively debates (it could not have been otherwise)', but Maisky appreciated Layton's determination to provide 'as objective material as possible about the Soviet Union'. In March 1927, at a particularly tense moment in Anglo-Soviet relations, Layton agreed to publish a 'Russian Supplement' to the *Economist*, giving 'a detailed picture of the economic development of our country at that time and its prospects. In those days this was a great achievement for us.' It was at that time 'an act of civic courage and political far-sightedness on Layton's part'.

In 1930 *The Economist* ran a second Russian supplement, this time examining the Five Year Plan, which was introduced with a typically open-minded and time-alone-will-show leader, which concluded:

> At present many Russian institutions are repugnant to the mind of democracy in Western Europe, and it would be a rash man who would assert either that contemporary Russia is a pleasant place in which to live, or that the stability of her present *régime* is assured. Human nature being what it is, we have still to discover whether an attempt to create a completely new order of society, based on a curious blend of Americanised hustle, idealistic propaganda and methods reminiscent of those of the tyrants of Syracuse, can be crowned with ultimate success ... All that can be said at present is that, whether Russia breaks under the strain or succeeds wholly or partly on her present lines of development, she is making an experiment which is of intense interest not only to herself but to the world at large.[7]

When Maisky became ambassador in London in 1932, he renewed and strengthened his association with Layton and remembered afterwards with gratitude that, at a time when *The Times*, *Daily Telegraph* and most of the other serious newspapers simply avoided any contact with Soviet embassy officials, the *News Chronicle* and its sister papers, as well as *The Economist*, maintained a friendly attitude to the USSR 'and more than once did valuable work in helping to bring the two countries closer together. [Indeed Maisky spoke at one of Layton's Liberal Summer Schools.] In addition to this, during the 'thirties, Layton played an important role in the League of Nations and in various other economic and financial institutions and organisations, both British and international. He was a veritable gold-mine of information of the most varied kinds concerning the economics and economies of the capitalist world.'[8] A significant encomium from the same stable came from St Loe Strachey's son John, an admirer of the Soviet Union, in the *Left News*, the organ of the fellow-travelling Left Book Club, when in 1937 he referred to 'the *Economist*, the leading and, on the whole, the best informed and most objective organ of capitalist economic thought in this country'.[9]

Layton had another great quality as editor: he saw the international scene not only from the British point of view, but synoptically. In his anxiety to communicate this vision to his readers, early in his editorship, he invited Arnold Toynbee to write on international affairs. Beginning in May 1922 with the occasional article, Toynbee's contributions increased steadily in number. From the end of 1925 he normally contributed a weekly leader and some notes and continued to do so until the outbreak of the Second World War; in the paper's history, the only outside contributor of comparable longevity and influence has been St Loe Strachey.[10]

Layton and Toynbee had had parallel careers. A brilliant classical scholar, Toynbee (five years Layton's junior) was a tutor in ancient Greek and Roman history at Balliol College, Oxford, before the war. Having contracted dysentery during his extensive travels, he was unfit for fighting and spent most of the 1914–18 war on public service, mainly in the Political Intelligence Department of the Foreign Office; in 1919 he was a member of the British delegation to the Paris Peace Conference. At the University of London he became, first, Professor of Byzantine and Modern Greek Language, Literature and History and then, in 1925, the first incumbent of a chair of International Affairs. He combined this research job with the Directorship of Studies at the Royal Institute of International Affairs (better known as Chatham House). As single-minded a worker as Layton, he produced annually a 500-page *Survey of International Affairs*, while setting out to acquire through reading and travel nothing less than an understanding of the complete history of the world for analysis and transmission to a wide public. Asked in his late seventies how he would like to be remembered, he replied: 'As someone who has tried to see it whole, and . . . not just in western terms'. During his time with *The Economist*, he was to publish the first six volumes of *A Study of History*, which rated Western civilisation as only one among 21 'philosophically equivalent' civilisations. In the 1950s, denounced by Hugh Trevor-Roper – with that savagery of which he is master – as guilty of determinism, obscurantism, self-adulation, illiberalism and much else, Toynbee tumbled out of fashion, but his rehabilitation now seems to be underway. The historian Jonathan Clark wrote recently with admiration of 'the power and range of his historical vision . . . [which] went far beyond anything being produced by his fellow historians in the 1930s, and lifted the profession out of its Anglocentric (or Eurocentric) parochialism'¹¹ – precisely what Layton was trying to do with political journalism.*

Layton was the practical man, Toynbee the theoretician. Layton sought for the facts that would lead to logical and reasonable solutions for the pressing problems of mankind. Toynbee sought for patterns in the past on which to base sweeping global prophecies. Layton liked every article to contain figures: Toynbee littered his text with classical quotations,† anglicised Greek words and cultural references of awe-inspiring variety. Two passages in one of his travel articles for *The Economist* illustrate the difference of style. 'What is the percentage of the world's dates that Iraq supplies?' he asks. 'You know better than I; for the *Economist*, which publishes statistics of everything – is sure to print the correct figure from time to time. Is it 83.46 per cent. or 84.63? I cannot remember, and you can look it up.' Later in that article came a classic Toynbee paragraph, as he embarked for the Arabian Sea and looked at a nearby sailing ship being towed up stream by a rowing boat.

> Have I not seen pictures of such boats paddling through the surf off the coast of Somaliland or Malabar? And then the ship herself. Did Sinbad sail in such a ship to find the roc's egg in Madagascar? Or those merchants of Siraf who traded to Canton when the Abbasids ruled in Iraq and the T'ang in China? No, perhaps not, for the lines of the poop suggest a Western galleon of the sixteenth century. Possibly those lines are the last vestige of

*A renegotiated contract with Chatham House in 1928 required Toynbee to refuse all outside journalism unless permission was obtained in advance from the Council: an exception was made for his weekly articles for *The Economist*.

†'*Caveant consules ne res publica aliquid detrimenti capiat*' ('Let the Consuls ensure that the state comes to no harm') was the last sentence in 'BRITISH INTERESTS', an article published at the end of August 1935, urging Britain to push for League action in the Abyssinian crisis: it was, of course, untranslated.

the Portuguese colony on the island of Ormuz, which dominated the Gulf for a century until Shah Abbas conquered the place with the help of his English allies.[12]

That passage also demonstrates another marked contrast with Layton: their different perspectives on 'abroad'. Layton might be internationally-minded, but he had no sensual or cultural feeling for the places to which he travelled. He was not unlike a modern academic on the conference circuit who travels from country to country for intellectual transactions and acquires no sense of place. Layton conscientiously studied conditions and structures, looking for 'ways to help', but he lacked any imaginative grasp of new societies. In Graham Hutton's view, despite their intellectual commitment to internationalism, Layton and Geoffrey Crowther were Little Englanders in their souls. Hutton, a polyglot and a man of many and great cultural enthusiasms, once persuaded his two colleagues to make a detour after a conference to visit his beloved Hungary. In Budapest, one of the most beautiful cities in the world, they saw the Prime Minister and the Foreign Minister and met people from the highly cultivated group of original thinkers who had long enhanced Hutton's life. Convinced that even they could not fail to be captivated by this experience, Hutton waited expectantly for his colleagues' return. When it emerged that they thought Budapest small and provincial, and had not visited even one museum, Hutton wrote them off as ineducable. He never even tried with Douglas Jay, whose main job was editing foreign correspondence; he likened Jay to Nancy Mitford's fictional Uncle Matthew, who thought 'abroad' was unutterably bloody and all foreigners were fiends. Hutton and Toynbee touched in their attitude to 'abroad', but Hutton lived mainly in the present and Toynbee, increasingly, either in the past or in an apocalyptic future.

Toynbee had been recruited to *The Economist* before he began to make his international reputation through his annual *Survey*s and while he was still acquiring the knowledge he needed before embarking on the huge enterprise he called his 'Nonsense Book'. At Chatham House he had the help of a group of competent women who clipped stories about international relations from leading Western newspapers and sorted them by subject. On this material, on his own scholarship and with the help of Foreign Office and other specialists, Toynbee built what an *Economist* reviewer in 1925 described as 'a truly tremendous mosaic of essential facts upon which he throws the searchlight of a brilliant intelligence'.[13] The emphasis of each *Survey* altered according to the events of the year and Toynbee's simultaneous historical reseaches. In one year, for instance, he wrote at such length on 'The Islamic World since the Peace Settlement' that the subject had to be given a volume of its own. 'In his writing', said his biographer, 'he always exceeded planned and projected limits. Words came tumbling from his pen, as fast as his fingers could move, and as he wrote his imagination provided a series of wide-ranging historical comparisons, together with striking metaphors and other embellishments.' His articles for *The Economist* were written in manuscript: that stickler for stylistic perfection, Douglas Jay, recalled that Toynbee was one of only two people he ever knew whose choice of words and punctuation were beyond criticism.

As a prophet, Toynbee was erratic. In 1924, two years after Mussolini had led his blackshirts to power, Toynbee was reporting in 'THE POSITION OF ITALY' that the ex-servicemen were now firmly in opposition and that 'Fascism has been left to depend upon the violence of inexperienced youths who have grown up since the war, and who are as ignorant of what they are doing as their contemporaries and fellow-dupes who have become the gladiators of Communism. This dependence, in the last resort, upon boys is characteristic of all the extreme reactionary movements in post-war Europe, and when it comes to a battle between the Young Guard and the Old Guard, the issue cannot be in doubt.' The signs were that a 'constitutional *régime* seems in a fair way to being restored; and, as convinced constitutionalists ourselves, we may legitimately hope for this development, in the belief that it will be in the truest interests of Italy and her people. The road to this goal may not be altogether a smooth one, but they will, we believe, surmount the roughnesses and obstacles, and as they do so they will have with them the sympathy of the British people.'[14]

That was Toynbee at his least effective, analysing the micro rather than the macro and indulging in wish-fulfilment along the way. But throughout the 1920s, as he accumulated his vast store of knowledge of world affairs past and current, his *Economist* contributions grew in authority. Toynbee's was the influence that lifted the eyes of *The Economist* beyond the walls of international conference rooms. Layton, writing his own valedictory in 1938, quoted briefly from two brilliant *Economist* articles of the late 1920s which were undoubtedly Toynbee's. The first, in September 1928, had observed of a speech by the French Foreign Minister, Aristide Briand, in the League of

Nations Assembly, that it was 'a pronouncement which condemns to failure the policy of international disarmament, and therewith, in the long run, the hope of international peace'. A forceful comparison was made with Napoleon's disarming of Prussia in 1807: the result of a process of disarmament 'cannot be perpetuated if the disarmed people is left with a sufficiently powerful incentive to arm itself again'.[15] The second, published six months later, had opened by saying that for a decade 'two incompatible systems of international relations have been in competition for mastery; and the same statesmen in the same countries have been promoting both with even-handed inconsistency. With one hand they have been preparing for perpetual peace; with the other for periodical war . . . Ten years hence we shall know which is going to prevail.'[16] More sombre and more sweeping was a classic piece, written for the tenth anniversary of the 1918 Armistice, in which Toynbee surveyed the span between the outbreaks of great and lesser wars and considered the possibilities for improving on the depressing pattern of history. Two concise paragraphs give some idea of the distinction he added to the paper:

> In the matter of political institutions, Parliamentary democracy – for which the world was to have been made safe by the victory of the Allies – has lost ground on two fronts, and the Fascist-Bolshevist alternative has proved more attractive to the awakening East, as witness Mustafa Kemal's party in Turkey, and the Wafd in Egypt, and the Kuomintang in China. On the other hand, the principle of nationality during these ten years has continued its triumphal march across the world.
>
> Perhaps the most astonishing movement in these ten years has been the world-wide self-assertion of 'under dog' – the successful reaction of 'proletarian' classes, people, and civilisations against the recent masters of the world. We see this everywhere, not only, as between classes, in the redistribution of wealth at home, but internationally and politically in Italy and in Mexico, in the Islamic world, and in China. 'Westernisation' is the watchword, pammixia [mingling] the probable goal.[17]

Until 1932, when recruitment of bright young men accelerated, Toynbee's is the identifiably dominant intellectual influence (apart from Layton's) on *The Economist*. Another key figure was Aylmer Vallance, a subtle manipulator with a hidden agenda, who wrote with the fluency and clarity of a fine classicist (with a liberal spattering of classical tags) and pushed the paper towards the left.

Vallance and Toynbee had coincided at Balliol, where Toynbee was a tutor in the year when Vallance was awarded a first in classics. Vallance later told a story about his own wartime career which, like much about him, was suspect and attractive.

> In 1914 at Balliol College he went to a farewell party for an undergraduate who was in the Yeomanry and was being called to the Colours. The farewells reached such an emotional pitch that they all got on the train to Taunton, where the Yeoman was to report. The drinking continued, and the next morning they all woke up to find that they had enlisted in the Somerset Light Infantry. Aylmer was sent to India, commissioned, and then transferred to the Intelligence Corps. He seemed to accept this story himself, rather liked it, and could not be faulted under the closest questioning.[18]

Nothing could be more respectable than his next incarnation: from 1919 to 1928 he was general secretary of the National Maritime Board. Shortly after Layton became editor Vallance offered him a monthly Index Number of tramp shipping tonnage rates, and thereafter he additionally provided notes on a wide range of other subjects. Layton remembered his brother's story of how he asked Vallance for a leader on shipping which he then presented to Walter. 'According to Gilbert, as soon as I had read it I asked him who had written it. "You can't have. It's much too good." Tall, sharp-featured, spare, and with a keen wit, Aylmer Vallance was one of the quickest and most intelligent of my early recruits. Before the twenties were out he had been appointed Assistant editor.'

Those words, written in 1965, were deadeningly prosaic even by Layton standards. They were also characteristically charitable, for in the 1930s Vallance's disreputable behaviour at the *News Chronicle* was to cause Layton great distress and embarrassment. At *The Economist*, however, he was a tremendous success. He could produce an intelligent and elegant leading article in an hour and he was an inspiration in discussion. Hutton described him as 'a devil for rational argument' who very quietly made one devastating point after another and completely outclassed everyone else.'

Two articles from 1930 mark the watershed of Layton's editorship, the year in which the *News Chronicle* replaced *The Economist* as his major journalistic concern, and the last year of a decade of whiggish optimism about the perfectability of man. First was 'THE CHANGES OF TWENTY YEARS', written – almost certainly by Vallance – to mark George V's completion of twenty years as King. It began with a vigorous setting out of the context:

> Twenty years! Has any full reign, even Queen Victoria's, sustained so great a shock of happenings or seen so great a degree of revolution and evolution, both political and economic, as have been crowded into the first two decades of this Georgian era? The Victorian age, it is true, saw the coming of steam and the great miracle of industrialisation. The Georgian period – not yet one-third of the span of the Victorian – has seen already such phenomena as the greatest war in history, the evolution of democracy, the passing of the world idea of nationality into one of internationalism, the giant strides of science and its application to industry, the maturing of the British Commonwealth of Nations, the world-wide enthronement of the Peace ideal, and the establishment of the basic machinery for its attainment.

What were the outstanding features of the scene in 1910, so often called '"those happy pre-war days"? The constitutional crisis over the House of Lords question was at its height and was threatening deadlock to the workings of the Parliamentary system; the Irish crisis was apparently at its bitterest, and yet grew more bitter day by day till the Great War alone averted civil strife; Europe was an armed camp and armament competition grew month by month, drawing the world nearer to the edge of the precipice; the suffragettes were using force to back their demand for a limited female suffrage.' By contrast, today there was no likelihood of reform of the Second Chamber creating internal strife, Ireland was 'a peaceful and loyal member of the British Commonwealth', 'Europe, and more than Europe, [was] concentrating slowly and painfully, not on armament rivalry, but on the means of securing peace' and British democracy boasted virtual universal suffrage.

Though war was yet to be banished, 'we may at least hail the steady discrediting of belligerency in favour of co-operative effort. This process is as visible in the domestic as in the international sphere. In 1910 Europe and the world were practically without the machinery of arbitration, conciliation or the peaceful settlement of international disputes.' The British trade unions had been organising themselves for 'the great struggle with unorganised capital', which had come to a climax in 1926.

In 1930 we have at Geneva the common consulting ground for the rulers of the nations and the means, at least, of the widest co-operation; on paper the Kellogg Pact* has outlawed war; the treaties of Washington and London have substituted restriction for unfettered competition in naval preparations; the economic activities of the League and such events as the establishment of the International Bank have not merely countered the dire effects of the world war, but have set the feet of the nations into the way of peaceful and co-operative self-help. At home the belief in brute force and 'direct action' as effective industrial weapons has given way to the realisation that, however difficult the road of give and take, and common pursuit of efficient and economic production, it is the only road by which Capital and Labour can reach the goal of prosperity.

While from 1919 to 1924 there had been 'spasmodic, often ill-directed efforts at "clearing up the wreckage"', there had followed 'six years of concentration (sometimes feeble, sometimes interrupted, but always gaining ground) on applying the lessons of the decade for the common good of the nations and their peoples'. This process was still going on.

In our own country, for instance, we are learning the new art of Minority Government;† and we are witnessing a great shift of the centre of gravity of British industry from North to South. We still face a surfeit of baffling problems. Events in India [nationalist discontent] and the long struggle in China [civil war] remind us of the clash of East and West, which demands a new evolution of political wisdom; the great world-wide slump in trade shows up luridly the gaps in economic organisation which wait to be filled.

(These were indeed baffling problems, and Layton had expended much labour on two of them. On the international economic-cooperation front he searched tirelessly for answers to the dire problems that appeared after the

---

*In 1927 Aristide Briand proposed to Frank Kellogg, the American Secretary of State, a Franco-American pact intended to contain any new German aggression. Kellogg succeeded in 1928 in substituting a multinational agreement renouncing war as an instrument of policy, which was signed by almost every government in the world. The Kellogg-Briand Pact was riddled with loopholes and devoid of teeth.

†The results of the May 1929 general election were: Conservative 260 seats, Labour 288, Liberal 59 and others 8. James Ramsay MacDonald, who had been Prime Minister in the first British Labour government (from January to November 1924), once again became head of a minority Labour government.

1929 Wall Street Crash. India had been a more temporary commitment. In 1927 the Secretary of State for India, Lord Birkenhead, had invited Layton to become the Finance Member of the Viceroy's Executive Council – the job that had killed James Wilson in 1860. Like Bagehot, Layton refused, but next year he agreed to be Financial Assessor to his friend Sir John Simon's Statutory Commission on the future of India, where M. K. Gandhi's campaign of civil disobedience was proving highly effective. Layton spent some months in India early in 1929, and wrote a report which *inter alia* proposed central government financing of essential social services in the provinces. The commission's report in June 1930 broadly accepted Layton's proposals, but by then its work had been overtaken by events and had no influence on the continuing negotiations between the British government and Indian politicians. Once again, a great deal of work went largely to waste, though *Economist* readers received much useful information on Indian matters as a by-product. In 1928 India had merited 9 leaders and 15 Notes of the Week: in 1930 the figures were up to 20 and 47. Layton's consolation prize was his second offer of a knighthood; this time, he accepted.)

'Yet as we look backward over the chequered years and forward into the uncharted future', went on Vallance gamely, 'we may claim some grounds for satisfaction and some for confidence. The net result of these dire years of victory and defeat, of progress and setback, of achievement and disappointment, has on balance been progress all round.'

> If we have not achieved the unachievable 'Parliament of Man and Federation of the World' we have yet gone some way towards substituting the co-operative for the competitive spirit in international and in industrial and social policies; if we have not found the key to prosperity – and who, indeed, would expect to find that key quickly amid the ruins of war-impoverishment – we have at least done something towards a better distribution of wealth, towards the establishment of higher standards of living, towards reaching a greater degree of material well-being for the greater number.

At this point the article embarked on a theme that would have made every previous editor blench. 'The task of the coming years is so to organise the system of production, credit and exchange that the means for the sustentation [sic] of higher standards are forth-coming. That and the gradual perfection of the newly and roughly forged instruments of international confidence and co-operation – these are the two supreme problems of the next decade.'

If responsible leaders in the political and economic spheres succumb to the spirit of 'defeatism' or surrender to frenzies engendered by the pressing troubles of the present, these problems will not be solved. But we are confident of their progressive solution – and this for three (if no more) reasons: – science and invention have placed and are placing in our hands new weapons of incalculable power; the cataclysms of the recent past have taught lessons which history sometimes takes centuries to teach; the peoples of civilised countries have had their eyes sufficiently opened to see the difference between the strait path of united effort that leads ultimately into the fertile valleys and the broad road of belligerency that leads directly into the inhospitable mountains of distress. We believe, therefore, that when the full tale of the reign of George V comes to be told – and far off may that time be – the final balance of progress and achievement over trial and failure will be greater than, amid our many troubles, we can realise to-day.[19]

The other seminal 1930 article was written in October of that year, almost certainly by Toynbee. Sixty-two years later, in January 1993, it was to be cited by Paul Kennedy, the historian (and *Economist* contributor), in the *New York Times* when he urged the world's present leaders to think hard and big about its key problems.[20] 'THE PROSPECTS OF THE LEAGUE', taking stock after a disappointing session of the League of Nations, insisted that participants and observers must take the long view, keeping in mind the League's whole history from its launch in 1920. The first question was: what task had it been created to perform? The answer was 'that it is a political task more difficult than any that the world has ever before set itself. The supreme difficulty of our generation – a difficulty which underlies the war problem, the unemployment problem, the gold problem, and every other problem with which we are beset – is that our achievements on the economic plane of life have outstripped our progress on the political plane to such an extent that our economics and politics are perpetually falling out of gear with one another.'

On the economic plane, the world has been organised into a single all-embracing unit of activity. On the political plane, it has not only remained partitioned into sixty or seventy sovereign national States, but the national units have been growing smaller and more numerous and the national consciousness more acute. The tension between these two antithetical tendencies has been producing a series of jolts and jars and smashes in the social life of humanity; and the smash which pushed us into founding the

League – the Great War of 1914–18 – was not a unique catastrophe. It was merely the worst that has occurred so far, and we know that worse will follow unless we succeed in putting our politics into gear with our economics again.

The minimum programme for the League was to prevent war and align the political and economic organisation of the world in such a way as to make progress towards worldwide economic efficiency and prosperity. A long list of League failures in the field of disarmament was admitted to be discouraging. 'The effort seems quite disproportionate to the achievement. But this is largely because the League does not acquiesce in its own failures. It goes on trying again and again.' One of the League's main points of strength was its permanent organisation and the continuity of its work. 'The ground for pessimism lies rather in the general temper and outlook of the statesmen and parties who are in the ascendant in certain great countries. The symptom that is really alarming is the persistence, or recrudescence, of the belief that national interests can be served best by a policy of "sacred egoism"; and the most ominous instance of this attitude is its prevalence in France.'[21]

Toynbee had come to feel intensely bitter against the French, believing that 'such clever people have no right to be so stupid'. But the French, in their anxiety to keep Germany disarmed while staying well-armed themselves, were merely (and characteristically) expressing overtly the principle of national self-interest that was maintained covertly by most other citizens of the League's member states. It was only a handful of the high-minded who truly believed the message that many politicians parroted unthinkingly – that peace would be maintained through collective security. In practice, governments preferred to hold on to their own armaments and when it came to the various crunches they failed to support collective action – for reasons both good and bad. In September 1931, when Japanese troops seized the Chinese province of Manchuria, Toynbee called Japan's aggression 'an "acid test" of collective security'. China appealed to the League, which, led by Britain, the only League Power (other than Japan) with large-scale interests in the region, chose a policy of investigation, conciliation and inaction. The way the League handled the affair was seen as a betrayal by those who, like Toynbee, were labelled 'idealists'; it was regarded as the only sensible thing to do by the self-styled pragmatists. Then, in 1935, came Mussolini's invasion of Abyssinia (Ethiopia). This time the League voted to impose economic sanctions on the aggressor, but they were so limited (oil was not withheld) that they had little effect. Toynbee, who had wanted Mussolini to be stopped by armed force, was devastated.

From time to time Toynbee evidently felt some hope that Hitler might see reason if Germany's stated grievances were generously addressed. In his attitude to Hitler he showed the same fatal flaw as Layton, the belief that within every dictator there is a statesman trying to get out. Discussing in *The Economist* a speech of May 1935 in which Hitler offered terms for rejoining the League of Nations, Toynbee saw it as bearing 'all the marks of sincerity of "the ex-service man" who has seen war and its aftermath at close quarters in a subordinate capacity'.

> He knows the horrors of war at first-hand; he knows that the harvest of war is Dead Sea fruit which mocks the heroism with which its horrors have been endured; and he knows that he and his kind have suffered intensely from the late war and its sequel without having been morally responsible for either. Herr Hitler is here speaking with the sane and simple voice of the common man.[22]

Toynbee's moment of truth came in the spring of 1936. Late in February he went to Germany by invitation to address some academic audiences, and in Berlin produced, in a lecture called 'Peaceful Change', a successful crowd-pleaser. 'We in England', Toynbee declared, 'are beginning to think very hard about possible ways and means of arriving at some peaceful adjustment between "have-nots" and "haves" – of whom we are the chief.' His proposals were for the return of former German colonies to a German administration, subject to various international safeguards. Hitler, on the verge of sending troops into the demilitarised zone of the Rhineland, was looking for someone impressionable who might have influence on British public opinion, and he found Toynbee. For nearly two hours, he 'discoursed to Toynbee about "his personal mission to be the saviour from Communism," on the importance of an understanding with Great Britain, and on the limited character of his aims in Europe and overseas'. He greatly impressed his visitor with the sweep and detail of his historical diatribe against the Stalinist menace, which he saw as the latest in the long series of assaults upon Europe by Asiatic barbarians. More importantly, Hitler convinced Toynbee that the Nazi government really wanted and needed a peaceable understanding with Britain and France. In a confidential memorandum to Baldwin, the Prime Minister, and Anthony

Eden, the Foreign Secretary, Toynbee summarised the interview and voiced his conviction that Hitler had been 'quite sincere' in what he had said about wanting Anglo-German friendship.

On 7 March the German army occupied the Rhineland and, rather to Hitler's surprise, there was no military reaction from France or any other country. 'What should this country do?' asked *The Economist*. 'We are now faced with a sharp and inescapable choice between a genuine European reconciliation and another European war. If appeasement does not emerge from this crisis, the alternative is war – in the short rather than the long run.' Logically, the League should take military action now. But would that be right, bearing in mind that the Rhineland belonged to Germany? The conclusion evaded the issue and showed the level of Toynbee's gullibility. Hitler had declared himself 'a good European' and was thus under an obligation 'to convince the rest of us that his own belief in European peace and solidarity is sincere'. A gesture was called for. 'Herr Hitler can still save a situation which threatens to become as tragic for him as for us, if he will . . . temporarily withdraw his troops again . . . in exchange for an understanding that they shall be allowed to return again as soon as a new European settlement has been negotiated on the terms which Herr Hitler himself has put forward. A temporary withdrawal which Herr Hitler might, for reasons of internal politics, be unable to make, under threat of external pressure, would still be possible to him on his own initiative. Let him open the way, by such an act, for negotiations on his terms. Then he may live in history as the maker, and not as the destroyer, of the peace of Europe.'[23] As Bagehot once noted: 'In the faculty of writing nonsense, stupidity is no match for genius.' To Graham Hutton and Douglas Jay, who viewed Hitler and Mussolini as thugs, this kind of innocence was very hard to bear.

Hitler kept his troops in the Rhineland and, in May, Italy formally annexed Abyssinia: 1936 was the year the League effectively died and the balance of power in Europe shifted dangerously with the forming of an alliance between Germany and Italy and their overt intervention on General Franco's side in the Spanish civil war. Toynbee's disillusion was total, his judgment erratic. Fundamentally he had come to believe that Western civilisation could be saved only if religion took the place of nationalism. He pondered whether Germany or Russia would create the new Roman Empire; sometimes he welcomed the idea as preferable to the parochialism of the nation state, sometimes he regarded it as unthinkable and to be resisted. He became a less

THE ECONOMIST

Vol. CXXX   JANUARY 1, 1938   No. 4923

CONTENTS

Faith or Works?

IT is a long time since New Year's day fell at a juncture when the immediate future was so hard to forecast as it is to-day. In the next article an attempt is made to probe some of the grim mysteries of the great international game of power politics; and on pages 11 to 17 of this issue of *The Economist* we inquire at some length whether the economic auspices point to continued prosperity or to onsetting decline.

The conclusions of our survey, which is concerned solely with diagnosis and makes no attempt to formulate policy, need only be briefly and dogmatically summarised here, since the full argument is within easy reference. It is becoming clearer each succeeding week that the economic climate has changed in the last few months. Between August and October British recovery reached its summer solstice, and there has been since then a slight but perceptible recession in almost all the different fields of enterprise. There is not, however, in economic affairs, any astronomical inevitability of decline from high summer to the dark days of midwinter. If some further upward stimulus can be provided there is no reason why the present high level of output in this country should not be broadly maintained, even though it is unlikely that there will be any considerable further increase. A successful economic policy, that is to say, may perform the biblical miracle of making the sun stand still, though it is unlikely to raise it still higher in the heavens. And in any case, even if this success cannot be achieved, there is no reason to anticipate a sudden eclipse, or anything more drastic than a gradual decline.

The obvious practical conclusion to be drawn from this analysis is that economic statesmanship should be preparing itself to fight a battle in defence of our present prosperity. The Government have hitherto chosen to wage this battle with the weapons of faith. Before Parliament adjourned, the PRIME MINISTER once more denied that there was any threat of a slump, declared that "this country is in a far better position to meet any temporary decline in trade than at any time since the War," and condemned talk of depression as "not only exaggerated but dangerous," and he has reiterated the same view this week in a New Year message to the Conservative Party.

This attitude has considerable logical justification. It is a commonplace that public psychology plays a very large part in the causation of economic fluctuations, and in the very earliest stages of a downward movement it is the soundest of policies to do nothing to disturb, and everything to maintain, the highest degree of public confidence in the continuance of recovery. It is becoming more and more questionable, however, whether the time for such a policy has not already passed. The disheartening returns of unemployment in November were only the most obvious of many signs which must by now have convinced the majority of thinking men that there is some change in the economic atmosphere. When, in such circumstances, the public authorities persist in declaring that

20. Hartley Withers

21. Walter Layton

22. Leonard Reid

23. Aylmer Vallance

28. Hargreaves Parkinson

29. Roland Bird

30. Graham Hutton

31. Douglas Jay

32. Presentation plate to Hargreaves Parkinson: Roland Bird, Albert H. Chapman, R. L. Clark, Geoffrey Crowther, N. Crump, Graham Hutton, Douglas Jay, Gilbert Layton, M. S. Rix, Donald Tyerman, Paul Winterton, Walter Layton and Nicholas Davenport

33. Barbara Ward

34. Geoffrey Crowther: editor

35. Geoffrey Crowther: chairman – in front of the *Economist* Building

36. Donald Tyerman

Left: **37**. Peter Dallas Smith

Below:
38. Editorial meeting,
circa 1961.
Left to right, anti-clockwise:
Marjorie Deane,
Roland Bird,
Margaret Cruikshank,
Nancy Balfour,
Brian Beedham,
John Midgley,
Donald Tyerman,
Pat Norton,
Donald Webster

Right: **39**. Alastair Burnet

Below, left: **40**. Norman Macrae

Below, right: **41**. Brian Beedham

Above: **42**. Paris, 1963
From left to right:
Daniel Singer,
Donald Tyerman,
Laurie Valls-Russell,
John Midgley
and Sam White

Left: **43**. Andrew Knight

44. David Gordon

45. Rupert Pennant-Rea

46. Henry Kissinger and Gordon Lee

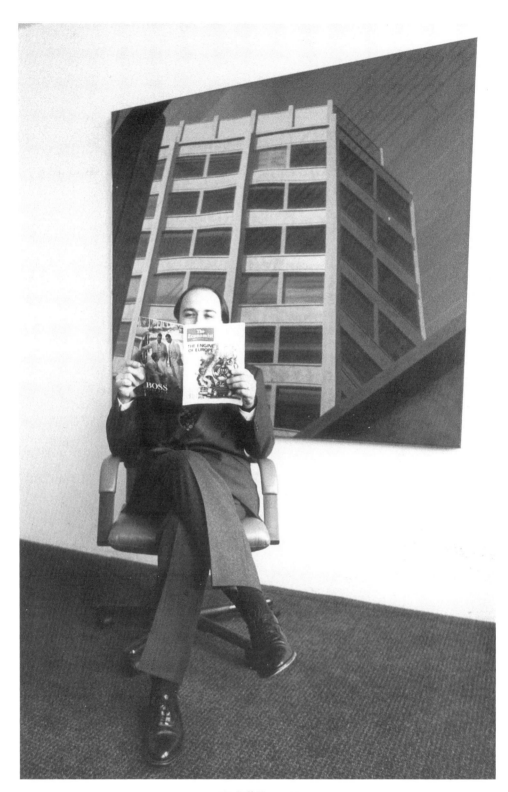

47. Bill Emmott

and less effective voice in *The Economist*; he was troubled and vacillating and it showed.

The times were just as dispiriting for Layton, whose biographer reckoned that he published in *The Economist*, between 1922 and 1935, almost 150 articles in favour of collective security. However, being Layton, he did not fall into despair but worked on, often behind the scenes, with other men of goodwill. Some of his activities were with the Anti-Nazi Council, later known as Focus, 'a secret network of journalists, politicians, businessmen, trade unionists and intellectuals'. Besides Layton, Focus included the editors of the *New Statesman* and the *Spectator* and was, in essence, 'a conspiracy to change the course of British foreign policy through propaganda, with Churchill as the chief publicist'; but its campaign lost momentum at the end of 1936 with the start of a period of relative quiet from Hitlerian aggression.[24]

CHAPTER XXXIX:

Standards? What standards?

I think it is a rule that can be derived almost without exception from
monetary history that no country has deliberately raised the value of its
currency without getting into trouble.[1] *Geoffrey Crowther, 1951*

Even before the hopes of a new international order based on the League were
dashed, the familiar world economic order collapsed in the aftermath of the
1929 Wall Street Crash. In 1925, wondering – presciently, as it turned out –
whether there was a danger that a boom followed by a slump in America
might 'draw us in its vortex if we attach ourselves to the gold standard',
Layton had concluded that 'we have to balance the advantages of exchange
stability against the risk of becoming associated with the other chief trading
countries of the world in international ups and downs of trade under those
conditions with which we had become familiar before the war. But even in
this respect there is room for hoping that the abnormal experiences of the
war and post-war years may have taught the world something in regard to
trade fluctuations, and that the resources of the science of finance may be
better able than before the war to mitigate the excesses of the trade cycle.'[2]

The deepening depression after 1929 rocked the free-trade faith of
many, but Layton did not budge. In March 1931 Keynes announced that, to
secure a breathing space, a limited tariff was necessary. 'A minor political and
fiscal sensation has been caused', began 'THE INCONSEQUENCES OF MR
KEYNES', 'by the publication in the *New Statesman and Nation* of an article by
Mr J.M. Keynes advocating a revenue tariff'. *The Economist* proceeded to
assail his argument from every direction. Particularly absurd was the
recommendation of a temporary tariff: 'The experience of our own country
in the last ten years – as well as that of every other country – makes it

abundantly clear that those who fondly believe we can introduce a substantial measure of protection to meet a crisis and remove it when the crisis is past are living in a fool's paradise.' The only answer was to balance the Budget by raising taxes and cutting expenditure. 'We shall neither solve our budget difficulty nor cure our economic ills by abandoning the open market policy on which the prosperity of this country depends.'[3] The free and frank exchange of views between Layton and Keynes continued in subsequent issues of both journals. 'When *The Economist*', observed Keynes tartly, 'complains against a revenue tariff that it will increase the cost of living of the working classes, I know that these are crocodile's tears. For in the same breath they propose alternative means of raising the same amount of revenue by taxes on beer, tobacco, sugar and tea, and demand a reduction of 10 to 15 per cent in the level of wages.'[4]

A run on sterling began in July 1931: 'When doubts, as to the prosperity of a currency, such as now exist about sterling, have come into existence, the game's up', wrote Keynes to Ramsay MacDonald,[5] but patriotism kept him silent in public. *The Economist* talked up sterling and refused to contemplate coming off the gold standard. Twelve years later, at *The Economist*'s centenary luncheon, the Labour Home Secretary, Herbert Morrison, spiced his warm congratulatory speech with the product of some mischievous research. His lengthy quotation from an *Economist* article of September 1931 began: 'Encouraged by the approval of the section of expert economic opinion led by Mr J.M. Keynes, organised Labour is inclined to toy with the idea of abandoning the gold standard.' Depreciation would be 'a disaster for the whole world. Any depreciation of the pound, however moderate, would be deplorable enough, and the deliberate adoption of such a policy a counsel of despair.'

> Even if we were prepared to face the resultant loss of London's earnings as an international banking centre, even if we were not impressed with the dangers of precipitate withdrawals of foreign capital, we should still unhesitatingly reject devaluation, for the reason that no country in the world except France and the USA would be able to maintain its currency at the gold parity if the pound sterling were allowed to find its own level. The upshot would be an international competition in the depreciation of currencies, a disastrous reversion destroying all the supposed advantages of our own devaluation and leading to exchange chaos.

It was interesting, remarked Morrison gleefully, 'to recall that about a week after the publication of that article the Government of the day, which was originally formed to worship at the shrine of those very orthodoxies so pungently set out in this *Economist* article, went off the gold standard amid loud applause, and nobody since that time, as far as I can recall, has ever had reason to regret it.'

There are striking parallels with what happened in 1992 over the exchange-rate mechanism (ERM). 'CRISIS? WHAT CRISIS?'* was extremely relaxed about 'what the media dubbed a "sterling crisis" . . . "Crisis" is a much abused word . . . The British, brought up on decades of economic mismanagement, are particularly fond of talking about sterling crises. But this one hardly makes the grade.' The government was prepared, if necessary, to raise interest rates. 'That, roar its critics, would be a disaster, turning the recession into a slump. Many of these same critics, including the Confederation of British Industry and leading industrialists, cheered when Mr Major, then Chancellor, took sterling into the ERM. As interest rates fell, they cheered even more. Now, at the first sign of trouble, they have jumped ship.'[6] Three weeks later, 'MAYHEM' began: 'Europe's monetary system now faces a test that puts its very survival in doubt, yet which challenges the old logic of a Europe of independent national currencies as never before. On September 16th overwhelming currency-market speculation forced Britain to suspend sterling's membership of the exchange-rate mechanism (ERM) that links the currencies of the European Community. What had, only weeks earlier, seemed a measured march towards a monetary union in Europe became a rout.' What had to be understood was that the government, 'though brought in the end to a clumsy and humiliating defeat, was right to try to defend sterling with high interest rates. Its mistake was in failing to do so earlier. More important, the near-breakdown of the ERM makes a strong case not for abandoning the system, still less for making it more flexible, but for striving all the more urgently to create a single European currency.'[7] As with the gold standard debate, *The Economist* believed that maintaining parity took precedence over levels of income and employment.

One other important link between the two crises needs highlighting: an essential element that contributed to the contrast between the before and

---

*This title referred back to a remark made in January 1979 by the then Prime Minister, James Callaghan, on returning from a conference abroad to a country paralysed by strikes; it was to help him lose the general election in May.

after articles in both cases was the sense of responsibility felt by both editors towards their country's currency. Asking why markets called for realignments, 'MAYHEM' dismissed the notion that it had to do with 'economic fundamentals': sterling had been 'correctly' valued.

> Mountaineers climb mountains because they are there; markets seek currency-realignments because they might happen. In recent days, the mere possibility of a currency realignment has been the ERM's most destabilising feature.

That is a constant dilemma for an influential and responsible newspaper, which in Alastair Burnet's time addressed the issue with feeling. In November 1967, in 'LIFE BEGINS AT $2.40', after reporting the details of a long-overdue devaluation by Harold Wilson's government, there came a *cri de coeur*: 'It is no good saying that Britain's long delaying fight against devaluation, fought with other people's money, has been obligatory in order to try to avoid default and dishonour. Once sterling had reached an obviously untenable position, every day's delay in devaluing has merely meant further losses to the reserves – and has also meant that the eventual devaluation would have to be bigger, and have to cause even more disturbance to the world monetary system.'

> For *The Economist* this has therefore been a beastly last three to four years. Whenever we have pointed out this central fact about the British economy, we have been told that we were bearing the national currency, and that the speculative drain of blank million dollars from the reserves in such and such a week was all this newspaper's fault. 'The value of these half crowns I hold in my hand,' it has been said, 'depends entirely on what people say it is, and if you go on implying that half a crown is worth less than half a crown you will bring down upon the British people hardships they do not deserve to bear.' The truth is that the men responsible for managing Britain's affairs in the last three years honestly have not understood that the level of a currency, like the level of the tide on King Canute's beach, really does not depend on what anybody . . . says it is.[8]

No more than with the ERM did *The Economist* apologise for its defence of the gold standard in 1931; on that occasion too it supported the Treasury's vain attempts to maintain sterling's exchange value. 'THE END OF AN EPOCH' was a spirited and constructive analysis of what had gone wrong, which culminated in a demand for the convening of an international conference of statesmen 'to ensure that the exchange standards of the future are worked out on the basis of a common international rule, whether related or not to gold . . . the question of currency values and exchange ratios is fundamental'.[9]

(Though Layton and Pennant-Rea, sixty years apart, were of the same mind, sandwiched between them were editors who saw monetary policy differently. Geoffrey Crowther addressed the matter in July 1944, after the conference at Bretton Woods.* 'Let us suppose that the worst happens, and that the postwar world is not one of balance and expansion, but of distortion and depression': America would risk only a modest loss in dollars and gold. 'As in the depression of the 1930s the American interest would be to prevent other countries from imposing exchange controls (which the strong dollar would not require), from depreciating their currencies, and from discriminating against purchase of American goods because they were shorter of dollars than of other currencies. The closer the approach to the gold standard – which, in these days, is a dollar standard – the better American interests are served, in prosperity and depression.' Britain, however, was in a different position: 'it is in the British interest to be free to make the best of a bad job if a bad job is what has to be faced . . . If the circumstances of 1931 were to recur, Britain would wish to be able to allow the pound sterling to find its level and to concert measures for stabilising trade within a group to which all countries that would abide by the rules should have access. A Bretton Woods system would not be in the British interest in times of crisis.' Nonetheless, the benefits of Bretton Woods were so great that on balance Crowther recommended ratification.[10]

In 1971 it was America that was in trouble: between the Vietnam war and domestic economic problems, debt was overtaking gold stocks. In August President Nixon devalued the dollar against gold. Alastair Burnet's *Economist* was delighted: 'COME ON, IT'S FINE', was the title of the leader. It was a golden opportunity: the time had come to float.[11] As it had taken two years

---

*At Bretton Woods in New Hampshire in 1944, the United States, Britain and some of their wartime allies agreed to set up two institutions to stabilise the post-war economic order: the World Bank to promote reconstruction and development, and the International Monetary Fund to keep order in the monetary system. IMF permission would be required for any changes in currency value exceeding 10%. Exchange rates would be fixed in terms of gold or the dollar, with the dollar the only currency convertible into gold.

for the gold standard to break down generally, so it was with Bretton Woods. It was not until 1973 that all the main currencies were floating, and the lack of system worked successfully for a time. In 1990, though, 'TIME TO TETHER CURRENCIES' re-examined the situation.

> Economic historians will look back on the 1980s as the decade in which the experiment with floating currencies failed. The starkest evidence of this failure is not, as it might seem, the dollar's sharp rise in the early 1980s followed by its equally spectacular fall after 1985. Those who advocated the move to floating rates through the 1960s and early 1970s – including, it should be said, this newspaper – did so precisely because they wanted exchange rates to shift. The price of a currency, on that view, should be free to act as a balancing mechanism: it ought to move about so that other things (wages, workers, productive capacity) would not need to. By themselves, the ups and downs of the major currencies during the 1980s settle nothing.

What mattered was that these swings had increased rather than reduced economic volatility, which in turn made currency changes self-defeating. 'Increasingly, exporters regard news from the foreign exchange market as noise rather than as a signal for action . . . By introducing inertia in this way, exchange-rate uncertainty not only acts as a tax on trade and foreign investment; it also leaves many firms, as currencies fluctuate, selling the same goods at widely different prices around the world. What might otherwise be a single global market is thus divided into national sub-markets. Competition is stifled.'[12]

In 1868 Bagehot wrote in *The Economist* a series of articles under the heading 'INTERNATIONAL COINAGE', published later in pamphlet form as 'A Universal Money'. Lugubriously predicting that 'Before long all Europe, save England, will have one money', he went on to explain why British conservatism about coinage should be overcome in favour of the adoption of a universal currency: whatever the differences between nations, 'commerce is everywhere identical; buying and selling, lending and borrowing, are alike all the world over, and all matters concerning them ought universally to be alike too . . . Ultimately the world will see one *code de commerce* and one money as the symbol of it.'[13] Simplification of trade was the aim. 'Commerce has very many and very natural difficulties. Distance of place, difference of speech, are irremovable impediments. We may conquer them, but we cannot remove them; nature made them, not man, and man cannot hope to foresee the time when they shall exist no longer. But the painful existence of real obstacles is the very reason why mankind should not invent artificial ones. We are encumbered in our commerce already; do not let us be more encumbered than we can help. Yet we voluntarily invent impediments if one set of us count in one fashion and the others count in different fashions.'[14] One-and-a-quarter centuries later, through *The Economist*, Pennant-Rea argued relentlessly for the same objective. The first step would be a single, low-inflation money for the European Community – 'a monnet'; the second, a single currency for big industrial countries – a 'phoenix'.

The Bagehot–Pennant-Rea link was strengthened in 1993. At the centenary luncheon, fifty years earlier, Montagu Norman had said that, as editor of *The Economist*, 'Bagehot more than any other single individual promoted and directed' the transformation of the Bank of England 'from being one commercial institution among others to its position as a central bank operating as a public institution with a unique function'. Through *The Economist*, Rupert Pennant-Rea, a Bank of England ex-employee, campaigned against weaknesses in the policies and organisation of the Bank and called for it to be made independent of government; indeed in January 1993 he felt obliged to publish a full-page apology for an allegation that the Bank had been involved in a conspiracy to 'hush up' a particular aspect of the Blue Arrow affair and that the National Westminster Bank (whose chairman is an *Economist* trustee) had attempted a 'whitewash'.*[15] That same week, in the year of the paper's sesquicentenary, he was appointed the Bank of England's deputy governor. In view of the government's opposition to independence for the Bank, this was a somewhat unexpected appointment. One explanation offered in the press was that the Prime Minister's policy unit was headed by Sarah Hogg, under whom Pennant-Rea had worked when he first joined the *Economist* staff, and that the government's main economic priority was the reduction of inflation: Robin Hood had been despatched to purify the Sheriff of Nottingham's council.

The week after his appointment to the Bank, Pennant-Rea faced the problem of what his own paper should say about the appointments of himself and of his predecessor and future boss, Eddie George. The report on 'THE BANK'S NEW BROOMS' described George, the new governor, as 'a shrewd and respected career central banker', but pointed out that the Bank had been

*See below, p.714.

under severe criticism for 'its performance as supervisor of Britain's banking system. Mr George was not directly involved in supervision but, as deputy governor, he supervised those who were.' All that was said about Pennant-Rea was: 'Perhaps because Mr George was seen as so much the insider, the government appointed an outsider to the deputy's job. Rupert Pennant-Rea, editor of *The Economist* for the past seven years, will return in July to the Bank, where he worked as an economist for four years in the mid-1970s.'[16]

In the 1943 centenary issue, Donald Tyerman summarised what brought about changes in *Economist* thinking: 'The 1931 crisis, the collapse of the gold standard, the Great Depression and the recovery under managed and cheap money blew away many cobwebs. *The Economist* was compelled, like many others, when faced by the problems of pre-war and war economics, to evolve a fresh monetary policy, based on a grasp of realities and an understanding of new techniques.' Progress was unsteady. Wartime experience had changed Layton, as it had changed Keynes, Salter, Stamp and those other young economists who proved highly successful in the civil service: all of them, to a greater or lesser extent, came to see a role for government in industry. How best to exercise this power was one of Layton's key concerns. He was, wrote his biographer, 'a leading member of the group of Liberal radicals who exercised a major influence on public opinion in the interwar years'.

> It is difficult to find a parallel in other times to this tightly knit group, members of which met each other constantly in Whitehall, in the Westminster lobbies, in clubs, in Fleet Street, the City and at the ancient universities. Layton, Keynes, Hubert Henderson and Dennis Robertson, all Cambridge economists, were at the centre of this network whose members included such remarkable ex-civil servants as William Beveridge, Josiah Stamp and Arthur Salter, businessmen with a strong social conscience such as Ernest Simon and Seebohm Rowntree, bankers such as R.H. Brand of Lazards, political thinkers such as Gilbert Murray, Graham Wallace and Ramsay Muir and idealistic politicians such as Philip Noel-Baker, Charles Masterman and Philip Kerr.
>
> The views of this remarkable group of people sometimes conflicted but more often they reinforced each other in their attempts to work out more rational and humane policies, both in home and overseas affairs.[17]

Layton's major contribution to this process was in putting together the huge Liberal Yellow Book, *Britain's Industrial Future*, an investigation into British industry intellectually driven by Keynes, which called for state intervention on a wide scale. Published in 1928, it fell flat. Complex, dense and here and there disturbingly novel, it repelled the press; its only important favourable review was in *The Economist*. Its strengths and weakness reflected Layton's. Few others would have had the patience to construct it out of what Keynes described as 'Liberal blather', yet most people would have jibbed at including so much stodge. '[It] has had rather a bad press,' Keynes told his wife, 'but I daresay it deserves it. Long-winded, speaking when it has nothing to say, as well as when it has, droning at intervals "Liberals, Liberals all are we, gallant-hearted Liberals." It would have been so much better at half the length splashing only what is new and interesting and important.' But to H.G. Wells he described it as 'a pretty serious effort to make a list of the things in the politico-industrial sphere which are practicable and sensible. It may therefore have a good deal of influence on future political programmes, whether or not there is a Liberal Party to put the matter through.'[18]

Politicians largely ignored the Yellow Book until, in mid-1935, the young, dissident Tory MP, Harold Macmillan, incorporated many of its ideas in *The Next Five Years*, produced with the help of Layton and Seebohm Rowntree. In 1936, in *The General Theory of Employment, Interest and Money*, Keynes produced the intellectual underpinning which was to bring about a sea-change in economic thinking: during and after the next war, Keynesianism became the new all-party orthodoxy.

What is Keynesianism? There is still no agreement. In December 1992, with Keynesianism coming rapidly back into fashion, 'THE SEARCH FOR KEYNES', making much of his inconsistencies, questioned whether Keynes was really a Keynesian.[19] An irritated economist, Professor Don Patinkin, was permitted to respond with a signed article in which he attacked the left and right for making common cause to deny that 'today's mainstream Keynesians are the legitimate heirs of the Master's policy views. In this way, the "zealous Keynesians" on the left are able to claim Keynes's support for their radical view that the problems of the capitalist system are so fundamental that they cannot be solved by the fiscal policy advocated by mainstream Keynesians. And the extreme conservatives on the right can claim Keynes's support for their view that opposes this policy because they regard it as endowing the government with too much discretionary power.'[20] Keynes's most recent biographer, describing the theological war between economists that began with the publication of the *General Theory*, says that much of the complexity of the doctrine was lost: the 'two things which survived were the idea that, for one reason or another, unmanaged capitalist economies were liable to collapse into slumps, and an efficient machine for action [was] waiting to be used when rulers were ready'.[21]

The *General Theory* was not easy and Layton avoided it. Taking issue with Keynes's popular articles was one thing; grappling with his dense and difficult polemic was another. He handed the job of reviewing the book to the Cambridge economist, Austin Robinson, who wrote many years later to Layton's biographer about the episode. Layton 'was so able and in a way one of the early creators of quantitative economics. But he was at the same time curiously anti-intellectual.'

> One of my most vivid memories of crossing swords with him was over the review in the *Economist* of Keynes's *General Theory*. He and Geoffrey Crowther (who was potentially more able but in practice very obstinate and anti-intellectual) were terrified of seeming to praise the *General Theory* or to say that it was important. They not only made me sign the review when the *Economist* normally published unsigned reviews.* They also cut out, without my agreement, the final paragraph in which I summed up the book. I never quite forgave Geoffrey Crowther and I still think that Layton ought to have had a little more perception and courage. He was a great man but he had rather severe limitations.[22]

Layton's caution does not surprise: nor should Crowther's. When the *General Theory* came out he was only 29 years old and hoping in due course to become Layton's successor; it was not a time to risk his reputation on a book which was wrinkling the foreheads of the greatest living economists. At the time it was unclear how long Layton would continue in the job. His editorship had been under attack from early in the 1930s on two counts: the scale of his other activities and the emphasis he gave to politics.

If not quite an absentee editor, Layton, like Wilson, Bagehot and Palgrave, was never full-time. Even in his most assiduous period, he was away quite frequently in Europe or America on various kinds of public service; early in 1929 he visited India as part of his work for the Simon Commission. And,

---

*Graham Hutton, however, thought they asked Robinson to sign – or rather, initial – because he was a colleague of Keynes's. In the modern *Economist*, reviews are always signed when the book's author is a member of staff.

from taking up less than an hour or so a day in 1927, the *Daily News* had rapidly become a major preoccupation. Layton was much involved in negotiations for its merger in January 1928 with the *Westminster Gazette* and in 1930 with the *Daily Chronicle*, bringing into being in 1930 the *News Chronicle*, of which he became chairman and editor-in-chief. Henceforward, he appeared at *The Economist* usually only for an editorial meeting on Monday, a check-up on Wednesday and to read the proofs on Thursday in the late afternoon and evening.

Once the process of buying *The Economist* was well under way, Layton had made a number of changes to enable the machine to run more efficiently. The first step was to move the office in the spring of 1928 from Arundel Street to premises opposite the *Daily News* in Bouverie Street, rented from the *News of the World*. By the standards to which the staff were accustomed, the new premises, consisting of 23 rooms, were palatial, although some of the space was sublet both to a publishing enterprise called the London General Press Ltd,* run by Gilbert Layton and Leonard Reid, and for a short period, to Hartley Withers. Net rent, lighting and fuel stayed at around £17 per week.

The accommodation has been variously described as 'dreary', 'grubby' and a 'mucky spot' that deserved to be bombed. 'The rooms were all along one corridor', remembered H.V. Hodson. 'It began with a couple of rooms into which I hardly ever penetrated which were occupied by Gilbert Layton who was the manager and his staff, then there was a sort of cubby hole where a famous character called Mr Chapman dwelt. Then behind him was the editor's office, which was a respectable size with a small office for the assistant editor who was Leonard Reid. Then there was a sort of general editorial office which was occupied by everybody else . . . Then opposite across the corridor was a boardroom where we had meetings, where anybody who

*Among the London General Press's activities was the publication of pamphlets, then a popular product. Examples include Walter Layton, 'The Economic Situation of Great Britain' (a translation and reprint of his response in the *Revue de Paris* to a critical view of Britain by a German); Nicholas Davenport, 'The Price of Tin: the problem of stabilisation' (with preface by Layton); P.E. Gourju and Hargreaves Parkinson, 'The Rubber Crisis'; and R.A. Lehfeldt, Professor of Economics, South African School of Mines and Technology, 'Controlling the Output of Gold' (with preface by Dr Schacht). *The Economist* often republished supplements or series as pamphlets. Examples include Sir Henry Strakosch, 'Monetary Stability and the Gold Standard' (1928); G.D. Rodeling, 'A British Index of National Prosperity, 1920–1927' (with foreword by Sir Josiah Stamp); and (anonymously) a 1942 series, 'The Reform of Accounts', and a 1944 series, 'The Principles of Trade'.

wanted to be quiet could get away and write, because it wasn't usually occupied.'

In June 1928 Gilbert Layton had been transferred from editorial to become general manager, taking over from Kirk. The folklore relayed to Reggie Forty, who joined in 1936, was that the transfer followed on Kirk's refusal to answer a summons from the editor until he had finished his tea; Kirk replaced Mike Flood (who retired) as advertising manager. Otherwise the London business staff stayed the same. In New York there was R.S. Farley, who was to stay in charge of advertising until 1954 and of subscriptions until 1959.

On the editorial side there was a considerable influx of talent. The approaches from Parkinson and Vallance had 'confirmed the opinion I had formed . . .', wrote Layton in the 1960s, 'that there would be little difficulty in persuading young men to join the staff as it was a splendid means of establishing contacts with all branches of City life'.

> I had myself discovered service on the paper to be a form of subsidised research to young men anxious to learn about affairs and to have the opportunity of carrying out some piece of economic research. The editor of *The Economist*, in fact, has the pick of the market. For example, Harry Hodson [Fellow of All Souls, later editor of the *Sunday Times*], who had already been working on figures of British investments overseas, came on to the staff with a view to completing a university thesis. The Deputy Governor of the Bank of England, Sir Humphrey Mynors . . . came in 1926 to help me in preparing the documentation for the World Economic Conference of 1927.

He omitted Lionel Robbins, later a distinguished economist, for a time a director of *The Economist* and always its great friend, who had come in 1924, two mornings a week, to read German newspapers for industrial information. 'I don't think I was much good at this – to be a good industrial journalist involves a degree of training and experience I had not had at that time. But it broadened my basis of knowledge in the applied field, made me much more aware of continental economic life than I otherwise should have been, and confronted me with problems of concise exposition with which the habits of academic life might have left me unacquainted.'[23] Henry Brooke, later to acquire fame as a Conservative Home Secretary, was there in the late 1920s; he was to be yet another ex-*Economist* Financial Secretary to the Treasury.

Layton had in fact adopted Hirst's recruitment policy, which had two essential elements: flexibility and a bias towards the academically-gifted young. Withers had applied this principle only once, when he took on Gerald Shove, Layton's ex-pupil and later Economics Fellow of King's, who stayed only a few months. Layton's recruits were numerous: part-time, full-time, temporary and permanent. They included David Bensusan-Butt, a student of Keynes's and the compiler of the index to the *General Theory*, later a Treasury mandarin, Brian Reddaway, later Professor of Political Economy in Cambridge, and Layton's daughter Margaret, an economist, who of his seven children was intellectually most like him.

Although there was some cross-over, editorial was essentially split in two, the general – if unstated – perception being then, as now, that politics was more cerebral than business. When Gilbert Layton was transferred to management, Hargreaves Parkinson, head of the Intelligence Branch, had become City editor and his place had been taken by a statistician, Walter Hill, who had come to *The Economist* in the first place in 1928 to do research work on company balance sheets. 'A keen young fellow who deserves to get forward', recorded Parkinson in the 1930s. 'He was "a wizard", said Graham Hutton. 'If he couldn't dig up at least some quotable and measured fact nobody else could.' Hill's assistant, Diana Rhodes (later by Lee Bolton), was a capable administrator and statistician, who left early in the 1930s, but was to return during the war.

Parkinson was short, red-faced and round, an unpretentious lover of books, cinema and music, equally enjoying Surtees's Jorrocks, Robert Louis Stevenson and Shakespeare, Beethoven and musical comedy: he was a solid, responsible and kindly middle-brow, middle-class family man. His largely factual diaries record a blameless life of intensely hard work, contentment at home, enjoyment of friends and occasional diversions and holidays. Yet they also show a professional life centred round financial journalism in a much more single-minded way than would be common on today's *Economist*. His regular lunch companions – often at the Reform Club – were colleagues on the paper, journalists like Collin Brooks, Harold Cowan and Oscar Hobson and good sources of information on gold, rubber, tea and any other commodities dear to the wallets of his readers. His circle respected and greatly liked him. Oscar Hobson, perhaps the most eminent financial journalist of his day, who fell out with Brendan Bracken and gave up the editorship of the *Financial News* in 1934, was happy to act as Parkinson's holiday relief on *The Economist*.

Contemporaries admired Parkinson for his hard work, dedication, absolute integrity and decency, but no one ever accused him of having flair. As a friend wrote after his death, 'he rarely sparkled: his quality was not brilliance; he was more of a steady plodder, but he had remarkable staying power and shrewdness; and patience and perseverance usually got him where he wanted'. Lionel Robbins shared a room with him, and, coming from a background of high theory, was interested 'to meet a down-to-earth chap who told me the way the world actually ran in his particular sector' of City and Stock Exchange: 'what he didn't know in those days about that side of the work of financial journalists, probably wasn't worth knowing'. He always, said Bensusan-Butt, knew 'what was happening to zinc'. Yet, as Crowther put it in *The Economist*'s very brief obituary: 'His service to the profession – and it was a great one – was to raise comment on investment matters from the level of Throgmorton Street tipstering to that of close and reasoned analysis.'[24] In that he was part of the team of friends and colleagues like Collin Brooks, Richard Fry, Oscar Hobson, Harold Wincott and the other participants in Reform Club discussions, who were in the forefront of cleaning up financial journalism in the 1930s.

From 1933 Parkinson had two jobs, combining his *Economist* work with being 'Lex' on the *Financial News*: 'Under the new conditions, it is clear that my motto will be the actor's "Never Dry Up"', he recorded early on in this arrangement. 'I dictated this morning part of an Economist leader, a Lex note, and an Economist note.'

> *9 February 1933* Thursday, under the new regime, is a bit of a brute. It is necessary to stick grimly to it, through morning and afternoon, and even so, the last hour at the 'Financial News' office tends to drag. Most of those fellows have only come on in the afternoon (working 1pm till midnight) and are full of pep. Still, there is a sort of pleasure in it. It is darned interesting, full and vivid and I definitely like it. The day finished with a poached egg at a Lyons and an hour or two at the 'Economist' printing works, seeing that paper through.

Parkinson's helpers included Chapman, who did all the statistical donkey-work, and Nicky Davenport, who had gone from full to part-time in January

1932. Davenport was to make a great deal of money in his main profession of stockbroking, and to make his journalistic reputation by writing a witty City column for the *New Statesman* under the pseudonym of 'Toreador'. 'He was', observed Hutton unchallengeably, 'the only man I know in any country as an economist who got his higher degree at Oxford on the pseudo-Isidorian decretals.' Waggish and ready for amusing diversion, he was, for example, the originator of a notion that spouses should be leased for a fixed period. Parkinson liked Davenport, as he liked almost everyone, but he features in the diaries as a frequent problem because of his unpunctuality and unpredictability. (Chapman reported that 'the presentation of his manuscript was calculated to break the heart of the printer'.) For instance:

> *Tuesday 7 November, 1933* – Davenport is writing the Economist leader this week, but I am not altogether convinced of his orthodoxy on the 'Fixed Terms' question. So I began the dictation this morning of a leader on Artificial Silk Companies as a second story in case he is late with his copy as usual and it isn't good enough . . .
>
> *Thursday 9* – The crisis I foresaw over Davenport's leading article matured this morning. I didn't like the article, nor did the Editor, so we'll put in my Rayon leader instead.

In October 1933 the over-worked Parkinson prevailed upon Layton to agree to his recruiting a replacement for his assistant, Paul Winterton, who had gone to the *News Chronicle*. The advertisement at the bottom of one of the Stock Exchange pages was appropriately anonymous:

> WELL-KNOWN WEEKLY NEWSPAPER
> requires University Graduate, under 25, with
> first-class scholastic record, literary ability, and
> specialised training in economics and (preferably)
> finance. Good prospects for suitable man.
> Apply, stating age, qualifications and recent
> experience (with copies only of testimonials), to –
> BOX 24, '*The Economist*,' 8, Bouverie St., London, E.C.4[25]

Applicants included nine holders of firsts from Cambridge and London, of whom the shortlist, at least, were asked to provide a sample piece on a choice of subjects. Roland Bird chose commercial motors, and used his experience as editor of a college magazine to good effect: 'I thought it needed some figures to go with it . . . and counted very carefully the number of characters in a column of *The Economist* – what the printers call "ems". Allowed, very cleverly, too, I thought, for the width that the rules would take in the table'. Bird succeeded in fitting in details of trading profits and earnings and yields on shares for five companies: laying out comparisons between companies like this was a novelty and 'obviously made a great hit with Hargreaves Parkinson'. Bird was then interviewed by Hutton and Parkinson, who recommended him in preference to the other shortlisted candidate, Otto Clarke, who went to the *Financial News* instead and later to the Treasury, of which he became permanent secretary. Bird, recorded Parkinson, was 'a man who seems almost too good to be true, so excellent are his qualifications'. The editor had to see him and approve: Roland Bird's recollection of the interview is a reminder that Layton lived his intensely public life with the handicaps of extreme shyness and inarticulateness.

> Hargreaves Parkinson shepherded me into his office. (Walter was always a great messer with paper . . . always fingering papers and rustling them about.) We went in. I expected this great man, Walter Layton, to be a dynamic character. There he was taking no notice of anything and fidgeting about with these papers; it was most embarrassing. Nothing happened for three minutes or so. I began to think we ought to back out. Eventually Hargreaves Parkinson said: 'This is Bird who we would like to take on as Stock Exchange assistant.' This didn't make much impression and there was another awkward pause. At the end of it all he uttered the remarkable words: 'Well, yes. I suppose so.'

(Layton's style was often compared to that of Clement Attlee. Geoffrey Crowther reported that when Attlee was Prime Minister, his Cabinet colleague Sir Stafford Cripps took Edwin (later Lord) Plowden to Downing Street on his appointment as government economic adviser. Cripps said: 'I have brought Mr Plowden to see you, Prime Minister.' After a long silence Attlee looked up and enquired: 'Have you seen any cricket recently?')

Bird's early life bears a close resemblance to a C.P. Snow novel. He had a first from the London School of Economics, which he had acquired the hard way. Born in 1908, into a poor background, he had left school at 16 and joined the accounts department of a Northampton shoe factory. His interest in economics was sparked off by reading Keynes, particularly his *Economic Consequences of the Peace*. The principal of the local technical school which he attended part-time encouraged him to sit in 1927 an economics examination for the Royal Society of Arts, for which he won a silver medal and an Exhibition to the LSE. The manager of the factory prevailed upon one of its owners to give Bird a job in his London accountancy firm, so he worked during the day, attended the LSE in the evenings and studied at weekends. The LSE, with which *The Economist* has had close personal links since the 1920s, was, in Bird's view, 'an absolutely magnificent place'. Evening students were given the same courses as their full-time counterparts. 'There were crowds of people who came from City and business and so on' and were treated by the staff 'with great consideration'. The staff in Bird's time included Lionel Robbins, George Schwarz (a regular *Economist* contributor of Gibb-like flights of fancy), T.E. Gregory and Dennis Robertson.

Bird went to see Robbins to learn his examination results.

> He said, 'You will not be surprised, my dear Bird,' in his rather orotund way, 'to learn that you have achieved a first.' I said, 'I think there must be some mistake somewhere.' 'Oh, but my dear Bird, I've thought for some time that the matter admitted of no doubt'.

('He was one of a crop of extraordinarily distinguished people in 1931 or 1932', Robbins recalled many years later, 'in which, with a comparatively small economics department, we had something like half-a-dozen firsts. Roland spoke at classes with authority about the goings on in the City; we hadn't anything to teach him there. We sent a man to teach him about the more abstract parts of economic theory but he gobbled them up and was then, as now, extremely lucid in writing.' He gained 'a very distinguished first'.)

Before Bird actually joined, not only had *The Economist* published his commercial motors piece, but it had done so under a new section that he had inspired: 'Company Notes' was a spin off from 'Investment Notes' which examined industries across the board. Bird was to spend the rest of his working life with *The Economist*, becoming deputy editor and, for a brief crisis period, managing director. Parkinson recorded his early progress.

> *Thursday 23 November 1933* – Even on his first Press Day I found my new man useful. He ought to do very well.
> *Tuesday 28 November* – Chapman down with bad chill and loss of voice. This is only Bird's second week here, and we have the Actuaries Index to do.

Fortunately, he looks like coming up trumps . . . Am involved in argument with Davenport over his page corrections.

Thursday 30 November – Bird has done yeoman service this week.

Thursday 21 December – Everything ran two to three hours earlier today at The Economist. Once again I thank the chance that threw Bird my way for he is a good man.

Thursday 4 January 1934 – Bird now invaluable.

Monday, 22 January – Am taking Bird this week on some of my City 'walks'. Today to Scrymgeours where we went up to have tea with the partners.

Thursday 25 January – We are running good Stock Exchange sections in The Economist now. Bird being worth his weight in gold to me. With his help, Press Days are transformed.

Tuesday 13 March – Bird took me to lunch to celebrate his definitive contract with Economist.

Wednesday 2 May – The absence of Davenport as a writer of notes and leaders is noticeable, but less so than I should have expected. Bird is now a tower of strength. He did his second leader for us this week.

Thursday 30 August – Had a rare luxury this morning of a quarter-of-an-hour's talk with Bird on Brahms violin concerto – which, on a Thursday, is wonderful.

In 1930 Norman Crump had been appointed banking editor and from 1932 was shared with the *Banker*. It was through him that his brother-in-law, Harry Hodson, was brought on to the paper, where he combined writing on Commonwealth affairs and investment with playing chela and bag-carrier to Walter Layton's guru.

Crump was exceptionally knowledgeable about money. He could have become a top-flight financial journalist, one well-informed contemporary believed, but he drank too much. Crumpled, with a sergeant-major moustache, he was unpopular with some of his colleagues, who found him lazy, overbearing, bad-tempered and always convinced he was right. A man for facts and figures, not policy, he was good at his job 'in a rather hard-boiled Fleet Street way', was a stickler for accuracy and was respected and trusted in the City; he was an early editor of the *Lloyds Bank Review*. He was kind to young David Bensusan-Butt, and took him on his weekly tour of the City, which would include one of the big five discount houses and the Bank of England.

Visiting the Bank of England used to be fun because we would go up in some grand silverplated lift, to go and see the Chief Cashier or somebody like that. We would enter some vast room in which some ten-foot man seated behind a fifty-foot desk would bow us to huge armchairs; it was usually something splendid in Sheraton round a very beautiful table. We would be given cups of tea and then he would say, 'Heard this one?' and tell some story of unspeakable indecency. Crump would say, 'No, but have you heard this one?' and produce another, then they'd both look at me, but I never knew stories of that or any other kind. Then the great man would say, 'Rates a bit soggy this week', or something like that, and then we'd say, 'Ah, mmm, yes, may not last' – something like that. Whereupon we would go and this small exchange of gnomic City utterances would become a column and a half of learned commentary on the state of the money market by the evening. But I hadn't a clue what was going on!

Bensusan-Butt described the contribution of the 'literate office boy', 'the wandering junior', who would be assigned some of the less interesting notes of the week. 'I remember this horrid feeling of being told to do a note of the week on something you knew damn all about. You went to their competent library and you looked up their previous notes on the subject and you wrote something on the first principles. And when you saw it in print it looked awfully solid, as if you really knew all about the subject. And I used to have a little private nightmare of somebody who really did know about the subject reading this thing and thinking: "Oh, I didn't think it was like that, but if *The Economist* say so, I suppose it must be." And feeling that there was something fraudulent about it. I think if one has that sort of qualm one is not a journalist.' The only long piece he remembered writing was one about the patent medicine industry. 'I still remember having included the phrase: "Whereas for all the public knows it might have been made of grass". And there was an extra line to get in and Norman Crump crossed out "made of grass" and put "might have been made of that comestible which so pleased Nebuchadnezzar". I was furious but it got him his extra line neatly fitted.'

In the pre-computer era, and one when *The Economist* was a key source of statistics, the business side required a ferocious attention to figures that made it extremely unattractive to many. Nor in the social climate of inter-war Britain was business or finance a glamorous subject of study; to some of the gilded youth on the political side, the business journalists, like the managerial staff, seemed barely to exist. 'Hutton and I were the only full-time members of the staff,' wrote Jay in his autobiography, 'apart from one statistician and those in the stock exchange section.'[26] With expansion and an increasing turn-over of staff, Chapman's notion of the staff as a small happy family was ceasing to have much basis in reality. The assistant editor, Leonard Reid, who after 18 years on the staff became first a part-timer and then went to the *Daily Telegraph*, was a substantial loss, but Vallance took his place with such success that by 1932 Sir Henry Strakosch, chairman of the board, wanted him to take over as editor.

Under the new proprietorship, Layton had to suffer editorial interference in a way that would have been unthinkable under the dear old ladies, and it came, not as might have been expected, from Brendan Bracken, who in this area behaved impeccably, but from Layton's most important backer, Henry Strakosch, chairman of the *Economist* board. When the board came into existence in 1929, it had five members. Two were *Financial News* nominees. Major-General Guy Payan Dawnay, managing director of Bracken's merchant bankers, Dawnay Day, described by T.E. Lawrence as 'the least professional of soldiers, a banker who read Greek history',[27] remained until 1947 and made little impact and no trouble. He was described by a colleague as 'an awfully nice man of absolute integrity', one of that breed who get added to boards to add a tone of decency and uprightness and are not required to contribute anything else.[28] Bracken himself was managing director until he went into government in 1941; he returned in 1947 for another eight years. Charles Garrett Ponsonby Moore, a viscount, and from 1957 Earl of Drogheda, took Bracken's place and job while he was away, but stayed as a full board member until 1985 (serving as an alternate from 1986 to 1989). Compton Mackenzie described Guy Dawnay as 'a fragile figure with something of an exquisitely fashioned porcelain in the finely chiselled features of his small face',[29] which strangely enough is a description that fits Moore brilliantly. But there was nothing fragile about the manner in which he conducted his highly successful career at *The Economist* and as Bracken's great ally in the *FN/FT* world. He played up all the aristocratic camouflage of languidness and charm to conceal a devastating mixture of shrewdness and determination to get what he wanted. Feline, subtle and sometimes mischievous, he was one of the more effective board members, but he rarely exerted himself for *The Economist* in the way that he did for the *FT*, of which he was managing director for thirty years. An astute observer of men and brilliant at picking up useful information, through long and loyal service with the obsessively private Bracken he acquired a habit of discretion that added to his effectiveness but frustrated colleagues and historians alike.

The three directors nominated by the independent shareholders were Layton, Strakosch and Walter Runciman, who had to resign in 1931 when he became President of the Board of Trade. Harold Pearson, Viscount Cowdray (who had been commendably determined that a paper owned partly by financial institutions should have its editorial independence guaranteed), replaced Runciman but died within two years. (Under the management of his son, Pearson's took over the *Financial Times* and hence its half-share in *The Economist*). In turn Cowdray was replaced by Eric Gibb, who stayed on for thirty years. Even by the 1940s he was 'sleepy', and Lionel Robbins, who joined in 1960, remembered him as 'an aged man . . . who didn't really take any part', to whom Crowther was very kind and of whom he said: 'Oh, I wouldn't do anything which upset poor Gibb's self-respect' – a typical example of Crowther's decency as well as of one of his inadequacies as chairman.

From the outset the composition of the board had major deficiencies, and indeed, despite strenuous recent efforts to broaden its membership, it has for most of its existence tended towards the ineffectual. Drogheda remembered it during the war as a very perfunctory, rubber-stamping affair with the tremendously thorough Strakosch absorbed in tiny details.

There is certainly no doubt about Strakosch's commitment to the paper, though he took it to a level which caused problems for Layton. There have been five chairmen since 1929 – Strakosch, Layton, Crowther, Evelyn de Rothschild and John Harvey-Jones – and only Strakosch and Crowther have ever strayed over the boundary into editorial concerns, and Crowther very rarely. Strakosch posed problems in two ways: first, through a personal conflict of interest; and second, through his hostility to aspects of Layton's politics, to his non-*Economist* activities and to the balance of interests reflected in his paper.

In 1943, Crowther's *Economist* obituary of Strakosch, describing him 'as a shrewd and successful business man and as a practical economist of great sense and clarity', remarked that it was perhaps natural in the chairman of the Union Corporation that his chief interest should be in the monetary uses of gold, but 'what was less to be expected was his open mind and his lack of producer's bias'.[30]

That was true up to a point: Strakosch had a much wider vision than might have been expected of the chairman of a South African gold-mining company. During many years of public service he made a major contribution to the devising of the South African currency system, was heavily involved in Indian affairs and laboured long and hard with the League of Nations. But intellectually respectable though his views undoubtedly were, it was somewhat unfortunate that he liked to express them forcefully and at length in *The Economist*. Strakosch seems always to have signed his contributions (the most substantial was a supplement in July 1930 on 'Gold and the Price Level'), but this device could not wholly distance the paper from its chairman, and meanwhile Layton knew that Strakosch was keeping a sharp eye out for heretical tendencies in the paper. Hutton, who had known Strakosch through a Chatham House committee on the international gold problem, remembered how difficult it was then and at *The Economist* to tell whether Strakosch was seriously striving to be a detached analytical economist or was covertly plugging the Union Corporation and his colleagues on the Rand: his constant refrain was: 'just keep gold production up and all will be well'.

This was no more than a minor nuisance for a man of Layton's principles and standing. He dealt with it by publishing (signed) what Strakosch wanted published if it was reasonable to do so, while encouraging opponents to respond with critical letters. In Hutton's observation, Layton could on occasion say 'Look, Henry – that I cannot do and you wouldn't expect me to, would you?', and being slightly uncertain in British society Strakosch would say, 'Of course not!'

More disturbing were Strakosch's behind-the-scenes activities. Towards the end of 1932 he tried to persuade Vallance to take over from Layton. Vallance wrote at the end of December 1932 that 'in such lucid intervals as are vouchsafed between Christmas meals, I have been thinking a lot about the various points you raised in our talk the other night about the Economist. May I try to sum up the position as I see it?'

> The situation, I suggest, is dominated by the fact that in the past few years The Economist has become no longer, as it once was, a staid and colourless City weekly, made up largely of 'routine' articles, but a very definite 'organ of opinion' associated throughout the world with the name of an editor who is not so much a journalist as an 'international public man'. From that situation in which, you must admit, the Economist's prestige has enormously increased – three consequences seem to follow:-

(1) The loss to the Economist of Layton's name would be a grievous blow.

(2) With the other interests inseparable from his role in the world, Layton cannot be expected to bear responsibility for all the minutiae of editorship, but these are very important.

(3) With its widened scope and new types of fresh readers, The Economist will best succeed if it is the fruit of as many of the best minds as its limited resources can command.

Are not these three conditions in fact furnished by the 'Layton Plan'?

Strakosch had suggested that while it should remain 'Layton's paper', Vallance would be in charge and have the full editorial salary. 'I do not', said Vallance, 'think the public would understand the title you propose that I should have. To outsiders unfamiliar with Layton's and my relationship it would suggest an uncomfortable dyarchy, bad for the Economist's influence.' And it would mean that the paper would be either starved of sub-editorial help or crippled financially. 'I should be so submerged in detail that I could not feel sure of being able to maintain City political contacts, or keep the paper's policy alive & fresh, no matter how generously Layton contributed ideas and advice from above.' Surely, then, the 'Layton Plan' held the field, since it would ensure that *The Economist* retained Layton's influence and control along with Vallance's cooperation, would be properly manned 'as it has not been for some time', and could expand in the way which was necessary if it was to hold its increased circulation.

> There remains only your objection that the Economist should not be too closely associated with a daily paper whose views are supposed to be identified with those of a particular political party. But surely in practice, this is not material. The Economist is known in every country as a 'liberal' journal, and 'Liberalism' is now so indeterminate, unattached a thing that – to say nothing of the fact that Layton and I are both very jealous of the tradition of the Economist – I can see little danger of the News Chronicle being ever regarded again as a party organ – especially since you would hardly call Layton, its controller, a 'party' [man].

It would be foolish for the paper not to avail itself of the 'unique chance of building up a really strong team, and retaining, at its head, in Layton and myself, two people who work together perhaps unusually well, are equally devoted to the paper, and can contribute to it, together, what no other form of control could'.

Vallance copied out his letter and sent it to Layton with a note: 'Herewith letter sent today to H.S. With what you told me of L.C.'s views in mind, I slightly stiffened the last paragraph. I take it you will not disclose to H.S. that you have this copy.'[31] 'L.C.' was Laurence Cadbury, substantial *Economist* shareholder, who as chairman of Daily News Ltd, proprietors of the *News Chronicle*, meddled ceaselessly, but, like Strakosch, was right to think that Layton took on far too much.

Within three months, Vallance had become editor of the *News Chronicle*.[32] Given what rapidly emerged there about his politics and his personal predilections, Strakosch should have felt considerable relief that he had not taken over at *The Economist*. Vallance was not the first or last journalist to combine austere and high-minded principles with looseness of living: the difficulty was that he was particularly uncompromising on the first and unusually public in his pursuit of the second. Layton had wanted him to use the paper to help 'reinvigorate the Liberal inheritance' and also to present Yellow Book-type policies in such a way as to capture moderate Labour politicians. Vallance insisted that he 'should be free to run the paper as an independent radical organ – opposed, naturally, to revolutionary socialism but not tied to any of the groups which once formed the Liberal Party and – *a fortiori* – hostile to Toryism'. At a time when the Liberal Party was falling apart, that was an understandable position, and the objective Layton had set was, as Stephen Koss observed, 'a tightrope, impossible for Vallance or any other editor to walk'. Yet Vallance's conduct was dishonourable. A communist fellow-traveller, he despised liberalism, whereas Layton was liberal to his core. Vallance claimed that 'the spirit of philanthropic radicalism' that George Cadbury had declared in 1911 to be the soul of the *Chronicle* was now to be found in the Labour Party, and he 'castigated "the elderly Reform Club Whigs", whose "bitter hostility" threatened to swing the paper "unmistakably to the Right"'. And to Vallance, the right was fascism. 'I do not know how long we have before the Fascist Revolution', wrote the worried editor of the *New Statesman*, Kingsley Martin, in his diary in May 1934, 'or in what form it is coming . . . Graham Hutton told me that Vallance is talking about machine guns, and prophesying the Revolution before two years are out'.[33]

Vallance's real ambition for the liberal inheritance was to see it dead at the hands of the left rather than the right, and to outsiders that seemed clear. 'If Sir Walter Layton has taken the decision that the "News Chronicle" shall turn Socialist,' commented the *Evening Standard* in 1934, 'then his own position becomes extremely interesting, for he is also editor of the "Economist".'

> The 'Economist' is owned half by Financial Newspaper Proprietors Limited, and half by leading financiers, including Sir Henry Strakosch, and, it is believed, Rothschild and Cowdray interests. There can be, therefore, no prospect of the 'Economist' turning Socialist, so Sir Walter Layton will have to ride two horses. It is a feat to which he is accustomed.[34]

While in effect using a Liberal newspaper to work towards the socialist new dawn, Vallance was also using its premises to fulfill more immediate objectives. 'Tongues were set wagging by his debaucheries,' records Stephen Koss, 'which took place after working hours and left the premises littered with empty bottles and occasionally pieces of ladies' apparel. Years later, Collin Brooks [Hargreaves Parkinson's great friend] savoured "the story of the Aylmer Vallance episode at the *News Chronicle*, when the austere Quaker newspaper office became a veritable brothel". The editor and his companions were said to have fornicated "all over the place!! Even Arthur Cummings's sacred desk was violated." Such scandals were particularly shocking in Bouverie Street, where . . . the traditional atmosphere was Puritan as well as Radical.' What would Chapman have made of it all?

Late in 1935, Vallance went too far on both the sexual and political fronts. Layton coped surprisingly well with finding him having sexual intercourse in the office ('And they did not even stop when I came in', he reported as he left the scene), but Vallance's performance at Layton's election-night office party in November 1935 upset him more. On a catastrophic night for Liberals,* an inebriated Vallance engaged in 'vindictive applause' as each Liberal lost deposit was announced: Herbert Samuel's defeat gave him particular pleasure. Recognising his brilliance as an editor, Layton had been defending

---

*The Liberal Party was split three ways, between the Liberal National Party – the Simonites (led by Sir John Simon) – who supported the National Government; the Samuelites (led by Herbert Samuel), who had resigned from the National Government in 1933 when it became protectionist; and the Lloyd Georgites, who were Independent Liberals. In the general election of November 1935 the Liberal Nationals were unopposed by Conservatives: together they won 432 seats; the Samuelites won 17, the Lloyd Georgites 4 and Labour 154.

Vallance for a long time against a deluge of attacks, but he had gone too often beyond any reasonable limits. He was fired and spent the rest of his professional life as deputy editor at the *New Statesman*, where his warmth, irreverence and wicked humour enlivened left-wing circles. History does not record if Layton was ever told about Walter Hill's discovery of Vallance's greatest crime: when under pressure he sometimes fabricated *Economist* statistics. For the early 1930s, even the sacred Index Number is suspect.

Before Vallance had moved mainly to the *News Chronicle*, in the spring of 1933, the main part of the team about which he had written to Strakosch was in place. It consisted of Hutton and Jay, who were full-timers, and Crowther, who spent most of his time at the *News Chronicle*, and who had been the first of the trio to arrive.

CHAPTER XL:

The new men

ARE ECONOMISTS HUMAN?

By overwhelming majority vote, the answer would undoubtedly be No. Practitioners of the dismal science have long grown accustomed to the popular picture of themselves as thin, sad men wrapt in gloom and eloquent only in prescribing misery; they have learnt not to expect faces to light up when they come upon the stage . . . This is a matter of sorrow to them, for there is no body of men whose professional labours are more conscientiously, or consciously, directed to promoting the wealth and welfare of mankind. That they tend to be regarded as blue-nosed kill-joys must be the result of a great misunderstanding.[1] *Geoffrey Crowther, 1952*

Crowther's father was Professor of Agricultural Chemistry at Leeds University, the first person from a line of Yorkshire woollen manufacturers to go to university and a staunch Lloyd George Liberal. He married a qualified though non-practising teacher, the daughter of a wholesale grocer, and they had four children; Geoffrey, born in 1907, was the second child and eldest son. The family lived in an academic world and had academic expectations for their children; two acquired PhDs and one became a doctor. Signs of precocity in the young Geoffrey included corresponding in Esperanto with adults abroad and inventing games that revolved around the interpretation of maps and the mastering of train time-tables. Having failed to flourish at Leeds Grammar School (where he was bored) he won a scholarship to Oundle, where he shone both academically and in debate. Years later he re-read a paper he wrote as a schoolboy called 'Some recent experiments in governance' – a survey of various new constitutions that were being introduced after 1918 – and was greatly impressed: his exceptional ability to grasp the conceptual had already been apparent.

With two brothers also at Oundle, family financial problems made it desirable for Crowther to go on to university as early as possible. He was thought to be ready to win a languages scholarship but to need another year to win one in history, so, although he had hoped to read history at Trinity College, Cambridge, instead he read modern languages at Clare. His disappointment about Trinity evaporated as he found success on the Cambridge scene, where he became President of the Union, but after taking a first in Part I of the Tripos, he burned his notes and turned to economics. Evaluating him some time after his death, Donald Tyerman wrote:

> Spender said that the most impressive thing about Auden at Oxford was 'that, at such an early age, he was so confident and conscious a master of his situation.' Spender's journalist uncle said that Auden was 'a remarkably self-possessed young man.' Contemporaries of Geoffrey Crowther at Cambridge said the same of him. Crowther and Auden were different young men in different contexts. Crowther's self-awareness and self-confidence were not so much asserted as taken for granted. But men who did well enough in life after Cambridge were in despair when they saw how sure it seemed that he would succeed in whatever he chose to do.[2]

The war had robbed Cambridge of some of its best economists and not until the late 1920s did the subject again attract many bright undergraduates. Crowther was there just at the start of the period when a younger generation began to challenge aspects of the Marshallian economics which, under Professor Pigou, still dominated the Cambridge School: 'very clear, very systematic, but at the same time very rooted in the Marshall tradition – "it's all in Marshall"', said Austin Robinson.[3] Marshall, the greatest of the neo-classical economists, had built on the basic principles of the classical economists but tinkered with the detail; Wilson would have found heretical his rejection of the notion that a purely *laissez-faire* system would be to the equal benefit of all.

When Crowther was there, Cambridge offered a thorough grounding in traditional economics, but there were signs of the approaching revolution, what have been called the 'years of high theory', which would end in a schism in the 1930s. Crowther heard Keynes developing his monetary ideas in his lectures on 'The Theory of Money'; Keynes's total dismissal of *laissez-faire* was inherent in his writings; and the belief that government had an important role in industry was elaborated most practically in the Yellow Book, which was published while Crowther was at Cambridge. So Crowther, who had an excellent theoretical mind, was tackling a subject which in Cambridge was taught in a highly theoretical way and was just becoming highly contentious. In his Economics Tripos 'Crowther wrote the most remarkable papers', recalled Lionel Robbins, who with T.E. Gregory, the other external examiner, fought hard for Crowther to be awarded an upper-first-class degree. 'I remember arguing for an hour and reading aloud the questions and saying "What would you give a 1:1 to?" I think they had given a 1:1 to Barbara Wootton, but, being a woman, she was not allowed to take a degree in those days . . . Eventually they yielded and Geoffrey got a 1:1. They were so stupid about that. They felt that you had to reserve the 1:1 for an archangel or a woman who wouldn't be allowed to take her degree.' Crowther was given a Commonwealth Fund Fellowship in 1929 and went for a year to Yale; the following year, although nominally attached to Columbia University, he spent in Wall Street, so he experienced at first hand the after-effects of the Wall Street Crash. From 1931 he worked in a London merchant bank, undertook a special study of the Irish banking system and became an adviser on banking to the Irish government. Next year he married Peggy Worth, a clever woman from a Quaker family in Wilmington, Delaware, who had won a scholarship to Yale Law School, but who henceforward devoted herself to family life. Chapman remembered him sending from America a contribution on banking which Layton accepted. 'This seemed in some way to lead up to his joining the paper.' Sometime in the second half of 1932, Crowther went to work for Walter Layton.

Graham Hutton came in January 1933. Born in 1904, he went as a boarder to Christ's Hospital School and from there went straight into the old family import-export business. He spent as much time as possible abroad travelling and acquiring languages and at home studied part-time at the City of London College, where his mentors told him his head was too full of literature and language, ancient and modern, and despatched him to the class on economic theory. Like Roland Bird two years later, Hutton was encouraged to take the Royal Society of Arts examination in economics and he, too, won the silver medal and an exhibition to the LSE. His father guaranteed him £1 a week for life so that he would never starve, and he waved the family business goodbye in October 1925.

Seven years later Davenport introduced him to Vallance, who had been commissioned by Layton to recruit likely talent and who offered Hutton the new job of assistant and foreign editor, for which he was by now exceptionally well qualified. He had taken an outstanding double first in economics and sociology, and was now in his third year at the LSE as a Research Fellow and Tutor; he had been called to the Bar; he was widely travelled and fluent in several languages; perhaps most important of all, he had worked half-time at Chatham House since 1929 as the resident economist. His freelance writing included regular articles for the *New Statesman* and a book on *Nations and the Economic Crisis*. Adventurous, gregarious and radiating curiosity about almost everything, at only 28 he had an extensive network of contacts at home and abroad. He already knew Keynes, Montagu Norman and other major figures in the world of economics and money as well as Layton, Strakosch, Toynbee, Davenport and others in the *Economist* circle. The General Strike had made Hutton a socialist, so he went for advice to the Professor of Politics at LSE, the far-left Harold Laski, who said, "'Don't hesitate for a minute." I said, "But they are liberals." He said, "It will do you all the good in the world.'"

Douglas Jay came a few months later. The same age as Crowther, he had arrived by the intensely intellectual route of Winchester, New College Scholar and All Souls. Winchester produces the most consistently strange products of the whole public school system: 'Well, you see, he's a Wyke-hamist', is a sufficient explanation of odd behaviour. Traditionally, Wyke-hamists are quirky, industrious, intellectually arrogant and lacking in doubt: Jay was no exception. Having taken a first in Greats (basically, classical studies) at Oxford, he had taught himself economics with the help of some advice from Lionel Robbins, and in 1930 won election to the most coveted of all intellectual prizes, an All Souls Fellowship, on the basis of his paper on 'political economy'. At All Souls at weekends he talked economics with Hubert Henderson and Arthur Salter and reviewed economics for the *Times Literary Supplement* and *The Times*, for which, during the week, he worked as a sub-editor. 'Meticulous care was then exercised by Times sub-editors', he remembered, 'not merely to abbreviate down to the bone, to check every fact, date and spelling, but to exorcize every form of grammatical or linguistic solecism.' His *bête noire* was Stephenson, the *Times* correspondent in Ottawa, who used to send telegrams of several feet which had to be edited down to a couple of inches. Bored, preoccupied with the deepening depression as well as with the rise of the Nazis, he was in the mood for a change of job when an

All Souls colleague intervened. Reggie Harris, a classicist and a leader-writer on both *The Economist* and *The Times*, walked into the sub-editors' room at Printing House Square one evening and asked if Jay felt that

> Shades of the Printing House begin to close
> About the growing boy.*

And on receiving a positive reply, Harris arranged with Layton to give Jay a job. 'On my first morning at the *Economist*, full of enthusiasm for the new venture, I found I was regarded as an expert on overseas news and politics, and the first task I was given was to edit a telegram from their Ottawa correspondent. It was from Stephenson, and was three feet long.'

Graham Hutton had been recruited to replace Vallance. 'Lunched with Hutton, the new man who will Assistant-Edit the front of the paper, now that Vallance is going mainly to the "News Chronicle"', recorded Parkinson. 'Very nice fellow', he concluded a few days later. 'I think though he takes things seriously. That is natural when one is starting at the "Economist".'

By *Economist* editorial standards Hutton was highly paid. In November 1935, for example, his annual salary was £900, Walter Hill and Douglas Jay received £500, Roland Bird £400 and Chapman, in his 38th year of service, £325. Crowther's half-time salary was £350, Crump's £450 and Walter Layton's £800. By that time Parkinson was a full-time associate editor earning £1,750, and, like Walter Layton, he had a share in the profits. Graham Hutton also had the unusual arrangement of a commission on circulation, which for 1935 amounted to £56.

Hutton's five years on *The Economist* were to be professionally 'the most creative and happiest and most constructive years' of his life. He shared with Chapman that sense of family that was no longer universally felt, though he was thinking in terms of journalists only: the cleavage between them and non-editorial staff was by now almost total. (In 1984 he wrote to thank Andrew Knight for a lunch (attended by Roland Bird and Douglas Jay) held at *The Economist* to celebrate his eightieth birthday: 'You and your colleagues carry on a very odd sense of membership in a creative (and critical!) family

---

*From Wordsworth's 'Intimations of Immortality':

Shades of the prison-house begin to close
  Upon the growing boy,
But he beholds the light, and whence it flows,
  He sees it in his joy.

which I still share; indefinable but deep and heart-warming.') It was typical of his impulsive enthusiasm that within two months of joining the paper he had become its largest staff shareholder.*

For that 1930s sense of family Hutton gave absolute credit to Walter Layton. For the young men Layton was a greatly admired headmaster. When Jay was sentenced to write every week on the Reichstag fire trial, his weekly report was referred to as 'Douglas's lines'. 'One always felt that one wasn't being chastised: one was being brought up in the way one should go.'

The paper's weekly cycle began with the after-lunch Monday editorial meeting, an innovation of Layton's, attended by the editorial staff, more often than not by Arnold Toynbee, Vallance, Harry Hodson and, by invitation, other outside contributors like Nicholas Davenport. In March 1933, the month when Hutton and Jay both arrived, Parkinson recorded: 'Our meeting at the Economist this afternoon produced a vigorous and entertaining discussion. The numbers are growing, for the array of writers on the general side of the paper is becoming formidable. Still, the discussions are particularly interesting.' In June: 'An entertaining and informative Economist meeting today.' In October: 'A long Economist meeting – they always are nowadays', and in November: 'A long "Economist" meeting (they *do* talk).'

At editorial meetings Layton was essentially a chairman. He presided 'scrupulously', seeing that matters were discussed in a logical order and that decisions were taken about who should write what and by when. He took little part in actual discussion on the political issues, but, said Hutton, 'he would say, "That's all right" or "Geoffrey had better do that"'. He understood 'pretty well what capacities we all had', and that determined whom he chose to do what. Leaders would be assigned according to areas of particular expertise or interest: Crowther, for instance, was the main writer on economics and on America. Layton did not often write leaders himself: as William Rathbone Greg had been to James Wilson, so Geoffrey Crowther was to Walter Layton. Layton would dictate the main points of an article and

---

*The following bought the special staff shares in 1929: Brooke 200, Crump 50, Hodson 50, Parkinson, 100 and Reid 1,000 (all described as 'Journalist'); Chapman ('Statistician') 100; Gilbert Layton ('Manager') 250; Kirk and Whitcomb ('Advt Manager') 250 each and H.R. Bernard ('Advt Canvasser') 500; Doris Ellen (aka Diana) Rhodes, 200, Pearl Wallace 25 and Miss E.M. Wadsworth 25 (all described as 'Spinster'). Hutton acquired 525 and Jay 50 in 1933; Crowther 50, Hill 25 and Ernest Stanley Tucker, a newcomer, 50. Bird bought his first 50 in 1938.

Crowther would produce the polished piece. Hutton's passion was Central Europe; he had to be held back from writing weekly at great length about Hungary. Vallance might contribute a leader every week or so, and Crowther wrote usually one leader a fortnight and a note or two every week, but, like Layton and Vallance, he gave more of his attention to the *News Chronicle*. Hutton and Jay were the front-of-the-paper workhorses, required to write on anything and everything. Hutton recalled a classic occasion. Searching for a subject to fill a gap, a participant in an editorial meeting said idly: 'It's the beginning of the oyster season; we could write something about that', and the job was handed over to a protesting Douglas Jay. The result was a quintessential *Economist* clever-young-man's piece. Starting on Monday from a position of total ignorance, and with much other writing as well as sub-editing to do, Jay produced an authoritative amalgam of elegantly merged fact, opinion and mandarin wit, which also showed the sheer intellectual pleasure he took in economics and the effortless quality of his writing.

In '... THOSE OF THE LARGEST SIZE', he used the oyster industry as a prime example of the new *Economist* thinking. It was an industry that needed more government control to save it from extinction. 'Fortunately, oysters are a luxury; and we need not accordingly shed too many walrus tears over the disorganisation that impedes home production, and the tariff that impedes imports in this sadly unplanned industry.' It was possible that if the tariff were removed 'and production properly organised, oysters would become so plentiful that they would be a luxury no longer'. In the days when 1,000,000,000 were landed every year, they had not been a luxury in Britain; nor were they now in some parts of the United States. 'But, in any case, they could hardly become a necessity. And may it not be that the epicure would lose his taste for the oyster if it was deprived of its comparative scarcity and became as common as the winkle or the shrimp? The elasticity of demand might prove to be negative and actually decrease in intensity as the price fell. At any rate, the demand and the price have been remarkably maintained throughout the present depression; which fact, like the record of cinema attendances in the last few years, seems to suggest that nowadays we save on necessities first and luxuries afterwards, or else, perhaps, that to those who are addicted to them, both cinemas and oysters are a necessity.'

On the face of it, admittedly, our treatment of the oyster trade is illogical.

We abstain from eating oysters from May to August, with the ostensible object of preserving them; but we allow them to be indiscriminately harvested throughout the rest of the year. We impose a tariff on imports with the ostensible object of encouraging home production; but we take no steps to encourage it. The more profound student of the national character, however, will perhaps discover some method in this madness. For may it not be that we thus gratuitously restrict the period of consumption and the cheapness of the supplies in order that we may have the extra pleasure, when the first month with an R in it comes round again, of enjoying a delicacy which is not only appetising, but also ephemeral and dear?[4]

(This was the kind of piece that particularly appealed to foreign readers. 'I most enjoyed the articles which dealt with everyday life in Britain which I found quaint and fascinating', recalled a Hungarian who had first started to read the paper in the 1930s, when working in the National Bank of Hungary. 'I still remember the short article "Stop me and buy one", describing the rights and taboos for ice-cream vendors and barrow-boys, the archaic rules and regulations. I felt I was back in the Dickensian era.'[5] The dottier aspects of Englishness which still attract foreigners exist mainly because stability has preserved into modern times what no one would ever now dream of inventing. And while *The Economist* laughs at the more idiotic anachronisms (sometimes with irritating superciliousness), it opposes them only when it considers they impede progress. For instance, although for more than a century anxious for radical reform of the House of Lords, and never uncritical of the monarchy, the paper has no republican agenda. Under that most radical of editors, Rupert Pennant-Rea, at the height of the disasters afflicting the royal family in 1992, a robust line was taken: 'The Head-of-State arrangements that a country has do not lend themselves to fruitful discussions. They are bequeathed by history, not by reason; they emerge from cataclysm, not from debate. For better or worse, Britain (like many other countries) has a Monarchy. Unless the House of Windsor chooses to dismiss itself, the Monarchy will remain.'[6])

The system of holding Monday editorial meetings still persists to the present day, though the meeting is now held in the morning. The atmosphere is often described as that of an Oxbridge senior common room – in the early 1980s a young participant described it as a senior common room of 1959. In theory everyone has an equal chance of making his views known; in practice, the race is to the most articulate and forceful. It is a system that favours the confident – not to say arrogant – male product of the major public school and Oxford debating society: the shy or less articulate, however well they write, are at a disadvantage in trying to get their ideas across. One result is that, if they have the right proponents, minority views can have a disproportionate effect. In the last few decades, Nick Harman and Stephen Hugh-Jones, both Old Etonians and both well to the left of most of their colleagues, have challenged homogeneous thinking with some success.

Three major factors differentiate editorial meetings of today from those of the 1930s: numbers of staff, their backgrounds and the sheer volume of subjects to be covered. A typical Layton conference would have had perhaps a dozen people (Layton, Crowther, Hutton, Jay, Bird, Parkinson, Crump, Walter Hill, Toynbee, Vallance, Reggie Harris or Hodson and an outsider or two), whereas nowadays the average attendance is more than three times as many. Though both groups would be dominated by extremely clever people, the Layton group had more ballast in the persons of solid specialists like Crump, Hill and Parkinson and more people (for example, Bird, Layton, Toynbee and Vallance) with non-journalistic experience. Post-1945 editors have increasingly tended to favour brains over experience: nowadays the vast majority of *Economist* people have no significant working background outside journalism, and this can make them ignorantly opinionated.

The 1930s *Economist* had only about 25 pages of political and economic coverage; today's *Economist* has more than 60. So there is inevitably a tendency for much of a modern editorial meeting to be taken up by section heads reading out lists of suggestions and answering queries: while there can be a lively argument about some particular issue, the logistics of fitting journalists to stories is the main consideration. In Layton's day there was more leisure to talk through a whole spectrum of issues. It was also a time when the paper was reflecting the centre-stage economic debate and some of Layton's radical young men were pressing for the adoption of a full-employment policy. The old certainties were going and were not to return until the 1980s, when once again the market ruled supreme.

Outsiders assigned topics in the Layton years were required to get their articles in by Wednesday morning. Toynbee wrote his at home in St John's Wood in time for the midnight post on Tuesday; it would reach Bouverie Street by 8.30 a.m. (The efficiency and speed of the postal system in those days was vital to the operation of the paper. Roland Bird recalled once sending a piece of copy to the printers at 4 o'clock in the afternoon by hand; it was set between 4.30 and 6 o'clock and the proof was posted to his Highgate flat where it arrived at 9.30; he made the necessary alterations, took it to the post office before midnight, and the printers received it in time to be able to have the corrected proof on Bird's desk when he arrived at *The Economist* at 9.30 a.m.) The foreign post was also highly effective; it took only one or two days for correspondence to arrive from Europe and five days from America. There was no airmail, so urgent material came by cable. It was impossible to ring Australia or South Africa, but in a crisis, with Foreign Office help, after 1935, Robert Warren, who provided financial coverage from New York, could be reached by telephone.

When a topic was assigned for a leader by a member of staff, it often became common property. At the front of the paper, usually Hutton or Jay – or even Crowther or Vallance – would produce a first draft, which others might enhance from their areas of particular strength; this did a great deal to build up the editorial *esprit de corps*. Walter Hill provided a useful rein on over-statement. "'You can't say that'", he might say. "'You will be torn to pieces by the statisticians in Geneva".'

Layton's major contribution was twofold. First was his ability to see subjects in the round: 'Don't forget so and so, put in so and so, you were wrong there, you have forgotten so and so'. Second were his contacts, which in Britain extended throughout academia, politics, the civil service and also industry. In his time in government, the difficulties of gathering statistical information sector by sector had revealed the importance of trade associations and brought many more into being. Layton had come to know all the key people: as Hutton put it, 'He'd whipped them all into line for the war.' By the 1930s the practice was well established that, when an important report came out on a particular industry, Layton would direct a member of staff to commission a piece from the administrator of the relevant trade association, who would give information off the record. Hugh Quigley, for instance, economist and statistician of the British Electrical and Allied Manufacturers Association, provided an annual brief; on occasion, he would even provide a draft leading article highly critical of his own organisation's annual report: a staff member would add two or three paragraphs, and someone would polish the style and clear the final version with Quigley. Others liked to provide only oral information. In the British film industry, a production manager called Simon Rowson was a tremendous source of copious information on exactly what people were spending, what was in jeopardy and what was solid, transmitted usually to Hutton over lunch in the Reform Club. Reggie Harris, who in 1935 somewhat improbably went from leader-writing and editing the *Nineteenth Century* to run the Argentine railway system, used to send notes to *The Economist* tipping it off about shady activities.

Having mapped out the shape of the paper at the editorial meeting, Layton would leave it to the permanent team to organise the writing, sub-edit, send material to the printers and have corrected proofs available by Thursday noon, when he would begin his extensive – and expensive – revisions. 'You got the proofs', remembered Hutton, 'and then Layton and you would disagree or Layton and Crowther and Toynbee on one side or perhaps Douglas when he was there and myself on the other side, dear old Hargreaves Parkinson loyally treading on the middle of the see-saw, Roland Bird quietly getting on with his high finance.'

Layton would spend the afternoon and evening reading the proofs, cutting out what he felt to be extravagances, and rewriting what he felt was too distinctive. Caution predominated: if he could not resolve his unease with a leader by tinkering with the concluding paragraph, Layton might distance the paper by adding the by-line, 'By a correspondent', even if the bothersome article was by a member of staff.

When Layton produced his pencil, which he would use until it became too small to manipulate, Bird, Jay and Hutton would speculate on whether it would last the evening out, 'as page after page of pencil-written stuff' was written in. Layton did not so much add as replace: 'He had to read every niggling word and justify himself to God and Man . . . Poor old Benney, the chief compositor, tore his hair. Sometimes he'd say, "Mr Hutton, for Gawd's sake go and deal with Sir Walter Layton."' Hutton coined a clerihew:

> Sir Walter Layton
> Has a passion for alterat'on
> Would to God someone could alter
> Sir Walter.

From Hargreaves Parkinson's diary comes a sample of the crises that could turn press day from a hard day into a terrible day: 'The fog greatly delayed our Paris and Berlin letters, but by hook and crook I got them in'; 'Company reports came thick and fast. The Treasury has butted in again with its embargo on foreign issues. "They cannot leave well alone, and their heads are wood.'"; 'City full of currency rumours. Much rewriting of Economist'; 'Press day was interrupted in the first hour by a snag in the Actuaries Index'; and so on. 'This was a long press day and rather a dreary one', noted one entry. 'They really are a test of physical endurance with lunch from 3–4 o'clock and work at printers to 11.45, leaving one just able to catch the last train home. We are not understaffed for three-quarters of the week, but we are on Wednesday and Thursday, and if anyone should fall ill we are for it.' Thursday entries ranged from 'A steady-going keep-at, dogged-as-does-it sort of press day' to 'A press day up to highest tradition of stress and strain'.

Those going to read the proofs at the printers would have tea in a tea-shop in Fleet Street on the way, where Douglas Jay added to his reputation for eccentricity by demanding dry brown toast, butter and blackcurrant jam. 'If the toast came buttered he would send it back, he wanted the butter separately. He would spread the butter on the toast, spread the jam on the butter, then he would seize the salt shaker and sprinkle salt until it was all white on top.'

With the exception of Crowther and Layton, all the senior staff went to the printers. 'The devoted and proud staff didn't mind what hours they kept', remembered Hutton. 'I often went down to the printer at two in the morning from my flat in Great Ormond Street.' The tradition of senior staff spending long periods at the printers may have pre-dated Layton; certainly from his time it became an enduring *Economist* tradition. Accuracy had always mattered to Wilson and Bagehot, even if Bagehot had to rely on others to counterbalance his own slipshod tendencies. Minor errors were quite frequent in the late-nineteenth-century paper, though Eliza Bagehot did her best to discourage them by sending her regular lists of misprints to Edward Johnstone. In the British newspaper world, proof-reading standards have dropped sharply since the Second World War: the age of the cultivated and rigorous sub-editor has gone. Yet, if anything, *Economist* standards of accuracy have risen, because the principle is maintained that everyone is involved in trying to produce a mistake-free paper and overall responsibility for the most trivial error lies with the most senior person present on Thursday night, who is usually the editor or his deputy.

(*The Economist* has one reader who cares as much about the eradication of its errors as do its staff. Franklin Phillips, an American doctor, has for several years scanned the entire paper for errors and infelicities. There has been an extremely friendly correspondence between him and the paper. 'Traitor', wrote Dudley Fishburn to him in 1985 on hearing that he had been in London. 'To come to London and not to drop by St James's Street to see us ... we continue to catch a host of literals every Thursday, only to see another host on Friday morning. Thanks for your letters.'[7] In the same year, Carol Mawer became proof-reader and began a correspondence with Phillips about whether standards were rising and falling, what English expressions like 'chuntered' or 'scrabbling' or 'cack-handed' meant, and why there had been a bumper crop of errors (eight) in one particular week. Many papers would regard Phillips as a nuisance; to *The Economist* he is an ally: copies of his findings are circulated to section heads to encourage ever-greater vigilance: 'terror and retribution stalk these corridors', Mawer informed him after the arrival of one 'appalling package'. 'Dear Dr Phillips,' wrote Pennant-Rea in May 1986, 'As the new Editor of *The Economist*, I am writing to say how much I appreciate your diligence in spotting our errors. I regard it as a sign of a good week when we produce an edition without any literals: your correspondence with Carol Mawer reminds me how far we have to go to achieve that standard. Thank you for taking the trouble: I hope you will carry on doing so.'[8] Phillips's happiest coup was finding 'Britain' misspelled – 'BEST YET' was his note, with an arrow pointing to the underlined error. He has not, however, found anything to compare with a literal of 1938, deemed sufficiently serious to cause the destruction of the 2,500 copies already printed. The dramatic opening to the first leader was supposed to begin: 'Almost seven months to a day after Signor Mussolini's visit to Herr Hitler in Berlin, two bullet-proof trains, bearing the Fuehrer of Great Germany and his retinue, arrived on Tuesday night at a special station in Rome, where he and his staff of nearly 150 were greeted by the King of Italy and the Duce.' No one spotted until expensively late in the proceedings that 'brains' had appeared in the place of 'trains'.[9])

In the 1930s, as now, Friday was an easy day during which those who were so minded could get on with outside activities. Moonlighting has always been a part of the *Economist* culture: it was accepted that such free time compensated for what was (until recently) relatively low pay. All of editorial were engaged in writing books or freelance articles and the paper hummed with intellectual excitement. Characteristically, Hutton's outside money-earning activities included translations and turning a Frederick Lonsdale play into a novel. '*The Economist* in those years under Walter Layton', recollected Jay, 'had principles, purposes and serious political ideals. We fought three major battles: first, in the tradition of Bagehot and F.W. Hirst for free trade, and above all free import into the UK of food and raw materials; secondly, defence of the League of Nations and the doctrine of collective security; and thirdly in favour of an internal expansionist policy to bring down the unemployment figures, which stood at their peak of nearly three millions when I joined *The Economist* . . . [We] often pointed out in 1933–5 that it was the fall in import prices of food and materials which made possible a cheap money policy and so the recovery in house-building and the steady drop in unemployment which began in 1933. It was in these years that I fully understood the fundamental wisdom of free importation of primary products for this country – as was again proved after 1951.' This training, coupled with his distaste for abroad, was to help make Douglas Jay as a senior politician one of the most savage opponents of Britain joining the European Economic Community, particularly because of the protectionism of the Common Agricultural Policy.

While he acknowledged that Layton and Toynbee provided the main inspiration for the paper's support of the League, Jay saw himself, Crowther and Vallance as the driving force on the third issue, expansionism. 'Layton was a moderate, but did not oppose reflationary moves, provided they operated in harmony with liberal imports. Crowther and I were even permitted to introduce the phrase "full employment". Here I believe that the backing of Arthur Salter and Josiah Stamp for cautious inflation influenced Layton. The *Economist* support for reflation in 1933–5, before Keynes's "General Theory" was published in 1936, helped a little, I believe, to make reflation respectable in those years.'[10]

Jay did not explain why he excluded Hutton from that list, but it was mainly because they were at odds politically. Jay in the mid-1930s was spending evenings and weekends writing *The Socialist Case*, which came out in late 1937. Hutton, by contrast, had been alienated during 1933 by the Labour Party's twists and turns over rearmament and had moved away from socialism to the liberalism which suited him temperamentally and which he was to champion for the rest of his life. He was to be an *éminence grise* behind the Institute of the Economic Affairs, founded in the 1950s to press the case of traditional economic liberalism at a time when both major parties believed – as Douglas Jay had always done – that Whitehall knew best. Typically, Jay concluded that Hutton had been ensnared by the *laissez-faire* dons at the LSE – Lionel Robbins and Friedrich von Hayek (Tooke Professor of Economic

Science and Statistics). He also believed that Hutton did not truly understand economics.

Yet *The Economist* went only some of the way with Douglas Jay. The extent to which it had moved by the mid-1930s is summed up by a survey of British economic prospects called '1936 and After'.[11] 'When a period of recovery enters its fifth year', wrote Crowther, 'it must, judging by past experience, be considered to have passed middle age and to be approaching senile decay.' Assuming there was no European war, what lay ahead? 'What is the criterion of an improving economic position? The classical economists would have answered, without hesitation, "a rising average real income"! Virtually all economic literature in our Grandfathers' and even in our Fathers' day was unconsciously founded upon that assumption, though politicians may have had other pre-occupations.'

> It was only in the first decade of the present century, however, that *a full volume of employment* achieved equality of status with a rising real income as a criterion of economic efficiency. Since the war we perhaps have gone too far in the opposite direction. There is a tendency to-day, among politicians and economists, to concentrate upon the reduction of unemployment, even at the cost not merely of the real income of those already employed but also of the average real income of the whole population. There are obvious dangers in such an undue concentration upon unemployment. Carried to its logical extreme, it would lead a country deliberately to seek out inefficient methods of production in order to employ a larger proportion of its labour force in producing the essential minimum of income. Certain Government policies, both in our own and in other countries, in recent years have not been far removed from this objective.

The sensible criterion of economic improvement was 'a reduction of unemployment, with the *caveat* that it must not be secured through the agency of a sharp fall in real incomes in the lower-income classes. Some rise in prices there will certainly be in the course of recovery. If we say, however, that real wages must not, in the process of recovery, fall below the pre-depression level, we shall probably err on the safe side.'

Hutton believed that he and Crowther were very close politically. 'If the younger Tories are only able to emancipate themselves from their class of origin', he wrote to Crowther in 1937, 'we have at last after fifteen years the opportunity to make that centre party along which alone in history our big progress has come. I would drop everything and work like a navvy in such a party, I guess so wd you. It wd avoid both myopias of Toryism and Socialism.'[12]

'Shut up, Graham, it's not your subject', said the socialist Davenport to Hutton once in the presence of Jay during an argument about economics. The polymath is ever regarded as superficial, and with Hutton, economics was only one of many subjects that he cared about. (Chapman judged him 'a veritable live wire capable of writing on almost any question . . . quickly'.) Twenty years later, in *Who's Who*, Hutton gave his recreations as 'ecclesiology, music and astronomy' and Jay offered none at all. Hutton was mercurial, intellectually effervescent and wildly enthusiastic in all sorts of directions. Jay was detached and single-minded. Yet they greatly liked each other and were happy colleagues. Respectively exotic and eccentric, they added greatly to the gaiety of an otherwise staid office. On one occasion Jay set fire to the copy of *The Times* which Hutton was reading and Hutton contributed his own brand of pyromania one November the 5th by placing a firework under Jay's chair. It shot around the room, laying burning trails all over the lino. Jay and Hutton enjoyed the spectacle mightily, but Crowther and Layton, also present, were not amused.

Hutton's relatively bohemian life dazzled some of his colleagues. Bird, Crowther and Jay were married and settled down. Hutton was separated from his first wife and falling in love with beautiful women all over the place; his holidays were spent with the Hungarian aristocracy; at weekends he rode or flew (he was always proud of having been the only assistant editor of *The Economist* to have flown a colleague – Jay – over the office building). The staff dressed soberly, Jay dressed scruffily, but Hutton wore made-to-measure silk shirts. Bird and Jay were plain, Crowther was ugly and Hutton was handsome. When the young men visited Layton and his family on holiday, all but Hutton were deeply embarrassed by being expected to swim naked in a group that might include some of Layton's four attractive daughters. More importantly, like Layton, Hutton brought to the paper a sense of a much wider world, though a much more cosmopolitan and raffish one than Layton's. Among the streams of Hutton's visitors at *The Economist* were two Hungarian economists who were to achieve fame in Britain as advisers to Harold Wilson, Tommy Balogh and Nicholas Kaldor.* Crowther and Jay

---

*Hutton was once forced into agreeing to act as Kaldor's second in a duel in Hungary after a row at an international naval conference with a Hungarian journalist. He had to point out to Kaldor that since he couldn't fence it was unwise of him to agree to swords, so revolvers were chosen instead. After much worry for Hutton, the protagonists made it up just before the appointed time.

used to make fun of Hutton and his 'entourage of failed economists and businessmen kicked out of their own countries', for he was a magnet for refugees from Nazi persecution. People came from Poland, Hungary, Czechoslovakia and Yugoslavia and all over Europe with confidential information. He had excellent networks too in the United States, Canada and Mexico. Abroad he saw prime ministers and foreign ministers with ease, for by then *The Economist*'s reputation was so high that its name opened most doors. The same is true today.

Jay was happy to stay in the office all week, while Hutton was there only at the absolutely necessary times. He spent the rest of the time picking up information and making contacts. The Reform Club was his main outside headquarters. It was there that he was tipped off about the pepper scandal of 1935, one of the two contributions he made to *The Economist* of which he was most proud.

In February 1935, Sir Andrew Macfadyean, one of Layton's public-service contemporaries and by then a distinguished businessman, ran into Hutton and said: 'There's something brewing in the City. There's a very nasty smell.' The smell came from a collapsed syndicate that had been formed to corner the pepper market. Also present was Bobby Stopford, a distinguished banker, and one of Layton's best friends and most constant informants, who predicted this would be the biggest scandal since the war and suggested Hutton check it out with Montagu Norman. Hutton went rushing excitedly down to the Bank of England, and was allowed in to see the Governor. Anxious to leak information, but equally anxious to protect himself, Norman rang Layton to see if it was safe to confide in Hutton and then did so.

What was rocking the City was not simply that the syndicate had crashed and that its prospectus had been clearly fraudulent but that Reginald McKenna, chairman of the Midland Bank, ex-Chancellor of the Exchequer, was tainted by association, as was Sir Hugo Cunliffe-Owen, chairman of the British-American Tobacco Company. 'It is all pepper, pepper, pepper, with a first-class scandal', wrote Parkinson, recording the following Monday: 'Afternoon on the pepper crisis at the Economist meeting. We are running some strong articles on this exciting question.' And by Layton's standards, strong they undoubtedly were – right in the tradition of Edward Johnstone. Layton might be cautious, but he was not cowardly and he was the last man to approve of Establishment wrongdoing. Hutton and Parkinson did their research thoroughly, and *The Economist* broke the story and led the field in the comprehensiveness of coverage and the severity of comment. 'Pepper is one of the commonest of culinary spices', began Hutton's first article. 'Long years ago we fought the Dutch for the Spice Islands where pepper was first obtained; for we consume more than half the world's supply of white pepper. It might be thought that, as the bulk of pepper comes from British Malaya for use in Britain, the market would be a quiet one. Clearly, it is not always so. For in the past year, when money has been extremely cheap and many of its possessors have been looking round for a more remunerative return than the few miserable shillings per cent yielded by Treasury bills, the pepper market, like that in shellac and some other raw materials, has attracted the attention of a group of speculators. The result, as all the world now knows, has turned out to be one of the less creditable episodes in our commercial history.' Having told the full story of how the venture had failed, Hutton went on to deal with Cunliffe-Owen and McKenna, who had turned out to be not only shareholders in James and Shakspeare, the speculators' brokers, but directors of companies that were likewise substantial shareholders. 'Whether these shareholdings and the direction of associated companies involved knowledge of the operations of the pool we do not know; but the association must, at least, have lent prestige to the agency by which it was conducted.'

> It is no doubt possible for the chairman of our largest joint-stock bank and for the head of one of our largest industrial companies to disassociate their personal interest as investors from their great public responsibility. And we hope that the public will shortly have an assurance that neither of these gentlemen was personally privy to the attempt artificially to force up the price of important commodities by speculative manipulations. But in any case there are some things which, though lawful, are not expedient. We regret that men in the position of trusteeship for the public should have placed themselves in a situation in which the market might infer, or might be led to believe, that they had some responsibility for what was happening.[13]

Hutton learned through his contacts at the Bar that McKenna and Cunliffe-Owen consulted lawyers and were told that all they could expect from *The Economist* if they took it to court was a halfpenny in damages.

A year later three of the principals in the syndicate were found guilty of conspiring to issue a false prospectus. Summing up 'PEPPER MORALS', Hutton once again discussed the involvement of McKenna and Cunliffe-

Owen, regretting that a name of such authority in the City as McKenna's 'could have been used to further purposes which were hardly compatible with the public interest, and involved the issue of a prospectus that a jury has found to be false'.

> All in all, the pepper story is not one of which the City can be proud. On the question of the prospectus, the law has taken its course . . . But on the wider issue public opinion has long since pronounced its verdict. Free enterprise and free financial institutions have not gained in prestige from the revelation that men of considerable wealth and of great influence with Government employ their time and their resources in 'cornering' pepper, forming syndicates in shellac, and organising private pools in tin.[14]

The pepper coup highlighted out the fact that experience and contacts are prerequisites for good investigative financial journalism. Hutton had the backup not only of Layton, but of the wise and well-informed Hargreaves Parkinson. Lacking the resources of the daily financial press, *The Economist* is rarely able to break stories of this importance, but an exception, just over 50 years after the pepper scandal, was the blowing of the whistle on County Nat West involvement in the Blue Arrow affair. In this case a member of staff, who happened to have more outside experience than is common nowadays in the *Economist* business pages, broke the story that County Nat West had breached the Companies Act and forced the resignation of its chairman and chief executive. This happened at a time when the paper's reputation was low in the City; for too long its financial coverage had been mainly the preserve of young, clever Oxbridge recruits who knew nothing about the world of money and did no legwork. The furore over Blue Arrow both raised the stock of *The Economist* and made it more courageous (though some wobble was evident in the perhaps unnecessary apology that ended the affair in 1993). For the last few years the quality of financial coverage has much improved.

(One famous 1930s scandal over which *The Economist* did not distinguish itself was that of Ivar Kreuger, the Swedish 'match king' who tried to create a world monopoly of match production. From 1925 his activities involved much speculative financing in the shape of long-term dollar loans to hard-up European and Latin American countries. The impact of the world depression on his complicated empire led him to shoot himself in 1932. *The Economist* was deeply distressed. 'THE KREUGER TRAGEDY' was vintage Vallance.

The Greek tragedians, with their unerring sense of values, rightly laid it down as an axiom of their art that a personage of the drama, whose downfall at the hands of Fate was to be regarded as possessing the significance of tragedy, must have been an inherently great man. Whatever defects in the way of overweening confidence or lack of vision and foresight could be laid at the doors of the tragic heroes of Aeschylus and Sophocles, they were essentially characters whose stature was such that the emotion of pity as well as terror was awakened by their ill-starred end. Not dissimilar are the feelings aroused by the fate of Mr Ivar Kreuger; his death in Paris last Saturday by his own hand represents the veritably tragic wreck of a career which in its sphere was unsurpassed by that of any individual in living memory.

Kreuger was 'no mere gambler on a gigantic scale in the world's bourses, no mere "promoter" in quest of personal profit at the expense of sucking dry the enterprises to which he laid his hand'. He was a man of 'great constructive intelligence and wide vision, who planned boldly, yet on a basis which seemed to be protected by carefully devised safeguards, and who for once seemed about to combine with the profits of private enterprise a real contribution to the welfare of nations'. A description of his career was followed by a reverent estimate of his motives, which included a desire 'to play whatever part he could in acting as a medium between nations with surplus reserves available for lending and countries in desperate need of such resources'. He sought to 'make good shortcomings which he saw in the world's borrowing-lending mechanism. His financial organisation functioned, in fact, in a manner complementary to and comparable with that of the Finance Committee of the League of Nations.' His 'endeavour' had broken down because 'he was crushed, in the words of Mr J.M. Keynes, "between the icebergs of a frozen world which no individual man can thaw and restore to the warmth of normal life."' Possibly he might have overborrowed. 'In the hands of a different man, too, the enormous power which he seemed on the way to acquire over the Governments of a score of countries might have been undesirable.' In this case, however, history would have to record 'that in a crisis created in the main by the blindness and unwisdom of statesmen, fostered by national jealousies, and ending in the almost universal breakdown of "capitalist" confidence and the severance of financial and commercial relations between countries, Ivar Kreuger, as the channel for the smooth flow of capital from country to country, was destroyed by the impingement of forces which even the financial mechanism of the League of Nations has not been able to withstand'.

> In setting before himself as his objective the refinancing of the debtor countries of Central Europe and South America – an òbjective that was neither predominantly self-seeking, nor ignoble, nor, on any reasonable assumption of world sanity, perilous for its pursuers – Kreuger made, like others who bent their influence towards that end, a bold bid to become a great force for good in the world. *Dis alitur visum*.* He failed; but he did not fail alone.[15]

Three weeks later there was a paragraph written in the light of 'the revelations of the chartered accountants', which 'disclose the stark fact that even a man who had the imagination and the courage to launch and develop an international financial system on so great a scale could not resist the temptation to follow the all too easy path of deception and manipulation of accounts when the pressure of world events became too strong for his hastily built structure'.

> It is a humiliating story, particularly for those who look to the salvation of the world from its super men, and may well cause us to ask whether such a concentration of power may safely be entrusted to any man – unless, indeed, it be exercised in conditions where every action is exposed to the fullest glare of an inconvenient but healthy publicity.[16]

(Even before the grisly truth emerged, Pennant-Rea's *Economist* was not disposed to mourn Robert Maxwell when he disappeared off his yacht in 1991. It too considered the system that produced such a phenomenon.

> The biggest question is this: are the Maxwells of this world A Good Thing? Keynes talked of 'animal spirits' driving economic progress. Schumpeter described a process of 'creative destruction', with capitalists laying waste even as they build. Paul Samuelson thought that if entrepreneurs were prevented from pursuing 'good clean money' they would become oppressive brutes, intent on 'bad dirty power'; happy the society that has billionaires rather than Brezhnevs.

---

*He will be viewed differently in heaven.

Good, as far as it goes. But that version of the entrepreneur dwells upon
success; what about excess and failure?

The answer was supervision: by accountant and bank manager rather than by
civil servant and regulator. 'Once bureaucrats get involved in saving capitalism from its excesses, they tend to kill it off, the good bits as well as the
bad ... Entrepreneurial capitalism always needs capital, but capital always
needs guardians. The swashbuckler is essential to the system's vitality, the
bean-counter essential to its survival. The men in dark suits will now have
their say. They should have had it sooner.'[17])

Hutton was also particularly proud of his achievements in updating the
paper's appearance. His first breakthrough came in January 1934, at a time
when British newspapers had began to change their layout and typography.
Even *The Times* was experimenting: Stanley Morison, the great typographer,
was designing for it the new typeface that became *Times* Roman. Layton –
pre-eminently a man for content, not style – had no ambition to make any
changes at all in *The Economist*. In its ninety years, various editors had
introduced subtle changes in, for instance, density and blackness of print, size
and quality of paper, numbers of columns, location of advertisements, layout
of contents lists and the use of ruled lines around text, but this was the first
serious overhaul.

It was inspired by Hutton's long-standing interest in calligraphy and
typography. He had come to know Stanley Morison and Beatrice Warde,
another expert who worked with the Monotype Corporation. One day,
shortly after he joined the paper, Warde remarked to Hutton that *The
Economist* was 'a disgrace. *The Times* is pulling its socks up. Hadn't you better
pull yours up?' Hutton hurled himself at the challenge, and with the help of
Morison, Warde and Benney,* head compositor at Eyre & Spottiswoode, he
put some ideas up to Layton and the board of directors. Brendan Bracken was
enthusiastic and introduced him to yet another typographer, and eventually
Hutton produced a draft layout that pleased everyone except Strakosch; he
feared that any change would reduce *The Economist*'s influence in foreign
capitals. Stage one of the revamp, introduced in January 1934, included
banishing from the front page the miscellaneous advertisements which had
appeared there for nearly 50 years and, most dramatically, dropping from the

---

*Benney, and Vedgen who followed him as 'clicker' at St Clement's Press, were able and friendly
craftsmen, who nursed *Economist* staff through fraught press days.

title its unnecessary verbiage '*Weekly Commercial Times, Bankers' Gazette, and Railway Monitor. A Political, Literary, and General Newspaper*'. *The Economist* has always been slow to talk about itself in its own pages, so the tone of the explanation verged on the coy.

> *Our New Dress.* – The unfamiliar appearance of the *Economist* this week, and the surprise which some readers may experience on finding certain features no longer in their accustomed places, call for a word of explanation. A new type-face has been employed throughout, with a clearer lay-out on each page, in the belief that the change will make the *Economist* easier to read. We hope that the verdict of our readers will approve this innovation.

While no change had been made in the substance of the paper, the order of the contents had been changed 'in one important respect. The Money Market report, together with those Notes of the Week which deal with banking and the money market and such articles as discuss these subjects from time to time, will be brought together in a self-contained section immediately preceding the section relating to the Stock Exchange. This means that, following the contents, the *Economist* will open with articles of general interest.' There were two minor changes: the Stock Exchange 'now contains a series of Company Notes, of which the first each week analyses the position of a particular industry or concern [Bird's innovation]; while "Commercial Reports" will be replaced by a section on Commerce and Trade, headed by a special weekly survey of the commodity markets. These, together with a number of small alterations in lay-out, constitute one of the greatest changes in the appearance of the *Economist* since its foundation over ninety years ago.'[18]

Despite Strakosch's disapproval and Montagu Norman's shocked reaction, the dropping of the Money Market from the front page did not bring civilisation as the City knew it to an end, so the process continued. For the next three years, Hutton went on having long consultations with his (unpaid) typographer friends and carrying out his experiments with Benney on the press. Parkinson recorded the next stage:

> *17 February 1936* At today's editorial conference we discussed new and far reaching changes in Economist format, etc. This will be the first of many such talks.
> *9 April* Had Morison along and discussed new 'makeup' for the paper. Rather a fruitful interview.

4 May This evening Graham Hutton and I had W.T.L to dinner at Reform, and we made much progress on discussing future layout and aims of the Economist.

4 December Showed W.T.L our suggested new cover, and he likes it.

28 December We now come to culmination of twelve months work with first issue of the Economist in a new dress.

The change was dramatic. The cover was grey, with the title, at Morison's suggestion, printed in red. 'At New Year three years ago *The Economist*, moving with the times, said farewell to a Gothic title which had appeared, both on and within the cover, for a nearly a century. To-day, a process which began three years ago is carried to what we may hope – save for minor alterations – will prove to be a long-lasting completion.' The British public had become type-conscious and demanded 'cleaner typography and clearer lay-out; a truce with Gothic and heavy glowering type-faces. It knows why it wants all this: easier and more pleasurable reading in a busier and busier world. To no journal, perhaps, is easier reading more important than to *The Economist* which, perforce in these days, must give its busy (often harassed) readers both news and comment, facts and figures, from a field as wide as the world, and on almost all topics, which vex, interest, or concern mankind.'

From now onwards this journal appears in a more serviceable, more handsome cover; it is printed on better and whiter paper; editorial matter is presented in narrower columns with wider margins; and 'leading articles,' properly so-called, together with a special weekly economic article of general interest, are set differently from those of a technical nature. The chief typographical improvement is the setting of titles and article-headings in bold 'upper and lower case' type, instead of, as hitherto, in solid capitals, i.e., 'upper case'. It has been demonstrated in psychological tests that the eye reads an 'upper and lower case' line more quickly and easily than the solid 'upper case' line.

The typeface chosen for the new headings of articles, sections of the paper, and correspondence was Eric Gill's elegant Perpetua. There was no change in content. 'And we would ask any of our regular readers whom the new format of *The Economist* shocks, because it *is* strangely new, to take last week's and this week's issues in his hand, to compare the two, and to decide which makes for easier reading.'[19]

'Favourable comments on new paper, which seems to have gone over with a bang', recorded Parkinson on New Year's Day. One exception, once again, was Montagu Norman, who disapproved mightily of the change and did not for a long time forgive *The Economist* for 'vulgarising itself'.

The red title on a grey cover lasted for less than three years. In October 1939, under a heading 'NAKED AND UNASHAMED', its disappearance was announced as a measure of wartime economy. *The Economist* regretted the loss of its 'practical and distinctive' dress and hoped it would soon be back. It was, in fact, to be 20 years before colour was again used, under the editorship of Donald Tyerman, the first editor since Wilson to care about the paper's appearance.

Parkinson had been much involved in the decision to restyle the paper, because in 1935, under pressure from Strakosch, Layton had promoted him.

> *Thursday 25 July*. A memorable day. Long negotiations, over at the Economist, between Editor and directors have resulted in my being offered position of Associate Editor – in fact, managing-editorship, with Sir Walter retaining ultimate control but devoting his energies to his heavy task at News Chronicle. £1,750 a year plus share in profits over a given figure. I feel intensely gratified. There could be no pleasanter consequence of twelve years service on the paper. Letter from W.T.L embodying offer arrived to-day.

It was a job which Hutton might have reasonably expected to be given, but Strakosch was determined to have somebody with City expertise to counter-act what he thought to be the unduly political slant of the paper. Not only was Parkinson promoted over Hutton, but Crowther moved up in the pecking-order; now he as well as Hutton was an assistant editor, forming with Parkinson a triumvirate which Parkinson called the 'Cabinet'. 'It may have been', reflected Chapman, 'that Sir Walter felt that there would come a time when he would retire from the Editorship and when this time came the promoters would have men available from whom they could choose to become Editor in his place. The three men chosen by Sir Walter Layton . . . were Hargreaves Parkinson, Graham Hutton and Geoffrey Crowther. It will be agreed that with Sir Walter Layton still Editor and with three such capable associates the strength of The Economist was undoubtedly further enhanced. It was a case of time would tell and it certainly did.'

Parkinson went about the job in his typically decent, solid and conscientious fashion and Hutton hid his disappointment. 'Had Graham, to whom I had written a personal letter over the weekend, to lunch and we discussed matters. He will heartily work in with me and his help will be more valuable than I can readily say.'

> *Tuesday 1 October* A milestone. To-day became Associate Editor of the Economist with a seat at THE Table. It will be very pleasant, though hard going for a while. The staff are loyal, and Graham Hutton, in particular, very likeable. Lex continues but is done by Clarke and Bird, both very able, under my direction.

> *Friday 4 October* First of our Cabinet meetings – Geoffrey, Graham and I – this morning. They will be Mondays and Fridays. Started first steps of the 'Budgetting' system for future articles after W.T.L's sanction. Discussed various matters with various people (there is going to be a great deal of 'discussing' in this new role of mine). On the whole, this first week suggests that life is to be full, but very varied and real as Associate Editor. Tonight gave a dinner at the Reform Club to W.T.L, Graham and Geoffrey. It was an exceedingly pleasant affair.

> *Monday 21 October* Am trying to write a Stock Exchange Leader for the Economist (Brewery Shares), which is really difficult with all the multifarious duties that now fall to me. Had Bird to lunch, and got out future S.E. articles. Usual Economist meetings – Cabinet at 12.00 and full conference at 2.30 and saw Editor to discuss various business matters, in the evening.

> *Tuesday 22nd October* Saw Bracken this morning. I want to maintain contact with all my directors. Two more callers before lunch, then finished Brewery Article. To Hobson's 'At Home' at 9.00 where I knew large majority of menfolk and had a pleasant time.

> *Wednesday 23rd October.* Saw Sir Henry Strakosch at 3.15, and stayed until nearly 5.15. Our chairman and an interesting man. I think I have a 'fair' idea of policy now. Saw W.T.L at six o'clock and discussed first leader for this week.

Four weeks into his new job he wrote his first political leader ever for *The Economist*. 'I know for certain nobody has ever done first leader and Stock Exchange leader in the same week before.' The article concerned the forthcoming general election: 'The Government has taken the grave responsibility of plunging the country into the vortex of a General Election in the middle of an unresolved international crisis. The party augurs have spoken; the Prime Minister has made up his mind. Parliament was dissolved on Friday, October 25. The nation will poll on November 14, and a new Parliament will be in session in the first week of next month.' There followed a competent and balanced analysis of the government's record, but it was pedestrian, long on facts and short on ideas. 'Which post-war precedent will be relevant to this month's result?' he wondered. 'The tradition that every election since 1923 has reversed the House of Commons majority established by its predecessor, or the historic fact that every administration during fourteen of the last seventeen years has drawn its voting power in the House of Commons predominantly from the Conservative Party? Will the results of 1935 fall half-way between those of 1929 and 1931? Or will the vagaries of our out-of-date and incalculable electoral system once again produce a lop-sided and unrepresentative Parliament? For good or ill, the events of the next fortnight will decide these questions.'[20]

Parkinson was far more out of his depth in international politics, yet he had many virtues. He was unquestionably the safe pair of hands that Strakosch had sought and he did far more than simply follow established procedures. He addressed himself to the area in which Layton was in Strakosch's view most neglectful – making *The Economist* more profitable. For Layton's mission to inform his readers – though in general terms good for *The Economist*'s image – was bad for its balance sheet: profits went down as the size of the paper went up without a proportionate rise in advertising. An announcement in April 1936 summarised the position.

> *The Economist: Quarterly Volumes.* – Beginning with this week's issue, volumes of the *Economist* will be numbered quarterly. The inexorable growth in the size of each weekly issue, and the increase in the number of special Supplements during recent years, have made our hitherto half-yearly volumes almost unmanageable in bulk. This is the first change in the volumes since the paper's foundation, ninety-three years ago. If any readers care to review the growth in the scope and content of the *Economist* during its ninety-three years of existence, they will find that in 1843 a half-yearly volume measured 1 in. in width; in 1850 it had risen to 1¼ in.; in 1875 to 2 in.; in 1900 to 3¼ in.; in 1913 to 4 in.; and in 1935 to just on 5 in. To be 'growing like a tree in bulk' is not necessarily a measure of merit. But in these days events crowd thicker and faster upon us than a mere generation ago. The *Economist* has had to expand in 'an expanding universe.'[21]

When Layton became editor in 1922 the paper consisted of 5,088 columns, of which 1,076 were advertisements or company meetings. The equivalent figures for 1929 were 6,000 and 1,164, so the unprofitable had risen by 18% and the profitable by only 8%. In the same period, expenditure had risen by 26% and revenue by only 10%. Other financial strains were caused by the creation of the new special Stock Exchange section in 1928 and an expansion of coverage (which had led to the unprecedented marketing ploy of a special poster for display in the City to advertise the new section). There were extra printing expenses because of a change of printers. As part of the deal with the *Financial News*, Eyre & Spottiswoode had acquired the right to print *The Economist*: St Clement's Press had lost the work after 50 years. (When the *Economist* office was bombed in 1941, Eyre & Spottiswoode went with it; St Clement's Press took over once again. As Chapman put it: 'time and events made The Economist go back to their old love'.)

The depression had not helped, although it increased demand. Noting in 1873 that the paper had had a poor period in the years after the 1866 panic, Bagehot attributed this to 'the dull state of the money market which was so motionless for nearly four years, that there was nothing to tell the public about it . . . when the money market began to afford points of interest, *The Economist* at once recovered its position and its profitableness'.[22] Almost a century later, writing his memoirs, Layton remarked that 'periods of bad trade are good for *The Economist*. People want to know why they are losing their money and how to get it back.' Circulation figures for the period of major economic crises of Layton's editorship confirm this, but the downside was that recession hit advertising. *The Economist* at this period relied mainly on financial advertising (particularly prospectuses) and company meeting reports. During the 1920s, company meetings had increased steadily as a proportion of advertising revenue – from 45% in 1923 to 64% in 1929.

Company meetings were the area of greatest competition. In City pubs, representatives of the financial press bought drinks for prospective clients and bonhomie was as important an element in acquiring business as was the reputation and circulation of one's newspaper. Layton understood that this form of advertising could not be acquired without expenditure on alcohol; what horrified him was the discovery that some 'appeared to stay longer than they had to and drink for drink's sake'.

Even as advertising revenue continued to decline in 1931, there was no cutback in expenditure on the product itself. At the 1933 annual general meeting Strakosch reported that 'during the year a number of special supplements were issued which, from the financial point of view, were not directly remunerative in that they carried no advertising matter, but they had attracted considerable attention and are still in steady demand and undoubtedly afford a medium of publicity, the benefits of which outweigh the additional costs entailed'. All that had a healthy effect on weekly circulation; in 1935, at 8,706 columns, it was 46% up on 1928.

Any breakthroughs on the advertising front were inevitably limited by the calibre of the staff. Kirk and Whitcomb (and after Whitcomb's death in 1936, Bernard) were ageing and set in their ways. Parkinson tried to help in January 1936 with a memorandum to the board on advertising prospects. 'I respectfully suggest', it began, 'that the consequences should be examined of the possibility that 1936 may correspond, in the present cycle, to the year 1929 in the last one.' The Stock Exchange had declined from February 1929, whereas the general trade recession had not began until 1930; 'this movement *in advance of* general industry is characteristic of the phenomenon of the City'. There was a possibility of a recession beginning in 1937. 'I should look therefore for "stickier" stock markets as the present year progresses – particularly in gilt-edged and high grade fixed-interest securities, which have made the running in the new issue market throughout the present up-grade movement.' In 1929 prospectuses had continued to flow for several months and then gradually dried up: this might or might not happen in 1936. There might be an imposition of 'an enforced "breathing space" on the new issue market ... The increasingly less favourable result of many new issues will itself check the activity of the market.' Industrial shares might continue to advance in price; his conclusion was 'that we should expect a fair number of new prospectuses in the first half of the year, but the latter months of the year may see much quieter conditions. It may be suggested that the susceptibility of Financial advertising to wide upward and downward swings, in short periods, emphasises the argument for the broadening of the basis of "The Economist" advertising revenue.'[23]

This was not the kind of document likely to galvanise the advertising staff into energetic action. Yet in Parkinson's time there was a sense of a sharper eye being kept on commercial realities. Supplements yielded advertising revenue. In 1936, for instance, there were 12 special supplements. In ascending order of popularity with advertisers, these were: United States of America (yielding £48), Engineering (£138), India (£185), Insurance (£220),

Building Societies (£275), Argentina (£320), *Commercial History of 1935* (£358), Argentina again (£485), Fixed Trusts (£515), Banking (£648), Banking again (£678) and Canada (£837). So instead of losing money, the supplements at least paid their way overall.

As manager, Gilbert Layton's perennial plea was for a reduction in the size of the paper. In 1933 he reported a decline over five years of 205 'paid-for advertisement pages' and an increase in total number of pages of 72. Parkinson was his greatest ally. Diary entries show him straining to cut editorial matter. For instance: 'Nearly got to a 52 page paper but had to let it go at 56 eventually'; 'Stiff going but we got the paper made up eventually to 48 pages'; 'Actually a 40 page paper today. Hope we are not overdoing it.'

But on the editorial side he was waging a rather forlorn battle. Hutton, for one, always wrote far too much, and at the front of the paper only Parkinson cared about such mundane matters as saving money. In October 1937 Gilbert Layton was writing to Parkinson: 'As the price of paper has risen by 16 per cent since June the cost of our paper is 26½ per cent higher than this time last year owing to the change in quality made last January. It is all the more unfortunate, therefore, that the size of the paper has been allowed to expand during the holiday period. Advertisement and company meetings account for not more than eight pages of the increase and I would urge that efforts to check the expansion in editorial matter be intensified during the current quarter.'

'I am anxious to reduce "*The Economist*" costs of production', responded Parkinson 'and to increase our commission on profits.' Most increases in outlay on paper were outside his control: paper prices, improved quality thereof and increased circulation. He had already reduced the statistical part of the paper by four pages: 'only a small part of the excess is due to the editorial or contributorial verbosity. The major part reflects:

(a) Special Features

(b) Leading, Double Headings, and reduced words per page

(c) Our inability to use any part of the cover, under the new regime, for editorial matters.

Thus, if we are to get the whole of the 'improved' paper into the same compact as the old, it means that special features will have to be reduced (though in fact we are planning to increase them), or that other parts of the paper will have to be cut down. Mere compression will not do it; definite omission will be necessary. But will this be good policy, seeing that we have had so encouraging a reception to our efforts already? Whatever decision may be reached in the high quarters, I will faithfully and cheerfully carry out, and in the meantime you may rely on me to keep the paper down as far as I possibly can. But the financial side, as you properly point out, is important, in view of rising costs, and for that reason I should welcome a ruling on the main question.

Parkinson's virtues were apparent to Layton and the board of directors, but they were not highly rated by the *jeunesse doré*. The morale of the young men collapsed, taking with it the *esprit de corps*. Jay accepted a job as City editor of the *Daily Herald* in December 1936* and was replaced the following month by Donald Tyerman, a young history lecturer at Southampton University. He was hardworking and liked by his colleagues, but he was a newcomer and less fun than Jay. Like Parkinson, Tyerman was unglamorous and easily underrated. In 1950, when deputy editor of *The Times*, he wrote a highly personal follow-up to Parkinson's obituary. 'I was one of the many whose first steps in journalism were taken under the kindly sagacious care of H.P. All of us – and journalism itself – owe him very much . . . He was a good friend and a wise, though always modest, mentor to all who worked with him; he knew them shrewdly and helped them continually, he sympathized with them in their setbacks and rejoiced without reserve in their successes. He hated only slipshod, pretentious, or prejudiced work.'

Hutton continued to back up Parkinson, organising a highly successful Coronation Supplement in 1937 (which used colour inside the paper for the first time), developing his ideas on layout, working hard, spending a weekend with Parkinson's family and building palaces of wooden bricks for his son, but he was inwardly chafing at the strain of working for someone he found limited and slow. In September 1937 he went on five months' leave of absence, sending back from the United States and from Mexico (where he spent three months covering the oil industry) an avalanche of excited letters, articles, notes and information gathered from an ever-expanding network.

'I am glad things are going all right in the inner ring,' he wrote to

*In 1941 he joined the wartime civil service and in 1946 became a Labour MP. His political career included periods as Financial Secretary to the Treasury and President of the Board of Trade. He received a peerage in 1987. One of his daughters married Rupert Pennant-Rea in 1986, making him, as Jay pointed out, the second editor of *The Economist* to be a son-in-law of a Financial Secretary to the Treasury.

Crowther in October. 'I thought they would if you had three days a week actually in the office. I am anxious to get Paul Bareau in N[orman] C[rump]'s place . . . If PB would come [he came in 1939], that would greatly assist our new layout, make-up, etc.' Hutton was tremendously enthusiastic about the typeface – 'chaste and modern, new and yet classic', and was visiting American offices to look at processes. He was fretting about Eyre & Spottiswoode. 'We seem doomed not to be able to shake off those old men of the sea because of one young man of the City [Bracken].'[24]

A long letter Hutton wrote to Layton in February 1938 was highly revealing.

> Geoffrey recounted the vexations of the paper's metamorphosis, to which I replied from Los Angeles. I think with you that the paper should be better and better turned out as E. & S. get used to it. But Geoffrey also added a penned memo. to the effect that he would be about 'haywire' by the time I returned, owing to the accumulating strain of what he termed petty discussions and arguments over detail with H.P. I expect H.P's Lancashire make-up would account for much of a Yorkshireman's annoyance, and the paper's change-over for the rest. But I *am* glad that another than I has had the occasion to sit in that office even for only three days a week or so, and to gauge atmosphere.

Hutton's views 'on what I personally should be ready to envisage after, say, the end of 1938 have not been "softened" by my long leave of absence. They have crystallised with sharper definition; for I have never had since my Finals year the opportunity to see what freedom from uncongenial personal relations can accomplish in one's intellectual energy and resources – except, I should add without reserve, during those two years Sept. 1933 to Sept. 1935 when I tried to do all I was capable of in the office, under your eyes alone.' Even then his marital troubles were at their height, and 'mainly due to them my health buckled up [he got ulcers]. The work was really the hardest I've ever put out in those two years, and, as you know, I was at the same time trying to get the best new dress for the paper and to get the internal office routine into easier working shape.' On re-reading his own articles from that period, he was surprised at their quality. 'I owe it to you to write (what one man scarcely ever tells another) my appreciation of the way you handled an impatient and scarcely-licked young writer. On this unforgettably valuable trip I have had my nose repeatedly rubbed in the realisation of your formative influence – in my current capacity to judge things economic as much as political and social. I write this here and now because, first, it is overdue, and, secondly, as I said, men are shy of saying these things openly to the right person's face. This is but one of the many realisations I have made from my recently-gained new perspectives. And I'll say no more lest you think it soft soap. It isn't, anyhow.'

One of Hutton's many engaging attributes was his candour. A man who talked rather than listened, he was often unaware of the impact he made on others. His next paragraph – intended to reassure – was highly unlikely with a man like Layton to strengthen the case for making him editor.

> One thing may interest you: this *Distanzierung* (a psycho-physical term for which we have no equivalent) has worked a power of good on my temperament; for, being most untypically temperamental and mercurial an Englishman, home political and economic passivity got my goat. After my fruitful wanderings I have gotten a modicum of balance into my judgment of things English. You and Dorothy are two of the rare few who will recall that young Rupert Brooke went through the same chastening in this country, and put it into his *Letters from America* just before the war. Here, I find with alarm that I tend to become more Tory in viewing home from afar. 'Home thoughts from abroad', with a vengeance!

> (N.B. This does not apply to foreign affairs!)

He had 'amassed so many volumes of notes that the very idea of writing a neat little Leader or two for the paper of 1,200 words each on – say – the American or Mexican scene is "just a laff", as they say here. You will understand why when, as I hope, we can spend a dinner together on my arrival. I've certainly got the low-down on a lot. I can't close without saying how grateful I am to you (not forgetting my colleagues in the breach) for the opportunity to be free to do something, the lack of which I so often felt. I honestly feel doubly-equipped, intellectually, compared with six months ago.'[25]

At the end of March 1938, Hutton returned to London *en route* to the Balkans: 'the same G.H. as of yore', recorded Parkinson. 'Has spent a lot of money, and earned £800 by lecturing and writing.' Within 24 hours he had resigned: Layton was unprepared to change the status quo or – presumably – promise him the editorship. When he came back to the office at the end of

April he wrote to confirm the conversation of 29 March, at which he had given the six months' notice required by his contract. 'However, I am, as I also told you on March 29th, ready to end my service with the paper at the close of any month after June next, if this is more convenient to you and to the rest of my colleagues here. I hope you will let me know in writing what you and they prefer. In no case, however, do I want to remain bound by my contract after September next.'[26]

CHAPTER XLI:

Geoffrey Crowther

Geoffrey Crowther happened to be born into a period in which the world had become preoccupied by problems of economic management, where neither extreme of dogma could evidently be relied on for solutions, but in which the qualities of analysis and reason which had sustained *The Economist* for a century had come to play a crucial part. His intellectual approach, as well as his mastery of the editor's technique, bore notable resemblance to Bagehot's. He was moved by the need to create a world of justice, freedom and economic welfare. He judged the instrumentalities of governments and the effectiveness of the market place from this broad standpoint.[1] *Roland Bird, 1972*

There is no evidence that Layton intended to give up the editorship at the time when Hutton resigned. Modest and unassuming though he might be, he was not a man who let go easily. In the late 1950s and early 1960s, as chairman of *The Economist*, he was to show no more urgency about letting that post pass to an increasingly desperate Geoffrey Crowther than he had done in the case of the editorship.

Brendan Bracken and Henry Strakosch, between them, forced the pace. In April 1938 Bracken offered Parkinson the editorship of the *Financial News* and he talked it over with Layton, who did not make a counter-offer. 'Saw Sir Henry Strakosch, our chairman, this morning', noted Parkinson a few days later. 'He seems sorry I am leaving the Economist, but will not stand in my way. He also leaves a little anxious about what is going to happen.'

Layton was almost ready to give up the editorship, if he could do so to the right person on the right terms. His 1965 recollections recorded that 'there were three men writing for the paper all of whom were candidates for the post of Editor. They were Prof. Arnold Toynbee, Graham Hutton and Geoffrey Crowther. Of these Toynbee already had an international reputation but administration was not one of his strong suits, and his historical writing was too valuable to spend his time on administration or supervising a growing staff; Graham Hutton's background knowledge almost rivalled that of Professor Arnold Toynbee, but it was not organised for quick or simple exposition. There was not room in some of his more complex sentences for all the ideas that sought refuge there. But Geoffrey Crowther had all the qualities of an ideal Editor, including a terse and simple gift of expression.' Or as Tyerman put it: 'The long head was on Crowther's thirty-year-old shoulders. He knew where he stood and what he stood for.'

By this time Crowther had in effect been Layton's personal assistant for five-and-a-half years and had become, in Layton's words, his 'spiritual son', with whom he had an easy relationship of a kind he was never to manage with any of his seven children. Crowther understood Layton's mind better than anyone else. He used to say that when he stood in for Layton he edited by interpreting his silences on the telephone. The services he performed for Layton included preparing the second edition to *An Introduction to the Study of Prices*, in recognition of which Layton added Crowther's name to the title page. In July 1938 Crowther wrote the preface to the third edition.

For his part, Crowther had found in Layton the mentor he sought. In Hutton's retrospective view, Crowther was at that time deeply impressed by people who had played a major role on the international stage. For Layton he had 'a profound respect that was nearly religious'. Yet Crowther was also intensely ambitious, aiming to become editor of *The Economist* while still young and then, at around 50, to move over into the world of business and become a multi-millionaire.

During Crowther's early years with the paper Hutton was the heir apparent. Yet despite all his achievements for the paper, and although he was very close to Layton and his family, the longer Hutton was there the less suitable he seemed for the editorship. Fifty years later, Hutton's judgment on himself was that he had probably seemed too unpredictable. He recalled Mark Abrams, a distinguished *Economist* contributor and friend, describing him as 'here there and everywhere like a parched pea in a pan'. Crowther, by contrast, had been completely single-minded; everything he learned and everything he did during his time with Layton made him a more credible candidate for his job. A prime example was his address in January 1934 to the Royal Statistical Society.

In October 1933 the paper had published a supplement called 'An Index of Business Activity', a brave innovatory attempt to show short-term variations in economic conditions, which was fraught with problems and highly controversial in the eyes of some members of the Royal Statistical Society.[2] Crowther described how he had constructed the index before an audience that included some of the greatest experts in the statistical field. In the chair was the RSS president, Lord Meston of Agra and Dunottar, one of James Wilson's successors in India. Immensely learned and technical, yet lucid, the address as published in the society's journal ended with a disclaimer: 'We make no claims of statistical perfection or of theoretical infallibility for our index. We regard it rather as a pioneer attempt to make this particular variety of bricks with a scanty and indifferent supply of straw.' Suggestions for improvements would be gratefully received. 'But our greatest hope is that in the next few years the starvation diet upon which statisticians in the country are at present forced to subsist may be transformed into the relative plenty of America.' Crowther was still finding his style; he would learn to coin phrases with more originality and *élan*, but he was already showing an almost Bagehotian desire to explain through the medium of the simple but apt phrase. He once remarked critically of a member of his staff that he had 'a certain tendency to write "professionally", i.e. in such a way as can only be understood by those who already know all about the subject'. A determination to make everything intelligible was to be a dominant feature of his editorship.

Among those who spoke at the meeting in response to his address, in addition to four members of the RSS Council, were Sir George Paish, retired adviser to the Chancellor of the Exchequer and ex-editor of the *Statist*; Norman Crump, who, like all the others, made a number of criticisms; and Hargreaves Parkinson, who helped Crowther out by putting the Index in a sensible perspective: its purpose was 'not to replace or refute any other index, but to give the readers of the paper the earliest possible intimation of how the seething mass inside the pot was boiling up'.

'I was well aware', responded Crowther to all his critics, 'that in accepting the invitation of your Secretary to come here to-night, I was adopting the position of one who attempted to expound the composition of a patent medicine to the General Medical Council, but I am still of the opinion that this index, imperfect though it is, inaccurate as it is, incorrect as it may be, is still worth publishing month by month.' Concisely, authoritatively and good-humouredly, he rejected the main criticisms and warned against defeatism: 'One critic said it was not possible to compile an index of business activity. In the narrowest statistical sense of course it is not possible, nor is it possible in that sense to compile an index of prices or of anything.' It was an astonishingly confident performance by a 26-year-old. Whatever he might say about Crowther's statistical orthodoxy, no one present, or reading the proceedings afterwards, could be in any doubt about his intellectual quality.[3]

In 1935, when Strakosch was trying to push Layton out, there is some evidence to suggest that Crowther influenced Layton towards the half-way measure with Parkinson that kept the succession open. Later, Hutton's five-month sabbatical gave Crowther the opportunity to establish himself at *The Economist*, dealing with routine administration, sub-editing and seeing the paper through the printers. By February 1938 he was experienced enough to be a credible editor, though Layton seemed no closer to giving up. That month Parkinson recorded that at lunch Crowther had seemed 'tired and dissatisfied with his future and the world generally'. The *Financial News* offer to Parkinson came at a perfect time for Crowther. The only obstacle to be overcome was Strakosch, whom Layton had to neutralise. Although Crowther unquestionably loved, admired and was always kind to Layton, he manipulated him brilliantly.

Strakosch was not pleased at the idea that *The Economist* should be handed over to a stripling, and an intellectual stripling at that, but Layton had used the time-honoured method of offering only unacceptable alternatives. Crowther was preferable to a bohemian polymath or an historian of ideas. The chairman concentrated on damage limitation, seeking a way of getting round *The Economist*'s guarantees of editorial freedom. Over the next few months Parkinson, and then Layton, tried to find some formula to reassure him. In May, after conversations with Bracken, Layton and Strakosch, Parkinson addressed the central issue: what happened in the event of a clash between 'editorial principle and immediate commercial interest . . . How far should a paper go in advocacy of an unpopular policy, which may seriously reduce its circulation?' *The Economist*'s editorial traditions were 'well-established and undisputed', but subject to adjustment.

> The dynamic of events, and changing currents of public opinion, must be closely followed by any newspaper which desires, directly or indirectly, to

influence either. 'The Economist's' devotion to liberal principles (in the widest sense) has been unquestioned for 95 years. But uncompromising opposition to the introduction of a general tariff for British industry, appropriate in 1923, had ceased to be possible in the changed conditions of 1931–32. In the very near future, again, the question may well arise as to how far cherished ideals of individual liberty should be subordinated to the interests of public safety, in a time of national emergency. To be over-hasty in compromising with a changed environment is to be attainted of extremism; to be laggardly is to forfeit the interest of readers. And that, for a newspaper, is fatal.

However, he said uncompromisingly: 'Whenever editorial principle and immediate commercial interest are not wholly coincident, the former must prevail.' Parkinson suggested the setting up of an editorial committee of five, comprising the new editor, Strakosch and Layton, with Parkinson himself and Harry Hodson as outsiders with an understanding of *The Economist*.

> I venture to think that, with such a membership, the committee would have a reasonable balance of interests and an array of accumulated knowledge and experience which could hardly be equalled. The two members of the Board, for example, would not merely form an invaluable link with the 'commercial' side of the paper; they would bring, in addition, a weight of authority as two of the foremost economists of their time.

It would be apparent that the editor could obtain a favourable vote on any policy he brought forward, provided he could convince two other members of the committee. 'In the last resort, a paper should, and must, bear the imprint, mainly, of its editor's personality. But a committee on these lines would, I believe, provide the one link which is missing in the present constitution.'[4]

Despite all the carefully-applied soft soap, Parkinson's compromise bit the dust. A month later, Strakosch circulated a memorandum on 'Editorial Policy', which addressed two issues. First, he and 'a number of influential readers of "The Economist" in whose judgement I have very great confidence' were critical of editorial policy. Too much space was devoted to foreign politics, which were presented 'in a manner which savours far too much of party politics'. There was too little technical coverage on high finance, and the investment notes were inadequate: 'what in my view "The

Economist" needs is a diminution of the space given to foreign and general politics, the avoidance of anything that would suggest political partisanship, both as regards leaders and second-hand news items relating thereto, and at the same time a stiffening on the technical side, particularly finance and investment, but also economic'.

In the course of his complaints, Strakosch had implicitly questioned whether Layton was doing the job required of him by the Articles of Association: 'to maintain to the best of his ability the general character and traditions of "The Economist"': he thus left himself wide open to a riposte. A devastating exoneration was produced – under Layton's name, but mainly prepared by Crowther. Liberally larded with statistics, it called the great names of the paper's past as witnesses for the defence. Excluding the Great War, the document divided the past into five main periods.

In Wilson's time, when his party was in office, 'The *Economist* policy was "semi-official" (Wilson's life speaks of writing his weekly Economist articles while sitting on the Treasury bench), and when the Tories were in, the Economist was frankly an opposition organ. The paper at that time, gave a great deal of space to agricultural and Commercial treaties.'

In Bagehot's time *The Economist* had given more space to politics than ever afterwards. 'Acute analyses and criticisms of political speeches occupied much space, and the proportion of articles dealing with the internal politics of foreign countries – particularly France – was very great. During this period, the circulation of the Economist rose steadily and its prestige was very high.'

In Johnstone's time the proportion of space given to politics fell. 'The cost of paper and composing was evidently low. Bulky supplements of statistics were printed (the trade returns were printed monthly in full!), articles of five or six columns containing columns of standardised tables were published month after month. The paper became dull and technical and its influence and circulation stood still and then began to sag. It was living on its past.'

Under Hirst the paper had been overhauled thoroughly and had resumed its political and general character. It was broadly supportive of the Liberal government, though critical of the armaments race. Non-economic articles dropped to a low figure of 29%, 'but this was due to the fact that the number of articles increased to a very high figure since almost everything was dealt with in Leaders'. There followed an elaborate demonstration of how a different method of analysing the figures showed that the number of articles on general topics was the same as in 1938.

'Since 1922 the proportion of space devoted to non-economic subjects remains about the same as that of the Johnstone period. In recent years, however, the effect of the greater amount of space devoted to business and technical matters has been deliberately minimised by layout and segregation of technical matter – so that the transition from the general and political part of the paper to the technical part is gradual.' This was wise from the point of view of broadening and extending circulation.

'The analysis, however, lends no support to the suggestion that the Economist has departed from its traditions by becoming more political. For my part, I think it would be a very great mistake to reduce the space devoted to home and foreign politics.' The paper was read widely and 'in important quarters' at home and abroad for its political articles.

> In my judgement there is a 20,000 or more circulation to be obtained by the Economist if it directs its appeal to the general reader who is also interested in Economic affairs and who recognises the interaction of Economics and politics. An economist's and banker's organ might have a circulation of 5,000. A more purely stock exchange organ could get a large circulation if it were better than the rivals already in this field. It is in the tradition of the Economist to appeal to as broad a section as possible of the intelligent classes at home and abroad.

It was Layton's hope that, with this end in view, 'the Economist will have more articles of general interest, employ the most modern technique of lay-out and illustration, and seek to ensure that everything from cover to cover is written in a good and attractive style'.

The statistical bombardment was appended.

ANALYSIS OF ECONOMIST LEADERS

The following table analyses the subject matter of the leading articles in the Economist in different calendar years from 1860 to 1935.

	1860	1866	1870	1875	1880	1891	1905	1910	1925	1935
					Percentages					
Home economics	37	50	31	41	32	43	48	53	50	40
Foreign economics	5	6	11	12	6	11	8	12	13	14
Imperial economics	5	2	2	2	6	6	6	6	3	3
Other economics									2	1
Total economics	47	58	44	56	44	60	62	71	68	58
Home politics	32	28	29	27	36	27	23	16	23	24
Foreign politics	15	11	26	14	14	10	12	8	5	12
Imperial politics	3	2	1	3	6	3	2	3	2	2
Miscellaneous	2	1	–	–	–	–	–	2	2	4
Total non-economic	53	42	56	44	56	40	38	29	32	42
Total articles on which percents. are based	396	371	242	266	248	315	362	497	369	369

The above figures are calculated according to the *number* of articles covering different subjects, not according to space. For 1860 and 1866 the figures include leaders, notes and long letters, as these are indistinguishable, but from that date they cover only leading articles.

(In 1987 Rupert Pennant-Rea and Dudley Fishburn analysed six issues according to a set of modern, but not dissimilar, criteria.

PERCENTAGES

International Politics	15.0
Internal Politics	31.6
International Economics	3.9
Internal Economics	12.3
Demography	4.7
Company, Sector Performance	13.1
Cross-Sector Business	1.3
Finance	6.7
Banks and Banking	3.0
Science and Technology	4.9
Arts	3.5

Strakosch would have been deeply upset.)

The allegation of political partisanship was then addressed. If this meant that editorial comment was 'unfair, imputes unworthy motives or is biassed by party considerations', that would be a very grave fault, which Layton strongly denied. If the criticism was that views were too strongly expressed, 'my reply is that forceful and forthright comments follow the best traditions of the paper. I have, for example, just picked up at random the volume for 1875. The first article that caught my eye was one dealing with "Parliament and the Press", the occasion being an attempt by a disgruntled member to stop the reporting of speeches on the ground that it was breach of privilege. Bagehot observes that "the debate . . . was a very helpless one, and helpless just because the natural adviser of the House abdicated his position and recommended it to do nothing, when it was evident to the least brilliant capacity that it was absolutely necessary to do something".' After two more examples from Bagehot, Layton continued: 'The other period in which the most outspoken articles will be found is during the Hirst regime.* At both periods *The Economist* was on the upgrade both in circulation and in influence. In both periods it was strongly criticised; but that was bound to happen to any journal that takes a definite line and does not sit on the fence.' The worst fault of an influential paper was to be 'neutral and dull. I maintain that *The Economist* should speak from conviction and put its views as forcefully as it can – provided always that its manner of expression does not overstep the boundaries – so impossible to define – of good taste.'

The second major issue which Strakosch had raised had been editorial responsibility. He objected to Article 105,† which gave the editor 'dictatorial powers in regard to the direction and control' of editorial policy, which were without precedent in the newspaper world and 'inconsistent with the duties of the Board'. He wanted it to be abolished and replaced by friendly

---

*Bearing in mind the invective to be found during Wilson's editorship, let alone what was said in Johnstone's day about Gladstone and Home Rule, it is clear that both periods had been written off as unworthy of investigation.

†The objectionable second sentence of Article 105 was: 'Provided that every such [editor's] Agreement shall contain similar provisions to those contained in the draft Agreement referred to in the last preceding Article entrusting to and conferring upon the Editor of the Economist Newspaper (to the exclusion of the Board of Directors) the sole direction and control of the editorial policy of the Economist Newspaper and also conferring upon the Editor the right to exercise all such of the powers exercisable by the Directors under these presents as may be necessary for rendering effective the Editor's control of the editorial policy of the Economist newspaper.'

collaboration between board and editor, with a gentleman's agreement that neither party would 'spring surprises on the other'.

Layton was firm: editorial independence was crucial. When the 1928 purchase was being organised, both Cowdray and Sir Josiah Stamp had insisted that *The Economist* should have no shareholders whom it might have to criticise, unless there was absolute independence. 'It is thus clear that when the constitution was drawn up, the public was intended to understand that the Board would not function as a body to control policy as is normal with an ordinary newspaper, but that ultimate responsibility would rest with independent trustees functioning through an Editor in whom they had confidence. I venture to think that these provisions have achieved their object and that it would be detrimental to the paper if they were whittled away. I personally may have been criticised as misguided or biassed, but no one has been able to say of the Economist that its policy has been subjected to external pressure, financial or otherwise.'

> I am opposed to the simple deletion of Article 105, because I think that however smoothly things may work in the immediate future, it will mean that ultimately it may be taken for granted that normal Board-room control over policy may be legitimately exercised. Indeed it seems likely that sooner or later it will be so exercised unless a particularly strong-minded Editor refuses to take instructions and shelters himself behind the Trustees.

It had never been intended that an editor should ignore the views of members of the board, whose 'directorship is not merely a trusteeship for the shareholders, but is a form of service to the public through the newspaper, and incidentally a most unremunerative one! Moreover an Editor who fell foul of his Board and of the Trustees would lose his job.' He therefore proposed modifying rather than deleting Article 105* to take account of this, and involving the trustees more.

In this crucial battle for the soul of the paper, Strakosch was vanquished on all fronts. Henceforward, *Economist* editors were protected by unchallenge-

*The revised second sentence was: 'Provided that every such Agreement shall impose on the Editor an obligation in directing and controlling the editorial policy of the Economist Newspaper to maintain to the best of his ability its general character and traditions and shall provide that with a view to so doing the Editor shall from time to time confer with the Board of Directors and that any such conference shall take place whenever either the Editor or the Board of Directors consider it desirable.'

able guidelines. Woolly though the paper has been about its past, since Layton's retirement there has never been any doubt about the relationship between editor and board. Nor has any serious challenge been mounted against the extent of the political coverage.

Layton made only two concessions, and both were more apparent than real. He admitted that business and industrial coverage was unimaginative, that there were insufficient technical articles and that the banking section had too often been 'humdrum' and 'stereotyped'. However the diminution in the coverage of monetary theory was 'because it plays a less dominating part in world affairs. Differences of view on this subject are in abeyance whereas commercial policy and political influences are clearly playing a great part over the whole field of economic activity. A survey of the history of *The Economist* brings out that this change of emphasis inevitably occurs from time to time.' Too much was being written by the staff and a narrow circle of outsiders. It would involve a little money, but the number of outside contributors should be increased. Crump had just left, and Crowther and Layton wanted to attract new talent, so this concession merely provided an excuse for investing yet more money in quality.

The second concession was an admission that it was desirable 'that the Editorship of the Economist should be regarded as a whole-time appointment, or at all events that it should be the Editor's sole important journalistic appointment'. Three weeks later, on 20 July 1938, citing his growing responsibilities elsewhere, Layton resigned formally. He expressed his very great regret, 'for those who are privileged to sit in the chair of Walter Bagehot fill one of the most enviable positions in British journalism'.

Hutton left in August. His last article, 'DANUBIA'S DILEMMA', was highly appropriate. Not only was it about Hungary, but its last two sentences made history. He had bet a few scoffing colleagues half-a-crown each that he would manage to sign an article before he left. 'And the Germans threaten to become for the non-Slavs', was the introduction to his veiled acronym, '– Greeks, Roumanians and Hungarians – alien masters. Helots usually turn traitors, or nuisances.'*[5] He got over his disappointment within a few

---

*In 1939 Hutton published the much acclaimed *Danubian Destiny*. He had worked informally for Intelligence during much of the 1930s, and when war broke out he was posted to its staff at Bletchley. From there he was sent to the American Mid-West to spearhead a propaganda campaign for the Ministry of Information which earned him an OBE. After the war he earned his living in London as a successful economics consultant, writer, and broadcaster.

months and was restored to his affectionate relationship with Layton. He stayed on warm terms with Crowther, always took a deep interest in the paper's progress and, having a freakishly good memory, was able to give tremendous help in providing information for the paper's history.

On 1 September, Strakosch wrote to the trustees advising them of the proposed amendment to the Articles and informing them of the appointment of Crowther, who 'as a part time assistant on the Editorial side . . . has proved himself sober in his judgment and efficient in his work'. 'In choosing Geoffrey Crowther the Board were right in their preference', wrote Layton in 1965, 'for in the seventeen years of his editorship *The Economist* made greater progress in every way than in any similar period in its history. For over thirty years Geoffrey has been my most brilliant and reliable colleague.' Crowther did not live long enough to write his memoirs, but in March 1956 he wrote to his chairman:

31 March, 1956

My dear Walter,

   This is the last day of my editorship and I don't want it to pass without some attempt to put on paper my grateful realisation of the fact that it was you who made it possible in the first place, and have supported me throughout. I have never been conscious of doing anything on The Economist beyond developing the conception of the paper that you first taught me.

With every good wish,
Yours ever,
Geoffrey

'I became Editor on the night of Munich', wrote Crowther in his valedictory, 'and my introduction to the duties of the office was to sit up the whole of that night, re-writing my leader over and over again as the reports came in.' He and Bird finally left the printers at 6am. While Layton havered across the street at the *News Chronicle*, Crowther analysed the information he had and summed up.

   The temptation is almost irresistible to thrust aside the precise details of the agreement arrived at in Munich, whatever they may be, and to treat them as of little account beside the magnitude of the universal relief that we have been saved, at the fifty-ninth minute of the eleventh hour, from destruction.

> But to-day's rejoicings will sound a little flat if it is soon discovered that the
> great crisis of our civilisation is merely postponed, soon to fall on us again.
> And they will appear downright foolish if it eventually transpires that this
> week's work has lessened our powers of resistance to aggression when we
> come to meet it again. The skeleton at the feast is not a lovable creature. But
> even at the risk of casting ourselves for this role we feel constrained once
> more to repeat what has been said so frequently in these columns: any
> agreement with the ambitious dictator-States, whatever its apparent terms,
> will turn out to be bad and dangerous in so far as it rewards aggression, good
> and beneficent in so far as it warns the aggressor for the future. We hope
> that the Munich Agreement, when it comes to be put to the touchstone of
> experience, will prove to have been a good day's work.[6]

If Crowther did not go as far as Churchill (or Hutton, who had wanted war
over the Rhineland), he was no appeaser: there was no doubting the firmness
of every line taken by the new editor. 'By the eve of the war', wrote Tyerman
in the centenary issue, '*The Economist* held clear views on rearmament
finance, full employment and inflation; the attempt was being made to place
the monetary policy in perspective against the wider economic background.'

> Then came the war, the single track of wartime journalism and the
> straitjacket of paper rationing. What contribution the paper may have made
> to war economics and war finance is recent and can be read.[7]

The paper proffered two main policies – one, the attack on inflation, was old;
the other, the crusade for central planning, was new. In 1941, a Tyerman
article provided a typical example of the novel approach. Discussing the need
to give proper incentives to managers and workers in their work for the war
effort, he explained that it was 'more state control, not less, that is probably
wanted, if the war effort is not to be resolved into a confusion of competing
claims; effective central planning and allocation in the technical field, if the
regional decentralisation . . . is to work; and a single centralised wages policy,
if the programme of wage adjustment is to mean anything'.[8]

Taking stock in the centenary issue, Crowther was urgently concerned to
justify change, for there was no denying that much had altered during his and
Layton's editorships. *The Economist*'s ideas had hardly altered for 80 out of
100 years, he explained, but had then had to move on from the Manchester
School. 'So many battles have been fought round the symbols of the liberal

faith that it is often forgotten that they were only symbols. The ultimate objects of nineteenth-century liberalism were part of that great awakening of the human spirit which marched in step with the developing technique of the modern world.'

> Opinions will naturally differ on precisely what, in any order of ideas, is a fundamental dogma and what is mere changeable expression. But the two dominant beliefs of the liberal philosophy are comparatively easy to identify. The first is freedom – the belief that it is not only just and wise but also profitable in politics and in economics to let people do what they want to do. The second is the principle of the common interest – that is, that human society need not be an arena of conflict, but that it can be an association for the welfare of all. Nearly all else in the beliefs of *The Economist* of a hundred years ago is merely incidental to these two grand principles.

Although the custodians of the modern *Economist* had come to have doubts about their forefathers' means, they still believed as passionately as ever in their ends. 'The problems of the national and the international society seem, in 1943, to be more complex and more difficult than they did in 1843, and less capable of solution by simple and embracing formulas. But the ultimate goals remain unchanged.' The policy of the paper could be expressed 'as being that of adhering to the fundamental objectives of 1843, but of modifying the means of attaining those objectives as time passes, as experience accumulates and as the climate of society changes'.

In 1843 there was only one economic objective: wealth creation. In 1943 there were three: 'They have been defined by Professor Pigou as being to increase the national income (the old policy of increasing the sum total of wealth), to improve the regularity of the national income and to improve its distribution among the individual members of the community. In more homely terms, they can be expressed as being to abolish poverty, to diminish unemployment and to reduce inefficiency.'

The development from the 1843 belief in complete *laissez-faire* 'to a belief that the organs of the state have a most important and positive function to perform in the national economy, as expressed in *The Economist* of 1943, is a necessary consequence of the widening objective'. *Laissez-faire* could not prevent economic fluctuations or reduce inequality of income: it was 'all but dead in the Britain of 1943'. (It had been thoroughly resurrected by 1993. 'Market-minded thinkers since Adam Smith have acknowledged that the case for intervention by governments is strong – in theory. That is because "market failure" . . . is indeed common and because – again in theory – governments are wise, disinterested and technically competent. In practice, as you may have observed, governments rarely measure up to those standards, least of all when trying to spur growth by intervening. That is why, in the real world, government failure has done more harm than market failure. Interventionists have been allowed their propaganda advantage too long. It is they who are the sellers of textbook theories. Those who favour markets are the pragmatists.'⁹)

Nothing was sacred to Crowther in 1943. While the paper was still a great believer in free trade, 'in a world that seeks regularity in its economic system, and that uses force in its political relationships, it is highly doubtful whether the best way to secure the maximum possible division of labour is simply to remove all controls and impediments. For example, there is no doubt that a country does far more harm to world trade by allowing itself to suffer a depression than by almost any imposition of obstacles to foreign trade. If a necessary part of a Full Employment policy is (as it would be in Great Britain) the taking of steps to prevent too sudden a rise in imports, does that mean that Full Employment must be forsworn, lest it infringe the Free Trade canon?' The answer was one of balance. 'The primary test of a country's commercial policy should not be the height of its tariffs, but whether on balance its foreign trade is expanding. And . . . if there must be restraints on freedom of trade, they should be restraints imposed in the general interest . . . Controlled expansion in the public interest is leagues apart from restrictive protectionism.' (Unfettered free trade is now also back in vogue. In a late 1992 issue of *The Economist* Edward Carr explained how, after repeal of the Corn Laws in 1846, 'Continental Europe soon followed Britain's lead into what was to become an era of rural prosperity built on the growing urban demand for meat. The prosperity did not last long. Within 30 years, recession and a war between Germany and France had driven most of Europe to abandon farm trade . . . The rest of the continent sought protection in the 1930s, during the Depression. So ended farming's sole exposure to free trade.' After a survey of the state of agriculture, he concluded: 'Farm protection is ubiquitous. It has a formidable history. It remains a potent emotional and political force. Without 30 years of free trade in 19th-century Europe, it would seem impossible to believe that reform were feasible. But it is. If voters are informed and leaders have the courage to confront farmers, the world can rid itself of the most regressive, wasteful and persistent folly in modern history.'[10])

Herbert Morrison mused in his centenary speech about the economic stance of the paper in 1943. 'Not many years ago, economists had a higher output of heat than of light. In plain English, they were like a collection of Kilkenny cats. Now, I gather, it is all different, and there is almost an official economic view, outside politics and in many respects above controversy, with which the great majority of economists agree; and to this more unified outlook in economics I think it will be agreed that Lord Keynes has made a principal contribution. This is very good for the authority and prestige of *The Economist* as the principal mouthpiece of doctrine; and I should like to congratulate the editor of *The Economist* on occupying something like the archbishop's chair at an episcopal synod. He does not claim infallibility – well, he does not claim infallibility in so many words – but he wears the panoply and wields the power of the head of a great system of established belief. He bears the keys of the kingdom – perhaps I should say the Keynes of the kingdom – and can hardly find a heretic to burn at the stake.'

A few heretics – or throwbacks – were present, including Francis Hirst and his ally Sir Ernest Benn, President of the Society of Individualists, who recorded the occasion in his diary.

> *September 2, 1943*: The *Economist* Centenary luncheon, a really wonderful exhibition of the decencies of English public life. A hundred or more of the leading figures in the City of London turned up to do honour to a great paper which has survived a hundred years. The Chancellor of the Exchequer and the Governor of the Bank of England both spoke to the main toast, skated round the subject, and left the company to infer that they were not happy about the present policy of the paper. Sir Walter Layton and Geoffrey Crowther displayed an impertinence which I rather envied. They both made long speeches, talked of Wilson, the founder, Bagehot, the most famous of the Editors, John Stuart Mill, Robert Giffen, Hartley Withers, Francis Hirst, Asquith, Milner and other orthodox economists; these two revolutionaries calmly assumed the mantle of the lot of them and claimed to be carrying on in the great tradition. They are, in fact, week by week, preaching every sort of financial heresy.[11]

One man's heresy, is, however, another man's orthodoxy. In the context of the paper's long history, another section of Morrison's entertaining speech is important: 'If I have amused myself by trotting out these skeletons from *The Economist*'s cupboard, it is only to show that *The Economist* today can rise superior even to the claims of consistency – the hobgoblins of little minds, and the plague, sometimes, of big ones – and I can say that in times when we ourselves know how greatly people can rise above controversy, even inconsistency and even in high places, *The Economist* possesses, in fact, the chief ingredient of human wisdom, an ability to learn from experience.'

CHAPTER XLII

Wartime

We have already gone a considerable way towards doing something that is unique in British journalism – namely, the collection into a single team of people who are primarily experts in their own fields but employ their expertise in journalism. All the other weeklies, for example, have a very small nuclear staff and rely on outside contributors to fill their space. Almost the whole of *The Economist* is now written in the office by our own staff. They use, of course, information obtained from outside, but the paper is produced as a consistent and coherent whole – to its very great advantage, as I think. As present we pursue this policy somewhat imperfectly. In particular, we are compelled by poverty to rely unduly either on part-timers or on juniors. But at comparatively little expense, we could build up a very fine team of informed, responsible and authoritative journalists.[1] *Geoffrey Crowther, 1943*

Economist wisdom has always been that Bagehot created the paper of the nineteenth century and Geoffrey Crowther that of the twentieth. In fact the creators were Wilson and Layton. It was Layton who saved Wilson's invention from any threat of corruption: it was his forethought that enshrined in legal form the tradition of editorial independence that has been the foundation of the paper's spectacular success in the post-1945 years.

What Bagehot and Crowther did, brilliantly, was to refashion their inheritance in the light of changing times. Seventy years after Bagehot had produced his memorandum on the state of *The Economist*, Crowther produced his. It was written almost five years after he became editor, a period during which – as with Crowther's whole career – there had been great highs and lows. He had inherited the paper in 1938 at the moment when it achieved the magical figure of 10,000 in circulation. Within a year the outbreak of war had cut away 2,000 readers, expansionist plans had been jettisoned, paper rationing had been introduced and key staff were lost. Roland Bird disappeared into Intelligence, some of the office staff disappeared into uniform and Crowther himself, in mid-1940, followed Walter Layton into the Ministry of Supply, later spending a period in the Ministry of Information and then as deputy head of the joint war production staff at the Ministry of Production.

The civil service, one of his contemporaries later remarked, was 'a sea in which Geoffrey couldn't swim': he was an individualist who could not fit into a large organisation. He performed at his absolute best at the centre of a small admiring team. While he could cope with a superior like Walter Layton, whom he could directly persuade and manipulate, he was driven to distraction by his inability to get ministers to do what they were told. He could make recommendations, not decisions, and they could be rejected by one of several levels further up. Apart from a short period in Washington with the Anglo-American purchasing commission, Crowther was very unhappy with his government work, his misery exacerbated by his family's move to America in 1940 for the duration of the war.

Fortunately, apart from his time in America, Crowther's wartime service was part-time and there were compensations in new contacts and friends and always in his circle at *The Economist*. He was released to go back full-time to the paper in the spring of 1943, having done a deal with the Ministry of Information which involved his being exempted from war service in exchange for bringing into being and editing, simultaneously with *The Economist*, a journal called *Trans-Atlantic*, 'an important organ of Anglo-American publicity'.[2]

The Economist's staff in 1943 consisted of four part-timers and 22 full-timers, including five secretaries and clerks and four advertising canvassers (Kirk, with 51 years of service, Harry Bernard with 23, Howard Cox with 8, and Lionel Grey with 6). Management consisted of Gilbert Layton (32 years of service) and E.M. Webb (29), who as office manager was to continue until the 1960s the frugal habits of an earlier age. Roland Bird recalled his refrain of 'I gave you paper yesterday, Mr Bird. Why should you need any more today?' Among Webb's duties was the counting of unsold copies. If the books said that 317 copies were left over, then 316 would not do; a hue and cry would be raised to find the missing *Economist*. Vera Andrews (10 years), whose library had been destroyed by German bombs two years earlier, struggled to provide some vestigial service to editorial, and Chapman (46 years) continued to perform as a human calculator.

The truncated paper ran to 28 or 32 pages, of which about four were advertising. If the wartime management side was the preserve of the old, with the exception of Crowther the editorial side was manned entirely by the halt, the women and the dispossessed. The rock of industry, loyalty and good sense on which the paper had relied until Crowther's return was the acting editor, Donald Tyerman, who by 1943 had been with the paper six years.

Tyerman had been born in Middlesbrough in 1908 and had contracted severe polio at the age of three, leaving him with completely paralysed legs, which nonetheless grew to almost their natural length: at 5′ 10″, he was only about four inches shorter than he would otherwise have been. From heaving himself and his leg calipers around on two sticks, he had acquired a mighty torso and arms 'that could lift a house'. He was 'splendid-looking, cheerful, ruddy, open and vital' and passionately fond of sport, particularly cricket (he could bowl, and bat with a runner). In his early married life, partnering his wife, he would play tennis serving from the base line.

Much of Tyerman's childhood was spent in hospital, where male patients played cards with him and he was taught to read. His widowed mother was a teacher and he managed to acquire a reasonable education before going at 15 to the local secondary school. Although Oxford was an almost mythological concept in that corner of the world, his headmaster encouraged him to apply and the local education authority matched the £150 that came with the scholarship he won to Brasenose College. Going up in 1926, he took a first in Modern History and then spent a year working on a BLitt. on 'The relation between the banks and industry in periods of depression', which was unfinished when he went in 1930 to a lecturership at Southampton University College in economic history and politics. There he married one of his students, Margaret Gray, an intelligent and tough woman with whom he had five children; she gave her life to making it possible for him to minimise the effects of his disability.

It was at Southampton that Tyerman first showed his exceptional gifts as an encourager of talent. His wife recalled the arrival at one of his evening extension-classes of a booking clerk who told Tyerman he wanted to go to Oxford. Tyerman's response was that if he wrote essays, he would get to Oxford. In due course this is what Walter Taplin succeeded in doing;

Tyerman later brought him on to the pre-war *Economist* and he eventually became editor of the *Spectator*.

As secretary of the Appointments Committee, Tyerman received a notice sent on by Cambridge of a vacancy at *The Economist* for a junior editorial assistant – Douglas Jay's job. The application date having passed, he threw the notice in the wastepaper bin – and then fished it out, sent a telegram asking if he could still apply, and was invited for interview. For his thesis he had read through most of the nineteenth-century *Economist*, and to demonstrate his familiarity with the paper he carried to the interview in a brown-paper parcel his manuscript, with its numerous *Economist* source references.

Tyerman was always to claim that without the challenge posed by being a cripple he might have ended up as a clerk at the Middlesbrough gasworks. Certainly, the way he chose to live his life demonstrated that he possessed an extraordinary well of courage. Although he suffered no pain, the sheer effort of heaving himself about a world of staircases and long corridors was exhausting, frustrating and sometimes humiliating. It was exacerbated by living in a society where the fear of saying or doing the wrong thing can prevent even nice people from offering practical help.

Alastair Burnet was to be one of those who instinctively got it right. After Tyerman had handed over the editorship to Burnet, the basement restaurant, targeted by a protection racket, was firebombed, filling the building with black smoke. Tyerman, who retained an office in the building, and was by then overweight and suffering from a bad chest, had to struggle down 13 flights of stairs. Burnet (supported by some of his colleagues) stayed with him throughout the whole agonising journey, putting up a creditable imitation of a man whose response to being told to evacuate a burning building is to amble down stairs at a snail's pace exuding affability.

Tyerman's physical courage was matched by his moral courage. A letter written in October 1942, when he was acting editor of *The Economist*, was a case in point. To Brendan Bracken, who was then effectively co-proprietor of *The Economist* and who, until he became Minister of Information the previous year, had been managing director, Tyerman wrote:

Dear Mr Bracken,

No-one at your Ministry knows better than you the difficulties under which I work in wartime with a war staff to produce *The Economist*. I think you will agree that, when I released the Foreign Editor, Barbara Ward, to visit the

United States on behalf of the Ministry of Information, it was a concession involving considerable sacrifice and hardship on the part of *The Economist*. I made the decision because the cause seemed a good one, and because the distinct understanding, as it appeared to me, was that the trip would be a short one and the same official efforts would be made to expedite Barbara Ward's return as were made to speed her departure. The implied condition of her release was that she should be back at work here in October.

I now learn that she has been refused air priority of any kind and that she will not be back, by sea, until December. Frankly, while I realise the tremendous difficulties of air transport at present, I regard this as a breach of faith. It may be, I know, that everything possible has been done, without success. But, in the circumstances, I do not think it is unreasonable for me to ask you, personally, to see whether still more cannot be done by the Ministry, even at this late hour, to honour its side of the bargain, which has already fallen onerously on *The Economist* – in money as well as in time and effort. Plainly, after this experience, there can be no question in the future of any member of *The Economist* staff leaving the country to do Government work.

'Dear Tyerman', responded Bracken. 'I am sorry that you should have had to write to me in such round terms about Barbara Ward. She is a remarkable woman and I am not surprised that you should be indignant at not getting her back here so soon as you had hoped.'[3] Bracken looked into the problem, but Barbara Ward was not returned to *The Economist* until the beginning of January 1943, after an absence of five months which had coincided with a period when Crowther had hardly been able to do anything for the paper.

A typical issue of that period (7 November 1942) explains Tyerman's testiness: as well as editing he wrote three leading articles and four notes. Patricia Norton (who had come in 1939 as Crowther's secretary and whom he had encouraged to write) was by now a stalwart on the home affairs side and provided four notes; Margaret Stewart, the trade union expert, wrote three; and Walter Hill, in addition to providing the statistics, supplied two notes and the business leader as well as a contribution to the 'Finance and Banking' section. Also on the staff was Pamela Matthews, who had taken a brilliant degree in economics, had worked at Chatham House under Toynbee when it was relocated to Oxford and had had to come to London for personal reasons. She helped the stand-in business editor, Waldo Forge, who was City editor of the *Glasgow Herald* and was simultaneously meticulous and neurotic. He and Pamela Matthews between them wrote the 'Investment' section; she also contributed one of the notes. American Survey that week was as usual mainly written by Margaret Cruikshank, whom Crowther had imported the previous year to clip American newspapers. She worked part-time and also wrote leaders for *The Times*, on one occasion delivering her copy to Printing House Square on her way to hospital to have a baby.

Finance and Banking was written almost entirely by Paul Bareau, whom Graham Hutton had been so anxious to recruit in place of Norman Crump; he was one of the most elegant financial writers of his day and was to become City editor of the *News Chronicle* and later the *Daily Mail*. (Paul Bareau was appointed editor of the *Statist* in 1961. Prompted by Don Ryder, the thrusting editor of the *Stock Exchange Gazette*, Cecil King, the driving force of the parent group, the International Publishing Corporation, decided to revamp the *Statist*, then on its last legs as an investment weekly. His ambition was to turn it into a domestic rival to *The Economist*. With a talented group of journalists, including at various times, Jock Bruce-Gardyne, Adam Fergusson and Hugh Haining, it was kept afloat, making a small loss on a circulation of between 20,000 and 30,000, until axed in 1967. By that time Bareau had become editor-in-chief, Colin Jones having taken over as editor in 1965. Jones had originally joined the *Statist* directly from *The Economist* as industrial editor. Eventually he ended his full-time career as editor of the *Banker*, yet another successful rider on the roundabout of economic journalism.

The significance of this episode, as with the *FT*'s short-lived *World Business Weekly*, is in its failure. *The Economist*'s success has inspired competitive emulation, but so far it has been too well-rooted domestically and internationally to be toppled from its perch: the going was too hard, the cost too high. Crowther's foresight, notably in giving Bird his head to create a modern business section and in establishing American Survey as a distinct entity, had made that sure.)

That particular week Bareau was helped out by Hill and Norton. 'Industry and Trade' was written by Hill and Mrs Desbrow, with a freelance contribution from David Evans, who had been commenting on the coal industry for many years. Other outside contributors were Denis Brogan, the distinguished historian of France and America, who provided a piece for

American Survey; George O'Brien, the long-standing Irish correspondent and Professor of Economics at University College, Dublin; and Rahmer, who wrote about Germany and Denmark. The only other contributors were two part-timers, Schleiter and Deutscher.

Schleiter had been writing for the paper since the 1930s. One of Graham Hutton's recruits, he was one of the luckier of the refugees who moved in and out of *The Economist* for a decade from the mid-1930s, desperate for opportunities to earn some money. As Hartley Withers had been with Paul Einzig 20 years earlier, so Hutton, Crowther and particularly Tyerman were with the victims of the Nazis. There was little money to spare, but tiny amounts were distributed in exchange for material which was frequently written in fractured English that required laborious sub-editing. Tyerman's kindness to refugees was legendary; he listened sympathetically and rewrote patiently. Among the life-long friends he made at that time were Eric Sosnow, who had arrived in 1935 as foreign correspondent of a Polish financial daily, and Isaac Deutscher, who was on the staff of the same paper.*

Deutscher was one of *The Economist*'s more remarkable and unlikely recruits. Born in 1907 into an orthodox Polish Jewish family, he abandoned his religion for communism. Having joined the party in 1927, he was expelled in 1932 for suggesting that it should make common cause with social democrats in Germany in order to defeat Nazism; this was heresy – at that moment – to the Stalinists. Deutscher arrived in London in 1939 as a correspondent, and when war broke out he found himself stranded, with no source of income. Like Einzig, he had always longed to write for *The Economist*, and with the help of a dictionary he wrote an article and sent it in. Tyerman wrote inviting him to come to the office, but he was afraid that since he could not understand spoken English, no one would believe he had written his article, so he did not pay the office a visit until his English was adequate. By then he was a regular contributor. Donald and Margaret Tyerman took a great interest in Deutscher and helped him to perfect his English.

When Deutscher was ordered to join the Polish army and found himself stuck in a remote part of Scotland, *The Economist* reclaimed him to join the staff part-time and to write on European politics. A Trotskyist anti-Stalinist

---

*Editorial salaries in 1943 were: Crowther £2,000, Tyerman £1,000, Hill £900, Ward £550, Matthews £400, Norton £300, Stewart £350, Desbrow £250, Chapman £375, Vera Andrews £168, and the part-timers Deutscher £260, Schleiter £260, Forge £480 and Cruikshank £180.

intellectual and a gifted writer, Deutscher was to become the greatest exponent of an anti-Stalinist brand of Marxism in the Western world, through his biographies of Stalin, Trotsky and Lenin.

'I have never known such a time for foreign politics and the more there is to write about, the less one knows about the real event', wrote Barbara Ward to an American colleague in January 1944. 'I have a marvellous assistant who is worth far more to the paper than I could be if I slaved every night for ten years. He is a man of great journalistic capacity coupled with the background of a real scholar. Son of a Polish Rabbi, ex-Communist (in the proper international CP set-up) now a confirmed but noble sceptic, he is probably the most interesting & stimulating companion one could possibly have. For me, he is a constant source of shame for when you meet people of real culture, then is the time for you to realise the abysmal secondrateness of your own – I mean in the context "When *I* meet" & "secondrateness of my own."'[4]

Deutscher made with Barbara Ward an extraordinary partnership. Psychologically, intellectually and doctrinally, they were absolutely at odds, yet for a long time they worked admirably together and hugely enjoyed the partnership. In 1950, long after Deutscher had left the staff, Ward asked *The Economist*'s editorial representative in America, Helen Hill Miller, to help the Deutschers on their forthcoming visit. 'It does seem to me to be worthwhile attempting to broaden so able a mind and give a wider picture to one whose writings are bound to be influential . . . I am always divided in my mind between love and exasperation with my dear Deutschers. I respect his character and detest his theories. I love his warmth and affection, but his intellectual assurance sticks in my gizzard.'[5]

Like Crowther and Tyerman, Barbara Ward was from Yorkshire, but she was brought up at Felixstowe. Educated at a convent until she was 15 and then at schools in France and Germany, she had fluent French and German by the time she reached Somerville, Oxford, in 1932 as an Exhibitioner. Always a performer, success in university opera made her contemplate a career as a singer, but a first-class degree in PPE (philosophy, politics and economics) put her on a different path. She was briefly a university extension-lecturer in politics and economics, during which time she wrote a study of colonial problems called *The International Share-out*, published in 1938. At this time she visited her brother, who was working in Turkey, and began a study of Kemal's programme of national regeneration which was published in 1941.

From Italy and Turkey Ward had sent two freelance pieces which had made Crowther determined to get her on his staff. When war broke out in 1939 she was already part of Arnold Toynbee's monitoring unit at Balliol. When Toynbee was told to reduce his staff by 10%, he offered Ward to Crowther. This was a sensible choice, for she did not have the temperament to do the backroom job of sifting and summarising mountains of information.

Ward came to *The Economist* on a fortnight's trial and stayed for 11 years. The impact of this pretty, fragile, sexy (though chaste) woman on that staid institution can be illustrated by the fact that, when she died in 1981, Andrew Knight gave Roland Bird five pages in which to commemorate her – roughly eight times as much obituary space as Walter Layton had rated and four times as much as Geoffrey Crowther.[6] She had left the staff in 1950, but, through occasional contributions (she was on a retainer for many years), through visits, letters and friendships, she kept the paper collectively in love with her.

There were a few exceptions among the men. Graham Hutton, who met her in America, and John Midgley, who was a colleague, thought her overrated intellectually, and Donald Tyerman, though fond of her, maintained his detached historian's eye; but most of the other men, from Crowther downwards, were besotted. Female responses to her were more varied. Some felt exploited by her but most felt affectionate, and those who knew her best were sorry for her, as her public life of increasing fame and distinction was clouded by a private life of disappointment and loneliness.

In a sense Barbara Ward was closer to James Wilson in temperament and approach than any of his more orthodox journalist successors, for she was both a crusader and a belief producer. As Tyerman observed: 'With her mother an irresistible Catholic and her father an immovable Quaker, she had the qualities of both. When she "lost" her faith at Oxford and recovered it, she added the zeal of the convert to the steadiness of the Catholic born.'

Ward's Catholicism was intensely spiritual yet very worldly, in that she was driven by a desire to apply political and economic ideas that would make the world a better place for everyone. Summing up her post-*Economist* career, Bird wrote:

> Barbara Ward, Baroness Jackson of Lodsworth, has been a conscience and provider of fresh ideas, a spur and enthuser, a phrasemaker, provoker and counsellor to one pope and handfuls of cardinals and archbishops, to two

American Presidents and handfuls of their senior advisers, to British and countless other prime ministers and ministers of rich and poor governments alike, to successive presidents of the World Bank and dozens of the world corporate fry, small and large. Deeply Roman Catholic, her role since the war as a policy catalyst to great men of every kind, and as a teacher at Harvard, Columbia and many other colleges, has been catholic in a wider sense.

A woman whose devoted fans included John F. Kennedy and Lyndon Johnson (who claimed hers were the only books he ever read) – men not exactly noted for their respect for women's intellect and spirit – was a star indeed. Although when she joined *The Economist* late in 1939 she did not yet know her own strength, she was swiftly to establish herself as Geoffrey Crowther's equal, if not intellectually, certainly in terms of personality and fluency: if she could not remotely match him as an academic economist, she was by far his superior in imagination.

David Astor recalled meeting her during the war, when she was still in her twenties and they were both members of a small circle who used to meet in the flat of Stafford Cripps.

> Barbara was easily the equal of the men in this group in assertiveness. But she looked more like the daughter of a country vicarage than a high-powered woman writer. Her manner was charming, her style direct and good-natured, and her expression had just a touch of the angelic.
>
> Already she showed an amazing intellectual self-reliance. When she told Cripps he was missing the point or accused Crowther of being spiritually lazy, she was giving a strongly-held view, not point-scoring.
>
> Yet she never seemed to lose her balance or humour, never became clumsy or superior, even though her convictions were strong ones.

'Her contributions and questioning at editorial conferences were a joy', wrote Bird; 'she and Geoffrey Crowther sparked each other off and stimulated all the rest of us. Her writing and her talk were as fluent as his, though perhaps less firm and analytical, and her output was prodigious. She could write anywhere on anything . . . and always with immense persuasiveness.'

First as an editorial assistant, and then, once Tyerman became acting editor, his replacement as foreign editor, she brought clarity and distinction to the reporting of the war itself and idealism to the debate about the post-war world, as, for example:

On April 6th, 1941, about half an hour before the official Notes declaring war had been delivered to the governments of Greece and Jugoslavia, Germany invaded both countries. The pretext – that the Greeks and Jugoslavs had frustrated Germany's peaceful intentions by bringing the British into the Balkans and that German troops must now restore peace, order, and independence – barely merits recording. It is difficult to imagine for whose benefit these masterpieces of blatant falsehood are compiled. It must be a matter of profound indifference to the German people whether or not there is an excuse for each new chapter of slaughter, and the outside world has long since ceased to listen.[7]

And a week later:

The spring campaigns have opened. Before the people of this country lies six grim months during which every resource of Germany's arms and propaganda will be devoted to crushing their resistance. For once more the problem of Britain is not how to win the war but how not to lose it. Germany still enjoys a great preponderance of manpower and military equipment; the initiative still rests with the German General Staff; the conquest of Europe has put a moat round Germany where its defences were most vulnerable; its centralised position allows it to strike out in all directions from its strong compact defences. Against these advantages, Britain has, so far, only three to set – the promise of American help, the proved superiority of the RAF, and the ubiquity of British seapower. The winter victories have perhaps given the country the feeling of having turned the corner. It is a false feeling. The corner is barely in sight.[8]

Of Vichy France: 'The Fourteenth of July has come and gone and the anniversary of France's freedom has been spent for a second time under the shadow of a regime which is both a denial of and a disgrace to the honour of France.'[9] 'Japan is proving even more adept than Italy in the art of pre-belligerency. The hour of destiny is always about to strike. Historic decisions are forever about to be taken. Every phase of emergency is achieved until it seems that no further move is possible in any direction save that of war. Yet again and again the nation is checked on the brink of the final choice. Its leaders halt under the signpost and take counsel. They reiterate that Japan is, indeed, at the crossroads, but they show an obvious hesitation in advancing down any of the diverging roads.'[10]

From 1943 the separate abilities of Crowther and Ward were on show to the British nation on the hugely popular Brains Trust radio programme where panellists were asked to give their opinions on questions from listeners. It was a programme tailor-made for those capable of instant and elegantly expressed opinions. Walter Layton would have been a disaster on it, and Donald Tyerman little better. It was no vehicle for those who suffered from intellectual doubt or who were preoccupied with the need to be even-handed. As chairman, Crowther exuded brilliance, authority and wit: as a panellist, Ward exuded charm, goodness and zest. A Crowther appearance would be followed by letters to *The Economist* from listeners who wished to become subscribers. In the case of Ward, recalled her *Economist* colleague, Elizabeth Monroe, 'she became the personal counsellor to thousands of listeners – into her post-box poured letters from eager sixth formers, frustrated housewives wanting an outlet, conscripts wanting to know how to get to Oxford from the Army of the Rhine; these letters she always answered if she thought she could help'.

As Bagehot's contemporaries were to lament the impossibility of reproducing his conversational brilliance, so were Barbara Ward's. Tyerman told an extraordinary story of the effect she had on Ernest Bevin, the tough working-class trade union leader who had been an outstanding success as wartime Minister for Labour and on whose behalf she was speaking in the 1945 general election:

> One very hot summer evening the candidate turned up sweating from every pore and sat on the steps outside a meeting which Barbara was keeping in play until he came. As his perspiration cooled and dried, his face became wet with tears. Barbara was talking about the need for, and the way to, full employment, coolly, logically, intensely, in her high, compelling voice, and the hard-bitten trade unionist could not bear it.

Two extracts from their *Economist* writings illustrate the essential difference between Crowther and Ward, the head and the heart. One was an article which Crowther wrote late in his editorship before the general election of 1955. He was talking about the difficulties of the Liberals, 'or, as they are better named (to avoid the still remaining hazard of identification with a party), the Radicals', who had to decide whether to vote Labour or Conservative. 'It is to the Radicals that *The Economist* still likes to think of itself as belonging. That is the paper's historical position; that is the place to which it is carried by the momentum of the ideas it strives to represent; that is the personal instinct of those who are the present servants of the paper's traditions.'

> It is not very easy to define what is meant to be a Radical; but the essence of it is surely a belief in change and progress. Surely that belief, among those who profess it, is stronger today than ever before. There was never a time when the British people had more to lose by passive tranquillity. If they are to keep their place in the world – if indeed, on their crowded island, they are still to live and to prosper – it was never more necessary than it is today to foster the former zeal, to be willing to probe down to the roots of every stalk of the national life and to cut and to graft wherever an improvement can be seen. There ought to be nothing timid or tepid, nothing cautious and not too much that is merely judicious, about a Radical policy. It should have the quality that was described some years ago in these columns as that of the Extreme Centre – moderate and catholic in its aims, but audacious in their pursuit.

The problem, explained Crowther, was that this habit of mind was more a characteristic of the left and that while the paper was distinctly inclined against conservatism yet it found equally repugnant any dogmatism such as socialism – 'especially when it is professedly supplied in the interest of one class alone'. Detailed analysis in that and preceding articles therefore forced Crowther to the conclusion that for pragmatic reasons the Radicals could not vote Labour: 'An elector who tries to reach his conclusion by reason based on observation has no choice. He may not like voting Tory. But there is nothing else he can do.'[11] Symbolically enough, that article was called 'IN THE SIGN OF THE BALANCE'.

The contrasting article by Barbara Ward, 'UNSORDID ACT', written in 1948, was singled out by Roland Bird as one of her finest *Economist* pieces. 'Men lose their capacity for astonishment very easily', it began. 'Let a thing be mentioned often enough and they begin to accept it as a normal unsensational fact. Few things have been mentioned more persistently in the last ten months than the chances and the hopes and the possibilities offered by the Marshall Plan. Insensibly people have grown used to it. Its fabulous quality has been stripped away. But this week, since the Plan is no longer just a hope or a chance but a concrete reality – an Act approved by Congress and signed by the President, provisional funds already granted, ships already sailing with supplies from American harbours – this week, it is fitting that the peoples of Western Europe should attempt to renew their capacity for wonder, so that they can return to the United States a gratitude in some way commensurate with the aid they are about to receive. For a day or two, the Marshall Plan must be retrieved from the realm of normal day-to-day developments in national affairs and be seen for what it is – an act without peer in history.'[12]

Added to the powerful combination of Crowther and Ward in the 1940s was the great talent of Deutscher. He wrote with authority on Central Europe, but his contributions on Soviet affairs had something of the depth and passion of a Solzhenitsyn. In 1943 'THE RED ARMY' began by recalling 1918, when Russia – in the throes of a civil war – had possessed no army. 'The old military structure had been destroyed; the old discipline had been abolished. All that remained, after the revolution had achieved its work of destruction, was a seemingly amorphous mass. The critical point, familiar from the history of other revolutions, was reached when the disappearance of authority coincided with the pressing need to set up a new authority and a new discipline. The first step had to be made to change the chaos of anarchic decentralisation into a new centralised order. Only in the process of that change could an army, by its nature the most centralised of institutions, be created. The transformation could only be achieved gradually; and all the stages of that evolution have been reflected in the composition and outlook of the Red Army.'[13]

The historical analysis that followed was typical of Deutscher in its intellectual depth. However it was also coloured by the Deutscher belief that the experience of fighting fascism together would lead to friendship and cooperation between Russia and the West after the war. Whatever his reservations about Stalin, he refused to take seriously contemporary fears of Soviet expansionism.

> Axis propaganda has once again been using the bogy of Europe falling a prey to Bolshevism with the connivance of the British. Sir Stafford Cripps's speeches have been especially exploited for this purpose; and, over the innumerable German-controlled wireless stations, broadcasting in all European languages, the prospect of the Bolsheviks 'sitting in Berlin' has been presented as the avowed war aim of Great Britain. The effectiveness of this scaremongering should not be under-rated . . . If the Allies win the war Soviet Russia, it is said, is bound to gain a decisive say in European affairs. The

question, for Europeans, is: What will Russia do? And what matters most is not the short-term diplomatic zig-zags, which merely reflect the pressure of changing events, but rather the long-term trend of Soviet foreign policy, viewed against its economic, social and ideological background.

Deutscher's conclusion was that Soviet expansionist aims were essentially local, so Europe need not worry. Yet it would, he admitted, 'be futile to say that there was no risk involved in the present situation. Whatever the extent to which Russia has given up expansionist ambitions, and whatever the political line taken by its Government, other factors, independent of the conscious will and the political aims of Soviet statesmen, may count.'

> The Red Army carries with it the legend of a international Soviet revolution. It may be out-moded; but it still influences the imagination of considerable sections of the European proletariat. It is impossible to foresee all the possible implications of the impact of that legend upon a Europe hollowed out of its old traditions and turned by the Nazis into an amorphous social and political chaos. Many of the old ways of European life are likely to have gone for ever. But all that can be said now is that whatever risk there may be is a matter of the future: it may or it may not materialise. It is the risk that has sprung from Nazi totalitarianism, spelling the doom of European civilisation, that is the hard reality of today.[14]

Writing of how they ran the paper without Crowther, Tyerman remembered: 'We did it over, say, coffee at eleven in the Brettenham House café, after 8 Bouverie Street was destroyed in May, 1941. It was a sort of brainstorming. We talked in dozens, with Barbara setting the pitch; then we went back with leaders to write . . . We thought and felt and argued our way to what to say, Catholic, Marxist or Liberal or what not.'

So among its tiny staff *The Economist* of the 1940s contained two intellects and one persuader of world class, and in Donald Tyerman the sympathetic, intelligent and industrious presence who kept the show going when his more glittering colleagues were off the premises. Tyerman's contribution was to be widely underrated. Because he was a modest and charitable man with a deep appreciation of other people's talents, his perceptive and generous verdicts on his colleagues enhanced their reputations and tended to diminish his own by comparison. Tyerman was never more than a competent stylist – indeed he could be rather leaden – but, as one of his obituarists said, 'What common-sense, the broad view and the historical perspective could bring to the analysis of affairs, he could be relied upon to give.' Just as important was what he did for comparable or greater talents. To Isaac Deutscher and Tamara Lebenhaft (who lived with Deutscher from 1942 and married him five years later), Tyerman was a mentor, a friend, an opener of doors and an incomparable encourager of talent. Patiently he extracted ideas from people and stimulated them to give of their best.

During the 1939–45 war Tyerman's contribution was heroic. Unable to join up himself, he encouraged his wife to join the ATS (the women's army corps). This left him for long periods alone in London in a boarding house, immobile during air raids. It was typical of him that when Crowther returned to the paper and the pressure lifted, Tyerman took on the additional job of being deputy editor of the *Observer*. In September 1944 he moved to the deputy editorship of *The Times*, where his *Economist* experience and inclinations would help him to make a memorable contribution to the development of a forward-looking approach to post-war Britain's social and economic problems.

Crowther was Ward's rein and her ballast. He wrote of her once in a note to Eric Gibb in the late 1940s that 'her writing is never bad and at its best is quite brilliant. Her chief defect from my point of view is a certain tendency to go overboard in support of her latest idea, forgetting she was arguing the contrary last week.' Without Crowther's ability to subject her ideas to analysis and to insist that her arguments be rooted in fact, she would never have achieved the solid body of distinguished work that she produced throughout her decade working full-time for *The Economist*.

Some of her jealous contemporaries found her prone to glibness; she herself referred to 'my fateful facility'. A quote from one article on the Marshall Plan illustrates how slick and almost meaningless she could be. 'It must be done quickly, but it cannot be done quickly. It must be big enough to take the breath away, but there is no time to construct even the simplest structure.'[15] Words used to run away with her. There was the occasion when on the death of Deutscher in 1967 Ward wrote a typically beautiful letter to Tamara in London. 'The ocean divides us', she wrote. 'If only I could be at your side.' Next day Tamara accidentally heard her live and in London on radio.

Like Crowther's, Barbara Ward's remarkable gifts were offset by some remarkable character flaws. She was an exploiter of people, she was greedy for fame and money, and there was some tart comment in her circle about her ingenuity in avoiding tax payments on the large sums she earned by lecturing about Western taxpayers' duty to provide more funds for the Third World. Yet on balance she was a great source of warmth and inspiration and her influence on the paper was rightly cherished. As Geoffrey Crowther's conscience, she lifted its moral tone and together they made it – despite its still relatively small circulation – influential in the corridors of power in Washington and Western Europe, as well as in London. Where Layton's *Economist* had been influential because of his sources and his reputation, Crowther's was influential because of its sheer intellectual force in a way not achieved since Bagehot's day.

A good example of the Crowther–Ward partnership in action was on the issue of what should be done with Germany after the war. True to all the paper's traditions, they railed against the idea of a Carthaginian peace. In August 1944, in 'TERMS FOR GERMANY', an article written jointly argued against any 'peace with indemnities, reparations, annexations of territory and transfers of population'. Disclaiming in true *Economist* style any moral or idealistic reasons for opposing such a peace, they explained:

> It is supremely necessary to insist this is not a question of being kind to the Germans. Let it be conceded for the purpose of the argument that all Germans are thoroughly and irremediably bad and that there is no distinction to be drawn between the general body of German citizens and the most brutal sadist the Gestapo has ever produced. Let us all agree to hate them for ever. But let us, for Heaven's sake, leave all such emotions out of the very serious business of peacemaking, which is matter for cold calculation, not for emotions of either hate or love.

The only aim of a peace treaty was to avoid the recurrence of war. 'The question is whether the treaty will work. An unenforced treaty is the worst kind of all. It may be sound policy to love your enemy and go on loving him, or to kick him and go on kicking; but to kick him and then let him get to his feet is certainly the least sound of all policies.' Hard facts, not morals, were 'the compelling reasons why, in a settlement with Germany, it is absolutely necessary to go the way of moderation. It is only the moderate that will be enforced – not now, but in fifteen or twenty years' time when the fat and lazy habits of peacetime have returned.'[16]

Authors of the flood of critical letters that followed included Laurence Cadbury, a major shareholder, and Major General Guy Dawnay, one of the four members of the board of directors, who commenced his attack with: '*The Economist*'s view of the ultimate results of terms for Germany are, of course, *The Economist*'s views. They are not, however, demonstrably nor even necessarily accurate; and to say that the inclusion of "strong" territorial terms would ultimately and disastrously weaken the settlement is to make a statement which must be qualified by the words "in the view of *The Economist*".'

Crowther was always fearless in the columns of his paper. 'It is, of course,' he answered, 'obvious that every matter of opinion which is stated editorially in *The Economist* is only *The Economist*'s opinion. We have never claimed that what we think to be true is gospel truth; it would be absurd to do so.'

> In this case, however, there is a great deal of past experience to go upon, and General Dawnay does not cite a single piece of evidence to support his own opinion that the rulers and people of this country will be more willing to act, and if need be to fight, to keep Germans under the rule of, say, Dutchmen or Poles, in ten or fifteen years' time, than they were between the wars. All he says is that they *ought* to be more willing, which is a very different matter. Our view, simply put, is that we must be desperately careful not to promise now what we will not perform then, because that is the way to provide the enemy with the opening for his Third Attempt. In other words, the Peace must be as strong as *possible*. – EDITOR[17]

Crowther and Ward returned to the attack. 'The article which appeared under this same title, in *The Economist* of August 12th, has aroused considerable controversy, both in these columns and outside. It is good that the issue on which the whole peace settlement will turn should be capable of stirring minds and pens. But it is disappointing that few of the critics should have been able to understand an article which was quite clearly written. The critics have written at length about the treatment that Germany deserves; *The Economist* wrote about the sort of settlement that would work. They have expatiated on German psychology; we were concerned about British psychology. They have accused *The Economist* of wanting to be kind to the Germans; our only desire was to be truthful about the British. They have attacked us for wanting a soft peace; but the argument was for the sternest peace that had any hope of being maintained.'[18]

Sir Henry Strakosch had died in 1943 and been replaced by Layton, and the conduct of the board as regards editorial independence was exemplary. As

Minister for Information, Bracken occasionally made official contact with Crowther, but never misused his personal influence with the paper. He passed on to Crowther in December 1944 a complaint about a searing attack in *The Economist* on the general manager of the Associated Press news agency, who was accused of cloaking his commercial ambitions in the language of 'Liberty and Rights of Man'. Crowther responded with a flat assertion of his right to say what he thought. He referred to 'what Disraeli said of Gladstone (I quote from memory): "I do not object more than the next man to being cheated at cards, but I do object when my opponent tries to tell me that it was the Almighty who put the ace of trumps up his sleeve".'[19]

Two months later Bracken sent him a translation of an article in *Pravda* attacking *The Economist* 'for its "armchair criticisms"'. The paper – 'reputed a very staid and responsible journal' – was attacked for its alleged blindness in commenting on the military situation and for promoting 'an indulgent attitude to the German people' which smacked 'of the ideas of Chamberlain . . . Despite its mistakes the journal has not confessed its blunder . . . it continues to gallop in its armchair with the same errors', which included peddling the line of the émigré Polish government in London. 'Dear Geoffrey', wrote Bracken. 'Having successfully stirred up Uncle Sam you have done something more than stir up Uncle Joe. BB'. At the bottom of the letter he scribbled: 'To call *The Economist* "staid" is the worst of insults.'

'Staid' it certainly was not. Richard Holt Hutton had once written of Bagehot's 'dash and doubt': Crowther demonstrated only dash. He gave the paper an opinionated tone which, ever since, has attracted many people and repelled many others. He used to say that the rule of effective journalism was 'first simplify , then exaggerate', and he was reluctant to weaken his argument by making unnecessary reservations. Besides, more often than not he was right. The fears that he and Ward had expressed in 1944 about the peace were to prove, if anything, an underestimate (though the annexations and reparations were Soviet, not Western, doing). In his signed valedictory article in April 1956, he reflected on foreign affairs: 'One is tempted to say that the big change since 1938 is the invention of nuclear fission as a weapon of warfare or, linked with that, the emergence of Soviet Russia as a potentially aggressive great power. But I do not think that either of these has made much difference to the conduct of foreign affairs. The problem for Britain has always been how to contain the potential master of the Continent, and the fact that he now speaks Russian, instead of German or French or Spanish, is not a fundamental change. Nor, alas, has the bomb, as yet, altered the nature of the nation-state or the way it conducts its affairs.' The really important change was the emergence of the United States 'as a full-time great power and its willingness to form and lead a Grand Alliance. That is, indeed, a change. True, the Americans fought in the Kaiser's War, but they relapsed thereafter into the most dogmatic neutrality.'

> It was not, in fact, very difficult, as the second war approached, to foresee that America would again be involved . . . But this was speculation; the European governments laid their plans, whether of offence or of defence, on the assumption that America would stay out. Had the United States been committed to intervene in full strength from the first moment of a European war, the first world war would probably, and the second world war would certainly, never have happened.

It had seemed unlikely at the end of the war that the United States 'would actually accept the obligations and commitments of a permanent formal alliance. But the miracle happened (thanks to Stalin) and the transformation it has brought about in the diplomatic position is revolutionary. It is not simply that Britain, itself so often the balancing factor in Europe, now for the first time has an immensely powerful reinforcement at its back. That would be a great deal, but it is not all. The essential point is that, for the first time in modern history, the defending powers are virtually as strong, and as ready, as the potential aggressors. That is the great, the overwhelming, difference between 1938 and 1956 and, though nothing is certain in this dangerous world, I see in it the best assurance of peace.'[20]

CHAPTER XLIII

Suez

The English nation cannot bear failure in war.[1] *Walter Bagehot, 1859*

Crowther 'never laid down the law doctrinally', said Tyerman, reflecting in *Encounter* on 'Crowther & the Great Issues'. 'He was open to, indeed he moved himself by, argument. He was never, crudely, a cold warrior. But he was as sure in the days of Stalin (and afterwards), as he had been in the days of Hitler, that a country must know – and certainly that *The Economist* must know, and say – who its real friends and potential enemies were.' It was the test that Crowther 'most applied to his successors and their colleagues after he ceased to be editor and remained as deputy-chairman and then chairman of the board of directors. He did not interfere at all with the paper's policy, just as he never had been interfered with himself; but he made it plain that this test was the first of his great issues – whether it was a question of offending the Americans over Suez or weakening towards the Russians over Cuba.' Donald Tyerman was in the hot seat to apply this test on both occasions.

When Disraeli had announced the expenditure of £4,000,000 on a large (but not a majority) holding of shares in the Suez Canal Company in 1875, Bagehot had disapproved. 'We have heard it said that our having these shares will enable the English people to seize on the Canal with a "safe conscience". "You may prove," it is said, "that they give no right, but Englishmen will always think they have". But we cannot consent to pay £4,000,000 for a bad argument, and we deny that the English are so insensible to just views of law and equity. They would quite understand that the purchase of half the shares of the Caledonian Canal by the French Government would not give French ships of war any right to go through it.'[2]

What precipitated the Suez crisis was that, in July 1956, Britain and America withdrew their offer of helping Egypt to finance the building of the Aswan High Dam, and President Gamal Abdul Nasser retaliated by expropriating the internationally-owned Suez Canal Company. This led many British people to think they had every right to 'seize on the Canal' (the last of the British troops who had been stationed there for more than 70 years had been withdrawn only in June). The United States, although suspicious of Nasser, urged restraint. Several weeks of discussion brought no agreement. The British and French governments then made a secret deal with Israel. On 29 October Israeli forces advanced across Sinai. Two days later Britain and France knocked out Egypt's air force; on 5 November they landed troops at the Canal's northern end. From the outset, *The Economist* was rootedly against a resort to force. 'The Suez Canal has become the Achilles heel of Britain and of Europe', it pointed out on 4 August. 'Their dependence on this one thread of water has been growing, with their growing dependence on Persian Gulf oil, at a rate which could have well caused alarm even if the world had been spared the alarming personality of Colonel Nasser. Checked in his scheme for the Aswan High Dam, the Colonel has retaliated against the Suez Canal Company, and in a manner calculated to offer the most ostentatious possible affront to the western world.' The real shock to the West had been 'the appalling discovery of its own vulnerability'. The British reaction had called to mind King Lear, with his confused threats 'which held more emotion than strength: "I will do such things – what they are yet I know not – but they shall be The terrors of the earth."'

> Government and public, caught off balance, have been threatening force without having apparently either defined the problem to be faced, or formulated the purpose of action. Enough force is to hand, it may be hoped, to deal with Colonel Nasser if the decision were taken to use it. But on what occasion would it be used, and with what intention? How far would it have to go to impose the will of the nations upon Egypt's dictator? Above all, what solution would it be expected to bring? Armed occupation was tried before; it solved no political problems, and was rightly given up.[3]

That leader was written by the new foreign editor, John Midgley, Tyerman's ally and friend. He had begun life as a lower-middle-class boy in Manchester who won scholarships to Hulme Grammar School and then to Trinity College, Cambridge, where he at first read history. After taking a 2.1 in Part

I, he had switched to modern languages, French and German. He was to attribute his failure to achieve the academic distinction of which he was capable to his 'idleness and inattention'. Although, in Europe and later in America, he became a highly distinguished journalist, much admired for shrewdness, intelligence, cultivation, wisdom and writing ability, he was conscientious but never single-minded about his work or career. In the rather puritan world of *The Economist*, as with Graham Hutton, Midgley's enjoyment of women, friends, food, wine and travel made him appear to be not quite an *homme sérieux*.

Although Midgley cultivated an exterior of *gravitas* and the wardrobe of a gentleman, his affectionate and sensual nature and his ironic view of life could not be long concealed from the discerning by the initially forbidding nature of his delivery. Like Tyerman, he was (and is) an unrepentant old radical whose views on foreign as well as domestic policy stayed left of centre.

After Cambridge, Midgley had worked freelance for the *Manchester Guardian* and had then become its labour correspondent. He spent his holidays in Central Europe; at home he agitated against appeasement and helped refugees. He spent his five-and-half war years in the army in Military Intelligence, dealing mostly with Germany, and emerged as a lieutenant-colonel. Demobbed early in 1946, he became German correspondent of the *Guardian*, and in 1947 was asked by Donald McLachlan, foreign editor of *The Economist*, to write an article called 'WILL GERMANS RESIST DISMANTLING?'.[4]

Midgley's line on the Germans was entirely in sympathy with that of *The Economist*. 'I was all for humane treatment of the Germans. My quarrel with them stopped more or less when their villainous government was overthrown. I was old enough and had read enough historically to know that you would not do any good by trying to crush or castrate the Germans: they were necessary.' The last paragraph of his first *Economist* article read: 'As General Clay has hinted in his sledgehammer way, the occupying authorities have in their hands powerful weapons of retaliation against any open disobedience. They can always withhold food and supplies. But who will benefit if they do?'

This article led to Crowther's offering Midgley the job of 'industrial specialist', working for Roland Bird, who was now deputy editor and virtually undisturbed monarch of the 'Business World' pages, which embraced business leaders, business notes, statistics and financial advertising. Crowther produced what was known as 'the front of the paper', Bird the 'back'. When Midgley expanded into more general subjects and wrote leaders for the front, he worked directly for Crowther and developed a deep admiration for his professional competence and intellectual stamina. 'When I took an article to him rather late on a Wednesday – perhaps seven or eight in the evening – he would find something in it which didn't quite measure up to the preceding material and he would apply his intelligence to thinking where my argument had been leading . . . He was a splendid journalist.'

After his first spell of almost three years with *The Economist*, John Midgley was lured across to *The Times* by Tyerman, who was then its deputy editor. Midgley became its foreign leader writer and then, three years later, its German correspondent. He returned to *The Economist* just when Tyerman was succeeding Crowther there.

Midgley's and Tyerman's attitude to the Suez conflict was shared by their paper's Middle Eastern expert, Elizabeth Monroe, historian and ex-colleague of Toynbee's on his *Surveys*, ex-director of the Middle East division of the Ministry of Information, ex-diplomatic correspondent of the *Observer*, and a member of the foreign staff of *The Economist* from 1945 until 1958. Witty, learned and well-informed, she knew the Middle East intimately, visiting the region in most years and maintaining close contacts with politicians and officials. In so far as she had any bias, she was pro-Arab, with, perhaps, a weakness for some of the region's royal families that was shared by other British Arabists of her generation. Throughout the Suez period, *The Economist* proceeded in its customary way by packing its pages with relevant information. In the issue of 4 August that contained Midgley's 'EUROPE'S ACHILLES HEEL' there was a box headed

What Suez Means

Different aspects of the Suez Canal dispute are discussed in this issue of *The Economist* under a number of headings. In addition to this leading article, *Via Suez* (page 419) considers the Suez Canal traffic in oil and dry cargoes and the financial and economic aspects of the seizure; and a note (page 391) deals with the two-way character of the Anglo-Egyptian trade.

Our Paris correspondent outlines the French attitude to the seizure and the Suez Canal Company's position (page 412).

'VIA SUEZ' was, in fact, a remarkable compilation, with graphs and maps and charts of everything any man of business could possibly want to know about the Suez Canal, presented in authoritative and digestible form.

The issue of 29 September, to take another example, had from the Cairo correspondent 'ASIAN PRESSURES FOR A SUEZ SETTLEMENT' which began: 'To most people here, the Suez Canal crisis appears to move inevitably towards negotiations with President Nasser and it is difficult to see what useful purpose is served by refusing to face the fact.' Kim Philby, then a special correspondent in Beirut, considered the possibilities of the Lebanese government emulating the actions of Nasser; and Taya Zinkin, the Indian correspondent, reported that India's attitude to the Suez dispute 'is quite cool and practical. It wants a solution which will at once avoid war and ensure free passage through the canal and it thinks it can be better obtained by talking to Colonel Nasser than by moving troops or forming users' associations.' India's difference with the Western powers was primarily 'not one of morality but of political judgement'.[5]

Andrew Boyd weighed in a week later. Having experienced a fairly strenuous war in the Far East, Boyd had come to the paper in 1951, recruited by the then foreign editor, Donald McLachlan, who had taught him German and Russian at Winchester in the 1930s; they had met again in 1950 while working in a Chatham House study group on the new-born Atlantic alliance. Like Midgley, Boyd was to be an *Economist* institution for almost the whole post-war period and a prop and stay for the foreign department. While keeping up with world politics in general – and especially with those problems that involved the United Nations, on which he wrote several books – he liked to make some particular part of the world his speciality for a few years and then switch to another one. He was a kind of multipurpose foreign correspondent usually working from London.

Gifted, gentle and unassuming, there were two unusual aspects to Andrew Boyd. Although a Wykehamist he was without arrogance, and although able he wanted no promotion. When Donald McLachlan left to go to the *Telegraph* in 1954, Boyd had been put in charge of the foreign department, a job which he hated and begged to be released from. He was haunted by the idea that one week the paper would come out with a blank page in his section. It was only his threat to leave if the burden was not removed from him that made Crowther relent and bring in Midgley in his stead.

One of Boyd's missions on the paper was to lighten it, as a counterbalance to the heavyweight intellects who tended to take themselves a touch too seriously. ('Even the men are bluestockings', commented one observer.) Boyd's 'CHANNEL CROSSING' was typical of his style. Discussing the statement by the Prime Minister, Sir Anthony Eden, that 'Anglo-French friendship has never been so firm', Boyd considered the state of the fifty-one-year-old *Entente Cordiale*, which appeared suddenly to be having a new lease of life. Could this be connected with America's failure to see eye to eye with the British and French about Suez? 'It is not surprising that some should claim to discern, behind all the heartening talk, merely the sight of "two aged colonialist ladies" standing skirt to skirt the better to wield their brollies against their young persecutors.'

> If that suspicion were justified, there would be little to say in favour of maintaining the *Entente*. The modern world has no place for a pair of petulant old ladies, unwilling to admit they are no longer strong enough, even in concert, to take on all comers, united only when challenged by Asian-African nationalism, and blind to the fact that by aligning their crinolines they simply provide a better target for anti-colonialist catapults.

The *Entente* revival and other trends, including a new German initiative on European unity, pointed to two alternative possibilities. One course would lead to an anti-American form of European isolationism: the second, 'far from alienating the United States, could transform into reality the vision which internationally minded Americans have begun to think delusive – the vision of a self-respecting Western Europe, a friend and partner of the United States, not its perennial suppliant. This is not only the path of idealism; it is the path of interest, too.'[6]

The British are not a naturally jingoistic people. It is not until hostilities are opened that emotion begins to run wild, as happened with the Anglo-French invasion of Egypt. Although the Suez *débâcle* was to be brief it was to be as divisive in Britain as the Vietnam war would be in America: in each case what wounded the national psyche was a discovery of national fallibility.

Up until this point the readership had been quiescent. They erupted over Elizabeth Monroe's 'SPLENETIC ISOLATION' on 3 November. 'Sir Anthony Eden has isolated Britain, except for the company of France.' He had asked the deeply-divided House of Commons not to impugn the government's motives. 'But that was precisely what must be done. What was the prime motive? Was it to stop the fighting which Israel had started by moving faster than the Security Council could move? Or was it to carry out a project cherished since July: the seizure of the Suez Canal and the forcible overthrow of Colonel Nasser?'

Instead of trying to send Israel back into its own territory, the British government had offered Egypt two alternatives: 'an Anglo-French occupation of the Suez Canal with Egyptian assent, or an Anglo-French occupation of the Suez Canal against Egyptian opposition. As a result, statesmen all over the world are bracketing Britain and France with Israel as aggressors.' Since Egypt had chosen the second alternative, 'Britain and France have attacked a state which, however great its recent misdemeanours, was at the time a victim of an armed assault. This is a gambler's throw; upon it the Prime Minister has hazarded not only his own political future and that of his Government, but, vastly more important, his country's position, interest, and reputation in the world. For an Opposition officially to oppose a war after hostilities have started is, in modern times, unprecedented; but so, too, is what Sir Anthony Eden has done.'

An examination of the events leading up to the invasion concluded that to 'attack Egypt against the reasoned urging of the world, and under cover of a smoke-screen of obfuscatory statements, can arouse no confident support in the country. The manner in which this crisis has been handled suggests a strange union of cynicism and hysteria in its leaders.'⁷

The letters page of the following week began with the statement: 'From a heavy postbag this week we have selected a few from the large majority which take an opposite point of view from that expressed in our leading article entitled 'Splenetic isolation' on November 3rd.' Those writing in protest included Eric Gibb. While his letter used moderate language, others were highly emotional. 'Your leading article of today has dealt a shattering blow to the respect with which I have hitherto regarded your opinions'; 'As an old and regular reader of your paper, I write today for the first time to any paper to say how deplorable I think your leading article of this week'; 'This is a sad day for one old and fond subscriber.'⁸

By the time that issue came out, the Anglo-French operation had been halted as a consequence of its condemnation by most of the Commonwealth governments, the United States and the United Nations and the plunge of sterling. John Foster Dulles, the American Secretary of State, had always been firmly opposed to military action against Egypt; and since early September Eden had known that President Eisenhower shared this view.

Donald Tyerman and Norman Macrae together wrote 'THE PRIME MINISTER': the only issue in domestic politics was 'should he go or stay?'

> Now that some sort of cease fire has sounded across the Middle East, there is a natural tendency to seek to sound some sort of political cease fire at home. Unfortunately, if one agrees with the views on the Suez adventure that are set down in subsequent articles in this issue, this is impossible. It would be a blessed relief to be able to say that by its belated wisdom on Tuesday the British Government had pulled its chestnuts out of the fire. But the Anglo-American alliance is badly hurt; the Commonwealth is at odds . . . the uncommitted nations are alienated; the canal is blocked; there is the searing question mark over Suez's effect upon Hungary.* Too many chestnuts have been burned already.

Sir Anthony Eden, the article concluded, 'has always been, in a career of long public service, a man of principle and patriotism. There may rest upon him a painful but inescapable decision.'[9]

The letters printed the following week made even more painful reading, and again, they were but a few of the many received. 'With your authority and the respect in which your paper is held, are you going to sit back and deride from the touchline or are you going to get your head down and really give a shove to public opinion?'; 'For many years your famous journal has been guide, philosopher and friend, in the sphere of public affairs to a host of readers who hold it in such esteem that they habitually quoted it as a shining example of impartial judgment and practical common sense in a world where these commodities were often at a premium. And so it came as a tremendous shock to us when – forsaking your traditional sense of values – you severely castigated the Prime Minister and virtually demanded his dismissal on the score of a political decision which – though admittedly unorthodox and distasteful to a man of his moral convictions – he adjudged to be the only effective means of averting the immediate danger of a world war – a judgement since endorsed by millions of his countrymen'; 'The views of the Labour Party on Middle East affairs are plainly based on political opportunism. Your motives for your unhelpful articles of the last two weeks are far more difficult to discern'; 'It has been said that the crisis has caused strange

---

*The global hullabaloo over Suez had made it easier for the Soviet Union to quell the Hungarian national rising which had began in late October; any possibility of intervention from the West had been stymied by the exactly simultaneous crisis over Suez.

bedfellows but none stranger than yourself, jew-baiters and police horse baiters in whose company you have placed yourself by your attack on the organisers of police whether operating in Egypt or Whitehall. How you must regret you cannot put back the clock and get the Austrian Corporal to make a four at your cosy little party.'[10]

Geoffrey Crowther was in America when this hurricane broke and the letters poured in. It was the first major crisis to challenge the concept of editorial independence, since so many of the letters continued to suggest that *The Economist* was being untrue to its traditions. Sending Walter Layton 'two angry letters' addressed to him and opened in error, Tyerman remarked that they were 'not dissimilar from 20 or 30 other letters which we have received . . . My withers are unwrung because I believe, ever since August 4th, we said no more and no less than we had to say from the facts as we saw them. Certainly our views in the last two weeks have followed perfectly logically and consistently from the views which we have argued ever since the Suez business began. It is in a way odd that these indignant gentlemen did not object to our earlier article; the explanation is, I suppose, that it is only now, when the political implications become manifest, and opinions become polarised, that people have began to feel strongly – and indignantly – one way or the other.'

> I should say, incidentally, for your information, that I've had a letter from Geoffrey on the subject. It came after our last issue and so didn't affect at all what we said; but it stands as interesting confirmation of the line which we have taken. The relevant extracts are:
>
> 1. Eden's worst crime was not using force. It was endangering the Anglo-American alliance by disloyalty, fraud and deceit . . .
>
> 2. To rebuild the alliance is now the great task of statesmanship. Fortunately, the omens are good especially if Dulles is out of the way. But it requires a repudiation of Eden's methods by the UK. Moreover, he himself – vain – petty – vindictive – is not the man to do the job. *He must go* . . .
>
> 3. Properly handled this could turn out for good. But not with Eden. There never was such a case when one man should make a sacrifice for his country.'[11]

Three days later Tyerman was able to send on an extract from another Crowther letter. 'I have now read last week's (Nov.10) issue and want to congratulate you on it. I agree with the substance of it *entirely*, and the expression of it is better, for being more temperate, than anything I could have achieved. It would be flattering to my vanity to believe I could contribute anything if I were in London, but the plain fact is that I could do nothing . . .'

Layton circulated the angry letters to the other members of the board, along with the extracts from the Crowther letter and his own reply to correspondents.

> I am sorry that you find yourself in disagreement with the paper. But it is not the practice of the Board to interfere with or dictate the opinions expressed in it week by week. Indeed, it would be contrary to the constitution of *The Economist* for them to do so. Nor would it be proper for the Board to make any comment upon what appears in the paper. It is the Board's responsibility to appoint, with the consent of the Trustees, an Editor in whom they have confidence. It is the Editor's responsibility when appointed to conduct the paper in accordance with *The Economist*'s tradition.
>
> This conception of editorial responsibility has been *The Economist*'s great strength. It would be wrong for the Board to depart from it in any way.

Thanking him, Tyerman said he was stressing Crowther's remarks 'because, as you know, Geoffrey is peculiarly and informally my link with the Board; and, although I take full responsibility for everything that we have done, and Geoffrey's comments have in each case been *after* the fact, I am at any rate relieved to find that his views are, if anything, more extreme than anything that I could have brought myself to publish! The important thing now, from your own personal point of view and from mine, is that we should take the first opportunity to show that, while the transatlantic alliance is crucial, the European connection is now made more valuable than ever before.'

A female critic provides the conclusion to the paper's most unpopular moment. 'I regret to hear that it is not the practice of the Board to take any responsibility for the contents of the paper, especially the Leader by the Editor.'

> It seems to me to be a strange state of affairs. I always thought that the chairman and the directors of a company or business were responsible finally for the policies of any enterprise in which they were engaged.
>
> Is yours the practice of the whole newspaper world?
>
> Possibly, in ordinary times, it works out fairly well on the whole, but

during the present grave state of affairs when Britain and the Common-wealth stand in great danger can you get off so easily? In England, except for the Labour Members under Gaitskell, the mass of the people, fortunately, are loyal to their country and the elected government. We have authority from *The Economist* itself as to the workers – as a member of the middle class I have questioned a number of them as to their views and not one of them is against the Suez action.

The army was solid, and a letter from a friend told her that 'New Zealand backs the Mother Country to a man and hopes that we carry right on.'

> We cannot all be wrong – who then is the editor of *The Economist* to deliver us up, hook, line and sinker to the vacillating and insufferable United States?
>
> It looks as though the statements in your paper, together with those of the Manchester Guardian and The Observer (owned by members of an American family) have had a disastrous affect abroad and may indeed finish us completely. Is it not the great strength of *The Economist*'s tradition that you should be concerned about the nation's life?
>
> I am indeed sorry about the dreadful trend of the paper. I have greatly enjoyed my reading hitherto – beautifully worded and clear as a bell even to me. Cannot you devote all your energies to evolve some way of living for us so that we can stand on our honour and be independent of our enemies?[12]

Eden resigned within two months. *The Economist* was able to look back on its stance over Suez with pride. It was never again to have such occasion to alienate the self-styled patriots, for it favoured the use of armed force against Argentina in 1982 over the Falklands and against Iraq in 1990–91 over Kuwait. Some might suggest that the paper's support for military action on those occasions reflected its drift to the right, but that is to miss one central fact. The paper never saw Nasser as being in the true mould of Mussolini or Hitler, but even if it had, the main point was that he could not be decisively defeated without the support of America. *The Economist* has never believed that a war should be fought for the sake of the grand gesture when it could not be won.

CHAPTER XLIV

The Philby interlude

The man was manifestly proved to have been a Soviet mole in the British Intelligence service. But the question remains with me to this day. How can anyone who was so dumb about practicalities and disturbed in his own emotional condition be of service in the spy business? John Midgley, 1986.

By the time the next major test of editorial independence came along, Crowther and Tyerman were no longer politically at one. As he moved into the world of business and became a tycoon, Crowther was moving to the right and was increasingly suspicious of what he saw as Midgley's and Tyerman's tendency to leftish anti-Americanism. Matters had not been helped by the paper's public embarrassment over Kim Philby.

John Midgley had known H.A.R. Philby when they both canvassed for the Labour Party in 1931 in Cambridge county. Philby was good-looking with a rather endearing stammer and Midgley found him a rather sweet man despite his touch of righteousness. Although Midgley was at Cambridge at a time when communism was fashionable there, he had never taken to the creed; he had noted its practitioners' 'combination of genuine bigotry and opportunistic bigotry, along with their ability to swallow the line they were given, whatever it was'. And he never thought Philby was a communist. Canvassing in 1931, Philby used to make straight 'Fabian-socialist-dogoodery' speeches.

They had also spent some time together in 1933 in Berlin, where Midgley had gone during his Easter vacation for a crash course in German. He came across Philby outside a shop which was being boycotted and picketed because of its Jewish ownership. Philby was expostulating with a policeman, explaining that 'we in England did not make a distinction between our own citizens and Jewish citizens; we treated everybody impartially as being equal'. The policeman was telling him to go home, which Midgley succeeded in persuading him to do.

What Midgley particularly recalled from that period was Philby's puritanism. On visiting Midgley's room, he was shocked to discover he had two dressing gowns.

> By curious chance I had a silk dressing gown which had been handed down by a neighbour of my mother's in Manchester, which was rather warm, very warm indeed. Then I had a very cool, thin, foulard thing, dark blue with white spots. In my vanity I brought both these garments. However they were not really very costly or indecent garments; I shouldn't think it was the first time that anyone has travelled with more than one dressing gown. Philby found this shocking. He was a man with an economic background far superior to my own, of course, but he was shocked over the two dressing gowns.

When Donald Maclean and Guy Burgess defected to the Soviet Union in May 1951, their friend Kim Philby came under suspicion as the 'third man'. Although the Foreign Secretary, Harold Macmillan, publicly cleared Philby in 1955, he was no longer wanted in MI6. A mutual friend told Midgley that Philby wanted to get into journalism, that the *Observer* would pay part of his costs in Beirut and he wondered if *The Economist* would pick up the rest of the bill. Midgley told the go-between to tell Philby to ask for the job in person, but, a few days later, on one of his regular visits to the head of the Foreign Office news department, he mentioned the approach and asked if it would be wise to employ Philby.

> The answer I got, which in retrospect had obviously been prepared but at the time seemed like a spontaneous response, was that they felt that Philby had had rather a raw deal when the parliamentary row had erupted . . . and they would not only not object but they would rather approve if somebody would put some employment in his way.

Midgley reported this to Tyerman, who a short while later found himself at dinner with a senior Foreign Office official whose view he canvassed. There was no reason why Philby should not be employed, was the advice – 'a perfectly sound idea'. What neither of them knew was that these same people were actually asking the kind-hearted David Astor at the *Observer* to employ Philby. Astor's biographer takes up the story. 'The Foreign Office official who called on David told him that Philby had been cleared, and was employable, but needed a helping hand. David, who knew as much about Philby as anyone could read in the papers, sympathised with him because he felt "an injustice was being done against Philby", as he had been declared innocent but could not find employment.'[1]

'What *we* got from the Foreign Office', wrote Tyerman to Crowther after Philby's defection, 'was neither a request to employ him (which we would automatically have jibbed at) nor a permission to employ him (which we would never have asked for) but simply the "assurance" from our various informal personal contacts, when we told them, (a) that there was no ground at all, politically, after his clearance by the Foreign Secretary, why he should not be employed and (b) that, on personal grounds, they were all glad that, after bad times, he was getting the break he deserved.'[2]

The Economist was happy to pay a third of the £500 per year. It wanted an extra correspondent in the Middle East, because it saw in the spring of 1956 that relations were breaking down between Egypt and the Americans and the British. The Cairo correspondent was a news agency man who provided *The Economist* only with the spinoff of his main work. In fact, when the Suez crisis broke all the foreign correspondents in Cairo were expelled, but *The Economist* had Philby in Beirut to fill the breach; and Kim Philby, son of the famous Middle Eastern traveller Harry St John Philby, was very well-connected there. Indeed finances were eased because he could live in his father's Beirut flat.

'It seemed like a very smart transaction', recalled Midgley thirty years later. 'For a quite modest price we assured ourselves of a good Middle Eastern correspondent during a time when our own Middle Eastern coverage would be falling apart and yet there was more demand for Middle Eastern news than ever before.' When Philby eventually came to ask Midgley to finance him, 'I said, "It rather looks as if Nasser might seize the Suez Canal, and I get the impression that the Eden government is rather thinking of some form of intervention, military intervention if they do." He said "Well it might not be a bad thing. It may well be that a sharp stroke would bring them to their senses."' Midgley was concerned about this and said 'Look, it doesn't seem to us that what ought to be administered is a sharp blow. You can see for yourself. Go and have a look, tell us what you think, tell us how it seems.'

During and after Suez, when the regular available sources of views and comments from Egypt and the Near East were cut off, Philby was indeed valuable and produced good material, for which *The Economist* got some kudos. But by the late 1950s he had become slipshod, unreliable and politically very sloppy. Around 1961 the Syrians started an agitation about a supposedly imminent American invasion, adducing as evidence the fact that Nato naval manoeuvres were being held in the Eastern Mediterranean.

Philby sent a message to *The Economist* which assumed this whole tale to be true. Midgley wrote to him sceptically, and Philby retreated and the story was not published. 'That would appear to be a left-wing deviation, but his deviations were not all left-wing by any means. They were just as likely to be right wing', as, for instance, when Philby went to cover the civil war in Yemen between royalists and leftists. Happening to go in with the royalists, 'he sent back a report so devoid of reality that I sent a message asking "Did you go there at all?"' Philby had been getting rather demanding about expenses, and it looked as if he was either pretending to travel or travelling pointlessly; Midgley was coming to believe that *The Economist* was wasting its money. Midgley wrote rebuking him, asking for explanations and appealing to him to pull himself together. He got 'a sweet apologetic letter back saying "Let's have a new beginning"', and for a while Philby seemed to pull himself together to some extent, but then his performance deteriorated again.

Some time after he went to Beirut, a group in MI6 had reactivated Philby as a British spy. What Midgley still found bewildering years later was that Philby was not only an agent but a double agent at a time when he was becoming incompetent even as a correspondent. In 1962 Midgley visited Iran, and on the way home he stopped in Beirut, wanting to talk to Philby about his unsatisfactory performance.

> As I came out of the gate there was Kim, obviously delighted to see me. So I marched across the hall to the guichet where the immigration department's officer was waiting to look at passports. Kim wouldn't leave me to fend for myself – not a bit of it. He took my passport out of my hand and waved it at the immigration officer. There happened to be a number of people ahead of us and they were being treated in rather a slow and sluggish manner and Kim evidently thought that by adopting a sharp foreign tone in a haughty English manner he could successfully browbeat the customs officer and make him deal with Mr Midgley's business quicker than anybody else's.
>
> This was not the case. As it turned out, they took much longer. Because I had Kim helping me, the customs officer insisted on dealing with every single entrant before he touched Kim and me.

So one thing that retrospectively struck Midgley as odd was that 'this international master of espionage didn't know when to keep his trap shut at a point of entry on a frontier'. Then there were his baffling difficulties in communicating with the locals, although he had by then been in Beirut for several years. Outside the airport there was waiting the taxi which had picked Philby up at a British Embassy party, taken him to the airport and waited during the altercation. 'Kim gave a brief, crisp order to the taxi driver and we took off. It turned out that the taxi driver didn't understand Kim's brief, crisp order and instead of taking us to the St George's Hotel where I was to stay, he took us back to the house where Philby had been at a party and where he'd been picked up. So this is another thing which gives me pause about the accomplished international spy; he couldn't give simple directions to a taxi driver.'

Eventually they reached the hotel, where they drank some of the whisky Midgley had brought with him and then had dinner on the terrace.

> By now Kim had been at the embassy party, and had been drinking whisky with me in my hotel room; then we had all this wine; so he was fairly drunk by the time we were through. We decided it was time to pack it up and call it a day and he would come and pick me up in the morning. I was going to stay a whole day in Beirut and be with him.
>
> We were on the terrace out-of-doors. There was a tiny opening with a wrought-iron gate in the garden wall and Philby decided to go through that, but it was locked. He became annoyed with that, so started to shake it. Seeing nearby an Arab boy who worked for the hotel he said, 'Open this gate'. The boy shook his head (he presumably didn't have a key). Philby raised his voice and said, 'Open this gate' – really like an 18th century Englishman visiting Venice – and so Philby shook the gate furiously. The boy had already pointed out that about three yards away in the same wall was a bigger gateway which was not locked or even closed. Philby was refusing to go through that; he wanted this gate. In other words he was drunken-paranoid. Eventually he gave it up and marched out through the bigger gateway.

So in that short visit, Midgley experienced from Philby 'a lot of conspicuous presence and radiation of tensions and so forth to no purpose'.

Philby disappeared from Beirut towards the end of January 1963, leaving no forwarding address. The 1963 *Economist* account book shows, opposite

'H.A.R. Philby, £52.18.0' in the March-to-July lists of retainers, a pencilled note: 'Hold payment'. In July Edward Heath, the Lord Privy Seal, had to summon David Astor and Tyerman to his office to reveal that Philby had defected to Russia and to apologise for the Foreign Office's role. John Midgley had the job of writing 'A LOST CORRESPONDENT'.

> When Mr Edward Heath told the Commons on Monday of information that puts a new light on the case of H.A.R.Philby, the Government was able to believe that this was not 'another security failure,' as television and press at once took it to be, but a security success. Since *The Economist* employed Philby, jointly with *The Observer*, as its Middle East correspondent from 1956 until his disappearance on January 23rd last, this newspaper has some duty to tell the facts as it knows them.

He took his readers through Philby's biography, including the period when he was cleared of being the suspected 'third man'. Describing his time with *The Economist*, Midgley remarked that during the Suez crisis Philby 'seemed to move from a degree of sympathy with Sir Anthony Eden's Middle Eastern policy (more than we had in the office) to severe comments on its effects in practice. He was an excellent Middle East correspondent in 1956, 1957, and 1958.'

> As the pressure of explosive crises began to ease off in 1959 and 1960, we began to notice that he failed to find non-crisis topics to write about. We had difficulty in getting him to respond to our general, as distinct from political, interest in the affairs of his part of the world, and we had a growing feeling of a lack of real communication with him. By the time he failed to turn up for a dinner in Beirut on January 23rd our contact with him had for some time been inadequate, so it was some weeks before we could establish (with no help from his family, from his many too-loyal friends, or from the British authorities, who knew) that he had in fact disappeared.[3]

'I have to confess that I have no bad conscience about this', wrote Tyerman to Crowther:

> Hindsight now puts the question whether it is worse, both being bad, to employ a man at the FO's request (which I would never do) or to take on the man *now* 'admitted' to be the 'third man'. Then, of course, he was officially *not* the 'third man'; his work for us in the first and longer part of his

engagement was excellent and, as Elizabeth [Monroe] herself told *The Observer* on Sunday, properly impartial and judgmatical. At the very end, he did flag, as we said in our piece, but for personal not political causes; and, when he went, we had for some time been wondering what to do about him, simply on journalistic grounds.[4]

Innocent though Tyerman and Midgley were in all this, Crowther seemed never quite to trust them again.

CHAPTER XLV

The Cuba crisis

Never in the history of journalism has so much been read for so long by so few. *Geoffrey Crowther re* The Economist, *n.d.*

The other 'great issue' of Tyerman's editorship and Midgley's foreign editorship came in 1962 with the Cuban missile crisis. This time there was a breach with Crowther.

Crowther's *Economist* was not driven by anti-communism but by the desire for some kind of world order that would give maximum stability and liberty to the maximum number of people. As Barbara Ward put it in 1950: 'Every responsible statesman in the Western world can have only one objective – to achieve lasting peace by agreement with Russia. To end "the hatreds and manoeuvres of the cold war" and to avoid the inconceivable horrors of a hot one are the overriding aims of Western diplomacy. The real question is not one of aims but of methods. Would a direct approach to Russia, designed to secure, by mutual concession, an agreement on atomic weapons, or possibly on all armaments, in fact bring genuine pacification nearer?'[1] She came down against premature negotiations which might weaken the West's position.

That was written in Ward's last year as a full-time member of the staff. From the beginning of 1947 she had shared the foreign editorship with Donald McLachlan. Before the war McLachlan had doubled school-mastering with writing for *The Times* and during the war he had been in Naval Intelligence. Conventional, dry of wit and sometimes quite lively in his writing, McLachlan was obliged by virtue of working with Barbara Ward to be rather more cautious than was his nature. Much more Eurocentric than Crowther or Ward, he was never particularly an *Economist* man, merely a good writer and editor who made a solid contribution during his eight years at the paper.

He was to achieve fame in January 1956 as deputy editor of the *Daily Telegraph* (he later became editor of the *Sunday Telegraph*) by making a savage attack on Sir Anthony Eden, nine months after he became Prime Minister. Critical, like most of the press, of Eden's indecisiveness and procrastination, McLachlan's 'WAITING FOR THE SMACK OF FIRM GOVERNMENT' included the famous passage: 'There is a favourite gesture of the Prime Minister which is sometimes recalled to illustrate this sense of disappointment. To emphasise a point he will clench one fist to smack the open palm of the other – but this smack is seldom heard. Most Conservatives ... are waiting to feel the smack of firm Government.'² According to contemporaries, this article was the last straw for the thin-skinned Eden and bears some of the responsibility for helping to push him into the psychological state that brought about his desperate and futile Suez initiative, of which McLachlan was a supporter.³

At *The Economist*, McLachlan was certainly – compared to Ward – a hardliner. In late 1950, considering the relationship which the free world should have with Stalin, he showed very much the thrust and the tone that would dominate the paper during the foreign editorship of Brian Beedham.

> There appear to be quite a number of people in the free world who are now taking fright at the cost of keeping it free – the cost not only in money and work but also in patience, political courage and self-denial. Both in the British and French parliaments there are men who refuse to acknowledge the challenge of Stalinism, and whose resolution falters as they see just what is involved in that once cherished idea, 'steady and collective resistance to aggression.'

An analysis of the state of East–West relations led to the conclusion that there was no room for compromise: 'So long as the fomenting of strikes, the encouragement of sabotage, the preaching of subversion, the appeals to peoples over the heads of their Governments go on; so long as the invasions of Korea, Tibet and Indo-China are regarded as incidents in the "liberating mission" of the Stalinist system, so long is any real understanding and settlement unlikely.'

If the dynamic of the Soviet system depended on the maintenance of its missionary spirit, only two possibilities existed. 'One is that its expansion is contained and contested in every part of the world where free peoples are threatened, until Stalinism gives convincing evidence of having abandoned aggression; that has been for two years the policy of the United States and the British Commonwealth. The other is that changes in the Soviet system eventually lead to a change in its attitude to the outside world': that was primarily the concern of the Russian people.

> The clear implication for present policy of either of these possibilities is to stand firm and wait. It will be said that this is a policy of rigidity, a counsel of despair. On the contrary, it is those who persist in thinking – as Mr Chamberlain persisted in thinking when dealing with Hitler – that the twentieth century generalissimo is open to persuasion by nineteenth century methods who are rigid; and it is those who want to abandon or modify a policy of resistance just when it is taking shape and effect who are guilty of despair. They are, surely, confuted by their own logic. If they are convinced that the Soviet Union does not intend war, then there is no point in urging the danger of war as a reason for premature appeasement. If, on the other hand, they believe that the Soviet Union will go to war rather than accept a fair and just ordering of the world's affairs, then they should be advocating the speediest and most resolute rearmament as the one way to prevent the recurrence of what has happened in Korea.[4]

The double standards of the left were addressed two years later by one of the 'semi-detached stand-bys', Geoffrey Hudson, a Fellow of All Souls, whose distinguished contributions used to arrive from Oxford by post, on sheets of foolscap paper, in the clearest of mandarin handwriting. If towards the end of an article he found he had more to say than he had expected, his writing and the space between lines would get more and more cramped. 'Before the House of Commons and public opinion,' he wrote in 1952, 'there has come lately from the battlefield of Korea a question which should have received an instantaneous answer from people of principle and conscience. Instead there have been trimming and shilly-shallying among some politicians and uneasy silence from those who normally leap into the battle of controversy.'

> Once again the suspicion has been created that there is one law for the Left and another for the Right: what Dr Malan [the hardline, apartheid-promoting South African Prime Minister] is doing is wrong – and it is, indeed, very wrong – but what Mao Tse-tung is doing may be right; the Russians are within their rights by organising Eastern Europe after their own design, but it is wrong for the Americans to seek any influence in Western Europe.[5]

McLachlan's old pupil, Andrew Boyd, in his brief tenure as foreign editor, grappled with the terminology. '"Cold war" is an even more misleading phrase than most of the monosyllabic slogans that headline writers love', he suggested in November 1955. 'It is commonly identified with such rudeness and crudeness as the Russians practised until lately. For those who make this over-simple identification, the "cold war" presumably ended when Vishinsky's diatribes gave place to Mr Khrushchev's waggery, and the first red carpets were laid down for the foreign statesmen who have thronged Moscow this year. "Cold war" in that sense need not now return, and it probably will not; even while Mr Molotov was slapping his bricks together at Geneva [he had announced a whole set of barriers to contact between the communist and free world], his masters were slapping Western backs in Moscow, and throwing still more footballers and fiddlers into their cultural offensive.'

> But the phrase 'cold war' was originally coined with reference not to a form of etiquette but to a policy – the policy of 'struggle,' to borrow a Communist key word. This 'struggle' is basically a contest for a power over men's minds, a political contest in which economic and military pressures are auxiliary. The 'cold war' in this deeper sense never ended, and can never end while the Communist rulers cling to their aim of worldwide victory – which they formally restated only last week. All that can change are the tactics employed, both by them and by the nations that are ready to defend their liberty.[6]

Under Tyerman and Midgley the process of guessing the intentions of the Soviet Union continued. 'Phases in world affairs overlap', wrote Daniel Singer in 1957; 'they cannot be timed with a stop-watch; but their overlapping still leaves it possible to distinguish when a new one has begun. International relations are now clearly entering their fourth postwar phase. The disintegration of the war alliance became complete with the Berlin blockade; the cold war, which had set in by then, lasted until Stalin's death. His successors initiated a more flexible policy which took its name from the fashionable slogan of "peaceful coexistence." This, too, collapsed under the combined shocks of the Budapest rising and Anglo-French intervention in Egypt. Neither of those two crises is over; but the shooting has stopped and it is time to peer through the dispersing smoke at the shape of things to come, to ponder what form international relations are now likely to take.' He saw a faint glimmer of hope that the Soviet Union might be interested in some disarmament deal.*⁷

Understanding the mind of the Kremlin and keeping an eye out for the next flashpoint was the predominant concern of every post-war foreign commentator. In 1960 Alastair Burnet addressed himself to the new ideological struggle between Russia and China. 'Tweedlenik and Tweedlemao are having another battle. Above the mêlée of dialectical blows and knocks rise hoarse cries and dire taunts befitting the struggle. The tenets of Marxism-Leninism, modern revisionism and peaceful co-existence all eddy and swirl in portentous tumult.'

> Within the flurry of debate, strange movements can be discerned. Mr Molotov is shifted from Ulan Bator to Vienna; Soviet technicians start homeward from China. The flailing convulsions are becoming more frequent and undisguised in the communist world. At two great gatherings of the clans this summer, the conference of the World Federation of Trade Unions in Peking and the Rumanian party congress at Bucharest, the argument has raged between the communisms of East and West. It is still rumbling in the Moscow and Peking papers. When Mr Khrushchev goes to North Korea in October it may well break out again, with or without a stopover to confront Chairman Mao in person. It is enough (borrowing a Russian proverb) to make even a shrimp whistle.
>
> None of this prevents Tweedlenik and Tweedlemao from continuing to link comradely arms whenever the outside world has become too interested or inquiring.⁸

The major flashpoint came over Cuba. Fidel Castro had toppled the dictator General Batista in January 1959 with the encouragement of the United States, but his wholesale expropriation of property and his acceptance of arms from China and the Soviet Union soon alienated the Americans. Diplomatic relations were broken off in January 1961, and three months later the CIA-organised invasion by 1,500 Cuban exiles at the Bay of Pigs failed to ignite the expected revolution; this fiasco gravely embarrassed President

---

*Daniel Singer and his father, Bernard, were Polish-Jewish and close friends of Isaac Deutscher, who introduced them to Crowther. Daniel remained with *The Economist* for about twenty years, often writing about France and becoming in his last years with the paper its Paris correspondent. Like his mentor, Deutscher, Daniel Singer was affable, affectionate, argumentative and unorthodoxly Marxist.

Kennedy, while it both enhanced Castro's stature and pushed him farther into the arms of the Soviet Union.

The extent of Russian involvement in Cuba became a source of speculation. In September 1962, Brian Beedham considered the scale of the problem. Beedham had first joined the paper briefly, in 1955; he rejoined it in 1957 after spending a year in America as a Harkness Fellow, and had been its Washington correspondent in 1958–60. He had gone to America leftish and moved rightish as he fell in love with the openness and kindness of American society. To a grammar-school, national-service and Oxford-scholarship boy of the grey, rationed and repressed 1950s, America was a massive liberation and one that made him an Atlanticist. It followed that he rejected everything that communism stood for – secrecy, repression of the individual and destruction of civil liberties.

Above all, Beedham was a romantic – an old-fashioned, romantic British patriot, whose patriotism was heightened by being in America at the time of Suez, with some of his Anglophile contacts expressing their distress at Dulles's treatment of Eden. As soon as it looked as if there might be a Suez war, Beedham, who was on the army reserve list, rang the military attaché at the British Embassy to request instructions. He encountered such a laid-back response as to make him believe that no military action was likely, so when it came, he was doubly shocked. He differed from almost all his future colleagues on *The Economist* in backing Eden's attack on Egypt.

By the time of the Cuba crisis Beedham was a senior figure on the paper, with two years as its Washington correspondent behind him. For all practical purposes, he was John Midgley's deputy in the foreign department: their political differences had not yet reached testing-point, as they were to do over Vietnam. 'Flying Dutchman, wandering Jew', he wrote in September 1962: 'the disembarking Russian, with snow on his army boots, is this century's recruit to the company of spectral travellers. The one thing known for sure about his latest manifestation, in Cuba, is the existence of a tented camp a dozen miles outside Havana containing a sizeable number of healthy-looking young Russians.'

> All else is speculation: that the young men are not technicians, as the
> Russians and Cubans say they are, but soldiers (Senator Keating); that there
> is evidence of four Russian intermediate-range missile bases on the island
> (Senator Thurmond); and that these developments require the United

States to invade Cuba instantly (Senator Capehart). Unless the Senators possess information denied to their government, there are still no solid grounds for believing that the Red Army has moved into Cuba as a combat force. Healthy-looking young Americans, after all, have been seen disembarking in various countries since President Kennedy took office; no one has yet suggested that the Peace Corps is a branch of the United States Army.

The only plausible explanation was that they were there to do 'more or less exactly what the Americans are doing in South Vietnam; that is, to train the local army to fight a more advanced kind of war than it has hitherto been used to', which could only be a defence of Cuba against another invasion. 'Doubtless, in a perfectly ordered world, the Monroe doctrine would require the removal of these alien intruders. But in the imperfect real world, where the Americans keep troops along the border of the communist block (in one case, within: remember Berlin) and claim an unhindered right of access to these outposts, it is going to be awkward, to say the least, to expel or blockade the Russians in Cuba. Mr Khrushchev has made the neatest of moves in the international chess game; take my pawn in Cuba, he says, and you risk your castle in South Vietnam – or your Berlin queen.'[9]

'OBSESSED BY CUBA' the following month was written by Barbara Smith. A comparative newcomer, she had come to the paper in 1958 via Chatham House and trade journals. In 1954 Roy Lewis, who was editing the magazine *New Commonwealth* during an interval between two spells of work for *The Economist*, published two of her articles and suggested she apply to the Economist Intelligence Unit. There she found herself becoming the expert on paper and pulp, editing one of the EIU commodity news magazines and doing random research on subjects about which she knew nothing. She began to provide an occasional note on commodities, her first published *Economist* piece being on fats and oils. A recommendation from a cousin who was a friend of John Midgley got her to see him and he took to her immediately. She was forever grateful to him because he helped her to improve her style. Where most *Economist* editors impatiently rewrite the work of their juniors and leave them to guess what is wrong, Midgley used rather brutally to tell its author to rewrite it in the light of his criticisms.

The prevailing custom in the foreign department at that time was that any new recruit who was not already a regional specialist would be told to take on Latin America, in which few people were interested. Smith was to become one of the stars as well as a linchpin of the paper: her Latin American coverage sparkled, especially after she had been allowed to travel there. ('A country that can cha-cha-cha to the "Internationale" wears its communism with a difference', she wrote after one of her Latin American tours. 'Neutral diplomats may call Cuba a communist paradise, but the tactful faces of the Russian experts carry a hint of their bafflement at the soaring hopes, the sunstruck lethargy, the eager conformism and the even more eager heresies of Caribbean socialism. At the Havana carnival, which astoundingly survives through all four weekends of March, the construction workers' syndicate was using its picks and shovels for makeshift music, and the builders' overalls glistened with the sweat of their dancing.'[10]

In early October 1962, like her superiors, Barbara Smith was not worrying about the Russian menace. 'There are plenty of good reasons for being worried about Cuba, and it may seem odd to put the correspondence columns of *Time* magazine and the *New York Herald Tribune* at the top of the list. But in fact the most disturbing thing about recent developments in Cuba is the effect they have had on the American state of mind; these two papers in particular (though not only they) convey the furious impatience – and the reluctance to see Cuba in context – that seem to mark the current mood in the United States. The widespread demand for President Kennedy to "do something," and damn the consequences, has reached the point when an outsider can fairly say what he thinks.' There was an immediate danger that the President might be pushed, against his will, 'into doing the wrong thing about Cuba'.[11]

This was written at a stage when it was generally known that Russia was supplying arms to Cuba. Ten days later Kennedy was shown aerial photographs which convinced him that nuclear missiles, capable of reaching American cities, were already being installed in Cuba and that more were on their way. On 22 October he announced a naval 'quarantining' of Cuba, stationed a line of warships across the path of the Soviet ships that were heading for Cuba with missiles stacked on their decks, and formally requested Khrushchev to remove all the missiles; on 26 October the Russians offered to withdraw their weapons if American equivalents were removed from Turkey. Kennedy rejected this proposal.

John Midgley was distrustful of the American case, and evidence from the Washington correspondent, Alex Campbell, corroborated his feeling that all this was related to aggressive American designs on Cuba; he believed on balance that the Americans were lying and the photographs were fakes. Beedham thought the photographs were probably genuine but agreed with Midgley that even so the issue was not worth bringing the world to the brink of nuclear war. Tyerman was also unconvinced by the Americans but less inclined than Midgley to voice his doubts. Almost seven years into his editorship, Tyerman's instinct for seeing several points of view was making him increasingly indecisive, so there was a lack of firm leadership at the top.

With some help from Andrew Boyd on the possible role of the United Nations, Midgley wrote 'CYCLONE CUBA', which spelled out the frightful consequences for Berlin if the Russians retaliated, or for the whole world if nuclear war resulted. Geoffrey Crowther read it and was so horrified that he breached the principle of editorial independence and told Tyerman to have it rewritten. On the morning of press day, Beedham was given it; he rewrote the first four or five paragraphs to reflect his own softer position, not condemning Kennedy but warning hardline Americans against trying to humiliate Khrushchev further. Tyerman added a few qualifiers, and the resultant implicitly contradictory mess must qualify as one of the most obfuscatory leaders ever to appear in a journal devoted to clarification. Even such an old hand as Gordon Lee, who had been away from the office that week, picked up *The Economist* on Friday at a news-stall and was so baffled by the contradictory nature of the leader that he rang the office to ask what was going on.

How useful the leader was can be illustrated by its last few lines, in which it said that, whether effective or not in defusing such a crisis, 'the United Nations was never more urgently needed than it is this week. If it did not exist, it would now be necessary to invent it – if there was time.'[12]

It is easy to mock in hindsight, but that week was one filled with dread for many millions of people. It was the kind of terrifying crisis where the most fortunate on-lookers are the blinkered, those who see no undesirable consequences flowing from decisive action. Much as a dedicated liberal like Walter Layton had spent the night of Munich in an agony of indecision, fearful of appeasement yet appalled by the nightmare of another terrible war, so there was much greater reason in the week of Cuba to agonise. This time the stakes were higher; there was the possibility of a war which could annihilate the human race. Nor could sceptical observers have anticipated that Kennedy would play his hand so skilfully.

The Economist made handsome amends the following week with three good leaders on the aftermath. In 'AFTER CUBA', John Midgley wrote: 'Foreign policy has been likened to a game of chess – wrongly, as Mr Hamilton Fish Armstrong points out in the fortieth anniversary number of *Foreign Affairs*, looking back on the whole dizzy period in which the United States has learnt to live with the responsibilities of world power. "There is no fixed book of rules to say that a certain move will be successful or that a contrary one will fail." The board is a patch of fluid afloat on the waters of time; the pieces, the vehicles of power, change their attributes without proper notice; and no contestant ever sees all of the board.'

> From many quarters, in the past twelve days, the Russians have been bitterly upbraided for the stealth of their action in deceitfully setting up missile bases on Cuba . . . What we must all hope is that they are upbraiding themselves mercilessly for the folly of it. Once they had done it and been found out, their position was irretrievably weak. Mr Kennedy, in the tense six days which began with his broadcast on October 22nd and ended last Sunday with Mr Khrushchev's promise to withdraw the offending weapons – 'Both you and I understand what kind of weapons they are' – from Cuba, was playing from strength.
>
> He played his hand as a strong hand should be played: the bid called exactly, the moves unhesitating, the objective, once stated, adhered to. Some people hoped, and many more in the world feared, that he would try to exceed his bid, perhaps by allowing the blockade of Cuba to become indiscriminate, perhaps by a direct blow to overthrow the Castro regime. Statements coming out of Washington last weekend did suggest that direct action against Cuba was very close. In the last phase of the crisis the pace was becoming hot, and the hours precious: as Mr Kennedy wrote to Mr Khrushchev last Sunday when it ended. 'You and I . . . were aware that developments were approaching a point where events could become unmanageable.'
>
> Perhaps only this can explain the astonishing speed and . . . the completeness of the Russian retreat. Mr Kennedy thereupon showed that he knew not only how far to go, but precisely where to stop. His acceptance of Mr Khrushchev's retreat was unreserved and handsome. His conditional offers made the day before – to call off the blockade, and to give assurances against an invasion of Cuba – were at once reaffirmed as 'firm undertakings.' There was not a touch of the intoxication that confuses success with victory.[13]

In 'SOVIET BRINKMANSHIP', Andrew Boyd began: 'Neither an idiot nor a devil, Mr Khrushchev has extricated himself, with the loss of a certain amount of skin, from a position that proved untenably brinkmanlike', and followed with an absorbing investigation of the underlying psychology behind it and the likely next step. 'At the height of the "Cuban crisis," no Cuban voice was heard or listened for', wrote Barbara Smith in 'CASTRO'S MORNING AFTER'. 'The island's identity vanished behind the storm. But as people blink their way back into the light, it is relevant to wonder in what shape Dr Fidel Castro and his men have survived the diplomatic battering that has been going on over their heads.'

> The mortification of the Cuban leaders at being demonstrably passed over while the decisions that mattered were being made has been taken for granted, perhaps too glibly . . . But face can be lost and won again, words eaten and forgotten, faster and more easily than logical minds suppose. The analogy with Egypt's victorious emergence from the Suez Canal crisis of 1956 is worth a tentative probe. Although the circumstances were very different, both leaders were powerless to control the events that thundered around them. Yet President Nasser was able to emerge not only with honour but with triumph.

No attention had been paid to the Cuban siege mentality. 'From the Cuban point of view, the technically "offensive" weapons were defensive; where the Cubans made their mistake was in thinking that their point of view mattered.'

'There is nothing like a good scare to make a man take a rosy view of life', wrote Brian Beedham a few weeks later. 'To judge from some recent comments, the fact that the world did not blow itself up about Cuba a month ago has sharply improved the chances that it will refrain from blowing itself up about anything else . . .'

> It is true that several people have learned a useful lesson this October and November. The United States has learned that, if it catches Mr Khrushchev far from home with his conventional trousers down, he is likely to back warily away without resorting to nuclear mayhem; those who were not at all sure that he would do this can indeed salute the coolness of Mr Kennedy's judgment. Mr Khrushchev himself has undoubtedly made a note not to get caught again in a situation where he is left with no choice except atomic war or backing down.

In the post-crisis world, 'the relationship between Russia and the United States, which is still the heart of the matter, has not been fundamentally changed in the last couple of months. The two sides have had a horrid shock at finding themselves on the brink of war, and have learned something about the techniques for scrambling back from the brink.' There might now be a possibility of reaching agreement on areas of common interest, like, for instance, a nuclear test ban.* Not on the cards, however, were 'the larger hopes that have been circulating since the euphoric day when the Russian missiles were pulled out of Cuba. These hopes range from the expectation that Mr Khrushchev is about to call a general truce in the East–West struggle, to the wild-eyed dream that he will fairly soon discover that he prefers capitalist Americans to Stalinist Chinese.'

> Not just yet, not just yet, one must regretfully say. To understand why such hopes are still totally unrealistic, it is necessary to appreciate what would have to happen before they could be fulfilled. It is sometimes suggested that when Russia gets at loggerheads with the West – over Berlin, say, or Cuba – it is because Mr Khrushchev has simply decided to 'cause trouble'. On this theory, he starts international crises at times and places of his own choosing for the purely offensive purpose of frightening and dividing his opponents. If this were really the case, a single decision by Mr Khrushchev could cause the flow of crises to be turned off at the Kremlin stopcock.

But this theory did not stand up. Though he enjoyed seeing his opponents being frightened and divided, 'another reason why he gets embroiled in rows with the West is that he wants to defend what he conceives to be the Soviet Union's vital interests. In the case of Berlin, these interests were to save the client regime in East Germany from collapse: in Cuba, one guesses, he wanted in addition to redress the missile balance by putting some medium-range rockets on the island.'

> In other words, East–West crises arise from real clashes of interest, not from Luciferic raids on what would otherwise be a world-wide Garden of Eden. But this means Mr Khrushchev is not entirely free to sound a general truce

---

*The Test Ban Treaty between Britain, the Soviet Union and the United States was signed in August 1963, prohibiting the testing of nuclear weapons everywhere but underground. Between 1963 and 1965 ninety other governments signed the treaty, though France and China continued to test nuclear weapons in the atmosphere.

in the cold war even if he wanted to. He is, to a certain extent, a prisoner of the national and ideological interests he champions; of the people in the Soviet Union who would attack him if he failed to champion those interests properly: and of communists outside Russia who would claim that they could do the job better. Mr Mao Tse-tung already makes it plain that he thinks Mr Khrushchev a pretty poor fellow for defining his interests in too defensive a way. The fact that very similar considerations apply to the leaders of the West merely makes things more complicated. There is no unilateral way to guarantee peace.

The real significance of Cuba was not any alteration in the status quo, 'but that Mr Kennedy and Mr Khrushchev have rediscovered for themselves in the most nerve-tingling way the simple truth that Marshal Bulganin and Mr Eisenhower lit upon at Geneva in 1955: that these arguments have got to be kept short of war. The leaders of 1962 seemed to have gone a stage further, by starting to set up the machinery of consultation and informal negotiation by which they may be able to prolong the peace. In this sense, and nothing grander, Cuba may have changed the weather.'[14]

CHAPTER XLVI

The evil empire

We believe . . . that the certain result of all communist schemes, in action, would be vastly diminished production, and, consequently, vastly diminished means of consumption; with the necessary further result of increased misery, want, and suffering; we believe them to be based on a total misconception of the nature of man, and the circumstances in which he is placed; and we believe them to draw much of their support, if not their origin, from an ignorant jealousy of the large share, which those who possess the accumulated fruits of their forefathers' industry, must ever obtain in the annual produce of land and labour, owing to those fruits being necessary instruments in its production.[1] The Economist, *1848*

Brian Beedham became foreign editor in 1963 when Midgley went to Washington. In his twenty-five years in the job he and *The Economist* were often accused of taking an inflexible cold-warrior stance. But there was never anything in common between Beedham and the 'Commie-bashers'. His end was the maintenance of the balance of power: his arguments with colleagues were over the means. Indeed, he saw the balance of power best protected by a duopoly. In 'THE FIFTY-YEAR ITCH', looking at the scene in 1967, under new players, Lyndon Johnson and Leonid Brezhnev, Beedham looked at the prospects for coexistence. There was no possibility of their proclaiming a policy of mutual non-intervention around the world; nor would it be desirable: 'if Russia and America are not going to retire from the world, they will have to do the opposite. They will have to make sure they have a real grip on things. This means, at the very least, agreeing that there are certain parts of the world which are too important to both of them to be allowed to fall wholly under the control of either, or of anybody else. It means a pretty precise definition of their essential spheres of influence in those areas, and an agreement to make these spheres stick.' It had already been done in Europe and needed to be done also in South-East Asia and the Middle East.

> It will not be easy, or quick. But it is the only alternative to an anarchic dog-fight that the great powers will one day inevitably get drawn into. What it amounts to is the beginning of a loose, informal, and indirect condominium over certain specified regions. Put it another way: it amounts to the beginning of a rudimentary form of international government. This is the proposition that Mr Brezhnev is now mulling over. A lot depends on which seems more important to him: the drum beat of communist evangelism or a world with some claim to peace and order.[2]

In 1965, it was the necessity of keeping the balance of power that made Beedham and the new editor, Alastair Burnet, swing the paper firmly behind American action in Vietnam. In 1954 the Geneva agreements had recognised a partitioned Vietnam: in the north Ho Chi Minh's republic, in the south a republic from 1955 under President Ngo Dinh Diem, whose repressive government was overthrown in November 1963, the month of President Kennedy's assassination. Fearful of encroaching North Vietnamese communism, the Kennedy administration tried to build up South Vietnam from 1961 onwards, but by the time Diem was overthrown communist guerrillas, known as Vietcong, had infiltrated many areas in the south. By mid-1964 the Americans were becoming militarily engaged, with heavy bombing of North Vietnam in operation early in 1965.

The Beedham-Burnet view was that the West could not sit 'unprotestingly by' while communist power was extended. 'What has to be avoided in South-East Asia is the uncertainty about Western intentions that disastrously drew the communists into their invasion of South Korea in 1950.'[3] To reach its objectives, America did not need to expunge North Vietnam. 'Winning this fight consists of denying victory to the other side. If and when it is clear that to commit the North Vietnamese army to the fighting in the south is to send it to its destruction, Hanoi will be faced again with a choice between escalation and negotiation. If it chooses escalation, then the United States will doubtless have to follow it to the new level, if necessary to a direct confrontation with China. But if North Vietnam chooses negotiation, then the independent existence of South Vietnam can be safeguarded and the myth of "wars of liberation" punctured. The essential condition is that Hanoi should abandon its belief that the east wind is bound to prevail over the west. For the time being, the east wind is blowing harder than ever. It might even blow away a paper tiger. But the Americans are not that.'4

By now there were well over 100,000 Americans on active service in Vietnam; the figure rose to 400,000 by the end of 1966. In December 1965 *The Economist* ran 'VIETNAM: AN ARGUMENT WITH THE POLES'. 'Some weeks ago', explained Beedham in introducing it, 'the foreign editor of *The Economist* and the foreign editor of *Polityka*, the Polish weekly, got into an argument about Vietnam. It led to an offer by *Polityka* to print the western point of view; so far as we know, it is the first such article to appear in the press of the communist world. Our foreign editor begins:' What followed was a classic Beedham exposition of his concept of coexistence.

'What does coexistence mean? If it means anything at all, it means that we must often refrain from using violence, or from supporting the use of violence, even in situations where we passionately believe we have justice on our side. You doubtless prefer your system of organising an economy and running a government. We prefer ours.' The existence of nuclear weapons meant that 'the only way to avoid total disaster is to control the conflict between the rival systems while we find out which of them really does satisfy man's material and spiritual needs best. I believe that on present evidence the western system looks the better bet. I do not expect you to agree. But I am prepared to wait for experience to decide the issue; neither of us should shove his solution on the other by force.'

It was necessary to be absolutely honest about what this involved. 'The idea of coexistence has been generally accepted as it applies to Europe. In the East German riots of 1953, and the Hungarian rebellion of 1956, the Western powers did nothing to help the rioters and rebels even though we believed that they represented the true feelings of most East Germans and Hungarians. In believing this we may have been right or wrong. The point is that we did believe it, passionately, but we swallowed our feelings while Russian tanks put down what we considered to be the just cause. We did this for the sake of peace.' In the same way, communists should refrain from supporting the recourse of the Vietcong to violence. 'For coexistence is going to break down very rapidly indeed if the rules of the game turn out to be one-sided. If we in the West accept the existence of a line in Europe beyond which there is no poaching, then you must accept a similar line in Asia. And if the Chinese refuse to accept such a line – if they reject coexistence, in other words – then you must dissociate yourselves from the Chinese, just as you would expect us to dissociate ourselves from anybody who tried to foment rebellions in eastern Europe.'

> This does not mean that the dividing line between the socialist and non-socialist camps must remain fixed forever as it is now. There are quite a few countries – including several in Africa – that could go communist tomorrow without our feeling desperately worried. I dare say you feel the same, the other way round, about Albania. But there are other places where for the moment the line is firmly drawn. Central Europe is one; and we accept it. South-east Asia is another. Will you accept that?

What both sides were trying to do was 'to work out a set of rules by which we can live in peace while we find the best economic and political system for men to live under. If, in the name of "wars of national liberation," you support the use of violence to change the régime in South Vietnam, how can we appeal to other people to refrain from violence in the pursuit of "liberation" elsewhere: the Pakistanis over Kashmir, the Austrians over South Tyrol – in the end, maybe, the West Germans over East Germany? Peace is indivisible, Mr Litvinov told us. Coexistence is a formula for keeping the peace. So coexistence, with the self-discipline it involves, is indivisible too. It has to be valid everywhere, or it will be valid nowhere.'

Johnson's decision to send a large American army into action into Vietnam made it unlikely that the Vietcong could win the total victory wanted by Mao and Ho Chi Minh, but 'I doubt whether the Vietcong, who are also strong and brave, can be totally defeated either. Here is a chance for a negotiated settlement, with no total victory for anybody, and with an independent and peaceful South Vietnam settling its political problems between "the people and the government," as President Johnson put it on March 25th. Can we help to arrange this between us?'[5]

Grimly, Beedham continued his support for the Americans in the teeth of a good deal of opposition within his own department. He had written to his predecessor, Midgley, at the end of 1964 to say that he would have found the job of foreign editor, 'totally and definitively unmanageable if the Foreign Department hadn't been as alive and smooth running as it is. Rest assured I shall do what I can to keep it that way, though I have been painfully – at times very painfully – aware that you have qualities to that end that I don't have, or at least haven't developed yet. Keeping eight bright people in the air simultaneously, some more fragile than others, is an art one doesn't appreciate until the original skilled hand steps away and you find yourself lunging all over the place in the effort to prevent disaster . . . in short, this is a very good department thanks to you; we'll see if we can maintain standards.'⁶ His team at the time included Barbara Smith, 'now looking after International Report, which has never been done so well (she is one of the best editors the paper has, in addition to having a real womanly sense of lay-out)'; Andrew Boyd, who was at the time taking on Africa; Wendy Hinde, who ran the foreign stringers and Eastern Europe; Joe Rogaly (who later became a columnist on the *Financial Times*) and Stephen Hugh-Jones, who at the time was editing Foreign Report.

Beedham has an automatic suspicion of the easy option. Indeed he surmises that his long and often lonely defence of American action in Vietnam made him tend towards the hard option. In 1977 he once wrote to an aspiring journalist about a piece she had submitted, 'I thought that at each difficult moment in the argument you opted for the "easy" train of thought: the result being a comfortable, rather Guardian-like, proposition that all can be the best in the best of all possible worlds, rather than the much harder-headed piece that was really needed.'⁷ Responding to her rewritten piece, he suspected 'that you started out with an instinctive judgment, and then proceeded to collect arguments to sustain it. This is by no means uncommon: we all do it from time to time, politicians, civil servants and journalists alike, and it is sometimes a way of breaking through to the truth. But I tend to cock an eyebrow when the instinctive judgment leans in favour of doing nothing rather than doing something; too much of our instinct – in politics, if not in other things – is in favour of pulling down the blinds and hoping things will turn out for the best without us.'⁸

Beedham went through agony over Vietnam, locked in a running battle with several of his most liked and trusted colleagues in his own department and additionally having to go through bitter arguments at editorial meetings. From the perspective of the colleagues who disagreed with him, he was blindly committed to America, following his instinct and refusing to face the facts, particularly about the way America was itself reacting. But Beedham is a ferocious logician. Once his premise is accepted no one can fault the development of his argument, and in debate he was unbeatable. Nobody doubted his integrity and his courage, although some believed him to have a massive blind spot.

Like James Wilson – and indeed like Pennant-Rea – Beedham is an unusually kind man in personal dealings, affectionate and generous of spirit. But he has an implacable streak that marks out the crusader from the mere journalist. Once committed he never lets go: he was no fair-weather friend to the United States. Not surprisingly, this led to some wishful thinking in the coverage of Vietnam. While the anti-war element were taking comfort in the peace movement and in what proved to be America's unsuitability to wage this particular jungle war, Beedham was sometimes clutching at straws. 'The past year came to the brink of disaster. Things are a bit brighter now', ran one sub-heading in June 1966.[9] And a few months later: 'The Johnson doctrine for Asia is starting to pay off. It has not yet passed its decisive test, which is the test of the battlefield; the North Vietnamese and the Vietcong can be expected to make another attempt this winter to demonstrate that they are willing to go on fighting in South Vietnam longer than the Americans and their allies.' But Johnson's actions were succeeding in building up a Pacific consensus on the non-communist side.[10]

Doubts crept in in mid-1967. 'Maybe the Americans don't have what it takes after all. What it takes in Vietnam is patience: the patience to slog on with a defensive war, and to accept the restraints on military action that this sort of war calls for. If the Americans can command enough patience, they can do what they set out to do in Vietnam. This is a bloody war, and an expensive one, but for the Americans the cost is a long way short of intolerable.' Johnson would not run short of money and men, but what he might be running short of 'is something else: patient public support for the whole idea of a limited war'.[11]

Later that year Beedham applied logic to the demonstrators who were besieging American embassies in Europe and various other parts of the world. The Marxist demonstrator's position on Vietnam was straightforward, but 'the others – the genuinely idealistic young students who do not start from the premise that a Marxist society is just what South Vietnam needs – might usefully ask themselves what they are demonstrating against.'

> It is not just the peculiar beastliness of a war in which both sides find themselves killing civilians. That is the result of the chosen tactics of the people who devised the idea of 'wars of national liberation.' What they are really demonstrating against is the fact that a war is happening in Vietnam at all. They might choose a different target for their protest if they remem-

bered Lenin's advice. If you want to get to the heart of any political problem, Lenin said, the essential question to ask is 'who, whom? Who is trying to do what to whom?'

The opponents of the American intervention in Vietnam used two different arguments. 'The first does not stand up to a moment's serious examination. This is the argument that the Americans are there to further their own selfish and presumably material interests. Those who believe this – the people who talk about "American imperialism" – would say that the answer to the who-whom question is that the United States is trying to take over south-east Asia from the local inhabitants for its own national advantage. But how can anybody this side of lunacy suppose that the American troops fighting in the paddy-fields of Vietnam can raise their real gross national product back home by a single cent?' Indeed the war was adding to America's inflationary pressures, 'so those who believe in the "imperialist" theory are reduced to arguments like those of Professor Gunnar Myrdal, who is recently reported to have said that the Americans find the Vietnam war useful because it works off the latent aggressiveness in their national character. That may seem an interesting speculation to a professor, but most other people will regard it as really rather scraping the bottom of the barrel.

'The alternative is to say that the Americans went into South-East Asia for unselfish reasons – to stop the communists taking over most of the area by force of arms – but they got their calculations horribly wrong.' But the critics cannot know who would come out on top in Vietnam. 'This has become, though it was not intended to be, a war of attrition; and the point about wars of attrition is that it is impossible to foresee with any confidence whose resources of men and fighting spirit are going to run out first.'

If the critics felt that the Americans had got their political calculations wrong, they had a better case. 'But it is quite certainly not an argument that anybody can be so certain about that he should be tempted to go and scream abuse in Grosvenor Square to show which side he is on. Our own judgment would still fall decisively on the other side.'[12]

What *The Economist* wanted for South Vietnam was to see it joining 'the chain of other economic success-stories – Hong Kong, Taiwan, South Korea and Singapore – that have sprung up on the eastern seaboard of Asia in the 1960s. They all happen to be pluralist, that is non-Marxist, economies . . . The problem is to define the place allotted to the communists in a peace settlement so that they cannot, while this is going on, haul Vietnam back into the dead end of a Marxist dictatorship.'[13]

That was written in 1968. By 1972, everything seemed to be slipping away. 'It has been its own sort of war from the start, and it is staying in character right to the end. Even when the basic terms of a settlement have been published by both sides, no one is quite sure whether the Vietnam war is over, or who has won it if it is. That is a measure of the failure that has dogged public understanding of this war.'[14]

The Economist fought hard against a fudged peace. 'There is no reason that a liberal should accept why the two Vietnams ought to be reunited until it has been shown that a majority of the people in both of them, or at least of those in the south, wish it to be so. Until that happens, a liberal would add, South Vietnam should have a government of its own based on some sort of reasonably accurate measurement of the preferences of the South Vietnamese. Most people in the west would accept those principles, as principles; after all, it is what they say about that other divided nation, Germany, and they would be outraged if one half of Germany sent its army into the other half in order to insist on putting its own preferred sort of government into power there. The difference in Vietnam is the reluctance of so many people to apply these principles as the necessary test of the terms on which the war has ended.'[15] But the fudging went ahead anyway, and in due course South Vietnam was overrun.

Beedham was to feel entirely vindicated in his stand on Vietnam when the exodus of boat people began. The first wave were the Chinese minority who were simply expelled; then came the desperate professional and trading people. *The Economist* urged that they be taken in. They would be good citizens, those people 'enterprising and determined enough to risk their lives on the high seas . . . Britain can testify that refugees from tyrannies tend to enrich, not impoverish, their host societies. The argument that Vietnam is America's problem – or China's or Russia's – will not wash. It is every decent human's problem, and will not be wished away.'[16]

(Because of *The Economist*'s consistency in pursuing to their logical conclusion even the most unpopular policies, the heartless label has hung around it for 150 years, yet it has never been without a heart. The paper's attitude to the dispossessed was summed up movingly in 1956 in 'UNFOR-GETTABLE PEOPLE'. 'Most of us are refugees from refugees', wrote Andrew Boyd. 'It is not really true that they are "forgotten people." They are, rather, people about whom we should like to forget.

> A vague feeling of guilt makes us recoil, in classic Freudian style, from the thought of our homeless and helpless fellows. It is less emotionally disturbing to turn mind and conversation on to Mrs Ponomareva's hats or Mr Liberace's clothes, even on to the more serious problems of navigation through Oxford and Suez. Mercifully, a few devoted people refuse to push all thought about refugees to the back of the mind, and instead give of their best to help them. But the mass of mankind grasps at excuses for its inaction. And some of the excuses are plausible: 'Surely an enormous amount has already been done for these people?' – 'But there are so many of them; where can you even begin?' – 'What's the good of talking about solving the problem when new refugees keep coming?'

Addressing himself particularly to the plight of displaced persons – those with no country who just needed some financial help to get them going – he ended: 'If we are not humane enough to heed the appeal of these tragic figures out of sheer charity, have we not reason at least to make one more effort to clear our own consciences – an absurdly small effort when seen against what has already been done? To spoil a ship for a ha'p'orth of tar is peculiarly mean when the ship happens to be an ark of refuge.'[17])

'Poor Brian', remarked a colleague towards the end of 1989, when the Berlin Wall finally went. 'What will he do now that someone has shot his fox?' The answer is of course that there are always other vermin and he is a more flexible man than he has often been given credit for.

In the Christmas issue of 1989, the year in which he ceased to be foreign editor, Beedham wrote a three-page article, 'GREAT YEARS OF HISTORY', which, though anonymous, was in its way a valedictory. The sub-heading ran: 'For those who like to roll the taste of history on their tongue, this has been a vintage year, though not one of the greatest. Our list of the really big years of the past, minus Adam Smith's birthday'.

'It has been a wonderful year,' he began, 'a year your great-grandchildren's schoolbooks will spend a whole chapter on; but it does not quite rank with the great years of history. In the great years, something new is written into the human ledger. This year has been an erasing year. It did a splendid job, clearing the page for whatever comes next; but that is not exactly the same thing.'

In a passage reminiscent of James Wilson's glorying in the dismantling of wicked legislation, Beedham described 1989 as the year in which 'one of history's bigger mistakes began to be rubbed out'.

Really great years were: 457 BC, when the Athenian democracy got firmly on its feet; 30 AD, when Christianity got going; 410, when the Visigoths took Rome; 622, when Islam took off with Muhammad's flight to Medina; 732 and 1683, when Islam was blocked, at Vienna, from advancing further into Europe. Destructive power took a great leap forward in 1249 with gun-powder and in 1945 with the atomic bomb explosion. The printing revolu-tion (1456) and television (1926) were great leaps forward, yet the biggest date of all was 1517, 'when Luther pinned up the case for free choice in religion on the church door at Wittenberg' and challenged the church's monopoly authoritarianism.

> One way of looking at the history of the past 2,500 years is to see it as a slow, uneven but relentless focusing of human consciousness. Out of the tribal collective of the distant past, men started to become aware of themselves as separate individuals. Each individual had to make up his own mind about the big choices in life, and carry the responsibility for the choice thus made.

Man began to look around him, examine, measure and reach conclusions. In 1613 Galileo concluded that the earth went round the sun and in 1666 Newton came up with the theory of gravity. They were the fathers of modern science.

> The quality they shared was objectivity, an insistence on the right to refer any issue to detached inspection. Authoritarians loathe objectivity, because it deprives them of their claim to lay down the law.

Then came the revolutions. In 1775 the American colonies fought 'for the simple principle that no small group of men could write the laws for a much larger number of people, especially if the small group lived in a country far away. The Americans wanted to run their own lives, in whatever way a majority of them saw fit. This is liberal democracy, plus self-determination.' In 1848 the European revolutions were fought on the same principle, and though they mostly failed, they made it easier for democracy eventually to come to these countries. 'The post-1945 freeing of the colonial empires was carried out in the name of self-determination and liberal democracy, though it achieved little of the second. And in 1989 yet another echo from Lexington has been crashing . . . round Eastern Europe.'

The American model has one drawback. It tends to produce a lot of nation-states, and a nation-state is no less keen on asserting its national interests when it is a democracy. This makes for an abrasive world; parts of Eastern Europe may soon be feeling the awkward side of liberated nationalism. For government by the consent of the governed, though, nothing has yet been invented to beat this definition of democracy. The majority decides how it wants to run the place – with luck, being gentle to the minority – until a new majority takes shape to replace it. No general rule applies, except that people must be free to make and re-make their own rules.

In 1789, the French Revolution had gone off in a different direction. Although the eighteenth century in some ways was the high point of European culture, 'it was also the century that produced the Idea . . . some people, particularly in France, got over-confident'.

> They thought they could work out, with the force of scientific certainty, a set of general rules for the well-being of mankind. Apply those rules, and a new world would have begun.
>
> The 1789 revolution, after a generous start, soon degenerated into the madnesses of ideological certainty. Not everybody agreed what the new rules were, so the slow-minded had to be coerced.

Revolutionary autocracy replaced royal autocracy both then and after 1917, 'when another revolution driven by a similar demon of an idea took place in Russia. The chief difference in Russia was that Lenin had prefaced his revolution by announcing that it would all be done by a single, certain-of-itself party, so the arrival of the new autocracy took no time at all.'

France had escaped from the idea quickly, because of Napoleon, who turned out to be an 'old-fashioned sort of dictator, and he also lost a war'. Russia and her empire had to wait for 70 years before finding a leader willing to admit to second thoughts.

> The upheaval of 1989 is the beginning of the end of Lenin's 1917 revolution. It may also be the end of the wider error that began exactly two centuries ago: the notion that politics is a science, that people can be governed out of a laboratory.

Nobody seemed to be clear about what the next entry in the ledger might be. 'For the first time in centuries, no novel political idea urgently offers itself.

The apparent triumph of the individual over ideology presumably leaves free-market democracy as the world's chief politico-economic system.'

> In fact, it would be odd if politics or economics were the issue that led to history's next great year. They were the subject of the last argument, which has just been settled. The next argument will probably be about something different: something out there in the misty ground beyond the now routine organisation of everyday life. Muslim fundamentalists know what they think the next hundred years will be about. So do the pushy new sects on the fringes of Christianity. Neither of them quite looks like the bringer of the future. But they may be pointing in the right direction. Unless, that is, the end of history really has arrived. How unlike history that would be.[18]

CHAPTER XLVII

The special relationship

If the British want to, they can give up the attempt to influence American policy. They can retire to the side-lines and blow raspberries instead . . . They will then be treated the way barrackers usually are treated, by being ignored. But if the British want to keep any influence over what the United States does, they must remember the basic rule for the only sort of relationship that gives Britain any pull in Washington. The rule is that Britain goes along with the main aims of American foreign policy in return for the right to nudge the Americans back on course when they seem to be deviating from those aims . . .

This right to dig the elbow into the Americans' ribs at critical moments is extremely valuable.[1] *Brian Beedham, 1966*

An unusual feature of *The Economist*'s coverage of Vietnam was the difference of emphasis between the leaders and the American Survey pages, caused by Beedham's eye being on Vietnam and the communist world, while the eyes of those running American Survey were on the United States itself. American Survey heard the sheer volume of sound from the peace movement, while the foreign department argued against its reasoning.

In 1966 John Midgley wrote from Washington in his report on the resumed bombing of North Vietnam: '"This war," said an unnamed Senator, emerging from one of the many conferences and hearings that have marked the past month, "is as popular as a rattlesnake." It is hard to imagine, let alone remember, a nation advancing into a major and certainly bloody military adventure with such resolute step and such total disenchantment of heart.'[2] And in 1967 Robert Novak wrote from Washington: 'Within the last two months leaders of the Democratic party have started coming around to the realisation that liberal intellectuals and left-wing trade union leaders may actually mean it when they threaten not to support President Johnson for re-election next year because of his Vietnamese policy. There are, indeed, increasing signs of the Democratic party's first left-wing revolt of any consequence since 1948 and potentially the most serious defection inside the party since William Jennings Bryan's disastrous campaigns 70 years ago.'³

One result of the different perspective was that there was relatively little coverage of Vietnam in the American Survey because Nancy Balfour wanted to avoid appalling rows. The two different parts of the paper could avoid straightforwardly contradicting each other, mainly because American Survey was much more factual than opinionated. But American Survey was run as an independent barony, and one where the foreign editor's writ did not run.

American Survey was invented by Geoffrey Crowther as a rapid response to the Japanese bombing of the American naval base at Pearl Harbor on 7 December 1941. Congress had declared war on Japan the following day and Japan's allies, Germany and Italy, had declared war on the United States on 11 December. American Survey was in place by 17 January 1942, with Margaret Cruikshank running the London end.

Cruikshank was typical of Crowther's brilliant recruiting technique. An American, she had been to Swarthmore (his wife's college), then Columbia, and had a degree in economic history. She had met Crowther while working on Wall Street and then had married Robin Cruikshank, an Englishman, in 1939. At the start of their married life he was editor of the *Star*, one of the newspapers under Layton's control. During the war he became director of the American division of the Ministry of Information and after the war editor of the *News Chronicle*.

At first Cruikshank was hired part-time to clip the newspapers that arrived from America every six weeks or so. She acquired more material from her husband, who brought home, for instance, Isaiah Berlin's reports from the British embassy in Washington. In the first week of American Survey Crowther wrote most of it with help from Paul Bareau, Walter Hill and outsiders like Denis Brogan and a couple of American correspondents. Cruikshank contributed her first piece the week after she joined, and by March 1942 she was writing most – sometimes all – of the section.

From America, material came in the early days mainly from Robert Warren and Helen Hill Miller. Warren, of the Institute for Advanced Studies at Princeton, had been for many years the New York correspondent of *The*

Economist. 'We have the very highest respect for his contributions,' wrote Crowther to Hill Miller in 1940, 'which give a running commentary on the financial and economic position in the United States, as illuminated by the current statistics, that is, in my opinion better than anything that is available anywhere else.'

Helen Hill Miller was a much more recent acquisition. Crowther had met her briefly in Washington in the mid-1930s, and in 1940 he had been impressed by a document she had written for a proposed 'Special Committee on Steps Toward a Durable Peace' which recognised 'what seems to me to be the central truth – that any durable peace settlement has got to be cynical'. He was in need of a Washington correspondent, for the veteran journalist Raymond Gram Swing had become too busy to contribute. '*The Economist* would like to have fuller coverage of political and social subjects, and matters of broad general interest', he told her. 'The European reader is not, of course, interested in the details of party manoeuvres or Congressional debate. But he is interested in the broad outlines of, say, the Presidential campaign and the more colourful personalities, state and federal. He can also be interested in such matters as agricultural policy, the food stamps, and so forth.' Crowther invited her to send contributions of about 1,200 words every two or three weeks as a complement to Warren.[4]

On 14 January 1942 Crowther wrote to her: 'As I cabled you yesterday, the Paper Control has now made it possible to run a special American section in *The Economist* every week. Most of it we shall write here, but there will also be more room for correspondence. I'm hoping to draw correspondence from a regular team of three writers and from other additional occasional contributors and, to prevent either overlapping or omissions, I have asked John Chapman of *Business Week* to act as co-ordinator. I very much hope that you will continue your Washington letters, which are much admired. So far as may prove practicable, would you consult with Chapman about subjects, and forward your letters through him?'

Robert Warren stopped writing for the paper at the end of 1941. His place as financial expert was eventually taken by Donald Woodward, the economist for Mutual Life Insurance of New York. Chapman had not done much for his money, so Crowther dropped him on a pretext and appointed Hill Miller co-ordinator in his stead.

Helen Hill Miller had been educated at Bryn Mawr, the University of Chicago (where she took a PhD in physics) and Oxford, where she earned a diploma in economics and political science. She was a freelance writer as well as being a writer on the staff of the US Department of Agriculture from 1934 to 1940.

'We want three things', wrote Barbara Ward (then in America) in October 1942, quoting Tyerman: '1. a supply of articles from Chapman's team somewhat more frequently than hitherto; 2. articles on social, human, local and administrative questions as well as on specific problems of production and finance; and 3. as many articles as the team can send (a), on industries and (b), on regions.'

> AS [American Survey] takes it for granted rather too much that people in this country really do understand the continental nature of American life and thought and the peculiar social and institutional ways of the American people. Anything that brings out by reference to current war problems the habits of thought and action and the variety of those habits in the US will be welcome here.

Hill Miller faced two main problems: how to find contributors who would work anonymously for almost nothing and how to write knowing that wartime copy would go to London slowly by ship convoy. 'Therefore you had the constant humiliation of reading six weeks after you wrote something, something which you wished you hadn't written.' Finding stringers, particularly in America, was done very much on Crowther lines, so *The Economist* tended to have a rather unexpected selection of people. Instead of established journalists, unknowns or the struggling young were often given a chance, as were friends and friends of friends, some of whom might never have written anything of consequence.

The fact that the paper always paid badly never posed a serious problem in getting stringers. For some it was a wonderful opportunity to prove what they could do, for others it was an honour to write for a paper of such distinction, and others again enjoyed the sense of belonging to a wide family. To say that one worked for *The Economist* gave one the entrée everywhere, particularly in America. (Indeed, one disadvantage of anonymity was that occasionally people who had no connection with the paper would claim to be writing for it. The industrial correspondent, Howard Banks, was once introduced at a party to the industrial correspondent of *The Economist*. 'There's a coincidence', he said. 'So am I.')

Stringers tended to stay for a very long time even when they became successful and well-known. Tony Lewis of the *New York Times*, twice winner of the Pulitzer Prize, is a case in point. For such people *The Economist* offered a great opportunity to express themselves in a more critical, more opinionated, way than would be allowed under their own by-line in a newspaper. Lewis covered the Justice Department, anything in Congress to do with law, and the Supreme Court. Ed Dale, also of the *New York Times*, liked writing for *The Economist* because he could be relaxed and amusing in a way he could not be on his own paper. Sandy Ungar liked writing about quirky things that would normally be off-limits. Other American correspondents included Ralph Nader, Gene Liechtenstein, Murray Rossant and Eileen Shanahan. American readers did not realise how much of American Survey was written by Americans.

Two anecdotes about Justice Felix Frankfurter of the US Supreme Court are revealing. He had been a contributor and friend of the paper in the 1930s, one of those people who used to drop into the office when he was in London. A devoted reader, he once went so far as to quote it in a Court opinion.

In order to head off a strike, President Truman had seized a number of steel mills in April 1952. This action had been ruled unconstitutional by a judge of the Washington District Court, a decision upheld by a majority of 6 to 3 in the Supreme Court. Frankfurter contributed a sparkling, subtle and broad-based reflection on the Constitution. 'Before the cares of the White House were his own,' he began, 'President Harding is reported to have said that government after all is a very simple thing. He must have said that, if he said it, as a fleeting inhabitant of fairyland. The opposite is the truth. A constitutional democracy like ours is perhaps the most difficult of man's social arrangements to manage successfully.' What was necessary in a case like this was 'rigorous adherence to the narrow scope of the judicial function [which] is especially demanded in controversies that arouse appeals to the Constitution'.

> The attitude with which this Court must approach its duty when confronted with such issues is precisely the opposite of that normally manifested by the general public. So-called constitutional questions seem to exercise a mesmeric influence over the popular mind. This eagerness to settle – preferably forever – a specific problem on the basis of the broadest possible constitutional pronouncements may not unfairly be called one of our minor national traits. An English observer of our scene has acutely described it: 'At the first

sound of a new argument over the United States Constitution and its interpretation the hearts of Americans leap with a fearful joy. The blood stirs powerfully in their veins and a new lustre brightens their eyes. Like King Harry's men before Harfleur, they stand like greyhounds in the slips, straining upon the start.' *The Economist*, 10 May 1952, p. 370.[5]

This was flattering to the paper, if slightly embarrassing in that the 'English' author of the quote was in fact an American stringer. Another manifestation of Frankfurter's devotion occurred when Tony Lewis was covering the Supreme Court in the late 1950s. He had written a quite critical piece about some action of the Court which was by-lined 'From a special correspondent in Washington', indicating that it was not by a member of staff. A page brought over to him a note signed 'F F' which asked playfully, 'Who do you think is the "special correspondent of *The Economist*" who dares to criticise the Supreme Court in the current issue?'

In the words of the American Survey editor in 1980, Dudley Fishburn, Mildred Adams Kenyon, who had just died, was 'our prime instance of a "stringer" who cared lovingly for the paper, and who established with us an almost familial relationship over the years. It was because Mildred's contribution was so valuable from the earliest days of the American Survey that we subsequently built up a network of writers throughout the United States, now perhaps numbered in the hundreds, modelled on her work with us. This has been the secret of our success . . . and it is a secret in which Mildred not only partook but, through her own success, made possible for us.'[6]

Mildred Adams Kenyon was recruited by Helen Hill Miller in 1946. Like Hill Miller and the other stringers of that generation, she was an enthusiastic supporter of President F.D. Roosevelt and the New Deal. She spent some time covering Spain for the *New York Times* in the early 1930s and then, in New York, ran a rescue committee for Spanish republican refugees. A translator and critic as well as journalist, she typified those remarkable women who made the American Survey what it was. Hill Miller, Cruikshank, Nancy Balfour, Mary Ellen Leary and so many more: they were liberal Democrats to a woman and all were, inevitably, opposed to American involvement in Vietnam.

Increasingly, expatriate Americans began to read *The Economist* to find out what was going on at home, and even in the United States it was winning a devoted readership. Though most of the American Survey was written in

London with the help of clippings from American newspapers, Hill Miller sought out stringers in unlikely places and the scope of its geographical coverage was greater than that of the Washington press. Around 1967, reported a contemporary, Secretary James Forrestal entered his Pentagon office to hold a press conference. 'Then his fist came down on his quarter-acre desk as he said, "Why in hell, gentlemen, do I have to read an English newspaper to find out what's happening in this country?" One or two of the press boys who were in the know leaked the story to Don Woodward, Helen Hill Miller and Mildred Adams, who then wrote most of each week's American Survey for *The Economist*.'

In 1947 Crowther pulled off what from his point of view was another fine opportunistic coup, but from Helen Hill Miller's point of view it caused problems. He did a personal deal with Robin Barrington-Ward of *The Times* to share their new American correspondent, John Duncan Miller (no relation), the condition being that no one was to know that he was writing for *The Economist*, since on principle *The Times* did not share correspondents. (There was a story that one of the later foreign editors of *The Times* fell down dead in the office because he discovered Johnny Miller was working for two papers.) This difficulty was circumnavigated by having Miller's wife Madeline registered as the correspondent.

Helen Hill Miller had not been consulted and was worried about the arrangement. Barbara Ward tried to reassure her. 'I've had an evening with Johnny and Madeline and Geoffrey and the Cruikshanks and I think the situation is much clearer and the difficulties ironed out. The Millers should make most useful and stimulating colleagues and I have the feeling that they have more "antennae" than some we know of! And in making partnerships work there are few things more important than sensitivity to atmosphere and ability to see what the other fellow feels and thinks.'[7]

Next month, Ward's 'belief in the Millers as able and cooperative people increased. I think Geoffrey feels in some way he mishandled the situation and is now content you should work it out without reference back to London which is inevitably out of touch. He and Margaret also feel that more could be done in London to keep the American editorial staff in touch with what British opinion is looking for and that letters with comment and suggestion might usually come from this end from time to time.' Ward suggested 'two things – the result of brooding away over *The Economist* on the Queen Elizabeth where I read 7 issues running'. It was impossible 'to spell out too much for the British reader' and the first article in the survey ought to deal with the series of great themes which ran right through the year, like a presidential campaign.[8]

Hill Miller accepted the comments; the 'great themes' idea parallelled closely a letter which Crowther wrote the Millers on their appointment. During the late 1940s the various Millers tried to cooperate with each other as well as with the London office. Madeline Miller worked for The *Economist*, sending clippings by air mail and doing research. The *Economist* office was in her house. Yet tensions were always there and the London–Washington relationship also had its deficiencies. As Crowther wrote in June 1947 to Johnny and Madeline Miller, 'I am very conscious of the fact that we send back to Helen and the group far fewer comments on their pieces than they deserve.'

> I think you know why this is. I am both lazy and busy, and Margaret is only in the office for the first three days of each week. Her time then is very fully occupied with getting the week's Notes ready. I realise that this is a defect in our present organisation and that, ideally, the head of our American department ought to be a full-timer. But I am willing neither to replace Margaret nor to demand more of her time than she can give. But we do appreciate how irritating it must be to Helen to be firing articles off without ever knowing whether they have hit the target.

There was no problem with the 'seconds', which showed an admirable variety of subject and source. It was the first pieces that they hadn't got right: 'Variety of topic and writer is an advantage for the second piece; but not for the first, which should aim at consistency both of topic and of writers. By consistency of topic, I mean that there are, in any year, a short list of not more than about half-a-dozen topics of American public affairs that are of continuous interest to European readers.'

> At present these are:–
> 1. The development of American foreign policy in its political mani-festations. The problem of Isolation or Not.
> 2. The development of American external economic policy. The problem of the Dollar Gap.
> 3. How the Recession was coming along.
> 4. What Congress is up to . . .

5. Who will win the next election.

6. Labour . . .

As I see it, the group should ask itself each week 'on which of the standard subjects is there something new to report' and decide accordingly. As to whether one member of the group always writes on one subject that is for the group to say.

Having picked the subject, the next point concerns the manner of treating it. I think the group, living as they do in America and reading thousands of words *per diem* on all these subjects, find it difficult to realise how little we, or at least the non-specialist reader of The Economist, know about them. It might almost be a sound rule to assume the reader knows nothing about what has happened to the subject since it was last discussed, and that he has probably forgotten most of what he was told . . . I therefore plead for the greatest simplicity in form as well as regularity in content in the first piece. Take nothing for granted. Assume the reader is a child – and indeed he is a child in American public affairs.

Mildred Adams tried to defuse the tensions between Helen Hill Miller and Madeline Miller, but the problem was now compounded by new tensions between Washington and London, for the gentle emollient Margaret Cruikshank was no longer in charge. The new boss was Nancy Balfour, who was half American, born in the United States but brought up in Britain.

Balfour had a degree in PPE. During the war she had worked with the Foreign Office research department in Oxford under Toynbee, reading the foreign press and summarising the twenty or so newspapers from cities across America that arrived every three or four weeks. In 1945 she got a job with the BBC North American Service as their intelligence expert, at which moment Crowther offered her a job on American Survey, but she thought it improper to break her contract.

Early in 1948 he offered her the job again, assuring her that she would be running the section but failing to convey that to Margaret Cruikshank, so they rubbed along for a time as equals until Cruikshank left temporarily to nurse her dying husband. Utterly honest, extremely direct, reliable, industrious and very well informed, Balfour could be inflexible and disconcerting in her dealings with correspondents: her nickname was 'Colonel Balfour'. American Survey became her kingdom. She almost never wrote anything for any of the other parts of the paper, in which she had little interest except where something impinged on her territory.

Like Crowther, Balfour had a clear vision of what American Survey should be: not centred on Washington and New York but, as Crowther had envisaged, taking an overview of the whole country. That was the rationale for having it edited in London from a more detached and therefore wider perspective. Typically, Crowther told Balfour she was to run the section from London, though Helen Hill Miller thought she was still running it from Washington.

In March 1950 Crowther wrote to Hill Miller about a reorganisation that they had discussed recently when she had been in London. The paper's profits were looking rather sick, 'that is to say, we are still well in the black, but the trend is quite definitely in the wrong direction. Later on today I am going to read the riot act to our monthly staff luncheon, and I am afraid that the pressure for economies in our American expenditure on the lines we discussed when you were over is not likely to be relaxed.'

> I think the way may be opening up for reorganisation on the lines then envisaged, and I may be able to bring it to a head when I am in Washington next month. In the meantime, you might perhaps be making estimates of minimum expenditure to cover (i) your own retainer; (ii) rent of the new room; (iii) a junior; (iv) retainers for the group; (v) payments for articles; (vi) a minimum on expenditure on travelling and meetings.

Hill Miller organised aspects of his and his daughter Judy's trip to America and they stayed with her for a weekend in April. In June he wrote from London to say that since returning home he had been 'brooding on the general organisation of our American affairs in the light of the talks that I had with you and all concerned. This letter is an attempt to put on paper the conclusions, and I am afraid that it is a most unpleasant letter both to write and to read, since I cannot find anything that would give me a valid excuse for dodging or postponing any further the painful decision to undertake a pretty far-reaching reorganisation of our American affairs.'

The impelling reason for this was financial. 'With the devaluation of the pound, our American operation has become very costly', and at the same time production costs were rising and competition for advertising and circulation was fully re-established, so revenue was going down. 'The American Survey has become one of the established features of the paper and one on which we get more compliments than any other. If there were no other way of running it than the present method, I think we should probably find the money from somewhere. But what I cannot dismiss from my mind is that it would be quite possible to run it much more cheaply, by having no resident editorial representative, no Washington office and no American editorial group.' He had to opt for the very much cheaper though second-best way. 'I think, looking back, I have known this for quite a time, but I have put the decision off, hoping something would happen to make it unnecessary. The devaluation and the proof that there is no quick way of increasing our dollar income removed my last excuses.'

> I have it rather on my conscience that I did not raise the matter with you verbally in April. I was on the point of doing so when the possibility of your running in the primary came up and to have done so when you were considering that would, it seemed to me, to have been rather a dirty trick. After that was disposed of, there was really no appropriate opportunity. Besides, I don't think my mind was one hundred per cent clear.

Crowther was going to keep the arrangement by which most of the leaders came from America and the notes were written in London, but the arrangements could be handled largely from London. 'For the first leader, I cling to my view, on which we had some arguments – was it three years ago? – that it should be done regularly by one or two or at the most three of the British correspondents in Washington (I don't say British for Nationalist reasons, but because the external observer is at an enormous and instinctive advantage in knowing what is interesting and intelligible outside, and the non-British foreigners in Washington don't write well in our language)'. So he would be asking Johnny Miller and one or two others to provide them. Second leader arrangements would be made directly from London and he hoped the present editorial group would be willing to contribute. 'To anticipate one remark that will occur to you, I appreciate that the handling of correspondence from this end will require qualities that are not at present always conspicuous, and I hope to do something about this. The data service will be more necessary than ever and I should propose to ask Madeline to continue it, possibly in modified form.'[9]

Helen Hill Miller stiffly proposed to close down the office within a few weeks. (His response to her question what to do about files was in the true tradition of *The Economist*. 'Not knowing exactly what is in the files, I find this a little difficult to answer but in case of doubt I would say destroy them.')

'I cannot escape the conclusion from your letters that you feel very hurt by the decision that I felt compelled to arrive at', he responded. 'I do ask you to believe that this makes me extremely sorry. I do not think that I have ever had a more distasteful job to do, or one that it took me longer to screw my resolution up to. I hope that if there is anything in the world that we can do to ease the transition you will not hesitate to let me know.'[10]

Geoffrey 'may have been his normal usual ineffective self over the Miller v Miller situation', wrote Elizabeth Monroe to Mildred Adams, 'but has been and is being sweetness and understanding itself over Barbara [Ward was waiting for an annulment of her fiancé's marriage], of whom he is as you know extremely fond.'

> As far as I can make out the Pope has capitulated or is about to but Robert is in the hands of his doctors. Barbara looks awful.[11]

'Now we are on our last official week of work as American staff', wrote Adams to Monroe, 'I can count my blessings and shed my tears with a more orderly mind – if minds ever help in shedding tears. I'm divided between regret and exasperation, a feeling of real achievement, and one of frustration. I know that from the American point of view we did a very good job – it has been highly ironic, in these last weeks, to be greeted withal by new people as doing the extraordinarily good job for *The Economist*, and to know that that job was in the process of being folded up. I'm taking Geoffrey's explanation of devaluation costs as unbearable and yet at the same time I know there were also problems of personality which really lay at the crux of the thing and made it impossible to find a less sweeping solution.' Helen Hill Miller had run it on a shoestring and they all had devoted a huge amount of time to what was from the American point of view paying very little. 'I don't regret one minute of it, and I've taken pleasure as well as pride from it, but there had been moments when I've wondered how long I could afford to continue.'[12]

'The one item that sticks in my gullet', wrote Monroe, 'is the hurt done to Helen personally by the fact that Geoffrey said nothing when he was over in April. Why did he lack the moral courage to drop a hint? She told him it seems some had been thinking of asking her to stand for Congress. How easy to answer "Well, why not. *The Economist* may have to draw in its horns etc." Lack of guts is a dreadful failing. How queer to me. How much better to give a gulp and get it over. When I talk to Geoffrey I always feel an inferiority in the sense of being bad at arguing with one so quick at repartee, but a superiority which is indefinable which I think is that I don't mind speaking out.'

Instances of Crowther's lack of moral courage always came as rather a shock to those who did not know him well; it seemed to sit oddly with his hard-hitting and critical journalism. Monroe was resigned to it. In 1950, when he had ruled that rather than Adams or Monroe, someone close to it should cover the United Nations, she wrote: 'He is a queer fish. He seemed to think I should be wounded to the quick by this decision, and beat about the bush so divertingly . . . that I was obliged to help him along in words of one syllable. Having realised, with a sigh of relief, that I am not wounded, he next thought you would be, and in his usual lily-livered style, asked me to write to you, which I have done . . . But as you fagged to do all that good work . . . simply for the honour of the paper and the good of the cause, I am going to make him also write to you this week. So if you get a letter from him you know that yours truly has won.'[13]

The arrangement with Johnny Miller began to falter in 1952 during the presidential election race between Eisenhower and Governor Adlai Stevenson. The eloquent and cultivated darling of the liberal intelligentsia, Stevenson was a close friend of Barbara Ward and king of the political world which *The Economist*'s American contributors and readers mainly inhabited. 'Among those who have been moved and inspirited by Governor Stevenson's eloquent liberalism', said the first leader in American Survey just before the election, 'there is a feeling that the United States will somehow be shamed in the eyes of the intelligent free world if it now fails to elect this Wilsonian symbol of the New American.'[14]

Johnny Miller was no exception. He wrote memorably in *The Times* of how Eisenhower's campaign was 'running like a dry creek'. 'He often writes well,' observed Bracken, 'but as a political correspondent he is about as impartial as Dr Johnson was when knocking the Whigs.'[15] Like the readers of *The Times*, *Economist* readers were also informed that Stevenson's victory was inevitable and since there were many who took *The Economist* as a kind of second opinion to *The Times* Crowther's conscience was a little troubled. He concluded that he would have to find new blood.

His options were to 'pay a rather third-rate established journalist who had some experience but was not highly regarded . . . or to employ a young man without experience who I consider to be a high flier'. He found Keith Kyle through Donald McLachlan.

Kyle, who had been briefly at Oxford reading history and then in the army for four years, had become a talks producer in the North American Service of the BBC. McLachlan had done a talk for him and had subsequently asked him for an article about a world Quaker conference he was to attend. The ensuing rather satirical article caught Crowther's eye and in 1953 he decided to offer Kyle a job.

To his horror, he later explained, as a member of the board of the Harkness Fellowship he found Kyle coming before him as an applicant. 'I came before the board', recalled Kyle, 'and the only member of it who was, I thought, rather hostile, and pursued me with this rather close examination was Geoffrey Crowther. It seemed to me that he was anxious to fail me, and I answered his questions with some tension. He was very agreeable to the others.'

Two or three days later Crowther rang and asked Kyle to come to see him and then explained and offered him the Washington job. Kyle accepted immediately and began his five-year stint working with Balfour and Cruikshank by spending three months with them in London 'learning to write'.

Kyle was the pioneer in a relationship between Washington and London that was run in the same way until 1972. His great strengths were his intelligence, his curiosity and his ability to strike up excellent relationships. He made many contacts among Republicans, attracted new talent and vastly broadened the base of American Survey. He was, for instance, extremely keen on getting to understand individual state legislatures and very happy to drive all over the country. The downside was that he was absent-minded and therefore unreliable.

A friend of his, Godfrey Smith, once described him as a 'tall, lean, pale, chronically absent-minded yet formidably gifted chap called Keith Kyle. When we were undergraduates he used to entertain us by presenting an entire budget on the eve of the Chancellor unveiling his in the Commons. He was blissfully impervious to the ordinary rules of life. He would, for example, when staying with friends, open a book at bedtime and still be sitting there reading it when they came down for breakfast the next morning', having simply forgotten to go to bed. He was the kind of man, observed an affectionate ex-colleague, whose reason for not filing his copy was that he had crashed his car crossing the Andes.

As Washington correspondent Kyle used to go missing and found it impossible to operate according to Nancy Balfour's strict and frugal sched-ules. He was forever missing air-mail deadlines and having to send cables with copy at his own expense. Yet Kyle stayed in America for five years and fully established the institution of *Economist* Washington correspondent. He then returned to London to cover parliament.

Kyle was replaced in 1958 by the ex-Harkness Fellow, Brian Beedham, whose view of America was consolidated by his two years in Washington. He loved the openness of American public life. A friend of Kyle whom he soon visited was Supreme Court Justice Felix Frankfurter. 'I went into his vast room, his desk was twenty yards from the door: this tiny figure came from behind this desk and said "I see *The Economist* continues its policy of sending children to represent it in Washington."' After that they used to lunch together every month.

The quality of the Washington coverage was high under Beedham and the administration ran more smoothly. But there followed two hiccoughs in the London–Washington system. Roy Lewis had first joined the paper as a part-timer in 1952, writing business features for Roland Bird in the back of the paper and, having a background of travel in Africa, he also contributed articles on colonial issues. After a short absence he rejoined full-time in 1955 to run the surveys and help with both home and colonial affairs, being nicknamed 'Mr Home and Colonial' after a famous grocery chain. (He also served as defence correspondent and in that capacity he had accompanied the British invasion force to Egypt in 1956.) Having succeeded Beedham in Washington, he left within a year because of an offer from *The Times* that he felt he could not refuse. Balfour was extremely angry; Tyerman gave Lewis advice on how to negotiate his *Times* contract.

At John Midgley's suggestion, Lewis was replaced by the widely experienced Alex Campbell, who had been *Time-Life* bureau chief in Africa, India, Japan and the Middle East. He arrived in Washington in 1961 and lasted for three years; but he and Nancy Balfour simply could not get on.

Although Campbell had often written for *The Economist* during his years with *Time-Life* and had worked amicably with the foreign department, he was too long in the professional tooth to adapt to a regime in which he had to follow tightly worded instructions. For her part, Balfour decided that she could not trust him. Despite Tyerman's sensitive and intelligent attempts to resolve the problem and persuade Balfour to treat Campbell more as an equal, the relationship was a disaster. Alex Campbell left at short notice at the end of 1963 to become editor of the *New Republic*, precipitating a crisis which was resolved by John Midgley.

Midgley was to remain Washington correspondent until 1976, bringing great authority and depth to the political coverage. 'My dear John,' wrote the usually reserved Roland Bird to him in August 1974.

> For several weeks, your reporting on Watergate and other misdeeds has been quite *outstanding* – and never more distinguished than last week, when you put together at high speed a fine piece of analysis and judgment.
>
> As one who now watches the editorial process from a distance but remembers all its joys and heartaches, I bow deferentially towards you.

Midgley's long tenure of the job gave it solidity and greatly strengthened the network of contributors and sources. The job expanded vastly. He was sent from London as assistants a series of young journalists (including David Gordon and Andrew Knight) who gained experience and partly learned their trade through Midgley. He was a tough but paternalistic figure, very shrewd in assessing the quality of his young staff and tending, as his extensive correspondence shows, to cover up their deficiencies with head office and excuse any egregious behaviour.

When Nancy Balfour retired in 1972 (she still runs the Arts Committee), for a time American Survey was edited by Midgley from Washington with Cruikshank anchoring in London, an arrangement which Balfour had bitterly opposed. Although she admired Midgley's professionalism and was unfailingly grateful for his loyalty to her, she saw him as Washington-centric and strove mightily to balance that with good local coverage. She and Cruikshank never lost sight of American Survey's great advantage over the competition – its recognition that in America there are fifty states (as well as the District of Columbia) and that all of them are different.

Control from Washington worked for a couple of years efficiently enough, but on Midgley's replacement by Edmund Fawcett the old arrangement returned. Since then Dudley Fishburn, Johnny Grimond, Matt Ridley and now Ann Wroe have exercised editorial control from London.

When Midgley first went to Washington, he communicated with Balfour primarily by air mail. It would be rare to have even one telephone call each month. By the time she left normal communication was telex. Now, of course, all communication is instantaneous, and in addition to the two correspondents in Washington there are two full-time staff members in New York reporting largely on business and finance and more recently another full-timer on the Pacific Coast.

An exchange of memoranda in 1984 gives an excellent illustration of how the *Economist* senior common room works in the face of tensions and policy differences. Andrew Knight was editor and he sent to the American Survey editor, Johnny Grimond, one of his lengthy memoranda, written after reading an edition of *The Economist* which had come out when he was away. 'I couldn't help being struck by the contrast between our leader (Here I go again) and American Survey's lead piece (Reagan is Reagan again).

'The leader is full of implied criticisms of what is being done in Reagan's first term and what will be likely to be done in the second term. And it constructively suggested a better way from November 7th onwards.

'Yet the whole tenor of the leader – rightly in my view – cheerfully recognised Reagan's strengths. He has reflected changes in America and, in terms of mood, answered an American need and provoked a good American reaction.' The world was better off with an America thus Reaganised (with reservations), 'than with one uncharacteristically searching its inner mind on every internal and external subject'. Indeed the leader had been slightly more cheerful than he would have been. 'By contrast, the underlying tone of our American lead piece was to say that "everything is wrong about Reagan, he is a phoney through and through, he doesn't represent what America needs, he shouldn't be going to win but – oh bother and damn – it looks as if he is going to."'

The lead piece made the paper look old fashioned and 'makes American Survey backward rather than forward-looking, and reduces the force of the criticisms we might have to offer editorially in leaders or in the section itself'. Anachronism seemed to be pervading the reporting. Knight had watched the Reagan–Mondale debate and thought Reagan won on virtually every count. 'If he did well in the average American front room, even though making patent errors, how and why does he manage it? Is he just a lucky buffoon, or is he (as I suspect) a highly shrewd politician whose cleverness and personality merge to reflect very closely what America is actually about? Such questions need addressing. Our notes, by contrast, tend to follow the dismissive conventional wisdom.'

Reagan had been authoritative, clear and not unsubtle. 'His contrast between not regretting what he feels about the Soviet Union's evil, yet a need to do business with it; his point about the Shah and other likely Shahs, and the revolutions against them being worse than they were, his unruffled ability to make distinctions – all these contrasted with Mondale's "briefcase

politician" feel, an almost Carteresque throwing of every conceivable consideration at every answer so that, while harping over and over again on the
words "tough" and "command", he managed to give the impression of
somebody who lacked it, and who wanted to be on every side of every
question.'

There was in that American Survey lead piece little of the feeling of
'"giving Reagan his due" . . . After the election I suspect one of the questions
that Europeans are going to be asking themselves is "Have we continued to
underestimate Reagan's sheer smartness and leadership as a President four
years after Americans have stopped doing so?" Our American Survey reaction
sometimes seems to be that such a question is beneath consideration.

'Reagan might be no more than a good con-man as we and other
newspapers seem to say. But he isn't simply a con-trick. He does represent
something, both in himself and in the huge demographic, economic and
generational changes that have taken place in America itself.'

> In failing to note or analyse this, we follow one particular Washington herd
> – so weakening the force of our criticisms when we have criticisms to make.
> All those who work for Reagan – even the cattiest of them – emphasise that,
> though Reagan is not too hot on detail, dozes off and procrastinates, there is
> no doubt whatever who is 'in charge', and that when it comes to decisions it
> is Reagan who makes them. He is no actor puppet, is my impression. I've
> never seen us – or others – say this, or ever discuss it.
>
> With our own American outpost so firmly placed on the eastern seaboard,
> our coverage does sometimes read like a Massachusetts Brahmin's last
> despairing protest. There are things going on. Reagan is in the middle of
> them. We should be describing what they are; pointing out what is good
> about them and criticising – with the credibility of a clear-eyed observer not
> the regret of an old-timer – the weakness and dangers inherent in them.
> Your leader did all these things to an extent. Our picky American Survey
> notes in my view often failed to do so.

The criticism of American Survey was by implication directed at the
Washington correspondent, Barbara Smith, and David Lawday, her number
two, and all the old stable of *Economist* stringers. It was also of course a
criticism of Grimond in his capacity as editor of American Survey, while
complimenting him as author of the relevant leader.

He had returned to a barrage of criticism, Grimond told his Washington colleagues. 'The first hit came from Andrew in the form of a memo, apparently both shorter and more temperate than its original . . . The comparison with the leader is odious and its conclusions probably misplaced, since I think Andrew did not see the leader before it was Brianised, so I guess I am as guilty as anyone else.'

Johnny Grimond disagreed with Knight about the debate but accepted he might have a point about 'our coverage in general, namely that it too often ignores the reality of America, which is at present a bustling Reaganite country, and that there are too many carping sideswipes'. This was certainly the view of Dudley Fishburn, his predecessor as American Survey editor, who felt that American Survey had lost its old detachment and that 'therefore the criticisms that we make lose their force. He [Fishburn] feels that it is too often written with an air of superciliousness and condescension, and that we risk turning off our readers by failing to accept the place as it is.'

> That does not mean approving of everything; on the contrary, part of American Survey's popularity is its habit of analysing events with at least implied criticism. But it has to be detached, otherwise it merely sounds *parti pris*; and it has to be offered with a basic sympathy towards the country and the system, otherwise it appears ignorant – the work of arrogant Europeans.

Grimond reported that his number two, Ann Wroe (now the American Survey editor), shared some of these views, feeling that the Republicans particularly were being neglected. During the campaign she had found herself writing in bits about the Republicans, who, when they were covered by correspondents in American, were treated in 'a sneering way'. If these accusations were fair things were rather serious.

> I think that some of the unhappiness comes from the fact that your, and my, political views are not Andrew's and the paper's, still less Brian's. But I don't think that is the basis of the complaint. And if it were, I would not be too worried. I am much more worried by the accusation that we appear carping, sniping, supercilious and out of touch – partly because one does not, in general, want to be such things, partly because I think American Survey's strength is that we can explain things better by being a bit detached from American conventional wisdom, which tends to be generated on the Bos–Wash axis. We can cover the week's news better than the American press by being discriminating, short and to the point . . . and we can put events in context better by being free of American prejudices. At a time

when power is ebbing away from the east coast, we are in a particularly strong position, as foreigners, to analyse and explain the rise of western Republicanism and all that goes with it.

Grimond went on to admit sometimes himself feeling that the American correspondents were too sneering, particularly one of the stringers, who was rather snide, and he blamed himself for most of this. 'The fact that three people all feel that we are at fault needs to be taken seriously, but I don't think we should exaggerate the problem. Our coverage this week, I thought, was excellent, and, although I have not looked back over the year's coverage in general I should expect it will stand up pretty well.'

He sent a copy of this to Knight.

Barbara Smith replied, admitting the justification of some of the criticism. 'Criticism is horrid but salutary, and will be taken to heart. But what is one man's snide sneer, is another's irreverent humour. The line between the two is narrow and also subjective. The criticism I hear on this side of the Atlantic, and not just from dyed-in-the-wool Democratic buddies, is why does *The Economist* feel that it can say what it likes about Mrs Thatcher but is so bland about Mr Reagan? I suppose that Andrew and Dudley would say that we criticise Mrs T as a clear-eyed friend and Mr R as an old-time opponent. But I would challenge that assumption.'

However, she would act on the criticism she accepted.

Midgley, now 73 and writing part-time for the paper, weighed in with a letter to Grimond in 'a spirit of helpfulness'. It was up to Grimond if he wanted to pass the remarks along.

It is altogether natural that the American situation should present a different appearance to people looking at it from Europe from that which it presents to us here. Western Europe is a depressing scene economically and politically, caught in the doldrums with no sign of a fresh breeze. The United States makes a lively, in many ways cheerful, contrast, brisk and bustling with its business revival. European investors are more inclined to put their money here than to put it to work in Europe. European non-investors have grown tired of their anti-American causes. Those Europeans who are pro-American enjoy an understandable feeling of relief that the Americans have stopped whining about American shortcomings. To the extent that these feelings come into focus on a figure, the figure is that of Reagan.

'It looks otherwise to me', he continued. 'What I see is the staggering insouciance with which at the highest level the government of the United States is being conducted, and the happy ignorance that is the reverse face of that self-confidence which reassures Europe.' *The Economist* would be failing in its job if it did not describe this 'in whatever polite and restrained language, as it appears to us . . . Take the recent Presidential election. Mondale was wrong on plenty of things – wrong on Israel, wrong on domestic content, wrong on immigration, wrong on the sacrosanctity of Social Security and Medicare, but what turned people off was none of that, it was the sight of him perpetually lecturing and fault-finding and warning: in short, as people felt, trying to depress them. Reagan stood there exuding charm, radiating warmth and reassurance, and people embraced him.'

> It was perfectly obvious that Reagan was too old, too lazy and too deeply superficial for the job, but they didn't care about that, they embraced him just the same because he made them feel better, he cheered them up, just as they had been warmed and cheered up in 1980 by the personal contrast he offered to Jimmy Carter. There is an interesting political fact here, and I would be very sorry if we kept it from our readers. If, through delicacy or collegiate loyalty or our sense of duties as allies, we felt constrained to represent Reagan as a master of the arts of government skilfully disguised, then we would in effect be giving them quite a different explanation for what has happened; we would be denying them the fascinating truth.
>
> Well, I suppose that in one way or another it all will become clear in the end.

Nobody ever got the last word in a debate with Andrew Knight. 'I enjoyed your note about the American controversy', he responded. 'But in my view we need to take a more historical view than your note does.' The essence of the issue was, first, that Reagan represented a change that America needed. 'When history is written I suspect that people will reckon it was good for America that Reagan beat Carter, and good also that he beat Mondale – and good, in addition, for both the Republican and particularly the Democratic parties that he should have done so. One day, of course, the pendulum will swing again; but we should not just ignore what has happened in the meantime.'

The second point was that, because of Reagan's 'undoubtedly insouciant, lazy and ignorant way of government, there is going to be a price paid for the fact that he rather than somebody else should have come along and been the representative of these necessary changes. Our role, surely, should be to assess how high that price will be and whether, in the eventual balance, it is likely to outweigh the benefits of the paragraph above.'

The paper had persistently attacked the deficit, though on foreign policy it had broadly agreed with Reagan, who was right in his handling of the Soviet Union, and more right on El Salvador and Nicaragua 'than any of us thought likely two years ago . . . in both of which change away from the worst likely outcomes has been achieved largely because of pressure from Washington'.*

That particular debate came to an end with the absence of bitterness that usually characterises even the paper's most explosive internal rows. It was a theme Andrew Knight picked up in his signed valedictory article. 'If we are truthful, we journalists have, as an estate, lagged behind the flow of opinion these past 12 years. Our function is to chase among the trees for every scent and piece of torn skin in the undergrowth. The forest above, the changing season, we press-hounds hardly see. Certainly we were slow on this paper to see the significance of Mrs Thatcher, and it has been an enjoyable irony (doubtless for her too) that *The Economist* should be so frequently classed as Thatcherite for the clarity of its liberal, free-market, reforming view, when its establishment has rarely been at ease with Britain's Prime Minister. The point of Mr Reagan we saw faster – perhaps because we could see, across the expanse of the Atlantic, and resisting the view of our own Washington office, how the great forest of America needed him for a while.'[16]

The pendulum swung from *The Economist*'s perspective eight years later in the Bush–Clinton contest, when Mike Elliott was Washington correspondent and Ann Wroe in charge in London. Having supported neither candidate in the 1988 Bush–Dukakis election, this time the paper concluded that 'The man is spent, and his party with him. The Republicans, tired to distraction, out of ideas, have become prey to a far right whose economic nostrums run to demonising taxes, and many of whose social ideas would rub salt in the country's wounds.'

The Democratic Party had spent twelve years trying to become a plausible modern party of government, and should be given a chance to try. Clinton

---

*The favourable coverage of events in Central America was in part due to the influence of the then Latin American specialist in the foreign department, Robert Harvey. A likeable Old Etonian, he was a Beedham import who was on the staff from 1974 to 1983, when he became a Conservative MP.

had shown himself far more than a token candidate. 'He is intelligent; he is diligent; he is energetic; he has grasped most of the issues, and found persuasive solutions to some. He could mark an end to divided government and could, if he used the Presidency well, begin to bring Americans, black and white, rich and poor, closer together. Despite the risks, the possibilities are worth pursuing. Our choice falls on him.'[17]

CHAPTER XLVIII

Home and business

Times change, even *The Economist* changes a little. Its format quite surprised me when it began. I used to remember it as rather a dull looking professorial paper that always rebuked me. Every article began, 'Mr Macmillan has now, in the last effort of this year, destroyed the British economy for ever.' But it didn't seem to matter very much. Now, however, I read it to get news about all parts of the world and it has become what is called a very readable paper.' Brilliantly edited and magnificently produced. When I was coming up today from Sussex I just wondered what Bagehot would have thought of it. I think on the whole he'd have liked it because it suits the age, it suits the time. It's practical, it's modern, it's objective, it's up to date. That's what he liked.[1]
Harold Macmillan, Prime Minister 1957–63, speaking in 1978

'In domestic politics', wrote Crowther in his valedictory, '1938–1956: A RETROSPECT', 'by far the most far-reaching change has been the assumption by the state of responsibility for the condition of the national economy. A government today thinks itself responsible, and is certainly held responsible by the opposition, for the state of trade, both in general and in particular.' Until the outbreak of war in 1939, 'the accepted philosophy was that, since the power of governments to determine general economic conditions was very limited, it would be foolish of them to accept responsibility for what happened'. Even the Labour party, daunted by their 'complete failure in 1929–31 to hold back the waves of depression' had very little idea of any 'practical policy to avoid economic fluctuations, beyond a generalised idea that nationalisation would perform this miracle among the many others that were expected of it'. Now both parties accepted responsibility 'for maintaining the economic health of the community', differing only on the methods they chose to employ.

The Crowther of 1956 was sadder and wiser than the young man who had been so impatient to see government putting things to rights. This new doctrine of responsibility 'is so universally accepted that one would be thought very eccentric, and very reactionary, even to question it'.

> Yet the odd thing is that this responsibility has been accepted without the slightest proof that anyone knows how, in fact, it is to be discharged. Indeed, the evidence is that neither party has had, at best, more than the most rudimentary control over the economic climate since the war. It is true that full employment has been steadily maintained, and as that is what matters most to the ordinary man, it perhaps accounts for the general illusion that governments have been successful in their economic policy. But full employment has persisted since the war all over the world, and it has certainly not been due to successful economic planning all over the world.

Was it not much more likely that British full employment had been mainly due to this worldwide conjuncture than to the policies of Labour and Conservative governments? Moreover, looking at such British problems as inflation and the balance of payments, it became obvious that the failure was pretty complete. 'What real reason is there to suppose that the degree of success will be any greater when, some day, through a shift in the wind, it is once again the forces of deflation against which a government finds itself battling? We may not inconceivably find ourselves back in the position of the thirties, and both sides, when in turn they have broken their teeth on the problem, may be ready to accept much more modest ideas about their ability to control the weather.'[2]

As between 'both sides' (with the Liberal Party no longer a serious political force) *The Economist* was non-aligned in the first post-war years, pursuing the vision that had been outlined in 1935 after the general election whose result had suggested 'that the common ground between the parties is of more permanent importance than the issues which divide them. And this prompts the question whether the nation is working towards a new political order in which, from a wide and common centre, the balance will shift now to the Right, now to the Left, instead of swinging from one extreme to the other? There is much that is desirable in such a development.'[3]

During the war, Eric Gibb had produced an exceptionally vituperative attack on the House of Commons, sparked off by a libel action brought by Captain Ramsay, MP, against the *New York Times*, for alleging 'that Captain Ramsay had by a circuitous route sent information to the enemy' and was therefore a traitor. Ramsay won his case – and one farthing in damages.

The trial had produced the information that Ramsay was close to known spies and traitors, including 'Lord Haw Haw' (William Joyce), as well as being a great admirer of Hitler. 'Whatever he be – whether disloyal or patriotic, fifth columnist or honest independent politician – there is one thing that Captain Ramsay undoubtedly and undeniably is. He is a complete fool.' Having proved this to be the case, Gibb went on to ask why such a fool should be an MP? 'How did Captain Ramsay persuade the Peebles Conservative Association to adopt him and a majority of the Peebles electors to vote for him? *Who's Who* supplies the answer:–'

> 'Captain Ramsay, MP for Peebles since 1931, o.s. of late Lieut.-Col. H.L. Ramsay, elder son of Gen. the Hon. Sir Henry Ramsay, KCIE, CB, m. Ismay Lucretia Mary, o.d. of 14th Viscount Gormanston and widow of late Lord Ninian Crichton-Stuart, MP, Educ. Eton, RMC Sandhurst, joined 2nd Battalion Coldstream Guards.'
>
> He is MP for Peebles because he comes of the right sort of family, because he married a daughter of the peerage and the widow of a very rich man, because he went to the right school and joined the right regiment. If his father had been a bank clerk and his wife the daughter of an insurance agent, if he had been educated at the local grammar school, gone with a scholarship to Oxford and made his way by his own brains to a moderate competence in a respectable trade or profession, then he might have bombarded every political association on the books of the Central Office for a constituency, and every time the odds against his getting into the House would have been 1,000 to 1.

He might well be the only fifth columnist in the House, but was certainly not the only 'silly ass . . . It is common knowledge – and many people can check it from their personal acquaintance – that the intellectual level of the House of Commons has been, since 1931, deplorably low; and when the historian of the future comes to write the story of the pre-war years, one of the things he will need to bear in mind (if he is to read aright the disastrous record) is this intellectual poverty of the men chosen as the people's representatives, this profusion of men who at the very best can only be described, in the words of

Jane Austen, as "persons of strong, natural, sterling insignificance."'

> These tenth-rate nonentities who have been jobbed into the House of
> Commons because they were men of the 'right type' provided just the
> background that the Front Bench required for its calamitous foreign policy
> and for its blindness to the danger in which the country stood. The
> Government needed behind it a solid block of MPs stupid enough to jeer at
> Mr Churchill, to admire the moral grandeur of Stanley Baldwin and to
> applaud the foresight of Mr Chamberlain; and the political bosses saw to it
> that the right men were provided in Captain Ramsay and others of the same
> intellectual and social build.

It was no answer 'to say that the selection of trade unionists by seniority also
filled the scanty benches opposite with mediocrities. Power lay on the Right:
and there is a long score to settle with the men who put Captain Ramsay and
the like into Parliament.'⁴

'Had lunch with Geoffrey Crowther, editor of *The Economist*', wrote Cecil
King in his diary in 1944. 'He opened by saying he thought we were in a bad
way politically: 5% of us had been to a public school and were inhibited by
the fear of showing bad form; the other 95% were inhibited through not
going to a public school! As a result we all suffer from an inferiority complex.'

> Crowther has a theory that the great moment will come when those born in
> the 20th century will take over. He said that only one cabinet minister in
> England, Germany, or France had been born since January 1, 1900 (and he
> was Malcolm MacDonald!) the point being that hitherto we have been ruled
> by the men who were over military age in 1914. Those who served in the
> war were either killed or, with their vitality sapped, have lost their way. Now
> we can look to a revolution under younger men who never knew the security
> before the last war, and have grown up in the insecurity of the years between
> the wars. A further point Crowther made was that in the 19th century most
> technical discoveries applied to processes in factories: since 1900 so many of
> them affect our daily lives. Those of us born since 1900 are completely
> familiar with bicycles, cars, airplanes, telephones, radio, and birth control.
> As a result, he said, he thought the distinction was no longer between Right
> and Left but between New and Old.⁵

Mostly, the post-war *Economist* was contemptuous of both alternative governments. 'All would agree', wrote Crowther before the 1945 general election,

'that the object should be to serve the common interest. But there are two quite different and largely incompatible doctrines about how the common interest is to be served.'

> One school would do it directly, by requiring the managers of economic policy to regard only the interests of the community in the round and to be no respecters of particular persons or groups. They would think of the national income in total, not of any constituents of it, and damage to the interest of particular groups would be recognised as part of the price to be paid – and to be settled generously – for the progress and security of the whole. The other school of thought would see the generality as the confederation of a number of special groupings, and would seek by protecting the livelihood of each of these to serve the common purpose. If the word had not already been misappropriated for a wholly different doctrine, the first might aptly be called Communism. The second doctrine is particularism or Protectionism, and in these columns it has often been christened the New Feudalism.[6]

There was no recommendation of how to vote in 1945; and in 1950 Crowther was very sniffy about the notion that the paper might express such an opinion. 'A journal that is jealous of its reputation for independence would . . . be foolish to compromise it by taking sides in a general election . . . Even if we had a decided preference, we should try to conceal it. In this particular election, however, there is another and more compelling reason for perching on the fence. However much one may admire the gallantry of the Liberal fight, the effective choice of the government lies between the Labour and Conservative parties, and their manifestos have made it clear that it is a choice of evils – which is always a difficult choice.'[7] (In a parody of *The Economist* which *Punch* published in 1955, the title given the paper was:

THE EC*N*M*ST
Incorporating Bagehot's Gazette,
and the Fence-sitter's Friend)*[8]

---

*The fence-sitting theme was emphasised by the publisher's note at the bottom declaring *The Ec*n*m*st* 'Registered as a Newspaper, Blue Book, White Paper, Monograph and House Organ of the LSE and Carlton Club.' Dullness and stolidity were the main targets of the parody, the best line of which came under *Corrections*: 'On page 978 of the same issue the line "Most Non-sterling OEEC countries . . ." should read "By and large, it is probably true to say . . ."'

'The temptation must be strong in the breast of any intelligent elector,' wrote Crowther five years later, 'after looking at what the parties have to say about the issues of foreign policy, to spoil his ballot paper.'[9] Yet it was on this occasion that Crowther abandoned his lofty position of neutrality, made his impassioned statement of the essential radicalism of *The Economist* and recommended for want of any reasonable choice that readers vote Conservative. Four years later Tyerman echoed Crowther: 'One is bound to confess to start with the reluctant preliminary belief – the exasperated, even angry, belief – that there is no better alternative in sight to the devil we have.'[10]

In 1964, after thirteen years of a Conservative government, the paper opted for Labour. 'An election is not only a decision', wrote Norman Macrae. 'It is also, always, a wager. The first question for Thursday is whether the Conservatives have surely earned an extra term; that must be doubted. The second is whether Labour offers the alternative. That, too, is far from sure.'

> There is no need for an independent journal to stand up to be counted. There is every excuse when the choice is so close to dodge it. That is precisely why it is honester, with every reservation made, not to leave it in the air. It does seem to *The Economist* that, on the nicest balance, the riskier choice of Labour – and Mr Wilson – will be the better choice for people to vote on Thursday.[11]

During Alastair Burnet's editorship there was never any doubt about which party the paper would support; Burnet was a Heath man through and through. In 1966 and 1970 the recommendation was the same: the Conservatives provided, said the paper in 1970, 'the better hope on at least three grounds: restoring some incentives to risk-taking, not destroying savings through Mr Crossman's pension schemes, and making some overdue advance towards trade union reform'.[12]

Harold Wilson gave Crowther a peerage. In 1968, as Prime Minister, he had attended one of the lunches to which came (and come) the famous and influential to converse with *Economist* staff. His Chancellor, James Callaghan, influenced by the Hungarian-born economists Thomas Balogh and Nicholas Kaldor, had brought in a Selective Employment Tax on workers employed in service industries. Crowther, then chairman of Trust Houses, a hotel company, was furious and complained about it bitterly in correspondence in public and in private. Barbara Ward recounted the story to Cecil King in July 1968 over lunch.

Recently Wilson . . . had lunch at *The Economist*. Having consumed half a bottle of brandy at lunch, he asked to be taken to the gents. When Crowther took him there, he asked him to come inside. While he did what was necessary, he asked Crowther if he would accept a peerage. Crowther asked who else was on the list; Wilson said he had forgotten. He had of course done nothing of the sort, but did not want to admit that Crowther's peerage was a set-off to Balogh's.[13]

In 1970 Edward Heath won, only to misjudge the mood of the country in 1974 and force a trial of strength with the miners. 'It may be that a majority of the British now want an easy way out. But if they want the resolution that they will win through one day, that the right decisions for winning through will be found and taken and that most of the right decisions will be adhered to, then there is no alternative to Mr Heath. He is the best man in British politics to go into a crisis with.'[14]

Later that year when Wilson's minority government went to the polls, the advice the paper gave was to reinforce 'the sensible centre wherever it can be managed: that includes social democratic Labour men, who may yet have a decisive part to play, as much as it excludes Conservatives who would rely on unemployment as their main policy'.[15]

There were two new players in the 1979 election. 'It is only the most remarkable of the many ironies of Britain's current general election that Mr James Callaghan should be campaigning so blatantly on the platform of middle-ground conservatism, Mrs Margaret Thatcher equally blatantly as the apostle of radical reform.'[16] Therefore '*The Economist* votes for Mrs Thatcher being given her chance.'[17] Knight was later to castigate himself for being slow to spot and back the Thatcher revolution.

Four years later, in 1983, there was much hand-wringing at the thought that a Tory government could be returned with a greatly increased majority while unemployment was over 3,000,000. *The Economist* had once entertained hopes of some new force like the Alliance Party

coming down the middle of British politics, wedded to the constitutional reform of proportional representation – provided that the disproportionate influence which that would give to the centre went to the daring extreme centre (ready to proffer constantly new ideas stemming from no political code-book, left or right) rather than to the dead centre (which runs away from any ideas, and preaches state control of incomes and that the frontier between the competitive and monopoly sectors must be stuck eternally wherever it is now for fear of annoying anybody).

During this election, however, the Alliance was destroying itself 'by adopting the policies of the dead centre which would send Britain back to sleep'.[18]

Pennant-Rea's paper was somewhat crisper four years later. 'Some day, the British electorate will want to turn out the Tories, and they – whether because of exhaustion, incompetence or corruption – may deserve to go. This day is not yet Thursday. Britain still needs more shaking up, more competition, more choice before it can face the twenty-first century with confidence. The Tories may not succeed; the Thatcher revolution may stall, unfinished. But to end its chances now would be folly, grand scale.'[19]

'MAY THE WORST LOT LOSE' was the message in the middle of the cover before the 1992 election, surrounded with pictures of three party leaders and assorted henchmen. 'The Britain that goes to the polls on April 9th is in fractious mood, a strange mixture of impatience and indifference . . . For a newspaper like *The Economist*, whose lifeblood is political economy, it would seem natural to say that the voters are wrong, that really there is much to argue about, much to move the heart as well as the head. Actually the voters are right. Although this election ought to be of great moment, the politicians have not risen to the occasion.' An analysis of what was wrong with all the parties led to the conclusion that a Liberal revival was what was wanted. This could come about only if the Labour Party and the Liberals 'overturned the history of the last 92 years' and rejoined each other.

> For that to happen, Labour must lose this election, and the bigger its loss the better.
> And that, given the depressing state of British politics, is the best reason for wanting the Conservatives to win next week.[20]

The Economist's radicalism and genuine absence of party loyalty lead to much misunderstanding of its position, particularly because of the often arrogant nature of its criticism and its gift for the wounding phrase. The British press in general is so partisan and so predictable that the concept of an independent organ is a difficult one to grasp. In the Crowther tradition, the tone is hypercritical and its victims tend to see the paper as their enemy: criticism rankles long after praise has been forgotten.

Brendan Bracken was one of those who often found the style irritating. In his 'Men and Matters' column in the *Financial Times* he used to refer to *The Economist* as the 'three-decker' pulpit. In 1952 he remarked, of the paper of which he was supposedly managing director, that 'Many readers of the *Economist* look upon that paper as an oracle, and so do its editorial writers; there is no subject on which they are unwilling to lay down the law.' 'I have no objection to being called three-tiered or even sermonical', wrote Crowther to him privately.

> Nor, on a dull Monday, do I very much mind your working off once again the old jest about inconsistency – even in a paragraph that is itself inconsistent. I know it isn't true, I know you know it isn't true, and we both know that nobody (including you and me) gives a damn whether it's true or not. It is not on any of those scores that my complacency is dented. I recognise that they are just pretty Fanny's way.
>
> What does make me cross is that you can't get our name right. For years I have been trying to get an admission from Printing House Square, who insist that the paper they publish is *The Times*, that we have an equal – indeed, a better – right to the definite article. Sometimes they agree and comply; usually they just forget. How can I hope to teach them newspaper manners if my own Managing Director forgets his?
>
> Next time you abuse us (next Monday, I hope) let it be *The Economist*, please.[21]

In his biography of Hugh Dalton, Chancellor of the Exchequer 1945–7, Ben Pimlott referred to *The Economist* as right-wing, the label being earned because it thought the country over-taxed; but it was right-wing only in the sense that it always put first of all economic priorities the need for sound money. Crowther's vicious attacks were designed to try to shock the government out of the pursuit of what he thought to be an inflationary policy.

Crowther undoubtedly saw himself much in the role of Walter Bagehot – 'the spare chancellor' – though their relationships with government were very different. Bagehot had been a friendly critic and almost uniquely influential: Robert Giffen believed that he played a very important part in persuading Gladstone not to abolish income tax. Both Liberal and Conservative Chancellors trusted Bagehot's judgment and listened to him or even consulted him. That was a product of an intimacy impossible 70 years later.*

---

*On one occasion a Cabinet minister quite happily lent Bagehot a set of Cabinet minutes in order to clear up one of his queries.

Crowther was seen as fierce, not friendly, destructive, not constructive. Hugh Dalton nicknamed *The Economist* 'the Prig's Weekly' because of its pessimistic forecasts. 'If, in the end,' observed Pimlott, 'Crowther got the better of the argument, this was partly because his prophecies were self-fulfilling.'[22] That is a judgment very flattering to the influence of Crowther's *Economist*.

When Sir Stafford Cripps was appointed Minister of Economic Affairs, the *New Statesman* feared that the government might become one 'not only of economists but of *The Economist*'. [23] Then there was the case of the historic devaluation announced by Cripps, Dalton's successor as Chancellor, on 18 September 1949, when the pound was devalued from $4 to $2.80. '*The Economist*,' wrote Pimlott, 'which had previously contrasted Cripps's courage and clarity with Dalton's alleged willingness to shirk unpalatable duty, declared that the decision should have been taken months before. Yet devaluation itself was a mainly technical matter delayed . . . because Cripps and the cabinet had been persuaded by the City and the Treasury to regard it "as a sign of fiscal irresponsibility if not of downright moral turpitude."'

What *The Economist* had to say was listened to. Sir Robert Hall of the Economic Section of the Treasury, a colleague of Crowther's great friend Sir Edwin Plowden, and one of the pro-devaluationist officials who believed that devaluation must be accompanied by an austerity package on Budget day 1949, reflected in his diary anxieties over the way Crowther would jump. 'I felt deeply enough to do what I hardly ever do, and I called at *The Economist* and found Roland Bird and Wilfred King writing their pieces. Fortunately they felt as I did, that it was a very fine budget so there was no need to go in for any argument. Edwin spoke later to Geoffrey on the same lines.'[24] Other quotations give the tone: '*The Economist* on Saturday was very bitter about the cuts being a "flea-bite".'[25] 'I have seen E.N.P. [Plowden] and he discussed the UK strength and how G. Crowther was so disappointed that there was no collapse that he had openly said in *The Economist* that we must *hope* for one. Both EP and I feel very disappointed about G as two years ago we felt we saw eye to eye about everything.'[26]

Crowther sometimes seemed critical for criticism's sake or perhaps for the sake of the wittily turned phrase: 'the British people more planned against than planning'; 'the song in the Chancellor's heart is the wind in the nation's stomach'. He was an alternative rather than a spare chancellor, 'working out week by week on paper to his own satisfaction what do to about balance of payments, exchange rates, wage inflation, industrial relations, investment and productivity, to say nothing of the problems of the wider world.'[27]

There was not to be another *Economist* editor capable of taking on the Treasury on their own ground until the next economist, Rupert Pennant-Rea, who had both the ability and self-confidence. Shortly before he left in 1993 to become the Bank of England's deputy governor, his paper severely criticised the budget for lack of fiscal prudence in leaving a dangerously large deficit. While praising what there was to be praised on the micro level, the leader concluded by declaring that it was the macro judgment that mattered most: 'A lesson of the past few years is that an unpredictable business cycle can make budget plans irrelevant in a flash. Mr Lamont dare not say he is counting on better economic news to cure his fiscal sickness but he is. That may be good politics, but it is not fiscal prudence.'[28]

Geoffrey Crowther's principle of encouraging independent compartments on *The Economist* allowed Roland Bird virtual autonomy at the back of the paper. There were tensions between the front and the back in the early days of Dalton's chancellorship, with Wilfred King working away on the small print of Treasury figures, but by 1947 front and back were united in opposition. Bird's job was to change the Business World from what Crowther described as 'a collection of articles and notes which at present sometimes defy reading into a really interesting, challenging and readable weekly review of everything that is happening in finance, investment, industry and trade. From being a number of technical appendices to the main body of the paper, it should become a consistent and balanced whole in its own right.'[29]

Roland Bird created modern business journalism, as opposed to City or economic journalism: it was not until the 1960s that the *Sunday Times* and gradually other newspapers began to emulate *The Economist* in this. He combined the solid qualities of the old-fashioned professional journalist with an openness to new ideas and a respect for young talent. Moreover, he had a vast range of contacts. Post-war insiders were much more prepared to open up than they had been in Parkinson's pre-war days. Bird had moles in the Stock Exchange, in pension funds, insurance companies and government departments. He also had excellent sources in industry. A prime example was Georg Tugendhat, *The Economist*'s former Austrian correspondent, who had arrived in England as a refugee and started an oil refinery business and was an excellent source of inside stories. Bird also had admirable informants in accountancy and taxation: 'It wasn't', he said, 'so much weekly journalism as research into fundamental issues which produced a kind of popularised green paper.'

While Bird and his colleagues initiated most of this from their own slender resources, occasionally other people made contact with them seeking a vehicle for their ideas. For instance, one long series on local authority finance was instigated by the treasurer of Bird's local county council. The business section and the front of the paper met at Monday morning conferences, swapped ideas and helped each other, but on Wednesday night and Thursday morning there was little working contact between them.

Towards the end of Crowther's editorship, though money was still tight, the back of the paper had an array of talent that was to raise its prestige steadily. Wilfred King (who simultaneously edited the *Banker* which was produced under *The Economist*'s auspices) used to drive Crowther mad because of his habit of writing about six pages of preliminary notes to every one printed – the very opposite of Crowther's approach. But King was a superb researcher to whom Norman Macrae, his deputy for a short time, was ever grateful for his training. Crowther wrote of him once in a confidential note to Eric Gibb that though he could never resist a red herring, in many ways King was 'in the true Bagehot tradition. He is a very profound thinker on the nature of the financial system, and from an academic point of view his work is of the highest order.'

King had joined in 1945. Next in seniority was Jack Hartshorn, who joined in 1950 and was to succeed Bird as business editor. Intellectually rarefied and immensely intelligent, Hartshorn wrote 'with calm good sense'. An expert on the oil industry, he was later to leave *The Economist* to go into management consultancy. Mary Goldring had by then been with the paper for four years and was making her name as a tough and newsy writer on aerospace and science.

Ronald Brech covered commodity markets until he took himself off to Unilever and was replaced by Barry Mortimer, who, in turn, went to South Africa to work for Harry Oppenheimer's Anglo-American Corporation. Chapman, with over half-a-century of service behind him, and now under the sceptical but kindly eye of George Webster, was still at work on investment statistics (which then included a self-balancing analysis of company accounts that Bird had ingeniously devised, and which later produced – under Bird's prompting and with Gordon Lee's enthusiastic backing – a comparatively short-lived rival to the *FT* ordinary share index).

Gordon Lee, born in 1925, was brought in straight from university to help the over-loaded Chapman and Webster. He was an atypical recruit, having been working class, having served in the army as a gunner, having had a torrid time in the Burma campaign and then having been to a redbrick university where he got a poor degree in economics, a subject he disliked (being, in fact, a historian *manqué*.) For a long time he stood 'in timid awe' of Bird, whom he found 'a stern, though much more often than not, a just, mentor'. Finally he was welded into the journalistic investment team by the convivial, avuncular John Marvin who, a member of the Reform Club circle, joined *The Economist* from the City columns of the *Daily Telegraph*, went to South Africa to be the founder-editor of the successful weekly, the *South African Financial Mail*, and then returned to London to edit the *Investors Chronicle* in succession to the doyen of his craft, Harold Wincott. It was Marvin's style and manner in dealing with the young and inexperienced that Lee adopted in his later career at *The Economist*, where under Burnet and his successors he combined the editing of Surveys with being the defence correspondent until in the latter role he was replaced by an American ex-naval commander, Jim Meacham. Lee then combined editing the book section with Surveys and, in that semi-detached situation away from the weekly bustle, he became a kind of uncle-confessor who dispensed advice on personal and professional problems to a cross-section of the staff, old and new alike.

In the background for many years was Marjorie Deane. A maths graduate, she had been a statistician at the Admiralty during the war. In 1948 she sent an advertisement to *The Economist* asking for job offers and got a letter from Crowther confirming that her advertisement was being published but also saying the paper might be interested. She found that it was.

Her first job was to summarise the national income and expenditure blue book, which she managed by sitting up all night drinking coffee. She then became the paper's – and for a time also the Intelligence Unit's – statistical guru and had a staff to produce the voluminous *Records and Statistics* that Crowther had introduced. As government statistics were becoming more comprehensive, *Economist* coverage diminished correspondingly and *Records and Statistics* died, but she kept the flag flying. One of her innovations, of which Harold Wilson was most approving, was the introduction of 'Key Indicators'. Another was the inclusion of statistics within different sections, instead of putting them all together in a separate block. Later, under Andrew

Knight, they were returned *en bloc* to the back and made easier to understand.

Then there was Fred Hirsch. Born in Vienna in 1931, Hirsch arrived in England three years later and was in his final year at the London School of Economics and on his way to his first-class honours in 1952 when he consulted his tutor on what to do next. He wanted to do practical research into industry or trade and was anxious to join *The Economist* or the Economist Intelligence Unit. 'This afternoon I went for the long awaited interview at the Economist', he wrote to his mother in March 1952. 'Geoffrey Crowther, who I saw, is a particularly nice chap; not at all patronising as so many Greats tend to be towards "smalls". Mind you of course, he realised it was quite an occasion for me and lived up to it – by way of "appalling frankness" and rather dreamy reminiscences . . . the general intimation seemed to be that if there *was* anything going there would be a good chance. He asked in which side I was interested; I said the international economic and business side – so I'm going to see the Editor of that section of the paper some time next week – Crowther said that there were no definite vacancies but he knew of some *possible ones.'*[30]

Nothing materialised at that stage. Hirsch applied for various other jobs, one of which, in the UN Department of Economic Affairs, fell through because he was not yet naturalised; but in March the next year he was summoned again by Crowther. 'What was so nice was the way they greeted me on Wednesday; Crowther waffled a bit at first, and I thought, my goodness, another one of these "nearly got the jobs", but then he said that *they* were quite sure *they* wanted *me*, the only question was whether I wanted to work with them.' His job was to work with King for both the *Banker* and *The Economist*. 'Altogether there seems a very nice atmosphere there; I asked what the hours were; they thought, and said they weren't quite sure. Start just after 10 and carry on till one has finished – which is earlyish at the beginning and end of the week and late in the middle . . . Holidays also seemed a bit vague: "about four weeks" . . . Of course, everyone at college is quite impressed. However modestly one answers the question on where one is to work it still sounds good. You see, I am in danger of becoming conceited; actually I'm not. When I read *The Economist* and compare it to the standard at which I write I wonder if I shall ever make the grade.'[31]

On his first day, Hirsch could report having been at 'the weekly conference attended by all the big pots to decide the next issue of the paper. 'Naturally, that was very interesting – particularly the way that decisions emerge out of light-hearted chatter, if you know what I mean. Everyone calls everyone else by their Christian names, by the way, from Geoffrey down.'

> As for the other points: I was sorry to see that *no-one* was wearing a sports jacket; which means that I ought to have another suit . . . as for meals, they have a system of separating staff from clericals by the price system – one can go in the cafeteria, but most of the staff go to the canteen, which has waitress service and very good food – steaks etc – with the main dish from anything over 3/–.[32]

A week later he felt himself 'getting into the swing of the work there. King is very helpful, and gets me to sit in with him while he organises things, and so gives me a chance to see how the wheels go round. There is none of that horrible "this bit of information is only for X" sort of atmosphere . . . The work itself consists mainly of reading proofs, preparing articles or information, editing etc . . . Of course, there is a lot to learn for me in the *technical* matters of High Finance – but they are very helpful and accept the fact that one can possess a reasonable amount of intelligence and still not know certain routine things.' He had just learned 'how much of the important work is done over the dinner table. There's hardly a day that King doesn't have lunch with some civil servant, banker or whatnot – i.e. see the people that *make* the news. He encourages me to do the same once I've got the hang of things.'[33]

In May Hirsch reported writing 'my first note for *The Economist* – appropriately enough on the Austrian devaluation. You could imagine what it was like trying to get any information out of the Embassy officials! The Bank of England were more help than the charming nincompoops in the "Foreign Trade Office".'[34]

By July he felt he was shaping up reasonably well on the writing side but had a long way to go on reliability – 'i.e. being fully reliable in checking figures, not forgetting things, etc. As soon as that is straight King wants me to be his effective deputy; that is, be able to rely on me without having to check afterwards. But I hope that this aspect will come on with time; he himself is very decent, and when I make a mistake his concern is only to point it out as a lesson. Because of this, I feel I'm learning pretty fast: I'm sure one learns more there in a few months than in other places in years.'[35]

By September the following year Hirsch was well on top of things, organising the makeup of the *Banker* in King's absence and writing a good deal for *The Economist*. 'I am now getting a much closer relationship to the

Deputy Editor (of *The Economist*, above King) [Bird]. He even brought me in something he'd edited and asked me to give it a second eye. Apart from everything else I like that because as a person he is very satisfactory, the complete opposite of King: goes about his work quietly, without fuss, and assumes you will do the same; doesn't talk all the time but when he does say something it's usually a peach of prose.'

He reported being taken by King to the Reform Club, where King 'bumped into gent in corridor who started talking to him about Chicago with a German accent. Then imagine my surprise when King introduced "Mr Hirsch, Professor Hayek". We all sat at one big table with Deputy Editor and some other wizards of the financial press. Hayek was amazingly mild and seemed far less interested in the Retreat from Serfdom than getting away from Chicago in the hot season.* King said afterwards, not without truth, that of course his stuff had an important basis of truth but only a Germanic mind could have carried it to such ridiculously "logical" conclusions. Which also, of course, applies to wallahs like Marx and Hegel. However. The great thing about the Reform is obviously the people just bumped across.'[36]

Hirsch's involvement with the *Banker* ended in 1958 and he went on to *The Economist* full-time, becoming financial editor in 1963. His second *Economist* editor, Donald Tyerman, was to perform for Hirsch in 1978 his frequent function of perceptive and generous obituarist. 'Only twice in our time has *The Economist* had a writer on money matters whose reports and comments, like those of Walter Bagehot a century before, were part of the monetary discussion itself. The first, of course, was Geoffrey Crowther; the second, only too briefly, was Fred Hirsch.'[37]

Hirsch had a happy argumentative relationship with Norman Macrae. They 'agreed on most tactics in macroeconomic policy,' wrote Macrae in 1977, 'and on some tactics in microeconomic policy. All through these years he and I have disagreed completely on nearly all aspects of economics.' But then Hirsch was a socialist who believed, said Tyerman, that 'the market was made for man, not man for the market, and it was a fallible exemplar'.

---

*Friedrich von Hayek had moved in 1950 from the University of London to a chair at the University of Chicago. His *The Road to Serfdom*, published in 1944, was an attack on the notion of the planned society – whether totalitarian or democratic – in the tradition of the classic liberal economists. The great guru of the Adam Smith Institute and the Institute of Economic Affairs, he became in the late 1970s a hero of the libertarian right and an intellectual pillar of Thatcherism.

Similarly, in his special bailiwick of money, Fred Hirsch right to the end saw both sides of the argument. He fastened on the truth that here as everywhere else in the fogged markets of modern economies there was still both a supply function and a demand function as well, that it was nonsense to make forecasts, and still less policy, simply from the supply of money alone (however defined) though that indeed was critically important, as he confessed in his latest thoughts. What was decisively important, nevertheless, was still the composition, the scale and the ramification of the demand on the money supply. Fred Hirsch was still in a straight line from those who had the task of reconciling the banking and currency schools of argument at the time of the Bank Charter Act and the foundation of *The Economist* four generations before.

Hirsch was an attractive and lovable colleague, his earnestness leavened by good humour and wit. 'Fred had a second self called by us and by him Fred Stag,' wrote Tyerman, 'the name he used to sign letters to newspapers, including his own. Fred Stag was a full-blooded radical bent on social justice and genuine individual choice, within the parameters of Fred Hirsch's own positive welfare economics and the real constraints of the market.'

(This was an interesting variation on the tradition of having *Economist* people complaining about the paper publicly in the letters column. The most recent example of the tradition has been provided by Hirsch's great friend David Gordon – who wrote with him in 1975 what Tyerman described as 'an acutely searching and sometimes impish and over-ingenious study of *Newspaper Money*'. The fact that Gordon was *The Economist*'s chief executive did not prevent him sending it, in 1993, in his capacity as deputy chairman of the Periodical Publishers Association, a detailed rebuttal of an *Economist* editorial suggestion that publications should be brought into the VAT taxation net.[38])

Fred Hirsch was lost to the paper in 1966 when Jack Hartshorn left and Alastair Burnet chose Mary Goldring as business editor. Hirsch, who by then was the intellectual equal and probably the superior of anyone on the paper, went off to be, first, a senior adviser in the research department of the International Monetary Fund; then a fellow of Nuffield College, Oxford; and finally, for the rest of his short life, Professor of International Studies at Warwick University, making with his fourth book, *Social Limits to Growth*, a huge international reputation as an economist. Marjorie Deane replaced him as finance editor and was to become one of the world's most respected international financial journalists.

Mary Goldring was much more Burnet's kind of journalist. She liked news, took risks and wanted blood on the carpet rather than intense intellectual discussion. Flouting the tendency of *The Economist* to bring in people who do not know much but are clever and can write, she more often imported people who knew a great deal but wrote badly. Indeed, she was so conscientious in rewriting the prose of her subordinates, that it was not until she left that it became clear that some of them were absolutely hopeless.

Among the Goldring stars was Howard Banks, who as a metallurgist had worked with the British Aircraft Corporation and then on a trade paper, and who came to report on industry. He worked on the journalistic principle that if you follow the money you will root out the wickedness. His image with some of his colleagues was that of the chap who goes out after a telephone tipoff, meets a man in a dirty raincoat on the corner of a dark street and comes back with an exclusive. That tradition of inquisitiveness was later maintained by Vince McCullough (the scourge of Lloyd's) and Charles Grant, who successfully maintained his ability to smell a rat when he was posted to Brussels to write on EC affairs.

David Gordon was an accountant who thought journalism would be more fun, and was knowledgeable about films and the entertainment industry. Lively and fertile with ideas, he had the great virtue as a business journalist of understanding how the books were cooked. Ian Coulter was brought from the *Sunday Times* to run Business Britain. He saw his job primarily as that of the non-commissioned officer who taught the rookies how to 'stick fingers in people's eyes'. (He was to marry his colleague Barbara Beck, the German-born European editor who later became the first woman chairman of the Reform Club.)

Business has presented more problems since 1945 than any other section of the paper. The first major difficulty came in the 1960s with competition for readers and staff from the new business pages of the quality newspapers. 'I should tell you', wrote Burnet to Crowther in 1968, 'that we must certainly expect more people leaving the Business World than in the past. The reason is simply: *The Times*, the *Sunday Times*, and even the *Financial Times*, continually cast offers – sometimes up to double the money we can afford to pay, over our young men. They are flattered, alert and slightly neurotic at being paid money well above what they could have expected before Thompson began his spending spree.'[39] Rising salaries and rapid staff-turnover put financial and editorial strains on *The Economist*, and there were dramatic lurches in emphasis. Investigative journalists such as Howard Banks, Ian Coulter and Mary Goldring – and later Iain Carson – wanted to break stories, but post-Burnet there was little sympathy for that approach. Knight was interested in business from the perspective of politics and power; Pennant-Rea's outlook was more that of the intellectual economist. Then there were the different views about City coverage, in which neither Burnet nor Goldring was really interested. Indeed under Burnet the finance section veered temporarily towards investment advice of the kind that James Wilson had eschewed from the beginning. It was also during the Burnet–Goldring period that *The Economist* missed the boat on the coverage of City and capital markets, allowing *Euromoney*, which started in 1969, to cover the London-based international capital markets unchallenged.

Part of the problem was that the business section, which had traditionally been almost entirely about Britain, could not match the staff or space resources of its newspaper competitors. Andrew Knight managed an important transition shortly after he became editor. When Mary Goldring, who had opposed his appointment, left to develop her already successful broadcasting career, he decided that the range of coverage must be greatly widened and he tempted Stephen Hugh-Jones back to the paper from the Paris-based business journal, *Vision*, of which he was deputy editor.

Hugh-Jones has an extraordinary ability both to get people to fly their kites and then brilliantly to sub-edit their material. With journalistic experience in India as well as Paris, he was well placed to widen the parameters of the business coverage. He excelled at playing to his people's strengths. Under his influence, Iain Carson produced first-rate coverage of the European chemical industry and several others were given their heads – Andrew Neil on British labour, and, more generally, Peter Martin (who sizzled with ideas) and John Plender (whose speciality was thoughtful in-depth coverage of individual companies and who fell out with Andrew Knight because he refused to let him do a critical analysis of GEC). Hugh-Jones was happy for people to go for the jugular, and Banks, Neil and Stephen Milligan were encouraged to run leaks; it was alleged at one time that Neil and Banks between them were causing more leak enquiries than the rest of Fleet Street put together. Another newcomer on the industrial side around that time was Nick Valéry, who had been deputy editor of *New Scientist*. (Only Valéry, later Tokyo and now United States West Coast correspondent, stayed with *The Economist*. Banks is now in Washington as deputy editor of *Forbes Magazine*, Carson is the BBC industrial correspondent, Peter Martin and John Plender are with the *Financial Times*, Stephen Milligan is a Conservative MP and Andrew Neil is editor of the *Sunday Times*.)

The Economist suffered a great loss when, in 1980, Hugh-Jones stormed out because Knight had announced his intention to move business leaders from the back of the paper to the front. Hugh-Jones's temper is legendary. A contemporary who worked in the room next door described, as typical of the sound effects, 'a tremendous thud on the wall behind and a booming voice shouting "God damn the bloody North Thames Gas Board"'. Folklore tells of his having thrown a typewriter (or perhaps a telephone) at the back of Alastair Burnet (or somebody else) through an intervening glass door. Hugh-Jones (who has once again returned to the paper) denies throwing anything at anybody, but admits there are reasons why such stories are believed.

The struggle to get the business section right goes on. World coverage has increased steadily, with a full-time business and finance correspondent in New York and a Tokyo correspondent heavily biased towards business. In the 1980s first Tony Thomas and then Bill Emmott struggled to get the formula right and keep *The Economist* playing to its strengths, producing enough international coverage to satisfy a global audience while paying enough attention to the needs of home readers. One important development was a change in emphasis from company news stories towards management and multinational themes.

Then there is the problem of classification of stories. What is business? What is finance? What is economics? What is politics? And, indeed, what is foreign affairs? Is a dramatic news story about IBM the province of the foreign department, American Survey or World Business? Such issues have caused a great deal of tension and argument over the years. And what about economics? The new post of economics editor was introduced under Burnet; in it, the forceful Brian Reading, Sarah Hogg, Rupert Pennant-Rea and later Clive Crook had other departmental battles to fight with colleagues on business or politics whose views might not be quite classically liberal.

Keeping the paper compartmentalised yet dovetailed is the editor's problem, and it is exacerbated by *The Economist*'s uniqueness as a global and multi-disciplinary newspaper with a strong local presence. That the divisions are contained, and are irritating rather than destructive, is primarily a consequence of two of the paper's most unusual characteristics: anonymity and the collegiate structure. Except for the surveys, the occasional signed article by an outsider, the occasional lengthy special and any review of a book by a member of staff, anonymity is adhered to rigidly; and it is defended stoutly by all but a tiny number of staff.

Two arguments are frequently used against anonymity. The first is one of straightforward individual self-interest. In the first post-1945 years Denis Healey, later Labour Chancellor of the Exchequer, was one of those freelancers for whom anonymity is a disadvantage: 'I also wrote occasionally for *The Economist*, though since they demanded high quality articles, paid little, and did not publish their writers' names, I found it unrewarding both financially and politically.'[40] Staff journalists are now well-paid, but as they are not permitted to write for directly competing journals, some want more public recognition than can be gained from writing books or broadcasting. Seeing by-lines tempt a few valued journalists away is painful, but not painful enough to raise doubts about preserving the status quo.

The second criticism seems more serious, as it is made by high-minded and disinterested believers in the principle of openness. One such is the Hon. William Plowden (son of Crowther's great friend Edwin), whose career, most notably as Director of the Royal Institute of Public Administration, has been largely concerned with bringing more reason and accountability into government. In 1987 he was provoked by the last paragraph of Andrew Knight's valedictory:

> In my time editors became too self-important. One of the most celebrated of them elevated the by-lines and photographs of the journalists working for his heavy-weight newspaper to a greater size than the headlines of the stories they were writing . . . Readers are interested in what journalists and editors report or have to say. They may seek out the names of good writers on a paper, and buy that newspaper again. Or they may want the newspaper itself to write well, anonymously, as *The Economist* so successfully does. Either way, the readers' interest is in the message not the messenger; they are justly uninterested in us. Which is why this tradition of asking departed editors to sign an article is a mistake – which will not be repeated, I trust, for about ten years.

'Not all readers', responded Plowden in a letter to the editor, '"want the newspaper to write . . . anonymously". It is high time you and your colleagues had the self-confidence to come out from behind your corporate cloak (including your book reviewers: the idea of a corporate book review is particularly nonsensical). It is precisely because I sheltered and sniped from behind it myself a quarter of a century ago that I, as a reader, want to know who is there now. After all, if the *Financial Times* – rightly praised by Mr Knight – can name names and distinguish its gurus from its novices, why cannot you?'[41]

The main reason, as St Loe Strachey pointed out 70 years ago, is that journalists who write 'in the name of their paper and not of themselves, are much less likely to yield to the foolish vanity of self-assertion': they can sink their individuality and speak for their paper.[42] For, as that great *Times* editor, Sir William Haley noticed, 'signed writing invites exhibitionism'.

One of the best defences of the principle of anonymity was made in 1915 by a great liberal journalist, Sir Edward Cook, ex-editor of the *Pall Mall Gazette*, the *Westminster Gazette* and the *Daily News*, in his biography of John Delane, editor of *The Times* from 1841 to 1877. Mourning the waning of anonymity, he observed:

> In many modern newspapers a reader may find almost as many expressions of opinion as there are special articles. The veiled personality of the editorial 'we' is swamped by a multitude of obtrusive persons, each giving his name and airing his individual opinion . . . The mystery of the unknown has gone. The power, the influence, the authority of the newspaper itself are sacrificed to the advertisement of its several contributors.

He took issue with Lord Morley's contention that

> as anonymity in journalism waned "a sense of responsibility" would wax. With all respect due to a master of the craft (and, as piety bids me add, to my own first editor), I must take leave to differ from his opinion. The corporate sense of responsibility, behind the veil of anonymity, was in the best days of Victorian journalism very strong.

On an important paper, especially if the editor inspired confidence, every member of the staff had the *esprit de corps*, and felt the professional pride, that belonged to members of a regiment. The writers worked not for the individual credit of each, but for the credit of the paper, which was in their minds something greater than the aggregate of themselves. They were not, it is true, individually and personally responsible, but they were responsible, each in his measure and sphere, for the honour of the institution which they served.'

It lent to the leader-writers 'a great responsibility to be speaking, not as a signed writer nor as one whose identity was generally known, but as the mouthpiece of an impersonal organ whose deliverance proceeded with the authority of accumulated traditions'. Under the newer system there was a tendency for a newspaper 'to become a vehicle for the expression of individual views, or a ladder for the promotion of individual ambitions'.[43]

For the true *Economist* person, there is no doubt. 'The policy of anonymity is not merely traditional', said Crowther in his speech at the 1943 centenary lunch; 'for myself I am convinced that it is one of the golden rules of sound and honest journalism.'

> It is also a deliberate policy, and it means that *The Economist* has acquired a corporate personality far stronger than any one mind. If an editor of *The Economist* wished to use the paper as his personal vehicle, the constitution . . . puts astonishingly few obstacles in his path; but I am sure that my predecessors will agree with me in saying that in fact there is everything in the world to prevent any such thing happening, for every editor of *The Economist* feels that he is not the master but the servant of something far greater than himself. You can call that ancestor-worship if you wish, but it gives to the paper an astonishing momentum of thought and principle.

That is the simplest and strongest virtue of anonymity, the glue that has held the fabric of the newspaper together for 150 years. Second is the certainty that the editor's authority stands over every fact and every expression of opinion. Third, and an enormous plus in producing a product of high quality, is that anonymity has engendered the collegiate approach. There is no incentive for any journalist to keep material close to the chest. Ideas are for sharing and arguing over; a colleague's prose is there to be improved whether he likes it or not. Many articles are the work of many hands but there is no by-line grabbing.

For a journalist with outside experience, the first exposure to the collegiate approach can be startling. At its best it can happen thus: a journalist suggests a subject and an approach, which is chewed over, sharpened and enriched at the editorial conference. Afterwards, someone from another section may drop by to discuss the thing and improve it with unexpected extra material. The journalist writes the piece, a section head improves it, somebody gifted subs it and just before it goes to print someone catches and corrects the only error.

On the other hand, his idea could be strangled at birth by people more articulate and forceful than he is; or, when he has written it, his section head disagrees violently and rewrites it so thoroughly as to turn the argument on its head; or a heavy subber removes every word of which he is proud; or (until recently) having cleared all the other obstacles, his piece falls into the hands of Norman Macrae, who sprinkles it with negatives.

During his four decades with the paper, Macrae is probably the person who has both most justified and most abused the system. At his worst, his absolute conviction about his ideological correctness has driven crazy the more junior colleagues whose copy he has altered with abandon. On the other hand, Macrae's generosity with his knowledge and his ideas over the years have added breadth and substance to his colleagues' arguments.

As with Andrew Boyd, *The Economist* has suited Macrae perfectly, having allowed him to follow his interests from subject to subject. Born in 1923, Macrae had a roving childhood, spending time as a member of a diplomatic family in several countries, including Nazi Germany (briefly) and Russia at the time of the pre-war Stalinist purges. Educated in England, he went up to Cambridge in 1941 and the following year became a navigator in the RAF. His last year of war-service was spent in Burma. He returned to Cambridge in 1945, where, after graduating with a first in economics in 1947, he stayed for two years to do research. Macrae wrote freelance for the *Banker*, which he joined in 1949 as Wilfred King's deputy, while writing simultaneously for *The Economist*. Crowther brought him in to fill a gap in the home department, for which he had constant trouble finding an editor. He had tried out Walter Layton's daughter-in-law Elizabeth in the hope that she could take over, and when this failed to work out, he took on Alastair Buchan, with whom he could not get on. Buchan (later a biographer of Bagehot) left to embark on a new career in which he became the widely esteemed Director of the International Institute for Strategic Studies, and was replaced by Tom Kent. After a couple of years, Kent decamped to Canada, where he became an influential journalist and public servant.

Increasingly bored with editing and writing, Crowther was particularly keen to find someone who, like Kent, could write fluently about economics. Kent had been slightly left of centre; Macrae was slightly right; he was to be an enthusiastic supporter of 'Rab' Butler in his attempt to become Conservative Prime Minister after Eden's 1957 resignation. During his first years with the paper Macrae wrote primarily about British politics, trade unions and the economy. Gradually, though, he began to turn his attention to other countries and disciplines, most notably through the medium of the Surveys, creating a great stir from the early 1960s onwards, particularly with his two prescient Surveys on Japan, 'Consider Japan' (1962) and the two-part 'The Risen Sun' (1967), both of which were turned into books.

Surveys, which had been steadily developing under Layton and then under Hargreaves Parkinson, sank under wartime paper rationing and did not really come into their own again until the 1960s, when Gordon Lee (who had been seduced away by his old *Economist* colleague, John Marvin, now editor of the *Investor Chronicle*) was brought back by Alastair Burnet mainly to make the Surveys work. They were to become a successful circulation booster in targeted markets, as well as an increasingly valuable source of advertising revenue. In common with the rest of the paper, the feature that distinguished *Economist* Surveys from those in competing newspapers was that they were editorial-led, not advertising-driven. There have been Surveys on countries, industries, transport, insurance, sport, media, defence, technology, travel, and institutions like the International Monetary Fund and the City of London.

Lee's role was to encourage journalists to write on their enthusiasms, match ideas for Surveys with suitable people, raise and then keep them to a high standard and encourage the advertising department to exploit what advertising potential they might possess; some Surveys carry no advertising. No more than with the rest of the paper is there any discussion with the advertising department about editorial content, though there is cooperation over layout and timing.

The lead having been set, notably by Macrae, in the mid-1960s, the Surveys became an integral, though distinct, part of the newspaper, being gradually turned, under Lee's guidance over long lunches and amid clouds of cigar smoke and snuff, from being loosely-strung-together collections of articles on a broad-ranging subject to thematic essays on a particular topic. At first they were unpopular with most editors, for a Survey took a journalist away from his desk for weeks. And some journalists found having to write at such length taxing. But, over time, the journalists began to appreciate their worth, and when, again following Macrae's lead, they began to carry the author's by-line, members of staff started to clamour to write them. Their being signed meant that the authors had more freedom than usual to express a somewhat individual point of view. The problem of allowing journalists to write about what excites them, while keeping the interests of the reader paramount and not ignoring advertising potential, has led to a balancing act unique in journalism.

It was with the Surveys that Macrae was to come into his own. He proved to have an extraordinary ability to go somewhere new or tackle a new subject in a very short space of time and come up with a Survey that even the jaded found fresh. He viewed a Survey as different from a report. 'You go out there saying there are twelve things I want to find out. You find six of them have very boring answers, four of them are new but there are a dozen other things that surprise you. If they surprise you, then they surprise the reader.'

What drove Macrae was passionate interest, made more effective by his ruthlessness. If he went to a country having arranged meetings with ten politicians and concluded after seeing three that he would be better seeing businessmen, he would cancel all appointments and start afresh.

Researching his first breakthrough, 'Consider Japan', he found he got little from talking to the British expatriates. Then, in a Mitsubishi factory, he accidently came across a machine-tool salesman from Britain who told him over several drinks that Japanese workers, although paid only a third of the wages of their British counterparts, were getting three times as much out of their machines. So, before anybody else, Macrae came out with an optimistic prognosis for a country that was generally seen in the world as medieval. His prediction of a Japanese export boom gave heart to the Japanese and in 1988, in gratitude for that, for subsequent Surveys and for his books on Japan, he was awarded the Order of the Rising Sun. Other Macrae subjects have included France, Germany, Latin America, the EEC, the United States and the future of international business; they almost always attract an immense amount of attention. As early as 1969, *Newsweek* described Macrae as having 'illuminated American problems with a brilliance seldom equalled by home-grown journals'.[44]

Deputy editor since 1965, Macrae twice failed to become editor. He has been much better suited to being a brilliant deputy and promoter of intellectual ferment, whose wilder ideas have been reined back by his editor and colleagues. Nor is man management or administration Macrae's forte. Quite apart from anything else, he is not an easy man to communicate with. On his travels and in search of information he will listen and he is an excellent public speaker, but at home on his own territory he talks continually and incomprehensibly. 'His words burst forth indistinctly and are chased out by cackling laughter', observed one newspaper profile. 'Yet all strain to decipher him: for this is the man who has for ages preached the economic liberalism that everyone now practises; who immediately pooh-poohed the food and other shortages wrongly promised by the Club of Rome; who saw 25 years ago where Japan would be today; who lost far too little sleep over OPEC's oil shock because he knew that an oil price slump must surely follow; who coined the words "Butskellism", "stagflation" and "privatisation"; who wrote a book prophesying that the Russian leadership would change its whole approach at the end of this decade.'[45]

Added to the problem with Macrae's speech is his handwriting, which is dishearteningly illegible. At *The Economist* for many years, he was able to function only because Elizabeth Methold, the only person in the world to be able to decipher his scrawl, translated it into typescript. When Macrae was seconded for three months to *Time*, his colleagues in London were mystified about how he could make himself understood. The secret, which he himself did not reveal, was that while there he used a typewriter (under compulsion). When the Atex computer system was introduced in 1982, it was assumed that every journalist would be able to adapt to it with the exception of Macrae. Then the word spread round the building: on being introduced to the keyboard, Macrae had gazed at it, suddenly crashed his immense hands down on it and within minutes was happily typing away.

What makes Macrae's writing – not just his Surveys – so extraordinary is his ear and eye for the one interesting idea and his ability to communicate that interest in print. He is *sui generis* in his sweep, his optimism and in his absolute faith in his own judgment. Once he has made up his mind, and a pattern has formed in his head, everything else he learns fits in with it. His critics accuse him of manipulating facts, though only the very disgruntled ever suggest that he does so consciously. He was a believer in the free market before almost anyone else in the post-war period and has taken his recommendations farther than most. An ideas man *par excellence*, he is capable of being, as one colleague put it, 'both brilliantly right and brilliantly wrong. There are no half-measures with Norman. He thinks in the long term. Remarkably, but perhaps not so remarkably for a man of such dazzling intellectual gifts, his awareness of the pains of economic and political transition and his sensitivity to others' ideas and opinions are minimal. There is a touch of the Old Testament prophet about him, an eccentric Deutero-Isaiah.' Always buoyant and vigorous, Macrae is never abashed by getting something wrong; he assumes that he will get it right next time.

Macrae has for many decades now been in great demand throughout the world as a lecturer, a consultant and a freelance writer, mainly in the realm of futurology: *The Economist*'s toleration of moonlighting has been a vital factor in keeping him on the paper. Over four decades, he has been the paper's leading maverick, a vital and original influence, a benign, stimulating and eccentric presence, rather as, in a lesser vein, was Thomas Hodgskin almost 150 years ago. Post-war, during the socialist and the corporate years, with an impact greater than any other journalist – possibly even than any editor – Macrae kept *The Economist* true to its roots by flying – with verve and style – James Wilson's *laissez-faire* and individualistic flag.

CHAPTER XLIX

Getting bored

Anyone who for long pursues the calling of a job in opinions eventually arrives at the condition of an intellectual slot machine. If the penny is inserted, either by the asking of a question or by the happening of an event, then the wheels will turn and a nicely packaged opinion will emerge.[1]
Geoffrey Crowther, 1956

Crowther's vision of how the paper could be improved and how it might develop was remarkably far-sighted. His recruiting policy was often inspired and his intellectual ability of the first rank. As the *Times* obituary (another appreciation written by Tyerman) said of his editorship:

> Although he was always perfectly ready to be shot at in the editorial chair and even on occasion to be shot down, Crowther had an extraordinary gift both for eliciting and for formulating consensus: in spite of the wide variety of political attitudes, of temperament and of expertise, represented at the weekly editorial conferences – which frequently had all the entertainment value of a combined Brains Trust and three-ring circus – *The Economist* spoke with a single voice, and its staff wrote with conviction because they were convinced.
>
> Under Crowther's editorship *The Economist* was revolutionised in format and in content. While retaining its specialist authority as a City periodical, it widened its appeal to the intelligent general public, lightened its style, and became one of the most influential weeklies in the world. Much of the achievement was undoubtedly due to Crowther's own writing; to his gift of getting to the heart of the matter, and to his blend of pungent common sense, steady principle, lucidity and pervasive wit. But his indirect influence was hardly, if at all, less important. He was in a special sense an inspired leader. *The Economist* was the model of a successful democracy.[2]

Crowther was always, of course, *primus inter pares*, as an editor needs to be. Norman Macrae had a vivid recollection of Crowther's habit of going around suggesting to his staff, along with helpful aphorisms, what to write in opinion pieces – short notes as well as leaders. 'As one example among many, when a Tory shadow minister said circa 1950 that sterling should float on the high seas of convertibility, Geoffrey put an evening newspaper on my desk with the words underlined, and said: "Quote that and say that on the high seas sterling would unfortunately turn sea-sick for the following reasons." He then gave the reasons in about three minutes, with every sentence including an aphorism or joke.'

He was also a gifted sub-editor; one of those rare people who leaves the person edited actually grateful: he could take a flabby argument and find within it the nugget that the author had missed.

'The paper', wrote Roland Bird, in his Crowther obituary, 'achieved its unity of expression and content from the presence of like-minded people who tried to absorb, by some sort of osmosis, the principles and practical methods that Crowther applied to his own work – the simple, utterly clear prose, the perfect analysis and the solution in words of one syllable. This was Crowther's style, and his colleagues did their best to emulate it.'[3]

His wit and his ability to bring it out in others was also integral to the paper's success. When Professor C. Northcote Parkinson sent in a long essay proving – with full statistical and mathematical backup – that 'work expands so as to fill the time available for its completion', it was thoroughly subbed and drastically shortened. After publication in the paper it was issued as an *Economist* pamphlet; later, Parkinson added other essays to create a best-selling book. Crowther had inserted a footnote to explain why this new law was being called 'Parkinson's Law', for of course anonymity forbade any mention of the writer's name. The footnote simply read 'Why? Why not? –Editor.'[4]

It was under Crowther's editorship that Andrew Boyd picked up the tradition of Eric Gibb and developed the light-hearted article full of learned and slightly dotty information. 'The medievalists will have their hour when the International Court hears the dispute between Britain and France over the Ecreho and Minquier islets, which lie between Jersey and the French coasts; for this dispute goes back some 750 years, to the French conquest of Normandy in 1204. In 1682 a distinguished Jersey man described the islets as "being of noe use at alle"; but his fellow-islanders have taken a very different view.' There followed an explanation why this case was unlikely to create any precedent which would bind other nations. 'But when the Attorneys-General of the United Kingdom and Jersey travel together to The Hague to plead their claims to the Pipettes, Gross Tete, La Vieille, Les Maisons, the Tas de Pois and a host of other charmingly named rocks, they will at least be setting a example of respect for international law in small things as in great. And if the Indian, Brazilian, Russian, Chinese and other judges of the Court are so bemused by the dog-Latin of the parchments on which much of the case turns that they deliver a judgment which seems unfair to British eyes, responsibility for the confusion can be placed squarely on King John, who originated the whole affair by losing Normandy and who, as every schoolboy knows, was a Bad King.'[5] (This piece was reprinted in full nearly two years later when the International Court was holding further hearings about the islets, to prompt 'some reflection on the speed – if that is the right word – at which the Court is accustomed to move'.)

The daft aspects of Englishness so beloved by Anglophiles were something Boyd was particularly good at pointing out. A review of *A Dictionary of English Weights and Measures: From Anglo-Saxon Times to the Nineteenth Century* began: 'Four-letter men were our forefathers. Never more so than when measuring things. With a bind and a bing, a fatt and a flyk, a shid and a swod and an unch. Meaning 250 eels, 8 cwt of lead, 4 bales of unbound books, a side of bacon, 4 feet of firewood, a bushel of fish, and either an ounce or an inch. They poured their wine by the aume or the fust, and cut their cloth by the goad – not to be confused with the gawd, which was a measure of steel. Their nook was not cosy; it covered 20 acres. Their idea of a glen, on the other hand, was either a bunch of teasels (in Essex and Gloucestershire) or 25 herrings. Take 15 glens and you had a rees. Take two pokes, and what you got was a gybe. Not that they ever agreed how much wool should go into a poke, or whether it should not rightly be a pook, a poik, a powk or a pock. But 240 dishes of lead were undoubtedly a boot, 28 lb of wood were a toad, a pint was of course a mugg, and a kade was a thousand sprats, though this could also be a gag.'[6]

Under other editors Boyd and some like-minded colleagues were to introduce literate frivolity into the paper where possible and particularly at Christmas, where spoofs and games and mock quizzes came in over the years. Another piece of harmless fun which he used to perpetrate in collusion with his friend Gordon Lee was to introduce rude words covertly into the paper.

Another book review by Boyd provided them with the opportunity to get 'bugger' in for the first time. So levity became enshrined as part of the paper's tradition, later to distinguish its covers, its captions, its headlines and, of course, its cartoons.

Crowther was such a towering figure, and he was there for so long, that hardly anyone had any consciousness of the paper before him, so he tended to get the credit for what in many cases his predecessors had made of the institution. But as the articulator of the paper's ethos he got it exactly right. However much the paper might preach about market forces, it was always, from the time Layton took over, a benevolent employer; pensions were paid to staff without any prior agreement; widows were given modest help; assistance was given to the ill and allowances made for them. And Crowther himself was personally kind. When Margaret Cruikshank's husband was ill and she was still coming to the office, Crowther would pick her up on his way in every morning. One journalist allegedly was given a job because she arrived in his office heavily pregnant and burst into tears. Crowther showed concern for sick children, and when he heard that Gordon Lee, then a new statistical clerk, was interested in the American Civil War, he borrowed some of his brother's book collection for him. When, around the same time, he heard that the then-unknown young man George Steiner had suffered an academic set-back, he created for him a temporary place in the foreign department, where Steiner hugely enjoyed himself in, for instance, castigating Picasso for his Marxist leanings in an article entitled 'THE CLAWS OF THE DOVE' while becoming a close friend of the staff Trotskyite, Daniel Singer.

Crowther continued the process of making *The Economist* an unusually agreeable place to work; as a rule, people helped each other to get the final product right, rather than indulging in rivalry. Rows there have been over the years, some of them vicious, but they have almost always been on points of principle. The institution does not easily lend itself to intrigue or back-stabbing.

Yet brilliant though Crowther was as an editor, he was never entirely content in the job. Boredom was to dog him on and off throughout his career. It had caused him problems at school, it had tormented him in Part I of his Tripos, it was a serious problem during parts of his wartime service and it was setting in as early as 1944 when he first began to hanker after outside activity.

The first episode was his request to the board to allow him to accept a directorship of the Commercial Union insurance company. 'I spoke on the telephone to Lord Moore [later Lord Drogheda] on May 22nd', noted Layton. 'He saw possible grounds for criticism, but did not feel sufficiently strongly to wish to influence the board.' Neither Guy Dawnay nor Eric Gibb had objected. 'My view, which I expressed to Geoffrey Crowther, is that my own membership of the Board of the National Mutual was an advantage', wrote Layton.

> It brought me in weekly touch with Keynes and Falk, both of whom are extremely valuable critics and contacts. The fact that it is a mutual society removed any possibility of taking advantage of market fluctuations of its shares. I had been a member of the board before accepting the *Economist* editorship. This case was, therefore, slightly different but not sufficiently so to make me feel any strong objection to G.C.'s proposal on grounds of association with a commercial enterprise which might come under criticism by *The Economist*. I did, however, tell G.C. that membership of the board did tend to involve the editor in a more detailed contact with City affairs than may be desirable in view of the very extensive field for *The Economist* in general politics, social and economic topics. I felt that G.C. ought to keep a close watch on this, and if the call on his time was too great, he should resign.[7]

(Drogheda was to say many years later that when Bracken heard about this he was furious and he never trusted Crowther again.)

'This is a purely personal note', wrote Crowther to Layton a couple of months later. 'You have referred twice recently to the possibility of my being tempted away from *The Economist*. I think you can set your mind entirely at rest about that. I find it very difficult to imagine anything for which I would willingly leave the editorship of *The Economist*, certainly not either the life of a company director or that of a Fleet Street prima donna.' But he did hope to increase his income.

> I never know whether to say that I have expensive ambitions or not. On the one hand I do not aspire after more than reasonable bourgeois comfort. If I could educate my children [there were six, one boy went to Eton, one to Winchester], have a simple place in the country, do a certain amount of travel, buy the books I want and save something for my old age, I should be quite content. But on the other hand, with twentieth century taxation, this simple catalogue requires a great deal of money.
>
> I am not, however, either discontented or impatient.

As for the future, he could foresee such prosperity for *The Economist* that 'there might be some more for me. And since even Quakers are mortal, there may, at some future date, be a need for directors of the Daily News Ltd – by which time the Board of *The Economist* may not consider it pollution to admit a connection. So I can foresee the possibility, by the time my children reach the expensive age, of such further modest increase of my already large income as to make me entirely sure that I shall never want to leave *The Economist*.' And of course Peggy, his wife, would have quite a lot of money some day.

> As for *The Economist*, perhaps I give the impression of desiring infinite expansion for it. That is not so at all. It would entirely lose its character if it ever became too big a business to escape from one man's intimate control. I would like to see it on such a basis of prosperity that it could attract and retain the best brains and for that I think it is reasonable to hope for an increase in the turnover of the business to about £100,000.[8]

In 1945 Crowther was asked to join the board of a new subsidiary of Barclays Bank, to be known as Barclays Overseas Development Corporation. It would take very little time, he explained to Layton. 'In some of the cases I refer to you (e.g. the parliamentary candidature), I am honestly on the margin of indifference. In this case, which I have thought over for a week, I want to accept.' The bank wanted him 'because I could apply knowledge of world economic tendencies to the particular problems of primary-producing countries'. Conversely, 'regular contact with the facts of economic life could hardly fail to be useful to the paper'. The fee did not concern him but he would enjoy visiting the parts of the world where the corporation would operate.

It might be argued that acceptance 'would be an improper thing for the Editor of *The Economist*. In view of the nature of the Corporation's objects, I don't think it would.' Although it was a pity that it was attached to just one bank, nonetheless the Governor of the Bank of England was anxious that Crowther should take it on. 'I think the Governor's approval – indeed, as I gather, rather more than approval of my name – really covers the point . . . I want to do it because it is interesting, because it will yield information of value to the paper, because it will bring me some personal benefit and because it will not be very burdensome on my energies . . . I don't think this is a matter which need come formally before the Board of *The Economist*, since a directorship is not an "employment", for which I am under a contractual obligation to seek approval. Nevertheless, I am sending a copy of this letter to Garrett [Moore].' He had, he assured Layton, taken to heart his admonition of the previous April about the use of his time. Three of his activities would be coming to an end by the end of the year: *Trans-Atlantic*, which would be ceasing publication; the Railway (London Plan) Committee, whose report was in draft; and Chatham House, where he would not seek re-election to the council. Other than that, he had occasional lunchtime meetings on advisory councils for the Home Office, the Ministry of Fuel and Power and Commercial Union. Unmoved by all this eloquence, Layton successfully discouraged Crowther from taking the job.

In 1947, Crowther, who by now had built up a substantial shareholding in *The Economist*, became a director, 'without, of course,' said Layton, 'creating a presumption that the editor should ever become *ex officio* a member of the Board'.

Crowther's acquisition of more and more outside interests proceeded steadily (at the peak of his post-editorial career, he held forty directorships) and he chafed at any restrictions. In a mid-1955 letter to Layton, he explained his state of mind. He had until quite recently expected to continue as editor for another few years, then intending 'to make way for a man fifteen or twenty years younger and, so far as *The Economist* is concerned, retire from the scene'.

> But more recently I have come to believe that this would be the wrong course – for three reasons. First, I am sorry to say (it is a confession of failure) that I know of no young man, on our own staff or elsewhere who looks to me as if he be the right man in a few years' time. Secondly, I find that the more I contemplate leaving *The Economist* and trying to find something else to do, the more horrified I am by the prospect. I don't want ever to have any other main job. And thirdly, it would be impossible just to hand over my job as it now is to someone else. Since I have grown up with it, and since I am not the worrying type, I scramble through most weeks without too much wear and tear. But I fear that anyone coming new to the job would find it a great strain. And, of course, scrambling is not good enough.

He was now responsible for far too much. 'In the old days, when *The Economist* was a very small show, the editor was also always the chief executive of the business. I inherited the position and have kept it. Though the responsibility of the job has perhaps not grown, the time-consuming elements undoubtedly have, and I find nowadays that I am far too busy to do my job as editor well. I no longer have all the time an editor should have to think or to read. My editorial colleagues have to make appointments to see me, instead of dropping in at any time (as used to be the case) to talk over a problem or the line to be taken.'

So the job of editor should be divorced from that of chief executive. Nobody ought to try both to be the effective head of a business with 160 employees (mostly in the Economist Intelligence Unit) and a turnover of £500,000 and also to supervise with the necessary care an output of 50,000 words a week. '(Let me parenthetically deal with the criticism – which I know is made – that my busyness arises from the purely extraneous things I do, having no connection with the paper. This is not so. No editor should be a hermit and to get out and about is an essential part of his job. I have done no broadcasting and very little public speaking for some years, and have not served on any official committee (all of which are useful things to do). My directorships burden my time only – or almost only – to the extent that they limit the number of free lunch dates. I don't think anybody holding my job could well do less outside the office than I do; I ought to get out much more than I do.)' Layton underlined 'much more than I do' and added in pencil '?But for *Economist* purposes'.

Crowther wanted to resign the editorship and keep the job as chief executive: 'I am quite sure that this is the right way round.' His negative reasons were 'that I feel nearly played out as an editor, in the strict sense of the word. Editing a paper like *The Economist* is not physically as arduous as editing a daily paper. But I think that it is, over time, mentally more exhausting. It is unremitting. There are so many subjects to keep abreast of; and unless one is ready to accept opinions ready-made, it involves so much thinking, the most exhausting of all pastimes.'

> I confess that often I find the weekly effort of mind wearisome, and observe myself resisting the need to make my mind up. I do still watch very closely what goes into the paper, but nearly all the writing I do nowadays is writing sentences and paragraphs into other people's work. I rarely find the time or energy to write something of my own and still more rarely am I pleased with what I write. Nor do I think I could recapture the pristine rapture by dropping everything else . . . In short, I am stale. Sixteen or seventeen years is probably as long as anyone can do this job well.

The positive reason was that, although he could not see how anyone could relieve him substantially of the administrative or representational side, 'there is somebody available, in the person of Donald Tyerman, who is fully capable of taking on the specifically editorial responsibilities, who could carry them better than I am nowadays able to do, and with whom I would be quite willing to divide my job in the conviction we could work together intimately and fruitfully'.

(Naming Tyerman creates one embarrassment for me. For if the editorship is to be vacant, it is only fair that my present deputy, Roland Bird, should have an opportunity to state his claims, if he wished to do so, which is not certain, and it would be wrong of me to queer his pitch in advance. But I must frankly say, first, that he would be extremely difficult to replace in his present job, and secondly that, though he has always behaved towards me with the most perfect loyalty, to put him in as editor with me as chief executive would be to exclude me from the paper far more than I wish or could stand. There is not, between him and me, the same interlocking of temperaments and capacities that there is between Donald Tyerman and me.)

Crowther would, he added, like to take a sabbatical year and then 'I think there would be plenty for me to do here. Nor do I mean simply in supervising the management departments and the Intelligence Unit (though there is much more to be done in both directions than I am now able to do). I should definitely not propose to disinterest myself in the editorial contents of the paper. I should hope to write for it more often than if I were less preoccupied with editing what other people write. The new editor would have the responsibility and must therefore have the final say about what goes in – including my own contributions. But I envisage myself as being in much the same position as what the Americans call the publisher.' The clause placing on the editor the duty of consulting the board when required to do so 'would be my mandate'.

He wanted also to be useful to the paper in 'the higher representation. At present our contacts are excellent at the second and third levels of industry and politics, but we are not as closely in touch as we might be with the people at the top, who really know what is happening in the world. This is the sort of work that only the head of the business – the editor or the publisher – can do.' He had been neglecting this and would hope to repair that neglect, to get out and about more.

'The usefulness of all this to the paper would, of course, depend on the right relationship with the editor. But if Donald Tyerman were editor I am as sure as one can ever be in advance that it would work well.' Although in 1952 Crowther had thought that someone else could be appointed associate or managing editor, he was now convinced such an arrangement would not work. 'The job of editing a journal of opinion is something of a seamless garment; it cannot be done at all without attending to all the details; and the man who in fact does the work has the responsibility and should have the authority and the credit. If there were two editors one of them would inevitably be bogus. If (as I devoutly wish) I can hand over the detailed work [these words were underlined by Layton with a note saying "This is wrong"] to someone else, I am entirely content that he should have the title and the privileges.'

This change had to happen now because Crowther needed a long break, he thought Tyerman was available and he felt 'personally at the watershed. With some such arrangement as I propose, I think I should be happy to go on being responsible for the paper and the business for an indefinite number of years.' But he could not go on as he was now. He would have to go. 'I would like you to look upon the proposal, as I do, not as a means by which I can run away from *The Economist*, but as a means by which I can stay with it for the rest of my working life.' Most of his time would be given to *The Economist*.[9]

Crowther, as in most of his dealings with Layton, got his way. Tyerman rejoined the staff on 1 January and formally took up the job of editor on 1 April 1956. He was delighted at last to be an officially gazetted editor. He had been cruelly disappointed twice in not being promoted to editor from the *de facto* editorship of *The Times*, which he had repeatedly exercised while ranking only as deputy editor. He had done his work there with distinction, bringing to it all the clarity of mind he had learned at *The Economist*. One colleague, John Pringle, decided later that some *Times* directors had thought that he was 'somehow too "uncouth" to be editor . . . One of them even invited him to dinner to observe his clothes and table manners – and then rang to let him know his conclusions!'[10] Another, Louis Heren, concluded that the *Times* proprietors had seen Tyerman 'as a kind of alien . . . they wanted the editor to wear the habit – Homburg hat, dark clothes and a grave demeanour – and to subscribe to their version of enlightened conservatism. Tyerman did not fit the part. He was too much of a Yorkshireman; despite his poor shrivelled legs, he was a bull of a man, pugnacious and forthright. His round face with its short nose and bold eyes did not suggest that he was a liberal Tory and an Establishment man. It could redden with anger or exasperation when a leader writer or correspondent was unwilling to oppose the Establishment view. His throaty voice also changed with his mood, but he could smile warmly and was generous with his congratulations when a job was well done.'[11]

Most journalists liked and admired Tyerman. He was a member of the Reform Club, but preferred to eat in Soho, where the company and conversation were often boisterous and lubricated with much wine. His Tuesday lunch club, which he had begun in the late 1940s, had such 'regulars' as Isaac Deutscher, John Midgley, David Low and Barbara Ward.

Some people said that Tyerman drank too much, but there was no sign of this in his writing. He was often found snoozing at his desk in the early afternoon, but he worked long hours. Passed over when Barrington-Ward died, Tyerman had kept *The Times* going loyally under the editorship of the ailing stop-gap, William Casey, who often left Tyerman to do all the work for days on end. Tyerman had, said Pringle, 'the responsibility without the position . . . He had to try to carry out Casey's policy while at the same time proving to the directors that he could do better. Eventually the strain told on him too and he became increasingly irritable. I was Donald's friend and sympathised deeply as I watched him drag himself to the conference room each night on his crutches, his powerful arms and chest in painful contrast to his withered legs, his heavy face scowling with determination.' In 1952 Tyerman was passed over again, this time in favour of William Haley, and a couple of years later, to Crowther's distress, Tyerman was rejected for the editorship of the *News Chronicle*. There is no doubt that part of Crowther's plan was the desire to give Tyerman some compensation for his disappointments.

Louis Heren was one of those who believed that *The Times* missed an opportunity, for Tyerman 'was a tough and talented journalist who could have exploited Barrington-Ward's partial break with the past'. Heren believed he could have been another Barnes if not a Delane: 'His physical disability prevented him from moving freely in political society, but Barnes had created the paper without moving far from his desk. Nor did drink affect his editorial judgment. *The Times* became the "Thunderer" under him, and Tyerman was capable of thundering. His mind was open to new ideas, and his enjoyment of the company of the young kept him in touch with the rising generation. His interests and imagination seemed to be as limitless as theirs.

This may have scared the proprietors; as did some of the bright young men he brought on to the paper, and who left soon after his eventual departure. On Tyerman's sixty-fifth birthday I attended a rather grand luncheon given him by an admirer. It was a large party because most of the guests were men he had launched into successful journalistic careers. The paper would have avoided some of its troubles if he and they had not left it.'

Among the journalists whom Tyerman so notably helped either to get started or to go down the right path were Henry Fairlie, James (now Jan) Morris, Peregrine Worsthorne and John Midgley. And in many people he inspired ferocious admiration and affection. On *The Economist*, with the existing staff, reactions were rather different. They were set in their ways, the majority having no experience of any editor except Crowther, and several of them could see only that an exceptionally brilliant mind had been replaced by one that by comparison seemed pedestrian; that where Crowther never wasted a word, Tyerman was prone to write discursively, and that where editorial meetings had been breathtaking because of Crowther's instinctive appreciation of the core of any argument, discussions were less stimulating and the whole event lacked the old sparkle. Where Crowther's intellectual slot machine had worked perfectly and instantly, Tyerman sometimes doubted and agonised. He was written off as second-rate by several of his more senior new colleagues, trained to measure an editor's effectiveness by comparison with Crowther. It became clear, too, that Tyerman had not been given the job on the same terms as Crowther.

However, Crowther was happy, for Tyerman loyally and uncomplainingly carried out the terms of their agreement. In February 1957, after returning from a long time away, Crowther wrote to Layton that 'this is perhaps a convenient time to report that the regime of consultation between the editor and the managing director has begun well and is working satisfactorily. I make a point of being here on Monday mornings for the editorial conference and on Thursday mornings to read the proofs, and though I have no fixed times in between, there are plenty of opportunities for talking to Donald. He shows me the drafts of leaders in which I am interested, or where he is in doubt.' And Crowther had begun writing again.

Crowther now wanted to join the board of Hazell Sun Ltd and perhaps that of Spicers, the paper firm. What would the *Economist* board think? He wrote a defensive letter a few days later. He had decided against Spicers and 'let me make it quite clear. In saying that Monday and Thursday mornings were my only fixed times at *The Economist*, I didn't mean to imply that they were the only times that I was to be found there. On the contrary, I am there when I am not anywhere else', almost certainly half his time. His other commitments took very little time: Commercial Union, the Cotman Investment Trust, Trust Houses, the Encyclopaedia Britannica in London, the Britannica in Chicago; Hazell Sun would take only two afternoons. He admitted, however, that the Central Advisory Council for Education, which was just one full day a month, might require more time, and he had obligations to a few other educational bodies. By mid-1958 even Crowther realised he was overstretched. He ceased to be managing director, becoming instead deputy chairman of the board, with some executive responsibilities for which he was generously paid. By then he had almost completely dropped out of editorial concerns, and Tyerman was left to run the paper his own way.

Alastair Burnet, who joined the paper in 1958, was one of those who admired Tyerman's great abilities as a newspaperman. Crowther was never primarily a newspaperman: he was interested in ideas. He saw *The Economist* as a pulpit, a journal of his opinions, a 'viewspaper'; indeed, he hated it to be called a newspaper. Tyerman, however, loved the whole process of bringing out the paper, from beginning to end. He cared about the ideas, the writing, the appearance, the typography and the people. He loved the company of other newspapermen, whom Crowther liked to avoid. Crowther liked 'champagne' people; he took against plodders. Tyerman enjoyed getting the best out of everyone.

In his valedictory article in 1974, Alastair Burnet referred to the paper in his own time as editor as having been 'conducting itself according to the inspiration and many of the ideas given to it by Walter Layton and Geoffrey Crowther, and according to the methods chiefly instituted by my immediate predecessor Donald Tyerman... The end of Crowther's editorship co-incided with the ending of the age of successful, individual editorships in British weekly journalism. Crowther, Kingsley Martin, and Wilson Harris, each in his way, personified the best of the weekly papers at a time when they were read for their originality. What Tyerman saw was that no paper could rely on having a succession of Crowthers; so, building on the paper's growing advertising revenue, he steadily increased the staff and the scope of the paper's interests, which in turn increased the circulation. He introduced a cover which was designed to attract attention; he pushed ahead with illustrations; but, again, it was the issues that mattered.' Burnet cited Suez and the recommendation to vote Labour in 1964. 'But above all he has encouraged young people throughout his life; he thereby secured for the paper a young, and able, staff.'

CHAPTER L:

Learning new ways

70,000 READERS — BUT WHO?

Statisticians and economic eggheads? Not a bit of it. Business and professional men with heads screwed on. Politicians with ears to the ground.
Investors looking ahead. People, busy people, who want to know just what is
happening in the world and why, and what is going to happen *next*. Ordinary
people – and not so ordinary. Not excluding Prime Ministers and Presidents. And many of them attach such importance to seeing *The Economist* in
a hurry that they pay £10 a year or more to have the air edition flown to
them each week – did you read a lead feature article in *Life* last March about
consternation in the White House when President Kennedy's air copy failed
to arrive? (There was consternation at *The Economist* too when we read about
it!) *Extract from 1963 sales leaflet*

By the time he handed over to Tyerman in 1956, Crowther had achieved his
main editorial objectives: the radical improvement and substantial development of American Survey, the World Overseas and the Business World.

Writing in 1943, when the paper's circulation was for the second time
about to exceed 10,000, Crowther's estimation was that after the war it would
be possible to regain most of the lost sales in Europe and overseas. 'With
some luck and with the assistance of air mail editions, etc.', circulation might
reach, but was unlikely to go beyond, 15,000 weekly. In fact circulation
growth was breathtaking, from 10,396 in 1943 to 17,744 in 1945 and then
almost doubling within two years. By 1956, when Crowther handed over to
Tyerman, it had reached 55,175.*

*Important milestones were to be passed when circulation exceeded 100,000 in 1970, 250,000 in
1984 and 500,000 in 1992.

As editor and manager after 1945 Crowther had coasted on his own brilliance and the paper's solid foundations, but from the mid-1950s onwards, as Tyerman was bringing the editorial side into a new and competitive age, *Economist* management was facing similarly fundamental changes. In *The Economist* as in Britain, management had been an occupation for amateurs. Other than Crowther, there was no new blood on the board until 1958 (although Roland Bird stood in as Bracken's alternate).

At its meetings, the board busied itself with minutiae. In October 1949 it sanctioned an expenditure of £1,500 on sales promotion; in December 1950 it was agreed that the company's Hillman Minx car should, for an experimental period of one year, be made use of by a circulation representative and for occasional visits to the provinces. In March 1952 circulation was going up so pleasingly along with printing and paper costs, that Crowther persuaded the board to agree to a 25% increase in advertisement rates. In the same year, he got their permission to undertake a complicated re-negotiation of commission rates, which had become far too high in the light of the increased advertising revenue.

Brendan Bracken had resumed his nominal position as managing director in 1947, though for most purposes he confined himself to signing cheques and baiting Geoffrey Crowther, who as editor did much of the managerial work. After taking over from Bracken in 1956, Crowther spent much of the next few years either travelling, working on his education report or adding to his business commitments. His interest in actually managing the paper was minimal; he just wanted to stay a central part of the organisation. Once acclimatised to the singular culture of *The Economist*, it becomes very difficult to leave.

In 1993, in his goodbye speech, Rupert Pennant-Rea observed that having been appointed editor in 1986, he had realised to his distress that this condemned him to having to leave *The Economist* at a relatively early date, rather than stay around and be wheeled out of the building when he grew too old to be useful. Layton and Crowther saw no such imperative; both of them died in office.

For practical purposes, Layton played little more than a nominal part in proceedings after 1945. Occasionally prudence or punctiliousness led him to exercise some kind of rein on Crowther's grand plans, but usually admiration and affection for a man whose gifts he regarded with awe inclined him to let Crowther have his head. One of the paper's biggest problems was that, corporately, it felt the same way. Crowther was a figure of legendary authority, and it was difficult for anyone to face the truth of the emperor's managerial nakedness.

Alastair Burnet once described *The Economist* as having been run by Crowther from the back of an envelope in his pocket and turned into an organisation by Tyerman. On the management side, the Tyerman equivalent was Peter Dallas Smith, an energetic moderniser and a highly intelligent enthusiast who did much to drag the paper into the second half of the twentieth century, before making some errors that had dramatic consequences and made him scapegoat for the board.

Peter Dallas Smith, who had been a lieutenant-commander in the Royal Navy, joined the paper after the war. When Gilbert Layton retired as manager in 1951 he was replaced both by Dallas Smith and by Gerald Andrews, husband of the librarian, who had joined as a cartographer before the war, and had spent some time managing the Intelligence Branch: they called themselves 'the joints' – short for joint managers. During the war Andrews, a major in the Royal Marines, had suffered a permanent injury to his leg and Dallas Smith had lost one of his. *Economist* folklore tells of the occasion when in the late 1950s the Ministry of Labour demanded to know if the paper was employing the appropriate disabled quota: it was informed that the editor (Tyerman) and the joint managers had only two good legs between the three of them. Dallas Smith and Andrews shared an office and sat opposite each other, got on extremely well and divided up the work amicably, Andrews being particularly good with production while Dallas Smith was the man of ideas.

There were several other ex-servicemen, mainly naval, on the post-1945 staff. Reggie Forty, a lowly secretary before the war, had returned with heightened status after becoming a naval lieutenant-commander. He was to take over from Gilbert Layton as the company secretary in 1957, when Layton retired completely, and to keep the job for almost thirty years, representing an important link with the pre-war paper and an object of general affection. George ('Whacker') Payne, an ex-petty officer and a pre-war naval boxing champion on the China station, who was taken on as a commissionaire and receptionist, became a much-loved court jester, given licence in those prim times to make loud, embarrassingly personal remarks in colourful language. Simultaneously rough and kind-hearted, Payne was plagued by a chest complaint caused by his having been sunk twice on the same West African convoy during the war, but that did not stop him carousing merrily with his friends from the post room and the garage, whom he described as 'hooligans'.

Howard Cox, who had spent the war placating frustrated advertisers, was inclined to intellectual hobbies such as astronomy and Pelmanism; but he liked going out to night clubs with the occasional colleague, where he sometimes performed spontaneously, and with skill, on the piano. He aroused resentment among his staff by his mystifyingly unfair treatment of John Thorne, who had been a prisoner of war in Germany and was one of the paper's best-ever salesmen. Cox was retired early in 1961, after a fiasco over a visit to America; going over on the *Queen Mary*, he arrived in New York on a Friday and was back in the office on Monday, having flown home because he did not like his hotel room. He was replaced by N.A. Gaunt (called 'Tiny' because of his great stature), another ex-naval officer and part-time river policeman, who in his bearded maturity looked remarkably like Edward VII.

In October 1953, Harry Bernard, head of the company meetings department, retired after 33 years' service and was replaced by the popular Parry Jones. Gaunt recalled how Jones varied his technique in dealing with lost business according to the psychology of the individual.

> He would ring the chairman of the company, not the advertising manager. In one case it would be, 'Oh hello, George. It's Parry here. How are you? How's Grace? Good, fine.' And he'd ramble on and then say, 'Oh, by the way, George. I think there must have been some mistake. Your man hasn't put your company meeting in the paper. I took it upon myself to put it in because I knew you'd want it in. If it's wrong, well too bad, but I didn't want you not to appear and be upset about it.' George would say 'Oh thank you very much, Parry. I'll put that right straight away.'
>
> Then the second one would be, 'Is that you, you so and so? What the bloody hell do you think you're doing? What? Your damn fool of a manager didn't put the thing in. All right, I'll take jolly good care that everyone knows that you're too damned hard up not to put the thing in. Oh, you'd like to put it in. I don't think I can put it in now. It's too late. No, you've been buggering about. No, I'm sorry. Well, I'll try. I'll do my best. All right.' Crash.

Because of their shock value, he was a liberal sender of telegrams, which were known in the trade as 'Parrygrams'.

The European printing sagas of the 1950s illustrate the amateur/military *esprit de corps* of the time at its best. A series of crises were precipitated by printing labour disputes – the chronic post-war problem. Before 1939 printing problems had been caused by machines, not by labour. The paper had been printed by St Clement's Press from a very early stage: Chapman believed that in Bagehot's time it was composed at Russell Court, Strand, and machined at St Clement's under the auspices of a Mr Dagnall. However, when the 1928 deal was done with Brendan Bracken, it was agreed that his parent firm's printing company would take over, 'subject to the Board being satisfied that the contract is made on competitive terms'.[1] Board minutes and internal reports on the change-over to Eyre & Spottiswoode in February 1929 complain about delays and below-standard work, compounded by the demands made by the revamp of the paper in 1934 and a move from flat-bed to rotary printing in 1938, forced by rising circulation. There were many teething troubles; as speed increased, so did expenses, but with wartime constraints on size and circulation the paper reverted to flat-bed printing.

The May 1941 bomb drove *The Economist* back to St Clement's but, although all but one item of copy had been lost, the staff cobbled together an issue which came out on time. As circulation went over 16,000 in 1945, there was a return to rotary printing.

The first rumbles of labour troubles came in August 1946. The *News Chronicle* recorded *The Economist*'s failure to appear at its normal weekend publication time because of a refusal to work overtime by members of the Printing and Kindred Trades Federation: 'The editorial staff of the Economist knew last week of this overtime ban and purposely sent their pages to be printed several hours earlier than usual . . . In one department the day shift refused to handle the work left over by the night workers, and the work awaited their return on Friday night. Further difficulties occurred in getting out the paper during the weekend.'[2] However, the issue came out eventually.

The government, not the trade unions, was responsible for a loss of production in the following year: a coal shortage had turned into a coal crisis. 'The point has been made *ad nauseam*', pronounced Crowther, 'that unless fuel supplies were more strictly allocated between essential and unessential users, all users, necessary and unecessary alike, would eventually have to go without.'

> Some Ministers, it is believed, urged this policy of elementary prudence in the Cabinet. But they were overborne. Rationing would be unpopular;

restriction of supplies to less essential users would cause unemployment; it might even interrupt the sacred nationalisation programme. It was far better to leave it alone – after all, there might be a mild winter. Never was there a clearer case of improvidence meeting its reward. Yet there is no note of contrition, not a hint of humility, in Ministers' statements. The responsibility is still laid on the weather and on the reprehensible desire of the public to keep warm. God and the Common Man are to blame; Ministers' consciences are clear.

What really hurt was a government decree that all periodicals must suspend publication for at least two consecutive issues. By virtue of an agreement with the Periodical Trade Press and Weekly Newspaper Proprietors' Association, no distinction was recognised between the periodicals. 'The Association, being the usual restrictive-minded trade body, will not admit that any considerations of the public welfare equal in importance the interests of its larger members.'

> The Government's attitude is that to discriminate most outrageously between newspapers and periodicals is permissible, since there are several Associations; to discriminate between different classes of periodicals is out of the question since there is only one Association which has agreed to the blanket prohibition. So *The Economist*, the *Spectator* and the *New Statesman* must be treated on a dead level with the astrologers, the pornographers and the trash-mongers. The daily organ of the licensed victuallers can continue to appear; we must stop.

The government was about to achieve what Göring had failed to do, by causing *The Economist* to miss an issue for the first time. The instruction would be obeyed 'under protest. This is not a time to suppress the free discussion of economic policy.'[3] In the event the paper did not miss publication. The next two issues appeared as a page of the *Financial Times* and were subsequently reprinted in four-page format.[4]

In September and October 1950 there were two work stoppages caused by an intra-union dispute which prevented the compositors from setting the paper; but Gerald Andrews, then manager of the Intelligence Unit, saved the day by employing a piece of the Unit's equipment. 'The Economist', wrote an historian of journalism, 'became the first British paper to be produced wholly by Varityper and litho-printing. This proportional spacing typewriter was first employed in the production of a journal by a Florida newspaper, the *Leesburg Commercial Ledger*, a few years earlier, and later several American daily newspapers used this process during printing employees' strikes.'[5] Winifred Glover, who was artistic and used to varitype the EIU *Newsletter*, laid out and typed the two emergency issues in September and the four in October 1950. 'This emergency edition', wrote Crowther as a preface to the first one, 'has . . . been produced without any type-setting whatever. We are painfully aware that it is only a token issue, but we take some pride in being able to preserve the tradition in a week that marks our 107th birthday . . .'

> It is perhaps natural, that we, as the victims of the dispute, should feel aggrieved against the union, who were its initiators. But even apart from this natural bias, we think any fair-minded person would deem the course of action taken by the London Society of Compositors to be so devious and disingenuous as to deprive them of any right to public sympathy. We have no better friends than the compositors who set out pages week by week. But their Union leaders would do well to observe that it is possible to get along without any compositors at all.[6]

Having managed sixteen pages in the two September issues, duplicated by several different firms, in October the size increased to twenty-four. The last strike-breaking issue was varityped in London and printed in Brussels, where it could be done on larger paper, the full edition being flown back to London early on Friday morning. 'The arrangements in Brussels had been carried out by Mr Gerald Andrews and the Board expressed their great appreciation of his efforts and of those of all other members of the staff in surmounting the obstacles in the production of the paper arising from the printing disputes.' Some £17,000 was lost in advertising revenue alone.

Gerald Andrews was again the prime organiser during the next strike, which hit in early 1956, just after Tyerman became editor. John Midgley was sent backwards and forwards to Switzerland for seven weeks in February and March carrying copy to Roland Bird, who was *in situ* at a Fribourg convent called Les Petites Soeurs de Saint Paul, where the nuns' secular activity was printing. One of the pieces he carried with him was a Tyerman leader in two forms, the first to be used if Eisenhower decided to run for the presidency again, the second if he decided against. The news of Eisenhower's candidature arrived at Fribourg just in time for the press to roll. (*The Economist* prepares alternative leaders every time there is a general election, since

British elections are always held on Thursdays. On occasion it goes wrong. In 1951 four versions had been plated up and ready to go. At 1.30 a.m. on Friday morning, when only a few constituency results were available, but the trend seemed clear, the printers were instructed by telephone to run version C in both the airmail and the main edition, but the message was misunderstood and they put version D into the main edition.) *The Economist* lost some money on the 1956 strike, but less than it would have lost if it not appeared at all, and its circulation increased.

The position in 1959 was much more theatrical. As 'HOME THOUGHTS FROM ABROAD' later explained,

> We have not during the stoppage found any printer still working in this country (whether 'black' or 'white' in the disputing unions' eyes) able to produce a paper suitable or punctual enough for *The Economist*'s worldwide readership . . . We have therefore had to print abroad, with the British unions pertinaciously stopping bolt-hole after bolt-hole by appeals to continental solidarity, and with the British masters themselves not too happy about it.[7]

They had been expecting the strike this time and the best foreign-language speakers were primed and ready to go. Midgley had spent a month living in Fribourg waiting for the strike to start. Every week he would receive copy from London and get it set in type ready for printing if required. When the strike began, however, the British unions prevailed on the Swiss laymen who ran the convent's machine room to 'black' the operation. Gerald Andrews flew in to try to enforce the contract, but they proved unpersuadable.

As Midgley observed later, what was most interesting about *The Economist*'s reaction was that 'the one option we never considered was just saving our money and not appearing'. Andrews, Bird and Midgley sped off in different directions – to Barcelona, Paris and Copenhagen respectively. The first issue ended up being half-composed in Belgium, half-composed in France, and printed in Brussels.

Tiny Gaunt was found to speak French and was drafted in the following week when production was scattered over half-a-dozen locations in Paris during a heat wave. He remembered being with Roland Bird on the first floor of a corrugated iron shack, under instructions to cut some copy. (Back home, instructions to staff were as far as possible to make their copy cuttable at any sentence.)

So I was reading it through and cutting out this and that bit from a Rolls Royce financial report. 'What the bloody hell are you doing?' I said, 'Well, you told me to.' 'No, no, no, that's not the way you cut the bloody thing. Like that – cut out a paragraph.'

In the same week, having succeeded in getting the paper printed in Paris, Bird and Gaunt arrived at the transport firm to find that virtually everyone had gone on holiday. 'We were petrified – no vans to take them away.' Bird recorded Gaunt's reaction. 'Tiny's impeccable French: "Où est les bloody camions [vans], you bastards?"'

At one stage Midgley flew the lead plates from one blacked firm in Copenhagen to Antwerp, where he had found a man in a basement with a linotype machine. The unions caught up with Antwerp. Gaunt, who had gone back to England, returned to Antwerp on the Thursday and met Gerald Andrews, who said '"Tiny, it's Thursday morning and we haven't got a place to print."'

> It was a proper undercover operation. You just didn't tell anybody what you were doing. You didn't use the hotel exchanges because the unions got the hotel exchange girls to tell them what we were doing. We went up to a little place on the German border. It was a terribly hot day; the temperature was 98.5 degrees, stinking hot and we drove up to the German border and saw this chap called Bart who ran this little paper there and asked if he could do it. He said as far as the Unions were concerned no union was going to stop him or his men but he wasn't quite sure if he could work it in. Peter Dunbar, the art director, meanwhile had gone to Bruges to get some plates, some matrix and it was the wrong diameter for Bart's machine. In the end they managed to cut and alter the matrices to fit and they did it all right and we waited and it worked.

The 65,000 copies used to arrive in London paginated but unstapled and unstitched. Then they would be sent over to where Peter Dallas Smith had got a man in a back street in west London to put them together. *Economist* staff then wrapped and despatched individual copies to subscribers and, since the paper was 'blacked' by the wholesale distributors, got all the copies out by van, car, bike and any available means to the retail outlets.

When the crisis was over, the paper celebrated with a presentational breakthrough. 'The least we can do after our eight-weeks' tour of friendly printing works in nearer Europe', began 'FROM BLACK TO WHITE – AND RED', 'is to greet our readers and advertisers (and our own London printers) with a heartfelt "hello." For those eight weeks we have been, by no wish of ours, "black" in the eyes of the British printing unions, because we have had to be printed beyond their pale. This week, thankfully back with them in London, we are "white" again. But, on the cover, we have also seized the moment to go "red".'[8]

The red title, introduced in 1937 and dropped along with the cover when war broke out (the cover had returned in 1952), came back, complemented by other improvements in the use of space. It was one of several of Tyerman's innovations, which had included the replacement of the old Eric Gill masthead by a new version by the great engraver, Reynolds Stone. The aim was businesslike: the guiding purpose of the new format was to lighten *Economist* readers' load. 'This will go on being the aim as other changes are brought in later on – to make reading still easier, while at the same time increasing the services that busy readers have a right to expect.'[9]

(Changing technology has involved the paper in frequent innovations in its appearance. The unsung heroes and heroines of this are the graphics department, who have had to keep up standards while adjusting to ever-changing computer technology. In Tyerman's day the key designers were the art director, Peter Dunbar, and Pip Piper, who brought a welcome whiff of Soho into *The Economist*. Their successors, Mike Kenny and then Penny Grundy (and, for much of the period, the cartographer Richard Natkiel) coped with an increasing staff and a huge explosion in demand from editorial. Aurobind Patel, whom Andrew Knight poached from *India Today*, is a philosophical typographer, who invented a new typeface, Ecotype, for the paper's last major redesign in 1989.)

The Economist lost less than £7,000 in the 1959 strike, and at the next board meeting Crowther made special mention of the efforts of Gerald Andrews, 'who organised the printing arrangements abroad and established a temporary home in Brussels', thus keeping costs down. It was not quite Andrews's swan song, but within a couple of years his tendency to drink too much began to affect his work and he was eased out of the joint managership. He spent some time as the advertising supremo, concentrating on increasing overseas revenue, but when his wife became an alcoholic and then terminally ill, the slide accelerated and he died soon after her.

Meanwhile, Peter Dallas Smith was gaining in authority and struggling to shift the paper in a sensible direction despite resistance and neglect from the top. Well ahead of most British businesses, he brought in consultants to advise on efficiency and savings in the accounts and subscription departments, introduced departmental budgets and brought in extra revenue, for instance, through distributing *Scientific American*. In 1961 he had Marplan undertake research on the American market. In 1960 the circulation department, under the highly competent Terry Holder, was directed to push hard to increase sales overseas and Dick Dyerson was recruited to canvass for more circulation everywhere east of Dover. Although company meetings still provided an important part of the revenue for advertisements, and there was expansion into classified advertising sold over the telephone, Dallas Smith's emphasis was on attracting lucrative display-advertising. By 1962, he was pushing hard for more representatives overseas and putting his reputation on the line about priorities. 'Everything,' he wrote to Crowther, 'and above all our own confidence in the rightness of the decisions we are taking, depends on the growth of international display advertising. Domestically, our rates are high; internationally, they are not. More international advertising at a high rate is the only way I can see of breaking back into an expansionary spiral.'

Seeing that an expansion of advertising revenue required an expansion of international readership, Dallas Smith also threw his weight behind making editorial more international, but there problems arose with some of the editorial barons. In 1960 Tyerman had asked for opinions about whether the digest of contents, the home department or the Business World should have more space. 'The disagreements within the paper can, I believe,' wrote Dallas Smith privately to Crowther, 'be summarized by saying that Norman Macrae is root and branch against any expansion of the Business World at all. Roland is in favour of the Business World expansion but visualises the weight mainly being Home, while the managerial view is that the most noticeable imbalance in the paper at the moment is that the front is international and that the back is too national. We would therefore wish the weight of Business World expansion to be thrown overseas.'

> Donald's position in the midst of these three conflicting views is not an easy one. I believe it would become immeasurably easier for him to take a decision if he could have the advantage of knowing where you personally stand . . . Against a background of protracted but not always productive

discussions of these issues over some years now decisions would be welcome. Since no decision would be likely to please everybody the fact that what was decided was seen to have your support would not only be a consolation to the loser but a great source of support to the Editor.

By now Tyerman's position *vis-à-vis* his senior colleagues was worse than ever. Because he had come in without full authority, he had never established supremacy over the old guard; and now that Crowther was no longer interested in being much involved, Tyerman had the full responsibility without the power. 'With considerable trepidation, could I express one general belief', wrote Dallas Smith to Crowther. 'I know how well aware you are of the difficulty of Donald's position with yourself as his predecessor above him and overwhelmingly your own team below him. But it sometimes seems to me that his problems are made more difficult rather than easier by your own unwillingness to "interfere". I think that editorially the paper really needs very little of your time, but if when modest changes of direction are contemplated you could give Donald a clear indication of where you stand (while of course making your usual comments about his freedom to go ahead) I believe that it would greatly strengthen his position.'

Dallas Smith had put his finger on the nub of the problem, but Crowther continued to let matters drift. He seems also to have been suffering from the classic symptom of the retired great man, a sneaking desire that his successors should not build too successfully on his achievements. 'I have more faith than you in the future of *The Economist*', wrote Dallas Smith to Crowther in 1962, 'but am less experienced and, by an uncomfortably wide margin, less able. And I know that my ideas could be wrong. As I told you recently, if you left *The Economist* I would not want to stay. I need your confidence and clearly could not have it if we disagreed at all seriously over too wide an area.'[10] About to be appointed managing director with a seat on the board, Dallas Smith wanted to develop a proper structure for running the paper. 'It seems to me that there must be close working relationships between the "proprietor" (who is in effect yourself), the Editor, and the Managing Director. The lack of these close links at the top I take to be one of the main reasons why papers lose a real sense of purpose and direction even though they can seem to be successful for a time.'

> This is not to say that you as 'proprietor' should give a lot of time to *The Economist*'s affairs. We need an Executive Board below the present Board

level. We have discussed this and I think it is absolutely necessary. I visualise four regular members: The Editor, Roland, Gerald and myself, but with the possibility of co-opting Alastair Burnet or Brian Beedham. If, as I rather believe, Alastair should be given a special title, with at any rate some connotations of Crown-Princeship, then he should become a permanent member of the Executive Board.[11]

The memorandum went on to sketch out methods of ensuring managerial–editorial cooperation that presaged the structures painstakingly developed throughout David Gordon's time. In his ideas on management as in his ideas on where the paper should be going, Dallas Smith was supremely perceptive. But Crowther remained courteously evasive and the board continued to turn a blind eye.

Still, if Crowther did not help, he did not actively obstruct; and Dallas Smith was able to bring about massive change in the culture of the management side, particularly by recognising and developing the formidable talents of Michael Alderson. Alderson, ex-RAF, had joined in 1962 as an advertising-space salesman, recruited by Robin Ludlow, ex-army and by now a salesman cum assistant general manager, from space-selling for George Newnes. The new breed of space-salesmen were predominantly ex-servicemen: personable ex-officers, without any formal qualifications, often drifted into sales. Hugo Meynell, like Ludlow an ex-Sandhurst man, began his *Economist* career in the company meetings department and then gravitated to management in the same way. Alderson was given the Newcastle territory. It having been decided to publish a survey on north-east England, Tiny Gaunt took Alderson down to Dallas Smith to talk about prospects. Alderson predicted that he would be able to sell ten pages of advertising, and Dallas Smith was delighted.

> We came out of Peter's office and Tiny turned to me in the passage outside and said, 'That was very stupid . . . You and I know there is no way you are going to get more than 4 to 6 . . . He is going to be very disappointed.'
>
> My heart sank, but I went up to Newcastle and worked out a plan which took even me by surprise. I took a rather grand attitude: I called a meeting of advertising agents and told them that this is going to be the greatest thing, and by the end of the meeting even I was surprised at the enthusiasm amongst these people. They were getting excited about almost nothing.

Alderson then proceeded to visit the head of development in the north-east, a

Labour MP, and persuaded him to send to all the chairmen of companies that had moved to the region a letter he had drafted which 'said in effect that we welcome the fact that *The Economist* of all papers was going to throw a spotlight on the north-east, and how important it was for the whole development of that area that a paper of such power was going to do this'. However, for commercial reasons, the space they could allocate would necessarily depend on the number of advertisements, and we want the maximum coverage of this area we can get, so I do ask you, etc, etc. I got 21 pages of advertising from the north-east.'

Dallas Smith sent Michael Alderson to Harvard Business School, and on his return he shook up first advertising and then circulation from top to bottom. Disciples like Ludlow (who went from *The Economist* to be a Buckingham Palace official and then a head-hunter) and Robert Logan, who went on to be a super-salesman, still believe him to have taken *The Economist* from amateurism to professionalism in one stride. It was Alderson who built on Andrews's and Dallas Smith's first experiments with market research, and made his colleagues understand readership, as opposed to circulation, and grasp research as an aid to selling. He was the ideal person to fulfil Dallas Smith's ambitions for development overseas; he saw the point – which most editorial people did not – of building up a presence in even the most unlikely countries. As he put it, he could sell an advertisement by pointing out that, though *The Economist* had only five readers in Dahomey, they were the people that mattered there.

Alderson recruited and trained well: his two most notable young acquisitions were David Hanger, the cornerstone since 1968 of the paper's great success in attracting international advertising, and Clive Greaves, who was to spearhead the huge circulation and advertising breakthrough in the United States in the 1970s.

Dallas Smith's role in modernising management was largely lost on the editorial staff, but his success in bringing the Economist Building into existence was lost on nobody. Accommodation had long been a continual problem. After being bombed out of Bouverie Street in 1941, the staff were lent space at the *News Chronicle*, and during that period accommodation was found in Brettenham House*, just west of Aldwych. As the staff grew in size

---

*Brettenham House, 15 Lancaster Place, turned out, to *The Economist*'s surprise, to be built on the site of 6 Wellington Street, its first office back in 1843.

after the war, the place became intolerably overcrowded and editorial were farmed out for a few months to 162A Strand. Against the opposition of Moore and Bracken, Crowther acquired a lease of 22 Ryder Street, an apartment building which before the war had a rather dubious name; it had also housed Sir Basil Zaharoff, a millionaire armaments dealer of equally shady reputation. 'I cannot believe', wrote Bracken, 'that it is wise for a newspaper company to spend more than half of its capital on a thirty-eight year lease.'[12] At one of the first board meetings held there he remarked darkly: 'Mr Crowther is set on ruining this small company, which will never be able to pay the rent for these lush West End quarters.'[13]

The five-storey building in Ryder Street met the immediate need but, towards the end of the 1950s, with the continued expansion of both the paper and the Economist Intelligence Unit (EIU), redevelopment came under discussion. By 1960 the staff were dispersed over five buildings, and the decision was taken to acquire a site that extended well beyond the dimensions of No. 22 and to redevelop it, creating a much taller structure ringed by open space (the 'Plaza'). It was Crowther's idea and he told Dallas Smith to achieve it. Crowther made two main stipulations: the builder was to be McAlpine's, because Edwin McAlpine was Crowther's old school friend and Crowther was about to join the board; and he wanted an apartment on the top floor. (There were to be 15 floors and two basements.)

Dallas Smith was left free to look for an architect. It was his doing that Alison and Peter Smithson, the young 'new brutalists', as their envious rivals dubbed them, were chosen. At a time when neo-Georgian was fashionable, the Smithsons produced a minimalist design which was to bring fame to them and celebrity in architectural circles to *The Economist*. The Smithsons described the building as 'a didactic building, a dry building', and so it is. It has now been listed as a building of architectural significance, and on the whole, the inmates are happy with it, but it has the serious disadvantage of encouraging departmental divisions in a company in which there is already little mixing.

Dallas Smith was a superb project manager of a job of extreme complexity. He had to persuade a disparate group of occupants, who included Martin's Bank, Lobb the bootmakers and Boodle's club, to agree to have their buildings restructured or knocked down. The architects were delighted because he was a problem-solver, who understood plans and knew how to deal with planners, builders and *Economist* people. The result was a money-spinner for *The Economist*, which found itself in possession of property so valuable that periodically it questions whether it can afford to occupy it itself. Every time this question is raised there is a staff outcry. The *Times* staff were packed off to Wapping, Andrew Knight took the *Telegraph* staff to the Isle of Dogs, but the *Economist* staff are a collection of people with more clout and with a board that treats them with much respect, so they remain one of the few papers still based in central London. Yet they too have suffered for the building, first, by having to work in uncomfortable temporary accommodation above a soap-and-toiletries concern while it was being built in 1962–64, and then by the miseries they endured when it was refurbished in the late 1980s.

For the success of the project Crowther deserves a great deal of credit, and Peter Dallas Smith even more. Yet there were worrying aspects to the manner in which it was carried out. The board paid little attention, costs were greatly underestimated and the building itself was not finished because of an untimely lack of funds. Another problem was that success bred hubris, and this led to the fiasco of the Latin American edition, which could provide a fascinating case study in the deficiencies of post-1945 British management.

The long sad story begins at the January 1965 board meeting, when it was reported 'that the production of a digest in Spanish of selected articles from *The Economist* for distribution in Central and South America was being considered. The project was at an early stage of its development, so a fuller report could be made at a later stage.' Peter Dallas Smith, fortified by the success of his building, was behind this idea. The inspiration had come from the time he had spent in South America as a young naval officer before the war, when he became intrigued by Britain's long history of a special connection with Latin America, now rapidly disappearing. What tipped the scales for him was that the paper's American advertising agents, Mr and Mrs Robert Kenyon (not to be confused with Mildred Adams and her husband Houston Kenyon), were so sure of making a packet that they insisted on taking a 30% minority stake in the project, so he thought the financial base was secure.

Classic mistakes were made. International banks and businesses were asked in general terms what they thought of the idea, and all pronounced it excellent. The Economist Intelligence Unit were asked to undertake market research in July 1965, but because their charges were high, they were asked to do only a modest investigation.

Norman Macrae, who was in Latin America in July writing 'No Crisis on the Andes', had been asked to keep his eyes open. He produced a report saying that the idea was lunatic. 'I said, "I gather that you are going to send it all by subscription, using stamps. Any foreign stamp is always stolen by the postman in Argentina and Brazil, as they can sell it at eight times its face value. Anyway, Brazil speaks Portuguese."' Macrae suffered the fate of those who tell people what they do not want to hear, and was encouraged to stay out of it. Burnet was very new and did not want a fight over something he thought might lose around £20,000. Macrae prophesied £100,000; actual losses were more like £300,000.

In December Dallas Smith was reporting on encouraging responses from his trip to Mexico and the newly appointed editor, Norman Macdonald, was despatched in the spring to discover if the project was viable editorially. In May 1966 the EIU reported favourably and in December a £50,000-budget launch was agreed. At the April 1967 board meeting, 'Mr Norman Macdonald, reporting as Editor of the Latin American edition, said that on receiving the "go-ahead" in November last it set out to recruit good translators, but that in the intervening period there had been a policy change and the need had become one of getting men who were first class journalists, capable of sub-editing, producing original material and translating material into a Spanish acceptable in the Latin American countries.' He had also found correspondents in the principal Latin American countries.

There is a long history of stout opposition from *Economist* editors to the idea of having regional editions with different texts for different parts of the world, so Macdonald's announcement sounded like an astonishing breach of precedent. But oddly, because the thing was to be in Spanish, no one seemed to care. Burnet was not going to be able to read it, so he shrugged his shoulders and left the problem to management. The only realist around was the business manager of the new edition, David Jamieson, who warned Dallas Smith about six weeks before the launch that they were heading for disaster. Dallas Smith was at this time plunged into a printing crisis and he saw no way out other than to go ahead and hope.

At the company's annual general meeting in July 1967 Crowther reported the launching in May 'of a fortnightly edition of *The Economist* in Spanish, designed for the countries of Latin America. At this very early date all that can be said is that the initial reception has been more favourable than we dared hope.' By February 1968 he was taking fright. The paper's profits were already down by £75,000 on the previous year because of massive increases in costs, and the deficit on the Latin American edition was higher than expected. Crowther 'expressed the view that it was our main duty to protect *The Economist* itself and, in incurring such losses, we were not now fulfilling this charge. We must not let other ventures undermine this basic principle. The Latin American edition losses, running at the rate of £70,000 p.a., were excessively high and a price we could not afford to continue to pay, even for an agreed excellent product.' A realistic estimate must be produced and a decision taken as to whether the project was to continue beyond May or June if advertisement revenue did not increase so as to reduce the annual loss for the next financial year to below £30,000.

There were difficulties with printing, with bad debts and with late billing of subscriptions because of computer-programming problems, yet the Kenyons attended the board and were 'quietly confident that the outlook was good'. The Latin American edition had given *The Economist* a higher ranking with advertisers: 'the two papers were helping each other'. Tiny Gaunt, by then advertisement director, concluded that the Latin American edition target of £60,000 in advertising revenue was achievable.

The July 1968 board meeting was chaired by Crowther, with Bird, Lord Drogheda, Lord (Lionel) Robbins, Dallas Smith, Tyerman and Evelyn de Rothschild present and Burnet and Gaunt in attendance. (Pat Gibson of the *Financial Times*, who had replaced Bracken on the board in 1958 and was to remain for twenty years, was absent. Wise and experienced, he used to ask penetrating questions, but he carried out the the the *FT* principle of not interfering.) The meeting provides a classic example of how the late-1960s board operated, with Crowther for the first time facing a challenge to his authority from a Young Turk, de Rothschild.* 'The case for continuing publication was put by Mr Rothschild, who was of the opinion that it was wrong to consider the operation a failure after only eighteen months: he would prefer to judge its performance after, say, three to five years. He recognised that there was a limit to how much *The Economist* could go on investing in this operation but thought it likely he could persuade other City institutions or individuals to support it'; in exchange they would probably expect a share in the equity and full support from *The Economist*. The sales

---

*In 1965, of 63,000 'A special' shares, Crowther had 14,500, de Rothschild 7,200, Cadbury and his children 8,320.

potential had not been fully tapped: 'A new approach was needed to meet the special requirements of the Latin American temperament', perhaps by adopting local sales techniques. Two major mistakes had contributed to the heavy costs: 'First, printing in the United Kingdom, and second, the failure of the computer to run subscription renewals at the intended time.' These errors had been recognised by the proposals to print in Panama and go over to an addressograph. 'On the editorial side it would seem that the shift from syndication of *The Economist* articles to a majority of original material had had a good initial response from intellectuals and others both in Latin America and North America.' The report had said nothing about the costs of closure.

Drogheda was in favour of continuing and 'was of the opinion that it would be in the interest of the country and would add to the prestige of the Company'.

'Lord Crowther said that after deep consideration he had come to the conclusion that the venture should be closed down. He was gravely concerned about the further demands put forward in the memorandum put forward from the Editor of the Latin American edition, and he apprehended from his report that a serious departure from the original intent had taken place and further that this process was to continue.' It had been his understanding that the paper was largely to consist of syndicated *Economist* articles and not, as had transpired, mainly of original materials.

> This present composition of editorial content was unacceptable to him: he could see that there might arise a divergence of opinion between the two papers and that this might raise the very serious danger of *The Economist*'s reputation being undermined both editorially and financially. The same association in the Latin American edition's title was a powerful selling point and we must be on our guard that it should not be misused or misunderstood.
>
> It was of the utmost importance that the Editor of *The Economist* should exercise a positive control over the editorial content of this edition.

Crowther seriously doubted the optimistic figures being presented to the board. He felt that 'to go to the City on such a basis would be to invite potential investors to lose their money. He could not support such a move.'

Lord Robbins explained that 'he had been persuaded by Mr Rothschild's argument for the continuance of the journal, although his earlier thoughts had been that it would not be worth carrying on. However, he also shared the doubts of other members of the Board about the reliability of the figures and the editorial difficulties.' A decision was therefore deferred.

The following month there was a report of an encouraging advertising intake, but an annual loss forecast of £100,000 for the current year was still the best available estimate. Crowther feared the estimates were still very optimistic; Pat Gibson asked 'whether, if we continued, and if more cash were to be needed, it would be forthcoming. He thought it would be sensible to plan on a long-term basis and to take further future cash requirements, if any, into account. Were we prepared if necessary to face greater costs and losses than the forecast implied?' Crowther thought it would be possible to reach a final decision in a year, and de Rothschild said he could raise $60,000 from Brazil. City merchant banks would help, but they were expressing doubt about whether the forecasts were accurate.

> The Chairman asked whether it was right to continue to put resources of *The Economist* into the Latin American edition. Mr de Rothschild considered there was great scope in Latin America. The Chairman questioned whether this applied to our particular product . . . Lord Robbins found difficulty in choosing between the views of the Chairman and Mr de Rothschild. Could we be sure of obtaining support from possible outside shareholders? Mr de Rothschild was convinced that it would be wrong to kill the Latin American edition without having given it a fair trial run which, he considered, it certainly had not yet had.
>
> The Editor [Burnet], when questioned, said that for reasons principally concerned with the language problem he was not capable of accepting full editorial responsibility for the edition. The Chairman wondered whether the title could be changed so as not to identify the edition so closely with *The Economist*. He felt that such a decision would be necessary if the edition reached the stage where its continuance was assured. He would not want to insist on a change at this point.

Cancellation costs would be about £60,000.

An attempt to attract outside shareholders failed, and at a special board meeting in September Crowther said that, in spite of news of improving advertising and circulation revenue figures, 'if left to ourselves we should have to close. But he was being asked to extend the life of the publication a little longer by the Permanent Under-Secretary of State for Foreign Affairs, Sir Paul Gore-Booth, who had said that termination of publication at this moment would cause the Government acute embarrassment both in respect of Her Majesty's forthcoming visit to South America and the holding of a British trade fair in Brazil.' Gore-Booth would see if funds could be made available to subsidise the edition: Crowther's own view was that it should be continued until March, 'when the glimmer of hope that was now beginning to show might become stronger'.

Much dithering ensued over the the next few months. Roland Bird, who had temporarily taken over as managing director, drove home to the board the strain that the Latin American edition was placing on managerial resources, thus weakening the main paper. In January 1970 the board agreed to close down the edition.

Well before then, Peter Dallas Smith had fallen on his sword.

CHAPTER LI

Vision and reality

The fallibility of boards of directors? My goodness, yes. *The Economist* all the
time – Geoffrey absent more often than not, frying other fish, Drogheda
mischievously irresponsible because Geoffrey was boss, Rothschild backing
the wrong horses and then sacking the managing directors (Peter and now
Trafford) who rode them – and so on. Better be a journalist.[1]
Donald Tyerman, 1980

To this day it is arguable that the Latin American edition might have been a
success if given a proper chance. Certainly the blame for its failure should sit
as, if not more, heavily on the board than on Peter Dallas Smith, but no more
than most cosy gentlemen's boards of the period did *The Economist*'s have a
clear understanding of its duties. Crowther's idea of a successful board
meeting was one which he got through in twenty minutes. He was not a
reflective man: he dealt with problems only when they forced themselves
upon him, and he had little regard for the advice of others, since in the areas
which he respected he was the intellectual superior of everyone he knew.

Dallas Smith, like most of his managerial colleagues, was in love with the
paper and his errors were caused by trying too hard. He had always tried to
get through to Crowther that he saw himself as a number two, but as a *de facto*
number one he had no one to rein him in. His main weakness was his
tendency to trust people unreservedly. The problems with the Latin
American edition had been compounded by his starry-eyed attitude to the
advertising representatives in America, the Robert Kenyons. He had not only
believed in their bullish forecasts about Latin American advertising, he had
let through a contract with them for American advertising which gave them
enormous rewards for minimal effort. Roland Bird bought out the contract at
great expense when he took over.

Dallas Smith's final nemesis was a maverick trade unionist called David Back, a poacher whom, in an imaginative but suicidal attempt to resolve a printing crisis, he appointed gamekeeper.

The Economist was not tortured by printing unions for as long or as intensely as were most of the daily newspapers, but it had its own war of attrition. From the mid-1960s, for almost twenty years, board meetings were dominated by news of fresh printing disasters. In the early 1960s Dallas Smith had tried to interest Crowther in long-term solutions to the inadequacies of St Clement's, but Crowther had shown little interest: he did not want to face the problem that Dallas Smith identified – that when there was a conflict between the interests of the *Financial Times* and *The Economist*, St Clement's favoured their bigger customer.

In 1967, with Gerald Andrews's retirement, Dallas Smith had found himself in charge of printing, about which he knew nothing. He had cleverly, he thought, resolved major trade union problems at St Clement's by lending £10,000 to David Back, a most difficult but plausible union official, to enable him to turn entrepreneur and set up a warehouse operation in which *The Economist* would be stitched and distributed without union difficulties.

That year St Clement's gave up printing periodicals, and *The Economist* had to switch hastily to the Electrical Press at Harlow. They were the only firm who could take on the job, but their machinery and organisation were simply not up to it, and like every other printer they had labour troubles. During negotiations, Dallas Smith reported to the board in October 1967, he had had 'the able assistance' of Mr David Back, managing director of Graphical & Allied Developments Ltd, who had successfully intervened in Electrical Press's union problems. He had taken Back on to the staff, he reported, to run production, distribution and publishing. The board agreed that Back should be given the title of 'Production Director'.

Dallas Smith not only wanted to get the paper out, he desperately wanted to give editorial the diminishing deadlines that were demanded for a paper which, under Burnet, was much more news-orientated than before: Dallas Smith passionately believed that editorial needs were paramount. Knowing that the speed, cost and labour constraints created a circle that could not be squared, he believed the answer would come from the input of raw energy which he thought he had found in David Back.

The Electrical Press could not meet the paper's ever more sophisticated demands for faster times, higher volumes and colour as well as black and white printing. The board agreed, hastily, with its chairman, that negotiations should go ahead with what appeared to be the only suitable printer in southern England, the British Printing Corporation at Slough. Crowther, a major shareholder in BPC and its ex-chairman, declared an interest, yet pushed the deal along, mainly, it would seem, through impatience. De Rothschild's query as to 'whether in view of the length and importance of this contract, it was wise to proceed at this speed without first getting competitive quotations', was brushed aside.[2]

Within *The Economist* itself, Dallas Smith was seen as being in thrall to Back, whose behaviour was causing consternation throughout the organisation. It would be truer to say that, at a time when the Latin American edition was going on the rocks, he was clinging to Back as the only hope of preventing disaster on the printing front. Crowther was one of the few who appeared to have a soft spot for Back, but then he never had to work with him. Back's temper was frightful, and there are on record many choice examples of the abuse that colleagues had to endure when he was out of sorts: he had a tendency to use language that would have made Whacker Payne blush. His spontaneous late-night parties in the Economist Building were boisterous, and it was not only the puritans who felt that as an ambassador for *The Economist* he was a disaster. Nor was he thought to be putting the paper's interests before his own. Ultimately, in desperation, Roland Bird went to his old tutor, Lionel Robbins, the deputy chairman, and explained what was happening.

The board minutes record, in the elliptical manner of such minutes, what happened next. In January 1969 Crowther 'informed the Board that during December he had felt it necessary to intervene in a situation involving senior members of the management staff. After speaking to certain members of the board and to senior members of the editorial and management staff, he had decided that the managing director should take leave of absence for a period of about three months.'

> The Production Director had been informed that his behaviour could be construed as a breach of contract and a letter had been written to him by the Chairman cautioning him as to his future behaviour. Roland Bird had accepted responsibility for the administration over the next few months and would take over the circulation and publishing departments.

Next month Back resigned, explaining that he wished to devote more time to his own company. In giving up his *Economist* job 'he expressed the wish to continue the warehousing of the paper', which was agreed subject to proper performance. Further investment in this undertaking would be considered. Mr de Rothschild said he wished to declare his interest in this matter as he had been acting in an advisory capacity to Mr Back.

Peter Dallas Smith resigned, and Roland Bird spent two years as caretaker managing director *cum* undertaker. As well as paying off the Kenyons and winding up the Latin American edition, he navigated the legal and union minefields necessary to buy out the paper's contracts with Back. One consequence of the new printing contract with the BPC firm, Hazell's Offset, in Slough, explained Crowther delicately in the 1971 report and accounts, 'has been the termination of a contract with Graphical and Allied Developments for binding and warehousing *The Economist*, for which agreed compensation of £30,000 has been paid and provided for in 1970–71 accounts. As part of this arrangement we have disposed of our one-third.'

The natural successor to Bird in 1972 was Michael Alderson, now marketing director, who had become even more ambitious in his plans for the paper after being sent by Dallas Smith to Harvard Business School. But the job went elsewhere. Alderson was told by Crowther that it had been necessary to take on Ian Trafford to sort out the EIU, but that he would have little to do with *The Economist* itself; Alderson could continue to operate as normal. Initially, at least, that was the case, for between printing and the paper's various ancillary activities Trafford had plenty to occupy him; yet later that year, to his utter devastation, Alderson was fired by Crowther's successor, Evelyn de Rothschild, with a £20,000 pay-off and no real explanation. (Years later, his reflections concur with the observations of others: he was a driven perfectionist who for personal and professional reasons made a number of key enemies, and his homosexuality offended some of the old guard.)

The managing directorship went to Ian Trafford on the recommendation of Lord Drogheda. Trafford (Charterhouse; St John's College, Oxford; Middle East army service in the Intelligence Corps) had been recruited in 1951 by the great *Financial Times* editor and talent spotter, Gordon Newton. He spent some years as the *FT* industrial correspondent, and in 1957 moved over to run a new *FT* subsidiary called Industrial and Trade Fairs Ltd, whose successes included the British Exhibition in Moscow in 1961. He was an excellent organiser and a good motivator, and Drogheda clearly thought he was the man to sort out both printing and the Economist Intelligence Unit, which was now in trouble.

Trafford was entirely Drogheda's idea; no one else was considered. Crowther was then engaged in his last losing boardroom battle and had little time to think about *The Economist*, so he invited Trafford to lunch and promptly offered him the job. Happy with trade fairs, where he had been very successful, Trafford was reluctant to move, but Drogheda leaned on him; and no one told him what had happened to Dallas Smith or that there were hideously difficult and immediate problems to be dealt with.

In 1943, in a lengthy memorandum, along with many excellent ideas for improving the editorial content of the paper, Crowther had spelled out for Layton methods of increasing income substantially through spin-offs. He was always anxious to develop profitable ancillary activities on the back of the paper's intellectual and physical resources, with a view to making further expansion of the paper possible. By the late 1940s, these ventures included 'confidential letters', diaries, a bookshop and a greatly enlarged Intelligence Branch (now known as the Intelligence Unit).

The successful confidential letter was *Foreign Report*, produced in the beginning from within the Intelligence Unit but always impinging on the foreign department. Since it was first launched people have tried to define the difference in content between this blue, 8-page, expensive newsletter and *The Economist*. Crowther was vague. 'There are things that one doesn't want to put into print and have quoted on the Moscow radio next day; or things that we think are correct but aren't sure; or which, for one reason or another, get displaced from a paper that is pretty rigid in size and form.'[3] A definition from Brian Beedham in 1964 is as good as any. 'It has always seemed to me that the good Foreign Report piece fell into one of two categories – *either* the under-the-bed piece, reporting something not yet known to the public press, or not properly, *or* the novel item of analysis and interpretation looking farther into the future than other human eye can see.'[4]

It is, in fact, exceedingly difficult to make the distinction. From the very beginnings of *Foreign Report*, which was developed and launched by two more female Crowther-discoveries, there were tensions with the foreign department, whose editor was nominally responsible for *Foreign Report*'s contents. Alison Outhwaite, who had been a European expert in the Political Intelligence Department during the war, and Jean Bird, an American who had served in the American embassy in London on similar work, did not necessarily see eye to eye with the *Economist* line. Outhwaite in particular was too much of a cold warrior for John Midgley's liking and her critics thought her sources were too 'Establishment'. *Foreign Report* used to go to press a day earlier than the *Economist* and therefore imposed a burden on the foreign editor on the day on which he was most vulnerable. But there was a hunger in the market for intelligence about the new post-war world, the founding editors were well-informed and well-regarded, many of their contributors had excellent sources, and they succeeded in winning for *Foreign Report* a solid subscription base.

Crowther had launched simultaneously a *London Letter*, which folded within a year. He never got round to his other proposals: an economic analysis for the British businessman; an international economic report; and a report on America. At various times *The Economist* tried some others. Those on communications and on Third World development collapsed quickly; Marjorie Deane's *Financial Report* was an excellent product that lasted for seven years and provided a splendid training ground for young journalists, but it was never really profitable. (Hugh Sandeman, later Tokyo and then New York correspondent until he left to make money on Wall Street, was one of those who benefited greatly from her rigorous training.) When *Financial Report* was axed in 1988, she privatised it.

Foreign Report survived, despite many enemies along the way, because it makes a profit. It even survived a period when it looked rather like a propaganda sheet for the CIA, and it has for many years now been in safe hands with Roland Dallas. Over the years, its outside contributors have been numerous (and many of them famous) and *Economist* staff have fed stories to it; but its critics complain that it takes up more editorial and management time than it is worth, and speak darkly of the libel actions that have caused much grief as well as expense. Critics of management complain in turn that none of the confidential letters was ever marketed properly.

The diaries were devised first by Gerald Andrews, who during the war had struck up a friendship with a member of the Letts family, the diary publishers, and had agreed to a joint fifty-fifty deal on producing *Economist* diaries. It was not entirely a new idea; Hargreaves Parkinson recorded his life in *Economist* diaries, which contained a good deal of information along the lines of the modern equivalent. However these appeared to have been for giving away rather than selling. The Letts–*Economist* product was a pioneer in the newspaper field. The diaries were profitable and easy to market. One of Roland Bird's tidying-up operations during his managing directorship had been to cut Letts out of the operation when they refused to renegotiate a better deal. Profitability therefore went up, but so, too, did management involvement. The production and selling of diaries and other executive paraphernalia have occupied over the years a great deal of the energies of talented people like Leslie Gardner and Hugo Meynell. And as other papers, notably the *Financial Times*, began to compete, marketing became increasingly demanding. Yet, up to now, the diaries, more than any other *Economist* ancillary, have fulfilled Crowther's aim of finding a relatively trouble-free way of making additional profits based on the paper's good name.

The bookshop came about in 1946. Crowther wanted 'a bookshop through which our readers – particularly those in foreign parts – could obtain books in which they are interested, at some profit to ourselves',[5] and he made a deal with the London School of Economics, of which he was a governor, to go 50/50 on setting up 'The Economist's Bookshop'. Until the late 1970s it went reasonably smoothly. There was then a long and bitter strike over union recognition. After that the business of bookselling became first more competitive and then cut-throat, and it was with a sigh of relief that the business was sold in 1992.

Along the way there have been other minor ventures and a number of projects that came to naught. In view of the failings of *Economist* senior management over the years, it is just as well that Crowther failed in 1960 to achieve his great aim of buying Penguin Books.

The biggest of all Crowther's projects turned out to be what became the Economist Intelligence Unit (EIU). His ambitions for the Intelligence Branch, as the embryo was styled, were described in his 1943 memorandum. 'There seem to me to be two possible ways of developing this work. One would be to revert to the pre-war methods, perhaps with a little more steam behind them, and see what happens. The other would be to make up our minds to do the business properly and set out from the start to equip ourselves with the staff and facilities necessary to handle efficiently a substantial volume of business.'

He proposed investing in the more ambitious course. 'I feel sure that there will be a return and that it will arrive promptly. The minimum objectives of the Intelligence Branch in relation to the rest of the paper should be to provide, gratis, a full library and statistical service, thus relieving the paper's overhead. The further objective should be to earn an independent profit.'

He suggested making the headship of the Intelligence Branch into a full-time job, and also appointing a full-time manager 'whose sole duty it would be to find business for the Branch'. There were four varieties of work this Branch could perform: individual *ad hoc* investigations; regular services performed for individual clients ('e.g. the writing of a weekly letter to a South American Central Bank, or a weekly cable on conditions in the cotton market for an Indian firm', both of which were actual pre-war examples); regular confidential analyses of the economic outlook; and the publication of reference books, including an *Economist Year Book*.

In October 1946 *The Economist* advertised for a Director of Intelligence and Crowther hired Geoffrey Browne, the head of the economics department of the National Farmers Union. Early Economist Intelligence Unit staff included Harold Gearson, who was to stay until retirement and was by common agreement the most valuable as well as sensible member of staff, and Gerald Andrews, who developed the diaries and marketed syndicated publications and confidential reports. Briefly housed in just two rooms in Brettenham House, the EIU moved in October 1947 with *The Economist* to 22 Ryder Street, where, according to Geoffrey Browne, 'cooperation between the two organisations became simpler . . . Or it should have been simpler, but Crowther's idea of employing editorial talents for profit did not work out quite as easily and fully as he intended.'[6]

The post-war appetite for business-related information was huge: 'War-time dislocation of industry, markets and supplies of raw materials gave business many headaches: there were problems arising from nationalisation; from trade and currency restrictions, and so on.' The research side grew fast. In 1947 alone, EIU studies included the economic and social effects of the oil industry in Trinidad, petrol distribution in Sweden and the market for Indian jute.

The Unit also successfully syndicated articles on economic and political topics, written in turn by Browne, Crowther, Roland Bird, Paul Bareau and Wilfred King: 'For this activity the link with *The Economist* was an asset both in reputation and cooperation.'

Early on, however, Browne became dissatisfied with reliance on *Economist* people, because the journalists gave priority to the paper's deadlines, increasingly found more profitable sources of income from freelance writing or broadcasting, or, most upsetting of all, 'EIU facilities and contacts were used by some as a means of getting jobs as consultants or contributors on a personal basis. This was embarrassing, and not only financially, but it gave impetus to the development of an EIU staffing programme.'

By 1950, the Unit had a staff of 30 – mostly young graduates – and business was booming; and Browne recruited a deputy director. 'Except for intelligence, Bill [Mills] was as unlike as could be the typical banking gentleman or product of Eton and Trinity, Cambridge. But he was energetic, a very fast worker and impatient with any inefficiency or unpunctuality, and a progress chaser who knew his job. Perhaps not suave enough for GC [Crowther] but even he became reconciled to growing EIU profits.'

Quarterly economic reports (QERs) on countries and industries and bulletins on particular fields like paper and motors and books spread the Unit's reputation rapidly. It went into the field of management consultancy early on and expanded rapidly overseas. Bill Mills was an extremely rough operator who was utterly dedicated to building it into a large-scale international organisation.

In 1956 it became a limited company with a nominal capital of £250,000. It was a wholly owned subsidiary of *The Economist* but no money was actually invested. 'I believe', wrote Browne bitterly in the early 1980s, 'that the main Board still cherish the myth that a quarter of a million pounds was poured into the EIU. It wasn't. The EIU did not need it, and *The Economist* had not got it to give.'

By that time the gap between parent and adolescent child, now in different buildings, was becoming a chasm. Within *The Economist*, people who had come over from the EIU had tales of being required to produce work for clients without having either expertise or guidance. The editorial culture tends to be naturally contemptuous. The thirteenth floor (politics) tends to look down on the twelfth floor (business) (and the feeling is too often mutual), and they mostly despise everyone else in the organisation, particularly management, whom they see as existing in order to throw away on idiotic projects the money editorial earns through its brilliance and hard work. The EIU was beneath contempt, full of 'slow typists, fast women, and silly little men', as one escapee described it. Crowther, the Unit's creator, endorsed that view. When in 1952 Fred Hirsch said he would be interested in working for the EIU, Crowther 'said quite frankly he thought it would be rather a bore for me (!), "That's where we usually put young women with Seconds". However, he said that it would be an advantage to have this routine work behind one (apparently the work consists mainly of looking up things for firms that they're too lazy to look up themselves)'.[7]

In turn, the EIU resented *The Economist*. While *Economist* people thought the Unit traded on the paper's name, the EIU believed the name to be a liability. The paper's stance on Suez, for instance, had enraged the City and businessmen and had been damaging. Crowther treated the Unit high-handedly when it suited him; there was much indignation when *Foreign Report* and the highly profitable diaries were transferred to the parent company. For the most part, Browne and Mills were left to their own devices. While the figures looked good, the main board adopted towards the Unit's activities an attitude of patronising neglect. In the early days Browne had sent a weekly report to Crowther and their relations were cordial. Later, there were regular bullish reports to the board which elicited little interest. Bringing in large profits year after year, the EIU felt the parent company to be parasitical.

In a couple of letters to Trafford in 1972, Browne's resentment was made plain. One referred to the 'grudging indifference we had to put up with from *The Economist* side – Board and otherwise', and another remarked *à propos* 'the interest shown by the independent Board members in the information they received. This I would prefer not to describe on paper.'[8]

By the time Trafford arrived, it had become clear to the parent board that the Unit was in deep trouble. For years it had been regarded primarily as a milch cow, producing useful profits to balance occasional lean *Economist* years. Neither on the parent nor the EIU board were there any directors who knew about the consultancy business, either as providers or users, or had substantial marketing experience in a service industry. Geoffrey Browne and Bill Mills were both amateur managers who were left to do what they liked, and not unnaturally, what they liked was to run after new business without considering if they could handle it properly.

The 100-odd EIU headquarters staff by now worked in St James's in Spencer House, the marvellous Georgian town residence of the family of the Princess of Wales. Largely driven by Mills's ruthless ambition to make the Unit a worldwide presence, they had a vast overseas network of subsidiary companies. Browne was later to admit that from the late 1960s he had lost control of the offices abroad and that at home he and Mills had failed to develop the right managers for the organisation, wrongly expecting research staff to be natural managers and administrators. 'Those we appointed from our own ranks were apt to be too specialised, too young, and lacking enough in *savoir faire* to deal readily with people of all levels of seniority. But they were the best available from our own family.' Internally people tended to complain about competition rather than try to defeat it. Departmental chauvinism reigned, middle management was weak and training was poor. To many excellent and dedicated individuals who worked for the Unit over the years, that had been all too clear for a long time.

When the truth began to emerge, and it became clear that much of the EIU's apparent health was due to vastly overvalued work in progress, Roland Bird took over. He persuaded Browne to retire in 1970, and Mills shortly afterwards, and the chief executive's job was given to Mike West, one of the EIU's best consultants, a man far too nice for the butchering job required. Of all the horrors that emerged around this time, the one that comes first to everyone's lips is Sudene, the open-ended fixed-price contract to investigate Brazilian fisheries which came back to haunt the Unit after five years' massive inflation.

Trafford worked ceaselessly to try to save the EIU, often hampered by the helpfulness of his colleagues, but the slide continued. One of the retrospectively amusing episodes for uninvolved onlookers was the appointment towards the end of the decade, at de Rothschild's instigation, of Sir Claus Moser, ex-head of the Central Statistical Office, as part-time chairman. An excellent administrator and a fine statistician, Moser was academically, not commercially, minded, and he, like West, was dangerously soft-hearted. Like West, Moser later felt that he had been quite the wrong man for the job. Under Moser, in a desperate effort to drum up business, the EIU went in in a big way for what Edward Johnstone would have called 'decorative' appointments. First to be hired at considerable expense was Bernard (later Lord) Donoughue, retired from being an adviser to Harold Wilson, and second was Peter Jay, retired from being British ambassador to Washington. Donoughue's appointment and his method of doing his job (he was a dedicated luncher of the influential) maddened the staff of the EIU. Jay's appointment caused an explosion at *The Economist*, for Moser had done a deal with Andrew Knight and with de Rothschild which involved sharing the enormous cost of having Jay contribute a very few days' work. The fall-out at *The Economist* was so appalling that it left Knight at one fraught point saying he would have to resign.

Trafford did his best and achieved much in the civilised winding-down of the EIU, which the board now treated with great hostility. As dedicated and as much in love with the paper as had been Dallas Smith (Trafford used to read it from cover to cover), he was a very different operator. As befitted an organiser of trade fairs, where 'the one thousand little decisions have to be correct', he tended to spend too much time over the detail of his job.

What brought Trafford down was printing. The BPC operation into which Crowther had rushed them was a nightmare: the press bought specially to print *The Economist* never worked properly. The problems of combining black-and-white sections with colour sections produced elsewhere, and the problems of binding lines and timings, became weekly agonies. All the board could see was that Hazell's was not working: the consensus was that anything else would be preferable.

David Brockdorff had made his name within *Financial Times* and *Economist* circles as a manager of a section of St Clement's and had the highly prized reputation of being able to deal successfully with the trade unions: in a world of overmanning, overpayment and inefficiency he could wheel and deal and get the most effective agreements. Driven by violent union troubles at Hazell's and weekly delays, errors and massive cost increases, *The Economist* decided to accept the rescue plan he offered and to go into the printing business with him. At the 1976 annual general meeting de Rothschild reported to shareholders the decision 'to transfer the printing of *The Economist* with effect from 10 July 1976 to a new plant managed by David Brockdorff Ltd in Brentford, which is an excellent location for us, halfway between London Airport and the Central London rail terminals. A further new plant in Camden will be established later in the year where the setting of the paper will take place. We are ourselves making a substantial investment in both of these projects.'

The sad first major cost of this decision was, on 19 June 1976, the loss of an issue for the first time in the paper's history, when the National Graphical Association blacked its printing because the Hazell's workers had not received what they considered adequate compensation for having the work removed.

By October 1976 there was a serious financial problem at West London Offset Litho (the Brentford printers) and a similar situation building up in Camden; in 1977–8 WLOL lost almost a million pounds. Camden had the most advanced electronic text editing system in the United Kingdom but losses continued there too.

In November 1978, at Andrew Knight's suggestion, David Gordon, the international business editor, was offered the chairmanship of both printing subsidiaries and became production director. A few years earlier he had been summed up by one of his bosses: 'He is bright, quick, effervescent, inclined to panic and get tied in such a knot of nerves that writing can be agony, but this is nothing like as bad as it was. Probably the only naturally witty individual on the back of the paper and potentially one of the best brains . . . Liberal and moderately leftish . . . very hard working; it's the self-confidence that needs the odd boost.' Almost twenty years on, his self-confidence seems in good repair and since he has little writing to do, he has no reason to panic. Critics complain that his attention span is 3.2 seconds ('So long?' he enquired, when this was reported to him). And as he remarks himself, his strength and his weakness is that he changes his mind. He did so over printing. To the horror of several of his colleagues, who thought he knew he was meant to close the place down, he spent a long time trying to save Brentford through agreement with the trade unions, but in the end one of the six unions opted to be completely unreasonable and printing was transferred to Garrod and Lofthouse at Crawley. De Rothschild, Drogheda, Trafford and Gibson (with reservations) had all been in favour of going into printing, while Alan Hare of the *Financial Times* had been strongly against it. Yet it was Trafford who was blamed for the Brentford affair and brutally sacked by de Rothschild, after a long period of unease between them, David Gordon being installed in his place.

Crowther had always said that de Rothschild would become deputy chairman over his dead body; in fact he became chairman. He had never got on with Trafford, to whom he was extremely abusive at times. Crowther had dominated the *Economist* board through the force of his intellect; de Rothschild dominated through the force of his will. No more than Crowther did he succeed in running an effective *Economist* board, but his business instincts were far superior to Crowther's. He often asked the right questions, where Crowther had asked none at all, he had the imagination to go for growth in America, and he backed Clive Greaves financially to the hilt. When he gambled, he gambled high and did not panic. Clive Greaves was a catalyst in the paper's expansion, his single most important achievement being to persuade the board to spend two or three million pounds on going for a 50,000 circulation in America in order to get the necessary advertising revenue: that was the beginning of the serious breakthrough.

De Rothschild was also brave about new technology. And his decision to hire a tyro as managing director turned out to be correct. He also broke the tradition of staying in office until death, and stepped down in 1989 in favour of Sir John Harvey-Jones, ex-chairman of ICI, an ebullient media business-guru who has done much to make the board more effective.

David Gordon learned on the job (he sent himself to Harvard Business School for three months after he had been managing director for a year and a half). The first of his big achievements was taking the hard decision to close down the ancillary activities which the firm simply could not get right – the consultancy side of the EIU, and the Camden typesetting plant. His critics, however, point to various unsuccessful developments (including some publishing ventures) and acquisitions (in particular, Business International) for, like Crowther, Gordon was preoccupied by the need for sensible diversification to cushion the lean years; and he had to axe several of his own mistakes. The problem of getting ancillaries right will not go away.

Printing has been a brilliant success. Building on Trafford's innovative work in Camden, Gordon made *The Economist* a technological world-beater, introducing direct input even before Rupert Murdoch did, and now having *The Economist* printed at six sites around the world.

As a manager of the paper he has proved excellent, strongly in the tradition of Dallas Smith in developing talent and thinking strategically. James Wilson once wrote that 'whether a journal can be sold to its readers for a penny or sixpence with profit to its proprietors depends . . . on the revenue it can obtain from advertisers. In addition to the financial and other advantages which advertising confers on the Government and the public, it sustains in wealth and independence that press that is the best guardian of the public liberty.'[9]

In the modern *Economist* advertising and circulation are separate departments with separate directors. Their common aim is to make money for the paper, but tensions arise over how best to do it. Circulation will not be thanked for delivering unprofitable readers if what the advertisers want is a higher proportion of big-spender 'ABs'. Circulation may resist a cover price rise which is welcomed by advertising, while advertising may resist a rise in its own rates that could make it hard to get advertisements. When Marjorie Scardino succeeded Clive Greaves as the paper's boss in America, she had difficulty in getting through to the London management the point that in the American market, unlike in Britain, *The Economist* was not cover-price sensitive.

In London Helen Alexander runs the team of circulation-drivers: their market research is highly professional, their advertising campaigns win awards and the subscriptions system is computerised and works. One floor up, David Hanger runs a team brightened up by young men in coloured braces. Behind the customary back-slapping and entertaining of customers there are, here too, highly professional research and marketing.

Circulation and advertising share offices in locations throughout the world. Together they sell what editorial stands for. David Hanger remarks that in selling *The Economist* there are two things that have to be lived with. First is that the title is terrible; second, that if you ever try to influence editorial you will be in trouble. You can almost guarantee that if you introduce a journalist to a company, he says he will instantly go away and write a fiercely critical article.

In 1993 David Gordon was the first managing director of *The Economist* since Crowther to leave the post of his own volition, to take up the chief executive's job in Independent Television News. He left behind him strong senior and middle management, and his successor was Marjorie Scardino, a Texan lawyer whose background had included running a shrimp-boat and a newspaper. Although in eight years she has become imbued with the paper's ethos, she has, like David Gordon, the toughness and humour necessary to avoid being intimidated by the board or the journalists. Editorial betrayed little concern about the changeover: they merely hope that Scardino will not throw around the money which, they feel, they, and they alone, earn.

CHAPTER LII:

The succession

An institution is the lengthened shadow of one man. *Ralph Waldo Emerson,*
Self-Reliance

From the beginning, Tyerman had agreed with Crowther that he would not
stay until retirement; in due course he would make way for a suitable young
successor. By the early 1960s, he was beginning to go downhill. Becoming
editor of *The Economist* after so many cruel disappointments had made
Tyerman feel he had arrived; he loved being editor. Quite apart from the
sheer enjoyment of getting the paper out, he luxuriated in the trappings – the
international conferences, the media attention, and, most of all, the *Economist*
lunches for outside luminaries. Naturally convivial, he revelled in the sheer
social enjoyment of these occasions. It is, however, one thing to drink too
much at a long, boozy, journalists' lunch; it was another to do so in front of
solemn, visiting dignitaries who regarded the occasion as one of business.
And Tyerman had that fatal flaw in a convivial man; a poor head for alcohol.
Increasingly, when he drank too much, he talked too much and bored his
guests. Public attention was focused on his drinking habits after a television
appearance that inspired the satirical magazine, *Private Eye*, to run the
headline 'Econopissed'. He wanted to resign the next day, but was dissuaded
by Dallas Smith.

As he got heavier as well as older, the strain on Tyerman of heaving
himself around became increasingly demanding. And while he remained an
excellent manager of people and never lost his courage, he agonised more
about which line the paper should take on new issues and often became,
especially on press day, a liability.

Crowther, still deputy chairman, was too much involved in his outside activities to pay consistent attention to conditions at the paper, though he did ask Alastair Burnet in 1962 if he were interested in becoming editor. (It was around this time that Dallas Smith made a passing reference to Burnet as the Crown Prince.) Burnet was then 34 and saw himself at about number ten or eleven in the pecking order. Those ahead of him, simply by seniority, included Beedham, Bird, Goldring, Hartshorn, Hirsch, Macrae and Midgley: he believed it would be foolish and wrong to promote him over all those others. In the same year, he left the paper to become political editor of Independent Television News.

It was Bird who forced Crowther to face up to the urgency of doing something about Tyerman's deteriorating condition. In March 1963 Crowther wrote to Layton that 'Donald is drinking pretty heavily and is not in a good state of health or mind. Morale in the editorial staff is low.' Tyerman should be persuaded to appoint a managing editor who could succeed him.

No more than last time was Crowther prepared to let Roland Bird have a run at the editorship. 'One preliminary step that can be taken almost at once with the full agreement of everyone is to relieve Roland Bird of the office of deputy editor and of responsibility for the back of the paper. The proposal is that he should become what the Americans call a Contributing Editor and that he should prepare for the paper special sections or supplements such as the two admirable ones he has done in recent years on Canada and India.' Bird could help Dallas Smith on the management side and could also go on the board of the EIU. 'All this is with his full agreement on the reasonable condition that he does not suffer financially.' Tyerman 'could easily be persuaded to the further step of appointing a managing editor if the chosen person were to be Norman Macrae. That course would also be favoured by Peter Dallas Smith. But I have grave doubts about the wisdom of such an appointment and Lionel Robbins is strongly against it. I think you would be too. Certainly there would not be unanimity on the board.

'Unfortunately, I fear there is no one else on the staff who can now be seriously put forward. We shall therefore have to canvass the other promising men in the profession, of whom there are not a few.' There would have to be much discussion. 'I think I am the best placed of the Board to undertake it and to try first to pick the winner and then to get agreement on him. But I could do this more authoritatively if I were the Chairman of the company. You know that I would not bring this up if I did not know that it was your intention to resign the Chairmanship before long. I suggest for your consideration that if it is to happen soon, there would be advantage in its happening now.'[1]

One of the young journalists who came to Layton's mind, and whose name he wrote at the bottom of this letter, was the City editor of the *Sunday Telegraph*, Nigel Lawson, later to be editor of the *Spectator* and Chancellor of the Exchequer; presumably Crowther rejected him as being too much to the right.

Crowther and Tyerman talked matters through in May. Thanking him for a quite delightful dinner and talk, Tyerman admitted only one reservation. 'You once said that Keynes was the only chap in whose presence you felt hypnotised into not saying frankly enough what you thought; even after all these years you have something of the same effect on me . . . I am unlimitedly glad that a new and fruitful niche has been found, and made real, for Roland, so that he at any rate will no longer be in a cul-de-sac, but will have a new chapter of usefulness for the paper and the Company until he wants to lay all the burdens down.' Tyerman did not want Bird's move to be announced until after August, when Bird would, as usual, stand in as editor. 'This is the more important because of the other verdict which you announced to me on the basis of Lionel's veto; namely that it wasn't worthwhile even to try out Norman in charge. This means, if I am to take this as final, that until we find the right deputy and editor-designate, it will be both emotive and misleading for me to leave the paper in the charge of somebody else while I am away, unless it is Roland.' Bird should keep the title until his replacement was agreed.

> It may be of course that, in view of your remark about John, you might wish John to take things over in my absence, with the view in mind of his taking over from me as caretaker at some point – though I strongly believe, as I think you ought to believe, that to follow one caretaker with another at this stage would intolerably delay the hand-over to the youngsters in which I have so firmly believed for seven and a half years now.

'John' was John Midgley, and Crowther had just succeeded in driving a wedge between him and Tyerman. The sequence was straightforward; the interpretation is less so. Crowther had talked to Midgley the previous autumn, in 1962, about Tyerman's condition and how and where a successor could be found, explaining that Midgley was too old to be considered.

Midgley thought there were quite a number of promising editorial people, but that it might take time to find the right candidate, and he suggested keeping Tyerman a little longer. When Crowther vetoed that idea, Midgley suggested Crowther consider appointing someone older for a short period, maybe two years, with the directive to move people about and find what young talent emerged. Crowther asked 'if he decided to do that, would I be willing to be the person to take the editorship for that short period? And I said that it wasn't what I was proposing, but I would not be unwilling to do it.'

Midgley heard no more of this for many months, during a time when, as Tyerman's most trusted and loyal friend, he was distressed by a coolness that appeared to have grown up between them. In June it was announced that Crowther and Layton were swapping jobs and that Roland Bird would be giving up the deputy editorship. Midgley received a letter from Crowther in July, just after the Philby story had broken:

Personal and Private

Dear John,

I find that the announcement of Roland Bird's retirement from the Deputy Editorship has to some extent brought into the open discussion of the future of the Editorship. I suppose this is inevitable.

I think it also makes it impossible for me to delay any longer giving you an answer to the proposal you put to me in the autumn, that you should yourself succeed as Editor for a limited period with the definite mandate to find a younger successor.

I assure you that the delay does not mean that I did not take the suggestion seriously. Quite on the contrary, it was obviously an idea that had to be taken very seriously indeed, and I did not want to close the door on it unless I had to.

In the last few weeks I have had several discussions with other Directors and I think I know the state of opinion better than I did. I have to report the almost unanimous view that, difficult though it may be to find the right young man, it would be wrong to defer the search for several years. I must say that my own reflections lead me to the same conclusions. Unless we act quickly, there is a real danger of *The Economist* being caught in the wrong generation.

In these circumstances I think it is only fair to tell you that there is not very much prospect of your suggestion being accepted, so that you should feel entirely free. I would most bitterly regret it if you decided to move elsewhere – indeed, I hope very much that you will not. But it would not be right to try to hold you back if, in your own interest, you decided to do so.

Writing this letter has not been a pleasant task and on all personal grounds I wish it could be otherwise. I think we are all trying to do what we think will be best for the paper.[2]

Outraged by the suggestion that he had proposed himself to Crowther, as well as by being implicitly encouraged to resign by someone other than the editor, Midgley instantly took the letter to Tyerman. Then it emerged that Crowther had told Tyerman that Midgley had asked for his job. Midgley concluded that Crowther was not trying to make mischief – that was not in character – but that the imbroglio was due to absolute insensitivity. Having misunderstood dramatically what Midgley was saying to him, he had compounded his offence by tactlessly informing Tyerman that his best friend was trying to replace him.

'Dear Geoffrey,' responded Midgley.

I don't remember intending, at my pleasant dinner with you, to make a proposal; I would prefer you to think of it as I did as an uninhibited airing of hypotheses. At all events I have not been expecting an answer, and if I had it would have been the one you have given.

I must say I wish you luck in your search and appreciate your telling me what is in your mind. As far as my own position, it is possibly a more complicated matter than simply going or staying. You are not going to get your young new paper with a full set of middle-aged assistant editors; on this level it is not so much a matter of finding young people as of giving the ones you have got more of a run.

In short, I don't think it is in the paper's interest that I, in particular, should stay on in my present job until the remote date of my retiring age. Nor do I feel I shall want to stay all that time without a change of position or activity.* Thus the paper's interest and my own may very well coincide.

*At Midgley's own request he became in December 1963 Washington correspondent for an initial period of one year. He then chose to stay on and hand the foreign editorship over to Brian Beedham, who had been acting in his absence.

However, I don't at this moment see what the solution is; maybe one will appear.[3]

In Tyerman's letter to Crowther, he fought a familiar case valiantly. 'On the question of Norman I remain rather more intransigent than I was able to say during your hypnotic hospitality. I still feel it an obligation of honour to press not for his appointment, but for his trial, whatever Lionel may say – even to the extent of feeling, though not deciding, that if this is not possible, then I ought to regard my usefulness as ended and go myself.'

> The only test of the paper is the paper itself, as it comes out of the weekly mincing machine. I don't think that anybody who reads this week's paper, dated June 1st, can possibly fail to find a unique intellectual and journalistic distinction in the combination of the article on housing and the political/economic articles on Russia, all of which Norman of course wrote. Your stock answer to this sort of comment is that Norman is all right as a leader writer, but not as an editorial prospect. But this is not a good argument as you present it (a) since most of your arguments about Norman relate to the articles he writes and (b) none of you now knows very much about the intellectual and stimulating contribution that Norman unremittingly makes to the ideas and the shape and the content of the paper as it has grown to be. I have never said that he is the man; I have said, and still say, that of all the men approximating to the choice he is certainly worth the trial and test that none of you has been willing to give him, beyond your own intelligent and partly informed outside gossip.
>
> But I am, as always, a servant of the paper, and I have always regarded it as my chief and last function to help in finding my successor. This indeed, as I said on Friday, I am entirely willing to do, provided I can be sure that my views are regarded as at any rate worth-while listening to.

'The new name that you mentioned on Friday', went on Tyerman, 'could be a stroke of genius; but it is just a gleam in the eye, given that the man concerned is, editorially, a complete novice, and his own record of uncertainty and instability about his own future. Intellectually, of course, he is outstanding; whether this can be latched onto the editorial task is something that cannot be assumed lightheartedly and has to be proved by whatever tests are appropriate to a newcomer into this particular field.' This 'new name' was Roy Jenkins, whose background was already quite impressive: a first-class PPE degree, wartime army service, two years with the Industrial and

Commercial Finance Corporation, director of financial operations at the John Lewis Partnership and a director of Morgan Grenfell, as well as being a Labour MP.

Then 42 years old, Jenkins was well regarded as a writer, having published successful biographies of Clement Attlee and Sir Charles Dilke as well as a Penguin Special on the Labour case for the 1959 general election. Later to be Chancellor in a Labour government, president of the European Commission and first leader of the Social Democratic Party, Jenkins was cultivated, clubbable and the Establishment's ideal left-of-centre man. In 1963 he was in a party that had been out of office since 1951 and he did not get on with Harold Wilson, who had just been elected leader of the Labour Party in succession to Jenkins's dead friend Hugh Gaitskell. 'In these circumstances,' he wrote in his autobiography, 'disenchanted with politics, detached from my new leader, keeping too many balls in the air, I was an obvious sitting target for the offer of a job outside politics. On 5 July 1963 one duly came, and very attractive it at least superficially was. I lunched that day with Norman Macrae, the assistant editor of *The Economist*. There was an old joke that all members of the *Economist* staff were assistant editors, on the ground that they all tried to assist the editor. But Macrae was the real McCoy.'

> Not only was he the one person indisputably entitled to the designation, but he was also the epitome of the internal spirit of *The Economist*, Willy Whitelaw to the Conservative party, Gubby Allen to the MCC. Although intellectually didactic, he was personally modest. Donald Tyerman, who had followed Geoffrey Crowther, the modern refounding editor, in 1956, ought to retire, he said. He did not think that he (Macrae) had the all-round qualities to replace him. His view and (he implied) that of the staff, and (he stated) that of Crowther, who was then Chairman, was that I should do so.
>
> I was surprised, flattered and excited . . . I became distinctly interested. Macrae was right about Crowther, with whom we dined at the end of that month, and who pressed me hard to accept. *The Economist* in 1963 did not have the vast international circulation and popularity of today, but it perhaps had greater prestige and influence in Britain, maybe in New York and Washington, and quite enough money to go on with. I was offered over twice a Cabinet Minister's salary (which is probably about the going ratio today), and more than expected perquisites. (There was a mention of an apartment in New York; I suppose they must have had one going.)

Tempted though he was, Jenkins still had a strong reservation. Since he had few expectations of a decent ministerial job, he was not concerned about giving up the prospect of office in a possible 1964 Labour government, but he did mind the idea of giving up his seat in the House of Commons. 'So I told Crowther that I would think it over during the long French writing holiday that I had planned for that August.' In September he told Wilson about it. 'I think he was genuinely impressed by the *Economist* offer, more than Hugh would have been . . . It was exactly the sort of institution that he respected.' Wilson then said that if he formed a government he would offer Jenkins a worthwhile job. 'He would understand if I accepted the *Economist* offer, but he would deeply regret it.'

Jenkins was cooling when he next saw Crowther. 'But so was he . . . Crowther was chairman and patron saint of *The Economist*, but Lionel Robbins was chairman of the *Financial Times*, which was the principal shareholder in the Economist Newspaper Ltd.'

> Perhaps to compensate for his current occupation of putting the finishing touches to one of the great 'state as provider' documents of the post-war consensus,* Robbins's half-free-market soul was rather shocked by the idea of having a Labour MP as editor of Bagehot's journal. I backed off and so did Crowther. Although we were still in some sort of vestigial (and friendly) discussions as late as January 1964, they were never serious after 17 September 1963.[4]

In fact Crowther had not given up. In November he was writing to Robbins suggesting another talk: 'For the present, I will content myself with saying that I do not think your apprehensions about meeting J. are justified. I doubt whether it could have taken place at any time without it being perfectly apparent to him what the purpose was. But now, for better or for worse, he knows what the position is, and you would find it very easy to talk to him. I shall certainly urge you to do so, but there again I see no harm in waiting a little, and I will therefore make no effort to fix an encounter until you have addressed the Labour education committee – which means, probably, until the end of January or February.'

---

*The Robbins Report recommended a vast increase in the number of universities and university places.

I shall certainly continue to think hard about other names. I have had several talks with Garrett [Drogheda] and one or two names have been mentioned that I would classify as 'not impossible' but I don't think I could put them any further, and that is why I am anxious not to exclude a candidate to whom (if he were willing) there would, in my opinion, only be a single objection – though that one – I grant you, a weighty one, which I do not underrate.[5]

There were more arguments against Jenkins than his being a Labour politician. *The Economist* was not his kind of paper. 'As it happens', he wrote some years later, 'I am not a dedicated reader of *The Economist*, despite the narrow margin by which I missed becoming its editor in 1963, regarding it as essentially a journal for foreigners.' He was writing about an occasion in the 1970s when a picnic 'was rather spoilt by buying *The Economist* on the way and reading a particularly disobliging article (it was not malevolent, which made it worse, just deeply discouraging) about my first six months [as president of the EC]'. Jenkins would have been far more suitable for a journal of politics and *belles-lettres*.

Above all, as Tyerman pointed out, Jenkins's lack of editing skills was a huge disadvantage. The sheer business of ensuring *The Economist* gets out without a blank page or a disastrous overlap or omission is intensely difficult. One of the reasons why there is a tendency to favour internal candidates is, first, because they understand the ethos and second, because they understand the mechanics which are unique to the paper. Each Thursday *The Economist* acts, in part, like a daily – without the staff resources. Its journalists, as Burnet once observed, know 'the paper isn't printed by fairies twelve miles away': the more senior they are the more frightful nights they have spent subbing and being subbed, panicking at the printers because a story is too long or too short or has just been overtaken by events or, until recently, because the printers have been on a go-slow and the distribution deadlines are going to be missed.

As Crowther was to demonstrate again and again in his business life, not only did he have poor judgment, he did not know he had poor judgment. He assessed people according to how they performed in the areas in which he shone and had little respect or understanding of other qualities. Burnet was one of the many people who felt that Crowther totally underrated Tyerman. On this occasion, in his long letter, as on so many occasions, Tyerman was giving excellent advice, to which Crowther simply did not listen. 'Other youngsters we mentioned', went on Tyerman, 'may not have his [Jenkins's] intellectual claim, but they have much else already proven to commend them. All of this means that the process of choice, in which I would wish to participate as much as you want, is going to be as difficult as it ought to be, given *The Economist*'s importance. My own part in the process, which would crown whatever work I may have been able to do, will necessarily be qualified by the extent to which you have confidence (a) in my own conduct of affairs, and (b) in my view of chaps, on which I have hitherto rather prided myself, if only through personal vanity. At any rate, I can agree that you and I and Peter ought to set about this task with a common will so that we, the paper's own chaps, can present some agreed plan in person to our colleagues in this matter.'[6]

A series of dinners had been held earlier that year for eligible young men, all of whom Crowther found wanting. Nick Harman, one of Tyerman's protégés and probably too much of a brilliant maverick to have been right for the editorship, attended one of these functions in a private room at the Dorchester, 'in circumstances of enormous grandeur – gilt lifts and that kind of thing. It was rather a sombre sort of occasion really, and I foolishly thought it my duty to try to keep the conversation going and kept on trying to discuss points rather than saying yes . . . and obviously bogged it up . . . I expressed various heterodox views about the notion of free enterprise and things like that; that was fatal. It was terrible.' Harman found Crowther ill-at-ease, pompous, uncommunicative and given to making rather 'flattening' and 'crushing observations'.

Harman had got to *The Economist* through an appropriately odd route. Coming straight out of university in 1956, he had been promised a job on the *Financial Times*, subject only to the apparent formality of seeing its managing director, Lord Moore (Drogheda). 'He had on his desk an enormous silver cigarette box and he took a cigarette out of it and cut it in half with a pair of scissors and smoked half of it himself and he didn't even offer me the other half.'

> He then, I suppose quite helpfully trying to make conversation, made some observation about my having rowed for the school at Eton – which at that moment I thought was an irrelevant part of my past. So I made some remark about the fact that I had been very young and didn't know any better or something, and great offence was caused.

Moore vetoed the job offer and Harman walked round all the newspapers in London looking for a job. He went into *The Economist* and met Frances Chadwick of the home department, who asked what he could do. He said '"I really have no idea." She said "Can you write?" I said "I'd like to", so she said "What would you like to write about?" I said, "I think strikes and things are interesting" and she said "Well, why don't you go away and produce an article by Tuesday. Buy *The Economist* on Friday and if your article is in, you've got a job."'

> So I went down to the docks and spent the whole weekend down there. There was a dock strike. There were always dock strikes. Every day there was a dock strike. I went down to the docks and wrote two pieces, one of which was deeply, balls-achingly serious, analysing the problems of redundancy, and the other was about how all they were really interested in was the Test Match but they were voting for the strike anyway. I handed these two articles in on the Tuesday and on the Friday I bought the paper and the one with the Test Match was in.

Tyerman duly gave him the job. (*The Economist*'s taste for the unorthodox approach to job-seeking continues; recently a job in the Science and Technology section went to Geoffrey Carr, a post-graduate student who included with his application an elaborate mock-up of the section, text, illustrations, diagrams and all.)

The impasse was broken by Alastair Burnet. Burnet had been introduced to *The Economist* by Beedham, who had been in America with him as a Harkness Fellow. With a history degree from Worcester College, Oxford, he had spent seven years on the *Glasgow Herald* as sub-editor and leader writer, joining *The Economist* in 1958 and leaving in 1963. By the time he ran into Dallas Smith in the street in the summer of 1964, he had acquired a wide public reputation as a trenchant television commentator. Dallas Smith asked him if he had any ideas about who would be a good editor, and Burnet said, 'Put my name down, if you like.' Shortly afterwards Crowther offered him the job.

'Burnet', observed Crowther to one of the trustees, 'has all the best qualities of the Scot.'[7] To all four trustees he wrote that the directors 'have not found it an easy task to find the right man. We early came to the conclusion that there was no one now on the staff who could be considered for appointment. A large number of names from outside was canvassed, but the search was narrowed down by the conviction that, in this rapidly changing world, we must have a young man, and that we would not therefore consider anyone over the age of about forty.'[8] The note on Burnet sent to the trustees from Crowther included:

> Burnet's views and opinions are (so far as I know them) exactly those that we would want. He is a liberal in a fairly exact sense of the word, without qualifying for the capital L by having any attachment to the Liberal (or any other) party. I should describe him as a man of the Left Centre. In foreign affairs, he is a very firm believer in the policy of the North American Alliance, without any of the leanings towards neutralism which (to my regret) have sometimes been apparent in *The Economist* in recent years.
>
> In character, Burnet has the seriousness, even the high-mindedness, of the Scot, though it is overlaid with a great deal of personal charm. I was already thinking of him as a potential Editor when he left us for ITN two years ago, and the chief reservation I had then was whether his modesty and diffidence would prevent him from imposing himself on his staff, as an Editor must do. I think (and my colleagues who know him confirm this) that two years before the cameras have removed the diffidence, and that in the interval the underlying firmness of his character has emerged.
>
> The great difficulty for *The Economist* is always to be sensible without being heavy, to be lively without being silly, to be original without being eccentric. I believe that Alastair Burnet is admirably qualified to achieve this balance.

On hearing the news Tyerman wrote Crowther a note.

> Always, since you called me back to take your place, I have (a) left the determination of events, and my practical and financial place in them, entirely to your friendly disposition, and have no regrets for it; (b) assumed, even on the basis of our first talk in May (?1955) that I would 'do my own more modest Crowther' well before I grew to be sixty – you have heard me often say how important young leadership, as well as the young followers I have tried to recruit (including Alastair), is especially, and always has been, to our odd *Economist*. Clearly, as you told me today, the next step is for me to make honest, easy-minded men, first of the directors and then of the Trustees, by voluntarily bowing myself out (asking for my release as from the end of March next year).[9]

At the end of 1964 Tyerman appointed Macrae 'my senior assistant editor', who would stand in for him taking the chair at meetings. Macrae coped generously with the appointment over his head of an editor who had at one stage been his number two in the home department.

Burnet arrived in January 1965 and took over formally in April. (Tyerman had no other job to go to, and he stayed on the board until 1969 and shared Burnet's office from time to time for a long period, wanting to keep in touch. He went on writing book reviews until shortly before his death in 1981. He was confined to a wheelchair for several years; the only *Economist* colleagues who found time to visit him were Burnet, Lee, Hugo Meynell and, when he came to Britain, John Midgley.)

Burnet's temperament and style were very different from Tyerman's. He never visibly agonised and his style was punchy, direct and challenging. He was driven by a desire to persuade as many people as possible to read *The Economist*: everything else took second place to that. As far as policy was concerned, although he was to Tyerman's right, they were very close on the central foreign policy issues of the Atlantic alliance and the future of Europe.

In his valedictory, Tyerman had quoted Crowther's statement in his own: '"The most important change is the emergence of the United States as a full-time great power and its willingness to form and lead a grand alliance." Nothing has been driven home again more ceaselessly, or more dramatically, in the years since than this; and nothing has made me despair more for human folly than the cries that still go up in this country from utopians as well as from gadarenes, catcalling the Americans as a threat to peace when they have become, as a matter of historic fact, its saviour. Fallible American policy can indeed be; candid criticism there should be from good (but only good) allies; but the alliance is and will go on being our ever present help, just as it is, whether he likes it or not, the ever-present help, in the still armed and contentious world, of General de Gaulle.'

Crowther had been very slow to see the point of Europe, but Tyerman had taken *The Economist* very early into the forefront of the Common Market campaign, won over by the combination of Midgley, whose feelings for Europe and Germany in particular were very strong, and Christopher Layton, Walter's youngest son, who like his father was a passionate 'European'.

Christopher Layton had joined the paper from the EIU just before Crowther left, and he pursued a single-minded educational crusade. Having

been much involved with his father in various abortive post-war manifestations of the European movement, Layton was exceptionally well-
informed and well-connected. One of his most useful articles – 'THE
EUROPEAN RIFT', written in 1959 – was a diary of the events since 1940 that
had led up to the split between Britain and the six countries of the European
Economic Community.[10] François Duchêne, a close colleague of Jean
Monnet, father of the Common Market, was another key foreign-department
crusader for Europe.

Beedham summarised the paper's line on Europe memorably in 1962: 'A
spectre is haunting Europe again; not Marx's this time, but the spectre of two
authoritarian old men trying to run Western Europe in a way which means
the exclusion of Britain. This impression is not wholly a figment of the
imagination of people like Lord Beaverbrook, who are disposed to think that
bogey men begin at Calais. Recent events have added just a little weight to
the possibility that Dr Adenauer and General de Gaulle might really be
coming to the joint conclusion that their ideas about the future of Europe are
incompatible with Britain's, and therefore Britain had better be kept out of
the common market.'

This was all the more reason for Britain to try and get in. Once inside, 'it
will then be able to encourage and support the forces favouring conciliation
in central Europe and the continued close attachment to the United States'.[11]

Five years later Britain applied to join the Common Market for the second
time. Burnet and his political editor, George Ffitch, wrote in 'ON THE
BRINK':

> Mr Wilson's way is very different from Mr Macmillan's; perhaps his Britain,
> too. It is not a country that is bidding ambitiously, and of right, to lead the
> Europeans. It is not telling itself this time that it must go in to ensure that
> the Somme and Passchendaele are never repeated. It does not like the
> common market's agriculture policy, but if the corn laws must come back
> and wildly profitable wheatfields must stretch up the hillsides, so be it. And
> by now it is pretty well bored with the Commonwealth. A great deal has
> changed since 1963.

'This paper has supported British entry into the common market for many
years', said 'THE YEAR FOR EUROPE' in 1971, 'and it would have supported
it whether entry was achieved under Labour or Tories. It has done so despite
a protectionist farming policy practised by the common market which

offends principles *The Economist* has long stood for. Fortunately, if the trends of recent years continue, it is reasonable to hope that Europe's farm problems, and the protectionist policy, will be on the way to a solution by 1980.'

It was under Burnet, too, that the young Andrew Knight set up the Brussels office, once Britain had been accepted into the EEC.

If Tyerman was content, Burnet was style. With the newspaper increasingly profitable, he could afford to buy in experienced talent. Two of those he imported to write about British politics were George Ffitch and Ian Trethowan, both of whom were hard-headed and practical and understood the nuts and bolts of British politics in a way that their predecessors on the paper had not. Norman St John-Stevas, the political and ecclesiastical writer in the home department who later went on to be a Tory minister and a peer, understood the Tory party profoundly but had no knowledge of Labour.

There was a tendency for *Economist* people to know those at the top, but not those in the second and third levels who would really talk about what made organisations, parties and institutions tick. Burnet was interested in breaking news stories: he was a news man more than an opinion man, encouraging investigative journalists such as Goldring, Coulter, Nicholas Faith and Howard Banks. At its worst, his *Economist* was seen as vulgar and pandering to a rather low common denominator. The more lighthearted approach of Burnet's editorship was symbolised by *The Economist*'s acquisition of a horse, which was even exhibited on the Plaza in its racing colours. In his valedictory, Rupert Pennant-Rea, whom Burnet's *Economist* might have described as 'Mr Fixed-Principle himself', took a side-swipe at *The Economist* of Burnet's period, warning against the tendency of journalists – like politicians – to give in to special interest groups. 'In the early stages of the sequence', he wrote, '– more spending, more taxes, more borrowing – it was easy to find a friendly journalist to back some scheme proposed by a suitably serious-sounding body. This paper was no exception. There are not many lines I could quote from *The Economist* of – what? – 20 years ago, but I vividly remember an article about some Yorkshire textile firms seeking a subsidy from an industry minister, Christopher Chataway. The piece ended with the words: "Give'em t'money, Chris lad." Jolly journalism; dreadful economics.'[12]

Burnet did not restrict himself to hard-nosed journalists. He liked horses for courses. As one colleague put it: 'You don't want all birds of a feather.

You want a parrot, a crow, a vulture and an eagle and then mix them all up.' It was, for instance, during his editorship that the Mistress of Lady Margaret Hall in Oxford wrote to say that she had among her pupils a girl with a first-class mind who unaccountably wanted to go into journalism and who therefore must join *The Economist*, and Burnet obediently recruited Sarah Hogg, an intellectual's intellectual. He did not, however, recruit Rupert Pennant-Rea, who wrote in April 1972 to enquire about job possibilities and received a response of typical Burnet courtesy.

> I appreciate your interest in *The Economist*, but I am sorry to have to reply that there is no present possibility of an early vacancy here. It is also only very seldom that we take people who do not have considerable journalistic experience.
>
> If you are going to be in London at any time in the months ahead and would like to talk about the prospects then, please give my secretary a ring.

Burnet had plenty of courage. In 1966 he had a problem with Crowther, who although broadly supportive and non-interfering was becoming increasingly vulnerable because of his business activities. During that year, Crowther was involved in a fearful mess with the British Printing Corporation, which had come into existence the previous year largely through his instigation. It came out of a merger of Hazell Sun, whose chairman was Crowther, and Purnell, whose chairman was Wilfred Harvey. Crowther sped the merger through to prevent a *News of the World* bid for Hazell. *The Economist* reported that it was not until after the merger that the Hazell Sun directors had looked at the service agreements of the Purnell directors. Having discovered that they were being paid at 'a grotesque and ridiculous level', Crowther and other directors were trying to get Harvey and two of his colleagues off the board.

Nicholas Faith covered the annual general meeting of the BPC the following January, describing the statement of Sir William Worboys, the chairman, as 'disappointing in both content and delivery'; he wrote an entertaining article on the supine behaviour of most of the shareholders and the silencing of one of them, 'an awkward fellow this and clearly right . . . the late H.L. Mencken's famous denunciation of the middle classes as the booboisie came readily to mind when looking at the behaviour of the shareholders present at the meeting.

'But what of the absentees? There has been no public squeak out of the investment institutions at any point since Mr Harvey's curious salary arrangements (and the liberty he enjoyed with Purnell's money) first became known some years ago. This is presumably because Mr Harvey did nothing to offend them ... why should they meddle? But they by their absence, as much as the smaller shareholders by their ineffectual presence, did a grave disservice to the notion that boards of directors are publicly accountable to the shareholders.' (Faith was memorably to put his principles into action in the late 1980s at an *Economist* AGM, where he enlivened the usually brief and well-behaved gathering by a series of sharp questions and criticisms.)

Crowther wrote to Burnet 'to express my anger at Faith's article on the BPC AGM'.

> I have never suggested in any way what *The Economist* should or should not say about any matter with which I am publicly concerned, and I do not now offer any comment on the substance of what Faith wrote. If that is what he thinks, and you agree, it is what *The Economist* ought to say.
>
> But when it comes to the tone and manner of its saying, it does not seem to me unreasonable to express the hope that, before deciding to be grotesquely offensive, Mr Faith should stop to reflect on the embarrassment and trouble he is likely to cause to the Chairman of the company that pays his salary. Five seconds' thought would have told him that comment of this kind, appearing in *The Economist*, would be very widely ascribed to my inspiration, and would cause bad blood between me and Sir Walter Warboys.
>
> I think it would be difficult to find a more considerate employer than *The Economist*, and when the only return is that these clever young men take what seems to be deliberate pleasure in causing trouble, I get very angry. This is not the first, or the second, time that Faith has done this, and I can no longer believe that it is accidental. If this is his attitude to *The Economist* and its owners, I suggest that he might be happier in another employment.
>
> Brendan Bracken used to have a rule for the *Financial Times*, that nothing with which he was associated was to be mentioned in the paper, or commented on either favourably or unfavourably. Perhaps we ought to have a similar rule for *The Economist*.[13]

'I was sorry to get your letter this morning', responded Burnet, 'even although I was kindly forewarned by you on Wednesday evening.'

The responsibility for the BPC article is, of course, not Nick Faith's but mine. I read it, amended it and said it should be published as amended. That may have been an error of judgement. I believe, though, that the facts were right and that the criticisms were justified. They have been levelled elsewhere; I think they would be levelled by *The Economist* at any other chairman and any other shareholders if their firm were caught in the same predicament.

I did not ignore your own situation, though you may well feel that I did. If the tone was wholly wrong then I apologise . . . questions of tone are obviously difficult in such a sensitive situation. So when you say there is an argument for *The Economist* not commenting on affairs in which its chairman is concerned I can see the force of it. With you, that might mean a fair number of affairs. But if you do feel strongly that way then I would agree with you, and we would announce the fact. I think it would be a pity, though, and I shall certainly try to see that unnecessary offence is not given in future.

The outward manifestation of the upheaval that Burnet caused within *The Economist* was the change in the covers. As the *New York Times* commented when he left, *The Economist*'s 'serious approach is leavened by trenchant writing and by hilarious covers, whose effect is that of an Oxford don clapping on a false nose, whiskers and blue spectacles'.[14] He had a better eye than any of his successors.

One of his most memorable covers was of a British passport lying amid a pile of rubbish, with the caption 'If That's What It's Worth'. Its meaning was was explained inside in 'THE COST OF WHITENESS', an explosion of fury at the decision to put a strict quota on the acceptance of East African Asians with British passports, then being forced out of Kenya.

The Economist's record on race and immigration has been consistently liberal. In 1891, for instance, during some of the worst Russian pogroms, it had argued against restricting Jewish immigration. 'There is an arguable case for limiting the entry of black-skinned people into this country', Burnet had written, in 1961, under Tyerman's editorship. 'It rests on the proposition that an apparently sizable minority of white-skinned people fear and resent them, publicly denigrate them (even from political platforms), disseminate racialist literature about them (even at party conferences) and, from time to time, have to be restrained by the police from physically assaulting them . . . There is no excuse whatever for the hypocrisy uttered, with few exceptions, by the Tories at Brighton to justify the very end they are, it seems, ashamed to admit.' The country was the better for the immigrants. There were better alternatives to 'bleakly putting up the shutter'.[15]

Burnet's *Economist* fought a spirited and passionate battle against racism, hypocrisy and ignorance. Nick Harman's article on the Kenyan Asians began:

> This week Britain's Labour government announced its intention of adopting a policy towards would-be coloured immigrants to Britain which is more restrictive than anybody except the right wing of the Conservative party would have advocated. This week . . . the Commons hastened to give effect to that intention. In its hurry to keep out brown-skinned men, government, parliament and the nation have achieved disgrace.
>
> The worst thing is the discrediting of the British passport. Certain British passports, duly and lawfully issued to subjects of the Queen, will not entitle their holders to enter the United Kingdom unless the fortunate holder happens to be British by descent . . . Britain has restricted the entry of many holders of British passports, simply and solely because they are brown.[16]

When Idi Amin threw the Asians out of Uganda in 1972, *The Economist* welcomed the government's 'prompt acknowledgement of responsibility for Uganda's Asian holders of British passports . . . [which] goes some way to wipe out the shame of the Commonwealth immigration act of 1968'.[17] The paper did not, however, underrate the problems faced in bringing about better race relations.

'MORE IMMIGRANTS, PLEASE' announced (the immigrant) Pennant-Rea's *Economist*. 'It is a quirk of human nature that a country's most successful wealth and job creators are often its most resented residents: the Jews in pre-war Germany, the Asians in Idi Amin's Uganda, the Chinese in South-East Asia, the Ibos in Nigeria.'

> Part of the explanation is, of course, that many self-made men are outsiders in the country where they make their money, including two of the three British entrepreneurs we look at this week . . . Derring-do and a willingness to upset the establishment come easier to the outsider than to people whose lives are so settled that they feel they have little to prove. The Hong Kong Chinese should be encouraged to come and live in Britain.[18]

As a manager of staff, Burnet was loyal and supportive, though impatient with intellectual argument, which he liked to wreck by the use of his considerable talents as a mimic. 'He would retail', recalled Macrae, ' – in the exact timbre of particular statesmen's voices – how he imagined Harold Wilson was negotiating with Ian Smith, how LBJ would react to the latest disasters in Vietnam, how Charles de Gaulle would react to the Paris '*Chien-en-lit*' in May of 1968, what Jim Callaghan would be saying as he tried too long to avert sterling's devaluation. The staff member whom he had asked to write each story, who had often come into the room intending to say something else, would find the summary so hilarious that he went out and wrote what Alastair wanted.'

Immensely courteous and naturally egalitarian, Burnet was hugely appreciated by the rank-and-file. It was typical of him that his chauffeur, Wally Stott, was never left waiting outside while Burnet had dinner with colleagues after the printers or went racing: Wally was his friend and companion. The negative side of this was an editorial perception of Burnet as cliquish; there was a small group with whom he enjoyed conversation and drinking in his office in the evening.

Above all, Burnet was a brilliant technician. His valedictory said little of policy, but much that was generous about his predecessors and his successor. 'If a paper is doing moderately well it is usually wise to pick someone who understands its roots. A new man will change things; that is what new men are for, but his changes are all the better when they are based on an understanding of the paper's ways and its people. In this sense of a common cause and a common understanding I have been singularly fortunate: of the dozen most senior journalists at the end of my time only three (one of them the new editor) joined the paper during my editorship. All twelve are a scarce commodity: they are all professionals. So we have had a continuity in our approach and in our argument.'

Burnet had made a huge public reputation outside *The Economist* by continuing television work throughout his time as editor. He combined the two effortlessly, and though there was some resentment about this within the paper and worries from the board, he was too valuable to lose. But he was ready to move on.

In March 1970, Crowther put out a staff notice: 'The Editor told me some months ago that he intended to resign after the General Election. The Board has been giving some consideration to the choice of a successor but no decision is expected to be reached for some time to come.' Brian Beedham looked like the natural heir, backed by Burnet and Crowther and approved by the board, but he was fated to remain foreign editor – a role which, indeed, he filled with distinction for a further 18 years.

'The whole place is in a tizzy over the question of the next editor', wrote Norman Macdonald to Midgley. 'As you will know, there have been various leakages and guesses in the press, which have continued since Crowther put round his odd notice. Discontent in the editorial ranks is pretty prevalent, not so much because of this or that candidate as because of the way the whole thing is being handled, so much so that there is a movement among some to approach the management at top level and complain of lack of consultation. I am on the sidelines, of course, but I do think the whole thing is being handled very badly, and without much regard to the fact that the place is not a car factory but something in which human emotions are much involved.' 'On the editorship question', wrote another in April, 'we have had a meeting of editorial staff and as a result sent a letter to Lord Crowther asking him to see us . . . the idea is that we should make it plain that we are not happy with the Olympians who occasionally condescend to think about the future of *The Economist*. We shall also try to press for more open consultation about the choice of editor than has so far existed.'[19]

The ensuing meeting with Crowther, reported one of the participants, 'was basically an exercise in non-communication. We voiced our complaint, that our views were totally ignored on the selection of the new editor and that there was no rapport between the editorial staff and the management. He said that he already had his own undivulged ways of knowing what we thought (though he immediately showed he didn't know what we thought). He did say that if anyone wanted to see him or communicate by letter he would be only too willing, but that he abhorred syndicalism, as he called it, and defended the right of the board to choose the next editor.' Yet his response to the meeting was to funk the issue and lean on Burnet to stay for another three years.

Burnet had observed in 1964 that 'when favourites for anything are exposed too long in the paddock, the money can move away from them and on to some dark horse. If you go on postponing the race for two or three years, as *The Economist* did, it's bound to be a dark horse that wins. That is how I see it, and it is pretty near the truth.'[20] On that occasion he was speaking of his seniors, but he was right on this occasion also: Beedham had lost his opportunity.

'As you know the issue is now in limbo', wrote one of the dissidents, 'since Alastair has decided to stay until the end of 1971. Neither he nor the management have noticeably distinguished themselves in this tawdry episode. But I expect it will take a sheer dip in the profits to make any impression on their mutual complacency.'

Geoffrey Crowther died suddenly in 1971 at Heathrow Airport after a long, bruising and losing boardroom battle with Charles Forte, the sad culmination to a business career of almost unqualified disaster. Anxious to be rich as well as anxious to prove that he could practise what he preached, he had thrown himself into the business world with his customary self-assurance and lack of regard for the non-intellectual virtues. Those with whom he had fallen out included Nigel Broackes, who went on to a highly successful career as chairman of Trafalgar House; but his downfall occurred over the merger of Trust Houses, the chain of which he was chairman, with the business of Charles Forte in 1970, the one being centred on up-market hotels and the other on mass catering.

From the start Forte had disliked Crowther, finding him arrogant and patronising. One anecdote from Forte illustrates the difference between them. 'I always remember a conversation with Geoffrey Crowther when we had merged with Trust Houses. I said to him, "You know, Geoffrey, it is an interesting business we are in, isn't it? Everything we do is made up of small things; taking shillings and pounds from customers and trying all the time to give them good value. That is the important part of our business, the individual small unit." And his reply to me was, "Oh, Charles, you are in a different business now. You have moved out of that. We are in the multi-million pound business."'[21]

It was Crowther who precipitated the conflict with Forte as the cultural differences between the two groups became clear. But he underestimated his enemy's street-fighting skills. His obituaries all lamented his move into business. In the late 1950s, he had put an enormous amount of work into a commission on education which had recommended the raising of the school leaving age and had produced excellent ideas for educating 15–18-year-olds. He had been, too, a passionate advocate of the Open University, of which he was the first chancellor. In public work, as leader of a team, he could succeed: in the private sector, he was outclassed.

Tyerman summed up later the man he had known so well: 'The humour, the wit, the gaiety, the stimulus, the humanity, the impishness beside the authority, the childishness sometimes beside the eminence, the will to manipulate people, plans and events, the obsession now with this-or-that and then the leap to new pastures, the struggle to keep so many balls in the air without being too forgetful of some, the stamp always of style and mind, and some egotism, on whatever he said and did. To his real colleagues he was always a friend. Most of all, encompassing all else that he did, he was an educator. That is why he was a great writing journalist. That was the great issue which held him all his life, from school and Cambridge to the Crowther report and the Open University: the open door to education and the human problem of getting it accomplished.'[22]

CHAPTER LIII

Continuing the line

Editors have to resist and impart – resist the great, the good and the scoundrels who lobby them, resist the space barons who run parts of their newspapers, resist the inevitable misjudgments of journalists as they emerge sometimes, not always, blinded from the thick of things. Resist, above all, the consensual conventional wisdom both in the running of their own newspapers and in the running of the world. Such wisdom is almost always wrong. What editors have to impart are daring, clarity, structure, common-sense, a view.[1] *Andrew Knight, 1987*

Evelyn de Rothschild was a particularly impatient new broom, who made it clear that he would like a new editor and handled the next change-over swiftly and efficiently. By 1974 the dark horse had come up on the rails beside Beedham and Macrae.

Then 34 years old, Andrew Knight came of New Zealand parents who had settled in Britain. A Roman Catholic, he was educated at Ampleforth and then Balliol College, Oxford, where, like Alastair Burnet, he took a second in history. Knight's first job, in 1961–63, was at J. Henry Schroder Wagg, the City merchant bankers, from which he tried to get on to *The Economist* and was turned down by Brian Beedham. He started to try again in 1964, this time from the *Investors Chronicle*.

After a lunchtime meeting, Beedham recorded that 'his interests at the moment are rather excessively economic, but he talks well enough about international affairs and I liked him. He has a slightiy brooding manner but has the large advantage of not being a smooth young man. He is bright and direct. All in all, well worth bearing in mind.' Eventually Beedham recommended him to Fred Hirsch. Apart from a brief period reading PPE at

Oxford and an abortive few months toying with a BSc at the London School of Economics, Knight had no knowledge of academic economics. Fred Hirsch was 'an extremely difficult and brilliant interviewer. He expected the very best from you and he expected total knowledge. Having told me what I would be paid, he completely tied me up in knots on fiscal policy . . . as I remember it, the impact of fiscal policy on the gilts market, which I was in no position to answer at all. So he said, "Well, I'm afraid I don't think very much of that", and I said, "Well, what do you expect for £1250 a year?" And I think that is more or less what got me in.'

Knight arrived at the beginning of 1966, very low down the pecking order in the investment section. His mentors were Hirsch, who was intellectually demanding and taught him how to use his critical faculty in dealing with numbers; like Macrae – and indeed James Wilson – Hirsch believed that articles grow out of figures. Knight's other mentor was David Kelly, whom he described as 'a born *Economist* editor – stimulating, full of ideas, very good at handling other people's copy and quite ruthless at it'.

Intensely ambitious, energetic, restless and critical of what he thought was being badly done, Knight homed in on the oil industry after the departure of Jack Hartshorn, the oil and energy expert. Knight was convinced that the oil companies were riding for a fall and that the governments of exporting countries would form a cartel (as indeed they did). He was briefly oil correspondent, and then in 1968 was despatched to Washington to work under Midgley, partly because it was felt that Midgley would channel Knight's energies and teach him his trade, for he had shown little talent as a writer.

The difficulty was that Knight had only one way of doing things and that was his way. He had absolutely no interest in sitting in the Washington office, acquiring written information, concentrating, as headquarters wanted, on business coverage, writing the pieces decreed by Nancy Balfour and making contacts and travelling in any time he had left. As far as Knight was concerned, everything else came second to making contacts; that he believed to be the primary role of a journalist. Critics saw his behaviour as a mixture of social climbing and career advancement.

Surviving correspondence between Washington and London shows how Midgley, though a patient man with difficult subordinates, was driven near to distraction. As a number two on the Washington staff Knight was an unproductive source of irritation – although he was an excellent ambassador for *The Economist*. In 1970 he was brought back to London. Not realising he was in semi-disgrace, Knight was baffled by being given what he considered to be a non-job, acting as number two to Gordon Lee and writing a few Surveys, one of which was on the European Economic Community.

One of the paper's strengths is its ability to tolerate difficult people if it sees in them real talent. Though as a writer Knight tended to be clotted, he had a passionate desire to understand international politics and there were enough senior people who saw that he had many inchoate gifts which needed the right circumstances in which to blossom. His break came when a gap in European coverage was created by Stephen Hugh-Jones's departure to become deputy editor of *Vision* in Paris. Knight threw himself into the gap with customary vigour, rushing back and forth across the Channel, making contacts and forming, as he had in America, a network of which the editor of *The Times* would not have been ashamed. He was industrious and assiduous in getting his coverage into the paper.

Appointed an assistant editor in October 1970, he was reporting from the London and European perspectives on the culmination of Britain's negotiations to join the EEC. In January 1973 Britain became a member of the Community and Knight set up *The Economist*'s European section and established an office in Brussels. It was during this period that he showed his real class.

First, and probably most important, he was not afraid of the departmental barons. Endless problems arise on *The Economist* over subjects that might reasonably be allotted to more than one section, and it requires great editorial vigilance to avoid overlapping, or even worse, the risk of an important item falling between stools. At the time of the frightful 1984 disaster at the Bhopal chemical works in India, the paper almost failed to cover it. So many sections had been fighting over it that everyone thought it was in someone else's hands, and it was only the intervention of Pennant-Rea that caused a leader to be written at the printers at the last minute.

The creation of a new section is a threat to all the others; the number of editorial pages can be increased only with great difficulty because of expense, so a new section means that the others have to cede some space. One of Knight's strengths, and one he believes to be crucial for an editor, is that he accepts the inevitability of unpopularity. From the moment he was given his own section he stood up to legendary seniors like Beedham and Goldring and fought them on equal terms, insisting, for instance, on freedom from foreign department control. At Knight's suggestion, his new section was placed right in the middle of the paper just before the Business World, so that it could be seen as being in neither the front nor the back. He was, however, realistic enough to limit his Europe section essentially to the EEC, recognising that his resources did not permit him to cover all European stories.

In Brussels, with the help of his superb contacts, Andrew Knight found a niche. No one else was covering the Community bureaucracy's manifold activities on a week-by-week basis. But while he showed great ability to form contacts at the top level, his reporting suffered, as it would always tend to do, from his lack of interest in the views of people at levels just below the top, who usually yield the deeper stories. Yet he knew some of his limitations, and was prepared either to rewrite his copy, or let it be rewritten, when he was told it was unreadable.

He showed himself excellent at handling staff. To Edmund Fawcett and Tony Thomas he was kind on a personal as well as a professional level. Recognising that there were three of them in an office which really required only two-and-a-half, he encouraged them to spread into other sections. The basic point about Knight, as one colleague observed, was that he was an excellent team player as long as you did not cut across his ambition.

Knight also cultivated people from the home base, inviting them to Brussels, entertaining them well and earning their respect and sometimes their liking; and he rushed to and fro between Brussels and London protecting his position. Foreign correspondents tend to become isolated from office politics and often suffer from the headquarters/regional office malaise of feeling unloved and neglected; paranoia develops when several stories get spiked. That never happened with Knight: he cultivated people in London and he kept up with all the gossip.

There is a prevailing belief that he got the editorship in 1974 because he had cultivated the new chairman for a long time. It seems, however, as if Knight had met de Rothschild only twice before Burnet's resignation was announced, at which stage he knew no other members of the board.

When it was revealed on the ITN news on a Sunday night that Burnet was going to go, David Gordon rang his friend Knight in Brussels and suggested that he come over quickly. But Knight was close to the winning post already. He was invited over to have dinner with the board, and shortly afterwards, with alacrity and enthusiasm, he was appointed. Mary Goldring, who had opposed his candidature, offered her resignation immediately and instead of

938 THE PURSUIT OF REASON

trying to cajole her into staying, Knight accepted it. That was the first assertion of his authority: the second was that, instead of appointing an internal candidate to succeed her as business editor, he brought back Stephen Hugh-Jones.

Knight recruited Hugh-Jones, fully expecting that he would walk out again in due course (he did, but has since returned again), and installed him as business editor deliberately to raise the standards of accuracy. To his gratification, Hugh-Jones's first action was to buy calculators for his staff, who had been using slide rules.

The assumption had been widespread that Macrae and Midgley would be squeezed out: in the event Macrae became Knight's strongest supporter and Midgley was pressed to remain as Washington correspondent, and later as a consulting editor. Both Macrae and Beedham were to outlast Knight's editorship.

Knight said in his valedictory that the only value of editors was

> to get the best out of journalists better informed than they are, to support them to the hilt when they are right; yet to set them in a clearer structure where everybody knows the line of authority, and never to fear the thought, when resisting a consensus among colleagues, that what seems obvious to journalists today will be wrong tomorrow.
>
> Editors are lucky because they derive from and work with journalists who are stimulating, interested and interesting people practising an under-appreciated profession and a wonderful walk of life. But editors have to learn to be unpopular and, as time goes by, lonely.

Knight found the daily thrust and parry of debate within *The Economist* the most stimulating and rewarding part of his editorship. Others, less resilient than he, have been known to find it wearisome, a matter of scoring points against one's colleagues. Intensely reserved and with a great sense of his own dignity, Knight is very difficult to know, yet he is notorious for his success in forming relationships with important and influential people. A relentless self-justifier, Knight indignantly refutes and clearly fails to understand his colleagues' view of him as a social climber on a breathtaking scale. The positive side of this is that it was very good for the paper and increased its influence in the most select circles. Knight was friendly with Henry Kissinger and George Shultz, with prime ministers and ambassadors. He was also an intellectual snob: his recruiting policy was almost the opposite of Burnet's.

He always pursued brains and talent rather than experience and, all things being equal, if the candidate in question was well-connected, so much the better.

Under Knight a first-class degree in PPE appeared to be the norm; indeed it is almost certain that he would never have recruited himself. Yet, narrow though his focus was, he undeniably found excellent people. R.W. Johnston, a talent-spotter at Magdalen College, Oxford, provided several excellent recruits including the present editor, Bill Emmott. Several young, bright people were brought on to the paper through the three-month intern system, sponsored by Knight and run by Lee, and through Marjorie Deane's *Financial Report*.* The system works best in the business sections, rarely in the political ones, where it is hard to find a suitable narrow subject to research and gain some expertise on. But Knight deserves credit for developing a training stable of economic and financial journalists. 'Whatever the method of recruitment,' observed Gordon Lee, 'the result was always the same. Those who succeeded were usually products of a middle-class, public-school, Oxbridge background with a good degree. What else can you expect when people have to survive in an atmosphere which combines an intellectual hot-house with a social freezer?'

Personally kind though Knight undoubtedly is, (he fully maintained the high standards of decency that mark *The Economist*'s normal treatment of its staff), he was a chilly presence on the paper, reinforcing a culture which over the past couple of decades has been a cruel one for newcomers to the editorial staff. A novice may be left to sink or swim. In most cases he will lack guidance and criticism of his products will often be expressed by a complete rewriting or, more frighteningly, by a silent spiking. The arrogant and precocious flourish in this environment, prove themselves quickly and then one day are accepted: the more diffident – those in need of encouragement – shrivel and depart within a few months or are sacked at the end of six. When accused of callousness in their treatment of newcomers, most established members of staff are baffled, thinking either that there is no other way to treat them since it is the only way they can prove themselves or responding indignantly, like

*Among those with little or no experience of journalism who joined *The Economist* the stayers, to date, are: Martin Giles (Paris), Ann Wroe (American Survey), Merrill Stevenson (finance), John Parker (Europe), Andrew Cowley (Moscow), John Micklethwaite (business), Ed Carr and Oliver Morton (science); the leavers include Chris Huhne and Tim Jackson (*The Independent*), Hugh Sandeman (Wall Street), John Browning (freelance), Anatole Kaletsky (*The Times*), Tim Hindle, Nigel Holloway and Jeremy Gavron.

Albert Chapman would, that *The Economist* is a wonderful happy family.

Knight's relentless pursuit of excellence was recognised in 1981 by the *World Press Review*, which chose him as International Editor of the Year. Important too was his restoration of the paper to the path of fiscal rectitude from which it had strayed during a period when Burnet and Macrae became carried away with enthusiasm for growth and stopped worrying about inflation. More specifically, perhaps his finest achievement as editor was the introduction of the science and technology pages in the teeth of opposition. The idea had been suggested by Richard Casement, the paper's great expert on transport, whose areas of competence Knight was anxious to expand. An extraordinarily original but obsessive journalist, Casement could apparently think of nothing but transport, so, to wean him, Knight made him science writer, believing firmly that anybody clever could pick up enough of any subject to write about it coherently. Casement went off to 'Silicon Valley' in California, and came back with what Knight considered the most important article ever published in *The Economist*. It was the lead piece to a special section devoted to the coming impact of the microchip and was accompanied by a photograph of a silicon chip on somebody's finger, accompanied by the explanation that the chip was powerful enough to drive a train.

Casement persuaded Knight that a science section was a good idea, and Knight forced the business section to cede the necessary space. Casement being prone to errors, Knight gave him the meticulous Alice Barrass as his deputy and they formed a stunningly successful partnership. Casement died suddenly at the age of 40 in 1982 and Barrass took over; she died of cancer in 1984 at the age of 48. But they had left a solid creation behind them, which has continued to thrive successively under Matt Ridley, Anthony Gottlieb and Oliver Morton. As in Casement's time, it is one of the most friendly corners of the paper.

Someone outside the mould who joined the paper during Knight's editorship (having been turned down during Burnet's) was Rupert Pennant-Rea. Born in Rhodesia, he was educated outside the golden circle at Trinity College, Dublin, where he took an upper second in economics, followed by an MA in economics from Manchester. Having graduated in 1970 at the height of the period of corporatist Britain, he worked as an economist first for a year at the Confederation of Irish Industry, then with a trade union in London for about 18 months and then in the Bank of England, during which time he wrote a thriller about a plot to return to the gold standard.

Fed up with institutions and having a natural facility for writing easily and well, Pennant-Rea applied for a vacancy as an economics correspondent at *The Economist*. He had lunch with Sarah Hogg, the section editor, who asked him to provide a trial piece by the following morning. He posted it that evening, it reached her by the deadline and she liked it. Pennant-Rea joined the staff in 1977, replaced Hogg as economics editor four years later, briefly combined it with editing the world business section and then carried on being economics editor. When Knight announced towards the end of 1985 that he was about to leave to become chief executive of the *Telegraph* empire, there were three obvious candidates: Simon Jenkins, imported by Knight to raise the level of political coverage, which he had done in a most stimulating and newsworthy way; Dudley Fishburn, who had been a successful executive editor for several years; and Pennant-Rea, whose experience as a journalist was far more limited than theirs. Yet most of the staff favoured Pennant-Rea, for his intellectual qualities were seen as having raised the paper's prestige in an area where it had been weak. Jenkins was not felt to be truly of *The Economist* (he was thought even to be in favour of introducing by-lines). Fishburn was liked but not seen as a reformer: by and large the staff believe in perpetual change.

On this occasion de Rothschild invited staff to make their views known to him in person or in writing, without compromising on the board's absolute right to make its own choice. The process went smoothly and without controversy, although the press had become excited and had thrown other names into the ring: Peter Jay is the perennial gossip columnist's tip, possibly because he is the only writer on economics that gossip columnists think their readers have heard of. As *The Economist* continues to expand even in a recession-plagued world, it becomes increasingly a subject of fascination. Its anonymity adds a certain frisson.

Pennant-Rea stayed only seven years – which he believes to be long enough, thinking that after seven years editors begin to think they can walk on water. He was a highly efficient editor, whose innovations included the Asia section, the three-page specials, the Bagehot and Lexington columns (plus the Economic Focus and Market Focus) and a page on sport, which he added to the arts pages introduced by Knight. Though approachable and pleasant, his ferocious efficiency (he rose at 4 a.m. to write) and his ideological rigour invited comparison with a machine, but like James Wilson, Pennant-Rea's tough exterior obscures his highly emotional centre. By common consent he was seen to have the best mind of any editor since Crowther and he certainly had his lucidity and his certainty, but also, more than any post-war editor he had an absolute clarity about the paper's principles.

What Wilson called *laissez-faire* is now called competition. 'It is competition', wrote Pennant-Rea in his valedictory,

> that delivers choice, holds prices down, encourages innovation and service, and (through all these things) delivers economic growth. It is competition that is the true target of the lobbyists; whatever they may claim to be doing, their real target is the pickings that exist when markets are uncompetitive. It is competition that is at the heart of political pluralism too, because it allows for differences of view as much as for differences of product. In short, it is competition, and only competition, that works for the general interest. And the more of it the better, which is why worldwide competition – global free trade – is the essence of intelligent political economy.
>
> Free trade is the principle to which *The Economist* has remained strikingly loyal throughout its 150 years. The paper has often been pigeon-holed as pro-business, as right-wing (and sometimes as left-wing), as backing a particular political party. All those labels are misleading: indeed, the aim of most label-stickers is to mislead. But the one badge we could wear with pride is that this is the paper of competition.

That of course was an abstract concept: 'The task of *The Economist*, week by week, is to apply its principles to a wide range of issues and events, not just to restate them. Even if its philosophy is timeless, it must always be a paper of its time. It must be full of the sap of reality; reduce it to a husk of theory and it will die. It should mostly be serious; it should never be solemn. Above all, it should be independent – and, thanks to its complicated constitution of checks and balances, it is. During my seven years as editor, I (and no doubt all my colleagues) received countless exhortations to write about this subject or that, to take this view or that; but not once did pressure come from the shareholders or directors of this company. What we wrote was what we, the journalists, chose to write. Few other publications are so lucky.'

> So there it is, this lucky paper: in its 150th year, kept on its toes by its readers, refreshing itself through internal debate and through occasionally changing its editor. I pass *The Economist* on to excellent hands, knowing that

the value of its history has seldom been more relevant. In 1843 we were founded to campaign for free trade and against the folly of the corn laws. In 1993 the struggle goes on.[2]

Pennant-Rea's successor was chosen by a board headed by the chairman, Sir John Harvey-Jones. This time the media were much more excited, partly because Pennant-Rea was leaving for a high-profile job and partly because *The Economist* was even better known than seven years previously. The less well-informed press tipped all sorts of outsiders from Peter Jay to Nigel Lawson, but the short list of nine was composed entirely of insiders. The *New York Times*'s coverage included an attack by Andrew Neil, in his time an editor of the Britain section of *The Economist* and at one stage with aspirations to be editor of the whole paper, on its declining 'domestic impact'. It had lost touch with its home base, he said: 'That is the price of being an international success story. Its coverage of domestic issues is very poor now'; and he thought that *The Economist* risked compounding its mistakes in Britain by choosing 'some unknown' as its next editor. 'I would have gone for a big-name outsider,' he added, 'someone to give it a personality and a direction in Britain.'

Harvey-Jones had no such intention. On settling down to deal with the succession, he called for the rules of procedure only to be told that there were none, so he drew them up. The staff were notified formally that all applications were welcome, and that they would not be publicised though confidentiality could not be guaranteed. Candidates were asked to submit a one-page manifesto on *The Economist* of the future and why they were best qualified to lead it. Members of staff were encouraged to make their views known to Harvey-Jones, in confidence and preferably in writing. It was an acknowledgement of how the staff's views have gradually become more important with each change of editor.

The board's selection sub-committee consisted of Harvey-Jones, Frank Barlow of the *Financial Times* and Dominic Cadbury, an independent shareholder and son of Laurence. Nine internal candidates were selected for the short list, which, after interviews, was reduced to two: Nico Colchester, who had joined as business editor in 1986 after an impressive career at the *FT*, becoming Pennant-Rea's deputy in 1988, and Bill Emmott, the business editor.

The job went to Emmott. Way back, when he was recommended to the paper by Bill Johnston of Magdalen, he had had a disappointing interview with Andrew Knight and Johnny Grimond, wrote a test piece which they quite liked, then saw Brian Beedham and had another interview which also went indifferently, and wrote another test piece which was not enough to win him a job. He heard nothing further until he was a year into a PhD on the French Communist Party and received a letter saying, 'Dear Mr Emmott, have you found yourself a job yet? Stephen Hugh-Jones, Business editor'.

When Emmott got in touch, Hugh-Jones said he did not himself have a job to offer, but that he had been looking through the files and noticed they had no record of where Emmott had gone to. Some confusing episodes later, Emmott was at last offered a job by Knight as number two in Brussels, writing about economics and the European Monetary System (EMS). After his spell in Brussels, he was economics correspondent (while Pennant-Rea was economics editor), then he spent two years working for the paper in Tokyo. He then rejoined the London staff, doing the job of finance editor with conspicuous success, which won him the business editorship. He is often described as inscrutable: his successor in Tokyo, Paul Maidment, composed a verse:

> How courteous is the Emmott-san
> He always says, 'Good day, my man.'
> He climbs into his Atex seat
> And smiles, and says 'Delete, Delete:'
> He bows and grins a friendly grin
> And calls his hungry writers in:
> He grins, and bows a friendly bow:
> 'So sorry, this story overmatter now.'

An answer sent to a reader while he was finance editor gives some impression of Bill Emmott's personality and attitudes:

> Thank you for your pink memo about Marx, 'socialism' and joint-stock companies. Thank you also for your comments that we are talented and hard-working: despite that, few of us favour by-lines or a masthead, mainly because by-lines in particular discourage genuine cooperation and encourage the development of prima donnas. It is a policy we have had since 1843, and there is no plan to change it.
> In this sense, at least, we believe in the workers' cooperative.[3]

Forward to the past

In his goodbye speech in 1988, Norman Macrae reminisced about Albert Chapman. 'He'd joined *The Economist* at the then school-leaving age of 12 under editor Johnstone in the 1890s. So you'll see that by 1949 he was qualifying for leaving parties like this.'

> There was only one problem. He would say at his leaving parties that he was really most touched at this kindness, and he couldn't think why people were giving him all this, and he did drink all their health, quite copiously. But then on Monday he'd come back and sit at his desk, and nobody quite liked to tell him even at his next leaving party that he wasn't meant to be there. And the young ones among us got quite cross about this. We said, 'How will this place ever amount to anything if senile old fools like that aren't made to realise that they've retired but come back and sit at their desk.'
>
> Anyway thank you all so much. I really am touched. And I do drink all of your healths quite copiously. And I'll be back at my desk on Monday. Thank you.

That was a link with 95 years ago. It falls to Macrae also to provide a suitable link with James Wilson and his *Economist* in an article he wrote in 1991, three years after his leaving party, in which, in looking at the future, he takes us back to the thinking of Wilson, Hodgskin and Spencer. It was a signed article, which can stand as Macrae's valedictory to a newspaper to which he made such a vast and vigorous contribution, for it brought together a number of ideas he had been advocating for years. 'A FUTURE HISTORY OF PRIVATI-SATION, 1992 TO 2022', had the subheading 'Norman Macrae looks forward to the end of politicians'.

First he took a look at the recent past. In America and Europe the position of the underclass had worsened as a result of huge, misdirected public expenditure. In Britain, nationalisation had 'plunged the great monopoly industries . . . into vast losses: they were operated in the interests of their unions instead of their customers'. Yet even as late as the 1960s, 'it was hard to persuade even sensible people how wrong were those like J.K. Galbraith, who told eager politicians that the interests of the poor could be served best by spending much more of GDP through politician-dictated monopolies instead of market-leading common sense'.

The Economist had come up with the word 'privatisation', to describe the returning 'to profitable private motivation of anything that had declined through unprofitable state intervention – in Europe usually through state ownership, in America usually through excessive regulation (including what Herman Kahn called "health and safety fascism")'.

The clear advantage of privatisation was that people got more money if their way of doing things succeeded and if they failed they went bust, whereas in the public services people learned 'that they got more money if their settled ways of doing things failed, because then they could wail that governments must pump still more money to them'.

During the 1970s, 'those of us who appealed for reform via privatisation were still generally regarded as nuts . . . Then it took off.' In the past dozen years, 1979–91, privatisation had become a real policy in more than 70 countries, aspired to 'in all the ex-communist countries as a means through which industries and services long buried under dead socialism can bring some springtime to the frozen earth above. The policy has taken wing in Japan (telecoms and railways) and the Asian dragons. It stumbles forward in the third world.'

The scope for further privatisation was everywhere enormous. Taking Britain as the example, Macrae then proceeded to sketch 'a plausible future history for privatisation'. Examples were: the diminution of safety regulations to allow some abandoned coalmines to be worked unofficially by teams of miners; the introduction of charges for road use; and the privatisation of railways. The Channel Tunnel would allow into Britain railway locomotives that were newer, cheaper and more varied in design. 'By the early 2000s the successful privatisation of British Rail will be followed by privatisation of the Bundesbahn, the trans-Siberian railway and every other railway on the Eurasian land mass.'

Telecommunications and television would leave the public sector completely and competition would be introduced into the other utilities, with entrepreneurs feeding electricity into a central grid, and cheap gas coming from Siberia and the Middle East. Food prices would fall along with those of energy, and 'after free trade with Russia, the European Community's common agricultural cartel will collapse'.

Worldwide, social services would be privatised, through the use of educational vouchers and the adoption of 'a system of health maintenance organisations (HMOs, or bodies that compete to get your capitation fee, and then seek to provide all your health-care needs as economically as possible)'. Similarly, the prisons, the police and the legal system would face competition.

In due course, commercial firms rather than politicians would be elected to run local services. 'By 2015 there will be only two main "public goods" left – in the sense economists use the term (things best provided by government rather than markets). These two remaining public goods will be redistribution and military protection. These will then become competitivised.'

Some people would be able to insure against falling into poverty. Those, like the handicapped, who were in need of special help could have it provided competitively by institutions on performance contracts. Eventually, poverty would be tackled in the same way. 'People will start to bid for contracts to try to help "endangered people" thus to avoid being long in poverty, and some of the contracts will work.'

In the case of defence, there was no need to develop more sophisticated weapons than were now available. Nato and the former Warsaw Pact states would get together to stop arms sales to poorer countries and gradually assume the role of a world policeman. 'It will equip itself at lowest price with stuff that actually works and will therefore probably buy much of its electronic hardware from the Japanese. It will recruit its soldiers in the cheapest high-quality markets: Gurkhas, Britain's SAS, sons of old soldiers from various villages round the world with fighting in their blood.'

> By the 2020s it will be recognised as absurd that only the Republican and Democratic parties should field serious candidates for (say) the 2024 election for president of the United States. A competing 'contractual' candidacy will be emerging – a cabinet team who say they will never raise income tax above 10% (watch their lips), but will contract to provide government of the following quality . . .'

Macrae's row of dots indicates that there will be further unthinkable thoughts to come. For thinking the unthinkable is what has made *The Economist* more than a record of fact. This piece of futurology was Macrae at his opinionated and radical best, four-square with the basic instincts and traditions of *The Economist*. In his early years, Wilson would have thought Macrae had not gone quite far enough, but later, tempered by political office, he might have raised an eyebrow. Bagehot would have grinned and asked 'But how?' Hirst would have been torn between horror at the technological predictions and approval of the ideological purity. Layton would certainly have added 'time alone will show'. Crowther would have said 'But Norman, some of your arguments are somewhat convoluted. Bearing in mind the following aphorisms . . . if we take this central idea and proceed to B, C and D, meeting the counter-arguments thus, thus and thus, I think that would strengthen it.' Without exception, they, and all of the other ten in the editorial pantheon, would have recognised and applauded Macrae's audacity in the pursuit of reason.

150 years ago, *The Economist* had a circulation of 1,750: now it is over half a million. Its readership then was composed mainly of British men of business; now over 80% of its circulation is abroad. Although still London-centred, it strives to report on the world without nationalistic bias, and it is this that makes it unique among news magazines. Firmly established as an international newspaper, it has no direct competitor, though there is plenty of indirect competition in one speciality or another from other journals around the globe. The revolution in telecommunications has enhanced the paper's strength, enabling it to disperse its printing and part of its editorial and management staff.

Geoffrey Crowther, whose later mistakes do not detract from his mighty contribution to the paper's history, provides the final word.

> The faiths and the hopes of 1843 still stand . . . It is still possible by social action to create a world of justice, freedom, and fraternity, and of material welfare . . . we have yet to see the best of the journey.
>
> In this great caravan, the journal of opinion, if it be humble and honest, has its place. *The Economist* has stayed with the caravan for longer than is given to most. It hopes to stay a great while longer.

Appendices

EDITORS

Name	From	To	Age on becoming editor
James Wilson	1843	1857	38
Richard Holt Hutton	1857	1861	30
Walter Bagehot	1861	1877	35
Daniel Conner Lathbury	1877	1881	46
R.H.I. Palgrave	1877	1883	49
Edward Johnstone	1883	1907	39
F.W. Hirst	1907	1916	34
Hartley Withers	1916	1921	49
W.T. Layton	1922	1938	37
Geoffrey Crowther	1938	1956	31
Donald Tyerman	1956	1965	48
Alastair Burnet	1965	1974	37
Andrew Knight	1974	1986	35
Rupert Pennant-Rea	1986	1993	37
Bill Emmott	1993		36

CHAIRMEN

Name	From	To
Sir Henry Strakosch	1929	1944*
Lord Layton	1944	1963**
Lord Crowther	1963	1972*
Sir Evelyn de Rothschild	1972	1989**
Sir John Harvey-Jones	1989	

* Deceased
** Resigned

(Titles as of the date of leaving office)

MANAGING DIRECTORS/CHIEF EXECUTIVES

Name	From	To
Brendan Bracken	1929	1941
Lord Moore (later Drogheda)	1941	1947
Lord Bracken	1947	1956
Sir Geoffrey Crowther	1956	1962
Peter Dallas Smith	1962	1969
Roland Bird	1969	1971
Ian Trafford	1971	1981
David Gordon	1981	1993
Marjorie Scardino	1993	

(Titles as of the date of leaving office)

TRUSTEES

Name	From	To
Sir Josiah Stamp	1929	1941*
Sir William Beveridge	1929	1963*
Sir Alan Anderson	1929	1952*
Sir Laurence Halsey	1929	1945*
Sir Charles Hambro	1941	1963*
Lord Franks of Headington	1946	1987**
Lord Sinclair of Cleeve	1953	1978**
Sir Frank Lee	1963	1971*
Viscount Harcourt	1964	1979*
Sir Patrick Dean	1971	1990**
Sir Campbell Fraser	1978	
Sir David Steel	1979	
Professor Sir James Ball	1987	
Lord Alexander of Weedon	1990	

* Deceased
** Resigned

WORLDWIDE CIRCULATION, 1843–1993

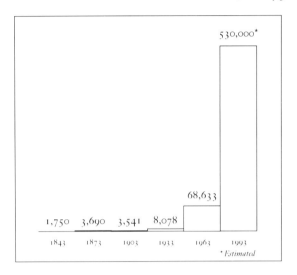

530,000*

68,633

1,750   3,690   3,541   8,078

1843   1873   1903   1933   1963   1993

*Estimated

WORLDWIDE DISTRIBUTION, 1958 and 1992

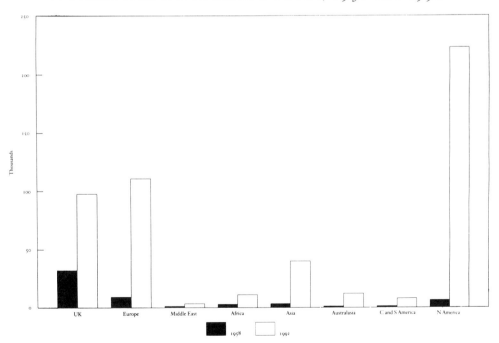

Notes

I have been fortunate throughout the writing of this book to have at home the complete run of *The Economist* on microfilm along with a microfilm reader that produces photocopies, so it has been possible to refer to the paper constantly. I have also had beside me the other major primary sources, the archives of *The Economist*.

The library and records of *The Economist* were almost completely wiped out by a bomb in May 1941. All that survived were the contents of a fire-proof safe which by the time I came on the scene had disappeared and been forgotten. By sheer luck some old account books were found by *Economist* accountants who were going through financial records in the basement in order to throw out what was more than seven years old. We conducted a thorough search through many black garbage bags which produced account books, circulation records and other invaluable material, including Albert Chapman's memoir, which in some instances went back to the 1870s.

After 1941 the paper had ceased consciously to keep any archives that were not required for legal purposes, but with the help of Gerry Stephens and his colleagues, I found some material from the 1950s and 1960s in old desks and filing cabinets in the further recesses of the basement; gradually, more material was found lurking in cabinets here and there around the building. When the Economist Intelligence Unit left Spencer House, I took away a lot of files that would otherwise have been thrown out. Then, in the mid-1980s, when refurbishment of the Economist Building required mass movement of staff, I was encouraged to go through everyone's files taking originals that would otherwise be jettisoned and copying anything I wanted. David Gordon, Andrew Knight and Rupert Pennant-Rea deserve special gratitude for making their files freely available to me.

For the later period covered by this book, I have drawn heavily on 300 or so interviews. All but a couple of these were recorded on tape and transcribed. At present the transcriptions are in my possession; some of them are subject to a thirty-year rule.

Because of promises of confidentiality, in many instances I do not quote the source of certain oral testimony. I have, however, used all such material circumspectly; any controversial views or recollections have been checked with other contemporaries.

The papers and transcriptions in my possession are here described as the *Economist* archives (*EA*); in due course they will find a permanent and accessible home.

References to the papers of Walter Layton crop up frequently from chapter XXXVI onwards. When I consulted them they were uncatalogued and temporarily in the custody of Layton's biographer, David Hubback. They have since been lodged at Trinity College, Cambridge.

I have read or used many books and papers not mentioned below. The scope of this book has been such that a bibliography would be both enormous and pointless. I cite below only the sources used directly.

The following abbreviations occur frequently throughout the endnotes.

CH	*The Economist 1843–1943: A Centenary Volume*, London, 1943
DNB	*Dictionary of National Biography*
E	*The Economist*
EA	*Economist* archives
GC	Geoffrey Crowther
JW	James Wilson
LWB	Mrs Russell Barrington, *The Life of Walter Bagehot*, London, 1914
Overstone	D. P. O'Brien (ed.), *The Correspondence of Lord Overstone*, three volumes, Cambridge, 1971
PEC	The six volumes of the *Political Economy Club*, published in London between 1860 and 1921
SA	Emilie I. Barrington, *The Servant of All Pages from the family, social and political life of my father James Wilson Twenty years of mid-Victorian life*, two volumes, London, 1927
WB	Walter Bagehot
WB	*The Collected Works of Walter Bagehot* (ed. Norman St John-Stevas, London, fifteen volumes, 1965–1986)

Westwater   Martha Westwater, *The Wilson Sisters: A Biographical Study of Upper-Middle-Class Victorian Life*, Ohio and London, 1984

CHAPTER 1: Why

1 *E*, 4 November 1843

2 *Ibid.*

3 'Memoir of the Right Honourable James Wilson', *WB*, iii, pp.323–64; *E*, 17 November 1860

4 *Yorkshire Evening News*, 7 September 1943

5 JW to George Wilson, 12 July 1845, Manchester City Library

6 *E*, 11 November 1843

7 *WB*, xi, p.236

8 Scott Gordon's brilliant essay, 'The London *Economist* and the High Tide of Laissez-Faire', in the *Journal of Political Economy*, December 1955, pp.461–88, persuasively makes the case

9 William D. Grampp, *The Manchester School of Economics*, London, 1960, *passim*

10 John Morley, *Life of Cobden*, i, London, 1908, p.153

11 *WB*, iii, p.334

12 JW to Cobden, 8 May 1839, British Library Add.Mss. 43667 f.33

13 *SA*, i, p.27

14 *WB*, iii, p.329

15 British Library Add.Mss. 43667, f.43/3

16 *E*, 25 November 1843

17 British Library Add.Mss. 35,151, ff.348, 349

18 Archibald Prentice, *History of the Anti-Corn Law League*, ii, London, 1853, p.58

19 *WB*, xii, pp.178–9

20 Henry Ashworth, *Recollections of Richard Cobden, M.P. and the Anti-Corn-Law League*, London, 1876, pp.268–80

21 *E*, 24 February 1844

22 JW to Cobden, 20 December 1843, West Sussex Record Office

23 *WB*, iii, p.297

24 9 November 1841, Manchester City Library

25 David Ayerst, *Guardian. Biography of a Newspaper*, London, 1971, pp.104–5

26 JW to Cobden, 20 December 1843, Cobden MS 961, West Sussex Record Office

27 11 June 1843, *SA*, i, pp.67–8

28 George Wilson papers, 21 June 1843, Manchester City Library

CHAPTER II: How

1 Sir Richard Temple, *Men and Events of My Time*, London, 1882, quoted in *SA*, ii, pp.230–31

2 *E*, 27 June 1992

3 *E*, 5 June, 1847

4 *SA*, i, pp.70–71

5 Arthur Taylor, *Laissez-faire and State Intervention in Nineteenth-Century Britain*, London, 1972, p.29

6 Wendy Hinde, *Richard Cobden*, London, 1987, p.132 or Cobden to George Wilson, 24 August, 1843, Manchester City Library

7 *EA*, August 1843

8 *SA*, i, p.71

9 *E*, 16 September 1843

10 Cf. e.g. *E*, 14 September 1985

11 *E*, 3 August 1985

12 *E*, 14 June 1986

13 *E*, 3 August 1985

14 *E*, 14 September 1985

15 *E*, 26 May 1990

16 *E*, 25 November 1843

17 JW to Cobden, 20 December 1843, Cobden MSS 961, West Sussex Record Office

18 Circulation figures from 1843 until the abolition of stamp duty in mid-1854 can be deduced from the relevant *Newspaper Stamps Returns*, House of Commons Accounts and Papers (I), 1844, vol. xxxii, pp.419–37; (I), 1852, vol. xxviii, pp.497–543; (I) 1854, vols. xxx, pp.509–15, xxxix, pp.479–93, 502–13

19 Overstone, i, pp.352–55

20 *E*, 28 July 1928

21 *E*, 18 July 1846

CHAPTER III: Setting the course

1 15 September 1860

2 *WB*, iii, pp.295–6 and 331

3 James A. Monsure, 'James Wilson and the Economist: 1805–1860', a 1960 Columbia University PhD thesis, has a full account

4 *The Times*, 10 January 1845

5 *E*, 11 January 1845
6 *E*, 21 December 1844
7 *E*, 24 February 1849
8 *E*, 18 March 1989
9 *E*, 11 January 1845
10 *E*, 12 July 1845
11 *E*, 6 January 1844
12 Circular of Belgian Association, quoted in *E*, 11 September 1847
13 *E*, 6 May 1848
14 *WB*, ix, p.298
15 13 September 1860
16 Denis Knight (ed.), *Cobbett in Ireland: A Warning to England*, London, 1984, p.257
17 *WB*, xi, pp.225–6
18 *E*, 5 July 1845
19 *E*, 11 November 1848
20 *E*, 17 January 1846
21 *E*, 15 March 1845

CHAPTER IV: The crucible: the Irish famine

1 Cormac Ó Gráda, *The Great Irish Famine*, Dublin, 1989, p.52
2 *E*, 7 November 1846
3 *E*, 17 June 1848
4 *E*, 21 May 1864
5 *PEC*
6 *E*, 28 October 1843
7 *E*, 28 October 1843
8 *E*, 14 September 1844
9 *E*, 4 January 1845
10 *E*, 19 April 1845
11 *E*, 4 January 1845
12 *E*, 28 June 1845
13 *E*, 6 September 1845
14 *E*, 18 October 1845
15 Norman Gash, *Sir Robert Peel*, London, 1972, pp.552–3
16 *E*, 29 November 1845
17 *E*, 21 March 1846
18 *E*, 4 April 1846
19 *E*, 18 April 1846

20 *E*, 13 March 1847
21 *E*, 28 October 1848
22 *E*, 23 September 1848
23 *E*, 30 September 1848
24 *E*, 18 December 1847

CHAPTER V: No quick fixes

1 *WB*, vii, 180–181
2 Cormac Ó Gráda, *The Great Irish Famine*, Dublin, 1989, *passim*
3 *E*, 27 February 1847
4 *E*, 26 December 1981
5 *E*, 26 June 1848
6 *E*, 23 December 1843
7 *E*, 28 June 1845
8 *E*, 15 August 1846
9 *E*, 19, 26 September and 3 October 1846
10 *E*, 13 February 1847
11 *E*, 11 December 1847
12 *E*, 4 September 1848
13 *E*, 3 August 1850
14 *E*, 2 November 1974
15 *E*, 5 July 1975
16 *E*, 29 January 1977
17 *E*, 29 July 1978
18 *E*, 8 November 1980
19 *E*, 11 February 1984
20 *E*, 16 March 1985
21 *E*, 20 July 1985
22 *E*, 21 November 1987
23 *E*, 14 March 1987
24 *E*, 14 October 1989
25 *E*, 2 December 1989
26 *E*, 5 January 1991
27 *E*, 11 May 1991
28 *E*, 23 May 1992
29 *E*, 4 April 1846
30 *E*, 15 August 1846
31 *SA*, i, p.108

32 *E*, 27 February 1847
33 *E*, 20 February 1847
34 February–March 1847, letters from Clarendon, Greg and Porter quoted in *SA*, i, pp.108–10
35 *E*, 30 October 1847
36 Scott Gordon, 'The London *Economist* and the High Tide of Laissez-Faire', in the *Journal of Political Economy*, December 1955, p.463
37 *E*, 3 August 1850
38 Interview with Al Senter, *Media Week*, 11 July 1986

CHAPTER VI: The pull of politics

1 *E*, 5 June 1847
2 *E*, 28 October 1843
3 *E*, 2 December 1843
4 *E*, 3 February 1844
5 *E*, 3 February 1844
6 *E*, 5 April 1845
7 *E*, 9 August 1845
8 *E*, 31 January 1846
9 *E*, 31 January 1846
10 *E*, 27 September 1845
11 *E*, 14 February 1846
12 *E*, 6 July 1850
13 *E*, 13 July 1850
14 *E*, 26 July 1845
15 *SA*, i, ch. viii; *WB*, iii, 342; JW to Cobden, 29 June 1846, Cobden MSS 182/3, West Sussex Record Office
16 *E*, 13 February 1847
17 *E*, 5 June 1847

CHAPTER VII: 'The Up-Line'

1 *E*, 17 February 1844
2 *E*, 29 November 1845
3 *E*, 6 July 1844
4 *WB*, x, pp.447–458
5 *E*, 23 January 1993

6 *E*, 8 February 1845
7 *E*, 5 April 1845
8 *E*, 31 January 1846
9 *E*, 27 September 1845
10 *E*, 27 September 1845
11 *E*, 22 November 1845
12 *E*, 28 March 1846
13 *E*, 18 September 1847
14 *E*, 21 October 1848

CHAPTER VIII: Why Lombard Street ceased being dull,
and became extremely excited

1 15 September 1860
2 Lionel Robbins, *Robert Torrens and the Evolution of Classical Economics*, London, 1958, pp.93–4
3 Overstone contains an excellent account
4 I am indebted for this to Scott Gordon, 'The London *Economist* and the High Tide of Laissez-Faire', in the *Journal of Political Economy*, December 1955
5 *E*, 9 September 1843
6 Frédéric Bastiat, *Cobden et la Ligue*, Paris, 1883, p.315
7 *E*, 11 May 1844
8 *E*, 22 March 1845
9 Torrens, quoted in Sir John Clapham, *The Bank of England*, ii, London, 1944, p.184
10 *E*, 3 May 1845
11 *SA*, ii, p.21
12 *SA*, i, pp.126–7
13 *Parliamentary Papers: Reports from Committees, 1847–8*, ii, Pt. l
14 *E*, 22 December 1855
15 Overstone, pp.632–5
16 Journal, 10 January 1855
17 Overstone, p.708
18 *Ibid.*, pp.719–20
19 *Ibid.*, pp.660–61
20 *Ibid.*, pp.683–4
21 See *WB*, iii, pp.379–403
22 *SA*, ii, p.26
23 *WB*, iii, p.340
24 Overstone, pp.898–9

25 *SA*, ii, p.64
26 *SA*, ii, pp.48–9
27 *SA*, ii, pp.50–51
28 *Report from the Select Committee on Bank Acts, 1857*, i, *passim*
29 Overstone, pp.748–9
30 *Ibid.*, *passim*
31 *Ibid.*, p.874
32 Cf. e.g. *SA*, ii, correspondence with Lewis
33 *SA*, ii, pp.185–6
34 *SA*, i, p.224

CHAPTER IX: Independent?

1 *E*, 13 July 1850
2 Westwater, p.16
3 *E*, 2 March 1844
4 *E*, 31 January 1846
5 *E*, 1 February 1845
6 *E*, 1 March 1845
7 See *SA*, *passim* and British Library Add.Mss.44,095, 44,577 and the substantial 44,346
8 *E*, 9 June 1855
9 Hansard, Vol. cxliv, col.1018
10 Quoted in Westwater, pp.19–20
11 *E*, 9 November 1850
12 *E*, 23 November 1850
13 *E*, 1 March 1851
14 Public Record Office 30/22 10C 16–18
15 *SA*, i, p.206
16 Grey of Howick papers, Department of Palaeography, Durham University
17 *SA*, i, pp.203, 205
18 *SA*, ii, pp.50–51
19 *SA*, i, p.208
20 *E*, 10 July 1852
21 Public Record Office 30/22 10C/181–6, 17 July 1852
22 *The Times*, 10 July 1848
23 *E*, 21 October 1848
24 *SA*, i, pp.206–7
25 14 January 1850, Grey of Howick papers
26 *SA*, i, p.168

CHAPTER X: Thomas Hodgskin

1 *E*, 21 October 1848

2 Sidney and Beatrice Webb, *The History of Trade Unionism*, London, 1911, p.147

3 Unless otherwise stated, the sources used for Hodgskin are M. Beer, *A History of British Socialism*, London, 1940; *DNB Missing Persons*; C.H. Driver, 'Thomas Hodgskin and the Individualists', in F.J.C. Hearnshaw (ed.), *The Social and Political Ideas of Some Representative Thinkers of the Age of Reaction and Reconstruction, 1815–65*, London, 1932; Scott Gordon, 'The London *Economist* and the High Tide of Laissez-Faire' in the *Journal of Political Economy*, December 1955; Elie Halévy, *Thomas Hodgskin, 1787–1869*, Paris, 1903, which has a bibliography that includes all the Hodgskin contributions to *The Economist* Halévy was able to identify; Graham Wallas, *The Life of Francis Place*, London, 1898

4 *E*, 16 September 1854

5 *E*, 28 October 1848

6 F.J.C. Hearnshaw, *A Survey of Socialism*, London, 1928, pp.182–3

7 See, for example, Graeme Duncan's *Marx and Mill: Two views of social conflict and social harmony*, Cambridge, 1973, p.53

8 *E*, 28 October 1848

9 *E*, 12 December 1846

10 *E*, 27 May 1848

11 *E*, 17 March 1849

12 *E*, 21 October 1848

13 *E*, 21 October 1848

CHAPTER XI: The case against the rope

1 *E*, 10 May 1845

2 *E*, 1 February 1845

3 *E*, 29 March 1845

4 *E*, 10 May 1845

5 *E*, 7 June 1845

6 *E*, 16 May 1846

7 *E*, 2 July 1983

8 *E*, 28 October 1848

9 *E*, 8 August 1846

10 *E*, 21 October 1848; 13 July 1850

11 *E*, 19 July 1879

12 *E*, 6 May 1916
13 *E*, 2 July 1983
14 *E*, 31 January, 28 February and 2 May, and probably also 14 February 1857
15 *E*, 16 May 1857
16 *WB*, xiii, p.441

CHAPTER XII: Herbert Spencer

1 *E*, 8 February 1851
2 David Duncan, *The Life and Letters of Herbert Spencer*, London, 1908
3 Quoted in *ibid.*, p.537
4 Herbert Spencer, *An Autobiography*, i, London, 1904. Unless otherwise attributed, the material in this section comes from this source. The autobiography contains an account from hearsay of the founding of *The Economist* which is wrong in almost every particular
5 Quoted in Duncan, *op.cit.*, p.57
6 Duncan, *op. cit.*; p.63 wrongly gives 20 December 1851 as the date on which this appeared: I have failed to find it
7 Evans to Sara Sophia Hennell, 29 June 1852, in Gordon S. Haight (ed.), *The George Eliot Letters*, ii, London, 1954, p.40
8 C.H. Driver, 'Thomas Hodgskin and the Individualists', in F.J.C. Hearnshaw (ed.), *The Social and Political Ideas of Some Representative Thinkers of the Age of Reaction and Reconstruction, 1815–65*, London, 1932, p.203
9 Cf. e.g. *E*, 13 March 1847
10 Duncan, *op. cit.*, p.5
11 Evans to Mr and Mrs Charles Bray, 27 April 1852, Haight, *op. cit.*, ii, p.22
12 Evans to Mrs Charles Bray, 27 May 1852 Haight, *op. cit.*, ii, p.29
13 Evans to Mrs Charles Bray, 16 April 1853, Haight, *op. cit.*, ii, p.98
14 *E*, 21 October 1854
15 Duncan, *op. cit.*, p.92
16 John Viscount Morley, *Recollections*, i, London, 1917, p.116

CHAPTER XIII: William Rathbone Greg

1 *SA*, i, p.84
2 David Duncan, *The Life and Letters of Herbert Spencer*, London, 1908, p.viii
3 John Morley, 'W.R. Greg: a sketch' in *Critical Miscellanies*, iii, London, 1909. Other principal biographical sources used are Eliza (Wilson) Bagehot's diaries (in the

possession of Lord St John of Fawsley); microfilm lent to me by Sr Martha Westwater); *WB, passim*; *Memorials of W.R.G.* in the possession of Joy Greg; *SA, passim*; Westwater; and the memoir and other prefatory material to the 1891 edition of Greg's *Enigmas of Life* (London). Virtually all of the attributions are mine alone, but since Greg's style is extremely distinctive, it is rare that there seems to be any doubt about his authorship

4 *E*, 21 November 1846

5 Adrian Desmond and James Moore, *Darwin*, London, 1991, p.32, and on Greg, *passim*

6 Quoted in John Viscount Morley, *Recollections*, i, London, 1917, p.234

7 *DNB*

8 Reprinted in W.R. Greg, *Essays on Political and Social Science*, ii, London, 1853

9 *SA*, i. p.212

10 Public Record Office 30/22, 10C/181–6, 17 July 1852

11 *E*, 3 July 1852

12 *SA*, i, p.212

13 *E*, 25 February 1871; *WB*, vi, p.400

14 *Spectator*, 19 November 1881: almost certainly Richard Holt Hutton

15 Annabel Huth Jackson, *A Victorian Childhood*, London, 1932, p.57

16 R.K. Webb, *Harriet Martineau*, London, 1960, pp.13–14

17 Gordon S. Haight (ed.), *The George Eliot Letters*, ii, London, 1954, p.21

18 *Ibid.*, p.66

19 'Why Women are Redundant' in Greg, *Literary and Social Judgments*, ii, London, 1877, pp.81–2

20 Unsigned memoir, probably by his widow, in Greg, *Enigmas of Life*

21 *E*, 3 July 1852

22 *E*, 1 April 1848; reprinted in Greg, *Essays on Political and Social Science*, ii

23 *E*, 7 September 1850

24 *E*, 6 December 1851

25 *The History of The Times*, ii, London, 1939, pp.147–8

26 *E*, 27 December 1851

27 *WB*, iv, pp.29–84

28 *WB*, iv, p.48

29 *WB*, iv, p.36

30 *WB*, iv, pp.50–51

31 *WB*, iv, p.52

32 *WB*, iv, p.77

33 *WB*, xii, p.326

34 *E*, 4 December 1852

35 See e.g. a rapturous leader 'KOSSUTH: HIS PRINCIPLES, APPEARANCE, AND ORATORY', *E*, 15 November 1851
36 *WB*, xiii, p.354
37 Cf. *SA*, i, pp.250–254 and *E*, 22 April 1854

CHAPTER XIV: Moving on

1 Cobden to Henry Richards, 16 June, 1857, quoted in John A. Hobson, *Richard Cobden, The International Man*, London, 1918, pp.218–19
2 *E*, 24 September 1853
3 *E*, 8 October 1853
4 *E*, 12 November 1853
5 *E*, 31 December 1853
6 *E*, 14 January 1854
7 *E*, 11 March 1854
8 *E*, 11 March 1854
9 *E*, 30 December 1854
10 *E*, 27 January 1855
11 *E*, 15 May 1852
12 *E*, 12 June 1852
13 Mrs Cannan in W.R. Greg, *Enigmas of Life*, London, 1891, p.lxviii
14 James Drummond and C.B. Upton, *Life and Letters of James Martineau*, i, London, 1902, p.269
15 8 February 1855 to Henry Crabb Robinson, *WB*, xiii, p.357
16 Drummond and Upton, *op. cit.*, *loc. cit.*
17 *E*, 21 July 1855
18 *E*, 6 October 1855
19 *E*, 5 January 1856
20 *WB*, xi, p.235
21 *E*, 6 February 1858

CHAPTER XV: Changing guard

1 *E*, 22 January 1916
2 Alastair Buchan, *The Spare Chancellor: The Life of Walter Bagehot*, London, 1959, p.127
3 Robert H. Tener and Malcolm Woodfield, *A Victorian Spectator: Uncollected Writings of R.H. Hutton*, Bristol, 1989. The other chief sources used here are *WB*, *passim*; *LWB*;

SA; *DNB*; James Drummond and C.B. Upton, *Life and Letters of James Martineau*, 2 vols, London, 1902; John Hogben, *Richard Holt Hutton of 'The Spectator': a monograph*, Edinburgh and London, 1899; Robert H. Tener, 'The Writings of Richard Holt Hutton: A Check-list of Identifications', in *Victorian Periodicals Newsletter*, No. 17 (September 1972) and 'R.H. Hutton: Some Attributions', *VPN*, No. 20 (June, 1973)

4 19 October 1859 to Sir George Cornewall Lewis, *SA*, ii, p.190

5 *LWB*, p.225

6 ?22 Dec 1856, *WB*, xiii, p.386

7 25 December 1856, *WB*, xiii, pp.387–8

8 John Viscount Morley, *Recollections*, ii, London, 1917, p.74

9 Tener and Woodfield, *op. cit.*, p.1

10 Andrew St George, 3 February 1990, reviewing Tener and Woodfield in the London *Independent*

11 Sir Owen Chadwick, quoted in Tener and Woodfield, *op. cit.*, *loc. cit.*

12 John St Loe Strachey, *The Adventure of Living: A Subjective Autobiography*, London, 1922, p.221

13 Quoted but unattributed in *Richard Holt Hutton of 'The Spectator'*, *op cit.*, p.39

14 *WB*, xi, pp.207–8

15 *WB*, xv, p.86

16 To Mrs J.S. Reynolds, 26 July 1843, *WB*, xii, p.173

17 *WB*, vii, pp.354–5

18 *WB*, xv, p.86

19 30 August 1846, *LWB*, pp.106–7

20 16 November 1846, *WB*, xii, p.258

21 *LWB*, p.108

22 10 December 1848, *WB*, xii, p.290

23 To Rev. W.R. Alger, 17 March 1858, Drummond and Upton, *James Martineau*, i, p.442

24 *DNB*

25 *WB*, xv, pp.106–7

26 17 August 1853, *WB*, xii, p.352

27 WB to Crabb Robinson, 5 April 1855, *WB*, xiii, p.370

28 *WB*, xiv, pp.416–19

29 *WB*, xiii, *passim*

30 29 November 1857, *WB*, xiii, p.413

31 *LWB*, pp.105–6

32 5 July 1857, George Ticknor, *Life, Letters, and Journals of George Ticknor*, ii, Boston, 1876, pp.361–2

33 *LWB*, p.237

34 17 September 1860, *LWB*, p.327

35 *LWB*, pp.326–7

36 *E*, 30 May 1857

37 *E*, 13 February 1858

38 *E*, 29 May 1858

39 *E*, 12 December 1868; *WB*, iii, p.496

40 *E*, 1 December 1860

41 *WB*, xiii, p.390

42 *WB*, xiii, pp.394–7

43 Mountstuart Grant Duff, *WB*, xv, p.137

44 29 November 1857, *WB*, xiii, p.413

45 1 December 1857, *WB*, xii, p.419

46 2 December 1857, *WB*, xiii, p.423

47 *E*, 23 January 1858

48 24 January 1858, *WB*, xiii, p.490

49 1 February 1858, *WB*, xiii, p.503

50 *E*, 6 February 1858

51 13 February 1858, *WB*, xiii, p.519

52 16 February, 1858, *WB*, xiii, p.525

53 *WB*, xiii, p.505

54 1 February 1858, *WB*, xiii, p.505

55 22 November 1857, *WB*, xiii, pp.402–3

56 11 January 1858, *WB*, xiii, p.455

57 1 February 1858, *WB*, xiii, p.505

58 Buchan, *op. cit.*, p.111

59 6 April 1860, *WB*, xiii, p.559

60 10 January 1858, *WB*, xiii, p.454

61 17 January 1858, *WB*, xiii, p.470

62 *LWB*, p.68

63 24 February 1858, *WB*, xiii, p.527

64 *SA*, ii, p.149

65 27 October, 1856, *WB*, xiii, p.445

66 *WB*, vi, pp.81–115

67 *WB*, vi, p.82

68 *WB*, vi, p.94

CHAPTER XVI: The politics of equilibrium

1 *WB*, iii, pp.25–6

2 *E*, 16 January 1858

3 *WB*, vi, pp.187–235 and cf. pp.181–6 for useful introductory note

4 *E*, 1 January 1859

5 10 January 1859, *WB*, xiii, pp.543–4

6 *WB*, xiii, p.545

7 12 March 1859, *WB*, xiii, pp.544–7

8 31 March 1859, *WB*, xiii, p.547

9 *E*, 16 April 1859

10 13 November 1856

11 'Saunters in the Strand. "*The Economist*" and its Editors.' The *British and Colonial Printer and Stationer*, 19 June 1884

12 *WB*, iii, 343

13 19 December 1858, *SA*, ii, p.105

14 21 June 1852, quoted in Westwater, p.39

15 14 May 1856, *The Letters of Queen Victoria: a selection from Her Majesty's Correspondence between the years 1837 and 1861*, A.C. Benson (ed.), iii, London, 1907, p.190

16 Westwater, p.60

17 *WB*, iii, p.352

18 Westwater, p.60

19 *E*, 17 October 1857

20 *E*, 7 November 1857

21 *E*, 21 November 1857

22 11 July 1859, *SA*, ii, p.171

23 22 July 1859, *WB*, xiii, p.552

24 19 October 1859, *SA*, ii, p.190

25 14 October 1859, *WB*, xiii, p.553

26 From *Men and Events of My Time in India*, quoted in *SA*, ii. pp.229–31

27 8 January 1860, *WB*, xiii, p.557

28 28 November 1859, *WB*, xiii, p.555

29 To William Halsey, ?8 October 1860, *WB*, xiii, p.567

30 *SA*, ii. p.233

31 *SA*, ii, p.237

32 *E*, 12 May 1860

33 Journal, 10 January 1855

34 *SA*, ii, p.252

35 Humphrey Trevelyan, *The India We Left: Charles Trevelyan 1826–65, Humphrey Trevelyan 1929–47*, London, 1972, p.82

36 10 June 1860, *WB*, xiii, pp.562–3

37 4 July 1860, *SA*, ii, p.255

38 Lord Canning to Sir Charles Wood, 12 August 1860, *SA*, ii, p.309

39 *SA*, i, pp.54–5

40 G. Findlay Shirras in *E*, 24 September 1927

41 *E*, 15 September 1860

42 *WB*, xiii, pp.566, 567–8

43 *LWB*, pp.326–7

44 *E*, 17 November 1860; *WB*, xiii, pp.323–364

45 To Clough, Frederick L. Mulhauser, *The Correspondence of Arthur Hugh Clough*, ii, Oxford, 1957, pp.538–9

46 *E*, 23 March 1861

47 *E*, 25 November 1843

48 *E*, 4 May 1861

CHAPTER XVII: 'He was like no one else'

1 October 1867, to R.W. Church, quoted in *WB*, xiii, p.628

2 Cf. *WB*, i, p.30, fn.

3 *WB*, xv, p.202

4 William Irvine, *Walter Bagehot*, London, 1939, p.52

5 *E*, 30 May 1914

6 Irvine, *op. cit.*, 1. For an excellent bibliography of works on Bagehot, see *WB*, xv, pp. 426–442. Of the biographies, that by his sister-in-law, Mrs Russell Barrington (*LWB*) is the most moving, Irvine's is the most stimulating and Alastair Buchan's (*The Spare Chancellor: The Life of Walter Bagehot*, London, 1959) the most efficient. *The Collected Works of Walter Bagehot* (fifteen volumes edited by Norman St John-Stevas, London, 1965–1986) (*WB*) is not only magnificent in its comprehensiveness but abounds with interesting assessments of Bagehot in his various intellectual manifestations by experts in their field, as well as a useful short biographical account and other essays by the editor.

7 'Bagehot as Historian', *WB*, iii, p.23

8 4 January 1858, *WB*, xiii, p.444

9 *WB*, iii, p.178

10 *WB*, xiv, pp.195–6

11 *WB*, xiv, pp.47–8

12 *WB*, iv, p.480

13 *WB*, xv, p.203

14 *WB*, xiv, p.268

15 *WB*, xi, p.225

16 *WB*, xiv, pp.153–4

17 *WB*, v, p.222

18 *WB*, iii, p.61

19 *WB*, v, p.338

20 To Lady Derby, 21 October 1877, *WB*, xv, p.54

21 For a superb assessment of Bagehot's mind, see the conclusion to Irvine, *op. cit.*

22 'Boscastle', *Spectator*, 22 September 1866, *WB*. xiv, p.117

23 1870, 'On the Emotion of Conviction', *WB*, xiv, pp.48–9

24 Edward Gibbon, *The Decline and Fall of the Roman Empire*, London, n.d., Chapter LI

25 n.d., almost certainly to Hutton, quoted by him in *WB*, xv, p.39

26 *WB*, xv, p.158

27 *LWB*, p.231

28 WB, xiv, p.53

29 *WB*, i, pp.278–9

30 *WB*, xii, p.199

31 *WB*, xii, pp.222–4

32 *LWB*, p.64

33 1851, To Edith Bagehot, *WB*, xii, p.331

34 *LWB*, p.66

35 *LWB*, p.73

36 *WB*, xii, p.166

37 *WB*, xii, pp.84–5

38 *WB*, xii, p.148

39 Buchan, *op. cit.*, p.32

40 *WB*, xv, p.89

41 *WB*, xv, p.90

42 *WB*, i, pp.108–41

43 *WB*, i, p.141

44 *WB*, i, p.110

45 *WB*, ix, pp.235–71

46 *WB*, ix, p.236

47 *WB*, ix, p.254

48 *WB*, xii, p.273

49 *WB*, xii, p.280

50 *WB*, xi, pp.157–94

51 *WB*, xi, p.177

52 *WB*, xi, p.182

53 *WB*, xi, pp.183, 193

54 *WB*, xii, p.342

55 See Irvine, *op. cit.*, pp.34–7 for a sensitive assessment of his frame of mind during this period

56 *WB*, xii, p.274

57 *WB*, vii, p.246
58 *WB*, ii, pp.241–60
59 *WB*, i, p.47
60 *WB*, xii, p.331
61 *WB*, iv, p.48
62 *WB*, i, p.405
63 *WB*, xii, p.327
64 *WB*, xii, p.329
65 *WB*, iv, p.36
66 *WB*, iv, p.81
67 *WB*, iv, p.81
68 *WB*, iv, p.52
69 *WB*, xii, p.344
70 *WB*, vii, pp.246–7
71 *WB*, i, pp.156–7
72 *WB*, xii, p.343
73 *WB*, xv, p.6
74 *WB*, ix, p.58
75 *WB*, ix, p.85
76 *WB*, iv, p.177
77 *WB*, ix, p.306
78 *WB*, x, p.53
79 *WB*, i, p.86
80 *WB*, iii, p.245
81 *WB*, iii, p.187
82 *WB*, iii, pp.159–60
83 *WB*, ix, p.272
84 *WB*, ix, p.274

CHAPTER XVIII: The changing face of *The Economist*

1 *WB*, xv, p.61
2 *WB*, xiii, p.575
3 *WB*, ii, p.225
4 *WB*, xiv, p.425
5 *WB*, xiii, p.599
6 *WB*, xiii, p.600
7 *WB*, xiii, p.602
8 *WB*, xiii, p.603

9 *WB*, iii, p.420
10 *WB*, vi, p.132
11 *WB*, xii, p.605
12 *WB*, xiv, p.347
13 *WB*, xiv, pp.123, 126
14 *WB*, xiii, p.619
15 *WB*, xiv, p.47
16 *WB*, xiv, p.424
17 *WB* to Cairns, 21 June 1874, *WB*, xiii, pp.653–4

CHAPTER XIX: Putting figures to it

1 *E*, 4 November 1843
2 *WB*, xi, pp.199–221
3 The main sources used here are the *DNB*, 'Records and Statistics' in CH; *E*, 25 March 1882; Robert Giffen, 'The Utility of Common Statistics' in *Essays in Finance*, London, 1887; Judy L. Klein, *The History of Practical Dynamics and Time Series Analysis*, to be published shortly by the Cambridge University Press; and *PEC*
4 Henry Higgs, *PEC*
5 *WB*, ix, p.303
6 *Journal of the Statistical Society*, xx, pp.ii–iii
7 *WB*, vi, p.187
8 Cf. Newmarch's obituary, *E*, 25 March 1882
9 W. Stanley Jevons, 'On the study of periodic commercial fluctuations', in *Investigations in Currency and Finance*, London, 1982, quoted in Klein, *op cit.*
10 *E*, 8 May 1869
11 *E*, Statistical Supplement, 4 November 1843
12 *WB*, xiii, p.608
13 *WB*, xiii, p.607
14 W. Stebbing, *PEC*
15 Lord Courtney of Penwith, *PEC*
16 *E*, 8 September 1877
17 *WB*, xi, pp.222–54

CHAPTER XX: 'A "new cut" into things'

1 *WB*, xv, p.71
2 *WB*, i, pp.351–2

3 *WB*, xiii, pp.456–7

4 *WB*, xi, p.258

5 *WB*, x, pp.341–71

6 *WB*, x, pp.49–76

7 *WB*, i, p.157

8 *WB*, xi, p.207

9 *WB*, iii, p.33

10 Walt Rostow, 'Bagehot and the Trade Cycle', in CH, is an excellent analysis.

11 *WB*, x, pp.20–22

12 *WB*, x, p.81

13 *WB*, x, pp.81–2

14 *E*, 9 September 1978

15 *E*, 15 October 1988

16 *E*, 13 July 1991

17 Overend, Gurney articles are in *WB*, x, pp.77–116

18 *WB*, x, pp.484–96; *E*, 15 December 1866, 12 January 1867

19 *WB*, x, p.419

20 *WB*, xiii, p.608

21 *WB*, x, p.94

22 Cf. particularly, Henry Higgs in the *DNB*; Roger S. Mason, *Robert Giffen and the Giffen Paradox*, London, 1989; Robert Giffen MSS, London School of Economics

23 Giffen to WB, 15 July 1861, Robert Giffen MSS, London School of Economics

24 Giffen to WB, 2 October 1861, *loc. cit.*

25 Giffen to WB, 9 January 1865, *loc. cit.*

26 Giffen to WB, 12 June 1865, *loc. cit.*

27 Henry Higgs's introduction to Giffen's *Statistics*, London, 1913, an unfinished book written in about 1898–1900 and published posthumously

28 *WB*, xi, p.201, 216–17

29 *WB*, xi, pp.201–2

30 Eliza (Wilson) Bagehot's diary

31 *WB*, iv, pp.136–7

32 *Lombard Street* is in *WB*, ix

33 *WB*, xv, p.35

34 *WB*, xi, p.214,

35 *WB*, ix, p.49

36 *WB*, xv, p.200

37 *WB*, xi, pp.207–208

38 Cf. 'The Genesis of the Treasury Bill (1876–7)', *WB*, xi, pp.405–14 and xv, pp.55–60

CHAPTER XXI: The experiencing nature

1 *E*, 2 April 1988

2 *E*, 28 June 1845

3 *E*, 21 May 1853

4 *E*, 10 July 1858

5 *E*, 17 July 1858

6 *E*, 2 March 1861

7 *WB*, iv, pp.295–6

8 *WB*, vii, pp.59–60

9 *E*, 15 February 1862

10 *WB*, xi, p.401

11 *E*, 1 March 1862

12 *The Economist*'s attitude to the American Civil War has been examined comprehensively in Alastair Burnet's *The Economist and America*, London, 1993. Hugh Brogan's 'America and Walter Bagehot', *American Studies*, ii, 3, pp.335–56 is a splendid analysis. Cf. also Michael Churchman, 'Bagehot and the American Civil War', in *WB*, iv, pp.179–94

13 *WB*, iv, p.316

14 *WB*, iv, p.321

15 *WB*, iv, pp.391–2

16 *WB*, xii, p.339

17 *WB*, iv, pp.97–8

18 *WB*, iii, p.403

19 *WB*, iv, p.336

20 *WB*, iv, p.369

21 *WB*, iv, p.409

22 *WB*, iv, p.281

23 *WB*, viii, pp.351–3

24 'The American Constitution at the Present Crisis', *WB*, iv, pp.235–313

25 *WB*, v, pp.203–4

26 Alastair Buchan, *The Spare Chancellor: The Life of Walter Bagehot*, London, 1959, p.161

27 *WB*, v, p.206

28 *WB*, v, p.210

29 *WB*, v, p.226

30 *WB*, v, pp.229–30

CHAPTER XXII: After Bagehot: trial and error

1 E.D.J. Wilson, 31 March 1877: *WB*, xv, p.41
2 6 April 1877, *WB*, xv, p.54
3 *WB*, p.457
4 The most important source for James Wilson's daughters is Westwater, a piece of splendidly exhaustive research
5 To John Neville Keynes, quoted in *WB*, ix, p.40
6 Walter Wilson Greg, *Biographical notes, 1877–1947*, Oxford, 1960, p.5
7 Mrs Russell Barrington, *Reminiscences of G.F. Watts*, London, 1905, p.73
8 Wilfred Blunt, *England's Michelangelo; a biography of George Frederick Watts, O.M., R.A.*, London, 1975, p.178
9 Mrs Russell Barrington, *Life, Letters and Works of Frederick Leighton*, London, 1906
10 *SA*, ii, p.191
11 *LWB*, p.68
12 *E*, 6 August 1927
13 *WB*, xv, pp.28–34
14 *WB*, xv, pp.41–2
15 *WB*, ix, pp.199–221
16 *WB*, xv, pp.64–8
17 *E*, 1 February 1919
18 *E*, 17 June 1922
19 *WB*, p.366
20 W.H. Bidwell, *Annals of an East Anglian Bank*, Norwich, 1900
21 *WB*, xv, p.47
22 *WB*, xiii, pp.657–8
23 *E*, 24 October 1874
24 *WB*, xiii, pp.665–6
25 *E*, 17 April 1875
26 *Who was Who*; Annual Register, 1922; H. Paul (ed.), *Letters of Lord Acton to Mary, daughter of the Right Hon. W.E. Gladstone*, London, 1909; obituaries: *Guardian*, 16 June 1922, *Spectator*, 17 June 1922 are my main sources here
27 *Guardian*, 16 June 1922
28 J. Robertson Scott, *The Life and Death of a Newspaper*, London, 1952, p.365
29 Hugh Tulloch, *Acton*, London, 1988, p.66
30 *Ibid.*, p.68
31 *The Annual Register 1923*, London 1922, p.152
32 *Guardian*, 16 June 1922
33 *E*, 23 March 1878

34 *E*, 17 May 1879
35 *E*, 3 April 1880
36 *WB*, viii, pp.129–31; *E*, 22 April 1876
37 *WB*, viii, p.132
38 *WB*, iii, pp.420–21
39 *E*, 24 April 1880
40 *E*, 23 July 1881
41 *E*, 20 January 1883
42 *E*, 6 September 1884

CHAPTER XXIII: Herbert Henry Asquith

1 The chief sources for the biographical details are The Earl of Oxford and Asquith, *Memories and Reflections, 1852–1927*, 2 volumes, 1928; *DNB*; Roy Jenkins, *Asquith*, London, 1964; J.A. Spender and Cyril Asquith, *Life of Herbert Henry Asquith, Lord Oxford and Asquith*, 2 volumes, London, 1932
2 Spender and Asquith, *op. cit.*, i, p.154
3 Oxford and Asquith, *op. cit.*, i, p.68
4 Spender and Asquith, *op. cit.*, i, p.46
5 Roy Foster, *Modern Ireland 1600–1972*, London, 1988, p.405
6 *E*, 11 December 1880
7 *E*, 11 December 1880
8 *E*, 15 January 1881
9 *E*, 29 January 1881
10 *E*, 19 and 26 March 1881
11 *E*, 28 May 1881
12 *E*, 10 September 1881
13 *E*, 24 September 1881
14 *E*, 22 October 1881
15 *E*, 22 October 1881
16 *E*, 7 January 1882
17 *E*, 31 December 1881
18 *E*, 8 April 1882
19 *E*, 22 April 1882
20 *E*, 22 April 1882

CHAPTER XXIV: Settling down

1 *WB*, vii, p.182
2 *The Scotsman*, 6 December 1913; *E*, 13 December 1913
3 *E*, 13 December 1913
4 *E*, 19 November 1881
5 *WB*, xiv, pp.423–40
6 See W.T.C. King, 'The Money Market', CH, pp.109–10
7 *E*, 21 May 1881
8 *E*, 9 February 1878
9 *E*, 23 February 1878
10 *E*, 9 March 1878
11 *SA*, i, p.93. Or there may have been two David Airds – father and son
12 J.W. Robertson Scott, *The Life and Death of a Newspaper*, London, 1952, *passim*
13 John Viscount Morley, *Recollections*, London, 1917, i, p.87, quoted in *WB*, xv, pp.24–5
14 *E*, 26 September 1908
15 *E*, 13 December 1913

CHAPTER XXV: The fallen idol

1 *WB*, iii, p.431
2 *E*, 6 May 1882
3 *DNB*
4 *E*, 10 September 1881
5 *E*, 10 June 1882
6 *E*, 15 December 1883
7 *E*, 28 March, 1908
8 *E*, 9 June 1855
9 *E*, 11 August 1855
10 *WB*, viii, p.311
11 *E*, 11 January 1879
12 *E*, 29 November 1879
13 *E*, 6 December 1879
14 *E*, 13 January 1883
15 *E*, 3 January 1885
16 *WB*, viii, p.90
17 *WB*, iii, p.459

18 *WB*, viii, pp.123–4
19 *E*, 29 August 1885
20 *E*, 29 August 1885
21 *E*, 12 December 1885
22 *E*, 19 December 1885
23 *E*, 26 December 1885
24 *E*, 23 January 1886
25 *E*, 6 February 1886
26 *E*, 6 February 1886
27 *E*, 13 March 1886
28 *E*, 6 March 1886
29 *E*, 27 March 1886
30 *E*, 3 April 1886
31 *E*, 10 April 1886
32 *E*, 17 April 1886
33 *E*, 8 May 1886
34 *E*, 5 June 1886
35 *E*, 19 June 1886
36 *E*, 26 June 1886
37 *E*, 26 June 1886
38 *E*, 3 July 1886
39 *E*, 10 July 1886
40 *E*, 17 July 1886
41 *E*, 27 May 1882
42 *E*, 31 July 1886

CHAPTER XXVI: St Loe Strachey

1 *Guardian*, 16 June 1922
2 The *Guardian* and the *Spectator* obituarists differ, the latter claiming that Lathbury followed Gladstone in the Home Rule split, but it is certain that the *Guardian* obituarist knew what he was talking about. The confusion may have arisen because Lathbury later returned to the Gladstonian fold.
3 The main biographical sources for St Loe Strachey are W.V. Cooper in the *DNB*; Amy Strachey, *St Loe Strachey; his life and his paper*, London, 1930; and Strachey's autobiography, *The Adventure of Living: A Subjective Autobiography*, London, 1922
4 St Loe Strachey, *op. cit.*, p.159
5 *Ibid.*, p.11
6 *Ibid.*, p.192

7 *Ibid.*, pp.179–81
8 *E*, 2 April 1887
9 *E*, 22 October 1887
10 *E*, 29 October 1887
11 *E*, 3 March 1888
12 *E*, 25 August 1888
13 *E*, 8 September 1888
14 *E*, 7 December 1889
15 *E*, 4 January 1890
16 *E*, 22 September 1888
17 *E*, 5 October 1889
18 CH, p.43
19 *E*, 5 October 1889
20 *E*, 22 November 1890
21 *E*, 3 January 1891
22 *E*, 10 October 1891
23 *E*, 4 June 1892
24 *E*, 1 April 1893
25 *E*, 29 July 1893
26 *E*, 30 September 1893
27 *E*, 3 March 1894
28 *E*, 21 May 1898
29 CH, pp.11–12
30 *E*, 18 April 1992

CHAPTER XXVII: Turning the century

1 Gibb reminiscences; *E*, 22 February 1964
2 Webb interview, 17 August 1982
3 Chapman memoir
4 James Mill *A Window in Fleet Street*, London, 1901, pp.35–6
5 Walter Wilson Greg, *Biographical Notes 1877–1947*, Oxford, 1960, p.6
6 *Spectator*, 11 September 1897
7 Stephen Koss, *The Rise and Fall of the Political Press in Britain*, i, London, 1981, p.420
8 *PEC*
9 *E*, 13 December 1913
10 John St Loe Strachey, *The Adventure of Living: A Subjective Autobiography*, London, 1922, pp.298–9
11 *WB*, xv, p.119

12 *WB*, vii, pp.266–267

13 *E*, 22 May 1886

14 St Loe Strachey, *op. cit.*, pp.298–9

15 *E*, 14 April 1894

16 *E*, 28 December 1895

17 *E*, 4 January 1896

18 *E*, 4 July 1896

19 *E*, 26 February 1898

20 *E*, 21 January 1899

21 *E*, 26 August 1899

22 Roy Jenkins, *Asquith*, London, 1964, p.116

23 *E*, 20 January 1900

24 *E*, 16 December 1899

25 *E*, 7 June 1902

26 *E*, 10 August 1901

27 *E*, 9 August 1902

28 Main sources *DNB*; St Loe Strachey, *op. cit.*, chs. xvi and xvii

29 *E*, 29 November 1879

30 *E*, 20 December 1879

31 *E*, 27 December 1879

CHAPTER XXVIII: Selling integrity

1 CH, pp.132–3

2 David Kynaston, *The Financial Times: A Centenary History*, London, 1988, p.1

3 Francis Hirst, *The Stock Exchange*, London, 1911, pp.80–81

4 Charles Duguid, *The Stock Exchange*, London, 1904, p.1

5 *E*, 22 August 1863

6 *E*, 28 June 1845

7 *E*, 15 October 1864

8 *E*, 3 March 1877

9 *E*, 13 December 1913

10 *E*, 6 September 1884

11 *E*, 2 May 1885

12 *E*, 22 November 1890

13 *E*, 1 November 1890

14 *E*, 7 May 1988

15 *E*, 9 March 1991

16 *E*, 27 July 1991

17 *E*, 22 February 1992
18 *E*, 29 February 1992
19 *E*, 23 November 1895
20 *E*, 23 March 1895
21 *E*, 15 June 1895
22 *E*, 22 November 1902
23 *E*, 2 May 1903
24 Aylmer Vallance, *Very Private Enterprise: An Anatomy of Fraud and High Finance*, London, 1955, *passim*
25 *E*, 18 February 1888
26 *E*, 23 February 1889
27 *E*, 31 October 1896
28 *E*, 11 March 1893
29 *E*, 26 December 1896
30 *E*, 1 April 1893
31 *E*, 15 July 1989
32 *E*, 10 July 1897
33 *E*, 30 June 1898
34 *E*, 15 January 1898
35 *E*, 20 May 1899
36 Quoted in *E*, 15 February 1902
37 *E*, 12 January 1901
38 *E*, 15 February 1902
39 *Sunday Times*, 12 July 1992
40 Kynaston, *op. cit.*, p.54
41 *E*, 1 November 1913
42 *E*, 28 January 1888
43 *E*, 10 September 1898
44 For a description of the relationship, see George H. Nash, *The Life of Herbert Hoover – The Engineer 1874–1914*, New York and London, 1983, *passim*
45 *E*, 7 April 1956

CHAPTER XXIX: Fighting the future

1 24 February 1953
2 *E*, 28 January 1905
3 *E*, 29 October 1904
4 *E*, 2 December 1905
5 *E*, 20 January 1906

6 *E*, 13 January 1906

7 *E*, 24 October 1903

8 *E*, 9 July 1904

9 *E*, 16 July 1904

10 *E*, 6 August 1904

11 *E*, 8 October 1904

12 *E*, 4 February 1905

13 *E*, 20 May 1905

14 *E*, 15 July 1905

15 *E*, 6 January 1906

16 *E*, 4 July 1914

17 *E*, 28 June 1845

18 *E*, 10 October 1936

19 *E*, 17 October 1936

20 *E*, 9 April 1949

21 *E*, 31 July 1948

22 *E*, 25 January 1958

23 *E*, 15 September 1956

24 *E*, 1 August 1987

25 *E*, 22 February 1964

26 C.M. Bowra, *Memories: 1898–1939*, London, 1966, *passim*

27 Mary Agnes Hamilton, *Remembering My Good Friends*, London, 1944, pp.80–81. The most important biographical sources for Hirst are *F.W. Hirst by his Friends*, Oxford, 1958; *DNB*; Hamilton, *op. cit.*; obituaries and the introductions to some of his numerous books

28 *DNB*

29 F.W. Hirst, *Gold, Silver & Paper Money*, London, 1933, Introduction

30 *F.W. Hirst by his Friends*, p.62

31 Hamilton, *op.cit.*, p.80

32 Douglas Jerrold, *Georgian Adventure*, London, 1937, p.79

33 *E*, 7 September 1907

34 *E*, 13 July 1912

35 *Yorkshire Evening News*, 8 January, 1945

36 *WB*, iii, p.317

37 *E*, 16 June 1883

CHAPTER XXX: The editorial dame

1 *E*, 9 December 1850

2 *E*, 10 December 1853

3 *WB*, ii, p.265

4 Cf. particularly, *WB*, i, p.208, ii, p.106 and his essay on Lady Mary Wortley Montagu in *WB*, ii, pp.208–36

5 *WB*, ii, p.226

6 *WB*, ii, p.304

7 *WB*, ii, p.209

8 *E*, 13 June 1868

9 *E*, 18 July 1868

10 *WB*, iii, pp.542–3

11 *E*, 19 September 1868

12 *WB*, vi, 396–397

13 *WB*, vi, p.398

14 *WB*, vii, pp.413–16

15 *E*, 12 May 1877

16 *E*, 26 January 1878

17 Cf. e.g. *E*, 11 August 1888

18 See Westwater, chapter 10, 'Tea and Anti-Suffrage Sympathy' for a full discussion of the Wilson sisters and female suffrage

19 Westwater, p.212

20 *E*, 10 July 1897

21 *E*, 27 June 1908

22 *E*, 4 July 1908

23 *E*, 12 December 1908

24 *E*, 19 December 1908

25 *E*, 13 April 1912

26 *E*, 1 February 1913

27 *E*, 10 May 1913

28 Mary Agnes Hamilton, *Remembering My Good Friends*, London, 1944, p.82

29 George Dangerfield, *The Strange Death of Liberal England*, London, 1935, pp.125–7

30 *E*, 23 June 1917

31 *E*, 5 December 1919

32 *E*, 16 April 1927

33 *E*, 29 November 1941

34 *E*, 1 April 1944

35 *E*, 27 March 1943

36 *E*, 9 December 1944

37 *E*, 28 November 1953

38 *E*, 21 April 1956

39 *E*, 23 March 1963
40 *E*, 29 August 1964
41 *E*, 23 April 1966
42 *E*, 20 February 1982
43 *E*, 14 August 1982
44 *E*, 2 April 1982
45 *E*, 8 February 1986
46 *E*, 9 July 1983
47 *E*, 10 November 1990
48 *E*, 8 August 1992

CHAPTER XXXI: The Oxbridge influx

1 *E*, 3 February 1923
2 *E*, 21 July 1928
3 *E*, 29 February 1908
4 Walter Layton, *Dorothy*, London, 1961, p.40
5 Quoted in David Hubback, *No Ordinary Press Baron*, London, 1985, p.32
6 Francis Hirst, *Gold, Silver and Paper Money*, London, 1933, Introduction
7 Quoted in Stephen Koss, *The Rise and Fall of the Political Press in Britain*, ii, London, 1984, p.211
8 Milo Keynes, *Essays on John Maynard Keynes*, Cambridge, 1975, p.153
9 *The Collected Writings of John Maynard Keynes*, vol. xv, *Activities 1906–1914*, (ed.) Elizabeth Johnson, London, 1971, p.17
10 *E*, 29 October 1938
11 *E*, 20 July 1912
12 The main sources for Mary Agnes Hamilton are her books *Dead Yesterday*, London, 1916, *Up-Hill All the Way*, London, 1953, and *Remembering My Good Friends*, London, 1944; Newnham College Register and obituary by Myra Curtis
13 She appears in Ben Pimlott's *Hugh Dalton* (London, 1985) as a friend of both Daltons
14 Hamilton, *Remembering My Good Friends*, pp.61–2
15 Hamilton, *Dead Yesterday*, pp.68–9
16 *Ibid.*, p.70
17 *E*, 3 April 1886
18 *E*, 2 January 1909
19 *E*, 16 January 1909
20 *E*, 28 February 1953
21 Business correspondence between Einaudi and *The Economist* exists in the Centro di Ricerca e Documentazione 'Luigi Einaudi' in Turin

22 *E*, 4 November 1961
23 Douglas Jay, *Change and Fortune: A Political Record*, London, 1980, p.52
24 *E*, 9 June 1934
25 Cf. *E*, 16 December 1934
26 *E*, 17 August 1946
27 *E*, 8 July 1916
28 *E*, 3 May 1913
29 *E*, 17 May 1913
30 *E*, 5 September 1992
31 *E*, 5 June 1909

CHAPTER XXXII: Peace, retrenchment and reform

1 *E*, 19 May, 1945
2 *E*, 21 September 1907
3 *E*, 6 February 1909
4 *WB*, viii, pp.45–58
5 *WB*, viii, pp.59–64; *E*, 26 April 1862
6 *E*, 26 October 1963
7 *E*, 2 November 1963
8 *E*, 28 January 1888
9 *E*, 15 July 1905
10 *E*, 19 May 1888
11 *E*, 19 February 1848
12 *E*, 7 February 1852
13 *E*, 18 September 1852
14 *E*, 16 October 1852
15 *E*, 30 October 1852
16 *E*, 30 July 1859
17 *E*, 6 December 1884
18 *E*, 28 July 1906
19 *WB*, viii, p.52
20 *E*, 8 April 1911
21 *WB*, viii, p.61
22 *WB*, viii, p.67
23 *E*, 5 December 1896
24 *E*, 28 April 1900
25 *E*, 7 October 1905
26 *WB*, iv, p.127

27 *E*, 16 November 1907

28 *E*, 13 February 1909

29 *E*, 15 February 1913

30 Mary Agnes Hamilton, *Remembering My Good Friends*, London, 1944, p.64

31 Mary Agnes Hamilton, *Dead Yesterday*, London, 1916, pp.19–21

32 *E*, 25 July 1914

33 *E*, 13 June 1992

34 *E*, 24 January, 1914

35 *E*, 30 May 1913

36 *E*, 25 July 1914

37 Hamilton, *Remembering My Good Friends*, p.65

38 *E*, 1 August 1914

39 *E*, 8 August 1914

CHAPTER XXXIII: Freedom and responsibility

1 London, 1935, p.354

2 Layton papers, unpublished memoir

3 Mary Agnes Hamilton, *Remembering My Good Friends*, London 1944, p.71

4 Mary Agnes Hamilton, *Dead Yesterday*, London, 1916, pp.255–6

5 Walter Layton, *Dorothy*, London, 1961, pp.57–8

6 Quoted in Stephen Koss, *The Rise and Fall of the Political Press in Britain*, London, 1984, ii, p.213

7 Hamilton, *Remembering My Good Friends*, p.80

8 *E*, 7 August 1915

9 Hamilton, *Dead Yesterday*, p.286

10 *Ibid.*, p.309

11 *E*, 8 August 1914

12 *E*, 22 August 1914

13 *E*, 21 November 1914

14 *E*, 2 January 1915

15 Bagehot to Crabb Robinson, 25 December 1851, *WB*, xii, pp.329–30

16 *WB*, iv, p.33

17 *E*, 17 May 1930

18 *E*, 21 May 1938

19 *E*, 10 December 1938

20 *E*, 28 October 1939

21 *E*, 2 December 1939

22 *E*, 20 November 1943

23 *E*, 16 January 1971
24 *E*, 26 July 1975
25 Hansard, 13 October 1975
26 *E*, 18 October 1975
27 *E*, 6 December 1975
28 *E*, 6 December 1975
29 *E*, 13 December 1975
30 *E*, 20 December 1975
31 *E*, 13 February 1982
32 *E*, 19 February 1983
33 *E*, 25 July 1987
34 *E*, 9 January 1988
35 *E* 29 October 1988
36 *E*, 27 November 1971
37 *E*, 1 February 1992
38 *WB*, iv, p.18
39 *E*, 24 April 1915
40 21 May 1915 in Trevor Wilson (ed.), *C.P. Scott Diaries 1911–1928*, London, 1970, pp.124–5
41 28 May 1915, *ibid.*
42 Hamilton, *Remembering My Good Friends*, p.80
43 *E*, 29 May 1915
44 *E*, 5 June 1915
45 *E*, 12 June 1915
46 Quoted in Koss, *op. cit.*, ii, p.282
47 21 August 1915
48 18 September 1915
49 16 October 1915
50 *E*, 20 May 1916
51 *E*, 1 July, 1916
52 *E*, 8 July 1916
53 *E*. 8 July 1916
54 Hamilton, *Remembering My Good Friends*, p.80
55 The main biographical sources for Hartley Withers are *DNB*; obituaries in *E*, 25 March 1950 and *The Times*, 22 March 1950; *Who's Who* and *Who was Who*
56 June 1909
57 Hartley Withers, *The Meaning of Money*, London, 1909, pp.189–90
58 *E*, 20 February 1909
59 Withers, *op. cit.*, p.207
60 *E*, 11 May 1918

61 Paul Einzig, *In the Centre of Things*, London, 1960, pp.11–19

62 *E*, 15 September 1923

63 David Kynaston, *The Financial Times*, London, 1988, pp.95–6

64 *E*, 16 December 1916

65 *E*, 6 October 1917

66 *E*, 6 October 1917

67 *E*, 24 November 1917

CHAPTER XXXIV: The wasting disease

1 Hartley Withers, *Bankers and Credit*, London, 1924, p.vi

2 Gibb reminiscences, *E*, 25 March 1950

3 *E*, 28 July 1917

4 *E*, 1 September 1917

5 *E*, 22 September 1917

6 Hartley Withers, *Our Money and the State*, London, 1917, pp.54–5

7 *E*, 22 September 1917

8 Economist Publications, London, 1983

9 Hartley Withers, *War-Time Financial Problems*, London, 1919

10 *E*, 15 April 1939

11 *E*, 29 July 1939

12 *E*, 27 January 1940

13 *E*, 28 September 1940

14 *E*, 22 March 1941

15 *E*, 21 June 1941

16 *E*, 8 September 1945

17 *E*, 10 August 1946

18 *E*, 17 March 1951

19 *E*, 30 May 1959

20 *E*, 19 January 1974

21 *E*, 26 April 1980

22 *E*, 5 May 1990

23 *E*, 8 September 1951

24 *E*, 22 August 1992

CHAPTER XXXV: War and peace

1 *E*, 11 October 1919

2 *E*, 14 September 1918
3 *E*, 12 October 1918
4 *E*, 14 November 1992
5 *E*, 16 November 1918
6 *E*, 16 November 1918
7 *E*, preliminary number
8 *E*, 12 May 1945
9 *E*, 16 November 1918
10 *E*, 23 November 1918
11 *E*, 9 December 1916
12 *E*, 10 May 1919
13 *E*, 11 October 1919
14 *E*, 3 January 1920
15 *E*, 27 December 1919
16 *E*, 27 December 1919
17 *DNB*
18 *E*, 18 October 1919

CHAPTER XXXVI: How can I help?

1 Letter to his sister, *circa* 1905, quoted in David Hubback, *No Ordinary Press Baron*, London, 1985, p.15
2 The chief biographical sources for Layton are his *Dorothy*, London, 1961; Hubback, *op. cit.*; Graham Hutton interviews, *DNB*; his private papers, Trinity College, Cambridge; and innumerable interviews with contemporaries and family.
3 *War Memoirs of David Lloyd George*, Odhams Press ed., n.d., pp.941–2
4 *New Republic*, 19 May 1917, quoted in Hubback, *op. cit.* p.46
5 *E*, 26 February 1966
6 *E*, 17 December, 1921
7 Layton papers
8 *E*, 1 May 1926
9 Layton papers
10 Charles Edward Lysaght, *Brendan Bracken*, London, 1979, p.99
11 J.W. Robertson Scott, *'We' and Me*, London, 1956, pp.213–14
12 *E*, 27 November 1976
13 *E*, 31 January 1981
14 *E*, 21 February 1981
15 *E*, 20 February 1982
16 *E*, 20 March 1982

17 *E*, 1 July 1989
18 *E*, 8 July 1989
19 *E*, 6 February 1988
20 23 July 1986
21 Layton papers
22 *E*, 27 December 1952
23 *E*, 4 July 1964
24 *E*, 10 July 1982
25 *E*, 22 January 1983
26 *E*, 28 July 1928
27 *E*, 18 March 1933

CHAPTER XXXVII: Keeping the faith

1 For two excellent accounts of the pros and cons of this debate, see Paul Addison, *Churchill on the Home Front 1900–1955*, London, 1992 and Robert Skidelsky, *John Maynard Keynes: The Economist as Saviour 1920–1937*, London, 1992
2 *E*, 3 January 1925
3 Skidelsky, *op. cit.*, p.205
4 *E*, 3 January 1925
5 Skidelsky, *op. cit.*, p.188
6 Skidelsky, *op. cit.*, p.198
7 Quoted in Addison, *op. cit.*, pp.248–9
8 *E*, 2 May 1925
9 Addison, *op. cit.*, p.244
10 *E*, 8 August 1925
11 'The Question of High Wages', *Political Quarterly*, January–March 1930, *The Collected Writings of John Maynard Keynes*, vol. xx, *Activities 1929–1931*, (ed.) Donald Moggridge, London, 1981, p.7
12 *E*, 30 August 1845
13 *E*, 10 April 1926
14 *E*, 15 May 1926
15 *E*, 30 April 1927
16 *E*, 18 May 1946
17 *E*, 26 January 1985
18 *WB*, viii, p.19
19 *E*, 17 October 1992
20 *E*, 16 January 1993
21 *E*, 30 April 1927

22 Quoted in David Hubback, *No Ordinary Press Baron*, London, 1985, p.103

23 *E*, 21 May 1927

24 *E*, 28 May 1927

25 *E*, 13 April 1929

26 *E*, 31 May 1924

27 Douglas Jay, *Change and Fortune*, London, 1980, p.50

28 *Daily Telegraph*, 15 February 1966

29 Quoted in Hubback, *op. cit.*, p.164

30 Layton to Strakosch, 7 July 1938, Layton papers

31 Centenary pamphlet

32 *E*, 20 December 1924

33 *E*, 27 December 1924

34 16 June 1965, Layton papers

CHAPTER XXXVIII: Unreason abroad

1 Douglas Jay, *Change and Fortune*, London, 1980, p.53

2 *E*, 2 September 1933

3 *E*, 7 May 1927

4 *E*, 23 September 1933

5 *E*, 11 November 1933

6 *E*, 30 December 1933

7 *E*, 1 November 1930

8 *Novy Mir*, 1968, No.4, pp.194–216; interview in the Soviet paper, "*The Journalist*", No.6, 1971: copies in Layton papers

9 April 1937

10 The main sources for Toynbee are *DNB*; William H. McNeill, *Arnold J. Toynbee: A Life*, Oxford, 1989; Toynbee, *Acquaintances*, London, 1967. S. Fiona Morton, *A Bibliography of Arnold J. Toynbee*, Oxford, 1980, locates *Economist* reviews of Toynbee's books, signed articles and a number of those by-lined 'By a Travelling Correspondent', but does not attempt to identify his anonymous writing

11 *Sunday Times*, 30 July 1989

12 *E*, 12 October 1929

13 *E*, 7 November 1925

14 *E*, 15 November 1924

15 *E*, 15 September 1928

16 *E*, 16 March 1929

17 *E*, 10 November 1928

18 C.H. Rolph, *Kingsley: The Life, Letters and Diaries of Kingsley Martin*, London, 1973, p.233

19 *E*, 17 May 1930

20 4 January 1993

21 *E*, 11 October 1930

22 *E*, 25 May 1935

23 *E*, 14 March 1936

24 Paul Addison, *Churchill on the Home Front 1900–1955*, London, 1992, pp.320–22

CHAPTER XXXIX: Standards? What standards?

1 GC to Al Hayes, 12 June 1951, *EA*

2 *E*, 17 January 1925

3 *E*, 14 March 1931

4 *The Collected Works of John Maynard Keynes*, vol. xx, *Activities 1929–1931*, (ed.) Donald Moggridge, London, 1981, p.500

5 Robert Skidelsky, *John Maynard Keynes: The Economist as Saviour 1920–1937*, London, 1992, p.393

6 *E*, 29 August 1992

7 *E*, 19 September 1992

8 *E*, 25 November 1967

9 *E*, 26 September 1931

10 *E*, 29 July 1944

11 *E*, 21 August 1971

12 *E*, 6 January 1990

13 *WB*, xi, p.66

14 *WB*, xi, p.73

15 *E*, 23 January 1993

16 *E*, 30 January 1993

17 David Hubback, *No Ordinary Press Baron*, London, 1988, p.64

18 Skidelsky, *op. cit.*, pp.264–5

19 *E*, 26 December 1992

20 *E*, 23 January 1993

21 Skidelsky, *op. cit.*, p.572

22 Quoted in Hubback, *op. cit.*, p.94

23 Lord Robbins, *Autobiography of an Economist*, London, 1970, p.97

24 *E*, 27 May 1950

25 *E*, 7 October 1933

26 Douglas Jay, *Change and Fortune*, London, 1980, p.51

27 Quoted in David Kynaston, *The Financial Times*, London, 1988, p.106

28 Lord Drogheda interview 23 September 1982, 3 August 1989

29 Quoted in Kynaston, *op. cit.*, p.106

30 *E*, 6 November 1943

31 Layton papers

32 Hubback, *op. cit.*, and Stephen Koss, *The Rise and Fall of the Political Press in Britain*, ii, London, 1984, are the main sources for this episode

33 C.H. Rolph, *Kingsley: The Life, Letters and Diaries of Kingsley Martin*, London, 1973, p.205

34 Quoted in Hubback, *op. cit.*, p.137

CHAPTER XL: The new men

1 *E*, 27 December 1952

2 *EA*, unidentified article

3 Robert Skidelsky, *John Maynard Keynes: The Economist as Saviour 1920–1937*, London, 1992, the main source here, is extremely informative and entertaining on the changes in the Cambridge School

4 *E*, 9 September 1933

5 Dr E.F. Papp, 15 October 1984, *EA*

6 *E*, 12 December 1992

7 *EA*

8 *EA*, 12 May 1986

9 *E*, 7 May 1938

10 Douglas Jay, *Change and Fortune*, London, 1980, pp.52–3

11 *E*, 13 June 1936

12 Hutton papers

13 *E*, 16 February 1935

14 *E*, 29 February 1936

15 *E*, 19 March 1932

16 *E*, 9 April 1932

17 *E*, 9 November 1991

18 *E*, 6 January 1934

19 *E*, 2 January 1937

20 *E*, 2 November 1935

21 *E*, 4 April 1936

22 *WB*, xiv, pp.423–4

23 *EA*

24 28 October 1937, Hutton papers

25 11 February, 1938, *loc. cit.*

26 Hutton to Layton, 28 April 1938, Layton papers

CHAPTER XLI: Geoffrey Crowther

1 'Geoffrey Crowther and *The Economist*', The Economist Newspaper Ltd Annual Report and Accounts, 31 March 1972
2 For a detailed account, see CH, 'Records and Statistics'
3 'The *Economist* Index of Business Activity', *Journal of the Royal Statistical Society*, vol. xcvii, Part ii, 1934
4 Parkinson to Strakosch, 26 May 1938, Layton papers
5 *E*, 20 August 1938
6 *E*, 1 October 1938
7 *E*, 4 September 1943
8 *E*, 27 September 1941
9 *E*, 9 January 1993
10 *E*, 12 December 1992
11 Deryck Abel, *Ernest Benn: Counsel for Liberty*, London, 1960, pp.119–20

CHAPTER XLII: Wartime

1 Memorandum to Layton, *EA*
2 GC to Bracken, 12 April 1943, Bracken papers
3 Bracken papers
4 To Helen Hill Miller, 15 January 1944, Miller papers
5 23 March 1950, *loc. cit.*
6 *E*, 6 June 1981. The reminiscences quoted in this chapter come from this source
7 *E*, 12 April 1941
8 *E*, 19 April 1941
9 *E*, 19 July 1941
10 *E*, 6 December 1941
11 *E*, 21 May 1955
12 *E*, 10 April 1948
13 *E*, 27 February 1943
14 *E*, 7 March 1942
15 Quoted in *E*, 6 June 1981
16 *E*, 12 August 1944
17 *E*, 2 September 1944
18 *E*, 30 September 1944
19 6 December 1944, Bracken papers
20 *E*, 7 April 1956

CHAPTER XLIII: Suez

1 *WB*, vi, p.19
2 *WB*, viii, pp.325–6
3 *E*, 4 August 1956
4 *E*, 25 October 1947
5 *E*, 29 September 1956
6 *E*, 6 October 1956
7 *E*, 3 November 1956
8 *E*, 10 November 1956
9 *E*, 10 November 1956
10 *E*, 17 November 1956
11 13 November 1956, Layton papers
12 November 1956, Layton papers

CHAPTER XLIV: The Philby interlude

1 Richard Cockett, *David Astor*, London, 1991, p.155
2 10 July, 1963, Layton papers
3 *E*, 6 July 1963
4 10 July 1963, Layton papers

CHAPTER XLV: The Cuba crisis

1 *E*, 18 February 1950
2 3 January 1956
3 David Carlton, *Anthony Eden: a biography*, London, 1981, p.389
4 *E*, 25 November 1950
5 *E*, 24 May 1952
6 *E*, 19 November 1955
7 *E*, 23 March 1957
8 *E*, 27 August 1960
9 *E*, 8 September 1962
10 *E*, 23 March 1963
11 *E*, 6 October 1962
12 *E*, 27 October 1962
13 *E*, 3 November 1962
14 *E*, 1 December 1962

CHAPTER XLVI: The evil empire

1 *E*, 11 March 1848
2 *E*, 15 July 1967
3 *E*, 27 February 1965
4 *E*, 4 December 1965
5 *E*, 11 December 1965
6 23 November 1964
7 6 October 1977, *EA*
8 3 November 1977, *EA*
9 *E*, 25 June 1966
10 *E*, 29 October 1966
11 *E*, 19 August 1967
12 *E*, 28 October 1967
13 *E*, 2 November 1968
14 *E*, 4 November 1972
15 *E*, 23 December 1972
16 *E*, 16 December 1978
17 *E*, 29 September 1956
18 *E*, 23 December 1989

CHAPTER XLVII: The special relationship

1 *E*, 9 July 1966
2 *E*, 5 February 1966
3 *E*, 24 June 1967
4 10 March 1940 – the correspondence from and to Mildred Adams Kenyon and Helen Hill Miller is at the Schlesinger Library, Radcliffe College, Cambridge, Mass.
5 *United States Reports*, vol 343, p.579. I am indebted to Tony Lewis for this
6 *E*, 11 November 1980
7 24 May 1947
8 18 June 1947
9 14 June 1950
10 5 July 1950
11 No date
12 24 July 1950
13 Sunday, ... 1950
14 *E*, 1 November 1952
15 23 March 1953, Bracken papers

16 *E*, 7 February 1987
17 *E*, 31 October 1992

CHAPTER XLVIII: Home and business

1 *E*, 30 December 1978; *WB*, xv, p.222
2 *E*, 7 April 1956
3 *E*, 16 November 1935
4 *E*, 9 August 1941
5 Cecil King, *With Malice Toward None*, (ed.) W. Armstrong, London, 1970, p.243
6 *E*, 23 June 1945
7 *E*, 4 February 1950
8 *Punch*, 5 January 1955
9 *E*, 14 May 1955
10 *E*, 12 September 1959
11 *E*, 10 October 1964
12 *E*, 6 June 1970
13 Cecil King, *Diary 1965–70*, London, 1972, 1968
14 *E*, 23 February 1974
15 *E*, 5 October 1974
16 *E*, 21 April 1979
17 *E*, 28 April 1979
18 *E*, 28 May 1983
19 *E*, 6 June 1987
20 *E*, 4 April 1992
21 Charles Edward Lysaght, *Brendan Bracken*, London, 1979, p.318
22 Ben Pimlott, *Hugh Dalton*, London, 1985, p.464
23 *Ibid.* pp.517–18
24 Sir Robert Hall, *The Robert Hall Diaries*, London, 1989, pp.55–6
25 *Ibid.*, 1 November 1949
26 *Ibid.*, 20 June 1950
27 Donald Tyerman, 'Crowther and the Great Issues' in *Encounter*, May 1972
28 *E*, 20 March 1993
29 Memorandum, 1943, *EA*
30 7 March 1952. All Fred Hirsch's letters are to his mother and are held privately
31 28 March 1953
32 20 April 1953
33 27 April 1953
34 6 May 1953

35 16 July 1953
36 23 September 1954
37 *Banker*, January 1978
38 *E*, 27 February 1993
39 25 September 1968, *EA*
40 Denis Healey, *The Time of My Life*, London, 1989, p.110
41 *E*, 28 February 1987
42 John St Loe Strachey, *The Adventure of Living*, London, 1922, pp.318–20
43 Edward Cook, *Delane of The Times*, London, 1915, pp.290–92
44 *Newsweek*, 26 May 1969
45 *The Independent*, 31 December 1988

CHAPTER XLIX: Getting bored

1 *E*, 7 April 1956
2 7 February 1972
3 *E*, 12 February 1972
4 *E*, 19 November 1955
5 *E*, 22 December 1951
6 *E*, 9 November 1958
7 29 May 1944, Layton papers
8 9 July 1944
9 28 June 1955, Layton papers
10 John Pringle, *Have Pen: Will Travel*, London, 1973
11 Louis Heren, *Memories of Times Past*, London, 1988, pp.93–4

CHAPTER L: Learning new ways

1 Memorandum of Agreement, 10 June 1928, Bracken papers
2 *News Chronicle*, 19 August 1946
3 *E*, 15 February 1947
4 *FT*, 21 and 28 February 1947
5 Harold Herd, *The March of Journalism – The Story of the British Press from 1622 to the Present Day*, London, 1952
6 *E*, 2 September 1950
7 *E*, 25 July 1959
8 *E*, 15 August 1959
9 *E*, 15 August 1959

10 *EA*, 14 May 1962
11 *EA*, 14 May 1962
12 23 January 1948, *EA*
13 Roland Bird, 'Geoffrey Crowther and *The Economist*', Economist Annual Report and Accounts, 1972

CHAPTER LI: Vision and reality

1 No date, Midgley papers
2 Board minutes, October 1968
3 11 February, 1946, Layton papers
4 4 August 1964, Midgley papers
5 8 May 1946, Layton papers
6 Browne memorandum on EIU is in *EA*
7 7 March 1952, Hirsch papers
8 Browne/Trafford correspondence is in *EA*
9 quoted in Centenary pamphlet, p.4

CHAPTER LII: The succession

1 14 March 1963, Layton papers
2 8 July 1963
3 9 July 1963, Midgley papers
4 Roy Jenkins, *A Life at the Centre*, London, 1991, pp.149–51
5 18 November 1963, Layton papers
6 29 May 1963
7 5 July 1964, *EA*
8 7 July 1964
9 July 1964, Layton papers
10 10 January 1959
11 *E*, 19 May 1962
12 *E*, 27 March 1993
13 5 January 1966
14 28 September 1974
15 *E*, 14 October 1961
16 *E*, 2 March 1968
17 *E*, 19 August 1972
18 *E*, 31 May 1986

19 24 April 1970
20 16 November 1964
21 *Forte: the autobiography of Charles Forte*, London, 1986, p.189
22 Donald Tyerman, 'Crowther and the Great Issues' in *Encounter*, May 1972

CHAPTER LIII: Continuing the line

1 *E*, 7 February 1987
2 *E*, 27 March 1993
3 *EA*, 26 February 1987 to AS

EPILOGUE: Forward to the past

1 *E*, 21 December 1991

Index

Shaftesbury, Anthony Ashley Cooper, 7th
  Earl of   50, 309
Shakespeare, William   195
Shanahan, Eileen   814
Shaw, George Bernard   413, 608
Shawcross Press Commission   627
Shelley, Percy Bysshe   182, 195, 198, 199,
  227
Sherrard, Clifton   504
Shipley, Orby   321, 325, 328, 357, 358, 406,
  618
Shove, Gerard   682
Shultz, George   938
Sibeth, John   7
Siepmann, H.A.   612n
Simon, Ernest   620n, 635n, 677
Simon, Sir John   461, 479, 565, 664, 694n
Simon Commission   664, 679
Simonites   694n
Sinclair, Sir Robert   627–30
Singer, Bernard   588n, 789n
Singer, Daniel   588n, 788–9, 864
Sir Robert Peel's Act of 1844, Regulating the Issue
  of Bank Notes, Vindicated (Arbuthnot)   101
Sisson, C.H.   228n
Six Panics and Other Essays, The (Hirst)   522,
  527
Skidelsky, Robert   635n
Skiold, Per   612n
Sky television   622
Slave Power, The (Cairns)   308
Slavery   27–9, 41, 142, 261, 300–310, 313,
  386, 414, 454
Smith, Adam   5–6, 8, 39, 45, 47, 69, 77, 128,
  242, 243, 294, 595, 743
Smith, Barbara   485, 791–2, 795, 802, 827,
  829
Smith, F.E. (Lord Birkenhead)   461, 544,
  639, 664
Smith, Godfrey   823
Smith, Ian   930
Smith, Octavius   146n
Smith, Sydney   463
Smithson, Alison   889
Smithson, Peter   889
Social Darwinism   165, 227
Social Discussion Society   492
Social Limits to Growth (Hirsch)   849
Social Statics (Spencer)   141, 147, 148, 149
Socialist-Case, The (Jay)   709
Society of Individualists   745
Socrates   647
Somalia   65–6
Some Leading Principles of Political Economy
  Newly Expounded (Cairns)   262
Sosnow, Eric   753
'Sound Banking' (Bagehot)   286
South Africa   30, 106, 139, 334, 411, 419–23,
  446, 528, 691
South America   106, 435, 446
South Korea   799
South Vietnam/South Vietnamese   799, 801,
  803, 804, 805
Soviet Union: and censorship 560; collapse of

68; and Cuba crisis 790–97; expansion of
  760; and Reagan 826, 831
Spain, and banning of TE   560
Spalding, William F.   612
Spanish Civil War   668
Speaker   464
Spectator   35n, 129–30, 144, 180, 224, 225,
  233, 293, 309, 320, 333, 334, 344, 381–3,
  409, 412, 417, 423, 424, 428, 568, 625, 669,
  880, 913
Spencer, Herbert   123, 141–53, 203n
Spencer, Thomas   141, 143, 144, 147
Spender, Stephen   697
Spring-Rice, Dominick   612
Spycatcher (Wright)   557–8
Stalin, Joseph   754, 760, 766, 786, 788
Stamp, Sir Josiah   606, 612n, 626, 637, 677,
  680n, 709, 739
stamp duty   15, 217, 259–60
Standard   55, 384, 518
Standard Chartered Bank   220
Star   459
Statesman (Calcutta)   452
Statist   260, 279, 280, 327, 333, 732, 752
Statistical Society   277, 280, 294, 329
statistics   273–83, 294, 493–5, 688, 695,
  845–6
Stead, W.T.   524
Steed, Wickham   620
Steiner, George   864
Stephenson (Times correspondent in
  Ottawa)   699, 700
Stevenson, Adlai   822
Stevenson, J.A.   612n
Stevenson, Merrill   939n
Stevenson, Robert Louis   384
Stewart, Alexander Mackay   491, 495
Stewart, Margaret   751, 753n
Stirling Journal   293
Stock Exchange: and 'A Merchant' 120; and
  Bagehot 431, 433; and Bird 843; closure of
  537, 538; decline of 724; and Johnstone
  428, 433; and railway mania 90, 91;
  stockbrokers operating outside 434; TE's
  coverage of 85–6, 430–31, 718, 723;
  wrongdoing in 436
Stock Exchange, The (Hirst)   516
Stock Exchange Committee   438, 439
Stock Exchange Gazette   752
Stocks, Mary (Lady Stocks)   617
Stocks and Shares (Withers)   568n, 569
Stone, Reynolds   884
Stopford, R.J.   617n, 712
Stott, Wally   930
Stowe, Harriet Beecher   309
Strachey, Amy (née Turner)   413
Strachey, Sir Edward   381–2, 383
Strachey, John   656
Strachey, Sir John St Loe   180, 381–6,
  388–9, 392, 393, 409, 428, 449, 450, 536,
  656, 854; autobiography 412; and
  Chamberlain 452; early life 381–3; and
  federalism 385–6, 416; and imperialism 413,
  415, 416, 417; starts to write for TE 384;